WEST'S LAW SCHOOL ADVISORY BOARD

JESSE H. CHOPER
Professor of Law and Dean Emeritus,
University of California, Berkeley

JOSHUA DRESSLER
Professor of Law, Michael E. Moritz College of Law,
The Ohio State University

YALE KAMISAR
Professor of Law Emeritus, University of San Diego
Professor of Law Emeritus, University of Michigan

MARY KAY KANE
Professor of Law, Chancellor and Dean Emeritus,
University of California,
Hastings College of the Law

LARRY D. KRAMER
President, William and Flora Hewlett Foundation

JONATHAN R. MACEY
Professor of Law, Yale Law School

ARTHUR R. MILLER
University Professor, New York University
Formerly Bruce Bromley Professor of Law, Harvard University

GRANT S. NELSON
Professor of Law, Pepperdine University
Professor of Law Emeritus, University of California, Los Angeles

A. BENJAMIN SPENCER
Professor of Law,
Washington & Lee University School of Law

JAMES J. WHITE
Professor of Law, University of Michigan

THE LAW OF THE WORLD TRADE ORGANIZATION (WTO)

DOCUMENTS, CASES & ANALYSIS

Second Edition

■ ■ ■

By

Petros C. Mavroidis
*Edwin B. Parker Professor Foreign and Comparative Law,
Columbia University School of Law, &
Professor of Law
University of Neuchâtel*

and

Mark Wu
*Assistant Professor of Law
Harvard Law School*

AMERICAN CASEBOOK SERIES®

WEST®

Mat #41405051

This publication was created to provide you with accurate and authoritative information concerning the subject matter covered; however, this publication was not necessarily prepared by persons licensed to practice law in a particular jurisdiction. The publisher is not engaged in rendering legal or other professional advice and this publication is not a substitute for the advice of an attorney. If you require legal or other expert advice, you should seek the services of a competent attorney or other professional.

Nothing contained herein is intended or written to be used for the purpose of 1) avoiding penalties imposed under the federal Internal Revenue Code, or 2) promoting, marketing or recommending to another party any transaction or matter addressed herein.

American Casebook Series is a trademark registered in the U.S. Patent and Trademark Office.

© 2010 Thomson Reuters
© 2013 LEG, Inc. d/b/a West Academic Publishing
    610 Opperman Drive
    St. Paul, MN 55123
    1–800–313–9378

West, West Academic Publishing, and West Academic are trademarks of West Publishing Corporation, used under license.

Printed in the United States of America

ISBN: 978–0–314–28721–2

ACKNOWLEDGMENTS

In the second edition of our Casebook, we continue to strive to offer a comprehensive, yet relatively accessible, book on WTO law that could be of use to both un-initiated students as well as those looking for the latest developments in a specific area of WTO law. The book would not have seen the light of the day without the help of many individuals who responded beyond the call of duty and helped us with their critical remarks. At the WTO, Cato Adrian, Rob Anderson, Willie Chatsika, Diwakar Dixit, Edwini Kessie, Mark Koulen, Juan–Alberto Marchetti, Andrea Mastromatteo, Wolf Meier-Ewert, Julie Pain, Maria Pereyra, Majda Petschen, Sergios Stamnas, Hannu Wager, Erik N. Wijkström, and Rhian-Mary Wood-Richards helped us immensely through their comments but also by pointing to us useful documents that we have referred to in this volume. Åke Linden, and Jan–Eirik Sørensen, both ex-WTO officials, shared with us their experience over the years working with in different divisions of the WTO. Their help has been invaluable as we learned a lot from them regarding the earlier stages of GATT integration. Kyle Bagwell, Jagdish Bhagwati, Chad P. Bown, Bill Davey, Daniel Gervais, Gene M. Grossman, Bernard M. Hoekman, Henrik Horn, Rob Howse, Doug Irwin, David Palmeter, Tom Prusa, Kamal Saggi, André Sapir, Bob Staiger, Alan Sykes, Jasper–Martijn Wauters, and Robert Wolfe, long time collaborators and friends, graciously shared their immense expertise with us. Steve Charnovitz, and Jeff Dunoff read drafts of chapters and provided us with valuable comments. Dozens of interviews with GATT 'old hands' helped us get a better grasp of the negotiating history of various provisions: at the risk of forgetting some we acknowledge the generous help we received in this respect from Julian Arkell, Bob Cassidy, John Croome, Dick Cunningham, Dorothy Dwoskin, Murray Gibbs, Tom Graham, John Greenwald, David Hartridge, Gary Horlick, Felipe Jaramillo, Mario Kakabadse, Abdel-Hamid Mamdouh, John Richardson, Gary Sampson, Jonathan Scheele, Dick Self, Harsha Singh, Jorge Vigano, David Walker, Bruce Wilson, and Rufus Yerxa. Finally, we thank our research assistants who have worked with us on this volume.

This book is meant for students of WTO law. The questions, comments, and suggestions of our students at Columbia and Harvard Law Schools have helped shape its content. It is to them and all future students of the WTO that this volume is dedicated.

PETROS C. MAVROIDIS
MARK WU

REFERENCES

Abbott, Frederick, Thomas Cottier, Francis Gurry. 2007. *International Intellectual Property in an Integrated World Economy*. Aspen Publishing: New York.

Anderson, Robert D. 2011. Reflections on Bagwell and Staiger in Light of the Revised WTO Agreement on Government Procurement. Mimeo.

Antras, Pol, and Robert W. Staiger. 2012. Offshoring and the Role of Trade Agreements, *American Economic Review*, 102(7): 3140–3183.

Arkell, Julian. 1990. *The Role of Services in Socio-economic Transformation and the Integration of Western and Eastern Europe*, Institute for World Economics: Budapest, Hungary.

Arrowsmith, Sue. 2005. *The Law of Public and Utilities Procurement*, Sweet and Maxwell: London.

Arvis, Jean-François, Monica Alina Mustra, Lauri Ojala, Ben Shepherd, Daniel Saslavsky. 2012. Connecting to Compete 2012, Trade Logistics in the Global Economy, The World Bank: Washington D.C.

Avi-Yonah, Reuben and J. B. Slemrod. 2002. (How) Should Trade Agreements Deal with Income Tax Issues? *Taxation Law Review*, 55: 533–554.

Bagchi, Sanjoy. 2001. *International Trade Policy in Textiles, Fifty Years of Protectionism*, ITCB: Geneva.

Bagwell, Kyle, and Petros C. Mavroidis. 2007. US-Section 129: Beating Around (the) Bush, pp. pp.315–338 in Henrik Horn and Petros C. Mavroidis (eds.), *The WTO Case-Law of 2001–3: The American Law Institute Reporters' Studies*, Cambridge University Press: Cambridge, UK.

Bagwell, Kyle, and Petros C. Mavroidis. 2010. Too Much, Too Little, ... Too Late? pp. 168–171 in Kyle W. Bagwell, George A. Bermann, and Petros C. Mavroidis (eds.), *Law and Economics of Contingent Protection in International Trade*, Cambridge University Press: Cambridge, UK.

Bagwell, Kyle, Petros C. Mavroidis and Robert W. Staiger. 2002. It is All About Market Access, *American Journal of International Law*, 96: 56–76.

References

Bagwell, Kyle, Petros C. Mavroidis and Robert W. Staiger. 2005. The Case for Tradable Remedies in the WTO, pp. 395–414 in Simon Evenett and Bernard Hoekman (eds.), *Economic Development and Multilateral Trade Cooperation*, Palgrave Macmillan and the World Bank: Washington, DC.

Bagwell, Kyle and Robert W. Staiger. 2002. *The Economics of the World Trading System*, MIT Press: Cambridge, MA.

Bagwell Kyle, and Robert W. Staiger. 2011. Can the Doha Round Be a Development Round? Setting a Place at the Table. *Mimeo*.

Bagwell, Kyle, and Alan O. Sykes. 2007. Chile-Price Band, pp. pp.436–460 in Henrik Horn and Petros C. Mavroidis (eds.), *The WTO Case-Law of 2001–3: The American Law Institute Reporters' Studies*, Cambridge University Press: Cambridge, UK.

Bagwell, Kyle, and Alan O. Sykes. 2007a. India-Measures Affecting the Automobile Sector, pp. pp.461–481 in Henrik Horn and Petros C. Mavroidis (eds.), *The WTO Case-Law of 2001–3: The American Law Institute Reporters' Studies*, Cambridge University Press: Cambridge, UK.

Balassa, Bela. 1966. Tariff Reductions and Trade in Manufactures among the Industrial Countries, *American Economic Review*, 56: 466–473.

Balassa, Bela. 1967. Trade Creation and Trade Diversion in the European Common Market, Economic Journal, 77: 1–21.

Balassa, Bela. 1975. *European Economic Integration,* North Holland: Amsterdam, The Netherlands.

Baldwin, Richard E. 1992. Measurable Dynamic Gains from Trade, *Journal of Political Economy*, 100 : 162–174.

Baldwin, Richard E. 1993. On the Measurement of Dynamic Effects of Integration, *Empirica*, 20: 129–145.

Baldwin, Richard E. 1995. A Domino Theory of Regionalism, pp. 25–48 in Richard E. Baldwin, Pertti Haaparanta, and Jiakko Kiander (eds.), *Expanding Membership of the European Union*, Cambridge University Press: New York.

Baldwin, Richard E. 1997. The Causes of Regionalism, *The World Economy*, 20: 865–888.

Baldwin, Richard E. 2008. Sequencing and Depth of Regional Economic Integration: Lessons for the Americas from Europe, *The World Economy*, 31: 5–30.

Baldwin, Richard, E. 2009. Integration of the North American Economy and New-Paradigm Globalisation, CEPR Discussion Papers 7523, C.E.P.R: London.

Baldwin, Robert E. 1970. *Non-tariff Distortions in International Trade*, Brookings Institution: Washington, DC.

Baltagi, Badi H., Peter Egger, and Michael Pfaffermayr. 2008. Estimating Regional Trade Agreement Effects on FDI in an Interdependent World, *Journal of Econometrics*, 145: 194–208.

Barfield, Claude. 2001. *Free Trade, Sovereignty, Democracy: The Future of the World Trade Organization,* American Enterprise Institute: Washington, DC.

Bartels, Lorand. 2002. Article XX of the GATT and the Problem of Extraterritorial Jurisdiction, *Journal of World Trade*, 36: 353–403.

Becker, Gary S. 1968. Crime and Punishment, *Journal of Political Economy*, 76: 169–217.

Berg, Terrence G. 1987. Trade in Services: Toward a 'Development Round' of GATT Negotiations Benefiting Both Developing and Industrialized States, *Harvard Journal of International Law*, 28: 1–30.

Berry, Steve, Jim Levinsohn, and Ariel Pakes. 1999. Voluntary Export Restraints on Automobiles: Evaluating a Trade Policy, *American Economic Review*, 89: 400–430.

Beviglia-Zampetti, Americo. 2000. Market Access through Mutual Recognition, pp. 283–306 in Pierre Sauvé, and Robert Stern (eds.), *The GATS 2000, New Directions in Services Trade Liberalization*, Brookings: Washington, DC.

Beviglia-Zampetti, Americo. 2000a. Mutual Recognition in the Transatlantic Context: Some Reflections on Future Negotiations, pp. 303–328 in Thomas Cottier and Petros C. Mavroidis (eds.), *Regulatory Barriers and the Principle of Non-discrimination in World Trade Law*, University of Michigan Press: Ann Arbor, MI.

Bhagwati, Jagdish. 1987. International Trade in Services and its Relevance for Economic Development, pp. 3–34 *in Orio Giarini (ed.). The Emerging Services Economy*, Pergamon Press: New York.

Bhagwati, Jagdish. 1989. *The Role of Services in Development*, pp. 5–8 in Services and Development, The Role of Foreign Direct Investment and Trade, United Nations Centre on Transnational Corporations, UN Doc. ST/CTC/95.

Bhagwati, Jagdish. 2002. The Unilateral Freeing of Trade Versus Reciprocity,' pp 1–30 in Jagdish Bhagwati (ed.), *Going Alone: The Case For Relaxed Reciprocity in Freeing Trade*, MIT Press: Cambridge, MA.

Bhagwati, Jagdish. 2008. *Termites in the World Trading System*, Oxford University Press: New York, NY.

Bhagwati, Jagdish and Petros C. Mavroidis. 2004. Killing the Byrd Amendment with the Right Stone, *The World Trade Review*, 3: 1–9.

Bhagwati, Jagdish and Arvid Panagariya. 1999. Preferential Trading Areas and Multilateralism—Strangers, Friends, or Foes, pp. 33–100 in Jagdish Bhagwati, Pravin Krishna and Arvind Panagariya, *Trading Blocks*, MIT Press: Cambridge, MA.

Bhala, Raj. 2004. Saudi Arabia, the WTO, and American Trade Law and Policy, *The International Lawyer*, 34: 741–812.

Blandford, David, and David Orden. 2011. United States, pp. 97–152 in David Orden, David Blandford, and Tim Josling (eds.), *WTO Disciplines on Agricultural Support: Seeking a Fair Basis for Trade*, Cambridge University Press: New York.

Blank, Annet and Gabrielle Marceau. 1997. A History of Multilateral Negotiations on Procurement: from ITO to WTO, pp. 31–56 in Bernard M. Hoekman and Petros C. Mavroidis (eds.), *Law and Policy in Public Purchasing*, University of Michigan Press: Ann Arbor, MI.

Bombach, Kara M. 2001. Can South Africa Fight AIDS? Reconciling the South African Medicines and Related Substances Act with the TRIPS Agreement. *Boston University International Law Journal.* 19: 273–306.

Bown, Chad P. 2010. China's WTO Entry: Antidumping, Safeguards, and Dispute Settlement, pp. 281–337 in Robert C. Feenstra, and Shang-Jin Wei (eds.), *China's Growing Role in World Trade*, University of Chicago Press: Chicago, IL.

Bown, Chad P., and Niall Meagher. 2010. Mexico-Olive Oil: Remedy Without a Cause? pp.85–116 in Henrik Horn and Petros C. Mavroidis (eds.), *The WTO Case-Law of 2008: The American Law Institute Reporters' Studies*, Cambridge University Press: Cambridge, UK.

Bown, Chad P. and Alan O. Sykes. 2008. The Zeroing Issue: a Critical Analysis of US—Softwood Lumber V, pp.121–142 in Henrik Horn and Petros C. Mavroidis (eds.), *The WTO Case-Law of 2004–5: The American Law Institute Reporters' Studies*, Cambridge University Press: Cambridge, UK.

Bown, Chad P., and Joel P. Trachtman. 2009. Brazil-Measures Affecting Imports of Retreaded Tyres: a Balancing Act, pp.85–136 in Henrik Horn and Petros C. Mavroidis (eds.), *The WTO Case-Law of 2006–7: The American Law Institute Reporters' Studies*, Cambridge University Press: Cambridge, UK.

Bradley, Jane A. 1987.Intellectual Property Rights, Investment, and Trade in Services in the Uruguay Round: Laying the Foundations, *Stanford Journal of International Law*, 23: 57–98.

Breene, John. 1993. Agriculture pp. 123–254 in *Terence P. Stewart (ed.), The GATT Uruguay Round: a Negotiating History (1986–1992)*, Kluwer Law: Deventer, the Netherlands.

Brenton, Paul and Miriam Manchin. 2003. Making EU Trade Agreements Work: the Role of Rules of Origin, *The World Economy*, 26: 755–769.

Brewster, Rachel. 2011. The Surprising Benefits to Developing Countries of Linking International Trade and Intellectual Property. *Chicago Journal of International Law*, 12: 1–54.

Brink, Lars. 2001. The WTO Disciplines on Domestic Support, pp. 23–60 in David Orden, David Blandford, and Tim Josling (eds.), *WTO Disciplines on Agricultural Support: Seeking a Fair Basis for Trade*, Cambridge University Press: New York.

Brittan, Leon. 2000. *A Diet for Brussels, The Changing Face of Europe*, Little, Brown and Company: London, UK.

Brock, William E. 1982. A Simple Plan for Negotiating on Trade in Services, *The World Economy*, 5: 229–240.

Broda Christian, Nuno Limão and David E. Weinstein. 2008. Optimal Tariffs and Market Power: the Evidence, *American Economic Review*, 98: 2031–2065.

Broda Christian, and David E. Weinstein. 2006. Globalization and the Gains from Variety, *Quarterly Journal of Economics*, 121: 541–585.

REFERENCES

Bronckers, Marco C.E.J. 1985. *Selective Safeguard Measures in Multilateral Trade Relations*, Springer: New York.

Bronckers, Marco C.E.J. 1987. A Legal Analysis of Protectionist Measures Affecting Japanese Imports into the European Community—Revisited pp. 57–120 in E.L.M. Völker (ed.), *Protectionism and the European Community*, Kluwer: Deventer, the Netherlands.

Bronckers, Marco C.E.J. 1997. Priviatized Utilities under the WTO and the EU Procurement Rules, pp. 243–260 in Bernard M. Hoekman and Petros C. Mavroidis (eds.), *Law And Policy In Public Purchasing*, University of Michigan Press: Ann Arbor, MI.

Brou Daniel, and Michele Ruta. 2011. *A Commitment Theory of Subsidies Agreements,* Mimeo.

Broude, Tomer. 2007. Genetically Modified Rules: an Awkward Rule-Exception-Right Distinction in EC-Biotech, *The World Trade Review*, 6: 215–232.

Brown, Winthrop. 1950. *The United States and the Restoration of World Trade: an Analysis and Appraisal of the ITO Charter and the General Agreement on Tariffs and Trade*, Brookings Institution: Washington, DC.

Büthe, Tim, and Walter Mattli. 2011. *The New Global Rulers*, Princeton University Press: Princeton, NJ.

Busch, Marc L. and Eric Reinhardt. 2001. Bargaining in the Shadow of the Law: Early Settlement in GATT/WTO Disputes, *Fordham International Law Journal,* 24 : 158–72.

Busch, Marc L. and Eric Reinhardt. 2002. Testing International Trade Law: Empirical Studies of GATT/WTO Dispute Settlement, pp.457–481 in Daniel M. Kennedy and James D. Southwick (eds.), *The Political Economy of International Trade Law: Essays in Honor of Robert Hudec,* Cambridge University Press: Cambridge, MA.

Busch, Marc L. and Eric Reinhardt. 2005. Three's a Crowd: The Influence of Third Parties on GATT/WTO Dispute Settlement. *Mimeo.* Georgetown University.

Cadot, Olivier, Céline Carrère, Jaime de Melo and Bolormaa Tumurchudur. 2005. Product Specific Rules of Origin in EU and US Preferential Trading Arrangements: an Assessment, *The World Trade Review*, 25: 199–224.

Cadot, Olivier, Jaime de Melo. 2008. Why OECD Countries Should Reform Rules of Origin, *The World Bank Research Observer*, 33 : 77–105.

Caliendo, Lorenzo and Fernando Parro. 2009. Estimates of the Trade and Welfare Effects of NAFTA. *Mimeo*, University of Chicago: Chicago, IL.

Candau, Fabie, and Sébastien Jean. 2009. What are European Union Trade Preferences Worth for Sub-Saharan African and Other Developing Countries ?, pp. 65–102 in Bernard M. Hoekman, Will Martin, and Carlos A. Primo Braga (eds.), *Trade Preference Erosion, Measurement and Policy Response,* Palgrave MacMillan and the World Bank: Washington, DC.

Chakravarthy, S., and Kamala Dawar. 2011. India's Possible Accession to the Agreement on Government Procurement: What are the Pros and Cons? pp. 117–139 in Sue Arrowsmith and Robert D. Anderson (eds.), *The WTO Regime on Government Procurement: Challenge and Reform*, Cambridge University Press: Cambridge, UK.

Chang, Ha-Joon. 2002. *Kicking Away the Ladder: Development Strategy in Historical Perspective.* Anthem Press: London.

Charnovitz, Steve. 1991. Exploring the Environmental Exceptions in GATT Article XX. *Journal of World Trade,* 25: 37–55.

Charnovitz, Steve. 1998. The Moral Exception in Trade Policy, *Virginia Journal of International Law*, 38: 689–732.

Charnovitz, Steve. 2002. The Law of Environmental PPMs in the WTO: Debunking the Myth of Illegality, *Yale Journal of International Law*, 27: 59–109.

Charnovitz, Steve. 2007. Exploring the law of WTO accession, pp. 855–944 in Merit E. Janow, Victoria Donaldson, and Alan Yanovich (eds.), *The WTO: Governance, Dispute Settlement, and Developing Countries,* Juris Publishing: Huntington, NY.

Chase, Kerry A. 2006. Multilateralism Compromised: The Mysterious Origins of GATT Article XXIV, *The World Trade Review* 5: 1–30.

Conconi Paola, and Robrt L. Howse. 2012. Panel Report on EC-IT, *The World Trade Review*, 11: 223–256.

Conrad, Christiane R. 2011. *Processes and Production Methods (PPMs) in WTO Law, Interfacing Trade and Social Goods*, Cambridge University Press: Cambridge, UK.

Conrad, Christiane R. 2007. The *EC-Biotech* Dispute and Applicability of the SPS Agreement: Are the Panel's Findings Built on Shaky Ground?, *The World Trade Review*, 6: 233–248.

Cooter, Robert. 1984. Prices and Sanctions, Columbia Law Review, 84: 1523–1560.

Coppens, Dominique. 2012. *WTO Disciplines on Subsidies and Countervailing Measures: Balancing Policy Space and Legal Constraints in International Law*, Cambridge University Press: Cambridge, UK.

Corden, Max W. 1971. *The Theory of Protection*, Oxford University Press: London.

Correa, Carlos M. 2007. *Trade Related Aspects of Intellectual Property Rights: A Commentary on the TRIPS Agreement.* Oxford Univ. Press: Oxford, UK.

Croley, Steve, and John H. Jackson. 1996. WTO Dispute Procedures, Sstandard of Review, and Deference to National Governance, *American Journal of International Law*, 90: 193–213.

Croome John. 1995. *Reshaping the World Trading System*, The World Trade Organization: Geneva.

Crowley, Meredith. 2010. Why are Safeguards Needed in a Trade Agreement? pp. 379–400 in *Kyle W. Bagwell, George A. Bermann, and Petros C. Mavroidis (eds.), Law and Economics of Contingent Protection in International Trade*, Cambridge University Press: Cambridge, UK.

Crowley, Meredith and Robert L. Howse. 2010. US-Stainless Steel (Mexico) pp.117–150 in *Henrik Horn and Petros C. Mavroidis (eds.), The WTO Case-Law of 2008: The American Law Institute Reporters' Studies*, Cambridge University Press: Cambridge, UK.

Crowley, Meredith and David Palmeter. 2009. US-Countervailing Duties on Dynamic Random Access Memories from Korea, pp.259–272 in *Henrik Horn and Petros C. Mavroidis (eds.), The WTO Case-Law of 2006–7: The American Law Institute Reporters' Studies*, Cambridge University Press: Cambridge, UK.

Curzon, Gerard. 1965. *Multilateral Commercial Diplomacy: The GATT and Its Impact on National Commercial Policies*, Martinus Nijhoff: Amsterdam.

Czako, Judith, Johan Human, and Jorge Miranda. 2003. *A Handbook on Anti-Dumping Investigations*, Cambridge University Press: Cambridge, UK.

Daly, Michael. 1998. Investment Incentives and the Multilateral Agreement on Investment, *Journal of World Trade*, 32: 5–41.

Dam, Kenneth W. 1963. Regional Economic Arrangements and the GATT: The Legacy of Misconception, *University of Chicago Law Review*, 30: 615–665.

Dam, Kenneth W. 1970. *The GATT: Law and International Economic Organization*, University of Chicago Press: Chicago, IL.

D' Andrea Tyson, Laura. 1992. *Who's Bashing Whom? Trade Conflict in High-Technology Industries,* Institute for International Economics: Washington, DC.

Das, Dilip K. 2001. *Global Trading System at the Cross-roads*, Routledge: London, UK.

Das, Kasturi. 2006.*GATS Negotiation and India: Evolution and State of Play*, Centre for Trade and Development (CENTAD): New Delhi.

Davey, William, J. 1988. Article XVII GATT : An Overview, pp. 17–36 in Thomas Cottier, and Petros C. Mavroidis (eds.), *State Trading in the Twenty-First Century,* University of Michigan Press: Ann Arbor, MI.

Davey, William J., and André Sapir. 2010. US-Subsidies on Upland Cotton Recourse to Article 21.5 by Brazil, pp.181–200 in Henrik Horn and Petros C. Mavroidis (eds.), *The WTO Case-Law of 2008: The American Law Institute Reporters' Studies*, Cambridge University Press: Cambridge, UK.

Davies, Gareth. 2007. Morality Clauses and Decision Making in Situations of Scientific Uncertainty: The Case of GMOs, *World Trade Review*, 6: 249–264.

Dean, Judith M., and John Wainio. 2009. Quantifying the Value of US Tariff Preferences for Developing Countries, pp. 29–64 in Bernard M. Hoekman, Will Martin, and Carlos A. Primo Braga (eds.), *Trade Preference Erosion, Measurement and Policy Response,* Palgrave MacMillan and the World Bank: Washington, DC.

Deardorff, Alan V. 1980. The General Validity of the Law of Comparative Advantage, *Journal of Political Economy*, 88: 941–957.

Deardorff, Alan V. and Robert M. Stern. 1998. *Measurement of Non-Tariff Barriers*, University of Michigan Press: Ann Arbor, MI.

De Bièvre, Paul, R. Dybkaer, A. Fajgelj, B. Hibbert. 2011. Metrological Traceability of Measurement Results in Chemistry–Concepts and Implementation. *Mimeo.*

Deere, Carolyn. 2009. *The Implementation Game.* Oxford Univ. Press: Oxford, UK.

Deese, David A. 2007. *World Trade Politics: Power, Principles, and Leadership*, Routledge: London and New York.

De Jong, David N. and Maria Ripoli. 2006. 'Tariffs and Growth: An Empirical Exploration of Contingent Relationships', *The Review of Economic Statistics*, 88: 625–40.

Delimatsis, Panagiotis. 2008. *International Trade in Services and Domestic Regulations: Necessity, Transparency and Regulatory Diversity, International Economic Law Series*, Oxford University Press: Oxford, UK.

Démaret, Paul and R. Stewardson. 1994. Border Tax Adjustments under GATT and EC Law and General Implications for Environmental Taxes, *Journal of World Trade*, 28: 5–65.

Demelo, Jaime, and David Tarr. 1992. A *General Equilibrium Analysis of US Foreign Trade Policy*, MIT Press: Cambridge, MA.

Diakantoni, Antonia, and H. Eskaith. 2009. Mapping the Tariff Waters, *WTO Working Paper Series*, ERSD: 2009–13.

Diakosavvas, Dimitrios. 2002. How to Measure the Level of Agricultural Support: Comparison of the Methodologies Applied by the OECD and WTO, pp. 217–245 in *Agricultural Policies in China After WTO Accession*, OECD: Paris.

Dickerson, Kitty G. 1995. *Textiles and Apparel in the Global Economy*, Second Edition, Merrill: Englewood Cliffs, NJ.

Diego-Fernandez Mateo. 2008. Trade Negotiations Make Strange Bed-Fellows, *The World Trade Review*, 7: 423–454.

Dinwoodie, Graeme and Rochelle Cooper Dreyfuss. 2009. Designing a Global Intellectual Property System Responsive to Change: The WTO, WIPO, and Beyond. *Houston Law Review.* 46: 1187–1234.

Drake, William J. and Kalypso Nicolaidis. 2000. Global Electronic Commerce and GATS: the Millennium Round and Beyond, in Pierre Sauvé and Robert Stern (eds.), *GATS 2000: New Directions in Services Trade Liberalization,* Brookings Institution Press: Washington, DC.

Drebentsov Vladimir, and Constantine Michalopoulos. 1998. State Trading in Russia, pp. 303–318 in Thomas Cottier, and Petros C. Mavroidis (eds.), *State Trading in the Twenty-First Century,* University of Michigan Press : Ann Arbor, MI.

Dunoff, Jeffrey. 1999. The Death of the Trade Regime, *European Journal of International Law,* 10: 733–760.

Dunoff, Jeffrey. 2006. Lotus Eaters: The Varietals Dispute, the SPS Agreement, and WTO Dispute Resolution, pp. 153–189 in George Bermann and Petros C. Mavroidis (eds.), *Trade and Health in the WTO,* Cambridge University Press: Cambridge, MA.

Ehring, Lothar. 2002. De facto Discrimination in World Trade Law: National and Most Favoured Nation Treatment—or Equal Treatment, *Journal of World Trade* 36: 921–77.

Ehring, Lothar. 2011. Article IV of the GATT: an Obsolete Provision or Still a Basis for Cultural Policy? pp. 96–118 in *Inge Govaere, Reinhard Quick, and Marco Bronckers (eds.), Trade and Competition Law in the EU and Beyond,* Edward Elgar: Cheltenham, UK.

Esserman, Susan and Robert Howse. 2004. Trade Disputes Require Fairer Arbitration, *The Financial Times,* 12 September 2004. **Estevadeordal, Antoni and L.J. Garay.** 1996. Protection, Preferential Tariffs, and Rules of Origin in America', *Integration and Trade:* 2–25.

Ethier, Wilfred J. 2001. *Punishments and Dispute Settlement in Trade Agreements,* Copenhagen: EPRU.

Evenett, Simon, and Bernard M. Hoekman. 2007. International Disciplines on Public Procurement: Teaching Materials. Mimeo.

Falkenberg, Karl. 1997. Comments, pp. 457–464 in Paul Démaret, Jean-François Bellis, and Gonzalo Garcia-Jimenez (eds.), *Regionalism and Multilateralism after the Uruguay Round,* European University Press: Brussels.

Feddersen, Christoph T. 1998. Focusing on Substantive Law in International Economic Relations: the Public Morals of GATT's Article XX(a) and "Conventional" Rules of Interpretation, *Minnesota Journal of Global Trade,* 7: 75–101.

Feenstra, Robert C., Benjamin R. Mandel, Marshall B. Reinsdorf, and Matthew J. Slaughter. 2009. Effects of Terms of Trade and Tariff Changes on the Measurement of US Productivity Growth, NBER Working Paper No. 15592.

Feinberg, Robert. 2005. US Antidumping Enforcement and Macroeconomic Indicators Revisited: do Petitioners Learn?, *Review of World Economics,* 141: 612–22.

Feketekuty, Geza. 1988. *International Trade in Services: an Overview and Blueprint for Negotiations,* American Enterprise Institute: Washington, DC.

Feketekuty, Gaza. 1988a. The Uruguay Round: the US Perspective, pp. 189–190 in *Dorothy I. Riddle (ed.), Information Economy and Development,* Friedrich-Ebert-Stiftung: Bonn, Germany.

Finger, Michael (ed.) 1993. *Antidumping: How It Works And Who Gets Hurt,* University of Michigan Press: Ann Arbor, MI.

Finger, Michael J. 2010. A Special Safeguard Mechanism for Agricultural Products: What Experience With Other GATT/WTO Safeguards Will Tell Us About What Might Work, *The World Trade Review,* 9: 280–318.

Finger, Michael J., and Julio J. Nogues. 2006. *Safeguards and antidumping in Latin American trading liberalization: fighting fire with fire,* World Bank: Washington, DC.

Fink, Carsten and Keith Maskus (eds.). 2005. *Intellectual Property and Development: Lessons from Recent Economic Research.* World Bank / Oxford Univ. Press: Washington, DC.

Footer, Mary E. 2007. Post-normal Science in the Multilateral Trading System: Social Science Expertise and the EC-Biotech Panel, *World Trade Review,* 6: 281–298.

Foster, Caroline E. 2011. *Science and the Precautionary Principle in International Courts and Tribunals,* Cambridge University Press: Cambridge, UK.

Francois, Joseph F., Douglas Nelson and David Palmeter. 1997. Public Procurement in the United States: a post-Uruguay round Perspective, pp. 105–124 in Bernard M. Hoekman and Petros C. Mavroidis (eds.), *Law and Policy in Public Purchasing,* University of Michigan Press: Ann Arbor, MI.

Francois, Joseph F., and David Palmeter. 2008. US-Countervailing Duty Investigation on DRAMS, pp.219–230 in *Henrik Horn and Petros C. Mavroidis (eds.), The WTO Case-Law of 2004–5: The American Law Institute Reporters' Studies,* Cambridge University Press: Cambridge, UK.

Garcia, Frank J. 2006. The Salmon Case: Evolution of Balancing Mechanisms for Non-Trade Values in WTO, pp. 133–152 in *George A. Bermann, and Petros C. Mavroidis (eds.), Trade and Human Health and Safety, Columbia Studies in WTO Law and Policy*, Cambridge University Press: Cambridge, UK.

Gardner, Richard N. 1956. *Sterling-Dollar Diplomacy*, Columbia University Press: New York.

Gay, Daniel. 2005. Vanuatu's Suspended Accession Bid: Second Thoughts? Pp. 590–606 in Peter Gallagher, Patrick A. Low and Andrew L. Stoller (eds), *Managing the challenges of WTO participation, 45 case studies*, Cambridge University Press: Cambridge, UK.

Genasci, Matthew. 2008. Border Tax Adjustments and Emissions Trading: the Implications of International Trade Law for Policy Design, *Carbon and Climate Law Review*, 2: 33–42.

Georgopoulos, Aris. 2000. The System of Remedies in Enforcing Public Procurement Rules in Greece, *Public Procurement Law Review*, 9:75–93.

Gerhart, Peter M. 2007. The Tragedy of TRIPS. *Michigan State Law Review*. 2007: 143–184.

Gervais, Daniel (ed.). 2007. *Intellectual Property, Trade, and Development: Strategies to Optimize Economic Development in a TRIPS-Plus Era*. Oxford Univ. Press: Oxford, UK.

Gervais, Daniel. 2008. *The TRIPS Agreement: Drafting History and Analysis* 3rd ed. Sweet & Maxwell: London.

Gibbs, Murray, and Mina Mashayekhi. 1991. Development in the Uruguay Round Negotiations on T*rade in Services, Services in Asia and Pacific: Selected Papers, Volume Two,* UNCTAD/ITP/151, UNCTAD/UNDP: Geneva.

Gill, Henry. 1988. The Uruguay Round: Perspectives from Latin America, pp. 184–188 in Dorothy I. Riddle (ed.), *Information Economy and Development*, Friedrich-Ebert-Stiftung: Bonn, Germany.

Ginsburg, Jane C. 1990. A Tale of Two Copyrights: Literary Property in Revolutionary France and America. *Tulane Law Review*. 64: 991–1031.

Goldstein, Paul and Bernt Hugenholtz. 2010. *International Copyright* (2d ed). Oxford Univ. Press: Oxford, UK.

Gopinath, Munisamy. 2011. India, pp. 277–309 in David Orden, David Blandford, and Tim Josling (eds.), *WTO Disciplines on Agricultural Support: Seeking a Fair Basis for Trade*, Cambridge University Press: Cambridge, UK.

Graham, Thomas J. 1978. The US generalized System of Preferences for Developing Countries: International Innovation and the Art of the Possible, *American Journal of International Law*, 72: 513–540.

Graham, Thomas R. 1979. Results of the Tokyo Round, *Georgia Journal of International and Comparative Law*, 9: 153–175.

Grando, Michelle T. 2009. *Evidence, Proof, and Fact-Finding in WTO Dispute Settlement*, Oxford University Press: Oxford, UK.

Green, Andrew, and Michael Trebilcock. 2010. The Enduring Problem of World Trade Organization Export Subsidies Rules, pp. 116–167 in Kyle W. Bagwell, George A. Bermann, and Petros C. Mavroidis (eds.), *Law and Economics of Contingent Protection in International Trade,* Cambridge University Press: Cambridge, UK.

Grossman, Gene M. 1986. Imports as a Cause of Injury: the Case of the US Steel Industry, *Journal of International Economics*, 20: 201–223.

Grossman, Gene M., and Elhanan Helpman. 1995. The Politics of Free Trade Agreements, *American Economic Review*, 85: 667–690.

Grossman, Gene M., Henrik Horn, and Petros C. Mavroidis. 2012. *Principles of World Trade Law: National Treatment*, ALI Study, Cambridge University Press: Cambridge, UK.

Grossman, Gene M., and Petros C. Mavroidis. 2007. Here Today, Gone Tomorrow ? pp. 183–213 in Henrik Horn, and Petros C. Mavroidis (eds.), *The American Law Institute Reporters' Studies on WTO Case Law*, Cambridge University Press: Cambridge, UK.

Grossman, Gene M., and Petros C. Mavroidis. 2007a. Would've or Should've? Impaired Benefits Due to Copyright Infringement, pp. 294–314 in Henrik Horn, and Petros C. Mavroidis (eds.), *The American Law Institute Reporters' Studies on WTO Case Law*, Cambridge University Press: Cambridge, UK.

Grossman, Gene M., and Petros C. Mavroidis. 2007b. The Sounds of Silence, pp. 367–380 in Henrik Horn, and Petros C. Mavroidis (eds.), *The American Law Institute Reporters' Studies on WTO Case Law*, Cambridge University Press: Cambridge, UK.

Grossman, Gene M., and Petros C. Mavroidis. 2007c. Recurring Misunderstandings of Non-Recurring Subsidies, pp. 381–390 in Henrik Horn, and Petros C. Mavroidis (eds.), *The American Law Institute Reporters' Studies on WTO Case Law*, Cambridge University Press: Cambridge, UK.

Grossman, Gene M., and Petros C. Mavroidis. 2007d. Not for Attribution, pp. 402–435 in Henrik Horn, and Petros C. Mavroidis (eds.), *The American Law Institute Reporters' Studies on WTO Case Law*, Cambridge University Press: Cambridge, UK.

Grossman, Gene and Esteban Rossi-Hansberg. 2007. The Rise of Offshoring: It's Not Wine for Cloth Anymore, Mimeo.

Grossman, Gene M. and Alan Sykes. 2005. A Preference for Development: the Law and Economics of GSP, *The World Trade Review*, 4: 41–68.

Grossman, Gene M., and Alan O. Sykes. 2007. EC – Antidumping Duties on Imports of Cotton-Type Bed Linen from India, pp. 581–600 in Henrik Horn, and Petros C. Mavroidis (eds.), *The American Law Institute Reporters' Studies on WTO Case Law*, Cambridge University Press: Cambridge, UK..

Grossman, Gene M., and Alan O. Sykes. 2011. 'Optimal' Retaliation in the WTO – a Commentary on the Upland-Cotton Arbitration, pp.133–164 in Henrik Horn and Petros C. Mavroidis (eds.), *The WTO Case-Law of 2009: The American Law Institute Reporters' Studies*, Cambridge University Press: Cambridge, UK.

Grossman, Gene M., and Jasper Wauters. 2008. Sunset Reviews of AD Measures on OCTG from Argentina: a Cloudy Sunset, pp.235–264 in Henrik Horn and Petros C. Mavroidis (eds.), *The WTO Case-Law of 2004–5: The American Law Institute Reporters' Studies*, Cambridge University Press: Cambridge, UK.

Gruszczynski, Lukasz. 2010. *Regulating Health and Environmental Risks under WTO Law: a Critical Analysis of the SPS Agreement*, Oxford University Press: New York City.

Guth, Eckart. 2012. The End of the Bananas Saga, *Journal of World Trade*, 46: 1–32.

Guzman, Andrew T., and Beth Simmons. 2005. Power Plays and Capacity Constraints: the Selection of Defendants in WTO Disputes, *Journal of Legal Studies*, 37: 557–580.

Hahn, Michael J. 1991. Vital Interests in the Law of the GATT, an Analysis of the GATT's Security Exception, *Michigan Journal of International Law*, 12: 558–584.

Haidt, Jonathan. 2001. The Emotional Dog and its Rational Tail: a Social Institutionist Approach to Moral Judgment, *Psychological Review*, 108: 814–834.

Helpman, Elhanan. 2011. *Understanding Global Trade*, The Belknap Press of Harvard University Press: Cambridge, MA.

Hemmendinger, Noel. 1969. Non-Tariff Trade Barriers, *American Society of International Law Proceedings*, 63: 204–211.

Hindley, Brian. 1980. Voluntary Export Restraints and the GATT's Main Escape Clause, *The World Economy*, 3: 313–341.

Hindley Brian. 1987. International Trade in Services: a Comment, pp. 35–39 *in* Orio Giarini (ed.). *The Emerging Services Economy*, Pergamon Press: New York.

Hoda, Anwarul. 2001. *Tariff Negotiations and Renegotiations Under the GATT and the WTO*, Cambridge University Press: Cambridge, UK.

Hoekman, Bernard M. 1995. Tentative First Steps: An Assessment of the Uruguay Round Agreement on Services, in Will Martin and L. Alan Winters (eds.), *The Uruguay Round and the Developing Economies,* World Bank Discussion Paper Series No. 307, Washington, DC.

Hoekman, Bernard M. 2005. Operationalizing the Concept of Policy Space in the WTO: Beyond Special and Differential Treatment, *Journal of International Economic Law*, 8: 405–424.

Hoekman, Bernard M., and Robert L. Howse. 2008. EC-Sugar, pp.149–178 in Henrik Horn and Petros C. Mavroidis (eds.), *The WTO Case-Law of 2004–5: The American Law Institute Reporters' Studies*, Cambridge University Press: Cambridge, UK.

Hoekman, Bernard M. and Michel Kostecki. 2009. *The Political Economy of the World Trading System*, (3rd ed.), Oxford University Press: Oxford, UK.

Hoekman, Bernard M. and Petros C. Mavroidis. 1996. Dumping, Antidumping and Antitrust, *Journal of World Trade* 30: 27–42.

Hoekman, Bernard M. and Petros C. Mavroidis. 1996a. Policy Externalities and High-Tech Rivalry, Competition and Multilateral Cooperation beyond the WTO, *Leiden Journal of International Law*, 9: 273–318.

Hoekman, Bernard M., and Petros C. Mavroidis. 2009. Nothing Dramatic (... Regarding Administration of Customs Laws), pp.31–44 in Henrik Horn and Petros C. Mavroidis (eds.), *The WTO Case-Law of 2006–7: The American Law Institute Reporters' Studies*, Cambridge University Press: Cambridge, UK.

Hoekman, Bernard M., and Joel P. Trachtman. 2008. Canada-Wheat: Discrimination, Non-Commercial Considerations, and the Right to Regulate State Trading Enterprises, pp.45–66 in Henrik Horn and Petros C. Mavroidis (eds.), *The WTO Case-Law of 2004–5: The American Law Institute Reporters' Studies*, Cambridge University Press: Cambridge, UK.

Hoekman, Bernard M., and Joel P. Trachtman. 2010. Continued Suspense: EC-Hormones and WTO Disciplines on Discrimination and Domestic Regulation pp.151–180 in Henrik Horn and Petros C. Mavroidis (eds.), *The WTO Case-Law of 2008: The American Law Institute Reporters' Studies*, Cambridge University Press: Cambridge, UK.

Hoekman, Bernard M., and Jasper Wauters. 2011. US Compliance with WTO Rulings on Zeroing in Antidumping, pp.5–44 in Henrik Horn and Petros C. Mavroidis (eds.), *The WTO Case-Law of 2009: The American Law Institute Reporters' Studies*, Cambridge University Press: Cambridge, UK.

Horlick, Gary and Peggy Clark. 1994. The 1994 WTO Subsidies Agreement, *World Competition*, 17: 41–54.

Horn, Henrik, Giovanni Maggi, and Robert W. Staiger. 2010. Trade Agreements as Endogenously Incomplete Contracts, *American Economic Review*, 100: 394–419.

Horn, Henrik, Louise Johannesson, and Petros C. Mavroidis. 2011. The WTO Dispute Settlement System (1995–2010): Some Descriptive Statistics, *Journal of World Trade*, 45: 1107–1138.

Horn, Henrik and Petros C. Mavroidis. 2001. Legal and Economic Aspects of MFN, *European Journal of Political Economy*, 17: 233–279.

Horn, Henrik and Petros C. Mavroidis. 2003. US—Lamb, pp.72–114 in Henrik Horn and Petros C. Mavroidis (eds.), *The WTO Case-Law of 2001: The American Law Institute Reporters' Studies*, Cambridge University Press: Cambridge, UK.

Horn, Henrik, and Petros C. Mavroidis. 2003a. National Health Regulations and the SPS Agreement: the WTO Case-Law of the Early Years, pp. 255–286 in Thomas Cottier and Petros C. Mavroidis (eds.), *The Role of the Judge in international Trade Regulation*, University of Michigan Press: Ann Arbor, MI.

Horn, Henrik and Petros C. Mavroidis. 2004. Still Hazy After All These Years: The Interpretation of National Treatment in the GATT/WTO Case-Law on Tax Discrimination, *European Journal of International Law*, 15: 39–69.

Horn, Henrik and Petros C. Mavroidis. 2005a. A Comment on US—Offset Act (Byrd Amendment), pp. in Henrik Horn and Petros C. Mavroidis (eds.), *The WTO Case-Law of 2003: The American Law Institute Reports' Studies*, Cambridge University Press: Cambridge, UK.

Horn, Henrik, and Petros C. Mavroidis. 2005b. What is a Subsidy?' pp. 220–47, in Henrik Horn and Petros C. Mavroidis (eds), *The WTO Case-Law of 2002, The American Law Institute Reporters' Studies*, Cambridge University Press: Cambridge.

Horn, Henrik and Petros C. Mavroidis. 2007a. EC – Tube or Pipe Fittings, pp. 657–699 in Henrik Horn & Petros C. Mavroidis (eds.) *The WTO Case Law*, Cambridge University Press: Cambridge, UK.

Horn, Henrik and Petros C. Mavroidis. 2008. The Permissible Reach of National Environmental Policies, *The Journal of World Trade*, 42: 1107–1178.

Horn, Henrik and Petros C. Mavroidis. 2009. Non-Discrimination, pp. 833–839 in Kenneth A. Reinert, R.S. Rajan, A.J. Glass and L.S. Davis (eds.), *Princeton Encyclopedia of the World Economy*, Princeton University Press, Princeton, NJ.

Horn, Henrik, Petros C. Mavroidis, and André Sapir. 2010. Beyond the WTO: An Anatomy of the EU and US Preferential Trade Agreements, *The World Economy*, 33: 1565–1588.

Horn, Henrik, Petros C. Mavroidis, and Erik N. Wijkstrom. 2013. In the Shadow of the DSU: Addressing Specific Trade Concerns in the WTO SPS and TBT Committees, IFN Working Paper No. 960.

Horn, Henrik, and Joseph H.H. Weiler. 2003. European Communities—Measures Affecting Asbestos and Asbestos-Containing Products, pp. 14–40 in Henrik Horn and Petros C. Mavroidis (eds.), *The WTO Case-Law of 2001: The American Law Institute Reports' Studies*, Cambridge University Press: Cambridge, UK.

Horn, Henrik, and Joseph H.H. Weiler. 2007. EC-Trade Description of Sardines: Textualism and its Discontent, pp. pp.551–578 in Henrik Horn and Petros C. Mavroidis (eds.), *The WTO Case-Law of 2001–3: The American Law Institute Reporters' Studies*, Cambridge University Press: Cambridge, UK.

Howse, Robert. 2010. Do the World Trade Organization Disciplines on Domestic Subsidies Make Sense? The Case for Legalizing Some Subsidies, pp. 85–102 in Kyle W. Bagwell, George A. Bermann, and Petros C. Mavroidis (eds.), *Law and Economics of Contingent Protection in International Trade*.

Howse, Robert L., and Henrik Horn. 2009. EC-Measures Affecting the Approval and Marketing of Biotech Products, pp.49–84 in Henrik Horn and Petros C. Mavroidis (eds.), *The WTO Case-Law of 2006–7: The American Law Institute Reporters' Studies*, Cambridge University Press: Cambridge, UK.

Howse, Robert L., and Damien J. Neven. 2007. US-Shrimp Recourse to Article 21.5 of the DSU by Malaysia, pp. pp.54–84 in Henrik Horn and Petros C. Mavroidis (eds.), *The WTO Case-Law of 2001–3: The American Law Institute Reporters' Studies*, Cambridge University Press: Cambridge, UK.

Howse, Robert L., and Damien J. Neven. 2007a. Mexico-Corn Syrup pp. pp.153–167 in Henrik Horn and Petros C. Mavroidis (eds.), *The WTO Case-Law of 2001–3: The American Law Institute Reporters' Studies*, Cambridge University Press: Cambridge, UK.

Howse, Robert L., and Damien J. Neven. 2007b. Argentina-Ceramic Tiles, pp. pp.168–182 in Henrik Horn and Petros C. Mavroidis (eds.), *The WTO Case-Law of 2001–3: The American Law Institute Reporters' Studies*, Cambridge University Press: Cambridge, UK.

Howse, Robert L., and Damien J. Neven. 2007c. US-Tax Treatment for FSC Recourse to Arbitration by the US under Article 22.6 of the DSU and Article 4.11 of the SCM Agreement pp. pp.339–366 in Henrik Horn and Petros C. Mavroidis (eds.), *The WTO Case-Law of 2001–3: The American Law Institute Reporters' Studies*, Cambridge University Press: Cambridge, UK.

Howse, Robert L., and Damien J. Neven. 2007d. Canada-Export Credits and Loan Guarantees for Regional Aircraft, pp. pp.391–401 in Henrik Horn and Petros C. Mavroidis (eds.), *The WTO Case-Law of 2001–3: The American Law Institute Reporters' Studies*, Cambridge University Press: Cambridge, UK.

Howse, Robert L., and Damien J. Neven. 2007e. US-Section 211 Omnibus Appropriations Act of 1998, pp. pp.472–522 in Henrik Horn and Petros C. Mavroidis (eds.), *The WTO Case-Law of 2001–3: The American Law Institute Reporters' Studies*, Cambridge University Press: Cambridge, UK.

Howse, Robert L., and Robert W. Staiger. 2007. US-Sunset Reviews of AD Duties on Corrosion-Resistant Carbon Steel Flat Products from Japan, pp. pp.601–621 in Henrik Horn and Petros C. Mavroidis (eds.), *The WTO Case-Law of 2001–3: The American Law Institute Reporters' Studies*, Cambridge University Press: Cambridge, UK.

Howse, Robert and E. Turk. 2001. The WTO Impact on Internal Regulations—A Case Study of the Canada-EC Asbestos Dispute, pp. 283–328 in G. de Búrca and J. Scott, *The EU and the WTO: Legal and Constitutional Issues*, Hart Publishing: Oxford, UK.

Hudec, Robert E. 1975. *The GATT Legal System and the World Trade Diplomacy*, Praeger: New York.

Hudec, Robert E. 1987. Developing Countries in the GATT Legal System, Gower Publishing Company: Aldershot, UK.

Hudec, Robert E. 1988. Tiger, Tiger in the House: a Critical Evaluation of the Case Against Discriminatory Trade Measures, pp. 165–196 in *Ernst-Ulrich Petersmann and Meinhard Hilf (eds.), The New GATT Round of Multilateral Trade Negotiations: Legal and Economic Problems*, Kluwer: Deventer, the Netherlands.

Hudec, Robert E. 1990. *The GATT Legal System and the World Trade Diplomacy*, Butterworth Legal Publishers: Salem, MA.

Hudec, Robert E. 1990a. Thinking About The New Section 301: Beyond Good and Evil, pp. 111–162 in *Jagdish Bhagwati and Hugh Patrick (eds.), Aggressive Unilateralism: America's 301 Policy and The World Trading System*, 1990, University of Michigan Press: Ann Arbor, MI.

Hudec, Robert E. 1993. *Enforcing International Trade Law*, Butterworth: London.

Hudec, Robert E. 1998. GATT/WTO Constraints on National Regulation: Requiem for an "Aims and Effect" Test, *International Lawyer*, 32: 619.

Hudec Robert E. 2000. "Like Product": the Differences in Meaning in GATT Articles I and III, pp. 101–123 in Thomas Cottier and Petros C. Mavroidis (eds.), *Regulatory Barriers and the Principle of Non-Discrimination in World Trade Law*, University of Michigan Press: Ann Arbor, MI.

Hull, Cordell. 1948. *The memoirs of Cordell Hull, volumes I and II*, Macmillan: New York.

Inama, Stefano. 2003. Trade Preferences and the WTO Negotiations on Market Access: Battling for Compensation of Erosion of GSP, ACP and Other Trade Preferences or Assessing and Improving their Utilization and Value by Addressing Rules of Origin and Graduation, *Journal of World Trade*, 37: 959–976.

Inama, Stefano. 2009. *Rules of Origin in International Trade*, Cambridge University Press: Cambridge, UK.

Irwin, Douglas A. 1995. The GATT in Historical Perspective, *American Economic Review*, 85: 323–328.

Irwin, Douglas A. 1996. *Against the Tide*, Princeton University Press: Princeton, NJ.

Irwin, Douglas A. 1998a. Changes in US Tariffs: the Role of Import Prices and Commercial Policies, *American Economic Review*, 88: 1015–1026.

Irwin, Douglas A. 1998b. The Smoot-Hawley Tariff: A Quantitative Assessment, *Review of Economics and Statistics,* 80: 326–334.

Irwin, Douglas A. 2003. Causing Problems? The WTO Review of Causation and Injury Attribution in U.S. Section 201 Cases, *The World Trade Review*, 2: 297–325.

Irwin, Douglas A., Petros C. Mavroidis, and Alan O. Sykes. 2008. *The Genesis of the GATT*, Cambridge University Press: Cambridge, UK.

Jackson, John H. 1967. The General Agreement on Tariffs and Trade in United States Domestic Law. *Michigan Law Review*, 66: 249–332.

Jackson, John H. 1969. *World Trade and the Law of the GATT*, Bobbs-Merril: Indianapolis, IA.

Jackson, John H. 1997. *The World Trading System: Law and Policy of International Economic Relations (2nd ed.)*, Cambridge University Press: Cambridge, UK.

Janow Merit, and Robert W. Staiger. 2003. Canada-Measures Affecting the Importation of Dairy Products and the Exportation of Milk, pp. 236–280 in Henrik Horn and Petros C. Mavroidis (eds.), *The WTO Case-Law of 2001: The American Law Institute Reporters' Studies*, Cambridge University Press: Cambridge, UK.

Janow, Merit, and Robert W. Staiger. 2007. US-Export Restraints, pp. pp.214–248 in Henrik Horn and Petros C. Mavroidis (eds.), *The WTO Case-Law of 2001-3: The American Law Institute Reporters' Studies*, Cambridge University Press: Cambridge, UK.

Jaramillo, Felipe. 1994. Las Negociaciones Sobre el Commercio de Servicios en la Ronda Uruguay, pp. 117–132 in *Patricio Leiva (ed.), La Ronda Uruguay y el Desarollo de America Latina*, Centro Latinoamericano de Economia y Politica Internacional,: Santiago, Chile.

Jimenez de Arréchaga, Eduardo. 1978. International Law in the Past Third of the Century, Receuil des Cours, 159, Brill Academic Publishers: The Hague, the Netherlands.

Johnson, Harry G. 1953–4. Optimum Tariffs and Retaliation, *Review of Economic Studies,* 1: 142–153.

Johnson, Harry, and Melvin Krauss. 1970. Border Taxes, Border Tax Adjustments, Comparative Advantage, and the Balance of Payments, *Canadian Journal of Economics*, 3(4): 595–602.

Josling, Timothy E., and Alan Swinbank. 2011. European Union, pp. 61–96 in David Orden, David Blandford, and Tim Josling (eds.), *WTO Disciplines on Agricultural Support: Seeking a Fair Basis for Trade*, Cambridge University Press: Cambridge, UK.

Josling, Timothy E., Stefan Tangerman and T.K. Warley. 1996. *Agriculture in the GATT*, Macmillan: Basingstoke, UK.

Kahneman, Daniel. 2011. *Thinking Fast and Slow*, Farrar, Straus and Giroux: New York City.

Kapczynski, Amy. 2009. Harmonization and its Discontents: A Case Study of TRIPS Implementation in India's Pharmaceutical Sector. *California Law Review.* 97: 1571–1649.

Karl, Joachim. 1998. Das multilaterale Investitionsabkommen, *Recht der internationalen Wirtschaft*, 44: 432 – 456.

Kathuria Sanjay, Will J. Martin and Anjali Bhardwaj. 2003. Implications of Multifibre Arrangement Abolition for India and South Asia, pp. 47–66 in Aaditya Mattoo and Robert M. Stern (eds.), *India and the WTO*, Oxford University Press and the World Bank Group: Washington D.C.

Kelly, Kenneth. 1988. The Analysis of Causality in Escape Clause Cases, *Journal of Industrial Economics,* 37: 187–207.

Kennedy, Matthew. 2010. When Will the Protocol Amending the TRIPs Agreement Enter into Force? *Journal of International Economic Law*, 13: 459–474.

Kessie, Edwini. 2007. The Legal Status of Special and Differential Treatment Provisions Under the WTO Agreements, pp. 12–35 in George A. Bermann, and Petros C. Mavroidis (eds.), *WTO Law and Developing Countries*, Cambridge University Press: Cambridge, UK.

Knetter, Michael and Tom Prusa. 2003. Macroeconomic Factors and Antidumping Filings: Evidence from Four Countries, *Journal of International Economics*, 61: 1–17.

Komuro, Norio. 2009. Japan's Generalized system of Preferences, pp. 103–130 in Bernard M. Hoekman, Will Martin, and Carlos A. Primo Braga (eds.), *Trade Preference Erosion, Measurement and Policy Response,* Palgrave MacMillan and the World Bank: Washington D.C.

Kono, Daniel Y. 2006. Optimal Obfuscation: Democracy and Trade Policy Transparency, *American Political Science Review*, 100: 369–384.

Kostecki, Michel. 1987. Export Restraint Arrangements and Trade Liberalization, *The World Economy*, 10: 425–453.

Kotschwar, Barbara. 2010. Mapping Investment Provisions in Regional trade Agreements: Towards an International Investment Regime? pp. 365–417 in Antoni Estevadeordal, Kati Suominen, and Robert Teh (eds.), *Regional Rules in the Global Trading System*, Cambridge University Press: Cambridge, UK.

Koulen, Mark. 2001. Foreign investment in the WTO, pp. 181–203 in E.C. Nieuwenhuys and M.M. T.A. Brus (eds.), *Multilateral Regulation of Investment*, Kluwer: Deventer, the Netherlands.

Kovacic, William E. 2010. Price Differentiation in Antitrust and Trade Instruments, pp. 264–275 in Kyle W. Bagwell, George A. Bermann, and Petros C. Mavroidis (eds.), *Law and Economics of Contingent Protection in International Trade,* Cambridge University Press: Cambridge, UK.

Kowalczyk, Carsten. 1990. Welfare and Customs Union, NBER Working Paper No 3476.

Kowalski, Przemyslaw. 2009. The Canadian Preferential Tariff Regime and Potential Economic Impacts of its Erosion, pp. 131–172 in Bernard M. Hoekman, Will Martin, and Carlos A. Primo Braga (eds.), *Trade Preference Erosion, Measurement and Policy Response,* Palgrave MacMillan and the World Bank: Washington, DC.

Krishna, Kala. 2006. Understanding Rules of Origin, pp. 19–34 in O.Cadot, A. Estevadeordal, A Suwa-Eisenmann, and T. Verdier (eds.), *The Origin of Goods: Rules of Origin in Regional Trade Agreements*, Oxford University Press: Oxford, UK.

Krishna, Pravin. 1998. Regionalism and Multilateralism: a Political Economy Approach, *Quarterly Journal of Economics*, 113: 227–251.

Krommenacker, Raymond J. 1987. Multilateral Services Negotiations: From Interest-Lateralism to Reasoned Multilateralism in the Context of the Servicization of the Economy, pp. 455–463 in Ernst-Ulrich Petersmann and Meinhard Hilf (eds.), *The New GATT Round of Multilateral Trade Negotiations, Legal and Economic Problems*, Kluwer: Dewenter, the Netherlands.

Krueger, Anne O. 1997. Free Trade Areas vs. Customs Unions, *Journal of Development Economics*, 54: 169–87.

Krugman, Paul. 1991. The Move Toward Free Trade Zones, *Economic Review, November–December 1991*: 1–24.

Kuran, Timur, and Cass Sunstein. 1999. Availability Cascades and Risk Regulation, *Stanford Law Review*, 51: 683–768.

Laborde David and Will Martin. 2011. Agricultural Market Access, pp. 35–54 in Will Martin and Aaditya Mattoo (eds.), *Unfinished Business? The WTO's Doha Agenda*, The World Bank Group: Washington, DC.

Lang, Andrew, and Joanne Scott. 2009. The Hidden World of WTO Governance, *European Journal of International Law*, 20: 575–614.

Lawrence, Robert Z. 2003. *Crimes and Punishment. Retaliation Under the WTO*, Institute for International Economics: Washington, DC.

Lawrence, Robert Z. 2006. Rule Making Amidst Growing Diversity: a Club of Club Approach to WTO Reform and New Issue Selection, *Journal of International Economic Law*, 6: 923–939.

Liang, Margaret. 2011. Antidumping Negotiations in the Uruguay Round: Reflections of a Singapore Negotiator, pp. 59–101 in C.I. Lim and Margaret Liang (eds.), *Economic Diplomacy, Essays and Reflections by Singapore's Negotiators,* Lee Kuan Yew School of Public Policy, Singapore.

Limão, Nuno. 2006a. Preferential Trade Agreements as Stumbling Blocks for Multilateral Trade Liberalization: Evidence for the U.S., *American Economic* Review,96: 896–914.

Linarelli, John. 2011. Global Procurement Law in Times of Crisis: New Buy American Policies and Options in the WTO Legal System, pp. 773–802 in Sue Arrowsmith and Robert Anderson, eds., *The WTO Regime on Government Procurement: Challenge and Reform*, Cambridge University Press: Cambridge, UK.

Lin, Li-Wen and Curtis Milhaupt. 2011. We Are the (National) Champions: Understanding the Mechanics of State Capitalism in China, *Columbia Law and Economics Working Paper Series* No. 409.

Lippoldt, Douglas. 2009. The Australian Preferential Tariff Regime, pp. 173–218 in Bernard M. Hoekman, Will Martin, and Carlos A. Primo Braga (eds.), *Trade Preference Erosion, Measurement and Policy Response,* Palgrave MacMillan and the World Bank: Washington, DC.

Long, Doris Estelle Long and Anthony D'Amato (eds.). 2000. *International Intellectual Property.* Thomson West: St. Paul, MN.

Low, Patrick A. 1993. *Trading Free.* Twentieth Century Fund: New York City, NY.

Low, Patrick A. 1995. Pre-shipment Inspection Services, *World Bank Discussion Paper No 278*, World Bank: Washington, DC.

Low, Patrick. 2007. Is the WTO Doing Enough for Developing Countries? Pp. 324–357 in George A. Bermann, and Petros C. Mavroidis (eds.), *WTO Law and Developing Countries*, Cambridge University Press: Cambridge, UK.

Maggi, Giovanni, and Andres Rodriguez-Clare. 1998. The Value of Trade Agreements in the Presence of Political Pressures, *Journal of Political Economy*, 106: 574–601.

Maggi, Giovanni and Andres Rodriquez-Clare. 2007. A Political Economy Theory of Trade Agreements, *American Economic Review,* 97: 1374–1406.

Malacrida, Reto. 2008. Towards Sounder and Fairer WTO Retaliation: Suggestions for Possible Additional Procedural Rules Governing Members' Preparation and Adoption of Retaliatory Measures, *Journal of World Trade*, 42: 3–60.

Marchetti, Juan A., and Petros C. Mavroidis. 2011. The Genesis of GATS, *European Journal of International Law*, 2011, 22: 1–33.

Marchetti, Juan A., and Petros C. Mavroidis. 2012. I Now Recognize You (and Only You) As Equal: an Anatomy of (Mutual) Recognition Agreements in the GATS, pp. 415–443 in Ioannis Lianos and Okeoghene

Odudu (eds.), *Regulating Trade in Services in the EU and the WTO, Trust, Distrust, and Economic Integration*, Cambridge University Press: Cambridge, UK.

Marchetti, Juan A., and Martin Roy. 2009. *Opening Markets for Trade in Services: Countries and Sectors in Bilateral and WTO Negotiations*, Cambridge University Press: Cambridge, UK.

Marconini, Mario. 1990. The Uruguay Round Negotiations on Services: an Overview, pp. 19–41 in Bernard M. Hoekman, Patrick Messerlin, and Karl Sauvant (eds.), *The Uruguay Round: Services in the World Economy,* The World Bank Group: Washington, DC.

Martin, William, and Christian Bach. 1998. State Trading in China, pp. 287–302 in Thomas Cottier, and Petros C. Mavroidis (eds.), *State Trading in the Twenty-First Century,* University of Michigan Press : Ann Arbor, Michigan.

Maruyama, Warren H. 1989. The Evolution of Escape Clause Section 201 of the Tariff Act of 1974 as Amended by the Omnibus Trade and Competitiveness Act of 1988, *BYUL Rev*: 393–430.

Marx, Axel. 2011. Global Governance and the Certification Revolution, pp. 590–603 in D. Levi-Faur (ed.) *Handbook of the Politics of Regulation*, Elgar Publishing: Cheltenham, UK.

Maskus, Keith and Carsten Fink (eds.). 2005. *Intellectual Property and Development: Lessons from Recent Research.* Washington, DC: World Bank Publications.

Matsushita, Mitsuo, Thomas J. Schonbaum and Petros C. Mavroidis. 2006. *The World Trade Organization, Law Practice, and Policy* (2nd edition), Oxford University Press: Oxford.

Mattoo, Aaditya. 1997. Economic Theory and the Procurement Agreement, pp 57–72 in Bernard M. Hoekman and Petros C. Mavroidis (eds.), *Law and Policy in Public Purchasing*, University of Michigan Press: Ann Arbor, MI.

Mattoo, Aaditya. 2000. MFN and the GATS, pp. 51–99 in Thomas Cottier and Petros C. Mavroidis (eds.), *Regulatory Barriers and the Principle of Non Discrimination*, University of Michigan Press: Ann Arbor, MI.

Mattoo Aaditya, Devesh Roy and Arvind Subramanian. 2003. The Africa Growth and Opportunity Act and its Rules of Origin: Generosity Undermined? *The World Economy*, 26: 829–851.

Mattoo, Aaditya and Arvind Subramanian. 1998. Regulatory Autonomy and Multilateral Disciplines: the Dilemma and Possible Resolution, *Journal of International Economic Law,* 1: 303–324.

Mattoo, Aaditya and Arvind Subramanian. 2009. Currency Undervaluation and Sovereign Wealth Fund: A New Role for the World Trade Organization, *The World Economy*, 32: 1135–1164.

Mavroidis, Petros C. 1993. Government Procurement Agreement; the Trondheim Case: the Remedies Issue, *Aussenwirtschaft*, 48: 77–94.

Mavroidis, Petros C. 2000. Remedies in the WTO Legal System: Between a Rock and a Hard Place, *European Journal of International Law*, 11: 763–813.

Mavroidis, Petros C. 2000a. Trade and Environment after the Shrimps-Turtles Litigation, *Journal of World Trade*, 34: 73–88.

Mavroidis, Petros C. 2004. *Amicus curiae* Briefs Before the WTO: Much Ado About Nothing, pp. 317–330 in Armin von Bogdandy, Petros C. Mavroidis and Yves Meny (eds.), *In Honour of Claus-Dieter Ehlermann*, Kluwer: Amsterdam.

Mavroidis, Petros C. 2004a. Proposals for Reform of Article 22 of the DSU: Reconsidering the 'Sequencing' Issue and Suspension of Concessions, pp. 61–74 in Federico Ortino and Ernst-Ulrich Petersmann (eds.), *The WTO Dispute Settlement System 1995–2003*: Kluwer, London, UK.

Mavroidis, Petros C. 2006. If I Don't Do it, Somebody Else Will (or Won't), *Journal of World Trade*, 40: 187–214.

Mavroidis, Petros C. 2006a.Highway XVI Re-Visited: the Road from Non-Discrimination to Market Access in GATS, *The World Trade Review*, 6: 1–24.

Mavroidis, Petros C. 2008. No Outsourcing of Law? WTO Law as Practised by WTO Courts, *American Journal of International Law*, 102: 421–474.

Mavroidis, Petros C. 2009. Crisis? What Crisis? Is the WTO Appellate Body Coming of Age?, pp. 173–183 in Terence P. Stewart (ed.), *Opportunities and Obligations: New Perspectives on Global and US Trade Policy*, Kluwer: Amsterdam.

Mavroidis, Petros C. 2012. *Trade in Goods, Second Edition*, Oxford University Press: Oxford, UK.

Mavroidis, Petros C., Patrick Messerlin and Jasper M. Wauters. 2008. *The Law and Economics of Contingent Protection*, Elgar: Cheltenham, UK.

Mavroidis, Petros C. and Damien J. Neven. 1999. Some Reflections on Extraterritoriality in International Economic Law: a Law and Economic Analysis, pp. 12997–1325 in *Mélanges en homage de Michel Waelbroeck*, Bruylant: Brussels.

Mavroidis, Petros C. and André Sapir. 2008. Mexico—AD Measures on Rice: Don't Ask Me No Questions and I Won't Tell You No Lies, pp.305–324 in Henrik Horn and Petros C. Mavroidis (eds.), *The WTO Case-Law of 2004–5: The American Law Institute Reporters' Studies*, Cambridge University Press: Cambridge, UK.

Mavroidis, Petros C., and Werner Zdouc. 1998. Legal Means to Protect Private Parties' Interests in the WTO: the Case of the EC New Trade Barriers Regulation, *Journal of International Economic Law*, 3: 407–432.

McDonough, Patrick J. 1993. Subsidies and Countervailing Measures, pp. 803–1008 in Terence P. Stewart (ed.), *The GATT Uruguay Round: a Negotiating History (1986–1992)*, Kluwer Law: Deventer, the Netherlands.

McCloskey Deirdre N., and Stephan T. Ziliak. 1996. The Standard Error of Regressions, *Journal of Economic Literature*, 34: 97–114.

McCulloch, Rachel. 1990. Services and the Uruguay Round, *The World Economy*, 13: 329–348.

McMahon, Joseph. 2011. *The Negotiations for a New Agreement on Agriculture*, Martinus Nijhoff: Leiden, the Netherlands.

Meade, James E. 1974. A Note on Border-Tax Adjustments, *Journal of Political Economy*, 82: 1013–1015.

Meagher, Niall. 2007. Representing Developing Countries in WTO Dispute Settlement Proceedings, pp. 213–226 in *George A. Bermann, and Petros C. Mavroidis (eds.)*, WTO Law and Developing Countries, Cambridge University Press: New York.

Meessen, Karl M. 1996. *Extraterritorial Jurisdiction in Theory and Practice*, Kluwer: London.

Meng, Werner P. 1990. The Hormones Conflict Between the EEC and the United States within the Context of GATT, *Michigan Journal of International Law*, 11: 819–839.

Mercurio. Bryan and Dianna Shao. 2010. A Precautionary Approach to Decision Making: the Evolving jurisprudence on Article 5.7 of the SPS Agreement, *Trade, Law and Development*, II: 195–223.

Messerlin, Patrick. 2001. *Measuring the Cost of Protection in Europe*, Institute of International Economics: Washington, DC.

Milner, Helen V. 1988. *Resisting Protectionism: Global Industries and the Politics of International Trade*, Princeton University Press: Princeton, NJ.

Mostashari, Shalam. 2010. *Trade Growth, the Extensive Margin, and Vertical Specialization,* Ph.D. Dissertation, University of Texas: Austin, Texas.

Müller, Anna Caroline. 2011. Special and Differential treatment and Other Special Measures for Developing Countries Under the Agreement on Government Procurement: the Current Text and the New Provisions, pp. 339–376 in Sue Arrowsmith and Robert D. Anderson (eds.), *The WTO Regime on Government Procurement: Challenge and Reform*, Cambridge University Press: Cambridge, UK.

Narlikar, Amrita. 2003. *International Trade and Developing Countries: Coalitions in GATT and the WTO*, Routledge: New York.

Nassar, André. 2011. Brazil, pp. 223–276 in David Orden, David Blandford, and Tim Josling (eds.), *WTO Disciplines on Agricultural Support: Seeking a Fair Basis for Trade*, Cambridge University Press: Cambridge, UK.

Neven, Damien J. and Petros C. Mavroidis. 2007. El Mess in TELMEX, pp. 758–789 in Henrik Horn, and Petros C. Mavroidis (eds.), *The American Law Institute Reporters' Studies on WTO Case Law*, Cambridge University Press: Cambridge, UK.

Neven, Damien J. and Joseph H.H. Weiler. 2007. Japan—Measures Affecting the Importation of Apples: One Bad Apple? Pp. 280–310 in Henrik Horn and Petros C. Mavroidis (eds.), *The WTO Case Law of 2000–2003, The ALI Reporters' Studies*, Cambridge University Press: Cambridge, UK.

Nicolaidis, Kalypso. 2000. Non-Discriminatory Mutual Recognition: an Oxymoron in the New WTO Lexicon? pp. 267–301 in Thomas Cottier and Petros C. Mavroidis (eds.), *Regulatory Barriers and the Principle of Non-Discrimination in World Trade Law*, University of Michigan Press: Ann Arbor, MI.

Nicolaidis, Kalypso, and Joel Trachtman. 2000. From Policed Regulation to Managed Recognition in GATS, pp. 241 – 282 in Pierre Sauvé, and Robert Stern (eds.), *The GATS 2000, New Directions in Services Trade Liberalization*, Brookings: Washington, DC.

Nyahoho, Emmanuel. 1990. Libéralisation multilateral dui commerce des services: enjeux et stratégie des négociations, *Etudes Internationales*, 21: 55–80.

O'Connor, Bernard. 2005. The Structure of the Agreement on Agriculture pp. 83–90 in Bernard O'Connor (ed.), *Agriculture in WTO Law*, Cameron May: London.

Olsen, Sven. 2005. The Negotiation of the Agreement on Agriculture, pp. 43–82 in Bernard O'Connor (ed.), *Agriculture in WTO Law*, Cameron May: London.

Orden, David. 2009. Farm Policy Reform in the United States: Past Progress and Future Direction, pp. 86–120 in Ricardo Melendez-Ortiz, Christophe Bellmann and Jonathan Hepburn (eds.), *Agricultural Subsidies in the WTO Green Box*, Cambridge University Press: Cambridge, UK.

Orden, David, David Blandford, and Tim Josling. 2011. Introduction, pp. 3–22 in David Orden, David Blandford, and Tim Josling (eds.), *WTO Disciplines on Agricultural Support: Seeking a Fair Basis for Trade*, Cambridge University Press: Cambridge, UK.

Özden, Czaglar and Eric Reinhardt. 2003. The Perversity of Preferences: GSP and Developing Country Trade Policies, 1976–2000, *World Bank Working Paper 2955*, The World Bank: Washington, DC.

Paemen, Hugo, and Alexandra Bentsch. 1995. *From the GATT to the WTO, The European Community in the Uruguay Round*, Leuven University Press: Leuven, Belgium.

Palmeter, David N. 1995. US Implementation of the Uruguay Round Antidumping Code, *Journal of World Trade,* 29: 39–82.

Palmeter, David N. 1998. The WTO Appellate Body Needs Remand Authority, *Journal of World Trade*, 32: 41–57.

Palmeter, David N. and Petros C. Mavroidis. 2004. *Dispute Settlement in the WTO, Practice and Procedure* (Second edition), Cambridge University Press: Cambridge, UK.

Panagariya, Arvind. 2010. *India: The Emerging Giant.* Oxford Univ. Press: Oxford, UK.

Panagariya, Arvind. 1999. TRIPS and the WTO: An Uneasy Marriage, pp. 3–41 in Keith Maskus, ed., *The WTO, Intellectual Property Rights and the Knowledge Economy*, Edward Elgar: Cheltenham, UK.

Perez, Oren. 2007. Anomalies at the Precautionary Kingdom: Reflections on the GMO Panel's Decision, *World Trade Review*, 6: 265–280.

Petersmann, Ernst-Ulrich. 1991. Non-violation Complaints in Public International Trade Law, *German Yearbook of International Law*, 34: 175–231.

Petersmann, Ernst-Ulrich. 1993. International Competition Rules for the GATT—MTO World Trade and Legal System, *Journal of World Trade*, 27: 35–86.

Potipiti, Tanapong. 2006. *Import Tariffs and Export Subsidies in the WTO: A Small Country Approach*, Proceedings of the 2th National Conference of Economists: Bangkok.

Preeg, Ernest H. 1995. *Traders in a Brave New World: The Uruguay Round and the Future of the International Trading System*, University of Chicago Press: Chicago, IL.

Priess, Hans-Joachim, and Pascal Friton. 2011. Designing Effective Challenge Procedures: the EU's Experience with Remedies, pp. 511–531 in Sue Arrowsmith and Robert D. Anderson (eds.), *The WTO Regime on Government Procurement: Challenge and Reform*, Cambridge University Press: Cambridge, UK.

Prusa, Thomas J. 1992. Why are so Many Antidumping Petitions Withdrawn?' *Journal of International Economics*, 33: 1–20.

Prusa, Thomas J., and Edwin Vermulst. 2009. A One-Two Punch on Zeroing, pp.187–242 in Henrik Horn and Petros C. Mavroidis (eds.), *The WTO Case-Law of 2006–7: The American Law Institute Reporters' Studies*, Cambridge University Press: Cambridge, UK.

Prusa, Thomas J., and Edwin Vermulst. 2010. Guilt by Association, pp.59–84 in Henrik Horn and Petros C. Mavroidis (eds.), *The WTO Case-Law of 2008: The American Law Institute Reporters' Studies*, Cambridge University Press: Cambridge, UK.

Puccio, Laura. 2012. *Building Bridges Between Regionalism and Multilateralism: Enquiries on the Ways and Means to Internationally Regulate Preferential Rules of Origin*, EUI: Florence, Italy.

Raffaelli, Marcelo and Tripti Jenkins. 1995. The Drafting History of the Agreement on Textiles and Clothing, ITCB: Geneva.

Randhawa, P. S. 1987. Punta del Este and After: Negotiations on Trade in Services and the Uruguay Round, *Journal of World Trade Law*, 21: 163–171.

Regan, Donald H. 2002. Regulatory Purpose and "Like Products" in Article III:4 of the GATT (With Additional Remarks on Article II:2), *Journal of World Trade* 36: 443–78.

Reichman, Jerome and David Lange. 1998. Bargaining Around the TRIPS Agreement: The Case for Ongoing Public-Private Initiatives to Facilitate Worldwide Intellectual Property Transactions; *Duke Journal of International and Comparative Law.* 9: 11–68.

Reyna, Jimmie V. 1993. Services, in Terence P. Stewart (ed.), *The GATT Uruguay Round: a Negotiating History*, Kluwer: Deventer, the Netherlands.

Richardson, John B., and Jonathan Scheele. 1989. *Appropriate Regulation and Other Concepts,* pp. 151–155 in Services and Development, The Role of Foreign Direct Investment and Trade, United Nations Centre on Transnational Corporations, UN Doc. ST/CTC/95.

Rodriguez, Francisco and Dani Rodrik. 2001. Trade Policy and Economic Growth: a Skeptic's Guide to the Cross-national Evidence, pp. 261–324 in Ben S. Bernanke and Kenneth S. Rogoff (eds.), *NBER Macroeconomics Annual 2000,* MIT Press: Cambridge, MA.

Rodrik, Dani. 2001. *The Global Governance of Trade as if Development Really Mattered*, UNDP: New York.

Rose, Andrew K. 2004. Do we Really Know that the WTO Increases Trade? *American Economic Review*, 94: 98–114.

Rosenow, Sheri, and Brian J. O'Shea. 2010. *A Handbook on the WTO Customs Valuation Agreement*, Cambridge University Press: Cambridge, UK.

Rubini, Luca. 2010. *The Definition of Subsidy and State Aid: WTO and EC Law in Comparative Perspective*, Oxford University Press: Oxford, UK.

Rutkowski, Aleksander. 2007. Withdrawals of Anti-dumping Complaints in the EU: a Sign of Collusion, *The World Economy*, 30: 470–503.

Sacerdotti, Giorgio. 1997. *Bilateral Treaties and Multilateral Instruments on Investment Protection*, Receuil des cours, 269.

Sacerdotti, Giorgio. 2005. The Role of Lawyers in WTO Dispute Settlement, pp. 125–131 in Rufus Yerxa and Bruce Wilson (eds.), *Key Issues in WTO Dispute Settlement*, Cambridge Univ. Press: Cambridge, UK: 125–131.

Sachs, Jeffrey D. and Andrew M. Warner. 1995. Economic Reform and the Process of Global Integration, *Brookings Papers on Economic Activity*, 1: 1–95.

Saggi, Kamal. 2010. The Agreement on Safeguards: Does it Raise More Questions than it Answers? pp. 374–378 in Kyle W. Bagwell, George A. Bermann, and Petros C. Mavroidis (eds.), *Law and Economics of Contingent Protection in International Trade*, Cambridge University Press: Cambridge, UK.

Sampson, Gary. 1988. Uruguay Round Negotiations on Services Issues and Recent Developments, pp. 274–287, in Detlev Chr. Dicke and Ernst-Ulrich Petersmann (eds.), *Foreign Trade in the Present and the New International Economic Order*, University Press Fribourg: Fribourg, Switzerland.

Sampson, Gary. 1989. Developing Countries and the Liberalization of Trade in Services, pp. 132–148 in John Whalley (ed.), *Developing Countries and the Global Trading System, Volume 1*, The University of Michigan Press: Ann Arbor, MI.

Sampson, Gary and Richard Snape. 1985. Identifying the Issues in Trade in Services, *The World Economy*, 8: 171–182.

Sapir, André. 1987. International Trade in Services: a Comment, pp. 49–54 in Orio Giarini (ed.). *The Emerging Services Economy*, Pergamon Press: New York.

Sapir, André. 2011. European Integration at the Crossroads: a Review Essay on the 50th Anniversary of Bela Balassa's Theory of Economic Integration, *Journal of Economic Literature*, 49: 1200–1229.

Sapir, André, and Joel Trachtman. 2008. Subsidization, Price Suppression and Expertise: Causation and Precision in US—Upland Cotton, pp.183–210 in Henrik Horn and Petros C. Mavroidis (eds.), *The WTO Case-Law of 2004–5: The American Law Institute Reporters' Studies*, Cambridge University Press: Cambridge, UK.

Sauvé, Pierre, and Christopher Wilkie. 2000. Investment Liberalization in GATS, pp. 331 – 363 in Pierre Sauvé, and Robert M. Stern (eds.), *GATS 2000: New Directions in Services Trade Liberalization*, Brookings: Washington, DC.

Schelling, Thomas. 1960. *The Strategy of Conflict,* Harvard University Press: Cambridge, MA.

Schepel, Harm. 2005. *The Constitution of Private Governance*, Hart Publishing: London, UK.

Schoenbaum, Thomas J. 2011. Fashioning a New Regime for Agricultural Trade: New Issues and the Global Food Crisis, *Journal of International Economic Law*, 14: 593–612.

Schott, Jeffrey. 1989. More Free Trade Areas? Pp. 1–58 in Jeffrey Schott (ed.), *Free Trade Areas and US Trade Policy,* Institute of International Economics: Washington, DC.

Schwarz, Warren F. and Alan O. Sykes. 1998. The Positive Economics of the Most Favored Nation Obligation and its Exceptions in the WTO/GATT System, pp. 43–75 in J. Bhandari and A. Sykes (eds.), *Economic Dimensions in International Law*, Cambridge Univ. Press: Cambridge, MA.

Schwarz, Warren F. and Alan O. Sykes. 2002. The Economic Structure of Renegotiation and Dispute Resolution in the WTO/GATT System, *Journal of Legal Studies*, 31: 179.

Segal, Adam. 2011. *Advantage.* W.W. Norton & Company: New York.

Self, Richard B. 1989. International Discussions on Trade in Services: The Perspective of Developed Countries, pp. 167–169 in *Services and Development, The Role of Foreign Direct Investment and Trade, United Nations Centre on Transnational Corporations,* UN Doc. ST/CTC/95.

Self, Richard B., and B.K. Zutshi. 2003. Mode 4: Negotiating Challenges and Opportunities, pp. 27–59 in Aaditya Mattoo and Antonia Carzaniga (eds.), *Moving People to Deliver Services,* Oxford University Press and the World Bank Group: Washington, DC.

Sell, Susan K. 1998. *Power and Ideas: North South Politics of Intellectual Property and Antitrust.* State University of New York Press: New York.

Sell, Susan K. 2003. *Private Power, Public Law: The Globalization of Intellectual Property Rights.* Cambridge Univ. Press: Cambridge, UK

Shaffer, Gregory, Michelle Ratton Sanchez, and Barbara Rosenberg. 2008. The Trials of Winning at the WTO: What Lies Behind Brazil's Success. *Cornell International Law Journal*, 41: 383–501.

Shukla, Shirnag, P. 1989. International Discussions on Trade in Services: the Perspective of Developing Countries, pp. 170–174 in *Services and Development, The Role of Foreign Direct Investment and Trade, United Nations Centre on Transnational Corporations,* UN Doc. ST/CTC/95.

Siegel, Deborah E. 2002. Legal Aspects of the IMF/WTO Relationship: the Fund's Articles of Agreement and the WTO Agreements, *American Journal of International Law,* 96: 561 – 599.

Simmonds, K.N. 1988. The Community and the Uruguay Round, *Common Market Law Review,* 25: 95–115.

Slovic, Paul. 2000. *The Perception of Risk,* EarthScan: Sterling, VA.

Slot, Piet-Jan. 2010. The Boeing-Airbus Dispute: a Case for the Application of the European Community State Aid Rules? pp. 172–184 in Kyle W. Bagwell, George A. Bermann, and Petros C. Mavroidis (eds.), *Law and Economics of Contingent Protection in International Trade,* Cambridge University Press: Cambridge, UK.

Smith Alasdair and Antony Venables. 1991. 'Counting the Cost of Voluntary Export Restraints in the European Market' pp. 187–220 in E. Helpman and A. Razin (eds), *International Trade and Trade Policy.* MIT Press: Cambridge, MA.

Staiger, Robert, W., and Alan O. Sykes. 2011. International Trade, National Treatment and Domestic Regulation, *The Journal of Legal Studies,* 40: 149–203.

Staiger, Robert W., and Alan O. Sykes. 2010. Currency Manipulation and World Trade, *The World Trade Review,* 9: 583–628.

Staiger, Robert W., and F. Wolack. 1994. *Measuring Industry Specific Protection: Antidumping in the United States,* Brookings Papers on Economic Activity: Microeconomics, Brookings Institution: Washington D.C.

Stancanelli, Nestor. 2009. The Historical Context of the Green Box, pp. 19–35 in Ricardo Melendez-Ortiz, Christophe Bellmann and Jonathan Hepburn (eds.), *Agricultural Subsidies in the WTO Green Box,* Cambridge University Press: Cambridge, MA

Stewart, Terence P., and Myron Brilliant. 1993. Safeguards, pp. 1711–1820 in Terence P. Stewart (ed.), *The GATT Uruguay Round: a Negotiating History (1986–1992),* Kluwer Law: Deventer, the Netherlands.

Stewart, Terence P., Susan G. Markel and Michael T. Kerwin. 1993. Antidumping, pp. 1383–1710 in Terence P. Stewart (ed.), *The GATT*

Uruguay Round: a Negotiating History (1986–1992), Kluwer Law: Deventer, the Netherlands.

Stewart, Terence P., and Amy S. Dwyer. 2010. Antidumping: Overview of the Agreement, pp. 197–240 in Kyle W. Bagwell, George A. Bermann, and Petros C. Mavroidis (eds.), *The Law and Economics of Contingent Protection in International Trade*, Cambridge University Press: Cambridge, MA.

Stewart, Terence P., Eric P. Salonen, Patrick J. McDonough. 2007. *More than 50 Years of Trade Rule Discrimination on Taxation: How Trade with China is Affected*, The Trade Lawyers Advisory Group, Washington, DC.

Stigler, George J. 1961. The Economics of Information, *The Journal of Political Economy*, 69:213–225.

Stirling, Andrew. 2001. On Science and Precaution in the Management of Technological Risk, (http://www.esto.jrc.es/detailshort:cfm?ID_report=809).

Subramanian, Arvind and Shang Jin Wei. 2007. The WTO Promotes Trade Strongly but Unevenly, *Journal of International Economics*, 72: 151–175.

Summers, Larry. 1991. Regionalism and the World Trading System, pp. 42–65 in *Policy Implications of Trade and Currency Zones*, The Federal Reserve Bank of Kansas City.

Sunstein, Cass. 2002. *Risk and Reason*, Harvard University Press: Cambridge, MA.

Sunstein, Cass. 2003. Beyond the Precautionary Principle, *University of Pennsylvania Law Review*, 151: 1003–1076.

Swinbank, Alan. 2009. The Reform of the EU's Common Agricultural Policy, pp. 70–85 in Ricardo Melendez-Ortiz, Christophe Bellmann and Jonathan Hepburn (eds.), *Agricultural Subsidies in the WTO Green Box*, Cambridge University Press: Cambridge, UK.

Swinbank, Alan and Carolyn Tanner. 1996. *Farm Policy and Trade Conflict*, University of Michigan Press: Ann Arbor, MI.

Swinnen, Jo F. M. 2008. The Perfect Storm: the Political Economy of the Fischler Reports of the Common Agricultural Policy, Centre for European Policy Studies: Brussels.

Swinnen, Jo F. M. 2009. The Growth of Agricultural Protection in Europe in the 19th Century, *The World Economy,* 32: 1499–1537.

Sykes, Alan O. 1990. GATT Safeguards Reform: the Injury Test, pp. 203–236 in Michael Trebilcock and R. York (eds.), *Fair Exchange: Reforming Trade Remedy Laws,* Policy Study 11, C.D. Howe Institute: Toronto.

Sykes, Alan O. 1995. *Product Standards for Internationally Integrated Goods Markets*, Brookings Institution: Washington, DC.

Sykes, Alan O. 2003. The Safeguards Mess: A Critique of WTO Jurisprudence, *The World Trade Review,* 3: 216–296.

Sykes, Alan O. 2003a. The Economics of the WTO Rules on Subsidies and Countervailing Measures, John M. Olin Program in Law & Economics working papers, No 186, University of Chicago.

Sykes, Alan O. 2006. *The WTO Agreement on Safeguards, A Commentary,* Oxford University Press: Oxford.

Sykes, Alan O. 2006a. Domestic Regulation, Sovereignty and Scientific Evidence Requirements: a Pessimistic View, pp. 257–270 in George A. Bermann and Petros C. Mavroidis (eds.), *Trade and Human Health and Safety,* Cambridge University Press: Cambridge, UK.

Tang, Xiaobing. 1998. The Integration of Textiles and Clothing into GATT and WTO Dispute settlement, pp. 171–205 in James Cameron and Karen Campbell (eds.), *Dispute Resolution in the World Trade Organisation*, Cameron May: London.

Tinbergen, Jan. 1962. Shaping the World Economy, The Twentieth Century Fund: New York City, NY.

Tokarick, Stephen. 2006. Does Import Protection Discourage Exports? IMF Working Paper WP/06/20, IMF: Washington, D.C.

Toye, Richard. 2008. *Cripps Versus Clayton*. Unpublished manuscript.

Trachtman, Joel. 1998. Trade and ... Problems, Cost-Benefit Analysis and Subsidiarity, *European Journal of International Law,* 9: 32–60.

Trebilcock, Michael J., Robert Howse, and Antonia Elliason. 2013. *International Trade Regulation* (4th edition), Routledge: London.

Trebilcock, Michael J., and Julie Soloway. 2002. International Trade Policy and Domestic Food Safety Regulation: the Case for Substantial Deference by the WTO Dispute Settlement Body Under the SPS Agreement, pp. 537–574 in Daniel M. Kennedy and James D. Southwick (eds.), *The Political Economy of International Trade Law, Essays in Honor of Robert E. Hudec*, Cambridge University Press: Cambridge, UK.

Trefler, Daniel. 2004. The Long and Short of the Canada-US Free Trade Agreement, *American Economic Review*, 94: 870–895.

Tumlir, Jan. 1985. *Protectionism: Trade Policy in Democratic Societies*. American Enterprise Institute: Washington, DC.

Van Damme, Isabelle. 2007. The Interpretation of Schedules of Commitments, *Journal of World Trade*, 41: 1–52.

Van den Bossche, Pieter. 2005. *The WTO, Texts, Cases and Materials,* Cambridge University Press: Cambridge, UK.

Vermulst, Edwin. 1992. Rules of Origin as Commercial Policy Instruments—Revisited, *Journal of World Trade*, 26: 61–102.

Vermulst, Edwin. 1996. *EC Antidumping Law and Practice*, Sweet & Maxwell: London.

Vermulst, Edwin and Hiroshi Imagawa. 2005. The Agreement on Rules of Origin, pp. 601–678 in Patrick Macrory, Arthur Appleton, and Michael Plummer (eds.), *The World Trade Organization: Legal, Economic and Political Analysis vol. I*, Springer: New York.

Vermulst, Edwin and Paul Waer. 1997. *EC Antidumping Law and Practice*, Sweet & Maxwell: London.

Viganó, Jorge. 1988. National Treatment in Trade in Services and Developing Countries, pp. 288–291, in Detlev Chr. Dicke and Ernst-Ulrich Petersmann (eds.), *Foreign Trade in the Present and the New International Economic Order*, University Press Fribourg: Fribourg, Switzerland.

Viner, Jacob. 1922. Dumping, A Problem in International Trade, reprinted by Reprints of Economics Classics (1966), Augustus M. Kelley: New York.

Viner, Jacob. 1924. The Most-Favored-Nation Clause in American Commercial Treaties, *Journal of Political Economy*, 32: 126–50.

Viner, Jacob. 1950. *The Customs Union Issue*, Carnegie Endowment for International Peace: New York, NY.

Vogel, David. 1997. *Barriers or Benefits? Regulation in Transatlantic Trade*, Brookings Institution: Washington, DC.

Von Dewitz, Wedige. 1987. Services and the Uruguay Round: Issues Raised in Connection with Multilateral Action on Services: a Comment, pp. 475–479 in Ernst-Ulrich Petersmann and Meinhard Hilf (eds.), *The New GATT Round of Multilateral Trade Negotiations, Legal and Economic Problems*, Kluwer: Dewenter, the Netherlands.

Waincymer, Jeff. 2002. *WTO Litigation: Procedural Aspects of Formal Dispute Settlement*, Cameron May: London.

Wang, Ping. 2011. Accession to the Agreement on Government Procurement: the case of China, pp. 92–116 in Sue Arrowsmith and Robert D. Anderson (eds.), *The WTO Regime on Government Procurement: Challenge and Reform*, Cambridge University Press: Cambridge, UK.

Wauters, Jasper M. 2010. The Safeguards Agreement-An Overview, pp. 334–366 in Kyle W. Bagwell, George A. Bermann, and Petros C. Mavroidis (eds.), *Law and Economics of Contingent Protection in International Trade*, Cambridge University Press: Cambridge, UK.

Wauters, Jasper M., and Hylke Vandenbussche. 2010. China-Measures Affecting Imports of Automobile Parts, pp.201–238 in Henrik Horn and Petros C. Mavroidis (eds.), *The WTO Case-Law of 2008: The American Law Institute Reporters' Studies*, Cambridge University Press: Cambridge, UK.

Wilcox, Clair. 1949. *A Charter for World Trade*, Macmillan: New York.

Wolf, Martin, Hans Heinrich Glismann, Joseph Pelzman, and Dean Spinanger. 1984. *Costs of Protecting Jobs in Textiles and Clothing*, Thames Essay no. 37, Trade Policy Research Centre: London.

Wood, Diane P. 1997. The WTO Agreement on Government Procurement: an Antitrust Perspective, pp. 261–272 in Bernard M. Hoekman and Petros C. Mavroidis (eds.) *Law And Policy In Public Purchasing*, University of Michigan Press: Ann Arbor, MI.

Wouters, Jan, and Dominic Coppens. 2010. An Overview of the Agreement on Subsidies and Countervailing Measures – Including a Discussion of the Agreement on Agriculture, pp. 7–84 in Kyle W. Bagwell, George A. Bermann, and Petros C. Mavroidis (eds.), *Law and Economics of Contingent Protection in International Trade*, Cambridge University Press: New York.

Wu, Mark. 2008. Free Trade and the Protection of Public Morals: an Analysis of the Newly Emerging Public Morals Clause Doctrine, *Yale Journal of International Law*, 33: 215–251.

Wu, Mark. 2010. Why Not Brussels? European Community State Aid Rules and the Boeing-Airbus Dispute, pp. 185–196 in Kyle W. Bagwell, George A. Bermann, and Petros C. Mavroidis (eds.), *Law and Economics of Contingent Protection in International Trade,* Cambridge University Press: Cambridge, UK.

Yeutter, Clayton. 1998. Bringing Agriculture into the Multilateral Trading System, pp. 61–78 in Jagdish Bhagwati and Matthias Hirsch (eds.), *The Uruguay Round and Beyond, Essays in Honour of Arthur Dunkel*, The University of Michigan Press: Ann Arbor, MI.

Yoffie, David B. 1990. Trade in Services and American Express, pp. 367–386 in *David B. Yoffie, International Trade and Competition: Cases and Notes in Strategy and Management*, McGraw-Hill Publishing Company: New York.

Yu, Peter. 2011. TRIPS and Its Achilles' Heel. *Journal of Intellectual Property Law.* 18: 479–531.

Zeiler, Thomas W. 1999. *Free Trade, Free World: the Advent of the GATT,* The University of North Carolina Press: Chapel Hill, NC.

Summary of Contents

Acknowledgments III
References V
Abbreviations LXXI
Table of Cases LXXXIII

Chapter 1. The WTO Institution 1
1. WTO, The Successor to the GATT 1
2. The Institutional Architecture of the WTO in a Nutshell 6
3. Participation in the WTO 8
4. Day to Day Operations 25
5. The WTO Law 32
6. Withdrawing From the WTO 53

Chapter 2. Quantitative Restrictions 59
1. The Legal Discipline 59
2. The Rationale for the Legal Discipline 60
3. Coverage of the Legal Discipline 61
4. Exceptions 68
5. Administration of Legally Permissible QRs 80

Chapter 3. Tariffs 87
1. The Legal Discipline 87
2. The Rationale for the Legal Discipline 88
3. The Coverage of the Legal Discipline 90
4. Withdrawing Concessions From Members Leaving the WTO 103
5. Renegotiating Tariffs 103

Chapter 4. Most Favored Nation (MFN) 121
1. The Legal Discipline 121
2. The Rationale for the Legal Discipline 121
3. Coverage of the Legal Discipline 122
4. Exceptions 130

Chapter 5. Preferential Trade Agreements (PTAs) 137
1. The Legal Discipline 137
2. The Rationale for the Legal Discipline 137
3. Coverage of the Legal Discipline 138
4. Enforcing Art. XXIV GATT 146

Chapter 6. Special and Differential Treatment for Developing Countries 165
1. The Legal Discipline 165
2. The Rationale for the Legal Discipline 165

3. Coverage of the Legal Discipline 168
4. Committee on Trade and Development (CTD) 190
5. Trade and Development 191

Chapter 7. Import Licensing, Customs Valuation, and Pre-shipment Inspection 197
1. The ILA (Import Licensing Agreement) 197
2. The Customs Valuation (CV) Agreement 201
3. The Agreement on Pre-shipment Inspection (PSI) 207

Chapter 8. National Treatment 215
1. The Legal Discipline 215
2. The Rationale for the Legal Discipline 215
3. The Coverage of the Legal Discipline 216
4. Internal Taxes and Other Internal Charges (Fiscal Measures) 224
5. Laws, Regulations, and Requirements Affecting Trade (Fiscal Measures) 235
6. Exceptions to the National Treatment Obligation 245

Chapter 9. Goods in Transit 251
1. The Legal Discipline 251
2. The Rationale for the Legal Provision 251
3. Coverage 251

Chapter 10. State Trading 257
1. The Legal Discipline 257
2. The Rationale for the Legal Discipline 257
3. Coverage 258
4. Exceptions 264

Chapter 11. The General Transparency Obligation 267
1. The Legal Discipline 267
2. The Rationale for the Legal Discipline 268
3. Coverage of the Legal Discipline 269

Chapter 12. General Exceptions 285
1. The Legal Discipline 285
2. The Rationale for the Legal Discipline 285
3. Coverage of the Legal Discipline 288

Chapter 13. National Security 319
1. The Legal Discipline 319
2. The Rationale for the Legal Discipline 319
3. Coverage of the Legal Discipline 320

Chapter 14. Antidumping 331
1. The Legal Discipline 331
2. The Rationale for the Legal Discipline 332
3. Coverage of the Legal Discipline 333
4. Imposition of AD Duties 363

5. Procedural Requirements	384
6. WTO Review of Anti–Dumping Determinations	409
7. Institutional Issues	417

Chapter 15. Subsidies and Countervailing Duties 423
1. The Legal Discipline 423
2. The Rationale for the Legal Discipline 424
3. Coverage of the Legal Discipline 425
4. Definition of a "Subsidy" 427
5. Prohibited Subsidies 445
6. Actionable Subsidies 456
7. Non–Actionable Subsidies 468
8. Countervailing Duties (CVDs) 469
9. Institutional Issues 498

Chapter 16. Safeguards 503
1. The Legal Discipline 503
2. The Rationale for the Legal Discipline 504
3. Coverage of the Legal Discipline 505
4. Special Safeguard Regime With Respect to China 536
5. Procedural Requirements 543
6. Institutional Issues 548

Chapter 17. Agriculture 549
1. The Legal Discipline 549
2. The Rationale for the Legal Discipline 550
3. Coverage of the Legal Discipline 554
4. Border Measures on Agricultural Goods 557
5. Domestic Subsidies for Agriculture 560
6. Agricultural Export Subsidies 569
7. Other Commitments 576
8. Institutional Issues 577

Chapter 18. The Agreement on Textiles and Clothing 581
1. The Legal Discipline 581
2. The Rationale for the Legal Discipline 581
3. Coverage of the Legal Discipline 583
4. Institutional Arrangements: The TMB 591

Chapter 19. Technical Barriers to Trade 593
1. The Legal Discipline 593
2. The Rationale for the Legal Discipline 593
3. Coverage of the Legal Discipline 594
4. Technical Regulations 599
5. Standards 615
6. Conformity Assessment 617
7. Recognition 621
8. Special and Differential Treatment for Developing Countries 622
9. Institutional Issues 622

Chapter 20. Sanitary and Phyto–Sanitary Measures ... 629
1. The Legal Discipline ... 629
2. The Rationale for the Legal Discipline ... 630
3. Coverage ... 630
4. SPS Measures Based on International Standards ... 632
5. Unilateral SPS Measures ... 635
6. Precautionary SPS Measures ... 649
7. Control Procedures ... 653
8. Special and Differential Treatment for Developing Countries ... 654
9. Expertise in SPS-related Dispute Adjudication ... 655
10. Standard of Review ... 658
11. Institutional Issues ... 658

Chapter 21. Trade Related Investment Measures (TRIMs) ... 663
1. The Legal Discipline ... 663
2. The Rationale for the Legal Discipline ... 663
3. Coverage of the Legal Discipline ... 663
4. Institutional Issues ... 669
5. Trade and Investment Re–Visited ... 669

Chapter 22. Government Procurement ... 675
1. The Legal Discipline ... 675
2. The Rationale for the Legal Discipline ... 675
3. Coverage of the Legal Discipline ... 675
4. Enforcing the GPA ... 684
5. Institutional Issues ... 688

Chapter 23. The Advent and Integration Model of GATS ... 689
1. Regulation of Trade in Services Before the Advent of GATS ... 689
2. The Road to Punta del Este and the Formal Negotiation of GATS ... 692
3. Negotiating the GATS ... 702
4. The Integration Model of GATS ... 707

Chapter 24. General Obligations ... 743
1. General Obligations: Identification and Function ... 743
2. MFN ... 744
3. Domestic Regulation ... 759
4. Recognition ... 762
5. Transparency ... 763
6. Competition–Related Disciplines ... 764
7. Payments and Transfers ... 767
8. Balance of Payments ... 767
9. GATS Rules ... 768

Chapter 25. Specific Commitments ... 773
1. The Legal Discipline ... 773
2. The Rationale for the Legal Discipline ... 773
3. Coverage ... 773
4. Modification of Schedules ... 793

5. Interpretation of Commitments 794

Chapter 26. Exceptions **801**
1. Preferential Trade Agreements (PTAs) 801
2. Labour Markets Integration Agreements... 802
3. General Exceptions 803
4. National Security 807

Chapter 27. TRIPS: Introduction and Basic Principles **809**
1. Overview of the TRIPS Agreement 809
2. The Advent of the TRIPS Agreement 812
3. Rationales for the TRIPS Agreement... 815
4. An Overview of the TRIPS Agreement 818
5. National Treatment 824
6. Most Favored Nation (MFN) Treatment 833
7. Exhaustion... 836
8. Institutional Arrangements... 839

Chapter 28. Copyright **843**
1. The Legal Discipline.. 843
2. The Rationale for the Legal Discipline 843
3. Coverage of the Legal Discipline 844

Chapter 29. Trademarks **857**
1. The Legal Discipline.. 857
2. The Rationale for the Legal Discipline 857
3. Coverage of the Legal Discipline 858

Chapter 30. Patents and Undisclosed Information **869**
1. The Legal Discipline.. 870
2. The Rationale for the Legal Discipline 871
3. Coverage of the Legal Discipline 873
4. TRIPS and Public Health 893

Chapter 31. Enforcement of IP Rights **903**
1. The Legal Discipline.. 904
2. The Rationale for the Legal Discipline 904
3. Coverage of the Legal Discipline 906
4. Post–TRIPS Developments: The Anti–Counterfeiting Trade Agreement (ACTA) 921

Chapter 32. From GATT to the WTO: History of Adjudication in the Multilateral Trading System & Presentation of the WTO DSU **925**
1. The (Original) GATT 925
2. Panel Procedures... 927
3. The Later GATT Years 928
4. The WTO Dispute Settlement Understanding (DSU) 930

Summary of Contents

Chapter 33. Consultations **941**
1. The Request for Consultations 941
2. No Panel Without Consultations 941
3. Multilateral Defense 942
4. Confidentiality Requirements 942
5. The Outcome of Consultations 943

Chapter 34. Panel Proceedings **945**
1. The Request for Establishment of a Panel 945
2. The Composition of Panels 952
3. The Terms of Reference (TOR) 953
4. Sources Restraining a Panel's Jurisdiction 953
5. The Measure Before the Panel 959
6. Rights and Duties of Parties Appearing Before Panels 962
7. The Duty of the Panel: To Perform an Objective Assessment ... 966
8. Evidence 978
9. The Outcome of the Panel Process 980

Chapter 35. The Appellate Body **991**
1. The Notice of Appeal 991
2. Establishment of the AB Division 993
3. Sources Restraining the Jurisdiction of the AB 995
4. The Parties Before the AB 995
5. The Duty of the AB 998
6. Duty of parties 1001
7. Evidence 1002
8. The AB Report 1004

Chapter 36. Alternative Proceedings **1009**
1. Alternative Dispute Settlement Proceedings 1009
2. Arbitration Under Art. 25 DSU 1009
3. Good Offices, Conciliation and Mediation 1014
4. Dispute Resolution Outside of the DSU 1014

Chapter 37. Enforcement **1017**
1. Recommendations and Suggestions 1017
2. Reasonable Period of Time (RPT) 1021
3. Compliance Panels 1026
4. Compensation and the Suspension of Concessions 1032
5. Monitoring Compliance Following Retaliation 1053

INDEX 1063

TABLE OF CONTENTS

ACKNOWLEDGMENTS III
REFERENCES V
ABBREVIATIONS LXXI
TABLE OF CASES LXXXIII

Chapter 1. The WTO Institution 1
1. WTO, The Successor to the GATT 1
2. The Institutional Architecture of the WTO in a Nutshell 6
   2.1 The Various Bodies 6
   2.2 The WTO Secretariat 7
3. Participation in the WTO 8
   3.1 Accession to the WTO 8
      3.1.1 The Legal Basis for Accession to the WTO 8
      3.1.2 The Procedure of Accession 9
      3.1.3 Procedures for Least–Developed Countries (LDCs) 11
   3.2 Membership of the WTO 14
      3.2.1 Original Members 14
      3.2.2 New Members 14
      3.2.3 The Current WTO Membership 14
   3.3 Observer–Status in the WTO 19
      3.3.1 States and Customs Territories 19
      3.3.2 International Organizations 22
      3.3.3 Participation of Non–Governmental Organizations (NGOs) 25
4. Day to Day Operations 25
   4.1 Organization of WTO Meetings 25
   4.2 Decision Making in the WTO 27
      4.2.1 The General Rule 27
      4.2.2 Special Procedures 28
   4.3 Groupings and Alliances in the WTO 32
5. The WTO Law 32
   5.1 Three Layers of WTO Obligations 33
   5.2 The Multilateral Agreements: A Single Undertaking 34
      5.2.1 The Annex 1 Agreements 35
      5.2.2 The Dispute Settlement Understanding (DSU) 38
      5.2.3 The Trade Policy Review Mechanism (TPRM) 39
   5.3 The Plurilateral Agreements 40
      5.3.1 Agreement on Government Procurement (GPA) 41
      5.3.2 The Agreement on Civil Aircraft 41
   5.4 Waivers 42
   5.5 Non–Application 48
   5.6 The Treaty–Making Power of the WTO 51

6. Withdrawing From the WTO 53
   6.1 The Right to Withdraw 53
   6.2 Withdrawal in the GATT Years 54
         Questions and Comments 55

Chapter 2. Quantitative Restrictions **59**
1. The Legal Discipline 59
2. The Rationale for the Legal Discipline 60
3. Coverage of the Legal Discipline 61
   3.1 General Prohibition on Quantitative Restrictions 61
   3.2 What Qualifies as a QR? The Treatment of Certain Specific Cases 62
       3.2.1 Export Taxes 62
       3.2.2 Minimum Export Prices 62
       3.2.3 Minimum Import Prices 63
       3.2.4 Production Quotas 63
   3.3 The Concept of *De Facto* QRs 63
   3.4 The Necessary Government Involvement 68
4. Exceptions 68
   4.1 Critical Shortages of Foodstuffs and Any Other Essential Product 69
   4.2 Standards for the Classification, Grading or Marketing of Commodities 70
   4.3 Necessary for the Enforcement of Governmental Measures 70
   4.4 Balance of Payments (Arts. XII and XVIII GATT) 72
   4.5 Exchange Restrictions 75
   4.6 Infant Industry Protection 77
   4.7 Other Exceptions 78
5. Administration of Legally Permissible QRs 80
         Questions and Comments 81

Chapter 3. Tariffs **87**
1. The Legal Discipline 87
2. The Rationale for the Legal Discipline 88
3. The Coverage of the Legal Discipline 90
   3.1 Expressing Goods in Common Language: The Harmonized System 90
   3.2 Ordinary Customs Duties and Other Duties and Charges 93
   3.3 Customs Valuation 96
   3.4 Multilateral Trade Negotiations (Trade Rounds) 97
   3.5 Trade Negotiations Outside Trade Rounds 98
   3.6 Certification, Modification, and Rectification of Schedules 99
   3.7 Exceptions to Art. II.1 GATT Obligations 101
       3.7.1 Charge Equivalent to an Internal Tax 101
       3.7.2 Antidumping and Countervailing Duties 101
       3.7.3 Fees and Charges for Services Rendered 102
4. Withdrawing Concessions From Members Leaving the WTO 103
5. Renegotiating Tariffs 103
   5.1 The Participants in a Tariff Renegotiation 104

	5.2	The Mechanics of the Negotiation	108
		5.2.1 No Prior Approval Required	110
		5.2.2 Prior Approval Required	113
		Questions and Comments	114

Chapter 4. Most Favored Nation (MFN) 121
1. The Legal Discipline 121
2. The Rationale for the Legal Discipline 121
3. Coverage of the Legal Discipline 122
   3.1 The Requirement of Art. I.1 GATT 122
   3.2 Any Advantage, Favor, Privilege or Immunity 123
   3.3 A WTO Member May Not Treat a Non–WTO Member Better Than the WTO Members 125
   3.4 The Origin of Goods 125
   3.5 Immediately and Unconditionally 126
   3.6 Non–Discrimination With Respect to "Like Products" 129
4. Exceptions 130
   Questions and Comments 131

Chapter 5. Preferential Trade Agreements (PTAs) 137
1. The Legal Discipline 137
2. The Rationale for the Legal Discipline 137
3. Coverage of the Legal Discipline 138
   3.1 Which PTAs Fall Under the Purview of Art. XXIV GATT? ... 138
   3.2 The Scope of the Art. XXIV GATT Exception 138
   3.3 Requirements of WTO Members Entering into a PTA 139
   3.4 Notification 139
   3.5 Substantially All Trade ('Internal Requirement') 141
   3.6 No New Protection Towards Other WTO Members ('External Requirement') 143
4. Enforcing Art. XXIV GATT 146
   4.1 The Nature of the Multilateral Review 146
   4.2 Litigating the Consistency of PTAs Before Panels 147
   Questions and Comments 160

Chapter 6. Special and Differential Treatment for Developing Countries 165
1. The Legal Discipline 165
2. The Rationale for the Legal Discipline 165
3. Coverage of the Legal Discipline 168
   3.1 Who Are the Beneficiaries? 168
   3.2 Who Are the Donors? 169
   3.3 Preferences Are One Way, Non–Reciprocal 169
   3.4 What Constitutes Preferential Treatment? 170
      3.4.1 Tariff Preferences 170
      3.4.2 Preferences on Non–Tariff Measures 170
   3.5 Non–Discrimination 174
      3.5.1 Statutory Distinction Between LDCs and Other Developing Countries 174

	3.5.2 Preferences Based on Objective Criteria 187

	3.6 Withdrawal of Benefits 189
	3.7 Litigating the Enabling Clause 189
4.	Committee on Trade and Development (CTD) 190
5.	Trade and Development 191
	Questions and Comments 193

Chapter 7. Import Licensing, Customs Valuation, and Pre-shipment Inspection 197

1. The ILA (Import Licensing Agreement) 197
   1.1 The Legal Discipline 197
   1.2 The Rationale for the Legal Discipline 197
   1.3 Coverage 197
       1.3.1 Automatic- and Non–Automatic Import Licensing 197
       1.3.2 Automatic Licensing 198
       1.3.3 Non–Automatic Licensing 198
       1.3.4 Transparency and Administration of Import Licensing 199
   1.4 Institutional Issues 200
2. The Customs Valuation (CV) Agreement 201
   2.1 The Legal Discipline 201
   2.2 The Rationale for the Legal Discipline 201
   2.3 Coverage 202
       2.3.1 Limits of Coverage 202
       2.3.2 The Primacy of Transaction Value 202
       2.3.3 Moving Away From the Transaction Value 203
       2.3.4 Confidentiality 206
       2.3.5 Special and Differential Treatment 206
       2.3.6 Institutional Issues 207
3. The Agreement on Pre-shipment Inspection (PSI) 207
   3.1 The Legal Discipline 207
   3.2 The Rationale for the Legal Discipline 208
   3.3 Coverage 208
       3.3.1 Pre-shipment Entity 208
       3.3.2 The Independent Entity 211
       3.3.3 Transparency and Administration of the Agreement 211
       3.3.4 Special and Differential Treatment 212
             Questions and Comments 212

Chapter 8. National Treatment 215
1. The Legal Discipline 215
2. The Rationale for the Legal Discipline 215
3. The Coverage of the Legal Discipline 216
   3.1 Introductory Remarks 216
   3.2 Statutory Delimitation of the Coverage 218
   3.3 Delimitation of the Coverage Through Re–Negotiation of the GATT 219
   3.4 Delimitation of the Coverage Through Case Law 221
   3.5 Summary Remarks on Scope of Coverage of Art. III GATT 223

4.	Internal Taxes and Other Internal Charges (Fiscal Measures)		224
	4.1	Directly Competitive or Substitutable (DCS) Goods	225
		4.1.1 What Is a DCS Good?	225
		4.1.2 So as to Afford Protection (SATAP)	228
	4.2	Like Products	232
		4.2.1 What Is a Like Product?	232
		4.2.2 Taxation in Excess	235
5.	Laws, Regulations, and Requirements Affecting Trade (Fiscal Measures)		235
	5.1	Laws, Regulations or Requirements	236
	5.2	Affecting Sale, Offering for Sale	236
	5.3	Like Products in Art. III.4 GATT	237
	5.4	Less Favorable Treatment (LFT)	240
6.	Exceptions to the National Treatment Obligation		245
	Questions and Comments		245

Chapter 9. Goods in Transit ... 251
1. The Legal Discipline ... 251
2. The Rationale for the Legal Provision ... 251
3. Coverage ... 251
   - 3.1 Reasonable Costs and Charges ... 252
   - 3.2 Use of Most Convenient Routes for International Transit ... 252
   - 3.3 Absence for Discrimination ... 253
   - 3.4 Jurisdictional Limits ... 253
      - Questions and Comments ... 255

Chapter 10. State Trading ... 257
1. The Legal Discipline ... 257
2. The Rationale for the Legal Discipline ... 257
3. Coverage ... 258
   - 3.1 Defining STEs ... 258
   - 3.2 The Legal Obligations Imposed on STEs in a Nutshell ... 259
   - 3.3 Non–Discrimination ... 259
   - 3.4 STEs and Quantitative Restrictions ... 263
   - 3.5 STEs and Tariff Concessions ... 263
   - 3.6 Transparency Requirements ... 264
4. Exceptions ... 264
   - Questions and Comments ... 264

Chapter 11. The General Transparency Obligation ... 267
1. The Legal Discipline ... 267
2. The Rationale for the Legal Discipline ... 268
3. Coverage of the Legal Discipline ... 269
   - 3.1 Laws and Other Acts of General Application ... 269
   - 3.2 Uniform, Reasonable and Impartial Administration of Laws ... 270
   - 3.3 The Obligation to Maintain Independent Tribunals ... 277
   - 3.4 Standard of Review ... 278
      - Questions and Comments ... 281

Chapter 12. General Exceptions — 285
1. The Legal Discipline — 285
2. The Rationale for the Legal Discipline — 285
3. Coverage of the Legal Discipline — 288
   - 3.1 Preliminary Remarks on Common Elements — 288
     - 3.1.1 Art. XX GATT Functions as an Exception to All GATT Provisions — 288
     - 3.1.2 Art. XX GATT Operates as a Two–Tier Test — 289
     - 3.1.3 Allocation of Burden of Proof — 290
   - 3.2 The Specific Exceptions Enumerated in Art. XX GATT — 292
     - 3.2.1 Public Morals — 292
     - 3.2.2 Human, Animal, or Plant Life or Health — 293
     - 3.2.3 Imports and Exports of Gold and Silver — 300
     - 3.2.4 Compliance With Laws Not Inconsistent With the GATT — 300
     - 3.2.5 Prison Labor — 303
     - 3.2.6 National Treasures — 303
     - 3.2.7 Conservation of Exhaustible Natural Resources — 303
     - 3.2.8 Intergovernmental Commodity Agreements — 308
     - 3.2.9 Government Stabilization Plans — 310
     - 3.2.10 Products in General or Local Short Supply — 311
   - 3.3 Complying With the Chapeau — 311
     - Questions and Comments — 316

Chapter 13. National Security — 319
1. The Legal Discipline — 319
2. The Rationale for the Legal Discipline — 319
3. Coverage of the Legal Discipline — 320
   - 3.1 Practice Outside Dispute Adjudication — 320
   - 3.2 Dispute Adjudication — 321
     - Questions and Comments — 328

Chapter 14. Antidumping — 331
1. The Legal Discipline — 331
2. The Rationale for the Legal Discipline — 332
3. Coverage of the Legal Discipline — 333
   - 3.1 Dumping — 334
     - 3.1.1 Calculating Normal Value — 334
       - 3.1.1.1 Use of the Home Market Price as NV — 334
       - 3.1.1.2 Circumstances for Disregarding Home Market Price as the Basis for Normal Value — 334
       - 3.1.1.3 Use of Export Price in a Third Country as the Basis for Normal Value — 336
       - 3.1.1.4 Constructed Normal Value — 337
       - 3.1.1.5 Non–Market Economies — 340
       - 3.1.1.6 Summary for Calcuating Normal Value — 341
     - 3.1.2 Establishing the Export Price — 341
     - 3.1.3 Comparison of the Export Price to Normal Value — 342
     - 3.1.4 Calculation of the Dumping Margin — 344

		3.1.5	Sampling (and Other Exceptions to the Duty to Establish Individual Margins) 346

- 3.1.5 Sampling (and Other Exceptions to the Duty to Establish Individual Margins) 346
- 3.1.6 Margin of Dumping: The Required Level 349
- 3.2 Injury 349
  - 3.2.1 What Constitutes "Injury"? 349
  - 3.2.2 Determination of Injury 349
    - 3.2.2.1 Volume of Dumped Imports 350
    - 3.2.2.2 Effects of Dumped Imports on Prices 352
    - 3.2.2.3 Effects of Dumped Imports on Domestic Industry 353
    - 3.2.2.4 The Meaning of the "Domestic Industry" and "Like Product" in the AD Context 355
  - 3.2.3 Cumulation 358
  - 3.2.4 Sampling 358
  - 3.2.5 Determination of a Threat of Material Injury 358
  - 3.2.6 Determination of Material Retardation 362
- 3.3 Demonstration of a Causal Link Between Dumping and Injury .. 362

4. Imposition of AD Duties 363
   - 4.1 Provisional Measures 364
   - 4.2 Price Undertakings 365
   - 4.3 Definitive Duties 366
     - 4.3.1 Prospective vs. Retrospective Assessment of Duties 366
     - 4.3.2 Who are Duties Imposed Against? 368
   - 4.4 Counteracting Dumping Through Other Measures Besides AD Duties 372
   - 4.5 Public Interest Clause 373
   - 4.6 Lesser Duty Rule 373
   - 4.7 Duration and Administrative Reviews of AD Duties 374
   - 4.8 Sunset Reviews 376
     - 4.8.1 Absent a Sunset Review, the AD Duty Will Lapse 376
     - 4.8.2 Standard of Review for Sunset Reviews 378
     - 4.8.3 Substantive Requirements for Sunset Reviews 381

5. Procedural Requirements 384
   - 5.1 Standing 385
   - 5.2 The Investigation Process 386
     - 5.2.1 The Content of the Request for Initiation 386
     - 5.2.2 The Discretion to Initiate 387
     - 5.2.3 Questionnaires 391
     - 5.2.4 Verifications 392
     - 5.2.5 The Period of Investigation 393
     - 5.2.6 Due Process 398
     - 5.2.7 Duty to Cooperate and Recourse to Best Information Available (BIA) 401
   - 5.3 Transparency 407
   - 5.4 Judicial Review of AD Decisions 408

6. WTO Review of Anti-Dumping Determinations 409
   - 6.1 The Standard of Review 409
   - 6.2 Remedies Against Illegally Imposed AD Duties 416

7. Institutional Issues 417
   Questions and Comments 417

Chapter 15. Subsidies and Countervailing Duties **423**
1. The Legal Discipline... 423
2. The Rationale for the Legal Discipline 424
3. Coverage of the Legal Discipline 425
   3.1 Subsidies and Countervailing Duties... 425
   3.2 Only CVDs are Permissible in Order to Address Subsidization ... 426
   3.3 Mutual Exclusion of AD Duties and CVDs (Double Remedies) 426
4. Definition of a "Subsidy".. 427
   4.1 Financial Contribution by Government or Public Body 427
       4.1.1 Definition of a Government or Any "Public Body".......... 428
       4.1.2 Forms of Financial Contribution 430
       4.1.3 Any Form of Income or Price Support 434
   4.2 Benefit to Recipient.. 435
       4.2.1 The Private Investor / Marketplace Test 436
       4.2.2 The Concept of a "Pass–Through" Benefit 437
       4.2.3 Calculating the Amount of the Benefit............................ 439
   4.3 Specificity.. 443
5. Prohibited Subsidies 445
   5.1 The Legal Discipline... 446
   5.2 *De jure* and *De facto* Export Subsidies 447
   5.3 Counteracting Prohibited Subsidies... 451
6. Actionable Subsidies 456
   6.1 Injury to the Domestic Industry 456
   6.2 Nullification or Impairment of Benefits...................................... 456
   6.3 Serious Prejudice 457
       6.3.1 Situations Giving Rise to Serious Prejudice 458
       6.3.2 Evidentiary Issues Regarding an Examination of
              Serious Prejudice 466
   6.4 Counteracting Actionable Subsidies With Adverse Effects 468
7. Non–Actionable Subsidies 468
8. Countervailing Duties (CVDs).. 469
   8.1 Substantive Requirements for a CVD 470
       8.1.1 Subsidy 470
       8.1.2 Injury 470
       8.1.3 Causation 477
   8.2 Imposition of a CVD 480
       8.2.1 Provisional CVDs 480
       8.2.2 Price Undertakings 481
       8.2.3 Definitive CVDs 482
       8.2.4 Duration of CVDs.. 484
       8.2.5 Administrative Reviews (Changed Circumstances
              Reviews) 485
       8.2.6 Sunset Reviews 489
   8.3 Procedural Requirements 490
       8.3.1 Standing 490

		8.3.2	The Content of a Request for Initiation of a CVD Investigation 491

        8.3.3   Compulsory Consultations 491
        8.3.4   Initiation of an Investigation 492
        8.3.5   Due Process Obligations.. 493
        8.3.6   Duty to Cooperate and Recourse to Facts Available 495
        8.3.7   Judicial Review of CVD Decisions 496
   8.4   Standard of Review 496
   8.5   No Double Dipping 497
9.   Institutional Issues 498
   Questions and Comments 499

Chapter 16. Safeguards 503
1. The Legal Discipline... 503
2. The Rationale for the Legal Discipline 504
3. Coverage of the Legal Discipline 505
   3.1   A Typology of Safeguard Measures 505
   3.2   The Conditions for Lawful Imposition of Safeguards 507
        3.2.1   Unforeseen Developments... 508
        3.2.2   Increased Quantities of Imports 510
        3.2.3   Injury to the Domestic Industry Producing the Like Product 516
        3.2.4   Causal Link Between Increased Imports and Injury 523
   3.3   Provisional Safeguards 529
   3.4   Application of Definitive Safeguards 529
        3.4.1   Application Only to the Extent Necessary 529
        3.4.2   Application on Non–Discriminatory Basis, Bar Quota Modulation 530
   3.5   The Duration of Safeguards.. 532
   3.6   Compensation 533
   3.7   Special and Differential Treatment for Developing Countries....... 534
   3.8   Standard of Review 534
4. Special Safeguard Regime With Respect to China 536
5. Procedural Requirements 543
   5.1   Initiation 543
   5.2   The Period of Investigation (POI).. 543
   5.3   An Active Investigating Authority 544
   5.4   Provision of Access to the File 544
   5.5   Confidential Information 545
   5.6   Publication and Notification 545
6. Institutional Issues 548
   Questions and Comments 548

Chapter 17. Agriculture 549
1. The Legal Discipline... 549
2. The Rationale for the Legal Discipline 550
3. Coverage of the Legal Discipline 554
   3.1   The Agreement in a Nutshell 554
   3.2   The Relationship Between the AG and the SCM Agreements...... 555

		3.3	Product Coverage 557
4.	Border Measures on Agricultural Goods 557		
	4.1	The Tariffication Requirement 557	
	4.2	Exceptions to Bound Tariff Rate 558	
		4.2.1	Special Safeguard Mechanism 558
		4.2.2	Special Treatment Cases 559
	4.3	Commitments to Reduce the Overall Level of Agricultural Tariffs 560	
5.	Domestic Subsidies for Agriculture 560		
	5.1	The Advent of AMS 560	
	5.2	Exceptions From Calculations of AMS 562	
		5.2.1	Development Subsidies 562
		5.2.2	De minimis Payments 562
		5.2.3	Direct Payments for Production–Limiting Programs (Blue Box Measures) 562
		5.2.4	Green Box Measures 563
	5.3	Calculation of AMS (and EMS) 567	
	5.4	Commitments to Reduce Total AMS 569	
6.	Agricultural Export Subsidies 569		
7.	Other Commitments 576		
	7.1	Peace Clause 576	
	7.2	Net Food–Importing Developing Countries 576	
	7.3	Transparency Requirements 577	
8.	Institutional Issues 577		
	8.1	Committee on Agriculture 577	
	8.2	The Cotton Initiative 578	
		Questions and Comments 579	

Chapter 18. The Agreement on Textiles and Clothing 581
1. The Legal Discipline 581
2. The Rationale for the Legal Discipline 581
3. Coverage of the Legal Discipline 583
   3.1 The Objectives Sought 583
   3.2 The Means in a Nutshell 584
   3.3 Product Coverage 584
   3.4 The Integration Process 585
       3.4.1 Integration in Ten Years 585
       3.4.2 No New Restrictions 585
   3.5 Special Transitional Safeguard Mechanism 586
   3.6 Obligations of WTO Members During the Transition Period 590
4. Institutional Arrangements: The TMB 591
   Questions and Comments 591

Chapter 19. Technical Barriers to Trade 593
1. The Legal Discipline 593
2. The Rationale for the Legal Discipline 593
3. Coverage of the Legal Discipline 594
   3.1 The Relationship With the GATT 594
   3.2 Definitions 596

		3.3	Scope of Application 598

        3.3 Scope of Application 598
        3.4 General Principles Applicable to Technical Regulations and Standards 598
4. Technical Regulations 599
        4.1 Confirmity With International Standards, if Possible 600
        4.2 Non–Discrimination 604
                4.2.1 Like Products 604
                4.2.2 Less Favorable Treatment 607
                4.2.3 Necessity 611
                4.2.4 Legitimate Objectives 612
                4.2.5 Transparency 614
5. Standards 615
6. Conformity Assessment 617
7. Recognition 621
8. Special and Differential Treatment for Developing Countries 622
9. Institutional Issues 622
        Questions and Comments 625

Chapter 20. Sanitary and Phyto–Sanitary Measures 629
1. The Legal Discipline 629
2. The Rationale for the Legal Discipline 630
3. Coverage 630
        3.1 The Relationship With the GATT and the TBT 630
        3.2 Scope of Measures Covered 630
        3.3 Key Questions in Examining a SPS Measure 632
4. SPS Measures Based on International Standards 632
        4.1 The Primacy of International Standards 632
        4.2 Who Issues International Standards? 633
        4.3 Deviating From International Standards 634
5. Unilateral SPS Measures 635
        5.1 Non–Discrimination 636
        5.2 Scientific Evidence 636
        5.3 The Necessity–Requirement 644
        5.4 Consistency 646
6. Precautionary SPS Measures 649
7. Control Procedures 653
8. Special and Differential Treatment for Developing Countries 654
9. Expertise in SPS-related Dispute Adjudication 655
10. Standard of Review 658
11. Institutional Issues 658
        Questions and Comments 658

Chapter 21. Trade Related Investment Measures (TRIMs) 663
1. The Legal Discipline 663
2. The Rationale for the Legal Discipline 663
3. Coverage of the Legal Discipline 663
        3.1 No Comprehensive Treatment of Investment in the GATT 663
        3.2 Measures Coming Under the Purview of TRIMs 664

		3.2.1	Art. III GATT–Type Measures Included in the Illustrative List 664

        3.2.2   Art. XI GATT–Type Measures Included in the Illustrative List 665
    3.3   Obligations During and After the Transitional Phase 666
    3.4   Procedural Obligations 667
    3.5   Special and Differential Treatment 667
    3.6   The Relationship Between TRIMs and the GATT 668
    3.7   The Relationship With Other Annex 1A Agreements 669
4.   Institutional Issues 669
5.   Trade and Investment Re–Visited 669
    5.1   The Working Group on Trade and Investment 670
    5.2   Attempts to Multilateralize Outside the WTO 670
    5.3   Investment Protection in BITs and PTAs 672
           Questions and Comments 672

Chapter 22. Government Procurement 675
1.   The Legal Discipline 675
2.   The Rationale for the Legal Discipline 675
3.   Coverage of the Legal Discipline 675
    3.1   A Plurilateral Agreement 675
    3.2   The GPA Membership 677
    3.3   The Entities Covered 678
    3.4   Non–discrimination 680
    3.5   Awarding a Contract 681
        3.5.1   The Procedure 681
        3.5.2   Kicking the Process Off: The Invitation to Submit 682
        3.5.3   Awarding the Contract 682
    3.6   The New GPA 683
    3.7   Transparency 684
4.   Enforcing the GPA 684
    4.1   Challenge Procedures 684
    4.2   WTO Dispute Settlement 687
5.   Institutional Issues 688
        Questions and Comments 688

Chapter 23. The Advent and Integration Model of GATS 689
1.   Regulation of Trade in Services Before the Advent of GATS 689
2.   The Road to Punta del Este and the Formal Negotiation of GATS 692
    2.1   The 1982 Ministerial Decision 692
    2.2   The CG 18 693
    2.3   Involving the OECD 694
    2.4   The Jaramillo Group 695
    2.5   Punta del Este (1986) 699
3.   Negotiating the GATS 702
    3.1   Organization of the Negotiations and the Players Involved 702
    3.2   Reaching Consensus 705
4.   The Integration Model of GATS 707
    4.1   Coverage of GATS 707

	4.1.1	All Encompassing Minus Two 707
	4.1.2	Services Supplied in the Exercise of Governmental Authority 709
	4.1.3	Air Transport Services 711
	4.1.4	Social Security, BITs, Labor Mobility, Judicial and Administrative Assistance 711
4.2	Positive List, Negative List 712
4.3	General Obligations, and Specific Commitments 716
4.4	The Modes of Supply 721
	4.4.1	The Current Regime 721
	4.4.2	How Did We Get Here? 722
	4.4.3	Cross–Border Supply (Mode 1) 723
	4.4.4	Consumption Abroad (Mode 2) 726
	4.4.5	Commercial Presence (Mode 3) 728
	4.4.6	Presence of Natural Persons (Mode 4) 730
4.5	Non–Retroactivity of Obligations Assumed Under the GATS 733
4.6	Measures Affecting Trade in Services 734
4.7	The Relationship Between GATT and GATS 738
	Questions and Comments 740

Chapter 24. General Obligations 743
1. General Obligations: Identification and Function 743
2. MFN 744
   2.1 The Legal Discipline 744
   2.2 The Rationale for the Legal Discipline 744
   2.3 Coverage 744
       2.3.1 Likeness of Services (and Services Suppliers) 744
       2.3.2 Less Favorable Treatment 746
   2.4 Deviations From MFN 751
       2.4.1 MFN Exemptions (Listed Exemptions) 751
       2.4.2 GATS Provisions Justifying a Deviation From MFN 759
3. Domestic Regulation 759
   3.1 The Legal Discipline 759
   3.2 The Rationale for the Legal Discipline 759
   3.3 Coverage 760
       3.3.1 Reasonable, Objective, and Impartial Administration ... 760
       3.3.2 Judicial Review of Domestic Regulation 760
       3.3.3 The Work Programme and the Transitional Obligations 760
4. Recognition 762
   4.1 The Legal Discipline 762
   4.2 The Rationale for the Legal Discipline 763
   4.3 Non–Discrimination 763
5. Transparency 763
   5.1 The Legal Discipline 763
   5.2 The Rationale for the Legal Discipline 763
   5.3 Coverage 763
6. Competition–Related Disciplines 764
   6.1 The Legal Discipline 764

	6.2 The Rationale for the Legal Discipline 764
	6.3 The Coverage of the Legal Discipline.. 765
7.	Payments and Transfers... 767
	7.1 The Legal Discipline.. 767
	7.2 The Rationale for the Legal Discipline 767
	7.3 Coverage... 767
8.	Balance of Payments... 767
	8.1 The Legal Discipline.. 767
	8.2 The Rationale for the Legal Discipline 768
	8.3 Coverage... 768
9.	GATS Rules 768
	Questions and Comments 768

Chapter 25. Specific Commitments... **773**
1. The Legal Discipline.. 773
2. The Rationale for the Legal Discipline 773
3. Coverage.. 773
   3.1 Issues Common to Market Access, National Treatment, and Additional Commitments... 773
       3.1.1 The List of Services Where Commitments Will Be Entered.. 773
       3.1.2 The 1993 and 2001 Scheduling Guidelines 776
       3.1.3 The Level of Commitments 779
       3.1.4 Horizontal and Sector–Specific Commitments 780
       3.1.5 Clarification of Commitments Entered 781
   3.2 Market Access.. 783
       3.2.1 Six Measures Prohibited, in Principle............................. 783
       3.2.2 Art. XVI GATS: An Exhaustive List of Market Access Restrictions?.. 785
       3.2.3 Art. XVI GATS and Domestic Services Suppliers 786
       3.2.4 Relationship With Art. VI GATS (Domestic Regulation)... 787
   3.3 National Treatment (NT)... 787
       3.3.1 The Test of Compliance With Art. XVII GATS 788
       3.3.2 Like Services/Services Suppliers 788
       3.3.3 Less Favorable Treatment (LFT)..................................... 789
       3.3.4 *De Jure* and *De Facto* LFT 790
   3.4 Additional Commitments... 790
       3.4.1 The Content 790
       3.4.2 Scheduling Additional Commitments.............................. 791
4. Modification of Schedules 793
5. Interpretation of Commitments 794
   Questions and Comments 797

Chapter 26. Exceptions **801**
1. Preferential Trade Agreements (PTAs)... 801
   1.1 Coverage... 801
   1.2 A Profile of Notified PTAs 802
2. Labour Markets Integration Agreements... 802

3. General Exceptions 803
   3.1 An Exhaustive List 803
   3.2 A Two–Tier Test (à la GATT) 804
   3.3 Public Order 804
   3.4 Measures Aimed at Securing Compliance With Laws 806
   3.5 Compliance With the Chapeau of Art. XIV GATS 807
4. National Security 807
   Questions and Comments 808

Chapter 27. TRIPS: Introduction and Basic Principles 809
1. Overview of the TRIPS Agreement 809
2. The Advent of the TRIPS Agreement 812
3. Rationales for the TRIPS Agreement 815
4. An Overview of the TRIPS Agreement 818
   4.1 A Baseline Agreement for Partial Harmonization 818
   4.2 Transitional Periods for Implementation 819
   4.3 Implementation Flexibility 821
   4.4 Structure of the TRIPS Agreement 823
5. National Treatment 824
   5.1 The Legal Discipline 824
   5.2 The Rationale for the Legal Discipline 825
   5.3 Coverage of the Legal Discipline 826
       5.3.1 Relationship to Other International IP Agreements 826
       5.3.2 Relationship to the GATT 829
       5.3.3 Conditional Reciprocity 829
       5.3.4 *De Jure* vs. *De Facto* Discrimination 832
6. Most Favored Nation (MFN) Treatment 833
   6.1 The Legal Discipline 833
   6.2 The Rationale for the Legal Discipline 833
   6.3 Coverage of the Legal Discipline 834
       6.3.1 General Remarks 834
       6.3.2 Exceptions to the MFN Principle 835
7. Exhaustion 836
   7.1 The Legal Discipline 836
   7.2 Rationale for the Legal Discipline 837
   7.3 Coverage of the Legal Discipline 837
8. Institutional Arrangements 839
   Questions and Comments 840

Chapter 28. Copyright 843
1. The Legal Discipline 843
2. The Rationale for the Legal Discipline 843
3. Coverage of the Legal Discipline 844
   3.1 Preliminary Remarks 844
   3.2 Relationship to the Berne Convention 845
   3.3 Scope of Coverage 845
   3.4 Rental Rights 847
   3.5 Term of Protection 848
   3.6 Related Rights 849

Chapter 29. Trademarks 857
1. The Legal Discipline 857
2. The Rationale for the Legal Discipline 857
3. Coverage of the Legal Discipline 858
   - 3.1 Paris Convention (1967) Obligations 858
   - 3.2 Protectable Subject Matter 859
   - 3.3 Grounds for Denial of Protection 861
   - 3.4. Minimum Rights Conferred Upon the Owner of a Mark 862
   - 3.5 Term of Protection 863
   - 3.6 Limitations on Cancellation of a Trademark 864
   - 3.7 Limitations on Compulsory Licensing and Other Government Requirements 865
   - 3.8 Exceptions 866
   - Questions and Comments 867

3.7 Limitations and Exceptions: The Three–Step Test 851
Questions and Comments 855

Chapter 30. Patents and Undisclosed Information 869
1. The Legal Discipline 870
2. The Rationale for the Legal Discipline 871
3. Coverage of the Legal Discipline 873
   - 3.1 Paris Convention (1967) Provisions 873
   - 3.2 Protectable Subject Matter and Permitted Exceptions 874
   - 3.3 Term of Protection 877
   - 3.4 Exclusive Rights Conferred on the Patent Owner 877
   - 3.5 Non–Discrimination Principle 878
   - 3.6 Disclosure Conditions on Patent Applicants 879
   - 3.7 Exceptions to the Rights Conferred 880
   - 3.8 Compulsory Licensing 884
   - 3.9 Protection of Test Data Necessary for Regulatory Approval 888
   - 3.10 Trade Secrets and Confidential Information 891
4. TRIPS and Public Health 893
   Questions and Comments 901

Chapter 31. Enforcement of IP Rights 903
1. The Legal Discipline 904
2. The Rationale for the Legal Discipline 904
3. Coverage of the Legal Discipline 906
   - 3.1 General Obligations 907
   - 3.2 Civil and Administrative Procedures and Remedies 910
   - 3.3 Border Measures 915
   - 3.4 Criminal Procedures 918
4. Post–TRIPS Developments: The Anti–Counterfeiting Trade Agreement (ACTA) 921
   Questions and Comments 923

Chapter 32. From GATT to the WTO: History of Adjudication in the Multilateral Trading System & Presentation of the WTO DSU 925
1. The (Original) GATT 925
2. Panel Procedures 927
3. The Later GATT Years 928
4. The WTO Dispute Settlement Understanding (DSU) 930
   4.1 Major Departures From the GATT System 930
   4.2 State to State Litigation 930
   4.3 An Exclusive Forum 931
   4.4 Two Phases of Adjudication 932
   4.5 The Types of Legal Complaints 933
       4.5.1 Violation Complaints 933
       4.5.2 Non–Violation Complaints 934
       4.5.3 Situation Complaints 938
             Questions and Comments 939

Chapter 33. Consultations 941
1. The Request for Consultations 941
2. No Panel Without Consultations 941
3. Multilateral Defense 942
4. Confidentiality Requirements 942
5. The Outcome of Consultations 943
   Questions and Comments 943

Chapter 34. Panel Proceedings 945
1. The Request for Establishment of a Panel 945
   1.1 The Test for Compliance With the Statutory Requirements 945
   1.2 The Legal Consequence for Violating Art. 6.2 DSU 948
   1.3 Attendant Circumstances 949
       1.3.1 Claims on Provisions Incorporated in Cited Provisions 949
       1.3.2 Provision Not Adequately Cited, but Claim Explained in Submission 950
       1.3.3 Provision Not Adequately Cited, but Obligations Are Interlinked 950
       1.3.4 Provision Not Adequately Cited, but Matter Was Discussed in WTO Committee 951
       1.3.5 WTO Practice 951
       1.3.6 Trade Custom 952
       1.3.7 Contribution to Vagueness by the Party Challenging It 952
   1.4 Moot Claims 952
2. The Composition of Panels 952
3. The Terms of Reference (TOR) 953
4. Sources Restraining a Panel's Jurisdiction 953
   4.1 A Panel's Authority Lapses 954
   4.2 Subject Matter in Consultations and Request for Establishment 954

	4.3 Res Judicata	955
	4.4 Mutually Agreed Solutions (MAS)	955
	4.5 Agreements Between Parties as to the Ambit of Their Dispute	956
	4.6 Estoppel	956
	4.7 Direct Effect of WTO Law in Domestic Legal Orders	959
5.	The Measure Before the Panel	959
	5.1 Mandatory Versus Discretionary Legislation	959
	5.2 Measures Challenged Must Be in Effect When the Panel Is Established	961
6.	Rights and Duties of Parties Appearing Before Panels	962
	6.1 Complainants and Defendants	962
	6.2 Third Parties	963
	6.3 Amici Curiae	965
7.	The Duty of the Panel: To Perform an Objective Assessment	966
	7.1 Working Procedures	966
	7.2 Respecting the Institutional Balance	968
	7.3 Non Ultra Petita	969
	7.4 Exercising Judicial Economy	969
	7.5 *De novo* Review	970
	7.6 Reweighing the Evidence	972
	7.7 Refusal to Take into Account Belatedly Submitted Evidence	972
	7.8 Discretion to Exercise the Right to Seek Information	973
	7.9 Discovery Powers	973
	7.9.1 Calling Upon Experts	973
	7.9.2 Questions to the Parties	974
	7.9.3 Drawing Inferences From Non–Cooperative Attitude by the Parties	975
	7.10 Reviewing Compliance With Art. 11 DSU	975
	7.10.1 The Generic Standard of Review	975
	7.10.2 Finding *Ultra Petita*	976
	7.10.3 Judicial Economy	976
	7.10.4 *De novo* Review	977
	7.10.5 Improper Examination of the Factual Record	977
	7.10.6 Absence of Reasoning	977
	7.10.7 Inconsistent Reasoning	977
	7.10.8 Panels Cannot Rely on Ex Post Facto Justifications	977
	7.10.9 Violating Due Process	978
8.	Evidence	978
	8.1 Timely Submission of Evidence	978
	8.2 No *Ex Parte* Communications	979
	8.3 Allocation of Burden of Proof	979
	8.3.1 Burden of Production	979
	8.3.2 Burden of Persuasion	979
9.	The Outcome of the Panel Process	980
	9.1 Interim Review	980
	9.2 The Final Report	981
	9.2.1 The Form	981

		9.2.2	The Obligation to Provide a Reasoned Explanation for the Findings.. 981
		9.2.3	Dissenting Opinions 982
		9.2.4	Timely Circulation of Panel Reports 983
		9.2.5	Adoption of Panel Reports... 983
		9.2.6	Special Procedures for Least Developed Countries (LDC) 984
	9.3	Multiple Complaints... 984
		Questions and Comments 985

Chapter 35. The Appellate Body **991**
1. The Notice of Appeal 991
2. Establishment of the AB Division.. 993
   2.1 A Permanent Body 993
   2.2 The Selection Process 993
   2.3 Duties and Responsibilities of Members of the AB 994
   2.4 The AB Division... 995
3. Sources Restraining the Jurisdiction of the AB 995
   3.1 Withdrawal of the Appeal 995
   3.2 Mutually Agreed Solutions (MAS) 995
4. The Parties Before the AB 995
   4.1 Appellant, Appellee 995
   4.2 Third Parties... 996
   4.3 Amici Curiae 996
   4.4 Passive Observers.. 998
5. The Duty of the AB.. 998
   5.1 Working Procedures 998
   5.2 Objective Assessment.. 999
   5.3 Discovery Powers... 1001
6. Duty of parties 1001
7. Evidence... 1002
   7.1 The Appellant's Submission(s) 1002
   7.2 The Appellee's Submission 1002
   7.3 Meeting With the Parties.. 1002
   7.4 No *Ex parte* Communications 1002
   7.5 Proceedings Are Confidential 1003
   7.6 Timely Circulation of AB Reports 1003
8. The AB Report 1004
   8.1 Dissenting Opinions 1004
   8.2 Judicial Economy... 1004
   8.3 No Appeal Against AB Reports 1005
   8.4 The Legal Value of AB Reports 1005
       Questions and Comments 1008

Chapter 36. Alternative Proceedings.. **1009**
1. Alternative Dispute Settlement Proceedings 1009
2. Arbitration Under Art. 25 DSU... 1009
   2.1 The Identity of the Arbitrators 1010
   2.2 Parties to an Art. 25 DSU Arbitration? 1010

	2.3	No Consultations Required	1010
	2.4	Notification Requirements	1010
	2.5	Jurisdiction	1010
	2.6	Designing the Procedures	1011
	2.7	Burden of Proof	1012
	2.8	Evidence	1012
	2.9	Confidential Information	1013
	2.10	Discovery Powers of Arbitrators	1013
	2.11	The Legal Effect of the Arbitral Award	1013
3.	Good Offices, Conciliation and Mediation		1014
4.	Dispute Resolution Outside of the DSU		1014
	Questions and Comments		1016

Chapter 37. Enforcement 1017

1. Recommendations and Suggestions 1017
   1.1 Recommendations 1017
   1.2 Suggestions 1018
2. Reasonable Period of Time (RPT) 1021
   2.1 Bilateral Agreement on the Extent of the RPT 1021
   2.2 Arbitration 1021
      2.2.1 The Identity of the Arbitrator 1021
      2.2.2 The Task of the Arbitrator 1022
      2.2.3 Deciding on the RPT 1022
3. Compliance Panels 1026
   3.1 The Identity of the Panelists 1026
   3.2 Duration 1027
   3.3 No Need for Consultations 1027
   3.4 Request for Establishment of a Compliance Panel 1027
   3.5 Standing 1028
   3.6 Sequencing 1028
   3.7 The Mandate of Compliance Panels 1030
   3.8 The Standard of Review of Compliance Panels 1032
   3.9 Compliance Panel Reports Can Be Appealed 1032
   3.10 More Than One Compliance Panels in the Same Dispute? 1032
4. Compensation and the Suspension of Concessions 1032
   4.1 A Preference for Compliance (Retaliation, Only if Necessary) 1032
   4.2 The Forms of Retaliation 1033
   4.3 Compensation 1033
   4.4 Suspension of Concessions 1033
      4.4.1 The Conditions for Lawful Recourse to Cross–Retaliation 1034
      4.4.2 The Legal Constraint of Art. 22.4 DSU 1040
      4.4.3 The Arbitrators' Decision: First and Last Resort 1052
   4.5 Suspension of Other Obligations 1052
5. Monitoring Compliance Following Retaliation 1053
   Questions and Comments 1058

INDEX 1063

ABBREVIATIONS

AB	Appellate Body
ABI	Argentina, Brazil, India
ACP	African, Caribbean, and Pacific
AD	Agreement on Antidumping
ADB	Asian Development Bank
ADICMA	Association of Industrial Producers of Leather, Leather Manufactures and Related Products
AG	Agreement on Agriculture
AGOA	Africa Growth and Opportunity Act
ALADI	Associacion Latinoamericana de Integracion
AMF	Arab Monetary Fund
AMS	Aggregate Measurement of Support
APEC	Asian–Pacific Economic Cooperation
ATC	Agreement on Textiles and Clothing
BCI	Business Confidential Information
BIA	Best Information Available
BIT	Bilateral Investment Treaty
BOP	Balance of Payments
BTN	Brussels Convention on Nomenclature for the Classification of Goods in Customs Tariffs
CA	Civil Aircraft
CAFC	US Court of Appeals for the Federal Circuit
CAP	Common Agricultural Policy

CARICOM	Caribbean Community
CBD	Convention on Biological Diversity
CCA	Clean Air Act (US)
CCCN	Customs Cooperation Council Nomenclature
CCFRS	Certain Carbon Flat Rolled Steel Products
CDSOA	Continued Dumping and Subsidies Offset Act
CEFTA	Central European Free Trade Area
CIF	Cost Insurance Freight
CITES	Convention on International Trade in Endangered Species of Wild Fauna and Flora
COCOM	Coordinating Committee for Multilateral Export Controls
CPC	Central Product Classification
CRTA	Committee on Regional Trade Agreements
CSD	United Nations Commission for Sustainable Development
CTD	Committee on Trade and Development
CTG	Council for Trade in Goods
CTS	Council for Trade in Services
CU	Customs Union
CUSFTA	Canada–United States Free Trade Area
CV	Customs Valuation
CVD	Countervailing Duty
DCS	Directly Competitive or Substitutable
DDG	Deputy Director General
DG	Director–General

DRAM	Dynamic Random Access Micro Chip
DSB	Dispute Settlement Body
DSU	Understanding on Rules and Procedures Governing the Settlement of Disputes
EBR	Enhanced Bond Requirement
EC	European Community
ECE	United Nations Economic Commission for Europe
EEC	European Economic Community
EFTA	European Free Trade Association
EMS	Equivalent Measurement of Support
EPA	Environmental Protection Agency (US)
ESCAP	United Nations Economic and Social Commission for Asia and the Pacific
ESCWA	United Nations Economic and Social Commission for Western Asia
ESTO	European Scientific Technology Observatory
EU	European Union
FA	Factual Abstract
FANs	Friends of Anti–Dumping Negotiations
FAO	Food and Agriculture Organization
FDI	Foreign Direct Investment
FOB	Free on Board
FOIA	Freedom of Information Act (US)
FOREX	Foreign Exchange Contract
FORSEC	South Pacific Forum Secretariat
FP	Factual Presentation

FSC	Foreign Sales Corporations
G–6	Group of Six
G–7	Group of Seven
G–20	Group of Twenty
G–33	Group of Thirty Three
G–90	Group of Ninety
GAAP	Generally Accepted Accounting Principles
GATS	General Agreement on Trade in Services
GATT	General Agreement on Tariffs and Trade
GC	General Council
GDP	Gross Domestic Product
GIR	General Interpretative Rule
GMO	Genetically Modified Organism
GN	Geneva Nomenclature
GNP	Gross National Product
GNS	Group of Negotiations on Services
GPA	Government Procurement Agreement
GRULAC	Group of Latin American and Caribbean Countries
GSP	Generalized System of Preferences
HHI	Herfindhal Hirschmann Index
HS	Harmonized System
IA	Investigating Authority
IADB	Inter–American Development Bank
IAWG	Inter–Agency Working Group
IBM	International Bovine Meat Agreement

ICA	International Commodity Agreement
ICAG	International Cotton Advisory Committee
ICC	International Chamber of Commerce
ICCAT	International Commission for the Conservation of Atlantic Tunas
ICCO	International Cocoa Organization
ICO	International Coffee Organization
ICJ	International Court of Justice
ICSG	International Copper Study Group
ICSID	International Centre for the Settlement of Investment Disputes
ICTB	International Customs Tariffs Bureau
IDA	International Dairy Agreement
IDLO	International Development Law Organization
IEC	International Electro-technical Commission
IF	Integrated Framework
IFIA	International Federation of Inspection Agencies
IFSC	Integrated Framework Steering Committee
IGBA	Illegal Gambling Act
IGC	International Grains Council
IGE	Informal Group of Experts
IHA	Interstate Horseracing Act
IJSG	International Jute Study Group
ILA	Agreement on Import Licensing
ILC	International Law Commission
ILZSG	International Lead and Zinc Study Group

IMF	International Monetary Fund
INR	Initial Negotiating Right
INSG	International Nickel Study Group
IOOC	International Olive Oil Council
IPGRI	International Plant Genetic Resources Institute
IRSG	International Rubber Study Group
IsDB	Islamic Development Bank
ISG	International Study Groups
ISO	International Organization for Standardization
ISO	International Sugar Organization
ISONET	ISO Information Network
IT	Information Technology
ITA	Information Technology Agreement
ITC	International Trade Centre
ITD	International Institute for Trade and Development
ITLOS	International Tribunal of the Law of the Sea
ITO	International Trade Organization
ITTO	International Tropical Timber Organization
ITU	International Telecommunications Union
JEFCA	Joint FAO/WHO Expert Committee on Food Additives
JITAP	Joint Integrated Technical Assistance Programme
LAN	Local Area Network
LCD	Liquid Crystal Display
LDC	Least Developed Countries
LFN	Least Favoured Nation

LFT	Less Favourable Treatment
LTFV	Less Than Fair Value
MAI	Multilateral Agreement on Investment
MAS	Mutually Agreed Solution (MAS)
MC	Ministerial Conference
MEA	Multilateral Environmental Agreement
MERCOSUR	Mercado del Sur
METI	Ministry of Economy, Trade, and Industry
MFA	Multi–Fibre Agreement
MFN	Most Favoured Nation Clause
MIGA	Multilateral Investment Guarantee Agency
MITI	Ministry of International Trade and Industry
Montreal Protocol	Montreal Protocol on Substances that Deplete the Ozone Layer
MOU	Memorandum of Understanding
MRA	Mutual Recognition Agreement
MTN	Multilateral Trade Negotiation
NAFTA	North Atlantic Free Trade Area
NAIC	National Association of Insurance Commissioners
NAMA	Non Agricultural Market Negotiations
NGO	Non Governmental Organization
NGTMS	Negotiating Group on Maritime Transport Services
NME	Non–Market Economy
NT	National Treatment
NTB	Non Tariff Barrier

NV	Normal Value
NVC	Non Violation Complaint
OCD	Ordinary Customs Duty
ODC	Other Duties or Charges
OECD	Organization for Economic Cooperation and Development
OECS	Organization of Eastern Caribbean Countries
OHCHR	Office of the United Nations Commissioner for Human Rights
OIE	Office International des Epizooties
OPEC	Organization of Petroleum Exporting Countries
PCIJ	Permanent Court of International Justice
PFC	Production Flexibility Contract
PGE	Permanent Group of Experts
PIF	Pacific Islands Forum
POI	Period of Investigation
PPM	Process and Production Method
PSE	Producer Subsidy Equivalent
PSI	Principal Supplying Interest
PSIA	Agreement on Preshipment Inspection
PTA	Preferential Trade Agreement
Q and A	Questions and Answers
QFTI	Qualified Foreign Trade Income
QR	Quantitative Restriction
RAMs	Recently Acceded Members
RBP	Restrictive Business Practice

ROO	Agreement on Rules of Origin
Rotterdam Conv.	Rotterdam Convention on the Prior Informed Consent Procedure for Certain Hazardous Chemicals and Pesticides in International Trade
RPT	Reasonable Period of Time
RTA	Regional Trade Agreement
SADC	Southern African Development Community
SAPTA	South Asian Association for Regional Cooperation
SATAP	So as to Afford Protection
SCM	Agreement on Subsidies and Countervaling Measures
SDoc	Supplier's Declaration of Conformity
SDR	Special Drawing Rights
SELA	Latin American Economic System
SG	Agreement on Safeguards
SG & A	Selling, General, and Administrative Expenses
SGS	Société Générale de Surveillance
SI	Substantial Interest
SPS	Agreement on Sanitary and Phyto-sanitary Measures
STE	State Trading Enterprise
Stockholm Conv.	Stockholm Convention on Persistent Organic Pollutants
TBR	Trade Barriers Regulation (EC)
TBT	Agreement Technical Barriers to Trade
TDM	Temporary Defence Mechanism
TED	Turtle Excluding Device
TMB	Textiles Monitoring Body

TNC	Trade Negotiations Committee
TOR	Terms of Reference
TPRM	Trade Policy Review Mechanism
TRIMs	Trade Related Investment Measures
TRIPs	Trade Related Intellectual Property Rights
TRP	Telecommunications Reference Paper
TRQ	Tariff Quota
TSB	Textiles Surveillance Body
T–T	Transaction to Transaction
UN	United Nations
UNCITRAL	United Nations Commission on International Trade Law
UNCLOS	United Nations Convention on the Law of the Sea
UNCTAD	United Nations Conference on Trade and Development
UNDP	United Nations Development Programme
UNEP	United Nations Environment Programme
UNESCO	United Nations Educational, Scientific and Cultural Organization
UNFCCC	United Nations Framework Convention on Climate Change
UNIDO	United Nations Industrial Development Organization
UPOV	International Union for the Protection of New Varieties of Plants
URM	Usual Marketing Requirements
USD	United States Dollars
USDOC	United States Department of Commerce
US ITC	United States International Trade Commission

USO	Universal Service Obligation
VAT	Value Added Tax
VCLT	Vienna Convention on Law of Treaties
VER	Voluntary Export Restraint
WA	Weighted Average
WB	World Bank
WCO	World Customs Organization
WHO	World Health Organization
WIPO	World Intellectual Property Organization
WP	Working Party

TABLE OF CASES

Cases

American Banana Company v. United Fruit Company.............................. 418
Argentina–Ceramic Tiles 344, 392, 400, 402, 403, 408
Argentina–Footwear (EC) 95, 103, 143, 333, 425, 503, 506, 508, 511, 516, 519, 523, 527, 528, 947
Argentina–Hides and Leather .. 65, 67, 268, 269, 271, 275, 276, 279, 280
Argentina–Poultry Antidumping Duties ..149, 344, 345, 356, 365, 388, 389, 394, 397, 405, 407, 408, 415, 956, 1019
Argentina–Preserved Peaches 509, 512, 516, 518, 520
Australia–Apples 631, 639, 645, 657, 953
Australia–Automotive Leather II . 417, 449, 1045
Australia–Automotive Leather II (Article 21.5–US)........................ 1030
Australia–Salmon ...637, 640, 644, 647, 648, 649, 656, 999
Australia–Salmon (Article 21.5–Canada) 966, 1031
Belgium–Family Allowances.. 124, 127
Berlyn Inc. v. Gazette Newspapers 661
Brazil–Aircraft (Art. 22.6—Brazil) 451
Brazil–Aircraft (Article 21.5–Canada II) 1032
Brazil–Desiccated Coconut 945, 953
Brazil–Patent Protection................ 887
Brazil–Retreaded Tyres 291, 294, 297, 312
Brazil–Retreaded Tyres (Article 21.3(c)) 1024
Canada/EC–Article XXVIII Rights 112
Canada–Aircraft 435, 436, 437, 447, 449, 451, 974, 975
Canada–Aircraft (Article 21.5–Brazil) 1030
Canada–Aircraft Credits and Guarantees (Article 22.6–Canada) 454, 455, 1041, 1044
Canada–Autos 124, 128, 431, 668, 669, 730, 735, 744, 750, 775, 788, 948, 970, 999
Canada–Dairy........555, 570, 575, 1001
Canada–FIRA 63, 221, 260, 663
Canada–Gold Coins 300, 738
Canada–Herring and Salmon . 70, 303, 306
Canada–Ice Cream and Yoghurt 71
Canada–Patent Protection of Pharmaceutical Products............ 832
Canada–Patent Term of Protection 877

Canada–Periodicals 248, 249, 738, 739, 977, 999, 1000
Canada–Pharmaceutical Patents (Article 21.3(c)) 1024
Canada–Provincial Liquor Boards (US) 738
Canada–Suspended Concession ... 1054
Canada–Wheat Exports and Grain Imports. 257, 258, 260, 261, 262, 953
Chile–Alcoholic Beverages (Article 21.3(c)).. 1025
Chile–Price Band System 962, 964, 976, 992
Chile–Price Band System (Article 21.3(c)).................... 1023, 1024, 1025
China–Audiovisual Services ... 292, 298
China–Electronic Payment Services 785, 789, 799
China–GOES........... 402, 408, 435, 491
China–Intellectual Property Rights 913, 917, 919, 920, 921
China–Raw Materials 62, 67, 68, 69, 213, 289, 290, 328
Colombia–Ports of Entry . 67, 201, 202, 251, 252, 948, 967
Colombia–Ports of Entry (Article 21.3 (c))................................... 1023, 1026
Daubert v. Merrell Dow Pharm 661
Daubert v. Merrell Dow Pharmaceuticals 661
Dominican Republic–Import and Sale of Cigarettes ... 77, 95, 102, 243, 244, 298, 760, 976
EC and Certain Member States–Large Civil Aircraft 356, 444, 445, 448, 495
EC–Approval and Marketing of Biotech Products.................. 631, 650
EC–Asbestos ... 233, 237, 240, 289, 291, 294, 295, 316, 596, 658, 935, 939, 966, 987, 996, 998, 1000, 1004
EC–Bananas III 44, 123, 200, 240, 249, 280, 733, 735, 739, 745, 746, 768, 775, 788, 789, 790, 948, 952, 963, 964, 965, 992, 1028, 1052
EC–Bananas III (Article 21.5–EC). 984
EC–Bananas III (Article 21.5–Ecuador II)........................... 29, 956, 1032
EC–Bananas III (Article 21.5–Ecuador) 992, 1020, 1028, 1029, 1031
EC–Bananas III (Article 21.5–US) 1028
EC–Bananas III (Article 22.6–EC) 1043
EC–Bananas III (Article 22.6–US) 1029, 1033
EC–Bananas III (Ecuador) (Article 22.6–EC) 1036, 1040, 1041, 1044, 1045, 1047, 1048, 1049, 1052, 1059

EC–Bed Linen. 338, 339, 346, 351, 354, 411, 412, 471, 472, 965, 972, 973, 993, 1030
EC–Bed Linen (Article 21.5–India) 354
EC–Chicken Cuts 776, 962, 976
EC–Chicken Cuts (Article 21.3(c)) 1021, 1022, 1025
EC–Citrus 138, 147, 148
EC–Computer Equipment 92, 118, 952
EC–Countervailing Measures on DRAM Chips 401, 433, 434, 435, 440, 441, 444, 472, 473, 474, 477, 478, 479, 493, 495
EC–Export Subsidies on Sugar..... 436, 557, 570, 571, 574, 976, 1020
EC–Export Subsidies on Sugar (Article 21.3 (c)).......................... 1025
EC–Export Subsidies on Sugar (Article 21.3 DSU(c)) 1023
EC–Export Subsidies on Sugar (Australia) 964
EC–Fasteners (China)... 348, 357, 368, 391, 400
EC–Hormones. 604, 657, 965, 970, 999, 1017
EC–Hormones (Article 22.6–EC) . 1043
EC–Hormones (US) 632, 633, 635, 636, 637, 638, 640, 642, 643, 647, 648, 650, 653, 656, 658, 660, 974, 975
EC–Hormones (US) (Article 22.6–EC) 1043, 1045
EC–IT Products 118, 268, 270, 947, 964
EC–Poultry 123, 198, 269, 280, 976
EC–Refunds on Exports of Sugar .. 569
EC–Salmon (Norway).... 338, 347, 356, 368, 393, 405
EC–Sardines ... 594, 596, 598, 599, 600, 601, 625, 635, 669, 952, 966, 970, 972, 976, 978, 979, 996, 997, 1002
EC–Tariff Preferences ... 127, 167, 187, 189, 963, 965, 979
EC–Trademark and Geographical Indications............................ 830, 832
EC–Tube or Pipe Fittings 338, 343, 344, 345, 351, 352, 354, 358, 362, 363, 375, 392, 393, 395, 397, 398, 412, 949
EEC (Member States)–Bananas I. 310, 957
EEC–Animal Feed Proteins 129
EEC–Apples (US) 70
EEC–Bananas II............................. 148
EEC–Cotton Yarn 336
EEC–Dessert Apples 71
EEC–Imports of Beef from Canada 747
EEC–Minimum Import Prices .. 62, 63, 128
EEC–Oilseeds 457, 934, 936, 937
EEC–Parts and Components 964
Egypt–Steel Rebar.. 344, 354, 363, 392, 402, 404, 411
EU–Footwear (China) ... 340, 347, 358, 382

European Communities–Measures Affecting the Importation of Certain Poultry Products........................... 66
EU–Seizure of Generic Drugs in Transit 254
Guatemala–Cement I.................... 1019
Guatemala–Cement II ... 363, 388, 390, 391, 393, 394, 396, 399, 400, 404, 405, 407, 408, 416, 1019
Hatters' Fur Sales.................. 504, 508
In re Linerboard Antitrust Litigation 661
India–Autos 64, 664, 665, 666, 668, 669, 955, 961, 970, 979, 1017
India–Patents (US) 822, 974
India–Quantitative Restrictions 61, 73, 74, 78, 955, 969
Indonesia–Autos 127, 458, 459, 461, 462, 463, 467, 476, 664, 665, 668, 669, 866
Japan–Agricultural Products I.. 71, 72, 301
Japan–Agricultural Products II 650, 652, 653, 654, 655, 656, 974
Japan–Apples.......... 642, 651, 659, 660
Japan–Apples (Article 21.5–US) ... 638, 645, 1031
Japan–Apples................................. 659
Japan–DRAMS (Korea) (Article 21.3(c))....................................... 1021
Japan–Film 68, 113, 236, 241, 936, 938
Japan–Procurement of a Navigation Satellite.. 687
Japan–Quotas on Laver.................. 956
Japan–Semiconductors .. 64, 68, 72, 78, 81, 236, 433, 571
Japan–SPF Dimension Lumber 129
Korea–Alcoholic Beverages ... 224, 226, 227, 245, 522, 999
Korea–Certain Paper..... 347, 368, 393, 398, 399, 402, 404, 406, 407, 963, 968, 981
Korea–Commercial Vessels ... 430, 457, 458, 461, 462, 463, 464, 465, 467, 495
Korea–Dairy... 509, 520, 531, 546, 547, 945, 946, 947, 980
Korea–Procurement........................ 687
Korea–Various Measures on Beef . 168, 241, 243, 244, 246, 259, 260, 289, 291, 295, 296, 298, 301, 569, 833, 949
Mexico–Antidumping Measures on Rice..... 346, 349, 366, 368, 370, 371, 375, 393, 395, 396, 397, 406, 407, 950
Mexico–Corn Syrup. 359, 364, 387, 475
Mexico–Corn Syrup (Article 21.5–US) 360, 942, 949, 969, 982, 1027
Mexico–Olive Oil 474, 477, 492, 495
Mexico–Steel Pipes and Tubes 357, 389, 390, 391, 398, 399, 400, 406, 1020
Mexico–Taxes on Soft Drinks 149, 300, 979

TABLE OF CASES

lxxxv

Mexico–Telecoms....724, 727, 741, 765, 779, 983
Norway–Trondheim Toll Ring....... 684
Paoli R.R. Yard PCB Litig.............. 661
Raskin v. Wyatt Co........................ 661
Roche Products Inc. v. Bolar Pharmaceutical Co..... 882, 896, 897, 898, 899
Spain–Unroasted Coffee.. 99, 123, 129, 130
Thailand–Cigarettes....................... 295
Thailand–Cigarettes (Philippines) 203, 204, 205, 206, 270
Thailand–H–Beams 339, 350, 354, 363, 387, 472, 950, 952, 980
Turkey–Rice.............199, 964, 970, 979
Turkey–Textiles 60, 138, 148, 585, 591, 968, 969
United States v. Ford...................... 661
United States v. Williams.............. 661
US/Canada–Continued Suspension 657
US–1916 Act (EC)......... 965, 980, 1059
US–1916 Act (EC) (Article 22.6–US) 1043, 1048
US–1916 Act (Japan).......... 1020, 1059
US–Antidumping and Countervailing Duties (China).....372, 426, 428, 441, 444
US–Antidumping Measures on OCTG 374, 382, 383, 384
US–Canadian Tuna...71, 306, 312, 315
US–Carbon Steel 377, 380, 381, 382, 485, 488, 489, 490, 947, 953, 972, 973, 982, 999
US–Certain EC Products...... 931, 954, 969, 998, 1017, 1029
US–Clove Cigarettes 29, 244, 595, 604, 605, 607, 610, 611, 613, 614, 622
US–Continued Dumping and Subsidy Offset Act of 2000 (CDSOA)....... 426
US–Continued Suspension.... 947, 967, 1054
US–Continued Zeroing.. 415, 947, 967, 977, 1000, 1007
US–COOL 270, 595, 596, 608, 612, 613, 626, 977, 1021, 1022, 1026
US–Corrosion–Resistant Steel Sunset Review 378, 382, 383, 413
US–Cotton Yarn 522, 534, 584, 588, 589, 971, 1004
US–Countervailing Duty Investigation on DRAMs ...433, 434, 436, 469, 472, 473, 478, 494, 977, 998
US–Countervailing Measures on Certain EC Products.. 437, 487, 991, 993, 1002
US–Customs Bond Directive.......... 417
US–Customs User Fee ... 102, 123, 124
US–DRAMS 374, 375, 376, 392
US–Export Restraints..................... 428
US–FSC 236, 430, 437, 574
US–FSC (Article 21.5–EC II)...... 1027, 1031
US–FSC (Article 21.5–EC).... 245, 290, 431, 432, 993, 1020

US–FSC (Article 22.6–US) 453, 454, 1051
US–Gambling. 290, 292, 293, 295, 298, 302, 725, 736, 767, 774, 775, 776, 778, 779
US–Gambling (Article 21.3(c)) 1023, 1025
US–Gambling (Article 22.6–US) .. 1034
US–Gasoline... 289, 290, 293, 303, 305, 311, 312, 315, 613
US–Hot–Rolled Steel 335, 344, 349, 350, 354, 363, 369, 394, 395, 397, 403, 404, 406, 411, 413, 414, 415, 493, 1023
US–Lamb 410, 509, 517, 518, 519, 520, 521, 522, 523, 524, 525, 526, 527, 534, 948, 951, 970, 972, 981
US–Large Civil Aircraft. 444, 460, 467, 953, 964, 992, 993, 1017
US–Lead and Bismuth I................ 483
US–Lead and Bismuth II 437, 486, 496, 996, 997, 1018
US–Line Pipe . 149, 333, 425, 507, 516, 521, 524, 525, 527, 530, 531, 532, 547, 951
US–Malt Beverages 246, 738
US–MFN Footwear.......................... 124
US–Nicaraguan Trade.................... 322
US–Non–Rubber Footwear............. 128
US–OCTG Sunset Reviews.... 279, 378, 379, 380, 381, 382
US–OCTG Sunset Reviews (Article 21.3(c))............................. 1022, 1025
US–Offset Act (Byrd Amendment) 365, 372, 385, 456, 457, 983, 985, 992, 1008
US–Offset Act (Byrd Amendment) (Article 21.3(c)) 1022, 1023, 1024
US–Offset Act (Byrd Amendment) (EC) (Article 22.6–US) 1041, 1044
US–Oil Country Tubular Goods Sunset Reviews.......................... 1005
US–Orange Juice 344
US–Procurement............................ 687
US–Salmon...................................... 954
US–Section 110(5) Copyright Act.. 852, 854, 867, 1009, 1033
US–Section 110(5) Copyright Act (Article 25).. 1009, 1010, 1011, 1012, 1013
US–Section 211 Appropriations Act 828, 829, 832, 834, 860, 861, 862, 863
US–Section 301 Trade Act.... 959, 1018
US–Shrimp..... 270, 287, 290, 304, 306, 307, 313, 317, 965, 992, 996, 997
US–Shrimp (Article 21.5–Malaysia) 288, 312, 1005, 1030
US–Shrimp (Thailand) 954
US–Shrimp and Sawblades.......... 1007
US–Softwood Lumber III 480, 483, 484
US–Softwood Lumber IV....... 483, 986, 1000
US–Softwood Lumber IV (Article 21.5–Canada).................. 1030, 1031

US–Softwood Lumber V 338, 339, 342, 346, 982
US–Softwood Lumber V (Article 21.5–Canada) 1026
US–Softwood Lumber VI 359, 361, 475, 478, 497
US–Softwood Lumber VI (Article 21.5–Canada) 361, 1059
US–Stainless Steel (Mexico) . 341, 342, 343, 345, 346, 967, 1005, 1018
US–Stainless Steel (Mexico) (Article 21.3(c)) 1024
US–Steel Safeguards..... 509, 511, 512, 523, 524, 526, 528, 529, 534, 535, 546, 980, 981, 985, 997, 1005
US–Sunset Review Carbon Steel.. 958, 960
US–Suspended Concession ... 638, 640, 641, 651, 656, 931, 949, 978, 983, 1017
US–Taxes on Automobiles 246
US–Textiles Rules of Origin........... 125
US–Tuna II (Mexico) 244, 595, 597, 603, 604, 605, 608, 609, 611, 612, 613, 626
US–Tyres (China).................. 538, 540
US–Underwear 268, 269, 584, 586, 589, 590
US–Upland Cotton .352, 443, 445, 457, 458, 460, 461, 462, 463, 464, 465, 466, 467, 479, 554, 555, 564, 574, 575, 576, 579, 817, 954, 1004
US–Upland Cotton (Article 21.5–Brazil) 967, 973, 984, 1027, 1031
US–Upland Cotton (Article 21.5–US) 480
US–Upland Cotton (Article 22.6–US) 455, 1040, 1043, 1051
US–Wheat Gluten ..520, 524, 525, 526, 533, 543, 544, 546, 547, 976, 977, 999
US–Wool Shirts and Blouses 290, 970, 979
US–Zeroing (EC)..................... 983, 991
US–Zeroing (EC) (Article 21.5–EC) 1027, 1031
US–Zeroing (Japan)........................ 346
US–Zeroing (Korea)........................ 980

THE LAW OF THE WORLD TRADE ORGANIZATION (WTO)

DOCUMENTS, CASES & ANALYSIS

Second Edition

CHAPTER 1

THE WTO INSTITUTION

■ ■ ■

1. WTO, THE SUCCESSOR TO THE GATT

The Agreement Establishing the World Trade Organization (WTO)[1] entered into force on January 1, 1995. The story of multilateral trade integration, however, starts over 50 years prior to this momentous date. The WTO is the successor institution to the GATT, which entered into force on January 1, 1948. The GATT was created as a response to the commercial policies of the 1930s that involved greater restrictions on and more discrimination in world trade. These anti-trade policies arose in part because countries sought to insulate their own economy from the Great Depression, and became known as "beggar-thy-neighbor" policies. Blocking imports proved to be a futile method of increasing domestic employment due to the economic slump because one country's imports were another country's exports. The combined effect of this inward turn of policy was a collapse in international trade, exacerbating the problems of the world economy and contributing to political frictions between countries.

The GATT grew out of discussions between government officials from the United States (US), and the United Kingdom (UK) during World War II. After seeing international trade stifled under the weight of protectionist policies during the 1930s, officials from both countries had a compelling interest in pursuing policies that would reduce trade barriers and help expand world trade after the war. They sought to foster these conditions by creating a rules-based framework for liberal trade policies that would reign in the use of trade restrictions as well facilitate the process of reducing those barriers. One of the first individuals to recognize the need for an international agreement was James Meade, then working for the British government and whose later work on trade policy earned him the Nobel Prize in Economics in 1977. In 1942, Meade drafted "A Proposal for an International Commercial Union" that influenced British policymakers and anticipated many features of the GATT.

While the US and UK governments agreed on the most important and basic principles to be included in a trade agreement, they differed on many substantive details that affected the shape of the GATT: The US

---

[1] Hereinafter, the 'WTO Agreement'.

adamantly opposed trade discrimination and wanted UK to dismantle its "imperial preferences", while UK wanted major reductions in US tariffs, which were much higher than UK tariffs as a result of the Smoot–Hawley Tariff Act of 1930. The UK also convinced the US to seek a multilateral trade agreement rather than continue its old bilateral approach under the Reciprocal Trade Agreements Act (RTAA) of 1934.

At the Bretton Woods Conference in 1944, the US, UK, and others recognized the need for an international institution governing international trade as a complement to the International Bank for Reconstruction and Development (i.e., the World Bank) and the International Monetary Fund (IMF). This gave birth to the idea of an International Trade Organization (ITO).[2] The ITO's scope was envisioned to extend beyond simply tariffs and quotas, to a host of other instruments (e.g., employment policy) that affect trade. It was an ambitious project intended to create an overarching institutional umbrella for liberalizing trade.

As government officials set forth to negotiate the charter of the ITO, simultaneous negotiations began on a General Agreement on Tariffs and Trade (GATT). The GATT was envisioned originally to be a part of the ITO. It had a much narrower focus and dealt only with state barriers to international trade, such as tariffs, quotas, and the drafting of general clauses related to the governing of trade. The expectation was that once the ITO charter was approved, the GATT would be subsumed under the ITO's auspices.

The GATT recipe for liberalization was quite straightforward. Its genius rested in the simplicity of the adopted approach: At the time, tariffs and quotas served as the primary impediments to trade in many markets. Thus, the most immediate pressing need was to secure commitments from governments to limit their use. At the same time, there was awareness that border measures, such as tariffs and quotas, were not the only instruments that governments could use to affect trade; domestic regulations could so as well, at least indirectly. Consequently, an agreement would need to extend beyond tariffs and quotas to discipline other instruments that had the potential to limit trade as well. This led the key negotiators (essentially the UK and US) to opt for the following approach: First, the GATT would engage in a frontal attack on border measures restricting trade. Quotas should be outlawed, and countries would agree to not raise tariffs above an agreed-upon ceiling for each good. These tariff ceilings then would be lowered through subsequent rounds of tariff negotiations. Second, countries would agree to not discriminate among goods from different sources. All goods from countries that were parties to the GATT would be treated by each GATT contracting party in the same way. Third, the GATT would not seek to negotiate one-by-one each of the domestic policies (such as tax systems, etc.) that could affect trade. GATT

---

[2] Also known as the Havana Charter.

contracting parties would be allowed to define them unilaterally but they would need to apply them in an even-handed manner to domestic and imported goods alike. In other words, once a foreign good paid the import tariff, it would be treated in the same manner as a domestically-produced good. The only way that a GATT contracting party could afford an advantage to their domestic goods would be through import tariffs. And the goal of the GATT was to get all parties to lower such tariffs through reciprocal concessions.

Once the UK and the US agreed upon a document that could serve as basis for negotiation, other countries were invited to participate in shaping the provisions of the ITO Charter and the GATT. At a conference in the Palais des Nations, in Geneva, Switzerland, representatives of 23 countries met from April to October 1947 and established two key pillars of the post-war world trading system: First, they created a legal framework for commercial policy by finalizing the text of the GATT. Second, the participants at the Geneva conference negotiated numerous bilateral agreements to reduce import tariffs, the benefits of which were extended to other GATT parties through the unconditional most-favored nation (MFN) clause. As a result, the landmark 1947 meeting produced an enduring framework for post-war commercial relations in which government-imposed trade barriers were contained and then gradually scaled back over time.

Under this system of multilateral cooperation, international trade flourished for over half a century. Cordell Hull, US Secretary of State from 1933 to 1944 and America's foremost champion of trade liberalization, presciently noted that the positive impact of trade cooperation extended far beyond its economic benefits. Hull emphatically stated:

> I have never faltered, and I will never falter, in my belief that enduring peace and the welfare of nations are indissolubly connected with friendliness, fairness, equality and the maximum practicable degree of freedom in international trade.[3]

Regarding post-war trade cooperation, Hull argued that:

> a revival of world trade [is] an essential element in the maintenance of world peace. By this I do not mean, of course, that flourishing international commerce is of itself a guaranty of peaceful international relations. But I do mean that without prosperous trade among nations any foundation for enduring peace becomes precarious and is ultimately destroyed.

How is it that the GATT came to serve as the key agreement governing international trade? What happened to the ITO? The ITO never entered into force.[4] Domestic political developments intervened between

---

[3] Quoted in Irwin et al. (2008).
[4] Wilcox (1949) discusses the ITO in detail, Irwin et al. (2008) report on its demise.

1946 and 1948 which made ratification of the ITO charter impossible; it was not even presented to the US Congress for approval. As a result, only the GATT entered into force on January 1, 1948.

The GATT suffered from birth defects: it was designed to be an agreement coming under the aegis of an institution (ITO) and not an institution itself; this is why participants to the GATT were called "contracting parties" and not "members". The non-advent of the ITO led trading nations to provide the GATT with the necessary institutional infrastructure to administer trade liberalization. Over the years, the GATT became the forum for a series of periodic multilateral negotiations on trade liberalization, known as "rounds" named after the location or event which precipitated the negotiations.[5] Between 1947 and 1994, eight rounds of multilateral negotiations were conducted. As the number of parties to each round grew and the subject matter of the negotiations became increasingly complex, the length of each round grew:

Table 1.1 GATT Rounds and Identity of Participants

Name of the Round	Years	Number of Participants
Geneva	1947	19
Annecy	1949	27
Torquay	1950	33
Geneva	1956	36
Dillon	1960–61	43
Kennedy	1962–67	74
Tokyo	1973–79	85
Uruguay	1986–94	128[6]

In Baldwin's (1970) classic account, the first five rounds (Geneva through Dillon Rounds) focused primarily on reducing tariffs. A key shift occurred in the Kennedy Round, which witnessed the incipient stages of the shift towards negotiations of non-tariff barriers (NTBs). Over time, as tariffs were reduced (and since quotas had been eliminated anyway), NTBs came to serve as an increasingly important barrier to trade. In subsequent rounds, negotiators would not only liberalize trade, but they would also sometimes add new agreements. At first, these other agreements were confined largely to codes regulating instruments authorized

---

[5] Wilcox (1949) discusses in detail the genesis of the GATT as do Hull (1948); Irwin et al. (2008); Jackson (1969), Dam (1970), Hudec (1975), Gardner (1956), Curzon (1965), Croome (1995) discuss the subsequent rounds.

[6] At the moment of writing, the ninth round of multilateral trade negotiations, the Doha round, is still on-going.

by the GATT (e.g., antidumping, countervailing duties and safeguards). Eventually however, parties began to negotiate rules disciplining NTBs adopted ostensibly for reasons of public policy (such as the protection of human health) that were prima facie not designed in order to improve the competitive position of domestic industries.

The Uruguay Round served as a watershed event in expanding the scope and nature of international trade law and governance. It expanded the scope of the law beyond goods to include services (through the GATS) and intellectual property (through the TRIPS Agreement). In addition, it led to the formation of the World Trade Organization (WTO).[7] Art. II of the WTO Agreement relevantly states:

> 1. The WTO shall provide the common institutional framework for the conduct of trade relations among its Members in matters related to the agreements and associated legal instruments included in the Annexes to this Agreement.
>
> 2. The agreements and associated legal instruments included in Annexes 1, 2 and 3 (hereinafter referred to as "Multilateral Trade Agreements") are integral parts of this Agreement, binding on all Members.
>
> 3. The agreements and associated legal instruments included in Annex 4 (hereinafter referred to as "Plurilateral Trade Agreements") are also part of this Agreement for those Members that have accepted them, and are binding on those Members. The Plurilateral Trade Agreements do not create either obligations or rights for Members that have not accepted them.
>
> 4. The General Agreement on Tariffs and Trade 1994 as specified in Annex 1A (hereinafter referred to as "GATT 1994") is legally distinct from the General Agreement on Tariffs and Trade, dated 30 October 1947, annexed to the Final Act Adopted at the Conclusion of the Second Session of the Preparatory Committee of the United Nations Conference on Trade and Employment, as subsequently rectified, amended or modified (hereinafter referred to as "GATT 1947").

The functions of the WTO are described in Art. III of the WTO Agreement as follows:

> 1. The WTO shall facilitate the implementation, administration and operation, and further the objectives, of this Agreement and of the Multilateral Trade Agreements, and shall also provide

---

[7] With the creation of the WTO, any hopes that one might have harboured that the ITO might one day see the light of day were now buried for good. Note that hope had persisted since Art. XXIX GATT did not exclude the advent of the ITO. On the advent of the WTO, see the detailed analysis in Croome (1995).

the framework for the implementation, administration and operation of the Plurilateral Trade Agreements.

2. The WTO shall provide the forum for negotiations among its Members concerning their multilateral trade relations in matters dealt with under the agreements in the Annexes to this Agreement. The WTO may also provide a forum for further negotiations among its Members concerning their multilateral trade relations, and a framework for the implementation of the results of such negotiations, as may be decided by the Ministerial Conference.

3. The WTO shall administer the Understanding on Rules and Procedures Governing the Settlement of Disputes (hereinafter referred to as the "Dispute Settlement Understanding" or "DSU") in Annex 2 to this Agreement.

4. The WTO shall administer the Trade Policy Review Mechanism (hereinafter referred to as the "TPRM") provided for in Annex 3 to this Agreement.

5. With a view to achieving greater coherence in global economic policy-making, the WTO shall cooperate, as appropriate, with the International Monetary Fund and with the International Bank for Reconstruction and Development and its affiliated agencies.

Art. VIII of the WTO Agreement makes it clear that the Members comprising the organization are required to accord legal personality to the institution, and, inter alia, the WTO has the legal capacity to enter into a Headquarters Agreement (which the WTO did sign with Switzerland, where its premises are). The staff of the WTO (i.e., the WTO Secretariat), as well as the national delegates accredited to the WTO, enjoy diplomatic privileges similar to those set out in the Vienna Convention on Consular Relations. The WTO is financed through the contributions of its Members through a formula based on a Member's percentage of world trade.

2. THE INSTITUTIONAL ARCHITECTURE OF THE WTO IN A NUTSHELL

2.1 THE VARIOUS BODIES

Art. IV WTO Agreement lays out the institutional structure of the WTO. The Ministerial Conference (MC) is the highest authority. It meets at least every two years and is composed of representatives of all Members. In the two year interim period, its tasks are carried out by the General Council (GC) which meets approximately on a monthly basis. Under the General Council's guidance, the Council for Trade in Goods (CTG), the

Council for Trade in Services (CTS), and the Council for Trade–Related Intellectual Property Rights deal with trade in goods, services and trade-related intellectual property rights, respectively. Various Committees and sub-Committees deal with more specific issues (like, for example, anti-dumping, safeguards, etc.).

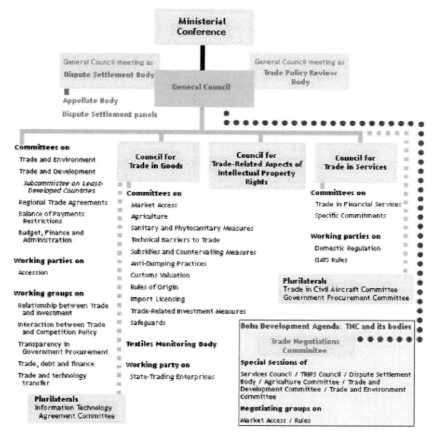

Source: WTO homepage (www.wto.org)

2.2 THE WTO SECRETARIAT

Art. VI of the WTO Agreement provides for a Secretariat headed by a Director–General (DG) appointed by the Members. A new DG is to be selected by the WTO Membership in 2013.[8] The previous DGs (including those during the GATT years) were: Eric Wyndham–White (United Kingdom); Olivier Long (Switzerland); Arthur Dunkel (Switzerland); Peter Sutherland (Ireland); Renato Ruggiero (Italy); Mike Moore (New Zealand), Panichpakdi Supachai (Thailand); and Pascal Lamy (France). The

---

[8] The procedures for electing a DG are reflected in WTO Doc. WT/L/509 of January 20, 2003.

tasks of the Secretariat are set forth in Art. VI.4 of the WTO Agreement in the following terms:

> The responsibilities of the Director–General and of the staff of the Secretariat shall be exclusively international in character. In the discharge of their duties, the Director–General and the staff of the Secretariat shall not seek or accept instructions from any government or any other authority external to the WTO. They shall refrain from any action which might adversely reflect on their position as international officials. The Members of the WTO shall respect the international character of the responsibilities of the Director–General and of the staff of the Secretariat and shall not seek to influence them in the discharge of their duties.

The Secretariat is sub-divided in various Divisions (e.g., Legal Affairs Division, Rules Division, Services Division, Trade and Environment Division, Agriculture and Commodities Division, etc.), corresponding to the subject-matter reflected in the WTO agreements. Currently, there are close to 700 individuals working for the WTO. WTO officials enjoy privileges and immunities necessary for the independent exercise of their functions by virtue of Art. VIII.3 of the WTO Agreement that have been reflected in the Headquarters Agreement signed between the WTO and Switzerland.

3. PARTICIPATION IN THE WTO

Participation in the WTO can take two forms of different intensity: full membership (which provides participants with the right to co-decide the issues coming under the mandate of the WTO), and observer-status (which grants parties with the right to participate in meetings but without voting rights).

3.1 ACCESSION TO THE WTO

3.1.1 The Legal Basis for Accession to the WTO

Art. XII of the WTO Agreement reads:

> 1. Any State or separate customs territory possessing full autonomy in the conduct of its external commercial relations and of the other matters provided for in this Agreement and the Multilateral Trade Agreements may accede to this Agreement, on terms to be agreed between it and the WTO. Such accession shall apply to this Agreement and the Multilateral Trade Agreements annexed thereto.
>
> 2. Decisions on accession shall be taken by the Ministerial Conference. The Ministerial Conference shall approve the

agreement on the terms of accession by a two-thirds majority of the Members of the WTO.

3. Accession to a Plurilateral Trade Agreement shall be governed by the provisions of that Agreement.

Art. XII of the WTO Agreement does not contain any procedural requirements. The procedural aspects of the accession process have been developed in practice (and in a relatively uniform manner). WTO Members must, by a two thirds-majority, (Art. XII WTO Agreement), vote in favor of accession. In practice, however, recourse to a formal vote is rare. Accessions have taken place only when a consensus to this effect has been already established.

3.1.2 The Procedure of Accession

A country or separate customs territory begins its accession process by submitting a formal communication to the DG of the WTO indicating its willingness to become a Member of the WTO and requests the establishment of a Working Party (WP). The communication is circulated to all WTO Members. The General Council will then consider the application and the establishment of a WP. Under its terms of reference, a WP will typically be requested:

> to examine the application for accession to the WTO under Article XII and to submit to the General Council / Ministerial Conference recommendations which may include a draft Protocol of Accession.

A Working Party will, typically, be established, in which all existing WTO Members can participate. The secretarial functions of the WP will be assumed by one or more officials of the WTO Accessions Division. The WP will examine the foreign trade regime of the acceding state or separate customs territory (since, as we will see *infra*, only states and customs territories enjoying independence in the formulation of their trade policies can become WTO Members). A Chairman of the WP will be appointed following consultations between the Chairman of the General Council, the applicant, and the Members of the WP. Upon formation of the WP, the WTO Secretariat will inform the applicant country of the procedures to be followed, and especially about the details of the requirement to submit its "Memorandum on Foreign Trade Regime" which covers, but is not necessarily limited to, a range of issues from the design and the operation of the trade instruments employed by the acceding country, to questions of a more general nature, such as those relating to overall economic policy (with specific questions on macroeconomic policies). The coverage of the Memorandum in the WTO-era extends to trade in goods and services as well as the protection of intellectual property rights covered by the TRIPs (but also, occasionally, in areas not covered by TRIPs).[9]

Upon submission of the Memorandum, the WTO Secretariat will check the overall consistency of the submitted text with the outline format (that is, the format reproduced in WTO Doc. WT/ACC/1). Although some differences with the outline format are tolerated, major deviations from it are not. At the same time, copies of the tariffs currently applicable by the applicant (in the Harmonized System nomenclature[10]) will be distributed. The WTO Secretariat will circulate the Memorandum (the consistency of which with the outline format it will have checked) to the Members of the WP. The Members of the WP will be invited to submit questions to the applicant. Depending on the responses and the trade interest involved, there could be more than one round of "Q & A sessions" organized between the Members of the WP and the applicant, where the former will ask questions that the latter will be called to respond to.

When the examination of the Memorandum is sufficiently advanced, Members of the WP will initiate bilateral market access negotiations with the applicant, i.e. negotiations between the applicant and particular WTO Members focusing on specific items (goods and services): in this context, the applicant will be requested to make tariff promises on goods (not to impose tariffs above an agreed level, as we will see in more detail in Chapter 3), and also to open up its services market; as noted, recently (post–1995) applicants have often been requested to assume obligations that incumbents did not have to assume and for this reason alone, Protocols of Accession constitute an important source of WTO law when it comes to delineating assumed obligations.

Upon their conclusion, the Schedule of Concessions of the applicant (for both goods and services) will be annexed to the "Draft Protocol of Accession", when the work of the WP has been successfully concluded. Eventually, post-verification of the agreed concessions, the terms for accession for the acceding country (or customs territory) will be annexed to its "Protocol of Accession".[11] Protocols of Accession have become voluminous over the years and especially since the advent of the WTO, and often reflect

---

[9] The WTO Doc. WT/ACC/1 of March 24, 1995 contains an outline format for the Memorandum on Foreign Trade Regime. Although occasionally differences across applicants are observable, the vast majority of its provisions are reproduced verbatim across national Memoranda.

[10] As we will see in Chapter 3, the Harmonized System (HS) expresses goods in two to six digits (two being the generic and six the more dis-aggregated category, 87 for example could correspond to textiles, while 870101 to polyester shirts).

[11] For a comprehensive description of the WTO relevant practice, from the moment when a WP is established until the end of the ensuing negotiations, see WTO Doc. WT/ACC/1 of March 24, 1995. The amount of technical capacity required in order to go through the accession process should not be underestimated. Gay (2005) for example, explains that Vanuatu had to suspend its accession process because of lack of technical expertise on issues under negotiation. Vanuatu came back to complete the negotiation later.

WTO+ obligations, that is, obligations that other WTO Members that had acceded before them do not have to observe.[12]

A summary of the discussions between the WP and the applicant is reflected in the Report of the WP to the General Council, along with a Draft Decision and the Protocol of Accession. The latter contains the terms of accession agreed by the applicant and Members of the WP. However, it is important to emphasize that, in many instances the Protocol of Accession contains cross-references to the Report of the WP that elaborate on significant issues of a substantive nature. There is no time set ex ante for the acceding country to ratify the Protocol and implement the negotiated market access commitments. In practice, in light of legal procedures and constraints, the applicant makes a proposal as to the period of time it envisages implementation will take (the proposed periods of implementation vary between 6–9 months). There are no reported cases where the deadline proposed has not been respected.

3.1.3 Procedures for Least–Developed Countries (LDCs)

On December 10, 2002, the General Council of the WTO adopted a decision[13] regarding procedures for the accession of LDCs to the WTO. Complying with the Memorandum might on occasion prove a daunting task for the some of the poorer developing countries. This prompted WTO Members to adopt a less rigorous procedure that LDCs could have recourse to when requesting accession to the WTO:

> 1. Negotiations for the accession of LDCs to the WTO, be facilitated and accelerated through simplified and streamlined accession procedures, with a view to concluding these negotiations as quickly as possible, in accordance with the guidelines set out hereunder:

Market access

> — WTO Members shall exercise restraint in seeking concessions and commitments on trade in goods and services from acceding LDCs, taking into account the levels of concessions and commitments undertaken by existing WTO LDCs' Members;
>
> — acceding LDCs shall offer access through reasonable concessions and commitments on trade in goods and services commensurate with their individual development, financial and trade needs, in line with Article XXXVI.8 of GATT 1994, Article 15 of the Agreement on

---

[12] One reason for this could be that those acceding after 1995 are often non-market economies (NMEs), see Charnovitz (2007).

[13] WTO Doc. WT/L/508 of January 20, 2003.

Agriculture, and Articles IV and XIX of the General Agreement on Trade in Services.

WTO Rules

— Special and Differential Treatment, as set out in the Multilateral Trade Agreements, Ministerial Decisions, and other relevant WTO legal instruments, shall be applicable to all acceding LDCs, from the date of entry into force of their respective Protocols of Accession;

— transitional periods/transitional arrangements foreseen under specific WTO Agreements, to enable acceding LDCs to effectively implement commitments and obligations, shall be granted in accession negotiations taking into account individual development, financial and trade needs;

— transitional periods/arrangements shall be accompanied by Action Plans for compliance with WTO rules. The implementation of the Action Plans shall be supported by Technical Assistance and Capacity Building measures for the acceding LDCs'. Upon the request of an acceding LDC, WTO Members may coordinate efforts to guide that LDC through the implementation process;

— commitments to accede to any of the Plurilateral Trade Agreements or to participate in other optional sectoral market access initiatives shall not be a precondition for accession to the Multilateral Trade Agreements of the WTO. As provided in paragraph 5 of Article IX and paragraph 3 of Article XII of the WTO Agreement, decisions on the Plurilateral Trade Agreements shall be adopted by the Members of, and governed by the provisions in, those Agreements. WTO Members may seek to ascertain acceding LDCs interests in the Plurilateral Trade Agreements.

Process

— The good offices of the Director–General shall be available to assist acceding LDCs and Chairpersons of the LDCs' Accession Working Parties in implementing this decision;

— efforts shall continue to be made, in line with information technology means and developments, including in LDCs themselves, to expedite documentation exchange and streamline accession procedures for LDCs to make them more effective and efficient, and less onerous. The Secretariat will assist in this regard. Such efforts will, *inter-alia*, be based upon the WTO Reference Centres that are already operational in acceding LDCs;

— WTO Members may adopt additional measures in their bilateral negotiations to streamline and facilitate the process, e.g., by holding bilateral negotiations in the acceding LDC if so requested;

— upon request, WTO Members may through coordinated, concentrated and targeted technical assistance from an early stage facilitate the accession of an acceding LDC.

Trade-related technical assistance and capacity building

— Targeted and coordinated technical assistance and capacity building, by WTO and other relevant multilateral, regional and bilateral development partners, including *inter alia* under the Integrated Framework (IF), shall be provided, on a priority basis, to assist acceding LDCs. Assistance shall be accorded with the objective of effectively integrating the acceding LDC into the multilateral trading system;

— effective and broad-based technical cooperation and capacity building measures shall be provided, on a priority basis, to cover all stages of the accession process, i.e. from the preparation of documentation to the setting up of the legislative infrastructure and enforcement mechanisms, considering the high costs involved and in order to enable the acceding LDC to benefit from and comply with WTO rights and obligations.

2. The implementation of these guidelines shall be reviewed regularly in the agenda of the Sub–Committee on LDCs. The results of this review shall be included in the Annual Report of the Committee on Trade and Development to the General Council. In pursuance of their commitments on LDCs' accessions in the Doha Ministerial Declaration, Ministers will take stock of the

3.2 MEMBERSHIP OF THE WTO

3.2.1 Original Members

The contracting parties to the GATT and the European Communities (now, European Union, EU) became original Members of the WTO (Art. XI of the WTO Agreement).

3.2.2 New Members

Art. XII of the WTO Agreement provides that:

(a) any state, or

(b) "separate customs territory" possessing full autonomy in the conduct of its external commercial relations and of the matters provided for in the WTO Agreement and Multilateral Trade Agreements may accede to the WTO on terms to be agreed between it and the WTO original Membership.

Note that entities that are part of the same political state (e.g., Hong Kong, Macao, People's Republic of China) may be entitled to separate WTO memberships if they operate as separate customs territories.

3.2.3 The Current WTO Membership

As of April 2013, the WTO had 159 Members.

Table 1.2 WTO Members and Their Date of Accession

Albania	8 September 2000
Angola	23 November 1996
Antigua and Barbuda	1 January 1995
Argentina	1 January 1995
Armenia	5 February 2003
Australia	1 January 1995
Austria	1 January 1995
Bahrain, Kingdom of	1 January 1995
Bangladesh	1 January 1995
Barbados	1 January 1995
Belgium	1 January 1995
Belize	1 January 1995
Benin	22 February 1996

Bolivia	12 September 1995
Botswana	31 May 1995
Brazil	1 January 1995
Brunei Darussalam	1 January 1995
Bulgaria	1 December 1996
Burkina Faso	3 June 1995
Burundi	23 July 1995
Cambodia	13 October 2004
Cameroon	13 December 1995
Canada	1 January 1995
Cape Verde	23 July 2008
Central African Republic	31 May 1995
Chad	19 October 1996
Chile	1 January 1995
China	11 December 2001
Colombia	30 April 1995
Congo	27 March 1997
Costa Rica	1 January 1995
Côte d'Ivoire	1 January 1995
Croatia	30 November 2000
Cuba	20 April 1995
Cyprus	30 July 1995
Czech Republic	1 January 1995
Democratic Republic of Congo	1 January 1997
Denmark	1 January 1995
Djibouti	31 May 1995
Dominica	1 January 1995
Dominican Republic	9 March 1995
Ecuador	21 January 1996
Egypt	30 June 1995
El Salvador	7 May 1995
Estonia	13 November 1999

European Community	1 January 1995
Fiji	14 January 1996
Finland	1 January 1995
Former Yugoslav Rep. of Macedonia (FYROM)	4 April 2003
France	1 January 1995
Gabon	1 January 1995
The Gambia	23 October 1996
Georgia	14 June 2000
Germany	1 January 1995
Ghana	1 January 1995
Greece	1 January 1995
Grenada	22 February 1996
Guatemala	21 July 1995
Guinea	25 October 1995
Guinea Bissau	31 May 1995
Guyana	1 January 1995
Haiti	30 January 1996
Honduras	1 January 1995
Hong Kong, China	1 January 1995
Hungary	1 January 1995
Iceland	1 January 1995
India	1 January 1995
Indonesia	1 January 1995
Ireland	1 January 1995
Israel	21 April 1995
Italy	1 January 1995
Jamaica	9 March 1995
Japan	1 January 1995
Jordan	11 April 2000
Kenya	1 January 1995
Korea, Republic of	1 January 1995
Kuwait	1 January 1995

Kyrgyz Republic	20 December 1998
Laos	2 February 2013
Latvia	10 February 1999
Lesotho	31 May 1995
Liechtenstein	1 September 1995
Lithuania	31 May 2001
Luxembourg	1 January 1995
Macao, China	1 January 1995
Madagascar	17 November 1995
Malawi	31 May 1995
Malaysia	1 January 1995
Maldives	31 May 1995
Mali	31 May 1995
Malta	1 January 1995
Mauritania	31 May 1995
Mauritius	1 January 1995
Mexico	1 January 1995
Moldova	26 July 2001
Mongolia	29 January 1997
Montenegro	29 April 2012
Morocco	1 January 1995
Mozambique	26 August 1995
Myanmar	1 January 1995
Namibia	1 January 1995
Nepal	23 April 2004
Netherlands[14]	1 January 1995
New Zealand	1 January 1995
Nicaragua	3 September 1995
Niger	13 December 1996
Nigeria	1 January 1995
Norway	1 January 1995

---

[14] For the kingdom in Europe and for the Netherlands Antilles.

Oman	9 November 2000
Pakistan	1 January 1995
Panama	6 September 1997
Papua New Guinea	9 June 1996
Paraguay	1 January 1995
Peru	1 January 1995
Philippines	1 January 1995
Poland	1 January 1995
Portugal	1 January 1995
Qatar	13 January 1996
Romania	1 January 1995
Russia	22 August 2012
Rwanda	22 May 1996
Saint Kitts and Nevis	21 February 1996
Saint Lucia	1 January 1995
Saint Vincent and the Grenadines	1 January 1995
Samoa	10 May 2012
Saudi Arabia	11 December 2005
Senegal	1 January 1995
Sierra Leone	23 July 1995
Singapore	1 January 1995
Slovak Republic	1 January 1995
Slovenia	30 July 1995
Solomon Islands	26 July 1996
South Africa	1 January 1995
Spain	1 January 1995
Sri Lanka	1 January 1995
Suriname	1 January 1995
Swaziland	1 January 1995
Sweden	1 January 1995
Switzerland	1 January 1995
Taipei, Chinese	1 January 2002

Tajikistan	2 March 2013
Tanzania	1 January 1995
Thailand	1 January 1995
Togo	31 May 1995
Trinidad and Tobago	1 March 1995
Tunisia	29 March 1995
Turkey	26 March 1995
Uganda	1 January 1995
Ukraine	16 May 2008
United Arab Emirates	10 April 1996
United Kingdom	1 January 1995
Uruguay	1 January 1995
Vanuatu	24 August 2012
Venezuela	1 January 1995
Vietnam	11 January 2007
Zambia	1 January 1995
Zimbabwe	5 March 1995

3.3 OBSERVER-STATUS IN THE WTO

3.3.1 States and Customs Territories

States and customs territories can be granted observer status pending their accession to the WTO: Annex 2 to the Rules of Procedure for Sessions of the Ministerial Conference and Meetings of the General Council[15] makes a distinction between observers to the Ministerial Conference sessions and observers to the General Council, and states that the latter form of participation was conceived as a means to familiarize non-Members of the WTO with the organization in view of their eventual accession. As a consequence, any country or separate customs territory upon submitting a request for accession to the WTO will be admitted on a provisional basis as an observer. We quote the relevant passage from Annex 2:

> 1. Governments seeking observer status in the Ministerial Conference shall address a communication to that body indicating their reasons for seeking such status. Such requests shall be examined on a case-by-case basis by the Ministerial Conference.

---

[15] WTO Doc. WT/L/161 of July 25, 1996.

2. Governments accorded observer status at sessions of the Ministerial Conference shall not automatically have that status at meetings of the General Council or its subsidiary bodies. However, governments accorded such status in the General Council and its subsidiary bodies in accordance with the procedures described below, shall be invited to attend sessions of the Ministerial Conference as observers.

3. The purpose of observer status in the General Council and its subsidiary bodies is to allow a government to better acquaint itself with the WTO and its activities, and to prepare and initiate negotiations for accession to the WTO Agreement.

4. Governments wishing to request observer status in the General Council shall address to that body a communication expressing the intent to initiate negotiations for accession to the WTO Agreement within a maximum period of five years, and provide a description of their current economic and trade policies, as well as any intended future reforms of these policies.

5. The General Council shall examine requests for observer status by governments on a case-by-case basis.

6. Observer status in the General Council shall be granted initially for a period of five years. In addition to being invited to sessions of the Ministerial Conference, governments with observer status in the General Council may participate as observers at meetings of working parties and other subsidiary bodies of the General Council as appropriate, with the exception of the Committee on Budget, Finance and Administration.

7. During its period of observership, an observer government shall provide the Members of the WTO with any additional information it considers relevant concerning developments in its economic and trade policies. At the request of any Member or the observer government itself, any matter contained in such information may be brought to the attention of the General Council after governments have been allowed sufficient time to examine the information.

8. (a) If, at the end of five years, an observer government has not yet initiated a process of negotiation with a view to acceding to the WTO Agreement, it may request an extension of its status as observer. Such a request shall be made in writing and shall be accompanied by a comprehensive, up-dated description of the requesting government's current economic and trade policies, as well as an indication of its future plans in relation to initiating accession negotiations.

(b) Upon receiving such a request, the General Council shall review the situation, and decide upon the extension of the status of observer and the duration of such extension.

9. Observer governments shall have access to the main WTO document series. They may also request technical assistance from the Secretariat in relation to the operation of the WTO system in general, as well as to negotiations on accession to the WTO Agreement.

10. Representatives of governments accorded observer status may be invited to speak at meetings of the bodies to which they are observers normally after Members of that body have spoken. The right to speak does not include the right to make proposals, unless a government is specifically invited to do so, nor to participate in decision-making.

11. Observer governments shall be required to make financial contributions for services provided to them in connection with their observer status in the WTO, subject to financial regulations established pursuant to Article VII:2 of the WTO Agreement.

Observers do not have the right to participate in the decision making process of the WTO and must start accession negotiation within five years from the date when they were granted observer-status. Currently (April 2013) the following governments have observer status:

Table 1.3: Observer Governments

1.	AFGHANISTAN	14.	IRAQ
2.	ALGERIA	5	KAZAKHSTAN
3.	ANDORRA	16.	LEBANON
4.	AZERBAIJAN	17.	LIBERIA
5.	BAHAMAS	18.	LIBYA
6.	BELARUS	19.	SAO TOME AND PRINCIPE
7.	BHUTAN	20.	SERBIA
8.	BOSNIA AND HERZEGOVINA	21.	SEYCHELLES
9.	COMOROS	22.	SUDAN
10.	EQUATORIAL GUINEA	23.	SYRIA
11.	ETHIOPIA	24.	UZBEKISTAN
12.	HOLY SEE	25.	YEMEN
13.	IRAN		

3.3.2 International Organizations

Observer status can be further granted to other international organizations. Art. V.1 of the WTO Agreement empowers the General Council of the WTO to:

> make appropriate arrangements for effective cooperation with other intergovernmental organizations that have responsibilities related to those of the WTO.

Annex 3 to the Rules of Procedure for Sessions of the Ministerial Conference and Meetings of the General Council,[16] regulates the modalities for participation of international organizations as observers at the WTO:

> 1. The purpose of observer status for international intergovernmental organizations (hereinafter referred to as "organizations") in the WTO is to enable these organizations to follow discussions therein on matters of direct interest to them.
>
> 2. Requests for observer status shall accordingly be considered from organizations which have competence and a direct interest in trade policy matters, or which, pursuant to paragraph V.1 of the WTO Agreement, have responsibilities related to those of the WTO.
>
> 3. Requests for observer status shall be made in writing to the WTO body in which such status is sought, and shall indicate the nature of the work of the organization and the reasons for its interest in being accorded such status. Requests for observer status from organizations shall not, however, be considered for meetings of the Committee on Budget, Finance and Administration or of the Dispute Settlement Body.
>
> 4. Requests for observer status shall be considered on a case-by-case basis by each WTO body to which such a request is addressed, taking into account such factors as the nature of work of the organization concerned, the nature of its membership, the number of WTO Members in the organization, reciprocity with respect to access to proceedings, documents and other aspects of observership, and whether the organization has been associated in the past with the work of the CONTRACTING PARTIES to GATT 1947.
>
> 5. In addition to organizations that request, and are granted, observer status, other organizations may attend meetings of the

---

[16] WTO Doc. WT/L/161 of July 25, 1996.

Ministerial Conference, the General Council or subsidiary bodies on the specific invitation of the Ministerial Conference, the General Council or the subsidiary body concerned, as the case may be. Invitations may also be extended, as appropriate and on a case-by-case basis, to specific organizations to follow particular issues within a body in an observer capacity.

6. Organizations with which the WTO has entered into a formal arrangement for cooperation and consultation shall be accorded observer status in such bodies as may be determined by that arrangement.

7. Organizations accorded observer status in a particular WTO body shall not automatically be accorded such status in other WTO bodies.

8. Representatives of organizations accorded observer status may be invited to speak at meetings of the bodies to which they are observers normally after Members of that body have spoken. The right to speak does not include the right to circulate papers or to make proposals, unless an organization is specifically invited to do so, nor to participate in decision-making.

9. Observer organizations shall receive copies of the main WTO documents series and of other documents series relating to the work of the subsidiary bodies which they attend as observers. They may receive such additional documents as may be specified by the terms of any formal arrangements for cooperation between them and the WTO.

10. If for any one-year period after the date of the grant of observer status, there has been no attendance by the observer organization, such status shall cease. In the case of sessions of the Ministerial Conference, this period shall be two years.

Table 1.4: Non-state Actors with Observer–Status

ACP	African, Caribbean and Pacific Group of States
Basel Convention	Control of Trans-boundary Movements of Hazardous Wastes and Their Disposal
CBD	Convention on Biological Diversity[17]
CITES	Convention on International Trade in Endangered Species of Wild Fauna and Flora
CSD	United Nations Commission for Sustainable Development
ECE	United Nations Economic Commission for Europe

---

[17] Not an observer at the TRIPs Council.

EFTA	European Free Trade Association
FAO	Food and Agriculture Organization
ICCAT	International Commission for the Conservation of Atlantic Tunas
IGC	International Grains Council
IMF	International Monetary Fund
IPGRI	International Plant Genetic Resources Institute
ISO	International Organization for Standardization
ITC	International Trade Centre
Montreal Protocol	Montreal Protocol on Substances that Deplete the Ozone Layer
OECD	Organization for Economic Cooperation and Development
OHCHR	Office of the United Nations High Commissioner for Human Rights
PIF	Pacific Islands Forum (former SPF–South Pacific Forum)
Rotterdam Convention	Rotterdam Convention on the Prior Informed Consent Procedure for Certain Hazardous Chemicals and Pesticides in International Trade
SELA	Latin American Economic System
Stockholm Convention	Stockholm Convention on Persistent Organic Pollutants (POPs or Stockholm Convention)
UN	United Nations
UNCITRAL	United Nations Commission on International Trade Law
UNDP	United Nations Development Programme
UNEP	United Nations Environment Programme
UNESCO	United Nations Educational, Scientific and Cultural Organization
UNFCCC	United Nations Framework Convention on Climate Change
UNIDO	United Nations Industrial Development Organization
UPOV	Int'l Union for the Protection of New Varieties of Plants

WB	World Bank
WCO	World Customs Organization
WHO	World Health Organization
WIPO	World Intellectual Property Organization

3.3.3 Participation of Non–Governmental Organizations (NGOs)

Art. V.2 of the WTO Agreement states that:

The General Council may make appropriate arrangements for consultation and cooperation with non-governmental organizations concerned with matters related to those of the WTO.

To date, no NGO has been granted observer status. In practice, NGOs participate in Ministerial Conference meetings as observers although they do not have the right to circulate documents or to take the floor. Accreditation of an NGO to a Ministerial Conference will typically entitle at least one representative of that NGO to access to plenary sessions in the official WTO conference center, where briefings on negotiations are typically provided by WTO Secretariat members, and selected delegations.

Note, however, that since each WTO Member has a sovereign right to determine the members of its delegation (subject obviously to considerations such as security), some Members have appointed non-governmental actors as delegates, although they are typically not included in secret negotiating sessions.[18]

4. DAY TO DAY OPERATIONS

4.1 ORGANIZATION OF WTO MEETINGS

On July 25, 1996, the WTO Members adopted Guidelines[19] dealing with the organization of meetings of the Ministerial Conference and the General Council. Below, we have excerpted a few of the most important provisions:

Rule 3

The provisional agenda for each regular session shall be drawn up by the Secretariat in consultation with the Chairperson and shall be communicated to Members at least five weeks before the opening of the session. It shall be open to any Member to propose items for inclusion in this provisional agenda up to six weeks be-

---

[18] Formally or informally dozens of international organizations and NGOs participate in the work of the various WTO Committees.

[19] WTO Doc. WT/L/161.

fore the opening of the session. Additional items on the agenda shall be proposed under "Other Business" at the opening of the session. Inclusion of these items on the agenda shall depend upon the agreement of the Ministerial Conference.

Rule 5

The first item of business at each session shall be the consideration and approval of the agenda.

Rule 7

Each Member shall be represented by an accredited representative.

Rule 8

Each representative may be accompanied by such alternates and advisers as the representative may require.

Rule 10

Representatives of States or separate customs territories may attend the meetings as observers on the invitation of the Ministerial Conference in accordance with paragraphs 9 to 11 of the guidelines in Annex 2 to these Rules.

Rule 11

Representatives of international intergovernmental organizations may attend the meetings as observers on the invitation of the Ministerial Conference in accordance with the guidelines in Annex 3 to these Rules.

Rule 12

During the course of each regular session a Chairperson and three Vice–Chairpersons shall be elected from among the Members. They shall hold office from the end of that session until the end of the next regular session.

Rule 16

A simple majority of the Members shall constitute a quorum.

Rule 23

Proposals and amendments to proposals shall normally be introduced in writing and circulated to all representatives not later than twelve hours before the commencement of the meeting at which they are to be discussed.

Rule 28

The Ministerial Conference shall take decisions in accordance with the decision-making provisions of the WTO Agreement, in particular Article IX thereof entitled "Decision–Making".

Rule 29

When, in accordance with the WTO Agreement, decisions are required to be taken by vote, such votes shall be taken by ballot. Ballot papers shall be distributed to representatives of Members present at the session and a ballot box placed in the conference room. However, the representative of any Member may request, or the Chairperson may suggest, that a vote be taken by the raising of cards or by roll call. In addition, where in accordance with the WTO Agreement a vote by a qualified majority of all Members is required to be taken, the Ministerial Conference may decide, upon request from a Member or the suggestion of the Chairperson, that the vote be taken by airmail ballots or ballots transmitted by telegraph or telefacsimile in accordance with the procedures described in Annex 1 to these Rules.

Rule 30

English, French and Spanish shall be the working languages.

Rule 31

Summary records of the meetings of the Ministerial Conference shall be kept by the Secretariat.

Rule 32

The meetings of the Ministerial Conference shall ordinarily be held in private. It may be decided that a particular meeting or meetings should be held in public.

4.2 DECISION MAKING IN THE WTO

4.2.1 The General Rule

In the GATT years, the contracting parties in practice always took decisions by consensus, although the GATT did provide for majority-decisions.[20] In fact, the Chair would presume consensus in the absence of any party present objecting or calling for a vote.[21] The WTO has not deviated from GATT practice. Art. IX WTO Agreement, which reflects the de-

---

[20] In the early years of GATT, voting occured either by "roll-call" vote (whereby the secretary to a meeting would ask participants to cast their vote), or through 'head-counting', whereby a proposal would be voted or not depending on the number of votes it would receive. Voting practice has essentially been discontinued since the early fifties.

[21] Hoekman and Kostecki (2009) at pp. 56ff. The authors anecdotally refer to a particular instance whereby a request for a vote by one GATT contracting party was followed by a pause and then a return to consensus procedures.

fault decision-making process used in the WTO, explicitly states that decisions will be taken following the traditional GATT consensus-based approach. A footnote to Art. IX of the WTO Agreement, makes it plain that consensus will not exist only when a WTO Member formally objects to a proposal that is under consideration; this provision does not make references to necessary "quorums": as a result, unless a specific provision to this effect exists, there is no need for quorum-based decisions in the WTO.

In the first fifteen years of the WTO, there has been no deviation from the consensus-rule. Informally, WTO Members have voted (intermediary vote) during the election of Mike Moore (the third DG of the WTO). Even on this occasion however, the final approval of his nomination was by consensus.

Art. IX of the WTO Agreement reads:

1. The WTO shall continue the practice of decision-making by consensus followed under GATT 1947. Except as otherwise provided, where a decision cannot be arrived at by consensus, the matter at issue shall be decided by voting. At meetings of the Ministerial Conference and the General Council, each Member of the WTO shall have one vote. Where the European Communities exercise their right to vote, they shall have a number of votes equal to the number of their member States which are Members of the WTO. Decisions of the Ministerial Conference and the General Council shall be taken by a majority of the votes cast, unless otherwise provided in this Agreement or in the relevant Multilateral Trade Agreement.

4.2.2 Special Procedures

(a) <u>Interpretations</u>: Art. IX.2 of the WTO Agreement provides for the possibility to adopt interpretations of the WTO Agreement. Recourse to Art. IX.2 of the WTO Agreement may be considered an option for various reasons: WTO Members might be willing to pre-empt an issue, or they might be willing to avoid repetition of a finding or interpretation by a WTO Panel or the Appellate Body (AB), that they consider goes further than what they are willing to accept. Art. IX.2 WTO Agreement states that a three-fourths majority of WTO Members is required in order to adopt an interpretation. This provision also imposes a quorum: at least three-fourths of the WTO Membership must be present for an authentic interpretation to be adopted:

> The Ministerial Conference and the General Council shall have the exclusive authority to adopt interpretations of this Agreement and of the Multilateral Trade Agreements. In the case of an interpretation of a Multilateral Trade Agreement in Annex 1, they shall exercise their authority on the basis of a recommendation by the Council overseeing the functioning of that Agree-

ment. The decision to adopt an interpretation shall be taken by a three-fourths majority of the Members. This paragraph shall not be used in a manner that would undermine the amendment provisions in Article X.

The question arose in *US–Clove Cigarettes* whether § 5.2 of the Doha Ministerial Decision which interpreted Art. 2.12 TBT could be regarded as an interpretation in the sense of Art. IX.2 of the Agreement Establishing the WTO or, alternatively, as subsequent agreement in the sense of Art. 31.3(a) VCLT (Vienna Convention on the Law of Treaties). In §§ 255–256, the AB rejected the view that the Doha Ministerial Decision was not an interpretation in the sense of Art. IX.2 of the Agreement Establishing the WTO because it had not adopted following a recommendation by the relevant Council. In § 249 of the same report, the AB, echoing prior case law and namely the report in *EC–Bananas III (Article 21.5–Ecuador II)*, held that a wedge must be driven between interpretations and amendments in the sense that the former can only clarify but cannot amend the agreement.

(b) <u>Amending the WTO Agreement</u>: Art. X of the WTO Agreement includes the specific procedure to be followed whenever a proposal to amend the WTO Agreement is tabled: if consensus is not possible, a qualified majority of the Ministerial Conference (two thirds of the Members[22]) is required for a proposal to be further submitted by the Ministerial Conference to WTO Members for acceptance. Amendments to five specific provisions set forth in Art. X.2 WTO Agreement (like the MFN clause) require unanimous acceptance of the WTO membership. We quote Art. X of the WTO Agreement in its entirety:

> 1. Any Member of the WTO may initiate a proposal to amend the provisions of this Agreement or the Multilateral Trade Agreements in Annex 1 by submitting such proposal to the Ministerial Conference. The Councils listed in paragraph 5 of Article IV may also submit to the Ministerial Conference proposals to amend the provisions of the corresponding Multilateral Trade Agreements in Annex 1 the functioning of which they oversee. Unless the Ministerial Conference decides on a longer period, for a period of 90 days after the proposal has been tabled formally at the Ministerial Conference any decision by the Ministerial Conference to submit the proposed amendment to the Members for acceptance shall be taken by consensus. Unless the provisions of paragraphs 2, 5 or 6 apply, that decision shall specify whether the provisions of paragraphs 3 or 4 shall apply. If consensus is reached, the Ministerial Conference shall forthwith submit the proposed amendment to the Members for acceptance. If consen-

---

[22] That is, not of the present Members, but of the total membership. Hence, once again we are in presence of a quorum-requirement.

sus is not reached at a meeting of the Ministerial Conference within the established period, the Ministerial Conference shall decide by a two-thirds majority of the Members whether to submit the proposed amendment to the Members for acceptance. Except as provided in paragraphs 2, 5 and 6, the provisions of paragraph 3 shall apply to the proposed amendment, unless the Ministerial Conference decides by a three-fourths majority of the Members that the provisions of paragraph 4 shall apply.

2. Amendments to the provisions of this Article and to the provisions of the following Articles shall take effect only upon acceptance by all Members:

Article IX of this Agreement;

Articles I and II of GATT 1994;

Article II:1 of GATS;

Article 4 of the Agreement on TRIPS.

3. Amendments to provisions of this Agreement, or of the Multilateral Trade Agreements in Annexes 1A and 1C, other than those listed in paragraphs 2 and 6, of a nature that would alter the rights and obligations of the Members, shall take effect for the Members that have accepted them upon acceptance by two thirds of the Members and thereafter for each other Member upon acceptance by it. The Ministerial Conference may decide by a three-fourths majority of the Members that any amendment made effective under this paragraph is of such a nature that any Member which has not accepted it within a period specified by the Ministerial Conference in each case shall be free to withdraw from the WTO or to remain a Member with the consent of the Ministerial Conference.

4. Amendments to provisions of this Agreement or of the Multilateral Trade Agreements in Annexes 1A and 1C, other than those listed in paragraphs 2 and 6, of a nature that would not alter the rights and obligations of the Members, shall take effect for all Members upon acceptance by two thirds of the Members.

5. Except as provided in paragraph 2 above, amendments to Parts I, II and III of GATS and the respective annexes shall take effect for the Members that have accepted them upon acceptance by two thirds of the Members and thereafter for each Member upon acceptance by it. The Ministerial Conference may decide by a three-fourths majority of the Members that any amendment made effective under the preceding provision is of such a nature that any Member which has not accepted it within a period specified by the Ministerial Conference in each case shall be free to

withdraw from the WTO or to remain a Member with the consent of the Ministerial Conference. Amendments to Parts IV, V and VI of GATS and the respective annexes shall take effect for all Members upon acceptance by two thirds of the Members.

6. Notwithstanding the other provisions of this Article, amendments to the Agreement on TRIPS meeting the requirements of paragraph 2 of Article 71 thereof may be adopted by the Ministerial Conference without further formal acceptance process.

7. Any Member accepting an amendment to this Agreement or to a Multilateral Trade Agreement in Annex 1 shall deposit an instrument of acceptance with the Director–General of the WTO within the period of acceptance specified by the Ministerial Conference.

8. Any Member of the WTO may initiate a proposal to amend the provisions of the Multilateral Trade Agreements in Annexes 2 and 3 by submitting such proposal to the Ministerial Conference. The decision to approve amendments to the Multilateral Trade Agreement in Annex 2 shall be made by consensus and these amendments shall take effect for all Members upon approval by the Ministerial Conference. Decisions to approve amendments to the Multilateral Trade Agreement in Annex 3 shall take effect for all Members upon approval by the Ministerial Conference.

9. The Ministerial Conference, upon the request of the Members parties to a trade agreement, may decide exclusively by consensus to add that agreement to Annex 4. The Ministerial Conference, upon the request of the Members parties to a Plurilateral Trade Agreement, may decide to delete that Agreement from Annex 4.

10. Amendments to a Plurilateral Trade Agreement shall be governed by the provisions of that Agreement.

On December 6, 2005, the General Council opened the way for the adoption[23] of the first amendment of the WTO Agreement regarding Art. 31 TRIPs (WTO Doc. WT/L/641 of December 8, 2005).

---

[23] See Part IV of this volume. To be sure, the amendment has not yet entered into force (at the moment of writing): 2/3 of the WTO Members must formally accept it first. (Art. X.3 of the WTO Agreement). The period for adoption originally expired in December 2007, but was extended to December 31, 2009 (WTO Doc. WT/L/711 of December 21, 2007) and then extended again. Until then, the temporary waiver first agreed upon in 2003 will continue to apply. Already during the launching of the Doha round, a Declaration on the TRIPs Agreement and Public Health (WTO Doc. WT/MIN(01)/DEC/2 of November 20, 2001) incorporated in § 6 the concern that special care must be taken to ensure developing countries were not prevented from meeting their public health needs because of obligations under TRIPs. § 6 was translated into operational language soon through a Decision by which it was agreed that Article 31(f) should be waived to al-

(c) <u>Waivers</u>:[24] ¾ of all WTO Members must vote in favour for a waiver to be lawfully granted (Art. IX.3 of the WTO Agreement).

(d) <u>Dispute Settlement</u>: the advent of the WTO marked the passage from positive- to negative-consensus when it comes to the settlement of disputes. In a nutshell:

   i. a dispute shall be submitted to a Panel which will be established to this effect even if the defendant objects its establishment ("negative" consensus, that is, it suffices that the complaining party requests establishment);

   ii. a Panel report will be adopted (unless unanimously the WTO Membership objects to its adoption);

   iii. if, an appeal has (eventually) been submitted, the AB report will be adopted (unless unanimously the WTO Membership objects to its adoption);

   iv. assuming non-implementation of the Panel and/or the AB report, the winning party will be allowed to suspend concessions irrespective whether the defendant has conceded to their adoption.

4.3 GROUPINGS AND ALLIANCES IN THE WTO

It is rarely the case that WTO Members will meet, all 159 of them, and negotiate a particular issue. WTO Members have formed various partnerships both regional groupings and negotiating alliances and usually pick a delegate that will represent them. Some of the groupings are permanent, some ad hoc, some cover a wide range of issues, some concern a specific subject-matter. In the first edition of this volume, we included a detailed description of these alliances and invite the interested reader to consult it.

5. THE WTO LAW

Compared to other bodies of international law, WTO law is a complex, wide-ranging body of law. The law is not contained within a single treaty, but rather a series of agreements that cover different subject area. These treaties are supplemented by a series of annexes as well as decisions and understandings passed by the WTO membership. The WTO it-

---

low pharmaceuticals manufactured under compulsory licenses ('generics') to be exported to developing countries with little or insufficient manufacturing capacity, to address public health needs. (WTO Doc. WT/L/540 and Corr. 1, of September 1, 2003). The Amendment closely mirrors the Decision, see Kennedy (2010).

[24] Through this procedure, following a request to this effect, the WTO Membership will waive the obligations of a WTO Member. We discuss waivers in detail infra in this Chapter.

self notes that the major legal texts which govern its membership is a "daunting list of about 60 agreements, annexes, decisions, and understandings." Below, we provide a bit of guidance of the structure overlaying this complex body of law.

5.1 THREE LAYERS OF WTO OBLIGATIONS

Upon accession,[25] a WTO Member must assume specific legal obligations. This can be divided into three layers of obligations:

First, there are a series of **multilateral agreements** that are obligatory for all WTO Members. These agreements constitute a single package that each WTO Member must accept; there is no possibility of opting out of any of these agreements.

- The umbrella agreement is the Marrakesh Agreement Establishing the World Trade Organization (the "WTO Agreement") concluded in April 1994. The WTO Agreement consists of sixteen articles that lay the foundations for how the WTO is to operate and a set of annexes that sets forth the legal agreements binding on all WTO Members.
- In addition, each of the three core areas—goods, services, and intellectual property—is governed by an agreement that establishes the broad principles for the rules governing trade in that area: the General Agreement on Tariffs and Trade (GATT) (for goods); the General Agreement on Trade in Services (GATS); and the Agreement on Trade–Related Aspects of Intellectual Property Rights (TRIPS).
- Included under the goods and services areas are a set of additional agreements and annexes that regulate specific issues or sectors. For example, the Agreement on Agriculture lays out specific rules governing trade in agricultural goods; the Annexes on Financial Services govern cross-border trade in financial services.
- The Understanding on Rules and Procedures for the Settlement of Disputes, commonly referred to as the Dispute Settlement Understanding (DSU), sets forth the rules for how disputes are to be settled within the WTO regime.
- In addition, the Trade Policy Review Mechanism (TPRM) sets forth the procedural rules to ensure transparency within the WTO regime, by allowing WTO Members the regular opportunity to review the trade policies of individual Members.

Second, the **plurilateral agreements**: participation in each of these agreements is optional for WTO Members. WTO Members that choose to accede to each plurilateral agreement need to extend the obligations required by the plurilateral agreement to only the other WTO Members

---

[25] On the institutional requirements of accession, see Williams (2008).

that have also acceded to that agreement; they not extend the benefits to all WTO Members. At present, there are only two such agreements: the Agreement on Government Procurement (GPA) and the Agreement on Trade in Civil Aircraft. When the WTO was established, two additional plurilateral agreements existed, but they expired at the end of 1997.

Third, there are a set of **ad hoc obligations** that apply only to an individual country. These are generally laid forth in that country's Protocol of Accession to the WTO and govern that country's relationships with incumbent WTO Members.[26] An ad hoc obligation may require that a WTO Member incur an obligation beyond that required of other WTO Members (commonly referred to as WTO+ obligation). For example, normally, when a WTO Member applies a safeguard measure to curtail imports, it must apply the safeguard measure to all imports and not just those from a particular country. However, China, in its Protocol of Accession, agreed to allow WTO Members to apply safeguard measures against only Chinese goods for the first twelve years following its WTO accession. Or an ad hoc obligation may allow a WTO Member to provide for less than what is required of all other WTO Members (commonly referred to as a WTO-obligation). For example, when Lithuania acceded to the WTO on May 31, 2001, it was allowed a grace period (until December 31, 2005) to bring its excise taxes on beer and mead into conformity with Art. III GATT.[27] WTO-obligations have a function comparable to "grandfathering" of obligations that the original GATT signatories practiced.[28]

In the sections that follow, we describe each of these three layers of agreements in greater detail.

5.2 THE MULTILATERAL AGREEMENTS: A SINGLE UNDERTAKING

The Uruguay Round agreements were concluded following the so-called "single undertaking"-approach: Membership of the WTO would be contingent upon accepting all of the treaties as a package. For instance, it would not be open for a country to accept the rights and obligations of the

---

[26] If there was any doubt as to the enforceability of obligations assumed under a protocol of accession, they were removed by the Panel report on *China–Auto Parts*. China joined the WTO in 2001, and agreed to a bound duty of 25% for vehicles, and a 10% for auto parts: in its Protocol of Accession, China had agreed that if it ever created a tariff line for certain types of motor vehicle kits, the duties would not exceed 10%. However, in 2004–2005, China adopted measures that imposed a 25% charge on auto parts that had been imported, and then assembled into vehicles inside China. The charge was being imposed following the assembly of the parts into the vehicle. The Panel held that the measure at hand was an internal measure and, since it was not being applied to domestic products as well, it was in violation of Art. III.2 GATT (§§ 7.220ff.). In an alternative finding, the Panel held that, had the measure been understood to be an import duty, it would still run afoul Art. II GATT (§§ 7.608ff.). The AB upheld.

[27] Report of the Working Party on the Accession of Lithuania to the WTO, WTO Doc. WT/ACC/LTU/52 of November 7, 2000 at § 66.

[28] Under grandfathering for example, the UK managed to keep its imperial preferences intact. The advent of the Uruguay round marks the end of the grandfathering practice.

GATT, while refusing the rules governing trade in intellectual property set forth in the TRIPS Agreement. This approach was a sharp break from the practices of the previous trade round (the Tokyo Round of 1973–79) where GATT contracting parties were given the option to decide whether to participate in a series of side agreements. The first edition of this volume reproduces a chart that describes the GATT à la carte-approach following the Tokyo round; those interested in the state of trade law prior to the Uruguay Round's approach of requiring a single undertaking may wish to consult it.

As noted above, the umbrella agreement governing the multilateral agreements is the WTO Agreement. Included at the end of the WTO Agreement is a series of three Annexes (referred to as Annexes 1, 2, and 3). Art. 2.2 of the WTO Agreement makes clear: "The agreements and associated legal instruments included in Annexes 1, 2, and 3 are integral parts of the Agreement, binding on all Members".

5.2.1 The Annex 1 Agreements

Much of the substantive law governing the WTO is found in Annex 1. This Annex is further sub-divided into three categories: Annex 1A includes the multilateral agreements on trade in goods; Annex 1B, the General Agreement on Trade in Services (GATS); and Annex 1C the Agreement on Trade–Related Intellectual Property Rights (TRIPs). Annex 2 reflects the Understanding on Rules and Procedures governing the settlement of Disputes (DSU) and, finally, Annex 3 reflects the Trade Policy Review Mechanism (TPRM).

The core agreement in Annex 1A is the General Agreement on Tariffs and Trade (GATT) 1994. The GATT 1994 sets forth the basic rules for trade in goods and is based on the original GATT drafted in 1947. However, Art. II.4 of the WTO Agreement makes clear that the GATT 1994 is its own agreement that is legally distinct from the GATT 1947. Besides encompassing the text of the GATT 1947, the GATT 1994 also includes a series of decisions and other legal instruments adopted during the GATT years (1947–94) prior to the WTO's establishment.[29] In addition, a number of Understandings and Agreements are annexed to the GATT 1994. As set out in Annex 1A of the WTO Agreement, the GATT 1994 includes the following:

1. The General Agreement on Tariffs and Trade 1994 ("GATT 1994") shall consist of:

(a) the provisions in the General Agreement on Tariffs and Trade, dated 30 October 1947, annexed to the Final Act Adopted

---

[29] The AB held that the issue of whether a specific 'decision' by the GATT CONTRACTING PARTIES should be considered as part of the GATT acquis is a question that can be determined through adjudication. For example, decisions adopting a Panel report were not considered to be 'decisions' covered by Art. 1(b)(iv) GATT 1994 (see AB report on Japan—Alcoholic Beverages II).

at the Conclusion of the Second Session of the Preparatory Committee of the United Nations Conference on Trade and Employment (excluding the Protocol of Provisional Application), as rectified, amended or modified by the terms of legal instruments which have entered into force before the date of entry into force of the WTO Agreement;

(b) the provisions of the legal instruments set forth below that have entered into force under the GATT 1947 before the date of entry into force of the WTO Agreement:

- (i) protocols and certifications relating to tariff concessions;

- (ii) protocols of accession (excluding the provisions (*a*) concerning provisional application and withdrawal of provisional application and (*b*) providing that Part II of GATT 1947 shall be applied provisionally to the fullest extent not inconsistent with legislation existing on the date of the Protocol);

- (iii) decisions on waivers granted under Article XXV of GATT 1947 and still in force on the date of entry into force of the WTO Agreement;

- (iv) other decisions of the CONTRACTING PARTIES to GATT 1947;

(c) the Understandings set forth below:

- (i) Understanding on the Interpretation of Article II:1(b) of the General Agreement on Tariffs and Trade 1994;

- (ii) Understanding on the Interpretation of Article XVII of the General Agreement on Tariffs and Trade 1994;

- (iii) Understanding on Balance-of-Payments Provisions of the General Agreement on Tariffs and Trade 1994;

- (iv) Understanding on the Interpretation of Article XXIV of the General Agreement on Tariffs and Trade 1994;

- (v) Understanding in Respect of Waivers of Obligations under the General Agreement on Tariffs and Trade 1994;

- (vi) Understanding on the Interpretation of Article XXVIII of the General Agreement on Tariffs and Trade 1994; and

(d) the Marrakesh Protocol to GATT 1994.

The basic principles governing trade in goods are all set forth in the GATT 1994, and we will concentrate primarily on these principles in the initial chapters of this book. We return to the GATT 1994 again when we examine the exceptions that it provides to the obligations incurred by WTO Members in Chapters 12–13.

In addition to the GATT 1994, Annex 1A lists a number of specific agreements that govern trade in goods for particular sectors or issues:

- the Agreement on Agriculture (AG), which establishes rules for the use of tariffs and quotas on agricultural goods and for the provision of domestic support and export subsidies for the agricultural sector (to be discussed in Chapter 17);
- the Agreement on Textiles and Clothing (ATC), which provides for the gradual elimination of quotas on textiles and clothing by 2005 (to be discussed in Chapter 18);
- the Agreement on Technical Barriers to Trade (the TBT Agreement) which regulates the enactment of technical regulations and standards by WTO Members (to be discussed in Chapter 19);
- the Agreement on the Application of Sanitary and Phytosanitary Measures (the SPS Agreement), which regulates domestic measures enacted by WTO Members to protect the lives of humans, animals, and plants and to ensure food safety (to be discussed in Chapter 20);
- the Agreement on Trade–Related Investment Measures (the TRIMS Agreement) which provides a small set of key principles that WTO Members must apply when regulating foreign investments (to be discussed in Chapter 21);
- the Agreement on the Implementation of Article VI of GATT 1994 (the Antidumping Agreement or AD), which elaborates on the rules that a WTO Member must follow when applying antidumping duties on imports (to be discussed in Chapter 14);
- the Agreement on the Implementation of Article VII of GATT 1994 (the Customs Valuation Agreement or CV), which establishes the rules that national customs officials must follow when valuing goods for customs purposes (to be discussed in Chapter 7);
- the Agreement on Pre-shipment Inspection (PSIA), which regulates the activities that a WTO Member may take with respect to inspecting a good to be exported (to be discussed in Chapter 7);
- the Agreement on Rules of Origin (ROO), which aims to harmonize the global rules to determine the origin of a good and sets forth disciplines that WTO Members are to enact in the transition period prior to such harmonization;

- the Agreement on Import Licensing Procedures (ILA), which sets forth rules governing the use of import licensing procedures by WTO Members; (to be discussed in Chapter 7);
- the Agreement on Subsidies and Countervailing Measures (SCM), which regulates the provision of subsidies by WTO Members and elaborates on the rules that a WTO Member must follow when applying countervailing duties on imports (to be discussed in Chapter 15);
- the Agreement on Safeguards (SG), elaborates on the rules that a WTO Member must follow when applying safeguard measures on imports (to be discussed in Chapter 16);

Annex 1B contains the General Agreement on Trade in Services (GATS). We discuss the GATS in detail in Chapters 23–26. Included within the GATS are a series of annexes that govern particular service topics or sectors. These include:

- the Annex on Article II Exemptions (for provision of most-favored-nation treatment);
- the Annex on Movement of Natural Persons Supplying Services under the GATS;
- the Annex on Air Transport Services;
- the First and Second Annexes on Financial Services;
- the Annex on Negotiations on Maritime Transport Services;
- the Annex on Telecommunications, and the Annex on Negotiations on Basic Telecommunications.

Finally, Annex 1C contains the Agreement on Trade–Related Aspects of Intellectual Property Rights (TRIPS). We discuss the TRIPS Agreement in Chapters 27–31. At present, the area of trade-related intellectual property is governed only by the TRIPS Agreement. Unlike goods or services, there are not any additional agreements or annexes.

5.2.2 The Dispute Settlement Understanding (DSU)

Annex 2 of the WTO Agreement makes clear that the Understanding on Rules and Procedures Governing Dispute Settlement (Dispute Settlement Understanding, or DSU) is an integral part of the WTO. The DSU (through Art. 23.2) establishes a compulsory third party-adjudication system for resolving all disputes that arise from the operation of the WTO Agreement. Each WTO Member must agree to submit all such disputes exclusively to the WTO dispute settlement body. The DSU represented a major innovation from dispute settlement procedures of the GATT era. It included a process for appellate review and stronger enforcement mechanisms. We discuss the DSU in detail in Chapters 32–37.

5.2.3 The Trade Policy Review Mechanism (TPRM)

The Trade Policy Review Mechanism (TPRM) was originally established in 1989 on a provisional basis. Pursuant to Annex 3 of the WTO Agreement, the TPRM became a permanent feature of the multilateral trading system.[30] The TPRM's objectives are:

> to contribute to improved adherence by all Members to rules, disciplines and commitments made under the Multilateral Trade Agreements and, where applicable, the Plurilateral Trade Agreements, and hence to the smoother functioning of the multilateral trading system, by achieving greater transparency in, and understanding of, the trade policies and practices of Members.

To this effect, the WTO Secretariat, which is entrusted with the responsibility to prepare the reports, is required to periodically review the trade policies and practices of all Members.[31] The WTO Secretariat's reports are written in close consultation with the authorities of the Member under review. Since the WTO Secretariat does not have the authority to interpret the covered agreements, a TPRM report on the trade policies and practices of a Member does not provide an assessment as to the legal consistency of particular policies with the multilateral agreements; it is a mere exercise in transparency. A WTO document[32] reflecting the record of the TPRM as of mid–2003 concluded that:

> while each review highlights the specific issues and measures concerning the individual Member, certain common themes emerged during the course of the reviews conducted in the period January–July 2003. These included:

> transparency in policy-making and implementation; economic environment and trade liberalization; implementation of the WTO Agreements; regional trade agreements and their relationship with the multilateral trading system; tariff issues, including peaks, escalation, preferences, rationalization and the difference between applied and bound rates; customs clearance procedures; import and export restrictions and licensing procedures; the use of contingency measures such as anti-dumping and countervailing duties; technical and sanitary measures and market access; standards and their equivalence with international norms; intellectual property rights legislation and enforcement; government

---

[30] The WTO Agreement required that the operation of the TPRM was to be evaluated by the Trade Policy Review Body (the WTO body administering the TPRM) in 1999. The evaluation concluded that the TPRM functions effectively, and as a consequence, the TPRM has become a permanent feature of the WTO legal edifice. WTO doc. WT/MIN(99)/2 of October 8, 1999.

[31] Occasionally, the WTO Secretariat reports will be prepared with the help of outside consultants; this has been the case for the reviews of Maldives, Niger, Senegal and the Southern African Customs Union.

[32] WTO Doc. WT/TPR/134 of June 27, 2003.

procurement policies and practices; state involvement in the economy and privatization programmes; trade-related competition and investment policy issues; incentive measures such as subsidies and tax forgone; sectoral trade-policy issues, particularly liberalization in agriculture and certain services sectors; GATS commitments; special and differential treatment, including market access and implementation, particularly for customs valuation, TRIPS and TRIMs; small-island and small landlocked Members; and technical assistance in implementing the WTO Agreements and the experience with the Integrated Framework.

By the end of 2011, 338 reviews had been conducted since the establishment of the TPRB: the reviews covered 141 Members, representing some 89% of world trade and 96% of the trade of Members.[33] All but three WTO Members (namely, Cuba, Guinea Bissau, and Myanmar) had been reviewed by February 2012.[34] Not all WTO Members are reviewed with similar frequency. The periodicity of the reviews depends on the relative weight that WTO Members have on world trade. Annex 3 of the WTO Agreement where the decision to establish the TPRM has been included pertinently reads in item C:

> The trade policies and practices of all Members shall be subject to periodic review. The impact of individual Members on the functioning of the multilateral trading system, defined in terms of their share of world trade in a recent representative period, will be the determining factor in deciding on the frequency of reviews. The first four trading entities so identified (counting the European Communities as one) shall be subject to review every two years. The next 16 shall be reviewed every four years. Other Members shall be reviewed every six years, except that a longer period may be fixed for least-developed country Members.

5.3 THE PLURILATERAL AGREEMENTS

Originally, four agreements were excluded from the single undertaking-approach: the Agreement on Civil Aircraft (CA), the Agreement on Government Procurement (GPA), the International Dairy Agreement (IDA), and the International Bovine Meat Agreement (IBM). These are the so-called plurilateral agreements, covered under Annex 4 of the WTO Agreement. Art. II.3 of the WTO Agreement defines the legal status of these Agreements:

> The agreements and associated legal instruments included in Annex 4 (hereinafter referred to as "Plurilateral Trade Agreements") are also part of this Agreement for those Members that

---

[33] WTO Doc. WT/TPR/287 of November 15, 2011.
[34] WTO Doc. WT/TPR/OV/14 of November 21, 2011 at p. 59.

have accepted them, and are binding on those Members. The Plurilateral Trade Agreements do not create either obligations or rights for Members that have not accepted them.

The terms for participation in the Annex 4 Agreements are spelled out in each of the four agreements (Art. XII.3 of the WTO Agreement).[35] These four Agreements are only open for accession to WTO Members, i.e. to states that have accepted all the multilateral agreements. Art. II.3 of the WTO Agreement reads to this effect:

> The agreements . . . (hereinafter referred to as "Plurilateral Trade Agreements") are also part of this Agreement for those *Members* that have accepted them . . . (emphasis added).

WTO Members (Art. X.9 of the WTO Agreement) can, through consensus-voting, add to the existing list of plurilateral agreements. They can also terminate the agreements. This has occurred with respect to two of four original plurilateral agreements—the International Dairy Agreement and International Agreement on Bovine Meats (IBM), which were terminated by decisions of the WTO General Council in December 1997.[36]

5.3.1 Agreement on Government Procurement (GPA)

Of the two remaining plurilateral agreements, the one that has attracted greater attention in recent years is the Agreement on Government Procurement (GPA). The GPA governs the regulation of government procurement by certain designated government entities. Art. XXIV GPA governs accession to this agreement. We discuss the GPA in detail in Chapter 22.

5.3.2 The Agreement on Civil Aircraft

The other plurilateral agreement is the Agreement on Civil Aircraft (CA), which entered into force on January 1, 1980.[37] Art. 9 CA regulates accession to this plurilateral agreement. The following WTO Members have acceded to the CA: all EU member states, Canada, Chinese Taipei, Egypt, Georgia, Japan, Macao (China), Switzerland, and the US. On January 1, 2002, an Additional Protocol dealing with customs duties and charges applied on products coming under the purview of the CA entered into force between its signatories. We quote:

---

[35] A series of provisions included in the WTO Agreement make it clear that the terms of participation in plurilateral agreements are the privilege of such agreements: accession (Art. XII of the WTO Agreement); acceptance and entry into force (Art. XIV.4 of the WTO Agreement); inclusion of reservations (Art. XVI.5 of the WTO Agreement); decision-making process (Art. IX.5 of the WTO Agreement); amendments (Art. X.10 of the WTO Agreement); non-application (Art. XIII of the WTO Agreement); withdrawal (Art. XV.2 of the WTO Agreement).

[36] For the agreements leading to the termination of the International Diary Agreement, see WTO Docs. IDA/8 of September 30, 1007, and WT/L/252 of December 17, 1997. For the agreements leading to the termination of the International Agreement on Bovine Meats, see WTO Docs. IMA/8 of September 30, 1997 and WT/L/252 of December 16, 1997.

[37] GATT Doc. BISD 34S/22.

1. The Annex attached to this Protocol shall, upon its entry into force pursuant to paragraph 3, replace the Annex to the Agreement as established heretofore by the Protocol (1986) Amending the Annex to the Agreement on Trade in Civil Aircraft.

2. This Protocol shall be open for acceptance by Signatories to the Agreement, by signature or otherwise, until 31 October 2001, or a later date to be decided by the Committee on Trade in Civil Aircraft.

3. This Protocol shall enter into force, for those Signatories who have accepted it, on 1 January 2002. For each other Signatory it shall enter into force on the day following the date of its acceptance.

4. This Protocol shall be deposited with the Director–General of the World Trade Organization who shall promptly furnish to each Signatory and each Member a certified copy thereof and a notification of each acceptance thereof pursuant to paragraph 2.

5. This Protocol shall be registered in accordance with the provisions of Article 102 of the Charter of the United Nations.

6. This Protocol deals only with customs duties and charges under Article 2 of the Agreement. Except with respect to requiring duty-free treatment for products covered by this Protocol, nothing in this Protocol or the Agreement, as modified thereby, changes or affects a Signatory's rights and obligations, as they exist on the day prior to the entry into force of this Protocol, under any of the WTO Agreements referenced in Article II of the Marrakesh Agreement Establishing the World Trade Organization.

Pursuant to Art. 2, signatories to this agreement are required to eliminate at the latest by the date when the agreement enters into force all customs duties for products listed in the Annex to the agreement (civil aircraft, repairs on civil aircraft). It also imposes obligations with respect to technical barriers to trade, government directed procurement, export credits, which to a large extent have been taken over by obligations assumed under the corresponding Uruguay round agreements.

5.4 WAIVERS

A WTO Member may, in exceptional circumstances, request that it be exempted from its obligations under the WTO. To this effect, a Member must submit a request for a "waiver" to the WTO Membership. Art. IX of the WTO Agreement sets out the procedure:

3. In exceptional circumstances, the Ministerial Conference may decide to waive an obligation imposed on a Member by this Agreement or any of the Multilateral Trade Agreements, provided that any such decision shall be taken by three fourths of the Members unless otherwise provided for in this paragraph.

> (a) A request for a waiver concerning this Agreement shall be submitted to the Ministerial Conference for consideration pursuant to the practice of decision-making by consensus. The Ministerial Conference shall establish a time-period, which shall not exceed 90 days, to consider the request. If consensus is not reached during the time-period, any decision to grant a waiver shall be taken by three fourths of the Members.
>
> (b) A request for a waiver concerning the Multilateral Trade Agreements in Annexes 1A or 1B or 1C and their annexes shall be submitted initially to the Council for Trade in Goods, the Council for Trade in Services or the Council for TRIPS, respectively, for consideration during a time-period which shall not exceed 90 days. At the end of the time-period, the relevant Council shall submit a report to the Ministerial Conference.

4. A decision by the Ministerial Conference granting a waiver shall state the exceptional circumstances justifying the decision, the terms and conditions governing the application of the waiver, and the date on which the waiver shall terminate. Any waiver granted for a period of more than one year shall be reviewed by the Ministerial Conference not later than one year after it is granted, and thereafter annually until the waiver terminates. In each review, the Ministerial Conference shall examine whether the exceptional circumstances justifying the waiver still exist and whether the terms and conditions attached to the waiver have been met. The Ministerial Conference, on the basis of the annual review, may extend, modify or terminate the waiver.

5. Decisions under a Plurilateral Trade Agreement, including any decisions on interpretations and waivers, shall be governed by the provisions of that Agreement.

A footnote to § 3 reads:

A decision to grant a waiver in respect of any obligation subject to a transition period or a period for staged implementation that the requesting Member has not performed by the end of the relevant period shall be taken only by consensus.

It follows that a waiver is a transitional multilateral authorization to deviate from agreed obligations. The transitional character is underlined by the fact that all waivers will be reviewed annually, irrespective of whether they have been granted for a multi-year period: WTO Members must satisfy themselves during the review that the rationale for granting the waiver is very much alive. Practice has led to conflicts across WTO Members as to the overall justiciability of waivers' decisions, as well as the terms under which waivers have been granted. Case law has provided some answers in both respects. The Panel in *EC–Bananas III* was called upon to address the EU argument that waivers[38] cannot form the subject-matter of a dispute before WTO adjudicating bodies. In rejecting this argument, the Panel held that it had the requisite jurisdiction to interpret the contents of a waiver granted by the WTO Members (§ 7.97). On appeal, the AB upheld this finding in the following terms (§ 167):

> The European Communities asserts that the Panel should not have conducted an objective examination of the requirements of the Lomé Convention, but instead should have deferred to the "common" EC and ACP views on the appropriate interpretation of the Lomé Convention. This assertion is without merit. The Panel was correct in stating:
>
>> We note that since the GATT CONTRACTING PARTIES incorporated a reference to the Lomé Convention into the Lomé waiver, the meaning of the Lomé Convention became a GATT/WTO issue, at least to that extent. Thus, we have no alternative but to examine the provisions of the Lomé Convention ourselves in so far as it is necessary to interpret the Lomé waiver.'
>
> We, too, have no alternative.

Having clarified that waivers are justiciable, the same Panel went on to provide its understanding on the manner in which the terms of a waiver should be interpreted. This Panel was requested, inter alia, to review whether the EU had respected the terms of the waiver that it had requested (and obtained) in order to treat imports of bananas from some WTO Members (the ACP countries, a group of countries from Africa, the Caribbean, and the Pacific with which it had signed a treaty, the Lomé Convention) better than imports from the rest of the world, in contravention of Art. I GATT. The precise question before the Panel was whether Art. XIII GATT, a provision that had not been explicitly included in the waiver granted to the EU, was covered by the terms of the waiver or not. Although the Panel was of the view that a waiver should be construed narrowly, it went on to hold that despite the fact Art. XIII GATT was not explicitly mentioned in the waiver granted to the EU, that provision should, nevertheless, be covered by the terms of the waiver in light of the *effet utile* of the waiver (§§ 7.105–108). On appeal, the AB reversed the Panel's findings and held that the waiver covered only what it had explic-

---

[38] The facts of this case which are reproduced in other parts of this volume are immaterial here, and hence omitted: the EU claimed that waivers, as general matter irrespective of the reasons underlying the granting of the request, are not justiciable.

itly been reflected into its body (§§ 182–188). The following Table provides the list of waivers that have been granted since the advent of the WTO and those waivers that are presently in force (February 2012):[39]

Table 1.5: List of Waivers

WAIVER	DECISION	DATE of ADOPTION of DECISION	GRANTED UNTIL	REPORT in 2010[i]
Granted in 2010				
Introduction of Harmonized System 2007 Changes into WTO Schedules of Tariff Concessions[ii]	WT/L/809	14 December 2010	31 December 2011	—
Introduction of Harmonized System 2002 Changes into WTO Schedules of Tariff Concessions[iii]	WT/L/808	14 December 2010	31 December 2011	—
Argentina—Introduction of Harmonized System 1996 Changes into WTO Schedules of Tariff Concessions	WT/L/801	29 July 2010	30 April 2011	—
Previously granted—in				

---

[39] WTO Doc. WT/GC/W/629 of February 8, 2011.

[i] Applicable if so stipulated in the corresponding waiver Decision.

[ii] The Members which have requested to be covered under this waiver are: Argentina; Australia; Brazil; Canada; China; Costa Rica; Croatia; El Salvador; European Union; Guatemala; Honduras; Hong Kong, China; India; Israel; Korea; Macao, China; Malaysia; Mexico; New Zealand; Nicaragua; Norway; Pakistan; Singapore; Switzerland; Thailand; United States and Uruguay.

[iii] The Members which have requested to be covered under this waiver are: Argentina; Australia; Brazil; China; Costa Rica; Croatia; El Salvador; European Union; Iceland; India; Republic of Korea; Mexico; New Zealand; Norway; Thailand; United States and Uruguay.

WAIVER	DECISION	DATE of ADOPTION of DECISION	GRANTED UNTIL	REPORT in 2010[i]
force in 2010				
Introduction of Harmonized System 2007 Changes into WTO Schedules of Tariff Concessions[3]	WT/L/787 and Add.1	17 December 2009	31 December 2010	—
Introduction of Harmonized System 2002 Changes into WTO Schedules of Tariff Concessions[4]	WT/L/786	17 December 2009	31 December 2010	—
Preferential Tariff Treatment for Least–Developed Countries— Decision on Extension of waiver	WT/L/759	27 May 2009	30 June 2019	—
Panama— Introduction of Harmonized System 1996 Changes into WTO Schedules of Tariff Concessions	WT/L/758	27 May 2009	30 April 2010	—
Argentina— Introduction of Harmonized System 1996 Changes into WTO Schedules of Tariff Concessions	WT/L/757	27 May 2009	30 April 2010	—
United States— Andean Trade	WT/L/755	27 May 2009	31 December 2014	WT/L/796

SEC. 5 THE WTO LAW 47

WAIVER	DECISION	DATE of ADOPTION of DECISION	GRANTED UNTIL	REPORT in 2010[i]
Preference Act—Renewal of waiver				
United States—African Growth and Opportunity Act	WT/L/754	27 May 2009	30 September 2015	WT/L/795
United States—Caribbean Basin Economic Recovery Act—Renewal of waiver	WT/L/753	27 May 2009	31 December 2014	WT/L/794
European Communities—Application of Autonomous Preferential Treatment to Moldova	WT/L/722	7 May 2008	31 December 2013	WT/L/800 and Corr.1
Mongolia—Export duties on raw cashmere	WT/L/695	27 July 2007	29 January 2012	—
United States—Former Trust Territory of the Pacific Islands	WT/L/694	27 July 2007	31 December 2016	WT/L/798
Cuba—Article XV:6 of GATT 1994	WT/L/678	15 December 2006	31 December 2011	WT/L/803
CARIBCAN	WT/L/677	15 December 2006	31 December 2011	WT/L/804
Kimberley Process Certification	WT/L/676	15 December 2006	31 December 2012	—

WAIVER	DECISION	DATE of ADOPTION of DECISION	GRANTED UNTIL	REPORT in 2010[i]
Scheme for rough diamonds[iv]				
European Communities' preferences for Albania, Bosnia and Herzegovina, Croatia, Serbia and Montenegro, and the Former Yugoslav Republic of Macedonia	WT/L/654	28 July 2006	31 December 2011	WT/L/799 and Corr.1
Least–Developed Country Members—Obligations under Article 70.9 of the TRIPS Agreement with respect to Pharmaceutical Products	WT/L/478	8 July 2002	1 January 2016	—

5.5 NON–APPLICATION

In order to facilitate accession to the GATT, Art. XXXV GATT provided flexibility in that, it allowed acceding countries not to enter into contractual arrangements at all with (one or more) incumbents (Art. XXXV GATT). Two countries could thus both acquire the status of a GATT contracting party without being bound by the GATT at all in their inter se relations. Historically, the rationale for its original inclusion in the GATT has to do with the fact that the world was emerging from World War II and, except for the neutral countries, many potential candidates to accede to the GATT had not healed the wounds: it would have been politically unacceptable for them to do "business as usual" with yesterday's enemies. For example, for decades following the war, a large number of GATT contracting parties invoked Art. XXXV GATT against

---

[iv] Annex: Australia; Botswana; Brazil; Canada; Croatia; India; Israel; Japan; Korea; Mauritius; Mexico; Norway; Philippines; Sierra Leone; Chinese Taipei; Thailand; United Arab Emirates; United States and Venezuela.

Japan.[40] Eventually, countries dis-invoked Art. XXXV GATT against Japan, although this often required the passing of time to heal history's wounds as well as persuasion from the Japanese government.[41]

During the Uruguay Round negotiations, the parties decided that the rationale for continued inclusion of the non-application-clause was still present. Consequently, the WTO Agreement includes Art. XIII, which states:

> 1. This Agreement and the Multilateral Trade Agreements in Annexes 1 and 2 shall not apply as between any Member and any other Member if either of the Members, at the time either becomes a Member, does not consent to such application.
>
> 2. Paragraph 1 may be invoked between original Members of the WTO which were contracting parties to GATT 1947 only where Article XXXV of that Agreement had been invoked earlier and was effective as between those contracting parties at the time of entry into force for them of this Agreement.
>
> 3. Paragraph 1 shall apply between a Member and another Member which has acceded under Article XII only if the Member not consenting to the application has so notified the Ministerial Conference before the approval of the agreement on the terms of accession by the Ministerial Conference.
>
> 4. The Ministerial Conference may review the operation of this Article in particular cases at the request of any Member and make appropriate recommendations.
>
> 5. Non-application of a Plurilateral Trade Agreement between parties to that Agreement shall be governed by the provisions of that Agreement.

The following is a list of the Members that have invoked the non-application clause under Art. XIII of the WTO Agreement as of the entry into force of the WTO:

---

[40] GATT Analytical Index, Geneva, 1995, at pp. 1034ff. Japan was the most frequent target of invocations of the non-application clause. Among the countries that invoked Art. XXXV GATT against Japan were: Australia (1964), Austria (1976), Barbados (1967), Belgium (1964), Benin (1972), Brazil (1957), Burundi (1972), Cameroon (1974), Central African Republic (1974), Chad (1971), Congo (1973), Cuba (1961), Cyprus (1962), France (1964), Gabon (1973), Gambia (1971), Ghana (1962), Guyana (1966), Haiti (1958), India (1958), Ireland (1975), Ivory Coast (1970), Jamaica (1972), Kenya (1977), Kuwait (1970), Luxembourg (1964), Madagascar (1969), Malaysia (1963), Maldives (1988), Mali (1993), Malta (1968), Mauritania (1968), Netherlands (1964), New Zealand (1962), Niger (1970), Nigeria (1975), Portugal (1972), Rhodesia and Nyasaland (1963), Rwanda (1970), Senegal (1975), Sierra Leone (1975), South Africa (1985), Spain (1971), Trinidad and Tobago (1966), Uganda (1970), United Kingdom (1963), and Upper Volta (1970).

[41] Japan, for example, had to threaten developing countries that it would not be providing them with tariff preferences since they had invoked Art. XXXV GATT against it. See GATT Doc. 2ss/SR.2 at p. 7.

Table 1.6: Instances of application of Article XIII of the WTO Agreement

Invoked by	In respect of	Date of General Council decision on accession	Date of invocation	Withdrawal
United States	Romania	N/A	WTO document dated 27 January 1995 indicates that the United States informed the Director–General on 30 December 1994 WT/L/11	WT/L/203
United States	Mongolia	18 July 1996 WT/ACC/MNG/10	Communication dated 11 July 1996 WT/L/159	WT/L/306
United States	Kyrgyz Republic	14 October 1998 WT/ACC/KCZ/28	Communication dated 9 October 1998 WT/L/275	WT/L/363
United States	Georgia	6 October 1999 WT/ACC/GEO/32/	Communication dated 30 September 1999 WT/L/318	WT/L/385
United States	Moldova	8 May 2001 WT/ACC/MOL/39	Communication dated 2 May 2001 WT/L/395	Still in force
El Salvador	China	10 November 2001 WT/ACC/CHN/49 and Corr.1	Communication dated 5 November 2001 WT/L/429	Still in force
Turkey	Armenia	10 December 2002 WT/L/ARM/23	Communication dated 29 November 2002 WT/L/501	Still in force

Invoked by	In respect of	Date of General Council decision on accession	Date of invocation	Withdrawal
United States	Armenia	10 December 2002 WT/L/ARM/23	Communication dated 3 December 2002 WT/L/505	WT/L/601
United States	Viet Nam	7 November 2006 WT/L/662	Communication dated 3 November 2006 WT/L/661	WT/L/679

5.6 THE TREATY–MAKING POWER OF THE WTO

The WTO possesses legal personality by virtue of Art. VIII of the WTO Agreement; it thus has treaty making power and, on this basis, can cooperate with other international organizations. Art. V of the WTO Agreement provides for the relationship of the WTO with other organizations. It reads:

> 1. The General Council shall make appropriate arrangements for effective cooperation with other intergovernmental organizations that have responsibilities related to those of the WTO.
>
> 2. The General Council may make appropriate arrangements for consultation and cooperation with non-governmental organizations concerned with matters related to those of the WTO.

The General Council is competent to decide on the parameters for international cooperation, and enjoys substantial discretion to this effect. By virtue of Art. III.5 of the WTO Agreement, however, the WTO must cooperate with the International Monetary Fund (IMF) and the World Bank (WB):

> With a view to achieving greater coherence in global economic policy-making, the WTO shall cooperate, as appropriate, with the International Monetary Fund and with the International Bank for Reconstruction and Development and its affiliated agencies.

Its cooperation with these institutions has recently reached new heights in the context of development aid that we are discussing infra in this volume.

The WTO has entered into formal international agreements, and sometimes into an MOU (memorandum of understanding) with other international organizations. We provide a complete list of arrangements in force as well as of those that have expired:

Table 1.7: MOUs and Agreements Currently in Force

	Abbreviation	Contracting party	Date of expiration
1.	ACP	African, Caribbean and Pacific Group of States	Indefinite period
2.	ESCAP	United Nations Economic and Social Commission for Asia and the Pacific	31/12/06
3.	FAO	Food and Agriculture Organization	Indefinite period
4.	FORSEC	South Pacific Forum Secretariat	03/04/11
5.	ICC/IFIA	International Chamber of Commerce/International Federation of Inspection Agencies	Indefinite period
6.	IDLO	International Development Law Organization	15/07/07
7.	IMF	International Monetary Fund	Indefinite period
8.	IsDB	Islamic Development Bank	18/02/2009
9.	ITD	International Institute for Trade and Development	28/02/07
10.	ITU	International Telecommunications Union	Indefinite period
11.	OIE	Office International des Epizooties	Indefinite period
12.	SINGAPORE	Republic of Singapore	Indefinite period
13.	UN	United Nations	Indefinite period
14.	UNCTAD	United Nations Conference on Trade and Development	27/02/10
15.	UNDP	United Nations Development Programme	Indefinite period
16.	UNEP	United Nations Environment Programme	Indefinite period

	Abbreviation	Contracting party	Date of expiration
17.	UNIDO	United Nations Industrial Development Organization	10/09/08
18.	WB	World Bank	Indefinite period
19.	WIPO	World Intellectual Property Organization	Indefinite period

(a) Integrated Framework missions not included.

Table 1.8: MOUs and Agreements that Have Expired

	Abbreviation	Contracting party	Date of expiration
1	ADB	Asian Development Bank	31/12/04
2	AMF	Arab Monetary Fund	31/12/04
3	CARICOM	Caribbean Community	01/07/05
4	ESCWA	United Nations Economic and Social Commission for Western Asia	31/12/04
5	IADB	Inter–American Development Bank	31/12/04
6	UoB	University of Barcelona	01/01/05
7	UoS	University of Salamanca	22/09/04

The WTO further cooperates with institutions such as the OECD (Organization for Economic Cooperation and Development), the WCO (World Customs Organization) and the standard setting institutions (such as the International Organization for Standardization, ISO).

6. WITHDRAWING FROM THE WTO

6.1 THE RIGHT TO WITHDRAW

Art. XIV of the WTO Agreement reflects the legal right of WTO Members to withdraw from the WTO. It reads:

1. Any Member may withdraw from this Agreement. Such withdrawal shall apply both to this Agreement and the Multilateral Trade Agreements and shall take effect upon the expiration of six months from the date on which written notice of withdrawal is received by the Director–General of the WTO.

2. Withdrawal from a Plurilateral Trade Agreement shall be governed by the provisions of that Agreement.

So far, no WTO Member has withdrawn from the WTO.

6.2 WITHDRAWAL IN THE GATT YEARS

The Republic of China (ROC) was an original contracting party to theGATT. After civil war led to the Communist takeover of the mainland China, the ROC government retreated to the island of Taiwan, but it continued to assert that it was the legitimate government for all of China. Through a letter addressed to the GATT on May 5, 1950, the ROC formally withdrew from the GATT. The newly-formed People's Republic of China (PRC) that ruled the mainland never acknowledged the legitimacy of this action, since doing so might acknowledge the ROC's claim that it was the rightful government of China. As a result, China's status in the GATT was left in limbo. Negotiations began in the 1980s to clarify China's status, with the Working Party established in 1987 carried the title "People's Republic China's Status as a Contracting Party". The PRC acceded to the WTO in 2001. The ROC also acceded to the WTO in 2002, but under the name of the Separate Customs Territory of Taiwan, Penghu, Kinmen and Matsu ("Chinese Taipei").

During the late 1980s, the Socialist Federal Republic of Yugoslavia (SFRY) began to disintegrate as a result of voices calling for independence of its various constituencies. By 1992, the SFRY had collapsed, as the "breakaway" republics of the Yugoslav Federation were widely being recognized as sovereign states on the international scene. The Federal Republic of Yugoslavia (FRY), a federation formed in 1992 by the republics of Serbia and Montenegro, claimed to be the successor of the SFRY; it requested to be acknowledged as such and preserve its status as a contracting party to the GATT. The rest of the GATT disagreed and moved to "freeze" the participation of the SFRY in the GATT. We quote the relevant excerpt from the discussions before the General Council:[42]

> The <u>Chairman</u> said that the break-up of the former Socialist Federal Republic of Yugoslavia had posed the question of its status as a contracting party. While the delegation speaking in the name of the Federal Republic of Yugoslavia (FRY) had laid claim to the status of successor to the former Socialist Federal Republic of Yugoslavia (L/7000), this claim had been contested by some contracting parties and some others had reserved their position on the issue. Some contracting parties had also suggested that the delegation claiming to represent the FRY as a successor to the Socialist Federal Republic of Yugoslavia (SFRY) in GATT

---
[42] GATT Doc. C/M/257 of July 10, 1992.

should not participate in GATT activities until the FRY had sought fresh membership, while others held the view that its participation should be without prejudice to the FRY's claim to successor status. He had held extensive informal consultations with contracting parties and believed there was agreement that this issue would need consideration by the Council. In these circumstances, without prejudice to the question of who should succeed the former SFRY in the GATT, and until the Council considered this issue, he proposed that the representative of the FRY should refrain from participating in the business of the Council. The Council so agreed.

The freezing of the participation effectively meant that the SFRY had been expelled: the SFRY was not recognized as a contracting party to the GATT at the moment of the advent of the WTO and, consequently, not as an original Member of the WTO as per Art. XI of the WTO Agreement. Later, Serbia and Montenegro (a state entity corresponding geographically to the Federal Republic of Yugoslavia) requested its accession anew to the WTO.[43] Other ex-Yugoslav republics, such as Croatia, the Former Yugoslav Republic of Macedonia (FYROM), and Slovenia, have since joined the WTO following their breakaway from ex-Yugoslavia. Montenegro acceded to the WTO in December 2011. Serbia's application remains in progress.

QUESTIONS AND COMMENTS

Theories for Explaining Trade Agreements: Economists do not dispute that there are gains from trade. The theory of comparative advantage, originally conceived by Ricardo (1818) and so eloquently reproduced in Deardorff (1980) is still widely accepted. In fact, the new trade theory suggests that because of the inherent advantages of specialization (which allows large scale production), trade liberalization is welfare increasing even across countries with similar endowments and production patterns as Balassa has explained in his many contributions (1966), (1967) and (1975); Broda and Weinstein (2007) have provided similar explanation. The obvious question against this background is why is there an agreement needed? If trade increases welfare, why not liberalize trade anyway? Economists have advanced two competing theories aiming to explain the rationale for the GATT (or a trade agreement): the commitment-theory suggests that a trade agreement like the GATT is necessary in order for governments to be in position to resist pressure from domestic lobbies ("I have tied my arms in the mast" would be the response to requests for protection, the "mast" being the GATT disciplines), see Tumlir (1985), and Maggi and Rodriguez–Clare (1998). The terms of trade-theory suggests that the rationale for a trade agreement like the

---

[43] Initially, only one Working Party (WP) was supposed to work on the accession of Serbia and Montenegro. Subsequently, Montenegro broke away from its federation with Serbia and, as a result, two WPs were formed.

GATT is not domestic but international externalities: countries when setting their tariff unilaterally will impose a negative external effect on foreign producers (since when setting tariffs hey will take into account domestic producers and consumers' welfare only); an international agreement will help internalize similar effects through reciprocal concessions, see Johnson (1953–54), and Bagwell and Staiger (2002). If the latter theory is correct why then would "small" states with little bargaining power impose tariffs in the first place, and why would they be welcome in a negotiation aiming to reciprocally reduce tariffs (that affect terms of trade)? If the former view is correct, what is the incentive for foreigners to enforce an agreement only to solve domestic problems of a third country? And how much of these rationales do you think actually explains the GATT as it was designed back in 1948?

Does the WTO Promote Trade Liberalization? In a provocative paper Rose (2004) has argued that it makes no difference if you are WTO Member or not, since trade patterns have not been affected by Membership. Subramanian and Wei (2007) show however, that the opposite is true: there are huge gains for developed countries trade, but maybe not so for developing countries' trade; in their view, this is so because the latter did not liberalize in significant manner. Moreover, Broda et al. (2008) find evidence for optimal tariff: they check tariffs of WTO Members before accession to the WTO and found that the larger the market the higher the tariff in specific goods before accession. With this paper the authors how that accession to the WTO led (for the countries in their sample) to tariff reductions and the ensuing expansion of trade.

What Explains Alliances at the WTO? Diego–Fernandez (2008), who used to represent Mexico in the WTO, takes the view that the dominant explanation for coalitions is pragmatism. In his study, he points to coalitions of countries that are, arguably, counter-intuitive but can be explained if one focuses on the objectives that a particular coalition seeks to achieve, which often are quite narrow. As a result, it is often the case that WTO Members might be allies when it comes to pursuing a certain objective, and opponents when the objective changes. In short, the author casts considerable doubt on the "permanent" character of some coalitions.

Law–Making by WTO Bodies: Have a look at the following decision adopted by the Council for Trade in Services on November 26, 1997 (WTO Doc. S/L/43 of December 2, 1997):

The Council for Trade in Services,

Having regard to the provisions of Article X of the General Agreement on Trade in Services (GATS),

Having regard to the proposal by the Chairperson of the Working Party on GATS Rules (S/C/W/28),

Decides as follows:

Notwithstanding the second sentence of paragraph 1 and paragraph 3 of Article X of the GATS, the first sentence of paragraph 1 and paragraph 2 of that Article shall continue to apply until 30 June 1999.

Is this decision, in your view, in accordance with Art. IX of the WTO Agreement? If not, why?

Waivers: Following the condemnation by a WTO Panel and the AB of its bananas regime, the EU requested and obtained a waiver for the very regime found to be WTO-inconsistent. Do you see anything in the language of Art. IX.3 of the WTO Agreement which could prevent a WTO Member from requesting waivers on practices already found to be inconsistent by WTO law? Do you think that the intended use of waivers was to cover similar requests?

Plurilaterals: Lawrence (2006) is one of the early (if not the earliest) advocates of extensive use of plurilaterals (what he terms a club of club approach). In his view, this approach offers a compromise in which diversity can co-exist with a more extensive set of commitments for willing members. Clubs should be chosen where they could help promote their central missions (lowering barriers to trade, reducing discrimination) and should be using the DSU. Do you share this view? Do you see any negatives in promoting proliferation of plurilaterals?

CHAPTER 2

QUANTITATIVE RESTRICTIONS

■ ■ ■

1. THE LEGAL DISCIPLINE

One means of restricting trade is to limit the access that a particular good has to a market. Restrictions may be imposed on the inbound end, by imposing a restriction on imports, or on the outbound end, by imposing a restriction on exports. Such restrictions can take on several different forms. Examples include:

- An outright prohibition or ban
- A quota, indicating the precise amount of a good that may be imported or exported
- A requirement for a license to import / export a good
- Voluntary export restraints

In WTO parlance, restrictions that limit the quantity of a good that may be imported or exported are referred to as quantitative restrictions ("QRs"). As we will see in this Chapter, case law has clarified that several other policy measures also qualify as QRs, including: minimum price requirements, a requirement to import through a state trading company, etc. In addition, WTO law has established the concept of a *de facto* QR, in which the government does not outright limit the quantity of a good, but nevertheless undertakes measures which result in this impact.

Art. XI GATT prohibits the use of QRs outright, on both imports and exports, irrespective of their rationale. The GATT, and now the WTO, seeks to encourage countries to use tariff duties rather than bans and quotas to regulate trade. Tariffs will be discussed in Chapter 3, including the rationale for why tariffs are preferable to QRs.

However, as we shall see, the principle that QRs are illegal is subject to a number of exceptions. This includes a number of specific exceptions noted in Art. XI GATT. For example, QRs may be maintained to alleviate food shortages or to address a balance-of-payments crisis, provided certain conditions are met. Such exceptions will be discussed in greater depth in this Chapter. In addition, the prohibition on QRs is also subject to a number of general exceptions spelled out in Articles XX and XXI GATT. For example, QRs may be maintained on national security grounds or to protect public morals. We will touch on some of these exceptions briefly in this Chapter but elaborate on them in greater detail in Chapter 12.

In instances where a WTO Member is authorized to maintain a QR on account of an exception in the law, the WTO Member nevertheless must follow certain principles in administering the QR:

- The QR must be administered in a non-discriminatory manner
- In applying an import restriction, the WTO Member must aim for a distribution of trade that approximates, as closely as possible, the shares which various trading partners would obtain in the absence of such restrictions.

We elaborate on these requirements in greater detail in this Chapter. In addition, we focus on how WTO law deals with a number of specific instances, such as the use of export taxes, production quotas, etc.

2. THE RATIONALE FOR THE LEGAL DISCIPLINE

In the aftermath of the Smoot–Hawley Act and other protectionist acts during the Great Depression, many countries resorted to QRs as a means to impede trade. The framers of the GATT wanted to introduce, as we saw in Chapter 1, non-discrimination in trade relations. Non-discriminatory trade is difficult to reconcile with a world where quotas are still in place: the concept of most-favored-nation (MFN) treatment (to be discussed in Chapter 4) is quite onerous to apply in a QR-setting, particularly where quotas may be set aside for particular trading partners. On the other hand, it is much easier to apply in a context where only tariffs exist. Thus, the GATT framers sought to eliminate or restrict the use of QRs and encourage the use of tariffs in their stead. As the Panel in *Turkey–Textiles* proclaimed (§ 9.63), "The prohibition against quantitative restrictions is a reflection that tariffs are GATT's border protection 'of choice.'"

Although the use of QRs was deemed illegal, in the later years of the GATT era, a number of countries sought to circumvent this requirement by pressuring their trading partners to accept voluntary export restraints (VERs). Through a VER, the exporting country voluntarily agrees to limit the number of exports to a given market. Why would a country agree to a VER? Most did so as a way to avoid other trade actions that they deemed would be even more punishing on their exporters. VER agreements were highly controversial, with their legality being a hotly-debated issue among lawyers. They also triggered much resentment from countries pressured to accept them. As part of the Uruguay Round negotiations, the GATT contracting parties clarified that VERs are also illegal, unless they conform to the Agreement on Safeguards (which we will discuss in Chapter 16).

Of course, it becomes difficult to require that all WTO Members accept trade in every good. For example, certain countries may wish to prohibit the availability of certain goods (e.g., alcohol, pornography) on religious or moral grounds. Others may wish to restrict the exports of certain goods deemed sensitive to national security (e.g., missiles, nuclear technology). For that reason, a number of exceptions have surfaced to the outright prohibition on QRs. Nevertheless, because the concept of non-discrimination is such a key principle of the post-war trade regime envisioned by the creators of the GATT, even QRs that may be lawfully maintained must be applied in a non-discriminatory manner.

3. COVERAGE OF THE LEGAL DISCIPLINE

3.1 GENERAL PROHIBITION ON QUANTITATIVE RESTRICTIONS

Art. XI GATT is entitled "General Elimination of Quantitative Restrictions." The meaning of the term "quantitative restriction"[1] is not exactly self-interpreting, and we will expound on its definition below. The requirement that QRs be eliminated is captured in the first provision of Art. XI which reads:

> No prohibition or restrictions other than duties, taxes or other charges, whether made effective through quotas, import or export licenses or other measures, shall be instituted or maintained by any contracting party on the importation of any product of the territory of any other contracting party or on the exportation or sale for export of any product destined for the territory of any contracting party.

Art. XI.1 GATT effectively prohibits measures other than "duties, taxes or other charges."[2] We will discuss the meaning and legal rules surrounding these terms in subsequent Chapters.

In some instances, what falls under the auspices of a QR is quite clear. For example, an outright ban is a QR. The same is true of a quota that sets an upper limit on the quantity of goods. The Panel in *India–Quantitative Restrictions* also made clear that a licensing scheme that is not automatically granted falls under the auspices of Art. XI.1 GATT (§ 5.130).[3] However, the concept of a QR is much broader than what is suggested by the illustrative examples included in Art. XI.1 GATT of quo-

---

[1] The term 'quantitative restriction' appears only in the heading of Art. XI GATT, while the terms 'restriction', and 'prohibition', appear in the body of the article. In light of the choice of terms, it seems reasonable to conclude (as case law has already done) that the three terms can be used interchangeably. The same is true for the term 'quota'. This is the manner in which they are being used in this volume.

[2] We discuss the treatment of import duties in Chapter 3, and of domestic taxes in Chapter 8.

[3] Non-automatic licensing schemes will be discussed in Chapter 7.

tas and licenses. In the next section, we will deal with a number of specific instruments that interface with QRs.

3.2 WHAT QUALIFIES AS A QR? THE TREATMENT OF CERTAIN SPECIFIC CASES

Case law has helped clarify what falls under the auspices of a QR and what does not. For example, with respect to import licenses, where the grant of such licenses is automatic, a GATT Panel held in *EEC–Minimum Import Prices* that such a scheme is not a QR (§ 4.1). Because every importer received a license, the scheme does not restrict the quantity of imports. Below, we discuss a number of other specific cases:

3.2.1 Export Taxes

The GATT contains a provision (Art. II) that deals with disciplining import duties (which we discuss in the next Chapter), but no provision that deals with export duties.[4] The absence of a corresponding provision disciplining export duties raises the question whether WTO Members are free to enact export duties as they see fit. Alternatively, could export duties be considered QRs? If set at a certain level, they might trigger an effect of limiting the quantity of exports. A Note prepared by the GATT Secretariat[5] during the Uruguay Round confirms the view that WTO Members are free to impose export taxes. WTO Members may negotiate restrictions on export taxes with other WTO Members as part of their Protocol of Accession,[6] but, in general, export taxes are not to be treated as QRs.

3.2.2 Minimum Export Prices

Minimum export prices have economic effects similar to export taxes; they both create a wedge between domestic and world prices. Consequently, like export taxes, a minimum export price, if set a certain level, could lead to a restricted quantity of exports. Yet, unlike export taxes, case law has established that a policy implementing a minimum export price may be inconsistent with Art. XI GATT. In *China–Raw Materials*, China established a minimum floor price for the exports of certain raw materials. Chinese producers that hoped to export a raw material below this price

---

[4] The absence of a corresponding provision is not on account of a lack of proposals. The reason for why provisions on export taxes have not carried the day is discussed in the Questions and Comments section of this Chapter.

[5] GATT Doc. MTN.GNG/NG2/W/40 of August 8, 1989.

[6] For example, China's Protocol Accession includes the following language: "China shall eliminate all taxes and charges applied to exports unless specifically provided for in Annex 6 of this Protocol or applied in conformity with the provisions of Article VIII of the GATT 1994." Annex 6 of the Protocol of Accession contains maximum export duties applicable on 84 products. China cannot levy an export tax on goods not included in the agreed list featured in Annex 6. See WTO Doc. WT/L/432, of November 23, 2001. Restrictions on export taxes are also found in Saudi Arabia's Protocol of Accession. See WTO Doc. WT/ACC/SAU/61 of November 1, 2005.

were prohibited from doing so. The Panel held that such a restriction violated Art. XI.1 GATT (§ 7.1081).

3.2.3 Minimum Import Prices

The case of minimum import prices falling under the legal discipline of Art. XI.1 GATT was dealt with in an earlier GATT-era case, *EEC–Minimum Import Prices*. In that case, importers of tomato concentrates into the European Community were required to provide additional security to guarantee that their product's price would equal or exceed a determined minimum import price. The GATT Panel found such a requirement to be a violation of Art. XI GATT (§ 4.9).[7]

3.2.4 Production Quotas

What about quotas that are applied on production rather than exports directly? Again, such quotas could directly impact the quantity of products to be exported. If a government restricts the amount of a product to be produced, then this also creates a ceiling as to the maximum amount that could be exported. For example, consider the case of OPEC (the Organization of Petroleum Exporting Countries), a cartel of countries that meets regularly to discuss oil production. Production quotas agreed upon by OPEC directly affect the quantity of oil available on world markets; they carry trade effects that affect a vast array of industries.

Do production quotas fall under the auspices of Art. XI GATT? Or are these purely domestic policies, and as such, governed by Art. III GATT (to be discussed further in Chapter 8)? Domestic measures, even if applicable at the border, are governed by Art. III GATT and evade the purview of Art. XI GATT.[8] The GATT Panel in *Canada–FIRA* suggested that with the exception of truly unique circumstances, such as state trading companies which often operate both as importers and distributors, a dividing line must be drawn between measures covered by Articles III and XI of the GATT.

3.3 THE CONCEPT OF *DE FACTO* QRS

The question has arisen in case law whether one should understand the term "QR" as referring only to measures that provide an explicit numerical target. Conversely, should the term extend to cover circumstances in which no explicit numerical target is set, but the policy instrument results in a *de facto* limitation on imports or exports?

---

[7] This is a form of variable levy that the EU practiced a lot before 1995: a variable component would be levied on all imports in order to equate their price to the EU price which was (almost always) higher than that of the world price for farm goods.

[8] The relationship between these two provisions is partly addressed in the Interpretative Note ad Art III.

In *Japan–Semiconductors*, a GATT Panel was asked to address a situation in 1980s in which the Japanese government, as a result of an agreement it had reached with the US (the US–Japan Semiconductor Pact), adopted a series of measures that induced, but did not require, Japanese companies producing semiconductors to raise their prices when exporting to the EU market. The ostensible goal of the Japanese government was to avoid a situation where the prices of Japanese exports were set too low, such that they might subject Japanese producers to an antidumping case in the EU market. (We will discuss the issue of "dumping" exports in Chapter 14.) The Ministry of International Trade and Industry (MITI)[9] instituted a supply-and-demand forecasting mechanism for Japanese semiconductor producers in order to influence the behaviour of private companies with respect to production and export. MITI also required Japanese producers to submit information on companies' product-specific costs and export prices, as a means to monitor the pricing policies of Japanese exporters (§ 113). Fines would be imposed for any failure to report information properly, but not for failure to follow suggested prices (§ 114). Japan, in a nutshell, using "administrative guidance", put in place a system that aimed at eliminating any dumping of semiconductors. However, the government did not impose any numerical target limiting the exports of semiconductors nor did it set an explicit minimum export price. However, MITI's measures allowed Japanese exporters to coordinate their actions to maintain a higher export price for semiconductors than would have otherwise been the case.

The EU asserted that the Japanese government's policies amounted to a violation of Art. XI GATT. It argued that Japanese producers would not have raised their export prices but for the incentive mechanism provided by the Japanese government. The EU suggested that the policies amounted to a *de facto* QR, since the government's actions, by facilitating a higher export price, triggered a lower quantity of exports. (Note that this is because demand falls with higher prices.) The Panel agreed (§§ 109ff.). In doing so, the Panel extended the coverage of Art. XI GATT to *de facto* QRs.

In *India–Autos*, the government measure at issue was a "trade balancing condition." Any automobile manufacturer in India wishing to import parts was required to sign a Memorandum of Understanding (MOU) that stipulated that the manufacturer's exports be equivalent in value to its imports over a certain period. In other words, the ability to import was conditioned on the manufacturer's balancing of its trade. The MOU did not specify a particular numerical target for imports, and the Panel was faced with the question as to whether it amounted to a QR. After first noting that "it is clear that a 'restriction' need not be a blanket prohibi-

---

[9] This is the predecessor to the Japanese ministry now known as METI (Ministry of Economy, Trade and Industry).

tion or a precise numerical limit" (§ 7.270), the Panel then added (§§ 7.277–7.278):

> With regard to the trade balancing condition, the Panel finds that . . . there would necessarily have been a practical threshold to the amount of exports that each manufacturer could expect to make, which in turn would determine the amount of imports that could be made. This amounts to an import restriction. The degree of effective restriction which would result from this condition may vary from signatory to signatory depending on its own projections, its output, or specific market conditions, but a manufacturer is in no free instance free to import, without commercial constraint, as many kits and components as it wishes without regard to its export opportunities and obligations.
>
> The Panel therefore finds that the trade balancing condition contained in Public Notice No. 60 and in the MOUs signed thereunder, by limiting the amount of imports through linking them to an export commitment, act as a restriction on importation, contrary to terms of Article XI:1.

The question before the Panel on *Argentina–Hides and Leather* was whether an Argentine law that allowed delegates of the downstream industry (leather products) to be present at the customs-clearance of hides was inconsistent with Art. XI GATT. Domestic downstream consumers preferred for the hides to remain in the country, as this would increase the domestic supply and keep prices low. Argentina contended that the presence of the downstream industry representatives was necessary in order to assist its customs officials with export clearance processes. The EU argued that the presence of downstream industry might inhibit exports, since domestic producers might be unwilling to export their products to Europe for fear that they would be blacklisted by the domestic downstream industry. This Panel held that Art. XI GATT should not be construed as an obligation to eliminate all potential for private parties to restrict trade (§ 11.19):

> . . . we do not think that it follows either from that panel's statement or from the text or context of Article XI:1 that Members are under an obligation to exclude any possibility that governmental measures may enable private parties, directly or indirectly, to restrict trade, where those measures themselves are not trade-restrictive.

The panel then noted that as a general matter, a complainant was not required to demonstrate actual trade effects in order to prove a violation of Art. XI.1 GATT (§ 11.20). However, in the particular context of a *de facto* case, the Panel requested that a complainant demonstrate, at the very least, a nexus between the challenged measure and the QR effect. The Panel justified this difference by noting that in circumstances where a complainant makes a *de facto* rather than a *de jure* claim, "greater weight attaches to the actual trade impact of a measure" (§ 11.20). It further noted that (11.21):

> Particularly in the context of an alleged *de facto* restriction and where, as here, there are possibly multiple restrictions, it is necessary for a complaining party to establish a causal link between the contested measure and the low level of exports. In our view, whatever else it may involve, a demonstration of causation must consist of a persuasive explanation of precisely how the measure at issue causes or contributes to the low level of exports. (italics in the original)

Importantly, in a footnote to § 11.22, the Panel noted:

> The Appellate Body in *European Communities–Measures Affecting the Importation of Certain Poultry Products* similarly required of the complaining party in that case a demonstration of a causal relationship between the imposition of an EC licensing procedure and the alleged trade distortion. See the Appellate Body Report on *European Communities–Measures Affecting the Importation of Certain Poultry Products* (hereafter "*European Communities–Poultry*"), adopted on 23 July 1999, WT/DS69/AB/R, at paras. 126–127. While this interpretation related to a claim under the Agreement on Import Licensing Procedures, it is not apparent why the logic should be any different in the case of a claim under Article XI:1 of the GATT 1994. (original emphasis)

After noting the above, the Panel rejected the EU claim, finding that the presence of representatives of the domestic industry was insufficient (or rather, the causal link too remote) for establishing a violation of Art. XI GATT (§ 7.35):

> We agree that it is unusual to have representatives from a downstream consuming industry involved in the Customs process of export clearance. As noted above, it seems to us that the levels of exports of raw hides from Argentina may be low. The European Communities has stated the matter to us in the form of a rhetorical question—what other purpose could these downstream industry representatives have in this government process of export clearance than restricting exports? However, it is up to the European Communities to provide evidence sufficient to convince us of that. In this instance, we do not find that the evidence is sufficient to prove that there is an export restriction made effective by the mere presence of tanners' representatives within the meaning of Article XI.

In subsequent cases, Panels have made clear that what is important is the *potential* for a measure to have a QR effect, rather than the actual effect of the measure. The Panel in *China–Raw Materials* noted the following (§ 7.35):

> The Panel consider the very *potential* to limit trade is sufficient to constitute a "restriction[] . . . on the exportation or sale for export of any product" within the meaning of Article XI:1 of the GATT 1994. The Panel considers this view is consistent with the panel on *Colombia–Ports of Entry* that any measure that creates uncertainty as to the ability to import/export and otherwise "compete" in the marketplace violates Article XI:1. (emphases in the original) (footnotes omitted)

How are we to reconcile the more recent Panel rulings with *Argentina–Hides and Leather*? The latter cases make clear that demonstration of an actual effect is unnecessary in order to prove a violation of Art. XI.1 GATT. But even the Panel in *Argentina–Hides and Leather* did not go so far as to impose an absolute effects-based test; it only asserted that great weight should be given to whether an actual causal effect emerges from the measure in question when the claim is one of a *de facto* QR. The relevant question is whether increased weight should continue to be given to the actual effects in the case of an alleged *de facto* QR, as suggested by the Panel in *Argentina–Hides and Leather*, in light of Panel holdings in subsequent disputes.

We suggest that the answer to this question is unclear; it depends on whether one chooses to interpret the holdings of the subsequent cases broadly or narrowly. One important factual distinction between *Argentina–Hides and Leather* and the subsequent cases is that the latter involve *de jure*, and not *de facto*, QRs. In *China–Raw Materials*, Chinese authorities applied an explicit export quota as well as minimum export prices. In *Colombia–Port of Entry*, Colombian authorities restricted the importation of textile, apparel and footwear produced in a Panamanian free trade zone to two ports. In both instances, the Panel held that the actual effect of the restrictions on trade was immaterial; what was important was that the measures had the potential to restrict trade. Yet, the measures involved explicit numerical targets, unlike *Argentina–Hides and Leather*. Therefore, a narrow reading would suggest that for *de facto* QR cases, the effects-based emphasis of *Argentina–Hides and Leather* still holds, as the case can be differentiated from the subsequent ones on a factual basis. A broader reading of the holding of *Colombia–Port of Entry* and *China–Raw Materials* would suggest that the jurisprudence extends to all Art. XI.1 cases. Until another *de facto* QR dispute surfaces that allows a Panel / the AB to clarify the law, the question remains open as to whether greater evidentiary weight should be given to actual trade effects, in instances where a WTO Member complains of a *de facto* (as opposed to a *de jure*) QR.

3.4 THE NECESSARY GOVERNMENT INVOLVEMENT

Art XI. GATT becomes, of course, irrelevant if the QR is not attributed to a WTO Member. The GATT Panel on *Japan–Semiconductors* stands for the proposition that providing incentives to private parties to act in a particular manner suffices for a measure to be attributed to government (§§ 109ff.). Importantly, in § 117 the Panel held that:

> The Panel considered that the complex of measures exhibited the rationale as well as the essential elements of a formal system of export control. The only distinction in this case was the absence of formal legally binding obligations in respect of exportation or sale for export of semiconductors. However, the Panel concluded that this amounted to a difference in form rather than substance because the measures were operated in a manner equivalent to mandatory requirements. The Panel concluded that the complex of measures constituted a coherent system restricting the sale for export of monitored semiconductors at prices below company-specific costs to markets other that the United States, inconsistent with Article XI:1.

Subsequent GATT and WTO case-law has consistently referred to this ruling, when deciding whether a particular measure should be attributed to government. For example, in *Japan–Film*, a measure endorsed by government was attributed to it (§§ 10.45); in *China–Raw Materials*, the Panel satisfied itself that a measure was attributable to the Chinese government because the government had delegated authority to CCCMC (Chinese Chamber of Commerce of Metals Minerals & Chemicals Importers & Exporters) (§ 7.1004–1005). Finally, in *US–Corrosion Resistant Steel Sunset Reviews*, the AB held that omissions as well, to the extent attributable to a government, can be challenged before a WTO Panel (§ 81).

4. EXCEPTIONS

The prohibition on QRs is not absolute. Instead, several exceptions exist within WTO law on this rule. Several are laid forth in Art. XI.2 GATT which notes that Art. XI.1 GATT does not apply to:

- Export prohibitions or restrictions temporarily applied to prevent or relieve critical shortages of foodstuffs or other products essential to the exporting contracting party;
- Import and export prohibitions or restrictions necessary to the application of standards or regulations for the classification, grading or marketing of commodities in international trade;

- Import restrictions on any agricultural or fisheries product, necessary to the enforcement of government measures to

    (a) restrict the quantity of the "like" domestic product to be produced or marketed

    (b) remove a temporary surplus of the "like" domestic product or a domestic product that is directly substitutable, provided certain conditions are met

    (c) restrict the production of any animal product whose production is dependent on the imported commodity

In what follows, we discuss each of the Art. XI.2 GATT exceptions in greater depth. We will then turn to a series of other exceptions that are enshrined in other parts of the GATT, including:

- Balance of payments exception of Arts. XII and XVIII GATT
- Exchange restrictions, authorized under Art. XV GATT
- Infant industry exception of Art. XVIII GATT
- General exceptions of Art. XX and XXI GATT
- Safeguards exception of Art. XIX GATT

4.1 CRITICAL SHORTAGES OF FOODSTUFFS AND ANY OTHER ESSENTIAL PRODUCT

In case a WTO Member experiences critical shortage of a foodstuff or any other essential product, it can temporarily impose export restrictions. The key terms of this provision were discussed in the Panel report in *China–Raw Materials*. The complainants challenged a number of export restrictions on products that China considered essential. In the view of the Panel, a product is "essential" if it is important, or necessary, or indispensable to a particular WTO Member (§ 7.282). The Panel added that substitutability across products could cast doubt on the essential character of one of them if those other substitutable products were available (§ 7.344). The Panel did not go so far and provide a specific numerical threshold requirement (e.g., the percentage of the GDP that is affected by the product) in order for a WTO Member to invoke this requirement. It did, however, hold (§ 7.213) that the burden falls on the WTO Member invoking the affirmative defense to provide the facts to support this defense. The Panel also clarified that a good that serves as inputs to another good may nevertheless be essential; consequently, it is immaterial whether or not the "essential" good is a final good. The Panel also emphasized that the temporal nature of this exception; it is to be used to address temporary shortages only (§ 7.297), as opposed to efforts to conserve limited exhaustible natural resources (§ 7.349).

4.2 STANDARDS FOR THE CLASSIFICATION, GRADING OR MARKETING OF COMMODITIES

Imposing a QR in order to comply with standards and regulations for the classification, grading or marketing of products is consistent with Art. XI.2(b) GATT. This concept was elaborated upon in the GATT-era case of *Canada–Herring and Salmon*. In that case, Canada applied certain quality standards on exports of pink salmon and herring and banned exports of those fish which did not meet this standard. Canada attempted to justify its export restrictions on the grounds of Art. XI.2(b). The Panel emphasized that the provision is meant to apply to government measures taken to further the marketing of a commodity by spreading supplies of the restricted exports over a longer period than would otherwise be the case, in the absence of a QR (§ 4.3). It is not meant to deal with or incorporate all regulations facilitating trade. Thus, the exception should be understood within the above-mentioned narrow reading. In that particular case, the Panel rejected Canada's attempt to invoke the exception, since even fish that met the quality requirements were prohibited (§ 4.2).

4.3 NECESSARY FOR THE ENFORCEMENT OF GOVERNMENTAL MEASURES

As noted earlier, Art. XI.2 includes a third exception, specifically for agricultural or fisheries product. This is an exception made for import restrictions that are made in conjunction with other governmental measures on agricultural or fisheries products, whereby restrictions on imports are necessary to ensure the success of the other measure.

Measures may be taken to restrict imports on the "like" product—a concept to be elaborated upon further in Chapters 3 and 4—in two circumstances spelled out in Art. XI.2:

(1) Where the government is seeking to restrict the production or marketing of an agricultural or fisheries product (Art. XI.2(a))

(2) Where the government is seeking to relieve a temporary surplus of an agricultural or fisheries product by making the surplus available free of charge or at below-market prices to certain groups of domestic consumers

One can see how the policy objectives of the government would be undermined if the domestic restrictions of the supply would be replaced by imports. Thus, under such circumstances, the import of the "like" product may also be restricted. The GATT Panel on *EEC–Apples (US)* echoing prior case law held that two goods are to be deemed "like products" in the context of this provision if they perform similar function for the consumer (§ 5.7); for example, an imported widget and a domestic widget that perform the same function for a consumer deemed "like" products. In instances where no domestic production of the "like" product occurs, a WTO Member may restrict the import of a good that acts as a direct substitute. To prevent this exception from becoming a quasi-protectionist instruments, in instances where an import restriction is enacted in conjunction with a restriction on domestic production or marketing, the effect of the import restriction must be such that the ratio of imports to domestic production is that which might be reasonably expected to be the case in the absence of such restrictions.

A third instance in which an import restriction may be legitimately enacted is when the government is seeking to limit the production of an animal. In such instances, the WTO Member may enact restrictions on not just the animal itself (as discussed above) but also on any agricultural or fisheries product that the animal depends upon for its production, subject to two qualifications: First, the domestic production of the restricted import must be "relatively negligible" (Art. XI.1(c)); the exact meaning of this term is not defined. Second, the WTO Member must give public notice of the total quantity or value of the product to be imported during the specified future period and of any changes in quantity or value.

The GATT Panel report on *Japan–Agricultural Products I* held that it is the trading nation imposing the restriction that carries the associated burden of proof underscoring thus the exceptional character of this provision (§ 5.1.3.7). Note that Art. XI.2(c) GATT refers to "restrictions" only, whereas the previous two provisions (Arts. XI.2(a) and (b)) refer to "prohibitions and restrictions". The linguistic difference suggests that outright bans on imports on exports are not covered by this provision; the GATT Panel on US–Canadian Tuna has confirmed this point (§ 4.6).[10]

The GATT Panel report in *Canada–Ice Cream and Yoghurt* laid out the requisite elements of the legal test under this provision (§ 62):

(a) The measure must be an import restriction;

(b) On agricultural or fisheries products;

(c) It must apply to 'like' products in any form;

(d) A governmental measure restricting the quantity of the domestic products to be marketed or produced must be in place;

(e) Public notice must be given as to the quantity that will be allowed during a future specified period;

(f) The restrictions in place should not defy the legitimate expectations regarding the proportion of domestic goods relative to imports.

The GATT Panel report in *Japan–Agricultural Products I* noted that, contrary to other provisions, no obligation to compensate for damage suffered is provided for in Art. XI.2(c) GATT; this is why, in the Panel's view, this provision requires similar restrictions on domestic goods (§ 12.15).

---

[10] See also, the GATT Panel reports on *Japan–Agricultural Products I* (§§ 5.3.1.2ff.), and *EEC–Dessert Apples* (§ 12.5).

During the negotiation of the GATT, the view was held that measures applying to seasonal goods at a time when like domestic goods were not available could not qualify as 'necessary' under this provision.[11] The GATT Working Party on Quantitative Restrictions in its report adopted a less stringent view, to the effect that similar measures would be GATT-consistent only if they were necessary to achieve the objectives of government measures relating to the control of domestic products.[12] Also, case law has established that the condition of a government program is fulfilled even if the measure at hand is not a compulsory government measure, provided that it gives sufficient incentives to traders to adopt a particular behaviour.[13]

Following the advent of the WTO, there is relative clarity as to the coverage of what products qualify as an agricultural or fisheries product[14]: The WTO Agreement on Agriculture explicitly deals with the products coming under its purview. Fisheries are not covered by the WTO Agreement on Agriculture, but there is convention that these products come under Chapters 3 and 16 of HS 2002.[15]

4.4 BALANCE OF PAYMENTS (ARTS. XII AND XVIII GATT)

Outside of the three specific exceptions enumerated within Art. XI.2 GATT, a number of other provisions within the GATT also provide an exception to the obligation of Art. XI.1 GATT to eliminate QRs. For example, WTO Members can legitimately deviate from their obligations under Art. XI GATT, if they encounter balance of payments (BoP) problems and, to this effect, can demonstrate that they have complied with the requirements of Art. XII GATT. Note that Art. XII was designed specifically as an exception for Art. XI GATT.[16]

Developing countries facing similar concerns may invoke Art. XVIII GATT, a provision that contains requirements less stringent than those of Art. XII GATT:

(a) Art. XVIII(b) can be used by WTO Members with inadequate monetary reserves, whereas Art. XII can be used by WTO Members with very low monetary reserves. Arguably, the former term leaves

---

[11] See § (e) of the London Conference report, cited in Irwin *et al.* (2008).

[12] GATT Doc. L/332/Rev. 1, adopted on March 5, 1955, BISD 3S/170 at §§ 67ff. On its legal value, see the discussion on GATT decisions in Chapter 1.

[13] *Japan–Agricultural Products I* (§ 5.4.1.4); see also the discussion *supra* on *Japan–Semiconductors*.

[14] Before 1995, the coverage of this provision was limited to Chapters 1–24 of the Customs Cooperation Council Nomenclature. See *Japan–Agricultural Products I* (§ 5.1.3.2)

[15] HS refers to Harmonized System.

[16] The opening sentence of this provision makes it clear beyond doubt that it was meant to function as exception to Art. XI GATT

more discretion to the state, and, consequently, would entail a more deferential standard of review, should litigation occur;

(b) Whereas Art. XII GATT requires WTO Members to progressively relax the restrictions imposed, Art. XVIII(b) GATT provides that no Member shall be required to modify restrictions on the ground that a change in its development policy would render such restrictions unnecessary;[17]

(c) While both Art. XII and XVIII(b) GATT require that the WTO Member invoking the BoP exception engage in consultations, the procedure is simplified in Art. XVIII(b) GATT.

At the time that the GATT was originally negotiated, a system of fixed (but adjustable) exchange rates (known as fixed parities) prevailed. As a result, countries with a payments deficit could not devalue its currency easily but would have to go through a multilateral process. The BoP exceptions were deemed necessary in light of the inflexibilities associated with the system of fixed parities. In the event that a party wishes to invoke a BoP restriction, a Balance of Payments Committee exists under the GATT/WTO to which a request must be made; the Committee will decide on the request.

Developed countries almost never made use of Art. XII GATT.[18] Developing countries, on the other hand, have made extensive use of Art. XVIII(b) GATT:

Table 2.1 Invocations of Art. XVIII(b) GATT

WTO Member	Period
Argentina	(1972–1978), (1986–1991)
Bangladesh	(1974–2008)[19]
Brazil	(1962–1971), (1976–1991)
Chile	(1961–1980)
Colombia	(1981–1992)
Egypt	(1963–1995)
Ghana	(1959–1989)
India	(1960–1997)

[17] Van den Bossche pp. 667–674. See also the AB report on *India–Quantitative Restrictions* at §§ 125ff.

[18] The GATT Analytical Index (6th edition, 1994) contains information about the invocations of Art. XII GATT at p. 361. Israel is the only developed country that invoked this provision in the past, but has ceased to do so.

[19] Bangladesh notified its intention to phase out its remaining restrictions by January 1, 2005 (WTO Doc. WT/BOP/N/54 of December 15, 2000, and WT/BOP/N/62 of 18 February 2004). Subsequent to this notification, Bangladesh imposed import restrictions under Art. XVIII(c) of the GATT, invoking *infant industry* protection, see WTO Doc. G/C/7 of January 16, 2002.

WTO Member	Period
Indonesia	(1960–1997)
Korea	(1969–1989)
Nigeria	(1985–1998)
Pakistan	(1960–2002)
Philippines	(1980–1995)
Peru	(1968–1991)
Sri Lanka	(1960–1998)
Tunisia	(1967–1997)

In the intervening years, most countries have now shifted to a system of flexible exchange rates. With this shift, manipulation of the exchange rate is now seen to be a more appropriate instrument to deal with BoP disequilibria. As a result, the GATT provisions on BoP have become largely redundant. All things being equal, WTO Members would rather devaluate and profit from the increase in export income than impose a QR and keep their exchange rate intact. Nevertheless, such an option continues to exist, through the BoP exception to QRs, should a WTO Member choose to resort to it.

In the WTO era, the most significant case involving the BoP exception for QRs is the *India–Quantitative Restrictions* dispute. Following the Uruguay Round, India attempted to leave in place QRs on over over 2,700 agricultural and industrial product tariff lines; it justified its QRs by invoking Art. XVIII(b) GATT. In 1991, India had suffered a BoP crisis which required that it turn to the IMF for assistance. By 1997–98, however, India's BoP situation had improved, and the Panel turned to the IMF for guidance on India's BoP situation. Based in part on this guidance, the Panel found India's measures to be inconsistent with Art. XI.1 GATT; it went on to also find that they could not be justified through recourse to Art. XVIII.11 GATT either.[20] Most importantly, the Panel found (and the AB upheld) that, in contrast to the argument advanced by India, BoP restrictions could be the subject of judicial review. On appeal, the AB noted the relevance of institutional balance within the framework of the WTO Agreement, and rejected India's argument that only the WTO BoP

---

[20] The US carried the burden of proof with respect to Art. XI GATT, and India then carried the burden of proof with respect to Art. XVIII GATT defense, an exception to the former provision. The Panel also held (and the AB upheld in § 138 of its report) that the burden of proof shifted back to the US with respect to the Interpretative Note ad Art XVIII.11 of the GATT. This note concerns the conditions under which a WTO Member should progressively relax import restrictions that have been in place. It is highly unlikely that a WTO member affected by such restrictions adequately knows the facts mandating similar behaviour. The Panel probably relied on the solemnity accompanying the IMF involvement on this score. Still, it would have been on safer grounds had it imposed the burden of proof on India.

Committee could review the consistency of its measures with the GATT, noting that (§ 105):

> such a requirement would be inconsistent with Article XXIII of the GATT 1994, as elaborated and applied by the DSU, and footnote 1 to the *BOP Understanding* which, as discussed above, clearly provides for the availability of the WTO dispute settlement procedures with respect to any matters relating to balance-of-payments restrictions.

The AB upheld this finding. The AB then went on to find against India, because India had not demonstrated that it had met its burden of proof in explaining why the removal of the QRs would lead to a change in its development policy and to a deterioration of India's overall BoP situation (§ 150).

4.5 EXCHANGE RESTRICTIONS

The relationship between the trade and the financial system was in the mind of negotiators already during the ITO negotiations,[21] and was eloquently presented in the Declaration of Ministers at the opening of the Tokyo round:[22]

> The policy of liberalizing world trade cannot be carried out successfully in the absence of parallel efforts to set up a monetary system which shields the world economy from the shocks and imbalances which have previously occurred. The Ministers will not lose sight of the fact that the efforts which are to be made in the trade field imply continuing efforts to maintain orderly conditions and to establish a durable and equitable monetary system.
>
> The Ministers recognize equally that the new phase in the liberalization of trade which it is their intention to undertake should facilitate the orderly functioning of the monetary system.

There are two key provisions in Art. XV GATT that deals with the issue of exchange restrictions, XV.4, and XV.9:

> Contracting parties shall not, by exchange action, frustrate* the intent of the provisions of this Agreement, nor, by trade action, the intent of the provisions of the Articles of Agreement of the International Monetary Fund.
>
> . . .
>
> Nothing in this Agreement shall preclude:

---

[21] Gardner (1956).
[22] GATT Doc. BISD 20S/19ff. at § 7.

(*a*) the use by a contracting party of exchange controls or exchange restrictions in accordance with the Articles of Agreement of the International Monetary Fund or with that contracting party's special exchange agreement with the CONTRACTING PARTIES, or

(*b*) the use by a contracting party of restrictions or controls in imports or exports, the sole effect of which, additional to the effects permitted under Articles XI, XII, XIII and XIV, is to make effective such exchange controls or exchange restrictions

The term "frustrate" appearing in Art. XV.4 GATT is further elaborated upon in an interpretative note as follows:

> The word "frustrate" is intended to indicate, for example, that infringements of the letter of any Article of this Agreement by exchange action shall not be regarded as a violation of that Article if, in practice, there is no appreciable departure from the intent of the Article. Thus, a contracting party which, as part of its exchange control operated in accordance with the Articles of Agreement of the International Monetary Fund, requires payment to be received for its exports in its own currency or in the currency of one or more members of the International Monetary Fund will not thereby be deemed to contravene Article XI or Article XIII. Another example would be that of a contracting party which specifies on an import licence the country from which the goods may be imported, for the purpose not of introducing any additional element of discrimination in its import licensing system but of enforcing permissible exchange controls

Consequently, WTO Members are entitled, by virtue of Art. XV.9 GATT, under certain conditions, to impose exchange restrictions in accordance with the IMF provisions so long as the restrictions do not frustrate the intent of the GATT provisions. For example, the intent of the GATT provisions would be frustrated by currency manipulations that confer an advantage to a Member's exports.[23]

There is scarce practice in this context, indicative of the fact that WTO Panels have shown considerable deference to the IMF when dealing

---

[23] BoP- and exchange restrictions could be related: it could be the case, for example, that a BoP restriction is complemented by an exchange restriction, where, for example, there is increased speculation about the exchange rate of the country imposing the restriction. It could also be that a WTO Member imposes only an *exchange restriction*, and thus could be opening the door to *barter trade*; if it does not want to practice *barter trade*, it will have to contemplate imposing a BoP restriction as well. In general, whether a measure is an *exchange restriction* has to do with the question of whether it involves a direct governmental limitation on the availability or use of foreign currencies. § 7.132 of the Panel report in *Dominican Republic–Import and Sale of Cigarettes* said as much. Exchange restrictions do not have to be recorded in the schedules of concession because they are a contingency that could have been unanticipated when concessions were scheduled.

with exchange restrictions. The Panel, in its report in *Dominican Republic–Import and Sale of Cigarettes,* dealt with an exchange restriction imposed by the Dominican Republic.[24] Essentially, the Dominican Republic had replaced an original exchange restriction that covered all transactions with one that covered only imports, thereby discriminating against imports. In the Panel's view, this change was evidence that the Dominican Republic was not genuinely addressing the issue that, in name, it was purporting to address. Despite the measure's apparent conflict with the intent of the GATT, the Panel decided to consult with the IMF to further cements its conclusion. This consultation reflects the growing strength of cooperation between the WTO and the IMF. For example, an agreement was signed[25] that provides for the establishment of a steady channel of information between the two institutions, and the WTO has invited the IMF to participate as an observer in meetings relating to its areas of competence, and vice-versa. In the Panel's view, if the IMF authorities held that the measures imposed by the Dominican Republic were in accordance with the IMF Articles of Agreement, these measures would *ipso facto* be deemed to be GATT consistent as well (§ 7.139). This result is the only one that, in the Panel's view, is consistent with a textual reading of Art. XV.2 GATT. The IMF responsed that the practice, because it targeted only imports, did not qualify as an exchange restriction in accordance with Art. XV GATT. Against this background, the Panel concluded that the Dominican Republic could not justify its measures through recourse to Art. XV.9 GATT (§§ 7.143–7.145). This finding was not appealed.[26]

4.6 INFANT INDUSTRY PROTECTION

Art. XVIII(c) GATT allows developing countries that are WTO Members to deviate from their obligations in order to protect their infant industry. The ideological basis for this exception is the notion that nascent industries often lack economies of scale that their established competitors have and therefore require protection in order to achieve an economy of scale. Infant industry protection was quite popular in the 1960s and 1970s, but has lost its luster. In many instances, attempts to nurture infant industries were hijacked by rent-seeking interest groups instead, and the infant industries never "grew up" into established competitors. In recent years, many developing countries have turned to other forms of industrial policy instead (e.g., subsidization of export-led industries). However, an exception continues to exist for QRs established to protect an infant industry.

In order to invoke this exception, a WTO Member must show that the measure favouring a particular industry is meant to raise the general

---

[24] The facts of the case are reflected in §§ 7.135–7.137 of the report.

[25] WTO Doc WT/L/195 of November 18, 1996.

[26] In the same report, the Panel held that the party invoking Art. XV GATT carries the burden of proof associated with this provision (§ 7.131).

standard of living (a judgment that can hardly been put into question by its trading partners). It also has to respect certain notification requirements, as well as an obligation to enter into consultations in case the measure envisaged concerns a commodity which has to respect a tariff binding.

The Panel in *India–Quantitative Restrictions* made it clear that an invocation of Art. XVIII(c) GATT is justiciable. At the time of writing, the only such restriction in place is by Bangladesh.[27]

4.7 OTHER EXCEPTIONS

In addition, as we will discuss in Chapters 14–16, the WTO allows its Members to implement policies to provide contingent protection to domestic industries. Such policies are also known as trade remedies. One form of such a contingent protection instrument is a safeguard. We will discuss safeguards in greater detail in Chapter 16, as it is governed by Art. XIX GATT and a separate Agreement on Safeguards. In a nutshell, safeguards can be imposed by an importing country where, as a result of an unforeseen development, an increase in imports causes injury to a domestic industry. Under such a scenario, one of the permissible forms of a safeguard that a WTO Member may impose is a quota. It therefore follows that where the requirements for a lawful imposition of a safeguard are met, this functions as a permissible exception to the Art. XI prohibition on QRs.

However, case law has made clear that QRs cannot be imposed by an exporting country in order to avoid an unfair trade practice that would result in its goods being subject to a contingent protection policy (i.e., trade remedy) by its trading partners. Two such practices are "dumping"[28] and the provision of subsidies, to be discussed in Chapters 14 and 15 respectively. Neither practice is outright condemned under WTO law, but actions can be taken by an importing country against trading partners that engage in such practices under certain circumstances to be elaborated upon *infra*. Recall that in *Japan–Semiconductors*, the Japanese government undertook actions that amounted to a *de facto* QR by enabling a scheme to guard against dumping and providing incentives for Japanese companies to participate. Japan argued before the Panel that, even if its actions were considered to be inconsistent with Art. XI GATT, it was still justified in acting this way since it was aiming to dissuade Japanese economic operators from dumping, a practice condemned by Art. VI GATT. The Panel was thus led to discuss the relationship between Art. VI, and

---

[27] WTO Doc G/C/7 of January 16, 2002. The United States first (WTO Doc G/C/8 of February 18, 2002) and the EU subsequently (WTO Doc G/C/9 of February 20, 2002) requested consultations with the government of Bangladesh. No subsequent notification took place.

[28] Dumping is a price differentiation scheme, whereby the export price is lower than the price practiced by economic operators in their home market. Dumping is not prohibited but is condemned. We discuss it in detail in Chapter 14.

Art. XI GATT. It held that Art. VI GATT did not address actions by exporting countries; it addressed only actions by importing countries, since it allowed them to impose AD duties in order to counteract dumping. It then went on to conclude that (§ 120):

> Article VI did not provide a justification for measures restricting the exportation or sale for export of a product inconsistently with Article XI:1.

Consequently, one cannot justify an export QR in the name of an effort to avoid dumping practices.

In addition to safeguards, there are a number of general exceptions embedded within Art. XX GATT. The legal requirements that need to be met in order to invoke such exceptions will be discussed in greater detail in Chapter 12. As a preview, please note some of the general exceptions most relevant for QRs are those that exist to:

- Protect public morals
- Protect human, animal or plant life or health
- Relating to the importation or exportation of gold or silver
- Protect national treasures of artistic, historical, or archaeological value
- Conserve exhaustible natural resources if such measures are made effective in conjunction with restrictions on domestic consumption
- Ensure essential quantities of domestic materials for a domestic processing industry when the domestic price of a material is held below the world price as part of a government stabilization plan

For example, as a result of these general exceptions, a WTO Member may lawfully impose a QR prohibiting the import of pornography or alcohol, or the export of rare national treasures. This is subject to the proviso that implementation of the QR complies with the requirements of Art. XX GATT. In that sense, the forthcoming discussion *infra* in Chapter 12 serves as a continuation, in part, of this discussion, and is of vital importance to understanding when a WTO Member can lawfully implement a QR.

Finally, Art. XXI GATT provides a general exception to GATT obligations for national security. For example, the Art. XXI GATT exception may be used to justify an export ban on certain technologies deemed essential for national security interests. We will discuss this exception in greater detail in Chapter 13.

5. ADMINISTRATION OF LEGALLY PERMISSIBLE QRS

Assuming one of the legal exceptions for the imposition of QRs has been met, the administration of the QR is subject to further discipline through Art. XIII GATT. That provision is entitled "Non–Discriminatory Administration of Quantitative Restrictions." The title of Art. XIII GATT leaves us with the impression that what is required is for lawfully permissible QRs to be administered on non-discriminatory basis. Art. XIII.2 GATT, however, which constitutes the operational arm of this provision, requires something slightly different:

> ... contracting parties shall aim at a distribution of trade ... approaching as closely as possible the shares that the various contracting parties might be expected to obtain in the absence of such restrictions.

Pursuant to Art XIII.2(d) GATT, a WTO Member lawfully imposing a QR is required to allocate quotas to various suppliers in a manner that respects their pre-QR market shares. A reference period (usually the previous 3–5 years) will be used as benchmark for the calculation of market shares. Hence, it is not non-discriminatory administration of quotas that is privileged through Art. XIII GATT; it is respect of historic market shares, a rather discriminatory policy (since new aggressive suppliers will not be put at equal footing with old suppliers).

Art. XIII GATT does not mention the period of time that a QR can remain in place. Ostensibly, the length of time a QR can be imposed depends on the rationale behind the QR: For instance, if a member experiences BoP problems for 2 years, a QR should logically be in place for the same period of time; conversely, as we shall see in Chapter 16, a safeguard action that takes the form of QRs can remain lawfully in place for maximum eight years, by virtue of Art. 7.3 SG.[29]

Finally, note that Art. XIV GATT allows WTO Members that have invoked a BoP exception to Art. XI GATT to deviate from their obligations under Art. XIII GATT. This exception exists to allow WTO Members to comply with their obligations with certain provisions of the IMF Agreement (namely Art. VIII or XIV, which are explicitly mentioned in Art. XIV.1 GATT). Art. XIV GATT permits a WTO Member to deviate from its Art. XIII GATT obligations if the following two conditions are met:[30]

(a) the quota must have been imposed to address problems relating to BoP;

(b) the discriminatory quota must affect a small part of its trade.

---

[29] This length may be increased to ten years in the case of developing countries, pursuant to Art. 9.2 SG.

[30] Report of the Working Party on Quantitative Restrictions, GATT Doc. BISD 3S/170ff. at § 26.

QUESTIONS AND COMMENTS

Why Treat Tariffs and QRs Differently? Krueger (1964) researches negative external effects associated with the administration of QRs: her work shows that there is need to monitor whether a QR has been filled; whether it has been filled in non-discriminatory manner; eventually, if (import- or export) licences have been issued, whether they have been issued in non-discriminatory manner, etc.[31] The administration of a tariff-based import system does not know of similar issues, and this is probably what explains their distinct treatment in the GATT. Negative external effects associated with QRs are thus, much more important than in a tariff-setting. Bhagwati (1965) on the other hand, shows that, in a perfect competition-context, tariffs have their QR-equivalent. Bhagwati shows that this is not necessarily the case in an imperfect competition-context: a monopolist in the market where a QR has been imposed will capture all residual demand (that is, demand after the QR has been exhausted); if a tariff is in place though, some competitive pressure will always be exercised on the monopolist who might not be in position to profit as much as it would had a QR (in lieu of a tariff) been in place. This point becomes even more persuasive if one factors in the considerable time span between rounds of trade liberalization: in the in between rounds-period, exporters facing tariffs (rather than QRs) will continue to exercise some pressure on the monopolist. For good reasons thus, the GATT framers decided to treat the two trade instruments in asymmetric manner.

Government Involvement / Monopoly Rents: Smith and Venables (1991) explain under what conditions private operators will raise their prices when facing trade barriers. In your view, does any of the scenarios discussed in this paper fit the facts of *Japan–Semiconductors*?

Government Involvement / Export Cartels: Following the *de facto* acceptance of the effects doctrine, an export cartel will be prosecuted in the market that it cartelizes (and not its home market). Antitrust authorities have anyway little, if any, interest to regulate the activities of their national export cartels, since the domestic market will not be affected by similar activities (*prima facie* at least, it will be affected positively since high export prices could be used to subsidize domestic sales and lead to more intense competition in the home market). In this vein, for example, the US Webb Pomerene Act of 1918 exempts (partially) export cartels from antitrust prosecution. In light of our discussion above, the question arises whether the US is violating Art. XI GATT through this law: the likelier scenario would be that an export cartel restricts output or increases prices. Recall, that following *Japan–Semiconductors*, providing incentives is enough for behaviour to be attributed to a government. Is the US government providing incentives to its economic operators to cartelize the world market by partially exempting them from antitrust prosecution?[32] A negative response is appropriate for the following

---

[31] Trading nations might have a strong incentive to do that: scarcity of the imported (or exported) goods will push (other things equal) its prices up, and through auctioning of import (or export) licences it will be effectively dividing rents with the private operator.

[32] Fox (1997).

reasons: first, the ultimate decision lies with the economic operators themselves, since the US government is not imposing cartelization; second, contrary to what is the case in *Japan–Semiconductors*, the US government is not incentivizing its economic operators so that they adopt a particular behaviour, it simply promises that it will not act against them if they do; and third, economic operators know that they might, anyway, have to face a foreign antitrust authority, if they decide to cartelize foreign markets. In light of the above, and especially because of the worldwide acceptance of the effects doctrine (and the increasing sophistication of antitrust authorities around the world which can now rely on legal assistance treaties etc.), it seems that lack of legal pursuit in the US market is an ancillary consideration, if at all.[33]

Devaluations: As import restrictions (in conjunction with export subsidies) are equivalent to a nominal devaluation, allowing (temporary) import barriers to deal with a balance of payments problem can make *some* sense, depending, of course, on the satisfaction of the *Marshall–Lerner* condition. According to the *Marshall–Lerner* condition, for a *currency devaluation* to have a positive impact in *trade balance*, the sum of *price elasticity* of exports and imports (in absolute value) must be greater than 1. The principle is named for economists *Alfred Marshall* and *Abba Lerner*. As a devaluation of the exchange rate means a reduction on the price of exports, demand for these will increase. At the same time, price of imports will rise and their demand diminishes. The net effect on the trade balance will depend on price elasticities. If goods exported are elastic to price, their quantity demanded will increase proportionately more than the decrease in price, and total export revenue will increase. Similarly, if goods imported are elastic to price, total import expenditure will decrease. Both will improve the trade balance. Empirically, it has been found that goods tend to be inelastic in the short term, as it takes time to change consumption patterns. Thus, the *Marshall–Lerner condition* is not met, and devaluation is likely to worsen the trade balance initially. In the long term, consumers will adjust to the new prices, and the trade balance will improve. This effect is called *J-curve effect*.

Exchange Rate Manipulation: The issue of exchange rates gained prominence recently with voices heard essentially in the US that China was engaging in currency manipulation keeping its domestic currency (*renminbi*, RMB) artificially low and thus boosting its exports. Many voices were heard and more forcefully that of Mattoo and Subramanian (2009) arguing for a role for the WTO to address similar practices. A number of possible legal bases have been offered as potentially relevant to attack the Chinese practices, although none of them seems appropriate: Art. XV GATT would lead Panels to defer to the IMF, an issue we discuss *infra*; the SCM-context is highly inappropriate since there is financial contribution by the government involved here, and since even if one extends the concept of 'financial contribution' to cover similar instances the specificity-requirement will not be met; finally, a WTO Member raising a non-violation complaint will have a mountain to climb when arguing that it legitimately expected China to act against its own

---

[33] Caution is warranted in light of total absence of case law dealing head on with this issue.

interests. Staiger and Sykes (2010) visit all literature to this effect and conclude that there is difficulty in identifying trade effects stemming from currency practices and, because of this factor, the role of WTO dispute settlement is limited. They note that, with respect to arguments raised under Art. XV GATT, there is not much a Panel could do in light of the high burden of proof ('frustrate' the intent) associated with this provision. This point is further supported by practice and the deference that Panels show to the IMF.[34] One could only add two points: first, it would be quite awkward to entrust Panels composed with trade delegates with the authority to decide on monetary issues: deference to IMF is highly warranted in this context; second, that the IMF itself, that is the body with the expertise on those issues, has found it difficult to conclude whether currency manipulation has occurred, although it has been treated similar questions on hundreds of occasions.

Tariff Quotas: WTO Members often have recourse to tariff quotas. A tariff quota (TRQ) is usually an import measure whereby a lower tariff will be applied for a certain volume of imports, and a higher tariff will be applied to any quota above and beyond the set quota: for example, a 5% *ad valorem* duty for the first 10,000 cars, and a 50% *ad valorem* duty for any additional entry. There should be no doubts as to the overall consistency of TRQs with the GATT, even though on their face, they seem to function as a QR[35]: Art. XIII.5 GATT (Restrictions to Safeguard the Balance of Payments), for example, calls for application of this provision to tariff quotas. By the same token, it becomes obvious when reading § 6 of the Understanding on the Interpretation of Art. XXVIII of the GATT 1994 that a TRQ can lawfully replace an unlimited tariff concession, provided that the conditions (payment of compensation) embedded in this paragraph have been met. In practice, most TRQs concern farm products: Australia, for example, has TRQs in place, *inter alia*, for fresh cheese (HS 0406.10.00); gated or powdered cheese (HS 0406.20.00); but also for tobacco for use in manufacturing of cigarettes (HS 2401.1012), and tobacco refuse (HS 2401.30.00). By the same token, Indonesia has TRQs in place for milk and cream of fat and its products (HS 0402 Ex), and rice (HS 1006 Ex). More generally, in 2006, 45 Members had in place 1,434 individual tariff quotas.[36]

Absence of Disciplines on Export Taxes: The interim report of the (US) Special Committee on Relaxation of Trade Barriers[37] recommended a provision should be made, in the context of a trade agreement like the GATT, to abolish all objectionable export taxes, with exceptions to be enacted for export taxes for revenue purposes, or enforced pursuant to international agreements, or imposed under the conditions of famine or severe domestic shortage in the exporting country, or even designed to regulate the trade in

---

[34] The authors identify a situation where acting consistently with the GATT and inconsistently with the IMF is possible, but fail to see functional consequence in their example.

[35] And they definitely operate as such in case the out of quota tariff rate is prohibitively high.

[36] See WTO Doc. TN/AG/S/22 of April 27, 2006.

[37] Report of December 8, 1943, International Trade Files, Lot File 57D–284, pp. 35ff.

military supplies under specified conditions.[38] This view did not carry the day for many good reasons. Lack of practice is probably the single most important reason explaining why the founding fathers did not spend time and effort designing a mechanism for negotiation of export tariffs *à la* Art. II GATT. We read, for example in the same report (p. 34):

> Except during wartime, governmentally-imposed export duties, and prohibitions and quantitative restrictions on exports have had relatively little influence in limiting the over-all movement of commodities in world trade, although they have seriously affected the movement of specific products. Export taxes and quantitative restrictions on exports have been instituted for a variety of reasons. Some, such as export taxes on coffee in certain Latin American countries, have been imposed for revenue purposes. Some have been imposed for indirect protective reasons: for example, the United States prohibition on commercial exports of tobacco seed for the purpose of preventing the cultivation abroad of American types of tobacco. In a different category are the Mexican export taxes, which are used for revenue purposes and, in combination with an export tax-rebate system to enforce membership in export cooperatives. Some, such as the United States control of helium exports, have been imposed for security reasons. Some have been imposed pursuant to international agreements; for example, the undertaking by Cuba, in connection with the trade agreement with the United States, to prohibit the exportation of avocados to the United States except during the months of July through September . . . [39]

In the absence of an agreement on outright prohibition, the GATT treats import- and export duties in symmetric manner: they are negotiable instruments that must anyway be applied in non-discriminatory manner, and can be bound following an agreement to this effect. Art. XXVIIIbis GATT reads:

> The contracting parties recognize that customs duties often constitute serious obstacles to trade; thus negotiations on a reciprocal and mutually advantageous basis, directed to the substantial reduction of the general level of tariffs and other charges on imports *and exports* and in particular to the reduction of such high tariffs as discourage the importation even of minimum quantities, and conducted with due regard to the objectives of this Agreement and the varying needs of individual contracting parties, are of great importance to the expansion of international trade.

---

[38] Dam (1977) discusses the US southern states' opposition to export taxes.

[39] Political economy considerations could also contribute to this outcome: exporters would not be necessarily interested in seeing their revenue divided between them and their government (that would pocket the export tax). Assuming that their lobby power matters to the government, one would expect few export taxes. The produces interests are of course the exact opposite when it comes to import tariffs and this probably explains proliferation of import- and almost total absence of export duties. On the other hand, producers could achieve the same outcome through other mechanisms such as export cartels; it is at best questionable whether a domestic antitrust authority can prosecute and some jurisdictions like the US explicitly exempt them from prosecution altogether.

The CONTRACTING PARTIES may therefore sponsor such negotiations from time to time. (emphasis added)

Nothing stops WTO Members from negotiating export concessions and in fact, they often do.[40] However, as noted in this Chapter, export taxes are not treated as QRs.

---

[40] See § 184 of the Working Party Report on the accession of Saudi Arabia to the WTO, WTO Doc. WT/ACC/SAU/61 of November 1, 2005.

Chapter 3

Tariffs

■ ■ ■

1. THE LEGAL DISCIPLINE

Unlike quotas and other forms of quantitative restrictions (QRs), the WTO permits the use of tariffs, sometimes referred to as import duties or customs duties. A tariff is a financial charge levied at the time of importation on a particular good.[1] As we will discuss in this Chapter, tariffs can take on various forms. The WTO distinguishes between the term "ordinary customs duties" (OCDs) and "other duties and charges" (ODCs). Both are negotiated multilaterally through negotiating rounds.

Although the WTO permits its Members to impose tariffs on imports, it recognizes that tariffs can constitute a barrier to trade. The WTO does seek to promote trade liberalization, and to that end, the WTO offers mechanisms whereby its Members can negotiate to lower tariffs through multilateral negotiating rounds. In order to do so, however, WTO Members must first agree on a common parlance to describe goods; this is done through the Harmonized System (HS), to be described further in this Chapter. The HS provides a numerical coding system that divides all goods into approximately 5,000 categories at a 6–digit level; these categories are commonly referred to as "tariff lines." Countries can sub-divide these further into even more granular categories.

Prior to the GATT, countries raised and lowered tariffs at will. During the Great Depression, a series of tit-for-tat tariff increases triggered a massive decline in trade, and left all parties worse off. To prevent such a recurrence, the GATT / WTO aims to have each country agree to not raise tariffs beyond a certain level for a given good. For each particular good (through use of the HS code for that good), each WTO Member must decide whether or not it wishes to commit to a maximum ceiling beyond which it will not raise tariffs for that particular good. If it decides to commit to such a ceiling, then the WTO Member is deemed to have "bound" that particular tariff line (i.e., 6–digit HS code). If it does not commit to such a ceiling, then the tariff line is said to be "unbound."

The agreed-upon ceiling is referred to, in WTO parlance, as the "bound" tariff rate. As this is the maximum ceiling, a WTO Member may choose to impose a tariff rate that is at the bound rate or at any rate low-

---

[1] Tariffs are governed by the GATT 1994, which as we discussed in Chapter 1, governs only trade in goods.

er than the bound rate. The actual rate that the WTO Member levies upon a particular good is what is known, in WTO parlance, as the "applied" rate.[2] Bound, applied and unbound tariffs must, in principle, respect the non-discrimination principle of most-favored-nation (MFN) treatment. (Note that we touched upon the MFN principle briefly in Chapter 1 and will discuss in extensive detail in Chapter 3.)

Each WTO Member offers a Schedule of Concessions in which it lays out the series of tariff bindings to which it has committed. Over the course of negotiating rounds, the tariffs can be modified—that is to say, they can switch from "unbound" to "bound" or the bound rates can be lowered. The hope is that over the course of time, countries will gradually lower their tariff protection through reciprocal concessions made to each other on products of interest.

Art. II.1 GATT obliges a WTO Member to commit to the bound tariff rates to which it has committed in its Schedule of Concessions with respect to tariffs, meaning both OCDs and ODCs. However, Art. II.2 GATT permits a series of exceptions. These include: taxes equivalent to an internal tax, antidumping duties, countervailing duties, and fees and services rendered in connection with importation. The first three of these exceptions are subject to elaborate rules which will be discussed in greater detail in subsequent Chapters, but the last of these exceptions is one that we will examine in this Chapter.

WTO law also provides WTO Members with the flexibility to increase the level of protection given to a particular tariff line beyond that to which it has committed in its Schedule. However, if a WTO Member chooses to do so, it must follow a series of complex rules which will be discussed in greater detail in this Chapter. These rules are embedded within Art. XXVIII GATT and ensure that trading partners that are seriously affected by this change are given compensation through decreased levels of tariff protection on other products in exchange.

2. THE RATIONALE FOR THE LEGAL DISCIPLINE

Before the advent of the GATT, trading nations were free to change the duty applied to imports (unless these were constrained through bilateral treaties[3]). Tariff volatility had a heavy impact on transaction costs which became unpredictable. As mentioned, they also could lead to devastating economic consequences through harmful tit-for-tat behaviour. The GATT put an end to all this by providing a forum to cap tariffs. The bound duties reflected in Schedules of Concessions (also referred to as

---

[2] The difference between the bound- and the applied level is called in GATT-parlance 'water'.

[3] The US for example, had signed a series of FCN Treaties (Friendship, Commerce and Navigation) with various other states.

Schedules of Commitments) represent legal commitments. By virtue of Art. II.7 GATT:

> The Schedules annexed to this Agreement are hereby made an integral part of Part I of this Agreement.

Why did the GATT privilege tariffs over other forms of import protection? In other words, why are quotas and other forms of QRs banned, while tariffs allowed? Unlike a QR, tariffs simply raise the transaction costs of trade, but do not act as an absolute barrier to importation. In addition, by forcing countries to reduce the level of protection down to a particular numerical bound rate, the hope was that this would make it easier for parties to negotiate with one another subsequently in order to further liberalize trade. At the very least, it provided increased transparency about the level of import protection.

Duties that have been bound cannot be unilaterally revised upwards; instead, a multilateral process is set forth in Art. XXVIII GATT and must be observed. In principle, compensation has to be agreed between the WTO Member wishing to revise upwards its bound duties and a sub-set of WTO Members particularly affected by the decision to revise bound duties. Reciprocity is very much behind the procedure established in Art. XXVIII GATT. The idea is that what is important is the preservation of the balance of rights and obligations established in the original negotiation, irrespective of the agreed level of duties. The mechanism laid out in Art. XXVIII GATT acts as insurance that the value of tariff promises (bindings) will not be altered unless both the promissor and the promissee agree that this should be the case.

Overall, the GATT was practical in its expecting that all countries, at some point, will want to have some level of protection for its domestic industry against certain imports. However, each country will also want increased access to markets for certain exports. The hope was that by encouraging tariffication and disallowing other forms of import protection, countries would find it easier to find mutually-beneficial trade-offs in which each country would agree to lower its tariffs further in exchange for tariff concessions from its trading partners. For nearly half a century, this prescription has worked wonders. Bound tariff rates have declined significantly worldwide. However, at some point, countries face a limit on what they are willing to give up. A relevant question for the Doha Round is whether we have come close to reaching this limit, with respect to tariffs, or whether there is more room for creative "win-win" solutions to further lower tariffs and liberalize trade.

3. THE COVERAGE OF THE LEGAL DISCIPLINE

3.1 EXPRESSING GOODS IN COMMON LANGUAGE: THE HARMONIZED SYSTEM

To bind duties, WTO negotiators first have to agree on a common language to describe goods and, based on this common language, exchange concessions. The Harmonized System (HS) supplies the common language. The HS is a document elaborated in the WCO (World Customs Organization),[4] an international organization with headquarters in Brussels, Belgium. Goods' descriptions are expressed in two-, four-, and six digits: the lower the number of digits, the more generic the product category; the higher the number of digits, the more specific the product category. For example, at the two-digit-level one might find the term 'vehicles', whereas, at the six-digit-level, the term 'passenger cars of less than 2 tons'. At the 6–digit level, the HS comprises of approximately 5,000 categories of goods.

The HS classification codes are updated every couple of years, as needed. In 2002, the changes made were mainly related to wood, paper, chemicals, pharmaceuticals, and metals. The 2007 amendments were mainly with respect to information technology and communication products. Each set of amendments affected approximately 10 percent of the HS categories.

What the HS ensures is that any given good will be classified under the same tariff line ('heading') across national jurisdictions. For example, bumpers will come under the heading 8708.10 which reads 'Bumpers and Parts Thereof' in the schedules of all WTO Members alike. What might change is the tariff treatment of bumpers: the US might impose a 2% import duty, whereas Pakistan 10%. The system is used by more than 190 countries as the basis for their customs tariffs. Not all WTO Members have formally adhered to the HS; however, either for legal reasons (formal adherence to the HS) or *de facto*, all WTO Members follow the HS classification up to the six-digit-level.

From the six-digit-level onwards, WTO Members are free to "shape" their concessions to their liking. Art 3.3 HS reads in this respect:

> Nothing in this Article shall prevent a Contracting Party from establishing, in its Customs tariff or statistical nomenclatures, subdivisions classifying goods beyond the level of the Harmonized system, provided that any such subdivision is added and coded at a level beyond that of the six-digit numerical code set out in the Annex to this Convention.

---

[4] This institution used to be known as the CCC (Customs Cooperation Council).

Assuming a WTO Member has made a concession at the four digit level, it can only treat sub-classifications more favourably. An example from the US Tariff Schedule can help explain this point: Chapter 87 of the HS is entitled 'Vehicles other than Railway Rolling–Stock, and Parts and accessories thereof'. 8708 is entitled 'Parts and Accessories of the Motor Vehicles of Headings 8701 to 8705' (the two categories corresponding to tractors, motor vehicles for the transport of ten or more persons and motor cars principally designed for the transport of persons). 8708.10 reads 'Bumpers and Parts thereof'. 8708.10.60 reads 'Bumpers' (i.e., stampings).[5] The US bound its tariffs in Chapter 87 at the eight-digit-level at 2.7%. This means that, if it enters a new sub-category (of 8708.10.60) at the 10– or 12–digit-level, it will be able to impose a maximum duty of 2.7%. A similar outcome would obtain had the US committed to observe a 2.7% ceiling at the four digit level, that is, for the entry 8708. Any sub-classification of this entry (i.e., 8708.01, 8708.02, but also 8708.0101) would have to observe this ceiling and goods classified under these entries could never be subjected to an import duty higher than 2.7%. Eight-digit descriptions are national classifications. They can be challenged before the WTO for not observing Art. 3.3HS.[6]

The legal status of the HS in WTO law is not addressed in the Agreement Establishing the WTO but has been clarified in case law. The Panel report in *EC—Chicken Cuts* held that the HS provides context[7] for the schedules of concessions submitted by WTO Members. As a result, Panels must always take the HS into account when the issue of interpretation of a particular concession arises.

At issue in *EC—Chicken Cuts* case was the proper tariff classification of exports of frozen boneless salted chicken cuts from Brazil to the EU. The dispute concerned whether such imports should fall under the tariff classification 0210.90 or 0207.41. The tariff heading 0207.41 referred to "Meats . . . fresh, chilled, or frozen of fowls of the species *Gallus domesticus*." The tariff heading 0210.90 referred to "Meat, . . . salted, in brine, dried, or smoked" that were not other animals other than bovine animals. Frozen chicken cuts, left unsalted, clearly fell into 0207.41. The question was whether once salted, they should be classified instead as 0210.90.

---

[5] It is not the case that in the pre-HS years, precise classifications and sub-classifications were unknown in customs practice. Irwin (2011, p. 35) refers to the following entry in the *Smoot–Hawley Tariff Act*: "bottle caps of metal, collapsible tubes, and sprinkler tops, if not decorated, colored, waxed, lacquered, enamelled, lithographed, electroplated, or embossed in color, 45 per centum ad valorem".

[6] As we will see *infra*, the process of certification of schedules of concessions does not at all immunize them from subsequent legal challenges. The AB report on EC—Bananas III made this point abundantly clear.

[7] This term is being used in the sense to which it is relevant for the Vienna Convention on the Law of Treaties (VCLT). The importance of the VCLT in interpreting WTO agreements will be discussed *infra* in this volume.

This mattered to Brazilian exporters because the import duties for 0210.90 were lower than those for 0207.41.[8]

The EU, in an attempt to prevent Brazilian exporters from simply adding salt to frozen chicken in order to obtain a lower tariff rate, changed its customs classification such that frozen salted chicken cuts would be treated as 0207.41. Brazil argued that this was a violation of the EU's tariff commitments. The EU maintained that meat would only count as salted if the salting was done for preservation purposes. This was not the case for Brazil's exports, which in the EU view, consisted of meat sprinkled with an amount of salt insufficient for preservation. The Panel rejected the arguments advanced by the EU, and agreed with Brazil.[9] In its view, nothing in the HS description conditioned the classification of salted meat under 02.10 (the relevant HS tariff heading) on the purpose of salting. In so ruling, the Panel turned to the HS as context for deciding the product's proper tariff classification (§§ 7.104ff). The AB upheld the Panel's findings in this respect (§§ 199ff).[10]

The view that the HS provides context for interpreting tariff concessions is reinforced by the LAN dispute (*EC–Computer Equipment*) between the US and the EU. At issue was the proper classification of certain computer equipment that the US was exporting to the EU market. The particular commodity (LAN equipment) could, conceivably, come under two different HS classifications; in light of the substantial discrepancy with respect to their tariff treatment, the US had a strong trade interest in seeing it classified under the heading with the lower import duty.[11] To make matters even more complicated, there was divergent practice with respect to the classification of LAN equipment among individual EU member states. The Panel was asked whether the legitimate expectations of the WTO Member which had negotiated the concession (the US) mat-

---

[8] As noted in § 7.3 of the Panel report: "The EC Schedule provides for a tariff of 102.4€/100kg/net for products covered by subheading 0207.14.10 and allows the European Communities to use special safeguard measures under Article 5 of the Agreement on Agriculture in respect of such products. The EC Schedule provides for a tariff of 15.4% *ad valorem* for products covered by subheading 0210.90.20 and there is no reservation for the use of special safeguard measures under Article 5 of the Agreement on Agriculture in respect of such products."

[9] Remarkably, in this case, as in *EC—Computer Equipment* before it, the parties to the dispute defended before the Panel the view that their dispute did not concern a classification issue (although this is precisely what this case was all about). The Panel did not disagree with the parties.

[10] The AB took a slightly different view on the use of the interpretative elements but did not disturb the Panel's findings on the proper classification of salted meat at all. The parties to the dispute could have submitted their dispute to the HS dispute settlement procedures (which we briefly discuss in the Questions and Comments at the end of this Chapter), which they did not. On the other hand, the Panel itself could have used its powers under Art. 13 DSU and request an expert testimony from HS officials. It did not do that either. It did address questions to the HS Committee, but exercised its own discretion when evaluating the responses granted.

[11] This was the first dispute concerning products covered by the Information Technology Agreement (ITA). We discuss its content in more detail *infra*; suffice to state here that classification of products coming under the purview of the ITA was not exact science, and considerable room for discretion was left in the importing states.

tered regarding the classification of the goods. The Panel agreed with the US, finding that legitimate expectations, in instances of textual ambiguity, matter. The AB rejected the Panel's interpretation. In its view, if at all, it should be the legitimate expectations of the WTO Membership *in toto* that could be relevant (§§ 80–96). In its words (§ 84):

> The purpose of treaty interpretation under Article 31 of the *Vienna Convention* is to ascertain the *common* intention of the parties. These common intentions cannot be ascertained on the basis of the subjective and unilaterally determines 'expectations' of *one* of the parties to a treaty. Tariff concessions provided for in a member's Schedule—the interpretation of which is at issue here—are reciprocal and result from a mutually advantageous negotiation between importing and exporting members. A Schedule is made an integral part of the GATT 1994 by Article II:7 of the GATT 1994. Therefore, the concessions provided for in that Schedule are part of the terms of treaty. As such, the only rules which may be applied in interpreting the meaning of a concession are the general rules of treaty interpretation set out in the *Vienna Convention*. (italics and emphasis in the original).

As a result of this case law, it follows that in instances where disputes may arise over tariff classifications, the proper place to turn for contextual guidance is the HS. Panels will seek the input and cooperation of the HS Committee, when presented with a question over tariff classification.

3.2 ORDINARY CUSTOMS DUTIES AND OTHER DUTIES AND CHARGES

Art. II GATT explains the process for binding tariff protection. Specifically, Art. II.1 GATT requires that WTO Members levy only those tariffs in conformity with its Schedule of Concessions. It states:

> (a) Each contracting party shall accord to the commerce of the other contracting parties treatment no less favourable than that provided for in the Part of the appropriate Schedule annexed to this Agreement.
>
> (b) The products described in Part I of the Schedule relating to any contracting party, which are the products of territories of other contracting parties, shall, on their importation into the territory to which the Schedule relates, and subject to the terms, conditions or qualifications set forth in the Schedule, be exempt from ordinary customs duties in excess of those set forth and provided therein. Such products shall also be exempt from all other duties and charges of any kind imposed on or in connection with the importation in excess of those imposed on the date of this Agreement or those directly and

mandatorily required to be imposed thereafter by legislation in force in the importing territory on that date.

Art. II.1 GATT makes reference to two terms when discussing tariffs: (1) "ordinary customs duty" (OCD), and (2) "other duties and charges" (ODC). Neither of the two terms is detailed any further in this provision. In *Chile–Price Band*, the Panel, and subsequently the AB, confirmed that a measure cannot simultaneously be both an OCD and an ODC.

At issue in *Chile–Price Band* was the Chilean practice of not imposing a fixed tariff duty rate on some imports; instead, Chilean officials assessed a duty rate that was calculated on the basis of difference between the world price and corresponding domestic price of a given commodity. Argentina complained that, when applying this system, Chile sometimes imposed duties beyond its bound level. The question facing the adjudicators in the case was whether the Chilean system qualified as an OCD, as the alleged violation was that of the bound OCD. The Panel defined OCDs as duties that took on a certain form[12] and that are levied without regard to exogenous factors such as fluctuating world market prices (§ 7.52 & fn. 64). The AB disagreed with the Panel's definition, but stopped short of providing its own definition.[13] In the AB's view, all that is required, anyway, for a measure to constitute an OCD is that it is expressed in a particular form that is commonly used (§§ 264–278).

In practice, an ordinary customs duty (OCD) is a duty which takes on one of the following forms:

(a) *ad valorem* duties;
(b) specific duties;
(c) compound duties;
(d) alternative duties (or mixed duties); and
(e) technical duties.

A duty is *ad valorem* when it is a percentage of the value of the imported product (e.g., 15% of a fax machine the import price of which is $400). A duty is specific when it is related to the weight, volume, surface, or other chararcteristic of the good at hand (e.g., $20 per ton of imported wheat). A duty is compound when it comprises an *ad valorem* duty to which the customs authority adds or from which it subtracts a specific duty (e.g., 10% on the import price of wheat plus $2 per imported kg of wheat). A duty is alternative or mixed when it ensures a minimum or maximum tariff protection through the choice between, in most cases, an *ad valorem* and a specific duty (e.g., 10% on the import price of or $2 per imported ton of wheat whichever is the maximum). Finally, particularly

---

[12] The Panel made reference to ad valorem and specific duties, which are discussed *infra*.
[13] The AB did so on account of judicial economy. It had already found that the Chilean price band scheme violated a provision (Art. 4.2) of the Agreement on Agriculture.

where agricultural products are concerned, a technical duty is determined by complex technical factors such as alcohol or sugar content.

Recall that WTO Members cannot apply duties above the bound level, but can of course apply duties at a lower than the bound level. The AB, in its report in *Argentina–Footwear*, faced the following situation: Argentina had bound its duties on footwear, during the Uruguay Round, as *ad valorem*. Subsequently, it had been applying on imports of footwear either an *ad valorem* duty of 35%, or a specific duty that was calculated on the basis of the world price. It later decided to apply specific duties only. Since, in its view, the case did not concern a change in the bound duties, it did not notify its decision as normally required. The complainant argued that such a change was not permissible because tariff bindings constituted an agreement both not to impose tariffs beyond a ceiling and not to change the type of duties. While the Panel agreed with the complainant's argument, the AB held that switching between different types of duties is perfectly legitimate as long as the overall ceiling of protection has not been violated (§§ 44–55). The AB did, nevertheless, find that Argentina had violated its obligations since, following the conversion, the resulting duty was higher than the negotiated ceiling.

If "ordinary customs duties" are the regular, plain-vanilla tariffs that are levied on imports, what then are "other duties and charges" (ODCs)? Practice, however, sheds light on the content of ODCs. Examples of an ODC include:

- An additional surcharge on imports (e.g., used to finance infrastructure improvements, etc.)
- A statistical tax imposed to finance the collection of trade statistics
- A customs processing fee
- A charge associated with the cost of public health controls on imports (e.g., quarantine)

Like the ordinary customs duties, ODCs are also levied at the point of importation on a particular good. During the Uruguay Round, negotiators concluded an Understanding on the Understanding on the Interpretation of Art. II:1(b) of the GATT, concluded during the Uruguay round. The *travaux preparatoires*, or negotiating history, of the Understanding reveal the willingness of negotiators to define ODCs by exclusion. The negotiators concluded that it would have been a daunting task to attempt to draw an exhaustive list of ODCs; this point was again emphasized by the Panel in *Dominican Republic–Import and Sale of Cigarettes* (§ 7.114). The Understanding provides that:

(a) ODCs have to be recorded in WTO Members' Schedules of concessions; otherwise they are *ipso facto* inconsistent with the GATT 1994. However, since ODCs are linked to customs duties, and since only bound customs duties appear in a schedule, in practice, ODCs applicable to unbound duties do not have to be included in schedules of concessions;

(b) ODCs are not by virtue of their inclusion in a schedule of concession automatically deemed GATT-consistent. WTO Members can, for a period of three years after the entry into force of the WTO, challenge ODCs reflected in a schedule of concessions, either because an ODC did not exist at the time of the original binding of the item in question, or because it exceeded its prior level (§ 4);

(c) Even after this period of three years, WTO Members can still challenge ODCs on grounds other than those mentioned above (i.e., challenge them for being GATT inconsistent) (§ 5).

In practice, ODCs are usually expressed in *ad valorem* terms.[14] The lack of precise definitions for both OCDs and ODCs has not hampered the negotiating process. Nowadays ODCs are being negotiated just like OCDs.

3.3 CUSTOMS VALUATION

For duties and other charges that are applied in *ad valorem* terms, the issue of customs valuation (CV) is of tremendous importance. CV is a customs procedure applied to determine the customs value of imported goods upon which import duties will be imposed. It is pertinent for both OCDs as well as ODCs. Art. VII GATT states that the value of imported merchandise for customs purposes should be based on its actual value and not on the value of comparable domestic merchandise or on any arbitrary or fictitious values. Art VII.2(b) GATT defines actual value in the following terms:

> 'Actual value' should be the price at which, at a time and place determined by the legislation of the country of importation, such or like merchandise is sold or offered for sale in the ordinary course of trade under fully competitive conditions. To the extent to which the price of such or like merchandise is governed by the quantity in a particular transaction, the price to be considered should uniformly be related to either (i) comparable quantities, or (ii) quantities not less favourable to importers than those in which the greater volume of the merchandise is sold in the trade between the countries of exportation and importation.

The value of goods can also be ascertained at the port of exportation: through pre-shipment inspection, one aims to ensure that the quantity and quality of the goods to be exported conform to the specifications reflected in a sales contract. Therefore, while the CV Agreement deals with

---

[14] ODCs feature under column 6 of the Uruguay Round schedules. Only Botswana, Côte d'Ivoire, Namibia, Swaziland, and South Africa have used compound ODCs.

the value of goods at the point of importation, pre-shipment inspection deals with similar issues (but with a wider range of issues as well) at the point of exportation. We discuss this agreement in more detail in Chapter 7 as well.

3.4 MULTILATERAL TRADE NEGOTIATIONS (TRADE ROUNDS)

GATT signatories, and now WTO Members, have periodically engaged in a round of multilateral trade negotiations designed to lower tariffs through reciprocal tariff concessions. These are known as "trade rounds" in which the full WTO Membership participates. Art. XXVIII*bis* GATT does not set a specific date on which rounds must start; it is the WTO Membership that will decide when to open up multilateral talks. At the moment of writing, we are in the middle of the ninth round since the inception of the GATT: the Doha Round.[15] The Trade Negotiating Committee, which includes representatives of all WTO Members, oversees the negotiations; it is usually headed by the Director–General of the WTO.

The various modalities for negotiating tariff cuts practised so far include:

(a) *Request–offer*: Pairs of WTO Members negotiate tariff cuts on certain product(s) or groups of products; this process continues, with different pairs and different products, until a mutually-advantageous solution has been reached and the WTO has been notified thereof;

(b) *Linear reduction*: All bound duties are reduced by the same agreed method;

(c) *Harmonized formula*: Reductions occur in a non-linear fashion with a greater reduction of higher tariffs than lower lower tariffs. This method is also sometimes referred to as a "Swiss formula" method.[16]

(d) *Tiered cuts*: Duties will be divided into bands (tiers) and the duties of the higher bands will be cut more drastically than those of the lower bands. This approach is reminiscent of the "Swiss formula" approach, but not identical.[17]

---

[15] Rounds, with few exceptions, tend to get their name from the place where negotiations are launched (exceptions include the Kennedy Round and the Dillon Round).

[16] Mathematically, linear reduction would look like this: $T^* = C \times T$ (where T^* is the new final rate, C the coefficient for agreed reductions, say 80%, and T, the base rate); the Swiss formula, in turn, would look like this: $T^* = C \times T / C + T$. The name "Swiss formula" is on account of a Swiss delegate having first proposed this approach during the Tokyo Round.

[17] The difference between (b) and (c) on the one hand, and (d) on the other, is that whereas the former is a formula applied on a tariff line by line basis, the latter is not. The latter can take different forms: *simple average reduction*, where one aims at reducing on the average the tariffs of various tariff lines; *reduction in the average*, whereby one compares the average base rates, the average final rates, and then determines the reduction of the latter vis-à-vis the former; *target average*, whereby a specific average that must be met by new bindings is agreed.

(e) *Sectoral approach*: Duties will be lowered only in a particular sector.

3.5 TRADE NEGOTIATIONS OUTSIDE TRADE ROUNDS

On occasion, WTO Members have attempted to negotiate tariff concessions outside of the multilateral trade rounds through negotiations in which only a sub-set of WTO Members participates. The results of these negotiations are subsequently "multilateralized." That is to say, any WTO Member, even those that did not participate in the negotiations, may choose to accept its results. Provided that the body of accepting Members exceeds a certain pre-determined threshold, the agreement enters into force. Moreover, WTO Members that choose to accept the terms of the agreement must apply the tariff concessions in a non-discriminatory manner.

The most prominent tariff concessions to have been negotiated in this manner are those associated with the Information Technology Agreement (ITA). The ITA concerned negotiations on tariffs for information technology (IT) goods. It resulted from negotiations concluded by a subset of WTO Members at the Singapore Ministerial Conference[18] in December 1996. At that time, 29 (including the then 15 member states of the EU) countries or separate customs territories signed the ITA. The ITA required that the WTO Members participating in the staged process of tariff reductions envisioned by the ITA must collectively account for at least 90 percent of world trade in IT goods in order for the tariff concessions to take effect. This threshold was met when a number of additional WTO Members agreed to join the original signatories (who accounted for only 83% of trade in IT goods) in participating in negotiating staged reductions. The first of a series of staged reductions in the tariff levels of IT goods took place on July 1, 1997. Since the original ITA, an ITA II was also successfully concluded. The ITA has now 70 members (counting the EU as 27), the majority of which are developing countries. Together, the 70 members of the ITA represent approximately 97% of world trade in IT products.[19]

With the outcome of the Doha Round still in doubt at the time of this writing, it is fair to say that in the WTO era (i.e., since the Uruguay Round), this approach of negotiating amongst a sub-set of Members has had more success than the full-scale multilateral approach. Note that disputes concerning tariff concessions arising out of the ITA have been

---

[18] According to Art. IV of the WTO Agreement, a *Ministerial Conference* is composed of representatives of all members and meets at least once every 2 years. The Ministerial Conference can take decisions on all matters under any of the multilateral trade agreements.

[19] Mexico, and Brazil are the most important non-ITA participants, accounting for more or less 3% of world ITA-trade. After its peak in 2000 (16.5%), the ITA now counts for approximately 12% of total world exports; the share of ITA products in world trade exceeds (in 2006) that of farm products.

the subject of WTO dispute settlement. We discuss these disputes in the Questions and Comments section of this Chapter.

3.6 CERTIFICATION, MODIFICATION, AND RECTIFICATION OF SCHEDULES

Once the WTO Membership is satisfied with the content of negotiations, the WTO Secretariat will circulate the Members' Schedules of Concessions for verification and certification. Until 1959, changes on the tariff level were incorporated into the GATT and its schedules through a series of Protocols.[20] In 1959, parties to the GATT agreed to adopt a procedure of certification for tariff schedules. In 1968, the GATT agreed that any modification or rectification would take place through the certification procedure. Then, in 1980, the GATT adopted the Declaration on Procedures for Modification and Rectification of Schedules of Tariff Concessions.[21] The 1980 Declaration was incorporated into the GATT 1994.[22]

The 1980 Decision confirms that modifications imply substantive change of the concession (§ 1 of the 1980 Decision), whereas rectifications imply no such change (§ 2 of the 1980 Decision). Modifications could be the outcome of action under various provisions, including Arts. II, XVIII, XXIV, XXVII, and Art. XXVIII GATT. The 1980 Decision requires multilateral review of both rectifications and modifications because of the admittedly fine line between the two, which might incentivize cheating by WTO Members who might claim rectification when something should be understood as modification. Modifications have to be communicated to the Director–General of the WTO within three months after the action (under one of the provisions mentioned above) has been completed. Rectifications must be communicated within six months after the amendment has been introduced in national legislation, or, in case of other rectifications, whenever the circumstances permit this to be the case. If no objection has been raised within three months from the communication, the notified modifications and/or rectifications become certifications (§ 3 of the 1980 Decision).

Unilateral actions, that have not been certified, risk being challenged before the WTO and eventually being deemed illegal. This issue was first tackled by a GATT Panel in *Spain–Unroasted Coffee*. Spain had originally made a tariff concession on unroasted coffee that did not differentiate be-

---

[20] There were five Protocols of rectification in total, one Protocol of modification, and nine Protocols of rectification and modification: the term 'rectification' essentially captures mundane changes (whereby e.g., the level of the tariff concession is not affected), whereas the term 'modification' refers to substantive changes, such as those resulting from a re-negotiation of duties conducted under Art. XXVIII GATT. Eventually, the Protocol would be registered in accordance with the provisions of Art. 102 of the UN Charter. See Jackson (1969, pp. 211ff.).

[21] Decision of March 26, 1980, L/4962, GATT Doc. BISD 27S/25–26, hereinafter the '1980 Decision'.

[22] This is by virtue of Art. 1(b)(iv) GATT 1994, which incorporated all formal decisions adopted by the GATT.

tween the various types of coffee.²³ It later modified its negotiated concession by reserving a tariff treatment of "unwashed Arabia" and "Robusta" coffees that was less favorable than that reserved for "mild" coffee (all three types being unroasted coffee): whereas it kept a 0% duty to the latter, it imposed a 7% duty to the former. Brazil complained due to this new, disparate treatment of its coffee exports to the Spanish market. The Panel found against the Spanish measure (§ 4.4):

> The Panel found that there was no obligation under the GATT to follow any particular system for classifying goods, and that a contracting party had the right to introduce in its customs tariff new positions or sub-positions as appropriate.

A footnote to this paragraph reads:

> Provided that a reclassification *subsequent* to the making of a concession under the GATT would not be a violation of the basic commitment regarding that concession (Article II:5). (emphasis added)

In this case, the Panel found that the various types of coffee were like products and that, in the absence of prior distinction across the three types, Spain was in violation of its obligations (§ 4.10).²⁴

Certification, however, does not confer legality. Consenting to a modified schedule means that the WTO Membership has conceded that the schedule at hand is *accurate*, but not necessarily *legal*. Accordingly, WTO Members have not, by virtue of the 1980 Decision, given up their rights to subsequently challenge the consistency of modified or rectified schedules with the multilateral rules.

An example of a case where a previously-certified Schedule was subject to a challenge is *EC—Bananas III*. In that case, the EU had included, in its Schedule, a condition that would allow some WTO Members²⁵ to benefit from a preferential tariff rate on bananas not afforded to other WTO Members. A series of banana-exporting WTO Members complained claiming that the measure at hand was inconsistent with the requirement that tariff concessions be enforced in a non-discriminatory measure. In response, the EU argued that its Schedule, with this controversial condition, had gone through the certification process without any WTO Mem-

---

²³ GATT Doc. BISD 28S/102ff.

²⁴ A similar to the *Spain—Unroasted Coffee* case arose recently: Panama eliminated from its schedule item 1901.10.10 (modified milk) to which it applied a 5% duty. It then created two new tariff items: 1901.10.11 (infant milk formula) with an import tariff of 0%, and 1901.10.19 (other) with an import tariff of 65%. Mexico complained since, in its view, this unilateral modification violated, *inter alia*, Art II of the GATT (WTO Doc WT/DS329/1). The parties to the dispute reached a mutually agreed solution (MAS) that they notified to the WTO, whereby Panama agreed to reduce the tariff on item 1901.10.19 to 5% (WTO Doc WT/DS329/2).

²⁵ These were countries that had signed a Framework Agreement with the EU. Note that a set of ACP (African, Caribbean, Pacific) countries could also benefit from the preferential tariff rates on bananas.

ber raising an issue as to its legality. It requested, consequently, from the Panel to dismiss all claims.[26] The Panel rejected the EU's argument; the AB later affirmed. In their view, a WTO Member can, through conditions attached to its Schedule, grant other WTO Members rights but it cannot, through this means, diminish its obligations (§§ 157–158). The fact that the WTO Membership had certified the Schedule did not confer upon it the status of being GATT-consistent.

3.7 EXCEPTIONS TO ART. II.1 GATT OBLIGATIONS

Art. II.2 GATT provides three exceptions to the obligation that OCDs and ODCs must conform to the obligations contained within each WTO Member's Schedule of Concessions. These are for:

- A charge equivalent to an internal tax imposed on a "like" domestic product
- Anti-dumping duties or countervailing duties
- Fees or other charges commensurate with the cost of services rendered

3.7.1 Charge Equivalent to an Internal Tax

WTO Members are allowed to impose a charge on imports that is equivalent to an internal tax imposed on domestic producers of the "like" good. This is subject to the internal tax being consistent with Art. III.2 GATT. We will discuss this further in Chapter 8 (*India-Additional Import Duties*).

3.7.2 Antidumping and Countervailing Duties

WTO Members are allowed to impose an additional duty on imports under two scenarios mentioned in Art. II.2(b):

- When an exporter is "dumping" its product into the market, causing injury to the domestic producer of the "like" product
- When an exporter is benefiting from subsidies that cause injury to the domestic producer of the "like" product

The WTO law contains elaborate rules on the use of antidumping duties to address the first scenario; we will discuss these rules in Chapter 14. The duties imposed in the second scenario are known as countervailing duties; again, WTO law contains elaborate rules on their use, which we will discuss in Chapter 15.

---

[26] The case concerned consistency with Art. 4.1 AG, which deals with farm goods only and is the parallel provision to Art. II GATT. There should be no doubt that, in light of the symmetric expression adopted in the two provisions and their identical function, the AB decision is relevant for all tariff concessions.

3.7.3 Fees and Charges for Services Rendered

As mentioned above, WTO Members may impose financial charges on imports that are not considered to be tariffs, but rather "fees" connected with importation. However, such fees must respect the requirements of Art. VIII GATT. Some examples include a statistical tax (i.e., a charge for the cost of maintaining trade statistics), the cost of public health controls on imports, and costs associated with consular transactions (such as invoicing and certification).[27]

Art. VIII.1 GATT imposes a limit on the amount that can be charged through such measures:

> All fees and charges of whatever character (other than import and export duties and other than taxes within the purview of Article III) imposed by contracting parties on or in connection with importation or exportation shall be limited in amount to the approximate cost of services rendered and shall not represent an indirect protection to domestic products or a taxation of imports or exports for fiscal purposes.

In *Dominican Republic–Import and Sale of Cigarettes*, the Panel confirmed that fees levied pursuant to Art. VII GATT do not overlap with those levied under Art. II GATT (§ 7.115). In other words, such fees and charges are not subject to the tariff disciplines for ODCs.

The GATT Panel report in *US–Customs User Fee* provided a series of additional clarifications regarding the ambit of Art. VIII GATT. The relevant facts are summarized in § 7 of the report:

> The term 'customs user fee' refers to a number of fees imposed by the United States for the processing by the US Customs Service of passengers, conveyances and merchandise entering the United States. Only one of these fees is at issue in this dispute. It is the 'merchandise processing fee,' an *ad valorem* charge imposed for the processing of commercial merchandise entering the United States. (italics in the original)

The Panel went on to explain that the services rendered, for which a charge would be imposed, did not have to be requested by the exporters, but could be unilaterally imposed by the importing state (§ 77). The Panel also explained that the service rendered must be linked to a particular transaction and not to the total cost of service (§ 81). Based on this analysis, the Panel went on to find that the US measure at hand was GATT-inconsistent, since, as an *ad valorem* duty, it was not linked to the cost of

---

[27] Art. VIII. 4 GATT provides that fees and formalities necessary to service an indicative list of measures come under its purview: consular transactions, such as consular invoices and certificates; quantitative restrictions; licensing; exchange control; statistical services; documents, documentation and certification; analysis and inspection; and quarantine, sanitation and fumigation.

the provided service, but to the cost of the good. Accordingly, minor value transactions would pay less than major value transactions for exactly the same service (§§ 84–86). As a result of this decision, fees and formalities coming under this provision cannot be expressed in *ad valorem* terms. Although this holding is from a GATT-era case, it has been affirmed in the WTO era by the Panel in *Argentina–Footwear*.

4. WITHDRAWING CONCESSIONS FROM MEMBERS LEAVING THE WTO

Art. XXVII GATT allows WTO Members to withhold or withdraw concessions that it negotiated with a government that has not become, or ceased to be, a contracting party. In the early days of the GATT, this provision was employed on several occasions. Following the withdrawal of the British Mandate for Palestine, the successor state was not regarded as being bound by obligations under the GATT. In 1992, following the breakup of the Socialist Federal Republic of Yugoslavia (SFRY), the GATT Membership refused to recognize the successor government governing Serbia and Montenegro as having assumed the SFRY's obligations; instead, the GATT General Council "froze" the SFRY's participation in the GATT.[28]

In recent years, there have been no cases concerning application of Art. XXVII GATT. Although there is a specific provision in the Agreement Establishing the WTO regulating withdrawal from the WTO (Art. XV), there are no reported cases of withdrawal.

5. RENEGOTIATING TARIFFS

What happens if a WTO Member wishes to raise its bound tariff rate (or undo a tariff binding altogether)? A WTO Member can increase its bound protection on a given tariff line provided that the multilateral process included in Art. XXVIII GATT has been followed. In the typical case, the Member wishing to raise its duties on a bound item will negotiate and agree on compensation with a sub-set of the WTO Membership that has been more severely affected by the tariff change. The agreed-upon compensation takes the form of tariff reductions on other product(s) and will be applied on MFN-basis. According to Art. XXVIII.2 GATT, the WTO Members participating in the renegotiation of the concession:

> shall endeavour to maintain a general level of reciprocal and mutually advantageous concessions not less favourable to trade than that provided for in this Agreement prior to such negotiations.

---

[28] GATT Doc. C/M/257 of July 10, 1992.

Art. XXVIII GATT epitomizes the idea that the GATT is about maintaining a level of reciprocally-negotiated concessions: Adjustments to bound tariff rates may be deemed necessary for a variety of reasons over time, but what matters most is that the initial balance of concessionary trade-offs is maintained throughout. Put differently, WTO Members must feel as if they "are getting their concessions' worth" at all times.

5.1 THE PARTICIPANTS IN A TARIFF RENEGOTIATION

The procedure starts with a WTO Member interested in renegotiating its bound level of duties on a tariff line making a request for a tariff renegotiation. A first question is which WTO Members should participate in these renegotiations. In principle, all WTO Members, either actually or potentially, will be affected by whatever new higher duty arises from the negotiation. Yet, to involve all WTO Members in a renegotiation of a tariff line for a single WTO Member would result in a cumbersome, unwieldy and prohibitively costly process.

In an effort to streamline the process, the WTO limits participation to a sub-set of its Members. These are:

- Members that hold an "Initial Negotiating Right" (INR)
- Members deemed to have a "principal supplying interest" (PSI)

A third category, WTO Members deemed to have a "substantial interest" (SI), will be consulted but have no legal right to participate in the negotiations.

In what follows, we describe how the composition of each of these categories is determined:

INR Holders: A WTO Member is an INR holder if it originally negotiated a specific concession with another WTO Member. The form that the international negotiations took, however, can prejudge the manner in which INR holders will be identified.

During some trade rounds, concessions were negotiated and concluded on a bilateral basis. In such cases, the identification of the INR holder is a simple factual question: these are the so-called *fixed INRs*. Fixed INRs are sub-divided into historic INRs and current INRs. Take the example of a concession on fax machines. Assume that during the Tokyo Round, India bound the duties on fax machines at 15% as a result of a negotiation that it conducted with Japan. Subsequently, during the Uruguay Round, India agrees to reduce the duty on fax machines to 10%. This time however, it negotiated the concession with Korea. In this example, Japan would be the historic INR holder and Korea would be the current INR holder (unless, of course, in the context of a new round, India agrees to further reduce its customs duty on fax machines due to negotiations with a third country, which would then become the current INR holder). Historic INR holders retain their legal right to participate in an Art.

XXVIII GATT-negotiation only if the proposed tariff increase exceeds the level of the duty at its historical level (in the example above, Japan would have negotiating rights if India requests, after the conclusion of the Uruguay round, an increase of its duty for fax machines beyond 15%).

During some other trade rounds (e.g., the Kennedy Round) concessions were not negotiated bilaterally. Trading nations agreed on tariff cuts using a formula (e.g., they all agreed to reduce tariff protection on industrial goods by 50% irrespective of the level of protection on these goods in each individual country.) In such cases, it is impossible to have fixed INRs. At the end of the Kennedy Round, the GATT contracting parties adopted the following decision to address this issue:

> In respect of the concessions specified in the Schedules annexed to the Geneva (1967) Protocol, a contracting party shall, when the question arises, be deemed for the purposes of the General Agreement to be the contracting party with which a concession was initially negotiated if it had during a representative period prior to that time a principal supplying interest in the product concerned.[29]

These are known as floating INRs. Floating INRs will be identified in subsequent to the Kennedy round-practice in the same way as PSI countries.

Note however, that because concessions may involve INRs at different levels of customs protection for different WTO Members, identification of INR holders is not always easy. Previously, INR holders were identified in the bilateral agreements deposited with the WTO Secretariat and in various informal working documents. However, this system was imperfect, as historic INRs were not always incorporated into successive schedules of concessions. The WTO membership has undertaken a series of initiatives to reduce uncertainty in this respect. For example, the Council for Trade in Goods (CTG) adopted the Decision on the Establishment of Loose–Leaf Schedules in November 1996 (WTO Doc G/L/138):

> Each Member shall include in its schedule all INRs at the current bound rate. Other Members may request the inclusion of any INR that had been granted to them. Historical INRs different from the current bound rate not specifically identified shall remain valid where a Member modifies its concession at a rate different from the rate at which the INR was granted.

---

[29] Recommendation adopted on 16 November 1967, GATT Doc. BISD 15S/67. Although the term 'recommendation' was privileged, there should be no doubt that this is a Decision by the GATT contracting parties and part of GATT 1994. As Mavroidis (2008) explains, contracting parties used different names when adopting decisions without ever clarifying why this had been the case. What mattered is whether they would in practice conform to whatever they had decided and this is what happened in this case as well.

The situation has further improved with the finalization of the Consolidated Tariff Schedules (CTS) Database, which provides consolidated information on the schedules of concessions of members.

PSI Countries: There are two definitions of a PSI. First, the Interpretative Note ad Art. XXVIII GATT defines a PSI as a member which:

> has had, over a reasonable period of time prior to the negotiations, a *larger share in the market of the applicant contracting party* than a contracting party with which the concession was initially negotiated or would, in the judgment of the CONTRACTING PARTIES, have had such a share in the absence of discriminatory quantitative restrictions by the applicant contracting party. (emphasis added)

Second, the same Interpretative Note ad Art XXVIII GATT provides a second (exceptional) definition of the term:

> the CONTRACTING PARTIES may exceptionally determine that a contracting party has a principal supplying interest if the concession in question affects trade which constitutes *a major part of the local exports of such contracting party*. (emphasis added)

During the Uruguay Round negotiations, an Understanding on the Interpretation of Art. XXVIII GATT was adopted which, *inter alia*, defines PSIs in § 1[30]:

> For the purposes of modification or withdrawal of a concession, the WTO member which has *the highest ratio of exports affected by the concession* (i.e., exports of the product to the market of the Member modifying or withdrawing the concession) to its total exports shall be deemed to have a principal supplying interest *if it does not already have an initial negotiating right or a principal supplying interest as provided for in paragraph 1 of Article XXVIII*. (emphasis added)

The rationale for including PSIs in the negotiation is explained in the Interpretative Note ad Art. XXVIII of the GATT which relevantly provides:

> The object of providing for the participation in the negotiation of any contracting party with a principal supplying interest, in addition to any contracting party with which the concession was

---

[30] The Understanding made clear that this clause would be reviewed within 5 years in order to check whether it has functioned in satisfactory manner or, whether it would have to be amended "with a view to deciding whether this criterion has worked satisfactorily in securing a redistribution of negotiating rights in favour of small and medium-sized exporting Members." No use of this possibility was made between 1995 and 2000. In early 2000, the WTO Committee on Market Access undertook a review in which it reported no basis to change the criterion. WTO Doc G/MA/111.

originally negotiated, is to ensure that a contracting party with a larger share in the trade affected by the concession than a contracting party with which the concession was originally negotiated shall have an effective opportunity to protect the contractual right which it enjoys under this Agreement.

The same document adds that:

It would . . . not be appropriate for the CONTRACTING PARTIES to determine that more than one contracting party, or in those exceptional cases where there is near equality more than two contracting parties, had a principal supplying interest.

Essentially, then, PSIs are the WTO Members that will suffer most from the change in tariffs.

Art. XXVIII GATT therefore aims to strike a balance between the old and the new market situation in terms of which WTO Members participate in the tariff renegotiations: The inclusion of INRs is justified on the grounds that historically, at least they had a strong export interest in this particular market. PSIs take a seat around the table because given the new market situation, they will be the ones who will suffer the larger damage are those who will be participating in the negotiated settlement. To what extent a balance of this sort should be maintained is open to discussion. Adoption of horizontal cuts, like the Swiss formula mentioned *supra*, wherein there are no historic INRs, suggest that we are probably moving towards an era where it is current market situation that matters most.

SI Countries: This term is defined in the Interpretative Note ad Art XXVIII:

The expression 'substantial interest' is not capable of a precise definition and accordingly may present difficulties for the CONTRACTING PARTIES. It is however, intended to be construed to cover only those contracting parties which have, or in the absence of discriminatory quantitative restrictions affecting their exports could reasonably be expected to have a significant share in the market of the contracting party seeking to modify or withdraw the concession.

In practice, WTO Members having a market share of 10% or greater in the market of the WTO Member seeking to renegotiate are deemed to have a substantial interest. A report of the Committee on Tariff Concessions dating from July 1985 confirms that the 10% share has been generally applied for the definition of SI countries.[31] Hence, SIs, unlike PSIs, need not have to have a market share larger than that of INRs in order to claim a right to participate in the negotiation.

---

[31] GATT Doc TAR/M/16.

The Uruguay Round Understanding on the Interpretation of Art XXVIII GATT states in § 3 that MFN trade (to be explained in Chapter 4) should be used as basis for defining PSIs and SIs:

> In the determination of which Members have a principal supplying interest . . . or substantial interest, only trade in the affected product which has taken place on a MFN basis shall be taken into consideration. However, trade in the affected product which has taken place under non-contractual preferences shall also be taken into account if the trade in question has ceased to benefit from such preferential treatment, thus becoming MFN trade, at the time of the negotiation for the modification or withdrawal of the concession, or will do so by the conclusion of that negotiation.

WTO Members that have some form of preferential arrangement with the requesting WTO Member can thus never become PSIs or SIs. In this context, a question arises regarding what do in the case of new products, where no trade statistics are available and thus, it is impossible to measure market shares to define PSIs and SIs. According to he Uruguay round Understanding on the Interpretation of Art. XXVIII GATT (§ 4), in similar cases recourse to other proxies such as production capacity and investment will be made:

> When a tariff concession is modified or withdrawn on a new product (i.e., a product for which three years' trade statistics are not available) the Member possessing initial negotiating rights on the tariff line where the product is or was formerly classified shall be deemed to have an initial negotiating right in the concession in question. The determination of principal supplying and substantial interests and the calculation of compensation shall take into account, *inter alia*, production capacity and investment in the affected product in the exporting Member and estimates of export growth, as well as forecasts of demand for the product in the importing Member. For the purposes of this paragraph, 'new product' is understood to include a tariff item created by means of a breakout from existing tariff line. (italics in the original).

5.2 THE MECHANICS OF THE NEGOTIATION

As mentioned above, only INRs and PSI(s) participate in tariff renegotiations. In exchange for a higher bound tariff rate (or the elimination of one altogether) on a particular product, the WTO Member seeking renegotiation is expected to offer compensation in the form of lower bound tariff rate on products of interest to those most affected by the tariff renegotiation. The INRs and PSIs derive, by virtue of their participation, an advantage since they can, in principle, either acting separately or collectively, identify the commodity (or list of commodities) where compensation will be paid.

Furthermore, there should be equivalence between the damage suffered because of the modification, and the compensation offered. Art XXVIII.2 GATT reads:

> In such negotiations and agreement, which may include provision for compensatory adjustment with respect to other products, the contracting parties concerned shall endeavour to maintain a general level of reciprocal and mutually advantageous concessions not less favourable to trade than that provided for in this Agreement prior to such negotiations.

The Interpretative Note ad Art XXVIII of the GATT adds (§ 4.6):

> It is not intended that provision for participation in the negotiations of any contracting party with a principal supplying interest, and for consultation with any contracting party having a substantial interest in the concession which the applicant contracting party is seeking to modify or withdraw, should have the effect that it should have to pay compensation or suffer retaliation greater than the withdrawal or modification sought, judged in the light of the conditions of trade at the time of the proposed withdrawal or modification, making allowance for any discriminatory quantitative restrictions maintained by the applicant contracting party.

Art. XXVIII GATT distinguishes between different scenarios under which tariff renegotiations occur. In essence, they depend on the following:

- Whether the WTO Member has reserved the right to renegotiate with respect to the particular tariff line
- Whether the renegotiation is taking place as a result of an initiated requested during a pre-designated period of time, to occur every three years

If the tariff renegotiation does not take place under one of these scenarios, then a WTO Member seeking renegotiation must first obtain approval from the WTO Membership through the Council on Trade in Goods (CTG). A request for authorization must include the elements specified in the Interpretative Note ad Art. XXVIII GATT (§ 4.1):

> Any request for authorization to enter into negotiations shall be accompanied by all relevant statistical and other data. A decision on such request shall be made within thirty days of its submission.

> The time-period within which the negotiation must be completed should be short (60 days), but could be extended. The Interpreta-

tive Note ad Art XXVIII of the GATT relevantly provides in this respect (§ 4.3):

> It is expected that negotiations authorized under paragraph 4 for modification or withdrawal of a single item, or a very small group of items, could normally be brought to a conclusion in sixty days. It is recognized, however, that such a period will be inadequate for cases involving negotiations for the modification or withdrawal of a larger number of items and in such cases, therefore, it would be appropriate for the CONTRACTING PARTIES to prescribe a longer period.

The CTG will determine the identity of the WTO Members that hold INRs as well as those that count as PSIs and SIs.[32] Assuming that, at the end of the renegotiations, a successful agreement has been reached between the participants (i.e., requesting WTO Member, the INRs and PSIs), the requesting WTO Member will notify the WTO of its new schedule of concessions, which will be applied on a non-discriminatory (i.e., MFN) basis.

However, what happens if the tariff renegotiations are unsuccessful? The answer to this question depends on whether or not prior approval was necessary for the tariff renegotiation in the first place. We explore each one of these scenarios below:

5.2.1 No Prior Approval Required

As mentioned above, a tariff renegotiation under Art. XXVIII GATT does not require prior approval if: (a) the requesting WTO Member reserved the right to renegotiate, or (b) the request to initiate a renegotiate is made during a pre-designated time period that recurs every three years. Under such a scenario, if the negotiations to modify the tariff are not successful, the requesting WTO Member can go ahead and unilaterally modify its concessions. If it decides to exercise this option, the WTO Member faces the risk of retaliatory withdrawal of concessions, not only from the Members participating in the negotiation, but from other WTO Members as well. Art. XXVIII.3 GATT(a) and (b) relevantly reads in this respect:

> If agreement between the contracting parties primarily concerned cannot be reached before 1 January 1958 or before the expiration of a period envisaged in paragraph 1 of this Article, the contracting party which proposes to modify or withdraw the concession shall, nevertheless, be free to do so and if such action is taken any contracting party with which such concession was initially negotiated, any contracting party determined under

---

[32] Art. XXVIII GATT states that it is the CONTRACTING PARTIES that will be entrusted with this task. However, following the advent of the WTO, this task has been entrusted to the CTG.

paragraph 1 to have a principal supplying interest and any contracting party determined under paragraph 1 to have a substantial interest shall then be free not later than six months after such action is taken, to withdraw, upon the expiration of thirty days from the day on which written notice of such withdrawal is received by the CONTRACTING PARTIES, substantially equivalent concessions initially negotiated with the applicant contracting party.

If agreement between the contracting parties primarily concerned is reached but any other contracting party determined under paragraph 1 of this Article to have a substantial interest is not satisfied, such other contracting party shall be free, not later than six months after action under such agreement is taken, to withdraw, upon the expiration of thirty days from the day on which written notice of such withdrawal is received by the CONTRACTING PARTIES, substantially equivalent concessions initially negotiated with the applicant contracting party.

This paragraph suggests that two categories of WTO Members can react when a WTO Member has decided unilaterally to modify its tariff concession following a negotiation in which prior approval was not necessary: (1) the participants in the negotiations (PSIs and INRs), and (2) the SIs, with the proviso that the retaliatory measures be taken on goods initially negotiated with the requesting WTO Member. The provision is nonetheless somewhat incomplete, and the following questions might legitimately arise:

(a) What if PSIs and SIs have no concessions initially negotiated with the requesting WTO Member? Should they lose their right to retaliate?

(b) Should the retaliation by PSIs and SIs be applied on a bilateral or multilateral basis? In other words, should the retaliatory tariffs be applied only vis-à-vis the requesting WTO Member with whom it was not conclude a successful negotiation? Or should the retaliatory tariffs be applied across the board, vis-à-vis the entire WTO Membership?

(c) What about other WTO Members, besides the INRs, PSIs or SIs, that are also affected by the unilateral modification of the concession? Should they not be entitled to react?

With the expansion in the number of WTO Members, it is nowadays increasingly likely that a INR, PSI, or SI will not have initially negotiated concessions with the requesting WTO Member. Practice suggests that retaliating WTO Members actually select the goods on which they intend to increase tariffs in retaliation, without regard to whether they have initially negotiated concessions on these goods with the applicant state.[33] Although such practice runs counter the explicit wording of Art. XXVIII GATT, there have been no formal challenge to it as of yet. Practice suggests that this condition has, *de facto*, been relaxed.

There are at least two instances in practice where the WTO Member reacting to a unilateral modification has threatened to withdraw concessions (i.e., apply higher retaliatory tariff rates) against not only the WTO Member modifying its tariffs unilaterally, but also across-the-board against all WTO Members. In the case of *Canada/EC–Article XXVIII Rights*, following a unilateral modification made by the EU, Canada threatened to apply the retaliatory tariffs on a multilateral basis and not just bilaterally vis-à-vis the EU. The Arbitrator noted that had Canada followed through on this threat, Canada would need to undertake "obligations to compensate third countries" that themselves have negotiating rights with respect to the products on which the retaliatory tariffs were being applied multilaterally.[34] The other instance where such a threat was made was in the instance of tariff modifications that needed to take place in light of the enlargement of EU membership from 12 to 15 countries.[35] Canada thought that the compensation offered for tariff modifications made during this process was inadequate and again threatened to apply the retaliatory tariffs on a multilateral basis.[36] Ultimately, an agreement was reached between the EU and Canada, whereby Canada was sufficiently satisfied with the concessions offered.[37] Canada's practice suggests that, for some WTO Members at least, retaliation against the whole Membership as response to unilateral modifications is very much in the cards.

What about the rights of WTO Members which do not belong to any of the two categories envisaged in Art. XXVIII.3 GATT? The current text does not explicitly acknowledge that they have a legal right to retaliate under this provision. On the other hand, they will, in all likelihood, be affected by a modification of the schedule, irrespective of whether an agreement between the primarily concerned parties has been reached, or not. What can be done if such an occasion arises? The most reasonable way out would be to acknowledge to such WTO Members the right to take a non-violation complaint (NVC) against the requesting WTO Member.[38]

---

[33] Such goods are known in WTO parlance as "products of interest." See, e.g., WTO Docs. G/SECRET/1 of March 1, 1995 (Canada reacting to EU enlargement); G/SECRET/18/Add. 1 of January 2005 (US reacting to EU enlargement); G/SECRET/20/Add. 3 of July 3, 2006 (Colombia reacting to EU withdrawal of concessions).

[34] GATT Analytical Index, p. 947.

[35] We will discuss in greater detail in Chapter 5 how compensation is required in instances where a Member joins a customs union (such as the EU) and needs to modify certain tariff lines in order to harmonize its tariff schedule with that of the customs union.

[36] WTO Doc G/SECRET/1 of March 1, 1995.

[37] WTO Docs G/SECRET/1 Add. 1 of March 7, 1995, and Add. 2 of February 5, 1998.

[38] According to case law, for an NVC to be successfully launched, the following must be cumulatively met: (a) a concession must have been negotiated; (b) a subsequent action has occurred

This solution seems warranted, in light of the explicit acknowledgement in Art. XXVIII.3 GATT, that the applicant WTO Member has the right to unilaterally modify its schedule of concessions, *even* in the absence of agreed compensation; hence, such behaviour cannot be deemed to be illegal.

5.2.2 Prior Approval Required

The process that follows in the event of an unsuccessful tariff renegotiation that requires prior CTG approval is different. In this case, according to Art. XXVIII.4 GATT:

> the applicant contracting party shall be free to modify or withdraw the concession, unless the CONTRACTING PARTIES determine that the applicant contracting party has unreasonably failed to offer adequate compensation.

Hence, under this scenario, the requesting WTO Member that failed to reach an agreement with the INRs and PSIs is allowed first to make a proposal for compensation, instead of being subject to whatever retaliatory tariffs the INRs, PSIs, and SIs choose to impose. This proposal is then reviewed by the CTG who will determine whether the proposed compensation is adequate. The Interpretative Note ad Art. XXVIII GATT states that the CTG must decide within thirty days from the submission of the matter before it, unless the applicant Member agrees to a longer period (§ 4.4). The Interpretative Note ad Art. XXVIII GATT further provides some useful information as to the elements that the CTG should take into account, when determining whether adequate compensation had indeed been offered (§ 4.5):

> In determining under paragraph 4 *(d)* whether an applicant contracting party has unreasonably failed to offer adequate compensation, it is understood that the CONTRACTING PARTIES will take due account of the special position of a contracting party which has bound a high proportion of its tariffs at very low rates of duty and to this extent has less scope than other contracting parties to make compensatory adjustment.

If the CTG determines that adequate compensation has indeed been offered, the modified tariff concessions will be allowed to stand.

What if the CTG determines that the compensation is inadequate, but the requesting WTO Member goes ahead and unilaterally modifies the desired tariff line anyways? In this case, INRs, PSIs, and SIs have the

---

which (c) could not have been reasonably anticipated by the affected WTO Members, and which (d) reduces the value of the tariff concession. Case law (*Japan–Film*) has clarified that it is the complainant that must show (c) above if the action occurs before the negotiation of the concession, whereas the burden shifts to the defendant in the opposite case. We discuss NVCs in detail in Chapter 46.

right to suspend substantially equivalent concessions (Art. XXVIII.4 GATT):

> If such action is taken, any contracting party with which the concession was initially negotiated, any contracting party determined under paragraph 4 (*a*) to have a principal supplying interest and any contracting party determined under paragraph 4 (*a*) to have a substantial interest, shall be free, not later than six months after such action is taken, to modify or withdraw, upon the expiration of thirty days from the day on which written notice of such withdrawal is received by the CONTRACTING PARTIES, substantially equivalent concessions initially negotiated with applicant contracting party.

Thus, the main difference between the two scenarios is that the latter envisions a more active role to be played by the CTG in evaluating the proposed concessions before retaliatory tariffs are legally authorized.

Questions and Comments

Why Tariff Ceilings and Not Rigid Tariffs? A ceiling is preferable to a rigid tariff because it allows for "downward flexibility" to preference shocks and permits efficiency enhancing tariff reductions. Maggi and Rodriguez–Clare (2007) explain that, from a political economy perspective, tariff ceilings and exact tariff commitments have very different implications: whereas when exact tariff commitments are being negotiated, lobbying effectively ends at the time of the agreement (since the agreement leaves no discretion for governments to choose tariffs in the future), when tariff ceilings are being negotiated, governments retain the option of setting tariffs below their maximum levels, and thus, they might be inviting lobbying and contributions after the agreement has been signed. Governments thus, might have a strong incentive to opt for ceilings rather than rigid commitments.

Reciprocity: Negotiations on tariff liberalization are based on reciprocal commitments. In the words of Eric Wyndham–White, one time DG of the GATT, speaking during the Torquay round:

> ... a number of European countries with a comparatively low level of tariff rates considered that they had entered the Torquay negotiations at a disadvantage. Having bound many of their rates of duty in 1947 and 1949, what could these low tariff countries offer at Torquay in order to obtain further concessions from the countries with higher level of tariffs?[39]

Reciprocity is often referred to as a GATT legal principle.[40] It does not, however, relieve WTO Members of their duty to observe the contract simply

---

[39] ICITO, 1952 at p. 9.

[40] On the role of reciprocity in the original negotiation of the GATT, see E/PC/T/33, Annexure 10.

because another WTO Member has failed to do so: if A violates the contract, B cannot, by invoking *non adimpleti contractus* unilaterally stop honoring its own commitments. B can, at most, challenge A's practices before the WTO adjudicating bodies, and A will, if found guilty, have to implement the rulings. In the meantime B will have to continue observing the contract. Only when A refuses to implement any multilateral adjudicatory decision can B request authorization to stop honoring its own commitments.

GATT Success in Reducing Tariff Protection: Tariff reduction is hailed as one of the biggest successes of the multilateral trading system, even though, as Irwin (1995), (1996), (1998a), and (1998b) has persuasively argued, the size of the success has probably been exaggerated: In his view, average duties across all goods calculated on dutiable imports stood at 19.34% in 1947 and 13.87% in 1948. However, were one to include duty free trade, the ration of duties collected to total imports amounted to 7.55% in 1947 and 5.71% in 1948. The average tariffs on dutiable imports (weighted with the 1939 trade values) in 1947 was 32.2% and 25.4% in 1948. As 60% of US imports were duty free in 1947, the average tariff for total imports was much lower. In addition, were tariff averages to be weighted with the 1947 trade weights (and prices and not with 1939 values) then the post-Geneva average tariff on dutiable imports drops from 25.4% to 15%. Including duty free imports, the pre-Annecy (GATT 1948) tariff average of all US imports was estimated by the US Tariff Commission to amount to 5.9%. This number fits unusually well with the ration of duties calculated to total imports (free and dutiable) of 5.97% in 1950.

Who Lowers Duties Most? Tariff reductions have been asymmetric in the sense that big important markets exhibit the highest number of bindings as well as the lowest level of bound tariffs.[41] During the Uruguay Round, LDCs for the first time agreed to bind many of their duties; Diakantoni and Eskaith (2009) note though, that, with respect to commitments entered by LDCs during the Uruguay round, their bound rate is higher than their applied rate.[42]

History of HS: The HS Convention originates in the Geneva Nomenclature (GN), which came into being on July 1, 1937. The GN was replaced by the Brussels Convention on Nomenclature for the Classification of Goods in Customs Tariffs (BTN) in 1959, and the BTN was, in turn, replaced in 1974

---

[41] It is almost always the case that developing countries exhibit nowadays (with few exceptions) higher tariffs than developed countries. Some researchers have cast doubt to the idea that high tariffs are universally detrimental to growth, arguing that policy prescriptions (such as low tariffs) designed to promote growth within developed economies may not be appropriate for universal adoption, see on this score, Rodriguez and Rodrik (2001), and more recently, de Jong and Ripoli (2006) who use a panel data set comprising 60 countries and spanning 1975–2000.

[42] That is, the binding of their duties did not generate any trade liberalization. It simply removed the possibility for tariff volatility above the bound level. The WTO webpage refers to the fact that all WTO Members increased their absolute number of tariff bindings: In percentage terms (out of 100 total tariff bindings), developed countries moved from 78 (pre-Uruguay round) to 99% (following the successful conclusion of the Uruguay round), developing, from 21 to 73%, and economies in transition, from 73 to 98%. The insight in Diakantoni and Eskaith (2009) is that these numbers might simply correspond to crystallization of prior practice, and sometimes even less than that.

by the Customs Cooperation Council Nomenclature (CCCN) in 1974 which was eventually replaced by the HS in 1988. The HS has been amended five times since 1988 (largely in order to account for changes in the technology): 1992, 1996, 2002, 2007, and 2011 (the last one will enter into force in 2012). The WTO Committee on Tariff Concessions established simplified procedures to implement these changes and any future changes in the HS relating to GATT concessions.[43] The HS is administered by the HS Committee, which is composed of representatives from each HS contracting party.

Dispute Settlement before the HS Committee: The language used in the various nomenclatures is quite generic in light of the fact that the intention was to subsume a large number of transactions into each one of them. As a result, disputes may arise as to the appropriate classification of a particular transaction. Art. 10 HS reflects the dispute settlement provisions available to its signatories. Disputes will be submitted to the HS Committee which will consider the dispute and make recommendations to the parties. The HS Committee will base its decision on the text of the HS Convention, but also, on the General Interpretative Rules (GIR) that it has adopted over the years, as well as, their Explanatory Notes. GIR 1, for example, subjects classification according to the terms of a heading, whereas GIR 3(a) stipulates that the heading which provides the most specific description shall be preferred to headings providing a more general description. There are specific GIRs for composite goods.[44]

How to Interpret GATT Schedules: Van Damme (2007) has argued that, although schedules of commitments are undeniably treaty language (and, consequently, it is only appropriate that the starting-point of interpretation is the VCLT) some adjustments are in order, in light of their special characteristics. She imports notions of public international law paying attention to the negotiating record that will help the WTO judge to develop future case-law in this field in coherent manner. She is probably right in that adjustments (in the sense of placing some additional weight to the negotiating record) are warranted in this context. As it stands, the VCLT does not include a coefficient for each of the elements reflected in Arts. 31–32 VCLT: we know that recourse to preparatory work is optional (hence, Art. 32 VCLT plays second fiddle to the elements included in Art. 31 VCLT), and we also know that a conscious attempt was made during the negotiation of the VCLT to downplay the importance of object and treaty, see Jimenez de Arréchaga (1978). The remaining elements of Art. 31 VCLT (text, context, subsequent treaty/practice, other relevant of public international law) are, *prima facie* at par, although good arguments can be made in favour of contextual interpretations: words are not a-contextual, and context (not only the 'historic' context) is informative of the rationale for signing a particular agreement.

ITA Disputes: The ITA has given rise to disputes regarding classification of products coming under its purview. This is probably due to the fact that it suffers from a birth defect: when concluded, its product coverage was

---

[43] GATT Doc. BISD 39S/300.
[44] GIR 3(b).

reflected in two attachments, only one of which contained HS numbers. The first, Attachment A, did include HS numbers, and was divided into two Sections: Section 1 dealt with specific products, the tariff classification of which was undisputed; Section 2 dealt with machinery necessary to produce specific products and contained some items which were to be handled in the same manner as the goods featured in Attachment B. The second, the notorious Attachment B included product descriptions where the tariff classification was disputed by the WTO Members. There were for example entries such as 'network equipment', or 'flat panel displays', or 'multimedia upgrade kits'. Such entries were prone to creating divergence of views across participants as to what precisely was covered. To make matters worse, technology moves faster than the relevant WCO Committee meets and adds new products to the existing HS list. Signatories to the ITA agreed to meet periodically in order to specify and update the coverage of the ITA, and ideally make unanimous suggestions to the WCO Committee.[45]

The *LAN* dispute (*EC—Computer Equipment*) quoted briefly above, between the US and the EU involved a disagreement between the two parties as to the proper classification of certain computer equipment. The products concerned were computers and network equipment. Computers are defined in the ITA as automatic data processing machines capable of storing the processing program or programs and at least the data immediately necessary for the execution of the program; being freely programmed in accordance with the requirements of the user; performing arithmetical computations specified by the user; and executing, without human intervention, a processing program which requires them to modify their execution, by logical decision during the processing run. The agreement covers such automatic data processing machines whether or not they are able to receive and process with the assistance of central processing unit telephony signals, television signals, or other analogue or digitally processed audio or video signals. Machines performing a specific function other than data processing, or incorporating or working in conjunction with an automatic data processing machine, and not otherwise specified under Attachment A or B, are not covered by this agreement. Network equipment is defined as Local Area Network (LAN) and Wide Area Network (WAN) apparatus, including those products dedicated for use solely or principally to permit the interconnection of automatic data processing machines and units thereof for a network that is used primarily for the sharing of resources such as central processor units, data storage devices and input or output units—including adapters, hubs, in-line repeaters, converters, concentrators, bridges and routers, and printed circuit assemblies for physical incorporation into automatic data processing machines and units thereof. One can immediately understand that a number of products can either totally or partially come under this definition. The classification issue is with respect to the latter category. Neither the Panel nor the AB decisively addressed the main issue at dispute and the final outcome could be described as 'pyrrhic'

---

[45] WTO Doc. WT/MIN(96)/16 of December 13, 1996; WTO Doc. G/L/160 of April 2, 1997. In EC–IT Products, the Panel held that the ITA was legal context to scheduling of concessions (§§ 7.304, and 384).

victory for the US, in the sense that practice by EU was not decisive for the classification of the goods concerned.

In *EC–IT Products*, the Panel dealt with a challenge against the EU classification of three goods that, in the complainants' opinion, were ITA goods that should have been benefiting from a tariff free-entry, as opposed to the 14% duty that the EU was levying on what it deemed to be consumer goods.[46] The Panel did not accept the EU view that the products were totally new and requested that the EU take corrective action. The Panel decided that if the disputed goods could come under one of the product descriptions already included in Attachment B, then the good would enjoy zero tariff treatment, but if not, then it would be subjected to the tariff treatment provided for in the national (EU member state) schedule.

Invocation of Art. XXVII GATT: The Table below provides a list of instances where a GATT Member withdrew concessions, pursuant to Art. XXVII GATT:

Table 3.1 Withdrawal of Concessions under Art. XXVII GATT

Concessions Granted by	Initially Negotiated with	Reference
Australia	China, Syria/Lebanon, Philippines	L/1266
Benelux: Section A—Metropolitan Territories	China, Syria/Lebanon, Liberia, Philippines	L/674
Benelux: Section C—Netherlands New Guinea	China	L/658 and Add.1
Canada	China, Liberia, Philippines, Korea	L/553
Ceylon	China	L/1102, L/1505
Chile	Colombia	L/3191
Czechoslovakia	Palestine	GATT/CP/23
Finland	China	L/659
France	China, Syria/Lebanon, Philippines	L/460 and L/1269

---

[46] This is what also happened in the *EC–Computer Equipment (LAN)* dispute: a new product appeared in the market and the various EU member states adopted different tariff policies, until the issue was resolved either through intervention of the EU Commission, or through the WTO's adjudicatory body. The latter is, of course, a substantially longer process and political economy might push resolution toward one or the other direction.

Concessions Granted by	Initially Negotiated with	Reference
Germany, Fed Rep	Philippines	L/1264
India	China, Colombia, Philippines	G/77 and L/1430
Pakistan	China	L/1293
Sweden	Colombia, Philippines, China	L/950
United Kingdom	China	L/786
United States	China	GATT/CP/115 and Add.3
Uruguay	China, Colombia	L/1613

CHAPTER 4

MOST FAVORED NATION (MFN)

■ ■ ■

1. THE LEGAL DISCIPLINE

The principle of most favored nation (MFN) treatment is one of the core principles underlying the trade regime: WTO Members must accord automatically and unconditionally to all WTO Members any trade advantage they have accorded to another nation, irrespective whether the latter is WTO Member or not.

Certain exceptions to the MFN principle are allowed under WTO law: For example, a WTO Member may give preferential treatment to those with whom it has a free trade agreement or customs union. It may also give market access preferences to certain developing countries. In addition, the MFN principle does not bar a WTO Member from taking action against products considered to be traded unfairly, as explained in the covered agreements, from a particular country. Finally, a WTO Member may seek an explicit waiver. We will mention the exceptions to MFN in brief in this Chapter and discuss a number of them in greater depth in subsequent Chapters.

2. THE RATIONALE FOR THE LEGAL DISCIPLINE

The commonplace explanation for MFN is that negotiators have a joint interest in avoiding concession diversion (or concession erosion, as it is often referred to): The value to A of a concession negotiated between A and B, risks being eroded through subsequent negotiation between B and C, assuming B has "conceded" to C more than it did to A.[1] A requirement of MFN treatment is the insurance policy against similar behaviour. Whatever B subsequently offers to another country beyond what it has given to A must then be extended to A, and vice versa. Without it, both A and B might be tempted to withhold certain concessions during the initial round of negotiations, so that it has something left to bargain after the subsequent concessions are made to other parties. The outcome of trade negotiations would be sub-optimal, as each side worries about concession diversion. With a MFN requirement in place, such worries disappear, and both A and B will have greater incentives to negotiate and liberalize trade beyond that which they would be willing to do without MFN.

---

[1] See on this score, Schwarz and Sykes (1998).

The negotiating record further reveals that US negotiators pushed hard for the post-war trade regime to be constructed in a non-discriminatory manner.[2] US negotiators were clear in their mind that preferential trade (e.g., the UK's imperial preferences to its colonies) should be eliminated. In Secretary Hull's mind, MFN was the US contribution to world peace.[3] As the ascendant power during the post-war years, the US could have extracted a better deal had it chosen to negotiate with its trading partners one-by-one on a reciprocal basis. But it recognized that by requiring MFN treatment, the trading order that it was seeking to construct would be built on a more solid foundation.[4]

3. COVERAGE OF THE LEGAL DISCIPLINE

3.1 THE REQUIREMENT OF ART. I.1 GATT

With respect to three categories of trade measures, Art I.1 GATT requires that:

> any advantage, favour, privilege or immunity granted by any contracting party to any product originating in or destined for any other country shall be accorded immediately and unconditionally to the like product originating in or destined for the territories of all other contracting parties.

The three categories of trade measures covered by this provision are:

(a) customs duties and charges of any kind imposed on or in connection with importation and exportation[5];

(b) rules and formalities in connection with importation and exportation;

(c) internal measures.

In what follows, we will discuss the meaning of certain terms employed within the core obligation of Art. I.1 GATT, as clarified through the jurisprudence. We will also turn to questions of how a WTO Member is to decide the country of origin for a given product as well as whether the MFN principle applies if the trade advantage is given to a country outside of the WTO.

---

[2] Wilcox (1949); Irwin et al. (2008).

[3] Hull (1948).

[4] Although definitely a secondary order-concern, one should not forget that MFN simplifies both customs procedures as well as the negotiation itself. The administration of discriminatory tariffs is costly because of the need to keep track of product origin; MFN significantly simplifies customs procedures. MFN also reduces the cost and complexity of negotiations by reducing the number of possible bids and outcomes.

[5] Also included are the methods of levying and collecting such duties and charges.

3.2 ANY ADVANTAGE, FAVOR, PRIVILEGE OR IMMUNITY

The wording chosen suggests that the intention of the drafters was to cast the net wide rather than narrowly. Case law has confirmed this much. Some examples include:

- In *US–Customs User Fee*, the WTO Panel that the term "customs duties and charges of any kind" covers not only transactions coming under the purview of Art. II, but also under Art. VIII GATT (i.e., "fees and formalities connected with importation and exporation").
- In *Spain–Unroasted Coffee*, a GATT Panel clarified that the MFN clause is equally applicable to both bound and to unbound customs duties (§ 4.3).
- In *EC–Poultry*, the AB confirmed prior case law (*EC–Bananas III*, § 207) that the MFN clause also covers tariff quotas, even though it is not explicitly mentioned in the body of Art. I GATT (§§ 96ff.). Note that a tariff quota[6] is a tariff structure in which a given tariff rate is applied on a fixed quota of goods and once this quota is exceeded, a higher tariff rate then applies.[7]

One of the categories of trade measures to which Art. I GATT applies is "rules and formalities in connection with importation and exportation." The meaning of this term, and the related question of what types of advantages might result from a given rule or formality is hardly self-interpreting. The GATT explicitly mentions one formality; Art IX GATT deals with marks of origin, and imposes the obligation that marks of origin be applied on an MFN basis. Case law has identified a number of other rules and formalities that come under the purview of Art. I GATT. In *EC—Bananas III*, the Panel found that the following measures were all advantages with respect to rules and formalities:

(a) The use of a less complicated licensing procedure (§§ 7.188ff.);[8]

(b) The incentive given to operators to purchase bananas of a particular origin (§ 7.194);

(c) The issuance of a license to import bananas of a particular origin upon the economic activity performed by the economic operator requesting the license (§§ 7.220ff.);

(d) The granting of licenses to operators representing producers from certain countries only (§§ 7.251ff.); and

---

[6] This is also sometimes referred to as a tariff rate quota.

[7] The unadopted Panel report in *EC–Bananas III* made clear that a tariff quota is not a quota and therefore not a QR. Only the tariff rate changes beyond a certain fixed quota, but there is no restriction on the quantity of the good that may be imported.

[8] Through its express wording, Art I.1 GATT states that the MFN clause does not extend only to duties and charges as such, but also to the methods of levying them.

(e) The imposition on certain bananas of the in-quota tariff rate provided that they originate in particular countries (§§ 7.235ff.)

These findings were confirmed by the AB (§§ 206ff.).[9]

Art I.1 GATT makes it clear that, by virtue of the explicit reference to Art. III.2 and III.4 GATT, MFN covers internal (e.g., behind the border, as opposed to border) measures as well. It was the GATT Panel in *Belgium–Family Allowances* that first found that internal tax exemptions for products purchased by public bodies were covered by Art. I.1 GATT. The Panel report on *EC—Bananas III* confirmed this holding (§ 7.239).

The MFN obligation extends to not only actions but also omissions, to the extent that an omission confers an advantage are covered by the discipline laid down in Art. I.1 GATT. The GATT Panel in *US–Customs User Fee* held that an exemption from the imposition of a customs fee should be considered to be an advantage in the sense of Art. I.1 GATT.[10]

In *Canada–Autos*, the AB held that both *de jure* as well as *de facto* discrimination are covered by the prohibition included in Art. I.1 GATT. Consequently, the scope of Art. I GATT is not limited to measures that are facially discriminatory (e.g., a law whereby an advantage is granted by using the origin of the good as an explicit criterion for its conferral). It also includes measures which on their face are origin-neutral, but discriminate in a *de facto*r manner in favor of particular sources of supply (§ 78):

> In approaching this question, we observe first that the words of Article I:1 do not restrict its scope only to cases in which the failure to accord an 'advantage' to like products of all other Members appears *on the face* of the measure, or can be demonstrated on the basis of the words of the measure. Neither the words '*de jure*' nor '*de facto*' appear in Article I:1. Nevertheless, we observe that Article I:1 does not cover only 'in law', or *de jure*, discrimination. As several GATT panel reports confirmed, Article I:1 covers also 'in fact', or *de facto*, discrimination. Like the Panel, we cannot accept Canada's argument that Article I:1 does not apply to measures which, on their face, are 'origin-neutral.' (italics in the original)

---

[9] In this context, the GATT Panel in *US–MFN Footwear* found that the automatic backdating of the revocation of a countervailing duty order without the need to have an injury review conducted in this respect is an advantage with respect to customs formalities in the sense of Art. I.1 GATT.

[10] §§ 121ff. The Panel did not formally rule on this issue since no claim had been made to this effect before it and, consequently, any ruling would be *ultra petita*. Still in § 123 of its report it left no doubt that it considered that exemptions as well could come under the purview of Art. I GATT.

3.3 A WTO MEMBER MAY NOT TREAT A NON–WTO MEMBER BETTER THAN THE WTO MEMBERS

Note that Art. I.1 GATT refers to

> any advantage, favour, privilege or immunity granted by any contracting party to any product originating in or destined for *any other country*. (emphasis added).

As a result, WTO Members cannot treat outsiders (non-WTO Members) better than they treat insiders (WTO Members). Although this provision refers to "country", there should be no doubt that it covers customs territories as well.[11]

3.4 THE ORIGIN OF GOODS

WTO Members have to extend any advantage granted to a product originating in one WTO Member, to all like goods originating in all other WTO Members. How are WTO Members to decide from what country a particular good originates? For example, suppose a widget is first manufactured in Country A (a WTO Member) and then tested (or packaged) in Country B (a non-WTO Member) before being shipped for consumption in Country C (a WTO Member). Should Country C consider the widget to be from Country A or B? The question is of relevance because Country C has to grant MFN treatment to a product from A but not B.

WTO law includes an Agreement on Rules of Origin (ROO). However, the ROO does not impose a harmonized set of rules that WTO Members must observe when it comes to conferring origin. WTO Members remain free to adopt their rules of origin, but, by virtue of the MFN principle, they must apply such rules in a non-discriminatory manner. The only reported case so far is the *US–Textiles Rules of Origin*, where the Panel (§§ 6.23–24) underscored the wide discretion that WTO Members enjoy when designing their rules of origin in the following terms:

> With regard to the provisions of Article 2 at issue in this case—subparagraphs (b) through (d)—we note that they set out what rules of origin should not do: rules of origin should not pursue trade objectives directly or indirectly; they should not themselves create restrictive, distorting or disruptive effects on international trade; they should not pose unduly strict requirements or require the fulfilment of a condition unrelated to manufacturing or processing; and they should not discriminate between other Members. These provisions do not prescribe what a Member must do.

---

[11] Recall that, by virtue of Art. XII of the WTO Agreement, a "separate customs territory possessing full autonomy in the conduct of its external commercial relations" can join the WTO. It would be odd to allow customs territories to be WTO Members bound by the MFN and then, thanks to a narrow reading of Art. I.1 GATT, allow them to profit from additional advantages.

By setting out what Members cannot do, these provisions leave for Members themselves discretion to decide what, within those bounds, they can do. In this regard, it is common ground between the parties that Article 2 does not prevent Members from determining the criteria which confer origin, changing those criteria over time, or applying different criteria to different goods.

One of, if not the most important, objective of the ROO is to eventually harmonize non-preferential rules of origin (Art. 9 ROO).[12] This requires work on 5,000 tariff lines. Some progress has been made, but a lot still needs to be done. Until then Art. 2(d) ROO condones regulatory diversity.

WTO Members have employed a variety of methods to confer origin. Some employ added value, where origin is conferred if a certain threshold value has been met. Others confer origin depending on where the last substantial transformation of a given commodity has occurred. To decide whether substantial transformation occurred, countries will have recourse to criteria such as the percentage criterion (where the question is whether a certain percentage of value added has been added), the change in tariff heading (as a result of the transformation),[13] or the so-called technical criterion, which prescribes certain production or sourcing processes that may (positive technical criterion) or may not (negative technical criterion) confer originating status. Some of the rules employed to decide whether substantial transformation has occurred leave substantial discretion to the administering authority and, as a result, disputes arise frequently.[14] Some WTO Members will employ a combination of the above-mentioned methods.

The ROO applies to not only the determination of MFN treatment in Art. 1 but also in other contexts (e.g., application of anti dumping duties and countervailing duties, to be discussed in Chapters 14–15). Just as the MFN principle allows for certain exceptions for preferential treatment, there are also preferential rules of origin. These are the rules used to determine whether a good qualifies for preferential treatment. We will not deal with them extensively in this volume, but we simply note that through Annex II of the ROO, WTO Members have an obligation to notify the WTO of its preferential rules of origin.

3.5 IMMEDIATELY AND UNCONDITIONALLY

WTO Members must extend any advantage, favor, privilege or immunity (as understood above) "immediately and unconditionally" to all other WTO Members. WTO adjudicating bodies will typically review the

---

[12] This is not the first multilateral initiative to this effect. The Kyoto Convention of 1977 pursues the same objective, but has had very little impact so far in WTO practice.

[13] It is usually substantial if the transformation leads to a change in the tariff classification say from one six digit- to another six digit classification.

[14] Some of the most notorious disputes are reported in Vermulst and Waer (1990).

consistency of a measure with the two terms simultaneously.[15] One might think that the meaning of the term "unconditionally" is simple enough: no conditions whatsoever may be attached. However, the term has led to a significant number of cases interpreting its meaning.

A number of cases suggest that a WTO Member may not condition a trade advantage on the exporting party (whether that be a WTO Member or a firm) "giving something in return" that would amount to reciprocity:

- The report of the Working Party on Accession of Hungary[16] noted that to condition a tariff treatment upon the prior acceptance of a cooperation agreement was a violation of Art. I.1 GATT
- In *Indonesia–Autos*, a WTO Panel held that the grant of tax advantages to only companies[17] that had entered into arrangements with Indonesian companies was inconsistent with the obligation under Art I.1 GATT (§§ 14.143ff.);

In addition, case law has suggested that a WTO Member may not condition a trade advantage on another WTO Member's adoption of certain policies:

- In *Belgium–Family Allowances*, whether imported products purchased by public bodies received a tax exemption depended upon whether the exporting country had a certain system of providing financial transfers to families; a GATT Panel found this conditional scheme to be inconsistent with Art I.1 GATT (§ 3);

Similarly, WTO Members may not impose a condition for which only a subset of WTO Members may qualify for the trade advantage.

- In *EEC–Imports of Beef*, a GATT Panel held that a duty waiver scheme conditional upon receipt of certification violated Art. I.1 GATT because the Annex governing this scheme only listed one entity (the US Department of Agriculture) as eligible for providing the certification necessary for obtaining the waiver (§ 4.1);
- In *EC–Tariff Preferences*, the Panel outlawed the EU policy to grant preferences based on prior adoption of a certain policy regarding trafficking of drugs (§ 7.60):

Because the tariff preferences under the Drug Arrangements are accorded only on the condition that the receiving countries are experiencing a certain gravity of drug problems, these tariff preferences are not accorded 'unconditionally' to the like products originating in all other WTO members, as required by Article I:1. The Panel therefore finds that the tariff advantages un-

---

[15] The AB report on Canada—Autos provides a good illustration to this effect (§§ 75–86).
[16] Report adopted on 30 July 1973, see GATT Doc BISD 20S/34.
[17] The companies to whom the advantages were granted were South Korean.

der the Drug Arrangements are not consistent with Article I:1 of GATT 1994.

Nevertheless, some case law has suggested that "unconditionally" does not mean that no conditions can be imposed altogether. This line of jurisprudence asserts that where the condition imposed is non-discriminatory, the measure does not arise to a violation of Art. I.1 GATT:

- In *EEC–Minimum Import Prices*, the EU authorities required a payment deposit from all countries that could not guarantee a specified minimum import price. However, because the payment of the deposit was requested by all exporting countries falling into this category, the GATT Panel ruled that the EC scheme was not considered to be a violation of Art. I.1 GATT;
- In *Canada–Autos,* a Panel held the view that the term 'unconditionally' refers to the notion that MFN treatment towards another WTO Member shall not be conditional on reciprocal conduct by that other WTO Member (§§ 10.22 and 10.24):

In our view, whether an advantage within the meaning of Article I:1 is accorded 'unconditionally' cannot be determined independently of an examination of whether it involves discrimination between like products of different countries.

. . .

In this respect, it appears to us that there is an important distinction to be made between, on the one hand, the issue of whether an advantage within the meaning of Article I:1 is subject to conditions, and, on the other, whether an advantage, once it has been granted to the product of any country, is accorded 'unconditionally' to the like product of all other Members. An advantage can be granted subject to conditions without necessarily implying that it is not accorded 'unconditionally' to the like product of other Members. More specifically, the fact that conditions attached to such an advantage are not related to the imported product itself does not necessarily imply that such conditions are discriminatory with respect to the origin of imported products. We therefore do not believe that, as argued by Japan, the word 'unconditionally' in Article I:1 must be interpreted to mean that making an advantage conditional on criteria not related to the imported product itself is *per se* inconsistent with Article I:1, irrespective of whether and how such criteria relate to the origin of the imported products.

Finally, conditional trade rebalancing schemes are not allowed. At issue in *US–Non–Rubber Footwear* was a US practice in which the US provided more favorable treatment to certain imports in order to offset the damage done to the same imports with respect to measures affecting them. The Panel held that a rebalancing scheme, whereby receipt of an advantage is conditional upon a certain disadvantage, violate Art. I GATT (§§ 6.10ff).

3.6 NON–DISCRIMINATION WITH RESPECT TO "LIKE PRODUCTS"

As noted above, Art. I GATT covers behaviour with respect to a number of trade-related measures, including internal measures (i.e., domestic instruments). We will be dealing with internal measures in Chapter 8, and simply note here that the term "like product" has been interpreted through an extensive jurisprudence in that context. We limit our commentary here to a discussion of the meaning of the term "like product" with respect to the other types of measures covered under Art. I GATT (i.e., tariff measures).

In this context, the dominant criterion that has emerged in case law as determinative of whether a good is a "like product" is its tariff classification.[18] In *EEC–Animal Feed Proteins*, a GATT Panel turned to this criterion to decide whether two goods were "like": The GATT Panel on *Japan–SPF Dimension Lumber* went further, explicitly acknowledging tariff classification as the dominant criterion for establishing likeness (§§ 5.11–12):

> ... if a claim of likeness was raised by a contracting party in relation to the tariff treatment of its goods on importation by some other contracting party, such a claim should be based on the classification of the latter, i.e., the importing country's tariff.
>
> The Panel noted in this respect that 'dimension lumber' as defined by Canada was a concept extraneous to the Japanese Tariff ... nor did it belong to any internationally accepted customs classification. The Panel concluded therefore that reliance by Canada on the concept of dimension lumber was not an appropriate basis for establishing 'likeness' of products under Article I:1 of the General Agreement.

GATT Panels have even gone so far as to dismiss the relevance of factors other than tariff classification. In *Spain–Unroasted Coffee*, for example, a Panel set aside the relevance of process-based distinctions in defining likeness (§§ 4.7–4.10):

> The Panel examined all arguments that had been advanced during the proceedings for the justification of a different tariff treatment for various groups and types of un-roasted coffee. It noted that these arguments mainly related to organoleptic differences resulting from geographical factors, cultivation meth-

---

[18] See on this issue the comprehensive analysis of Davey and Pauwelyn (2000).

ods, the processing of the beans, and the genetic factor. The Panel did not consider that such differences were sufficient reason to allow for a different treatment. It pointed out that it was not unusual in the case of agricultural products that the taste and aroma of the end-product would differ because of one or several of the above-mentioned factors.

The Panel furthermore found relevant to its examination of the matter that un-roasted coffee was mainly, if not exclusively, sold in the form of blends, combining various types of coffee, and that coffee in its end-use, was universally regarded as a well-defined and single product intended for drinking.

The Panel noted that no other contracting party applied its tariff regime in respect of un-roasted, non-decaffeinated coffee in such a way that different types of coffee were subject to different tariff rates.

In light of the foregoing, the Panel *concluded* that un-roasted, non-decaffeinated coffee beans listed in the Spanish Customs Tariff . . . should be considered as like products within the meaning of Article I:1. (original emphasis)

Note, however, in today's world, distinctions like the one in *Spain–Unroasted Coffee* could well be part of a national schedule of commitments. Recall that the HS extends up to the six-digit level, but WTO Members can shape their tariff bindings using eight and more-digit classifications. Although the HS at the six-digit level may not differentiate between unroasted and roasted coffee, countries can do so at the eight-digit level, provided they specify a six-digit classification for coffee generally. Yet, it is not clear that differences beyond the six-digit level are relevant for determining likeness; to date, no Panel has pronounced this to be the case.

4. EXCEPTIONS

There are numerous exceptions to the MFN clause. Among them are:

- Waivers (already discussed in Chapter 1);
- The general exceptions under Art. XX GATT (previewed in Chapter 2 and to be discussed in Chapter 12);
- Art. XXI GATT exception for national security (also previewed in Chapter 2 and to be discussed in Chapter 12);

In the next two Chapters, we will examine two other exceptions:

- Preferences granted under a preferential trade agreement (i.e., a free trade agreement or an agreement establishing a customs union) (to be discussed in Chapter 5)

- Special and differential treatment for developing countries (to be discussed in Chapter 6)

There is one more exception of historical value by now: the so-called 'grandfathering' clause (Art. I.2 GATT). GATT contracting parties agreed to exempt from the coverage of the MFN first the imperial preferences (granted by the UK to countries and territories participating in its Commonwealth), and then other preferences in place before January 1, 1948 across other GATT contracting parties. Annexes A–F to the GATT contain the list of the grandfathered preferences.[19] Their dismantlement had to await almost fifty years: only with the advent of the WTO did the end that signalled the end of grandfathering.

QUESTIONS AND COMMENTS

History of MFN Trade: Non-discriminatory trade liberalization is not an invention of the GATT-system: Hudec (1988) writes that, even in Medieval times, the city of Mantua (Italy) obtained from the Holy Roman Emperor the promise that it would always benefit from any privilege granted by the Emperor to 'whatsoever other town'. Jackson (1997, p. 158) notes that the term as such appears for the first time at the end of the seventeenth century. During the nineteenth century, the provision appeared in a number of treaties across European states. For instance, the *Cobden–Chevalier* Treaty of 1860, liberalizing trade between Great Britain and France, included an MFN clause guaranteeing that a signatory would not be treated worse than any other state with which the other signatory had, or would assume, trade relations. Such schemes, however, were not tantamount to worldwide non-discriminatory trade. Moreover, it is questionable whether, except for the very general idea of non-discrimination, they can provide guidance for the understanding of the term MFN. The drafters of the MFN clause were inspired by the formulation of the MFN clause as developed by the League of Nations. In turn, the League of Nations based its formulation of the MFN clause on the numerous bilateral trade treaties during the 1920s and before World War I.[20] Many of those treaties were signed by the US.[21]

Economists' Views on MFN: There is wide-spread view among policy-makers, lawyers, and many economists, that there are a number of strong economic rationales for non-discrimination. However, a general theoretical prima facie case for non-discrimination is not as easily advanced as might be thought. Indeed, Johnson (1976, p.18) goes as far as arguing that:

---

[19] See on this score, Jackson (1969), and Irwin et al. (2008).

[20] E/PC/T/C/33 at p. 9.

[21] In the 1942 reciprocal trade agreement with Mexico, Art. I read: "With respect to customs duties and charges of any kind imposed on or in connection with the importation or exportation, and with respect to the method of levying such duties and charges . . . any advantage, favor, privilege or immunity which has been or may hereafter be granted by the United States of America or the United Mexican States to any article in or destined for any third country shall be accorded immediately and unconditionally to the like article originating in or destined for the United Mexican States or the United States of America, respectively." 57 Stat. 835.

... the principle of non-discrimination has no basis whatsoever in the theoretical argument for the benefits of a liberal international trade order in general, or in any rational economic theory of the bargaining process in particular.

One fundamental role of trade agreements is to prevent negative externalities from nationally pursued trade policies. These international externalities may work through a number of different routes. For instance, they may take the form of changes in terms of trade, or through domestic prices affecting import demand. Bagwell and Staiger (2002) suggest that a central role of MFN is to channel these externalities through the terms of trade. This is important, since tariff negotiations can directly address terms of trade externalities, but are less effective to address other forms of externalities. A survey of the economics of MFN is provided by Horn and Mavroidis (2001), and a brief overview by Horn and Mavroidis (2009).

Bananas Saga: On the reaction of European courts to this decision, see Snyder (2003). The bananas saga ended on December 15, 2009. The EU agreed to gradually cut its import tariff on bananas from Latin America from € 176/ton to € 114/ton. The Latin American bananas exporters promised not to make any additional demands for tariff cuts on bananas during the Doha round. ACP (African, Caribbean, Pacific) exporters will continue to enjoy duty- and quota-free access to the EU market while the EU will mobilize up to $200 million from the EU budget to support the main ACP exporters' adaptation to the changing conditions of competition in the EU market, see Guth (2012).

Harmonizing Rules of Origin: The work was originally due to end in July 1998, but several deadlines have been missed since that date and conclusion of the negotiation is still elusive. The negotiation is being conducted under the aegis of the WTO Committee on Rules of Origin,[22] and the Technical Committee operating under the auspices of the WCO. A Work Programme is in place aiming, in principle, to provide for some sort of harmonized rules in this respect (Art. 9 ROO). The Committee on Rules of Origin has been actively pursuing this endeavour, known as HWP (Harmonization Work Programme), since 1995. Although meaningful discussions did take place, trading partners are still quite far from agreeing on a harmonized way to conferring origin.[23] It is reported that Members have made some progress: they have reached consensus on rules of origin for 55% of the products negotiated; some core policy issues have been heavily negotiated; product specific rules of origin are also being negotiated. Still, some hard issues remain open: the rules of origin applied to antidumping, countervailing, safeguards, SPS, TBT, and labelling figure among the thorniest issues where no consensus has

---

[22] As is the case with all WTO Committees, all WTO Members are represented in this committee.

[23] See for example, some of the discussions as reflected in WTO Doc. WT/GC/M/109 of October 24, 2007.

been reached as yet.[24] The question has been repeatedly raised whether the Committee of Rules of Origin is the appropriate forum for the negotiation of the HWP, in view of the fact that some of the issues involved are not purely technical, but also of political nature.[25] Negotiations were ongoing at the moment of writing.[26]

Rules of Origin and Trade in Tasks: Questions regarding rules of origin do not arise at all if a product is wholly obtained or produced in one country. Issues arise only if more than one country is involved in its production. This is a very likely scenario in today's world. The following picture (copied from Richard Baldwin, 2009, Integration of the North American Economy, and New Paradigm Globalisation, CEPR Discussion Paper 7523, London) of the origin of a Volvo car is quite telling in this respect:

Table 2.3

Production chain of a Volvo car

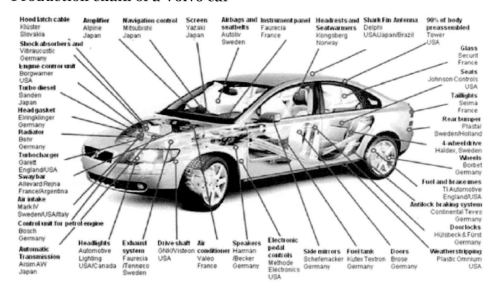

The picture above is the natural outcome of the current explosion of 'outsourcing', or 'off-shoring',[27] or, less colloquially, 'trade in tasks'. Information

---

[24] Discussions are ongoing on other issues as well, for example, on the so-called 'dual-rule approach', whereby, although each product must have one rule of origin, exceptionally for machinery, a WTO Member shall be allowed to choose either a value-added rule (where a fixed percentage of value confers origin) *or* a tariff-shift (where, because of value added, a product changes tariff line) rule.

[25] WTO Doc. WT/GC/M/126 of June 22, 2010.

[26] WTO Doc. G/RO/M/55 of December 17, 2010; see Vermulst and Imagawa (2005) for a discussion on the main themes.

[27] The terms 'outsourcing' and 'offshoring' refer to different activities but have not been used in the same manner across the literature: a recent WTO study uses *outsourcing* to denote activities that a company outsources in general, whereas *off-shoring* for activities outsourced in a foreign country, see *Trade Patterns and Global Value Chains in East Asia: from Trade in Goods to Trade in Tasks*, the WTO, 2011; Helpman (2011, p. 127) uses 'outsourcing' to refer to the acquisition of goods or services from an unaffiliated party, and independently of whether the unaf-

technology has certainly contributed in the rise of fragmentation of the production process across firms and countries. It is definitely not wine for cloth anymore, the transaction that Ricardo had in mind when constructing his theory of comparative advantage. Tempest (1996) shows how and why China, Indonesia, Japan, Malaysia and Taiwan were all participating in the production process of a Barbie doll along with the US.[28] The WTO Annual World Trade Report of 1998 explains that a typical US car includes 30% Korean added value, 17.5% Japanese, 7.5% German etc. The explosion of off-shoring is the outcome of economically rational decisions,[29] but it does pose new problems regarding the identification of the origin of a good.[30]

Preferential Rules of Origin: There is a panoply of similar schemes, a real mess which increases transaction costs often in highly disproportionate manner.[31] Preferential rules of origin are often more restrictive than non-preferential rules. This aspect, as well as many other negative aspects of preferential rules of origin have been highlighted in literature: Vermulst (1992, pp. 37ff) cites numerous EU court judgments in support of this claim; Brenton and Manchin (2003) investigate EU preferential schemes (such as 'Everything But Arms'), and suggest that for them to generate substantial improvements for developing countries, the EU should reconsider its current rules of origin;[32] Mattoo et al. (2003) estimate the medium-term benefits for

---

filiated party is located at home or abroad, and the term 'offshoring' to refer to the sourcing of goods or services in a foreign country, either from an affiliated or from an unaffiliated party.

[28] Ron Tempest, Barbie in the World Economy, The Los Angeles Times, September 22, 1996. See also Friedman (2005).

[29] Grossman and Rossi–Hansberg (2007), introduce a 'productivity-effect' and provide the theoretical framework to explain gains from trade thanks to off-shoring. Before their contribution, analysts focused on the 'labour-supply'- and the 'relative price' effects. Grossman and Rossi–Hansberg show that the 'productivity effect' can dominate the other two: put simply, improved opportunities for off-shoring low skill jobs will raise wages for domestic workers performing similar jobs. This is so because the companies that will profit from off-shoring are those companies that perform similar tasks intensively. Their increased profitability will enhance their labour demand and some of it will fall on domestic workers that perform tasks that cannot be moved easily.

[30] Of course, rules of origin is one and probably not the most important challenge posed by the rise in off-shoring. Antras and Staiger (2012) show that, whereas only trade policies get distorted in Nash equilibrium (terms of trade), both trade and domestic policies get distorted because of off-shoring. They thus, contemplate that the rise in off-shoring may necessitate a reorientation from shallow market access to deep integration. They thus, argue in favour of positive integration in the WTO. The WTO officials are fully aware of the issue: they recognize the challenges posed by off-shoring and have no trouble admitting that they are still in search of responses. In a recent speech (available at www.wti.org) DirectorGeneral Lamy publicly stated:

. . . we have not yet figured out how to deal with the interdependent world economy we have created. This (GATT) system was initially designed to tackle problems specific to the mid-twentieth century. . . . The basic architecture of the system reflected its origins in an Atlantic-centric world of shallow integration. The question now is what is needed to manage a globalized world of deep integration.

[31] See Inama (2003), and Krueger (1997) on this issue.

[32] The new EU GSP (Commission Regulation EU 1063/2010, in force as of January 1, 2011) includes a simplification of rules of origin especially for LDCs (least developed countries): a uniform local content rule of 30% is applied and this threshold confers LDC-origin for most manufactured goods (the percentage being 50% for developing countries which are not LDCs). The percentages are calculated on the basis of the ex-works price (including profits and general expenses). *Ex-works price* means the price to be paid for the product obtained to manufacturer in whose undertaking the last working or processing is carried out. The same regulation divides

African exporters stemming from the US AGOA (Africa Growth and Opportunity Act), and argue that the gains would be five times as much, were the US to relax the current stringent rules of origin.[33] There is ample empirical evidence that preferential rules of origin have substantially contributed to trade diversion.[34] Cadot and Demelo (2008) explain how rules of origin oblige developing countries to buy inefficient intermediate goods from developed countries in order to qualify for favourable treatment. Cadot et al. (2005) look at the EU—(the PANEURO) and US NAFTA regimes and conclude that the rules employed are tailor-made to fit protectionist requests by EU and US lobbies. The low utilization rate is explained in their view by a number of product specific rules of origin.[35]

Imperial Preferences: Imperial preferences involved both higher duties on non-British Empire goods, and lower duties on Dominion goods and drew the ire of excluded countries for discriminating against their trade. Cordell Hull was an especially sharp critic of imperial preferences because of their adverse effect on US exports, particularly to the UK and Canada, two of America's most important markets. Testifying before Congress in 1940, Cordell Hull called imperial preferences:

> the greatest injury, in a commercial way, that has been inflicted on this country since I have been in public life.[36]

Hull thought that the GATT was desirable also as a means to reduce the discriminatory effect against US exports. In 1938, the US and the UK signed a reciprocal trade agreement, but the negotiation was difficult and the results were limited. Despite Hull's best efforts, the agreement failed to put a dent in Britain's system of tariff preferences. Britain's entry into World War II in September 1939 and the ensuing trade controls reduced its value even further. The negotiation of MFN was intimately linked to the issue of imperial preferences. As Brown (1950, pp. 70ff.) points out, the MFN was the principle and the imperial preferences the exception: the latter could not be increased beyond the level existing on July 1, 1939, or July 1, 1946, whichever was lower. We briefly noted in Chapter 1, the widespread agreement in the literature that there was an implicit *quid pro quo* throughout the negotiation between the US and the UK that the extent of the MFN (the US commitment) would

---

LDCs into four groups (based on geographic proximity-considerations, Art. 85), and allows for *regional cumulation* if the working in the beneficiary country goes beyond minimal operations (defined in Art. 78.1 and in Annex 16 of the Regulation). Still, there are some features that continue to be debated, such as *'double jumping'*, whereby a country that produces garment from imported fabric from imported yarn can be the country of origin of the final exported good. As explained in detail *infra*, a UN list reflects all LDCs, whereas non-OECD countries are usually considered to be developing countries. LDCs have tabled their own proposal in this respect (WTO Doc. TN/MA/W/74/Rev. 1 of February 10, 2011) where they advocated even lower percentage thresholds for conferring LDC-origin.

[33] Similar evidence concerning the US trade with other American countries is provided in Estevadeordal and Garay (1996).

[34] For a survey of the literature not only on this score, but on all other aspects concerning rules of origin, see Inama (2009), Krishna (2006), and Puccio (2012).

[35] Compare the analysis by Inama (2009) who arrives at similar conclusions.

[36] Quoted in Gardner (1956) at p.19.

be in function of the reduction of the imperial preferences (the commitment by the UK):[37] during the London Conference, it was agreed that in addition to imperial preferences, other long-standing preferences, such as those between Cuba and the US, would be permitted temporarily.[38] Eventually, others joined in: the various Annexes (A–F) to the GATT refer to colonial preferences by France, Belgium as well as other bilateral preferences like US–Cuba; in this vein, § 3 was added to Art. I GATT at the Havana Conference: this paragraph deals with preferences across certain countries of the Near East (Ottoman Empire).[39] Other annexes were added so that some preferences could qualify for exemption. The annexes concerned Portuguese territories, and the special regime between Italy, San Marino, and the Vatican.

Clayton was very much in line with Hull with respect to their attitude towards imperial preferences. The presidential decision to override Clayton's council to abandon hopes of an agreement with the UK because of the latter's refusal to reduce its imperial preferences, ultimately ensured the success of the Geneva tariff negotiations and the advent of the GATT: to Clayton's disappointment, Britain's imperial preferences remained largely intact.[40]

---

[37] Irwin et al. (2008).
[38] E/PC/T/C/30 at p. 3.
[39] The GATT Analytical Index, 3rd revision, The GATT: Geneva, 1970 at p. 3ff.
[40] See Zeiler (1999) and Toye (2008) for details on the conclusion of the negotiations.

Chapter 5

Preferential Trade Agreements (PTAs)

■ ■ ■

1. THE LEGAL DISCIPLINE

WTO Members can grant tariff preferences to a sub-set of the WTO Membership through what we term a "preferential trade agreement" (PTA)[1] to create a free trade area (FTA) or a customs union (CU), conditional upon the satisfaction of legal requirements of Art. XXIV GATT: They must liberalize "substantially all trade" among themselves, and they must also not raise the level of protection towards the rest of the WTO Membership. An FTA involves opening up to trade between the constituents without adopting a common trade policy vis-à-vis outsiders; a CU adds common trade policy to 'internal' (e.g., between its members) trade liberalization.

2. THE RATIONALE FOR THE LEGAL DISCIPLINE

Arguably, one reason for the inclusion of a provision on CUs is that the GATT negotiators were presented with a *fait accompli*: Two CUs participated in the negotiation, the Syro–Lebanese customs union (Syria, Lebanon) and Benelux (Belgium, Netherlands, Luxembourg). Institutional arrangements would have to be made anyway in order to accommodate these contracting parties. But what explains the extension of the original provision (which was limited to CUs only) to cover FTAs as well? Drawing from a series of archival records, Chase (2006) demonstrates that it was the US negotiators that sought inclusion of FTAs in the provision in order

---

[1] Throughout this volume we privilege the use of the term 'PTA' over the term 'regional integration': the former captures the essence of these schemes, since participants in such arrangements will be treated better than outsiders; the latter term reflects a historical feature. The title of Art. XXIV GATT [Frontier Traffic, Customs Unions(CUs), Free Trade Areas(FTAs)], the relevant legal discipline, denotes geographic proximity. Sapir (2011) notes though, that the origin of the term 'regional integration' is uncertain as the term does not appear in the body of Art. XXIV GATT. He notes that this term was first used in an official GATT document in February 1996 when the WTO established the Committee on Regional Trade Agreements to examine the consistency of FTAs and CUs with the WTO. Dam (1963) is credited by Sapir as the first author to use the term 'regional trade agreements' probably because in the early sixties all preferential schemes were across regional partners. Nowadays, one third of FTAs are among countries that are not in geographic proximity: the number of cross-regional schemes has risen from six in 1995 to 80 in 2008. The FTAs between EU and Mexico, Australia and Chile, and Mexico and Japan underscore this point.

to accommodate a trade agreement that they had secretly reached with Canada.[2]

3. COVERAGE OF THE LEGAL DISCIPLINE

3.1 WHICH PTAS FALL UNDER THE PURVIEW OF ART. XXIV GATT?

To be clear, this Chapter concerns only the legal requirements for PTAs that fall under Art. XXIV GATT. PTAs that are concluded exclusively between developing countries are subject to a looser set of requirements outlined in the Enabling Clause (to be discussed in the next Chapter). Thus, the requirements of Art. XXIV GATT apply to a PTA where at least one party is a developed country. In addition, our discussion concerns PTAs covering trade in goods; PTAs for trade in services is governed by Art. V GATS.

3.2 THE SCOPE OF THE ART. XXIV GATT EXCEPTION

Art. XXIV.4 GATT leaves no doubt that there is room for PTAs under the aegis of the multilateral framework:

> The contracting parties recognize the desirability of increasing freedom of trade by the development, through voluntary agreements, of closer integration between the economies of the countries parties to such agreements. They also recognize that the purpose of a customs union or of a free-trade area should be to facilitate trade between the constituent territories and not to raise barriers to the trade of other contracting parties with such territories.

Art. XXIV GATT was designed as conditional exception to requirement for MFN treatment embedded within Art. I GATT. Case law during the GATT years (e.g., *EC–Citrus*) supports this view.

With the advent of the WTO (and the ensuing expansion of the coverage of legal disciplines to include various other multilateral rules, as discussed in Chapter 1), the question arises whether Art. XXIV may also function as an exception to other provisions as well. The AB, in *Turkey–Textiles*, responded in the affirmative. At issue in that case was whether Art. XXIV GATT could justify a deviation from Art. 2.4 of the Agreement on Textiles and Clothing (to be discussed in Chapter 18). The AB (§ 58), without naming one-by-one the provisions for which Art. XXIV GATT serve as an exception, held generally that:

---

[2] References to FTAs were thus included in Art. 44 of the Havana Charter, the corresponding provision to Art. XXIV GATT, and appear for the first time only in 1948. The US–Canada FTA, alas, was never ratified.

Article XXIV may justify a measure which is inconsistent with certain other GATT provisions.

In the same passage, the AB explained the conditions under which this exception can be successfully invoked:

> First, the party claiming the benefit of this defence must demonstrate that the measure at issue is introduced upon the formation of a customs union that fully meets the requirements of sub-paragraphs 8(a) and 5(a) of Article XXIV. And, second, that party must demonstrate that the formation of that customs union would be prevented if it were not allowed to introduce the measure at issue.

3.3 REQUIREMENTS OF WTO MEMBERS ENTERING INTO A PTA

To qualify for the exemption provided by Art. XXIV GATT, WTO Members must notify the WTO of any PTAs into which they enter. They must also fulfill two substantive requirements:

(1) Liberalize "substantially all trade" between constituents of a PTA (the "internal" requirement)

(2) Not raise the level of protection vis-à-vis outsiders (the "external" requirement)

In what follows, we discuss the nature of each of these requirements.

3.4 NOTIFICATION

WTO Members deciding to enter into a PTA have to notify the WTO of their intention to do so (Art. XXIV.7 GATT).[3] Notifications will be submitted to the CRTA (Committee on Regional Trade Agreements). There is standard notification format for PTAs irrespective under which provision (GATT, GATS, Enabling Clause)[4] the WTO has been notified (WTO Doc. G/L/834 of November 8, 2007). The CRTA was established through a decision by the WTO General Council on February 7, 1996.[5] The role of the CRTA is:[6]

> to carry out the examination of agreements in accordance with the procedures and terms of reference adopted ... and thereafter present its report to the relevant body for appropriate action

---

[3] WTO Members will notify a CU, an FTA, or an interim agreement leading to a FTA or a CU. In this latter case there is a requirement to report in set periods the implementation of the PTA, WTO Doc. TN/RL/W/8/Rev. 1 of August 1, 2002.

[4] We discuss PTAs in the realm of services trade in the Chapters dedicated to the study of GATS. Our discussion of PTAs between developing countries (Enabling Clause) is included in the next Chapter.

[5] The CRTA is the successor to Art. XXIV GATT Working Parties, the organ that would examine the consistency of notified PTAs with the multilateral rules in the GATT years

[6] WTO Doc. WT/L/127.

The CRTA adopts its decisions by consensus as per Rule 33 of the Rules of Procedure for Meetings of the Committee on Regional Trade Agreements:[7]

> Where a decision cannot be arrived at by consensus, the matter at issue shall be referred, as appropriate, to the General Council, the Council for Trade in Goods, the Council for Trade in Services or the Committee on Trade and Development.

There is no reported case of referral to a higher body. In principle, one cannot exclude the possibility that the CRTA concludes that a notified PTA is WTO-inconsistent. This conclusion is underscored by the explicit wording of Art. XXIV.7(b) GATT, which explains the powers of the CRTA when it reviews an interim agreement leading to the establishment of a CU or an FTA:

> If . . . the CONTRACTING PARTIES find that such agreement is not likely to result in the formation of a customs union or of a free-trade area . . . the CONTRACTING PARTIES shall make recommendations to the parties to the agreement. *The parties shall not maintain or put into force, as the case may be, such agreement if they are not prepared to modify it in accordance with these recommendations.* (emphasis added).

As we will see *infra* however, when we discuss the Transparency Mechanism, the CRTA falls short of discussing the consistency of PTAs with the WTO rules. The CRTA will circulate two documents: a factual abstract (an executive summary of the discussions held in the CRTA), and a factual presentation (the final report, which will provide factual information on various aspects of the notified PTA).

Note that PTAs concluded under the Enabling Clause (to be discussed in the next Chapter) are to be notified instead to the Committee on Trade and Development (CTD).

What about PTAs between WTO Members and non-Members? Art. XXIV.5 reads:

> Accordingly, the provisions of this Agreement shall not prevent, *as between the territories of contracting parties*, the formation of a customs union or of a free-trade area or the adoption of an interim agreement necessary for the formation of a customs union or of a free-trade area; (emphasis added).

Yet, practice has developed in a different way. WTO Members, irrespective of whether developed or developing, notify the CRTA and/or the CTD of their PTAs with non-WTO Members as well: EC–CARIFORUM (Bahamas is part of the agreement, but not a WTO Member) is an exam-

---

[7] WTO Doc WT/REG/1 of August 14, 1996.

ple of the former, and Ukraine–Uzbekistan of the latter.[8] As a result, WTO Members now, when signing PTAs with non-WTO Members do not have to automatically and unconditionally extend benefits to all other WTO Members (by virtue of Art. I GATT).

Art. XXIV:7(a) GATT addresses the timing of notification:

> Any contracting party *deciding to enter* into a customs union or free-trade area, or an interim agreement leading to the formation of such a union or area, shall *promptly* notify the CONTRACTING PARTIES and shall make available . . . such information . . . as will enable them to make such reports and recommendations to contracting parties as they may deem appropriate. (emphasis added).

This language suggests that the CRTA should be notified of a prospective action.[9] The WTO Secretariat (the TPRM Division) will then prepare a factual presentation of the PTA that would be circulated to all WTO Members.[10] It is quite frequent, however, that PTAs be notified with substantial delays. For example, NAFTA was signed on December 17, 1992, entered into force on January 1, 1994 and a Working Party to examine its consistency with the GATT rules was established only on March 23, 1994. The EC—Visegrad Agreements (an FTA between the EU on one hand, and Hungary, Poland, and the Czech and Slovak Federal Republic on the other) entered into force on December 16, 1991, and the Working Party was established only on April 30, 1992. A General Council decision regarding the content of notifications formally accepted that notifications can take place after the entry into force of the notified PTA:

> The required notification of a PTA shall take place as early as possible; it will occur when practicable before the application of preferential treatment by the notifying Member and, at the latest, three months after the PTA is in force.[11]

3.5 SUBSTANTIALLY ALL TRADE ('INTERNAL REQUIREMENT')

The internal requirement applies to FTAs and CUs alike: According to Art. XXIV.8 GATT, WTO Members wishing to enter into a CU or an FTA, will have to eliminate duties and other restrictive regulations of

---

[8] The WTO was also notified of the FTAs between Turkey–Syria, and EFTA–Lebanon, although neither Syria nor Lebanon are WTO Members.

[9] Art. XV.3 of the ITO was even clearer in this respect: The Organization shall examine the proposal and, by a two-thirds majority of the Members present and voting, may grant, subject to such conditions as it may impose, an exception to the provisions of Article 16 to permit the *proposed* agreement to become effective. (emphasis added).

[10] WTO Doc. TN/RL/18 of July 13, 2006.

[11] WTO Doc. WT/L/806 of December 16, 2010.

commerce with respect to substantially all trade in products originating in the constituents of the PTA.[12]

The meaning of "substantially all" remains largely un-interpreted. The GATT Analytical Index (vol. 2, p. 824, footnote 162) provides an exhaustive list of Working Party reports dealing with this issue; the inescapable conclusion is that trading partners did not manage to clarify this term in subsequent practice. In a series of papers that the WTO Secretariat prepared for the CRTA,[13] this conclusion was re-confirmed: Notwithstanding 50 years of practice, WTO Members have failed to come up with a workable definition of the term.

A General Council decision implicitly at least suggests that the requirement does not require liberalization of all trade involved.[14] But does it require a certain percentage to be liberalized? And what if a particular sector (such as agriculture) is excluded altogether? Some have suggested that a certain threshold percentage of trade must be liberalized.[15] Others have suggested that the exclusion of a sector, no matter what its percentage of trade, runs contrary to the spirit of Art. XXIV GATT.[16] The exact answers to both of these questions, however, remain unclear and ill-defined.

The other term featured in this provision is "duties and other restrictive regulations of commerce" whose elimination is required by Art. XXIV GATT. Although the provision does not define this term any further, there is little doubt that the term "duties" refers to customs duties. Hence, interpretative issues arise only with respect to the term "other restrictive regulations of commerce." In a notorious parentheses for Art. XXIV.8 GATT, measures coming under the purview of Arts. XI, XII, XIII, XIV, XV, and XX GATT are exempted from its coverage. However, practice suggests that this list is only an indicative list and not an exhaustive one. Some have suggested that the term excludes measures coming under the purview of the national security exception of Art. XXI GATT, even though it is not explicitly acknowledged.[17] Case law also suggests that

---

[12] Grossman and Helpman (1995) have argued that, absent this requirement, WTO Members might have the incentive to conclude preferential deals on commodities where the largest possible trade diversion could result.

[13] WTO Docs. WT/REG/W/17 of October 31, 1997; WT/REG/W/17/Add 1, of November 5, 1997; WT/REG/W/17/Corr. 1, of December 15, 1997; WT/REG/W/17/Rev. 1, of February 15, 1998.

[14] WTO Doc. WT/L/806 of December 16, 2010.

[15] For example, in the EEC Working Party, various EU member states expressed the view that "a free-trade area should be considered as having been achieved for substantially all trade when the volume of liberalized trade reached 80 per cent of total trade." GATT Analytical Index, pp. 824–5. On the other hand, the Working Party Report on EFTA takes the view that "the percentage of trade covered, even if it were established to be 90 per cent, was not considered to be the only factor to be taken into account."

[16] See, e.g., Working Party report on EEC—Agreements with Finland, GATT Doc. BISD 29S/79, § 12; Working Party report on Free Trade Area between Canada and the US (CUSFTA), GATT Doc. BISD 38S/73, § 83.

[17] In the EEC Working Party Report, the EEC member states expressed a view that "it would be difficult, however, to dispute the right of contracting parties to avail themselves of that

measures pertaining to the regulation of safeguards through Art. XIX GATT are also excluded, when the concept of "parallelism" is followed (to be discussed in greater detail in Chapter 16).[18]

In the context of deliberations at the 1970 Working Party on EEC—Association with African and Malgasy States, the opinion was raised that trade had not been substantially liberalized, in view of the continued imposition by certain parties to the Convention (the Association of EEC with African and Malgasy States) of fiscal charges on imports from other members. The members of the PTA responded arguing that:

> the provisions of Article XXIV, concerning the concept of a free-trade area concerned only protective measures. The taxes referred to were of a fiscal character, not protective.[19]

The question of whether fiscal charges on imports are excluded from the scope of "other restrictive regulations of commerce" has not been clarified through case law.

3.6 NO NEW PROTECTION TOWARDS OTHER WTO MEMBERS ('EXTERNAL REQUIREMENT')

WTO Members must not, when entering into a PTA, raise their protection vis-à-vis the remaining WTO Membership: They must liberalize trade between members of the PTA without increasing protection towards the rest of the WTO. Contrary to what is the case with respect to the internal requirement, the conditions for meeting the external requirement are different for FTAs and CUs.

Concerning FTAs, Art. XXIV.5(b) GATT requires that:

> ... duties and other regulations of commerce ... shall not be higher or more restrictive than the corresponding duties and other regulations of commerce existing in the same constituent territories prior to the formation of the free-trade area ...

The Understanding on the Interpretation of Article XXIV of the GATT clarifies that WTO Members entering into an FTA can raise their level of duties from the applied rate to the bound rate without violating Art. XXIV.5(b).

Note that in contrast to Art. XXIV.8 GATT, this provision refers to "other regulations of commerce," and not to "other restrictive regulations of commerce." This suggests that the former encompasses a broader set of

---

provision which related, inter alia, to traffic in arms, fissionable materials, etc., and it must therefore be concluded that the list was not exhaustive." GATT Doc. BISD 6S/70, p. 97.

[18] See *Argentina—Footwear (EC)*; *US–Wheat Gluten*. Parallelism is the concept that WTO Members can impose a safeguard measure against a WTO Member with whom it has a PTA if they have counted PTA-imports when assessing injury; they cannot do so, however, in the opposite case (when they have not counted PTA-imports when assessing injury).

[19] GATT Doc. BISD 18S/133, pp. 135–7.

measures than the latter. Art. XXIV.5(b) GATT does not contain a list of regulations of commerce (other than duties). There should be no doubt that ODCs are covered, but the question of what else falls under this term remains unclear.[20]

With respect to CUs, Art. XXIV.5(a) GATT reads:

> ... duties and other regulations of commerce ... shall not *on the whole* be higher or more restrictive than *the general incidence* of the duties and regulations of commerce applicable in the constituent territories prior to the formation of such union ... (emphasis added).

The italicized words mark the difference between the text of Art. XXIV.5(b) GATT, and that of Art. XXIV.5(a) GATT: "on the whole" and "general incidence" invite a comparison of the general (and not item by item) situation before and after the formation of the CU. This was indeed the intention of the drafters:

> The phrase 'on the whole' ... did not mean that an average tariff should be laid down in respect of each individual product, but merely that the whole level of tariffs of a customs union should not be higher than the average overall level of the former constituent territories.[21]

> The Sub–Committee recommended that the words 'average level of duties' be replaced by 'general incidence of duties' in paragraph 2(a) of the new Article. It was the intention of the Sub–Committee that this phrase should not require a mathematical average of customs duties but should permit greater flexibility so that the volume of trade may be taken into account.[22]

Subsequent practice sides with the view that an item-by-item approach is unwarranted in the context of Art. XXIV.5(a) GATT; there is, nonetheless, disagreement as to the precise level on which comparisons will take place. The report of the 1983 Working Party on Accession of Greece to the European Communities reflects the view expressed by the EU, that:

> Article XXIV.5 required only generalized, overall judgment on this point.[23]

---

[20] Rules of origin are of particular interest in the FTA-context, and have on occasion been discussed in the context of Art. XXIV.5 GATT, but no coherent approach has emerged. See WTO Doc. TN/RL/W/8/Rev. 1 of August 1, 2002. The General Council decision mentioned *supra* (WTO Doc. WT/L/806 of December 16, 2010) explicitly refers to the obligation to notify rules of origin when notifying a PTA.

[21] GATT Doc. EPCT/C.II/38 at p. 9 reproduced in the GATT Analytical Index: Guide to GATT Law and Practice, Updated 6th Edition (1995) at p. 803.

[22] Havana Reports reproduced in the GATT Analytical Index, at p. 803.

[23] See GATT Doc. BISD 30S/168, p. 184.

By the same token, the report of the 1988 Working Party on Accession of Portugal and Spain to the European Communities includes the view of the EU that:

> Article XXIV.5 only required an examination on the broadest possible basis.[24]

This view, however, failed to convince other members of the Working Party. One member:

> could not accept the Communities' contention that the extension of the tariff of the EC/10 to the EC/12 was compatible with their obligations under Article XXIV.5(a) regardless of the effect on the tariffs of Spain and Portugal. Article XXIV.5(a) required a comparison with the pre-accession tariffs of the constituent territories and the relative size of those territories was not a relevant factor.[25]

Disagreements appeared often among members of the Working Party as to whether bound or applied rates should be used in the context of Art. XXIV.5(a) GATT.[26] This issue has been clarified with the entry into force of the WTO Understanding on the Interpretation of Article XXIV of the GATT:

> The evaluation under paragraph 5(a) of Article XXIV of the general incidence of the duties and other regulations of commerce applicable before and after the formation of a customs union shall in respect of duties and charges be based upon an overall assessment of weighted average tariff rates and of customs duties collected. This assessment shall be based on import statistics for a previous representative period to be supplied by the customs union, on a tariff-line basis and in values and quantities, broken down by WTO country of origin. The Secretariat shall compute the weighted average tariff rates and customs duties collected in accordance with the methodology used in the assessment of tariff offers in the Uruguay Round of Multilateral Trade negotiations. For this purpose, the duties and charges to be taken into consideration shall be the *applied rates* of duty. It is recognized that for the purpose of the overall assessment of the incidence of other regulations of commerce for which quantification and aggregation are difficult, the examination of indi-

---

[24] See GATT Doc. BISD 35S/293, pp. 295–6.
[25] Idem, p. 311.
[26] See for example the discussions of the Working Party examining the compatibility of the EEC with Art XXIV, GATT Doc SR.18/4, pp. 46–54 and also in C/M/8, SR.19/6–7; see the Working Party report on Accession of Greece to the European Communities, op. cit., p. 175; see also the 1991 Working Party report on Free Trade Agreement Between Canada and the United States, BISD 38S/47, p. 66.

vidual measures, regulations, products covered and trade flows affected may be required. (emphasis added).[27]

There is an additional provision for CUs embedded in Art. XXIV.6 GATT:

> If, in fulfilling the requirements of subparagraph 5(a), a contracting party proposes to increase any rate of duty inconsistently with the provision of Article II, the procedure set forth in Article XXVIII shall apply. In providing for compensatory adjustment, due account shall be taken of the compensation already afforded by the reduction brought about in the corresponding duty of the other constituents of the union.

Compliance with Art. XXIV.5(a) GATT is, in other words, a necessary but not sufficient condition for compliance with Art. XXIV.6 GATT. Art. XXIV.6 GATT comes into play any time a member of a CU has to raise its pre-CU duty to meet the duty at the CU-level. In such cases, Art. XXVIII GATT-negotiations will kick in. This means that WTO Members which qualify as INRs or PSIs will participate in the negotiations with the members of the CU. Art. XXIV.6 GATT, second sentence makes it clear that built-in compensation will be taken into account.

4. ENFORCING ART. XXIV GATT

4.1 THE NATURE OF THE MULTILATERAL REVIEW

Recall that the CRTA has wide powers and can, in principle, go so far as to declare a PTA GATT-inconsistent. As of April 2013, the WTO has been notified of over 500 PTAs, the vast majority of which come under the aegis of Art. XXIV GATT; almost 2/3 of them are now in force.[28] Schott (1989) identifies four cases where PTAs were judged broadly consistent with the GATT. Since his study saw the light of day, the CU between the Czech and the Slovak republics has been judged GATT-consistent. A sea change occurred nevertheless with the advent of the Transparency Mechanism on December 14, 2006:[29] no discussion on the consistency of particular aspects of the PTA with the multilateral rules takes place since

---

[27] It is interesting that the Understanding focuses on *applied* as opposed to *bound* duties. By adopting this focus, it is going further than simply stating that WTO Members cannot use a CU to undo tariff obligations that were previously bound; it is also stating that WTO members cannot use a CU to jointly raise applied tariffs. This is interesting because one prediction of the theory would be that a CU would have the incentive to set higher external tariffs than the members would acting individually (i.e., before the CU) and that this would be one bad thing about the CU in terms of its multilateral effects. So from the multilateral perspective, this rule makes sense.

[28] According to the WTO 2011 World Trade Report dedicated to PTAs ('The WTO and Preferential Trade Agreements: From Coexistence to Coherence'), 300 PTAs were in force in 2010, whereas only 70 in 1990.

[29] WTO Doc. WT/L/671 of December 18, 2006.

then.[30] The Transparency Mechanism was originally supposed to complement the existing legal arsenal dealing with PTAs; in practice, however, it has not complemented, but substituted the previous arsenal.

4.2 LITIGATING THE CONSISTENCY OF PTAS BEFORE PANELS

The view that the consistency of PTAs with the multilateral rules can be the subject of judicial review was endorsed by GATT contracting parties, much before the AB explicitly accepted that is the case. A representative view is offered by the EU delegate, and is reflected in the report issued by the 1978 Working Party on the Agreement between the EEC and Egypt:

> ... as regards the possibility of consultations with the contracting parties concerning the incidence of the Agreement on their trade interests ... nothing prevented these countries from invoking the relevant provisions of the General Agreement, such as Articles XXII and XXIII.[31]

During the GATT years (1948–1994), three Panels were established to examine claims relating to the consistency of a PTA with the multilateral rules.[32] Two reports were issued and they both remain un-adopted. The first of these, the *EC–Citrus* Panel report argues in favor of an examination (by Panels) of individual measures only, and, based on this position, refused to pronounce on the overall consistency of the PTA with the multilateral rules:

> The Panel noted that at the time of the examination of the agreements entered into by the European Community with certain Mediterranean countries, there was no consensus among contracting parties as to the conformity of the agreement with Article XXIV.5
>
> . . .
>
> The agreements had not been disapproved, nor had they been approved. The Panel found therefore that the question of conformity of the agreements with the requirements of Article XXIV and their legal status remained open.[33]

---

[30] For a typical illustration, see the CRTA report on the FTA between Thailand and New Zealand, WTO Doc. WT/REG207/3 of January 3, 2007.

[31] GATT Analytical Index, p. 781.

[32] The first, after a request by Canada in 1974 in connection with the accession to the European Community of Denmark, Ireland, and the United Kingdom (GATT Doc. C/W/250) was not activated because the parties to the dispute reached an agreement (GATT Doc. C/W/259). The second, led to an un-adopted Panel report in EC—Citrus, GATT Doc. L/5776. The third report is on *EEC—Bananas II*, GATT Doc. DS38/R of 11 February 1994 which also remains un-adopted.

[33] GATT Doc. L/5776, dated February 7, 1985 at § 4.6 and at § 4.10.

This report remains un-adopted, and hence, of limited legal relevance.

In *EEC–Bananas II*, the Panel held that one way preferential arrangements are per se inconsistent with Art. XXIV GATT (§ 159):

> This lack of *any* obligation of the sixty-nine ACP countries to dismantle their trade barriers, and the acceptance of an obligation to remove trade barriers only on imports into the customs territory of the EEC, made the trade arrangements set out in the Convention substantially different from those of a free trade area, as defined in Article XXIV:8(b).

This Panel went on to conclude (§ 164) that the Lomé Convention (the agreement between the EU and a series of African, Caribbean, and Pacific states) did not meet the requirements of Art. XXIV GATT. This report remains un-adopted as well.[34]

At issue in the WTO-era *Turkey–Textiles* case was the erection of QRs on a broad range of textile and clothing imports by Turkey following the entry into force of a CU between Turkey and the EU. India filed a complaint arguing that the new QRs violated several WTO obligations, including Art. XI GATT. Turkey did not deny that this was the case, but tried to invoke Art. XXIV GATT as an exception to justify its actions. The Panel held that WTO adjudicating bodies are competent to examine PTA-related issues, but should stop short of providing an overall assessment regarding the consistency of a PTA with the WTO. This Panel followed the findings in the Panel report on *EC–Citrus* (§§ 9.52–9.53). On appeal, the AB held a different view arguing that those availing themselves of justifying their measures through recourse to Art. XXIV GATT must explain why their PTA is GATT-consistent (§§ 58–59):

> First, the party claiming the benefit of this defense must demonstrate that the measure at issue is introduced upon the formation of a customs union that *fully meets the requirements of sub-paragraph 8(a) and 5(a) of Article XXIV*. And second, that party must demonstrate that the formation of that customs union would be prevented if it were not allowed to introduce the measure at issue.
>
> . . .
>
> We would expect a panel, when examining such a measure, to require a party to establish that both of these conditions have been fulfilled. It may not always be possible to determine whether the second of the two conditions has been fulfilled without initially determining whether the first condition has been fulfilled. (emphasis added).

---

34 In the WTO-era the AB report on *EC–Bananas III* reproduced almost *verbatim* this view.

More recently, the Panel in *US–Line Pipe* faced an argument by the US that, as a member of NAFTA, it was entitled to treat imports from NAFTA differently than imports from non-NAFTA sources when imposing a tariff quota. The Panel repeated that the US had the burden of proof to show consistency of NAFTA with Art. XXIV GATT (§ 7.142); it then addressed the issue of the quantum of proof (burden of persuasion) that the party carrying the burden of proof has to provide in order to establish a prima facie case of the consistency of a PTA with the multilateral rules (§ 7.144):

> In our view, the information provided by the United States in these proceedings, the information submitted by the NAFTA parties to the Committee on Regional Trade Agreements ("CRTA") (which the United States has incorporated into its submissions to the Panel by reference), and the absence of effective refutation by Korea, establishes a prima facie case that NAFTA is in conformity with Article XXIV:5(b) and (c), and with Article XXIV:8(b).

The information provided by the US in the proceedings is confined to a statement (§ 7.142) that duties on 97% of the NAFTA parties' tariff lines would be eliminated within 10 years from the inception of NAFTA, whereas, with respect to other regulations of commerce, a reference to the principles of national treatment, transparency, and a variety of other market access rules is made. In the Panel's view, the submitted information was enough to make a prima facie case of consistency of NAFTA with Art. XXIV GATT. In subsequent cases as well (*Argentina–Poultry Antidumping Duties*, *Mexico–Taxes on Soft Drinks*), Panels have confirmed the view that they have the power to decide on the overall consistency of notified PTAs with the multilateral rules.

It follows from the discussion above that if review of the consistency of a PTA with the relevant GATT rules is to occur, it will most likely only take place before a Panel.

Table 5.1 Preferential Trade Agreements Notified Under Art. XXIV GATT

Name	Coverage	Type	Date of notification	Notification	Date of entry into force
Armenia—Kazakhstan	Goods	FTA	17–Jun–2004	GATT Art. XXIV	25–Dec–2001
Armenia—Moldova	Goods	FTA	17–Jun–2004	GATT Art. XXIV	21–Dec–1995

Name	Coverage	Type	Date of notification	Notification	Date of entry into force
Armenia—Russian Federation	Goods	FTA	17–Jun–2004	GATT Art. XXIV	25–Mar–1993
Armenia—Turkmenistan	Goods	FTA	17–Jun–2004	GATT Art. XXIV	07–Jul–1996
Armenia—Ukraine	Goods	FTA	17–Jun–2004	GATT Art. XXIV	18–Dec–1996
ASEAN—Australia—New Zealand	Goods & Services	FTA & EIA	08–Apr–2010	GATT Art. XXIV & GATS V	01–Jan–2010
ASEAN—China	Goods & Services	PSA & EIA	21–Sep–2005(G) 26–Jun–2008(S)	Enabling Clause & GATS Art. V	01–Jan–2005(G) 01–Jul–2007(S)
ASEAN—Japan	Goods	FTA	23–Nov–2009	GATT Art. XXIV	01–Dec–2008
ASEAN—Korea, Republic of	Goods & Services	FTA & EIA			01–Jan–2010(G) 01–May–2009(S)
Australia—Chile	Goods & Services	FTA & EIA	03–Mar–2009	GATT Art. XXIV & GATS V	06–Mar–2009
Australia—New Zealand (ANZCERTA)	Goods & Services	FTA & EIA	14–Apr–1983(G) 22–Nov–1995(S)	GATT Art. XXIV & GATS V	01–Jan–1983(G) 01–Jan–1989(S)
Australia—Papua New Guinea PATCRA)	Goods	FTA	20–Dec–1976	GATT Art. XXIV	01–Feb–1977
Brunei Darussalam—Japan	Goods & Services	FTA & EIA	31–Jul–2008	GATT Art. XXIV & GATS V	31–Jul–2008
Canada—Chile	Goods & Services	FTA & EIA	30–Jul–1997	GATT Art. XXIV & GATS V	05–Jul–1997

Name	Coverage	Type	Date of notification	Notification	Date of entry into force
Canada—Costa Rica	Goods	FTA	13–Jan–2003	GATT Art. XXIV	01–Nov–2002
Canada—Israel	Goods	FTA	15–Jan–1997	GATT Art. XXIV	01–Jan–1997
Canada—Peru	Goods & Services	FTA & EIA	31–Jul–2009	GATT Art. XXIV & GATS V	01–Aug–2009
Caribbean Community and Common Market (CARICOM)	Goods & Services	CU & EIA	14–Oct–1974(G) 19–Feb–2003(S)	GATT Art. XXIV & GATS V	01–Aug–1973(G) 01–Jul–1997(S)
Central American Common Market (CACM)	Goods	CU	24–Feb–1961	GATT Art. XXIV	04–Jun–1961
Central European Free Trade Agreement (CEFTA) 2006	Goods	FTA	26–Jul–2007	GATT Art. XXIV	01–May–2007
Chile—China	Goods & Services	FTA & EIA	20–Jun–2007(G) 18–Nov–2010(S)	GATT Art. XXIV & GATS V	01–Oct–2006(G) 01–Aug–2010(S)
Chile—Colombia	Goods & Services	FTA & EIA	14–Aug–2009	GATT Art. XXIV & GATS V	08–May–2009
Chile—Costa Rica (Chile—Central America)	Goods & Services	FTA & EIA	16–Apr–2002	GATT Art. XXIV & GATS V	15–Feb–2002
Chile—El Salvador (Chile—Central America)	Goods & Services	FTA & EIA	29–Jan–2004(G) 05–Feb–2004(S)	GATT Art. XXIV & GATS V	01–Jun–2002

Name	Coverage	Type	Date of notification	Notification	Date of entry into force
Chile—Japan	Goods & Services	FTA & EIA	24–Aug–2007	GATT Art. XXIV & GATS V	03–Sep–2007
Chile—Mexico	Goods & Services	FTA & EIA	27–Feb–2001	GATT Art. XXIV & GATS V	01–Aug–1999
China—Hong Kong, China	Goods & Services	FTA & EIA	27–Dec–2003	GATT Art. XXIV & GATS V	01–Jan–2004
China—Macao, China	Goods & Services	FTA & EIA	27–Dec–2003	GATT Art. XXIV & GATS V	01–Jan–2004
China—New Zealand	Goods & Services	FTA & EIA	21–Apr–2009	GATT Art. XXIV & GATS V	01–Oct–2008
China—Singapore	Goods & Services	FTA & EIA	02–Mar–2009	GATT Art. XXIV & GATS V	01–Jan–2009
Colombia—Mexico	Goods & Services	FTA & EIA	13–Sep–2010	GATT Art. XXIV & GATS V	01–Jan–1995
Common Economic Zone (CEZ)	Goods	FTA	18–Aug–2008	GATT Art. XXIV	20–May–2004
Commonwealth of Independent States (CIS)	Goods	FTA	29–Jun–1999	GATT Art. XXIV	30–Dec–1994
Costa Rica—Mexico	Goods & Services	FTA & EIA	17–Jul–2006	GATT Art. XXIV & GATS V	01–Jan–1995
Dominican Republic—Central America—United States Free Trade Agreement (CAFTA–DR)	Goods & Services	FTA & EIA	17–Mar–2006	GATT Art. XXIV & GATS V	01–Mar–2006
East African Community (EAC)	Goods	CU	09–Oct–2000	Enabling Clause	07–Jul–2000
EC—Albania	Goods &	FTA &	07–Mar–2007(G)	GATT Art. XXIV	01–Dec–

Name	Coverage	Type	Date of notification	Notification	Date of entry into force
	Services	EIA	07–Oct–2009(S)	& GATS V	2006(G) 01–Apr–2009(S)
EC—Algeria	Goods	FTA	24–Jul–2006	GATT Art. XXIV	01–Sep–2005
EC—Andorra	Goods	CU	23–Feb–1998	GATT Art. XXIV	01–Jul–1991
EC—Bosnia and Herzegovina	Goods	FTA	11–Jul–2008	GATT Art. XXIV	01–Jul–2008
EC—Cameroon	Goods	FTA	24–Sep–2009	GATT Art. XXIV	01–Oct–2009
EC—CARIFORUM States EPA	Goods & Services	FTA & EIA	16–Oct–2008	GATT Art. XXIV & GATS V	01–Nov–2008
EC—Chile	Goods & Services	FTA & EIA	03–Feb–2004(G) 28–Oct–2005(S)	GATT Art. XXIV & GATS V	01–Feb–2003(G) 01–Mar–2005(S)
EC—Côte d'Ivoire	Goods	FTA	11–Dec–2008	GATT Art. XXIV	01–Jan–2009
EC—Croatia	Goods & Services	FTA & EIA	17–Dec–2002(G) 12–Oct–2009(S)	GATT Art. XXIV & GATS V	01–Mar–2002(G) 01–Feb–2005(S)
EC—Egypt	Goods	FTA	03–Sep–2004	GATT Art. XXIV	01–Jun–2004
EC—Faroe Islands	Goods	FTA	17–Feb–1997	GATT Art. XXIV	01–Jan–1997
EC—Former Yugoslav Republic of Macedonia	Goods & Services	FTA & EIA	23–Oct–2001(G) 02–Oct–2009(S)	GATT Art. XXIV & GATS V	01–Jun–2001(G) 01–Apr–2004(S)
EC—Iceland	Goods	FTA	24–Nov–1972	GATT Art. XXIV	01–Apr–1973

Name	Coverage	Type	Date of notification	Notification	Date of entry into force
EC—Israel	Goods	FTA	20–Sep–2000	GATT Art. XXIV	01–Jun–2000
EC—Jordan	Goods	FTA	17–Dec–2002	GATT Art. XXIV	01–May–2002
EC—Lebanon	Goods	FTA	26–May–2003	GATT Art. XXIV	01–Mar–2003
EC—Mexico	Goods & Services	FTA & EIA	25–Jul–2000(G) 21–Jun–2002(S)	GATT Art. XXIV & GATS V	01–Jul–2000(G) 01–Oct–2000(S)
EC—Montenegro	Goods & Services	FTA & EIA	16–Jan–2008(G) 18–Jun–2010(S)	GATT Art. XXIV & GATS V	01–Jan–2008(G) 01–May–2010(S)
EC—Morocco	Goods	FTA	13–Oct–2000	GATT Art. XXIV	01–Mar–2000
EC—Norway	Goods	FTA	13–Jul–1973	GATT Art. XXIV	01–Jul–1973
EC–Overseas Countries and Territories (OCT)	Goods	FTA	14–Dec–1970	GATT Art. XXIV	01–Jan–1971
EC—Palestinian Authority	Goods	FTA	29–May–1997	GATT Art. XXIV	01–Jul–1997
EC—South Africa	Goods	FTA	02–Nov–2000	GATT Art. XXIV	01–Jan–2000
EC—Switzerland—Liechtenstein	Goods	FTA	27–Oct–1972	GATT Art. XXIV	01–Jan–1973
EC—Syria	Goods	FTA	15–Jul–1977	GATT Art. XXIV	01–Jul–1977
EC—Tunisia	Goods	FTA	15–Jan–1999	GATT Art. XXIV	01–Mar–1998
EC—Turkey	Goods	CU	22–Dec–1995	GATT Art. XXIV	01–Jan–

Name	Coverage	Type	Date of notification	Notification	Date of entry into force
					1996
EC (10) Enlargement	Goods	CU	24–Oct–1979	GATT Art. XXIV	01–Jan–1981
EC (12) Enlargement	Goods	CU	11–Dec–1985	GATT Art. XXIV	01–Jan–1986
EC (15) Enlargement	Goods & Services	CU & EIA	22–Dec–1994(S)	GATT Art. XXIV & GATS V	01–Jan–1995
EC (25) Enlargement	Goods & Services	CU & EIA	26–Apr–2004	GATT Art. XXIV & GATS V	01–May–2004
EC (27) Enlargement	Goods & Services	CU & EIA	27–Sep–2006(G) 26–Jun–2007(S)	GATT Art. XXIV & GATS V	01–Jan–2007
EC (9) Enlargement	Goods	CU	07–Mar–1972	GATT Art. XXIV	01–Jan–1973
EC Treaty	Goods & Services	CU & EIA	24–Apr–1957(G) 10–Nov–1995(S)	GATT Art. XXIV & GATS V	01–Jan–1958
EFTA—Albania	Goods	FTA	07–Feb–2011	GATT Art. XXIV	01–Nov–2010
EFTA—Canada	Goods	FTA	04–Aug–2009	GATT Art. XXIV	01–Jul–2009
EFTA—Chile	Goods & Services	FTA & EIA	03–Dec–2004	GATT Art. XXIV & GATS V	01–Dec–2004
EFTA—Croatia	Goods	FTA	14–Jan–2002	GATT Art. XXIV	01–Jan–2002
EFTA—Egypt	Goods	FTA	17–Jul–2007	GATT Art. XXIV	01–Aug–2007
EFTA—Former Yugoslav Republic of Macedonia	Goods	FTA	11–Dec–2000	GATT Art. XXIV	01–Jan–2001
EFTA—Israel	Goods	FTA	30–Nov–1992	GATT Art. XXIV	01–Jan–1993
EFTA—Jordan	Goods	FTA	17–Jan–2002	GATT Art. XXIV	01–Sept–2006
EFTA—Korea,	Goods &	FTA &	23–Aug–2006	GATT Art. XXIV	01–Sep–

Name	Coverage	Type	Date of notification	Notification	Date of entry into force
Republic of	Services	EIA		& GATS V	2006
EFTA—Lebanon	Goods	FTA	22–Dec–2006	GATT Art. XXIV	01–Jan–2007
EFTA—Mexico	Goods & Services	FTA & EIA	25–Jul–2001	GATT Art. XXIV & GATS V	01–Jul–2001
EFTA—Morocco	Goods	FTA	20–Jan–2000	GATT Art. XXIV	01–Dec–1999
EFTA—Palestinian Authority	Goods	FTA	23–Jul–1999	GATT Art. XXIV	01–Jul–1999
EFTA—SACU	Goods	FTA	29–Oct–2008	GATT Art. XXIV	01–May–2008
EFTA—Serbia	Goods	FTA	24–Nov–2010	GATT Art. XXIV	01–Oct–2010
EFTA—Singapore	Goods & Services	FTA & EIA	14–Jan–2003	GATT Art. XXIV & GATS V	01–Jan–2003
EFTA—Tunisia	Goods	FTA	03–Jun–2005	GATT Art. XXIV	01–Jun–2005
EFTA—Turkey	Goods	FTA	06–Mar–1992	GATT Art. XXIV	01–Apr–1992
EFTA accession of Iceland	Goods	FTA	30–Jan–1970	GATT Art. XXIV	01–Mar–1970
EU—San Marino	Goods	CU	24–Feb–2010	GATT Art. XXIV	01–Apr–2002
EU—Serbia	Goods	FTA	31–May–2010	GATT Art. XXIV	01–Feb–2010
Eurasian Economic Community (EAEC)	Goods	CU	21–Apr–1999	GATT Art. XXIV	08–Oct–1997
European Economic Area (EEA)	Services	EIA	13–Sep–1996	GATS Art. V	01–Jan–1994
European Free	Goods &	FTA &	14–Nov–1959(G)	GATT Art. XXIV	03–May–

SEC. 4 ENFORCING ART. XXIV GATT 157

Name	Coverage	Type	Date of notification	Notification	Date of entry into force
Trade Association (EFTA)	Services	EIA	15–Jul–2002(S)	& GATS V	1960(G) 01–Jun–2002(S)
Faroe Islands—Norway	Goods	FTA	12–Feb–1996	GATT Art. XXIV	01–Jul–1993
Faroe Islands—Switzerland	Goods	FTA	12–Feb–1996	GATT Art. XXIV	01–Mar–1995
Georgia—Armenia	Goods	FTA	08–Feb–2001	GATT Art. XXIV	11–Nov–1998
Georgia—Azerbaijan	Goods	FTA	08–Feb–2001	GATT Art. XXIV	10–Jul–1996
Georgia—Kazakhstan	Goods	FTA	08–Feb–2001	GATT Art. XXIV	16–Jul–1999
Georgia—Russian Federation	Goods	FTA	08–Feb–2001	GATT Art. XXIV	10–May–1994
Georgia—Turkmenistan	Goods	FTA	08–Feb–2001	GATT Art. XXIV	01–Jan–2000
Georgia—Ukraine	Goods	FTA	08–Feb–2001	GATT Art. XXIV	04–Jun–1996
Gulf Cooperation Council (GCC)	Goods	CU			01–Jan–2003
Honduras—El Salvador and the Separate Customs Territory of Taiwan, Penghu, Kinmen and Matsu	Goods & Services	FTA & EIA	06–Apr–2010	GATT Art. XXIV & GATS V	01–Mar–2008
Hong Kong, China—New Zealand	Goods & Services	FTA & EIA	03–Jan–2011	GATT Art. XXIV & GATS V	01–Jan–2011

Name	Coverage	Type	Date of notification	Notification	Date of entry into force
Iceland—Faroe Islands	Goods & Services	FTA & EIA	10–Jul–2008	GATT Art. XXIV & GATS V	01–Nov–2006
India—Singapore	Goods & Services	FTA & EIA	03–May–2007	GATT Art. XXIV & GATS V	01–Aug–2005
Israel—Mexico	Goods	FTA	22–Feb–2001	GATT Art. XXIV	01–Jul–2000
Japan—Indonesia	Goods & Services	FTA & EIA	27–Jun–2008	GATT Art. XXIV & GATS V	01–Jul–2008
Japan—Malaysia	Goods & Services	FTA & EIA	12–Jul–2006	GATT Art. XXIV & GATS V	13–Jul–2006
Japan—Mexico	Goods & Services	FTA & EIA	31–Mar–2005	GATT Art. XXIV & GATS V	01–Apr–2005
Japan—Philippines	Goods & Services	FTA & EIA	11–Dec–2008	GATT Art. XXIV & GATS V	11–Dec–2008
Japan—Singapore	Goods & Services	FTA & EIA	08–Nov–2002	GATT Art. XXIV & GATS V	30–Nov–2002
Japan—Switzerland	Goods & Services	FTA & EIA	01–Sep–2009	GATT Art. XXIV & GATS V	01–Sep–2009
Japan—Thailand	Goods & Services	FTA & EIA	25–Oct–2007	GATT Art. XXIV & GATS V	01–Nov–2007
Japan—Viet Nam	Goods & Services	FTA & EIA	01–Oct–2009	GATT Art. XXIV & GATS V	01–Oct–2009
Jordan—Singapore	Goods & Services	FTA & EIA	07–Jul–2006	GATT Art. XXIV & GATS V	22–Aug–2005
Korea, Republic of—Chile	Goods & Services	FTA & EIA	08–Apr–2004	GATT Art. XXIV & GATS V	01–Apr–2004
Korea, Republic of—India	Goods & Services	FTA & EIA			01–Jan–2010
Korea, Republic of—Singapore	Goods & Services	FTA & EIA	21–Feb–2006	GATT Art. XXIV & GATS V	02–Mar–2006
Kyrgyz Republic—Armenia	Goods	FTA	12–Dec–2000	GATT Art. XXIV	27–Oct–1995

Name	Coverage	Type	Date of notification	Notification	Date of entry into force
Kyrgyz Republic—Kazakhstan	Goods	FTA	29–Jun–1999	GATT Art. XXIV	11–Nov–1995
Kyrgyz Republic—Moldova	Goods	FTA	15–Jun–1999	GATT Art. XXIV	21–Nov–1996
Kyrgyz Republic—Russian Federation	Goods	FTA	15–Jun–1999	GATT Art. XXIV	24–Apr–1993
Kyrgyz Republic—Ukraine	Goods	FTA	15–Jun–1999	GATT Art. XXIV	19–Jan–1998
Kyrgyz Republic—Uzbekistan	Goods	FTA	15–Jun–1999	GATT Art. XXIV	20–Mar–1998
Mexico—El Salvador (Mexico—Northern Triangle)	Goods & Services	FTA & EIA	23–May–2006	GATT Art. XXIV & GATS V	15–Mar–2001
Mexico—Guatemala (Mexico—Northern Triangle)	Goods & Services	FTA & EIA	03–Jul–2006	GATT Art. XXIV & GATS V	15–Mar–2001
Mexico—Honduras (Mexico—Northern Triangle)	Goods & Services	FTA & EIA	10–Jul–2006(G) 20–Jun–2006(S)	GATT Art. XXIV & GATS V	01–Jun–2001
Mexico—Nicaragua	Goods & Services	FTA & EIA	17–Oct–2005	GATT Art. XXIV & GATS V	01–Jul–1998
New Zealand—Singapore	Goods & Services	FTA & EIA	04–Sep–2001	GATT Art. XXIV & GATS V	01–Jan–2001
Nicaragua and	Goods &	FTA &	09–Jul–2009	GATT Art. XXIV	01–Jan–

Name	Coverage	Type	Date of notification	Notification	Date of entry into force
the Separate Customs Territory of Taiwan, Penghu, Kinmen and Matsu	Services	EIA		& GATS V	2008
North American Free Trade Agreement (NAFTA)	Goods & Services	FTA & EIA	29–Jan–1993(G) 01–Mar–1995(S)	GATT Art. XXIV & GATS V	01–Jan–1994
Pakistan—China	Goods & Services	FTA & EIA	18–Jan–2008(G) 20–May–2010(S)	GATT Art. XXIV & GATS V	01–Jul–2007(G) 10–Oct–2009(S)
Pakistan—Malaysia	Goods & Services	FTA & EIA	19–Feb–2008	Enabling Clause & GATS Art. V	01–Jan–2008
Pakistan—Sri Lanka	Goods	FTA	11–Jun–2008	Enabling Clause	12–Jun–2005
Panama—Chile	Goods & Services	FTA & EIA	17–Apr–2008	GATT Art. XXIV & GATS V	07–Mar–2008
Panama—Costa Rica (Panama—Central America)	Goods & Services	FTA & EIA	07–Apr–2009	GATT Art. XXIV & GATS V	23–Nov–2008
Panama—El Salvador (Panama—Central America)	Goods & Services	FTA & EIA	24–Feb–2005	GATT Art. XXIV & GATS V	11–Apr–2003

QUESTIONS AND COMMENTS

Different Forms of Integration: Balassa (1967) provided a classification of "stages of integration" where FTA and CU were the two "shallowest" forms of market integration; next would come the common market, where factors of production (and not only trade restrictions) would be eliminated;

then, the economic union, where some form of harmonization of economic policies would occur, and finally a complete economic integration which would entail unification of monetary, fiscal, social policies and where a central authority entrusted with the capacity to issue binding rules would be established. Balassa, like Viner (1950), did see some sequence across the various stages. Sapir (2011) does not: in his view, there is no reason to believe that there is some form of automaticity in the integration process that leads from FTAs to CUs.

Why Go Preferential? Tinbergen (1962) was first to explain that the formation of PTAs was in some ways quite natural: he developed the gravity equation, aimed to predict trade in the absence of distortions: trade is an increasing function of the gross national product (GNP) of both the exporting, and the importing country; trade is further negatively influenced by the distance between the countries. Krugman (1991), and Summers (1991) have gone one step further and have argued that PTAs among countries in geographic proximity should be encouraged, whereas PTAs among countries which are not neighbours (in a geographic sense) should be discouraged. In their analysis, the former are more likely to avoid the adverse possibility of welfare reduction and to lead to a larger improvement in welfare. Krugman (1991) also observes that a trading block could be formed in order to improve the terms of trade for its participants. Beyond static, there are dynamic gains as well which are difficult to quantify, see Baldwin (1992) and (1993). Employing terms of trade and volume of trade analysis, Kowalczyk (1990) has shown that trade creation and trade diversion do not necessarily equate with welfare gains and losses. WTO Members might be deriving important political benefits by association with their preferential partners: in the account by Galiendo and Parro (2009), NAFTA was beneficial to Mexico not simply because the US lowered its tariff barriers to Mexican goods and services, but also because Mexico benefitted from other dynamic benefits, such as, increased investment over the years as a result of rationalization of its policies etc. In similar vein, Baltagi et al. (2008) discuss the relationship between PTAs and FDI (foreign direct investment) and conclude in an empirical paper regarding the Europe Agreements that removal of trade barriers has led to substantial flows of FDI for those participating. See Baldwin (1997) for a survey of this literature, and Baldwin (1995) for a theoretical model predicting who will form a PTA with who.

Costs of PTA–Formation: But of course, PTAs come at a cost. Viner (1950) was the first to explain why PTAs are welfare reducing in light of the resulting trade diversion (deflection).[35] Grossman and Helpman (1995) and Krishna (1998) established the incentive for PTA-partners to choose integration in these sectors where the possibility for preference (and thus, trade de-

---

[35] It is not the case that trade diversion is a necessary evil stemming from the creation of PTAs: the Kemp–Wan theorem posits that trade diversion can be eliminated by reducing external tariffs so as to keep trade with non-members unchanged, keeping, in other words, prices constant. The result in the Kemp–Wan theorem applies in a set of given circumstances. The Kemp–Wan theorem, nonetheless, is not a *passage obligé* in order to support a claim that PTAs can be welfare improving.

flection) is the greatest possible. Bhagwati (2002), (2008), Krishna (1998) and Limão (2006a) have all shown that, besides trade diversion generated through the establishment of PTAs, members of PTAs behave as enemies of non-discriminatory trade liberalization in the future as well, since they are unwilling to cut tariffs on MFN basis for fear of eroding the margin of preference that they have already granted to their PTA-partners: they become thus, as Bhagwati and Panagariya (1999) put it, stumbling blocks (as opposed to building blocks) in the multilateral trading system, opposing MFN trade liberalization, and frustrating the achievement of the basic WTO objective.

Certificates of Origin: They are necessary to avoid cases where an exporter attempts to circumvent high tariffs in one of the constituents of an FTA by exporting to the FTA member with the relatively lower import duty.

Dual Notifications: When MERCOSUR was established, it was notified under the Enabling Clause only, since all participants were developing countries. It was later agreed that the terms of reference of the Working Party should, in this particular case, also include an examination of the consistency of MERCOSUR with Art. XXIV GATT as well. Both the CTD and the CRTA were also notified of the CU established by the members of the GCC (Gulf Cooperation Council), the India–Korea and Korea–ASEAN FTAs. A number of developing countries raised concerns regarding the legality of this practice. A General Council decision did not manage to clarify this issue:

> Notifying Members shall specify under which provision or provisions in paragraph 1 their PTAs are notified.[36]

Substantially All Trade: After the conclusion of the Uruguay round, Australia tabled a proposal, to clarify the term 'substantially all trade'.[37] It proposed that, to comply with this requirement, WTO Members should be requested to liberalize 95% of all the six-digit tariff lines listed in the HS. In its response to questions by other WTO Members,[38] Australia accepted that the 95% figure was an arbitrary benchmark; in its view nonetheless, coming up with a number was an appropriate device intended to move negotiations out of a deadlock and provide a workable and reasonable rule of thumb.

Domestic Instruments and PTAs: Mavroidis (2012) takes the view that the disciplining of domestic instruments in a PTA must respect the MFN clause anyway. Do you agree?

Why So Little Litigation? Finger (1993) argued that no one wanted to question the wider European integration process though, by putting into question the GATT-consistency of ECSC. Contracting parties, having committed the original sin (by demonstrating benign attitude towards the European integration), refrained from changing attitude subsequently for fear of being inconsistent. Mavroidis (2006) has argued that WTO Member would rationally choose not to challenge a PTA: there is a collective action problem;

---

[36] WTO Doc. WT/L/806 of December 16, 2010.
[37] WTO Doc. WT/REG/W/18, November 17, 1997.
[38] WTO Doc. WT/REG/W/22/Add. 1 of April 24, 1998.

strategic reasons might argue against a challenge; the agency design for WTO adjudicating bodies probably does not inspire challenges of this sort (it would be unrealistic to trust Panelists with questions that Membership failed to answer after long practice). In an accompanying paper, Mavroidis (2011) argues that the absence of enforcement of Art. XXIV GATT should not be perceived as a major threat for the multilateral system. What do you think of these views?

Subject–Matter of Modern PTAs: Horn et al. (2010) examine the subject matter of PTAs concluded by two hubs (EU, US) with various spokes between 1992–2008, and divide it into WTO+ ('WTO plus', say tariff cuts beyond the MFN-level), and WTOx ('WTO extra', issues that do not come under the mandate of the WTO, say positive integration in fields such as environmental policy, fight against corruption etc.). The WTOx part of the PTAs is quite substantial. This paper thus suggests that the rationale for going preferential should also be sought in WTOx-type of obligations. The problem however, is that we lack a test (other than MFN) to measure the consistency of WTOx provisions with the WTO. What is, in your view, the WTO relevance for the WTOx component of PTAs?

CHAPTER 6

SPECIAL AND DIFFERENTIAL TREATMENT FOR DEVELOPING COUNTRIES

■ ■ ■

1. THE LEGAL DISCIPLINE

Goods originating in developing countries that are Members of the WTO can benefit from lower tariffs (and other preferences) when exported to the markets of developed countries that have unilaterally decided to accord similar preferences.

2. THE RATIONALE FOR THE LEGAL DISCIPLINE

The original GATT membership was a rather homogeneous group of 23 countries. Following decolonization, a number of newly-independent, developing countries joined the GATT in the 1960s. From the early days of their participation, developing countries sought preferential tariffs for their products.[1] In their view, the MFN tariff rate amounted to an impediment to their export trade, since they were competing for markets with other, more productive nations. They requested the establishment of a new mechanism that would allow them to access their export markets at preferential (when compared to developed countries' exports) tariff rates. Already during the negotiation of the GATT, Lebanon had argued in favor of introducing tariff preferences for trade across developing countries, although it was not accepted.[2] And, as Irwin et al. (2008) note, India (before partition) had a hostile reaction when it was presented with the Suggested Charter and was requested to comment upon it; its criticism focused on MFN, arguing that this instrument was ill-equipped to deal with countries at different stages of development.

The first time a comprehensive discussion on trade and development took place in the GATT was in 1958 with the circulation of the Haberler report. Haberler, professor of economics at Harvard, was requested by the

---

[1] Hudec (1987) should be credited with the most compelling narrative.

[2] In the words of the Lebanese delegate: "Members recognize that the development of industry in small nations is hampered by the lack of a sufficiently large market for manufactured goods. Consequently, the Organization shall give the most favourable consideration to any proposal for preferential tariff arrangements presented to it by small Member nations belonging to one economic region, aiming at the development of that region, with a view to releasing from their obligations under Chapter V." This proposal did not concern North–South preferences, but rather, South–South preferences aiming at developing industries within regional blocks, see E/PC/T/C.6/W/25 at p. 14.

GATT to examine the validity of claims by the less developed trading partners to the effect that MFN liberalization was not working to their advantage. He concluded, *inter alia*, that existing protectionist policies in the farm sector by developed (industrialized) nations, as well as tariff escalation practices by many developed nations were contributing factors to lack of growth in developing countries. On the other hand, Hans Singer, a German professor of economics at Cambridge, and Raoul Prebisch, an Argentine economist, were advocating industrialization through import substitution policies as the safest way to development. The view that development essentially equalled industrialization provided developing countries with the necessary impetus to adopt a negotiating strategy aimed at achieving non-reciprocal preferential access to developed countries' markets. Over time, the argument was that, thanks to increasing economies of scale resulting from non-reciprocal preferential access, developing countries would gradually become more competitive in their production of industrial goods.

A Working Party on Commodities was established to review trends and developments in international commodity trade; the Singer–Prebisch thesis was reflected therein, as the quoted passage from the report in 1961 evidences:

> ... in the long term, only the industrialization of the less-developed countries would enable these countries to overcome the present difficulties in their external trade; in turn, this industrialization and the economic development generally of the less-developed countries would only be achieved through an increase in their exports, including exports of manufactured and semi-manufactured goods. Direct investment and financial aid alone would not solve this problem.[3]

During the Kennedy Round of international trade negotiations (1962–1967) the Committee on Legal and Institutional Framework of GATT in Relation to Less–Developed Countries (one of the negotiating groups), worked on a Chapter on Trade and Development. This chapter was finalised in a Special Session of the CONTRACTING PARTIES, held from November 17, 1964 to February 8, 1965. It was annexed to the GATT as an amending protocol. It now appears as Part IV. Part IV came into effect on June 27, 1966, and consists of three new legal provisions: Principles and objectives (Art. XXXVI GATT); Commitments (Art. XXXVII GATT); Joint action (Art. XXXVIII GATT). A look at the wording of each provision leaves the reader in no doubt that these were meant to be "best endeavours" clauses aiming at opening the door to discriminatory (preferential) trade. An additional mechanism was needed to make the

---

[3] GATT Doc. L/1656, of December 4, 1961, published in GATT Doc. BISD 10S/83ff., at p.93. During the 1955 review of the GATT, Art. XXVIII GATT was redrafted in order to help the quest for import substitution policies which was largely reflected in Art. XXVIII(c) GATT.

language included in these provisions operational. This mechanism was, initially, a 10–year waiver allowing for preferential rates applicable to imports originating in developing countries only; this was subsequently replaced by the Enabling Clause.[4] The Enabling Clause reproduces the non-reciprocity idea, first embedded in Art. XXXVI.8 GATT, and provides for the possibility to make commitments in this vein.[5] The Panel on *EC–Tariff Preferences* recounts the advent of the Enabling Clause in the following terms:

> During the Second Session of UNCTAD, on 26 March 1968, a Resolution was adopted on expansion and Diversification of Exports and Manufactures and semi-manufactures of Developing Countries' (Resolution 21 (II)). In this Resolution, UNCTAD agreed to the 'early establishment of a mutually acceptable system of generalized, non-reciprocal and non-discriminatory preferences which would be beneficial to the developing countries' and established a Special Committee on Preferences as a subsidiary organ of the Trade and Development Board, with a mandate to settle the details of the GSP arrangements. In 1970, UNCTAD's Special Committee on Preferences adopted Agreed Conclusions which set up the agreed details of the GSP arrangement. UNCTAD's Trade and Development Board took note of these Agreed Conclusions on 13 January 1970. In accordance with the Agreed Conclusions, certain developed GATT contracting parties sought a waiver for the GSP from the GATT Council. The GATT granted a 10–year waiver on 25 June 1971. Before the expiry of this waiver, the CONTRACTING PARTIES adopted a decision on 'Differential and More Favourable Treatment, Reciprocity and Fuller Participation of Developing Countries' (the 'Enabling Clause') on 28 November 1979.

The Enabling Clause is the decision of the GATT contracting parties which allowed ("enabled") deviations from the MFN rate in favor of goods originating in developing countries to become a permanent feature of the GATT- and now the WTO legal order. Through the Enabling Clause, WTO Members can now legitimately accord tariff preferences to developing countries.

The most common vehicle by which a WTO Member provides tariff preferences to products from developing countries is a national GSP (Generalized System of Preferences) scheme. A GSP scheme lists a series of products and a set of beneficiary countries for which tariffs are reduced

---

[4] Decision on Differential and More Favourable Treatment Reciprocity and Fuller Participation of Developing Countries, of November 28, 1979 (GATT Doc. L/4903), GATT BISD 26S/203ff.

[5] A GSP is a list of products for which a tariff preference is accorded in favor of goods originating in developing countries.

(or eliminated altogether). It is administered by national governments, subject to WTO law.

3. COVERAGE OF THE LEGAL DISCIPLINE

3.1 WHO ARE THE BENEFICIARIES?

WTO Members have not managed to agree on the question of which Members qualify as a developing country. As a result, it is left to individual WTO Members to decide on their status; the WTO has a self-election principle. Unilateral declarations (to the effect that a WTO Member is a developing country) can, in principle, be challenged before a WTO Panel. No formal challenge has been launched so far in this context. While negotiating on the implementation of TRIPS, the US and the EU voiced their wish that WTO Members like Singapore, Korea and Hong Kong, China be considered as developed nations at least for the purposes of complying with TRIPS. The discussions in the TRIPS Council suggest that, although a mutually satisfactory solution was agreed among the interested parties, the principle of self-election as such was not questioned.[6] The EU delegate, to cite another example, during the discussions before the Dispute Settlement Body (DSB) regarding the adoption of the AB report on *Korea–Various Measures on Beef*:

> ... noted with surprise that Korea had been treated as a developing country for the purposes of the Agreement on Agriculture. Although this issue did not seem to have been in dispute, the EC was compelled to underline its disagreement with Korea's self-characterization as a developing country.[7]

While the WTO does not define which Members are "developing country," the question as to which are "least developed countries" (LDCs) is easily answered: The WTO recognizes as LDCs those countries which have been designated as such by the UN. There are currently 48 LDCs on the UN list.[8] Of this set, 33 are WTO Members: Angola; Bangladesh; Be-

---

[6] WTO Doc. IP/C/M/8, August 14, 1996, pp. 58ff.

[7] WTO Doc. WT/DSB/M/96, February 22, 2001, p.14.

[8] http://www.unohrlls.org/en/ldc/related/62/. In this webpage we find the UN criteria for including a country among the LDCs. We quote: In its latest triennial review of the list of LDCs in 2009, the UN Committee for Development Policy used the following three criteria for the identification of the LDCs: (i) A low-income criterion, based on a three-year average estimate of the gross national income (GNI) per capita (under $905 for inclusion, above $1,086 for graduation); (ii) A human capital status criterion, involving a composite Human Assets Index (HAI) based on indicators of: (a) nutrition: percentage of population undernourished; (b) health: mortality rate for children aged five years or under; (c) education: the gross secondary school enrolment ratio; and (d) adult literacy rate; and (iii) An economic vulnerability criterion, involving a composite Economic Vulnerability Index (EVI) based on indicators of: (a) population size; (b) remoteness; (c) merchandise export concentration; (d) share of agriculture, forestry and fisheries in gross domestic product; (e) homelessness owing to natural disasters; (f) instability of agricultural production; and (g) instability of exports of goods and services. To be added to the list, a country must satisfy all three criteria. In addition, since the fundamental meaning of the LDC category, i.e. the recognition of structural handicaps, excludes large economies, the population must not exceed 75

nin; Burkina Faso; Burundi; Cambodia; Central African Republic; Chad; DR Congo; Djibouti; Gambia; Guinea; Guinea Bissau; Haiti; Lesotho; Madagascar; Malawi; Mali; Mauritania; Mozambique; Myanmar; Nepal; Niger; Rwanda; Samoa, Senegal; Sierra Leone; Solomon Islands; Tanzania; Togo; Uganda; Vanuatu; and Zambia,[9] with another (Laos) expected to join in 2013. Nine more LDCs are currently negotiating their accession to the WTO: Afghanistan, Bhutan, Comoros, Equatorial Guinea, Ethiopia, Liberia, Sao Tomé & Principe, Sudan, and Yemen. Geographically, of the 48 LDCs, 33 are located in Africa, 14 in Asia, and only one (Haiti) in the Caribbean.

3.2 WHO ARE THE DONORS?

The Enabling Clause enables but does not oblige developed countries to grant preferences. Those that do are primarily a subset of the OECD countries. The best-known GSP schemes are those offered by the EU, US, Japan, Canada, and Australia.[10]

3.3 PREFERENCES ARE ONE WAY, NON–RECIPROCAL

Art. XXXVI.8 GATT provides the foundation for non-reciprocity:

> The developed contracting parties do not expect reciprocity for commitments made by them in trade negotiations to reduce or remove tariffs and other barriers to the trade of less-developed contracting parties.

The Interpretative Note to this provision sheds some additional light:

> It is understood that the phrase "do not expect reciprocity" means, in accordance with the objectives set forth in this Article, that the less-developed contracting parties should not be expected, in the course of trade negotiations, to make contributions which are inconsistent with their individual development, financial and trade needs, taking into consideration past trade developments.

During the Kennedy Round, this provision was further interpreted as follows:

---

million. To become eligible for graduation, a country must reach threshold levels for graduation for at least two of the aforementioned three criteria, or its GNI per capita must exceed at least twice the threshold level, and the likelihood that the level of GNI per capita is sustainable must be deemed high.

[9] Graduation applies here. The UN removed as of January 1, 2008 Cape Verde from this list where it previously featured, see UN GA Res. A/Res/59/210 of December 20, 2004. Donors followed suit: the EU, for example, removed Cape Verde from its list of LDCs beneficiaries of preferences through Regulation 1547/2007 of December 21, 2007 published in the Official Journal (OJ) of the EU L 337/70.

[10] Descriptions of the various schemes can be found in the following sources: EU: Canada and Jean (2009); US: Dean and Wainio (2009); Japan: Komuro (2009); Canada: Kowalski (2009); and Australia: Lippoldt (2009).

There will, therefore, be no balancing of concessions granted on products of interest to developing countries by developed participants on the one hand and the contribution which developing participants would make to the objective of trade liberalization on the other and which it is agreed should be considered in the light of the development, financial and trade needs of developing countries themselves. It is, therefore, recognized that the developing countries themselves must decide what contributions they can make.[11]

3.4 WHAT CONSTITUTES PREFERENTIAL TREATMENT?

Art. XXXVII GATT is a general clause recommending various actions that developed countries may, but again are not required to, undertake in order to help promote issues of interest to developing countries. Some of the recommended actions concern tariffs: For example, the provision includes an incitation to reduce the gap between (high) barriers on processed goods, and (low) barriers on primary products. Others deal with non-tariff barriers: For example, when imposing a contingent protection measure (to be discussed in Chapters 14–16), developed countries were to "have special regard to the trade interests" of developing countries and "explore all possibilities of constructive remedies before applying such measures."[12] The Enabling Clause in § 2 clarifies that preferences can be given for both tariff and non-tariff barriers.

Enabling Clause § 7 reflects an acknowledgement that developing countries are expected to participate more fully in the multilateral trading system as long as their economic situation improves.

3.4.1 Tariff Preferences

Enabling Clause § 1 and § 2a provide the legal means to provide tariff preferences in favor of developing countries. The margin of tariff preferences depends on the will of the donor.[13]

3.4.2 Preferences on Non–Tariff Measures

One such preference has already been discussed: In considering whether to apply contingent protection instruments (*i.e.*, antidumping

---

[11] GATT, COM.TD/W/37, p 9. § 5 of the Enabling Clause also reproduces the one way character of preferences.

[12] In the Anti–Dumping Agreement concluded during the Uruguay round, WTO Members agreed to transform this into a binding legal obligation. It has since been consistently interpreted as an obligation to examine the feasibility of introducing price undertakings on dumped imports originating in developing countries, before anti-dumping duties are imposed. This will be discussed further in Chapter 14.

[13] See, for example, the distinction between sensitive- semi-sensitive and non-sensitive products in the EU GSP as reported in Grossman and Sykes (2005).

duties, countervailing duties, or safeguards—to be discussed in Chapters 14–16), Enabling Clause § 2(c) subjects preferential trade agreements between developing countries to less onerous requirements than those established by Art. XXIV GATT:

> Regional or global arrangements entered into amongst less-developed contracting parties for the mutual reduction or elimination of tariffs and, in accordance with criteria or conditions which may be prescribed by the CONTRACTING PARTIES, for the mutual reduction or elimination of non-tariff measures, on products imported from one another.

PTAs negotiated and concluded pursuant to the Enabling Clause are to be notified to the Committee on Trade and Development (CTD) There are very few completed reports, such as the report concerning the Bangkok Agreement, and hence no meaningful conclusion can be drawn on the nature of multilateral review of preferential trade between developing countries.[14]

Table 6.1
Preferential arrangements notified under § 2(c) of the Enabling Clause

RTA Name	Coverage	Type	Date of notification	Notification	Date of entry into force
Andean Community (CAN)	Goods	CU	01–Oct–1990	Enabling Clause	25–May–1988
ASEAN—China	Goods & Services	PSA & EIA	21–Sep–2005(G) 26–Jun–2008(S)	Enabling Clause & GATS Art. V	01–Jan–2005(G) 01–Jul–2007(S)
ASEAN—India	Goods	FTA	19–Aug–2010	Enabling Clause	01–Jan–2010
ASEAN—Korea, Republic of	Goods & Services	FTA & EIA			01–Jan–2010(G) 01–May–2009(S)
ASEAN Free Trade Area (AFTA)	Goods	FTA	30–Oct–1992	Enabling Clause	28–Jan–1992
Asia Pacific Trade Agree-	Goods	PSA	02–Nov–1976	Enabling Clause	17–Jun–1976

---

[14] GATT Doc. BISD 25S/109.

RTA Name	Coverage	Type	Date of notification	Notification	Date of entry into force
ment (APTA)					
Asia Pacific Trade Agreement (APTA)—Accession of China	Goods	PSA	30–Apr–2004	Enabling Clause	01–Jan–2002
Common Market for Eastern and Southern Africa (COMESA)	Goods	FTA	04–May–1995	Enabling Clause	08–Dec–1994
East African Community (EAC)	Goods	CU	09–Oct–2000	Enabling Clause	07–Jul–2000
Economic and Monetary Community of Central Africa (CEMAC)	Goods	CU	21–Jul–1999	Enabling Clause	24–Jun–1999
Economic Community of West African States (ECOWAS)	Goods	CU	06–Jul–2005	Enabling Clause	24–Jul–1993
Economic Cooperation Organization (ECO)	Goods	PSA	10–Jul–1992	Enabling Clause	17–Feb–1992
Egypt—Turkey	Goods	FTA	05–Oct–2007	Enabling Clause	01–Mar–2007
Global System of Trade Preferences among Developing Countries (GSTP)	Goods	PSA	25–Sep–1989	Enabling Clause	19–Apr–1989
Gulf Coopera-	Goods	CU			01–Jan–2003

RTA Name	Coverage	Type	Date of notification	Notification	Date of entry into force
tion Council (GCC)					
India—Afghanistan	Goods	PSA	08–Mar–2010	Enabling Clause	13–May–2003
India—Bhutan	Goods	FTA	30–Jun–2008	Enabling Clause	29–Jul–2006
India—Nepal	Goods	PSA	02–Aug–2010	Enabling Clause	27–Oct–2009
India—Sri Lanka	Goods	FTA	17–Jun–2002	Enabling Clause	15–Dec–2001
Korea, Republic of—India	Goods & Services	FTA & EIA			01–Jan–2010
Lao People's Democratic Republic—Thailand	Goods	PSA	26–Nov–1991	Enabling Clause	20–Jun–1991
Latin American Integration Association (LAIA)	Goods	PSA	01–Jul–1982	Enabling Clause	18–Mar–1981
Melanesian Spearhead Group (MSG)	Goods	PSA	03–Aug–1999	Enabling Clause	01–Jan–1994
MERCOSUR—India	Goods	PSA	23–Feb–2010	Enabling Clause	01–Jun–2009
Pacific Island Countries Trade Agreement (PICTA)	Goods	FTA	28–Aug–2008	Enabling Clause	13–Apr–2003
Pakistan—Malaysia	Goods & Services	FTA & EIA	19–Feb–2008	Enabling Clause & GATS Art. V	01–Jan–2008
Pakistan—SriLanka	Goods	FTA	11–Jun–2008	Enabling Clause	12–Jun–2005

3.5 NON–DISCRIMINATION

Enabling Clause § 2a provides for the possibility to accord tariff preferences for products originating in developing countries are to be non-discriminatory. A note to this provision (note 3) states:

> As described in the Decision of the CONTRACTING PARTIES of 25 June 1971, relating to the establishment of "generalized, non-reciprocal and non discriminatory preferences beneficial to the developing countries" (BISD 18S/24).

3.5.1 Statutory Distinction Between LDCs and Other Developing Countries

Despite this requirement for non-discrimination, the Enabling Clause does allow WTO Members to make a distinction regarding the treatment across beneficiaries: In § 2(d), the Enabling Clause allows for the possibility of a WTO Member granting additional preferences in favor of LDCs:

> Special treatment on the least developed among the developing countries in the context of any general or specific measures in favour of developing countries

In 1999, WTO Members adopted a waiver that allows developing countries

> to provide preferential tariff treatment to products of least-developed countries, designated as such by the United Nations, without being required to extend the same tariff rates to like products of any other Member.[15]

This waiver allows for one way preferential treatment for products originating in LDCs.

Preferences given for products from LDCs vary across donors. The EU initiative aimed at helping LDCs is the so-called EBA (Everything But Arms). In February 2001, the Council adopted Regulation (EC) 416/2001, granting duty-free access to imports of all products from LDCs, except arms and ammunitions, without any quantitative restrictions (with the exception of bananas, sugar and rice for a limited period). The EBA initiative was later incorporated into the GSP Council Regulation (EC) No 2501/2001. The Regulation foresees that the special arrangements for LDCs should be maintained for an unlimited period of time and not be subject to the periodic renewal of the EU GSP.[16] There is not perfect absolute overlap between the list of LDCs and the EBA beneficiaries;

---

[15] WTO Doc. WT/L/304 of July 17, 1999.

[16] The current EU GSP is reflected in Regulation 732/2008 (July 22, 2008) published in the Official Journal (OJ) of the EU, L 211/1.

SEC. 3 COVERAGE OF THE LEGAL DISCIPLINE 175

for example, the EU has kept Maldives among the beneficiaries, although as of January 1, 2011 Maldives is no longer a LDC.[17]

Table 6.2 Preferences in Favor of LDCs[a]

Preference granting country	Description	Beneficiary(ies)	Coverge/margin of preference	References
Australia	Duty- and quota-free entry. Entry into force: 1 July 2003	LDCs	All products	WT/COMTD/N/18
Belarus	Harmonized System of preference by the Eurasian Economic Community (EAEC) Entry into force: May 2001	47 LDCs	Duty-free access for all products	WT/TPR/S/170
Brazil	Duty-free and Quota-free scheme for LDCs	LDCs	Duty-free and Quota-free access for products from LDCs covering 80 per cent of all tariff lines to be granted by mid–2010.	WT/COMTD/LDC/M/55
Canada	GSP–Least-developed Countries' Tariff Programme (LDCT) Entry into force: 1 January 2003, extended until 30 June 2014	LDCs	With the exception of over-quota tariff items for dairy, poultry and egg products, Canada provides duty-free access under all tariff items for imports from LDCs	WT/COMTD/N/15/Add.1 and Add.2 WT/COMTD/W/159
China	Asia–Pacific Trade Agree-	Bangladesh Lao PDR	In addition to 1,697 products	WT/COMTD/N/22

---

[17] Commission Regulation (EU) 1127/2010 of December 3, 2010, published in the Official Journal (OJ) of the EU, L 318/15.

Preference granting country	Description	Beneficiary(ies)	Coverge/margin of preference	References
	ment (APTA)[b]—amendment to the Bangkok Agreement Entry into force: 1 September 2006		(with average margin of preference of 26.7 per cent) available to all APTA members, tariff concessions granted exclusively to LDC members on 161 products with average margin of preference of 77.9 per cent	
		Bangladesh	On top of Asia–Pacific Trade Agreement (APTA), unilateral special preferential tariffs (zero rated) are offered on additional 87 tariff lines	Information received from the Government of China
	Framework Agreement on Comprehensive Economic Co-operation between ASEAN and China Entry into force: 1 January 2006	Cambodia	Duty-free treatment on 418 tariff lines	Information received from the Government of China
		Cambodia	On top of Framework Agreement on Comprehensive Economic Co-operation between ASEAN and China, unilateral special preferen-	Information received from the Government of China

Sec. 3   Coverage of the Legal Discipline   177

Preference granting country	Description	Beneficiary(ies)	Coverge/margin of preference	References
			tial tariffs (zero rated) are offered on additional 420 tariff lines	
	Framework Agreement on Comprehensive Economic Co-operation between ASEAN and China Entry into force: 1 January 2006	Lao PDR	Duty-free treatment on 330 tariff lines	Information received from the Government of China
China (cont'd)		Lao PDR	On top of Framework Agreement on Comprehensive Economic Co-operation between ASEAN and China, unilateral special preferential tariffs (zero rated) are offered on additional 399 tariff lines	Information received from the Government of China
	Framework Agreement on Comprehensive Economic Co-operation between ASEAN and China Entry into force: 1 January 2006	Myanmar	Duty-free treatment on 220 tariff lines	Information received from the Government of China
		Myanmar	On top of Framework Agreement on Comprehensive Economic Co-	Information received from the Government

Preference granting country	Description	Beneficiary(ies)	Coverge/margin of preference	References
			operation between ASEAN and China, unilateral special preferential tariffs (zero rated) are offered on additional 226 tariff lines	of China
	Forum on China–Africa Co-operation	African countries including LDCs having diplomatic relations with China	As of 1 July 2010, China grants zero-tariff to 4762 tariff lines imported from 33 LDCs which had completed the exchange of letters for that purpose. Eight more LDCs will enjoy the same treatment once the exchange of letters is completed. The 4762 tariff lines account for roughly 60 per cent of China's total tariff lines, and represented 98.2 per cent of all LDC exports to China in value in 2008. Zero tariff treatment will be expanded with an aim of achieving the final objective of including 95 per cent of China's total tariff lines.	WT/COMTD /W/164 WT/COMTD /M/77 WT/COMTD /LDC/M/57
China (cont'd)	Special preference tariff	Afghanistan, Maldives, Samoa,	Unilateral special preferential tariffs	Information received

Preference granting country	Description	Beneficiary(ies)	Coverge/margin of preference	References
		Vanuatu and Yemen	(zero rated) are offered on 286 categories of products	from the Government of China
EU	GSP—Everything But Arms (EBA) initiative Entry into force: 5 March 2001	LDCs	Since 1 October 2009, the EBA has been granting DFQF access for all products from all LDCs (except arms and ammunitions). The EU introduced revised rules of origin for the GSP, as of 1 January 2011, simplifying rules specially for the LDCs	WT/COMTD/N/4/Add.2 and Add.4 WT/TPR/S/214/Rev.1 ec.europa.eu
	Economic Partnership Agreements (EPAs)	79 African, Caribbean and Pacific (ACP) countries, 40 of which are LDCs	EPAs include provision for duty-free and quota-free market access. As of February 2011, a full EPA was signed by the 15 countries in the Caribbean Forum of ACP states (CARIFORUM), of which Haiti is an LDC. Interim EPAs are signed by the following LDCs: (i) Southern African Development Community (SADC): Lesotho and Mozambique; (ii) Eastern and	WT/TPR/S/214/Rev.1 WT7COMTD/LDC/W/46/Rev.1/Corr.1 http://ec.europa.eu/trade/index_en.htm

Preference granting country	Description	Beneficiary(ies)	Coverge/margin of preference	References
			Southern Africa (ESA): Madagascar (signatures by Comoros and Zambia are pending). Interim EPAs are initialled with the East African Community (EAC), which includes four LDCs: Burundi, Rwanda, Tanzania and Uganda.	
Iceland	GSP–Tariff Preferences in Regard to the Importation of Products Originating in the World's Poorest Developing Countries Entry into force: 29 January 2002	LDCs	Essentially all products with some exceptions in agricultural products (HS chapters: 04, 15, 18, 19, 21 and 22) and non-agricultural products (HS sub-headings: 3502 and 3823, and all of HS 16 with the exception of sub-headings 1603 to 1605)	WT/COMTD /N/17 and Corr.1 WT/TPR/S/1 64
India	Asia–Pacific Trade Agreement (APTA)– amendment to the Bangkok Agreement Entry into force: 1 September 2006	Bangladesh Lao PDR	In addition to 570 products (with average margin of preference of 23.9 per cent) available to all APTA members, tariff concessions granted exclusively to LDC members on 48 products with average margin of	WT/COMTD /N/22

SEC. 3 COVERAGE OF THE LEGAL DISCIPLINE 181

Preference granting country	Description	Beneficiary(ies)	Coverge/margin of preference	References
			preference of 39.7 per cent	
	Duty–Free Tariff Preference Scheme (DFTP)	LDCs	DFTP Scheme announced in April 2008. Duty-free access on 85 per cent tariff lines at HS 6–digit level within a five-year time frame.	WT/COMTD /M/69
India (cont'd)	South Asian Free Trade Agreement (SAFTA)c Entry into force: 1 January 2006	Bangladesh Bhutan Maldives Nepal	In addition to tariff concessions on 2,940 line at the HS 6–digit level to all SAFTA members, special concessions exclusively granted to LDC members. In 2006/2007, preferential rates were granted on 84.4 per cent of all tariff lines at average rate of 10.6 per cent (while 15 per cent for non-LDC members)	WT/COMTD /10 WT/TPR/S/1 82.Rev.1 and WT/COMTD /N/26
	Bilateral agreement Entry into force: 13 May 2003	Afghanistan	Tariff reductions on 38 HS 6–digit lines, with margins of preferences of 50 per cent or 100 per cent of MFN tariff	WT/TPR/S/1 82.Rev.1
	Bilateral agreement Entry into force: extended on 29 July	Bhutan	All products	WT/TPR/S/1 82.Rev.1 and WT/COMTD /N/28

Preference granting country	Description	Beneficiary(ies)	Coverge/margin of preference	References
	2006 for 10 years			
	Bilateral agreement	Nepal	Tariff exemptions for all goods subject to rules of origin. Imports of certain goods (vanaspati, copper products, acrylic yarn and zinc oxide) are subject to annual quota.	WT/TPR/S/182.Rev.1
Japan	GSP—Enhanced duty- and quota-free market access Entry into force: 1 April 2007	LDCs	Duty-free access on 8,859 tariff lines (or 98 per cent of the tariff line level), covering over 99 per cent in terms of the import value from LDCs.	WT/COMTD/N/2/Add.14
Kazakhstan	Harmonized System of preference by the Eurasian Economic Community (EAEC) Entry into force: May 2001	47 LDCs	Duty free for all products	WT/TPR/S/170
Korea, Rep. of	Presidential Decree on Preferential Tarriff for LDCs Entry into force: 1 January 2000	LDCs	Duty-free access is granted on 87 tariff items (HS 6–digit).	WT/COMTD/N/12/Rev.1 WT/TPR/S/137
	Asia–Pacific Trade Agreement (AP-	Bangladesh Lao PDR	In addition to 1,367 products (with average	WT/COMTD/N/22

Preference granting country	Description	Beneficiary(ies)	Coverge/margin of preference	References
	TA)—amendment to the Bangkok Agreement Entry into force: 1 September 2006		margin of preference of 35.4 per cent) available to all APTA members, tariff concessions granted exclusively to LDC members on 306 products with average margin of preference of 64.6 per cent	
Kyrgyz Republic	Harmonized system of preference by the Eurasian Economic Community (EAEC) Entry into force: May 2001	47 LDCs	Duty free for all products	WT/TPR/S/170
Morocco	Preferential tariff treatment for LDCs Entry into force: 1 January 2001	33 African LDCs	Duty-free access on 61 products (at the HS 4 to 10-digit level)	WT/LDC/S WG/IF/18 and G/C/6
New Zealand	GSP—Tariff Treatment for LDCs Entry into force: 1 July 2001	LDCs	All products	WT/COMTD /27 WT/TPR/S/1 15
Norway	GSP—Duty- and quota-free market access Entry into force: 1 July 2002	LDCs	All products	WT/TPR/S/1 38 WT/COMTD /N/6/Add.4
Pakistan	South Asian Free Trade	Bangladesh Bhutan	Special concessions available for	SAARC Secretariat

Preference granting country	Description	Beneficiary(ies)	Coverge/margin of preference	References
	Area (SAFTA) Entry into force: 1 January 2006	Maldives Nepal	least-developed contracting states.	website (www.saarc-sec.org) WT/TPR/S/193
Sri Lanka	South Asian Free Trade Area (SAFTA) Entry into force: 1 January 2006	Bangladesh Bhutan Maldives Nepal	Special concessions available for least-developed contracting states	SAARC Secretariat website (www.saarc-sec.org)
	Asia–Pacific Trade Agreement (APTA)—amendment to the Bangkok Agreement Entry into force: 1 September 2006	Bangladesh Lao PDR	In addition to 427 products (with average margin of preference of 14 per cent) available to all APTA members, tariff concessions granted exclusively to LDC members on 72 products with average margin of preference of 12 per cent	WT/COMTD/N/22
Switzerland	GSP—Revised Preferential Tariffs Ordinance Entry into force: 1 April 2007	LDCs	Duty-free access for all products originating from all LDCs as of September 2009.	TN/CTD/M/28 WT/COMTD/N/7/Add.2 and Add.3
Tajikistan	Harmonized System of preference by the Eurasian Economic Community (ECEA) Entry into force: May 2001	47 LDCs	Duty free for all products	WT/TPR/S/170

Preference granting country	Description	Beneficiary(ies)	Coverge/margin of preference	References
Turkey	GSP Entry into force: 31 December 2005	LDCs	Duties are eliminated for LDCs on the basis of EU's Everything But Arms (EBA) Initiative	WT/TPR/S/192
Russia	Harmonized System of preference by the Eurasian Economic Community (ECEA)	47 LDCs	Duty free for all products	WT/TPR/S/170
United States	GSP for least-developed beneficiary developing countries (LDBDC) Entry into force: 1 January 1976, extended until 31 December 2010 (further extensions are currently being considered)	43 designated LDCs[d]	In addition to the standard GSP coverage of nearly 5,000 products, 1,450 articles exclusively available for LDC beneficiaries for duty-free treatment	WT/COMTD/N/1/Add.4 & Add.5 WT/TPR/S/235 www.ustr.gov
	African Growth and Opportunity Act (AGOA) Entry into force: May 2000, extended until 30 September 2015[e]	38 designated Sub–Saharan African Countries (including 25 LDCs[f])	1,835 products, including textiles and apparel[g], available for duty-free treatment, in addition to duty-free treatment on products benefitting from GSP.	WT/COMTD/N/1/Add.3 WT/TPR/S/235 WT/L/754
	Caribbean Basin Trade Partnership	19 designated beneficiaries (including one LDC,	Duty free for most products, including textiles and	WT/TPR/S/235 WT/L/753

Preference granting country	Description	Beneficiary(ies)	Coverge/margin of preference	References
	Act (CBTPA) Entry into force: 1 October 2000, extended until 30 September 2020	i.e. Haiti) in Central America and the Caribbean	apparels. The Haitian Hemispheric Opportunity through Partnership Encouragement Act enhanced Haiti's benefits under CBERA. The Haiti Economic Lift Program Act of 2010 further expanded Haiti's benefits, including broadening duty-free access for Haitian textile and apparel exports.	www.ustr.gov
Uzbekistan	Harmonized System of preference by the Eurasian Economic Community (ECEA)	47 LDCs	Duty free for all products	WT/TPR/S/170

a This table, which represents a non-exhaustive list of market access initiatives untaken in favour of LDCs, updates the information contained in the previous report by the Secretariat (WT/COMTD/LDC/W/46/Rev.1). For those measures taken in favour of exports originating from LDCs prior to 2001, please see document WT/COMTD/LDC/W/38.

b Members of the APTA are: Bangladesh, China, India, Lao PDR, Republic of Korea and Sri Lanka

c Members of SAFTA which superseded the South Asian Preferential Trade Agreement (SAPTA) in 2006 are: Bangladesh, Bhutan, India, Maldives, Nepal, Pakistan and Sri Lanka.

d Afghanistan, Angola, Bangladesh, Benin, Bhutan, Burkina Faso, Burundi, Cambodia, Central African Republic, Chad, Comoros, Democratic Republic of Congo, Djibouti, East Timor, Equatorial Guinea, Ethiopia, The Gambia, Guinea, Guinea–Bissau, Haiti, Kiribati, Lesotho, Liberia, Madagascar, Malawi, Mali, Mauritania, Mozambique, Nepal, Niger, Rwanda, Samoa, São Tomé and Principe, Sierra Leone, Solomon Islands, Somalia, Tanzania, Togo, Tuvalu,

Preference granting country	Description	Beneficiary(ies)	Coverge/margin of preference	References

Uganda, Vanuatu, Yemen and Zambia.

ᵉ The Africa Investment Incentive Act of 2006 or AGOA IV extended the third-country fabric provision from September 2007 until September 2012; added an abundant supply provision; designated certain denim articles as being in abundant supply; and allows lesser developed beneficiary Sub–Saharan African countries to export certain textile articles under AGOA. Sec.3 of the Andean Trade Preference Extension Act of 2008 (Public Law 110–436) removed the abundant supply provisions, and re-designated Mauritius as a lesser developed beneficiary Sub–Saharan African Country for AGOA apparel benefits. See more information on the official AGOA website at www.agoa.gov.

ᶠ Angola, Benin, Burkina Faso, Burundi, Chad, Comoros, Democratic Republic of Congo, Djibouti, Ethiopia, The Gambia, Guinea–Bissau, Lesotho, Liberia, Malawi, Mali, Mauritania, Mozambique, Rwanda, São Tomé and Principe, Senegal, Sierra Leone, Tanzania, Togo, Uganda and Zambia.

ᵍ Twenty-five Sub–Saharan African countries, including 15 LDCs (Benin, Burkina Faso, Chad, Ethiopia, The Gambia, Lesotho, Malawi, Mali, Mozambique, Rwanda, Senegal, Sierra Leone, Tanzania, Uganda, Zambia), are eligible for AGOA apparel benefits.

3.5.2 Preferences Based on Objective Criteria

In *EC–Tariff Preferences*, the Panel and the AB faced the following issue: India and Pakistan both benefited from the EU GSP program. Pakistan, however, received extra preferences because it qualified under the so-called "Drug Arrangements", a scheme aimed at compensating those WTO Members that had adopted active policies against drug production and trafficking. India complained that, by discriminating in favor of Pakistani imports, the EU was in violation of Art. I GATT, a claim upheld by the Panel (§ 7.60). The Panel went on to examine to what extent recourse to the Enabling Clause could be offered as justification. In the Panel's view, the Enabling Clause requires that developed countries, must, by virtue of the term "non-discriminatory" featuring in Note 3 of the Enabling Clause, give identical tariff preferences to all developing countries. The AB reversed the Panel's findings in this respect. It started its analysis (§ 157) pointing to the terms used in § 3(c) of the Enabling Clause, which specifies that 'differential and more favorable treatment' provided under the Enabling Clause:

> ... shall in the case of such treatment accorded by developed contracting parties to developing countries be designed and, if necessary, modified, to respond positively to the development, financial and trade needs of developing countries.

In its view, this paragraph made it plain that development needs are not necessarily shared to the same extent by all developing countries (§ 162). As a result, differentiation might be warranted, indeed, necessary in order to respect the *effet utile* of this provision (§ 165). Consequently, the grant of additional preferences to a sub-set of developing countries cannot be outright excluded (§ 169). The AB further ruled that:

> in granting such differential tariff treatment, however, preference-granting countries are required, by virtue of the term 'non-discriminatory', to ensure that identical treatment is available to all similarly-situated GSP beneficiaries, that is, to all GSP beneficiaries that have the 'development, financial and trade needs' to which the treatment in question is intended to respond. (§ 173)

Applying its test to the specific case, the AB found that the Drug Arrangements were not WTO-consistent, only because the EU had included in it a closed list of beneficiaries (§§ 180 and 187). In § 183, we find the core of the AB argument:

> What is more, the Drug Arrangements themselves do *not* set out any clear prerequisites—or "objective criteria"—that, if met, would allow for other developing countries "that are similarly affected by the drug problem" to be *included* as beneficiaries under the Drug Arrangements. Indeed, the European Commission's own Explanatory Memorandum notes that "the benefits of the drug regime . . . are given without *any* prerequisite." Similarly, the Regulation offers no criteria according to which a beneficiary could be *removed* specifically from the Drug Arrangements on the basis that it is no longer "similarly affected by the drug problem". Indeed, Article 25.3 expressly states that the evaluation of the effects of the Drug Arrangements described in Articles 25.1(b) and 25.2 "will be without prejudice to the continuation of the [Drug Arrangements] until 2004, and their possible extension thereafter." This implies that, even if the European Commission found that the Drug Arrangements were having no effect whatsoever on a beneficiary's "efforts in combating drug production and trafficking", or that a beneficiary was no longer suffering from the drug problem, beneficiary status would continue. Therefore, even if the Regulation allowed for the list of beneficiaries under the Drug Arrangements to be modified, the Regulation itself gives no indication as to how the beneficiaries under the Drug Arrangements were chosen or what kind of considerations would or could be used to determine the effect of the "drug problem" on a particular country. In addition, we note that the Regulation does not, for instance, provide any indication as to how the European Communities would assess whether the Drug

Arrangements provide an "adequate and proportionate response" to the needs of developing countries suffering from the drug problem. (emphasis in the original).

For its scheme to be WTO-consistent, the EU would have to modify its Regulation so as to ensure that it reflects:

criteria or standards to provide a basis for distinguishing beneficiaries under the Drug Arrangements from other GSP beneficiaries. (§ 188)

As a result, donors can "scale" their preferences. In practice, similar schemes are referred to as GSP+, or even GSP++, with the number of + signs denoting the margin of preference.

In *EC–Tariff Preferences*, the AB speaks of a requirement for "identical treatment for similarly-situated GSP beneficiaries" (§ 173). Some WTO Members, such as the US, have tacked on a number of criteria to be taken into account in determining which developing countries qualify as a beneficiary under its GSP program. Presumably the addition of such criteria is legal since it still allows for the set of beneficiaries to be "similarly situated." There is nothing that requires that a GSP preference must be extended to all developing countries. However, an unanswered question is whether the added criterion needs to be one related to development.

3.6 WITHDRAWAL OF BENEFITS

WTO Members may choose to unilaterally withdraw benefits offered under the Enabling Clause. For example, the EU has removed Myanmar from the list of beneficiaries following charges that Myanmar was violating the ILO (International Labour Organization) conventions on forced labour (Council Regulation 552/97). In a press release dated December 15, 2009 by the Commission of the EU (DG Trade)[18], it was announced that In December 2009, the EU also removed Sri Lanka from the list of GSP+ beneficiaries for failure to implement three UN Human Rights Conventions, namely, the ICCPR (International Covenant on Civil and Political Rights); the CAT (Convention Against Torture); and the CRC (Convention on Rights of the Child). In other words, while the Enabling Clause may grant developing countries preferential treatment, it also gives the developed country providing the GSP preferences with leverage to pursue non-trade policy objectives with respect to the beneficiary country.

3.7 LITIGATING THE ENABLING CLAUSE

The AB, in its report on *EC–Tariff Preferences*, held that the Enabling Clause has become an integral part of the GATT, by virtue of Art. 1(b)(iv) GATT 1994. In the same report it notes that, since the Enabling

---

[18] See DG Trade Press Release (Dec. 15, 2009), http://trade.ec.europa.eu/doclib/press/index.cfm?id=499.

Clause enables WTO Members to grant tariff preferences to a sub-set of the WTO Membership (namely, developing countries), it constitutes a legal exception to Art. I GATT (§ 99). The legal implication, in the AB's view, is that the Enabling Clause takes precedence over Art. I GATT (§ 102). As to the allocation of the burden of proof, the AB, reversing the Panel in this respect, held that it is insufficient for a complaining party, when challenging a measure taken pursuant to the Enabling Clause, to simply claim violation of Art. I GATT (§ 110). Due process considerations (§ 113) require that the complaining party:

> *identify* those provisions of the Enabling Clause with which the scheme is allegedly inconsistent, without bearing the burden of *establishing* the facts necessary to support such inconsistency. (§ 115, emphasis in the original).

4. COMMITTEE ON TRADE AND DEVELOPMENT (CTD)

In 1964, the GATT contracting parties agreed on the establishment of the Committee on Trade and Development (CTD). Art. IV.7 of the Agreement Establishing the WTO, which describes the current mandate of the CTD, provides:

> The Ministerial Conference shall establish a Committee on Trade and Development . . . which shall carry out the functions assigned to them by this Agreement and by the multilateral trade agreements, and any additional functions assigned to them by the General Council. . . . As part of its function, the Committee on Trade and Development shall periodically review the special provisions in the multilateral trade agreements in favour of LDC members and report to the General Council for appropriate action.

All WTO Members may participate in the CTD. Over time, the CTD has evolved into a forum where the discussion on issues pertaining to trade and development, in the widest possible sense of the term, takes place under the aegis of the WTO. The CTD performs a multitude of functions:

(a) It is depositary for all GSP schemes;

(b) It is the forum where the notification of and the discussion about preferential arrangements under § 2(c) of the Enabling Clause takes place;[19]

(c) It supervises the implementation of provisions favouring developing countries (special and differential treatment);

---

[19] WTO Docs. WT/L/671 and 672 of December 14, 2006.

(d) It issues guidelines for technical cooperation. The CTD serves as a focal point for consideration and coordination of technical assistance work on development in the WTO and its relationship to development-related activities in other multilateral agencies;

(e) It adopts measures aiming to increase participation of developing countries in the trading system, paying particular attention to the position of LDCs.

5. TRADE AND DEVELOPMENT

The International Trade Centre (ITC) was established in 1964, with the aim of promoting trade of developing countries. The ITC became later a joint agency of United Nations Conference on Trade and Development (UNCTAD) and GATT (and eventually the WTO). In 1998, the WTO together with UNCTAD and the ITC established the Common Trust Fund, meant to finance technical capacity in developing countries.

At the Doha Ministerial Conference, in November 2001, Trade Ministers mandated the CTD to identify which special and differential treatment provisions are mandatory, and to consider the implications of making mandatory those which are currently non-binding. During this meeting, the Sub–Committee on LDCs saw the light of the day: This institution (again one in which all WTO Members participate), focuses on the implementation of the WTO Work Programme for the LDCs, namely:

(a) market access for LDCs;

(b) trade-related technical assistance and capacity building initiatives for LDCs;

(c) providing, as appropriate, support to agencies assisting with the diversification of LDCs' production and export base;

(d) mainstreaming, as appropriate, into the WTO's work the trade related elements of the LDC–III Programme of Action, as relevant to the WTO's mandate;

(e) participation of LDCs in the multilateral trading system;

(f) accession of LDCs to the WTO; and, follow-up to WTO Ministerial Decisions/Declarations.[20]

At the Hong Kong Ministerial Conference Members (2005), the CTD adopted five decisions in favour of the LDCs, including a decision to grant duty-free and quota-free (DFQF) market access for at least 97% of LDC exports. It has further been quite active in implementing a number of development-related initiatives, such as the WTO Work Programme for Small Economies. The Doha Declaration mandated the WTO General

---

[20] WTO Doc. WT/COMTD/LDC/11 of February 13, 2002. This Work Programme was thought to be one of the main pillars of the ongoing negotiations since the round was initiated with the aim of addressing development-related issues on a priority basis; hence, it was deemed the Doha Development Agenda (DDA).

Council to examine this issue, and to make recommendations regarding measures that could improve the integration of small economies into the multilateral trading system. On March 1, 2002, the WTO General Council agreed that:

> The question of small economies would be a standing agenda item of the General Council; The Committee on Trade and Development (CTD) would hold Dedicated Sessions on this question and report regurlaly to the General Council.[21]

In similar vein, § 55 of the Hong Kong Ministerial Declaration instructed the CTD to intensify its work on commodity issues in cooperation with other relevant international organizations and to report to the General Council with possible recommendations. The CTD has also been active in promoting electronic commerce,[22] and Aid for Trade. Besides the CTD, during the Doha round, ministers set up working groups on Trade, Debt and Finance, and on Trade and Technology Transfer, the former under the influence that the discussion on the impact of the financial crisis in the first years of the new century would have had on trade liberalization. The WTO now cooperates with other international organizations in programmes of common interest. The two most prominent initiatives aimed at providing technical assistance to developing countries are the Integrated Framework (IF) and the Joint Integrated Technical Assistance Programme (JITAP).[23] The IF, or EIF (Enhanced Integrated Framework) as it has become (1997),[24] is an inter-agency coordination mechanism for the delivery of technical assistance, promotion of economic growth and sustainable development, and more generally in helping lift LDCs from the poverty trap, among six multilateral agencies—ITC, IMF, UNCTAD, UNDP (United Nations Development Programme), World Bank, in partnership with bilateral donors and LDC beneficiaries. Only LDCs can take advantage of the IF-facility. The WTO serves as coordinator of the IF and accommodates a Secretariat, with a view to taking maximum advantage of each agency's expertise, to ensure optimal coordination.

Aid for Trade has been hailed as the single most important contribution of the WTO so far in the debate on Trade and Development. This is its description in the WTO webpage:

> part of overall development aid, but with the specific objective of helping developing countries, in particular the least developed,

---

[21] The CTD issued a report to this effect, see WTO Doc. WT/COMTD/SE/5, September 29, 2006.

[22] WTO Doc. WT/L/274, of September 30, 1998.

[23] WTO Doc. WT/COMTD/W/102 of 16 July 2002.

[24] The move from IF to EIF signaled a wider portfolio for the established entity and substantial 'ownership' by the beneficiaries (LDCs) who would now have more of a say in shaping the agenda and the programmes that should be financed.

to play an active role in the global trading system and to use trade as an instrument for growth and poverty alleviation.

Aid for Trade concentrates on trade policy and regulation, economic infrastructure, productive capacity building, and adjustment assistance. There are four main areas where Aid for Trade is relevant:

(a) Capacity building: participation of developing countries in trade negotiations has been severely damaged by scarcity of negotiating resources and lack of expertise. While there is not much that can be done, in the short run, to address the former-, a lot can be probably done with respect to the latter;

(b) Infrastructure: construction of roads, ports, airports, upgrading of existing infrastructure on telecommunications, and energy networks emerge as key issues in expanding on the current participation of developing countries in world trade;

(c) Increase productivity: very often it is the case that developing countries cannot compete in product-markets and some of the Aid for Trade money is meant to address this type of concerns;

(d) Adjustment assistance: as a result of the reduction of MFN tariffs worldwide, developing countries have suffered from preference erosion, that is, the margin of preference that they previously enjoyed has been gradually curtailed. Aid for Trade money could provide some sort term relief. Most importantly, it could go some way towards avoiding the risk that those who have suffered from preference erosion turn into enemies of trade liberalization (because of the ensuing preference erosion).

QUESTIONS AND COMMENTS

Singer–Prebisch Thesis: The argument for import substitution was justified as the adequate response to what was termed 'terms of trade pessimism', the idea that exports of developing countries were progressing at a slower pace than total exports.[25] Note that during that time, liberal market economies were discredited in the eyes of many observers especially in developing countries, and a strong argument in favour of government-driven economies was falling onto fertile ground. Prebisch and Singer concluded that the terms of trade for primary commodity exporters (the commodities were developing countries had comparative advantage) had a tendency to decline. Their explanation for this was that, for manufactured (industrial) goods, the income elasticity of demand is greater than it is for farm goods: as incomes rise, the demand for the former increased more rapidly than did demand for the latter.

---

[25] A related idea was what became known as *'elasticity pessimism'*: devaluation will improve trade balance assuming the Marshall–Lerner condition holds, that is, the sum of import and export demand elasticities exceeds one in absolute value. If elasticities are too low, other means (possibly QR) are needed to change an adverse trade balance. There is almost no evidence that the elasticities are so low, but that was the post-war fear of many developing countries.

Consequently, the argument goes, it is the structure of the market that creates inequality in the world system.

Special and Differential in WTO: A WTO Secretariat document classifies the various provisions regarding the special and differential treatment as follows:

(a) provisions aimed at increasing the trade opportunities of developing country Members;

(b) provisions under which WTO Members should safeguard the interests of developing country Members;

(c) flexibility of commitments, of action, and use of policy instruments;

(d) transitional time periods;

(e) technical assistance;

(f) provisions relating to least-developed country Members.[26]

Low (2007) expresses reservations regarding the well-founded of an approach that preaches 'one size fits all': it is quite true that developing countries present a very diverse group of countries which is becoming increasingly diverse over the years. The various provisions echo the very basic developing countries/LDCs distinction first reflected in the Enabling Clause. Rodrik (2001) has forcefully argued in favour of adding to the existing arsenal, pointing to the very limited usefulness (and even to the total uselessness) of some of the existing provisions: technical capacity, for example, as nowadays practised, has come under a lot of criticism, a point to which we return later. On the other hand of the spectrum, Hoekman (2005) warns against the dangers of an over-expanded class of provisions coming under the heading 'special and differential-treatment': WTO could become an irrelevant policy prescription for beneficiaries and thus, all gains from trade liberalization and participation in the negotiating process could be severely undermined.

Advisory Centre for WTO Law: The Advisory Centre for WTO Law (ACWL) aims at providing legal expertise to developing countries at non market (e.g., subsidized) rates.[27] The WTO also provides similar services, albeit in more limited manner, by making two legal experts available to developing countries on part-time basis (Art. 27.2 DSU).

Do GSP Schemes Work? There are dozens of papers pointing to the direction that the benefits from GSP schemes should not be exaggerated. Grossman and Sykes (2005), citing abundant empirical evidence to this effect, conclude that the flame is not worth the candle: there is little support to the

---

[26] WTO Doc. WT/COMTD/W/77/Rev.1 of September 21, 2001. Compare Kessie (2007).

[27] Meagher (2007) discusses its mandate in extenso. The WTO also provides similar services, albeit in more limited manner, by making two legal experts available to developing countries on part-time basis (Art. 27.2 DSU).

proposition that the EU GSP scheme has had substantial positive welfare effects on recipients. They calculate that developing countries roughly receive tariff reductions of 100% (for non-sensitive-), 65% (for semi-sensitive-), 30% (for sensitive-), and 15% (for very sensitive products) from the usual MFN rate for goods in each category. The export interest of most developing countries is of course, concentrated on the very-sensitive category of products, the one that receives the smallest preference margin. Dean and Wainio (2009) discuss the effects of US GSP to beneficiaries and conclude that high utilization rates should not hide the fact that preference margins for non-agricultural goods are low (preference erosion here is the direct result of the low US MFN tariffs), whereas preference margins are low for agricultural goods largely because of the exclusion of products that face high tariffs from GSP schemes. Their data supports the view that the US is more generous towards its PTA partners than it is to its GSP beneficiaries. Candau and Jean (2009) conclude that the EU GSP scheme is quite important for sub-Saharan LDCs, but not so for South Asian LDCs essentially because of the constraints imposed by rules of origin on textile and clothing exports. In a similar vein, Kowalski (2009) concludes that the welfare impact of Canadian preferences is very small for developing countries. Lippoldt (2009) concludes that the Australian GSP scheme has had unambiguous beneficial effects only for those developing countries in geographic proximity to the donor. Why is it so? GSP schemes simply do not reproduce a negotiation based on reciprocal concessions, as Bagwell and Staiger (2011) point out: developing countries are not there to request the opening up of the export markets they are interested in; they are at home waiting for donors to draw their GSP lists. Donors will do so discussing with their domestic lobbies and the opening up of their markets corresponds to the question 'where and how much would my lobbies want me to open up to international trade?' rather than 'where would you developing countries want me to open up?' This is the simple truth. This explains the distinction between sensitive and semi-sensitive products for example in the EU GSP list and the other distinctions in other lists as well. Özden and Reinhardt (2003), in an empirical study, point to yet another disturbing factor linked to GSP schemes: countries that gradually extricated themselves from GSP schemes, subsequently undertook greater liberalization than those that chose to retain their eligibility to participate in them. It is some sort of a wicked version of the Jevons paradox: preferences were supposed to help beneficiaries graduate to the non-beneficiaries status. Instead, beneficiaries become 'hooked' to the benefit granted, use it more than before (or as much as they can), and never graduate. The WTO becomes an irrelevance to them, as they live within the WTO world but outside the WTO legal disciplines. The countries that got out of this vicious circle are those that liberalized and enjoyed gains from trade. And recall that Sachs and Warner (1995) have shown that developing countries with more liberal trade policies have achieved higher rates of growth and development than countries that are more protectionist. A number of more recent studies point to the same result: Trefler (2004) shows how tariff cuts can increase the industry level-productivity of the country performing similar cuts. Tokarick (2006) examines import protection in 26 developing countries. The sample is quite disparate and hence largely representative of the situation prevailing across all developing countries: Argentina, Brazil, Botswana, Malawi, China, India, but also Albania and Romania are being reviewed. His main objective is to quantify the extent to which import protection acts as (implicit) tax on a country's export sector. He finds that this is indeed the case and arrives at a rather substantial tax level, 12% for the 26 countries in his sample.[28] Mostashari (2010) shows that tariff cuts by countries exporting to the US market are more important in explaining the success that these countries have enjoyed than the US import tariff cuts.

Is There a Firewall between PTAs and Special and Differential Treatment? The new EU GSP (applicable as of 2014) reduces the number of beneficiaries. One of the criteria for reduction is participation of former beneficiaries to an FTA with the EU. In your view, is this criterion consistent with WTO law, namely, the obligation to provide benefits on non-discriminatory basis to all developing countries?

---

[28] The equivalence between import tariffs and export taxes was first established by the economist Abba Lerner and is known as the *Lerner symmetry theorem*. Based on an assumption of a zero balance of trade (that is, the value of exported goods equals the value of imported goods for a given country), Lerner showed that an *ad valorem* import tariff would have the same effects as an export tax. The effect thus, on relative prices is the same, regardless of which policy, import duties or export taxes, has been privileged.

Chapter 7

Import Licensing, Customs Valuation, and Pre-shipment Inspection

■ ■ ■

1. THE ILA (IMPORT LICENSING AGREEMENT)

1.1 THE LEGAL DISCIPLINE

Licensing schemes must not constitute a restriction: The ILA simplifies and brings transparency to import licensing procedures in an effort to ensure their fair and equitable application and administration.

1.2 THE RATIONALE FOR THE LEGAL DISCIPLINE

While Art XIII.3(a) GATT imposes transparency-obligations that apply to the administration of import licenses, the provision was considered to be at a level of aggregation that was ill-suited to regulate import licensing. During the Tokyo Round, GATT members concluded the first ILA; this was later superseded by the Uruguay Round ILA. The current agreement contains stronger disciplines on transparency and notifications.

1.3 COVERAGE

The ILA deals with import—and not with export—licensing. Art. 1 ILA defines import licensing:

> For the purpose of this Agreement, import licensing is defined as administrative procedures used for the operation of import licensing regimes requiring the submission of an application or other documentation (other than that required for customs purposes) to the relevant administrative body as a prior condition for importation into the customs territory of the importing Member.

1.3.1 Automatic- and Non–Automatic Import Licensing

There are two forms of licensing provided for in the ILA: automatic licensing (Art. 2 ILA), that is, a licensing scheme has been enacted when no (legitimate) restriction (e.g., a QR on balance of payments grounds) is in place; and non-automatic licensing (Art. 3 ILA), when a scheme has been introduced in order to distribute import licences when a lawful restriction is in place.

1.3.2 Automatic Licensing

Automatic licensing is defined in Art. 2.1 ILA:

> Automatic import licensing is defined as import licensing where approval of the application is granted in all cases, and which is in accordance with the requirements of paragraph 2(a).

Art. 2 ILA states that automatic import licensing may be maintained as long as the circumstances which gave rise to its introduction are still present, provided that the reason for adopting it in the first place cannot be achieved in a more appropriate way. In practice, a WTO Member will usually have recourse to automatic licensing in order to monitor imports, that is, get statistical information.

There is a presumption that automatic import licensing has restrictive effects. This is not, however, the case if the three conditions mentioned in Art. 2.2(a) ILA have been met:

> (a) Any person, firm or institution which fulfills the legal requirements of the importing Member for engaging in import operations involving products subject to automatic licensing is equally eligible to apply for and to obtain import licences;
> (b) Applications for licences may be submitted on any working day prior to the customs clearance of the goods;
> (c) Applications for licences when submitted in appropriate and complete form are approved immediately on receipt, to the extent administratively feasible, but within a maximum of 10 working days.

Although the Agreement is not explicit in this respect, it should be the case that the three conditions must be met cumulatively.

1.3.3 Non–Automatic Licensing

Non-automatic import licensing can occur any time a restriction (a quota, usually) is in place. Non-automatic import licensing is defined in Art. 3.1 ILA as follows:

> Non-automatic import licensing procedures are defined as import licensing not falling within the definition contained in paragraph 1 of Article 2.

Non-automatic licensing is, in practice, the more frequently used type of licensing. The AB, in its report on *EC–Poultry*, held that WTO Members have to ensure that, when applying import licensing schemes, no distortive effects will be caused neither for the trade covered by the scheme at hand, nor for the trade not covered by the scheme (§ 67):

These arguments, however, do not address the problem of establishing a causal relationship between imposition of the EC licensing procedure and the claimed trade distortion. Even if conceded *arguendo*, these arguments do not provide proof of the essential element of causation. (italics in the original)

Art. 3.5 ILA further requests from WTO Members applying non-automatic licensing that:

(a) The period of application should not be excessively long;

(b) The period of validity of the license should not be unreasonably limited in time;

(c) They should not discourage full utilization of quotas;

(d) The desirability for issuing licenses for products in economic quantities must be taken into account by the WTO Member issuing an import license;

(e) When allocating import licenses, the previous import performance of the petitioner must be taken into account;

(f) In the case where a quota is administered through a license which is not country of origin-specific, importers shall be free to choose the source of imports;

(g) In case of variations between the amount designated in the license and the amount actually imported (which can occur, as Art. 1.4 ILA itself acknowledges), Art. 3.5(l) ILA calls for compensatory adjustments to ensure that trade flows continue un-impeded; and finally,

(h) They undertake, in accordance with Art. 1.9 ILA, the obligation to make foreign exchange available to petitioners for an import license under the same terms as importers of goods for which no import licensing scheme is in place.

In *Turkey–Rice*, the Panel had to entertain a claim by the US to the effect that Turkey was running afoul its obligations under Art. 3.5 ILA by restricting access to in quota-rice to traders who had previously purchased a larger quantity of domestic rice. This was, in the view of the complainant an impermissible distortive effect. The Panel for reasons of judicial economy did not formally rule on this issue, yet the overall context and discussion in the Panel report lend strong support to the view that similar practices are inconsistent with the obligations assumed under the ILA (§§ 7.294ff.).

1.3.4 Transparency and Administration of Import Licensing

Art. 1.4 ILA imposes a general obligation of transparency: the conditions for obtaining a licence become public and a notification is transmitted to the WTO at the very least 21 days before the effective date of the imposition of the requirement. WTO Members are further obliged to complete on an annual basis the "Questionnaire on Import Licensing Procedures" by September 30, each year.[1] WTO Members are, further, under the duty to notify the WTO (Committee on Import Licensing) of all laws, regulations, and the like, that regulate import licensing as well as initiations of licensing procedures. Art. 5.5 ILA allows for the possibility of cross notifications of licensing procedures instituted by other WTO Members.

Art. 1.3 ILA imposes a general obligation on WTO Members to the effect that:

> The rules for import licensing procedures shall be neutral in application and administered in a fair and equitable manner.

The AB in its report on *EC–Bananas III* clarified that this legal provision should be understood as imposing on WTO Members the obligation to apply the same procedures for import licensing to all WTO Members (§§ 196–198).

Art. 1.5 ILA requests that WTO Members guarantee that application and renewal forms are "as simple as possible"; the same obligation is imposed by virtue of Art. 1.6 ILA with respect to application and renewal procedures. Finally, Art. 1.7 ILA makes it clear that applications will not be rejected for minor documentation errors.

The treatment of confidential information is regulated in Art. 1.11 ILA:

> The provisions of this Agreement shall not require any Member to disclose confidential information which would impede law enforcement or otherwise be contrary to the public interest or would prejudice the legitimate commercial interests of particular enterprises, public or private.

Reservations to the ILA are possible, assuming the other WTO Members have provided their consent to this effect (Art. 8 ILA).

1.4 INSTITUTIONAL ISSUES

The Committee on Import Licensing is in charge of administering the ILA. It has adopted procedures for notification: a questionnaire must be completed by WTO Members every year, whereby the purpose and coverage of licensing, the applied procedures, the criteria for eligibility to apply for a licence, and its period of validity are, inter alia, reported.[2] Recently, the WTO Secretariat proposed a simplified formulary that could be used for notification purposes:[3] information regarding the publication of the import licencing scheme, a translation in one of the three WTO official

---

[1] Art. 7.3 ILA and WTO Doc. G/LIC/3.
[2] WTO Doc. G/LIC/3 of November 7, 1995.
[3] WTO Doc. G/LIC/22 of August 2, 2011.

languages (English, French or Spanish) if necessary, as well as the domestic institution in charge is provided. The new format will be used on a voluntary basis by the WTO Members.[4] A soft conciliation procedure is established where Members bring forward their complaints.[5] If submitted complaints do not get resolved at this stage, then the complaining party can always submit its concern to a WTO Panel.

2. THE CUSTOMS VALUATION (CV) AGREEMENT

2.1 THE LEGAL DISCIPLINE

The CV Agreement aims at streamlining the conditions under which specific methods for customs valuation will be legitimately used, while, at the same time, taking an active step towards transparency: traders have the right to request and receive explanations (Art. 16 CV), whereas all customs laws etc. must be published (Art. 12 CV). In *Colombia–Ports of Entry*, the Panel provided the following definition of customs valuation (§ 7.83):

> Essentially, customs valuation involves the process of determining the monetary worth or price of imported goods for the purpose of levying customs duties.

2.2 THE RATIONALE FOR THE LEGAL DISCIPLINE

Customs valuation is discussed in the original GATT (Art. VII GATT) but this provision does not contain a comprehensive definition of the term "customs valuation". First, during the Tokyo Round, an agreement on customs valuation (CV) was adopted, which aimed to complement Art. VII GATT, and introduced new disciplines to this effect. This agreement has since been superseded by the Uruguay Round's Agreement on Customs Valuation.[6]

Customs authorities might have legitimate reasons to doubt the accuracy of the invoice price and reject it. The CV Agreement wants to impose some limits in their exercise of discretion when they reject the invoice price. It thus, provides for five methods that can be used for the purposes of customs valuation:

(a) transaction value of identical goods (Art. 2 CV);

(b) transaction value of similar goods (Art. 3 CV);

(c) deductive method (Art. 5 CV);

(d) computed method (Art. 6 CV); and, finally,

(e) fall-back method (Art. 7 CV).

---

[4] See the Chinese notification along these lines, WTO Doc. G/LIC/23 of October 21, 2011.

[5] WTO Docs. G/LIC/Q and G/LIC/M are precious source of information on import licensing.

[6] Rosenow and O'Shea (2010) provide a comprehensive account of this Agreement, its function and its history.

2.3 COVERAGE

2.3.1 Limits of Coverage

The CV Agreement explains in detail how use of the five methods mentioned above will be legitimately made. Customs authorities cannot use anything other than the above-mentioned methods. Art. 7 CV contains a list of methods that cannot be used as basis for deciding on the customs value under any circumstances. The best known in practice was minimum customs value, whereby the customs value would not fall below a certain threshold under any circumstances. Developing countries nevertheless, can have recourse to them, if they have made a reservation to this effect and have shown good cause: the Decision on Texts Relating to Minimum Values and Imports by Sole Agents, Sole Distributors and Sole Concessionaires adopted during the Uruguay round says as much.[7] Customs authorities must, by virtue of Art. 7 CV, further refrain from using:

(a) Arbitrary or fictitious values: this term appears in Art. VII.2(a) GATT as the opposite to actual value;

(b) Price of goods in other export markets;

(c) Price of goods in the exporting market;

(d) Cost of production calculated without recourse to the computed value;

(e) The highest of two alternative values;

(f) Selling price of goods in the importing market.[8]

In *Colombia–Ports of Entry*, the Panel found that Colombia, by basing its customs valuation of imported goods on indicative prices, was in violation of Arts. 1, 3, 5 and 7 CV, (§§ 7.152ff.)

The CV Agreement does not contain obligations concerning valuation for purposes of determining export duties, or quota administration based on the value of goods, nor does it lay down conditions for the valuation of goods for internal taxation or foreign exchange control: its sole preoccupation is valuation of imported goods.

2.3.2 The Primacy of Transaction Value

The five methods described above must be applied in the prescribed hierarchical order[9] in cases where there is no transaction value, or where the transaction value has been rejected. The starting point nevertheless, is the transaction value: the CV Agreement confirms that valuation shall, with the exception of circumstances mentioned in the agreement, be

---

[7] See also Annex III to the CV Agreement at § 2.

[8] The rationale for this prohibition has to do with the decision to eliminate a US practice, the so-called 'American Selling Price' (ASP), which functioned almost like a variable import levy that would equate the world to the domestic price.

[9] That is, (a) before (b) before (c) before (d) before (e), as we explain in more detail *infra*.

based on the actual price paid or payable for the goods to be valued, which generally appears on the invoice. This price, adjusted for certain elements featured in Art. 8 CV, constitutes the "transaction value".

Transaction value is understood as the value of imported goods upon which the buyer and the seller have agreed for the purposes of a particular transaction. Activities that the buyer might undertake on behalf of the seller which relate to the sold goods (such as advertising) will not be taken into account for customs valuation purposes.[10] By the same token, internal taxes etc. cannot be added to the invoice price.

Art. 8 CV leaves it to the discretion of WTO Members to privilege a f.o.b (free on board) or a c.i.f (cost, insurance, freight) price as basis for valuing imported goods: in § 2, it provides:

> In framing its legislation, each Member shall provide for the inclusion in or the exclusion from the customs value, in whole or in part, of the following:
>
> (a) the cost of transport of the imported goods to the port or place of importation;
>
> (b) loading, unloading and handling charges associated with the transport of the imported goods to the port or place of importation; and
>
> (c) the cost of insurance.

2.3.3 Moving Away From the Transaction Value

The Panel in *Thailand–Cigarettes (Philippines)* entertained a claim to the effect that Thailand was violating its obligations under Art. 1, and 2(a) CV by enacting a general rule rejecting the transaction- and requiring the application of the deductive value. It first established the appropriate in its view standard of review to entertain this claim (§ 7.105) upholding:

> the Appellate Body's reasoning that panels need not necessarily confine their review of a domestic authority's determination to an examination of that determination in terms of the factual and legal arguments put forward by the interested parties during the domestic investigation. The Appellate Body in *US— Countervailing Duty Investigation on DRAMS* also stated, "this is not to say that a panel is prohibited from examining whether the agency has given a reasoned and adequate explanation for its determination, in particular, by considering other inferences that could reasonably be drawn from—and explanations that could reasonably be given to—the evidence on record. Indeed, a panel must undertake such an inquiry.]

---

[10] Interpretative Note ad Art. 1 CV.

The Panel went on to observe that the transaction value can be discarded if the buyer and seller are related (Art. 1.1(d) CV), and if the relationship has affected the price. So, there is no automaticity resulting from the relationship between buyer and seller that would lead to the rejection of the transaction value. It must be demonstrated that the relationship did not influence the price for the transaction value to be maintained. The duties of the customs authority and the importer in making this demonstration have been clarified in the Panel report on *Thailand–Cigarettes (Philippines)* (§§ 7.169–171):

> The particular nature of the examination to be conducted by the customs authorities can further be inferred from Case Study 10.1 on the application of Article 1.2 of the Customs Valuation Agreement by the WTO Technical Committee on Customs Valuation:
>
>> "Under Article 1.2 of the Agreement the responsibility for demonstrating that relationship [between buyer and seller] has not influenced price [sic] lies with the importer. While the Agreement requires Customs to provide reasonable opportunity to the importer to provide information that would indicate that prices are not influenced by the relationship, it does not require the Customs administration to conduct an exhaustive enquiry for the purpose of justifying the price difference. Thus, any decision in this regard must, to a significant degree, be based on the information provided by the importer."
>
> The WTO Technical Committee's comment supports the understanding that while customs authorities are responsible for providing a "reasonable opportunity" to the importer to provide information, once given this opportunity, importers are in principle liable for supplying the customs authorities with information that would indicate that the relationship did not influence the price.
>
> In sum, we consider that the customs authorities and importers have respective responsibilities under Article 1.2(a). The customs authorities must ensure that importers be given a reasonable opportunity to provide information that would indicate that the relationship did not influence the price. Importers are responsible for providing information that would enable the customs authority to examine and assess the circumstances of sale so as to determine the acceptability of the transaction value. Provided with such information, the customs authorities must conduct an "examination" of the circumstance of sale, which would require an active, critical review and consideration of the information before them.

The grounds for rejecting the transaction value must be communicated to the importer by virtue of Art. 1.2(a) CV.[11] The Panel in *Thailand–Cigarettes (Philippines)* explained that this obligation is distinct from the obligation to provide an explanation for how the customs authority had proceeded with customs valuation under Art. 16 CV; in its view communicating the grounds would entail communicating (§ 7.218):

> the customs authorities' *reasons for considering*, in the light of information provided by the importer or otherwise, that the relationship influenced the price. (emphasis in the original)

A customs authority would be required under Art. 16 CV to provide:

(a) The reason for rejecting transaction value: and
(b) The basis for the alternative valuation determination.

The Panel in *Thailand–Cigarettes (Philippines)* endorsed this standard (§ 7.237). WTO Members must provide affected parties with a forum to launch an appeal against this type as well as any other decision customs authorities adopt in the context of customs valuation (Art. 11 CV).

If the transaction value has been rejected, customs authorities must first make an attempt to locate prior transactions of "identical" goods (Art. 2 CV). If this has proven impossible, then they can legitimately use previous transactions of "similar" (a wider category than "identical") goods (Art. 3 CV): The five methods will be applied to different classes of goods depending on whether we are in an Art. 2 CV-scenario, or an Art. 3 CV-scenario. The term "identical" is defined in Art. 15 CV as referring to goods which:

> are the same in all respects, including physical characteristics, quality and reputation. Minor differences in appearance would not preclude goods otherwise conforming to the definition from being regarded as identical.

The same provision identifies "similar" goods as:

> goods which, although not alike in all respects, have like characteristics and like component materials which enable them to perform the same functions and to be commercially interchangeable. The quality of the goods, their reputation and the existence of a trademark are among the factors to be considered in determining whether goods are similar.

If none of the above is feasible, customs authorities can legitimately have recourse to the deductive value loosely defined as the price at which the importer (and not the seller) sells the imported good to an unrelated buyer (arm's length transaction). Customs authorities can deduct from

---

[11] In case they do reject the presented value, they should provide parties with a right to appeal the decision to reject the presented value (Art. 11 CV).

this price a percentage reflecting the profit of the importer as well as expenses relating to the same of the good to the buyer.

If recourse to the deductive value is not feasible, then customs authorities must rely on the computed value. This reflects a calculation by the customs authorities which must ascertain the production cost of the seller to which they can add general expenses, profit, and transport costs to the port of entry.[12]

Assuming all prior methods cannot be used, customs authorities can use the fall-back method. This method would allow customs authorities to devise their own procedure as long, however, as it is reasonable, and consistent with the principles of Art. VII GATT and the CV Agreement. This method is used in practice mostly when importations concern repaired (abroad) items, damaged goods etc. In its report on *Thailand–Cigarettes (Philippines)*, the Panel concluded that the Thai Customs' failure to properly consult the importer on the information necessary for the requested deductions rendered its decision not to deduct sales allowances, provincial taxes and transportation costs in the determination of the customs value of the entries at issue inconsistent with Article 7.1 CV (§ 7.332).

2.3.4 Confidentiality

Protection of confidential information submitted is guaranteed by Art. 10 CV. In *Thailand–Cigarettes (Philippines),* the Panel held that disclosure by the customs authorities of information regarding the pricing of a company and its overall volume of imports that had been submitted and classified as confidential constitutes a violation of this provision (§§ 7.405ff.).

2.3.5 Special and Differential Treatment

Art. 20 CV allows a developing country Member to delay the application of the CV Agreement for a period of five years from the date of entry of the WTO Agreement. This right could not be availed of by those WTO Members who had been signatories to the Tokyo Round CV Code. Several WTO Members, including Bahrain, Boliva, Jamaica, Kuwait, Senegal, Tunisia and Sri Lanka, have had recourse to this provision. Paragraph 2 of Annex III also permits developing Members to retain minimum values (prohibited by Art 7.2(f) CV) on a limited and transitional basis under terms and conditions to be agreed to by WTO Members. WTO Members

---

[12] The Interpretative Note to the CV Agreement requests from customs authorities that they use information prepared in a manner consistent with the Generally Accepted Accounting Principles (GAAP.) The GAAP has been defined in paragraph 1 of the Note.

having been granted this reservation include Colombia, Gabon, Honduras, Morocco and Nicaragua (see WTO Doc. G/VAL/2 and its revisions)[13].

2.3.6 Institutional Issues

The WCO has agreed on a template "Model Bilateral Agreement on Mutual Administrative Assistance in Customs Matters" the use of which it encourages by all customs authorities. The WTO membership has further adopted a Decision during the Doha Ministerial Conference, which allows customs authorities to inquire about the accuracy of the importer's declaration in case of reasonable doubt; the inquired authority can legitimately refuse to respond if the request is not consistent with its domestic public order.[14] A Committee on Customs Valuation is established where all WTO Members participate, and which is entrusted with the administration of the CV Agreement (Art. 18 CV). The same provision gave birth to the Technical Committee, also composed of representatives by all WTO Members (usually customs experts) and which meets twice a year in Brussels in the headquarters of the WCO. The Technical Committee reports to the Committee on Customs Valuation and prepares technical documents aimed at helping WTO Members when dealing with customs valuation issues[15]. Its output comes under different denominations (explanatory notes, advisory opinions) and is included in a publication issued by the WCO, the WCO Compendium.[16]

3. THE AGREEMENT ON PRE-SHIPMENT INSPECTION (PSI)

3.1 THE LEGAL DISCIPLINE

Through pre-shipment inspection, traders aim at ensuring that the value of exported goods conforms to the specifications reflected in a sales contract, as well as other relevant information such as the quality and quantity of goods shipped: while the CV Agreement deals with the value of goods at the point of importation, pre-shipment inspection deals with

---

[13] India, which was a signatory to the Tokyo round Customs Valuation Code, views itself as still being covered by this reservation. This view is not shared by others. This situation explains why the Annual Review documents from 1998 to 2009 prepared by the Secretariat for the purpose of assisting the Committee carry out the review under Art. 23 CV remain un-adopted; they do not list India as being covered by this reservation.

[14] Decision of November 14, 2001, WTO Doc. WT/MIN(01)/17 of November 20, 2001, at § 8.3. This matter has been discussed in the Committee since early 2000. However, to date discussions have not concluded partly because the same subject was introduced in the Trade Facilitation negotiation which in the view of some Members was the more appropriate forum for addressing this issue. In this connection, see also WTO doc. G/VAL/49 which provides a report of the Committee to the Trade Negotiations Committee on the outstanding implementation issues.

[15] See for example the response (VAL/W/54) of the Technical Committee to the terms of reference sent by the Committee on Customs Valuation in connection with its work on § 8.3 of the Ministerial Declaration (WT/MIN(01)/17).

[16] Its tasks are laid out in detail in Annex II of the CV Agreement.

similar issues at the point of exportation. In fact, footnote 4 of the PSI Agreement reads as follows:

> The obligations of user Members with respect to the services of pre-shipment inspection entities in connection with customs valuation shall be the obligations which they have accepted in GATT 1994 and other Multilateral Trade Agreements included in Annex 1A of the WTO Agreement.

3.2 THE RATIONALE FOR THE LEGAL DISCIPLINE

Through this agreement, exporters obtain the necessary certainty regarding the overall duty that will be imposed at the destination market, which they would not necessarily have if inspection took place in the importing market following the CV procedures. In this latter case, customs officers might put into question the invoice price. They will not do, or rarely do so, if the invoice price has been certified by a pre-shipment inspection entity.

3.3 COVERAGE

3.3.1 Pre-shipment Entity

Inspections are performed by private companies, the pre-shipment inspection entities.[17] The inspecting companies will perform essentially two functions:

(a) Ensure conformity of goods with the terms of the sales contract; and

(b) Verify the invoice price.

Government contracts with pre-shipment inspection companies have been either foreign exchange contracts (FOREX), where the basic objective of the government is to prevent exodus of capital through over-invoicing, and/or customs contracts, where the main aim is to ensure that there is no loss in customs revenue as a result of under-valuation, or misclassification of the good. A pre-shipment inspection company might also provide a number of subsidiary services which include, inter alia, the verification of origin of the product, maintenance of data for statistical purposes, technical assistance and training. Expertise by companies is not binding on customs authorities. They might decide to neglect it, and perform their own evaluation.

---

[17] SGS (Société Générale de Surveillance) is the company most frequently used.

(1) Physical inspection (quantity/quality only) for foreign exchange purposes.

(2) Including reporting for foreign exchange purposes. No programmes now include intervention on invoiced price.

(1) "Selective": only certain shipments subject to physical PSI based on risk assessment.

(2) Cargo destination inspection which may include price verification and classification on a preshipment or post-shipment basis.

The Agreement on Pre-shipment Inspection (PSI)

The table below has been sourced from WTO doc. G/VAL/W/63/Rev. 14 dated November 8, 2011 and lists countries using PSI regimes. It reproduced information compiled by the IFIA (International Federation of Inspection Agencies) Pre-shipment Inspection Committee. According to IFIA, the recent trend of PSI programmes shows a reduction in traditional programmes (ex. PSI programmes for customs purposes) with considerable growth in more modern programmes (ex. Customs support services) that are less intrusive for exporters.

Table 7.1 PSI Programmes for Customs Purposes

PSI Programmes for Customs Purposes (Revenue Protection)		
Country	Mandated Member(s) of IFIA PSI Committee	Basis of Member Choice
Angola	BIVAC, Cotecna, SGS	Importer
Bangladesh	BIVAC, Intertek, SGS, OMIC	Geographical
Central African Rep.	BIVAC	—
Chad	BIVAC	—
Dem. Rep. of Congo	BIVAC	—
Iran[1]	BIVAC, Cotecna, OMIC, SGS	Importer
Mauritania	SGS	—
Uzbekistan[2]	BIVAC, CUI, Intertek, OMIC, SGS	Importer/Exporter

(1) Physical inspection (quantity/quality only) for foreign exchange purposes.

(2) Including reporting for foreign exchange purposes. No programmes now include intervention on invoiced price.

Customs Support Services (including Destination inspection and/or Selective PSI)		
Country	Mandated Member(s) of IFIA PSI Committee	Basis of Member Choice
Burkina Faso[1][2]	Cotecna	—
Burundi[1]	SGS	—
Cameroon[1][2]	SGS	—
Chad[1]	Cotecna	—
Congo[1][2]	Cotecna	—
Côte d'Ivoire[1][2]	BIVAC	—
Equatorial Guinea	Cotecna	—
Ghana[2]	BIVAC, Cotecna	Air & land / sea-freight
Guinea (Conakry)[1][2]	BIVAC	
Haiti[1]	SGS	—
Liberia[1][2]	BIVAC	
Mali[1][2]	BIVAC	
Mozambique[1][2]	Intertek	—
Niger[1]	Cotecna	—
Nigeria[2]	Cotecna, SGS	Port of Arrival
Senegal[1][2]	Cotecna	—
Togo[2]	Cotecna	—

3.3.2 The Independent Entity

Disputes might arise between the pre-shipment entities and exporters concerning the evaluation by the former. Note that such disputes are between private parties, and not between state entities. In such cases, the complaining party can refer the dispute to the so-called Independent Entity (Art. 4 PSI).[18] The Independent Entity is a three-person body, including a member nominated by the pre-shipment entities, a member nominated by the exporters' organization, and an independent trade expert.[19] Its decisions, as per Art. 4(h) PSI, are binding on their addressees and cannot be appealed.[20]

3.3.3 Transparency and Administration of the Agreement

Members, be they Exporter Members or User Members[21] are obliged to ensure transparency and non-discriminatory application of all their laws relating to pre-shipment inspection (Arts. 2 and 3 PSI). They are further obliged to submit to the WTO Secretariat copies of the laws and regulations by which they have implemented the PSI Agreement, any other laws and regulations relating to pre-shipment inspection, as well as changes in the laws and regulations relating to pre-shipment inspection which must be notified immediately after their publication (Art. 5 PSI).[22]

Unlike other multilateral agreements in Annex 1A of the WTO Agreement, the PSI Agreement does not establish a Committee to monitor the implementation of the Agreement. Monitoring of the Agreement takes place in the Committee on Customs Valuation where pre-shipment inspection is a standing agenda item. This was one of the recommendations by the Working Party on Pre-shipment Inspection established by the General Council in November 1996 for the purposes of conducting the review provided for in Art.6 PSI, which states that:

> At the end of the second year from the entry into force of the WTO Agreement and every three years thereafter, the Ministerial Conference shall review the provisions, implementation and operation of the Agreement. . . . .

---

[18] The Independent Entity was established by a decision of the WTO General Council adopted on December 13, 1995, see WTO Doc. WT/L/125 Rev. 1 of February 9, 1996.

[19] One expert is nominated by the list provided by the International Federation of Inspection Agencies (IFIA) (WTO Doc. G/PSI/IE/1/Rev. 1), one by the list provided by the International Chamber of Commerce (ICC), and one by the administrator of the Independent Entity, that is, the WTO Secretariat.

[20] At the time of writing, two such decisions had been issued, WTO Docs. G/PSI/IE/R/1 and 2.

[21] The obligations of User Members are stipulated in in twenty-two paragraphs under Art. 2 PSI. They are expected to ensure that PSI activities abide by obligations covering matters such as the site of inspection, protection of confidential business information, delays and appeals procedures. Obligations of Exporter Members are covered in three paragraphs under Art. 3 PSI.

[22] For example, see WTO Doc. G/PSI/N/1 Add. 15 of June 27, 2011.

The Working Party submitted a first report in December 1997 (WTO Doc. G/L/214), but its life was extended by a year on two occasions. At the end of each of those extensions, a report was submitted to the General Council (WTO Docs. G/L/273, in 1998; G/L/300, in 1999). In the last report, a recommendation that future monitoring of the Agreement should be undertaken initially by the Customs Valuation Committee and that PSI should be a standing agenda item was adopted by the General Council. Another brief review of the PSI Agreement took place in 2006 in the Committee on Customs Valuation and the report of the review was issued in WTO Doc. G/L/809. The Working Party report contained in G/L/300 also states that:

> All Members have accepted that recourse to PSI is a transitional measure to be used only until their national customs authorities are in the position to carry out these tasks on their own.

3.3.4 Special and Differential Treatment

The PSI Agreement does not contain provisions on special and differential treatment. A paragraph on technical assistance entitled 'Obligations of Exporter Members' notes that (Art. 3 PSI):

> Exporter Members shall offer to provide User Members, if requested, technical assistance directed toward the achievement of the objectives of this Agreement on mutually agreed terms".

A footnote to this paragraph further specifies that technical assistance could be bilateral, plurilateral or multilateral. So technical assistance can be provided by even developing country Members to other developing country Members, unlike the CV Agreement which, as noted earlier, in its Art. 20.3 provides that developed country Members are to furnish technical assistance to developing country Members that so request.

QUESTIONS AND COMMENTS

Auctioning Import Licences: Should auctioning of import licences be considered as consistent with the ILA or not?

Export Licensing: The ILA deals with import- and not with export licences. In fact, there is no agreement on export licences, since WTO Members have refused to enter into a similar negotiation. During the Tokyo Round, there was an attempt to negotiate on export restrictions. Following a proposal in 1976 by the then Brazilian Ambassador, George A. Maciel, a negotiating group was established: the Framework Group. This group was, *inter alia*, requested to negotiate an agreement on export licensing. It is clear from the record that a negotiation on export restrictions was not a priority-issue.[23] Yet, trading nations were, in principle, unwilling to commit on this score fearing the repercussion of similar commitment on their sovereignty over natural

---

[23] GATT Activities in 1978, May 1979, The GATT: Geneva.

resources.[24] The end product of the negotiation was that an "Understanding Regarding Export Restrictions and Charges" was issued that dealt head on with this issue,[25] but which essentially called for treating export restrictions as priority issue for the negotiators in the post-Tokyo Round era.[26] The discussion continued for some time immediately after the conclusion of the Tokyo Round, and the Consultative Group of Eighteen (CG 18) was asked to advise the GATT Council on the forum and modalities of the negotiation. This body issued a document explaining the impact of export restrictions on international trade and added an Annex reflecting illustrative examples.[27] This provided the impetus for further work in this area. During the preparations leading to the GATT Ministerial Meeting in 1982, one delegation suggested the inclusion in the agenda of export restrictions with a view to pointing to the trade-distorting effects of similar practices. The matter was not included in the Declaration adopted at the end of the meeting.[28] Trading nations spent little time nevertheless negotiating this issue in the context of the Uruguay Round which was initiated in 1986. The GATT Secretariat issued a very elaborate document[29] where it discussed the rationale for imposing export restrictions as well as some illustrative examples: improving terms of trade, protection of processing industries, raising revenue, domestic price stabilization, and conservation of exhaustible natural resources were the reasons mentioned for restricting exports. Following the discussion mentioned above, nothing much happened and the Uruguay round did not include an agreement on export licences. Export licences do on occasion occur. So the question arises how should export licences be treated in WTO law? The Panel in *China–Raw Materials* held that export licences must be assessed in the context of Art. XI GATT: they do not necessarily violate this provision, unless they have restrictive effects of their own; for example, an authority that requests from (potential) exporters a document attesting the right to export is not violating Art. XI GATT (§§ 7.881, 7.917–7.918), but an authority that retains discretion to request a number of un-identified documents as a pre-condition for issuing a licence is acting inconsistently with this provision (§§ 7.957–7.958).[30]

Pre-shipment Inspection: For a comprehensive account of this topic, see Low (1995).

---

[24] The Tokyo Round of Multilateral Trade Negotiations, Report by the Director–General of the GATT, April 1979, The GATT: Geneva at pp. 98ff.

[25] GATT Doc. MTN/FR/W/20/Rev. 2 of March 30, 1979.

[26] See also GATT Doc. L/4885 of November 23, 1979 pp. 21ff. which contains a detailed discussion of the various GATT provisions dealing with export restrictions.

[27] GATT Doc. CG.18/W/43 of October 10, 1980.

[28] GATT Doc. BISD 29S/9.

[29] GATT Doc. MTN.GNG/NG2/W/40 of August 8, 1989.

[30] During the Doha round negotiations, Japan tabled a proposal entitled Protocol on Transparency in Export Licensing to the GATT 1994 (TN/MA/W/15/Add.4/Rev.7), and the EU a proposal to discipline export restrictions (TN/MA/W/101). At the time of writing the Doha negotiations were at a stalemate.

Trade Facilitation: The WTO webpage defines it as follows:

> Once formal trade barriers come down, other issues become more important. For example, companies need to be able to acquire information on other countries' importing and exporting regulations and how customs procedures are handled. Cutting red-tape at the point where goods enter a country and providing easier access to this kind of information are two ways of "facilitating" trade.

The Singapore Ministerial Declaration reflected in § 22, entitled "Trade Facilitation":[31]

> In the organization of the work referred to in paragraphs 20 and 21, careful attention will be given to minimizing the burdens on delegations, especially those with more limited resources, and to coordinating meetings with those of relevant UNCTAD bodies. The technical cooperation programme of the Secretariat will be available to developing and, in particular, least-developed country Members to facilitate their participation in this work.

Trade facilitation was thus originally conceived as an integral part of measures in favor of developing countries. The negotiation on trade facilitation has been taking place in the context of the Doha round. Defining the scope of the negotiation represented a challenging feature of the endeavor in and of itself: at one of the continuum, one could conceive the term to cover a very broad discussion of the (customs and regulatory) environment within which transactions take place, some sort of trade facilitation efforts 'inside the border'; at the other end, a narrow definition would call for addressing issues related directly with moving goods through ports. The agreement, as it now stands,[32] is essentially a clarification of Arts. V, VIII, and XX GATT, and an elaboration of some additional but related provisions. The focus on developing countries has not dwindled over the years: capacity building, technical assistance, and more generally special and differential treatment figure prominently on the agenda.[33]

Logistics Performance Index (LPI): The WB has developed an LPI, which provides a simple, global benchmark to measure logistics performance. It includes six components: efficiency of customs clearance process; quality of transport infrastructure; ease of arranging shipments; competence and quality of logistics services; ability to trace consignments; and frequency with which shipments reach the consignee within the expected delivery time. As expected OECD countries rank much higher than developing countries. There is thus, a "logistics gap", see Arvis et al. (2012).

---

[31] WTO Doc. WT/MIN(96)DEC of December 18, 1996.
[32] WTO Doc. TN/TF/W/165/Rev. 10 of July 25, 2011.
[33] WTO Docs. TN/TF/1 of November 16, 2004; TN/TF/2 of July 15, 2005.

CHAPTER 8

NATIONAL TREATMENT

■ ■ ■

1. THE LEGAL DISCIPLINE

An imported product that has entered a market after paying the price of entry (e.g., a tariff) should be treated in the same way as a domestically-produced version of the product. This principle is captured in Art. III GATT: a WTO Member may not impose a fiscal measure that taxes an imported good more than a domestically-produced good. Moreover, a WTO Member may not implement a law, regulation or requirement affecting the sale, purchase, transportation, distribution or use of a product (i.e., a non-fiscal measure) that treats domestically-produced goods more favorably than an imported good.

The specific rules governing fiscal measures are enumerated in Art. III.2 GATT, whereas those governing non-fiscal measures are enumerated in Art. III.4 GATT. As you will see in this Chapter, there are a number of notable differences in the legal requirements of these provisions. Consider the following example: Art. III.2 GATT refers to both "like" products as well as "directly competitive substitutes." Art. III.4 GATT, on the other hand, only refers to "like" products. To make matters even more confusing, case law has confirmed that, on the basis of this distinction, the meaning of the term "like products" is not exactly identical when used in Art. III.2 GATT as opposed to Art. III.4 GATT. Therefore, when examining questions of national treatment, an important question to ask is whether the measure at issue is a fiscal or non-fiscal measure. Depending on the answer to that question, the legal rules will vary.

2. THE RATIONALE FOR THE LEGAL DISCIPLINE

During the course of trade negotiations, trading partners agree to give each other concessions on tariffs. Put differently, they agree to lower the cost of entry for certain imports of their trading partner in order to secure lowered entry costs for certain of their own exports. The value of these tariff concessions, however, would be undermined, if upon entry, the imported good faced discriminatory internal policies. Negotiators worry that their trading partners, after giving up tariff concessions, might be tempted to introduce new internal policies as a way to re-protect their domestic producers.

The negotiating record reveals[1] that nations emphasized making national treatment (NT) a core principle of the post-war trade regime as a way to safeguard the value of their tariff concessions. The principle of NT ensures that no protection would be afforded through unilaterally designed domestic instruments (policies). As the GATT Secretariat has previously noted, "In the case of Article III, the rules were designed to safeguard tariff concessions and to prevent hidden discrimination".[2]

More recently, the AB in *Japan–Alcoholic Beverages II* confirmed this understanding of NT (p. 16):

> The broad and fundamental purpose of Article III is to avoid protectionism in the application of internal tax and regulatory measures. More specifically, the purpose of Article III 'is to ensure that internal measures not be applied to imported or domestic products so as to afford protection to domestic production.' Toward this end, Article III obliges Members of the WTO to provide equality of competitive conditions for imported products in relation to domestic products.

3. THE COVERAGE OF THE LEGAL DISCIPLINE

3.1 INTRODUCTORY REMARKS

What exactly does the national treatment obligation of Art. III GATT cover? Art. III.1 GATT reads:

> The contracting parties recognize that internal taxes and other internal charges, and laws, regulations and requirements affecting the internal sale, offering for sale, purchase, transportation, distribution or use of products, and internal quantitative regulations requiring the mixture, processing or use of products in specified amounts or proportions, should not be applied to imported or domestic products so as to afford protection to domestic production.

The language of Art. III.1 makes clear that the obligation covers:

- Internal taxes and other internal charges
- Laws, regulations and requirements affecting the internal sale, offering for sale, purchase, transportation, distribution or use of products
- Internal QRs requiring the mixture, processing or use of products in specified amounts or proportions

---

[1] See Irwin et al. (2008), and Jackson (1969).
[2] See the Working Party Report on Border Tax Adjustments, GATT Doc. L/3039 of July 11, 1968.

How exactly does one determine whether a particular policy measure is an "internal" measure, as opposed to one which is levied at the border? What if, for example, a certain good is barred at the border because it does not meet the product requirements for that market? Are the product requirements an internal measure, subject to the obligations of Art. III GATT, because they also apply to domestically-produced goods? Or are they not an internal measure because the policy is applied at the border and the imported good has never entered into the country? The Interpretative Note ad Art. III GATT Note clarifies:

> Any internal tax or other internal charge, or any law, regulation or requirement of the kind referred to in paragraph 1 which applies to an imported product and to the like domestic product and is collected or enforced in the case of the imported product at the time or point of importation, is nevertheless to be regarded as an internal tax or other internal charge, or a law, regulation or requirement of the kind referred to in paragraph 1, and is accordingly subject to the provisions of Article III.

In other words, even if the measure is applied at the border at the time of importation, it is to be considered an "internal" measure if it applies to imports and domestic goods alike.

The other term that we wish to highlight is "affecting," as used in Art. III GATT to qualify laws, regulations and requirements. Many policies "affect" trade, and so a question arises as to how broadly should we interpret this term. Clarifying the scope of this provision was not an easy exercise: the Chairman of the Technical Sub-committee in charge of preparing the draft provision on national treatment during the London Conference (1946) noted:[3]

> Whatever we do here, we shall never be able to cover every contingency and possibility in a draft. Economic life is too varied for that, and there are all kinds of questions which are bound to arise later on. The important thing is that once we have this agreement laid down we have to act in the spirit of it. There is no doubt there will be certain difficulties, but if we are able to cover 75 or 80 or 85 per cent of them I think it will be sufficient.

Furthermore, for some trading nations it was unthinkable to transfer sovereignty regarding behind the border measures. We quote from Hudec (1990, p.24):

> Governments would have never agreed to circumscribe their freedom in all these other areas for the sake of a mere trade agreement.

---

[3] UN Doc. E/PC/T/C.II/PRO/PV/7.

Against this background, the scope of the national treatment-provision has been somewhat clarified in three ways: through statutory language; through subsequent re-negotiation of the contract; and through case law. We discuss each one in turn.

3.2 STATUTORY DELIMITATION OF THE COVERAGE

The wording of several provisions in WTO law itself has helped clarify the scope of what falls within, as opposed to outside, the confines of the national treatment requirement of Art. III GATT. We discuss some examples below:

Mixing Requirements: Art. III.5 GATT refers to mixing requirements (a form of a local content-requirement in which a product is required to have a certain amount or proportion of domestically-produced input). Therefore, they clearly fall within the scope of the coverage. Mixing requirements, as well as any other form of an internal QRs related to the processing or use of products, are explicitly outlawed. Note that other forms of local content requirements are regulated in the Agreement on Trade Related Investment Measures (TRIMS), to be discussed in Chapter 21.

Subsidies: On the other hand, subsidies are excluded from the coverage of the national treatment-obligation by virtue of Art. III.8 GATT. They are instead regulated by the WTO Agreement on Subsidies and Countervailing Measures (SCM), to be discussed in Chapter 15.

Government Procurement: By virtue of Art. III.8 GATT, laws, regulations, and requirements pertaining to government procurement are also excluded from the coverage of Art. III GATT. Instead, they are governed by the WTO Agreement on Government Procurement (GPA), to be discussed in Chapter 22. Recall from Chapter 1 that the GPA is a plurilateral agreement for which participation is optional for WTO Members.

Film Quotas: By virtue of Art. IV GATT, screen quotas for cinematographic films of national origin (or originating in another specific contracting party) are also not subject to the national treatment obligation of Art. III GATT.[4] Art. IV GATT makes clear that film quotas are allowed.[5] The advent of the GATS had as consequence that, when it comes to cinematographic films, it is the commitments made on audiovisual services that matter in this respect.

---

[4] The rationale for this extension could be that two countries share common cultural factors such as language and in this vein it would be appropriate say for Canada to keep screen quotas for French speaking films originating in France.

[5] Ehring (2011, p. 114) has taken the view that this provision should be considered as lex specialis and not as exception to Art. III GATT: this understanding of the provision is not void of legal consequences since in the former case (lex specialis) it is still the complainant that carries the burden of proof, whereas in the latter, it is the defendant, that is, the WTO Member imposing the film quota. This issue is unresolved in case law.

3.3 DELIMITATION OF THE COVERAGE THROUGH RE-NEGOTIATION OF THE GATT

One question that emerged in the 1960s was whether a border tax adjustment was allowed under the GATT. A border tax adjustment is a fiscal measure that may take on the following forms:

- At the time of importation, an importer is charged all or a portion of a given tax that is charged on similar products produced domestically
- At the time of exportation, an exporter is refunded all or a portion of a given tax consumption

Border tax adjustments were especially popular in European countries. The US expressed concern over their legality, and the GATT formed a Working Party on Border Tax Adjustments.[6]

Recall from Chapter 3 (Tariffs) that Art. II.2(a) GATT granted an exception to Art. II.1 GATT for a charge equivalent to an internal tax, provided that tax was consistent with Art. III.2 GATT.[7] By tasking the Working Party with the question of which fiscal measures qualify for a border tax adjustment, the GATT Membership, through the process of negotiations within the Working Party, was clarifying the scope of coverage for Art. III GATT. The Working Party issued its report in 1971. It was not able to reach full agreement, but did manage to agree on the following (§ 4 of the final report):

> [T]he Working Party concluded that there was convergence of views to the effect that taxes directly levied on products were el-

---

[6] The definition adopted by the Working Party of a border tax adjustment was "... as any fiscal measures which put into effect, in whole or in part, the destination principle (i.e. which enable exported products to be relieved of some or all of the tax charged in the exporting country in respect of similar domestic products sold to consumers on the home market and which enable imported products sold to consumers to be charged with some or all of the tax charged in the importing country in respect of similar domestic products.)" See § 4 of of the final Working Party Report. The destination principle was taken over from bilateral agreements negotiated in the 1930s, such as the agreement of 6 May 1936 between the US and France. See § 10 of the Annex to the Working Party report on Border Tax Adjustments,; see also Irwin et al. (2008). Note that economists have also used more or less the same definition for the term BTA. This is, for example, how Johnson and Krauss (1970) describe border tax adjustments (pp. 596–597): "A border tax, properly interpreted, is a tax imposed when goods cross an international border, and as such must be inimical to international trade and therefore to the achievement of the economic benefits of international specialization and division of labor. A border tax adjustment, on the other hand, is an adjustment of the taxes imposed on a producer when the goods he produces cross an international border. . . . Under the origin principle, a tax is imposed on the domestic production of goods, whether exported or not, and under the destination principle, the same tax is imposed on imported goods as on domestically-produced goods destined for consumption by domestic consumers, while domestically-produced goods destined for consumption by foreigners enjoy a rebate of the tax. The origin principle involves no tax adjustment, but the destination principle involves a border tax adjustment to the full extent of the tax." Compare Meade (1974).

[7] In addition, on the export side, Interpretative Note ad Art. XVI GATT allows for tax exemptions from consumption taxes for products which will be exported. We do not touch on this issue in great depth here because the focus of this Chapter is on NT. Nevertheless, please recognize that in examining border tax adjustments on the export side, this is of importance.

igible for tax adjustment. Examples of such taxes comprised specific excise duties, sales taxes and cascade taxes and the tax on value added. It was agreed that [a Value Added Tax], regardless of its technical construction (fractioned collection), was equivalent in this respect to a tax levied directly—a retail or sales tax. Furthermore, the Working Party concluded that there was convergence of views to the effect that certain taxes that were not directly levied on products were not eligible for tax adjustment. Examples of such taxes comprised social security charges whether on employers or employees and payroll taxes.[8]

Based on the above, it is clear that a Value Added Tax (VAT) does fall within the scope of Art. III GATT. On the other hand, social security taxes and payroll taxes do not. Also, GATT Members had already previously made clear that income taxes, as well, do not fall under the scope of coverage for Art. III GATT[9]

On the other hand, the Working Party was not able to reach an agreement on certain areas (§ 15 of the final report):

> The Working Party noted that there was a divergence of views with regard to the eligibility for adjustment of certain categories of tax and that these could be sub-divided into
>
> (a) "Taxes occultes" which the OECD defined as consumption taxes on capital equipment, auxiliary materials and services used in the transportation and production of other taxable goods. Taxes on advertising, energy, machinery and transport were among the more important taxes which might be involved. It appeared that adjustment was not normally made for taxes occultes except in countries having a cascade tax;
>
> (b) Certain other taxes, such as property taxes, stamp duties and registration duties . . . which are not generally considered eligible for tax adjustment. Most countries do not make adjustments for such taxes, but a few do as a few do for the payroll taxes and employers' social security charges referred to in the last sentence of paragraph 14.
>
> It was generally felt that while this area of taxation was unclear, its importance—as indicated by the scarcity of complaints reported in connexion with adjustment of taxes occultes—was not such as to justify further examination.[10]

Re-negotiations, in the form of Working Party discussions, were able to clarify the scope of coverage only in part. The Report of the Working

---

[8] See § 14 of the Working Party's Final Report.

[9] This was done at the Havana Conference (1947). See § 12 of the Working Party's Final Report.

[10] On the extent of disagreement, see also Genasci (2008).

3.4 DELIMITATION OF THE COVERAGE THROUGH CASE LAW

In *Canada–FIRA*, a GATT Panel made clear that Art. III GATT applies to only laws, regulations and requirements that affect imported products. It does not encompass regulations on foreign investment or foreign investors, even though such regulations undoubtedly "affect" trade. As the GATT Panel explained (§§ 5.1, 5.9, 6.5):

> [The GATT] does not prevent Canada from exercising its sovereign right to regulate foreign direct investments
>
> . . .
>
> The purpose of Article III:4 is not to protect the interests of the foreign investor but to ensure that goods originating in any other contracting party benefit from treatment no less favourable than domestic goods . . .
>
> . . .
>
> [T[he national treatment obligations of Article III of the General Agreement do not apply to foreign persons or firms but to imported products.

Subsequently, during the Uruguay Round, the Agreement on Trade-Related Investment Measures (TRIMS) was concluded. Art. 2.2 TRIMS and the Annex includes an illustrative list of practices that are deemed inconsistent with Art. III.4 GATT's requirement for national treatment. We will discuss examine this issue further in Chapter 21.

Case law has also clarified the scope of what constitutes an "internal charge". The AB, in *China–Auto Parts*, remarked (§§ 163–165):

> . . . a key indicator of whether a charge constitutes an "internal charge" within the meaning of Article III:2 of the GATT 1994 is "whether the obligation to pay such charge accrues because of an *internal* factor (e.g., because the product was *re-sold* internally or because the product was *used* internally), in the sense that such 'internal factor' occurs *after the importation* of the product of one Member into the territory of another Member." We also observe that the Harmonized System does not serve as relevant

---

[11] There is a debatable question as to whether this on account of Art. 1(b)(iv) GATT 1994 (incorporating decisions of contracting parties to the GATT 1947) or Art. XVI of the WTO Agreement (GATT acquis). For a detailed discussion of this issue, see Mavroidis (2008). We believe that it falls under the former, but even if it were under the latter, it would still qualify as part of WTO law.

context for the interpretation of the term "internal charges" in Article III:2.

In sum, we see the Harmonized System as context that is most relevant to issues of classification of products. The Harmonized System complements Members' Schedules and confirms the general principle that it is "the 'objective characteristics' of the product in question when presented for classification at the border" that determine their classification and, consequently, the applicable customs duty. The Harmonized System, and the product categories that it contains, cannot trump the criteria contained in Article II:1(b) and Article III:2, which distinguish a border measure from an internal charge under the GATT 1994. Among WTO Members, it is these GATT provisions that prevail, and that define the relevant characteristics of ordinary customs duties for WTO purposes. Thus, even if the Harmonized System and GIR 2(a) would allow auto parts imported in multiple shipments to be classified as complete vehicles based on subsequent common assembly, as China suggests, this would not *per se* affect the criteria that define an ordinary customs duty under Article II:1(b). In any case, the Panel did not accept the broad interpretation of GIR 2(a) suggested by China. Rather, the Panel remarked that its findings on the meaning of "as presented" in GIR 2(a) did not appear to contradict its finding as to the meaning of "on their importation" in Article II:1(b).

In our view, accepting that a charge imposed on auto parts following, and as a consequence of, their assembly into a complete motor vehicle can constitute an ordinary customs duty would significantly limit the scope of "internal charges" that fall within the scope of Article III:2 of the GATT 1994. We also share the concerns expressed by the Panel to the effect that the security and predictability of tariff concessions would be undermined if ordinary customs duties could be applied based on factors and events that occur internally, rather than at the moment and by virtue of importation, and that this, in turn, would upset the carefully negotiated and balanced structure of key GATT rights and obligations, including the different disciplines imposed on ordinary customs duties and internal charges.[12]

---

[12] Following this reasoning the Panel and the AB found that a 25% duty imposed by China on auto parts was an internal charge in violation of Art. III.2 GATT, see Wauters and Vandenbussche (2010).

3.5 SUMMARY REMARKS ON SCOPE OF COVERAGE OF ART. III GATT

To recap, Art. III.1 GATT speaks of three different categories of measures that are prohibited when "applied to imported or domestic products so as to afford protection":

- Internal taxes and other internal charges
- Laws, regulations and requirements affecting the internal sale, offering for sale, purchase, transportation, distribution or use of products
- Internal QRs requiring the mixture, processing or use of products in specified amounts or proportions

The last of these categories is perhaps the easiest to discuss. Anything that amounts to a requirement to use a designated volume or percentage of locally-produced product (i.e., a local content requirement) is likely to violate Art. III.4 GATT. This is applicable even if the local content requirement takes the form of a mixing or processing requirement.

With respect to "internal taxes, and other internal charges," a large number of fiscal charges clearly fall into this category. For example, a direct sales tax or excise tax levied on a specific product (e.g., alcohol, cigarettes, etc.) clearly falls within the scope of Art. III GATT. The same is true of other types of internal charges (e.g., processing fee) that are levied on a specific product. Customs duties, on the other hand, do not fall within the scope of the national treatment obligation, because as discussed, they are not "internal." On the other hand, certain forms of taxes do not fall under Art. III GATT because they are not applied on a "product": for example, income taxes, social security tax, payroll taxes. A general value-added tax (VAT), however, does fall under Art. III GATT. With respect to border tax adjustments, the Working Party Report provides specific guidance. Finally, Art. III.8 GATT makes clear that a subsidy (even if its form involves taxes or fiscal charges, and even if it is specific to a product) does not fall under the purview of Art. III GATT. Subsidies are separately disciplined through the SCM Agreement (to be discussed in Chapter 15).

What about the category of "laws, regulation, or requirement affecting the internal sale, offering for sale, purchase, transportation, distribution or use of products"? Film quotas or screen requirements, clearly affect the distribution and use of a product (audiovisual films), but are not subject to national treatment obligations. Measures affecting investment only fall under the scope of Art. III GATT (unless they have been included in the illustrative list featured in the TRIMS Agreement). The vast majority of measures regulating products fall under the scope of Art. III GATT. For example, this is true of a measure that limits the transportation or distribution of a product to certain channels, regulates advertising for a product, or limiting the portion size of a product that may be sold. Determining whether a particular measure falls under the scope of the national treatment obligation is only the first step. With respect to the two categories (i.e., besides internal QRs), there are a number of additional legal tests that need to be considered in examining whether a particular measure complies with the national treatment obligation. We begin by discussing the requirements for fiscal measures (i.e., internal taxes and internal charges) before turning to non-fiscal measures.

4. INTERNAL TAXES AND OTHER INTERNAL CHARGES (FISCAL MEASURES)

Art. III.2 GATT reflects the discipline with respect to internal taxes and internal charges of any nature, that is, fiscal measures. The two sentences contained within Art. III.2 GATT create a distinction between two classes of goods: directly competitive substitutes (DCS) goods and "like" goods. Why does this distinction exist? The records of the Havana Conference[13] suggest that negotiators were concerned that, trading partners might try to use policies to benefit domestically-produced goods that functioned as imperfect substitutes of the imports:

> During the drafting of the Havana Charter, and thus the GATT, it was felt that this might occur where there was no, or negligible, domestic production of the imported product. Various examples were quoted; it was for instance suggested that a country which did not produce coffee could not impose tax on coffee, unless it placed a similar tax on chicory, a competitive product.[14]

Case law has established that "like" goods are a sub-set of DCS goods (in the sense that sharing a DCS-relationship is a necessary but not sufficient condition for likeness), The AB, in *Korea–Alcoholic Beverages*, held (§ 118):

> 'Like' products are a subset of directly competitive or substitutable products: all like products are, by definition, directly competitive or substitutable products, whereas not all 'directly competitive or substitutable' products are 'like'.

The first sentence of Art. III.2 GATT includes the national treatment obligation with respect to the narrower category of "like" goods: WTO Members shall not subject imports to internal taxes or other internal charges *in excess of* those applied to like domestic products.

The second sentence of Art. III.2 GATT includes the national treatment obligation with respect to the broader category of DCS goods: WTO

---

[13] Havana Reports at pp. 61–67. The Havana Conference signals the end of the negotiation on NT: Art. III GATT has remained unchanged since the last negotiations in the early months of 1948 in Havana.

[14] Working Party Report on Border Tax Adjustment § 17 (quoting from the preparatory work of the GATT).

Members shall not apply internal taxes or other internal charges *so as to afford protection* to domestically-produced DCS goods.

Note the difference in language between the two legal requirements. We will discuss its significance in what follows. Because like goods are a subset of DCS goods, we will begin our discussion by examining the legal requirement for the broader category first, which carries relevance for the narrower category of like goods as well.

4.1 DIRECTLY COMPETITIVE OR SUBSTITUTABLE (DCS) GOODS

4.1.1 What Is a DCS Good?

In *Japan–Alcoholic Beverages II*, the AB provided its understanding of the term "DCS" products. This dispute arose because of a Japanese tax which, while on its face neutral, subjected predominantly Western products to a heavier taxation than predominantly Japanese products: shochu (an alcoholic beverage predominantly produced in Japan) was subjected to less burdensome taxation than, inter alia, whisky (an alcoholic beverage predominantly produced in Europe and the US). The EU and the US protested arguing that the products at hand were at least DCS-, if not like products. The AB upholding the Panel's findings in this regard, held (p. 25):

> In this case, the Panel emphasized the need to look not only at such matters as physical characteristics, common end-uses, and tariff classifications, but also at the 'market place.' This seems appropriate. The GATT 1994 is a commercial agreement, and the WTO is concerned, after all, with markets. It does not seem inappropriate to look at competition in the relevant markets as one among a number of means of identifying the broader category of products that might be described as 'directly competitive or substitutable.
>
> Nor does it seem inappropriate to examine elasticity of substitution as one means of examining those relevant markets. The Panel did not say that cross-price elasticity of demand is '*the* decisive criterion' (footnote omitted) for determining whether products are directly competitive or substitutable. The Panel stated the following:
>
> > In the Panel's view, the decisive criterion in order to determine whether two products are directly competitive or substitutable is whether they have common end-uses, *inter alia*, as shown by elasticity of substitution.
>
> We agree. And, we find the Panel's legal analysis of whether the products are 'directly competitive or substitutable products' in

paragraphs 6. 28–6.32 of the Panel Report to be correct. (italics and emphasis in the original).

In a subsequent case (*Korea–Alcoholic Beverages*), the AB held that a decision that two goods are DCS can be based on either econometric-or non-econometric indicators, the two methods being of equal value in the eyes of the AB. In this case, the facts were similar to those in *Japan–Alcoholic Beverages II*: soju (an alcoholic beverage predominantly produced in Korea that is similar to Japanese shochu, but with noticeable differences) was hit by a substantially lower tax burden than their counterparts which were predominantly produced in the EU, Canada, and the US (vodka, whisky, etc.). The EU, Canada, and the US complained, arguing that the Korean regime was GATT-inconsistent. Korea argued that its system could not be held to be GATT-inconsistent since, the products concerned were not DCS in the first place: the price of (diluted) soju was only a small fraction of the price of the Western drinks at hand, claiming thus that changes in the price of soju would not lead its consumers to consumption of Western drinks. Consequently, following the analysis in *Japan–Alcoholic Beverages II*, and the relevance of econometric indicators in deciding whether two products are DCS, Korea argued that with respect to (diluted) soju at least, no claim under Art. III.2 GATT could be sustained. The complainants asserted that the fact that in another market (Japan), a product similar to soju (i.e., shochu) held a DCS relationship with Western drinks provided sufficient evidence that soju too was DCS product to the same Western drinks. The Panel essentially upheld the complaining parties' view, holding that the products were indeed in DCS-relationship: Only a reading of the AB report on *Japan–Alcoholic Beverages II* whereby cross-price elasticity would be elevated to *the* decisive criterion conferring DCS-status, would lead the Panel to rule otherwise; such a reading of Art. III.2 GATT, however, was in the Panel's eyes unwarranted. The AB upheld the Panel's findings (§§ 114 ff. and especially 133–134, 135–138):

1. Potential Competition

... In our view, the word 'substitutable' indicates that the requisite relationship *may* exist between products that are not, at a given moment, considered by consumers to be substitutes but which are, nonetheless, *capable* of being substituted for one another....

2. Expectations

As we have said, the object and purpose of Article III is the maintenance of equality of competitive conditions for imported and domestic products.

3. 'Trade Effects' Test

... the Panel stated that if a particular degree of competition had to be shown in quantitative terms, that would be similar to requiring proof that a tax measure has a particular impact on trade. It considered such an approach akin to a 'type of trade effects test.

We do not consider the Panel's reasoning on this point to be flawed.

4. Nature of Competition

The Panel considered that in analyzing whether products are 'directly competitive or substitutable,' the focus should be on the *nature* of competition and not on its *quantity* ... For the reasons set above, we share the Panel's reluctance to rely unduly on quantitative analyses of the competitive relationship. In our view, an approach that focused solely on the quantitative overlap of competition would, in essence, make cross-price elasticity *the* decisive criterion in determining whether products are 'directly competitive or substitutable.' We do not, therefore, consider that the Panel's use of the term 'nature of competition' is questionable.

5. Evidence from the Japanese Market

... It seems to us that evidence from other markets may be pertinent to the examination of the market at issue, particularly when demand on that market has been influenced by regulatory barriers to trade or to competition. Clearly, not every other market will be relevant to the market at issue. But if another market displays characteristics similar to the market at issue, then evidence of consumer demand in that other market may have some relevance to the market at issue. This, however, can only be determined on a case-by-case basis, taking account of all relevant facts. (emphasis in the original).[15]

Thus, while cross-price elasticity is important, it is not the decisive criterion in examining whether two products are DCS. As the AB in *Korea–Alcoholic Beverages* makes clear, recourse to non-econometric indicators is legitimate when considering whether two products are DCS.

---

[15] In the case at hand, the argument was made that demand in Korea was latent because of the regulatory barriers that impeded access for Western drinks. It did not however, beyond the generic references in the passage included above, refer specifically to these barriers. Hence, evidence from third country markets was necessary to establish whether soju and a series of Western beverages were indeed *DCS* products. Korea pointed out that the price of shochu was higher than that of soju, and closer to that of the Western drinks. Note also that there have not been any *serious* challenges regarding likeness in subsequent case law.

4.1.2 So as to Afford Protection (SATAP)

Art. III.2 GATT makes it clear that taxation of two DCS products violates the national treatment principle and is GATT-inconsistent, if it is applied so as to afford protection (SATAP) to domestic goods. In *Japan–Alcoholic Beverages II*, the AB noted (§ 118):

> Unlike that of Article III:2, first sentence, the language of Article III:2, second sentence, specifically invokes Article III:1. The significance of this distinction lies in the fact that whereas Article III:1 acts implicitly in addressing the two issues that must be considered in applying the first sentence, it acts explicitly as an entirely separate issue that must be addressed along with two other issues that are raised in applying the second sentence. Giving full meaning to the text and to its context, three separate issues must be addressed to determine whether an internal tax measure is inconsistent with Article III:2, second sentence. These three issues are whether:
>
> (1) the imported products and the domestic products are *'directly competitive or substitutable product' which are in competition with each other*;
>
> (2) the directly competitive or substitutable imported and domestic products are *'not similarly taxed'*; and
>
> (3) the dissimilar taxation of the directly competitive or substitutable imported domestic products is *'applied . . . so as to afford protection to domestic production.'* (emphasis in the original).

Hence, in the AB's view, Art III.1 GATT is relevant for the whole of Art. III.2 GATT; however, the impact of Art. III.1 GATT on the interpretation of the first sentence (dealing with like products) is not symmetric to its impact on the second sentence (dealing with DCS products):

> (a) With respect to like products, any taxation in excess of the imported like product amounts to *ipso facto* to a finding that a measure operates so as to afford protection;
>
> (b) Whereas with respect to DCS products, establishment of taxation in excess of the imported product is a necessary, but not sufficient, condition for finding that a measure operates so as to afford protection.

With respect to DCS goods, the AB further noted:

> The dissimilar taxation must be more than *de minimis*. It may be so much more that it will be clear from that very differential that the dissimilar taxation was applied 'so as to afford protection.' In some cases, that may be enough to show a violation. In this case, the Panel concluded that it was enough. Yet in other cases, there may be other factors that will be just as relevant or

more relevant to demonstrating that the dissimilar taxation at issue was applied 'so as to afford protection.' (italics in the original).

Provided that differences in the taxation scheme of DCS goods are more than de minimis, the AB (§ 119) then spelled out the relevant test:

> [W]e believe that an examination in any case of whether dissimilar taxation has been applied so as to afford protection requires a comprehensive and objective analysis of the structure and application of the measure in question on domestic as compared to imported products. We believe it is possible to examine objectively the underlying criteria used in a particular tax measure, its structure, and its overall application to ascertain whether it is applied in a way that affords protection to domestic products.
>
> Although it is true that the aim of a measure may not be easily ascertained, nevertheless its protective application can most often be discerned from the design, the architecture, and the revealing structure of a measure.

When it comes to fiscal measures covering DCS goods, WTO adjudicators will evaluate whether the design, architecture, and revealing structure of the measure, as well as the import regime for the particular goods to ascertain a violation of Art. III.2 GATT.

Chile–Alcoholic Beverages offers an example of how these factors play into an analysis of DCS goods. At issue in the case was a Chilean tax scheme for alcohol that used alcoholic content as the distinguishing criterion: Any alcohol, imported or domestic, with an alcohol strength of 35° or lower, was taxed at 27% ad valorem. The rate then increased gradually at 5% for each degree of alcohol strength until it reaches the top rate of 47% for any alcohol above 39° in strength. Any alcohol that was 40° or more was taxed at this top rate.

The complaining party (EU) noted that many Western alcohol products had a strength greater than 39° were DCS products to Chilean products of less than 35° (e.g., pisco). They argued that the tax differential operated so as to afford protection because it favored predominantly locally-produced alcoholic beverages. Chile responded that its scheme did not condition the payment of the higher tax on the origin of the product, and, moreover, that in the 39° and above tax category, the majority of the products hit by high taxation were domestic. As a result, in Chile's view, no protection could result from such a taxation scheme (§ 58). The AB, upholding the Panel's findings, condemned the Chilean fiscal scheme. It held that the tax differential (27% and 47%) across the two categories of lower and higher alcoholic content drinks was more than de minimis (§§ 44ff.). It then asked the question whether the dissimilar taxation supported the conclusion that it was applied SATAP to the domestic product (§§ 64–66):

> We note, furthermore, that, according to the Panel, approximately 75 per cent of all domestic production has an alcohol content of 35° or less and is, therefore, taxed at the lowest rate of 27 per cent *ad valorem*. Moreover, according to figures supplied to the Panel by Chile, approximately *half* of all domestic production has an alcohol content of 35° and is, therefore, located on the line of the progression of the tax at the point *immediately before* the steep increase in tax rates from 27 per cent *ad valorem*. The start of the highest tax bracket, with a rate of 47 per cent *ad valorem*, coincides with the point at which most imported beverages are found. Indeed, according to the Panel, that tax bracket contains approximately 95 per cent of all directly competitive or substitutable imports.
>
> Although the tax rates increase steeply for beverages with an alcohol content of more than 35° and up to 39°, there are, in fact, very few beverages on the Chilean market, either domestic or imported, with an alcohol content of between 35° and 39°. The graduation of the rates for beverages with an alcohol content of between 35° and 39° does not, therefore, serve to tax distilled alcoholic beverages on a progressive basis. Indeed, the steeply graduated progression of the tax rates between 35° and 39° alcohol content seems anomalous and at odds with the otherwise linear nature of the tax system. With the exception of the progression of rates between 35° and 39° alcohol content, this system simply applies one of two fixed rates of taxation, either 27 per cent *ad valorem* or 47 per cent *ad valorem*, each of which applies to distilled alcoholic beverages with a broad range of alcohol content, that is, 27 per cent for beverages with an alcoholic content of *up to 35°* and 47 per cent for beverages with an alcohol content of *more than 39°*.
>
> In practice, therefore, the New Chilean System will operate largely as if there were only two tax brackets: the first applying a rate of 27 per cent *ad valorem* which ends at the point at which most domestic beverages, by volume, are found, and the second applying a rate of 47 per cent *ad valorem* which begins at the point at which most imports, by volume, are found. The magnitude of the difference between these two rates is also considerable. The absolute difference of 20 percentage points between the two rates represents a 74 per cent increase in the lowest rate of 27 per cent *ad valorem*. Accordingly, examination of the design, architecture and structure of the New Chilean System tends to reveal that the application of dissimilar taxation of directly com-

petitive or substitutable products will "afford protection to domestic production." (italics and emphasis in the original).

The AB agreed that, as a matter of fact, most of the alcoholic drinks hit by the higher taxation were of Chilean origin. It dismissed the relevance of this observation for the interpretation of the SATAP-requirement in the following terms (§ 67):

> It is true, as Chile points out, that domestic products are not only subject to the highest tax rate but also comprise the major part of the volume of sales in that bracket. This fact does not, however, by itself outweigh the other relevant factors, which tend to reveal the protective application of the New Chilean System. The relative proportion of domestic versus imported products within a particular fiscal category is not, in and of itself, decisive of the appropriate characterization of the total impact of the New Chilean system under Article III:2, second sentence, of the GATT 1994. This provision, as noted earlier, provides for equality of competitive conditions of *all* directly competitive or substitutable imported products, in relation to domestic products, and not simply, as Chile argues, those imported products within a particular fiscal category. The cumulative consequence of the New Chilean System is, as the Panel found, that approximately 75 percent of all domestic production of the distilled alcoholic beverages at issue will be located in the fiscal category with the lowest tax rate, whereas approximately 95 percent of the directly competitive or substitutable imported products will be found in the fiscal category subject to the highest tax rate. (emphasis in the original).

It seems that, the sharp increase in the taxation-level was the quintessential element in the design, structure, and architecture of the challenged measure that made a prima facie case of violation of the GATT, which Chile did not rebut (§ 71):

> In the present appeal, Chile's explanations concerning the structure of the New Chilean System—including, in particular, the truncated nature of the line of progression of tax rates, which effectively consists of two levels (27 per cent *ad valorem* and 47 per cent *ad valorem*) separated by only 4 degrees of alcohol content— might have been helpful in understanding what *prima facie* appear to be anomalies in the progression of tax rates. The conclusion of protective application reached by the Panel becomes very difficult to resist, in the absence of countervailing explanations by Chile. The mere statement of the four objectives pursued by

Chile does not constitute effective rebuttal on the part of Chile. (italics in the original)[16]

4.2 LIKE PRODUCTS

4.2.1 What Is a Like Product?

Once goods are determined to be DCS, a second question arises as to whether or not, they fall under the sub-category of "like products." The term "like product" appears in various provisions of the GATT and was not judged self-interpreting by the negotiators: Irwin et al. (2008) reveal a discussion whereby GATT negotiators had originally planned for the ITO to establish a clarification of the meaning of the term.[17]

The non-advent of the ITO left it to GATT/WTO Panels to provide an understanding of this term. The GATT Working Party on Border Tax Adjustments (BTAs) established four criteria to define likeness (§ 18):

(a) the properties, nature and quality of the products;

(b) the end-uses of the products;

(c) consumers' tastes and habits; and

(d) the tariff classification of the products.

It did not assign a particular weight on each one of the four criteria it employed. It did not even explain whether all four criteria must be cumulatively met. Relying on three out of the four criteria, the Panel report on *Japan–Alcoholic Beverages I* held that, shochu and some western drinks (§ 5.6):

> should be considered as 'like products' in terms of Article III:2 in view of their similar properties, end-uses and usually uniform classification in tariff nomenclatures.

The AB in an oft-quoted passage from its report on Japan—Alcoholic Beverages II, used an accordion-metaphor to explain its views on this issue (p.21):

> No one approach to exercising judgment will be appropriate for all cases. The criteria in *Border Tax Adjustments* should be examined, but there can be no one precise and absolute definition of what is 'like'. The concept of 'likeness' is a relative one that evokes the image of an accordion. The accordion of 'likeness' stretches and squeezes in different places as different provisions of the WTO Agreements are applied. The width of the accordion

---

[16] Chile invoked four grounds to explain its measure including revenue collection but did not elaborate on any of them (§ 69). In § 72 of its report, the AB held that there was necessity-requirement in Art. III.2 GATT: Chile did not have to demonstrate that its measures were necessary (e.g., least restrictive) in order to be consistent with Art. III GATT.

[17] UN Doc. E/PC/T/A/PV/40(1) at p. 14.

in any one of those places must be determined by the particular provision in which the term 'like' is encountered as well as by the context and the circumstances that prevail in any given case to which that provision may apply. (italics in the original)

For example, alcoholic drinks such as shochu, beer, wine, vodka, and whiskey are all considered to be DCS products. However, within this category, shochu and vodka might be considered to be "like" products based on the circumstances of the marketplace. Both are versions of distilled alcohol that are clear in color. Consumers in certain countries also tend to drink both frequently as small shots or mix it with other drinks to hide its sharp flavor. On these points, both shochu and vodka hold similarities apart from other alcohol such as beer, wine, or whiskey.

In *EC–Asbestos*, the AB underscored this point when it ruled that Panels which are called to pronounce on likeness must examine "the evidence relating to each of those four criteria and, then, weigh all of that evidence, along with any other relevant evidence, in making an overall determination of whether the products at issue could be characterized as 'like' " (§ 109).

Note that earlier, during the GATT era, two cases had taken an alternate approach. Instead or resorting to the marketplace as the relevant criterion, the GATT Panels applied an "aims and effects" test to determine likeness.[18] According to this view, consequently, likeness will not be defined by reference to prevailing perceptions in the marketplace about the products concerned but, instead, by reference to the regulatory aims pursued by the intervening government. The approach was explicitly rejected by the Panel in *Japan—Alcoholic Beverages II* (§§ 6.15–19). The AB endorsed the Panel's approach holding that it is the marketplace that defines if two goods are DCS and/or like (pp. 16ff.). But where should one draw the line between like and DCS goods? In the AB's view, two DCS goods will be "like" if they share the same tariff classification, and if the classification is precise enough:

> If sufficiently detailed, tariff classification can be a helpful sign of product similarity.
>
> . . .
>
> It is true that there are numerous tariff bindings which are in fact extremely precise with regard to product description and which, therefore, can provide significant guidance as to the identification of 'like products.'

---

[18] These cases are *US–Malt Beverages* and on *US–Taxes on Automobiles* ('Gas Guzzler', as it is widely known). The latter is an unadopted GATT Panel Report, and therefore of limited value. The contours of the "aims and effects" test are discussed in greater depth in the Questions and Comments section of this Chapter.

This would be usually the case when two goods shared the same six-digit tariff classification. But then in *Philippines–Distilled Spirits*, the relevance of this finding was somewhat eviscerated. Philippines reserved a lower tax treatment for sugar-based alcoholic drinks (typically local) as opposed to drinks with no sugar basis (typically imported). The question arose whether the two sets of drinks could be considered like. The AB first held that the difference in physical characteristics across the two sets of products did not in and of itself disqualify a finding of likeness (§ 121). It then went on to find that for two products to be like, significant competitive relationship is not enough and a higher threshold should be required (§ 145). It noted that the products at hand did not share the same tariff classification at the six digit-level (§§ 106ff., and 159ff.). The AB did not stop there however: It went so far as to state that very high competitive relationship would suffice for a finding of likeness, even if a six digit tariff classification did not suggest that the goods in question were like (§§ 163–164):

> We observe that the six-digit HS subheading for brandy refers to spirits obtained by distilling grape wine or grape marc. The six-digit HS subheading for whisky contains no reference to the raw material from which this spirit is produced. However, the HSENs to the six-digit HS codes for both brandy and whisky specify the material from which the spirit is distilled, namely, grape wine or grape marc for brandy and mash of cereal grains for whisky. This, in our view, provides an indication that tariff classification would not suggest that domestic brandies and whiskies made from designated raw materials are "like" imported brandies and whiskies made from non-designated raw materials. Accordingly, we do not agree with the Panel's conclusion that at the six-digit level the HS classification provides no "conclusive guidance" as to the similarity of brandies and whiskies made from designated and non-designated raw materials.
>
> We observe, however, that tariff classification is only one of the criteria that the Panel reviewed in its analysis of "likeness" under Article III:2 of the GATT 1994. We have already agreed with the Panel's conclusions that the criteria of products' physical characteristics and consumers' tastes and habits do support a finding that the products at issue are "like" within the meaning of Article III:2. Moreover, we recall that the Panel's finding that the end-uses of the products at issue are similar was not appealed. Thus, the fact that the Panel overlooked the significance of HS six-digit level classification for brandy and whisky does not, in our view, undermine its overall finding that the products at issue are "like". Therefore, we do not consider that this is an error that rises to the level of a failure by the Panel to comply with its duties under Article 11 of the DSU.

Although this passage is not crystal-clear, it definitely suggests that sharing a tariff classification is but one of the criteria to decide on likeness. In the AB's words, the other criteria continue to be relevant and anyway a (§ 181):

> finding of "likeness" under the first sentence requires a degree of competition that is higher than merely *significant*. (emphasis in the original).

It follows that the most recent case-law suggests that two goods are "like" goods if they are in intense competitive relationship.

4.2.2 Taxation in Excess

The tax scheme or other fiscal charge on imports must not be in excess of that imposed on like domestic product. When it comes to determining what constitutes "taxation in excess", the AB has held that even a minimal tax differential, will suffice to satisfy this criterion. We quote from *Japan–Alcoholic Beverages II* (p. 23):

> Even the smallest amount of 'excess' is too much. 'The prohibition of discriminatory taxes in Article III:2, first sentence, is not conditional on a 'trade effects test' nor is it qualified by a *de minimis* standard. (italics in the original).

In the same report the AB held that, with respect to like products, taxation in excess should be understood as an instance of a measure meeting the requirement of being applied "so as to afford protection." Consequently, a complainant who has established that taxation on imported products is in excess of that on domestic like products, does not have to also establish that the measure at hand meets the SATAP-requirement as well (pp. 18–19).

5. LAWS, REGULATIONS, AND REQUIREMENTS AFFECTING TRADE (FISCAL MEASURES)

For non-fiscal measures, the requirements to provide national treatment are spelled out in Art. III.4 GATT. A complainant aiming to establish that this provision has been violated, will have to demonstrate that:

(a) with respect to laws, regulations or requirements;

(b) affecting internal sale, offer for sale, purchase, transportation, distribution or use;

(c) a foreign good is afforded in comparison to a domestic like good;

(d) less favorable treatment (LFT).

We discuss each of these elements required for a claim under Art. III.4 GATT in what follows below.

5.1 LAWS, REGULATIONS OR REQUIREMENTS

GATT/WTO case law has understood the term "laws, regulations and requirements" featured in Art. III.4 GATT as equivalent to the term "measure" featured in Art. XXIII.1b GATT, and Art. XI GATT. That is, the term assumed a rather all-encompassing notion.[19] Since it is only government measures that can be challenged before a WTO Panel, case law has had to address the issue of attribution in the context of Art. III.4 GATT as well. It followed an approach similar to that followed in the context of Art. XI GATT (*Japan–Semiconductors*): What matters is whether government has provided private parties with enough incentives to act in a particular way.[20] In *US–FSC*, the Panel noted (§ 10.376):

> A literal reading of the words *all laws, regulations and requirements* in Article III:4 could suggest that they may have a narrower scope than the word *measure* in Article XXIII:1(b). However, whether or not these words should be given as broad a construction as the word *measure*, in view of the broad interpretation assigned to them in the cases cited above, we shall assume for the purposes of our present analysis that they should be interpreted as encompassing a similarly broad range of government action and action by private parties that may be assimilated to government action. In this connection, we consider that our previous discussion of GATT cases on administrative guidance in relation to what may constitute a 'measure' under Article XXIII:1(b), specifically the panel reports on *Japan—Semiconductors* and *Japan—Agricultural Products*, is equally applicable to the definitional scope of 'all laws, regulations and requirements' in Article III:4. (italics and emphasis in the original).

5.2 AFFECTING SALE, OFFERING FOR SALE

Measures that not only actually, but also potentially and/or indirectly affect trade have been subjected to judicial review. The AB, in *US–FSC*, had the opportunity to confirm the wide interpretation of the term "affecting" (§§ 208–210):

> ... the word 'affecting' assists in defining the types of measure that must conform to the obligation not to accord 'less favourable treatment' to like imported products, which is set out in Article III:4.

---

[19] See for example, the Panel report on Japan–Trade in Semiconductors, discussed in Chapter 2, and the Panel report on Japan–Film (Kodak/Fuji) on this score. The framers of the GATT must have had this intention and this is probably what explains the inclusion of the term 'requirements' in the body of Art. III.4 GATT, see Irwin et al. (2008), and Jackson (1969).

[20] Note that the issue of attribution is a non-issue in the context of Art. III.2 GATT: fiscal impositions can only be imposed by governments, or by non-governmental organs, following delegation of authority by governments.

The word 'affecting' serves a similar function in Article I:1 of the *General Agreement on Trade in Services* (the 'GATS'), where it also defines the types of measure that are subject to the disciplines set forth elsewhere in the GATS but does not, in itself, impose any obligation. . . .

In view of the similar function of the identical word, 'affecting', in Article III:4 of the GATT 1994, we also interpret this word, in this provision, as having a 'broad scope of application." (italics in the original).

5.3 LIKE PRODUCTS IN ART. III.4 GATT

Art. III.4 GATT does not, in contrast to Art. III.2 GATT, distinguish between like and DCS products. The question, hence, arises whether the term "like product" should have the same meaning across the two paragraphs. The AB decided that this should not be the case. In *EC–Asbestos*, a WTO Panel, and later the AB, was confronted with a French decree that banned the sale of all construction material containing asbestos, irrespective of its origin. The question before the Panel (and the AB) was whether all construction materials were "like" products, irrespective of whether or not they contained asbestos. The AB held that the term "like products" in Art. III.4 GATT should be interpreted in light of the over-arching purpose of Art. III GATT, which was to punish protectionism with respect to both fiscal-and non-fiscal measures. Absent some parallelism in the scope of coverage across the two paragraphs (III.2 and III.4 GATT), WTO Members would be incurring obligations of different scope with respect to fiscal and non-fiscal instruments. In the eyes of the AB, this could not have been the case of what the negotiators' intentions. Thus, the AB explicitly held that the scope of products coming under the purview of Art. III.4 GATT was broader than the coverage of like products alone as understood in the Art. III.2 GATT context, but no broader than the combined coverage of like products and DCS products as understood in Art. III.2 GATT (§§ 98–100).

At issue in *EC–Asbestos*[21] was France's prohibition (administrative decree) of sales of asbestos-containing construction material was based on scientific evidence: asbestos-containing construction material contributed to mesothelioma, a form of cancer. The asbestos-containing construction material was chrysotile fibers (an input to the final product), heavily produced in the province of Québec in Canada. Canada had argued that there was no difference between construction material containing chrysotile fibers on the one hand, and construction material containing PCG fibers (which is an asbestos-free input to the final product), on the other. Since construction material containing PCG fibers was being legally sold in France, Canada argued that the French ban on construction material

---

[21] Horn and Weiler (2003) discuss this report in detail.

containing chrysotile fibers amounted to according to the Canadian good a less favorable treatment than that accorded to the French like good.

The question arose as to whether asbestos-free and asbestos-containing construction materials were like products. In making its likeness determination, the Panel paid particular attention to the end uses of the two products, which were the same: They were used for construction. The Panel therefore found that the two goods to be like products. As a result, France, by according imports less favorable treatment, was in violation of Art. III.4 GATT. (The Panel then went on to examine defenses under Art. XX GATT.)

On appeal, the AB reversed the Panel's findings with respect to likeness. In its view, the Panel should have examined all four criteria used in the evaluation of an Art. III.2 claim:

(a) the properties, nature and quality of the products;

(b) the end-uses of the products;

(c) consumers' tastes and habits; and

(d) the tariff classification of the products.

The AB found that the Panel focused only on one criterion (end uses) to its detriment. Had it expanded its inquiry, the Panel would, in the AB's view, have observed the differences in physical characteristics between the two products. Chrysotile fibers and PCG fibers are not the same: the former are carcinogenic, whereas the latter are not. This difference in physical characteristics, in the AB's view, most likely would have led reasonable consumers to stop purchasing material containing chrysotile fibers. The likelihood that these differences in physical composition might affect consumers' purchasing decisions was sufficient reason to raise a presumption that the two products not unlike (§§ 101–154). What more, these buyers of the imported material would often not be exposed themselves to the health risk, but would be indirectly affected, since their customers could be affected: the finding of non-likeness was hence based on the construction companies' assessment of how consumers' perceptions of risks would affect their choices. The burden of proof for Canada, in light of the difference in physical characteristics, would be now, in the words of the AB, much higher. The AB effectively held that the presence of health risk in asbestos containing-construction material raised a presumption that the two products were unlike. Canada was called to rebut this presumption (Canada did not and consequently, its original legal challenge against the French decree was rejected). Note that the AB did not rely on studies or information concerning actual buyer behavior; the AB uses its own interpretation of what reasonable buyers would do, if facing a choice between the two products (§ 122):

> In this case especially, we are also persuaded that evidence relating to consumers' tastes and habits would establish that the health risks associated with chrysotile asbestos fibres influence consumers' behaviour with respect to the different fibres at issue. We observe that, as regards *chrysotile asbestos and PCG fibres*, the consumer of the fibres is a *manufacturer* who incorporates the fibres into another product, such as cement-based products or brake linings. We do not wish to speculate on what the evidence regarding these consumers would have indicated; rather, we wish to highlight that consumers' tastes and habits regarding *fibres*, even in the case of commercial parties, such as manufacturers, are very likely to be shaped by the health risks associated with a product which is known to be highly carcinogenic. A manufacturer cannot, for instance, ignore the preferences of the ultimate consumer of its products. If the risks posed by a particular product are sufficiently great, the ultimate consumer may simply cease to buy that product. This would, undoubtedly, affect a manufacturer's decisions in the marketplace. Moreover, in the case of products posing risks to human health, we think it likely that manufacturers' decisions will be influenced by other factors, such as the potential civil liability that might flow from marketing products posing a health risk to the ultimate consumer, or the additional costs associated with safety procedures required to use such products in the manufacturing process. (italics in the original).

In the preceding recital to the above quoted passage, the AB had however, noted:

> Furthermore, in a case such as this, where the fibres are physically very different, a panel *cannot* conclude that they are "like products" if it *does not examine* evidence relating to consumers' tastes and habits... (italics in original).

The AB made clear that although the scope of "like" products in Art. III.4 GATT is broader than that in Art. III.2 GATT, the same four-factor test is to be used to analyze likeness. The AB stressed that these four factors were not a definitive or exhaustive list; instead, "all pertinent evidence" must be examined (§ 102). The AB elaborated this point in§ 103:

> The kind of evidence to be examined in assessing the 'likeness' of products will, necessarily, depend upon the particular products and the legal provision at issue. When all the relevant evidence has been examined, panels must determine whether that evidence, as a whole, indicates that the products are 'like' in terms of the legal provisions at issue. We have noted that, under Article III:4 of the GATT 1994, the term 'like products' is concerned with the competitive relationships between and among products.

Accordingly, whether the [four-factor] framework is adopted or not, it is important under Article III:4 to take account of evidence which indicates whether, and to what extent, the products involved are—or could be—in a competitive relationship in the marketplace.

In short, to determine likeness in the context of Art. III.4 GATT, what matters are any factors that may reveal information about the nature of the competitive relationship (or lack thereof) between the products.

5.4 LESS FAVORABLE TREATMENT (LFT)

A violation of national treatment arises under Art. III.4 GATT where the law, regulation or other requirement affecting trade gives rise to less favorable treatment to imports, as compared to domestic like goods. But what exactly constitutes "less favorable" treatment?

The concept that imports be subject to treatment "no less favorable" than that of domestic products is tied closely to the concept enshrined in Art. III.1 GATT that national treatment principle bars any measures granted "so as to afford protection" to domestic products. In *EC–Bananas III*, the AB made clear that these are related concepts, rather than two separate requirements:

> Article III:4 does *not* specifically refer to Article III:1. Therefore, a determination of whether there has been a violation of Article III:4 does *not* require a separate consideration of whether a measure afford[s] protection to domestic production. (emphasis in the original).

In its report on *EC–Asbestos*, the AB repeated in even clearer terms that the LFT-requirement echoes the principle set forth in Art. III.1 GATT (§ 100):

> The term 'less favourable treatment' expresses the general principle, in Article III:1, that internal regulations 'should not be applied . . . so as to afford protection to domestic production.' If there is 'less favourable treatment' of the group of 'like' imported products, there is, conversely, 'protection' of the group of 'like' domestic products. However, a Member may draw distinctions between products which have been found to be 'like,' without, for this reason alone, according to the group of 'like' *imported* products 'less favourable treatment' than that accorded to the group of 'like' *domestic* products. (emphasis in the original).

Earlier, a GATT Panel report, *US–Section 337*, had described the "treatment no less favorable" requirement as "an expression of the underlying principle of equality of treatment" (§ 5.11). It added that this amounted to a "call for effective equality of competitive opportunities for imported products" (§ 5.11). The notion that Art. III.4 GATT requires "effective equality of competitive opportunities" for imports as compared to domestic products has been repeated in several subsequent GATT and WTO decisions.[22]

Instances where an additional regulatory hurdle is placed on imported goods may lead to the creation of unequal competitive opportunities; this can serve as proof of "less favorable treatment" for imports as compared to domestic like products.[23] But what about instances where the measure, on its face, demonstrates formal equality? Could there be a violation nevertheless?

At issue in *Korea–Various Measures on Beef* was a Korean law that imposed a "dual retail system." The law allowed Korean retailers to sell only domestic or imported beef, but not both. On its face, the law was origin-neutral. Retailers were allowed to make their own choice, based on their own strategies of the customer segment that they wished to serve. As a result of this dual retail system, there were only 5,000 points of sale for imported beef, whereas there were over 45,000 points of sale for domestic beef. By forcing retailers to choose, the US argued that the law imposing the dual retail system amounted to a national treatment violation.

Korea made several arguments in its defense,[24] but we focus on two: First, Korea argued that the dual retail system had no detrimental effects on foreign imports. Korea also had implemented an import quota on foreign beef, invoking the balance-of-payments exception for QRs; the legality of the quota was not challenged. Korea pointed out that the full quota for imported beef had been met in every year but 1997 (during the Asian financial crisis). Therefore, even if foreign beef could be sold in more retail outlets, it was not as if foreign producers would have sold more beef. Second, Korea also argued the dual retail system was not discriminatory. Retailers were free to choose between selling domestic or foreign beef; there was no legal compulsion obliging them to choose one category of beef over the other. Furthermore, after a decision had been made, retailers subsequently could switch at no cost. Should imported beef become more popular in the market and/or offer greater profits, nothing prevented a retailer that previously had been selling domestic beef to switching over to selling imported beef. The dual retail system, Korea argued, estab-

---

[22] See, e.g., GATT Panel Report in *US–Malt Beverages* (§ 5.30); WTO Panel Report in *US–Gasoline* (§ 6.10); WTO Panel Report in *Canada–Periodicals* (§ 75); WTO Panel Report in *Japan–Film* (§ 10.379);

[23] As discussed in Howse and Neven (2007e), at issue in *US–Section 211 Appropriations Act* was a US law that imposed an additional administrative hurdle for foreigners seeking to register a trademark. This additional step made the law inconsistent with Art. III.4 GATT.

[24] Korea also made claims under Art. XX GATT, and argued that the system was in place in order to combat tax fraud: traders had the incentive to sell imported beef for domestic, in light of the very substantial price-differential between imported and domestic beef (the latter being substantially more expensive than the former).

lished equality of competitive conditions for domestic and imported like goods,[25] and consequently fulfilled the requirements of Art. III.4 GATT.

The Panel rejected all of Korea's asserted defenses and found in favor of the complainants. On appeal, the AB held that this system, although formally non-discriminatory, still modified the conditions of competition to the detriment of the imported product and found Korea's practices to be inconsistent with Art. III.4 GATT since it afforded LFT to imported like products. The modification of conditions of competition was evident, in the AB's view, by the fact that fewer retailers decided to sell imported beef (§§ 143–151). The AB accepted that the choice to distribute domestic or imported beef was in the hands of private retailers. It held that LFT resulted from Korea's decision not to stick to the prior regime (§ 146):

> We are aware that the dramatic reduction in number of retail outlets for imported beef followed from the decisions of individual retailers who could choose freely to sell the domestic product or the imported product. The legal necessity of making a choice was, however, imposed by the measure itself. The restricted nature of that choice should be noted. The choice given to the meat retailers was *not* an option between remaining with the pre-existing unified distribution set-up or going to a dual retail system. The choice was limited to selling domestic beef only or imported beef only. Thus, the reduction of access to normal retail channels is, in legal contemplation, the effect of that measure. In these circumstances, the intervention of some element of private choice does not relieve Korea of responsibility under the GATT 1994 for the resulting establishment of competitive conditions less favourable for the imported product than for the domestic product. (emphasis in the original).

The AB was quick to highlight what it had not been prejudging through its decision (§ 149):

> It may finally be useful to indicate, however broadly, what we are *not* saying in reaching our above conclusion. We are *not* holding that a dual or parallel distribution system that is *not* imposed directly or indirectly by law or governmental regulation, but is rather solely the result of private entrepreneurs acting on their own calculations of comparative costs and benefits of differentiated distribution systems, is unlawful under Article III:4 of the GATT 1994. What is addressed by Article III:4 is merely the *governmental* intervention that affects the conditions under which like goods, domestic and imported, compete in the market within a Member's territory. (emphasis in the original).

---

[25] Korea did not contest before the Panel the assertion of complainants that domestic and imported beef were like goods.

Subsequently, the AB has clarified that a negative disparate impact on imports resulting from a facially-neutral measure does not, by itself, automatically give rise to a national treatment violation. Instead, the less favorable treatment must arise on account of the foreign origin of the imported products. At issue in *Dominican Republic–Import and Sale of Cigarettes* was a requirement that all producers of cigarettes needed to post a bond of five million pesos in order to ensure the payment of taxes. The bond had a larger negative impact on foreign producers than domestic producers because they sold fewer cigarettes in the DR; as a result, the bond requirement amounted to a higher charge, on a unit basis (i.e., per cigarette), for foreign producers. The AB upheld the Panel's rejection of Honduras's claim under Art. III.4 GATT. It agreed with the Panel that a detrimental effect of a measure on a given imported product does not necessarily imply that the measure accords less favorable treatment to imports if the effect is explained by factors unrelated to the foreign origin of the product. In this case, the AB found that origin of the product was not the determinative factor for the disparate impact[26] (§ 96):

> The Appellate Body indicated in *Korea–Various Measures on Beef* that imported products are treated less favourably than like products if a measure modifies the conditions of competition in the relevant market *to the detriment of imported products*. However, the existence of a detrimental effect on a given imported product resulting from a measure does not necessarily imply that this measure accords less favourable treatment to imports if the detrimental effect is explained by factors or circumstances unrelated to the foreign origin of the product, such as the market share of the importer in this case. In this specific case, the mere demonstration that the per-unit cost of the bond requirement for imported cigarettes was higher than for some domestic cigarettes during a particular period is not, in our view, *sufficient* to establish "less favourable treatment" under Article III:4 of the GATT 1994. Indeed, the difference between the per-unit costs of the bond requirement alleged by Honduras is explained by the fact that the importer of Honduran cigarettes has a smaller market share than two domestic producers (the per-unit cost of the bond requirement being the result of dividing the cost of the bond by the number of cigarettes sold on the Dominican Republic market). In this case, the difference between the per-unit costs of the bond requirement alleged by Honduras does not depend on the foreign origin of the imported cigarettes. Therefore, in our view, the Panel was correct in dismissing the argument that the bond requirement accords less favourable treatment to imported ciga-

---

[26] The inclusion of the word 'however' in the fourth line of the quoted passage should leave little room for doubt that the AB was reversing its previous report on *Korea–Various Measures on Beef*.

rettes because the per-unit cost of the bond was higher for the importer of Honduran cigarettes than for two domestic producers. (italics and emphasis in the original).

Following this case, the AB was asked to pronounce on the consistency of a Thai tax measure with Art. III.4 GATT. Thailand had argued before the Panel and the AB that its measures were not origin-related and hence not in violation of Art. III.4 GATT. In § 126 of its report, the AB discussed LFT referring time and again to *Korea–Various Measures on Beef* while avoiding references to *Dominican Republic–Import and Sale of Cigarettes*. But in subsequent cases under the TBT Agreement (*US–Clove Cigarettes*, §§ 175ff; *US–Tuna II* (Mexico), §§ 215ff.), the test that has been applied has been that set forth in *Dominican Republic–Import and Sale of Cigarettes*.

In *US-Clove Cigarettes*, the AB held that the quoted passage from its report on Dominican Republic-Import and Sale of Cigarettes had been misread (§372):

> We disagree with the United States to the extent that it suggests that *Dominican Republic – Import and Sale of Cigarettes* stands for the proposition that, under Article III:4, panels should inquire further whether "the detrimental effect is unrelated to the foreign origin of the product". (United States' appellant's submission, para. 101 (referring to Appellate Body Report, *Dominican Republic – Import and Sale of Cigarettes*, para. 96)) Although the statement referred to by the United States, when read in isolation, could be viewed as suggesting that further inquiry into the rationale for the detrimental impact is necessary, in that dispute the Appellate Body rejected Honduras' claim under Article III:4 because:
>
>> ... the difference between the per-unit costs of the bond requirement alleged by Honduras is explained by the fact that the importer of Honduran cigarettes has a smaller market share than two domestic producers (the per-unit cost of the bond requirement being the result of dividing the cost of the bond by the number of cigarettes sold on the Dominican Republic market).
>
> (Appellate Body Report, Dominican Republic – Import and Sale of Cigarettes, para. 96)
>
> Thus, in that dispute, the Appellate Body merely held that the higher *per unit* costs of the bond requirement for imported cigarettes did not conclusively demonstrate less favourable treatment, because it was not attributable to the specific measure at issue but, rather, was a function of sales volumes. In *Thailand – Cigarettes (Philippines)*, the Appellate Body further clarified that for a finding of less favourable treatment under Article III:4 "there must be in every case a genuine relationship between the measure at issue and its adverse impact on

competitive opportunities for imported versus like domestic products to support a finding that imported products are treated less favourably". (Appellate Body Report, *Thailand – Cigarettes (Philippines)*, para. 134) The Appellate Body eschewed an additional inquiry as to whether such detrimental impact was related to the foreign origin of the products or explained by other factors or circumstances.

Finally, note that while there is no need to review the actual trade effects of a measure for the complainant to discharge its burden, a careful analysis of the implications of the measure in the marketplace must be performed all the same. In *US–FSC (Article 21.5–EC)*, the AB held (§ 215):

> The examination of whether a measure involves "less favourable treatment" of imported products within the meaning of Article III:4 of the GATT 1994 must be grounded in close scrutiny of the "fundamental thrust and effect of the measure itself". This examination cannot rest on simple assertion, but must be founded on a careful analysis of the contested measure and of its implications in the marketplace. At the same time, however, the examination need not be based on the *actual effects* of the contested measure in the marketplace. (emphasis in the original).

6. EXCEPTIONS TO THE NATIONAL TREATMENT OBLIGATION

The general exceptions of Art. XX GATT and the national security exception of Art. XXI GATT have been construed in case law as exceptions to Art. III GATT. We will turn to this discussion in Chapters 12 and 13.

QUESTIONS AND COMMENTS

DCS Products: Do you see any difference in the approach followed in *Japan–Alcoholic Beverages II* and *Korea–Alcoholic Beverages*?

So As To Afford Protection: Ehring (2002) critically discusses the AB report on *Chile–Alcoholic Beverages* and asks the question whether it makes sense to find against Chile when the bulk of the tax burden fell on the shoulders of Chilean producers? Compare with Regan (2002), Horn and Mavroidis (2004), Hudec (1998) and (2000), and Howse and Turk (2001).

Like Products: Hudec (1990) mentions that non-discrimination as such was considered as a non-satisfactory discipline to apply on domestic instruments. He refers to pre-GATT/ITO discussions across trading nations which reveal that non-violation complaints (NVCs) were thought to be the necessary complement to the contracted obligation not to discriminate. NVCs go of course beyond non-discrimination.

Less Favorable Treatment: Should exclusivity contracts between private suppliers and buyers be considered as running afoul Art. III GATT following the AB ruling on *Korea–Various Measures on Beef*?

Market-vs. Policy-"Like" Products: Grossman et al. (2012) advance a proposal whereby the term "like products" should be understood to cover both market-as well as policy-like goods, that is, identical goods, whereas DCS should correspond to market-like goods only. Thus, in their view, a WTO Member should not have any reason to distinguish between domestic and foreign like goods, whereas distinctions between domestic and foreign DCS goods will be permissible to the extent necessary to address the objective pursued by the domestic regulation.

The "Aims and Effects" Test for "Like" Products: As mentioned, during the GATT era, two Panels resorted to an "aims and effects" test to determine likeness. In *US–Malt Beverages*, the Panel defines likeness in § 5.25 in the following manner:

> Consequently, in determining whether two products subject to different treatment are like products, it is necessary to consider whether such product differentiation is being made 'so as to afford protection to domestic production'. While the analysis of 'like products' in terms of Article III:2 must take into consideration this objective of Article III, the Panel wished to emphasize that such an analysis would be without prejudice to the 'like product' concepts in other provisions of the General Agreement, which might have different objectives and which might therefore also require different interpretations.

In *US–Taxes on Automobiles*,[27] the Panel had the opportunity to elaborate this test further on (§§ 5.7, 5.10):

> In order to determine this issue, the Panel examined the object and purpose of paragraphs 2 and 4 of Article III in the context of the article as a whole and the General Agreement.
>
> . . .
>
> The Panel then proceeded to examine more closely the meaning of the phrase 'so as to afford protection.' The Panel noted that the term 'so as to' suggested both aim and effect. Thus the phrase 'so as to afford protection' called for an analysis of elements including the aim of the measure and the resulting effects. A measure could be said to have the *aim* of affording protection if an analysis of the circum-

---

[27] In this case, the EU had challenged the consistency of US tax scheme applicable to cars, according to which, the total fleet of passenger vehicles produced by an individual producer would be taken into account in order to decide on the tax that would be imposed on specific items. Producers with a fleet that consisted of large cubism cars (gas guzzlers) would suffer most, as a result. Many European producers belonged to this category. Note that the US regime was enacted at a time when those suffering most were US producers: it was a legislative effort to dissuade consumers eager to buy gas guzzlers. See Mattoo and Subramanian (1998).

stances in which it was adopted, in particular an analysis of the instruments available to the contracting party to achieve the declared domestic policy goal, demonstrated that a change in competitive opportunities in favour of domestic products was a desired outcome and not merely an incidental consequence of the pursuit of a legitimate policy goal. A measure could be said to have the *effect* of affording protection to domestic production if it accorded greater competitive opportunities to domestic products than to imported products. The effect of a measure in terms of trade flows was not relevant for the purposes of Article III, since a change in the volume or proportion of imports could be due to many factors other than government measures. (emphasis in the original).

As discussed, this test was rejected in the WTO era in *Japan–Alcoholic Beverages II*.

History of the Exclusion of Film Quotas from NT: It was the UK delegation that initially proposed (what later became Art. IV GATT) the exclusion of films from the coverage of Art. 15 of the London Draft. In the words of the UK delegate (Mr. Rhydderch):

> he would prefer a note to the Article to say it did not apply to films. There were cultural, as well as commercial, considerations to be taken into account in the case of films.[28]

And the same UK delegate:

> In the case of films it is not merely an economic and not even material question; it brings in a very important cultural consideration such as does not come in the case of other commodities. We think it is quite clear that countries will not allow their own film production which affects their own culture and ideas, to be swamped by imported films simply because the latter happen to be better organised commercially. Some perfectly reliable method of safeguarding domestic film production is needed and will in fact be insisted on by a great many countries. The method of the screen quota is much the most effective, perhaps the only effective method of attaining this desired object. We must therefore preserve our right to use this method.[29]

Eventually, a separate provision applicable only to films would be agreed to in subsequent negotiations (the current Art. IV GATT). We quote from Wilcox (1949) pp. 44–45:

> Almost without exception, the changes that had been suggested in the United States were accepted and the draft was amended accordingly. Of particular importance was the inclusion of two new articles, one limiting the freedom of nations to discriminate against foreign motion-picture films and the other dealing with the treatment of foreign investment.

---

[28] E/PC/T/C.II/E.14 of November 4, 1946 at p. 5.
[29] E/PC/T/A/SR/10.

The latter article, while unacceptable in substance, did serve to bring the subject of foreign investment within the scope of the Charter.

Overlap Between NT Provision of GATT and GATS and the Diminishing Significance of Art. IV GATT: The advent of the WTO, however, signaled the advent of GATS as well. The question of overlap between GATT and GATS in the audiovisual sector occupied the minds of the negotiators during the Uruguay round and was vividly discussed on more than one occasion.[30] There is certainly an overlap. In theory, though, the GATS regime may be less liberalizing than the GATT, as we will see in detail in the Chapters dedicated to trade in services, WTO Members can, under GATS, take MFN exemption and avoid commitments, thus keeping not only their markets closed but also the possibility of discriminating among different sources; Art. IV GATT though, was not meant as exception to MFN. So the question, with the advent of GATS, is whether Art. IV GATT still means something. The issue of the boundary between GATT and GATS is far from obvious and has been addressed in Canada–Periodicals: the issue arose whether the 'Canadian Excise Tax Act' should come under the purview of GATT or GATS since, as Canada had argued, the tax (equal to 80% of the value of all the advertisements contained in the so-called split-run magazines) was imposed on a service (advertising), and was therefore only subject to the disciplines of the GATS. Canada further argued that the measure at hand could only be reviewed under the national treatment obligation of the GATS (Art. XVII) in respect of which no specific commitments on advertising had been taken. Both the Panel and the AB disagreed with the Canadian argument, stating that the measure at hand (a tax) was also a measure affecting trade in goods. On the wider issue regarding the frontier between GATT and GATS, the AB provided a rather non-committal statement along the following lines (p. 19):

> The entry into force of the GATS, as Annex 1B of the *WTO Agreement*, does not diminish the scope of application of the GATT 1994. Indeed, Canada concedes that its position 'with respect to the inapplicability of the GATT would have been exactly the same under the GATT 1947, before the GATS had ever been conceived'.
>
> We agree with the Panel's statement:
>
> The ordinary meaning of the texts of GATT 1994 and GATS as well as Art. II:2 of the WTO Agreement, taken together, indicates that obligations under GATT 1994 and GATS can co-exist and that one does not override the other.
>
> We do not find it necessary to pronounce on the issue of whether there can be potential overlaps between the GATT 1994 and the GATS, as both participants agreed that it is not relevant in this appeal. (italics in the original).

---

[30] See for example, MTN.GNS/AUD/1 of September 27, 1990; MTN.GNS/AUD/2 of December 20, 2010; MTN:GNS/W/1, of October 4, 1990.

Further to its determination in Canada–Periodicals, the AB, in EC–Bananas III, reaffirmed that in certain circumstances GATT and GATS may overlap (p. 221):

> there is yet a third category of measures that could be found to fall within the scope of both the GATT 1994 and the GATS. These are measures that involve a service relating to a particular good or service supplied in conjunction with a particular good. In all such cases in this third category, the measure in question could be scrutinized under both the GATT 1994 and the GATS. However, while the same measure could be scrutinized under both agreements, the specific aspects of that measure examined under each agreement could be different. Under the GATT 1994, the focus is on how the measure affects the goods involved. Under the GATS, the focus is on how the measure affects the supply of the service or the service suppliers involved. Whether a certain measure affecting the supply of a service related to a particular good is scrutinized under the GATT 1994 or the GATS, or both, is a matter that can only be determined on a case-by-case basis.

Against this background, WTO Members made commitments in the audio-visual sector that represent retrogression even from the MFN clause (and not simply from national treatment as does Art. IV GATT). We quote from the relevant document at § 69:[31]

> Many Members (48) have scheduled one or more MFN exemptions pertaining to audiovisual services. Most of these Members have no specific commitments in the sector. Overall, 114 MFN exemptions have been listed for audiovisual services, making it the sector with most exemptions. These often relate to the conferring of national treatment to works covered by co-production agreements, support programmes, or, in the case of European countries, the Council of Europe Convention on Transfrontier Television. Some MFN exemptions also reserve the right to retaliate against adverse, unfair or unreasonable trading conditions abroad. MFN exemptions in the sector are often justified by the relevant Members on the basis of cultural policy purposes.

This practice should be evidence that Art. IV GATT does not mean anything anymore.

---

[31] WTO Doc. S/C/W/310 of January 12, 2010.

CHAPTER 9

GOODS IN TRANSIT

∎ ∎ ∎

1. THE LEGAL DISCIPLINE

WTO Members must allow transit for goods to or from the territory of other WTO Members. According to Art. V.1 GATT, a good is in transit if the passage through a territory is only a portion of a complete journey that begins and terminates beyond the borders of a WTO Member. The wording and the negotiating record of this provision[1] make it clear that WTO Members incur three obligations with respect to transit:[2]

(a) All costs and charges imposed on traffic in transit must be reasonable (Art.V.3, and V.4 GATT);

(b) A WTO Member shall allow transiting goods to use "the routes most convenient for international transit" (Art. V.2 GATT);

(c) A WTO Member cannot discriminate, with respect to "all charges, regulations, and formalities in connection with transit," for goods to or from other WTO Members (Art. V.5 GATT, MFN).

2. THE RATIONALE FOR THE LEGAL PROVISION

The negotiating record suggests that the negotiators included this provision so as to ensure that transiting goods will not be unduly burdened in the process of reaching their final destination.[3]

3. COVERAGE

Below, we elaborate on the legal obligations of certain key provisions in Art. V GATT.

---

[1] Irwin *et al.* (2008). Art. V.1, as well as the second sentence of Art. V.2 GATT are based on the corresponding provisions (Arts. 1 and 2) of the Convention and Statute on Freedom of Transit, signed in Barcelona, on April 29, 1921, see UN doc. E/PC/T/C.II/54/Rev.1.

[2] Actually, Art. V.6 GATT applies to WTO Members whose territory is the final destination for goods in international transit, and not to WTO Members through which goods are transiting. The Panel in Colombia–Ports of Entry concluded that much (§ 7.475). The rest of the provision concerns transiting goods.

[3] UN doc. E/PC/T/C.II/54/Rev.1.

3.1 REASONABLE COSTS AND CHARGES

Art. V.3 GATT states that goods in transit shall not be subject to customs duties; it places limitations on the charges that a WTO Member may impose:

> Any contracting party may require that traffic in transit through its territory be entered at the proper custom house, but, except in cases of failure to comply with the applicable customs laws and regulations, such traffic coming from or going to the territory of other contracting parties shall not be subject to any unnecessary delays or restrictions and shall be exempt from customs duties and from all transit duties or other charges in respect of transit, except for charges for transportation or those commensurate with administrative expenses entailed by transit or with the cost of services rendered.

Art. V.4 GATT adds: "All charges and regulations imposed by contracting parties on traffic in transit to or from the territories of other contracting parties shall be reasonable, having regard to the conditions of the traffic."

What is meant by "reasonable" in Art. V.4 GATT? There is no case law on this issue, but the negotiating record suggests that costs should correspond to services rendered and should not exceed whatever is required to pay for similar services.[4]

3.2 USE OF MOST CONVENIENT ROUTES FOR INTERNATIONAL TRANSIT

Art. V.2 GATT requires WTO Members to ensure that transiting goods may use the "routes most convenient for international transit" for traffic. In *Colombia–Ports of Entry*, a Panel clarified that a WTO Member may not make this allowance conditional on fulfillment of another requirement, such as trans-shipment (described below).

Recall that in *Colombia–Ports of Entry*, Panama had challenged Colombian restrictions on the ports through which certain goods (e.g., textiles, apparels, and footwear) coming from the Free Trade Zone of Colon in Panama must use. For Panamanian goods to be exempted from the port of entry restrictions, Colombia had required that the good be trans-shipped: trans-shipment is the process in which goods are transferred from one conveyance to another, for movement onward to another destination; for example, trans-shipment occurs at a port, when a set of containers are consolidated into one large container for movement beyond that port (or when one large container is broken down into a series of smaller containers). Goods were required to pass through designated

---

[4] UN doc. E/PC/T/C.II/54/Rev.1.

ports. Panama argued that "Article V:2, first sentence, as informed by Article V:1, obliges WTO Members to grant freedom of transit to traffic in transit to a territory of a third country regardless of whether the goods are trans-shipped or warehoused, or whether the importer breaks bulk or whether changes are made in the mode of transport" (§ 7.368).

The Panel sided with the argument advanced by Panama (§ 7.396):

> In the Panel's view, the definition of "traffic in transit" provided in Article V:1 seems sufficiently clear on its face. When applied to Article V:2, "freedom of transit" must thus be extended to all traffic in transit when the goods' passage across the territory of a Member is a only a portion of a complete journey beginning and terminating beyond the frontier of the Member across whose territory the traffic passes. Freedom of transit must additionally be guaranteed with or without trans-shipment, warehousing, breaking bulk, or change in the mode of transport.

Hence, the Panel held that a requirement for trans-shipment in order for certain Panamanian goods to secure passage through any Colombian port was a violation of Art. V.2 GATT (§ 7.423):

> Accordingly, the Panel concludes that by requiring that goods undergo trans-shipment in order to proceed in international transit, Colombia has failed to extend freedom of transit via the most convenient routes to goods arriving from Panama in international transit within the meaning of Article V:2 as informed by Article V:1 of the *GATT 1994*.

Furthermore, in § 7.431 the Panel found that the requirement for trans-shipment was in violation of Art. V.2 GATT, because it violated MFN (it applied only to goods originating in Panama).

3.3 ABSENCE FOR DISCRIMINATION

Art. V.5 GATT simply reflects the MFN provision embedded in Art. I GATT.

3.4 JURISDICTIONAL LIMITS

In recent years, a question has arisen over whether transiting goods should be subjected to laws and regulations of the country through which they are transiting, which are not intimately linked to customs procedures. Consider a case where a certain good is on its way from Country A to Country C via Country B. The good is legal in both the original source and final destination countries (A & C) but illegal in the country through whose territory it is transiting (B). Is the good in transit subject to the domestic laws of Country B? Or must Country B provide for freedom of transit, even if the good is illegal under its own laws?

In the context of goods, the general exceptions of Art. XX and XXI GATT (which we discuss in greater detail in Chapter 12) provide a possible justification, if a Panel were to hold that B, in our example, would be violating Art. V GATT had it denied transit. For example, a WTO Member could use the national security exception to justify why it need not allow a North Korean missile to transit through its port on the way to Syria.

This issue is of particular relevance to the TRIPS Agreement. Could, for example, counterfeit goods be subjected to domestic laws regarding protection of intellectual property rights, even if they are simply transiting through a WTO Member? Or must that WTO Member grant freedom of transit for such goods, even if its own intellectual property laws deem the goods to be counterfeit?

The issue of goods in transit has been discussed in the TRIPS Council since May 2009. WTO Members however, have been unable to arrive at a common answer to clarify this question through agreed-upon wording for an interpretation/amendment of the current TRIPS Agreement.[5]

This question came to a head in the *EU–Seizure of Generic Drugs in Transit* cases (DS/408 and DS/409) filed in May 2010 by India and Brazil. In that case, certain generic drugs produced in India were seized when transiting through the Netherlands on their way to Brazil and other destinations. The generic drugs were not subject to patent protection in India or Brazil, and therefore were perfectly legal in those WTO Members' jurisdictions. However, the drug was subject to patent in the Netherlands and the European Union. Dutch authorities seized the shipment at Amsterdam airport and ports in the Netherlands on the grounds that the generic drugs infringed patents and therefore were illegal. India and Brazil challenged the right of Dutch authorities to do so, on the grounds that this violated Art. V GATT, along with other provisions.

The question of whether goods, such as Indian generic drugs, are subject to other laws and regulations of the transiting country, such as EU patent laws, remains unresolved. In July 2011, India and the EU reached an understanding whereby Dutch customs authorities would stop seizing shipments of generic drugs simply on the grounds that such drugs violated an existing patent in the EU. Both sides clarified that a situation in which there is adequate evidence to suggest that there is a substantial likelihood that such drugs might be diverted to the EU market may constitute grounds for customs authorities to act. As a result of this understanding, neither India nor Brazil has proceeded to a request to establish a panel, although India iterated its future option to revive this dispute should the EU not conform to the understanding's terms.

---

[5] There is a record of these discussions in the respective TRIPS Council minutes—originally under "Public Health Dimension of the TRIPS Agreement", and later under "Enforcement Trends".

QUESTIONS AND COMMENTS

Most Convenient Routes: who in your view, should decide on which route is most convenient? Should it be the state through which goods are transiting, or traders?

Jurisdictional Limits: Can a WTO Member impose its public order on transiting goods, or does this provision impose a jurisdictional halt with respect to some transactions? It would be quite odd to accept that there are no exceptions to freedom of transit: a similar construction of the GATT would be elevating trade liberalization in a higher hierarchical value than public order, a thesis that Art. XX GATT (as we will see in more detail in Chapter 4) blatantly refutes: Art. XX GATT is a general exception to all obligations assumed under the GATT; recourse to this provision would thus, suggest that WTO Members can deny freedom of transit if they can successfully invoke one of the grounds mentioned therein. In a similar vein, Art. XXI GATT would allow WTO Members to invoke national security and deny freedom of transit.

CHAPTER 10

STATE TRADING

∎ ∎ ∎

1. THE LEGAL DISCIPLINE

State trading enterprises (STEs) operating within WTO Members must, by virtue of Art. XVII GATT, not discriminate. To the extent that an STE is acting as an importer only, respecting the non-discrimination principle is tantamount to respecting MFN; consequently, a STE should not discriminate across products because of their origin. To the extent, however, that a STE acts as a distributor as well, it must not only observe MFN, but also NT.

2. THE RATIONALE FOR THE LEGAL DISCIPLINE

Irwin et al. (2008) report, that the inclusion of a provision on STEs was very much a request by the UK government which, *inter alia*, aimed at preserving the role of the state within a context of liberal trade policy. Negotiators feared that, unless disciplined, STEs could be used in order to circumvent concessions (concession erosion), since they might have little incentive to act in accordance with commercial considerations, and might instead advance national industrial policy goals. This led them to negotiate Art. XVII GATT.

The AB, in its report on *Canada–Wheat Exports and Grain Imports*,[1] confirmed that the rationale for this provision is to operate as an anti-circumvention device in the following terms (§ 85):

> Subparagraph (a) seeks to ensure that a Member cannot, through the creation or maintenance of a State enterprise or the grant of exclusive or special privileges to any enterprise, engage in or facilitate conduct that would be condemned as discriminatory under the GATT 1994 if such conduct were undertaken directly by the Member itself. In other words, subparagraph (a) is an "anti-circumvention" provision.

---

[1] Hoekman and Trachtman (2008) discuss this case in detail.

3. COVERAGE

3.1 DEFINING STES

Art. XVII GATT does not contain a definition of STEs, other than the examples mentioned in the Interpretative Note ad Art. XVII GATT:

(a) Marketing Boards are covered;

(b) Standards aimed at ensuring quality or efficiency, or privileges granted for the exploitation of natural resources, but which do not empower the government to exercise control over the trading activities of the enterprise in question, do not constitute exclusive or special privileges.

The essence of the above was reproduced in the Understanding on the Interpretation of Art. XVII GATT, adopted during the Uruguay Round, which reads (§ 1):

> governmental and non-governmental enterprises, including marketing boards, which have been granted exclusive or special rights or privileges, including statutory or constitutional powers, in the exercise of which they influence through their purchases or sales the level or direction of imports or exports.

The added value here is that it suffices that STEs influence (as opposed to regulate) the level or direction of imports and exports and that the form regarding their establishment is not prejudged at the WTO level.

Finally, Art. XVII.2 GATT reflects a caveat which is critical for the understanding of the term 'STE': the legal obligations assumed do not concern government procurement. Hence, STEs must be entities which buy and resell, and not entities which buy for governmental use.[2]

Monopolies should be regarded as STEs, since monopolies by definition influence the level or direction of exports and/or imports: the GATT Panel in *Korea–Beef (US)* held that, a producer-controlled import monopoly for beef should be subjected to the discipline of Art. XVII GATT. By the same token, the Canadian Wheat Board, entrusted with the exclusive right to purchase and sell western Canadian wheat for export and human consumption, was considered to be a STE by a WTO Panel (*Canada–Wheat Exports and Grain Imports*).

The WTO webpage, which reproduces notified entities, mentions the following types of STEs:

(a) Statutory marketing boards (also referred to as statutory marketing authorities, or control boards): quite common in the agricultural sector, they often combine a monopoly in international trade and management of domestic production and distribution;

---

[2] See on this issue, Blank and Marceau (1997).

(b) Export marketing boards: these are enterprises which manage exports of domestic goods;

(c) Regulatory marketing boards: they look like statutory marketing boards, except that they do not participate in the conduct of international trade operations;

(d) Fiscal monopolies: they cover trade in goods for which domestic demand is (relatively speaking) price-inelastic, and foreign demand is (relatively speaking) price-elastic, and with respect to which the government has an active public health policy in place (e.g., tobacco, matches, etc.);

(e) Canalizing agencies: developing countries use them in order to channel specific goods particularly to domestic producers;

(f) Foreign trade enterprises: non market economies (NMEs) often use this term instead of STEs to denote entities entrusted with state trading;

(g) Boards of nationalized industries: to the extent that they get involved in the production/trade of goods, they come under the purview of Art. XVII GATT.

The Working Party on State Trading Enterprises is currently developing a more elaborate (hopefully) illustrative list of STEs. In case of disagreement between two WTO Members as to whether a particular entity should be regarded as a STE, it is ultimately WTO adjudicating bodies that will decide this issue.

3.2 THE LEGAL OBLIGATIONS IMPOSED ON STES IN A NUTSHELL

Art. XVII.2 GATT requests WTO Members ensure that their STEs:

(a) Observe the obligation not to discriminate;

(b) Behave in accordance with commercial considerations; and

(c) Afford companies (with respect to their purchases or sales) adequate opportunities to compete.

3.3 NON–DISCRIMINATION

Korea–Various Measures on Beef concerned a quota on beef imposed on balance of payments grounds. Korea had established a producer-controlled import monopoly for the importation and distribution of beef: the monopoly was the sole importer and distributor of beef, in times when the price of imported beef was substantially lower than that of domestic beef. The Korean measure was under attack for various reasons, one of them being its alleged inconsistency with Art. XVII GATT. The Panel held that the legal obligation not to discriminate included in Art. XVII.1 GATT, covered both MFN and NT, since the Korean monopoly operated not only on the importation, but also on the distribution of beef (§ 7.53):

Article XVII.1(a) establishes the general obligation on state trading enterprises to undertake their activities in accordance with the GATT principles of non-discrimination. The panel considers that this principle of non-discrimination includes at least the provisions of Articles I and III of the GATT.

The question arose whether the obligation to behave in accordance with commercial considerations, and the obligation to afford adequate opportunities to compete are mere illustrations of the non-discrimination obligation, or, conversely, whether they should be understood as obligations additional to the obligation not to discriminate. The Panel in *Canada–FIRA* held that the obligations embedded in Art. XVII.1(b) GATT are a mere illustration of the non-discrimination obligation (§ 5.16). As a result, STEs do not incur any obligations additional to the obligation not to discriminate. The Panel in *Korea–Various Measures on Beef* contained a statement that seemed to cast doubt on this view (§ 7.57):

> A conclusion that the principle of non-discrimination was violated would suffice to prove a violation of Article XVII; similarly, a conclusion that a decision to purchase or buy was not based on "commercial considerations", would also suffice to show a violation of Article XVII.

Any doubts on this score were put to rest by the AB: in its report in *Canada–Wheat Exports and Grain Imports,* the AB held that, the two obligations reflected in Art. XVII.1(b) GATT are a mere illustration of the obligation not to discriminate (§§ 89–106). As a result, the AB was unwilling to extend its review to any issues beyond claims of discriminatory behaviour (§ 145):

> The disciplines of Article XVII:1 are aimed at preventing certain types of discriminatory behaviour. We see no basis for interpreting that provision as imposing comprehensive competition-law-type obligations on STEs, as the United States would have us do.[3]

This approach can be traced back to the GATT Panel in *Belgium–Family Tax Allowance* (§ 4):

> As regards the exception contained in paragraph 2 of Article XVII, it would appear that it referred only to the principle set forth in paragraph 1 of that Article, i.e., the obligation to make purchases in accordance with commercial considerations and did not extend to matters dealt with in Article III.[4]

---

[3] Hoekman and Trachtman (2008) discuss this litigation: In their view, it is not unthinkable that private operators could behave in a similar manner as the Canadian STE.

[4] There was a fair number of cases dealing with Art. XVII GATT in the GATT years. Very often though, Panels had condemned challenged measures under other provisions of the GATT and, exercising judicial economy, did not pronounce on claims under Art. XVII GATT, see for example, Canada–FIRA at § 5.16, and Canada–Provincial Liquor Boards (EEC) at § 4.27.

The Interpretative Note ad Article XVII GATT provides an illustration of a practice that should be considered consonant with the obligation to act solely on commercial considerations:

> A country receiving a 'tied loan' is free to take this loan into account as a 'commercial consideration' when purchasing requirements abroad.

The Panel in *Canada–Wheat Exports and Grain Imports* dealt with a number of claims by the US to the effect that a Canadian STE was not acting in accordance with commercial considerations: the US had claimed that the law required from the relevant Canadian STE (the Canadian Wheat Board) not to sell with the objective of maximizing sales, but with the objective of maximizing profits. Although the first type of behaviour might be viewed as rational, to the US, it was not per se a commercial consideration. Continuing this line of thinking, the US also claimed that Canada should not allow its STE to use its privileges in order to maximize sales. The privileges of the Canadian Wheat Board were:

> (a) The exclusive right to purchase and sell Western Canadian wheat for export and domestic human consumption;
>
> (b) The right to set, subject to government approval, the initial price payable for Western Canadian wheat destined for export or domestic human consumption;
>
> (c) The government guarantee of the initial payment to producers of Western Canadian wheat;
>
> (d) The government guarantee of its borrowing; and
>
> (e) government guarantees of certain of its credit sales to foreign buyers.

The US added two more claims: the Canadian Wheat Board was acting inconsistently with its obligations because, when selling, it should not be discriminating across markets, and it should not be selling below market rates anyway; the Canadian STE's behavior was GATT-inconsistent, since it was seeking to maximize revenue and not profit, and was, hence, not acting like a private grain trader (a profit maximizing firm). The Panel rejected all US claims and arguments in this respect. It took the view that the STE at hand could legitimately use its privilege to the disadvantage of commercial actors (§ 6.106), that selling below market prices was perfectly legitimate as well (§ 6.129) and that not selling for its own profit should not be equated to acting without respecting commercial considerations (§ 6.133). In the view of the Panel (§ 6.60):

> In our view, the circumstance that STEs are not inherently 'commercial actors' does not necessarily lead to the conclusion that the 'commercial considerations' requirement is intended to make STEs behave like 'commercial' actors. Indeed, we think it should lead to a different conclusion, namely that the require-

ment in question is simply intended to prevent STEs from behaving like 'political' actors.

And in a footnote it added:

We use the term 'political actors' here merely to contrast our understanding of the first clause with that of the United States. Non-commercial considerations include, but are not limited to, political considerations.

Following an appeal by the US, the AB had the chance to explain its own understanding of the term 'commercial considerations'. Stating first the Panel's understanding of the term (§ 140), it went on to state that, as long as they do not discriminate, STEs can be deemed to have acted in accordance with commercial considerations and thus, can make use of their privileges which they do not have to undo in order to be deemed to be acting consistently with Art. XVII GATT (§§ 146–151).

An un-appealed finding of the same Panel (*Canada–Wheat Exports and Grain Imports*) concerns the interpretation of the term 'solely': in the Panel's view, were an STE to make purchases or sales on the following considerations:

(a) The nationality of potential buyers or sellers;

(b) The policies pursued;

(c) Or the national (economic or political) interest of the Member maintaining the STE,

it would not be acting solely in accordance with commercial considerations (§ 6.88).

In *Canada–Wheat Exports and Grain Imports*, the US had also complained about the practices of the Canadian STE vis-à-vis other enterprises, arguing that, it did not afford other companies adequate opportunities to compete and was thus, in violation of the second clause embedded in Art. XVII.1(b) GATT. The US was arguing that the obligation to afford adequate opportunities to other enterprises to compete extended to cover enterprises in competition with an STE, that is, enterprises which could substitute the STE, as a purchaser or a seller. The Panel had already rejected this claim, and the AB confirmed this finding (§ 157):

In other words, the second clause of subparagraph (b) refers to purchases and sales transactions where: (i) one of the parties involved in the transaction is an STE; and (ii) the transaction involves imports to or exports from the Member maintaining the STE. Thus, the requirement to afford an adequate opportunity to compete for participation (*i.e.*, taking part with others) in "such" purchases and sales (import or export transactions involving an STE) must refer to the opportunity to become the STE's counterpart in the transaction, *not* to an opportunity to replace the STE as a participant in the transaction. If it were otherwise, the transaction would no longer be the type of transaction described by the phrase "*such* purchases or sales" in the second clause of Article XVII:1(b), because it would not involve an STE as a party. Thus, in transactions involving two parties, one of whom is an STE seller, the word "enterprises" in the second clause of Article XVII:1(b) can refer *only* to buyers. (italics and emphasis in the original).

In § 161 it added:

the panel's findings that the terms 'enterprises of the other Members' in the second clause of paragraph (b) of Article XVII:1 includes 'enterprises interested in buying the products offered for sale by an export STE' but not 'enterprises selling the same product as that offered for sale by the export STE in question (i.e., the competitors of the export STE).

3.4 STES AND QUANTITATIVE RESTRICTIONS

The Interpretative Note ad Articles XI, XII, XIII, XIV and XVII GATT suggests that STEs should not be used as conduits to circumvent the obligation to impose QRs:

Throughout Articles XI, XII, XIII, XIV and XVII, the terms 'import restrictions' or 'export restrictions' include restrictions made effective through state-trading operations.

The WTO website (http://www.wto.org/english/tratop_e/statra_e/statra_e.htm) mentions one example of a law that would run afoul this provision:

a law which granted a state trading enterprise exclusive import rights in a certain product, and a decision by that enterprise to refuse to import at all, would appear to be a violation of article XI.

3.5 STES AND TARIFF CONCESSIONS

The Interpretative Note ad Art. XVII.3 GATT includes a reference to Art. II.4 GATT: this provision requires from WTO Members to ensure that any monopoly in the importation of a product will not result in protection which is on average in excess of the amount of protection provided for in the relevant schedule of concessions. Art. XVII.4 GATT deals with import monopolies on products which are not subject to concessions in accordance with Art. II GATT: it provides that the WTO Member concerned shall, upon request, provide information on the import mark up for any given product coming under its purview during a previous representative period.[5]

3.6 TRANSPARENCY REQUIREMENTS

All STEs must be notified to the WTO. But in light of the uncertainty regarding the definition of the term, it is highly likely that (some) notifications are deficient. The Understanding on the Interpretation of Art. XVII GATT (§ 4) allows for the possibility to cross-notify STEs, but there is no record of cross-notifications so far. To facilitate notifications, the Council for Trade in Goods (CTG) has adopted a series of decisions relating to the periodic notifications-requirement that WTO Members must observe.[6]

Furthermore, a Working Party on State Trading Enterprises has been established following the advent of the Understanding on the Interpretation of Art. XVII GATT (§ 5). This body will review all notifications (and updating of notifications) of STEs; it will meet, at the very least, once a year, and reports to the CTG. It has revised the 1960 Questionnaire (that has been used for notification purposes), and, as stated above, is in the process of elaborating an Illustrative List of STEs. Updating notifications for 1999 and 2000 were received from 47 and 44 Members, respectively. New and full notifications were received from 54 Members for the year 2001 and updating notifications for 2002 and 2003 were received from 42 and 33 Members, respectively. New and full notifications for 2004 and 2006 were received from 34 and 22 Members, respectively.[7] Participation is open to all WTO Members.[8]

4. EXCEPTIONS

Art. XX(d) GATT explicitly mentions STEs and states that nothing in the GATT shall prevent the adoption of measures necessary to secure compliance, inter alia, with laws or regulations relating to the enforcement of STEs.

QUESTIONS AND COMMENTS

Commercial considerations: Do you agree with the AB findings on the interpretation of this term? Should it be equated to the obligation not to discriminate?

---

[5] Drebentsov and Michalopoulos (1998) discusses STEs in Russia; Martin and Bach (1998) STEs in China. Davey (1998) raises questions regarding the adequacy of the current disciplines to deal with Chinese and eventually Russian STEs.

[6] WTO Docs. G/C/M/1, G/STR/N/1 and all subsequent numbers in this series.

[7] WTO Doc. G/L/829 of October 10, 2007. An Annex to this document contains information about all STEs notified so far.

[8] The most recent notifications appear in WTO Doc. G/L/223/Rev. 18 of March 9, 2011 at pp. 66–67.

Adequate opportunities to compete: Is this obligation effectively asking from monopolies to behave as if they were not monopolies? How can it happen? And what does the adjective 'adequate' mean in this context?

STEs and subsidies: When you have discussed in class the Chapter on Subsidies, come back to this Chapter and ask yourself the question whether the two disciplines taken together can guarantee that enterprises in NMEs will behave exactly like enterprises in market economies.

CHAPTER 11

THE GENERAL TRANSPARENCY OBLIGATION

■ ■ ■

1. THE LEGAL DISCIPLINE

Transparency covers both notifications as well as publication of laws. WTO Members have to observe 176 distinct obligations to notify information to the WTO. Of these, 42 are recurring obligations, in the sense that WTO Members are expected to provide notification reports on a regular basis (e.g., semi-annual, annual, bi-annual, triennial, etc.). For example, pursuant to Art. 25.1 of the SCM Agreement, each WTO Member is expected to provide a new and full list of specific subsidies every three years. During the intervening time period, each WTO Member is expected to provide update notifications. Similarly, each WTO Member is expected to provide reports twice a year on the status of anti-dumping investigations and include a list of all anti-dumping duties in effect. The remaining are obligations to provide ad hoc notifications as necessary.

The Overview Secretariat Document classifies the breakdown of the various types of notification-obligations as follows (p. 51):

	Regular	Ad hoc	Total
Development	0	7	**7**
Government Procurement	3	8	**11**
Intellectual Property	3	23	**26**
Services	3	11	**14**
Trade in Goods			
Agriculture	8	7	**15**
Market Access	9	27	**36**
Rules	7	34	**41**
Technical Barriers to Trade	1	13	**14**
TRIMs	1	2	**3**
General			
Balance of payments	1	1	**2**
RTAs	6	0	**6**

	Regular	Ad hoc	Total
TPRM	0	1	1
Total	42	134	176

One of the key mechanisms for ensuring transparency is each country's Trade Policy Review Mechanism (TPRM), which we have already discussed in Chapter 1.

For agreement-specific transparency requirements, we refer to the transparency obligations in the corresponding chapter discussing that agreement. In this Chapter, we focus on Art. X GATT, the general transparency obligation embedded in GATT.

Art. X GATT imposes the following obligations:

(a) All laws, regulations, administrative rulings and judicial decisions of general application affecting trade must be published (Art. X.1 GATT);

(b) State acts covered by the aforementioned legal discipline will not be enforced before their publication if they represent a new or more burdensome requirement on imports (Art. X.2 GATT);

(c) State acts coming under the purview of Art. X.1 GATT must be administered in 'uniform, reasonable, and impartial' manner, and a (national) forum must be provided where claims regarding the administration of customs laws can be adjudicated (Art. X.3 GATT).

2. THE RATIONALE FOR THE LEGAL DISCIPLINE

Transparency is a key first step in ensuring that WTO Members respect their obligations. By requiring that information be made published and made public, traders can easily access the national laws that implement WTO obligations and accommodate their trade-related activities accordingly.

The AB in *US–Underwear* understood the transparency-obligation embedded in Art. X GATT as a due process-obligation (p. 21).[1] In *EC–IT Products*, the Panel found that the EU had violated its obligations by publishing documents ten months after they had been made effective (§ 7.1076).

---

[1] See also the Panel report in *Argentina–Hides and Leather* noted in this respect (§ 11.76).

3. COVERAGE OF THE LEGAL DISCIPLINE

3.1 LAWS AND OTHER ACTS OF GENERAL APPLICATION

Art. X.1 GATT requires the publication of "all laws, administrative and judicial decisions of general application". The meaning of the term 'general application' is not self-evident. The Panel, in *US–Underwear*, asserted that a key criterion for evaluating this term is whether the measure at hand applied, in principle, to an un-identified number of economic operators as opposed to specific set of operators (§ 7.65):

> The mere fact that the restraint at issue was an administrative order does not prevent us from concluding that the restraint was a measure of general application. Nor does the fact that it was a country-specific measure exclude the possibility of it being a measure of general application. If, for instance, the restraint was addressed to a specific company or applied to a specific shipment, it would not have qualified as a measure of general application. However, to the extent that the restraint affects an uni-dentified number of economic operators, including domestic and foreign producers, we find it to be a measure of general application.

On appeal, the AB upheld this finding (p. 21). The AB in *EC–Poultry* provided the explicit confirmation to this effect. In that case, the Panel had found that import licenses issued by the EU to specific companies interested in importing poultry products, and/or import licenses applied to specific shipments (poultry products) to the EU, were not measures of general application, and thus, not justiciable under Art. X GATT. The AB upheld the Panel's findings. It held that (§ 113):

> We agree with the Panel that "conversely, licences issued to a specific company or applied to a specific shipment cannot be considered to be a measure 'of general application' " within the meaning of Article X.[2]

Art. X GATT mentions four categories of measures of general application: laws; regulations; judicial decisions; and administrative rulings. In *Dominican Republic–Importation and Sale of Cigarettes*, the Central Bank of the defendant (Dominican Republic) was publishing price surveys for imported cigarettes. In the Panel's view, these surveys could not, in principle, come under any of the categories envisaged by Art. X.1 GATT. However, they constituted an essential input to the final determination of the duty imposed on imported cigarettes: duties are of course measures of general application by any reasonable standard. Consequently, although price surveys lacked, in the Panel's view, the formal characteristics of the

---

[2] See also the Panel report in *Argentina–Hides and Leather* at §§ 11.73ff.

categories envisaged by Art. X GATT, because they functioned as input to a measure of general application, they should come under Art. X.1 GATT anyway (§§ 7.404–7.408). In *US–COOL*, the Panel held that (§ 7.840):

> The act of providing guidance on the meaning of specific requirements under a measure, for instance by publishing "frequently asked questions", is an act of administering such measure within the meaning of Art. X:3(a).

The same report held that a letter by the US Secretary of Agriculture, Thomas J. Vilsack (quoted in § 7.123 of the Panel report), providing details regarding the implementation of a US statute regarding the origin of goods also qualifies as a measure covered by Art. X GATT (§ 7.840).

In *Thailand–Cigarettes (Philippines)*, the AB confirmed the Panel's finding to the effect that providing a guarantee in order to release goods through customs was a measure covered by Art. X GATT (§§ 215–216).

In *EC–IT Products*, the Panel held that a measure does not have to be binding to be covered by Art. X GATT; it suffices that it is 'authoritative.' At issue in the case was the question of whether an Explanatory Note to an EU Council Regulation fell within the auspices of Art. X GATT.[3] The Panel held that the Explanatory Notes were authoritative because they were issued by the European Commission and were meant to help the EU member states to achieve uniformity with the EU Council Regulation (§§ 7.1023ff., and especially 7.1027). Therefore, they were covered by Art. X GATT.

3.2 UNIFORM, REASONABLE AND IMPARTIAL ADMINISTRATION OF LAWS

Laws, regulations, administrative rulings and judicial decisions that fall under Art. X.1 GATT are required, by virtue of Art. X.3 of the GATT, to be administered in a 'uniform, impartial, and reasonable' manner. The exact meaning of this requirement has been the subject of several disputes as well.

In *US–Shrimp*, several nations filed complaints challenging the consistency of the administration of US certification procedures for imported shrimp under Section 609, designed to ensure that foreign shrimp trawling practices did not lead to increased mortality of sea turtles, with the GATT. They asserted that the process violated Art. X.3 GATT because the internal governmental certification procedures applied by several US agencies was non-transparent; countries whose applications had been denied did not receive formal notice of denial, nor of the reasons for the denial; and there was no formal legal procedure for review of, or appeal from, a denial of an application.

---

[3] The Council Regulation 2658/87 of July 23, 1987 on Tariffs and Statistical Nomenclature and on the Common Customs Tariff, published in OJ L 256/1, September 7, 1987.

The AB held that Art. X GATT should be understood as imposing minimum transparency requirements, implying that WTO Members were free to go beyond the established standards, provided of course that their actions were otherwise GATT-consistent (§§ 182–183):

> The provisions of Article X:3 of the GATT 1994 bear upon this matter. In our view, Section 609 falls within the "laws, regulations, judicial decisions and administrative rulings of general application" described in Article X:1. Inasmuch as there are due process requirements generally for measures that are otherwise imposed in compliance with WTO obligations, it is only reasonable that rigorous compliance with the fundamental requirements of due process should be required in the application and administration of a measure which purports to be an exception to the treaty obligations of the Member imposing the measure and which effectively results in a suspension *pro hac vice* of the treaty rights of other Members.
>
> It is also clear to us that Article X:3 of the GATT 1994 establishes certain minimum standards for transparency and procedural fairness in the administration of trade regulations which, in our view, are not met here. The non-transparent and *ex parte* nature of the internal governmental procedures applied by the competent officials in the Office of Marine Conservation, the Department of State, and the United States National Marine Fisheries Service throughout the certification processes under Section 609, as well as the fact that countries whose applications are denied do not receive formal notice of such denial, nor of the reasons for the denial, and the fact, too, that there is no formal legal procedure for review of, or appeal from, a denial of an application, are all contrary to the spirit, if not the letter, of Article X:3 of the GATT 1994.

The Panel in *Argentina–Hides and Leather* held that the obligation to administer laws in uniform, reasonable and impartial manner included three distinct requirements that would have to be interpreted separately (§ 11.86). The natural conclusion emerging from this finding is that WTO Members must satisfy all three separate requirements to be consistent with their obligations under the GATT.

<u>Uniform Administration</u>: The Panel in *Argentina–Hides and Leather* discussed the consistency of an Argentine measure allowing for representatives of the Argentine producers of leather products during customs clearance of hides with the multilateral rules: recall that Argentina had enacted Resolution 2235/96 which, *inter alia*, made it possible for representatives of the Argentine tanning industry (Association of Industrial Producers of Leather, Leather Manufactures and Related Products), or ADICMA, to be present during customs clearing procedures concerning

exports of bovine hides. In the view of the EU, the presence of ADICMA representatives amounted to a *de facto* export restriction prohibited by Art. XI GATT (since ADICMA representatives would have had an interest in keeping bovine hides in the Argentine market and would thus, have had an incentive to affect the total volume of exports). The bulk of the complaint by the EU focused on the inconsistency of the said practice with Art. XI GATT. The claim under Art. X GATT focused on the administration of Resolution 2235/96. More specifically, the EU claimed that, in administering Resolution 2235/96 in an unreasonable, impartial and not uniform manner, Argentina was violating its obligations under Art. X.3 GATT. We quote the EU claim as reproduced in the AB report (§ 11.58):

> The European Communities argues that the presence of "partial and interested" representatives of the tanning industry makes an impartial application of the relevant customs rules impossible. The European Communities also considers that it is not "reasonable" within the meaning of Article X:3(a) that the interested industry is informed of all attempts at exports by those from whom they wish to obtain the exclusive right to purchase hides. The European Communities argued that the Argentinean administration of its laws also was not "uniform". According to the European Communities it was improper for Argentina to construct a special set of procedures for administering its export laws for only one type of product. Other products are subject to export duties or are eligible for export "refunds". In light of this, hides should not be singled out.

The EU claimed that the Argentine measure was not uniformly administered, and, thus, in contradiction with Art. X.3 GATT, because, it was applied to bovine hides only and not to other products. The Panel dismissed this claim. In its view, what mattered when reviewing the consistency of the challenged measure with Art. X.3 GATT was not whether the measure was discriminatory or not, but whether it provided traders with predictability as to future transactions (§§ 11.83–11.85):

> It is obvious from these uses of the terms that it is meant that Customs laws should not vary, that every exporter and importer should be able to expect treatment of the same kind, in the same manner both over time and in different places and with respect to other persons. Uniform administration requires that Members ensure that their laws are applied consistently and predictably and is not limited, for instance, to ensuring equal treatment with respect to WTO Members. That would be a substantive violation properly addressed under Article I. This is a requirement of uniform administration of Customs laws and procedures between individual shippers and even with respect to the same person at different times and different places.

We are of the view that this provision should not be read as a broad anti-discrimination provision. We do not think this provision should be interpreted to require all products be treated identically. That would be reading far too much into this paragraph which focuses on the day to day application of Customs laws, rules and regulations. There are many variations in products which might require differential treatment and we do not think this provision should be read as a general invitation for a panel to make such distinctions.

In our view, there is no evidence that Argentina has applied Resolution 2235 in a non-uniform manner with respect to hides. All hides exports are uniformly subject to the possibility of ADICMA representatives being present. Indeed, the European Communities' complaints are about Resolution 2235's application across the board. The difficulties of Argentina's administration of its Customs laws pursuant to Resolution 2235 are adequately dealt with under the other provisions of Article X:3(a).

The Panel in *EC–Selected Customs Matters* held that the obligation for uniformity covers, inter alia, geographic uniformity.[4] This Panel stated that, because identical products within its sovereignty were subjected to different customs treatment, the EU was in violation of Art. X GATT, (§§ 7.135 ff.). By the same token, the same Panel found that differential customs administration of LCD monitors (Liquid Crystal Display) within the EU was tantamount to a violation of Art. X GATT (§ 7.305).[5] In this Panel's view, 'uniformity' should not be confused with 'identity'. Some differentiation might be appropriate, and the degree of uniformity should be determined on a case by case basis: the narrower the challenge (that is, the more specific the aspects of the administrative action complained about), the higher the degree of uniformity required (and, consequently, the lower the burden for the complainant to make a prima facie case). More specifically, with respect to the tariff classification of LCD monitors with a digital video interface (hereinafter, LCD monitors), the situation was as follows: video monitors were classified under tariff heading 8528 and were subjected to a 14% import duty in the EU market, whereas computer monitors were classified under tariff heading 8471 and paid 0% import duty. The Netherlands classified LCD monitors under tariff heading 8528, whereas other EU member states under 8471. As a result, there was discrepancy as to the import duty that LCD monitors exported to the EU market were subjected to, depending on whether the destination was the Netherlands or another EU member state. The Panel had originally found that this discrepancy amounted to non-uniform application and, consequently, run afoul Art. X.3(a) GATT, and the EU appealed this find-

---

[4] Hoekman and Mavroidis (2009) approvingly discuss this issue in more detail.
[5] The Panel held that Art. XXIV.12 GATT is not an exception to Art. X.3(a) GATT.

ing. It did not contest that divergence indeed existed across the various EU member states; it did argue, however, that it had taken action since 2004 to address this phenomenon (§ 246, AB report). It submitted that the adoption of EC Reg. 2171/2005 combined with the withdrawal of the Dutch measure (classifying LCD monitors under 8528) were two measures that amply demonstrated that it had addressed the discrepancy and regretted that the panel did not take either into account. The Panel had refused to take such evidence into account because it had been submitted belatedly so, that is, after the interim review-stage. The EU believed that the Panel's handling of this evidence was DSU-inconsistent, since the evidence submitted directly related to the interim report that had been circulated to the parties to the dispute (§ 248, AB report). Additionally, the Panel had violated, in the eyes of the EU, its duty under Art. 11 DSU to make an objective assessment, since, it took into account actions (the classification of LCD monitors by the Dutch authorities) that post-dated its establishment (§ 249, AB report). The AB was, thus, confronted with two issues:

(a) Could the Panel have legitimately relied on evidence that post-dated its establishment?

(b) Was the Panel's decision not to take into account the evidence submitted by the EU at the interim review stage correct?

The AB responded affirmatively to the first question. In its view, the Panel could legitimately rely on data which post-dated its establishment in order to understand how a measure, which was in place when the Panel was established, was being administered. The AB found support for this conclusion in the fact that the EU did not point to any evidence that pre-dated the establishment of the Panel which could contradict the evidence on which the panel relied (§ 254, AB report). Hence, absence of uniform administration can be established using data that post-dates the establishment of the Panel. The AB responded affirmatively to the second question as well. In prior case-law, the AB had established that evidence submitted for the first time at the interim review-stage is legitimately rejected (§ 259, AB report). The requirement for uniformity has, consequently, been interpreted so far, as tantamount to a requirement to ensure predictability (for the handling of future transactions), and a requirement for geographic uniformity.

<u>Reasonable Administration</u>: In *Dominican Republic–Importation and Sale of Cigarettes*, the Panel found that not only positive actions, but omissions too can come under scrutiny in the context of the review regarding the consistency of a specific law, regulation etc. with Art. X.3 GATT (§ 7.379). Honduras challenged a practice by Dominican Republic to avoid calculating the imposition of tax on imported cigarettes based on one of the three methods reflected in the Dominican law (§ 7.387); instead, the Dominican Republic, on its own admission, had been calculat-

ing the amount of imposition based on variables other than those published in the relevant generally applicable law. That is, the Dominican Republic had not included in its publication of laws the various variables used for the calculation of the imposition. Such an omission constituted, in the Panel's view, an unreasonable administration of its laws (§ 7.388).

The Panel in *Argentina–Hides and Leather* addressed, *inter alia*, a claim by the EU to the effect that the Argentine measure was in breach of Art. X.3 GATT, since it provided representatives of ADICMA with possibility to have access to business-confidential information: namely, they could learn the names of the exporters, and their pricing schemes. In the Panel's view, similar information could then be used to confer an advantage to the Argentine tanning industry, when negotiating with the upstream segment of this market. To reach its conclusion, the Panel first turned to the objective of the challenged Argentine law (§§ 11.90):

> In considering this requirement, we first turn to the stated objective for Resolution 2235 offered by Argentina. Argentina stated that it required assistance in the classification of bovine hides when exported in order to ensure there were no mistakes or fraud regarding the proper payment of export duties and awarding of export "refunds". While a manifestly WTO-inconsistent measure cannot be justified by assertions of good intentions, we consider it reasonable in this instance to accept for purposes of analysis the proffered explanation in light of all the facts of the dispute.

It subsequently concluded that an administration of laws which allowed for this possibility to occur was unreasonable, and thus, in contradiction with Art. X GATT, since it allowed for the dissemination of business confidential information which could be used to the commercial advantage of the Argentine producers of leather goods (§§ 11.92–11.94):

> To provide some specific examples, ADICMA representatives should not be able to see the pricing information of the suppliers to ADICMA's members. This is information which ADICMA members could use to their commercial advantage in negotiations with the *frigoríficos*. We should note in this regard that Argentina bases its export duties on prices of hides quoted in the United States. Thus, even if we were to consider it reasonable for the tanners to be involved in the export clearance process, there would be no reason whatever for them to see the prices as these would be irrelevant to the assessment of export duties. We also see no need for them to be made aware of the destination or quantities involved as these data are irrelevant to the tasks ADICMA representatives are involved in.
>
> We think it is particularly important for the reasonable administration of Argentina's export laws that the tanners not be pro-

vided the name of exporters. Argentina claims that this is no longer possible. However, as it was part of the European Communities' claims and was unarguably possible as recently as May of 1999 that such written information was supplied to ADICMA, we consider it necessary to specifically find that it is unreasonable for such information to be provided to ADICMA or its members. However, this question goes beyond just supply of the name in writing. Argentina has stressed in its arguments under all three conditions of Article X:3(a) that the process is balanced because the exporters may be present during the Customs process. However, it necessarily follows that exercising this right would reveal the identity of the exporter. While it could be argued that the exporter could send a representative or agent and may thereby conceal his identity, imposing such a burden with respect to an exporter's own products would be unreasonable.

Therefore, we must conclude that a process aimed at assuring the proper classification of products, but which inherently contains the possibility of revealing confidential business information, is an unreasonable manner of administering the laws, regulations and rules identified in Article X:1 and therefore is inconsistent with Article X:3(a). (italics in the original).

It follows that, so far, the requirement for reasonable administration has been understood as a requirement not to confer a commercial advantage to domestic producers.

<u>Impartial Administration</u>: The Panel in *EC–Selected Customs Matters* held that the requirement for impartiality meant that the reviewing agency (tribunal) should be independent from the agency the acts of which were being challenged (§ 7.519). In *Argentina–Hides and Leather*, the EU had argued that the Argentine measure was not being administered in an impartial manner, since there was absolutely no legitimate reason why ADICMA-representatives should be present during customs clearance of bovine hides. Moreover, information obtained by their mere presence, could potentially be used to their own advantage (as already discussed supra). Hence, there was at least potentially a case of conflict of interest. The Panel upheld this claim, since it agreed that the mere possibility that the Argentine industry present in customs clearance could use confidential information to its own advantage, amounted ipso facto to a violation of the impartial administration-requirement embedded in Art. X GATT (§§ 11.99–11.102):

> The only private parties that have a contractual legal interest in the product and transaction are the exporter (and his agent) and the foreign buyer. The government also has a relevant legal interest in the transaction based on the sovereign right to regulate and tax exports. In contrast with this, the ADICMA representa-

tives have, outside of the measure in question itself, no legal relationship with either the products or the sales contract. ADICMA, in fact, represents an adverse commercial interest in that the exports are not in its members' interests as such exports potentially drive up the costs of hides. Furthermore, ADICMA members are competitors of the foreign buyers of the hides.

Much as we are concerned in general about the presence of private parties with conflicting commercial interests in the Customs process, in our view the requirement of impartial administration in this dispute is not a matter of mere presence of ADICMA representatives in such processes. It all depends on what that person is permitted to do. In our view, the answer to this question is related directly to the question of access to information as part of the product classification process as discussed in the previous Section. Our concern here is focussed on the need for safeguards to prevent the inappropriate flow of one private person's confidential information to another as a result of the administration of the Customs laws, in this case the implementing Resolution 2235.

Whenever a party with a contrary commercial interest, but no relevant legal interest, is allowed to participate in an export transaction such as this, there is an inherent danger that the Customs laws, regulations and rules will be applied in a partial manner so as to permit persons with adverse commercial interests to obtain confidential information to which they have no right.

While this situation could be remedied by adequate safeguards, we do not consider that such safeguards presently are in place. Therefore, Resolution 2235 cannot be considered an impartial administration of the Customs laws, regulations and rules described in Article X:1 and, thus, is inconsistent with Article X:3(a) of the GATT 1994.

A very demanding standard was thus established and WTO Members, following this case law, will have to ensure adherence to it.

3.3 THE OBLIGATION TO MAINTAIN INDEPENDENT TRIBUNALS

WTO Members must, by virtue of Art. X.3(b) GATT, establish (judicial, arbitral, administrative) tribunals (or procedures) that will be independent from the agency the acts of which they will be reviewing. Traders should have recourse to such tribunals or procedures. The Panel in *EC–Selected Customs Matters* underscored this requirement for impartiality of tribunals (§ 7.519). In this report, the Panel dealt with the question to what extent a decision should govern the practice of all agencies entrusted with administrative enforcement throughout the territory of the WTO Member concerned. The Panel held that reading Art. X.3(b) GATT in this way was unwarranted. It based its finding on its understanding that tribunals mentioned in Art. X.3(b) GATT were in all likelihood first instance tribunals and requiring similar effect of their decisions could raise public order-type concerns: in the Panel's view, the courts viewed by this provision should be typically first instance courts, and as such, it is only normal that in some national jurisdictions they might have been assigned a specific territorial scope.[6] The US appealed this finding (that WTO Members need not, by virtue of the obligation included in Art. X.3(b) GATT, establish courts which will have the authority to bind all agencies entrusted with administrative enforcement throughout the territory of a WTO Member). The US had recourse to predominantly textual arguments. In its view, the Panel had not paid sufficient attention to the term 'agencies' appearing in Art. X.3(b) GATT which, unless understood to cover all administrative agencies throughout the territory of a WTO Member, could not guarantee uniform application of laws as required by this provision. The AB was thus presented with the opportunity to clarify its understanding of the obligation included in Art. X.3(b) GATT. The AB upheld the Panel's finding to the effect that the tribunals envisaged in the first sentence of this provision are first instance tribunals (§ 294): based on textual and contextual arguments (first instance courts do not extend their jurisdiction throughout the territory of a WTO Member; the existence of second instance courts supports this thesis,) it sided with the Panel (§§ 298–299). It then went on to also find that the obligation is limited to first instance courts and not all administrative agencies as the US had argued, upholding the Panel's findings on this score in the following terms (§ 303):

> For these reasons, we are of the view that Article X:3(b) of the GATT 1994 requires a WTO Member to establish and maintain independent mechanisms for prompt review and correction of administrative action in the area of customs administration. However, neither text nor context nor the object and purpose of this Article require that the decisions emanating from such first instance review must govern the practice of *all* agencies entrusted with administrative enforcement *throughout the territory* of a particular WTO Member. (emphasis in the original).

3.4 STANDARD OF REVIEW

WTO adjudicating bodies must, by virtue of Art. 11 DSU, make an objective assessment of the factual record before them; case law has clarified that, with respect to disputes coming under the purview of Art. X GATT, this duty will, more specifically, entail that they:

---

[6] See the analysis leading to the final ruling in § 7.539.

(a) Are satisfied that a violation has occurred in cases where there is likely impact on the competitive situation across domestic and foreign products, due to the unreasonableness, lack of uniformity, and/or partiality in the administration of a law;

(b) Will not be questioning the substantive consistency of a law with the multilateral rules; rather, their review should be confined to the consistency in the administration of laws in accordance with the obligations included in Art. X GATT.

In *Argentina–Hides and Leather*, one of the questions before the Panel was, to what extent, in order to observe its burden of proof, the EU had to show actual effects (trade damage) for its producers and traders, as a result of the administration of the contested legislation. The Panel dismissed this thesis; in its view, it sufficed that the EU demonstrated the likelihood that the interests of traders would be negatively affected, as a result of the administration of Resolution 2235/96, and no actual trade damage had to be shown (§ 11.77):

> Thus, it can be seen that Article X:3(a) requires an examination of the real effect that a measure might have on traders operating in the commercial world. This, of course, does not require a showing of trade damage, as that is generally not a requirement with respect to violations of the GATT 1994. But it can involve an examination of whether there is a possible impact on the competitive situation due to alleged partiality, unreasonableness or lack of uniformity in the application of customs rules, regulations, decisions, etc.[7]

How much examination is required to observe the established standard of review under Art. X GATT is to be decided on a case-by-case basis. The AB in *US–OCTG Sunset Reviews* confirmed that some explanation is necessary for a claim to succeed and that a mere submission of data, which could be interpreted in more than one way, is not sufficient. In this case, Argentina argued that the US had not been administering its sunset reviews of antidumping duties in a reasonable manner, since the domestic industry recorded 223 wins in 223 cases, that is, there was no case where the exporters prevailed (§ 218). The AB refused to accept the Argentine claim in this respect since, in its view, for a claim under Art. X.3 GATT to be successful, solid evidence was required. Mere statistical evidence which could be interpreted in various ways did not suffice (§§ 217–219). It follows that what Argentina should have done was to demonstrate that the outcome was due to unreasonable, or non-uniform, or partial administration of laws.

---

[7] The potential for non-uniform administration of laws sufficed for the Panel to find against the EU in its report on *EC–Selected Customs Matters*. In this case, the Panel held that the defendant was in breach of its WTO obligations because of the possibility that blackout drapery lining was treated in German customs different than it was in other EU customs (§§ 7.276ff.).

Art. X GATT is not concerned with the substantive consistency of a particular act with the GATT rules either. This is the subject matter of other GATT provisions. For example, as discussed by the AB in *EC–Bananas III* (§ 200), Art. X GATT is concerned with the administration of laws:

> The context of Article X:3(a) within Article X, which is entitled "Publication and Administration of Trade Regulations", and a reading of the other paragraphs of Article X, make it clear that Article X applies to the *administration* of laws, regulations, decisions and rulings. To the extent that the laws, regulations, decisions and rulings themselves are discriminatory, they can be examined for their consistency with the relevant provisions of the GATT 1994.

The Panel in *Argentina–Hides and Leather* reached a similar conclusion (§§ 11.60) as that of the AB in in *EC–Bananas III*.

In the same vein, the AB reached a similar conclusion in *EC–Poultry*. The AB entertained a claim by Brazil, to the effect that an EU measure relating to imports of frozen poultry meat, did not allow Brazilian traders to know whether a particular shipment would be subjected to the rules governing in-quota trade, or to rules relating to out-of-quota trade. Brazil maintained that this was a violation of Art. X GATT. The AB held the view that in part, this claim concerned the substantive consistency of the EU measure at hand with the pertinent GATT rules, and, this part of the claim lied outside the coverage of Art. X GATT. It stated in § 115:

> Thus, to the extent that Brazil's appeal relates to the *substantive content* of the EC rules themselves, and not to their *publication* or *administration*, that appeal falls outside the scope of Article X of the GATT 1994. The WTO-consistency of such substantive content must be determined by reference to provisions of the covered agreements other than Article X of the GATT 1994. (emphasis in the original).[8]

In *EC–Selected Customs Matters*, the AB provided a noteworthy precision: the substantive content of the instrument that regulates administration of a measure can of course be challenged. It is the substantive content of instruments being administered that cannot be challenged (§§ 200–201):

> The statements of the Appellate Body in *EC—Bananas III* and *EC—Poultry* do not exclude, however, the possibility of challenging under Article X:3(a) the substantive content of a legal instrument that regulates the administration of a legal instrument of the kind described in Article X:1. Under Article X:3(a), a dis-

---

[8] For additional confirmation, see § 7.113 of the Panel report in *EC–Selected Customs Matters*.

tinction must be made between the legal instrument being administered and the legal instrument that regulates the application or implementation of that instrument. While the substantive content of the legal instrument being administered is not challengeable under Article X:3(a), we see no reason why a legal instrument that regulates the application or implementation of that instrument cannot be examined under Article X:3(a) if it is alleged to lead to a lack of uniform, impartial, or reasonable administration of that legal instrument."

This distinction has of course implications with respect to the type of evidence that the complainant must submit to support a claim of a violation of Article X:3(a) GATT. If a WTO Member challenges, under Article X:3(a) GATT, the substantive content of a legal instrument that regulates the administration of a legal instrument of the kind described in Article X:1, it will have to prove that this instrument *necessarily* leads to a lack of uniform, impartial, or reasonable administration. It is not sufficient for the complainant merely to cite the provisions of that legal instrument. The complainant must discharge the burden of substantiating how and why those provisions necessarily lead to impermissible administration of the legal instrument of the kind described in Article X:1.

QUESTIONS AND COMMENTS

Number of Notifications: The Overview Secretariat Document contains information regarding the number of notifications received between 1995–2010:

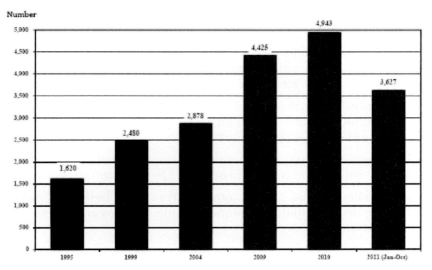

Source: Overview Secretariat Document p. 52.

Origins of Transparency Obligations: Originally, that is, in the GATT-era, there were obligations to publish trade-related information and notify the GATT of measures coming under its purview: this is what the Overview Secretariat Document terms 'the first generation transparency provisions' (pp. 50ff.); during the Tokyo round, the right to request information became a legal possibility ('second generation transparency provisions'). The Tokyo round Understanding Regarding Notification, Consultation, Dispute Settlement and Surveillance mentions to this effect (§ 3):

> Contracting parties which have reasons to believe that such trade measures have been adopted by another contracting party may seek information on such measures bilaterally, from the contracting party concerned.

During the Uruguay round, arguably the third generation transparency provisions were agreed and came to effect: cross-notifications became widely used, and the role of the WTO Secretariat was upgraded significantly. For example, recently the US cross-notified the WTO of dozens of (alleged) Chinese and Indian subsidy schemes, that China and India had failed to notify the WTO about: with respect to Chinese schemes, the US notified the WTO of 42 green technology schemes, 92 export subsidies, and 52 other schemes belonging to various categories;[9] it further notified the WTO of 23 Indian schemes.[10] Most of the activity regarding cross-notifications is in the subsidies-context, as should be expected in light of the corresponding (dis-)incentives to notify.

The WTO Secretariat saw an increase in its powers to become an international 'watchdog' monitoring transparency obligations. It established the Central Registry of Notifications (CRN) with the following mandate:

> A central registry of notifications shall be established under the responsibility of the Secretariat. While Members will continue to follow existing notification procedures, the Secretariat shall ensure that the central registry records such elements of the information provided on the measure by the Member concerned as its purpose, its trade coverage, and the requirement under which it has been notified. The central registry shall cross-reference its records of notifications by Member and obligation.
>
> The central registry shall inform each Member annually of the regular notification obligations to which that Member will be expected to respond in the course of the following year.
>
> The central registry shall draw the attention of individual Members to regular notification requirements which remain unfulfilled.
>
> Information in the central registry regarding individual notifications shall be made available on request to any Member entitled to receive the notification concerned.

---

[9] WTO Doc. G/SCM/Q2/CHN/42 of October 11, 2011.
[10] WTO Doc. G/SCM/Q2/IND/20 of October 10, 2011.

The Working Party on Notifications Obligations and Procedures was established in order to streamline the various transparency obligations: its final report is the first clear statement on where the WTO stood on this issue following the many agreements signed during the Uruguay round.[11] This report contained an Annex (Annex III) which reflected the type of information that should be included in notifications by WTO Members as well as a mandate to review at the multilateral level the consistency of notified information. Following lengthy negotiations, the Integrated Database (IDB) was established in 1997 through a decision by the General Council which requested from WTO Members to notify information relevant to tariffs and import trade;[12] following practice judged un-satisfactory, the WTO Members adopted a decision in 2009 which enabled the WTO Secretariat to gather information on its own initiative on the issues covered by the original decisions.[13]

The G 20 in their April 2, 2009 meeting called on the WTO to adopt monitoring mechanisms regarding trade measures, and included a plea to avoid recourse to protectionist measures as response to the financial crisis and a

> call to the DG to continue to monitor and report publicly on our adherence to these undertakings on a quarterly basis.[14]

The WTO Secretariat started issuing a series of documents concerning the manner in which WTO Members had been complying with their obligations to notify the WTO in accordance with the substantive content of Annex III that we saw *supra*: It started issuing the G/L/223 documents where it would "name and shame" the WTO Members that had been neglecting their notification obligations. The reports are entitled "Updating of the Listing of Notification Obligations and the Compliance Therewith as Set Out in Annex III of the Report of the Working Group on Notification Obligation and Procedures" and reflect manner in which WTO Members have been complying over the years with their notification obligation.[15]

---

[11] Report of the Working Party on Notifications Obligations and Procedures, WTO Doc. G/L/112, October 7, 1996.

[12] WTO Doc. WT/L/225 of July 18, 1997, and WTO Doc. G/MA/IDB/1/Rev. 1 of June 27, 1997 which explains the modalities and operation of the IDB and the kind of information requested.

[13] WTO Doc. G/MA/239 of September 4, 2009.

[14] WTO Doc. WT/GC/W/604 of May 22, 2009.

[15] See for example, WTO Doc. G/L/223/Rev. 18 of March 9, 2011.

CHAPTER 12

GENERAL EXCEPTIONS

■ ■ ■

1. THE LEGAL DISCIPLINE

WTO Members can justify violations of their obligations assumed under the GATT through recourse to one of the grounds mentioned in Art. XX GATT. This list covers a variety of exceptions, including:

- Public morality
- Protection of public heath
- Conservation of natural resources
- Protection of national treasures
- Securing compliance with laws not inconsistent with the agreement
- Particular issues related to trade in silver and gold
- Prison labor

Art. XX GATT establishes a two-tier test that a WTO Member must meet in order to successfully invoke an exception to its GATT obligations:

- A WTO Member must demonstrate that the measure taken conforms to the requirements of one of the enumerated exceptions in paragraphs (a)–(j) of Art. XX GATT;
- Furthermore, a WTO Member must meet the requirements of the chapeau of Art. XX GATT.

If both requirements have been met, then the opening sentence of this provision ("Nothing in this agreement . . .") leaves no doubt that the GATT framers' intent was for all of the grounds mentioned in this provision to "trump" all obligations to liberalize trade reflected in the rest of the GATT.

2. THE RATIONALE FOR THE LEGAL DISCIPLINE

Art. XX GATT provides WTO Members with the flexibility to regulate their markets unilaterally in order to protect certain important societal priorities, provided that the measures enacted conform with the requirements specified within the law. Inclusion of a flexibility-providing provision is important because certain priorities may well take precedence over trade liberalization in any given society; without the ability to place these priorities ahead of trade obligations, countries would have been reluctant to agree to conform to multilateral rules governing trade. In that sense, Art. XX GATT provides a hierarchy between trade commitments and (national) social preferences: public morals, protection of human health, and all the other grounds mentioned in the body of this provision "trump" trade commitments.

This understanding of GATT commitments is of course, perfectly consistent with the negative integration-character of the GATT.[1] Trading partners agree on a set of actions that they will not take; they do not necessarily oblige themselves to follow a common path-of-action or harmonize their regulatory regimes. Art. XX GATT seeks to strike a balance between providing WTO Members with continued flexibility to regulate their markets and societies unilaterally, on the one hand, and ensuring that such regulations do not function as a protectionist tool, on the other.

The fact that the GATT supports regulatory flexibility was made clear in a jurisprudential shift that occurred over the interpretation of Art. XX GATT in a series of environment-related disputes in the late 1980s / early 1990s. During the GATT years, two Panels outlawed legislation aimed at protecting dolphins caught in the nets of tuna fishermen, simply because the measure had been unilaterally decided. This reasoning construed the GATT contrary to its negotiating intent. At issue in the so-called *Tuna/Dolphin* case (formally known as *US–Tuna (Mexico)*) was unilaterally-enacted US legislation (Marine Mammal Protection Act) that required from all fishermen (domestic and foreigners alike) wishing to sell tuna in the US to observe a regulation requiring them to avoid fishing for tuna using purse seine nets. This fishing technique greatly increased the risk that dolphins would accidentally be caught and killed; the risk was particularly high in areas where tuna and dolphin swam together. Mexican fishermen did not adapt and, as a result, were left out of the lucrative US tuna market. Mexico protested that the regulatory ban amounted to a QR and thus violated Art. XI GATT. The US attempted to justify its actions under Art. XX GATT, but the GATT Panel rejected this defense because of the unilateral character of the US measure (§ 5.27):

> The Panel considered that if the broad interpretation of Article XX(b) suggested by the United States were accepted, each contracting party could unilaterally determine the life or health protection policies from which other contracting parties could not deviate without jeopardizing their rights under the General Agreement. The General Agreement would then no longer constitute a multilateral framework for trade among all contracting parties but would provide legal security only in respect of trade

---

[1] See the corresponding discussion in Chapter 8.

between a limited number of contracting parties with identical internal regulations.²

This case law was overturned by the AB in its landmark *US–Shrimp* report. This dispute triggered a jurisprudential sea change. At issue in this case was yet again the consistency of unilaterally-enacted US legislation with the GATT: this time US wished to prevent the accidental death of sea turtles, several categories of which were acknowledged as an endangered species by CITES (Convention on the International Trade of Endangered Species). CITES is a multilateral convention that prohibits trade of endangered species coming under its purview. The US prohibited the sale of shrimp that had not been fished with TEDs (turtle excluding devices), a US technology that allowed sea turtles to swim out of the net where shrimp had been caught. The US, therefore, was regulating trade in a good (shrimp) whose production process affected the incidence on the life of an endangered species (sea turtles). The US submitted ample proof that TEDs were considered an effective means to protect the life of sea turtles, since sea turtles and shrimp often swim together.³ Some producers/exporters of shrimp (Malaysia, Thailand, India, and Pakistan) complained. In their view, the US measure was effectively denying them access in the US market since they would have to change their production methods and incur substantial adjustment costs in order to comply with the US standard. Referring to prior GATT case law, the complainants challenged the consistency of the US measure with the GATT, arguing that it was inconsistent since it had been unilaterally defined.

The Panel that dealt with this dispute followed the ruling on *US–Tuna (Mexico)*, and condemned the US measure because of its unilateral character. The AB overturned the Panel, holding that WTO Members remained free to unilaterally regulate their market, provided that they respect the relevant GATT disciplines; in other words, a measure would not be judged to be GATT-inconsistent, simply because it had been unilaterally defined. In § 121 of its report, the AB importantly proclaimed:

> ... conditioning access to a Member's domestic market on whether exporting Members comply with, or adopt, a policy or policies unilaterally prescribed by the importing Member may, to some degree, be a common aspect of measures falling within the scope of one or another of the exceptions (a) to (j) of Article XX. Paragraphs (a) to (j) comprise measures that are recognized as *exceptions to substantive obligations* established in the GATT 1994, because the domestic policies embodied in such measures have been recognized as important and legitimate in character.

---

[2] This ruling sparked the discussion whether the GATT allows for PPMs (product process)—based distinctions, that is, regulatory distinctions based on process and production methods. The literature discussed in the previous Chapter largely addresses this issue as well, since regulatory distinctions will typically be made through domestic instruments.

[3] See the discussion in Howse and Neven (2007), and Mavroidis (2000a).

It is not necessary to assume that requiring from exporting countries compliance with, or adoption of, certain policies (although covered in principle by one or another of the exceptions) prescribed by the importing country, renders a measure *a priori* incapable of justification under Article XX. Such an interpretation renders most, if not all, of the specific exceptions of Article XX inutile, a result abhorrent to the principles of interpretation we are bound to apply. (italics and emphasis in the original).

This case law has been consistently re-produced and emphasized in subsequent reports.[4] As a result, it is now uncontested that Art. XX GATT condones and does not suppress regulatory diversity.[5]

3. COVERAGE OF THE LEGAL DISCIPLINE

3.1 PRELIMINARY REMARKS ON COMMON ELEMENTS

Art. XX GATT covers a series of grounds that, if successfully invoked, will provide WTO Members with a lawful escape route from their GATT-obligations. The substantive requirements that must be met for successful invocation of one of the grounds mentioned are not identical across the various sub-paragraphs of Art. XX GATT. There are nevertheless, some elements common to all grounds, namely:

(a) Art. XX GATT is an exception to all GATT provisions;

(b) Art. XX GATT operates as a two-tier test in which the chapeau of Art. XX GATT must always be complied with;

(c) The allocation of the burden of proof when Art. XX GATT is invoked, and the ensuing standard of review;

3.1.1 Art. XX GATT Functions as an Exception to All GATT Provisions

The framers of the GATT, when drafting Art. XX GATT, initially had intended for the provision to operate as exception to import and export restrictions only, and not to internal measures:

> The undertakings in Chapter IV of this Charter relating to import and export restrictions shall not be construed to prevent the adoption or enforcement by any member of measures for the following purposes, provided that they are not applied in such a manner as to constitute a means of arbitrary discrimination between countries where the same conditions prevail, or a disguised restriction of international trade.[6]

4　See, for example, §§ 137–138 of the AB report in *US–Shrimp (Article 21.5–Malaysia)*.
5　See on this score Howse and Turk (2001), and Mavroidis (2000a).
6　E/PC/T/C.II/50, pp. 7ff.; E/PC/T/C.II/54, pp. 32ff.

GATT/WTO case law has accepted that recourse to Art. XX GATT can be made in order to justify violations assumed with respect to all trade-related instruments, including internal measures. In *EC–Asbestos* (discussed in Chapter 8), the AB held that Art XX GATT could serve as legal basis to justify measures that had been previously found to be inconsistent with Art. III GATT (§ 115).[7]

Art. XX GATT can also serve as exception to obligations assumed under a Protocol of Accession; nevertheless, this would be the case only if there is explicit or even implicit reference to this provision in the relevant protocol (Panel Report, *China–Raw Materials*, §§ 7.158–160).

3.1.2   Art. XX GATT Operates as a Two–Tier Test

The AB has constructed Art. XX GATT akin to a two-tier test. In *US–Gasoline*, the AB stated (p. 22):

> In order that the justifying protection of Article XX may be extended to it, the measure at issue must not only come under one or another of the particular exceptions—paragraphs (a) to (j)—listed under Article XX; it must also satisfy the requirements imposed by the opening clauses of Article XX. The analysis is, in other words, two-tiered: first, provisional justification by reason of characterization of the measure under XX(g); second, further appraisal of the same measure under the introductory clauses of Article XX.

In the same report, the AB held that the choice of words should imply that the legal test chosen should not be identical across the various subparagraphs of this provision, whereas the same test always applies when discussing the conformity of a measure with the chapeau (pp. 17–18):

> In enumerating the various categories of governmental acts, laws or regulations which WTO Members may carry out or promulgate in pursuit of differing legitimate state policies or interests outside the realm of trade liberalization, Article XX uses different terms in respect of different categories:
>
> "necessary"—in paragraphs (a), (b) and (d); "essential"—in paragraph (j); "relating to"—in paragraphs (c), (e) and (g); "for the protection of"—in paragraph (f); "in pursuance of"—in paragraph (h); and "involving"—in paragraph (i).
>
> It does not seem reasonable to suppose that the WTO Members intended to require, in respect of each and every category, the same kind or degree of connection or relationship between the measure under appraisal and the state interest or policy sought to be promoted or realized.

---

[7] For confirmation, see the AB report in *Korea–Various Measures on Beef* §§ 152 ff.

In *US–Shrimp*, the AB provided the rationale for the two-tier approach in the following manner (§§ 119–120):[8]

> The sequence of steps indicated above in the analysis of a claim of justification under Article XX reflects, not inadvertence or random choice, but rather the fundamental structure and logic of Article XX.
>
> . . .
>
> The task of interpreting the chapeau so as to prevent the abuse or misuse of the specific exemptions provided for in Article XX is rendered very difficult, if indeed it remains possible at all, where the interpreter (like the Panel in this case) has not first identified and examined the specific exception threatened with abuse.

The Panel in *China–Raw Materials* added that the legal consequence of the two-tier test is that, unless compliance with a sub-paragraph has been shown, there is no need to examine the consistency of the challenged measure with the chapeau of Art. XX GATT (§ 7.469).

3.1.3 Allocation of Burden of Proof

Case law has consistently held that the party invoking an exception carries the associated burden of proof. The AB, citing prior case law to this effect (*US–Gasoline*, pp. 22–23; *US–Wool Shirts and Blouses*, pp. 15–16; *US–FSC* (Article 21.5–EC), § 133) has confirmed this view in its report in *US–Gambling* (§ 309):

> It is well-established that a responding party invoking an affirmative defence bears the burden of demonstrating that its measure, found to be WTO-inconsistent, satisfies the requirements of the invoked defence.

The AB in *US–Shrimp* expressed the view that it is the language of the chapeau that makes it clear that all exceptions appearing in Art. XX GATT are limited and conditional (§ 157):

> In our view, the language of the chapeau makes clear that each of the exceptions in paragraphs (a) to (j) of Article XX is a *limited and conditional* exception from the substantive obligations contained in the other provisions of the GATT 1994, that is to say, the ultimate availability of the exception is subject to the compliance by the invoking Member with the requirements of the chapeau. (emphasis in the original).

---

[8] In this case, the AB faced a US measure banning sales of shrimps that had been caught in a way that led to accidental taking of the life of sea turtles, an endangered species that featured in the list of CITES (Convention on International Trade of Endangered Species), a multilateral convention banning trade in similar commodities, see Howse and Neven (2007).

The word "limited" in the above quoted passage denotes that the list of exceptions mentioned in Art. XX GATT is exhaustive. The AB, in its report on *Brazil–Retreaded Tyres*, eliminated any doubts on this score, by holding the following (§ 139):

> First, a panel must examine whether the measure falls under at least one of the ten exceptions listed under Article XX.

The AB, in *Korea–Various Measures on Beef,* clarified that its judicial review has to be confined to the means used to achieve a particular objective, and cannot extend to an examination of the legitimacy of the ends themselves (§ 176):

> It is not open to doubt that Members of the WTO have the right to determine for themselves the level of enforcement of their WTO-consistent laws and regulations. We note that this has also been recognized by the panel in *United States–Section 337*, where it said: "The Panel wished to make it clear that this [the obligation to choose a reasonably available GATT-consistent or less inconsistent measure] does not mean that a contracting party could be asked to change its substantive patent law or its desired *level of enforcement* of that law. . . . "." (italics and emphasis in the original).

Over the years, however, the AB made it clear that it would be more deferential when human (life and) health was at stake, and less so when WTO Members were pursuing other regulatory objectives mentioned in the body of Art. XX GATT. The AB first announced in *Korea–Various Measures on Beef* that it would take into account the importance of the objective sought when measuring the necessity of the means employed to attain it. In *EC–Asbestos*, the AB confirmed that this was indeed the case (§ 172):

> We indicated in *Korea–Beef* that one aspect of the "weighing and balancing process . . . comprehended in the determination of whether a WTO-consistent alternative measure" is reasonably available is the extent to which the alternative measure "contributes to the realization of the end pursued". In addition, we observed, in that case, that "[t]he more vital or important [the] common interests or values" pursued, the easier it would be to accept as "necessary" measures designed to achieve those ends. In this case, the objective pursued by the measure is the preservation of human life and health through the elimination, or reduction, of the well-known, and life-threatening, health risks posed by asbestos fibres. The value pursued is both vital and important in the highest degree. (italics in the original).

3.2 THE SPECIFIC EXCEPTIONS ENUMERATED IN ART. XX GATT

As already noted, Art XX GATT operates akin to a two-tier test. When examining whether a particular measure that violates a GATT provision can nevertheless be excused on the basis of Art. XX GATT, the first step in the inquiry is to determine whether the measure conforms to the substantive requirements of one of the ten exceptions listed within the provision. Below, we discuss each of the ten exceptions enumerated in the paragraphs following the chapeau of Art. XX GATT.

Before doing so, we draw attention to the point that the term "necessary" is employed at the start of the description of three exceptions: XX(a) on public morals; XX(b) on human, animal, plant life or health; and XX(d) on laws and provisions not inconsistent with the GATT. The nature of the legal test for determining "necessity" is elaborated upon in our discussion of the Art. XX(b) GATT exception for public health; yet, it is of relevance for the other two exceptions as well.

Similarly, the term "relating to" is employed when describing three other exceptions: XX(c) on imports / exports of gold and silver; XX(e) on products of prison labor; and XX(g) on conservation of exhaustible natural resources. The jurisprudence on the meaning of the term "relating to" is described in our discussion of the Art. XX(g) GATT exception; yet, it too is of relevance for the two other exceptions in which the term is employed.

3.2.1 Public Morals

WTO Members can adopt measures necessary to protect their "public morals". This term is not defined any further in Art. XX(a) GATT, but has been defined through case law. The first case to address the public morals exception was *US–Gambling*, a GATS case to be discussed *infra*, where the term "public morals" is also employed in the text of the corresponding provision (Art. XIV(a) GATS), albeit in conjunction with the term "public order." Subsequent case law has clarified that the definition established for Art. XIV(a) GATS also applies to Art. XX(a) GATT. In *China–Audiovisual Services*, the Panel remarked (§ 7.759):

> We note that the panel and Appellate Body in *US–Gambling* examined the meaning of the term "public morals" as it is used in Article XIV(a) of the GATS, which is the GATS provision corresponding to Article XX(a). The panel in *US–Gambling*, in an interpretation not questioned by the Appellate Body, "found that the term 'public morals' denotes standards of right and wrong conduct maintained by or on behalf of a community or nation." The panel went on to note that the "content of these concepts for Members can vary in time and space, depending upon a range of factors, including prevailing social, cultural, ethical and religious

values." The panel went on to note that Members, in applying this and other similar societal concepts, "should be given some scope to define and apply for themselves the concepts of 'public morals'" ... in their respective territories, according to their own systems and scales of values." Since Article XX(a) uses the same concept as Article XIV(a) and since we see no reason to depart from the interpretation of "public morals" developed by the panel in *US–Gambling*, we adopt the same interpretation for purposes of our Article XX(a) analysis.

Only measures that are "necessary to protect public morals" will be deemed GATT-consistent. We discuss the necessity requirement in the sub-section that immediately follows.

3.2.2   Human, Animal, or Plant Life or Health

Art. XX(b) GATT has been used in order to justify measures that aim to protect not only human, animal or plant life or health, but also environment, although the latter is not explicitly mentioned in its body. The Panel in *US–Gasoline* clarified that the party seeking to invoke the Art. XX(b) GATT exception must demonstrate[9] (§ 6.20):

1. that the *policy* in respect of the measure for which the provision was invoked fell within the range of policies designed to protect human, animal or plant life or health; [and]

2. that the inconsistent measure for which the exception was being invoked were *necessary* to fulfill the policy objective (emphasis in the original)

The first part of this requirement has been quite straightforward and has not been the subject of much interpretative controversy. The necessity requirement has been interpreted by various GATT/WTO Panels to mean that WTO Members must use the measure that is least restrictive (on international trade). We engage in what immediately follows, in a discussion of the case law as it has evolved not only in the context of Art. XX(b) GATT, but also that of Art. XX(d) GATT which employs the same term, to the extent of course that the latter is relevant for the interpretation of Art. XX(b) GATT as well.[10]

Case law has clarified that WTO Members have the right to choose the level of regulatory enforcement that they see fit; a Panel cannot call

---

[9] The Panel report also makes reference to a third requirement which is that the party must satisfy the requirements of the chapeau.

[10] We reproduce here all of the case law regarding this requirement, irrespective of the sub-paragraph invoked. Although there is no guarantee that case law under Art. XX(d) GATT will be reproduced 'lock, stock, and barrel' in case law regarding Art. XX(b) GATT, case law so far suggests that adjustments might be warranted only in light of the relative importance of the objective sought. With this caveat, case law under Art. XX(d) GATT regarding the necessity-requirement is legally relevant for the understanding of the same requirement in Art. XX(b) GATT.

into question a WTO Member's desired regulatory outcome. (AB reports in *EC–Asbestos* and *Brazil–Retreaded Tyres*). The AB ruled in this respect in *EC–Asbestos* (§ 174):

> In our view, France could not reasonably be expected to employ *any* alternative measure if that measure would involve a continuation of the very risk that the Decree seeks to "halt". Such an alternative measure would, in effect, prevent France from achieving its chosen level of health protection. On the basis of the scientific evidence before it, the Panel found that, in general, the efficacy of "controlled use" remains to be demonstrated. Moreover, even in cases where "controlled use" practices are applied "with greater certainty", the scientific evidence suggests that the level of exposure can, in some circumstances, still be high enough for there to be a "significant residual risk of developing asbestos-related diseases." The Panel found too that the efficacy of "controlled use" is particularly doubtful for the building industry and for DIY enthusiasts, which are the most important users of cement-based products containing chrysotile asbestos. Given these factual findings by the Panel, we believe that "controlled use" would not allow France to achieve its chosen level of health protection by halting the spread of asbestos-related health risks. "Controlled use" would, thus, not be an alternative measure that would achieve the end sought by France.

The facts of *Brazil–Retreaded Tyres* are reproduced in § 118 of the report:

> Tyres are an integral component in passenger cars, lorries, and airplanes and, as such, their use is widespread in modern society. New passenger cars are typically sold with new tyres. When tyres need to be replaced, consumers in some countries may have a choice between new tyres or "retreaded" tyres. This dispute concerns the latter category of tyres. Retreaded tyres are used tyres that have been reconditioned for further use by stripping the worn tread from the skeleton (casing) and replacing it with new material in the form of a new tread, and sometimes with new material also covering parts or all of the sidewalls. Retreaded tyres can be produced through different methods, one of which is called "remoulding".[11]

In this report, the AB held that for a measure to pass the consistency-test of Art. XX(b) GATT, there is no need to quantify the contribution of means to ends; a qualitative analysis, by and large, suffices (§ 146). However, there is a presumption that recourse to drastic measure, e.g. an import embargo, should be allowed only in exceptional circumstances.

---

[11] Bown and Trachtman (2009) discuss this case in detail.

The AB held that, in principle, such a measure would be accepted only if it was proven that it has made a material contribution to the attainment of the stated objective (§ 150):

> As the Panel recognized, an import ban is "by design as trade-restrictive as can be". We agree with the Panel that there may be circumstances where such a measure can nevertheless be necessary, within the meaning of Article XX(b). We also recall that, in *Korea–Various Measures on Beef*, the Appellate Body indicated that "the word 'necessary' is not limited to that which is 'indispensable' ". Having said that, when a measure produces restrictive effects on international trade as severe as those resulting from an import ban, it appears to us that it would be difficult for a panel to find that measure necessary unless it is satisfied that the measure is apt to make a material contribution to the achievement of its objective. Thus, we disagree with Brazil's suggestion that, because it aims to reduce risk exposure to the maximum extent possible, an import ban that brings a marginal or insignificant contribution can nevertheless be considered necessary.

In the same report, the AB explained the relative importance of the social preference pursued and how its social ordering affects its standard of review (§ 143):

> In *US–Gambling*, the Appellate Body addressed the "necessity" test in the context of Article XIV of the GATS. The Appellate Body stated that the weighing and balancing process inherent in the necessity analysis "begins with an assessment of the 'relative importance' of the interests or values furthered by the challenged measure", and also involves an assessment of other factors, which will usually include "the contribution of the measure to the realization of the ends pursued by it" and "the restrictive impact of the measure on international commerce". (italics in the original).[12]

When the choice is between using a GATT-consistent, and a GATT-inconsistent measure, assuming the two are equally efficient, the WTO Member concerned must use the GATT-consistent option. In *Thailand–Cigarettes*, Thailand had argued that its trade embargo on the importation of cigarettes, while restricting the overall quantity sold in its market, was justified by the fact that it aimed to ensure the quality of cigarettes imported. The GATT Panel felt that Thailand could have ensured both objectives through the use of non-discriminatory, and hence GATT-consistent, measures (§ 75):

---

[12] Compare with § 172 of the AB report in *EC–Asbestos*.

The Panel concluded from the above that the import restrictions imposed by Thailand could be considered to be 'necessary' in terms of article XX(b) only if there were no alternative measure consistent with the General Agreement, or less inconsistent with it, which Thailand could reasonably be expected to employ to achieve its health policy objectives.

When the Panel satisfied itself that Thailand could indeed have reached its objectives by employing GATT-consistent measures (e.g., ban on advertising, non-discriminatory labelling requirements, etc.), it found that Thailand had violated its obligations under Art. XX(b) GATT (§ 81).

In a similar vein, the GATT Panel in *US–Section 337* held (§ 5.26):

It was clear to the Panel that a contracting party cannot justify a measure inconsistent with another GATT provision as "necessary" in terms of Article XX(d) if an alternative measure which it could reasonably be expected to employ and which is not inconsistent with other GATT provisions is available to it. By the same token, in cases where a measure consistent with other GATT provisions is not reasonably available, a contracting party is bound to use, among the measures reasonably available to it, that which entails the least degree of inconsistency with other GATT provisions.

The AB held that "necessary" should not be equated with "indispensable" since, in its view, the term 'necessary' in Art. XX(d) GATT refers to a range of necessary options. The AB explained that it understood "making a contribution to" to be on one end of a logical continuum, and indispensability, on the other: necessary measures are closer to the latter than the former, but how much closer will depend on factors as their contribution in realizing the objective sought, their relative impact on international trade etc. In *Korea–Various Measures on Beef*, the AB noted (§§ 161, 163, 164):

We believe that, as used in the context of Article XX(d), the reach of the word "necessary" is not limited to that which is "indispensable" or "of absolute necessity" or "inevitable". Measures which are indispensable or of absolute necessity or inevitable to secure compliance certainly fulfill the requirements of Article XX(d). But other measures, too, may fall within the ambit of this exception. As used in Article XX(d), the term "necessary" refers, in our view, to a range of degrees of necessity. At one end of this continuum lies "necessary" understood as "indispensable"; at the other end, is "necessary" taken to mean as "making a contribution to." We consider that a "necessary" measure is, in this continuum, located significantly closer to the pole of "indispensable" than to the opposite pole of simply "making a contribution to".

> . . .
>
> There are other aspects of the enforcement measure to be considered in evaluating that measure as "necessary". One is the extent to which the measure contributes to the realization of the end pursued, the securing of compliance with the law or regulation at issue. The greater the contribution, the more easily a measure might be considered to be "necessary". Another aspect is the extent to which the compliance measure produces restrictive effects on international commerce, that is, in respect of a measure inconsistent with Article III:4, restrictive effects *on imported goods*. A measure with a relatively slight impact upon imported products might more easily be considered as "necessary" than a measure with intense or broader restrictive effects.
>
> In sum, determination of whether a measure, which is not "indispensable", may nevertheless be "necessary" within the contemplation of Article XX(d), involves in every case a process of weighing and balancing a series of factors which prominently include the contribution made by the compliance measure to the enforcement of the law or regulation at issue, the importance of the common interests or values protected by that law or regulation, and the accompanying impact of the law or regulation on imports or exports. (emphasis in the original).

In *Brazil–Retreaded Tyres*, the AB added that the contribution of the measure to the overall objective could be critical in cases where a very restrictive measure, like a trade embargo, is being used (§ 210):

> In this respect, the fundamental principle is the right that WTO Members have to determine the level of protection that they consider appropriate in a given context. Another key element of the analysis of the necessity of a measure under Article XX(b) is 3the contribution it brings to the achievement of its objective. A contribution exists when there is a genuine relationship of ends and means between the objective pursued and the measure at issue. To be characterized as necessary, a measure does not have to be indispensable. However, its contribution to the achievement of the objective must be material, not merely marginal or insignificant, especially if the measure at issue is as trade restrictive as an import ban. Thus, the contribution of the measure has to be weighed against its trade restrictiveness, taking into account the importance of the interests or the values underlying the objective pursued by it.

It seems that the message that the AB wanted to convey here is that it will not accept light-heartedly the most egregious cases of market segmentation, but will do so when their contribution to the objective sought is meaningful.

In its report on *Korea–Various Measures on Beef*, the AB held that the necessity requirement should not be interpreted as requiring from WTO Members to employ the absolutely least restrictive measure in order to attain their objectives. What is required is to employ the least restrictive option among those reasonably available to the WTO Member availing itself of this possibility (§ 166):

> In our view, the weighing and balancing process we have outlined is comprehended in the determination of whether a WTO-consistent alternative measure which the Member concerned could 'reasonably be expected to employ' is available, or whether a less WTO-inconsistent measure is 'reasonably available'.

To evaluate the reasonable availability of a measure, the AB, in *Dominican Republic–Import and Sale of Cigarettes*, held that the following may be taken into account (§ 70):

> factors such as the trade impact of the measure, the importance of the interests protected by the measure, or the contribution of the measure to the realization of the end pursued, should be taken into account in the analysis"

In *China–Audiovisual Services*, the AB stated that a hardship test might be appropriate to decide on reasonable availability of a specific option. In its view a measure would be reasonably available if it did not impose an undue burden on the regulating state (§ 327). This test would imply that adjudicating bodies retain some leeway to impose a 'costlier' measure than the chosen option if the gains for trade would be substantial. Where exactly they will draw the line and what kind of methodology they will choose in deciding similar cases is an issue that only future practice can respond to.

Case law has clarified issues concerning the allocation of the burden of proof in the context of the necessity test: Assuming the regulating WTO Member has made a *prima facie* case[13] that its measures are necessary, the burden will shift to the original complainant to demonstrate the existence of another (equally efficient) alternative measure that should have been used. If the original complainant is successful in this endeavor, then the burden will shift back to the WTO Member invoking Art. XX GATT to show that the alternative invoked is not reasonably available to it. In *US–Gambling*, while discussing the necessity test in the context of Art. XIV

---

[13] We discuss this term in detail in the Chapters dedicated to Dispute Settlement. Suffice to say for the time being that, in GATT/WTO case law, this term has been understood as equivalent to a "preponderance of evidence"—standard, and not a standard akin to proving something beyond reasonable doubt.

GATS[14], the AB held that, with respect to the allocation of the burden of proof (§§ 309–311):

> It is well-established that a responding party invoking an affirmative defence bears the burden of demonstrating that its measure, found to be WTO-inconsistent, satisfies the requirements of the invoked defence.... In our view, however, it is not the responding party's burden to show, in the first instance, that there are no reasonably available alternatives to achieve its objectives. In particular, a responding party need not identify the universe of less trade-restrictive alternative measures and then show that none of those measures achieves the desired objective. The WTO agreements do not contemplate such an impracticable and, indeed, often impossible burden.
>
> Rather, it is for a responding party to make a prima facie case that its measure is "necessary" by putting forward evidence and arguments that enable a panel to assess the challenged measure in the light of the relevant factors to be "weighed and balanced" in a given case. The responding party may, in so doing, point out why alternative measures would not achieve the same objectives as the challenged measure, but it is under no obligation to do so in order to establish, in the first instance, that its measure is "necessary". If the panel concludes that the respondent has made a prima facie case that the challenged measure is "necessary"—that is, "significantly closer to the pole of 'indispensable' than to the opposite pole of simply 'making a contribution to' "—then a panel should find that challenged measure "necessary" within the terms of [the general exception being invoked].
>
> If, however, the complaining party raises a WTO-consistent alternative measure that, in its view, the responding party should have taken, the responding party will be required to demonstrate why its challenged measure nevertheless remains "necessary" in the light of that alternative or, in other words, why the proposed alternative is not, in fact, "reasonably available". If a responding party demonstrates that the alternative is not "reasonably available", in the light of the interests or values being pursued and the party's desired level of protection, it follows that the challenged measure must be "necessary" within the terms of [the general exception being invoked].

---

[14] Refer to the earlier discussion in Art. XX(a) GATT as to how, given the similarity between the general exceptions provisions of the GATT and GATS, the jurisprudence concerning the GATS is also likely to be relevant in this context.

3.2.3 Imports and Exports of Gold and Silver

WTO Members can justify their deviations from obligations assumed under the GATT, if they "relate to" the importation or exportation of gold or silver. The coverage of this provision is clear: only measures relating to the importation and exportation of two commodities, gold, and silver, are covered. The GATT Panel in *Canada–Gold Coins* emerges as the only case in this context so far: Canada (the province of Ontario) had in place a retail tax on gold coins which was applicable on *Krugerrand* (South African gold coin) but not to Maple Leaf gold coins struck by the Canadian Mint. The Panel found that gold coins were not only means of payment but also goods and thus covered by Art. III GATT (and consequently, by Art. XX GATT as well). The report remains un-adopted.[15]

The question is how one should understand the term "relating to" appearing in the body of Art. XX(c) GATT. There is no case law to draw on, but the same term appears in Art. XX(g) GATT. Our discussion of the term there provides useful inspiration for the understanding of the term here.

3.2.4 Compliance With Laws Not Inconsistent With the GATT

The Panel and the AB faced in the context of *Mexico–Taxes on Soft Drinks* a question regarding the coverage of Art. XX(d) GATT. The situation they faced is clearly described in § 68 of the AB report:

> the central issue raised in this appeal is whether the terms "to secure compliance with laws or regulations" in Article XX(d) of the GATT 1994 encompass WTO-inconsistent measures applied by a WTO Member to secure compliance with another WTO Member's obligations under an international agreement.

Mexico had raised its domestic taxes on some products (soft drinks) and was found to be violating Art. III.2 GATT (since it was treating imported goods in a manner that was affording protection to domestic DCS products): Mexico was in fact taxing the process (inputs) of soft drinks in a manner that led soft drinks originating in the US to pay a higher tax burden than Mexican soft drinks which contained different inputs. Mexico claimed before the Panel that its measures were necessary to enforce domestic laws covered by Art. XX(d) GATT. In Mexico's view, the differential taxation was necessary to enforce its rights under the NAFTA agreement: Mexico felt that the US had not complied with its obligations under NAFTA, and that it had the right, as a result, to retaliate under the relevant NAFTA provisions. The Panel dismissed Mexico's defense. It held that the indicative list in Art. XX(d) GATT, as well as its preparatory work were pointing to an understanding of this provision as covering only

---
[15] GATT Doc. L/5863, September 17, 1985 see especially §§ 50ff.

domestic and not international measures (§§ 8.162ff.). On appeal, the AB upheld the Panel's findings, arguing, however, that its reason for doing so was that Art. XX(d) GATT was not designed to cover obligations of other (than the enforcing) WTO Member. Since at stake here was US compliance with NAFTA, the measures at hand were found to fall outside the coverage of Art. XX(d) GATT.

The GATT Panel in *Japan–Agricultural Products I* dismissed an argument by Japan to the effect that a GATT-inconsistent monopoly for the import of farm goods could be justified through recourse to Art. XX(d) GATT, since the justification was unrelated to enforcement of otherwise GATT-consistent laws (§ 5.2.2.3).

WTO adjudicating bodies have understood the necessity requirement featured in Art. XX(d) GATT in the same way as in Art. XX(b) GATT. In *Korea–Various Measures on Beef*, Korea had adopted a dual retail system, whereby retailers could sell either domestic or foreign beef but, in principle, not both. In Korea's view, this practice was necessary to secure compliance with the Korean Unfair Competition Act, a law which was not inconsistent with the GATT and, consequently, came under the purview of Art. XX(d) GATT. The Panel and the AB recognized that the dual retail system was:

> ... established at a time when acts of misrepresentation of origin were widespread in the beef sector. (§ 158, AB report).

The question before the AB was, to what extent the dual retail system was necessary (§ 176):

> It is not open to doubt that Members of the WTO have the right to determine for themselves the level of enforcement of their WTO-consistent laws and regulations. We note that this has also been recognized by the panel in *United States—Section 337*, where it said: "The Panel wished to make it clear that this [the obligation to choose a reasonably available GATT consistent or less inconsistent measure] does not mean that a contracting party could be asked to change its substantive patent law or its desired *level of enforcement* of that law ... (emphasis in the original).

The importance of the ends sought mattered in the appraisal of the necessity-requirement (§ 162):

> It seems to us that a treaty interpreter assessing a measure claimed to be necessary to secure compliance of a WTO-consistent law or regulation may, in appropriate cases, take into account the relative importance of the common interests or values that the law or regulation to be enforced is intended to protect. The more vital or important those common interests or val-

ues are, the easier it would be to accept as "necessary" a measure designed as an enforcement instrument.

In §§ 180–182, the AB invoked two grounds to dismiss the Korean defense:

> We are not persuaded that Korea could not achieve its desired level of enforcement of the *Unfair Competition Act* with respect to the origin of beef sold by retailers by using conventional WTO-consistent enforcement measures, if Korea would devote more resources to its enforcement efforts on the beef sector. It might also be added that Korea's argument about the lack of resources to police thousands of shops on a round-the-clock basis is, in the end, not sufficiently persuasive. Violations of laws and regulations like the Korean *Unfair Competition Act* can be expected to be routinely investigated and detected through selective, but well-targeted, controls of potential wrongdoers. The control of records will assist in selecting the shops to which the police could pay particular attention.
>
> There is still another aspect that should be noted relating to both the method actually chosen by Korea—its dual retail system for beef—and alternative traditional enforcement measures. Securing through conventional, WTO-consistent measures a higher level of enforcement of the *Unfair Competition Act* with respect to the retail sale of beef, could well entail higher enforcement costs for the national budget. It is pertinent to observe that, through its dual retail system, Korea has in effect shifted all, or the great bulk, of these potential costs of enforcement (translated into a drastic reduction of competitive access to consumers) to imported goods and retailers of imported goods, instead of evenly distributing such costs between the domestic and imported products. In contrast, the more conventional, WTO-consistent measures of enforcement do not involve such onerous shifting of enforcement costs which ordinarily are borne by the Member's public purse.
>
> For these reasons, we uphold the conclusion of the Panel that Korea has not discharged its burden of demonstrating under Article XX(d) that alternative WTO-consistent measures were not "reasonably available" in order to detect and suppress deceptive practices in the beef retail sector, and that the dual retail system is therefore not justified by Article XX(d).

In *US–Gambling*, a subsequent GATS case, the AB adopted a different approach regarding the allocation of burden of proof (discussed *supra*) which should be regarded as the prevailing approach nowadays.

3.2.5 Prison Labor

WTO Members can justify their deviations from obligations assumed under the GATT, if they relate to products of prison labor. The term "prison labor" can be understood in a narrow sense (products wholly originating in prisons), or in a wide sense (products with inputs produced in prisons and other detention establishments). In the latter case of course, the term 'prison' could be understood as encompassing all sorts of state offices depriving humans of their freedom etc. There is total absence of practice in this area so these questions remain unanswered. The rationale for this provision is clear: as prisoners receive no salary for their work, exports of similar goods would be benefitting from lower prices and the ensuing competitive advantage. There is probably, on occasion, a social preference as well not to transact with goods made in prison. The term "relate to" appearing in the body of Art. XX(e) GATT describes the legal relationship between the challenged measure and the protection against imports of goods originating in prisons. Since this term appears also in Art. XX(g) GATT where it has been interpreted on a number of occasions, we will discuss it there, with the caveat we mentioned about the necessity-requirement (appearing in two sub-paragraphs) being applicable here as well.

3.2.6 National Treasures

The qualification of an item as "national treasure" depends on the satisfaction of one of the three criteria included in Art. XX(f) GATT: artistic-, historic-, or archeological value. This should not be a difficult test to meet since historic value has a much wider coverage than archeological value. There is absence of dispute settlement practice in this context.

3.2.7 Conservation of Exhaustible Natural Resources

The GATT negotiating history imparts an impression that the framers had in mind commodities such as petrol and minerals (i.e., non-living resources) when they drafted Art XX(g) of the GATT: the examples used during the negotiation point to the direction of constructing this term as referring to non-living organisms.[16] Charnovitz (1991) though, correctly observes that this is not a water-tight observation since some references might argue for a wider understanding of the term.[17]

GATT practice evidences a clear trend towards understanding this term as encompassing both living and non-living organisms. In the GATT years, the Panel in *Canada–Herring and Salmon* agreed with the parties that salmon and herring stocks are exhaustible natural resources (§ 4.4). In the WTO years, in *US–Gasoline*, the Panel held that clean air was an exhaustible natural resource (§ 6.37). The dispute related to the imple-

---

[16] E/PC/T/C.II/50, pp. 5ff.
[17] See also Matsushita *et al.* (2006).

mentation by the US of its domestic legislation known as the US Clean Air Act of 1990 (CAA) and, more specifically, to the regulation enacted by the US Environmental Protection Agency (EPA) pursuant to that Act, to control toxic and other pollution caused by the combustion of gasoline manufactured in or imported into the United States. The CAA had established two gasoline programs to ensure that pollution from gasoline combustion did not exceed 1990 levels, and that pollutants in major population centers were reduced. A preliminary question was raised by the US at the oral hearing concerning arguments made by Venezuela and Brazil in their respective appellees' submissions on the issues of whether clean air was an exhaustible natural resource within the meaning of Art. XX(g) GATT. The AB agreed with the US that the issue was not properly before it (pp. 10ff.). As a result, the AB did not rule on this issue, and the Panel's ruling stands.

Then, in *US–Shrimp*, the AB held that the term "exhaustible natural resources" should not be confined to non-living resources. At dispute was a US measure which banned the import of shrimp fished in a manner that led to the accidental taking of the life of endangered sea turtles. The US had argued that the measure at hand was in full conformity with the requirements of Art. XX(g) GATT, and if not, with the requirements of Art. XX(b) GATT. The complainants (India, Malaysia, Pakistan, and Thailand) argued that the negotiating history of the term "exhaustible natural resources" pointed to the conclusion that this term was meant to cover non-living resources only, such as minerals (§ 127, AB report). The question, thus, arose whether the US measure should come under the purview of Art. XX(b) or Art. XX(g) GATT. In the view of the AB, the term had to be given a meaning in accordance with today's perceptions (§ 130):

> ... the generic term 'natural resources' in Article XX(g) is not 'static' in its content or reference, but is rather 'by definition, evolutionary'.

The AB went on to state that sea turtles, a living organism, could very well be regarded as an exhaustible natural resource. International conventions (CITES) recognized sea turtles as endangered species, and others which used the term natural resources to cover both living- and non-living organisms (UNCLOS, United Nations Convention on the Law of the Sea) were cited (§§ 130ff., AB report) in support.[18] The defining criterion (which distinguishes exhaustible from non-exhaustible natural resources) was, in the AB's view, the response to the question: whether the item at hand was being depleted faster than it is being reproduced (§§ 128, 130 and 153):

---

[18] Although the AB did not prescribe in definitive manner the precise legal relevance of similar instruments in the WTO legal order, it used them in support of an opinion it had already reached hence, extra-WTO international treaties were used in this case as supplementary means of interpretation. For a more extensive analysis of this point, see Mavroidis (2008).

Textually, Article XX(g) is *not* limited to the conservation of "mineral" or "non-living" natural resources. The complainants' principal argument is rooted in the notion that "living" natural resources are "renewable" and therefore cannot be "exhaustible" natural resources. We do not believe that "exhaustible" natural resources and "renewable" natural resources are mutually exclusive. One lesson that modern biological sciences teach us is that living species, though in principle, capable of reproduction and, in that sense, "renewable", are in certain circumstances indeed susceptible of depletion, exhaustion and extinction, frequently because of human activities. Living resources are just as "finite" as petroleum, iron ore and other non-living resources.

. . .

From the perspective embodied in the preamble of the *WTO Agreement*, we note that the generic term "natural resources" in Article XX(g) is not "static" in its content or reference but is rather "by definition, evolutionary". It is, therefore, pertinent to note that modern international conventions and declarations make frequent references to natural resources as embracing both living and non-living resources.

. . .

The language [of the Preamble of the *WTO Agreement*] demonstrates a recognition by WTO negotiators that optimal use of the world's resources should be made in accordance with the objective of sustainable development. As this preambular language reflects the intentions of negotiators of the *WTO Agreement*, we believe it must add colour, texture and shading to our interpretation of the agreements annexed to the *WTO Agreement*, in this case, the GATT 1994. We have already observed that Article XX(g) of the GATT 1994 is appropriately read with the perspective embodied in the above preamble. (emphasis in the original).

The recognition that living organisms could be considered to be exhaustible natural resources further opened the door to the possibility of using Art. XX(g) GATT to address environmental disputes.

Two requirements must be cumulatively met for a measure protecting exhaustible natural resources to be judged GATT-consistent:

(a) It must relate to the conservation of exhaustible natural resources; and

(b) It must be made effective in conjunction with restrictions on domestic production or consumption.

We take each point in turn. The Panel in its report on *US–Gasoline*, went on to apply the GATT Panel's reasoning and conclusion in *Canada–*

Herring and Salmon as to the interpretation of the term 'relating to' used in this and other provisions. In this Panel's view, this term was tantamount to the term "primarily aimed at." In other words, a measure relates to protection of exhaustible natural resources if its primary aim is to protect such resources, but not if this is an ancillary or even accidental effect. The AB disagreed; it noted that although past case law had construed the term in this way, the AB was not comfortable with this understanding, even though the parties to the dispute seemed to endorse it (pp. 18–19):

> All the participants and the third participants in this appeal accept that a measure must be "primarily aimed at" the conservation of exhaustible natural resources in order to fall within the scope of Article XX(g). Accordingly, we see no need to examine this point further, save, perhaps, to note that the phrase "primarily aimed at" *is not itself treaty language and was not designed as a simple litmus test for inclusion or exclusion from Article XX(g)*. . . . (emphasis added)

In *US–Shrimp*, the AB confirmed this approach. The AB held that "relating to" implied a rational connection between a measure and the conservation of exhaustible natural resources, and nothing beyond that (§ 141):

> In its general design and structure, therefore, Section 609 is not a simple, blanket prohibition of the importation of shrimp imposed without regard to the consequences (or lack thereof) of the mode of harvesting employed upon the incidental capture and mortality of sea turtles. Focusing on the design of the measure here at stake, it appears to us that Section 609, *cum* implementing guidelines, is not disproportionately wide in its scope and reach in relation to the policy objective of protection and conservation of sea turtle species. The means are, in principle, reasonably related to the ends. The means and ends relationship between Section 609 and the legitimate policy of conserving an exhaustible, and, in fact, endangered species, is observably a close and real one. (emphasis in the original).

Art. XX(g) GATT further requires that, when imposing trade restrictions to protect exhaustible natural resources, WTO Members also adopt measures aimed at restricting domestic consumption or production (as the case may be). The GATT Panel in *US–Canadian Tuna* outlawed US measures restricting imports of some tuna because similar measures had not been adopted with respect to domestic tuna of the same kind (§§ 4.5ff.). The AB, in its report on *US—Gasoline*, explained that the requirement to demonstrate that import-restricting measures are taken in conjunction with domestic measures aimed at the conservation of exhaustible natural resources was an even-handedness requirement. It went on to stress that there was no need for an effects-test in order to comply with Art. XX(g) GATT in this respect (pp. 20–21):

> ... the clause "if such measures are made effective in conjunction with restrictions on domestic product or consumption" is appropriately read as a requirement that the measures concerned impose restrictions, not just in respect of imported gasoline but also with respect to domestic gasoline. The clause is a requirement of *even-handedness* in the imposition of restrictions, in the name of conservation, upon the production or consumption of exhaustible natural resources.
>
> ... if *no* restrictions on domestically-produced like products are imposed at all, and all limitations are placed upon imported products *alone*, the measure cannot be accepted as primarily or even substantially designed for implementing conservationist goals. The measure would simply be naked discrimination for protecting locally-produced goods.
>
> We do not believe ... that the clause "if made effective in conjunction with restrictions on domestic production or consumption" was intended to establish an empirical "effects test" for the availability of the Article XX(g) exception. (emphasis in the original).

The AB, in its report on *US–Shrimp* faced, *inter alia*, the question whether Art. XX(g) GATT included a jurisdictional limit, in the sense that WTO Members could intervene to protect exhaustible natural resources only within their jurisdiction, as the latter is defined by public international law.[19] In § 133, the AB held:

> We do not pass upon the question of whether there is an implied jurisdictional limitation in Article XX(g), and if so, the nature or extent of that limitation. We note only that in the specific circumstances of the case before us, there is a sufficient nexus be-

---

[19] Nationality and territoriality are the two most common bases, in public international law, for exercising jurisdiction: under the former, a state can regulate the behavior of its nationals; under the latter, a state can regulate transactions taking place in its territory. Public international law practice gives the edge to the latter, when a conflict between the two arises. On the other hand, one can further distinguishes between *objective* and *subjective* territoriality: the former captures activities occurring within national frontiers; the latter captures activities which occur in state A, but which affect state B. B could legitimately, by virtue of *subjective* territoriality (*effects doctrine*) punish, for example, A's *export cartels* which cartelize its own (B's) market. Indeed, except for some extreme cases, state A would have little incentive to regulate the behaviour of an *export cartel* operating from its market but affecting the rest of the world. Antitrust advocacy usually attributes such inactivity to the fact that domestic antitrust laws are there to protect domestic (as opposed to foreign) consumers' welfare. On this issue, see the various contributions in Meessen (1996) regarding the status of these principles in public international law; Mavroidis and Neven (1999), for a discussion on antitrust; and Bagwell *et al.* (2002), Bartels (2002), Charnovitz (1998), and (2002), and Horn and Mavroidis (2008) for a discussion regarding the status of these principles in WTO law.

tween the migratory and endangered marine populations involved and the United States for purposes of Article XX(g).

This question, its undeniable importance nowithstanding (climate change policies for example, typically address global as opposed to local externalities) has not been elaborated any further in case law.

3.2.8 Intergovernmental Commodity Agreements

WTO Members can justify their deviations from obligations assumed under the GATT, if their measures have been undertaken under one of the international commodity agreements (ICA) submitted to the WTO Members and not disapproved by them. ICAs are signed by governments in order to promote cooperation between producers and consumers of particular commodities. The following ICAs are currently in place: International Cocoa Organization (ICCO); International Coffee Organization (ICO); International Cotton Advisory Committee (ICAC); International Grains Council (IGC); International Olive Oil Council (IOOC); International Sugar Organization (ISO); International Tropical Timber Organization (ITTO).

Initially, ICAs were aimed at stabilizing international prices for commodities. Over time, only three of them were successful in doing so: the ICAs for coffee, cocoa (through retention schemes), and natural rubber (through a buffer stock). At present, none of the existing ICAs attempts to regulate markets through management of supply or price. All ICAs now exhibit a pure administrative nature; each provides a forum for producer-consumer cooperation and consultations, market transparency, development projects, and sources for statistical information. In practice, ICAs have now a function very comparable to that of ISGs (International Study Groups), the other forum for cooperation between producers and consumers. The following ISGs are currently in place: International Rubber Study Group (IRSG); International Lead and Zinc Study Group (ILZSG); International Nickel Study Group (INSG); International Copper Study Group (ICSG); International Jute Study Group (IJSG).

The Interpretative Note ad Art. XX(h) GATT makes it clear that this exception extends to any ICA which conforms to the principles approved by the UN Economic and Social Council (ECOSOC) in its resolution 30(IV) of 28 March 1947. This resolution reads as follows:

The Economic and Social Council,

Noting that inter-governmental consultations are going forward actively with respect to certain internationally trade commodities, and

Considering the significant measure of agreement regarding commodity problems and the co-ordination of commodity consultations already reached both in the First Session of the Preparatory Committee of the United Nationals Conference on Trade and Employment, and in the Preparatory Commission on World Food Proposals of the Food and Agriculture Organization of the United Nations.

Recommends that, pending the establishment of the International Trade Organisation, Members of the United Nations adopt as a general guide in inter-governmental consultation or action with respect to commodity problems the principles laid down in Chapter VII as a whole—i.e., the chapter on inter-governmental commodity arrangements of the draft Charter appended to the Report of the First Session of the Preparatory Committee of the United Nations Conference on Trade and Employment— although recognizing that discussion in future sessions of the Preparatory Committee of the United Nations Conference, as well as in the Conference itself, may result in modifications of the provisions relating to commodity arrangements, and

Requests the Secretary–General to appoint an interim co-ordinating committee for international commodity arrangements to keep informed of and to facilitate by appropriate means such inter-governmental consultation or action with respect to commodity problems, the committee to consist of a chairman to represent the Preparatory Committee of the United Nations Conference on Trade and Employment, a person nominated by the Food and Agriculture Organization of the United Nations to be concerned in particular with agricultural primary commodities, and a person to be concerned in particular with non-agricultural primary commodities.[20]

ICAs were included in Chapter VI of the Havana Charter which, as we saw in Chapter 1, never entered into force. WTO Members have, nevertheless, incurred an obligation, by virtue of Art. XXIX GATT, to

observe to the fullest extent of their executive authority the general principles of Chapters I to VI inclusive and of Chapter IX of the Havana Charter.

For the reasons developed in Chapter 1, this provision is of limited value. Conformity with the principles approved by the ECOSOC resolution 30(IV) of 28 March 1947 is one of the three ways in which an ICA can be legally relevant in the GATT (and, consequently, a WTO Member can invoke it by virtue of Art. XX(h) GATT). The other two ways mentioned in Art. XX(h) GATT are:

(a) either the ICA conforms to criteria which have been submitted to the WTO Members and not disapproved by them; or

---

[20] The text has been reproduced on p. 588 of the *GATT Analytical Index*, Geneva: 1995.

(b) the agreement itself is submitted to and not disapproved by the WTO Members.

The GATT Panel in *EEC (Member States)–Bananas I* faced, *inter alia*, an argument to the effect that the Lomé Convention, an agreement between the EU and a series of developing countries should be regarded as an ICA. Despite the fact that the GATT Panel report has never been adopted and is, hence, of limited legal value, it did clarify that: (1) No ICA was ever submitted for approval to GATT contracting parties, and (2) no criteria to review conformity of ICAs were submitted wither. Hence, the only way an ICA could be successfully invoked under Art. XX(h) GATT is if it conformed to the principles approved by ECOSOC resolution 30(IV) of March 28, 1947. These principles required that participation to ICAs were open to trading nations and not limited to a select group of countries. For this reason the GATT Panel found that the Lomé Convention could not qualify as an ICA in the sense of Art. XX(h) GATT (§ 166):

> Turning to the principles in the ECOSOC Resolution 30(IV), the Panel noted that this Resolution required, *inter alia*, that the negotiation of, and participation in, an international commodity agreement must be open to all interested countries and must avoid, as also stipulated in the requirements set out at the beginning of Article XX of the General Agreement, unjustifiable discrimination between countries. The Panel, noting the limited membership of the Lomé Convention and noting further that the EEC had never claimed the Lomé Convention to be a non-discriminatory commodity agreement open to all banana producer and consumer countries, found that the criteria of the ECOSOC Resolution 30(IV) had not been met. The Panel therefore concluded that Article XX(h) could not justify the inconsistency with Article I:1 of the EEC's banana preferences. (italics in the original).

3.2.9 Government Stabilization Plans

WTO Members can justify deviations from obligations assumed under the GATT if the measures are part of a government stabilization plan (of prices). Through this exemption, WTO Members can legitimately impose, for example, export quotas, and provide the domestic processing industry with essential quantities of material at prices held below the world price which, otherwise would have been exported to the world market where prices were higher. New Zealand, one of the initiators of this provision, explained that, unless an exemption was provided, those with government stabilization plans (of prices) in place, would be forced to either dismantle their domestic processing industry, or their stabilization plan altogether: if for example, the price of leather were below the world price, then New Zealand producers would be selling all production abroad and any attempt by the government to stop them would run afoul Art. XI

GATT: this is where this exception kicks in.[21] For such a scheme to be judged GATT-consistent, the WTO Member concerned must not use it in order to increase its exports, and it must respect the non-discrimination principle.[22]

3.2.10 Products in General or Local Short Supply

WTO Members can justify their deviations from obligations assumed under the GATT, if their measures are essential to the acquisition or distribution of products in general or local short supply. Only measures which are essential, that is, indispensable, for the acquisition or distribution of goods in general or local short supply, a rather stringent requirement indeed, will be exempted. This provision was meant to address the post-World War II observed short supply of goods, and it was intended to be eliminated at the latest by January 1, 1951.[23] Following a series of meetings where trading nations found it impossible to decide this issue in definitive manner, it was decided, within the context of the Working Group on Other Barriers to Trade convened during the Review Session of 1954–1955, to maintain this provision. The rationale for retaining it had to do with the awareness that this provision was considered relevant not only for the post war-period of short supply of various goods, but also for cases of natural disaster which could occur at any time.[24]

The WTO Member invoking this provision must ensure that all WTO Members will be entitled to an equitable share of the international supply of products the same of which is being restricted, and that any measure which is GATT-inconsistent will cease to exist as soon as the conditions giving rise to it have ceased to exist.

3.3 COMPLYING WITH THE CHAPEAU

In *US–Gasoline*, the AB made clear that a WTO adjudicating body cannot review the substantive consistency of a measure with Art. XX GATT under the chapeau of Art. XX GATT. This is to be done within the first part of the two-tier analysis of Art. XX GATT, in which the WTO adjudicating body confirms that the measure conforms to the substantive requirements of one of the ten enumerated provisions discussed above. When moving to the chapeau, the only remaining question is to what extent the measure at hand is applied in a GATT-consistent manner (p. 22):

> The chapeau by its express terms addresses, not so much the questioned measure or its specific contents as such, but rather the manner in which that measure is applied. It is, accordingly, important to underscore that the purpose and object of the intro-

---

[21] EPCT/A/PV/36 at pp. 22ff., and Irwin et al. (2008).
[22] GATT Doc. GATT/CP.4/33.
[23] EPCT/A/PV/30 at p. 20.
[24] GATT Doc. BISD 3S/249 at § 42.

ductory clauses of Article XX is generally the prevention of "abuse of the exceptions".

The AB, in *US–Shrimp (Art 21.5–Malaysia)*, explained the three conditions that must be cumulatively met for a measure to be chapeau-consistent (§ 118):

> The chapeau of Article XX establishes three standards regarding the *application* of measures for which justification under Article XX may be sought: first, there must be no "arbitrary" discrimination between countries where the same conditions prevail; second, there must be no "unjustifiable" discrimination between countries where the same conditions prevail; and, third, there must be no "disguised restriction on international trade". (emphasis in the original).

The AB, in *US–Gasoline*, discussed the term "between countries where the same conditions prevail": the question was whether it should be understood as referring only to exporting countries or, conversely, whether it should encompass the importing country as well. Although the AB did not formally rule on this issue on this occasion, it saw no reason to deviate from the prevailing practice which privileged the latter interpretation (pp. 23–4):

> It was asked whether the words incorporated into the first two standards "between countries where the same conditions prevail" refer to conditions in importing and exporting countries, or only to conditions in exporting countries. The reply of the United States was to the effect that it interpreted that phrase as referring to both the exporting countries and importing countries and as between exporting countries. . . . At no point in the appeal was that assumption challenged by Venezuela or Brazil.
>
> . . . we see no need to decide the matter of the field of application of the standards set forth in the chapeau nor to make a ruling at variance with the common understanding of the participants.

The GATT Panel in *US–Canadian Tuna* found that the US had been violating its obligations under the chapeau by subjecting Canada to import restrictions while exempting Costa Rica (§ 4.8). In *Brazil–Retreaded Tyres*, the AB clarified that there is no effects-test in the chapeau; consequently, all WTO Members must, in principle, be subjected to the same regulatory requirements, even if their respective volumes of trade are highly asymmetric. The question before the AB was whether, by allowing for imports of retreaded tyres from its MERCOSUR partners while banning similar imports from all other sources, Brazil was violating Art. XX GATT; Brazil's defense was that MERCOSUR countries exported a very small volume of retreaded tyres to Brazil (§§ 228–229):

In this case, the discrimination between MERCOSUR countries and other WTO Members in the application of the Import Ban was introduced as a consequence of a ruling by a MERCOSUR tribunal. The tribunal found against Brazil because the restriction on imports of remoulded tyres was inconsistent with the prohibition of new trade restrictions under MERCOSUR law. In our view, the ruling issued by the MERCOSUR arbitral tribunal is not an acceptable rationale for the discrimination, because it bears no relationship to the legitimate objective pursued by the Import Ban that falls within the purview of Article XX(b), and even goes against this objective, to however small a degree. Accordingly, we are of the view that the MERCOSUR exemption has resulted in the Import Ban being applied in a manner that constitutes arbitrary or unjustifiable discrimination.

The Panel considered that the MERCOSUR exemption resulted in discrimination between MERCOSUR countries and other WTO Members, but that this discrimination would be "unjustifiable" only if imports of retreaded tyres entering into Brazil "were to take place in such amounts that the achievement of the objective of the measure at issue would be significantly undermined". The Panel's interpretation implies that the determination of whether discrimination is unjustifiable depends on the quantitative impact of this discrimination on the achievement of the objective of the measure at issue. As we indicated above, analyzing whether discrimination is "unjustifiable" will usually involve an analysis that relates primarily to the cause or the rationale of the discrimination. By contrast, the Panel's interpretation of the term "unjustifiable" does not depend on the cause or rationale of the discrimination but, rather, is focused exclusively on the assessment of the *effects* of the discrimination. The Panel's approach has no support in the text of Article XX and appears to us inconsistent with the manner the Appellate Body has interpreted and applied the concept of "arbitrary or unjustifiable discrimination" in previous cases.

In the same report, the AB held that, although Brazil's import ban of some (all but MERCOSUR) retreaded tyres was the direct outcome of orders by Brazilian courts to allow imports from MERCOSUR countries, this fact in and of itself did not exonerate Brazil from responsibility; it concluded that Brazil was in violation of the requirements of the chapeau of Art. XX GATT (§§ 232–233, 246).

GATT/WTO case law has often examined the "arbitrary or unjustifiable discrimination"—requirement in tandem, without distinguishing between its two elements (AB report in *US–Shrimp,* § 150). It has, on occasion, though, proceeded the other way and examined the two elements separately. In *US–Shrimp*, the AB held that measures must result in discrimination and that the resulting discrimination must be unjustifiable or arbitrary (§ 150). This sounds like tautology. But it went further and held that, actively accounting for differences among various WTO Members is a necessary component of the obligation imposed on WTO Members not to discriminate in an unjustifiable or arbitrarily manner. Flexibility becomes thus a necessary component, otherwise compliance with the chapeau cannot be achieved (§§ 164–5 and 177):

> It may be quite acceptable for a government, in adopting and implementing a domestic policy, to adopt a single standard applicable to all its citizens throughout that country. However, it is not acceptable, in international trade relations, for one WTO Member to use an economic embargo to *require* other Members to adopt essentially the same comprehensive regulatory program, to achieve a certain policy goal, as that in force within that Member's territory, *without* taking into consideration different conditions which may occur in the territories of those other Members.
>
> We believe that discrimination results not only when countries in which the same conditions prevail are differently treated, but also when the application of the measure at issue does not allow for any inquiry into the appropriateness of the regulatory program for the conditions prevailing in those exporting countries.
>
> . . .
>
> Section 609, in its application, imposes a single, rigid and unbending requirement that countries applying for certification . . . adopt a comprehensive regulatory program that is essentially the same as the United States' program, without inquiring into the appropriateness of that program for the conditions prevailing in the exporting countries. Furthermore, there is little or no flexibility in how officials make the determination for certification pursuant to these provisions. In our view, this rigidity and inflexibility also constitute "arbitrary discrimination" within the meaning of the chapeau. (emphasis in the original).

The AB had the opportunity to further explain itself on this score during the compliance stage of this litigation. The original US measure conditioning market access for shrimp upon a particular fishing method (the use of TEDs), had been found to be in substantive compliance with Art. XX(g) GATT; it was judged, however, inconsistent with the requirements of the chapeau. In the AB's view, the US measure should be modified to allow exports of shrimp fished through other (than TEDs) fishing methods, of comparable, to the TED, effectiveness. Subsequent to the original condemnation of its measure, the US modified its statute so as to allow for certification of other fishing methods. The AB held that this amendment brought the US measure into compliance with its obligations in this respect (§§ 144 and 149–50). The US measures were also judged to be in violation of the chapeau-requirements, because international negotiations to resolve the problems encountered by the enactment of US Section 609 had been offered to some (Caribbean countries), but not to all WTO Members. This behavior was judged inconsistent with the requirements of the chapeau, because of its inherent discriminatory content. Subsequently, the US offered the same opportunity to all other (including Malaysia, the complainant in this case) shrimp-exporters affected by the US measure. The AB found that, in so doing, the US had effectively complied with its obligations in this respect. Wisely, the AB added that, in its view, the US could not have been asked to achieve through international negotiations with Malaysia an outcome comparable to that achieved with other WTO Members (as Malaysia indeed had argued): some were prepared to accept fishing using a particular technique which minimizes the incidental taking of sea turtles, others were not (§§ 122, 123 and 130).

The GATT Panel report in *US–Canadian Tuna* held that measures publicly announced could not, for this reason alone, be judged a "disguised restriction of trade" (§ 4.8).[25] On p. 25 of its report in *US–Gasoline*, the AB rejected the interpretation that the term "disguised restriction" (of trade) is not limited to concealed or unannounced restrictions only. In other words, the obligation to avoid disguised restrictions of trade is not a mere exercise in transparency:

> "Arbitrary discrimination", "unjustifiable discrimination" and "disguised restriction" on international trade may, accordingly, be read side-by-side; they impart meaning to one another. It is clear to us that "disguised restriction" includes disguised *discrimination* in international trade. It is equally clear that *concealed* or *unannounced* restriction or discrimination in international trade does *not* exhaust the meaning of "disguised restriction. (emphasis in the original).

That much should be obvious. On p. 25 of the same report, the AB went on and provided its view, of this term: the framers of GATT wanted to outlaw abusive invocations of Art. XX GATT:

> It is equally clear that *concealed* or *unannounced* restriction or discrimination in international trade does *not* exhaust the meaning of "disguised restriction." We consider that "disguised restriction", whatever else it covers, may properly be read as embracing restrictions amounting to arbitrary or unjustifiable discrimination in international trade taken under the guise of a measure formally within the terms of an exception listed in Arti-

---

[25] The Canadian delegate expressed his disappointment with this interpretation during the discussion regarding the adoption of the report see GATT Doc. C/M/155. This should not be considered good law anymore.

cle XX. Put in a somewhat different manner, the kinds of considerations pertinent in deciding whether the application of a particular measure amounts to "arbitrary or unjustifiable discrimination", may also be taken into account in determining the presence of a "disguised restriction" on international trade. The fundamental theme is to be found in the purpose and object of avoiding abuse or illegitimate use of the exceptions to substantive rules available in Article XX. (emphasis in the original).

The Panel in *EC–Asbestos* held that the term "disguised restriction" should be understood as outlawing interventions, which, under the guise of protection of one of the grounds mentioned in the sub-paragraphs of Art XX. GATT, aim at promoting other interests (§ 8.236):

> Referring also to the remark made by the Appellate Body in the same case according to which "the provisions of the chapeau [of Article XX] cannot logically refer to the same standard(s) by which a violation of the substantive rule has been determined to have occurred", we consider that the key to understanding what is covered by "disguised restriction on international trade" is not so much the word "restriction", inasmuch as, in essence, any measure falling within Article XX is a restriction on international trade, but the word "disguised". In accordance with the approach defined in Article 31 of the Vienna Convention, we note that, as ordinarily understood, the verb "to disguise" implies an *intention*. Thus, "to disguise" (*déguiser*) means, in particular, "conceal beneath deceptive appearances, counterfeit", "alter so as to deceive", "misrepresent", "dissimulate". Accordingly, a restriction which formally meets the requirements of Article XX(b) will constitute an abuse if such compliance is in fact only a disguise to conceal the pursuit of trade-restrictive objectives. However, as the Appellate Body acknowledged in *Japan—Alcoholic Beverages*, the aim of a measure may not be easily ascertained. Nevertheless, we note that, in the same case, the Appellate Body suggested that the protective application of a measure can most often be discerned from its design, architecture and revealing structure. (emphasis in the original).

QUESTIONS AND COMMENTS

Origins of the Provision: This provision has been modelled after the corresponding provision included in the 1927 International Convention for the Abolition of Import and Export Prohibitions and Restrictions (World Economic Conference of 1927), the first attempt to multilateralize international trade.[26]

---

[26] On the content of the negotiations, and the reasons for the non-ratification of the final text, see Charnovitz (1991), and Irwin *et al.* (2008).

Art. XX GATT and Annex 1A Agreements: Mavroidis (2012) discusses the relationship between Art. XX GATT and all Annex 1A Agreements. Howse (2010) and Rubini (2010) disagree with Mavroidis' vews on the relationship between Art. XX GATT and the SCM Agreement. Where do you stand on this issue?

Exhaustible Natural Resource: Do you agree with the AB interpretation of the term in its report on US–Shrimp?

Art. III and Art. XX GATT: Should the latter be an exception to the former in your view?

CHAPTER 13

NATIONAL SECURITY

■ ■ ■

1. THE LEGAL DISCIPLINE

The title of Art. XXI GATT (Security Exception)[1] leaves no room for doubt that this provision was intended to function as an exception to all obligations assumed under the GATT. The express wording of Art. XXI GATT makes clear that a WTO Member is not required "to furnish any information the disclosure of which it considers contrary to its essential security interests." In addition, Art. XXI GATT exempts WTO Members from taking an action which it unilaterally "considers necessary for the protection of security interests" as it relates to "fissionable materials or the materials from which they are derived," "traffic in arms, ammunitions and implements of war," and "other goods and materials as is carried on directly or indirectly for the purpose of supplying a military establishment." Similarly, Art. XXI GATT provides an exception for WTO Members for actions taken for national security interests "in times of war or other emergency in international relations." Finally, Art. XXI GATT provides an exception for WTO Members that take action in order to comply with obligations under the United Nations Charter for the maintenance of international peace and security.

2. THE RATIONALE FOR THE LEGAL DISCIPLINE

The negotiating history reveal that participants had a wide understanding of national security in mind: theyfound it unreasonable, for example, to request from contracting parties to continue to do business with firms that transferred all or part of their profits from their sales to the enemy. The discussions focused on the delineation of a security exception that everyone was willing to accept:

> We recognized that there was a great danger of having too wide an exception and we could not put it in the Charter simply by saying: 'by any Member of measures relating to a Member's security interests,' because that would permit anything under the sun. Therefore we thought it well to draft provisions which

---

[1] The term exception is used in the title of two provisions only: Art. XX, and Art. XXI GATT.

would take care of real security interests and, at the same time, so far as we could, to limit the exception so as to prevent the adoption of protection for maintaining industries under every conceivable circumstance. ... It is really a question of balance. We have got to have some exceptions. We cannot make it too tight, because we cannot prohibit measures which are needed purely for security reasons. On the other hand, we cannot make it so broad that, under the guise of security, countries will put on measures which really have a commercial purpose.[2]

3. COVERAGE OF THE LEGAL DISCIPLINE

3.1 PRACTICE OUTSIDE DISPUTE ADJUDICATION

There have been a few instances where, although no Panel was established, national security claims have been raised as defence for trade restricting measures. In 1949, Czechoslovakia complained that the US administration of its export licensing controls discriminated between destination countries, contrary to Arts. I and XIII GATT. The US delegate responded, *inter alia*, that the challenged measures were restrictions imposed for security reasons.[3] The complaint was rejected by a roll-call vote of 17 to 1 with 3 abstentions.[4] In 1961, when Portugal acceded to the GATT, Ghana imposed an import embargo on Portuguese goods, arguing that it justified pointing to the situation in Angola which posed (in the eyes of the government in Ghana) if not an actual, at least a potential threat to its own national security. In Ghana's view:

> ..., under this Article each contracting party was the sole judge of what was necessary in its essentially security interest.[5]

In 1970, the United Arab Republic (UAR) (Egypt) defended its boycott against Israel (both its primary boycott against Israel and its secondary boycott against firms having relations with Israel), before the members of the Working Group on the Accession of the United Arab Republic, arguing that it was necessary to defend its national security since, otherwise, it would be contributing to the financing of Israel. Several members of the Working Group expressed sympathy for the view that the boycott was of political-, and not of commercial nature.[6] In November 1975, Sweden introduced an import quota for some footwear products. It sought to justify its measure through recourse to Art. XXI GATT, arguing that the

---

[2] EPCT/A/PV/33 at pp. 20–21, and also EPCT/A/SR/33 at p. 3.
[3] GATT CP.3/SR.22 at pp. 4ff.
[4] See the decision of 8 June 1949 published in GATT Doc. II/28. The roll-call vote was a system of voting whereby the secretary to a meeting would call those present in a meeting individually to cast their vote. It has been discontinued in the GATT/WTO-context, like voting in general, since the early fifties.
[5] SR.19/12 at p. 196.
[6] GATT Doc. BISD 17S/40 at pp. 22f.

country's security policy necessitated the maintenance of minimum production capacity in vital industries. During the discussions that followed at the GATT General Council,[7] many delegations expressed doubts as to the applicability of Art. XXI GATT in this context, and Sweden eventually notified the termination of its measures.[8] In April 1982, the member states of the EU (then EEC, European Economic Community), Australia, and Canada suspended imports of products originating in Argentina into their territories. They all claimed that their measures were justified by Art. XXI GATT, and that they had been taken in light of the situation addressed in the UN Security Council Resolution 502, namely the Falkland/Malvinas war.[9] Argentina complained that the measures violated a series of GATT provisions, namely, Arts. I, II, XI, XIII, and Part IV.[10] During the discussions before the GATT General Council, the representative of the EU argued that it was the sole judge of the exercise of its rights under Art. XXI GATT; he added that the measures coming under the purview of this provision did not require notification, justification or approval. The Australian delegate held similar views, adding that the GATT contracting parties had no powers to question that judgment. In the same vein, the Canadian delegate took the view that the GATT had neither the competence nor the responsibility to deal with the political issue that had been raised.[11] Argentina requested an interpretation of Art. XXI GATT, which was decided in November 1982, five months after the challenged measures had been removed. On November 30, 1982, the GATT contracting parties adopted a Decision Concerning Article XXI of the General Agreement, which reads as follows:

> 1. Subject to the exception in Article XXI:a, contracting parties should be informed to the fullest extent possible of trade measures taken under Article XXI.
>
> 2. When action is taken under Article XXI, all contracting parties affected by such action retain their full rights under the General Agreement.
>
> 3. The Council may be requested to give further consideration to his matter in due course.[12]

3.2 DISPUTE ADJUDICATION

The dispute between the US and Nicaragua concerning the US import-and export-embargo against Nicaragua is the first time that a dis-

---

[7] GATT Doc. C/M/109.
[8] GATT Doc. L/4250/Add. 1.
[9] GATT Doc. L/5319/Rev. 1.
[10] See the discussions before the GATT General Council reflected in GATT Doc. C/M/157, and C/M/159.
[11] Idem.
[12] GATT Doc. BISD 29S/23.

pute where national security was an issue was submitted to a Panel.[13] The US measure came as response to the establishment of the Sandinistas in Nicaragua and their overall attitude which in the eyes of the US government was hostile to the US. Nicaragua was facing a two-way embargo from the US, which practically ended any trade relations between the two countries. Nicaragua complained that the measure at hand was in violation of Art. XI GATT. Even before the Panel had been established, the US argued that the measure was necessary to protect its national security interests. The US also claimed that an invocation of Art. XXI GATT was not justiciable. Before the Panel, the US repeated the same arguments. The Panel report in *US–Nicaraguan Trade* which dealt with the complaint by Nicaragua was never adopted, and, hence, remains of limited legal value. It reveals, however, the *opinio juris* of an influential WTO Member, with respect to Art. XXI GATT. The motivation for the trade embargo is reflected in § 3.1 of the report, and in § 3.3 the impact that the US embargo had on trade between the two countries is discussed:

> 3.1 On 1 May 1985 the President of the United States issued an Executive Order which reads:
>
>> ... I, RONALD REAGAN, President of the United States of America, find that the policies and actions of the Government of Nicaragua constitute an unusual and extraordinary threat to the national security and foreign policy of the United States and hereby declare a national emergency to deal with that threat.
>>
>> I hereby prohibit all imports into the United States of goods and services of Nicaraguan origin; all exports from the United States of goods to or destined for Nicaragua, except those destined for the organized democratic resistance, and transactions relating thereto.
>>
>> I hereby prohibit Nicaraguan air carriers from engaging in air transportation to or from points in the United States, and transactions relating thereto.
>>
>> In addition, I hereby prohibit vessels of Nicaraguan registry from entering into United States ports, and transactions relating thereto.
>>
>> The Secretary of the Treasury is delegated and authorized to employ all powers granted to me by the International Emergency Economic Powers Act to carry out the purposes of this Order.

---

[13] On this issue, see the excellent analysis offered in Hahn (1991) who discusses the case-law and pays particular attention to the standard of review employed in national security cases.

The prohibition set forth in this Order shall be effective as of 12:01 a.m., Eastern Daylight Time, May 7, 1985 and shall be transmitted to the Congress and published in the <u>Federal Register.</u>

3.3 According to calculations made by the GATT Secretariat almost all imports (more than 99 per cent) from Nicaragua into the United States are items for which the duties are bound under the General Agreement.

The parties agreed on special terms of reference for this Panel, reproduced in §§ 1.4–1.5:

1.4 At the meeting of the Council on 12 March 1986, the Chairman announced that the following terms of reference of the Panel had been agreed:

> To examine, in the light of the relevant GATT provisions, of the understanding reached at the Council on 10 October 1985 that the Panel cannot examine or judge the validity of or motivation for the invocation of Article XXI:(b)(iii) by the United States, of the relevant provisions of the Understanding Regarding Notification, Consultation, Dispute Settlement and Surveillance (BISD 26S/211–218), and of the agreed Dispute Settlement Procedures contained in the 1982 Ministerial Declaration (BISD 29S/13–16), the measures taken by the United States on 7 May 1985 and their trade effects in order to establish to what extent benefits accruing to Nicaragua under the General Agreement have been nullified or impaired, and to make such findings as will assist the CONTRACTING PARTIES in further action in this matter (C/M/196, page 7).

1.5 Following this announcement, the representative of the United States said the terms of reference had been drafted specifically for this case and would govern the Panel in this particular dispute. However, this should not imply that panels in other cases would not have to determine whether nullification or impairment existed. Only in this case did the United States not dispute the effects of a two-way trade embargo. Furthermore, the above terms of reference should not be interpreted to mean that any further action by the CONTRACTING PARTIES in this matter was necessary or appropriate. The representative of Nicaragua replied that, in his view, this Panel was not an exception; its functions would be those described in the 1979 Understanding (BISD 26S/211–218). Consequently, the CONTRACT-

ING PARTIES would have to take appropriate action on the Panel's report (C/M/196, page 8).

The main arguments of the parties focused on the standard of review to be applied by the Panel:

4.5 Nicaragua stated that the United States could not properly rely on Article XXI:(b)(iii) in this case. This provision could be invoked only if two conditions were met: first, the measure adopted had to be necessary for the protection of essential security interest and, second, the measure had to be taken in time of war or other emergency in international relations. Neither of these conditions were fulfilled in this present case. Obviously, a small developing country such as Nicaragua could not constitute a threat to the security of the United States. The embargo was therefore not necessary to protect any essential security interest of that country. Nor was there any "emergency" in the sense of Article XXI. Nicaragua and the United States were not at war and maintained full diplomatic relations. If there was tension between the two countries, it was due entirely to actions by the United States in violation of international law. A country could not be allowed to base itself on the existence of an "emergency" which it had itself created. In that respect, Article XXI was analogous to the right of self-defence in international law. This provision could be invoked only by a party subjected to direct aggression or armed attack and not by the aggressor or by parties indirectly at risk. Nicaragua added that it must be borne in mind that GATT did not exist in a vacuum but was an integral part of the wider structure of international law, and that the General Agreement must not be interpreted in a way inconsistent with international law. The International Court of Justice had found that the embargo was one element of a whole series of economic and military actions taken against Nicaragua in violation of international law and that it was not necessary for the protection of any essential security interest of the United States, and it had declared that the United States must make reparation for the damage caused. The Security Council (Resolution 562) and the General Assembly (Resolution 40/188) of the United Nations had also condemned the embargo for infringing the principles of free trade and had explicitly demanded its rescinding. Consequently, Nicaragua held that the United States could not base itself on Article XXI in the particular case, and that the trade measures under consideration constituted coercive measures applied for political reasons in contravention of paragraph 7(iii) of the Ministerial Declaration of November 1982, which obliged contracting parties to "abstain from taking restrictive trade measures, for reasons of a non-economic character, not consistent with the General Agreement.

4.6 The United States said that Article XXI applied to any action which the contracting party taking it considered necessary for the protection of its essential security interest. This provision, by its clear terms, left the validity of the security justification to the exclusive judgement of the contracting party taking the action. The United States could therefore not be found to act in violation of Article XXI. In any case, the Panel's terms of reference made it clear that it could examine neither the validity of, nor the motivation for, the United States' invocation of Article XXI:(b)(iii). The United States' compliance with its obligations under the General Agreement was therefore not an issue before the Panel. The United States added that it disagreed with Nicaragua's assessment of the security situation but it did not wish to be drawn into a debate on a matter that fell outside the competence of the GATT in general and the Panel in particular.

4.7 Nicaragua, while recognizing that it was not within the competence of the Panel to examine or judge the validity of or motivation for the invocation of Article XXI:(b)(iii), nevertheless felt that the Panel had sufficient legal material and other information before it to arrive at a conclusion on the consistency of the embargo with the provisions of the General Agreement.

The Panel report is of particular interest when discussing the standard of review that Panels should employ in similar cases:

5.16. . . The Panel recognized that the General Agreement protected each contracting party's essential security interests through Article XXI and that the General Agreement's purpose was therefore not to make contracting parties forego their essential security interests for the sake of these aims. However, the Panel considered that the GATT could not achieve its basic aims unless each contracting party, whenever it made use of its rights under Article XXI, carefully weighed its security needs against the need to maintain stable trade relations.

5.17. The above considerations and the conclusions to which the Panel had to arrive, given its limited terms of reference and taking into account the existing rules and procedures of the GATT, raise in the view of the Panel the following more general questions: If it were accepted that the interpretation of Article XXI was reserved entirely to the contracting party invoking it, how could the CONTRACTING PARTIES ensure that this general exception to all obligations under the General Agreement is not invoked excessively or for purposes other than those set out in this provision? If the CONTRACTING PARTIES give a panel the task of examining a case involving an Article XXI invocation without authorizing it to examine the justification of that invocation, do they limit the adversely affected contracting party's right to have its complaint investigated in accordance with Article XXIII:2? Are the powers of the CONTRACTING PARTIES under Article XXIII:2 sufficient to provide redress to contracting parties subjected to a two-way embargo?

5.18. The Panel noted that in 1982 the CONTRACTING PARTIES took a "Decision Concerning Article XXI of the General Agreement" which refers to the possibility of a formal interpretation of Article XXI and to a further consideration by the Council of this matter (BISD 29S/23–24). The Panel recommends that the CONTRACTING PARTIES, in any further consideration of this matter in accordance with that Decision, take into account the questions raised by the Panel above.

The essence of the Panel's approach is captured in § 5.17: although not explicitly stating it, the Panel seemed opposed to the view that the invocation of Art. XXI of the GATT was not justiciable. However, in light of its limited mandate (special terms of reference), the Panel did not have the opportunity to explore the appropriate standard of review any further.

In 1991, first the EU and then a host of other countries withdrew preferential benefits from Yugoslavia, in light of the prevailing situation there (civil war), invoking Art. XXI GATT to justify these measures.[14] Yugoslavia reacted arguing that the measures could not be justified under Art. XXI GATT. A Panel was established to discuss the dispute.[15] In light of the decision to freeze Yugoslavia's membership in the WTO, the Panel was discontinued.[16]

The notorious US Helms/Burton Act (Cuban Liberty and Democratic Solidarity Act)[17] emerges so far as the only dispute in the WTO-era where Art. XXI GATT has been invoked. Through this Act, the US imposed trade sanctions on products of Cuban origin, but also on products of other (than Cuban) origin, a percentage of the value added of which was Cuban (primary embargo). Eventually, the US, through a secondary embargo, stopped trading with nations trading with Cuba. The EU complained that the US measure violated a series of GATT provisions. The official description of the EU complaint is reproduced here:

> The European Community and its Member States wish to convey to you a request for consultations with the United States of

---

[14] GATT Doc. L/6948.
[15] GATT Doc. C/M/255 at p. 18.
[16] GATT Doc. C/M/264 at p. 3.
[17] Sometimes referred to as LIBERTAD.

America pursuant to Article 4 of the Understanding on Rules and Procedures Governing the Settlement of Disputes (DSU), Article XXIII:1 of the General Agreement on Tariffs and Trade 1994 (GATT 1994) and Article XXIII:1 of the General Agreement on Trade in Services (GATS) concerning the Cuban Liberty and Democratic Solidarity (LIBERTAD) Act of 1996, other legislative provisions consolidated therein, and any implementing measures taken thereunder.

The European Community and its Member States wish to express their profound concern about the apparent lack of conformity of certain aspects of this Act, including other legislative provisions consolidated therein and any implementing measures taken thereunder, to the international obligations of the United States under GATT 1994 and GATS. This concern relates in particular, but not necessarily exclusively, to the following aspects:

The Cuban Democracy Act and its companion the Cuban Liberty and Democratic Solidarity Act contain a number of provisions which have the intent and effect to restrain the liberty of the EC to export to Cuba or to trade in Cuban origin goods, as well as to restrict the freedom of EC registered vessels and their cargo to transit through US ports.

In addition, there are provisions which require the provisions of certificates in respect of trade in Cuban sugar. If such certificates are not provided, access to the US sugar quota is denied.

Finally, there are measures which may lead to the refusal of visas and the exclusion of non-US nationals from US territory in a way which may contravene US commitments under GATS.

The European Community and its Member States are of the view that these and comparable measures taken under the two laws mentioned above may not be in conformity with at least the following provisions: Articles I, III, V, XI and XIII of GATT 1994 and Articles I, III, VI, XVI and XVII of GATS and in particular in relation to the Annex on Movement of Natural Persons Supplying Services under the Agreement.[18]

Following inconclusive consultations, a Panel was established to adjudicate the EU complaint. Subsequent to the establishment of the Panel, the EU requested, in accordance with Art. 12.12 DSU, the suspension of the Panel's work, in order to allow it to reach a mutually acceptable solution with the US.[19] The Panel suspended its work on April 21, 1997, and since then no request has been tabled to reconvene the proceedings; the authority of the Panel, as per Art 12.12 of the DSU, lapsed on April 22,

---

[18] See WTO Doc. WT/DS38/1 of May 13, 1996.
[19] WTO DocWT/DS38/5 of 25 April 1997.

1998.[20] The WTO was never notified of any mutually acceptable solution. The EU has not resurrected the original Panel either.[21]

The key question remains what is the standard of review that Panels will employ in similar cases? Recently, the Panel in *China–Raw Materials* suggested that a very deferential standard is appropriate in national security cases (§ 7.276). The Panel's reasoning is very much in line with a line of thought that emerges from AB jurisprudence that a more deferential standard should be given to WTO Members in instances where the competing value being pursued is of grave importance. Arguably, in international relations, nothing is more sacrosanct to a state than its national security. Thus, despite the limited jurisprudence on Art. XXI GATT, most WTO Members consider the exception to provide it with cover for actions taken to advance national security.

This seems to be in line with the AB line of thinking to adopt a more deferential standard of view the higher the value that is being pursued: arguably, nothing is more sacrosanct than national security in state to state international relations.

QUESTIONS AND COMMENTS

Responses to Communism: The rise of Communism provided these feelings with additional ammunition. Some Communist regimes joined either as original members or later the GATT. Western states had put in place COCOM, an acronym for Coordinating Committee for Multilateral Export Controls: COCOM was established in 1947, during the Cold war to put an embargo on Western exports to East Bloc countries, and counted 17 member states, namely, Australia, Belgium, Canada, Denmark, France, Germany, Greece, Japan, Luxembourg, Netherlands, Norway, Portugal, Spain, Turkey, the United Kingdom, and the US. In addition there were a number of cooperating countries, such as Austria, Finland, Ireland, New Zealand, Sweden, and Switzerland. COCOM ceased to function on March 31, 1994, and the then-current control list of embargoed goods was retained by the member nations until the successor, the Wassenaar Agreement, was established. The Wassenaar Arrangement (Wassenaar Arrangement on Export Controls for Conventional Arms and Dual–Use Goods and Technologies) is an arms control convention with 40 participating states. It was established on May 12, 1996, in Wassenaar (the Netherlands). A Secretariat for administrating the agreement is located in Vienna, Austria. As of December 2006, the 40 participating states are: Argentina, Australia, Austria, Belgium, Bulgaria, Canada, Croatia, Czech Republic, Denmark, Estonia, Finland, France, Germany, Greece, Hungary, Ireland, Italy, Japan, Latvia, Lithuania, Luxembourg, Malta, the Netherlands, New Zealand, Norway, Poland, Portugal, Republic of Korea, Romania, Russia, Slovakia, Slovenia, South Africa, Spain, Sweden Switzerland, Turkey, Ukraine, the United Kingdom, and the United States. These

---

[20] WTO Doc.WT/DS38/6 of 24 April 1998.

[21] See the chapter dedicated to this issue in Matsushita *et al.* (2006).

arrangements were limited to exports of arms on which no tariff concessions occur; arms nonetheless, are often produced through a variety of inputs of pure commercial character, and the legal vehicle permitting COCOM and later the Wassenaar Arrangement countries to lawfully impose export restrictions on similar goods is Art. XXI GATT.

CHAPTER 14

ANTIDUMPING

■ ■ ■

1. THE LEGAL DISCIPLINE

"Dumping" is what happens when a producer exports a product at a price less than the "normal value" of the product. The concept of a "normal value" (NV) is a constructed legal term under WTO law, and it will be discussed in greater detail in this Chapter. Ordinarily, the NV is considered to be the price of the good in the producer's home market. However, under a number of circumstances, the home-market price is considered to be unreliable, and the NV is based on the export price of the good in a third country or constructed from scratch.

WTO law does not ban "dumping" outright nor does it attempt to regulate it fully. Instead, Art. VI GATT and the WTO Agreement on Antidumping (AD)[1] deal with the conditions that must be met in order for a WTO Member to impose duties to redress instances of dumping. Such duties are known as anti-dumping (AD) duties. In order for a WTO Member to impose anti-dumping duties, it must demonstrate that dumping has caused injury to the domestic industry producing the like product being dumped or materially retards the establishment of such an industry. In other words, there are three key cumulative requirements:

(1) dumping;

(2) injury; and

(3) a causal link between the dumping and injury.

To determine whether all three requirements exist for any particular instance, a WTO Member must appoint an investigating authority (IA) to conduct an investigation into the matter. In most WTO Members, anti-dumping cases proceed as administrative adjudications. WTO law requires that certain procedural and due process requirements be followed

---

[1] Consistently, WTO adjudicating bodies have held that antidumping is governed not only by the WTO AD Agreement, but also by Art. VI GATT (see for example, the AB report on US–1916 Act). The consequence of the current construction of the regulatory framework applicable to antidumping is two-fold: dumping is recognized as unfair practice (there is no statement regarding its unfairness in the context of the WTO AD Agreement), and the obligations of investigating authorities (IAs) when examining dumping practices originating in NMEs (non-market economies), an issue we will be discussing *infra*. Czako et al. (2003), Mavroidis, Messerlin, and Wauters (2008), Palmeter (1995), Stewart and Dwyer (2010) provide extensive discussions of the WTO AD Agreement, its negotiating record, and objectives.

during the course of the investigation. Provided all legal requirements are met, the WTO Member may impose an additional duty on goods from a particular producer or particular WTO Member to offset the dumping margin calculated during the investigation.[2] Or it may require that the foreign producer raise its prices so as to eliminate the dumping margin.

2. THE RATIONALE FOR THE LEGAL DISCIPLINE

Support for trade liberalization is conditioned on an expectation that all trading partners will play "fairly." WTO law provides mechanisms for countries to take action against unfair trade. In addition, trade liberalization can sometimes lead to unexpected adverse consequences, both economic and non-economic, for domestic producers. WTO law therefore provides its Members with a series of policy instruments to deal with such circumstances. These instruments are often referred to as instruments of "contingent protection": "contingent", in the sense that certain conditions must be fulfilled in order for these instruments to be deployed; "protection", in the sense that they allow a WTO Member to reintroduce a tariff, quota, or combination thereof that had been previously withdrawn so as to protect a domestic industry. They are also sometimes referred to as trade remedies, as they are policy instruments that help remedy certain adverse consequences resulting from trade.

The three most popular forms of contingent protection, or trade remedies are: antidumping duties, countervailing duties, and safeguards. Of the three, anti-dumping duties emerge as the most popular form in practice by far. To some extent, a common rationale exists for the inclusion of all three of these contingent protection instruments. This is the need to provide for a "safety valve" to deal with the negative economic and political consequences of trade liberalization. Each of the three contingent protection instruments provides a means for WTO Members to rollback, under certain limited circumstances, prior trade liberalization commitments. Knowing that these safety valve mechanisms exist, a government may be prone to make greater trade concessions at the negotiating table than would be the case if the concessions were absolutely permanent. The safety valve mechanisms also make it easier for a government to sell trade concessions to reluctant constituencies by allowing the government to note the possibility of a rollback of these concessions should certain adverse impacts occur. In other words, the existence of contingent protection mechanisms helps to facilitate greater trade liberalization, even if it means that concessions will need to be periodically rolled back.

Beyond the safety valve rationale (relevant for safeguard action), another rationale proffered is that of ensuring "fair" trade (relevant for both antidumping, as well as countervailing measures). On this score, a con-

---

[2] This results in a violation of the non-discrimination requirements of the GATT. However, an exception is authorized under Art. II.2(b) GATT, as mentioned briefly in Chapter 4.

tentious normative debate rages. Is "dumping" bad? Some would contend yes, drawing analogies to the dangers of predatory pricing under competition law. Others argue that while such dangers do exist, competition law, by itself, should suffice to regulate such activity. Finally, some suggest that firms may have solid reasons to engage in price differentiation across market segments; so long as firms do not price a good below its cost, the fact that it may charge more overseas than it does at home should not be worrisome. A related question is whether anti-dumping laws, as drafted, help to ensure greater "fairness" in trade or simply serve as a quasi-protectionist instrument. We leave it up to you to decide your own views on this question, after you learn about the relevant legal discipline.

The inclusion of Art. VI in the original GATT 1947 was largely at the insistence of the US, which sought a mechanism to deal with unfair trade. However, because of the vague language of the provision, by the 1960s, multiple parties expressed concerns that anti-dumping duties simply served as a means to re-introduce protection against lower-cost imports from Japan and developing countries. At the same time, countries that were resorting increasingly to anti-dumping duties sought reassurances that the measures that they were taking were legal under Art. VI GATT. As a result, the rules governing anti-dumping measures were further elaborated upon in subsequent negotiation rounds. At first, these took the form of an Anti-dumping Code whose adoption was optional. The first Code was issued following the Kennedy Round in 1967, and was replaced atthe Tokyo Round in 1979. After the Uruguay Round, the rules were enshrined in the WTO Anti-dumping Agreement, which became part of the mandatory single-undertaking that resulted from the round.

3. COVERAGE OF THE LEGAL DISCIPLINE

Art. VI GATT states, *inter alia*:

The contracting parties recognize that dumping, by which products of one country are introduced into the commerce of another country at less than the normal value of the products, *is to be condemned* if it causes or threatens material injury to an established industry in the territory of a contracting party or materially retards the establishment of a domestic industry." (emphasis added).[3]

It is by virtue of this provision that antidumping duties can be imposed. Dumping, although not illegal per se, is an unfair trade practice and can be counteracted.[4]

---

[3] Irwin *et al.* (2008) mention that this sentence was added at a late stage of the negotiation of the GATT, following a proposal by the Cuban delegation to this effect.

[4] Case law has recognized as much (§ 87 of the AB report on *Argentina–Footwear (EC);* and § 81 of the AB report on *US–Line Pipe*).

Based on Art. VI GATT, in order to impose an anti-dumping duty, a WTO Member must prove:

(1) Dumping;

(2) Existence, or threat, of injury to the domestic industry (or the material retardation of the establishment of such an industry)

(3) A causal link between the dumping and injury (or material retardation)

Of these three requirements, the most complicated is the determination of dumping, which is extremely technical, in nature.

3.1 DUMPING

According to Art. VI:1 GATT and Art. 2.1 AD, "dumping" occurs when the export price of a good is less than its "normal value." The difference between the two prices is the dumping margin. We begin by examining how the two prices are to be calculated.

3.1.1 Calculating Normal Value

As noted earlier, the "normal value" (NV) is a constructed legal term used specifically within the realm of anti-dumping law. Art. 2.1 AD defines NV as "the comparable price, in the ordinary course of trade, for the like product when destined for consumption in the exporting country."

3.1.1.1 *Use of the Home Market Price as NV*

The NV should normally be the actual price of the allegedly dumped good in the home market of the producer / exporter.

3.1.1.2 *Circumstances for Disregarding Home Market Price as the Basis for Normal Value*

In some circumstances, however, the price of a good in the home market may not be the right basis for comparison. The AD Agreement allows an IA to disregard the price of the good in the home market as the NV if one of the following situations occur (Art. 2.2 AD):

(a) There are no sales of the like product in the *ordinary course of trade*;[5] or

(b) A proper comparison between the normal value and the export price cannot be made, because of

   (i) the *particular market situation*, or

   (ii) the *low volume of sales* in the home market.

---

[5] The AB, in its report on *US–Hot–Rolled Steel* clearly stated that sales outside the ordinary course of trade must be excluded by the IA from the calculation of NV (§ 139).

Where either of these situations hold, the AD Agreement provides for two alternative methods for calculating NV:

(a) The use of a *third-country price;* or

(b) The use of a so-called *constructed normal value.*

We focus in this sub-section on the particular situations in which the home market price may be disregarded by the IA and an alternative approach may be used. We then turn in the next sub-section to the technical details of these alternative approaches.

Ordinary course of trade: The first situation mentioned in Art. 2.2 AD is when there are no sales of the like product in the "ordinary course of trade" in the home market of the producer / exporter. This leads to the question: When does a sale not occur in the "ordinary course of trade"?

Art. 2.2.1 AD permits an IA to treat a sale as not having been made in the "ordinary course of trade" if several conditions cumulatively hold:

- Sales were made at a price below the per unit (fixed and variable) cost of production plus selling, general and administrative (SG & A) expenses;
- Sales were made within an extended period of time (normally one year but in no case less than six months);
- Sales were of a substantial quantities, meaning either:
  - The weighted average selling price of the transactions under consideration for the determination of NV is below the weighted average per unit costs, or
  - The volume of sales at a loss represents at least 20% of the volume sold in the transactions under consideration for the determination of NV

Note that sales made at prices which are below per unit costs at the time of sale, but above weighted average per unit costs for the period of investigation, shall be considered to provide for the recovery of costs within a reasonable period of time. This might occur when there is a large, but temporary, fluctuation in the cost of factor inputs. Such sales are not to be considered outside the "ordinary course of trade."

In *US–Hot–Rolled Steel*, the AB identified sales between parties with common ownership as a case of sales outside the ordinary course of trade. However, the AB was quick to point out that, even where the parties to a sales transaction are entirely independent, a transaction still fall outside of the ordinary course of trade (§ 143). The example provided by the AB was that of a liquidation sale made by an enterprise to an independent buyer that did not reflect normal commercial principles (§ 148).

The AB also emphasized that when deciding which sales fall outside of the ordinary course of sales, the IA must apply its criteria in an even-handed manner. In *US–Hot Rolled Steel*, the US excluded all sales transactions between related parties[6] which were marginally low-priced, on the grounds that these sales fell outside the normal course of trade. The US had not excluded transactions between related parties that were high-priced sales, except for those proven, upon request, to be aberrantly high priced. The exclusion of only low-priced, but not high-priced, transactions between related parties resulted in an artificially-inflated NV. The AB ruled against the US on the grounds that the US did not apply its criteria in an even-handed manner (§ 154).

Low volume of sales: Footnote 2 to the AD Agreement indicates that sales shall be considered sufficient in volume, if they represent at least 5% of the sales of the product in the importing/investigating country. It is, nevertheless, clear from the text of this footnote that the 5% benchmark is not an absolute criterion. Assuming evidence that sales at a lower ratio are still of sufficient magnitude to provide for a proper comparison, a lower number of sales should be acceptable for the purposes of the NV-determination.[7]

Particular market situation: There is paucity of case law in this context. The GATT Panel report in *EEC–Cotton Yarn* suggests that the particular market situation must be of a form that prevents the home market from serving as the proper basis of comparison. In that case, the Panel held that the combined existence of hyper-inflation and a fixed exchange rate in Brazil did not render home market prices as an inappropriate basis for NV.

When one of these three circumstances holds, the IA may use one of two alternative approaches: (1) the use of a *third-country price*, or (2) a *constructed normal value* approach. The IA is free to choose between the two alternatives; there is no hierarchy between the two.

3.1.1.3 *Use of Export Price in a Third Country as the Basis for Normal Value*

Art. 2.2 AD notes that one alternative is to use "a comparable price of the like product when exported to an appropriate third party." This is qualified by the requirement that the price must be representative. At present, much discretion is given to the IA in selecting a third country. There is not extensive case law as to what would be an inappropriate third party. Nor has the case law elaborated upon when an export price would not be representative.

---

[6] Prusa and Vermulst (2010) discuss this concept as it has been interpreted across cases in WTO case law.

[7] The AD Agreement does not specify whether the sufficient volume-test relates to all domestic sales by an investigated exporter, or to only those sales by the exporter which are made in the ordinary course of trade, see WTO Doc. TN/RL/GEN/9.

3.1.1.4 *Constructed Normal Value*

The other approach that the IA may be use, when one of the circumstances in Art. 2.2 AD apply for disregarding home market price as the basis for NV, is to construct the normal value itself. To do so, it must add together the following elements:

- The cost of production in the country of origin,
- A reasonable amount for selling, general and administrative (SG & A) expenses, and
- A reasonable amount for profits.

The constructed NV approach is subject to manipulation by the IA to arrive at a NV in line with its desired outcome. To limit this possibility, the discretion of the IA when using this approach has been curtailed by provisions of the AD Agreement as well as case law.

<u>Cost of production in the country of origin</u>: In principle, the cost data to be used as a basis for constructing the NV are those of the exporter or producer in question. Questionnaires are typically sent by the IA to the exporter alleged to be dumping to obtain this data. The discretion of the IA in determining the cost of production is limited. Art. 2.2.1.1 AD requires that:

(a) Costs shall normally be calculated on the basis of records kept by the exporter or producer[8], provided that

    a. such records are in accordance with the generally accepted accounting principles (GAAP) of the exporting country; and

    b. they reasonably reflect the costs associated with the production and sale of the product under consideration;

(b) Authorities shall consider all available evidence on the proper allocation of costs including the information provided by the exporter or producer, provided that such allocations have been historically utilized by the exporter or producer in its own accounting for depreciation, amortization, capital expenses, etc.[9];

(c) Costs shall be adjusted appropriately for non-recurring items which benefit future and/or current production or for circumstances in which costs during the period of investigation are affected by start-up operations.

---

[8] The term 'on the basis of', which is reflected in this provision, arguably leaves some room for discretion. The Panel in its report in *Egypt–Steel Rebar* emphasized that only those costs recorded in the books in accordance with GAAP which reasonably reflect the costs associated with the production and sale of the product under consideration are to be included in the cost calculation (§ 7.393). In the same vein, the Panel in its report in *US–Softwood Lumber V* underscored the fact that these provisions are not absolute and apply only to the extent that the statutory conditions for their application have been met(§ 7.237).

[9] Reversing the Panel's findings in this respect, the AB, in its report on *US–Softwood Lumber V*, held that occasionally, at least, this sentence would oblige an IA to compare alternative methodologies on cost-allocation and privilege the one that better suits the facts of the case (§§ 138–139)

SG & A and Profit: The Panel in *US–Softwood Lumber V* noted that Art. 2.2.2 AD does not define what constitutes selling, general, and administrative expenses. In its view, all costs affecting all or nearly all products manufactured by a company should be considered "general" costs, while "administrative" costs were defined as costs concerning or relating to the management of the company's affairs (§ 7.263). When constructing SG & A and profits, an IA must, in accordance with Art. 2.2.2 AD, base its calculations on the investigated exporter's actual data pertaining to the production and sales in the ordinary course of trade of the like product.

In *EC–Tube or Pipe Fittings*,[10] the question arose whether data relating to sales that had been discarded by an IA under Art. 2.2 AD could still be used for the purposes of constructing SG & A and profits in the context of Art. 2.2.2 AD. Specifically, Brazil complained that the European IA used in its calculations under Art. 2.2.2 AD data relating to sales previously discarded under Art. 2.2 AD (low volume sales). The AB, upholding the Panel finding in this respect made it clear that an IA, which has discarded the market price for one of the reasons reflected in Art. 2.2 AD, other than for the reason that such sales were made outside the ordinary course of trade, can still use market data for the calculation of SG & A when constructing the NV (§ 101).

The Panel in its report on *EC–Salmon (Norway)* added that actual data about domestic profit, and actual SG & A data should not be excluded because of the low volume or the low level of profitability of the sales to which they pertain (§§ 7.309, 7.318).

IAs are not free to decide on the methodology that they can use to allocate reasonable amounts for SG & A expenses and profits. Paragraphs (i)–(iii) of Art. 2.2.2 AD provide for three alternative methods for calculating the SG & A and profit amount (when actual data regarding the production and sales in the ordinary course of trade cannot be used), which, in the words of the Panel in *EC–Bed Linen* (§ 6.60):

> are intended to constitute close approximations of the general rule set out in the chapeau of Article 2.2.2. These approximations differ from the chapeau rule in that they relax, respectively, the reference to the like product, the reference to the exporter concerned, or both references, spelled out in that rule.

In this Panel's view (§ 6.96), if one of these methods is properly applied, the results are by definition reasonable, as required by Art. 2.2 AD. The same Panel held that the three methods are at equal footing (§ 6.66).

The first alternative methodology is reflected in paragraph (i), which provides that the amounts can be based on the actual amounts incurred and realized by the investigated exporter for the same general category of

---

[10] Horn and Mavroidis (2007a) discuss this report.

products (which may include the like product). How broad the general category of products may be, is not defined in the Agreement. The Panel, in *Thailand–H–Beams*, found that the text of Art. 2.2.2 AD does not provide (§ 7.111):

> precise guidance as to the required breadth or narrowness of the product category.

It did note, however, that sticking to a narrower definition makes the methodology used fully consistent with the objectives of the Agreement (§ 7.113).

Paragraph (ii) provides for a second alternative: SG & A and profit may be based on the weighted average (WA)[11] of actual amounts incurred and realized by other investigated exporters or producers, rather than by the specific investigated exporter or producer, but for the same like product. The AB (*EC–Bed Linen*, § 80) clarified that all sales of other exporters or producers of the like product are to be included for determining SG & A and profit data, whether made in the ordinary course of trade or not.

Finally, as a third alternative methodology, paragraph (iii) provides that SG & A and profits may be based on any other reasonable method, with the proviso that the amounts shall not exceed the amounts incurred and realized by other investigated exporters for the same general category of products. The reference to any other reasonable method in paragraph (iii), led the Panel in *EC–Bed Linen* to the conclusion that (§ 6.98):

> in case a Member bases its calculations on either the chapeau or paragraphs (i) or (ii), there is no need to separately consider the reasonability of the profit rate against some benchmark'.

SG & A costs have to be based on actual data pertaining to production and sales of the like product. The Panel in *US–Softwood Lumber V* was of the view that, since SG & A costs benefit the production and sale of all goods that a company may produce, they must certainly relate or pertain to those goods, including to the product under investigation (§ 7.265). It, thus, concluded that (§ 7.267):

> unless a producer/exporter can demonstrate that the product under investigation did not benefit from a particular G & A cost item, an investigating authority is not precluded from attributing at least a portion of that cost to the product under investigation.

The Panel went on to find that it was not unreasonable for the US IA to allocate part of a large settlement amount relating to claims concerning

---

[11] The Panel in its report on *EC–Bed Linen (Article 21.5–India)* held that the weighting can be performed on a volume- or value-basis (§ 6.81). The use of data from one exporter only is not permitted, see AB report on *EC–Bed Linen* at § 76, see on this score, Grossman and Sykes (2007).

hardwood to the production and sale of softwood lumber as this settlement was a cost borne by the company as a whole.

3.1.1.5 *Non–Market Economies*

. When the producer alleged to be dumping is exporting from a non-market economy an IA may disregard the home market price as the basis for NV. Interpretative Note ad Art. VI GATT defines a non-market economy as:

> a country which has a complete or substantially complete monopoly of its trade and where all domestic prices are fixed by the state.[12]

The Interpretative Note allows WTO Members to deviate from the obligations imposed in Art. VI GATT (as further explicated in the AD Agreement) but does not explain what methodology exactly they should be following in similar cases:

> It is recognized that, in the case of imports from a country which has a complete or substantially complete monopoly of its trade and where all domestic prices are fixed by the State, special difficulties may exist in determining price comparability for the purposes of paragraph 1, and in such cases importing contracting parties may find it necessary to take into account the possibility that a strict comparison with domestic prices in such a country may not always be appropriate.

Normally, an IA, in the absence of legislative guidance as to what to do in such cases, will either use data from third-country producers, or construct the NV. The WTO Member most affected by its NME status is China, which is also the target of the greatest number of anti-dumping actions. Between 2005 and 2010, over one-third of all AD investigations worldwide were targeted against Chinese exporters.

In *EU–Footwear (China)*, the Panel affirmed the wide latitude given to IAs when adjudicating an anti-dumping charge against a producer from an NME. In that case, China challenged the EU's selection of Brazil as third-country surrogate country for China as violative of the AD

---

[12] The delegate of Czechoslovakia explained in the 1954–55 Review Session why there was a need to introduce alternatives to market prices for establishing NV in AD disputes:

[D]ifficulties caused by the application of certain standards relating to the definition of normal value ... are due to the fact that no comparison of export prices with prices in the domestic market of the exporting country is possible when such domestic prices are not established as a result of fair competition in that market but are fixed by the State.

Review Working Party II on Tariffs, Schedules and Customs Administration, Article VI, Proposal by the Czechoslovak Delegation, Revision W.9/86/Rev. 1 p. 1. Note that as Czechoslovakia was a socialist country at the time, its delegate likely made this proposal in order to avoid application of an even more radical approach by its trading partners in their formulation of the NV of Czechoslovakian exports in AD investigations. The first case involving an NME was the 1960 US investigation concerning 'Bicycles from Czechoslovakia' 25 Federal Register (1960) at p. 6657.

Agreement. The Panel ruled in the EU's favor, underlining the wide discretion IAs have when choosing surrogate countries for NMEs (§§ 7.253ff.).

3.1.1.6 *Summary for Calcuating Normal Value*

To summarize, when determining the NV of a product alleged to be dumped, one ordinarily relies upon the home market price of the like product. However, under three circumstances, the IA may deviate from this rule and instead rely on the export price in a third country or construct the NV on the basis of cost data provided plus reasonable amounts allocated for SG & A and profit. In addition, where the producer / exporter alleged to be dumping is from a NME, the IA has wide latitude to use an alternative approach.

Despite all the technical detail that we have discussed, one should take note of the fact that all that we have covered so far about the legal discipline is a small, albeit important, part of the overall legal requirement. Recall that dumping is but one of three key legal requirements, and that the calculation of NV is only half of the equation required to determine whether the dumping requirement is met. The other half of the equation is the export price, which must be less than the NV, in order for dumping to exist. We turn next to its calculation.

3.1.2 Establishing the Export Price

As is the case with NV, ordinarily, the IA will use the market price as the basis for the export price.

However, Art. 2.3 AD notes that an alternative approach may be used if:

- There is no export price
- The export price is unreliable because of association or a compensatory arrangement between the exporter and the importer or a third party (i.e., the export transaction is not an arms-length transaction).

Under such circumstances, Art. 2.3 AD allows the IA to construct the export price. The constructed price is "the price at which the imported products are first resold to an independent buyer." If this does not occur, or if the product is resold in a different condition, then the export price may be constructed "on such reasonable basis as the authorities may determine."

In *US–Stainless Steel (Mexico)*, the Panel noted that when using the price of the first independent resale as the basis for constructed export price, costs incurred between importation and resale can only be deducted if they were foreseen (§ 6.100). Interestingly, the same Panel highlighted that there does not exist an obligation to make such adjustments (§ 6.93):

because the failure to make allowance for costs and profits could only result in a higher export price—and thus a lower dumping margin.

3.1.3 Comparison of the Export Price to Normal Value

Once the export price and normal value have been determined, they are to be compared with each other. Art. 2.4 AD requires that this be a fair comparison, meaning:

(a) The two prices must be at the same level of trade; and

(b) Due allowances for any differences affecting price comparability must be made in accordance with the AD Agreement;

The purpose of this provision is, in the words of the Panel in *US–Stainless Steel (Mexico)* (§ 6.77):

> to neutralise differences in a transaction that an exporter could be expected to have reflected in his pricing.

Art. 2.4 AD does not require that an adjustment be made automatically in all cases where a difference is found to exist, but only where (based on the merits of the case) that difference is demonstrated to affect price comparability. The Panel in *US–Softwood Lumber V* explained as much (§§ 7.357–358):

> Comparability is a term which, in our view, cannot be defined in the abstract. Rather, an investigating authority must, based on the facts before it, on a case-by-case basis decide whether a certain factor is demonstrated to affect price *comparability*. We can imagine of situations where although differences exist, they do not affect price *comparability*. For instance, this could occur where in the exporting country all cars sold are painted in red, while cars exported are all black. The difference is obvious; in fact, it is one of those differences listed in Article 2.4 itself—a difference in physical characteristics. However, there might be no variable cost difference among the two cars because the cost of the paint—whether red or black—might be the same. If instead of differences in cost, we were looking at market value differences, we might reach the same conclusion if, either the seller or the purchaser, would be willing to sell or purchase at the same price, regardless whether the car is red or black.

> It is also important to note that there are no differences 'affect[ing] price comparability' which are precluded, as such, from being the object of an *allowance*. In addition, we consider that the obligation on an investigating authority is to examine the merits of each claimed adjustment and to determine whether the difference affects price comparability between the allegedly

dumped product and the like product sold on the domestic market of the exporting country." (emphasis in the original).[13]

Same level of trade: Art. 2.4 AD notes that the comparison of the export price with NV is normally made at ex-factory level.[14] However, an IA could compare the export price and NV at the wholesale- or retail-level. For the comparison to be fair, what matters is that prices are at the same level of trade.

Due allowances: Art. 2.4 AD provides an indicative list of the types of due allowances that may be made when comparing the normal value and export price:

> ... differences in conditions and terms of sale, taxation, levels of trade, quantities, physical characteristics, and any other differences which are also demonstrated to affect price comparability.

Any difference which affects price comparability must be accounted.[15] The Panel in *EC–Tube or Pipe Fittings* clarified that due allowances could also be made for items outside of the indicative list; in that case, an adjustment was made for packaging expenses, an item not explicitly mentioned in Art. 2.4 AD (§ 7.184). The Panel in *US–Stainless Steel (Mexico)* clarified that only differences that the exporter could reasonably have anticipated and could have taken into account in his price determination may be the subject of adjustments (§ 6.77).

The method to use when making due allowances is not prejudged in the AD Agreement. In *EC–Tube or Pipe Fittings*, the Panel clarified that as long as the AD Agreement does not specify a particular approach to account for differences, any methodology used, to the extent reasonable, should be considered WTO-consistent (§ 7.178).

Art. 2.4 AD also includes special rules for adjustments to be made when the export price is constructed: Under this circumstance, allowances should be made for costs, including duties and taxes, incurred between importation and resale, and for accrued profits. In addition, Art. 2.4.1 AD provides specific rules to be followed when the comparison between export price and normal value requires conversion of a currency.[16]

---

[13] In *Korea–Certain Paper*, the Panel (§ 7.147) rejected the need for an adjustment, as it was not convinced that there were sales-related services rendered by the trading company with respect to domestic sales of the exporters' products in the domestic market which were not rendered in the exporters' export sales to the importing country.

[14] This is also known as 'netting back': IAs establish an *ex factory* export price, and an *ex factory* normal value.

[15] In *EC–Fasteners (China)*, the AB found that a failure to indicate clearly what was necessary to perform fair comparison was inconsistent with Art. 2.4 AD (§ 527).

[16] Currency conversions should be done on the basis of the rate of exchange on the date of sale, provided that when a sale of foreign currency on forward markets is directly linked to the export sale involved, the rate of exchange in the forward sale shall be used. Also, fluctuations in exchange rates shall be ignored and in an investigation, the IA should allow exporters at least 60 days to have adjusted their export prices to reflect sustained movements in exchange rates during the period of investigation.

Burden of proof: It is now well settled in case law that Art. 2.4 AD places the obligation to ensure a fair comparison on the IA.[17] Hence, it is incumbent upon the IA to evaluate and decide whether an adjustment is required.[18] In *EC–Tube or Pipe Fittings*, the parties did not agree on the nature of the evidence that should be submitted in support of a claim for adjustment, and whether it is the IA or the exporter that bears the burden of identifying and substantiating the claimed adjustment. According to the Panel, it is for the IA to make due allowances and abide by the disciplines of Art. 2.4 AD; the IA retains discretion as to items to be included as well as the manner in which they will be evaluated. To this effect, it could very well be the case that an IA does not accept each and every claim presented under Art. 2.4 AD. It might request clarity from the party making the argument and, if this is the case, the party concerned is under a duty to cooperate (§ 7.158). The Panel in *Argentina–Poultry Antidumping Duties* held in the same vein that an IA must indicate to the parties concerned the type of information that is necessary to ensure a fair comparison, and it must not impose an unreasonable burden of proof on the interested party; if it does that, it is not violating the Agreement even if it refuses to make an adjustment for certain differences for which no such sufficient evidence has been presented by the party concerned (§ 7.239). With respect to a request to make adjustments for differences in packaging costs of the product when sold domestically compared to when exported, the Panel, in its report on *EC–Tube or Pipe Fittings* considered that no documentary evidence had been supplied by the Brazilian producer in spite of a clear request by the IA to provide such evidence. In such circumstances, the Panel was of the view that there was no obligation on the IA to establish the need for an adjustment through on-site verification, as argued by Brazil (§ 7.192). The Panel in *Egypt–Steel Rebar* held that the process of determining what kind or types of adjustments need to be made is something of a dialogue between interested parties and the IA. This Panel also seemed to accept that an IA may be required to make adjustments even when not explicitly requested or identified by the interested parties, in case it is demonstrated "by the data itself" that a given difference affects price comparability (§ 7.352). It thus appears that, even in the absence of a request for adjustments by an interested party, the IA has an independent obligation to make all reasonable adjustments as are necessary to ensure a fair comparison between normal value and export price.

3.1.4 Calculation of the Dumping Margin

The difference between the export price and normal value is the margin of dumping. This would seem straightforward enough, but controver-

---

[17] *US–Hot–Rolled Steel* at § 178, AB report. For a concise history of the zeroing case law, see the Panel report on *US–Orange Juice* §§ 7.89–136.

[18] *Argentina–Ceramic Tiles* at § 6.113, Panel report.

sies have arisen over the methodologies applied by IAs. Specifically, when comparing the export price and normal value, one could make comparisons on the basis of individual transactions or on the basis of a weighted average of a set of transactions.

Art. 2.4.2 AD states that the IA generally should normally employ one of two approaches. The existence of margins of dumping should normally be established on the basis of:

(a) A comparison of the weighted average NV with a weighted average of prices of all comparable export transactions (WA–WA); or

(b) A comparison of NV and export price on a transaction-to-transaction basis (T–T)

The AB in *EC–Tube or Pipe Fittings* made clear that WTO Members are free to choose between the two alternatives.

Note that when using the WA–WA methodology, the weighted average NV should be compared to a weighted average of prices of all comparable export transactions, and not of all sales. The Panel in *US–Stainless Steel (Mexico)* held that differences in timing may be considered to give rise to a comparability problem, only in case two elements exist:

(a) a change in prices; and

(b) differences in the relative weights by volume within the POI (period of investigation) of sales in the home market as compared to the export market (§ 6.123).

In *Argentina–Poultry Antidumping Duties*, the Panel also made clear that the weighted average NV must be established on the basis of all domestic transactions, other than those which may be disregarded pursuant to Art. 2.2.1 AD; the IA may not employ a weighted average based just on data from the domestic sales of the producers providing information to the IA (§§ 7.272ff).

The T–T methodology does not involve an evaluation of all sales either: there could be a discrepancy in the number of sales in the home and the export market. As a result, in such cases, in practice, an IA will look for the domestic sale as close in time as possible to each of the export transactions. In other words, it will compare the two transactions which are as close time-wise to each other as possible, and will neglect the remaining transactions.

Art. 2.4.2 AD permits the comparison of the weighted average NV to the export price of individual transactions (WA–T) in exceptional circumstances. One such circumstance is when there is "targeted dumping." For example, if during the period of investigation, an exporter dumps substantial volumes of exports during, say, one month only, then, an IA can, for the calculation of dumping margins, legitimately take into account the export prices as reflected in the transactions during this month. The AB, in its report on *EC–Bed Linen*, recognized as much (§ 62).[19] Use of the WA–T methodology is appropriate whenever the IA finds "a pattern of export prices which differ significantly among different purchasers, regions, or time periods."

<u>Zeroing</u>: Certain IAs, the most prominent example being the US, adopted an approach whereby for transactions in which the export price exceeded the normal value for the product (i.e., there was a negative dumping margin), they either completely disregarded the transaction or attributed a fictitious dumping margin of zero to the transaction. This resulted in a dumping margin that was higher than would have been the case, had the transaction(s) with the negative dumping margin been included. Zeroing has been used with recourse to calculation of dumping margin at various different stages of the original and subsequent investigations: original investigations (Art. 5.3 AD); administrative reviews (Art. 9.3.1 AD); sunset reviews (Art. 11.3 AD); interim or changed circumstances reviews (Art. 11.2 AD); and new shipper reviews (Art. 9.5 AD). (Note that these different types of reviews will be discussed *infra* in this Chapter.) It has resulted in over 20 WTO disputes, with the US as the respondent on the vast majority of cases. The ensuing case law is made up of diverging Panel reports, dissenting opinions,[20] a Panel overturning itself,[21] and the AB changing its reasoning to deal with the issue on several occasions. It even includes two Panel reports which openly disagreed with the AB and refused to follow its reasoning,[22] a very rare occurrence in WTO practice indeed. Since *EC–Bed Linens*, the AB has consistently held that zeroing is not permitted under the AD Agreement under any circumstances. It seems though that this discussion is water under the bridge by now, as a result of changes in the US's practice of calculating dumping margin.[23]

3.1.5 Sampling (and Other Exceptions to the Duty to Establish Individual Margins)

The NV must be established for each "known exporter" individually. As a result, Art. 6.10 AD states that IAs "shall, as a rule, determine an individual margin of dumping for each known exporter or producer concerned of the product under investigation." In *Mexico–Antidumping Measures on Rice*, the AB held that the term "known exporter" refers to

---

[19] See on this score, Janow and Staiger (2007), and Grossman and Sykes (2007).

[20] *US–Zeroing (EC)*, and *US–Softwood Lumber V*; See Bown and Sykes (2008); Prusa and Vermulst (2009), (2011); Crowley and Howse (2010); Crowley and Palmeter (2009); Hoekman and Wauters (2011).

[21] The reasoning in *US–Softwood Lumber V*, and *US–Softwood Lumber V (Article 21.5–India)* is not the same.

[22] *US–Zeroing (Japan)*; *US–Stainless Steel (Mexico)*.

[23] The US did initiate a procedure to repeal some forms of zeroing, see Federal Register, vol. 75 no 248, at pp. 81533ff., Tuesday December 28, 2010; see also Federal register, vol. 77 no 30, at pp. 8101ff., Tuesday February 14, 2012.

all exporters that have been identified in the petition, as well as those who have voluntarily appeared before the IA.

However, the AD Agreement permits exceptions to this rule: Where there are a large number of exporters, the IA may make recourse to "sampling" (Art. 6.10 AD), in which it restricts its investigation to a only limited number of companies (a sample). The IA will then determine an individual dumping margin for each of the sampled companies. Non-sampled exporters will be burdened, by virtue of Art. 9.4 AD, by a duty corresponding to the WA of the dumping margins of the sampled exporters.[24] An IA can either limit the examination to a reasonable number, or investigate a statistically valid sample. The two alternatives are, from a pure legal perspective, substitutes.

The Panel in *EC–Salmon (Norway)* has discussed what constitutes a "statistically valid sample" (§ 7.162):

> Thus, the "statistically valid" sample referred to in the second sentence of Article 6.10 is a "statistically valid" sample of all of the "known exporter[s] or producer[s] concerned" for whom it is "impracticable" to calculate an individual margin of dumping. Likewise, the "largest percentage of the volume of the exports . . . which can be reasonably investigated" is the "largest percentage of the volume of the exports . . . which can be reasonably investigated" in respect of all of the "known exporter[s] or producer[s] concerned" for whom it is "impracticable" to calculate an individual margin of dumping.

It is up to each WTO Member to determine the criteria to be used in its sampling. In *EU–Footwear (China),* China challenged the EU's criteria for sampling, which focused on those producers with the largest volume of sales both in the domestic as well as the export markets. The Panel held that the EU's criteria were consistent with Art. 6.10 AD (§§ 7.221ff.).

Sampling is not the only exception to the obligation to calculate individual dumping margins. In *Korea–Certain Paper*, the AB had held that an IA can legitimately calculate the same margin for a group of companies that together constitute one economic entity. The Panel addressed the question whether the practice of "collapsing" is consistent with the clear obligation in Art. 6.10 AD Agreement to calculate an individual margin of dumping for each known exporter or producer concerned: in this case, Korea had calculated a single margin of dumping for three legally independent Indonesian companies which it considered to constitute one entity for purposes of its antidumping investigation (collapsing); collapsing is intended to ensure the efficiency of the antidumping measure. The fear is that, if separate companies are sufficiently closely linked, they

---

[24] Note that the dumping margins for some sampled exporters may be calculated on the basis of facts available; the WA will be calculated by excluding such margins.

may be able to start selling through the company for which the lowest duty has been calculated, once the duty has been put in place. In other words, collapsing functions as a sort of pre-emptive anti-circumvention device. The Panel was of the view that Art. 6.10 AD does not define the term "exporter", or "producer", but that, when read in context, Art. 6.10 AD does not necessarily preclude treating distinct legal entities as a single exporter or producer for purposes of dumping determinations in AD investigations (§ 7.161). The Panel added, however that (§ 7.161):

> in order to properly treat multiple companies as a single exporter or producer in the context of its dumping determinations in an investigation, the IA has to determine that these companies are in a relationship close enough to support that treatment.

In other words, according to the Panel, only when the (§ 7.162):

> structural and commercial relationship between the companies in question is sufficiently close to be considered as a single exporter or producer

could collapsing be permissible. In the case at hand, the Panel accepted Korea's decision to treat the three independent Indonesian exporters as a single exporter and calculate a single margin of dumping for them in light of the following factors:

(a) The commonality of management and shareholding;

(b) The use of the same trading company by all three exporters; and

(c) The existence of cross-sales of the subject product among the three companies which, according to the Panel, evidenced (§ 7.168):

> the ability and willingness of the three companies to shift products among themselves.

In *EC–Fasteners (China)*, the AB went one step further. In § 376, it explained that, in cases where companies were "controlled" by the same entity, a single duty could be calculated for all of them:

> These situations may include: (i) the existence of corporate and structural links between the exporters, such as common control, shareholding and management; (ii) the existence of corporate and structural links between the State and the exporters, such as common control, shareholding and management; and (iii) control or material influence by the State in respect of pricing and output.

And later, when discussing the criteria for state control it noted (§ 381):

> ... evidence of State control or instruction of, or material influence on, the behaviour of certain exporters in respect of pricing and output. These criteria could show that in the absence of for-

mal structural links between the State and specific exporters, the State in fact determines and materially influences prices and output.

In this report, the AB closed the door to the possibility for similar calculations when companies originating in NMEs are being investigated, but opened it for companies "controlled" by the state where they originate.

3.1.6 Margin of Dumping: The Required Level

Dumping margins which fall under 2% are considered, by virtue of Art. 5.8 AD, to be de minimis. Any case against an exporter of a product which results in a dumping margin exceeding this threshold fulfills the dumping requirement necessary for imposition of an AD duty. Recall, however, that a finding of dumping is but only one of the requirements necessary. We turn now to a discussion of the other legal requirements.

3.2 INJURY

3.2.1 What Constitutes "Injury"?

Dumping, by itself, does not suffice for duties to be lawfully imposed. An IA has to demonstrate that dumping results in injury to the domestic industry producing the like product (Art. 3.5 AD). The term "injury" is used in the AD Agreement to refer to one of three situations:

- Current material injury to the domestic industry
- Threat of material injury to the domestic industry
- Material retardation in the establishment of a domestic industry.

Note that the concept of "material retardation" should not be confused with the concept of protecting an infant industry. A WTO Member may only rely on this situation for the injury prong when a domestic industry does not exist. Once a domestic industry has been established, the IA must find injury to exist under one of the first two situations.

3.2.2 Determination of Injury

Art. 3.1 AD makes clear that to show injury, an IA must provide "positive evidence" that injury has indeed occurred as a result of dumping.[25] The AB, in its report on *US–Hot–Rolled Steel,* elaborated that this meant that the evidence must be objective and verifiable (§ 192). The positive evidence-standard does not eliminate the possibility for an IA to resort to assumptions. But, as the AB pointed out in *Mexico–Antidumping Measures on Rice* (§ 204):

---

[25] In *Thailand–H Beams,* the AB stated that it considered Art. 3.1 AD to be an overarching provision that informed the more detailed obligations in the succeeding paragraphs of Art. 3 AD (§ 106).

these assumptions should be derived as reasonable inferences from a credible basis of facts, and should be sufficiently explained so that their objectivity and credibility can be verified.[26]

Art. 3.1 AD also requires that the IA undertake an "objective examination" of:

- The volume of the dumped imports;
- The effects of dumped imports on prices in the domestic market for like products; and
- The consequent impact of these imports on domestic producers of like products.

In *US–Hot–Rolled Steel*, the AB explained that the term "objective examination" relates to the way in which evidence is gathered, and requires from an IA to conduct the process without favoring the interests of any interested party in the investigation (§ 193).

We turn now to the elements of the "objective examination" required by Art. 3.1 AD. Note that AD 3.2 notes: "No one or several of these factors can necessarily give decisive guidance."

3.2.2.1 *Volume of Dumped Imports*

For an AD duty to be imposed, Art. 5.8 AD requires that the volume of dumped imports be above a de minimis level: If imports originate in one country, they must represent at least 3% of total imports. If imports originate from several countries whose individual share of total imports are each below 3%, then they must cumulatively represent at least 7% of total imports. AD duties may not be imposed in instances where the volume of dumped imports fall below these statutory thresholds.

Provided that the threshold has been met, Art. 3.2 AD requires that the IA examine whether there has been a significant increase in dumped imports:

- In absolute terms
- Relative to production in the importing WTO Member
- Relative to consumption in the importing WTO Member

The Panel in *Thailand–H–Beams* was of the view that Art. 3.2 AD required an IA to consider whether there had been a significant increase, rather than requiring it to make an explicit finding or determination as to whether the increase was significant (§ 7.161). The AB in its report on

---

[26] In the same report, the AB, upholding the Panel's findings, held in § 205:

An investigating authority that uses a methodology premised on unsubstantiated assumptions does not conduct an examination based on positive evidence. An assumption is not properly substantiated when the investigating authority does not explain why it would be appropriate to use it in the analysis.

EC–Tube or Pipe Fittings accepted this approach in explicit manner (footnote 114):

> Brazil's thesis is further predicated on the assumption that if no significant increase in dumped imports (either in absolute terms or relative to production and consumption in the importing Member) were found originating from a specific country under Article 3.2, then those imports would have to be excluded from cumulative assessment under Article 3.3. (Brazil's response to questioning at the oral hearing.) However, we find no support for this argument in the text of Article 3.2 itself: significant increases in imports have to be 'consider[ed]' by investigating authorities under Article 3.2, but the text does not indicate that in the absence of such a significant increase, these imports could not be found to be causing injury.

An IA cannot cherry pick among imports from a source that sometimes dumps and sometimes not. It must take into account the whole volume, as the AB clearly stated in its report on *EC–Bed Linen (Article 21.5–India)* as follows (§ 115):

> if a producer or exporter is found to be dumping, all imports from that producer or exporter may be included in the volume of dumped imports, but, if a producer or exporter is found not to be dumping, all imports from that producer or exporter must be excluded from the volume of dumped imports'.

In *EC–Bed Linen (Article 21.5–India)*, the AB dealt with injury analysis in a sampling scenario. The EU had sampled Indian exporters, and of the five sampled exporters, three were found to be dumping. The EU did not impose duties on the two exporters found not be dumping, but it did impose the WA (of the duties imposed on the three "dumpers") on the non-sampled Indian exporters. India protested, noting that during the investigation of Indian exporters of bed linen, 53% of imports in the EU market (the volume represented by the two non-dumping Indian exporters) were found not to be dumped. India did not put into question the methodology used by the EU for sampling. In India's view, it was the injury analysis of the EU that was questionable: since Art. 3.2 AD required investigating authorities to focus on the effects of dumped imports only, the EU should have kept as a working hypothesis that 53% of total Indian imports were not dumped, and, hence, could not be taken into account for the purpose of the injury analysis. The EU disagreed. In its view, the working hypothesis of the AD Agreement was that there was no need to make a separate injury analysis for non-sampled known exporters: the very fact that Art. 6.10 AD allowed sampling and Art. 9.4 AD allowed the imposition of the WA on non-sampled known exporters, amounted, in the EU's view, to a presumption that injury had been caused by such exporters. The AB rejected all EU arguments (§§ 132–133). In the view of the AB, Art. 9.4 AD does not provide justification for considering all imports from non-examined producers as dumped for purposes of Art. 3 AD (§ 127). The AB did not explicitly state how to determine the volume of dumped imports in the case of a sample, but it did indicate that it was difficult to perceive of any other way than to do this on the basis of some extrapolation of the evidence relating to the investigated producers/exporters (§ 137).

3.2.2.2 *Effects of Dumped Imports on Prices*

Art. 3.2 AD also requires that the IA must inquire whether, as a result of increased dumped imports, any of the following has occurred to a significant degree:

(a) price undercutting;

(b) price suppression;

(c) price depression

Price undercutting: This term refers to a situation where imported products are priced below domestic products. Note that price undercutting must be significant; a 20% differential was judged substantial in *EC–Tube or Pipe Fittings* (§ 7.268ff.).

In *EC–Tube or Pipe Fittings*, the Panel rejected the suggestion that an IA must base its analysis of price on a methodology that offset transactions with price undercutting prices must be offset by transactions with overcutting prices. The proposed methodology would require the IA to calculate one single margin of undercutting based on an examination of every transaction involving the product concerned and the like product. According to the Panel, to do so would have the result of requiring the IA to conclude that no price undercutting existed when, in fact, there might be a considerable number of sales at prices which might have had an adverse effect on the domestic industry (§ 7.276). This would not have been in line with the purpose of the price-undercutting analysis (§ 7.277).

Price suppression / depression: These terms were the subject of interpretation by the AB in its report on *US–Upland Cotton*.[27] Although this case dealt with the interpretation of the two terms as they appear in the SCM Agreement, Panels dealing with the interpretation of these terms in the context of the AD Agreement should defer to this report since the terms are identical and serve the same function (§§ 423–424):

> In explaining this term, the Panel stated, in paragraph 7.1277 of the Panel Report:
>
>> Thus, "*price suppression*" refers to the situation where "prices"—in terms of the "amount of money set for sale of upland cotton" or the "value or worth" of upland cotton—either are prevented or inhibited from rising (i.e. they do not increase

---

[27] See the discussion in Davey and Sapir (2010); see also Grossman and Sykes (2011).

when they otherwise would have) or they do actually increase, but the increase is less than it otherwise would have been. *Price depression* refers to the situation where "prices" are pressed down, or reduced.

Although the Panel first identified "price suppression" and "price depression" as two separate concepts in paragraph 7.1277, footnote 1388 of the Panel Report suggests that, for its analysis, the Panel used the term "price suppression" to refer to both price suppression and price depression. We recognize that "the situation where 'prices' . . . are prevented or inhibited from rising" and "the situation where 'prices' are pressed down, or reduced" may overlap. Nevertheless, it would have been preferable, in our view, for the Panel to avoid using the term "price suppression" as short-hand for both price suppression and price depression, given that Article 6.3(c) of the *SCM Agreement* refers to "price suppression" and "price depression" as distinct concepts. We agree, however, that the Panel's description of "price suppression" in paragraph 7.1277 of the Panel Report reflects the ordinary meaning of that term, particularly when read in conjunction with the French and Spanish versions of Article 6.3(c), as required by Article 33(3) of the *Vienna Convention on the Law of Treaties* (the "*Vienna Convention*"). (italics in the original).

3.2.2.3 Effects of Dumped Imports on Domestic Industry

Art. 3.4 AD requires from IAs to evaluate "all relevant economic factors and indices having a bearing on the state of the domestic industry" producing the liked product of the allegedly dumped good. The indicative list mentioned in Art. 3.4 AD includes:

• Actual and potential decline in sales, profits, output, market share, productivity, return on investments, and capacity utilization of the domestic industry

• Actual and potential negative effects on cash flow, inventories, employment, wages, growth, ability to raise capital or investments

In addition, IAs must also consider elements which may be relevant in resolving the causation question, as part of its examination of the impact of the dumped goods on domestic industry. Among those mentioned in the indicative list of Art. 3.4 AD are:

- Factors affecting domestic producers
- The magnitude of the margin of dumping

The Panel, in its report on *Egypt–Steel Rebar* held that Art. 3.4 AD does not require a full causation analysis, and stated that "as a whole, these factors are more in the nature of effects than causes" (§ 7.62).[28]

Art. 3.4 AD explicitly states that none of these factors by itself, or in combination with other factors mentioned therein is necessarily decisive for the outcome of the analysis. In other words, it is not necessary for each and every factor to be negative in order for injury to occur.[29] Instead, the listed factors, as a whole, should provide an indication of the extent of the injurious impact of dumped goods on the domestic industry.

A number of Panel[30] and AB reports[31] have held that all factors included in Art. 3.4 AD must be addressed in an investigation. What is important is that IAs engaged in comprehensive analysis of all factors; mere reference to a factor is insufficient.[32] In deciding whether an IA has examined all factors reflected in Art. 3.4 AD, it is the overall record of the investigation, and not just the final decision, that matters.[33] Finally, the AB, in *EC–Tube or Pipe Fittings*, held that explicit reference to a factor is not necessary if it is clear that the IA has implicitly examined it.[34]

Note, finally, that an IA must examine all relevant economic factors, and not only those mentioned in Art. 3.4 AD. In the words of the AB (*US–Hot–Rolled Steel*, § 194):

> Article 3.4 lists certain factors which are deemed to be relevant in every investigation and which must always be evaluated by

---

[28] In similar vein, the Panel in *EC–Tube or Pipe Fittings*, rejected a number of Brazilian arguments which, in its view, blurred the boundaries between Art. 3.4 AD, and Art. 3.5 AD, the forum for causation analysis (§ 7.335).

[29] See the Panel report on *EC–Bed Linen (Article 21.5–India)* at § 6.213.

[30] See e.g., *Egypt–Steel Rebar* at § 7.36; *EC–Bed Linen* at § 6.159; *Mexico–Corn Syrup* at § 7.128; *EC–Tube or Pipe Fittings* at § 7.304.

[31] See the AB report on *Thailand–H–Beams* at § 125.

[32] In *EC–Tube or Pipe Fittings*, the Panel made it clear that mere mention without analysis was WTO-inconsistent (§ 7.310), as an evaluation of the data is required (§ 7.314).

[33] Note, however, that in previous cases, Panels had expressed the view that the consideration of the factors in Art. 3.4 AD must be apparent in the determination, so as to enable the Panel to assess whether the IA acted in accordance with Art. 3.4 AD at the time of the investigation, see the Panel reports on *Guatemala–Cement II*, (§ 8.283); *EC–Bed Linen*, (§ 6.162). It is in *Egypt–Steel Rebar*, where the Panel first emphasized the importance of the written record even outside the final determination(§ 7.49):

> If there is no such written record—whether in the disclosure documents, in the published determination, or in other internal documents—of how certain factors have been interpreted or appreciated by an investigating authority during the course of the investigation, there is no basis on which a Member can rebut a prima facie case that its 'evaluation' under Article 3.4 was inadequate or did not take place at all. In particular, without a written record of the analytical process undertaken by the investigating authority, a panel would be forced to embark on a post hoc speculation about the thought process by which an investigating authority arrived at its ultimate conclusions as to the impact of the dumped imports on the domestic industry. A speculative exercise by a panel is something that the special standard of review in Article 17.6 is intended to prevent.

[34] In the case at hand, the EU had not reflected in its order a separate examination of growth, a factor listed in Art. 3.4 AD. It was clear from the record, however, that the IA had taken into account this factor (§§ 161–162).

the investigating authorities. However, the obligation of evaluation imposed on investigating authorities, by Article 3.4, is not confined to the listed factors, but extends to 'all relevant economic factors'.[35]

3.2.2.4 The Meaning of the "Domestic Industry" and "Like Product" in the AD Context

The analysis required by Art. 3.4 AD focuses on potential injury to the "domestic industry" producing the "like product." As we have already seen in other contexts of WTO law, these terms carry particular legal meaning. We discuss their meaning in the context of the AD Agreement below.

Art. 4.1 AD reads:

> For the purposes of this Agreement, the term "domestic industry" shall be interpreted as referring to the domestic producers as a whole of the like products or to those of them whose collective output of the products constitutes a major proportion of the total domestic production of those products, except that:

It contains two exceptions: related producers will not be taken into account, as will cases where a national market is segmented (and in this latter case it is the major proportion of each segment that counts). A footnote to this provision defines the term "related":

> For the purpose of this paragraph, producers shall be deemed to be related to exporters or importers only if *(a)* one of them directly or indirectly controls the other; or *(b)* both of them are directly or indirectly controlled by a third person; or *(c)* together they directly or indirectly control a third person, provided that there are grounds for believing or suspecting that the effect of the relationship is such as to cause the producer concerned to behave differently from non-related producers. For the purpose of this paragraph, one shall be deemed to control another when the former is legally or operationally in a position to exercise restraint or direction over the latter.

The term "like product" is in turn defined in Art. 2.6 AD as follows:

> Throughout this Agreement the term 'like product' ('produit similaire') shall be interpreted to mean a product which is identical, i.e. alike in all respects to the product under consideration, or in the absence of such a product, another product which, although not alike in all respects, has characteristics closely resembling those of the product under consideration.

---

[35] We will discuss the obligation of an IA to look for factors other than those mentioned in the body of Art. 3.4 AD, and examine their impact in the context of our discussion on the causality requirement, *infra*.

Panels have adopted restrictive interpretations of this term.[36]

More recently, however, in *EC and Certain Member States–Large Civil Aircraft*, the AB followed a different attitude when discussing like products. Although the case involved subsidies and not AD duties, the jurisprudence is relevant because AB first noted the "like product" definition in the SCM Agreement is identical to that in the AD Agreement (§ 1118). The AB noted that in examining whether two products are "like," an assessment should be made of their competitive relationship (§§ 1119–1120):

> ... Indeed, whether two products compete in the same market is not determined simply by assessing whether they share particular physical characteristics or have the same general uses; it may also be relevant to consider whether customers demand a range of products or whether they are interested in only a particular product type. In the former case, when customers procure a range of products to satisfy their needs, this may give an indication that all such products could be competing in the same market.

The AB then went on to state that both demand substituability as well as supply substitutability is relevant in establishing whether two goods are like (§ 1121).

In addition, we are left with the interpretation of the term "major proportion" as mentioned in Art. 4.1 AD: the Panel in *Argentina–Poultry Antidumping Duties,* rejected the argument that the term "major proportion" implies that such producers must account for at least 50% of total domestic production; it sufficed that the domestic producers that constitute the domestic industry for purposes of the AD investigation represent (§ 7.341):

> an important, serious or significant proportion of total domestic production.

In *US–Hot Rolled Steel*, the AB held that an IA cannot investigate the part of the industry that better suits its case (§ 204):

> Different parts of an industry may exhibit quite different economic performance during any given period. Some parts may be performing well, while others are performing poorly. To examine only the poorly performing parts of an industry, even if coupled with an examination of the whole industry, may give a misleading impression of the data relating to the industry as a whole, and may overlook positive developments in other parts of the industry. Such an examination may result in highlighting the neg-

---

[36] See the Panel reports in *EC–Salmon (Norway)* at §§ 7.13–76; *US–Softwood Lumber V* at §§ 7.139–158.

ative data in the poorly performing part, without drawing attention to the positive data in other parts of the industry. We note that the reverse may also be true—to examine only the parts of an industry which are performing well may lead to overlooking the significance of deteriorating performance in other parts of the industry.[37]

In *EC–Fasteners (China)* the AB found that the EU had inappropriately linked the percentage of the major industry in Art. 4.1 AD to that in Art. 5.4 AD.[38] The AB understood "major industry" as tantamount to a "relatively high proportion" of the sector concerned (§ 419). The AB however, did not give a precise number; it went as far as to state that a major proportion could be less than 50% on occasion and as low as 25% in case of fragmented industries (§§ 415ff.). It specifically acknowledged that the percentage may be lower in fragmented industries (than otherwise) (§ 419):

> In sum, a proper interpretation of the term "a major proportion" under Article 4.1 requires that the domestic industry defined on this basis encompass producers whose collective output represents a relatively high proportion that substantially reflects the total domestic production. This ensures that the injury determination is based on wide-ranging information regarding domestic producers and is not distorted or skewed. In the special case of a fragmented industry with numerous producers, the practical constraints on an authority's ability to obtain information may mean that what constitutes "a major proportion" may be lower than what is ordinarily permissible in a less fragmented industry. However, even in such cases, the authority bears the same obligation to ensure that the process of defining the domestic industry does not give rise to a material risk of distortion.

The Panel in *Mexico–Steel Pipes and Tubes* found that Mexico had failed to comply with this requirement as it had analyzed a number of factors with respect to three firms representing 88% of the national production, while its analysis of financial injury-factors was based on only one firm constituting 53% of national production only (§ 7.322). In other words, once a determination has been made as to which producers constitute the domestic industry for purposes of the investigation, and assuming of course that they represent a major proportion of the industry, it is the data from all of these producers that must be used to assess the impact of the dumped imports on the domestic industry.

---

[37] See also the AB report on *US–Cotton Yarn* at §§ 100–101.
[38] Which concerns the part of the industry that must support a petition for the process to start in the first place; we discuss standing-requirements *infra*.

3.2.3 Cumulation

Injury analysis will normally take place with respect to dumped imports originating in a particular WTO Member. It could be the case though, that injury is caused by dumped imports originating in various WTO Members, and in this case an IA might want to perform cumulative injury analysis: in this case, Art. 3.3 AD imposes certain disciplines on an IA that conducts similar analysis. It provides that an IA may only cumulate the effects of imports simultaneously subject to an AD investigation if it determines that:

> (a) The margin of dumping established in relation to the imports from each country is more than de minimis (*i.e.*, >2% of the export price), and the volume of imports from each country is not negligible (*i.e.*, >3% of imports of the like product in the importing product); and
>
> (b) Such a cumulative assessment of the effects of the imports is appropriate in light of the conditions of competition between the imported products from the various countries examined and the conditions of competition between the imported products and the like domestic product.

The AB, in its report on *EC–Tube or Pipe Fittings,* upheld the Panel's finding that cumulation is only possible after a prior country-specific analysis of volume and price effects of dumped imports, that is, after checking the conditions of competition in the marketplace. The AB justified its approach by looking at the rationale for cumulation (§§ 116–117).[39]

3.2.4 Sampling

Note that there is no provision in the AD Agreement allowing for sampling in the context of injury-analysis. Yet this is what happened in an EU investigation. In *EU–Footwear (China)*, the Panel held that the absence of a specific provision does not per se outlaw sampling. However, the sampled companies must be representative of the whole; in this vein, the volume of production is a relevant, but should not be the sole, criterion. The Panel, alas, did not identify other criteria (§§ 7.368ff., and especially 7.381ff.).

3.2.5 Determination of a Threat of Material Injury

Although most injury determinations proceed with examining whether dumped goods are causing actual material injury to the domestic industry, recall that, as discussed earlier, the concept of injury under the AD Agreement is broader. Another possible examination in which the IA may engage instead is whether the dumped goods present a threat of material injury to a domestic industry.

---

[39] See also, the Panel report on *EU–Footwear (China)* at §§ 7.404ff.

Art. 3.7 AD sets forth the requirements that an IA has to comply with in the case of a threat of injury examination:

(a) A determination of threat of injury must be based on facts, and not merely on allegations, conjecture or a remote possibility;

(b) The expected injury must be imminent and clearly foreseen;[40]

(c) A certain number of factors be considered by the authority concerning

> a. whether dumped imports have been increasing at a significant rate which indicates the likelihood of substantially increased importation;
>
> b. whether there is sufficiently freely disposable or an imminent substantial increase in the capacity of the exporter indicating a likelihood of substantially increased dumped exports;
>
> c. whether the prices of the dumped imports are such that they have a significant price depressing or suppressing effect on domestic prices and would therefore likely increase demand for further imports; and
>
> d. the state of the inventories of the subject product.[41]

The totality of these factors must lead to the conclusion that further dumped exports are imminent and that, unless protective action is taken, material injury would occur. According to the Panel in *US–Softwood Lumber VI*, an IA is required to consider these factors, in the same way as it is required to consider the volume and price effects of dumped imports in Art. 3.2 AD (§ 7.67). The Panel in *Mexico–Corn Syrup* held that the factors listed in Art. 3.7 AD relate specifically to the question of the likelihood of increased imports, and do not relate to the consequent impact of the dumped imports on the domestic industry. Limiting the examination to the factors listed in Art. 3.7 AD does not, consequently, suffice to reach a threat determination. In this construction, Art. 3.7 AD sets out factors that must be considered in a threat case, but does not eliminate the obligation to consider the impact of dumped imports on the domestic industry in accordance with the requirements of Art. 3.4 AD (§ 7.126). This Panel summarized the relationship between Arts. 3.1, 3.4 and 3.7 AD in the following manner (§§ 7.131–132):

---

[40] According to the Panel in *US–Softwood Lumber VI*, the change in circumstances that would give rise to a situation in which injury would occur encompasses a single event, or a series of events, or developments in the situation of the industry, and/or concerning the dumped or subsidized imports, which led to the conclusion that injury which has not yet occurred can be predicted to occur imminently (§ 7.57).

[41] Because the AD Agreement uses the term 'should' in the context of the factors listed in Art. 3.7 AD, the Panel in *US–Softwood Lumber VI* was of the view that, unlike the situation under Art. 3.4 AD, consideration of each of the factors listed in Art. 3.7 AD is not mandatory. According to this Panel, whether a violation of Art. 3.7 AD exists, would depend on the particular facts of the case, in light of the totality of the factors considered and the explanations given, see § 7.68.

In sum, we consider that Article 3.7 requires a determination whether material injury would occur, Article 3.1 requires that a determination of injury, including threat of injury, involve an examination of the impact of imports, and Article 3.4 sets out the factors that must be considered, among other relevant factors, in the examination of the impact of imports on the domestic industry. Thus, in our view, the text of the AD Agreement requires consideration of the Article 3.4 factors in a threat determination. Article 3.7 sets out additional factors that must be considered in a threat case, but does not eliminate the obligation to consider the impact of dumped imports on the domestic industry in accordance with the requirements of Article 3.4.

... an investigating authority cannot come to a reasoned conclusion, based on an unbiased and objective evaluation of the facts, without taking into account the Article 3.4 factors relating to the impact of imports on the domestic industry. These factors all relate to an evaluation of the general condition and operations of the domestic industry—sales, profits, output, market share, productivity, return on investments, utilization of capacity, factors affecting domestic prices, cash flow, inventories, employment, wages, growth, ability to raise capital. Consideration of these factors is, in our view, necessary in order to establish a background against which the investigating authority can evaluate whether imminent further dumped imports will affect the industry's condition in such a manner that material injury would occur in the absence of protective action, as required by Article 3.7.

The Panel in *US–Softwood Lumber VI* agreed with this view, but did not consider that an IA, once it had examined and evaluated the factors mentioned in Art. 3.4 AD, was required to make projections as to the likely impact of future dumped imports on each of these factors (§ 7.105). Nor would it be necessary, according to this Panel, for an IA to re-examine the factors mentioned in Art. 3.2 AD, concerning volume and price effect of dumped imports in a predictive context in making a threat of material injury determination (§ 7.111). In sum, it suffices for an IA to conduct an injury examination on the basis of Arts. 3.2 and 3.4 AD, and consider in addition some or all of the factors mentioned in Art. 3.7 AD in order to be able to conclude that further dumped imports are imminent and that, unless protective action is taken, material injury would occur.

The AB, in its report on *Mexico–Corn Syrup (Article 21.5–US)*, provided its understanding as to the applicable standard of review (§ 136):

In our view, the 'establishment' of facts by investigating authorities includes both affirmative findings of events that took place during the period of investigation as well as assumptions relating to such events made by those authorities in the course of their analyses. In determining the existence of a threat of material injury, the investigating authorities will necessarily have to make assumptions relating to 'the "occurrence of future events" since such *future* events "can never be definitively proven by facts" '. Notwithstanding this intrinsic uncertainty, a 'proper establishment' of facts in a determination of threat of material injury must be based on events that, although they have not yet occurred, must be 'clearly foreseen and imminent', in accordance with Article 3.7 of the *Antidumping Agreement.* (italics and emphasis in the original).

Consequently, the AB takes the view that an IA can lawfully have recourse to threat of injury in order to justify imposition of AD duties, only if the injury is imminent in the short-run and not an event which could, speculatively, occur in the distant future. According to the Panel in *US–Softwood Lumber VI*, this implies that (§ 7.33):

a degree of attention over and above that required of investigating authorities in all antidumping and countervailing duty injury cases is required in the context of cases involving threat of material injury.

In the same vein, the AB in *US–Softwood Lumber VI* (Article 21.5–Canada) held that any conclusion that there is a greater likelihood that a Panel will uphold a threat of injury-determination, rather than a determination of current material injury, when those determinations rest on the same level of evidence would be erroneous (§ 110). In its view, a Panel, when reviewing the factual basis for a threat of injury determination must determine (§ 98):

whether the investigating authority has provided 'a reasoned and adequate explanation' of:

a) how individual pieces of evidence can be reasonably relied on in support of particular inferences, and how the evidence in the record supports its factual findings;

b) how the facts in the record, rather than allegation, conjecture, or remote possibility, support and provide a basis for the overall threat of injury determination;

c) how its projections and assumptions show a high degree of likelihood that the anticipated injury will materialize in the near future; and

d) how it examined alternative explanations and interpretations of the evidence and why it chose to reject or discount such alternatives in coming to its conclusions.

3.2.6 Determination of Material Retardation

A third category of "injury" under the AD Agreement is that in which dumping leads to the "material retardation" of the domestic industry. As noted earlier, this should not be confused with infant industry protection. Beyond mention in footnote 9, the AD Agreement contains no further discussion of this concept. This concept of injury is rarely invoked, and the specific requirements necessary have not been elaborated upon in the case law.

3.3 DEMONSTRATION OF A CAUSAL LINK BETWEEN DUMPING AND INJURY

Beyond a showing of dumping and injury, before an AD duty may be imposed, a third requirement must be upheld: Art. 3.5 AD requires that the IA must show a causal link between the dumped imports and the injury. The causality analysis is to be based on all relevant evidence before the IA.

As part of this analysis, Art. 3.5 AD requires that the IA examine any other known factors, other than the dumped imports, which may be contributing to the injury of the domestic industry at the same time. The injury caused by such factors must be separated as part of the causality analysis and cannot be attributed to the dumped goods. The last sentence of Art. 3.5 AD contains an indicative list of factors that may appropriately be taken into account in the context of this exercise:

> Factors which may be relevant in this respect include, *inter alia*, the volume and prices of imports not sold at dumping prices, contraction in demand or changes in the patterns of consumption, trade restrictive practices of and competition between the foreign and domestic producers, developments in technology and the export performance and productivity of the domestic industry. (italics in the original).

Case law has confirmed that this list is of indicative character.[42] Case law has also clarified a factor is known as soon as it has been raised by a party.[43] In its report on *EC–Tube or Pipe Fittings*, the AB added that it is irrelevant if an interested party has raised a factor at one stage of the investigation only and not consistently throughout the investigation; what matters is whether a factor was raised or not (§ 178).[44]

The non-attribution obligation requires from an IA to separate and distinguish the effects of dumped imports on the domestic industry producing the like product from the effects of any other factor (*US–Hot–*

---

[42] Panel report on *EC–Tube or Pipe Fittings* at § 7.359.

[43] *EC–Tube or Pipe Fittings*, Panel report at § 7.359.

[44] Note nonetheless, that in *US–Wheat Gluten*, a safeguard case, the AB suggested that an IA cannot remain passive and rely only on evidence produced by the parties to the dispute.

Rolled Steel, AB, § 223). This implies that the nature and extent of the injurious effects of the other known factors need to be identified (§ 227).[45] The AB conceded that the discipline imposed is quite demanding for any bureaucracy (§ 228). The AB (*US–Hot–Rolled Steel*, § 224) was of the view that an IA can choose any methodology it deems useful in order to disentangle the effects of the various factors causing injury.[46] In *EC–Tube or Pipe Fittings*, the AB faced the question of whether the impact of factors other than dumped imports should be examined both individually and collectively. The AB noted that the answer to this question depends on the circumstances of the case, but did not provide any examples of circumstances where such an evaluation would be compulsory (§§ 191–192).[47]

The AD Agreement does not set forth any particular methodology for conducting the price effect and causation analyses when it comes to determining the injury caused by dumped imports as a result of price undercutting, price depression, or price suppression. Panels have, so far, rejected arguments that the analysis is to take place at a particular level of trade [*Egypt–Steel Rebar* (§ 7.73)], on a quarterly basis [*Thailand–H–Beams* (§ 7.168)], or over a particular period of time [*Guatemala–Cement II* (§ 8.266)].

At the end of the day, as dozens of reports have confirmed, what matters is whether there is a genuine and substantial relationship of cause and effect between dumping and injury. Dumping need not be the only cause of injury, nor even the principal cause. It only needs to be *a* cause of injury. Once this is the case, as we will discuss *infra*, AD duties can be imposed to counteract the entire dumping margin and not just the resultant injury caused by the dumped good.

4. IMPOSITION OF AD DUTIES

Provided that the key legal requirements of dumping, injury, and causal link are met, a WTO Member may take one of three types of measures as redress:

- Provisional measures
- Price undertakings
- Definitive anti-dumping duties

This section will first elaborate on the requirements that WTO Members must follow when imposing each of these three forms of AD measures. We will then discuss some particular variations and nuances followed by some individual WTO Members when imposing AD measures.

---

[45] Implicitly the agreement requests economic, and not statistical significance, on the difference between the two terms, see McCloskey and Ziliak (1996).

[46] In this vein, see also the Panel report on *EC–Tube or Pipe Fittings* at § 7.366.

[47] On EC AD practice in this respect, see Vermulst (1996).

Finally, we will turn to the question of how long AD measures may be maintained.

4.1 PROVISIONAL MEASURES

Art. 7 AD allows WTO Members to impose provisional AD measures, while the IA proceeds with its full-blown investigation of an allegation of dumping by a foreign producer. To do so, the IA must first conduct a preliminary investigation that results in an affirmative preliminary determination of dumping and consequent injury to the domestic industry (Art. 7.1(ii)AD).

In addition to preliminary affirmative determinations of dumping, injury, and causation, the following conditions must also be cumulatively met:

(a) No provisional duties can be imposed sooner than 60 days from the date of initiation of the investigation (Art. 7.3 AD);

(b) Parties must have had an opportunity to present their views during the course of the investigation up to that stage (Art. 7.1(i) AD);

(c) Preliminary duties are judged necessary to prevent injury caused during the investigation (Art. 7.1(iii)AD);

Note that there is no absolute requirement for an IA to make preliminary findings. The IA may choose to skip this step and proceed directly to a final determination. However, absent preliminary determinations, a WTO Member may not apply provisional duties.

Duties imposed should be preferably in the form of security (cash deposit, or bond), although additional customs duties remain a possibility (Art. 7.2 AD). The level of such duties shall not be higher than the provisionally estimated margin of dumping.

Art. 7.4 AD limits the time period for the application of a provisional measure to "as short a period as possible" with upper bounds: Provisional measures should not be applied for more than four months, in principle, with extension to six or nine months under certain circumstances.[48] The Panel in *Mexico–Corn Syrup*,[49] found that the application of provisional measures by Mexico for more than six months was inconsistent with Art. 7.4 AD(§ 7.183).

---

[48] Provisional measures may be applied for up to six months upon request of exporters requesting a significant percentage of the trade involved and on decision of the IA concerned. Note that exporters may wish for a longer period so as to have more time to provide the information required in an AD investigation. Provisional measures may also be applied for up to six months where the IA examines whether a duty lower than the margin of dumping would be sufficient to remove the injury (i.e., applies a lesser duty rule, to be discussed *infra*). The provisional measures may be extended up to nine months under such circumstances upon request of exporters requesting a significant percentage of the trade involved and on decision of the IA concerned.

[49] Howse and Neven (2007a) discuss this report in detail.

AD duties can take on various forms, including ad valorem, fixed, or variable.[50] In the case of a fixed duty, the AD duty will be charged on the basis of a pre-determined unit. In the case of a variable duty, the IA will determine a reference price (e.g., a minimum export price or reference normal value), and an AD duty will be imposed, based on a comparison between the actual export price and this reference price.

4.2 PRICE UNDERTAKINGS

Instead of imposing AD duties, WTO Members can request and/or accept price undertakings from willing exporters (Art. 8 AD). Through a price undertaking, an exporter agrees to raise prices up to the level of the dumping margin, or up to a level established in application of the lesser duty rule, if the investigating authority agrees to this latter level. Price undertakings may not be offered to exporters until a preliminary affirmative determination of dumping, injury and causal link has been made. There is no obligation to offer price undertakings, neither is there an obligation to accept such undertakings when offered by exporters, if the authorities consider their acceptance impractical, or for other reasons including reasons of general policy. The Panel in *US–Offset Act (Byrd Amendment)*, emphasized the freedom of IAs to accept or reject price undertakings, holding that an IA is not required to examine a proposed price undertaking in an objective manner (§ 7.81). The Panel thus rejected the argument that the incentive provided through the so-called "Byrd payments"[51] combined with the important role given to the US domestic industry in accepting an undertaking from exporters in tandem violated Art. 8 AD (§ 7.80).

The acceptance of a price undertaking puts an end to the investigation with respect to the exporter concerned, unless this exporter wants the IA to continue with the investigation. In case of continuation, if the investigation ultimately leads to a negative finding of dumping or injury, the undertaking shall automatically lapse, except in cases where a negative determination is in large part due to the price undertaking itself, in which case the undertaking may be maintained for a reasonable period of time.

Art. 8.6 AD provides for a monitoring device and allows an IA to request exporters to provide information periodically relevant to the fulfillment of the undertaking, thus permitting verification. In case of a violation of an agreed undertaking, IAs are entitled to take expeditious actions, which may include the immediate application of provisional measures using best information available. Definitive duties may be lev-

---

[50] See the Panel Report for *Argentina–Poultry Antidumping Duties* (§ 7.364)

[51] We discuss the incentive in more detail *infra*. Suffice to state here that according to the challenged measure, only US companies supporting a petition to impose AD duties would subsequently profit from disbursement of duties if the end of the process would lead to the imposition of AD duties.

ied retroactively up to 90 days before the application of such provisional measures. No duties may be levied on imports pre-dating the violation.

4.3 DEFINITIVE DUTIES

A duty becomes definitive when an IA concludes its investigation and issues its final determination (*Mexico–Antidumping Measures on Rice*, AB, § 345). As the AB noted in the same report (§ 346):

> the [AD and SCM] Agreements use the term 'definitive' to distinguish duties imposed after a final determination (following an investigation) from 'provisional' duties that may be imposed under certain conditions during the course of an investigation, namely, after a preliminary determination.

The AD duty collected may not exceed the dumping margin found in the final determination (Art. 9.3 AD). As we will discuss *infra*, a WTO Member is free to decide not to impose an AD duty if it decides that it is not in the public interest. It is also free to set the AD duty at a level lower than the dumping margin, if it should choose to follow the so-called lesser-duty rule.

4.3.1 Prospective vs. Retrospective Assessment of Duties

Almost all WTO Members that are active users of AD duties employ what is known as 'prospective method' for assessing AD duties. Once the AD investigation has been finalized and the dumping margin calculated, all future imports will be burdened with the established AD duty. Under the prospective assessment, the importer pays the AD duty upon importation. The WTO Member assessing the duty is under no obligation to review whether the duty rate is correct. Instead, Art. 9.3.2 AD only requires from WTO Members to maintain a procedure whereby an importer may request a refund if the importer can demonstrate that the AD duty paid was in excess of the actual margin of dumping. As the AB stated in *Mexico–Antidumping Measures on Rice* (§ 346): "The refund of duties is conditioned solely on (i) the request being made by an importer of the product subject to the antidumping duty; and (ii) the request having been 'duly supported by evidence.' " Although procedures for the refund review vary across WTO Members employing the prospective approach, in general, the review will not result in a revised duty for future imports. Instead, for the AD duty rate to be revised under a prospective system, the party must request an interim or changed circumstance review, pursuant to Art. 11.2 AD (discussed *infra*).

The US is the only major WTO Member to employ what is known as the 'retrospective method' for assessing AD duties. Upon importation, the importer pays only a provisional duty,[52] which may take the form of a cash deposit or guarantee. The IA itself will automatically review the duties in light of actual prices observed the preceding year in the US market to determine the definitive duty. This is known in US parlance as an "administrative review." Like the refund review under the prospective system, if the AD duty charged is higher than the actual dumping margin, the difference will be refunded. However, unlike the prospective system, if the AD duty charged is too low, then the IA will assess the additional difference upon the importer with the bill for the definitive duty. The newly-calculated definitive duty then serves as the basis for the provisional duty for the following year, and the process described above starts all over again.[53]

In a nutshell, the key differences between the two approaches concern whether:

(a) The importer pays the AD duty upon importation or only a cash deposit;

(b) The importer must request review of the AD duty, or the review takes place automatically;

(c) The review results in higher AD duty being charged for the goods that have already been imported;

(d) The review results in a higher AD duty rate assessed for future goods imported into the country

Irrespective of whether a prospective or retrospective approach is followed, AD duties cannot be imposed retroactively except under two very limited conditions provided for in Art. 10 AD:

(a) Duties can be imposed retroactively up to the moment when provisional measures had been imposed, if, following a finding of injury, provisional duties had been imposed; or, following a finding of threat of injury and a demonstration that in the absence of provisional measures, injury would have materialized, provisional measures had been imposed (Art. 10.2 AD);[54]

---

[52] A proposal has been made during the Doha Round to eliminate the requirement that a request be made, thereby making it mandatory for the authorities to refund any excessive duties collected. Linked to this is the proposed amendment of Art. 9.3 AD introducing a requirement to establish, upon request, the margin of dumping based upon normal values contemporaneous with the export transactions, see WTO Doc. TN/RL/GEN/131.

[53] Although the level of dumping may vary, there is no requirement to conduct a new injury analysis, unless a specific request is made to this effect. Proponents of the retrospective system note that the fear of higher definitive duties each year imposes a pricing discipline on exporters to the US market.

[54] The retroactive application is actually only a partial retroactivity: if the definitive antidumping duty is higher than the provisional duty paid, the difference shall not be collected, but if the definitive duty is lower, the difference shall be reimbursed (Art. 10.3 AD). In the case of a determination of threat of injury without the additional demonstration of the preventive effect of the measure, the provisional duties paid shall be refunded and any bonds released in an expeditious manner (Art. 10.4 AD). It goes without saying that were a negative final determination

(b) Duties can be imposed retroactively until 90 days prior to the imposition of provisional measures, but in no case prior to the initiation of investigation[55], if there is a history of dumping and injury, or if the importer was aware of dumping practices, and, in either case, the injury was caused by 'massive dumped imports' in a short period which, because of, *inter alia,* timing and volume of the dumped imports, are likely to seriously undermine remedial effects that AD duties might have (Art. 10.6 AD).[56]

In order to be able to collect duties retroactively to the period preceding the application of provisional measures, the Agreement provides in Art. 10.7 AD that the authorities, may, after initiation, take such measures as the withholding of appraisement or assessment as may be necessary for that purpose. The one condition is that the authorities must have sufficient evidence that the conditions for such extended retroactive application are satisfied.

4.3.2 Who are Duties Imposed Against?

In principle, individual dumping margins should be assessed for each known exporter. Art. 6.10 AD states that:

> The authorities shall, as a rule, determine an individual margin of dumping for each known exporter or producer concerned of the product under investigation.

The term 'known exporter' has been interpreted by the AB as referring to all exporters that have been identified in the petition, as well as those who have voluntarily appeared before the IA (*Mexico–Antidumping Measures on Rice*).

The Panel in *EC–Salmon (Norway)* held that it was legitimate for an IA to exclude exporters non-producing at the moment when the investigation was being held (§ 7.167).

However, under certain circumstances, IAs may legitimately assess non-individualized dumping margins, including when an IA:

- Engages in the practice of "collapsing" when calculating dumping margins, as discussed earlier for the *Korea–Certain Paper* case
- Treats companies "controlled" by the same entity collectively when calculating dumping margins, as discussed earlier for the *EC–Fasteners (China)* case

---

made, any cash deposits made during the period of provisional measures shall be refunded, and any bonds released (Art. 10.5 AD).

[55] As per Art. 7.3 AD, provisional measures may be applied as of 60 days following initiation.

[56] The rationale for this provision is to address cases where, exporters quickly dump their exports after the initiation of an investigation and stop exporting thereafter. For further discussion of the meaning of "massive dumped imports" requirement, see the Panel Report for *US–Hot Rolled Steel* (§§ 7.166–67).

- Engages in the practice of sampling (already discussed earlier, but elaborated upon below)
- Performs a new shipper review (Art. 9.5 AD)
- Assesses an AD duty on "unknown exporters" that were not identified by the IA at the time of the original investigation

We discuss the latter three scenarios below.

(a) Sampling: Art. 9.4 AD explains the maximum permissible AD duty that an IA can apply to non-sampled exporters or producers when it has sampled in accordance with Art. 6.10 AD:

> When the authorities have limited their examination in accordance with the second sentence of paragraph 10 of Article 6, any antidumping duty applied to imports from exporters or producers not included in the examination shall not exceed:
>
> (i) the weighted average margin of dumping established with respect to the selected exporters or producers or,
>
> (ii) where the liability for payment of antidumping duties is calculated on the basis of a prospective normal value, the difference between the weighted average normal value of the selected exporters or producers and the export prices of exporters or producers not individually examined,
>
> provided that the authorities shall disregard for the purpose of this paragraph any zero and de minimis margins and margins established under the circumstances referred to in paragraph 8 of Article 6. The authorities shall apply individual duties or normal values to imports from any exporter or producer not included in the examination who has provided the necessary information during the course of the investigation, as provided for in subparagraph 10.2 of Article 6.

Consequently, an IA will calculate individual dumping margins for all exporters that have been sampled, and will apply at most, the WA to all other known exporters. An individual exporter who has not been included in the investigation can, under Art. 6.10.2 AD, submit evidence and request from an IA to apply an individually calculated duty on his exports, if practicable. Importantly, when calculating the maximum duty for non-sampled producers or exporters, an IA must disregard de minimis and zero dumping margins, and cannot base itself on margins established through recourse to the facts available provision of Art. 6.8 AD:[57] the AB in its report on *US–Hot–Rolled Steel*, held that, whenever recourse was made to Art. 9.4 AD, an IA could not include in the average the results of

---

[57] We discuss recourse to best information available *infra*. Suffice to say here that, when facing non-cooperative behavior on behalf of exporters, an IA can, assuming certain statutory conditions have been met, disregard submitted evidence and make its own assessment regarding dumping margin.

a margin based even in part on facts available, that is, through recourse to Art. 6.8 AD (§ 122).

(b) New shippers: Art. 9.5 AD allows exporters who did not export any products during the period of investigation (or, who simply did not produce at all during the same period), to request from the IA to calculate an individual margin of dumping in order to determine their duty rate. These are the so-called "new shippers". Art. 9.5 AD provides for them as follows:

> If a product is subject to antidumping duties in an importing Member, the authorities shall promptly carry out a review for the purpose of determining individual margins of dumping for any exporters or producers in the exporting country in question who have not exported the product to the importing Member during the period of investigation, provided that these exporters or producers can show that they are not related to any of the exporters or producers in the exporting country who are subject to the antidumping duties on the product. Such a review shall be initiated and carried out on an accelerated basis, compared to normal duty assessment and review proceedings in the importing Member. No antidumping duties shall be levied on imports from such exporters or producers while the review is being carried out. The authorities may, however, withhold appraisement and/or request guarantees to ensure that, should such a review result in a determination of dumping in respect of such producers or exporters, antidumping duties can be levied retroactively to the date of the initiation of the review.

The Panel and the AB, in *Mexico–Antidumping Measures on Rice,* held that Art. 9.5 AD:

> clearly does not subject the right to an expedited new shipper review to a showing of a "representative" volume of export sales.[58]

(c) Unknown exporters: Practice reveals the existence of another category of exporters, not foreseen in the AD agreement: "unknown exporters" that were not identified by the authorities at the time of the investigation. Exporters could be unknown because they managed to hide (let us call this, un-cooperative behavior), or because the authority did not take any reasonable efforts to identify them (for example, they continued to export and were never requested to appear before the authority), or for other reasons as well. With respect to unknown exporters, the AD Agreement is silent as to whether they should pay a duty at all, and if yes, how much. Practice suggests that a 'residual rate' is calculated and imposed on their exports.

---

[58] See § 7.266 of the Panel report, and § 323 of the AB report.

In *Mexico–Antidumping Measures on Rice*, the WTO adjudicating bodies had the opportunity to pronounce on the consistency of some national practice in this respect. The Mexican IA (Economía) imposed duties on unknown exporters equalling the amount of the highest individual dumping margin. The question raised by the US claim was whether the AD Agreement imposes any limits on the amount of the residual duty. In US practice, the residual rate (WA) found in the context of an Art. 9.4 AD determination must be applied to new shipments as well as other unknown exporters. The US had put forward a claim to the effect that Mexico had violated its obligations under the AD Agreement: in its view, Mexico should impose on new shipments, prior to the expedited review, a maximum AD duty which should not exceed the WA of duties imposed: the residual rate should equal the 'all others rate', calculated in accordance with Art. 9.4 AD for exporters not included in the sample. In fact, the US was requesting Mexico to adopt the US practice in this respect. The Panel was not convinced by this argument, as it considered that Art. 9.4 AD provided a specific methodology with regard to the calculation of the duty for those interested parties that did not form part of the sample, but that there existed no requirement to apply that methodology in a case which did not involve sampling (§ 7.158). We quote from § 7.159:

> The US argument that the placement of this provision immediately preceding Article 9.5 of the *AD Agreement* dealing with new shipper reviews implies that its rules also apply to non-shipping exporters is not convincing, as we do not find that anything can be deduced in and of itself from the sequence of provisions in the *Agreement*, particularly when the provision in question relates to an exceptional situation, while the subsequent provision does not. The United States also argues that the non-sampled interested parties and the new shippers dealt with by Article 9.5 are in a similar position and that by analogy the same Article 9.4 methodology for the calculation of a residual duty rate should apply. We are not convinced that the text of the *Agreement* supports this view. In this respect, we find particularly relevant the absence of any cross-referencing in Article 9.5 of the *AD Agreement* dealing with new shippers to the calculation methodology of Article 9.4 of the *AD Agreement*. This absence of cross-referencing is particularly conspicuous if one were to accept, arguendo, the analogous situation of non-sampled and non-shipping exporters. Indeed, especially in such a situation, one would expect the drafters to have explicitly referred to Article 9.4 of the *AD Agreement*. As on other occasions, where the drafters intended to see obligations apply in similar circumstances, they explicitly provided for such cross-referencing. We recall in this respect that the AB also found that the absence of such cross-referencing to obligations contained in other provisions is

revealing of the absence of such an obligation. We find that Article 9.4 of the *AD Agreement* does not refer to non-shipping exporters outside a sampling situation, and that there was therefore no obligation for the Mexican authorities to calculate a residual duty margin for Producers Rice based on the 'neutral' methodology set forth in Article 9.4 of the *AD Agreement*. We therefore reject the US claim in this respect. (italics in the original).

The AB, on appeal, did not uphold this Panel finding, and, instead, went on to state that an authority is not permitted to impose a residual duty rate based on facts available. According to the AB, an authority which imposes a duty on unidentified exporters based on facts available, including facts from the petition, is acting in violation of Art. 6.8 AD, and Annex II, (§§ 259–260); putting exporters on notice that facts available will be used is a pre-condition for the use of facts available. For obvious reasons, this can never be met in the case of unidentified exporters. The AB did not however, establish the maximum amount of duty to be imposed in similar cases.

4.4 COUNTERACTING DUMPING THROUGH OTHER MEASURES BESIDES AD DUTIES

May a WTO Member enact another measure, besides AD duties, to counteract dumping? Art. 18.1 AD provides an answer to this question:

> No specific action against dumping of exports from another Member can be taken except in accordance with the provisions of GATT 1994, as interpreted by this Agreement.

A footnote to this Article (footnote 24) pertinently adds:

> This is not intended to preclude action under other relevant provisions of GATT 1994, as appropriate.

In *US–Offset Act (Byrd Amendment)*, the Panel was asked to interpret the meaning of this provision. At issue in the dispute were the Byrd Amendment[59] payments which allowed US domestic producers that had supported the AD petition to receive monetary compensation from the collection of AD duties. The Panel found that such payments constituted a "specific action against dumping" under Art. 18.1 AD and were hence illegal (§ 7.18). On appeal, the AB affirmed the Panel's findings (§§ 255–256 and 265).[60]

More recently, in *US–Antidumping and Countervailing Duties (China)*, the AB held that a WTO Member cannot impose both AD and coun-

---

[59] Its official acronym is CDSOA (Continued Dumping and Subsidies Offset Act).

[60] The heart of the issue here was whether Byrd Amendment payments to the injured US industry would dis-incentivize exporters to the US market who would stop dumping as a result. Horn and Mavroidis (2005a), and Bhagwati and Mavroidis (2004) discuss this report.

tervailing duties to address the same transaction (§§ 550ff. and especially 583 and 591). In other words, when an injury arises to a domestic industry as a result of dumping by a subsidized exporter, a WTO Member may not "double dip"; it must choose between using AD and countervailing duties to redress the same injury.

4.5 PUBLIC INTEREST CLAUSE

Although the imposition of an AD duty will benefit injured domestic producers, it may harm downstream consumers of dumped good. Such consumers will face higher prices as a result of the AD duty being imposed.

As a result, Art. 6.12 AD requires:

The authorities shall provide opportunities for industrial users of the product under investigation, and for representative consumer organizations in cases where the product is commonly sold at the retail level, to provide information which is relevant to the investigation regarding dumping, injury and causality.

Some WTO Members go a bit further than that: In particular, the EU[61] and Canada have imposed an additional requirement on themselves to examine whether the imposition of duties would not be against the public interest.

4.6 LESSER DUTY RULE

The level of AD duties can, but does not have to be equal to the established dumping margin; it can be lower, if a lower duty can adequately take care of the injury caused by dumping. Art. 9.1 AD permits a WTO Member to follow the so-called "lesser duty rule":

It is *desirable* that the imposition be permissive in the territory of all Members, and that the duty be less than the margin if such lesser duty would be adequate to remove the injury to the domestic industry (emphasis added).

The decision to impose a lesser (than the dumping margin) duty, depends solely on the investigating authority. The lesser duty rule is consequence of the fact that dumping is not illegal but simply unfair, and it should not always be punished in full as such as long as its nefarious consequences (i.e., injury) have been eliminated. The EU has adhered to this rule and consistently observed it in their antidumping practice.[62]

---

[61] Hoekman and Mavroidis (1996) discuss in detail the EU practice.

[62] On EU practice on this score, see Vermulst and Waer (1997). A proposal has been tabled in the Doha round in favor of mandatory application of the lesser duty rule, see WTO Doc. TN/RL/GEN/99, of March 3, 2006. The US issued a negative reaction, see WTO Doc. TN/RL/GEN/58.

4.7 DURATION AND ADMINISTRATIVE REVIEWS OF AD DUTIES

AD duties can be imposed for, in principle, five years (Art. 11.3 AD). At the end of the five-year period, a WTO Member may conduct a sunset review, discussed *infra*, to decide whether to continue the AD duties.

During the five-year period, the IA may choose to conduct an administrative review,[63] (sometimes referred to as "changed circumstances review"). This can take place either on the initiative of the IA (usually referred to as "self-initiated" or ex officio review), or upon request by any interested party which submits positive information substantiating the need for a review (Art. 11.2 AD). The former will take place when warranted, but the latter, only after a reasonable lapse of time has passed. The term "reasonable period of time" has not been interpreted by Panels so far.

An IA, when conducting an administrative review, must (Art. 11.2 AD):

> examine whether the continued imposition of the duty is necessary to offset dumping, whether the injury would be likely to continue or recur if the duty were removed or varied, or both.

The ambit of the administrative review can vary: It suffices, as the Panel in *US–DRAMS* underscored (§ 6.28), that the IA has shown continuation or recurrence of one of the two elements (dumping, injury). The IA has the option to review of continuation or recurrence of both elements, but is not obliged to do so. The extent of the review has, nevertheless, important repercussions for the remaining life of the AD duties in place:

> (a) If a narrow review (continuation or recurrence of either dumping or injury) takes place, and no sunset review takes place,[64] duties will remain in place for a maximum period of five years counting from the date of the original imposition;
>
> (b) If a comprehensive review (continuation or recurrence of both dumping and injury) takes place, duties will remain in place for five years counting from the end of the administrative review. In this case, the administrative review entails the same consequences as a sunset review.

Various Panels have discussed the conditions under which it is warranted to conduct an administrative review ex officio. In *US–Antidumping Measures on OCTG*, the Panel discussed the US system, where a request for a 'changed circumstances'-review can be based on the

---

[63] This should not be confused with the annual review conducted by the US IA under its retrospective approach of assessing AD duty, which is also referred to as an "administrative review."

[64] As we explain in more detail *infra*, unless a sunset review takes place, AD duties lapse five years after their imposition.

general review provisions, or on the basis of no dumping for three years. In the latter case, a company seeking revocation on the basis of no dumping for three years must demonstrate that it had made sales in the US market in commercial quantities during that period. The Panel held that a company which did not satisfy the additional requirements for revocation on the basis of no dumping was nonetheless entitled to seek revocation of the antidumping duty order as applied to it under the general changed circumstances provision, provided it could supply information substantiating the need for review, in accordance with Art. 11.2 AD (§§ 7.164–165). Both in this case (§§ 7.173–174), as well as in *US–DRAMS* (§§ 6.58–59),[65] WTO Panels have held that, absence of dumping for a period of three years and six months did not in and of itself mandate a self-initiated review. This is probably too much of a sweeping statement: duties are imposed if dumping causes injury for five years. If review is not warranted after 70% of the life-time of duties has lapsed and no dumping has occurred, then one might legitimately wonder whether a review, in the Panels' understanding, is warranted only in case where the health of the industry has improved. Recall however, that no AD duties can be imposed in the first place if injury is the outcome of factors other than dumping.

The AB in *Mexico–Antidumping Measures on Rice* agreed with the Panel that, to require that a 'representative volume of export sales' has taken place as a condition for conducting a changed circumstances review was inconsistent with the Agreement (§ 316):

> Article 68 of the Act requires as a rule that each time an interested party is unable to show that volume of exports during the review period was representative, such a review is to be denied. . . . The change in circumstances is unrelated to the export side of the equation. An interested party is entitled to a changed circumstances review under Article 11.2 of the *AD Agreement* and 21.2 of the *SCM Agreement*, if it submits positive information substantiating the need for a review. What such positive information relates to will depend from case to case, and such positive information does not, in our view, necessarily include that a representative number of exports sales were made. We consider that, by requiring the authority to reject a review each time the volume of export sales was not representative, even in cases where the change in circumstances is unrelated to the export price, Article 68 of the Act requires the authority to reject reviews in a manner which is inconsistent with Article 11.2 of the *AD Agreement*. (italics in the original).

The Panel in *EC–Tube or Pipe Fittings* dealt, *inter alia*, with the argument by Brazil regarding whether the devaluation of Brazil's national

---

[65] See Francois and Palmeter (2008).

currency (which time-wise coincided with the last weeks of the investigation) was, in and of itself, a reason for the EU to launch on its own initiative a review of the necessity to keep in place the antidumping duties. The Panel responded in the negative (§ 7.116), and concluded as follows (§ 7.118):

> The findings of the panel in US–DRAMS are relevant here. In examining the nature of a review conducted under Article 11.2 AD, that panel rejected the view that Article 11.2 'requires revocation as soon as an exporter is found to have ceased dumping, and that the continuation of an antidumping duty is precluded a priori in any circumstances other than where there is present dumping'. This reasoning would suggest to us that the *Antidumping Agreement* does not require a decision to be made by the investigating authorities after the end of the IP not to impose duties, nor to review the imposition of a duty immediately after it is imposed based on events between the end of the IP and the time of imposition, much less on the basis of events occurring before the end of the IP. (italics in the original).

In the same case, the Panel had also rejected a claim by Brazil to the effect that the determination could not have been made on the basis of positive evidence as the data from before the devaluation were not informative of the situation that prevailed at the time the duties were imposed, that is, when the devaluation occurred. The Panel rejected this argument, holding that these types of changes could be dealt with in subsequent reviews of the measure (§ 7.106).

The Panel in *US–DRAMS* held that, since the subject-matter of an administrative review was a forward-looking analysis, which necessarily entailed uncertainty, one could not require mathematical certainty from an IA when formulating its conclusions. Some degree of imprecision would thus, be unavoidable, and therefore, permissible (§ 6.43).[66] Finally, a public notice must be issued any time a review is initiated (Art. 12.3 AD).

4.8 SUNSET REVIEWS

4.8.1 Absent a Sunset Review, the AD Duty Will Lapse

AD duties last for five years, in principle, unless the IA determines as per Art. 11.3 AD:

> in a review initiated before that date on their own initiative or upon a duly substantiated request made by or on behalf of the domestic industry within a reasonable period of time prior to that date, that the expiry of the duty would be likely to lead to

---

[66] Compare Howse and Staiger (2007).

continuation or recurrence of dumping and injury. The duty may remain in force pending the outcome of such a review.

The five-year period counts from:

(a) The date of the original imposition; or

(b) From the date of the most recent administrative review under Art. 11.2 AD, if the review at hand covered both dumping and injury; or

(c) From the date of the most recent sunset review.

Since duties can stay in place after the five year-period only following a review, it is inferred that, absent such a review, any AD duties imposed will have to be eliminated. In the words of the AB in *US–Carbon Steel*[67] dealing with the sunset provision in the SCM Agreement, which is identical to that of the AD Agreement (§ 88):

> An automatic time-bound termination of countervailing duties that have been in place for five years from the original investigation or a subsequent comprehensive review is at the heart of this provision. Termination of a countervailing duty is the rule and its continuation is the exception.

A sunset review may be initiated either ex officio, or upon a duly substantiated request. When the latter occurs, the request must be deposited within a reasonable period of time prior to the expiry of the five-year period. The last sentence of Art. 11.3 AD clarifies that duties will remain in place during the review process.

The AD Agreement does not impose an obligation to start ex officio sunset reviews on a specific date. As a result, WTO Members retain some discretion on this score. Since the imposed duties will remain in place while the review is going ahead, there is a risk that WTO Members might keep duties in place for a period longer than the statutory five year-period, by starting a review at as late a stage as possible. This risk is somewhat addressed through the discipline included in Art. 11.4 AD which stipulates that a review should normally be completed within 12 months. US law provides for an automatic initiation of sunset reviews. The statutory requirements of the US law in this respect were clarified as follows by the AB in *US–Carbon Steel* (§ 101):[68]

> Section 751(c)(2) of the Tariff Act directs USDOC to publish a notice of initiation of a sunset review no later than 30 days before, *inter alia*, the fifth anniversary of the date of publication of a countervailing duty order. Section 351.218(b) of Title 19 of the Regulations confirms that USDOC will conduct a sunset review

---

[67] Grossman and Mavroidis (2007b) discuss this respect in detail and underscore the consequences of automaticity in this respect.

[68] This case concerned a sunset review of CVDs.

of each countervailing duty order. Both the Sunset Policy Bulletin and the SAA describe the initiation of sunset reviews by USDOC as *'automatic'*. (emphasis in the original).

The AB held that this law was not inconsistent with the requirements of the SCM Agreement (§ 118). Confirmation in the antidumping context as well, came with the Panel report in *US–Corrosion–Resistant Steel Sunset Review*: facing the same issue, the Panel held that automatic self-initiation procedures in the context of a sunset review were not inconsistent with the AD Agreement, because they did not necessarily[69] result in continuation of the duties in place (§ 7.55).

4.8.2 Standard of Review for Sunset Reviews

For an IA to lawfully keep the duties in place, it will have to demonstrate at the sunset review-stage that revocation of AD duties would be likely to lead to continuation or recurrence of dumping and injury (Art. 11.3 AD). The terms "continuation" and "recurrence" appearing in the body of this provision refer to two different factual situations: the first term presupposes that dumping and/or injury have not ceased to exist during the period of imposition of AD duties; the latter presupposes that the opposite has happened during the same period. Continuation or recurrence should be "likely", and this term has been understood by the AB as equivalent to the term "probable" (*US–Corrosion–Resistant Steel Sunset Review*, § 111). As a result, the ensuing standard of review applied by WTO adjudicating bodies cannot be overly demanding in this respect. The methodology used to demonstrate the likelihood of continuation or recurrence is not prejudged by the AD Agreement: in this regard, Art. 11.3 AD imposes an obligation of result, rather than of specific conduct (and thus, leaves discretion in the hands of the IA with the ensuing consequence for the standard of review). The Panel, in its report on *US–Corrosion–Resistant Steel Sunset Review*, dealt with the consistency of a US statute, which expressed the likelihood-standard in negative formulation: duties would be removed, only if it was unlikely that their removal would lead to recurrence or continuation of dumping and injury. It did not find the US statute to be inconsistent with Art. 11.3 AD (§§ 7.227–228), and the AB did not disturb this finding either. In *US–OCTG Sunset Reviews*, the AB, while agreeing with Argentina that the IA's likelihood-determinations under Art. 11.3 AD must be based on positive evidence, it made it clear that, since a review is by definition a forward-looking exercise, some speculation about future events cannot be avoided; in other words, the requirement to show likelihood on positive evidence should not be understood as a requirement to completely eliminate uncertainty about the course of future events (§§ 340–341).

---

[69] See the analysis of Howse and Staiger (2007) on this score.

The AB in *US–OCTG Sunset Reviews* addressed, *inter alia*, an argument by the complainant (Argentina) to the effect that an IA is obliged, by virtue of Art. 11.3 AD, to establish a precise time-frame within which continuation or recurrence of dumping and injury would likely occur. The US statute did not specify the time-horizon within which the likelihood of recurrence or continuation should occur, and in Argentina's view, this was unlawful since Art. 11.3 AD imposes a temporal limitation which must be imminent (§ 358). The AB rejected Argentina's argument. It underscored the Panel's finding that likelihood should be evaluated within the reasonably foreseeable future (with no further precision being required), and cautioned that an assessment whether injury is likely to recur that focuses too far in the future would be highly speculative and hence unhelpful for the purposes of sunset reviews (§ 360).[70] In its view, a determination of injury can be properly reasoned and rest on a sufficient factual basis even though the time-frame for the injury determination is not explicitly mentioned (AB, *US–OCTG Sunset Reviews*, § 364).

The likelihood of continuation or recurrence of dumping and/or injury must be determined by the IA. The term "determine" appearing in the body of Art. 11.3 AD has been interpreted in case law as dictating a standard that obliges authorities to reach their conclusions on positive evidence, and to justify them as well (AB, *US–OCTG Sunset Reviews*, §§ 179–180). To understand what the "positive evidence"-standard entails, we refer to the measures challenged in *US–OCTG Sunset Reviews*, which offer a very appropriate illustration to this effect. The US law on sunset reviews contained two types of waivers:

> (a) Those applicable in situations where an interested party (exporter) has provided incomplete information to questions asked by the IA during the review process (in US parlance, "deemed waiver"); and
>
> (b) Those applicable in situations where the exporter has declared that it will not participate in the proceedings ("affirmative waiver").

Where an interested party waives its right to participate in the review process (either through affirmative-, or deemed waiver), the US IA will presume likelihood of continuation or recurrence of dumping, without having to investigate to what extent this has actually been the case. The Panel, in its report on *US–OCTG Sunset Reviews*, had found both types of waivers to be WTO-inconsistent (§§ 7.91–99). On appeal, the US argued that the Panel erred since it had not sufficiently taken into account the process followed by US authorities: waivers were used when a company-specific review was being conducted; company-specific reviews, however, were only the first leg of the sunset review. Subsequent to this exercise, the US IA would examine the likelihood of recurrence or continuation of

---

[70] Grossman and Wauters (2008) concur offering other reasons to support this conclusion.

dumping on an order-wide basis.[71] The AB rejected the US argument and confirmed the Panel in this respect. In its view, even though reviews were order-wide, the input to the final determination was flawed by virtue of the fact that a determination was based on waivers, that is, not on positive evidence. We quote from § 234 of the AB report:

> We agree with the Panel's analysis of the impact of the waiver provisions on order-wide determinations. Because the waiver provisions require the USDOC to arrive at affirmative company-specific determinations without regard to any evidence on record, these determinations are merely assumptions made by the agency, rather than findings supported by evidence. The United States contends that respondents waiving the right to participate in a sunset review do so 'intentionally', with full knowledge that, as a result of their failure to submit evidence, the evidence placed on the record by the domestic industry is likely to result in an unfavourable determination on an order-wide basis. In these circumstances, we see no fault in making an unfavourable order-wide determination by taking into account evidence provided by the domestic industry in support thereof. However, the USDOC also takes into account, in such circumstances, statutorily-mandated assumptions. Thus, even assuming that the USDOC takes into account the totality of record evidence in making its order-wide determination, it is clear that, as a result of the operation of the waiver provisions, certain order-wide likelihood determinations made by the USDOC will be based, at least in part, on statutorily-mandated assumptions about a company's likelihood of dumping. In our view, this result is inconsistent with the obligation of an investigating authority under Article 11.3 to 'arrive at a reasoned conclusion' on the basis of 'positive evidence'.

The AB in *US–OCTG Sunset Reviews* specified that, when conducting its review, an IA could use information from the record of the original investigation or subsequent reviews, provided that it took a fresh look at it. The AB did not specifically address the question raised by the complainant (Argentina), whether an IA could base its conclusions solely on already-used information, as it considered that this was not what the US had done in the case at hand. The AB did, however, agree with the views expressed by another AB Division[72] in the countervailing duty case, *US–Carbon Steel*, that mere reliance on the determination made in the original investigation would not be sufficient (§ 328). In the same report, the AB also clarified that a decision to continue the imposition of duties could

---

[71] This term refers to all companies investigated and, in practice, is synonymous to country-wide determinations.

[72] This term refers to the three (out of seven) AB members who adjudicate a particular dispute.

be based on limited observations: in the case at hand, Argentina complained that the US IA did not base its decision on positive evidence since, following the imposition of AD duties, there were only a few transactions between Argentina and the United States. The AB, upholding the Panel's view in this respect, held that the small volume of export sales to the US market was not an impediment towards a finding that dumping would continue to occur were the duties in place to be revoked (§ 346).[73] Consequently, limited observations, in the sense of a small volume of export sales, might suffice for the purposes of conducting a lawful review; moreover, facts that have already been evaluated in the original investigation can be re-evaluated at the review stage. It appears, however, that a fresh determination, based on credible evidence will be necessary to establish that the continuation of the duty is warranted.[74]

Art. 11.4 AD provides that the provisions of Art. 6 AD (regarding evidence and certain procedural requirements) shall apply to sunset reviews: Reviews shall be carried out expeditiously, and shall, normally, be concluded within 12 months of initiation of the review. The due process rights of interested parties must be respected also in the context of a sunset review. With respect to the applicability of the basic due process provisions (Arts. 6.1, and 6.2 AD), the AB, in its reports on *US–Corrosion Resistant Steel Sunset Reviews*, and *US–OCTG Sunset Reviews*, stated that these procedural rules clearly applied to sunset reviews because of the cross-reference in Art. 11.4 AD, and that it was, therefore, very important to allow, also in a sunset review, interested parties to present evidence and defend their case. In the words of the AB in its report on *US–Corrosion Resistant Steel Sunset Reviews* (§ 152):

> Article 6 requires all interested parties to have a full opportunity to defend their interests. In particular, Article 6.1 requires authorities to give all interested parties notice of the information required and ample opportunity to present in writing evidence that those parties consider relevant. Articles 6.2, 6.4 and 6.9 provide other examples of the kind of opportunities that investigating authorities must give each interested party . . . They therefore confirm that investigating authorities have certain specific obligations towards each exporter or producer in a sunset review.

4.8.3 Substantive Requirements for Sunset Reviews

We start with the question of whether the standards applied during the original investigation are relevant at the review stage as well. In a nutshell, the answer by Panels and the AB has been that, since sunset reviews and original investigations are distinct processes with different

---

[73] See also the Panel report on *US–OCTG Sunset Reviews* at § 7.303.
[74] See the AB report on *US–Carbon Steel* at § 88.

purposes, the disciplines applicable to original investigations cannot be automatically imported into review processes.[75] In this vein, the Panel in *US–Corrosion–Resistant Steel Sunset Review*, held that the de minimis-thresholds applicable during the original investigation, in the absence of explicit language or cross-referencing to this effect are not applicable in the context of a review (§§ 7.70–71). The Panel concluded (§ 7.85):

> On the basis of this textual analysis of the relevant provisions of the *Antidumping Agreement*, we conclude that the 2 per cent *de minimis* standard of Article 5.8 does not apply in the context of sunset reviews. In this context, we again observe that, in light of the qualitative differences between sunset reviews and investigations, it is unsurprising that the obligations applying to these two distinct processes are not identical. (italics in the original).[76]

The AB in *US–OCTG Sunset Reviews* went on to find that, when it comes to establishing injury, an IA does not have to respect the standards included in Art. 3 AD (§ 280).[77] The AB did not go the full nine yards and establish what exactly is required to observe for an injury determination at the sunset-stage to be WTO-consistent.[78] The AB did add, on the other hand, that an IA may, without being obliged to do so, borrow from its analysis under Art. 3 AD (the original investigation), when conducting its review analysis (§ 284): however, in this case, if the injury analysis is inconsistent with Art. 3 AD, it will be deemed inconsistent with Art. 11.3 AD as well: the Panel report in *EU–Footwear (China)* held as much (§§ 7.337ff.). This finding does not seem to totally square with the finding in the AB report on *US–OCTG Sunset Reviews* that the injury-standard is not the same in the original investigation and the sunset review; eventually it is only through clarifications as to what exactly the injury standard entails at the sunset review-stage that inconsistencies in case law will be avoided.

The Panel in *US–OCTG Sunset Reviews* faced, *inter alia*, a claim that, in the absence of specific language to this effect, cumulation was not permissible; consequently, the US, by cumulating imports from various sources, was acting inconsistently with its obligations under the AD Agreement. The Panel, based on textual and contextual arguments, held

---

[75] See the AB reports on *US–Corrosion–Resistant Steel Sunset Review* at §§ 106–107, *US–Carbon Steel* at § 87, and *US–OCTG Sunset Reviews* at § 359.

[76] The AB reached a similar conclusion in the countervailing duty context in its report on *US–Carbon Steel* (§§ 81–84).

[77] Same findings are reported in the Panel report on *EU–Footwear (China)* at §§ 7.330ff. Note however, that the opposite is true in EU law: in Euroalliages, T–188/99 (2001), the Tribunal found that the standards applicable in the original investigation are applicable at the sunset-stage as well; in Europe Chemi Com, C–422/02 (2005), the Court confirmed the Tribunal's case law, invoking the EU interest as justification for its decision.

[78] Also see the Panel report on *US–Antidumping Measures on OCTG* at § 7.117. In this case, the Panel went on to examine whether the USITC determination of the likely volume of dumped imports, their likely price effects, and their likely impact was that of an unbiased and objective investigating authority (§§ 7.122–7.143).

that various provisions in the AD Agreement make it clear that cumulation was permissible throughout the investigation and the review processes, but that the standards regarding cumulation during the original investigation reflected in Art. 3.3 AD were not applicable in the context of reviews (§§ 7.323–336).[79] The AB confirmed this finding (§§ 300–302).[80] In *US–Antidumping Measures on OCTG*, the AB confirmed its view that Art. 3.3 AD did not apply to sunset reviews, but emphasized that on occasion a cumulative assessment might be inappropriate in light of the conditions of competition in the market place (§ 171).

With respect to the calculation of dumping duties at the review stage, the obligations imposed on an IA have also been interpreted to be less stringent than the corresponding obligations during the original investigation. The Panel in *US–Corrosion–Resistant Steel Sunset Review* held that during the review, an IA need not calculate in precise manner the dumping margins which would result in case it removed the duties in place. Rather, because uncertainty is inherent in any forward-looking study, some reasonableness-standard was warranted and, consequently, an IA should not be requested to make a determination of dumping in the sense of Art. 2 AD, or provide a precise amount of dumping margins (§§ 7.162–180). This did not mean, according to the Panel, that evidence of dumping was not relevant for likelihood of recurrence or continuation of dumping determination (§ 7.180). On appeal, the AB confirmed this view (§§ 123–124), albeit adding that, where a WTO Member goes ahead and does calculate dumping margins (although no such requirement exists in the AD Agreement), it should do so only in accordance with Art. 2 AD (§§ 127–128). The same Panel faced the question whether an IA would be required, by analogy with the obligation included in Art. 6.10 AD, to calculate an individual margin of dumping for each exporter or producer investigated, and to make a determination of likelihood of recurrence or continuation of dumping and injury for each exporter or producer under review. The Panel considered that no such company-specific likelihood determination was required, and a determination could thus be made on an order-wide basis (§§ 7.207–208). The AB confirmed this view. It acknowledged that Art. 11.4 AD contained an explicit cross-reference to the provisions of Art. 6 AD (regarding evidence and procedure) making these rules applicable to review situations. Art. 6.10 AD, which requires from IAs to calculate individual margins of dumping, could not apply in a review because, according to the AB, an IA was not required under Art. 11.3 AD to calculate dumping margins in the first place (§ 155). This finding has, of course, the important consequence that a company can remain subject to an antidumping order even though it is no longer dumping, and its sales will continue to be monitored and remain under threat of antidumping action for another five years.

---

[79] See also the Panel report on *US–Corrosion–Resistant Steel Sunset Review*, at § 7.102.

[80] See also the Panel report on *US–Antidumping Measures on OCTG*, at §§ 7.147–151.

The single most important case law contribution in this respect concerns the absence of necessity to demonstrate causal link between future dumping and future injury. The AB held that Art. 11.3 AD requires from an IA to make a determination concerning likelihood of dumping and injury but not of a causal link between the two: in *US–Antidumping Measures on OCTG*,[81] the AB first confirmed that a causal link between dumping and injury was fundamental to the imposition and maintenance of an antidumping duty under the AD Agreement. The AB was of the view, however, that, because the review contemplated in Art. 11.3 AD was a distinct process with a "different" purpose (than the original investigation), a causal link between dumping and injury did not need to be established anew. We quote from §§ 123–124:

> Therefore, what is essential for an affirmative determination under Article 11.3 is proof of likelihood of continuation or recurrence of dumping and injury, if the duty expires. The nature and extent of the evidence required for such proof will vary with the facts and circumstances of the case under review. Furthermore, as the Appellate Body has emphasized previously, determinations under Article 11.3 must rest on a 'sufficient factual basis' that allows the investigating authority to draw 'reasoned and adequate conclusions'. These being the requirements for a sunset review under Article 11.3, we do not see that the requirement of establishing a causal link between likely dumping and likely injury flows into that Article from other provisions of the GATT 1994 and the *Antidumping Agreement*. Indeed, adding such a requirement would have the effect of converting the sunset review into an original investigation, which cannot be justified.
>
> Our conclusion that the establishment of a causal link between likely dumping and likely injury is not required in a sunset review determination does not imply that the causal link between dumping and injury envisaged by Article VI of the GATT 1994 and the *Antidumping Agreement* is severed in a sunset review. It only means that re-establishing such a link is not required, as a matter of legal obligation, in a sunset review. (italics in the original).

5. PROCEDURAL REQUIREMENTS

So far, we have discussed only the substantive legal requirements involved in the imposition of AD duties. The AD Agreement also includes a significant number of requirements as to how a WTO Member is to decide whether its IA should initiate an AD investigation, and if so, how the investigation should be conducted. This section highlights a number of the key procedural requirements.

---

[81] Bown and Wauters (2008) critically discuss this case.

5.1 STANDING

An AD investigation can be launched either ex officio or upon request. The former is highly exceptional. Most AD investigations are initiated upon the request of the domestic industry through submission of a petition to the IA.

Art. 5.4 AD lays down the standing requirements that the domestic industry filing an application must fulfill. The existence of a standing requirement is meant to prevent WTO Members from initiating an investigation unless a certain percentage of the domestic industry producing the like product supports the application; if this is not the case, the application cannot be considered to have been made "by or on behalf of the domestic industry". There are two thresholds that must be met:

- First, the application needs to be supported by those producers whose collective output is more than 50% of the total production of that portion of the domestic producers expressing an opinion in favor or against the initiation;[82]
- Second, the producers expressly supporting the initiation need to represent at least 25% of total production.

The Panel in *US–Offset Act (Byrd Amendment)* faced the following situation: The US administration promised all US companies that actively backed a petition to impose AD duties, a re-distribution of proceeds from (the eventually imposed) AD duties (the notorious "Byrd payments" discussed earlier). The Panel found this measure to be inconsistent with the terms of Art. 5.4 AD since, in its view, it violated the principle of good faith (bona fides). By providing operators with an incentive to support an application, the US authority reduced a statutory requirement (Art. 5.4 AD) to redundancy. The Panel noted that Art. 5.4 AD had been introduced, *inter alia*, in response to the controversial US practice of presuming that an application was made by or on behalf of the domestic industry, unless a major proportion of the domestic industry expressed active opposition to the petition. It considered that the Offset Act undermined the value of the standing requirement (§§ 7.59–65). On appeal, the AB reversed the Panel's conclusions in this respect (§ 283):

> A textual examination of Article 5.4 of the Antidumping Agreement and Article 11.4 of the SCM Agreement reveals that those provisions contain no requirement that an investigating authori-

---

[82] The Agreement does not explicitly require individual producers' support and appears to allow the authority to consider as sufficient the support expressed by a producers' association on behalf of its members. Support expressed by associations is usually considered as equivalent to support expressed by all producers represented by this association, even though the association perhaps only supported the application following a small majority vote within the association. It has, therefore, been suggested to clarify the Agreement in this respect, by requiring that the standing determination be based on the positions expressed by individual domestic producers, and that representation by trade associations should not be counted collectively when such determinations are being made, see WTO Docs. TN/RL/GEN/23; TN/RL/GEN/69.

ty examine the motives of domestic producers that elect to support an investigation. Nor do they contain any explicit requirement that support be based on certain motives, rather than on others. The use of the terms 'expressing support' and 'expressly supporting' clarify that Articles 5.4 and 11.4 require only that authorities 'determine' that support has been 'expressed' by a sufficient number of domestic producers. Thus, in our view, an 'examination' of the 'degree' of support, and not the 'nature' of support is required. In other words, it is the 'quantity', rather than the 'quality', of support that is the issue.

Consequently, in the AB's view, Art. 5.4 AD imposed a mere formal requirement to ensure that a certain percentage of the domestic industry supported an application. The AB responded to the claim that Byrd payments under the controversial Byrd Amendment (i.e., "CDSOA") might lead to more initiations (§ 292):

> The Panel found that the CDSOA 'will result' in more applications having the required level of support from domestic industry than would have been the case without the CDSOA and stated that 'given the low costs of supporting a petition, and the strong likelihood that all producers will feel obliged to keep open their eligibility for offset payments for reasons of competitive parity', it 'could conclude that the *majority of petitions will achieve the levels of support required* under AD Article 5.4/SCM Article 11.4'. The evidence contained in the Panel record, however, does not support the overreaching conclusion that 'the majority of petitions will achieve the levels of support required' under Articles 5.4 and 11.4 as a result of the CDSOA. Indeed, we note that, in its first written submission to the Panel, the United States explained that 'it is rare for domestic producers in the United States not to have sufficient industry support in filing antidumping or countervailing duty petitions.' In support of its statement, the United States submitted to the Panel a survey that shows, for example, that during the year prior to the enactment of the CDSOA, all of the applications that were filed met the legal thresholds for support. (italics and emphasis in the original).

5.2 THE INVESTIGATION PROCESS

5.2.1 The Content of the Request for Initiation

An investigation will be initiated if the IA decides that the evidence submitted through the application of the domestic industry is adequate, and justifies the initiation of the process. Art. 5.2 AD reflects the elements that an application must contain:

> An application under paragraph 1 shall include evidence of (a) dumping, (b) injury within the meaning of Article VI of GATT 1994 as interpreted by this Agreement and (c) a causal link between the dumped imports and the alleged injury. Simple assertion, unsubstantiated by relevant evidence, cannot be considered sufficient to meet the requirements of this paragraph.

Art. 5.2 AD further specifies that "the application shall contain such information as is reasonably available to the applicant" concerning the domestic industry, the allegedly dumped product and the alleged dumpers, the normal value and export price, the volume and price effect of the imports, and their consequent impact on the domestic industry. The term "simple assertion" denotes that what must be avoided is unsubstantiated information. On the other side of the spectrum, the term "evidence", used in Art. 5.2 AD should not be equated to full proof, or proof beyond reasonable doubt: the Panel in *Mexico–Corn Syrup* clarified that the application need not contain information on all of the injury related factors listed in Art. 3.4 AD (§ 7.73).[83] In the same vein, the Panel in *Thailand–H–Beams* held that (§ 7.77):

> raw numerical data would constitute 'relevant evidence' than merely a 'simple assertion' within the meaning of this provision.

More generally, according to the Panel in *Mexico–Corn Syrup* (§ 7.76):

> ... Article 5.2 does not require an application to contain analysis, but rather to contain information, in the sense of evidence, in support of allegations. While we recognize that some analysis linking the information and the allegations would be helpful in assessing the merits of an application, we cannot read the text of Article 5.2 as requiring such an analysis in the application itself.

Similarly, the Panel in *US–Softwood Lumber V* rejected the argument that the "reasonably available" language included in Art. 5.2 AD is there to toughen the obligation to provide evidence in the application. The opposite, in its view, is the case (§ 7.54).

5.2.2 The Discretion to Initiate

When presented with an application (petition), an IA is not obliged to initiate an investigation; it retains discretion to this effect: Art. 5.3 AD provides that, even in cases where the application contains evidence on dumping, injury and the casual link as required by Art. 5.2 AD, no investigation may be initiated unless the IA has examined the record and verified the accuracy and adequacy of the information contained therein. When the IA is persuaded as to the accuracy of the information provided and the well-founded nature of the allegations, it may decide to launch a

---

[83] Howse and Neven (2007a).

formal investigation. In other words, a petitioner that has satisfied the requirements embedded in Art. 5.2 AD is not guaranteed an investigation. An IA has a duty to actively check the accuracy and adequacy of the information submitted under Art. 5.2 AD. The Panel in *US–Softwood Lumber V* held as much (§§ 7.74ff.). Now what does this duty specifically entail? The Panel in *Guatemala–Cement II* (§ 8.31), as well as the Panel in *Argentina–Poultry Antidumping Duties* (§ 7.60) were of the view that, while the accuracy and adequacy of the evidence are relevant to the authorities' determination whether there is sufficient evidence to justify initiation:

> it is however the sufficiency of the evidence, and not its adequacy and accuracy per se, which represents the legal standard to be applied in the case of a determination whether to initiate an investigation.

Art. 5.3 AD does not expressly provide that the evidence in question should relate to the questions of dumping, injury and the casual link, but Panels, reading Art. 5.3 AD in the context of Art. 5.2 AD, have consistently held that this is the kind of evidence required to justify initiation.[84] In order to determine whether there is sufficient evidence of dumping and injury, an IA cannot entirely disregard the elements that configure the existence of that practice as outlined in Arts. 2 and 3 AD.[85] In other words, even though the various provisions of Art. 2 AD relating to normal value and export price do not apply, as such, to the initiation determination, they are certainly relevant to the authorities' determination regarding the sufficiency of evidence.[86] According to the Panel in *US–Softwood Lumber V* (§ 7.80):

> this does not, of course, mean that an investigating authority must perform a full-blown determination of dumping in order to initiate an investigation. Rather, it means simply that an investigating authority should take into account the general parameters as to what dumping is when inquiring about the sufficiency of the evidence. The requirement is that the evidence must be such that an unbiased and objective investigating authority could determine that there was sufficient evidence of dumping within the meaning of Article 2 to justify initiation of an investigation.

So less than full proof suffices, for an investigation to be lawfully initiated, but how much less? Practice provides some responses in this respect. In *Guatemala–Cement II*, the Panel held that the Guatemalan IA was not justified in initiating an investigation based on an application which presented data for normal value and export price at different levels

---

[84] See, for example, the Panel report in *Guatemala–Cement II* at § 8.35.
[85] See the Panel report in *Guatemala–Cement II* at § 8.35.
[86] See the Panel report in *Guatemala–Cement II* at § 8.36.

of trade, and with important differences in the sales quantities, without examining the possible effects of such differences on price comparability (§§ 8.37ff.). The Panel in *Mexico–Steel Pipes and Tubes* held that the information contained in a request for initiation was not sufficient if the information regarding normal value presented therein consisted of one invoice and one price quote which did not even pertain to the known exporter but to a distributor, related only to a small subset of the product under investigation, and concerned one single day. By contrast, the export price information reflected the full spectrum of products imported by Mexico from Guatemala over the entire period of investigation, at the level of the Guatemalan producer or exporter. The Panel found that differences of this kind typically lead to a distortion of the normal value vis-à-vis the export price, and thus, if not adjusted, could give rise to apparent margins of dumping where no dumping in fact exists (§ 7.42). The Panel in *US–Softwood Lumber V* held that the following information was sufficient:

> (a) Cost-related evidence from smaller surrogate domestic producers (as a proxy for cost data from the exporters/producers allegedly dumping) satisfies the requirements of Art. 5.3 AD (§ 7.95);
>
> (b) Cost-allocation to specific products can legitimately not take place at this stage, and hence absence of evidence concerning such cost-allocation is not at odds with the requirements of Art. 5.3 AD (§ 7.97);
>
> (c) If cost data from various surrogate companies cover the whole year and costs data of one company covers the whole period, Art. 5.3 AD has not been violated (§ 7.99);
>
> (d) The fact that evidence of dumping is found only with respect to some categories of the product among those for which an initiation of investigation has been requested is not at odds with the requirements of Art. 5.3 AD (§ 7.101);
>
> (e) Prices for domestic sales (home market) can legitimately be taken from a specialized magazine, even though it reflects a number of sales and is not related to a specific sale (§ 7.105);
>
> (f) An affidavit which reflects deleted (confidential) information can legitimately be taken into account (§ 7.120);
>
> (g) Price information on only two out of seven categories of lumber products under investigation suffices to meet the requirements of Art. 5.3 AD, as long as the evidence concerns more than an insignificant subset of the imported product (§ 7.123);
>
> (h) Freight cost information which related to truck freight only does not violate Art. 5.3 AD as nothing before the authority indicated that only rail was used to transport lumber or even that rail was mostly used (§ 7.126).

In *Argentina–Poultry Antidumping Duties* the Panel held that the Argentine IA had not justifiably initiated an investigation, even though the application contained evidence on at least a number of transactions that were dumped: since not all comparable export transactions had been included in the preliminary dumping analysis, the Panel considered that there was not sufficient evidence for initiation. Similarly, in *Guatemala–Cement II*, the IA was faulted for initiating an investigation involving a claim of threat of injury which contained information on dumping, injury and the causal link, but did not provide information on the additional threat factors of Art. 3.7 AD. The Panel in *Mexico–Steel Pipes and Tubes* held that the Mexican IA could not have initiated an investigation on the basis of volume of import data at the tariff line level without any breakup of such data at the specific product level. Interestingly, the Mexican IA had acknowledged this problem, and stated, at the time of initiation, that this was one of the issues it was going to investigate in the course of the investigation in order to determine the exact trend in the volume of imports of the subject product as part of its injury analysis. Actually, the investigation confirmed that the subject product constituted a substantial portion of the imports under this more general tariff line, thus confirming the reliability of the data. The Panel did not consider any of this to be relevant in its assessment of whether, at the time of initiation, the Mexican IA was in possession of information sufficient to justify the investigation (§§ 7.58–60). The Panel in *US–Softwood Lumber V* is an outlier in this respect since it seems to be of the view that the complexity of the case lowers the evidentiary threshold for initiation (§ 7.95). This Panel appeared to give an IA the benefit of the doubt in complex cases, even where, the complexity was, as in this case, largely self-imposed by the applicants. Tension regarding the standard of review exists between the deferential approach of the Panel in *US–Softwood Lumber V*, and the rather demanding approach of Panels in all other cases discussed *supra*.

An IA, which is not persuaded by the record before it, can go ahead and complete it, and, using the additional information it has gathered, initiate an investigation; it has, however, no obligation to do so: the Panel held as much in *US–Softwood Lumber V* (§ 7.75). Consequently, the decision whether to initiate an investigation can be taken on the basis of information submitted by the applicants, and completed ex officio by the IA: according to the Panel in *Guatemala–Cement II* (§ 8.62), this is one of the consequences of the difference between Art. 5.2 AD (where the reasonably available-standard refers to the applicant), and Art. 5.3 AD (where the sufficiency of evidence-standard is applicable to the IA). It is important to point out that the exporters or producers alleged to have been dumping the product are not involved at all in this pre-initiation phase. Art. 5.5 AD expressly provides that the IA shall avoid publicizing the application for initiation of an investigation, unless if a decision has been made to initiate an investigation. It must notify though, the government of the exporting country of the receipt of a properly documented application prior to initiation of the investigation. The reason for this is to avoid the chilling effect on trade, which even the submission of an application may have, given the likelihood that it may lead to the initiation of an investigation and subsequent imposition of AD duties.

Art. 5.7 AD further requires from the IA that:

> The evidence of both dumping and injury shall be considered simultaneously *(a)* in the decision whether or not to initiate an investigation, and *(b)* thereafter, during the course of the investigation, starting on a date not later than the earliest date on which in accordance with the provisions of this Agreement provisional measures may be applied.

It is noteworthy that the few cases in which Panels have called for revocation of antidumping measures following a successful challenge of such measures before the WTO, have all involved disputes in which, *inter alia*, the determination of initiation under Art. 5.3 AD was considered flawed.[87] It appears that Panels are of the view that in cases of a flawed initiation, there can be no justification for maintaining antidumping measures that were based on an investigation that should not even have taken place. This has certainly added to the bite of Art. 5 AD.

Assuming that the decision is taken to initiate an investigation, the IA investigating authority will have to issue a public notice to this effect. When issuing this notice, the IA concerned will have to observe the requirements reflected in Art. 12.1 AD.

5.2.3 Questionnaires

The first act of the IA wishing to initiate an investigation is to send out questionnaires to the domestic industry (requesting information on the injury-side) and the exporters (requesting information regarding the dumping margin). The AD Agreement does not provide for a definition of or a mandatory table of contents for questionnaires. The AB in *EC–Fasteners (China)* rejected the idea that an EU formulary requesting information regarding the market economy-status of individual exporters was a questionnaire, because of its limited scope. It provided in brief its understanding of the term "questionnaire" (§ 613):

> Based on these considerations, we conclude that the meaning and scope of the term "questionnaires" in Article 6.1.1 of the *Anti–Dumping Agreement*, and its application to specific kinds of documents, must reflect a balance between the due process requirement to provide parties with an "ample opportunity" to submit all information they consider responsive to a questionnaire request in an anti-dumping investigation, and the overall timeframe imposed on the investigation under Article 5.10, along

---

[87] See, for example, the Panel reports in *Guatemala–Cement II* at § 9.6; *Argentina–Poultry* at §§ 8.6–8.7; *Mexico–Steel Pipes and Tubes* at §§ 8.9–8.13.

with the need for authorities to proceed expeditiously as contemplated in Article 6.14. We therefore find that the "questionnaires" referred to in Article 6.1.1 are a particular type of document containing substantial requests for information, distributed early in an investigation, and through which the investigating authority solicits a substantial amount of information relating to the key aspects of the investigation that is to be conducted by the authority (that is, dumping, injury, and causation). While in many investigations one "questionnaire" may be employed to solicit such information on these aspects of the investigation, we consider that, depending on how different Members organize the conduct of the investigation process, a party may receive several substantial requests soliciting such comprehensive information that are "questionnaires" within the meaning of Article 6.1.1. (italics in the original).

5.2.4 Verifications

The authorities must of course during the course of the investigation satisfy themselves as to the accuracy of the supplied information upon which their findings will be based (Art. 6.6 AD). This may imply an on-the-spot verification of the information, although there certainly does not appear to exist any obligation on the authorities to conduct such (an often costly) verification. In the view of the Panel in *US–DRAMS*, authorities (§ 6.78):

> could "satisfy themselves as to the accuracy of the information" in a number of ways without proceeding to some type of formal verification, including for example reliance on the reputation of the original source of the information.[88]

The Panel in *EC–Tube or Pipe Fittings* even seemed to consider on-site verification as the exception rather than the rule. According to this Panel, verification is an essentially documentary exercise that may be supplemented by an actual on-site visit (§§ 7.191–192). Authorities must inform the exporters/foreign producers of the information required for verification purposes (*Argentina–Ceramic Tiles*, Panel report, § 6.57).[89] On-the-spot verification may only take place in cases where the firms to be verified agree, and the authorities of the exporting Member have been notified and have not objected to their conduct (Art.6.7 AD). Annex I of the Agreement contains further details relating to on-the-spot verifications. Although the Agreement does not prescribe the conduct that must be followed in case of objections by firm(s) or the government in question, it appears that best information available can be used in this case (Art.

---

[88] See also the Panel report in *Argentina–Ceramic Tiles* at footnote 65; the Panel report on *Egypt–Steel Rebar* at §§ 7.326–327.

[89] Howse and Neven (2007b) discuss these requirements in detail.

6.8 AD); it is not clear though, how to treat government objection and there is lack of relevant practice in this respect.

Verification is not limited to information submitted prior to the visit, but may also include information to be provided during the course of verification: the Panel in *Guatemala–Cement II* ruled as much (§ 8.203). Note in this vein that, the Panel in *EC–Salmon (Norway)* held that recourse to facts available could not be justified solely on the basis that information provided at the time of the on-the-spot verification was not verifiable (§ 7.360).

The results of verification must be made available to the verified firms as well as to the applicants. The Panel in *Korea–Certain Paper* held that this disclosure does not necessarily have to be made in writing (§ 7.188); this holding is not totally unproblematic in light of evidentiary problems in case of challenge regarding whether disclosure occurred or not.

Art. 6.7 AD deals with foreign exporter-related verification. The obligation to disclose the results of the verification is intended to ensure that exporters can structure their cases for the rest of the investigation in light of those results. The Panel in *Korea–Certain Paper* held that such disclosure must contain adequate information regarding all aspects of the verification, including a description of the information which was not verified, as well as of the information that was successfully verified, since both could be relevant to the presentation of the interested parties' case (§ 7.192). It is not clear whether an obligation to make the results of verification available to the exporters exists in cases where verification takes place with respect to the domestic industry's questionnaire responses.

5.2.5 The Period of Investigation

The period of investigation (POI) refers to the period for which dumping- and injury-related data are collected and analyzed. The importance of this choice cannot be overstated. The Panel in *Mexico–Antidumping Measures on Rice* noted (§ 7.56):

> The choice of the period of investigation is obviously crucial in this investigative process as it determines the data that will form the basis for the assessment of dumping, injury and the causal relationship between dumped imports and the injury to the domestic industry.

The AD Agreement does not expressly discuss the POI for which the data with respect to dumping and injury should be collected, although, as the Panel in *EC–Tube or Pipe Fittings* acknowledged (footnote 116):

> The concept of a set period of investigation to examine the existence of dumping has been present in the GATT system for over 40 years. Indeed, a 1960 Report by a Group of Experts concern-

ing antidumping and countervailing duties considered the use of a "pre-selection system".' See Group of Experts, Second Report on Antidumping and Countervailing Duties, adopted on 27 May 1960 (L/1141) BISD 9S, 194.

The WTO Committee on Anti-dumping Practices (ADP Committee) has adopted a Recommendation Concerning the Periods of Data Collection for Antidumping Investigations (hereinafter, the "POI Recommendation"), which regulates the period of the POI. The POI Recommendation[90] distinguishes between a period of data collection for the dumping-, and a period of data collection for the injury investigation. It provides, *inter alia*, that:

> (a) The period of data collection for dumping investigations normally should be twelve months, and in any case no less than six months;
>
> (b) This period should end as close to the date of initiation as is practicable;
>
> (c) The period of data collection for injury investigations should normally be at least three years, unless a party from whom data is being gathered has existed for a lesser period; and
>
> (d) The period of data collection for injury investigations should include the entirety of the period of data collection for the dumping investigation.

The Panel in *US–Hot–Rolled Steel* held that the POI Recommendation was a non-binding instrument (footnote 152 of the report).[91] Subsequent Panels nevertheless, have shown considerable deference to the substantive part of the POI Recommendation, its non-binding nature notwithstanding. In its report on *Argentina–Poultry Antidumping Duties*, the Panel held (§ 7.287):

> Furthermore, we note that the issue of periods of review has been examined by the Antidumping Committee. It has issued a recommendation to the effect that, as a general rule, 'the period of data collection for injury investigations normally should be at least three years, unless a party from whom data is being gathered has existed for a lesser period, and should include the entirety of the period of data collection for the dumping investigation'. It would appear, therefore, that the period of review for injury need only 'include' the entirety of the period of review for dumping. There is nothing in the Antidumping Committee's recommendation to suggest that it should not exceed (in the sense of including more recent data) the period of review for dumping.

---

[90] WTO Doc. G/ADP/6, adopted by the ADP Committee on May 5, 2000. On its legal value, see Mavroidis (2008).

[91] A similar view has been expressed in the Panel report in *Guatemala–Cement II* at § 8.266.

The Panel in *Mexico–Antidumping Measures on Rice*, while recognizing its non-binding nature uses the POI Recommendation as support for its findings (§ 7.62). On appeal, its approach was upheld in its totality by the AB (§ 169):

> It appears to us that the Panel referred to the Recommendation, not as a legal basis for its findings, but simply to show that the Recommendation's content was not inconsistent with its own reasoning. Doing so does not constitute an error of law.

POI normally precedes the initiation of the investigation. The investigation itself normally runs for a period of 12 to a maximum of 18 months (Art. 5.10 AD). The Panel in *EC–Tube or Pipe Fittings*, explained the rationale for using a POI which ends before the initiation of the investigation in the following terms (§ 7.101):

> There are practical reasons for using an investigation period, the termination date of which precedes the date of initiation of the investigation. This ensures that the data that will form the basis for the eventual determination are not affected in any way by the initiation of the investigation and any subsequent actions of exporters/importers. The rationale is thus to acquire a finite data set unaffected by the process of the investigation. This can form the basis for an objective and unbiased determination by the investigating authority. The period of investigation terminates as close as possible to the date of initiation of the investigation in order to ensure that the data pertaining to the investigation period, while historical, nevertheless refers to the recent past. The use of a sufficiently long period of investigation is critical in order to ensure that any dumping identified is sustained rather than sporadic.

In *US–Hot–Rolled Steel*, the Panel considered whether an injury analysis which revolved around an evaluation of two years of data would be inconsistent with the requirement to conduct an objective examination based on positive evidence. In this case, the US IA had gathered data for a three-year period and acknowledged that this was required for injury purposes. The US did not compare the data, and argued that the reason the authority did not compare data for 1996 with that for 1998 was that 'changes created a new economic context for the performance of the industry'. The US did not explain why it considered the data no longer relevant in light of the changed economic circumstances. Nevertheless, the Panel did not consider it inappropriate for the IA to examine only data from two years, as such data related to the most recent period and included the period of alleged dumped imports (§ 7.234). The Panel emphasized that no end-point-to-end-point comparison was required, and that, in certain circumstances, it would be reasonable for an IA to examine only part of the data covering a two-year period. As long as three years of data were gathered, and such three-year data have at least in part been used, the authority would seem to be able to get away with the fact that it did not analyze part of the data for certain of the factors mentioned in Art. 3.4 AD. In *Guatemala–Cement II*, the Panel rejected the idea that the use of a one-year period of data collection would be *a priori* inconsistent with the requirement of Art. 3.2 AD (to consider whether there has been a significant increase in the volume of dumped imports). The Panel considered that no provision in the Agreement specified the precise duration of the period of data collection. In this case, Guatemala argued that the reason for the short period of data collection was that exports by the Mexican producer, Cruz Azul, did not become significant until the year of data collection, a conclusion supported by the record of the investigation; while the Panel was of the view that a longer data collection period might have been preferable, it was unable to find that the use by Guatemala of a one-year data collection period was inconsistent with Guatemala's obligation under Art. 3.2 AD (§ 8.266).

In *Mexico–Antidumping Measures on Rice*, the US claimed that the AD Agreement had been violated because the Mexican IA had analysed data pertaining to only six months for each of the three years of data collection. Mexico asserted that it was necessary to examine these particular six months of every year, instead of the full year, in order to ensure that the period of injury analysis paralleled the six-month period chosen for the analysis of dumping, so as to avoid any distortions. The Panel saw no *a priori* reason why the period of investigation for injury analysis should be chosen to fit the period of investigation for the dumping analysis, in case the latter covers a period of less than 12 months. The Panel considered that the choice of the POI was crucial, as it determined the data that would form the basis for the assessment of the impact of dumping, and that an examination or investigation could only be objective if it was based on data which provided an accurate and unbiased picture of what it was that one was examining. The Panel thus reached the following conclusion (§ 7.86):

> In sum, we find that the injury analysis of the Mexican investigating authority in the rice investigation, which was based on data covering only six months of each of the three years examined, is inconsistent with Article 3.1 of the AD Agreement as it is not based on positive evidence and does not allow for an objective examination, as it necessarily, and without any proper justification, provides only a part of the picture of the situation. In addition, we find that the particular choice of the limited period of investigation in this case was not that of an unbiased and objective investigating authority as the authority was aware of, and accepted, the fact that the period chosen reflected the highest import penetration, thus ignoring data from a period in which it can be expected that the domestic industry was faring better.

Similarly, the Panel in *EC–Tube or Pipe Fittings* was of the view that an IA is precluded from limiting its dumping analysis to a selective subset of data from only a temporal sub-segment of the POI. The Panel relied on the requirement of Art. 2.4.2 AD, which generally calls for comparison between a WA normal value and a WA of prices of all comparable export transactions, or a comparison of normal value and export prices on a T–T basis. According to the Panel, these methodologies would generally seem to require that data throughout the entire investigation period would necessarily be consistently taken into account. In *Argentina–Poultry Antidumping Duties*, the use of different time-periods to review the data for different injury factors was found to be inconsistent with the requirement to conduct an objective examination (§ 7.283). To examine only a part or a segment of the domestic industry was also considered to be inconsistent with the requirement to conduct an objective examination. The AB stated in its report on *US–Hot–Rolled Steel* that, where an IA undertakes an examination of one part of a domestic industry, it should, in principle, examine, in a like manner, all other parts that make up the industry, as well as the industry as a whole. A partial examination of the domestic industry could make it easier to find injury. This led the AB to conclude that such a practice was inconsistent with the AD Agreement (§ 204).

The requirement that the POI for injury purposes at least include the POI for dumping purposes was discussed by the Panel in its report on *Argentina–Poultry Antidumping Duties*. This Panel rejected the argument that the POI for dumping and the POI for injury should also end at the same time. Brazil had argued that such an identity was required in order to be able to establish a causal link between dumped imports and injury to the domestic industry as required by Art. 3.5 AD. According to the Panel, there was nothing in the POI Recommendation to suggest that the POI for injury should not exceed (in the sense of including more recent data) the period of review for dumping. The Panel added that there may be a time-lag between the entry of dumped imports and the injury caused by them, and that it may, therefore, not be appropriate to use identical periods of review for the dumping and injury analyses in all cases (§ 7.287).

In *Mexico–Antidumping Measures on Rice*, the US challenged the decision by the Mexican IA to use a POI for injury, which ended more than 15 months prior to the initiation of the investigation. The Panel considered that, while the AD Agreement does not contain any specific and express rules concerning the period to be used for data collection in an antidumping investigation, this does not mean that the authorities' discretion in using a certain period of investigation is boundless (§ 7.57). The Panel was of the view that there was necessarily an inherent real-time link between the investigation leading to the imposition of measures, and the data on which the investigation was based. In spite of the fact that an antidumping investigation out of necessity relies on historical data gathered during a past POI, such information should be the most recent information reasonably available (§§ 7.58ff.). The Panel considered that a 15–month gap between the end of the period of investigation and the initiation of the investigation was sufficiently long as to impugn the reliability of the evidence. In the Panel's view, Mexico had thus failed to use data that met the criterion of positive evidence pursuant to Art. 3.1 AD (§ 7.64). The AB fully upheld the reasoning of the Panel (§§ 163–172). It emphasized that the determination of whether injury exists should be based on data that provides indications of the situation prevailing when the investigation takes place, because the conditions to impose an antidumping duty are to be assessed with respect to the current situation (§ 165). The Panel in *Mexico–Steel Pipes and Tubes* agreed with the statements of the Panel and AB in their respective reports on *Mexico–Antidumping Measures on Rice*, concerning the real-time link between the POI and the imposition of measures, but considered that an eight-month gap between the end of the POI and the initiation of the investigation was reasonable. It acknowledged that this 8–month gap implied that the IA did not have "the most pertinent, credible and reliable information", but considered that "practical time constraints inherent in the production of data that must then be collected and analyzed by the applicant (in order to be relied upon and submitted in the application), and then analyzed by the investigating authority", and the fact that "the investigation occurred within the overall time constraints envisaged by the Agreement", were sufficient reasons to conclude that the temporal gap did not preclude the authority from making a determination of injury based on positive evidence and which involved an objective examination (§ 7.239).

The Panel in *EC–Tube or Pipe Fittings* rejected the argument that the POI would need to be adjusted in the case of important developments, such as a devaluation occurring towards the end of the POI. In other words, the Panel was of the view that, once an appropriate POI was chosen, i.e. a POI which relates to the recent past, there was no need to re-examine the issue (§ 7.102).

5.2.6 Due Process

The framers of the AD Agreement, mindful of the potential influence that domestic constituencies might exercise on IAs, opted for institutional guarantees that would reduce similar risks. In this vein, interested parties are to be given timely opportunities to see all information that is:

(a) Relevant to the presentation of their cases;
(b) Not confidential;[92] and

---

[92] As the Panel in *Korea–Certain Paper* noted however, Art. 6.4 AD cannot be interpreted to deny an interested party access to its own confidential information used, for example, in the calculation of a constructed normal value (§ 7.201). In this sense, disclosure under Art. 6.4 AD

(c) Used by the investigating authorities.

Interested parties must be allowed to prepare presentations on the basis of this information and authorities must keep a public record of the investigation to serve this duty (Art. 6.4 AD). For example, in the case of a constructed normal value, the actual figures for cost of manufacture, SG & A expenses or profits used in the calculation of the constructed normal value are to be disclosed to the interested party requesting such information.[93] This provision thus relates to information submitted by other interested parties, as well as information from other sources or documents prepared by the authorities. It is sometimes referred to as the access to file-obligation, although an IA can ensure compliance with Art. 6.4 AD through means other than by providing access to the file as well.[94]

During antidumping investigations, a substantial amount of information requested (and often submitted) is of a confidential nature. There is nothing specific in DSU regulating the provision and treatment of business confidential information (BCI), other than Art. 4 DSU (which states that proceedings are confidential). To provide interested parties with the incentives to submit such information, the AD Agreement guarantees that it will be disclosed only with the permission of the party submitting it (Art. 6.5 AD). According to the Agreement, there are two types of confidential information:

(a) Information which is confidential by nature; and

(b) Information which is confidential because confidential treatment has been requested by the party supplying the information.

Panels (*Guatemala–Cement II*; *Korea–Certain Paper*) have held that, in both cases, good cause must be shown for confidential treatment to be granted by the IA. These Panels found that good cause must be shown by the interested party submitting the confidential information at issue, and not by the IA itself.[95] When confidential information has been submitted, a non-confidential summary will be requested and, in principle, disclosed. The summary should be sufficiently detailed to permit a reasonable understanding of the substance of the information submitted in confidence.

---

differs clearly from the public notice requirements under Art. 12 AD, which do not allow the disclosure of any confidential information (§ 7.208).

[93] See the Panel report in *Korea–Certain Paper* at § 7.199.

[94] See the Panel report in *Guatemala–Cement II* at § 8.133.

[95] See the Panel report in *Guatemala–Cement II* at §§ 8.219–8.220; the Panel report in *Korea–Certain Paper* at § 7.335. The *Korea–Certain Paper* Panel did add that in its view, while some showing of good cause is necessary for both categories of confidential information, the degree of that requirement may, however, depend on the type of information concerned (§ 7.335). The Panel in *Mexico–Steel Pipes and Tubes* agreed with such conclusions and added that (§ 7.378):

a showing of 'good cause' for information that is 'by nature confidential' may consist of establishing that the information fits into the Article 6.5 (chapeau) description of such information: 'for example, because its disclosure would be of significant competitive advantage to a competitor or because its disclosure would have a significantly adverse effect upon a person supplying the information or upon a person from whom that person acquired the information'.

The Panel in *Argentina–Ceramic Tiles* held that the purpose of non-confidential summaries was to inform interested parties of the information provided, and to enable them to defend their interests. An IA is, therefore, not allowed to reject an exporters' response, simply because the summary was not sufficiently informative to allow the calculation of normal value, export price and the margin of dumping (§ 6.39). If, however, in exceptional circumstances, parties indicate that the information provided cannot be summarized, they will be requested to justify their opinion (Art. 6.5.1 AD).[96] Failure by the IA to request from those providing confidential information an explanation as to why it is impossible to supply a non-confidential summary amounts to a violation of Art. 6.5.1 AD: the AB found this to be the case in *EC–Fasteners (China)* at §§ 556ff. Investigating authorities retain discretion and they can refuse to adhere to a request to treat some information as confidential. In similar cases, they can disregard the information, unless it has been demonstrated that it is correct (Art. 6.5.2 AD). Interestingly, the Panel, in its report on *Mexico–Steel Pipes and Tubes*, found that an IA is complying with Art. 6.5 AD where it accepts without any explanation or analysis a request for confidentiality which is accompanied by a statement that a non-confidential summary is not possible for certain reasons. The Panel based its view on the fact that Art. 6.5 AD does not explain exactly how an IA should evaluate a request for confidential treatment; how it should indicate the manner and the extent to which it assessed an applicant's assertion to conclude that good cause existed for the information to be treated as confidential within the meaning of Art. 6.5 AD; or the extent to which it assessed an assertion that summarization was not possible within the meaning of Art. 6.5.1 AD.[97] In other words, where an IA accepts a request for confidentiality, no justification is required under Art. 6.5 AD (§ 7.380):

> We see that that Article 6.5.1 strikes a balance between the interests of the interested parties submitting confidential information to have that confidentiality maintained during the investigation and the interests of the rest of the interested parties to be reasonably informed about the substance of that information in order to be able to defend their interests.106 We are aware that the designation of information as 'confidential' might affect the ability of interested parties to have full access to that information, and therefore might affect their ability to defend their interests in the course of an antidumping investigation. We are further aware of the potential for abuse of the possibility to designate information as confidential so as to consciously place other interested parties at a disadvantage in the investigation. We consider that the conditions set out in Article 6.5, chapeau, and 6.5.1 are of critical importance in preserving the balance be-

---

[96] See the Panel report in *Guatemala–Cement II* at § 8.213.
[97] See the Panel report in *Mexico–Steel Pipes and Tubes* at § 7.393.

tween the interests of confidentiality and the ability of another interested party to defend its rights throughout an antidumping investigation. For precisely this reason, we consider it paramount for an investigating authority to ensure that the conditions in these provisions are fulfilled. We consider it equally important for a WTO Panel called upon to review an investigating authority's treatment of confidential information strictly to enforce these conditions, while remaining cognizant of the applicable standard of review.

It appears that this Panel ultimately adopted a deferential standard of review conceding that the IA had lawfully accepted important aspects of the information submitted by the domestic industry as confidential information, even though it had not examined whether good cause existed, or whether it was indeed not possible to provide a non-confidential summary as alleged by the applicant.

5.2.7 Duty to Cooperate and Recourse to Best Information Available (BIA)

Interested parties are under a duty to cooperate with the IA. If this is not the case, an IA can, when facing un-cooperative behavior by the addressee of its request for information, base its findings on the facts available, or, as is widely known, the best information available (BIA): Art. 6.8 AD and Annex II provide the legal basis for recourse to BIA and enables the IA to continue with the investigation in spite of the lack of cooperation from an interested party. The AD Agreement does not explain in a detailed manner what the duty to cooperate in an antidumping investigation actually means, except for the reference to BIA in Art. 6.8 AD, and in Annex II, § 7:

> It is clear, however, that if an interested party does not cooperate and thus relevant information is being withheld from the authorities, this situation could lead to a result which is less favourable to the party than if the party did cooperate.

The AB, in its report on *US–Hot Rolled Steel*, held that an IA is entitled to expect a very significant degree of effort—to the "best of their abilities"—from investigated exporters (§ 102). Based on this finding, the Panel in *EC–Countervailing Measures on DRAM Chips* (a case dealing with the application of Art. 12.7 SCM),[98] considered that a duty to cooperate exist. This Panel went on to find that an authority can draw adverse inferences, in case interested parties fail to cooperate (§§ 7.60–61). Recourse to BIA is permissible under Art. 6.8 AD when the requested party:

(a) Refuses access to necessary information; or

---

[98] This is the corresponding provision in the SCM Agreement dealing with recourse to best information available which has identical wording and function as the corresponding provision in the AD Agreement.

(b) Fails to provide necessary information within a reasonable period of time; or

(c) Significantly impedes the investigation.

However, as the Panel in *China–GOES* noted, the purpose of Art. 6.8 AD is not to punish non-cooperative parties who did not produce information (§ 7.302). An IA must include the information that is required in its request; it cannot ask in general about information relating to value and volume of exports. Similar behavior does not meet the Art. 6.8 AD-threshold for the kind of information that is necessary and required (§§ 7.446–447).

Refusing access: The Agreement does not specify what is meant by "necessary information". It is clear in case law by now that if an IA has not clearly requested certain information, the failure to submit such information cannot automatically be considered as failure to provide necessary information. This would be the case only if the IA has first sufficiently specified the kind of information it is after. The Panel in *Argentina–Ceramic Tiles* noted to this effect (§ 6.55):

> Thus, the first sentence of paragraph 1 [of Annex II] requires the investigating authority to 'specify in detail the information required', while the second sentence requires it to inform interested parties that, if information is not supplied within a reasonable time, the authorities may make determinations on the basis of the facts available. In our view, the inclusion, in an Annex relating specifically to the use of best information available under Article 6.8, of a requirement to specify in detail the information required, strongly implies that investigating authorities are not entitled to resort to best information available in a situation where a party does not provide certain information if the authorities failed to specify in detail the information which was required.

But does the mere fact that information was requested or required by the authorities suffice to label such information as necessary? This seems to have been the view of the Panel in *Egypt–Steel Rebar* (§ 7.155). A similar view was held by the Panel in *Korea–Certain Paper*: a certain percentage of the domestic sales of two exporters was made through a related company (called CMI), and the IA, for this reason, had considered that it needed the financial statements of CMI for purposes of verifying the completeness of the normal value data submitted. In spite of the fact that the two exporting companies and CMI submitted all of their domestic sales data, the IA considered that the failure to provide CMI's financial statements implied that necessary information had not been provided (§ 7.51). On this basis, the IA decided to reject all of the domestic sales data submitted. Deferring to the IA, the Panel upheld this approach. In this particular case, it was the IA's decision to base its normal value determination on the prices charged by the related company (CMI) to independent buyers which gave prominence to the financial statements of CMI. The Panel expressed the view that necessary information included information which was important in verifying information actually submitted, and was not limited to the actual data needed to calculate normal value and export price (§§ 7.43–44). A legitimate question can be raised here as to whether supporting evidence (like that requested from CMI) actually constitutes necessary information, and hence whether facts available may be used simply because no, or no sufficient supporting documents had been provided, when requested. The Panel in *Argentina–Ceramic Tiles* did not address this issue head on but linked it to the duty of an IA to specify the information requested (§ 6.66). One would expect nonetheless, that recourse to BIA should not be a matter of discretion when irrelevant or auxiliary information is requested and not provided. Problems might arise in similar cases (assuming a challenge before the WTO), because they might invite borderline de novo review by Panels.

Failure to provide information: the Agreement calls for a "reasonable period of time" that must be set by the IA during which information must be provided. The Panel in *US–Hot–Rolled Steel* dealt with a challenge by Japan against a US decision to reject submitted information: the US authority (DOC) had rejected information by NSC (a Japanese company) because it was submitted after the deadline it (DOC) had unilaterally fixed. NSC did not respect the deadline, but still sent its responses to the DOC before the initiation of the verification process. In the Panel's view, what mattered was not the respecting of unilateral deadlines, but rather whether the process had suffered as a result of NSC's behavior. In its view this was not the case, since there was ample time to verify the submitted information (§ 7.57). On appeal, the AB confirmed the Panel's finding, and explained in some detail how the term "reasonable period of time" (within which information must be provided) should be understood (§ 85):

> In considering whether information is submitted within a reasonable period of time, investigating authorities should consider, in the context of a particular case, factors such as (i) the nature and quantity of the information submitted; (ii) the difficulties encountered by an investigated exporter in obtaining the information; (iii) the verifiability of the information and the ease with which it can be used by the investigating authorities in making their determination; (iv) whether other interested parties are likely to be prejudiced if the information is used; (v) whether acceptance of the information would compromise the ability of the investigating authorities to conduct the investigation expeditiously; and (vi) the numbers of days by which the investigated exporter missed the applicable time-limit.

The Panel in *Korea–Certain Paper* first examined whether information was provided within the deadline set by the IA, and then whether it was nevertheless submitted within a reasonable period by applying the criteria set forth by the AB in the above quoted *US–Hot–Rolled Steel* report (§§ 7.48–55). This approach has become standing case law. Note that the effort made by the requested party does not necessarily matter, in the sense that requested parties might in good faith try to supply information and still fall short of the expectations of the IA. Information which was not verifiable or not appropriately submitted does not have to be taken into consideration if the party submitting it acted to the best of its abilities. The Panel in *Egypt–Steel Rebar*, noted to this effect that (§ 7.242):

> ... an interested party's level of effort to submit certain information does not necessarily have anything to do with the substantive quality of the information submitted' and thus the fact of acting to the best of one's ability by itself does not preclude the investigating authority from resorting to facts available in respect of the requested information.

Annex II provides in its § 5 that an IA is not justified to disregard all submitted information simply because there is no absolute overlap between what was requested and what was eventually supplied by a party acting in due diligence.[99]

Significantly impeding the investigation: according to the Panel in *Korea–Certain Paper*, Annex II, § 6 should not be understood as the means to provide the interested party a second chance to submit information (§ 7.85). The Panel in *Guatemala–Cement II* considered that a failure to cooperate with a verification visit due to a disagreement concerning the composition of the verification team and the presence of nongovernmental experts with a possible conflict of interest did not necessarily constitute a significant impediment of the investigation within the meaning of the Agreement. According to the Panel, the Agreement "does not require cooperation by interested parties at any cost" (§ 8.251). Annex II further provides in its § 3:

> All information which is verifiable, which is appropriately submitted so that it can be used in the investigation without undue difficulties, which is supplied in a timely fashion, and, where applicable, which is supplied in a medium or computer language requested by the authorities, should be taken into account when determinations are made. If a party does not respond in the preferred medium or computer language but the authorities find that the circumstances set out in paragraph 2 have been satisfied, the failure to respond in the preferred medium or computer

---

[99] See the AB report in *US–Hot–Rolled Steel* at § 81.

language should not be considered to significantly impede the investigation.

According to the Panel in *US–Steel Plate*, an IA is only required to take into account information which satisfies all of the applicable criteria of § 3 of Annex II (§ 7.57). According to this Panel (§ 7.71), information is verifiable if the:

> accuracy and reliability of the information can be assessed by an objective process of examination.

The fact that verifiable information was not actually verified is irrelevant in this respect (*Guatemala–Cement II*, Panel report, § 8.252). The Panel in *EC–Salmon (Norway)* added that, merely because information was not provided at the time of the on-the-spot verification does not imply that such information is not verifiable (§ 7.360).

Information which has not been submitted in accordance with a WTO Member's domestic laws is not appropriately submitted (*Argentina–Poultry Antidumping Duties*, Panel report, § 7.191): this Panel held that the information submitted by Brazilian exporters without respecting the Argentine accreditation requirements was not appropriately submitted. Submitted information does not necessarily have to be used even if it is verifiable. This would be the case when the use of the submitted information cannot be done without undue difficulties, hardly a self-interpreting term. The Panel in *US–Steel Plate* held that it is not possible to determine in the abstract whether information can be used without undue difficulties (§ 7.74):

> We consider the question of whether information submitted can be used in the investigation 'without undue difficulties' is a highly fact-specific issue. Thus, we consider that it is imperative that the investigating authority explain, as required by paragraph 6 of Annex II, the basis of a conclusion that information which is verifiable and timely submitted cannot be used in the investigation without undue difficulties.

Even where the authority is entitled or forced to make determinations on the basis of facts available, it is not entirely free to make its determinations on whatever basis it chooses: the determination should still be based on facts, not merely on assumptions or conjecture. The Agreement imposes two distinct obligations in this respect:

> (a) First, in light of the requirements set forth in §§ 3 and 5 of Annex II, an IA must use as much as possible the information submitted by the interested parties. There is a caveat here: as acknowledged by the Panel in *US–Steel Plate*, for certain parts of the information requested, the failure to provide such information may have ramifications beyond that particular item. For example, in the absence of cost of

production data, the IA will not be able to determine whether sales were made in the ordinary course of trade (§ 7.60);

(b) Second, Annex II, § 7 requires the IA to use "special circumspection" when basing its determination on secondary sources of information: it should check the information it receives from independent sources at their disposal (such as published price lists, official import statistics and customs returns), and from other interested parties. If the IA uses information from the petitioner without verifying its accuracy, it will be running afoul its obligations under Annex II (*Mexico–Steel Pipes and Tubes*, Panel report, § 7.193). On the other hand, an IA cannot claim that it does not need to verify the information it receives simply because it verified it at a prior stage of the investigation in order to comply with Art. 5.3 AD. The Panel in *Korea–Certain Paper* underscored this point in § 7.124 of its report. In *US–Hot-Rolled Steel*, the AB warns IAs that confuse willful non-cooperation, that could allow an IA to use adverse inferences, with cases of genuine difficulty to procure the requested information (§§ 99–100). Therefore, the AB concludes (§ 104):

> if the investigating authorities fail to "take due account" of genuine "difficulties" experienced by interested parties, and made known to the investigating authorities, they cannot . . . fault the interested parties concerned for a lack of cooperation.

The Panel in *Mexico–Antidumping Measures on Rice* faulted Mexico for having legislation in place which required its IA to always apply the highest (facts available)-margin in case of non-cooperation: according to Mexican laws, the IA would always apply the highest margin (assuming a range of margins) based on facts available to all those exporters that refused to cooperate with it. The Panel held that this law was based on a misunderstanding of Art. 6.8 AD, which was not aimed at punishing non-cooperative parties; in fact, in the Panel's view, case law made it clear that, even when presented with imperfect responses, an IA must always try to make good use of them (§ 7.238). The AB agreed with the explanation of the Panel concerning the term "best information available": in its view, this term required an evaluative, comparative assessment in order to determine which facts are best suited to fill in the missing information (§ 297):

> The use of the term 'best information' means that information has to be not simply correct or useful per se, but the most fitting or 'most appropriate' information available in the case at hand. Determining that something is 'best' inevitably requires, in our view, an evaluative, comparative assessment as the term 'best' can only be properly applied where an unambiguously superlative status obtains. It means that, for the conditions of Article 6.8 of the *AD Agreement* and Annex II to be complied with, there

can be no better information available to be used in the particular circumstances. Clearly, an investigating authority can only be in a position to make that judgment correctly if it has made an inherently comparative evaluation of the 'evidence available'. (italics in the original)

The AB, in its report on *Mexico–Antidumping Measures on Rice* held that an IA must not use data from secondary sources without ascertaining for itself the reliability and accuracy of such information; it must check it, where practicable, against information obtained from other independent sources at its disposal, including material submitted by interested parties (§ 289). Note however, in this context, that the Panel in *Korea–Certain Paper* upheld the Korean authorities' decision to construct NV based on facts available because of a failure by the related third party to provide the necessary information. According to the Panel, without this information from the related party, the authority could not possibly determine whether the sales made were in the ordinary course of trade. As a consequence, the authority was entitled to assume that they were not. In addition, the constructed NV did not simply consist of the exporters' cost of production plus the exporters' SG & A expenses and profits, but also included the constructed SG & A expenses for the trading company, since the decision had been made to determine NV on the basis of the trading company's resale price (§ 7.94). It appears that the authority never examined whether the remainder of the exporters' domestic sales which were not made through the related trading company were of sufficient volume to allow for a proper comparison.

5.3 TRANSPARENCY

Before making a final determination, IAs must inform all interested parties of the "essential facts" which formed the basis for the decision to apply AD measures. This disclosure should take place in sufficient time for the parties to defend their interests (Art. 6.9 AD). Case law reveals that the duty to inform embedded in Art. 6.9 AD does not imply that the IA is required to inform the parties of their legal determinations during the course of an investigation, or of the reasons for accepting or rejecting certain arguments:[100] the disclosure obligation under Art. 6.9 AD, as is the case under Arts 6.1 and 6.2 AD for that matter, relates only to factual information. Thus, in *Guatemala–Cement II*, the Panel rejected Mexico's claim that the Guatemalan IA had violated Art. 6.9 AD by changing its injury determination from a preliminary determination of threat of material injury to a final determination of actual material injury during the course of the investigation, without informing Cruz Azul, the Mexican producer, of that change (§§ 8.238–239).

---

[100] See the Panel report in *Argentina–Poultry Antidumping Duties* at § 7.225.

Different from the access to file-obligation included in Art. 6.4 AD, the disclosure obligation in Art. 6.9 AD requires from an IA to identify the facts that it considers essential.[101] Art. 6.9 AD imposes an obligation of result on IAs; the aim of disclosure is to allow interested parties to defend their interests, and it is in light of this aim that the means of disclosure may be examined, the modalities of performing disclosure being left to the discretion of IAs (*Argentina–Ceramic Tiles,* Panel report, § 6.125).

What should be considered essential facts? In *Argentina–Poultry Antidumping Duties* (§ 7.224), the fact that certain export price—and normal value data, which had been supplied by one of the parties but had not been used by the IA, was not considered by the Panel to be an essential fact that should have been disclosed to the interested party. Note, nonetheless, that the Panel in *Argentina–Ceramic Tiles* held that exporters should have been informed of the fact that their information, as submitted, was not going to be used for the final determination (§ 6.129).

In *China–GOES*, the AB held (§ 240) that the term "essential facts" should be understood to mean facts significant in the process of reaching a decision as to whether AD duties should be applied or not. In that case, the AB noted that it does not suffice for an IA to note simply that prices have dropped (§ 247). Without further disclosure about the price comparisons that the IA used, exporters were left with insufficient information about the essential facts underlying the IA's decision.

Art. 12.2 AD requests an IA to make public any preliminary, or final determination, or acceptance of price undertakings. Art. 12.2.1–3 AD reflects the elements that should figure in the public notice.

5.4 JUDICIAL REVIEW OF AD DECISIONS

Art. 13 AD requires each WTO Member to provide for review of all administrative actions relating to the final determinations of AD investigations and sunset review. This may be done through a judicial, arbitral, or administrative tribunals. However, the review tribunals and procedures must be independent of an IA.

The provision of judicial review through a domestic forum, therefore, creates a possibility for individual parties to directly appeal a final determination of an AD matter, without resort to assistance from one's government through the multilateral channel of the WTO. For losing petitioners, domestic judicial review is the key mechanism to challenge the legal determinations of an IA. However, respondents that believe that an IA has committed a substantive or procedural error have a choice: They can challenge the determination first through the domestic judiciary of the importing country; or they can proceed directly with requesting that their government file a challenge against the WTO Member imposing the

---

[101] See the Panel report in *Guatemala–Cement II* at §§ 8.229–230.

AD duty through WTO dispute settlement. The two options are not mutually-exclusive, and there is no requirement that a party must exhaust the appeals process through national courts first before filing a WTO challenge.

6. WTO REVIEW OF ANTI–DUMPING DETERMINATIONS

6.1 THE STANDARD OF REVIEW

A WTO Member may challenge the AD determination or practice of another WTO Member through the multilateral dispute settlement system. Normally, when reviewing another WTO Member's administrative determinations, WTO adjudicating bodies observe the generic standard of review included in Art. 11 DSU. The AD Agreement is the only covered agreement with its own standard of review embedded in Art. 17.6 AD:

In examining the matter referred to in paragraph 5:

(i) in its assessment of the facts of the matter, the panel shall determine whether the authorities' establishment of the facts was proper and whether their evaluation of those facts was unbiased and objective. If the establishment of the facts was proper and the evaluation was unbiased and objective, even though the panel might have reached a different conclusion, the evaluation shall not be overturned;

(ii) the panel shall interpret the relevant provisions of the Agreement in accordance with customary rules of interpretation of public international law. Where the panel finds that a relevant provision of the Agreement admits of more than one permissible interpretation, the panel shall find the authorities' measure to be in conformity with the Agreement if it rests upon one of those permissible interpretations.

WTO adjudicating bodies will consequently evaluate whether facts were properly established and evaluated in an unbiased manner, and whether the overall conclusion reached rests on a permissible interpretation of the AD Agreement.[102] Art. 17.6(i) has been understood in case law as statutory requirement not to engage in a "de novo" review. GATT and WTO adjudicating bodies have understood that a de novo review includes a certain degree of deference towards the establishment and evaluation of facts by an IA. They can, of course, sanction WTO Members for not properly establishing the record, and can find that conclusions reached by them are inconsistent with the requirements of the AD Agreement; they will refrain, however, from substituting their own judgment for that of the IA concerned. Total deference (towards the findings of an IA) and de

---

[102] See Francois and Palmeter (2008).

novo review are the two ends of the spectrum; the question is at what point in the continuum will WTO Panels intervene? Case law has provided some clarifications.

First, absence of reasoned and adequate explanation of the decision is fatal for the order (*US–Lamb*, AB report, §§ 106–107).[103] In *US–Softwood Lumber VI (Article 21.5–Canada)*, the AB went one step further and held that it was not the mere existence of plausible alternatives that rendered the IA's determination implausible. A Panel must examine the IA's determination in light of these plausible alternatives rather than in the abstract. This did not imply, according to the AB (§ 117, and footnote 176), that a Panel must reject the IA's explanation, if it did not agree with the opinion of the IA. What is important is that the IA has taken account of and responded to plausible alternative explanations that were raised before it and that, having done so, the explanations provided by it in support of its determination remain "reasoned and adequate". This Panel faced a re-determination by the USITC of a threat of injury-determination that had been found to be inconsistent with the AD Agreement by the original Panel.[104] The Panel emphasized that the fact that an alternative explanation of the data was possible did not ipso facto lead to the conclusion that the USITC had committed a violation. Canada had offered an alternative explanation but, in the eyes of the Panel had failed to also demonstrate that an unbiased and objective IA could not have reached the conclusions reached by the USITC (§ 7.35ff. and especially 7.56). In this Panel's view, hence successful complainants must not only provide an alternative explanation; they must also demonstrate that the explanation offered by the IA is not reasonable. On appeal, the AB reversed the Panel in this respect. In the AB's view, the Panel had shown total deference to the IA in this case. After explaining what it considered to be the Panel's obligation when reviewing a determination of an IA (§ 106), the AB went on to hold the Panel had failed to abide by the proper standard of review for the following reasons (§ 138):

> In sum, the Panel's analysis, viewed as a whole, reveals a number of serious infirmities in the standard of review that it articulated and applied in assessing the consistency of the Section 129 Determination with Articles 3.5 and 3.7 of the *Antidumping Agreement* and Articles 15.5 and 15.7 of the *SCM Agreement.* First, the Panel's repeated reliance on the test that Canada had not demonstrated that an objective and unbiased authority 'could not' have reached the conclusion that the USITC did, is at

---

[103] *US–Lamb* dealt with a dispute under the SG Agreement. Its standard of review however, soon found application in cases coming under other contingent protection instruments.

[104] We discuss dispute settlement and the DSU in subsequent Chapters. Suffice to state here that a compliance Panel is the judicial entity that might be entrusted, in case of disagreement between complainant and defendant, with the question of whether the latter has complied with the findings of the original Panel (assuming of course that the original Panel had accepted the original complaint).

odds with the standard of review that has been articulated by the Appellate Body in previous reports. As we noted earlier, the standard applied by the Panel imposes an undue burden on the complaining party. Secondly, the 'not unreasonable' standard employed by the Panel at various reprises is also inconsistent with the standard of review that has been articulated by the Appellate Body in previous reports, and it is even more so for ultimate findings as opposed to intermediate inferences made from particular pieces of evidence. Thirdly, the Panel did not conduct a critical and searching analysis of the USITC's findings in order to test whether they were properly supported by evidence on the record and were 'reasoned and adequate' in the light of alternative explanations of that evidence. Fourthly, the Panel failed to conduct an analysis of whether the totality of the factors and evidence considered by the USITC supported the ultimate finding of a threat of material injury. (italics in the original).

There is thus an obligation imposed on Panels to examine the explanation offered by the IA in light of alternative explanations offered by the complaining party. Panels cannot take into consideration evidence that was not submitted to the IA or that was not appropriately submitted to the IA, and which the IA had refused to take into account (*Egypt–Steel Rebar*, Panel report, § 7.21). In the words of the Panel in *US–Hot–Rolled Steel* (§ 7.6):

> Thus, for example, in examining the USITC's determination of injury under Article 3 of the *AD Agreement*, we would not consider any evidence concerning the price effects of imports that was not made available to the USITC under the appropriate US procedures. (italics in the original).

The question of what constitutes new facts and evidence was comprehensively addressed in the Panel report in *EC–Bed Linen*[105] in the following manner (§ 6.43):

> Article 17.5(ii) of the *AD Agreement* provides that a panel shall consider a dispute under the *AD Agreement* 'based upon: . . . the facts made available in conformity with appropriate domestic procedures to the authorities of the importing Member'. It does not require, however, that a panel consider those facts exclusively in the format in which they were originally available to the investigating authority. Indeed, the very purpose of the submissions of the parties to the Panel is to marshal the relevant facts in an organized and comprehensible fashion in support of their arguments and to elucidate the parties' positions. Based on our review of the information that was before the European Com-

---

[105] Janow and Staiger (2007) discuss this issue in detail and raise critical remarks regarding the internal consistency of WTO case law.

munities at the time it made its decision, in particular that presented by India in its Exhibits, the parties' extensive argument regarding this evidence, and our findings with respect to India's claim under Article 5.4, we conclude that the Exhibit in question does not contain new evidence. Thus, we conclude that the form of the document, (that is, a new document) does not preclude us from considering its substance, which comprises facts made available to the investigating authority during the investigation. There is in our view no basis for excluding the document from consideration in this proceeding, and we therefore deny India's request. (italics in the original).

Note though that in *US–Softwood Lumber V*, for example, the Panel excluded a regression analysis based on data that were before the IA, because it considered that such an analysis constituted new evidence that went beyond a mere mechanical re-formatting of appropriately submitted facts (§§ 7.40–41). The same Panel accepted, nonetheless, charts which were not before the IA, since they only (§ 7.168):

> display in graphical form data which was before DOC during the course of the investigation.

Still, both the regression analysis and the graph were based on evidence that had already been submitted to the IA so some additional explanation for the differential treatment would be warranted in this case. To quote the Panel report in *EC–Bed Linen* discussed above, it seems there is a thin line between evidence which is merely marshalling the already submitted evidence, and hence, can be taken into account by a Panel, and evidence which constitutes "a manipulation of already submitted facts and evidence", on which the Panel would not be allowed to base its review if it wants to avoid a de novo review. The Panel in *US–Steel Plate* considered that an affidavit based on data that were before the IA at the time of the investigation was acceptable as it did not constitute new information (§ 7.13):

> What the affidavits do is present the information submitted in a different manner than originally submitted, and adjust and sort it in various ways.

This criterion is what distinguishes acceptable from unacceptable evidence. An IA will be required to make public only the essential elements of the investigation which led it to its decision (Art. 12 AD). The question may arise whether such non-disclosed information should be considered as being part of the record and, if so, under what conditions. The Panel in *EC–Tube or Pipe Fittings*, made the following distinction: Facts which have not been submitted to the IA are not properly before the Panel. However, facts which have not been disclosed by the IA, but on which the authority has relied to reach its decision can (and should) be reviewed by a WTO Panel (§§ 7.35 and 7.45). On appeal, the AB upheld the Panel's approach in this respect(§§ 125ff., and especially 133).[106]

A Panel will review whether an IA has properly established the factual record before it. In practice, this amounts to examining whether the IA has diligently assembled the facts. It is against this background that Panels will evaluate whether the IA's appreciation was unbiased and objective. It is worth recalling that this latter test should not lead Panels to re-open the investigation process and re-do the whole procedure, substituting their judgment for that of the IA. The Panel in *US–Hot–Rolled Steel* expressed the view that the requirement to examine whether the facts had been properly established and evaluated in an unbiased and objective manner, as stipulated in Art. 17.6(i) AD, should be understood in the following manner (§ 7.26):

> The question of whether the establishment of facts was proper does not, in our view, involve the question whether all relevant facts were considered including those that might detract from an affirmative determination. Whether the facts were properly established involves determining whether the investigating authorities collected relevant and reliable information concerning the issue to be decided—it essentially goes to the investigative process. Then, assuming that the establishment of the facts with regard to a particular claim was proper, we consider whether, based on the evidence before the US investigating authorities at the time of the determination, an unbiased and objective investigating authority evaluating that evidence could have reached the conclusions that the US investigating authorities reached on the matter in question. In this context, we consider whether all the evidence was considered, including facts which might detract from the decision actually reached by the investigating authorities.

The relationship between Art. 11 DSU (the default standard of review applied to all cases) and Art. 17.6(ii) AD (the idiosyncratic standard of review applied in antidumping litigation) is the question that has occupied most of the case law. The argument is often made that the AD standard of review is more deferential (than Art. 11 DSU) towards WTO Members.[107] Practice shows that typically Panels have preferred to apply simultaneously the two standards of review, that is, they see no contradiction between them: For example, the Panel in *US–Corrosion–Resistant Steel Sunset Review*, held that the standard of review applicable in the context of sunset reviews would require it to apply both Art. 11 DSU, and Art. 17.6 AD to the factual and legal issues before it (§§ 7.4–7.5). The

---

[106] Horn and Mavroidis (2007a) find this distinction useful but point to evidentiary problems that might arise in this context.

[107] See on this score Croley and Jackson (1996), and Palmeter (1995).

Panel in *US–Softwood Lumber VI* reflects its understanding of the relationship between the generic and the AD standard of review in the following manner (§ 7.22):

> Thus, it is clear to us that, under the *AD Agreement*, a panel is to follow the same rules of treaty interpretation as in any other dispute. The difference is that if a panel finds more than one permissible interpretation of a provision of the *AD Agreement*, it may uphold a measure that rests on one of those interpretations. It is not clear whether the same result could be reached under Articles 3.2 and 11 of the DSU. However, it seems to us that there might well be cases in which the application of the Vienna Convention principles together with the additional provisions of Article 17.6 of the *AD Agreement* could result in a different conclusion being reached in a dispute under the *AD Agreement* than under the *SCM Agreement*. In this case, it has not been necessary for us to resolve this question, as we did not find any instances where the question of violation turned on the question whether there was more than one permissible interpretation of the text of the relevant Agreements. (italics in the original).

The Panel in *US–Hot–Rolled Steel* held that, in order to evaluate whether the interpretation reached was a permissible one, the starting point of its analysis should be the VCLT[108] (§ 7.27). On appeal, the AB confirmed that, to reach a conclusion whether more than one interpretation could be permissible, exhaustion of the interpretative elements reflected in the VCLT was the necessary first step (§§ 59–60):

> This second sentence of Article 17.6(ii) *presupposes* that application of the rules of treaty interpretation in Articles 31 and 32 of the *Vienna Convention* could give rise to, at least, two interpretations of some provisions of the *Antidumping Agreement*, which, under that Convention, would both be 'permissible interpretations'. In that event, a measure is deemed to be in conformity with the *Antidumping Agreement* 'if it rests upon one of those permissible interpretations'.
>
> It follows that, under Article 17.6(ii) of the *Antidumping Agreement*, panels are obliged to determine whether a measure rests upon an interpretation of the relevant provisions of the *Antidumping Agreement* which is *permissible under the rules of treaty interpretation* in Articles 31 and 32 of the *Vienna Convention*. In other words, a permissible interpretation is one which is found to be appropriate after application of the pertinent rules of the *Vienna Convention*. We observe that the rules of treaty interpretation in Articles 31 and 32 of the *Vienna Convention* ap-

---

[108] The Vienna Convention on the Law of Treaties (VCLT) is the legal instrument that Panels use to interpret the WTO Agreement. We discuss it in the Chapters on dispute settlement.

ply to any treaty, in any field of public international law, and not just to the WTO agreements. These rules of treaty interpretation impose certain common disciplines upon treaty interpreters, irrespective of the content of the treaty provision being examined and irrespective of the field of international law concerned. (italics and emphasis in the original).

In *US–Continued Zeroing*, the AB finally explained what exactly this standard entails: In its view, recourse to the VCLT should allow for more than one interpretation to be declared permissible, but cannot lead to conflicting interpretations.

So far, there is little evidence of "permissible interpretations". The Panel in *Argentina–Poultry Antidumping Duties* was requested to judge whether 46% of all domestic producers should be considered as a major proportion of the total domestic production, in accordance with Art. 4.1 AD. Without delving too much into a thorough discussion of this issue, the Panel accepted that this was indeed a permissible interpretation of the term (§ 7.341).[109] This is probably the only case where a Panel insinuated that this was one of a range of permissible interpretations, and since it was in the range, it was acceptable.

The relationship between Art. 11 DSU and 17.6(ii) AD was debated in the AB report in *US–Hot–Rolled Steel* (§ 62):

> Finally, although the second sentence of Article 17.6(ii) of the *Antidumping Agreement* imposes obligations on panels which are not found in the DSU, we see Article 17.6(ii) as supplementing, rather than replacing, the DSU, and Article 11 in particular. Article 11 requires panels to make an 'objective assessment of the matter' as a whole. Thus, under the DSU, in examining claims, panels must make an 'objective assessment' of the legal provisions at issue, their 'applicability' to the dispute, and the 'conformity' of the measures at issue with the covered agreements. Nothing in Article 17.6(ii) of the *Antidumping Agreement* suggests that panels examining claims under that Agreement should not conduct an 'objective assessment' of the legal provisions of the Agreement, their applicability to the dispute, and the conformity of the measures at issue with the Agreement. Article 17.6(ii) simply adds that a panel shall find that a measure is in conformity with the *Antidumping Agreement* if it rests upon one permissible interpretation of that Agreement." (italics and emphasis in the original).

---

[109] Mavroidis (2009) discusses this issue in detail.

6.2 REMEDIES AGAINST ILLEGALLY IMPOSED AD DUTIES

In the GATT-era, a series of Panels had recommended that, in the case of illegally imposed (antidumping and countervailing) duties, the GATT contracting party imposing such duties has the obligation to reimburse the injured exporter.[110] The Panel in *Guatemala–Cement II*, facing a specific request by Mexico to suggest reimbursement of illegally imposed antidumping duties, acknowledged that in the specific circumstances of the case, a request for reimbursement may be justifiable. However, ultimately, the Panel refused to pronounce on this score (§§ 9.6–7):

> We have determined that Guatemala has acted inconsistently with its obligations under the *AD Agreement* in its imposition of antidumping duties on imports of grey portland cement from Mexico. We have found these violations to be of a fundamental nature and pervasive. Indeed, in general terms we have found that:
>
> a) An unbiased and objective investigating authority could not properly have determined, based on the evidence and information available at the time of initiation, that there was sufficient evidence to justify initiation of the antidumping investigation;
>
> b) Guatemala conducted the antidumping investigation in a manner inconsistent with its obligations under various provisions of the *AD Agreement*;
>
> c) An unbiased and objective investigating authority could not properly have determined that the imports under investigation were being dumped, that the domestic producer of cement in Guatemala was being injured and that the imports were the cause of that injury.
>
> In light of the nature and extent of the violations in this case, we do not perceive how Guatemala could properly implement our recommendation without revoking the antidumping measure at issue in this dispute. Accordingly, we suggest that Guatemala revoke its antidumping measure on imports of grey portland cement from Mexico.
>
> In respect of Mexico's request that we suggest that Guatemala refund the antidumping duties collected, we note that Guatemala has now maintained a WTO-inconsistent antidumping measure in place for a period of three and a half years. Thus, we fully understand Mexico's desire to see the antidumping duties repaid and consider that repayment might be justifiable in circum-

---

[110] On GATT-practice in this context, see Petersmann (1993), and Mavroidis (1993), (2000).

stances such as these. We recall however that suggestions under Article 19.1 relate to ways in which a Member could implement a recommendation to bring a measure into conformity with a covered agreement. Mexico's request raises important systemic issues regarding the nature of the actions necessary to implement a recommendation under Article 19.1 of the DSU, issues which have not been fully explored in this dispute. Thus, we decline Mexico's request to suggest that Guatemala refund the anti-dumping duties collected. (italics in the original).

The Panel in *Australia–Automotive Leather II* held that the DSU did not exclude the possibility for retroactive remedies. These two Panel reports, nonetheless, are outliers: No other report goes that far. Typically a finding that duties have been illegally imposed will be accompanied by a statement that the WTO Member concerned should bring its measure into compliance; that is to say, prospective action only (eliminating the AD duties from the end of the compliance period[111]) will suffice.

7. INSTITUTIONAL ISSUES

A Committee on Anti-dumping Practices (ADP Committee) has been established, by virtue of Art. 16 AD. WTO Members must, by virtue of Art. 18.5 AD, notify the Committee of any changes in their laws. In *US–Customs Bond Directive*, the Panel found that the US, by not notifying the Committee of its new legislation, had acted inconsistently with its obligations under this provision (§ 7.285). In addition, WTO Members are required to file semi-annual reports with the Committee with information about its AD actions.

The ADP Committee is not simply a depository of national AD-related initiatives. Recall that the ADP Committee has produced recommendations, like the one on the duration of the period of investigation (POI), that WTO adjudicating bodies have used in case law.

QUESTIONS AND COMMENTS

Negotiating History: The father of Canada's AD legislation was the Finance Minister William S. Fielding who is quoted saying back in 1904:

> It was unscientific to meet special and temporary cases of dumping by a general and permanent raising of the tariff wall and that the proper method was to impose special duties upon dumped goods.[112]

So, AD was thought as the means to avoid punishing innocent bystanders. The relevant Australian statute is the 1906 Industries Preservation Act and it protects against international predation, as is made clear in

---

[111] As we will see in the Chapters discussing dispute settlement, WTO Members are usually allowed a period during which they should comply with adverse rulings.

[112] Viner (1922) at p. 193.

§ 19.[113] Protecting against international predation, and not simply price discrimination, seems to have been the thrust of the US laws to this effect. Stewart et al. (1993, p. 1401) reflect the following opinion by US Congressman Fodney, expressed in 1921:

> We have no law and we have no means of preventing concerns in a foreign country combining to sell their goods at a sacrifice in this country until competition here has been destroyed and thus control our markets at such prices as they wish to charge.

Indeed, in *American Banana Co v. United Fruit Co*[114] judge Oliver Wendell Holmes writing for the US Supreme Court held that one could not use domestic laws to attack foreign price discrimination. Citing prior case law to the effect that all legislation is prima facie territorial,[115] he went on to write (p. 357):

> Words having universal scope, such as "every contract in restraint of trade," "every person who shall monopolize," etc., will be taken as a matter of course to mean only everyone subject to such legislation, not all that the legislator subsequently may be able to catch. In the case of the present statute, the improbability of the United States' attempting to make acts done in Panama or Costa Rica criminal is obvious, yet the law begins by making criminal the acts for which it gives a right to sue. We think it entirely plain that what the defendant did in Panama or Costa Rica is not within the scope of the statute so far as the present suit is concerned. Other objections of a serious nature are urged, but need not be discussed.

The negotiation of the Uruguay round AD Agreement has been discussed in several publications.[116]

Antidumping Duties on Goods, the Duties of Which Are Unbound: Arguably, importing states will have little incentive to incur administrative costs and initiate an AD procedure on goods the duties of which have not been bound. It could, however, be the case that a law needs to be formally amended for a tariff change to occur, even in cases where the practiced tariff is not bound. In such case, an AD procedure could be less costly. For what it is worth as proxy, note that, as Bown (2010) shows, a number of WTO Members imposed AD duties on imports from China before 2001, that is, before the Chinese accession to the WTO, at a time when they could simply have raised their import duties. More generally, raising unbound duties faces the additional limitation that the tariff increase would have to apply on an MFN basis when the importer would rather punish one source of production. It might legitimately want to avoid alienating a number of its trading

---

[113] INDUSTRIES PRESERVATION, V Austl. C. Acts 19 (1906).
[114] 213 US 347 (1909).
[115] Ex parte Blain, LR 12 Ch. Div 522 at 528.
[116] See *inter alia*, Croome (1995), Liang (2011), Paemen and Bentsch (1995), Preeg (1995), Stewart *et al.* (1993).

partners, and therefore decide to have recourse to AD duties, even though it has not bound the duties of the (allegedly) dumped import.

Antidumping and Offshoring (Trade in Tasks): Increasingly outsourcing has been imposing a strain on antidumping and has provoked intense discussions; domestic industry using input produced elsewhere has become an enemy of antidumping.[117]

Antidumping as Safeguard: Finger and Nogues (2006) provided some empirical support for the argument that AD can be put to good use as a safeguard mechanism, by researching the MERCOSUR experience. In their account, national administrations in the MERCOSUR countries used the potential for AD as a carrot to persuade domestic lobbies to support trade liberalizing commitments.

Antidumping and Antitrust: Kovacic (2010) provides a great overview.

Dumping and Injury: The AD Agreement does not condition the initiation of injury analysis on a prior finding of dumping. In practice the two legs of the analysis, that is, the investigation of dumping margins and of injury, often take place in parallel. In fact, it is not unheard of that dumping follows injury analysis. Depending on what takes place first, the signaling to the market regarding the probability that AD duties will be imposed could be different. Knetter and Prusa (2003) note, for example, that of 800 cases investigated in the period 1980–1998, the DOC (US Department of Commerce), in charge of establishing dumping margin, issued a negative dumping decision only in 28 cases (3.5% of the total); on the other hand, the ITC (US International Trade Commission), in charge for establishing injury, made negative injury decisions in 37.5% of all cases submitted to it during the same period.

Nuisance Claims: Prusa (1992) looks at a wide sample of cases that includes cases where a petition has been withdrawn. His data shows that these withdrawn cases have at least as great an effect on trade as cases which resulted in duties. What he terms 'nuisance suits', that is, petitions with low probability of success, can confer large gains to the domestic industry supporting the petition.[118] Actually, an effect on the market might exist from the moment an announcement of a petition is made public. Rutkowski (2007) examines 45 such withdrawals in EU practice (between 1992 and 2004) and tests this hypothesis with similar results. Art. 5.4 AD goes some way towards restricting access to the "petitioners market".[119]

---

[117] See pp. 6 and 7 in Commission of the European Communities, Global Europe, Europe's Trade Defense Instruments in a Changing Global Economy, A Green Paper for Public Consultation, Brussels, 6 December 2006, COM (2006).

[118] Staiger and Wolak (1994) also find that the mere filing of a complaint aiming to open up an AD investigation can significantly reduce trade flows during the period of investigation even though no duties are in place during this period. Their explanation rests on legitimate expectations of exporters as to the outcome of investigation.

[119] The timing of the filing might have something to say about the chances to succeed: Feinberg (2005), and Knetter and Prusa (2003) discuss how business-cycle effects might affect the chance to prevail when filing for antidumping duties. Feinberg (2005), using financial health of

Public Interest Clause: the Extramet jurisprudence of the ECJ is the leading case in the EU legal order.[120]

Causality: In contingent protection cases, economists will often have recourse to Granger causality, whereby they will test whether one variable consistently precedes another. This method requires many observations of both the dependent and the independent variables, otherwise it might not be statistically reliable. It could thus be used in the context of AD, where, usually,[121] many transactions are observed, but not in the context of subsidization. So, instead of asking the question did A cause B, we try to show that if A had not occurred, B would not have occurred either.[122] Granger tests could also be used to check both directions (e.g., A->B, or B->A). One lesson from Grossman's paper cited above is that we really need to know if there is a third variable (say, C) which causes both A and B. Now, from an economic perspective this point is correct, and the question arises whether that is the case from a legal perspective as well. In other words, is there a legal statutory requirement to treat imports as endogenous? Consider the following example. Suppose we know that bad union contracts are weakening the steel industry, and that, as a result, the unions make the domestic industry unprofitable and inefficient. The contracts make it hard for the firms to upgrade their technology (perhaps because they cannot lay off workers). The union contracts also result in 'import pull' as consumers turn to foreign countries for more technologically advanced steel. As a result, policy makers see both negative profits and higher imports. By themselves, imports are not sufficient to cause injury. But, absent imports the industry might seek out a small profit. Does the law require the investigating authorities to consider that imports are endogenous? The correct response seems to be negative as we will see in what immediately follows.

Country–Wide Orders: Mavroidis and Sapir (2008) cast doubt on the underlying idea that AD orders can be imposed on country wide-basis, explaining that here are essentially two reasons why the 'law of one price' does not hold. The trivial reason is that products may not be identical either because they are differentiated or because differences in the services offered by competing firms might lead them to charge different prices for the same product. But even if products are truly homogeneous, price dispersion is likely to be the rule rather than the exception to the 'law of one price'. As Stigler (1961) argued 50 years ago, price dispersion is related to the existence of imperfect information and search costs of consumers. Product differentiation and imperfect information imply that firms might be able to exert some degree of market power and hence to price discriminate. Moreover, different firms can be expected to face different circumstances and to have different

---

the domestic industry as proxy for (lack of) injury, showed why in a booming market it will be hard to demonstrate that injury has occurred as a result of dumping.

[120] C–358/89, Judgment of the Court of June 11, 1992, ECJ Reports I–3843ff.

[121] Its relevance in the context of targeted dumping, that is, in cases for example, of dumped seasonal goods, might be questionable. In such cases, we might be observing one or very few export transactions.

[122] There are limits in the usefulness of this method if three or more variables are at stake.

capabilities that result in different costs and therefore different prices—unless they operate under perfect competition in which case prices have to be the same for all firms and the different costs simply translate into different profits.

China's NME Status: Not surprisingly, the NME-status of China was an important issue in the Chinese accession process (Accession Protocol), which starts from the principle that WTO Members have a choice either to use Chinese prices or costs for the industry (that is, to treat China as any other market economy country), or to use a methodology based on the general rule that it is up to the producers under investigation to:

> clearly show that market economy conditions prevail in the industry producing the like product with regard to the manufacture, production and sale of that product.[123]

If this has been the case, the importing WTO Member is obliged to use Chinese prices. In the opposite case, a methodology that is not based on a strict comparison with domestic prices or costs in China may be used. If this methodology is applied, it has to be notified to the WTO Antidumping Committee. At the same time, China's Accession Protocol provides that, as soon as China is able to establish that it is (either as a whole or with regard to a particular industry) a market economy according to the criteria set forth in the importing WTO Member's national law, China (e.g., the Chinese industry in question) must be treated as a normal market economy/industry. In order to benefit from market economy status, the criteria conferring it must have existed in the importing WTO Member's law at the time of China's accession in 2001; it is not entirely clear what happens if similar criteria were not in place at the time of China's accession, and it is an open question whether WTO Members finding themselves in this situation are precluded from treating China as an NME. This will be, if at all, a short-lived situation, since the NME-status of China will expire at the latest 15 years after accession, that is, by 2016.

---

[123] WTO Doc. WT/L/432 at § 15.

CHAPTER 15

SUBSIDIES AND COUNTERVAILING DUTIES

■ ■ ■

1. THE LEGAL DISCIPLINE

The SCM Agreement addresses two issues:

(a) It imposes obligations on WTO Members with respect to subsidization. Except for two particular forms, subsidies are not prohibited outright. However, WTO Members should avoid imposing subsidies which cause an adverse effect to the interests of other WTO Members.[1]

(b) It regulates the imposition of countervailing duties (CVDs), should a WTO Member choose to make recourse to this instrument to address the subsidies of a trading partner. Note that like anti-dumping duties, CVDs are a unilateral instrument that may imposed by a WTO Member after an investigation has been conducted by that Member that satisfies the criteria laid forth in the SCM Agreement.

Under WTO law, a subsidy involves:

- A *financial contribution* by a government or any "public body"
- That confers a *benefit*
- To a *specific* recipient (beneficiary)

The two forms of subsidies that are illegal per se, (i.e.. there is no need to show adverse effects) are:

- Local content subsidies; and
- Export subsidies

All other forms are subsidies are considered, in WTO parlance, *actionable* subsidies: they can be challenged if they cause one of three types of adverse effects (defined in Art. 5 SCM) to another WTO Member:

- Injury to the domestic industry
- Nullification or impairment of benefits

---

[1] The Agreement on Trade in Civil Aircraft also imposes disciplines on WTO Members with respect to financial support on civil aircraft (it also eliminates duties in civil aircraft and provides for conditions regarding procurement decisions). It counts 31 Members today. We will not be discussing it in detail in this volume since its disciplines overlap with those of the GATT (Art. II), the SCM Agreement discussed here, as well as the Agreement on Government Procurement discussed in Chapter 22.

- Serious prejudice

In order for a WTO Member to impose a CVD, it must demonstrate that subsidized imports have caused injury to the domestic industry producing the like product. In other words, there are three requirements that must be met cumulatively:

(1) the existence of a subsidy;

(2) injury; and

(3) a causal link between the subsidized imports and injury.

To determine whether all three requirements exist for any particular instance, a WTO Member must appoint an IA to conduct an investigation into the matter.

2. THE RATIONALE FOR THE LEGAL DISCIPLINE

Subsidies are one of the most sensitive and contentious matters in international trade. Many governments employ them in order to pursue certain economic and/or political objectives. They can feature prominently in industrial policy support for a particular industry or as targeted support for a certain constituency (i.e., a particular region, sector, class, etc.). Some subsidies can be welfare-enhancing, particularly when they are designed to address the market's failure to account for certain externalities. Many more subsidies, however, are welfare-reducing in that they involve inefficient transfers of rent. Because of their economic impact, subsidies have the potential to alter trade outcomes.

The main objective of the SCM Agreement is to discourage subsidies that might harm producers' interests. To this effect, some types of subsidies are prohibited outright, while others can be counteracted (irrespective whether they might be beneficial to consumers' interests). Various provisions can help us understand the rationale for the legal discipline: For example, Art. 12.9 SCM specifies that the domestic producers of a like product must be invited by the investigating authority to offer their views about an alleged subsidy and proposed countervailing measures, whereas the authority has discretion to decide whether or not to allow consumers of the subsidized good to do so. The focus of the SCM is on producers' interests. Art. 15.1 SCM requires that:

> a determination of injury . . . shall be based on positive evidence and involve an objective examination of both (a) the volume of the subsidized imports and the effect of the subsidized imports on prices in the domestic market for like products and (b) the consequent impact of these imports on the domestic producers of such products.

Arts. 14 and 19 SCM require the size of the CVD to be set so as to just offset the adverse effects of the subsidy on conditions in the domestic industry. This latter provision can only be understood as an attempt to restore competitive conditions in the industry to what they would have been absent the subsidy. This is the element of 'unfairness' that case law has underscored. We quote from § 87 of the AB report *Argentina–Footwear (EC)*:

> In perceiving and applying this object and purpose to the interpretation of this provision of the *WTO Agreement*, it is essential to keep in mind that a safeguard action is a "fair" trade remedy. The application of a safeguard measure does not depend upon "unfair" trade actions, as is the case with anti-dumping or countervailing measures. Thus, the import restrictions that are imposed on products of exporting Members when a safeguard action is taken must be seen, as we have said, as extraordinary. (italics in the original).

In the same vein, the AB confirmed in its report on *US–Line Pipe* (§ 81):

> Before turning to the first issue raised in this appeal, it is useful to recall that safeguard measures are extraordinary remedies to be taken only in emergency situations. Furthermore, they are remedies that are imposed in the form of import restrictions in the absence of any allegation of an unfair trade practice. In this, safeguard measures differ from, for example, anti-dumping duties and countervailing duties to counter subsidies, which are both measures taken in response to unfair trade practices. If the conditions for their imposition are fulfilled, safeguard measures may thus be imposed on the "fair trade" of other WTO Members and, by restricting their imports, will prevent those WTO Members from enjoying the full benefit of trade concessions under the *WTO Agreement*. (italics in the original).

3. COVERAGE OF THE LEGAL DISCIPLINE

3.1 SUBSIDIES AND COUNTERVAILING DUTIES

As stated *supra*, the SCM Agreement includes disciplines for both subsidies and CVDs. Subsidies are divided into actionable and prohibited, whereas a third category (non-actionable) that was originally part and parcel of the SCM Agreement was removed from the Agreement in 2001. It is by now commonplace in case law that Panels will examine the consistency of a challenged measure with both the SCM Agreement as well as Art. XVI GATT (which regulated subsidies in the GATT-era).

3.2 ONLY CVDS ARE PERMISSIBLE IN ORDER TO ADDRESS SUBSIDIZATION

Art. 32.1 SCM states that:

No specific action against a subsidy of another Member can be taken except in accordance with the provisions of GATT 1994, as interpreted by this Agreement.

The interpretation of this provision was the core subject-matter of the dispute between the US and a host of WTO Members regarding the *US–Continued Dumping and Subsidy Offset Act of 2000 (CDSOA)*, the notorious "Byrd Amendment" that we have already discussed in Chapter 14. The AB upheld the Panel's findings to the effect that CVDs are the only permissible action against subsidies (§ 256). In a subsequent case (*EC–Commercial Vessels*), the Panel faced, *inter alia*, an argument by Korea that the EU TDM (Temporary Defence Mechanism) Regulation violated Art. 32.1 SCM. Korea and the EU had reached an agreement on subsidization of their respective shipyards whereby they had agreed to stop similar practices: through the TDM, the EU deviated from its commitments and granted subsidies to the ship-building sector. In the EU's view, the TDM was necessary since Korea had not respected its own commitments in this regard.[2] The Panel agreed with the view that the TDM was a specific action relating to subsidization, but distanced itself from the view that it was against subsidization (§§ 7.154–174). In its view, a counter-subsidy (like the TDM) is not, in and of itself, against subsidization. For the Panel, a scheme would run against subsidy, in the sense of Art. 32.1 SCM, if it contained some element *additional* to the potential impact on competition (§§ 7.160ff.). This Panel thus, did not repeat the ruling of the AB with respect to Byrd payments, where the potential disbursement of CVDs to US economic operators sufficed for the measure to be judged WTO-inconsistent.

3.3 MUTUAL EXCLUSION OF AD DUTIES AND CVDS (DOUBLE REMEDIES)

In *US–Antidumping and Countervailing Duties (China)*, the AB was asked to respond to the question whether double remedies were consistent with the WTO. Double remedies are explained in § 541 of the report:

"[D]ouble remedies", also referred to as "double counting", refers to circumstances in which the simultaneous application of antidumping and countervailing duties on the same imported products results, at least to some extent, in the offsetting of the same subsidization twice. "Double remedies" are "likely" to occur in

---

[2] The TDM Regulation is described in detail in § 7.43 of the Panel report.

cases where an NME methodology is used to calculate the margin of dumping.

As discussed in Chapter 14, the AB found this practice to be WTO-inconsistent (§§ 560ff). The AB ultimately held (§ 583):

> We find instead that the imposition of double remedies, that is, the offsetting of the same subsidization twice by the concurrent imposition of anti-dumping duties calculated on the basis of an NME methodology and countervailing duties, is inconsistent with Article 19.3 of the *SCM Agreement.* (italics in the original)

4. DEFINITION OF A "SUBSIDY"

Neither Art. XVI GATT, nor the 1979 Agreement on Interpretation and Application of Articles VI, XVI and XXIII of the General Agreement on Tariffs and Trade (the Tokyo Round Subsidies Code) included a definition of the term "subsidy". One of the most import innovations of the WTO SCM Agreement is that it provides, for the first time, a definition of a subsidy as follows:

(a) A financial contribution by a government or any public body;

(b) Which confers a benefit;

(c) To a specific recipient.

The first two elements are included in Art. 1 SCM,[3] whereas the latter in Art. 2 SCM.

4.1 FINANCIAL CONTRIBUTION BY GOVERNMENT OR PUBLIC BODY

The SCM Agreement considers that a financial contribution is provided by a government or public body in the following cases (Art. 1.1 SCM):

(a) In case of direct transfer of funds (such as grants, loans, and equity infusions), or potential direct transfer of funds or liabilities (e.g., loan guarantee);

(b) When government revenue that is otherwise due is foregone or not collected (such as fiscal incentives in the form of tax credits);

(c) Where the government provides goods or services other than general infrastructure, or when it purchases goods;

(d) The government entrusts a private body to do the activities mentioned above;

---

[3] The negotiating history of Art. 1 SCM is described in §§ 8.64–74 of the Panel report in *US–Export Restraints*. See, on this score, Janow and Staiger (2007), and Rubini (2010).

In addition to the above forms of financial contribution, the SCM Agreement also considers "any other form of income support as spelled out in Art. XVI GATT" as a "subsidy" (Art. 1.1(a)(2) SCM).

The wording of this provision makes it clear that it deals in exhaustive manner with the types of government involvement that constitute financial contribution. The Panel in *US–Export Restraints* (§ 8.69) underscored this point.

In what follows, we will first discuss what is meant by the term "government" and "any public body." We will then turn to discuss the four forms of financial contribution that are discussed in Art. 1.1(a)(1) SCM. Finally, we will briefly discuss what qualifies as "any other form of income support" in the sense of Art. XVI GATT.

4.1.1 Definition of a Government or Any "Public Body"

The term "government", which appears in Art. 1 SCM, refers to all types and layers of government within a country, whether they are acting at the federal, state, or provincial level. Recall that under Art. XXIV.12 GATT:

> Each contracting party shall take such reasonable measures as may be available to it to ensure observance of the provisions of this Agreement by the regional and local governments and authorities within its territories.

Art. 1.1 SCM also makes clear that the SCM Agreement governs financial contributions made by a "public body." The inclusion of the term "public body" is, in part, an anti-circumvention device. It is designed to ensure that governments do not try to skirt the obligation by simply channeling the subsidy through an entity outside the formal structures of government. In *US–Antidumping and Countervailing Duties (China)*, the AB clarified the meaning of the term (§ 317):

> A public body within the meaning of Article 1.1(a)(1) of the SCM Agreement must be an entity that possesses, exercises or is vested with governmental authority. Yet, just as no two governments are exactly alike, the precise contours and characteristics of a public body are bound to differ from entity to entity, State to State, and case to case.

Case law has made clear that state ownership, by itself, is insufficient to render an entity a public body. In *US–Antidumping and Countervailing Duties (China)*, the AB held that the Panel had mistakenly characterized Chinese state-owned enterprises as public entities by simply focusing on the fact that the government had, in financial terms, a "controlling interest" in an entity. (§ 320–21) In that case, the Panel had sided with the US argument that the term "public body" "refers to entities owned or controlled by the government" (§ 8.134). The AB reversed the

Panel's definition of a public body as "as any entity controlled by the government" (§ 322). It reiterated (§ 318):

> [T]he mere existence of formal links between an entity and government in the narrow sense is unlikely to suffice to establish the necessary possession of government authority. Thus, for example, the mere fact that the government is the majority shareholder of an entity does not demonstrate that the government exercises meaningful control over the conduct of that entity, much less that the government has bestowed it with governmental authority.

If financial control by itself is insufficient, then what other factors should be considered in determining whether or not an entity is a public body? The key question, according to the AB, is whether the entity "possesses, exercises, or is vested with government authority" (§ 317). The AB noted that in some instances, this determination is quite straightforward because of an express statute or legal instrument vesting such an authority upon the entity. However, the absence of such a statutory delegation of authority is not fatal. As the AB noted (§ 318):

> What matters is *whether* an entity is vested with authority to exercise governmental functions, rather than *how* that is achieved. There are many different ways in which government in the narrow sense could provide entities with authority. Accordingly, different types of evidence may be relevant to showing that such an authority has been bestowed on a particular entity.

Besides the presence of an express statutory delegation of authority, the AB noted that another way of demonstrating that an entity is a public body is "evidence that an entity is, in fact, exercising government authority . . . particularly when such evidence points to a sustained and systematic practice" (§ 318).

In addition, the AB emphasized the concept of "meaningful control over the conduct" of the entity (§ 318). It noted that in evaluating this question, the US had previously relied upon a multi-factor test and suggested that such a test should be re-instated. Among the other factors considered, besides government ownership and the presence of a statutory delegation are: government presence on the board of directors, government control over activities, and pursuit by the entity of governmental policies or interests (§ 343). Where the IA had considered a broader range of factors in its consideration of the issue of meaningful control, the AB approved of the IA's determination on the public body issue. For example, the AB found nothing wrong with the treatment by the US of Chinese state-owned commercial banks as public bodies where the IA, in applying a multi-factor test, emphasized the banks' role in carrying out Chinese industrial policies in addition to the ownership stake (§ 355). This line of reasoning is in keeping with an earlier Panel determination in *Korea–*

Commercial Vessels that Korean Export–Import Bank (KEXIM) functioned as a public body, despite pursuing some activities of a commercial nature, because of government control over main appointments and KEXIM's mandate (§ 7.53).

4.1.2 Forms of Financial Contribution

Art. 1.1(a)(1) mentions the four particular circumstances mentioned *supra* where a "financial contribution" exists; the financial contribution does not have to be restricted to a transfer of monetary resources. The AB in *US–Softwood Lumber IV* held that (§ 51):

> the concept of subsidy defined in Article 1 of the SCM Agreement captures situations in which something of economic value is transferred by a government to the advantage of a recipient.

"Something of economic value" needs to be transferred thus, and not necessarily monetary resources. The Panel in *US–Softwood Lumber III*, held that in-kind transfers of resources, such as goods or services which can be valued and which represent a value to the recipient, as well (§ 7.24).

<u>Direct transfer of funds or liabilities</u>: The SCM Agreement provides an illustrative list of what qualifies as a direct transfer of funds or liabilities: This includes instances where the government directly provides a grant or loan to an entity or where the government makes an equity infusion. The illustrative list is not exhaustive.

In addition, the SCM Agreement notes that direct transfer need not actually occur for a government measure to qualify as a "financial contribution" under WTO law; what is important is the potential for such a direct transfer. For example, consider the example where a government guarantees the loan of a private entity. Whether the government will actually transfer funds or not will depend on circumstances that transpire following the loan guarantee. But by assuming this arrangement, the government is deemed to have made a "financial contribution" under the SCM Agreement.

<u>Revenue otherwise due</u>: A financial contribution also exists when a government does not collect, or foregoes revenue which is otherwise due. In *US–FSC*,[4] the AB held that the basis for the comparison must be the tax rules applied by the Member in question. In this case, the EU had challenged the consistency of US tax practices with the SCM Agreement. As a result of the Foreign Sales Corporation (FSC) Act, companies earning income outside the US were exempted from the obligation to pay US taxes. The EU argued that the FSC amounted to an export subsidy since absent enactment of the FSC, companies would have been obliged to pay taxes for income made both in the US and outside the US market. The

---

[4] Howse and Neven (2007c) discuss this case.

EU asserted that the US, by not collecting taxes on income earned outside of the US, was subsidizing its producers' exports. The Panel and the AB agreed with the complainant, holding that national law would serve as the benchmark to determine whether income was otherwise due (§§ 90ff. and especially 98). This principle was further affirmed by the AB in *US–FSC (Article 21.5–EC)* (§§ 86, 91–92).[5]

In *Canada–Autos*, an import duty exemption granted to certain cars was considered to be revenue otherwise due. This exemption meant that the normal MFN import duty of 6.1% would not have to be paid. Consequently, the Canadian government had, in the eyes of the AB, foregone revenue it otherwise would have raised (§ 91).

Footnote 1, and Annexes I–III to the SCM Agreement identify certain situations when revenue foregone will not confer a benefit and thereby will not result into subsidization. Footnote 1 to the SCM Agreement explains that exempting exported domestic goods from say consumption taxes is not a financial contribution by a government in the sense or foregone income otherwise due, if it conforms with the requirements included in Annexes I-III: instruments aiming at avoiding double taxation, an issue to which we will turn in more detail *infra*, constitute an instance of income foregone that is not considered to be a financial contribution by a WTO Member (Annex I); so are some drawback schemes (remission of import charges levied on inputs consumed in the production of exported goods, Annexes II, and III).

The SCM Agreement explicitly deals with the issue of double taxation only to make the point that instruments aiming to avoid that a transaction is taxed twice by two different jurisdictions will not be assimilated to financial contributions by governments even though in similar instances income is foregone. The same transaction can be taxed twice, assuming that one country imposes taxes by virtue of the nationality of the economic operator, and, another, by virtue of the territoriality-principle (where a transaction is taxed where it takes place irrespective of the nationality of the parties involved). To avoid this, a number of WTO Members have signed treaties aimed at avoiding double taxation. It is the Illustrative List of Export Subsidies (Annex 1 to the SCM) that discusses the treatment of double taxation; paragraph (e) of that list reads as follows:

---

[5] This was a compliance Panel which dealt with the legality of the so-called ETI, a measure the US had enacted in order to conform with the findings of the original Panel. The AB concluded that there appeared to be a marked contrast between the 'other rules' of taxation applicable to foreign-source income, and the rules of taxation applicable to foreign source income as qualified in the FSC/ETI measure, so-called Qualified Foreign Trade Income (QFTI): for US citizens and residents, all foreign-source income (subject to permissible deductions) was taxed; under the ETI measure, QFTI was definitively excluded from US taxation. This, together with the fact that taxpayers could elect to have their income treated more favorably as QFTI or see the normal rules for foreign source income applied to them, led the AB to conclude that the US forewent revenue on QFTI which was otherwise due (§ 105).

The full or partial exemption, remission, or deferral specifically related to exports, of direct taxes or social welfare charges paid or payable by industrial or commercial enterprises.

Footnote 59 explicitly excludes measures taken to avoid double taxation from the scope of this paragraph.[6] It pertinently reads:

Paragraph (e) is not intended to limit a Member from taking measures to avoid the double taxation of foreign-source income earned by its enterprises or the enterprises of another Member.

Consequently, remission of taxes in order to avoid double taxation should not be understood to be an export subsidy in the SCM-sense of the term. The AB on *US–FSC (Article 21.5–EC)*,[7] held that a measure falls under footnote 59 if it exempts from taxation only foreign-source income. If it further exempts other (than foreign-source) income, then it cannot benefit from this provision (§§ 184–186).

<u>Government provision of goods or services</u>: A government provision of goods or services other than general infrastructure, or purchase of goods can constitute financial contribution by virtue of Art. 1.1(a)(1)(iii) SCM.

In *US–Softwood Lumber III*,[8] as well as in *US–Softwood Lumber IV*, the question before the WTO adjudicating bodies was whether the Canadian stumpage arrangements amounted to a provision of goods in the sense of the SCM Agreement. Through these arrangements, Canadian harvesters of timber would rent land at less than market value. As a result, their exported products would benefit from a substantial cost advantage vis-à-vis the corresponding US products, since US harvesters had to pay a market price for renting land where they would harvest timber. The AB concluded that, since the Canadian stumpage arrangements gave tenure holders the right to enter onto government lands, cut standing timber, and enjoy exclusive rights over the timber that was harvested, such arrangements represented a situation in which provincial governments provided standing timber to harvesters. It disagreed with Canada's argument that the granting of an intangible right to harvest standing timber could not be equated with the act of providing that standing timber. According to the AB, by granting a right to harvest, the provincial governments put particular stands of timber at the disposal of timber harvesters and allowed those enterprises alone to make use of those resources. The stumpage programs amounted thus to the provision of goods or services other than general infrastructure (§ 75).

<u>Government entrusts or directs a private entity</u>: Art. 1.1(a)(1)(iv) notes that a "financial contribution" is also considered to have been made

---

[6] For an excellent discussion on tax issues in trade agreements, see Avi–Yonah and Slemrod (2002).
[7] See, on this score, the analysis by Howse and Neven (2007c).
[8] See the analysis by Horn and Mavroidis (2005b).

where a government "makes payments to a funding mechanism, or entrusts or directs a private body to carry out" one or more of the types of financial contributions discussed above, and where "the practice, in no real sense, differs from practices normally followed by governments".

The AB noted in its report on *US–Countervailing Duty Investigation on DRAMs,* that the purpose of this provision was to act as an anti-circumvention device (§ 113):

> Paragraph (iv), in particular, is intended to ensure that governments do not evade their obligations under the SCM Agreement by using private bodies to take actions that would otherwise fall within Article 1.1(a)(1), were they to be taken by the government itself. In other words, Article 1.1(a)(1)(iv) is, in essence, an anti-circumvention provision.

The Panel in *EC–Countervailing Measures on DRAM Chips* held that for the "entrust"- or "direct"-test to be met, an entity must be acting on behalf of a government, since purely private actions escape the purview of the WTO Agreement (§§ 7.52–53). This test, hence, is a quest to decide whether an activity can be attributed to a government. In the words of the AB on *US–Countervailing Duty Investigation on DRAMs* (§ 108):

> identify the instances where seemingly private conduct may be attributable to a government for purposes of determining whether there has been a financial contribution within the meaning of the SCM Agreement.

Echoing the case law on *Japan–Semiconductors*,[9] the AB held in the same case that it is not necessary that the government threatens sanctions in case of non-compliance; it suffices that it provides private parties with sufficient incentives to act in a particular way. The AB did not go so far as to establish a "but for"-test here (e.g., ask the question whether an activity would have taken place even absent government involvement) (§ 116).

Evidence of entrustment or direction does not have to be beyond reasonable doubt. The Panel in *EC–Countervailing Measures on DRAM Chips* stated in this vein that it did not (§ 7.109):

> want to be seen as requiring an investigating authority to come up with the smoking gun in the sense of a written order by the government to a private body to provide a financial contribution. We understand that, in most cases, the authority will have to base its decision on a number of arguments and pieces of evidence which perhaps when considered in combination may all point in the direction of government entrustment or direction,

---

[9] See the relevant discussion in Chapter 2.

especially in cases where the level of cooperation by the interested parties is low.

The AB on *US–Countervailing Duty Investigation on DRAMs* confirmed this point when it held that there was no need for compelling evidence for a finding that financial contribution has been made (§§ 175ff.). In *EC–Countervailing Measures on DRAM Chips*, the EU IA had relied on circumstantial evidence to reach the conclusion that the government of Korea was entrusting or directing private bodies to participate in the restructuring of a failing Korean DRAMs producer: alleged non-commercial behavior and government ownership were two factors that weighed heavily in the IA's decision and the Panel found this approach reasonable. This Panel also held that, even if an IA decides not to treat as a public body an entity with important government control, this does not imply that government control or shareholding becomes irrelevant—quite the contrary: government shareholding in a private body may lower the evidentiary threshold for establishing that the government exercised its shareholding power. The Panel also expressed the view that a significant degree of cooperation is to be expected of interested parties in a countervailing duty investigation. In the absence of any subpoena or other evidence gathering powers, the possibility of resorting to the facts available and also the possibility of drawing certain inferences from the failure to cooperate, can play a crucial role in inducing interested parties to provide the necessary information to the authority (§§ 7.60–61). This Panel report was not appealed. However, in the appeal concerning the parallel[10] proceedings (*US–Countervailing Duty Investigation on DRAMs*), the AB reversed the Panel's ruling regarding the impact of circumstantial evidence, since the Panel had examined pieces of evidence in isolation, rather than in their totality as the IA had indeed done. The AB emphasized the importance of a holistic approach in countervailing duty cases, as the only way in which important circumstantial evidence could be appropriately taken into consideration by an IA (§ 150). The AB noted that this approach was particularly relevant in cases of entrustment or direction under Art. 1.1(a)(1)(iv) SCM, where much of the evidence that is publicly available, and therefore readily accessible to interested parties and the IA, would likely be of a circumstantial nature (footnote 277). The AB (*US–Countervailing Duty Investigation on DRAMs*) added that Panels cannot base their findings on evidence that was not reasonably before the IA. In its words, Panels would be violating the standard of review embedded in Art. 11 DSU if they operated with the "benefit of hindsight" (§ 175).

4.1.3 Any Form of Income or Price Support

Outside of the particular forms of financial contribution discussed above, a subsidy may also exist when "there is any form of income or price

---

[10] These two cases are quasi identical: the US and the EU countervailed the same Korean practice.

support in the sense of Article XVI of the GATT 1994" (Art. 1.1(a)(2) SCM). The concept of "any form of income or price support" is taken directly from the first paragraph of Art. XVI GATT. Income or price support mechanisms play an important role in farm goods, and commodities in general.

In *China–GOES*, the Panel held that a voluntary restraint agreement (VRA) cannot be considered a form of price support. Although a VRA benefits the industry by keeping prices artificially high, in the Panel's view, it cannot be that all that results in a benefit is considered a subsidy; rather, the form of the financial contribution is relevant (§§ 7.85–86, and § 7.93). In footnote 104, it cites a GATT Panel, which had speculated on the circumstances under which "a system which fixes domestic prices to producers at above the world price level might be considered a subsidy in the meaning of Article XVI". That Panel had agreed that "a system under which a government, by direct or indirect methods, maintains such a price by purchases and resale at a loss is a subsidy". However, the Panel had speculated that "where a government fixes by law a minimum price to producers which is maintained by quantitative restrictions . . there would be no loss to government" and consequently, no subsidy.[11] The Panel in *China–GOES* noted that the conclusion regarding the latter example was less relevant in the context of the SCM Agreement, under which the benefit of a subsidy was defined by reference to market benchmarks, rather than by the cost to government. However, both examples used by the GATT Panel at least illustrate that it envisaged "price support" to involve a case where governments set and maintain a fixed price, rather than a random change in price merely being a side-effect of any form of government measure.

4.2 BENEFIT TO RECIPIENT

In order for a government measure to constitute a subsidy, a second requirement is that the measure must confer a "benefit" (Art. 1.1(b) SCM). The AB in *Canada–Aircraft* made it clear that (§ 157):

> the issues—and the respective definitions—of a "financial contribution" and a "benefit" as two separate legal elements in Article 1.1 of the SCM Agreement, which together determine whether a subsidy exists.

In this vein, the Panel in *EC–Countervailing Measures on DRAM Chips*, clarified that whereas the requirement to show that a financial contribution has been made is a question that needs to be addressed from the perspective of the donor, the response to the question whether a benefit has indeed been conferred needs to be assessed from the perspective of the recipient (§§ 7.212ff., and especially § 7.175). There is, however, a se-

---

[11] GATT Panel in Subsidies and State Trading, Report on Subsidies, L/1160, 23 March 1960.

quence between financial contribution and benefit. As the AB stated in its report on *US–Countervailing Duty Investigation on DRAMs*, if no contribution took place, no benefit can result either (§ 205).

4.2.1 The Private Investor / Marketplace Test

The SCM Agreement does not define the term "benefit". Art. 14 SCM deals with the calculation of the amount of a subsidy bestowed. Inspired by this provision, in *Canada–Aircraft*,[12] the AB set out its understanding of the term "benefit" that has since been reproduced in subsequent Panel[13] and AB reports (§§ 157–158):

> [T]he word 'benefit', as used in Article 1.1(b), implies some kind of comparison. This must be so, for there can be no 'benefit' to the recipient unless the 'financial contribution' makes the recipient 'better off' than it would otherwise have been, absent that contribution. In our view, the marketplace provides an appropriate basis for comparison in determining whether a 'benefit' has been 'conferred', because the trade-distorting potential of a 'financial contribution' can be identified by determining whether the recipient has received a 'financial contribution' on terms more favourable than those available to the recipient in the market.
>
> Article 14, which we have said is relevant context in interpreting Article 1.1(b), supports our view that the marketplace is an appropriate basis for comparison. The guidelines set forth in Article 14 relate to equity investments, loans, loan guarantees, the provision of goods or services by a government, and the purchase of goods by a government. A 'benefit' arises under each of the guidelines if the recipient has received a 'financial contribution' on terms more favourable than those available to the recipient in the market.

Case law has consistently held that a benefit is conferred whenever an entity receives a "financial contribution" on terms better than it would have been able to obtain on the market.[14] To evaluate whether this has indeed been the case, adjudicators must compare the situation prevailing under the government measure and that which would have normally prevailed under market conditions. This gives rise to the notorious "private investor" test to determine whether a benefit has been conferred: Did the

---

[12] See the discussion of Howse and Neven (2007d).

[13] See for example, the Arbitrators' report in *Canada–Aircraft Credits and Guarantees (Article 22.6–Canada)* at § 3.60.

[14] There are two exceptions: *Canada–Dairy* and *EC–Export Subsidies on Sugar*. Both cases involve farm subsidies and were adjudicated under the Agreement on Agriculture. For a discussion of the former case, see Janow and Staiger (2003). For a discussion of the latter case, see Hoekman and Howse (2008).

recipient receive terms that are favorable to those that are obtained by a private investor on the market?

Sometimes, the benefit is quite obvious and does not even require examination against a market benchmark. This is likely to be the case in instances where the financial contribution consists of revenue foregone or not collected. For example, the Panel, in its report on *US–FSC*, noted that the tax exemption granted to foreign sales corporations amounted to a savings as great as "15 to 30 per cent on gross income from exporting" and therefore a benefit was clearly conferred (§ 7.103).

4.2.2 The Concept of a "Pass–Through" Benefit

Has a benefit been bestowed when a financial contribution hass been made to an entity (let's call this original recipient "A") and then that entity (or its product) is purchased by another entity (let's call the subsequent purchaser "B")? In similar instances, whether or not B has benefited from the original contribution depends on whether (or not) the original benefit was "passed through" to B.[15] WTO case law originally held that so long as the transaction between A and B took place at arm's length and a fair market value had been paid, no benefit had been conferred. On the other hand, if the price paid by B to A was below fair market price, then benefit "passed through" from A to B (AB, *US–Lead and Bismuth II*, § 68).

In a subsequent case, the AB nuanced this position, holding that payment of fair market value does not in and of itself exhaust all previously bestowed benefits. We quote from the AB report in *US–Countervailing Measures on Certain EC Products* (§ 103):

> We agree with the United States that, irrespective of the price paid by the new private owner, privatization does not *remove* the equipment that a state-owned enterprise may have acquired (or received) with a financial contribution and that, consequently, the same firm may 'continue[]' to make the same products on the same equipment. However, this observation serves only to illustrate that, following privatization, the *utility value* of equipment acquired as a result of a financial contribution is not extinguished, because it is transferred to the newly-privatized firm. But, the utility value of such equipment to the newly-privatized firm is legally irrelevant for purposes of determining the continued existence of a 'benefit' under the *SCM Agreement*. As we found in *Canada–Aircraft*, the value of the 'benefit' under the *SCM Agreement* is to be assessed using the marketplace as the basis for comparison. It follows, therefore, that once a fair market price is paid for the equipment, its *market value* is redeemed,

---

[15] See, e.g., *US–Lead and Bismuth II* and *US–Countervailing Measures on Certain EC Products*. These two cases are comprehensively discussed in Grossman and Mavroidis (2007), and (2007c).

regardless of the utility the firm may derive from the equipment. Accordingly, it is the market value of the equipment that is the focal point of analysis, and not the equipment's utility value to the privatized firm. (emphasis and italics in the original).

The AB disagreed in this respect with the Panel, which had held that there is an irrebutable presumption to the effect that every time a fair market value has been paid, the benefit disappears. The AB held that the presumption is rebuttable even in case of payment of the market value and that the facts of the case will reveal whether a benefit continues to exist post-privatization (§§ 121–124). The AB gave no indication at all regarding the nature of circumstances that can successfully rebut such a presumption.

In *US–Softwood Lumber III*, and *US–Softwood Lumber IV*, WTO adjudicating bodies faced a related question: is it possible to impose CVDs on products if their current producers did not themselves receive a financial contribution? The US had imposed CVDs on imports of softwood lumber from Canada based on a determination of subsidization of the lumber producers through the stumpage programs discussed *supra*. Recall that, through these programs, a good (standing timber) was provided to the tenured timber harvesters at less than market price. The timber harvesters sold the trees to the log producers, who sold logs to lumber producers who turned them into lumber products. It was neither the trees, nor the logs, which were exported or countervailed, but only the lumber products. The question before the Panel was thus whether the lumber producer nevertheless benefited from the cheap trees that were provided by the government to the harvester/log producers? In other words, did the benefit pass through to the lumber producer? The key question for the WTO Panel and the AB was whether a fair market price had been paid by the downstream to the upstream producer for the allegedly subsidized input. This was the view of the Panels and the AB dealing with this question. We quote from § 144 of the AB report on *US–Softwood Lumber IV*:

> Thus, for a potentially countervailable subsidy to exist, there must be a financial contribution by the government that confers a benefit on a recipient. Where a subsidy is conferred on input products, and the countervailing duty is imposed on processed products, the initial recipient of the subsidy and the producer of the eventually countervailed product, may not be the same. In such a case, there is a direct recipient of the benefit—the producer of the input product. When the input is subsequently processed, the producer of the processed product is an indirect recipient of the benefit—provided it can be established that the benefit flowing from the input subsidy is passed through, at least in part, to the processed product. Where the input producers and producers of the processed products operate at arm's length, the

pass-through of input subsidy benefits from the direct recipients to the indirect recipients downstream cannot simply be presumed; it must be established by the investigating authority. In the absence of such analysis, it cannot be shown that the essential elements of the subsidy definition in Article 1 are present in respect of the processed product.

4.2.3 Calculating the Amount of the Benefit

Art. 14 SCM reflects a list of benchmarks that can be used in order to calculate the amount of benefit.

- Where the government provides equity capital, the relevant benchmark is the usual investment practice (including the provision of risk capital) of private investors in the territory of the subsidizing WTO Member (Art. 14(a) SCM);
- Where the government provides a loan, the relevant benchmark is the amount that the loan recipient would pay if the loan could actually be obtained on the market (Art. 14(b) SCM);
- Where the government provides a loan guarantee, the relevant benchmark is the amount that the loan guarantee recipient would pay on a comparable commercial loan absent the government guarantee, with an adjustment made for the difference in fees (Art. 14(c) SCM);
- Where the government provides a good or service or where the government purchases a good, the relevant benchmark is the prevailing market conditions for the good or service in question (Art. 14(d) SCM);

The relevant benchmark is important, not only because it determines whether or not a "benefit" exists, but also the size of the "benefit." As we shall discuss *infra*, calculating the precise amount of benefit bestowed serves two purposes:

(a) It provides the maximum amount of CVDs that may be used to counteract injury caused by a subsidy;

(b) It also provides the maximum amount of countermeasures that may be taken by a WTO Member should the subsidy (or its adverse effects) not be removed, following the conclusion of multilateral dispute settlement. (Note that there is a potential exception in the case of prohibited subsidies)

The question of the calculation of a benefit is separate and distinct from the question whether a benefit exists:[16] a benefit will be calculated

---

[16] Of course the title of Art. 14 SCM suggests that this provision deals with the calculation of the amount of the subsidy in terms of benefit to the recipient, and it deals with the method for calculating the benefit to the recipient as becomes clear from the chapeau of Art. 14 SCM. However, the guidelines set forth in paragraphs (a)–(d), with which the calculation methodology has to comply, also clearly deal with the existence or non-existence of a benefit. Whether it is the

only after a Panel has satisfied itself that the three elements of the subsidy definition (financial contribution, benefit, and specificity) are present. The Panel in *EC–Countervailing Measures on DRAM Chips* underscored this point (§§ 7.187–179). The same Panel emphasized the importance of approaching the question from the perspective of the recipient, rather than from the provider of the financial contribution (§§ 7.211–212).

The wording of Art. 14 SCMleaves the reader with the impression that all benchmarks for calculating a benefit have been exhaustively provided in this provision. Yet, case law followed the opposite route. The Panels on *US–Softwood Lumber III*, and *US–Softwood Lumber IV* examined the DOC calculation of the benefit conferred on the lumber producers by the Canadian government. The US had used US prices, since, in its view, none of the benchmarks mentioned in the body of Art. 14 SCM was reasonable. The US claimed that it would be meaningless to use Art. 14(d) SCM (which refers to the "prevailing market conditions" in the subsidizing country), since there were not market conditions at all in Canada with respect to the lumber market: the price of land was heavily subsidized. The Panel disagreed and held that the US should have used the price for trees on private land prevailing in Canada as benchmark for the calculation of benefit. The Panel's analysis was based on the language of Art. 14 SCM (§ 7.45). It concluded that (§ 7.60):

> as long as there are prices determined by independent operators following the principle of supply and demand, even if supply or demand are affected by the government's presence in the market, there is a "market" in the sense of Article 14(d) [of the] *SCM Agreement*. (italics in the original).

The Panel explicitly acknowledged that, as a matter of economic logic, the US argument was on strong grounds. However, in the Panel's view, its role was not to amend the clear content of a provision, a role reserved to the WTO Membership (§§ 7.58–60). The AB overturned the Panel's decision. The AB noted that it is not the case that any market may form the appropriate benchmark for measuring a benefit conferred. Instead, it could well be the case that a market is so distorted by the government's financial contribution that taking the distorted market as the benchmark would not reveal the true trade distortion caused by the subsidies. According to the AB, it suffices that the benchmark relates to the prevailing market conditions in the country of provision. The AB held that, while market prices will generally represent an appropriate measure of the ad-

---

provision of equity capital, a loan, a loan guarantee or a good or service, each of the paragraphs provides that the financial contribution shall not be considered as conferring a benefit, unless if one of the contingencies mentioned therein happens. Only in the case of loans and loan guarantees (Art. 14 (b) and (c) SCM) does the text actually state what the amount of the benefit is. So, Art. 14 SCM, on its face, seems to be as much about the existence of a benefit as it is about the calculation of the amount of the benefit.

equacy of remuneration for the provision of goods, this may not always be the case (§ 90):

> investigating authorities may use a benchmark other than private prices in the country of provision under Article 14(d), if it is first established that private prices in that country are distorted because of the government's predominant role in providing those goods.

Only this interpretation was, in the eyes of the AB, consistent with the objective of Art. 14(d) SCM, which is to establish whether the recipient is better off than it would have been absent the government financial contribution (§ 93):

> Under the approach advocated by the Panel (that is, private prices in the country of provision must be used whenever they exist), however, there may be situations in which there is no way of telling whether the recipient is 'better off' absent the financial contribution. This is because the government's role in providing the financial contribution is so predominant that it effectively determines the price at which private suppliers sell the same or similar goods, so that the comparison contemplated by Article 14 would become circular.

Thus, the AB considered that the Panel's interpretation frustrated the object and purpose of the SCM Agreement, which disciplines the use of subsidies while, at the same time, enabling WTO Members whose domestic industries are harmed by subsidized imports to institute countervailing measures (§ 95). In sum, the AB concluded that the Canadian market was too distorted to be used as benchmark, and, more generally, that it would not be possible to use in-country market prices to calculate the benefit where the government's participation in the market as a provider of the same or similar goods is so predominant that private suppliers will align their prices with those of the government-provided goods (§ 101). The AB added, nevertheless, a caveat to the effect that determination of whether private prices are distorted because of the government's predominant role in the market, as a provider of certain goods, must be made on a case-by-case basis, according to the particular facts underlying each countervailing duty investigation (§ 102).

The Panel in *EC–Countervailing Measures on DRAM Chips*, in line with the AB in this respect, held that, when facing problems with the prescribed methodology, an IA is entitled to considerable leeway in adopting a reasonable methodology (§ 7.213).

In *US–Antidumping and Countervailing Duties (China)* the US IA refused to use Chinese interest rates as benchmark to examine whether loans by SOCBs (state owned commercial banks) were subsidized (§ 470):

... because of pervasive government intervention in the banking sector, which created significant distortions, restricting and influencing even foreign banks within China. Having rejected interest rates in China as benchmarks, the USDOC resorted to an external benchmark. Specifically, the USDOC constructed, using a regression-based methodology, an interest rate benchmark based on inflation-adjusted interest rates of a group of countries with a gross national income ("GNI") similar to that of China.

The AB explained that the government being a significant supplier of a commodity does not necessarily lead to the conclusion that prices in the exporting market are unreliable and hence recourse to another benchmark is warranted. In its words (§ 441):

We read that Appellate Body report as indicating that, if the government is a significant supplier, this fact alone cannot justify a finding that prices are distorted. Instead, where the government is the predominant supplier, it is *likely* that private prices will be distorted, but a case-by-case analysis is still required. (emphasis in the original).

In this case, the Chinese state company possessed a 96.1% market share and 3% of total imports. In the AB's view, this information was enough for it to find that the US IA had the right to move away from the four corners of Art. 14 SCM and use another standard to calculate the benefit granted to the Chinese companies (§§ 455ff.). The AB went on to examine whether the US had exercised its discretion in reasonable manner. To do that, the external loan chosen should be comparable to that investigated (§ 476):

Thus, a benchmark loan under Article 14(b) should have as many elements as possible in common with the investigated loan to be comparable. The Panel noted that, ideally, an investigating authority should use as a benchmark a loan to the same borrower that has been established around the same time, has the same structure as, and similar maturity to, the government loan, is about the same size, and is denominated in the same currency. The Panel, however, also considered that, in practice, the existence of such an ideal benchmark loan would be extremely rare, and that a comparison should also be possible with other loans that present a lesser degree of similarity.[17] We agree with both of these observations by the Panel.

It went on to state that loans do not lose their character as "commercial" loans simply because they have been provided by a government; an IA must show how government presence altered the commercial character of the loan (§ 479). In establishing whether a loan is not "commercial", the

---

[17] Panel Report, § 10.115.

IA must show how because of government presence the loan provided is at odds with market reality (§ 480).

4.3 SPECIFICITY

For a government measure to constitute a "subsidy" under the SCM Agreement, the financial contribution which confers a benefit must be "specific" (Art. 2 SCM). Otherwise, the measure—which might be considered a subsidy in economics parlance—does not amount to a subsidy, as the term is legally construed by the SCM Agreement.

The rationale for the specificity-requirement reflects the view that only specific financial contributions can lead to inefficient resource allocation, and, eventually, to trade distortions. If a subsidy is generally available, then all productive units in a country can benefit from it, and there will be no diversion of resources to certain enterprises which would not otherwise have attracted such resources. In the words of the Panel in *US–Upland Cotton,* subsidies will not be specific if they are (§ 7.1142):

> sufficiently broadly available throughout an economy as not to benefit a particular limited group of producers of certain products.

For two types of subsidies, there is no need to satisfy the specificity-requirement, as they are considered specific per se: (1) export subsidies, and (2) local content subsidies (Art. 2.3 SCM). These are the so-called *prohibitive* subsidies to be discussed *infra*. The Panel in *US–Upland Cotton* underscored this point (§ 7.1153). In similar vein, subsidies limited to certain enterprises located within a designated geographical region are specific by virtue of Art. 2.2 SCM.

In contrast, two government activities are considered non-specific:

(a) The setting or change of generally applicable tax rates by all levels of government (Art. 2.2 SCM);

(b) The granting of subsidies according to objective criteria or conditions (Art. 2.1(b) SCM).

The former is the natural consequence of the fact that the WTO Agreement does not prescribe common tax policies. The latter is defined in footnote 2 to the SCM Agreement as follows:

> Objective criteria or conditions, as used herein, mean criteria or conditions which are neutral, which do not favour certain enterprises over others, and which are economic in nature and horizontal in application, such as number of employees or size of enterprise.

To determine whether a subsidy is specific to an "industry" or "enterprise" or a group of enterprises, an IA must review whether the challenged scheme is (Art. 2.1(c) SCM):

(a) Used by a limited number of certain enterprises;

(b) Predominantly used by certain enterprises;

(c) Disproportionately large amounts are granted to certain enterprises;

(d) Specific because of the manner in which discretion has been exercised by the granting authority in the decision to grant a subsidy.

There is no obligation to examine all four factors, as the Panel in *US–Softwood Lumber IV* made clear (§ 7.123): in this case, Canada had argued that the Canadian government had never intentionally limited access to the stumpage programs to lumber producers. In its view, the predominant use of the stumpage programs by lumber producers could be explained by the fact that the alleged financial contribution consisted of the provision of trees, which, thanks to inherent characteristics, are of interest mainly to a limited number of log and lumber producers. The Panel was of the view that there was no need to show intent in order to satisfy the *de facto* specificity-requirement although deliberate action by the government might be revealing (§ 7.116). What matters is that one (at least) of the four criteria mentioned in Art. 2.1(c) SCM has been met.[18]

Subsidies are specific either *de jure* (because they are by law limited to a group of industries and/or enterprises), or *de facto* (because, although by law generally available, their use is in fact confined to a group of industries and/or enterprises).

The Panel in *EC and Certain Member States–Large Civil Aircraft* understood the term "explicitly limits" appearing in Art. 2.1(a) SCM as equivalent to the establishment of the existence of a limitation that expressly and unambiguously restricts the availability of a subsidy to certain enterprises, and thereby does not make the subsidy sufficiently broadly available throughout an economy. The AB confirmed (§ 949). In similar vein, in *US–Large Civil Aircraft*, the Panel held that (§ 7.190):

> The express limitation can be found either in the legislation by which the granting authority operates, or in other statements or means by which the granting authority expresses its will.

In *US–Antidumping and Countervailing Duties (China)* the AB held that a subsidy will be specific if access is limited to either the financial contribution or the benefit (§ 378).

The SCM Agreement does not define "industry" in a particular way. The Panel in *US–Softwood Lumber IV*, rejected the argument that the term "industry" should be defined with reference to a particular and specifically defined product. The subsidy may be specific to an industry such as the steel industry or, in the case in question, the lumber industry, even

---

[18] Note nonetheless, that an IA is not precluded from examining all four criteria, as the Panel in *EC–Countervailing Measures on DRAM Chips* confirmed.

when this industry produces a wide variety of slightly different products. In this case, Canada had argued, that more than 200 separate products are manufactured by companies holding harvesting rights, together forming about 23 separate industries: in Canada's view, the wooden door and window industry should, for example, be distinguished from the wooden kitchen cabinet and bathroom vanity industry. A subsidy that is being granted to all those different industries was hardly, in Canada's view, being granted to a limited number of industries. Rejecting Canada's approach, the Panel expressed the view that specificity under Art. 2 SCM must be determined at the enterprise or industry level, and not at the product level: the text of Art. 2 SCM did not require a detailed analysis of the end-products produced by the enterprises involved; nor did Art. 2.1 (c) SCM provide that only a limited number of products should benefit from the subsidy (§§ 7.120–121).

The question nevertheless remains how big can an industry be? Is, for example, a subsidy specific if it is limited to the farm industry, or should it be confined say to wheat producers only? The Panel in *US–Upland Cotton*[19] avoided answering head on this question. It held that the breadth of industry may depend on several factors. In its view, the breadth or narrowness of specificity is not susceptible to rigid quantitative definition (§ 7.1142). It, thus, came to the following conclusion (§ 7.1151):

> In our view, the industry represented by a portion of United States agricultural production that is growing and producing certain agricultural crops (and certain livestock in certain regions under restricted conditions) is a sufficiently discrete segment of the United States economy in order to qualify as 'specific' within the meaning of Article 2 of the *SCM Agreement*. (italics in the original).

The Panel in *EC and Certain Member States–Large Civil Aircraft* addressed *inter alia*, the question of regional subsidies: should a subsidy be deemed specific if it is restricted to a certain region? Or, as the EU had argued, it should be specific only if it is also specific to certain enterprises within that region? The Panel refuted the EU argument (§§ 7.974 ff. and especially 7.1223).

5. PROHIBITED SUBSIDIES

Once a government measure is found to constitute a "subsidy" pursuant to the legal requirements of the SCM Agreement, the next step is to determine whether it falls under the category of a "prohibited" or "actionable" subsidy. A third category, "non-actionable" subsidy, originally exist-

---

[19] Sapir and Trachtman (2008) note that the specificity-requirement can be met when a scheme is limited to use by specific industries and/or enterprises, and the narrower the list of beneficiaries, the likelier that the requirement will be met.

ed, but has since expired. These three categories have sometimes been analogized to a "traffic lights" scheme: Prohibited subsidies are "red light" subsidies that are illegal under all circumstances. Actionable subsidies are "yellow light" subsidies, whose legality depends on the circumstances that arise from their effect. The now-expired non-actionable subsidies were once referred to as "green light" subsidies that are legal under all circumstances.

We begin in this Section with a discussion the rules pertaining to the category of prohibited subsidies. We then turn to the larger category of actionable subsidies in the subsequent Section.

5.1 THE LEGAL DISCIPLINE

Two forms of subsidies are expressly prohibited under Art. 3 SCM:

(1) Local content subsidies; and

(2) Export subsidies.

Local content measures have been outlawed since the inception of the GATT (Art. III.5); hence, outlawing subsidies conditional upon the use of domestic value added should not come as a surprise. Art. III SCM makes clear that it does not matter whether this is the sole condition or one of several conditions.

The attitude of the world trading system towards export subsidies, on the other hand, has remarkably evolved since the inception of the GATT. The GATT initially followed a much more lenient approach than the SCM-Agreement on this score.[20] Art. VI GATT implicitly recognized that subsidies may be a legitimate instrument of domestic public policy by specifying that countervailing duties to offset the subsidy can only be imposed if the effect of subsidization has resulted in material injury to a domestic industry. Art. XVI GATT in its original formulation did not ban export subsidies. It was in the context of the 1955 Review Session of the GATT that trading nations agreed to amend Art. XVI: they introduced § 4 (Section B) which banned export subsidies on manufactured goods; however, export subsidies on farm goods were not banned. The Working Party on Subsidies (1960) aimed *inter alia*, at ensuring faithful implementation of Art. XVI.4 GATT, and included an agreed-upon list of illegal subsidies.[21] The US continued to seek tougher measures against export subsidies,[22] which then led to the issuance of the 1987 "Declaration Giving Ef-

---

[20] Sykes (2003a); Janow and Staiger (2003); Trebilcock, Howse, and Elliason (2013).

[21] GATT Doc. L/1381 at para 5 adopted on November 19, 1960, GATT Doc. BISD 9S/185. The list of illegal subsidies mentioned in § 5 included: illegal currency restriction, direct subsidies, remission of direct taxes, exemption of charges in connexion with import or export other than indirect taxes, charging of prices below world prices for delivery by governments of raw materials, export credit guarantees at manifestly inadequate rates, export credits at non market rates, and government borne costs for obtaining credit.

[22] Hemmendinger (1969) at p. 206; Stewart *et al.* (2007) reflect in detail the US dissatisfaction with the results of the Working Party on Subsidies as well as the planning of the next steps.

fect to Provisions of Art. XVI.4" promising action within set deadlines.[23] Art. III of the SCM Agreement, banning export subsidies outright for non-agricultural goods, subsequently followed.

5.2 *DE JURE* AND *DE FACTO* EXPORT SUBSIDIES

Annex I of the SCM Agreement contains in an Illustrative List twelve types of export subsidies. Among some of the examples listed are:

- Direct subsidies contingent upon export performance
- Currency retention schemes or similar practices that involve a bonus on exports
- Government provision of (or government-mandated rates for) internal transport and freight charges on terms more favorable than those provided for domestic shipments
- Government provision of goods or services for use in the production of exported goods on terms and conditions more favorable than those for the production of goods for domestic consumption
- Full or partial exemption, remission, or deferral of direct taxes or social welfare charges, specifically related to exports
- Allowance of special deductions for exports, beyond those granted for production related to domestic consumption
- Provision of export credit guarantee or insurance programs, at premium rates which are inadequate to cover the long-term operating costs and losses of the programs
- Provision of export credit at rates below those which the government actually had to pay for the funds (subject to certain additional conditions)

The AB report in *Brazil–Aircraft (Art. 21.5–Canada)* held that a scheme that falls under the purview of the Illustrative List is *ipso facto* prohibited. There is no additional requirement to demonstrate that it is contingent upon export performance under Art. 3.1(c) SCM. Assuming a scheme is not reflected in the Illustrative List, the complainant must demonstrate that it is either *de jure* or *de facto* export subsidy.[24] A case where the law conditions the payment of a subsidy upon exportation would amount to *de jure* export subsidy. *De facto* export contingency operates as an anti-circumvention provision against attempts by WTO Members to link benefits to exports without explicitly stating that this has indeed been the case. The AB in *Canada–Aircraft* accepted this premise and discussed the different evidentiary standards required to demon-

---

In particular, the US was upset with the fact that some export refunds were not outlawed as well.

[23] 17 GATT contracting parties adhered, see GATT Doc. MTN.GNG/NG10/W/4 of September 28, 1987.

[24] The letter of Art. 3.1 SCM ("either in law or in fact") leaves no doubt that this is the correct conclusion.

strate the existence of a *de jure* or a *de facto* subsidy. It explained why, in its view, the latter was a more demanding standard in the following terms (§ 167):

> In our view, the legal standard expressed by the word 'contingent' is the same for both *de jure* and *de facto* contingency. There is a difference, however, in what evidence may be employed to prove that a subsidy is export contingent. *De jure* export contingency is demonstrated on the basis of the words of the relevant legislation, regulation or legal instrument. Proving *de facto* export contingency is a much more difficult task. There is no single legal document which will demonstrate, on its face, that a subsidy is 'contingent . . . in fact. . . . Upon export performance.' Instead, the existence of this relationship of contingency, between the subsidy and the export performance, must be inferred from the total configuration of the facts constituting and surrounding the granting of the subsidy, none of which on its own is likely to be decisive in any given case. . . . We note that satisfaction of the standard for determining *de facto* export contingency set out in footnote 4 requires proof of three different substantive elements: first, 'the granting of a subsidy'; second, 'is . . . tied to . . .'; and third, 'actual or anticipated exportation or export earnings.' (original emphasis)

In *EC and Certain Member States–Large Civil Aircraft*,[25] the AB explained that for a scheme to be *de facto* export subsidy it must incentivize producers towards exporting rather than selling in the domestic market even though similar behavior does not correspond to the market conditions of supply and demand (§ 1102):

> We find that the factual equivalent of *de jure* conditionality between the granting of a subsidy and anticipated exportation can be established where the granting of the subsidy is geared to induce the promotion of future export performance of the recipient. The standard for *de facto* export contingency under Article 3.1(a) and footnote 4 of the *SCM Agreement* would be met when the subsidy is granted so as to provide an incentive to the recipient to export in a way that is not simply reflective of the conditions of supply and demand in the domestic and export markets undistorted by the granting of the subsidy. (italics in the original).

It follows that inducement suffices for a subsidy to be considered an export subsidy and it is not necessary to impose a legally binding obligation to export. The AB explained its understanding of the evidentiary standard associated with proof of *de jure* export subsidy in § 112 of its report on *US—FSC (Article 21.5—EC)*:

---

[25] Compare Slot (2010) and Wu (2010) on this issue.

> ... a subsidy is contingent "in law" upon export performance when the existence of that condition can be demonstrated on the basis of the very words of the relevant legislation, regulation or other legal instrument constituting the measure.... [F]or a subsidy to be *de jure* export contingent, the underlying legal instrument does not always have to provide *expressis verbis* that the subsidy is available only upon fulfilment of the condition of export performance. Such conditionality can also be derived by necessary implication from the words actually used in the measure. (original emphasis)

The evidentiary standard associated with a demonstration of *de facto* export subsidy was discussed in the Panel report in *Australia–Automotive Leather II* (§§ 9.36–9.66). In this case the Panel found that a subsidy was *de facto* an export subsidy based on the following factors:

> (a) Australia had agreed to pay Howe (a private economic operator) 30 million Australian dollars in three instalments, if Howe were to meet certain sales and investment targets;
>
> (b) The terms of the contract between Australia and Howe did not require Howe to export, though it provided the latter with incentives to do so;
>
> (c) The government's awareness, at the time the contract was concluded, that Howe earned the majority of its income from exports was crucial in the Panel's evaluation;
>
> (d) For Howe to meet the targets set, exporting was *passage obligé*, since the Australian market was too small to absorb its production.

This Panel concluded that an export subsidy had been paid based on the totality of the evidence before it. A subsequent report clarified that at least one of the factors mentioned in *Australia–Automotive Leather II* by itself had no probative value that an export subsidy has been paid: the AB in *Canada–Aircraft* was dealing with a subsidy paid by TPC (a Canadian entity) to Canadian aircraft producers. The AB paid particular attention to footnote 4 to Art. 3.1 SCM, and held that mere knowledge that the beneficiary is exporting does not suffice for the *de facto* threshold to be met. Something more is required. Footnote 4, which interprets the term "subsidies contingent [...] in fact" reads:

> This standard is met when the facts demonstrate that the granting of a subsidy, without having been made legally contingent upon export performance, is in fact tied to actual or anticipated exportation or export earnings. The mere fact that a subsidy is granted to enterprises which export shall not for that reason alone be considered to be an export subsidy within the meaning of this provision.

We quote from §§ 172—174 of the report:

The second substantive element in footnote 4 is "tied to". The ordinary meaning of "tied to" confirms the linkage of "contingency" with "conditionality" in Article 3.1(a). Among the many meanings of the verb "tie", we believe that, in this instance, because the word "tie" is immediately followed by the word "to" in footnote 4, the relevant ordinary meaning of "tie" must be to "limit or restrict as to . . . conditions". This element of the standard set forth in footnote 4, therefore, emphasizes that a relationship of conditionality or dependence must be demonstrated. The second substantive element is at the very heart of the legal standard in footnote 4 and cannot be overlooked. In any given case, the facts must "demonstrate" that the granting of a subsidy is *tied to* or *contingent upon* actual or anticipated exports. It does *not* suffice to demonstrate solely that a government granting a subsidy *anticipated* that exports would result. The prohibition in Article 3.1(a) applies to subsidies that are *contingent* upon export performance.

We turn now to the third substantive element provided in footnote 4. The dictionary meaning of the word "anticipated" is "expected". The use of this word, however, does *not* transform the standard for "contingent . . . in fact" into a standard merely for ascertaining "expectations" of exports on the part of the granting authority. Whether exports were anticipated or "expected" is to be gleaned from an examination of objective evidence. This examination is quite separate from, *and should not be confused with*, the examination of whether a subsidy is "tied to" actual or anticipated exports. A subsidy may well be granted in the knowledge, or with the anticipation, that exports will result. Yet, that alone is not sufficient, because that alone is not proof that the granting of the subsidy is *tied to* the anticipation of exportation.

There is a logical relationship between the second sentence of footnote 4 and the "tied to" requirement set forth in the first sentence of that footnote. The second sentence of footnote 4 precludes a panel from making a finding of *de facto* export contingency for the sole reason that the subsidy is "granted to enterprises which export". In our view, merely knowing that a recipient's sales are export-oriented does not demonstrate, without more, that the granting of a subsidy is tied to actual or anticipated exports. The second sentence of footnote 4 is, therefore, a specific expression of the requirement in the first sentence to demonstrate the "tied to" requirement. We agree with the Panel that, under the second sentence of footnote 4, the export orientation of a recipient may be taken into account as *a* relevant fact, provided that it is one of several facts which are considered and is not the only fact supporting a finding. (original emphasis)

Panels can request the help of the Permanent Group of Experts (PGE), established in order to evaluate whether a scheme is a prohibited subsidy. The PGE comprises trade experts and, if requested to pronounce on a case, its opinion binds the Panel (Art. 4.5 SCM). So far, Panels have refused to make use of this institutional facility.

5.3 COUNTERACTING PROHIBITED SUBSIDIES

Assuming the complainant has prevailed in demonstrating that a government measure constitutes a prohibited subsidy, the Panel and/or the AB will recommend that the subsidy be withdrawn without delay (Art. 4.7 SCM).[26] Panels that are asked to pronounce on this issue are requested, in deviation of their usual procedures, to reach a speedy judgment within 90 days (Art. 4.6 SCM). In case of refusal to implement the recommendation, the injured party can have recourse to appropriate countermeasures (Art. 4.10 SCM). A footnote to Art. 4.10 SCM explains that "appropriate" means not disproportionate (sic).[27] Recall that Art. 7.9 SCM provides that in case of actionable subsidies, commensurate countermeasures, that is, countermeasures commensurate with the degree and nature of the adverse effects determined to exist, may be authorized. WTO adjudicating bodies have originally held that the punishment of prohibited subsidies through countermeasures should be harder than the punishment of any other breach of the WTO Agreement. The report on *Brazil–Aircraft (Art. 22.6—Brazil)* was the first that had the opportunity to clarify the ambit of the term "appropriate", and explain the relationship between Art. 4.10 SCM and Art. 22.4 DSU.[28] This case (and its "twin" dispute, *Canada–Aircraft*) concerned (export) subsidization by Canada and Brazil of their respective national aircraft producers. A duopoly producing regional jets (that is, short to medium haul: Embraer for Brazil, Bombardier for Canadawas in place). To base its finding that the quantification of appropriate countermeasures should be linked to a benchmark other than the damage suffered by the complainant (as is the case under Art. 7.9 SCM), the Arbitrators first explained the difference they saw in the function of the remedy against a prohibited subsidy, as opposed to remedies to address any other nullification or impairment of WTO Members' rights. Important to their reasoning was the fact that

---

[26] This is the only case where the content of a Panel recommendation is specific; normally, WTO adjudicating bodies will recommend that the concerned party bring its measures into compliance, leaving addressees thus with substantial discretion as to the implementing activities (Art. 19 DSU).

[27] Footnotes 9 and 10 provide as follows with respect to the term 'appropriate countermeasures': 'This expression is not meant to allow countermeasures that are disproportionate in light of the fact that the subsidies dealt with under these provisions are prohibited'.

[28] Report of the Arbitrators, *Brazil–Aircraft (Art. 22.6—Brazil)*, §§ 3.42–3.60.

they considered that the purpose of Art. 4 SCM is to achieve the withdrawal of the prohibited subsidy (§ 3.48):

> . . . the purpose of Article 4 is to achieve the withdrawal of the prohibited subsidy. In this respect, we consider that the requirement to withdraw a prohibited subsidy is of a different nature than removal of the specific nullification or impairment caused to a Member by the measure. The former aims at removing a measure which is presumed under the WTO Agreement to cause negative trade effects, irrespective of who suffers those trade effects and to what extent. The latter aims at eliminating the effects of a measure on the trade of a given Member; the fact that nullification or impairment is established with respect to a measure does not necessarily mean that, in the presence of an obligation to withdraw that measure, the level of appropriate countermeasures should be based only on the level of nullification or impairment suffered by the Member requesting the authorisation to take countermeasures.[29]

The focal point of the exercise for the Arbitrators was thus not the injury suffered by the payment of an illegal subsidy. They consequently rejected arguments by Brazil to the effect that their proposed benchmark (the amount of the subsidy) was not reasonable. The Arbitrators argued that anyway the subsidy benchmark was not too onerous since, in all likelihood, Brazil gained much more from its subsidies than it had actually invested. They also rejected an argument to the effect that their benchmark amounted to punitive damages. We quote from §§ 3.54 and 3.55:

> Our interpretation of the scope of the term 'appropriate countermeasures' in Article 4 of the SCM Agreement above shows that this would not be the case. Indeed, the level of countermeasures simply corresponds to the amount of subsidy which has to be withdrawn. Actually, given that export subsidies usually operate with a multiplying effect (a given amount allows a company to make a number of sales, thus gaining a foothold in a given market with the possibility to expand and gain market shares), we are of the view that a calculation based on the level of nullification or impairment would, as suggested by the calculation of Canada based on the harm caused to its industry, produce higher figures than one based exclusively on the amount of the subsidy. On the other hand, if the actual level of nullification or impairment is substantially lower than the subsidy, a countermeasure based on the actual level of nullification or impair-

---

[29] Report of the Arbitrators, *Brazil–Aircraft (Art 22.6—Brazil)*, at § 3.48. Similar issues were raised in the Panel and AB reports on *EC and Certain Members States–Large Civil Aircraft*, the dispute concerning the subsidization of Airbus, see the analysis of Slot (2010) and Wu (2010).

ment will have less or no inducement effect and the subsidizing country may not withdraw the measure at issue.

Brazil also claimed that countermeasures based on the full amount of the subsidy would be highly punitive. We understand the term 'punitive' within the meaning given to it in the Draft Articles. A countermeasure becomes punitive when it is not only intended to ensure that the State in breach of its obligations bring its conduct into conformity with its international obligations, but contains an additional dimension meant to sanction the action of that State. Since we do not find a calculation of the appropriate countermeasures based on the amount of the subsidy granted to be disproportionate, we conclude that, a fortiori, it cannot be punitive.[30]

The same logic was followed in the Arbitrators' report on *US–FSC (Article 22.6–US)*. The Arbitrators, extensively referring to public international law and the International Law Commission (ILC) reports on state responsibility,[31] held that the EU (complainant) should be authorized to adopt countermeasures up to US$4,043 million, that is, the amount of subsidies paid by the US to its national producers (beneficiaries under the Foreign Sales Corporation (FSC) scheme).[32] One should, however, add a caveat here: the Arbitrators claimed that, had they used an injury to EU-standard as benchmark (trade effects), they would have ended up anyway with a similar number.[33] The Arbitrators clarified that trade effects are not *a priori* ruled out as benchmark. They were simply of the view that Art. 4.10 SCM does not require a trade effects-test.[34]

To allow one complaining member to take countermeasures of an amount equal to the full amount of the subsidy may prove problematic in cases of sequential enforcement, where more than one WTO Members decide to challenge the same measure in subsequent WTO proceedings. In *US–FSC (Article 22.6–US)*, the Arbitrators added a few words to address the situation where, subsequent to the EU challenge, another WTO Member decided to attack the same US measure (the FSC scheme):

> Understandably, it would be our expectation that this determination will have the practical effect of facilitating prompt compliance by the United States. On any hypothesis that there

---

[30] Report of the Arbitrators, *Brazil–Aircraft* (Art 22.6—Brazil), §§ 3.54–3.55.

[31] Report of the Arbitrators, *US–FSC (Article 22.6–US)*, §§ 5.30–5.62.

[32] Report of the Arbitrators, *US–FSC (Article 22.6–US)*, §§ 6.1–6.30. With respect to the term 'not disproportionate', the arbitrators considered that 'the entitlement to countermeasures is to be assessed in light of the legal status of the wrongful act and the manner in which the breach of that obligation has upset the balance of rights and obligations as between Members. It is from that perspective that the judgment as to whether countermeasures are disproportionate is to be made', Arbitrator, *US–FSC (Article 22.6–US)*, § 5.24.

[33] Report of the Arbitrators, *US–FSC (Article 22.6–US)*, § 6.57.

[34] Report of the Arbitrators, *US–FSC (Article 22.6–US)*, §§ 6.33–6.34.

would be a future complainant, we can only observe that this would give rise inevitably to a different situation for assessment. To the extent that the basis sought for countermeasures was purely and simply that of countering the initial measure (as opposed to, e.g., the trade effects on the Member concerned) it is conceivable that the allocation issue would arise (although due regard should be given to the point made in footnote 84 above). We take note, on this point, of the statement by the European Communities:

... it may well be that the European Communities would be happy to share the task of applying countermeasures against the United States with another member and voluntarily agree to remove some of its countermeasures so as to provide more scope for another WTO member to be authorized to do the same. This will be another fact that future arbitrators could take into consideration.[35]

Interestingly, the Arbitrators in *Canada–Aircraft Credits and Guarantees (Article 22.6–Canada)*, saw force in the argument that there was need to induce Canada to comply in light of its statements before the panel that it did not intend to do so. The Arbitrators used the amount of the subsidy as the benchmark[36] and calculated the amount of countermeasures to be US$206,497,305.[37] They then continued, however, to examine whether adjustments needed to be made to this amount to make it "an appropriate level of countermeasures". In their view, an upward adjustment of this amount was justified in order to induce compliance, in light of Canada's statements that it would not withdraw the subsidy.[38] So, the Arbitrators added 20% to the level of the countermeasures in order to induce compliance:

---

[35] Report of the Arbitrators, *US–FSC (Article 22.6–US)*, §§ 6.28–6.29. The Arbitrators' claim that that they would have ended up with the same amount, had they used trade effects as benchmark to quantify the appropriateness of countermeasures, and this passage seem hard to reconcile. The Arbitrators calculated total trade effects (something which is discernible from the report): if their calculation is correct, this is a case where (total) trade effects yield a number as high as the amount of subsidy paid. However, since the number chosen is a number within a range of possibilities, we simply do not know if the EU injury is within the lower or the higher ebb of the range. In other words, the EU might have been over- or under-compensated depending on the placement of its injury within the range calculated in the Arbitrators' report. Be it as it may though, Esserman and Howse (2004) voiced their dissatisfaction with this report, arguing that the ultimate remedy was clearly disproportionate, in violation of the standard enshrined in Art. 4.10 SCM.

[36] Report of the Arbitrators, *Canada–Aircraft Credits and Guarantees (Article 22.6–Canada)*, § 3.51. The amount of the subsidy was calculated on the basis of the benefit to the recipient, that is, the benefit conferred by the loan, rather than the amount of the loan as such. Report of the Arbitrators, *Canada–Aircraft Credits and Guarantees (Article 22.6–Canada)*, § 3.60.

[37] Report of the Arbitrators, *Canada–Aircraft Credits and Guarantees (Article 22.6–Canada)*, § 3.90.

[38] Report of the Arbitrators, *Canada–Aircraft Credits and Guarantees (Article 22.6–Canada)*, § 3.107.

Recalling Canada's current position to maintain the subsidy at issue and having regard to the role of countermeasures in inducing compliance, we have decided to adjust the level of countermeasures calculated on the basis of the total amount of the subsidy by an amount which we deem reasonably meaningful to cause Canada to reconsider its current position to maintain the subsidy at issue in breach of its obligations. We consequently adjust the level of countermeasures by an amount corresponding to 20 per cent of the amount of the subsidy as calculated in Section III.E above, i.e.: US$206,497,305 x 20% (US$41,299,461) = US$247,796,766.

As we have noted in paragraph 3.120, adjustments such as the one we are making cannot be precisely calibrated. There is no scientifically based formula that we could use to calculate this adjustment. In that sense, the adjustment might be viewed as a symbolic one. Even so, we are convinced that it is a justified adjustment in light of the circumstances of this case and, in particular, the need to induce compliance with WTO obligations. Without such an adjustment, we would not be satisfied that an appropriate level of countermeasures had been established in this case.[39]

This is the only genuine case of punitive damages, that is, damages dissociated from the legal wrong that has been recommended in WTO case law. But then a sea change occurred: In *US–Upland Cotton (Article 22.6–US)*, the Arbitrators abandoned the subsidy-benchmark and decided that it is appropriate to use trade effects as benchmark when calculating countermeasures for refusal to withdraw a prohibited subsidy. We quote the relevant passage (§ 4.114):

> In conclusion, we have found that the terms "appropriate countermeasures", as informed by footnote 9 of the *SCM Agreement*, entitle the complaining party to countermeasures that are suited to the circumstances of the case. This can lead to a countermeasure being authorized at a level that is within the range of the *trade-distorting impact* that can fairly be said to arise for the complaining Member from the failure to withdraw the illegal measure. We have also determined that footnote 9 further invites us to ensure that the countermeasures to be authorized are not *excessive*, having regard to the extent to which the trade of the complaining party has been affected, and taking into account also the prohibited nature of the subsidy. (italics in the original).

Paying only lip service to prior case law, this report introduced the trade effects-test as benchmark to calculate appropriate countermeasures

---

[39] Report of the Arbitrators, *Canada–Aircraft Credits and Guarantees (Article 22.6–Canada)*, §§ 3.121–3.122.

and as a result equated the level of appropriate-to that of commensurate countermeasures. To defend their choice, the Arbitrators argued that otherwise WTO Members that could have suffered little injury would have been compensated as much as those who had suffered substantially more (§ 4.60).

6. ACTIONABLE SUBSIDIES

The vast majority of government measures that amount to a "subsidy" under the SCM Agreement fall under the category of actionable subsidies. Such subsidies are not outright illegal. Instead, actionable subsidy is impermissible under WTO law only if it causes one of the three types of *adverse effects* to the interests of other WTO Members included in Art. 5 SCM:

(a) Injury to the domestic industry;

(b) Nullification or impairment of benefits; and

(c) Serious prejudice.

Therefore, to prevail in WTO litigation, the complainant must demonstrate that an actionable subsidy results in one of these three "adverse effects." We discuss these in greater detail below.

6.1 INJURY TO THE DOMESTIC INDUSTRY

The term "injury" is used here in the same way as in the CVD-context (footnote 11 to Art. 5 SCM). We will examine this concept in greater detail in the section, *infra*, of this Chapter discussing CVDs. For now, it will suffice to note that the term "injury" carries the same legal meaning in the context of WTO multilateral dispute settlement of an actionable subsidy as it does in the context of a CVD investigation conducted unilaterally by a WTO Member.

6.2 NULLIFICATION OR IMPAIRMENT OF BENEFITS

Art. 5(b) SCM states that adverse effects can take the form of nullification or impairment of benefits accruing either directly or indirectly to other WTO Members, in particular, the benefits of concessions bound under Art. II GATT; a footnote to this provision explains that the term "nullification or impairment" should be understood as synonymous to the term included in Art. XXIII.1(b) GATT 1994. There is, nonetheless, an important difference regarding the evidence of nullification and impairment under the GATT, and in the SCM-context. The Panel, in its report in *US–Offset Act (Byrd Amendment)* held that, whereas nullification or impairment of benefits may be presumed under the GATT (since, any violation of a provision presumably leads to nullification of benefits according to standing case law), no similar presumption exists in the SCM Agreement where nullification must be proven (§ 7.119). The Panel held that three elements must be established in order to uphold a claim to this effect (§ 7.120):

(a) The existence of a benefit accruing under the applicable agreement;

(b) The application of a measure by a WTO Member;

(c) The nullification or impairment of a benefit as a result of the application of a measure.

The GATT Panel in *EEC–Oilseeds* considered that nullification or impairment would arise when the effect of a tariff concession is systematically offset or counteracted by a subsidy programme. The Panel in *US–Offset Act (Byrd Amendment)* confirmed this approach (§ 7.127).

6.3 SERIOUS PREJUDICE

Art. 6.1 SCM reads:

Serious prejudice in the sense of paragraph (c) of Article 5 shall be deemed to exist in the case of:

(a) the total ad valorem subsidization of a product exceeding 5 per cent;

(b) subsidies to cover operating losses sustained by an industry;

(c) subsidies to cover operating losses sustained by an enterprise, other than one-time measures which are non-recurrent and cannot be repeated for that enterprise and which are given merely to provide time for the development of long-term solutions and to avoid acute social problems;

(d) direct forgiveness of debt, i.e. forgiveness of government-held debt, and grants to cover debt repayment.

A footnote to the text (Footnote 16) reads:

Members recognize that where royalty-based financing for a civil aircraft programme is not being fully repaid due to the level of actual sales falling below the level of forecast sales, this does not in itself constitute serious prejudice for the purposes of this subparagraph.

Art. 6.1 SCM provides the complainant with an important evidentiary advantage, since it is relieved of the difficult burden to demonstrate the prejudicial effects of a subsidy. As this provision was enacted to serve on provisional basis, and since WTO Members could not agree on its extension, it has been repealed by virtue of Art. 31 SCM. This does not mean that it is totally irrelevant nowadays. The Panel in *US–Upland Cotton* took the view that it could still provide useful guidance in interpreting serious prejudice (footnote 1487 of the report), even if the evidentiary advantage has ceased. The Panel in *Korea–Commercial Vessels* evidences a similar attitude (§ 7.583). Its legal relevance, however, should not be overstated since, it is now up to individual Panels to draw inspirations from Art. 6.1 SCM.

6.3.1 Situations Giving Rise to Serious Prejudice

Art. 6.3 SCM is now the provision used to decide whether "serious prejudice" exists. It notes that "serious prejudice" may arise in any case where one or several of the following situations apply:

(a) The effect of the subsidy is to displace from or impede in the market of the subsidizing Member the exports of a like product originating in another Member;

(b) The effect of the subsidy is to displace from or impede in a third country market the exports of a like product originating in another Member;

(c) The effect of the subsidy is a significant price undercutting or significant price suppression, price depression or lost sales in the same market;

(d) The effect of the subsidy is an increase in the world market share of the subsidizing Member in a particular subsidized primary product or commodity as compared to the average share it had during the previous period of three years and this increase follows a consistent trend over a period when subsidies have been granted.[40]

The Panel in *Korea–Commercial Vessels* held that the use of the words "may arise" in the chapeau of Art. 6.3 SCM is an indication that the list in this provision is not exhaustive (§ 7.601). The list appearing in Art. 6.3 SCM nevertheless, covers a wide array of cases. The same Panel though, rejected the argument that, to demonstrate the existence of serious prejudice, the SCM Agreement requires additional elements beyond those referred to in Art. 6 SCM: The importance of that industry to the overall interests of the complaining party was thus judged irrelevant for the purposes of demonstrating serious prejudice (§§ 7.578–579).[41] The words "serious prejudice to the interest of another Member" appearing in the body of this provision do not go so far as to allow a WTO Member to claim serious prejudice based on effects felt by a company of that WTO Member but with regard to products not originating in the complaining WTO Member; the Panel in *Indonesia–Autos* (§ 14.201) held as much.

---

[40] Art. 6.3(b) SCM is further detailed in Art. 6.4 SCM (change in relative shares of the market to the disadvantage of the non-subsidized like product); Art. 6.3(c) SCM is further detailed in Art. 6.5 SCM (comparison of prices between subsidized and non-subsidized goods at the same level of trade to quantify the size of price undercutting). Annex V SCM, entitled 'Procedures for Developing Information Concerning Serious Prejudice', includes a special procedure for assisting parties involved in dispute settlement in obtaining information and evidence concerning serious prejudice claims. Art. 27.9 SCM contains special rules for determining serious prejudice in case of subsidies provided by developing countries.

[41] See also the Panel report in *US–Upland Cotton* at §§ 7.1370–1371.

Displacement or Impediment of Imports: Art. 6.3(a) SCM, and Art. 6.3(b) SCM provide that a subsidy has an adverse effect if it has the effect of displacing or impeding imports into the market of the subsidizing WTO Member or a third country market. The Panel in *Indonesia–Autos* examined claims relating to both displacement and impediment of cars exports to the Indonesian market, in particular with respect to cars from Japan, the EU, and the US, due to subsidization of the Indonesian carmaker (producing the "Timor"). To decide whether displacement had occurred, the Panel reviewed data concerning market share and sales: it appeared that, while market share of the European cars had fallen, sales volume in absolute figures did not go down (§ 14.210); the explanation was that the size of the Indonesian market expanded after the introduction of the Indonesian Timor (§§ 14.216–217). The data regarding the question, whether sales of EU models in absolute terms would have been higher than the actual had the Indonesian model not been introduced, were inconclusive; as a result, the Panel rejected the claim of displacement (§ 14.220), since, in its view, serious prejudice must be demonstrated on positive evidence (§ 14.222). The same Panel understood the term "impediment" as follows (§ 14. 218):

> the question before us is therefore whether the market share and sales data above would support a view that, *but for* the introduction of the subsidized Timor, sales of EC C Segment passenger cars *would have been greater* than they were while impedance relates to a situation where sales which otherwise would have occurred were impeded. (emphasis added).

The Panel considered that it had to review the information concerning plans to introduce new EU models in the Indonesian market, and to what extent their non-introduction was due to the Indonesian subsidization of its motor industry(§ 14.227). Once again, the Panel was of the view that the complainants failed to adduce sufficient positive evidence (§ 14.236). The Panel gave an indication of the kind of evidence it was expecting (§ 14.234):

> We do not mean to suggest that in WTO dispute settlement there are any rigid evidentiary rules regarding the admissibility of newspaper reports or the need to demonstrate factual assertions through contemporaneous source information. However, we are concerned that the complainants are asking us to resolve core issues relating to adverse trade effects on the basis of little more than general assertions. This situation is particularly disturbing, given that the affected companies certainly had at their disposal copious evidence in support of the claims of the complainants, such as the actual business plans relating to the new models, government documentation indicating approval for such plans (assuming the 'approval' referred to by the complainants with

respect to the Optima means approval by the Indonesian government), and corporate minutes or internal decision memoranda relating both to the initial approval, and the subsequent abandonment, of the plans in question.

Increase in World Market Share of a Subsidized Primary Product or Commodity: Art. 6.3(d) SCM states that, with respect to primary products or commodities, the subsidy has an adverse effect if it leads to an increase in world market share of this commodity as compared to the average share it had had during a previous period of three years; it adds that this increase has to follow a consistent trend over a period when subsidies had been granted. The Panel in *US–Upland Cotton* held that the term "world market share" (§ 7.1464):

> refers to share of the world market supplied by the subsidizing Member of the product concerned.

The Panel defined world market as the global geographical area of economic activity, in which buyers and sellers come together and the forces of supply and demand affect prices. It saw no force in the argument that this term would necessarily not include the domestic market of the subsidizing WTO Member (§§ 7.1431–1432). It, consequently, rejected Brazil's argument that world market share refers to the world market share of exports only (§§ 7.1434–1435).

Price Suppression, Price Depression, and Price Undercutting: Art. 6.3(c) SCM lists price suppression, price depression, and price undercutting as three forms of adverse effects. Information regarding these issues typically involves a fact-finding process in the subsidizing country, the complaining WTO Member, as well as third countries. To this effect, Annex V of the SCM Agreement organizes the fact-finding process and even makes room for the participation of a DSB representative to serve the function of facilitating the information-gathering process: Art. 6.8 SCM indicates that the existence of serious prejudice, pursuant to Arts. 5(c) and 6.3(c) SCM, is to be determined on the basis of information submitted to or obtained by the Panel, including information submitted in accordance with Annex V.[42]

The differences in content across the three terms are not obvious: In case law, price undercutting is equated to selling below a certain price; price suppression refers to the situation where prices are either prevented or inhibited from rising (that is, they do not increase when they otherwise would have, or they do actually increase, but the increase is less than it otherwise would have been); price depression refers to the situation where prices are pressed down or reduced (AB, *US–Upland Cotton*, § 423). Yet, all three terms refer to effects on the pricing policy of the non-

---

[42] In *US–Large Civil Aircraft (Second Complaint)*, the AB ruled that an Annex V procedure will be established automatically when a request has been places at a DSB session, § 549.

subsidized traders, and one might question the wisdom of using three terms for essentially the same purpose.

Price undercutting must occur in the same market; the Panel in *Indonesia–Autos* ruled as much (§ 14.239). Art. 6.3(c) SCM however, does not specify any further which market that is. In *Indonesia–Autos*, the Panel did not have to address this issue any further, since the Panel could anyway reject the US claim because of the fact that that the US and the Indonesian product were not competing in the same geographic market. In *US–Upland Cotton*, the AB agreed with the Panel that, in absence of specification in Art. 6.3(c) SCM, the market in question could be any national, regional or other market, including the world market (§ 406). The market could, consequently, be the world market, if it can be demonstrated that the subsidized product and the other product compete in it (AB, *US–Upland Cotton*, § 409). A geographic product market is of course, one where the same conditions of competition prevail. The Panel, and the AB on *US–Upland Cotton* accepted that much (AB, § 408 referring to § 7.1237 of the Panel report):

> the scope of the "market", for determining the area of competition between two products, may depend on several factors such as the nature of the product, the homogeneity of the conditions of competition, and transport costs.

For some products (such as airplanes) this is indeed the world market; for other products, conditions of competition might be affected through notably trade barriers and a narrower definition might be appropriate.

For two products to be considered to be in the same market, they must engage in actual or potential competition in that market, even if they are not necessarily sold at the same time and in the same place or country (AB, *US–Upland Cotton*, § 408). The subsidized product and the other product necessarily have to be directly competitive products in order to be able to be in the same market. Whether they have to be like products as well, was a question that the AB felt it did not need to resolve. The Panel in *Korea–Commercial Vessels* was more outspoken on this issue. It concluded (§ 7.553):

> that "like product" as defined in footnote 46 to Article 15 of the *SCM Agreement* is not a legal requirement for claims of price suppression/price depression pursuant to Article 6.3(c)." (italics in the original).

This Panel was dealing with a case of price suppression/depression. It based this conclusion on the absence of an explicit reference to like product for claims concerning price suppression/depression in Art. 6.3(c) SCM. The same provision nevertheless, requests that the effects of price undercutting must be on the like product (§§ 7.545–553). This is probably clumsy shorthand on behalf of the framers: the three phenomena (undercutting, suppression, depression) refer to essentially the same issue, and it would be odd to accept that the net is cast wider for the latter two. This is probably an issue that could easily be resolved at the negotiating table, unless of course, if WTO adjudicating bodies resolve it first by adopting the attitude that they did when interpreting Art. 14 SCM in the softwood lumber litigation discussed *supra*.

Interestingly, the AB, in its report on *US–Upland Cotton*, siding with the Panel, held that a suppression effect of the world price for cotton sufficed for making the price suppression-determination, and that it was not necessary to also determine whether prices of Brazilian cotton, the like product in this case, had been suppressed as a consequence of US subsidies. In its view, if world prices had been suppressed, so would Brazilian cotton prices (§ 417).

Price undercutting (like price suppression and price depression) must be significant; otherwise, it is not punished. The Panel in *Indonesia–Autos* upheld a claim that the subsidized Indonesian car, the Timor, significantly undercut the prices of EU products in the Indonesian market, because the level of undercutting was 42–54% (§§ 14.251–254). A quantification is certainly helpful, although, it appears, not strictly necessary. In *US–Upland Cotton*, the Panel understood the term "significant price depression or suppression" as "important, notable or consequential" (§ 7.1326).[43]

The same Panel added that (§ 7.1330):

a relatively small decrease or suppression of prices could be significant because, for example, profit margins may ordinarily be narrow, product homogeneity means that sales are price sensitive or because of the sheer size of the market in terms of the amount of revenue involved in large volumes traded on the markets experiencing the price suppression.

The Panel had found that price suppression indeed existed, based on three factors (§ 7.1280):

(a) The relative magnitude of the US production and exports in the world upland cotton market;

(b) General price trends (in the world market); and

(c) The nature of the subsidies at issue, and in particular, the fact that they had discernible price suppressive effects.

The Panel did not consider it necessary to quantify the suppression to conclude that it was significant. Rather, these three factors, as well as the readily available evidence of the order of magnitude of the subsidies, led the Panel to the conclusion that the price suppression in question was

---

[43] See also the Panel report in *Korea–Commercial Vessels* (§ 7.571).

indeed significant (§ 7.1333). The AB upheld all of the Panel's conclusions, and pointed to the relevance of such factors as the general price trends, the nature of the subsidies and the relative magnitude of the subsidized product share of the market (§ 434):

> In the absence of explicit guidance on assessing significant price suppression in the text of Article 6.3(c), we have no reason to reject the relevance of these factors for the Panel's assessment in the present case. An assessment of 'general price trends' is clearly relevant to significant price suppression (although, as the Panel itself recognized, price trends alone are not conclusive). The two other factors—the nature of the subsidies and the relative magnitude of the United States' production and exports of upland cotton—are also relevant for this assessment.

When examining price suppression, the effects of recurring subsidies may be allocated over time and are not limited to the year in which the subsidy was granted. The AB held as much in its report in *US–Upland Cotton* (§ 482):

> we are not persuaded by the United States' contention that the effect of annually paid subsidies must be 'allocated' or 'expensed' solely to the year in which they are paid and that, therefore, the effect of such subsidies cannot be significant price suppression in any subsequent year. We do not agree with the proposition that, if subsidies are paid annually, their effects are also necessarily extinguished annually.

Art. 6.3 SCM states that serious prejudice must be the effect of the subsidy. There must be, in other words, a causal relationship between the subsidy and its effects. The term "price suppression/depression" appeared in the Tokyo Round AD Agreement as well. During the GATT-era, Panels equated price depression to serious prejudice.[44] WTO Panels have used a finding of price suppression or depression (as the case may be) as determinative that serious prejudice has occurred. This has been the case in *Indonesia–Autos* (§ 14.238) and in *US–Upland Cotton* as well, where the Panel stated (§ 7.1390):

> the Article 6.3(c) examination is determinative . . . for a finding of serious prejudice under Article 5(c). That is, an affirmative conclusion that the effects-based situation in Article 6.3(c) exists is sufficient basis for an affirmative conclusion that 'serious prejudice' exists for the purposes of Article 5(c) of the SCM Agreement.

In this vein, both the Panel in *Korea–Commercial Vessels* (§ 7.534) and the AB on *US–Upland Cotton* found that price suppression contains

---

[44] See also WTO Panels in *EC–Sugar Exports (Australia)* (§ 4.26) and in *EC–Sugar Exports (Brazil)* (§§ 4.14–15).

some sort of built-in causation-requirement, and the factors that lead to a determination of the existence of price suppression may also be relevant to the question regarding its cause: in other words, it may be difficult to separate the existence of any suppression from its cause. There is an example suggesting the opposite though: the Panel report in *US–Upland Cotton*. On appeal, the AB noted the problems inherent in the Panel's approach (§ 433):

> However, the ordinary meaning of the transitive verb 'suppress' implies the existence of a subject (the challenged subsidies) and an object (in this case, prices in the world market for upland cotton). This suggests that it would be difficult to make a judgment on significant price suppression without taking into account the effect of the subsidies. The Panel's definition of price suppression, explained above, reflects this problem; it includes the notion that prices 'do not increase when they otherwise would have' or 'they do actually increase, but the increase is less than it otherwise would have been'. The word 'otherwise' in this context refers to the hypothetical situation in which the challenged subsidies are absent.

Irrespective however, of the question regarding the stage when the causation-analysis must take place, it is clear that it must take place anyway. The Panel in *Korea–Commercial Vessels* found that the text of Art. 6.3 SCM implies a "but for"-approach to causation, and would thus require a Panel to examine the counterfactual (§ 7.612): the complainant should demonstrate that, but for the subsidy, it could have expected to participate in a growing market (in case of displacement of its shipments from a particular market); or in the case of impeding exports, that, but for the subsidies, its sales and/or market share would have increased, or would have increased more than they actually did. This framework of analysis requires an evaluation of the various factors contributing to the particular market situation forming the subject of the complaint, that is, supply and demand factors, production costs, relative efficiency of the market actors, etc. (§ 7.615). By way of example, we refer to the Panel's decision in *US–Upland Cotton*. In this case, the Panel found a causal link to exist between the price-contingent subsidies and the significant price suppression for four reasons (§§ 7.1347–1355):

> (a) The US had exerted substantial influence on the world upland cotton market;
>
> (b) The price-contingent subsidies were directly linked to world prices for upland cotton, thereby insulating US producers from low prices;
>
> (c) There was a discernible temporal coincidence of suppressed world market prices, on the one hand, and the price-contingent US subsidies, on the other; and, finally,

(d) Credible evidence on the record concerning the divergence between US producers' total costs of production, and revenue from sales of upland cotton since 1997 supported the proposition that US upland cotton producers would not have been economically capable of remaining in the production of upland cotton, had it not been for the US subsidies, and that the effect of the subsidies was to allow US producers to sell upland cotton at a price lower than would otherwise have been necessary to cover their total costs.

The AB upheld the Panel's reliance on these factors (§§ 449–453): it emphasized that the nature of the subsidy, as well as the magnitude of the subsidy, played an important role in establishing price suppression, but that, ultimately, all relevant factors had to be taken into consideration (§ 461):

> However, in assessing whether 'the effect of the subsidy is . . . significant price suppression', and ultimately serious prejudice, a panel will need to consider the effects of the subsidy on prices. The magnitude of the subsidy is an important factor in this analysis. A large subsidy that is closely linked to prices of the relevant product is likely to have a greater impact on prices than a small subsidy that is less closely linked to prices. All other things being equal, the smaller the subsidy for a given product, the smaller the degree to which it will affect the costs or revenue of the recipient, and the smaller its likely impact on the prices charged by the recipient for the product. However, the size of a subsidy is only one of the factors that may be relevant to the determination of the effects of a challenged subsidy. A panel needs to assess the effect of the subsidy taking into account all relevant factors.

Art. 6.3 SCM does not, on its face, impose a non-attribution requirement, as that appearing in the CVD-context (Art. 15.5 SCM). Nevertheless, two Panels, (*US–Upland Cotton*, § 7.1344, and *Korea–Commercial Vessels*, § 7.618) considered it logical and appropriate to analyze other possible factors, with a view to determining whether such factors would have had the effect of attenuating the causal link, or of rendering insignificant the effect of the subsidy. In its report on *US–Upland Cotton*, the Panel concluded that the condition of a causal link requires from a Panel to ensure that significant price suppression is the effect of the subsidy, within the meaning of Art. 6.3(c) SCM; in this Panel's view, this requirement calls for an examination of US subsidies within the context of other possible causal factors, otherwise an appropriate attribution of causality cannot take place (§ 7.1344). The AB endorsed this approach (§§ 436–437):

> As the Panel pointed out, 'Articles 5 and 6.3 . . . do not contain the more elaborate and precise "causation" and non-attribution

language' found in the trade remedy provisions of the *SCM Agreement*. Part V of the *SCM Agreement*, which relates to the imposition of countervailing duties, requires, *inter alia*, an examination of 'any known factors other than the subsidized imports which at the same time are injuring the domestic industry'. However, such causation requirements have not been expressly prescribed for an examination of serious prejudice under Article 5(c) and Article 6.3(c) in Part III of the *SCM Agreement*. This suggests that a panel has a certain degree of discretion in selecting an appropriate methodology for determining whether the 'effect' of a subsidy is significant price suppression under Article 6.3(c).

Nevertheless, we agree with the Panel that it is necessary to ensure that the effects of other factors on prices are not improperly attributed to the challenged subsidies. Pursuant to Article 6.3(c) of the *SCM Agreement*, '[s]erious prejudice in the sense of paragraph (c) of Article 5 may arise' when 'the effect of the subsidy is . . . significant price suppression' (emphasis added). If the significant price suppression found in the world market for upland cotton were caused by factors other than the challenged subsidies, then that price suppression would not be 'the effect of' the challenged subsidies in the sense of Article 6.3(c). Therefore, we do not find fault with the Panel's approach of 'examin[ing] whether or not 'the effect of the subsidy' is the significant price suppression which [it had] found to exist in the same world market' and separately 'consider[ing] the role of other alleged causal factors in the record before [it] which may affect [the] analysis of the causal link between the United States subsidies and the significant price suppression'. (italics in the original).

The Panel in *US–Upland Cotton* examined the impact of other (than subsidized imports) factors (§ 7.1363), and held that they had contributed to the price suppression. However, the Panel found that even in the presence of these other factors, the challenged subsidy schemes still had had a significant price suppressing effect. The AB found no legal error in the Panel's causation analysis, although it expressed its disappointment about the fact that in its reasoning, the Panel did not offer a detailed enough analysis (§ 458). The key here is that as long as subsidies have caused significant price suppression, it is irrelevant if other factors have added to this effect.

6.3.2 Evidentiary Issues Regarding an Examination of Serious Prejudice

Any time serious prejudice has been caused as a result of subsidization, and WTO Members cannot find a mutually agreed solution, the matter can be referred to a Panel (Art. 7.4 SCM). Following a request to the DSB, recourse can be made to the procedures established in Annex V to the SCM: § 2 of Annex V reads:

> In cases where matters are referred to the DSB under paragraph 4 of Article 7, the DSB shall, upon request, initiate the procedure to obtain such information from the government of the subsidizing Member as necessary to establish the existence and amount of subsidization, the value of total sales of the subsidized firms, as well as information necessary to analyze the adverse effects caused by the subsidized product.

The Panel in *US–Large Civil Aircraft (2nd Complaint)* held that the DSB will decide on negative consensus whether to initiate this procedure; hence, the request by the WTO Member interested in initiating this procedure suffices. Nevertheless, total inaction by the DSB entails as sole consequence that the procedure has not been initiated (§§ 721ff.).

Annex V regulates the manner in which the information-gathering process will take place. A representative is appointed by the Panel, the so-called "Designated Representative" (DR), who will be in charge of the process and ensure it is completed in timely manner (Annex V, § 5). The DR could be the Chair of DSB or another person. The complainant will present facts, ask questions, and request for clarifications. The DR has discretion when replying to requests presented. If the complainant disagrees with the exercise of discretion it can assert a claim that Art. 11 DSU (the duty of Panels to provide an objective assessment of the matter before them) has been violated. Questions can, of course, also be asked through the Panel.

This process cannot last more than 60 days (Annex V, § 6). The Panel will decide based on the information gathered and may even draw inferences in case of non-cooperation (Annex V, § 7). No recourse to best information available (BIA) is permissible, unless the DR's opinion on the reasonableness of the requested information has been heard, as well as the reasons why the requested information could not have been supplied (Annex V, § 8). The Panel remains free to seek information additional to that gathered through this process (Annex V, § 9). The Panel in *Korea–Commercial Vessels* had recourse to this procedure.[45]

---

[45] See Attachment 1 to the Panel report where it is made clear that the DR retains discretion on issues not explicitly covered in Annex V. See also pp. 159–164 of the Panel report on *Korea–Commercial Vessels*, where the Working Procedures for the Designated Representative are explained. For a first application of this institutional facility, see §§ 1.17–1.19 of the Panel report on *Indonesia–Autos*. Information gathering under Annex V was also initiated in *US–Upland Cotton* (see § 1.3 of the Panel report).

6.4 COUNTERACTING ACTIONABLE SUBSIDIES WITH ADVERSE EFFECTS

Art. 7.8 SCM requires from the WTO Member causing adverse effects through its subsidies undertake one of two options: "to remove the adverse effects or . . . withdraw the subsidy."

Irrespective of whether adverse effects result in serious prejudice, nullification and impairment or injury, a WTO Member, that has proved their existence, can request from a Panel to recommend that the subsidizing WTO Member removes the effects, or withdraws the subsidy altogether (Art. 7.8 SCM). In case of non-compliance, the affected WTO Member can take countermeasures commensurate with the degree and nature of the adverse effects determined to exist. Art. 7.9 SCM reads in this respect:

> In the event the Member has not taken appropriate steps to remove the adverse effects of the subsidy or withdraw the subsidy within six months from the date when the DSB adopts the panel report or the Appellate Body Report, and in the absence of agreement on compensation, the DSB shall grant authorization to the complaining Member to take countermeasures, commensurate with the degree and nature of the adverse effects determined to exist, unless the DSB decides by consensus to reject the request.

In case of disagreement between the parties as to whether the proposed countermeasures are indeed commensurate, recourse will be made to an Arbitrator, who will define their level (Art. 7.10 SCM). There has been no practice so far in the context of Art. 7.9 SCM. There are good arguments to construe the term "commensurate" in parallel with the term "equivalent", which appears in Art. 22.4 DSU. Thus, the benchmark for calculation should be the injury suffered by the affected party.

7. NON–ACTIONABLE SUBSIDIES

The SCM Agreement, as originally drafted, provided for a third category of subsidies: non-actionable subsidies (Art. 8 SCM). Three types of subsidies were deemed non-actionable: regional aid, environmental subsidies, and subsidies for research and development (R & D) purposes. They were initially contracted for a 5 year provisional period. In the absence of agreement to keep this category in place, non-actionable subsidies ceased to exist as of January 1, 2000 (Art. 31 SCM). Consequently, a scheme which qualifies as subsidy under the SCM Agreement is, nowadays, either a prohibited or an actionable subsidy.

8. COUNTERVAILING DUTIES (CVDs)

Recourse to multilateral dispute settlement is not the only option available to a WTO Member when its domestic producers are confronted with competition from subsidized imports within its own market. In such a circumstance, a WTO Member may also make recourse to a specific contingent protection instrument (i.e., trade remedy) designed to tackle "unfair" trade caused by subsidization: a countervailing duty (CVD).

The process of imposing a CVD is undertaken unilaterally through a domestic administrative procedure (similar to that of anti-dumping); it is generally more expeditious than WTO dispute settlement. However, success through the CVD channel only results in the imposition of higher (than MFN) duties for the subsidized good within one's own market. A CVD is not effective at countering the negative impact that one's domestic producers may face in third-country markets from subsidized foreign competitors.

It should come as no surprise that many of the provisions discussing CVDs in the SCM Agreement are very similar to those of the AD Agreement. This is because both AD and CVD involve domestic administrative adjudicatory processes, and the two share several similar legal requirements. Case law reveals that Panels and the AB consider that the interpretations of AD provisions provide good guidance for the interpretation of similar provisions in the SCM Agreement, and vice versa. The Panel report on *US–Countervailing Duty Investigation on DRAMs* is an appropriate illustration to this effect (§ 7.351):

> The non-attribution requirement in antidumping investigations has been addressed by the Appellate Body in several recent cases. Although it has not been specifically considered in a countervailing duty case, given that the relevant provisions in the two Agreements are identical, and in light of the 'need for the consistent resolution of disputes arising from antidumping and countervailing duty measures' (Ministerial Declaration on Dispute Settlement Pursuant to the Agreement on Implementation of Article VI of the General Agreement on Tariffs and Trade 1994 or Part V of the Agreement on Subsidies and Countervailing Measures), it is clear to us that the requirement is the same in the context of both antidumping and countervailing duty investigations.

This approach is consistent with the "Ministerial Declaration On Dispute Settlement Pursuant to the Agreement on Implementation of Article VI of the General Agreement on Tariffs and Trade 1994 or Part V of the Agreement on Subsidies and Countervailing Measures" adopted at Marrakesh at the conclusion of the Uruguay Round which recognized the need for a consistent resolution of disputes arising from antidumping and countervailing duty measures.

8.1 SUBSTANTIVE REQUIREMENTS FOR A CVD

A WTO Member wishing to impose a CVD must demonstrate that:

(a) A subsidy

(b) Is causing injury

(c) To the domestic industry producing the like product.

8.1.1 Subsidy

The legal requirements for a subsidy are the same, regardless of whether one pursues multilateral dispute settlement or unilateral CVD. Our discussion supra regarding the content of this term finds application here as well.

8.1.2 Injury

The legal requirements regarding demonstration of injury are addressed in Art. 15 SCM. As in the AD context, the term "injury" is used to refer to a situation of "material injury", "threat of material injury", or "material retardation" in the establishment of an industry. The latter situation knows of no practice so far. Arts. 15.1–6 SCM deal with injury in general, while Arts. 15.7 and 15.8 SCM contain special additional obligations in cases of threat of injury. For injury to be shown, a WTO Member must conduct an objective examination based on positive evidence regarding (art. 15.1 SCM):

(a) The volume of the subsidized imports;

(b) Their effect on prices in the domestic market for like products; as well as

(c) The consequent impact of these imports on the domestic producers of such like products.

Art 15.3 SCM provides that, an injury analysis may be conducted on cumulative basis under the following conditions:

(a) Imports of a product from more than one country are simultaneously subject to CVD investigations;

(b) The amount of subsidization established in relation to the imports from each country is more than de minimis as defined in Art. 11.9 SCM;

(c) The volume of imports from each country is not negligible; and

(d) A cumulative assessment of the effects of the imports is appropriate in light of the conditions of competition between the imported products and the conditions of competition between the imported products and the like domestic product.

All this is quite similar to Art. 3.3 AD. The amount of subsidy is de minimis, if it is less than 1% ad valorem (Art. 11.9 SCM). For developing countries this threshold is set at 2%, and for least developed countries (and so-called Annex VII countries), at 3%. There is no definition of the term "negligible" volumes. Art. 27.10 SCM does so for imports originating in developing countries only: if subsidized (by developing countries) imports are less than 4% of total imports, they are negligible; if subsidized imports from developing countries whose individual shares represent less than 4% and collectively account for less than 9% of total imports, they are negligible as well.

A finding that injury has occurred must be based on positive evidence following an objective examination by the IA. The Panel in *US–Softwood Lumber VI*, dealt, *inter alia*, with the interpretation of the terms "positive evidence" and "objective examination". It quoted verbatim § 114 of the AB report on *EC–Bed Linen (Article 21.5–India)*, which dealt with an AD investigation (§ 7.28):

> The term 'positive evidence' relates, in our view, to the quality of the evidence that authorities may rely upon in making a determination. The word 'positive' means, to us, that the evidence must be of an *affirmative, objective* and *verifiable* character, and that it must be *credible*.

The Appellate Body has defined an 'objective examination':

> The term 'objective examination' aims at a different aspect of the investigating authorities' determination. While the term 'positive evidence' focuses on the facts underpinning and justifying the injury determination, the term 'objective examination' is concerned with the investigative process itself. The word 'examination' relates, in our view, to the way in which the evidence is gathered, inquired into and, subsequently, evaluated; that is, it relates to the conduct of the investigation generally. The word 'objective', which qualifies the word 'examination', indicates essentially that the 'examination' process must conform to the dictates of the basic principles of good faith and fundamental fairness.

The Appellate Body summed up the requirement to conduct an 'objective examination' as follows:

> In short, an 'objective examination' requires that the domestic industry, and the effects of dumped imports, be investigated in an *unbiased* manner, *without favouring the interests of any interested party*, or group of interested parties, in the investigation. The duty of the investigating authorities to conduct an 'objective examination' recognizes that the determination will be influ-

enced by the objectivity, or any lack thereof, of the investigative process. (emphasis in the original).[46]

An evaluation of the volume of imports requires an IA to consider whether there has been a significant increase in subsidized imports, either in absolute terms, or relative to production or consumption in the importing Member. No number quantifying significance is provided, and Panels have avoided doing so. A typical illustration is offered by the Panel report in *EC–Countervailing Measures on DRAM Chips*, where the Panel held that the ordinary meaning of the term "significant", encompasses "important", "notable", "major", as well as "consequential", which all suggest something more than just a nominal or marginal movement but are not at all precise (§ 7.307). The evaluation of the volume of subsidized imports is not, by itself, determinative in an injury determination, but forms part of an overall assessment (§ 7.290 of the Panel report on *EC–Countervailing Measures on DRAM Chips*). The Panel in *US–Countervailing Duty Investigation on DRAMs*, held (§ 7.233) that Art. 15.2 SCM included three alternative ways in which an IA could comply with this provision, suggesting that it sufficed for an IA to consider:

(a) Either an absolute increase;

(b) Or an increase relative to production;

(c) Or an increase relative to consumption.

The term "subsidized imports" refers to all imports from a source found to have been subsidized above the *de minimis* level. The Panel in *EC–Countervailing Measures on DRAM Chips* approvingly referred to findings by Panels and the AB in the AD-context, and, in particular to § 113 of the AB report in *EC–Bed Linen (Article 21.5–India)*, and held as much (§ 7.298, and footnote 227). In other words, imports from exporters not found to have been receiving subsidies are to be excluded from a determination. In fact, the level of non-subsidized imports will be one of the other factors that will need to be examined in the context of the causation and non-attribution analysis under Art. 15.5 SCM. The fact that imports from subsidized and non-subsidized sources are discussed side by side by the authority is not inconsistent with the Agreement. What matters is the use made of the data and whether the consideration required by Art. 15.2 SCM was made on the basis of data concerning imports found to have been subsidized (Panel report in *EC–Countervailing Measures on DRAM Chips*, at § 7.298). Neither is it relevant under Art. 15.2 SCM that subsi-

---

[46] See also the Panel report on *US–Countervailing Duty Investigation on DRAMs* (§ 7.218). Panels have consistently considered that Art. 15.1 SCM is a provision which informs the more detailed obligations set forth in the remainder of Art. 15 SCM, see, e.g., the Panel report on *EC–Countervailing Measures on DRAM Chips* at § 7.275, quoting from § 106 of the AB report in *Thailand–H–Beams*. For that reason, Panels have first examined the consistency of the measures with the specific obligations contained in Arts. 15.2–5 SCM: see the Panel report in *US–Countervailing Duty Investigation on DRAMs* at § 7.217; Panel report in *US–Softwood Lumber VI*, at § 7.26.

dized imports decreased in relative terms compared to non-subsidized imports, since this is not the focus of the volume determination under this provision (Panel report in *US–Countervailing Duty Investigation on DRAMs*, at § 7.243).

The Panel in *US–Countervailing Duty Investigation on DRAMs* found that, the fact that the greatest increase in subject imports took place prior to the provision of subsidies was not considered determinative, since (§ 7.245):

> Article 15.2 does not require an investigating authority to demonstrate that all of the subject imports covered by the period of injury investigation are subsidized.

An evaluation of the effects of the subsidized imports on prices requires an IA to consider whether there has been significant price undercutting, price depression, or price suppression. The SCM Agreement makes clear that the overall evaluation can be based on one or several factors. Art. 15.2 SCM does not impose any particular methodology for analyzing prices. What is important is that the methodology chosen is reasonable and objective (§§ 7.334–336 of the Panel report on *EC–Countervailing Measures on DRAM Chips*).

Art. 15.4 SCM requires that the examination of the impact of the subsidized imports on the domestic industry includes an evaluation of all relevant economic factors and indices having a bearing on the state of the industry, including actual and potential decline in output, sales, market share, profits, productivity, return on investments, or utilization of capacity, factors affecting domestic prices, actual and potential negative effects on cash flow, inventories, employment, wages, growth, ability to raise capital or investments and, in the case of agriculture, whether there has been an increased burden on government support programs.[47] It adds that this list is not exhaustive, nor can one or several of these factors necessarily give decisive guidance. The SCM Agreement, thus, reflects an indicative list of proxies, recourse to which should demonstrate injury. Case-law makes it clear that all factors mentioned in the body of Art. 15.4 SCM must be evaluated by the IA (§ 7.356 of the Panel report on *EC–Countervailing Measures on DRAM Chips*). The obligation of evaluation imposed by Art. 15.4 SCM is not confined to these listed factors, however, but extends to all relevant economic factors. Whether a factor is relevant depends, *inter alia*, on the nature of the industry being examined (§ 7.363 of the Panel report on *EC–Countervailing Measures on DRAM Chips*). The Panel in *EC–Countervailing Measures on DRAM Chips* stated that, relevant economic factors are not to be confused with other causal factors, such as the general economic downturn or the export performance of the domestic industry, which are to be examined as part of the causation and

---

[47] This list is very similar, although not identical to the list included in Art. 3.4 AD.

non-attribution analysis of Art. 15.5 SCM (§ 7.365). What is ultimately required is that these various factors be examined in their overall context. It is not required that each and every factor shows a negative trend. A proper evaluation of the impact of the subsidized imports on the domestic industry is dynamic in nature and should take account of changes in the market that determine the current state of the industry (§ 7.372 of the Panel report on *EC–Countervailing Measures on DRAM Chips*).

With respect to the period of data collection, the Panel in *EC–Countervailing Measures on DRAM Chips* rejected the argument that a pricing analysis must include the most recent period prior to initiation: the data on which the injury analysis is based should be sufficiently recent in order for these data to be relevant and probative such as to constitute positive evidence; the Panel considered that, since the EU had gathered data which covered three years, including the last full year for accounting purposes prior to the initiation, its analysis was clearly based on the recent past (§ 7.341). The Panel in *Mexico–Olive Oil* faced a claim by the EU to the effect that Mexico had been acting inconsistently with its obligations under Art. 15.5 SCM, by using data from some months every year only (April–December) and for the whole 12 months of the years under investigation. The Panel agreed with the complainant that Mexico was indeed running afoul its obligations, since it offered no explanation for its approach (§§ 7.273ff., and especially 7.289).

If CVDs are imposed on "threat of injury", the SCM Agreement requires that a demonstration that a threat of injury exists be based on facts and not merely on allegation, conjecture or remote possibility. In addition, the change in circumstances which would create a situation in which the subsidy would cause injury must be clearly foreseen and imminent (Art. 15.7 SCM). In making a determination regarding the existence of a threat of material injury, the IA should consider, *inter alia*, such factors as:

(a) The nature of the subsidy or subsidies in question and the trade effects likely to arise therefrom;

(b) A significant rate of increase of subsidized imports into the domestic market indicating the likelihood of substantially increased importation;

(c) Sufficient freely disposable or an imminent substantial increase in capacity of the exporter indicating the likelihood of substantially increased subsidized exports to the importing WTO Member's market, taking into account the availability of other export markets to absorb any additional exports;

(d) Whether imports are entering at prices that will have a significant depressing or suppressing effect on domestic prices, and would likely increase demand for further imports; and

(e) Inventories of the product being investigated.

The Agreement adds that not one of these factors by itself can necessarily give decisive guidance, but that the totality of the factors considered must lead to the conclusion that further subsidized exports are imminent and that, unless protective action is taken, material injury would occur. In a threat of injury-situation, the application of CVDs must be considered and decided with special care (Art. 15.8 SCM).[48] The Panel in *US–Softwood Lumber VI* held that authorities do not have to go so far as to specify one particular event that will cause injury in the future; indicating a progression of circumstances by and large suffices to meet the requirements of the SCM Agreement in this respect (§ 7.60). This Panel agreed with the views expressed by the Panel in *Mexico–Corn Syrup* that, in every case in which threat of injury is found, it is necessary to proceed to an evaluation of the condition of the industry in light of the factors included in Art. 15.4 SCM to establish the background against which the impact of future dumped/subsidized imports must be assessed, in addition to an assessment of the specific threat factors (§ 7.105). But the same Panel added that this requirement should not be interpreted as if a second predictive injury-analysis is required (§§ 7.105, 111).

With regard to the factors that must be examined in order to show threat of injury (Art. 15.7 SCM), the Panel in *US–Softwood Lumber VI* found that the IA has an obligation to consider these factors, but is not obliged to make a finding or determination with respect to the factors considered (§ 7.67). Moreover, the failure to consider a factor, or to adequately consider a particular factor would not necessarily demonstrate a violation of this provision; all will depend on the particular facts of the case, the totality of the factors considered and the explanations given (§ 7.68).

The Panel in *US–Softwood Lumber VI (Article 21.5–Canada)* discussed the applicable standard of review in threat of injury-cases, and held that it would be more deferential to the IA when examining a threat of injury determination compared to a material injury determination (§ 7.13):

> The possible range of reasonable predictions of the future that may be drawn based on the observed events of the period of investigation may be broader than the range of reasonable conclusions concerning the present that might be drawn based on those same facts. That is to say, while a determination of threat of material injury must be based on the facts, and not merely on allegation, conjecture, or remote possibility, predictions based on the observed facts may be less susceptible to being found, on review by a panel, to be outside the range of conclusions that might be

---

[48] On the special care-requirement, see the Panel report on *US–Softwood Lumber VI* at §§ 7.33–37.

reached by an unbiased and objective decision maker on the basis of the facts and in light of the explanations given.

Injury (or threat of injury) must be caused to the domestic industry producing the like product. In perfect symmetry with the AD Agreement, the SCM Agreement provides that the term "domestic industry" refers to the domestic producers as a whole of the like products, or to those producers whose collective output of the products constitutes a major proportion of the total domestic production of those products. In cases where producers are "related" to the exporters or importers, or are themselves importers of the allegedly subsidized product or a like product from other countries, they may be excluded from the investigation (Art. 16.1 SCM). The term "related" is explained in footnote 48 to Art. 16.1 SCM:

> producers shall be deemed to be related to exporters or importers only if (a) one of them directly or indirectly controls the other; or (b) both of them are directly or indirectly controlled by a third person; or (c) together they directly or indirectly control a third person, provided that there are grounds for believing or suspecting that the effect of the relationship is such as to cause the producer concerned to behave differently from non-related producers. For the purpose of this paragraph, one shall be deemed to control another when the former is legally or operationally in a position to exercise restraint or direction over the latter.

The term "like product" is defined in footnote 46 to the SCM Agreement:

> Throughout this Agreement the term 'like product' ('produit similaire') shall be interpreted to mean a product which is identical, i.e. alike in all respects to the product under consideration, or in the absence of such a product, another product which, although not alike in all respects, has characteristics closely resembling those of the product under consideration.

This definition is identical to that provided for in the AD Agreement, and evidences a statutory preference for a narrow definition of the term. The Panel in *Indonesia–Autos* established a parallelism between Art. III.2 GATT, first sentence, and the SCM Agreement and held that the following criteria should be pertinent in evaluating likeness (§ 14.173):

> In our view, the analysis as to which cars have 'characteristics closely resembling' those of the Timor logically must include as an important element the physical characteristics of the cars in question. This is especially the case because many of the other possible criteria identified by the parties are closely related to the physical characteristics of the cars in question. Thus, factors such as brand loyalty, brand image/reputation, status and resale value reflect, at least in part, an assessment by purchasers of the

physical characteristics of the cars being purchased. Although it is possible that products that are physically very different can be put to the same uses, differences in uses generally arise out of, and assist in assessing the importance of, different physical characteristics of products. Similarly, the extent to which products are substitutable may also be determined in substantial part by their physical characteristics. Price differences also may (but will not necessarily) reflect physical differences in products. An analysis of tariff classification principles may be useful because it provides guidance as to which physical distinctions between products were considered significant by Customs experts. However, we do not see that the SCM Agreement precludes us from looking at criteria other than physical characteristics, where relevant to the like product analysis. The term 'characteristics closely resembling' in its ordinary meaning includes but is not limited to physical characteristics, and we see nothing in the context or object and purpose of the SCM Agreement that would dictate a different conclusion.

This Panel went on to find that a kit car is a like product to a finished car (§ 14.197). This definition could be an unreasonable constraint when it comes to injury suffered not by the like product, but by the upstream or downstream product. For example, assume imports of subsidized wine; actually assume that it is production of foreign grapes that has been subsidized and not the final product (itself). Could in this case domestic wine producers successfully argue that they have been injured as a result of subsidization to foreign grapes? The Panels in *US–Softwood Lumber III*, and *US–Softwood Lumber IV* acknowledged that subsidies to an input (upstream subsidies) can result in benefits for the final product (downstream benefits). As a result, an IA can lawfully impose CVDs on the final product, even though such product might not be considered a like product to one of its inputs that has benefited from the subsidy.[49]

8.1.3 Causation

The general requirement to establish a causal link between the subsidized imports and injury is expressed in Art. 15.5 SCM.[50] It contains two obligations:

(a) A positive obligation to demonstrate that it is the subsidized imports which are causing the injury; and, in addition,

---

[49] See for example, § 163 of the AB report on *US–Softwood Lumber IV*. Note also that the Panel in *Mexico–Olive Oil* held that there is no requirement that a particular producer be producing the like product at the moment an application is filed. This view (voiced by the EU) could lead to absurd results, since, if accepted, it could, for example, exclude operators that had exited the market because of the subsidies from filing a petition (§§ 7.188ff., and especially 7.203).

[50] There are specific rules as well: for example, Art. 15.2 SCM requires from an IA to establish what caused the price undercutting; the Panel in *EC–Countervailing Measures on DRAM Chips* acknowledged that (§ 7.338).

(b) It sets forth a negative obligation, namely, not to attribute to subsidy injury caused by factors other than subsidized imports (non-attribution).

In this respect, Art. 15.5 SCM requires from an IA to examine any known factors, other than subsidized imports, which are injuring the domestic industry:

> Factors which may be relevant in this respect include, *inter alia*, the volumes and prices of nonsubsidized imports of the product in question, contraction in demand or changes in the patterns of consumption, trade restrictive practices of and competition between the foreign and domestic producers, developments in technology and the export performance and productivity of the domestic industry.

The Panel in *US–Softwood Lumber VI* held that wrong facts, assumptions, and absence of any discussion of specific factors appearing in the body of this provision are fatal; a WTO Member committing such errors is deemed not to have respected the causality requirement (§ 7.122). A causal link may be established between subsidized imports and the injury to the domestic industry, even in the absence of any increase in subsidized imports. Increased imports are not a condition for imposition of a CVD measure but merely an element in the overall assessment of injury and causation. This led the Panels on *EC–Countervailing Measures on DRAM Chips* (§ 7.320), and *US–Countervailing Duty Investigation on DRAMs* (§ 7.399) to find that there is no generalized requirement to establish a temporal correlation between increased subsidized imports and injury in the context of a countervail investigation. According to the Panel in *EC–Countervailing Measures on DRAM Chips* (§ 7.399, footnote 277):

> the absence of a temporal correlation certainly raises a flag, but it is not an absolute barrier to a finding of injury.

The Panel in *US–Softwood Lumber VI* dealt with the issue of other factors, that is, factors not mentioned in the body of Art. 15.5 SCM and which could be causing injury. The question before it was whether and if yes under what conditions an IA should examine them. The Panel condemned the fact that the IA had itself acknowledged the relevance of one other factor (future effects of subsidization on the domestic supplies of lumber) and yet failed to evaluate its impact. In the Panel's view, this failure was a glaring omission and constituted a breach of the obligation to respect non-attribution. (§§ 7.135–137). Recall that case law in the context of antidumping supports the view that the treatment of other factors should not be equated to an obligation to look beyond the list of Art. 15.5 SCM: factors brought to the attention of the authority during the investigation process, and factors otherwise explicitly acknowledged by the authority (as was the case here) must be analyzed though. The Panels in *US–Countervailing Duty Investigation on DRAMs* (§§ 7.351–353), and

EC–Countervailing Measures on DRAM Chips (§ 7.404) are illustrations to this effect. According to the latter Panel, while the AB had not provided guidance as to how an IA should examine other known factors, it was of the view that an IA must do more than simply list other known factors, and then dismiss their role with bare qualitative assertions such as:

> the factor did not contribute in any significant way to the injury.

In the Panel's view (§ 7.405):

> an investigating authority must make a better effort to quantify the impact of other known factors, relative to subsidized imports, preferably using elementary economic constructs or models.

It thus faulted the EU IA for acknowledging the negative impact on the industry of certain other factors, such as the economic downturn in the market, overcapacity of the domestic industry, and other non-subsidized imports, without examining the extent of this negative impact. The Panel was of the view that a mere assertion that the effect was not such as to break the causal link between subsidized imports and injury without any quantitative or thorough qualitative support did not suffice to separate and distinguish the injury that might have been caused by the subsidized imports (§§ 7.408, 413, 420, 427, 434).

In *US–Upland Cotton*, the AB, confirming the Panel in this respect, held that, when dealing with the causation-requirement, an IA must ensure that it does not attribute injury to subsidies when this has not been the case; the absence of explicit non-attribution language in the SCM Agreement was no obstacle for the Panel first, and the AB subsequently to reach this finding. We quote from §§ 436–437 of the AB report:

> As the Panel pointed out, "Articles 5 and 6.3 . . . do not contain the more elaborate and precise 'causation' and non-attribution language" found in the trade remedy provisions of the *SCM Agreement*. Part V of the *SCM Agreement*, which relates to the imposition of countervailing duties, requires, *inter alia*, an examination of "any known factors other than the subsidized imports which at the same time are injuring the domestic industry". However, such causation requirements have not been expressly prescribed for an examination of *serious prejudice* under Articles 5(c) and Article 6.3(c) in Part III of the *SCM Agreement*. This suggests that a panel has a certain degree of discretion in selecting an appropriate methodology for determining whether the "effect" of a subsidy is significant price suppression under Article 6.3(c).
>
> Nevertheless, we agree with the Panel that it is necessary to ensure that the effects of other factors on prices are not improperly attributed to the challenged subsidies. Pursuant to Article 6.3(c) of the *SCM Agreement*, "[s]erious prejudice in the sense of para-

graph (c) of Article 5 may arise" when "the effect of *the subsidy* is ... significant price suppression". (emphasis added) If the significant price suppression found in the world market for upland cotton were caused by factors other than the challenged subsidies, then that price suppression would not be "the effect of" the challenged subsidies in the sense of Article 6.3(c). Therefore, we do not find fault with the Panel's approach of "examin[ing] whether or not 'the effect of the subsidy' is the significant price suppression which [it had] found to exist in the same world market" and separately "consider[ing] the role of other alleged causal factors in the record before [it] which may affect [the] analysis of the causal link between the United States subsidies and the significant price suppression." (italics and emphasis in the original).

Non-attribution complicates the analysis by Panels as well, and yet, this is precisely what the AB has requested them to do. In § 357 of its report on *US–Upland Cotton (Article 21.5–US)*, it noted:

The relative complexity of a model and its parameters is not a reason for a panel to remain agnostic about them. Like other categories of evidence, a panel should reach conclusions with respect to the probative value it accords to economic simulations or models presented to it. This kind of assessment falls within the panel's authority as the initial trier of facts in a serious prejudice case.

8.2 IMPOSITION OF A CVD

8.2.1 Provisional CVDs

Art. 17 SCM allows for the possibility of imposing provisional measures when the IA judges it necessary to prevent injury being caused during the investigation. These measures may only be imposed after a preliminary affirmative determination has been made that a subsidy exists, and that there is injury to a domestic industry caused by subsidized imports. The SCM Agreement provides that provisional measures are not to be applied sooner than 60 days from the date of initiation of the investigation (Art. 17.3 SCM), and can be lawfully imposed for a period not extending beyond four months (Art. 17.4 SCM). The four months-period does not refer to the period during which cash deposits or bonds are taken, but to the period during which the affected imports enter for consumption. The Panel in *US–Softwood Lumber III* faulted the US for having imposed provisional measures less than 60 days after initiation and for a period of more than four months (§ 7.101).

8.2.2 Price Undertakings

The investigation may come temporarily or permanently to a halt, an affirmative preliminary determination of subsidization and injury caused by such subsidization notwithstanding, if satisfactory voluntary undertakings have been received (Art. 18.1 SCM). Art. 18.4 SCM provides that the investigation may be continued at the request of the exporting WTO Member, or simply when the importing WTO Member so decides, in spite of the acceptance of any voluntary undertakings:

> If an undertaking is accepted, the investigation of subsidization and injury shall nevertheless be completed if the exporting Member so desires or the importing Member so decides. In such a case, if a negative determination of subsidization or injury is made, the undertaking shall automatically lapse, except in cases where such a determination is due in large part to the existence of an undertaking. In such cases, the authorities concerned may require that an undertaking be maintained for a reasonable period consistent with the provisions of this Agreement. In the event that an affirmative determination of subsidization and injury is made, the undertaking shall continue consistent with its terms and the provisions of this Agreement.

The undertaking may originate in the exporting country government which undertakes to eliminate or limit the subsidy or take other measures concerning its effects. But it may also concern a commitment by one or more of the exporters under investigation to revise prices so that the investigating authorities are satisfied that the injurious effect of the subsidy has been eliminated: exporter undertakings require the prior consent of the exporting Member, though. The Agreement caps the price increase as it caps the amount of a countervailing duty. The price increases shall not be higher than necessary to eliminate the amount of the subsidy, and it is desirable that the price increases be less than the amount of the subsidy if such increases would be adequate to remove the injury to the domestic industry. Once accepted, compliance with an undertaking may be monitored, and any government or exporter who made an undertaking may be requested to periodically provide information relevant to to permit verification of pertinent data. Art. 18.6 SCM provides that, in the case of a violation of an undertaking, the authorities of the importing WTO Member may take expeditious actions such as immediate application of provisional measures using the best information available. In addition, definitive duties may be levied retroactively up to 90 days before the application of such provisional measures, except that any such retroactive assessment shall not apply to imports before the violation of the undertaking.

Undertakings are completely voluntary both when the initiative is that of the exporters or exporting Members, and when it is that of the importing country's authorities. Not offering or not agreeing to an undertaking cannot be held against the exporter, nor can an IA be forced to accept undertakings (Art. 18.5 SCM). An IA may refuse to accept undertakings, because of their impracticality: for example, if the number of actual or potential exporters is too great, or for other reasons, including reasons of general policy. Where practicable, an IA should provide the reasons for rejecting an offered undertaking, and, to the extent possible, give the exporter an opportunity to comment (Art. 18.3 SCM).

8.2.3 Definitive CVDs

Art. 19 SCM provides that, upon completion of an investigation, and where a final determination is made confirming the existence and amount of the subsidy causing injury, CVDs may be imposed (Art. 19.2 SCM). The maximum amount of CVDs is the amount of the subsidy found to exist, calculated in terms of subsidization per unit of the subsidized and exported product. The SCM Agreement also contains a "lesser duty rule", providing that it is desirable that the duty be less than the total amount of the subsidy, if such a lesser duty would be adequate to remove the injury to the domestic industry. Two provisions deal with the calculation of the amount of the subsidy:

(a) Art. 14 SCM concerns the calculation of the subsidy in terms of benefit to the recipient;

(b) Annex IV deals with the calculation of the total ad valorem subsidization (Art.6.1(a) SCM), and is based on a cost-to-government approach.

There is no legislative preference for one or the other method: Annex IV explicitly refers to Art. 6 SCM (serious prejudice), while Art. 14 SCM expressly refers to any calculation of the amount of benefit in Part V (CVD); this seems to suggest that the latter has a wider application. Neither of the two provisions addresses difficult calculation questions concerning, for example, allocation of subsidies over productive assets and/or over time, or the difficulties in calculating the subsidy amount in the case of non-recurring subsidies. A report by the Informal Group of Experts (IGE) to the Committee on Subsidies and Countervailing Measures (SCM Committee) discusses the various technical problems relating to the calculation of the amount of the subsidy:[51] it distinguishes between non-recurring subsidies, the benefits of which may have to be allocated over time, and recurring subsidies which are fully expanded in the course of the year of receipt. It makes a number of recommendations concerning, *inter alia*, the average useful life of the physical depreciable assets that

---

[51] WTO Doc. G/SCM/W/415/Rev. 2 of May 15, 1998.

could be used as basis for allocating the subsidy benefits;[52] the time value of money; the need to take account of inflation, and so on.[53]

The SCM Agreement also contains a public interest-test in providing that it is desirable that procedures be established which would allow the IA to take due account of representations made by domestic interested parties, including consumers, and industrial users of the imported product subject to investigation (Art. 19.2 SCM, and footnote 50). The SCM Agreement does not set forth an express obligation to calculate individual duties for each exporter, like Art. 6.10 AD does. Still, it appears that, as the amount of subsidization will be different for each exporter, an individual duty will normally be imposed: in *EC–Countervailing Duty on DRAM Chips*, for example, the EU IA calculated individual margins, and ended up imposing duties on Hynix, but not on Samsung (the two Korean companies subject to investigation).[54] While exceptional in practice, Art. 19.3 SCM allows WTO Members to impose duties on an aggregate basis; that is, all imports originating in a country found to be granting subsidies will be burdened with CVDs, irrespective of whether all individual exporters have benefited from subsidies. In this case, individual non-investigated exporters have the right to request an expedited review to establish their rate (if any) of subsidies received (AB, *US–Softwood Lumber IV*, §§ 152–153). An application of duties on aggregate basis does not imply that there is no longer any need to establish the basic conditions for the imposition of CVDs, that is, subsidy, injury to the domestic industry, and causation. In case of subsidies to upstream producers, this implies that it must in any case first be established that the subsidy was passed through to the downstream producers (AB, *US–Softwood Lumber IV*, § 154).

In principle, CVDs, whether provisional or final, may not be imposed retroactively. This means that where the final determination is negative, any provisional duties shall be refunded and any bonds released in an expeditious manner (Art. 20.5 SCM). There are two exceptions to this general principle, which are similar to the corresponding provisions in the AD context:

(a) Definitive CVDs may be levied retroactively back to the date of application of provisional measures in case of a finding of current material injury: the Panel in *US–Softwood Lumber III* underscored that the possibility to impose retroactive duties exists only with re-

---

[52] The un-adopted GATT Panel report in *US–Lead and Bismuth I* discussed this issue.

[53] The recommendations made by the IGE have formed the basis for a number of proposals that were made in the course of the negotiations to introduce technical guidelines on subsidy calculations.

[54] A proposal has been tabled by the EU to introduce a requirement to calculate an individual duty in the CVD-context as well, with the possibility of sampling. The level of the duty to be paid by non-sampled exporters would, as in the AD context, be the weighted average of the duty of the sampled exporters, see WTO Docs. TN/RL/GEN/93, and TN/RL/GEN/96.

spect to definitive, and not provisional duties (§§ 7.93–94). In case a determination is made of threat of injury, duties may be applied retroactively if it can be shown that the provisional measures prevented the injury from materializing; final duties may in such circumstances be applied retroactively for the period for which provisional measures, if any, have been applied. Retroactivity is therefore limited by the period of application of provisional measures, and by the amount collected as provisional duties. Indeed, the SCM Agreement provides that, if the definitive CVDs are higher than the amount guaranteed by the cash deposit or bond, the difference shall not be collected. Moreover, if the definitive duty is less, the excess amount shall be reimbursed, or the bond released in an expeditious manner. It is clear that, if no provisional measures had been applied to start with, the definitive duties may not be applied retroactively;

(b) Art. 20.6 SCM allows for the retroactive application beyond the period of application of provisional measures, in certain critical circumstances where the authorities find that injury which is difficult to repair is caused by massive imports in a relatively short period of a product benefiting from subsidies paid or bestowed inconsistently with the provisions of SCM and GATT. When the IA deems it necessary, the definitive CVDs may, in order to preclude the recurrence of such injury, be assessed on imports which were entered for consumption up to 90 days prior to the date of application of provisional measures. The SCM Agreement does not, unlike the AD Agreement, explicitly allow WTO Members to take such measures as the withholding of appraisement, or assessment. Nevertheless, it appears that a WTO Member *de facto* is entitled to take such measures. This has been the view of at least one Panel (*US–Softwood Lumber III*) which held (§ 7.95):

> We agree with the United States that a Member is allowed to take measures which are necessary to preserve the right to later apply definitive duties retroactively. In our view, an effective interpretation of the right to apply definitive duties retroactively requires that a Member be allowed to take such steps as are necessary to preserve the possibility of exercising that right. What kind of measures may thus be taken by the Member concerned will have to be determined on a case-by-case basis.[55]

8.2.4 Duration of CVDs

Art. 21.1 SCM states that CVDs can remain in place as long as, and to the extent necessary to counteract injurious subsidization. However,

---

[55] In § 7.98 of its report, this Panel held that requiring the posting of a bond or cash deposit went beyond necessary conservatory measures.

unless a review is conducted, a CVD must be withdrawn five years after its imposition. Two types of review, as in the AD Agreement, are provided for in the SCM system:

(a) Administrative review (Art. 21.2 SCM).[56]

(b) Sunset review (Art. 21.3 SCM).

Both types can put an end on the continued imposition of CVDs.

8.2.5 Administrative Reviews (Changed Circumstances Reviews)

Art. 21.2 SCM makes provision for an administrative review to examine whether the continued imposition of the duty is necessary. It can be initiated:

(a) *Ex officio*, provided that a reasonable time since the imposition of the CVD has passed; or

(b) Upon request by an interested party, at any time following the original imposition, provided that the interested party submits positive information substantiating the need for a review.

If, as a result of a review, the IA determines that CVDs are no longer warranted, their imposition shall be terminated immediately. The subject-matter of an administrative review does not necessarily overlap with that of a sunset review; irrespective of whether it has been initiated ex officio or upon request, an IA could investigate whether:

(a) The continued imposition of duties is necessary to offset subsidization; or

(b) Whether the injury would be likely to recur if the duty in place were removed or varied; or

(c) Whether subsidization resulting in injury will continue/recur, assuming that the duties in place were to be varied or removed.

From the three options listed above only (c) corresponds to the subject-matter of a sunset review. Where a review covers both subsidization and injury, it may form the basis for extension of the measure for another five years. In its report on *US–Carbon Steel*, the AB held that, whereas in the context of an administrative review the submission of positive evidence is a threshold issue to initiate the review at the request of an interested party, an *ex officio* initiation does not know of a similar requirement

---

[56] An explanation is warranted here in order to avoid creating confusion: the term administrative review should not be confused with its homonym in US practice. In US practice this term aims to capture the review undertaken in order to liquidate entries. As we explained *supra*, in the US system, goods that have been found to be subsidized will be burdened with a provisional deposit pending definitive calculation at the end of the year. Then, in the context of a US administrative review, or duty assessment review, the goods concerned will either have to be further burdened or the opposite. What we have termed here administrative review is sometimes referred to as 'changed circumstances review'. In the absence of an official term for the procedure under Art. 21.2 SCM, various nominations compete for prominence.

(§ 108). There is no case law concerning administrative reviews in the SCM-context. Recall however, that in the AD-context, the Panel in *US–CVDs on DRAMs* had held that a period of three years of no dumping did not, in and of itself, warrant an ex officio review (§ 6.60).

In an original investigation, the IA must establish that all conditions set out in the SCM Agreement for the imposition of CVD have been fulfilled; in an administrative review, however, the IA only need address those issues which have been raised before it by the interested parties or, in the case of an investigation conducted on its own initiative, those issues which warranted the examination: the AB held as much in its report on *US–Lead and Bismuth II* (§ 63). This case concerned the decision by the US IA to continue with the imposition of duties imposed on economic operators which had previously (for example, pre-privatization) benefited from non-recurring subsidies. The AB, in its report, made a distinction between the obligation of WTO Members to show existence of a benefit conferred by a subsidy during the original investigation, and in subsequent reviews. It concluded that, in the context of an administrative review under Art. 21.2 SCM, an IA need not always establish the existence of a benefit during the period of review. Rather, an IA might legitimately presume that a benefit continues to flow from an untied, non-recurring financial contribution. However, this presumption is not irrebuttable. In a case of change of ownership, as the case before it, an IA should review whether a benefit would continue to exist (§§ 61–62):

> We have already stated that in a case involving countervailing duties imposed as a result of an administrative review, Articles 21.1 and 21.2 of the *SCM Agreement* are relevant. As discussed above, Article 21.1 allows Members to apply countervailing duties 'only as long as and to the extent necessary to counteract subsidization ...'. Article 21.2 sets out a review mechanism to ensure that Members comply with this rule. In an administrative review pursuant to Article 21.2, the investigating authority may be presented with 'positive information' that the 'financial contribution' has been repaid or withdrawn and/or that the 'benefit' no longer accrues. On the basis of its assessment of the information presented to it by interested parties, as well as of other evidence before it relating to the period of review, the investigating authority must determine whether there is a continuing need for the application of countervailing duties. The investigating authority is not free to ignore such information. If it were free to ignore this information, the review mechanism under Article 21.2 would have no purpose.
>
> Therefore, we agree with the Panel that while an investigating authority may presume, in the context of an administrative review under Article 21.2, that a 'benefit' continues to flow from an

untied, non-recurring 'financial contribution', this presumption can never be 'irrebuttable'. In this case, given the changes in ownership leading to the creation of UES and BSplc/BSES, the USDOC was required under Article 21.2 to examine, on the basis of the information before it relating to these changes, whether a 'benefit' accrued to UES and BSplc/BSES. (italics in the original).[57]

There are nevertheless, limits to the exercise of discretion by IAs in this context and the deferential standards that WTO adjudicating bodies have adopted in this respect. In *US–Countervailing Measures on Certain EC Products,* WTO adjudicating bodies had to deal with the so-called "same person methodology" applied by the US when reviewing the need for continued imposition of CVDs following privatization of a previously subsidized firm. The factual aspects of the method are described in detail in § 145 of the report; the Panel made clear that the US had relied upon certain irrebutable presumptions that affected parties could not challenge under any circumstance. The review was thus, not based on facts but on fiction. In § 146, the AB explained that this method was inconsistent with US obligations under Art. 21.2 SCM: according to the AB, Art. 21.2 SCM sets forth an obligation to take into account positive information substantiating the need for a review (§§ 145–146):

> The Panel stated, and the United States agreed before the Panel and on appeal, that the 'same person' method requires the USDOC to 'consider'[] that the benefit attributed to the state-owned producer can be automatically attributed to the privatized producer without any examination of the condition of the transaction when the agency determines the post-privatization entity is not a new legal person. It is only if the USDOC finds that a new legal person has been created that the agency will make a determination of whether a benefit exists, and, in such cases, the inquiry will be limited to the subject of whether a new subsidy has been provided to the new owners.
>
> Thus, under the 'same person' method, when the USDOC determines that no new legal person is created as a result of privatization, the USDOC will conclude from this determination, without any further analysis, and irrespective of the price paid by the new owners for the newly-privatized enterprise, that the newly-privatized enterprise continues to receive the benefit of a previous financial contribution. This approach is contrary to the obligation in Article 21.2 of the *SCM Agreement* that the investigating authority must take into account in an administrative review 'positive information substantiating the need for a review'. Such information could relate to developments with respect to the

---

[57] See also the AB report in *US–Countervailing Measures on Certain EC Products* at § 141.

subsidy, privatization at arm's length and for fair market value, or some other information. The 'same person' method impedes the USDOC from complying with its obligation to examine whether a countervailable 'benefit' continues to exist in a firm subsequent to that firm's change in ownership. Therefore, we find that the 'same person' method, as such, is inconsistent with the obligations relating to administrative reviews under Article 21.2 of the *SCM Agreement.* (italics in the original).

In other words, as the US IA would never be in a position in the context of an administrative review or a sunset review for that matter, to examine whether a benefit continued to exist, even if presented with evidence to this effect, what should be a rebuttable presumption, becomes an irrebuttable presumption in US law. This is why the AB found that the US legislation at hand violated Art. 21.2 SCM as well as Art 1 SCM (§ 147):

In our view, this finding, relating to administrative reviews, leads inevitably to the conclusion that the 'same person' method, as such, is also inconsistent with the obligations of the *SCM Agreement* relating to original investigations. In an original investigation, an investigating authority must establish all conditions set out in the *SCM Agreement* for the imposition of countervailing duties. Those obligations, identified in Article 19.1 of the *SCM Agreement*, read in conjunction with Article 1, include a determination of the existence of a 'benefit'. As in the administrative reviews, the 'same person' method necessarily precludes a proper determination as to the existence of a 'benefit' in original investigations where the pre- and post-privatization entity are the same legal person. Instead, in such cases, the 'same person' method establishes an irrebuttable presumption that the pre-privatization 'benefit' continues to exist after the change in ownership. Because it does not permit the investigating authority to satisfy all the prerequisites stated in the *SCM Agreement* before the imposition of countervailing duties, particularly the identification of a 'benefit', we find that the 'same person' method, as such, is inconsistent with the WTO obligations that apply to the conduct of original investigations." (italics in the original).

Recall that the AB, in *US–Carbon Steel*, underscored the non-applicability of *de minimis* standard in sunset or administrative reviews (§ 71). The US legislation governing reviews imposed a 0.5% ad valorem-threshold for a subsidy to be countervailable. The Panel had agreed with the complainants that the *de minimis* threshold (1% ad valorem) applicable to the original imposition of CVDs was legally relevant for reviews as well. The US appealed this finding, arguing that legislative silence had to mean that a *de minimis* standard did not apply. The AB concurred with the US and reversed the Panel's findings on this score (§§ 88–89).

8.2.6 Sunset Reviews

All CVDs must be withdrawn five years after their imposition, unless the WTO Member has conducted a review, and has concluded that the expiry of the duty would be likely to lead to continuation or recurrence of subsidization and injury (Art. 21.3 SCM). The AB, in *US–Carbon Steel*, underlined that (§ 88):

> termination of a countervailing duty is the rule and its continuation is the exception.

In other words, absent a sunset review, all CVDs in place must immediately be withdrawn (§ 63). The starting point for counting the five-year period is not necessarily that of the original imposition: Art. 21.3 SCM makes it clear that:

> (a) If an administrative review has taken place, and
>
> (b) If this review covered both subsidization and injury, then the date when such a review took place becomes the starting point to count the five-year period.

The mere fact that the last duty assessment review (as used in retrospective systems) led to the conclusion that no duty should be levied, does not necessarily require from the authorities to terminate the definitive duty (Art. 21.3 SCM, footnote 52). The Agreement does not require the termination of the duty after the subsidy allocation period has ended either: in other words, it seems possible that, although an IA allocated the subsidy over a four-year period of time, CVDs could remain in place for the full five-year period (Art. 21.3 SCM).

A sunset review may be initiated:

> (a) On the importing Member's own initiative before the five-year deadline; or
>
> (b) Upon a duly substantiated request made by or on behalf of the domestic industry within a reasonable period of time before the five-year deadline expires.

There are no specific evidentiary requirements for sunset reviews: unlike the original investigation, where Art. 11.6 SCM requires from the IA to have sufficient evidence of subsidization, injury and a causal link to justify initiation of an investigation, sunset reviews may be automatically initiated every five years (AB, *US–Carbon Steel*, §§ 103, 116). If, in the context of the sunset review, an IA has demonstrated that withdrawal of CVDs would be likely to lead to continuation or recurrence of subsidization and injury, then the CVDs may remain in place. The Agreement does not set forth any precise methodology for making such a determination of likelihood of continuation, or recurrence of subsidization and injury. The Panel in *US–Carbon Steel* considered that such a determination, although inherently prospective, must nevertheless rest on a sufficient factual basis (§§ 8.95–96); in this case, the US IA had taken the CVD rate established in the original investigation as a starting point, and then subtracted from that rate the share of two subsidy programs that had been terminated after the imposition. In other words, the factual basis of the DOC determination was limited to the original rate of subsidization, and the fact that two of the original subsidy programs were terminated after the imposition of the original CVD order (§ 8.116). The Panel found that the DOC determination, which did not go beyond simple arithmetic calculation, lacked sufficient factual basis, in particular because the DOC refused to accept information that would have been relevant to the assessment of the likelihood of subsidization (§ 8.117): in particular, the DOC declined the request made by the German exporters that a calculation memorandum from the original investigation be placed on the record of the sunset review on the grounds that the submission was untimely, while it concerned information that was actually in the IA's possession and which was clearly relevant to the likelihood determination.

In *US–Carbon Steel*, the AB considered that the mere fact that a review leads to a rate of subsidization below the *de minimis* level, as set forth in Art. 11.9 SCM (applicable to original investigations), does not require an IA to terminate the measure. The AB came to this conclusion on the basis of the absence of any *de minimis* standard in the text of Art. 21 SCM, in general, and Art. 21.3 SCM in particular, as well as the fact that original investigations and sunset reviews are distinct processes with different purposes, and thus different rules may well apply in these circumstances (§§ 87–88). The AB added, however, that this does not imply that a likelihood determination should not be based on sufficient factual evidence (§ 88).

8.3 PROCEDURAL REQUIREMENTS

The procedural obligations included in the SCM Agreement concerning a CVD investigation are very similar and, on occasions, identical to those included in the AD Agreement.

8.3.1 Standing

Art. 11 SCM deals with the initiation of an investigation: Except in special circumstances, an investigation to determine the existence, degree and effect of any alleged subsidy shall be initiated upon a written application by or on behalf of the domestic industry. The standing requirements for a CVD petition are identical to those of an AD petition. There are two thresholds that must be met (Art. 11.4 SCM):

- First, the application needs to be supported by those producers whose collective output is more than 50% of the total production of that portion of the domestic producers expressing an opinion in favor or against the initiation;
- Second, the producers expressly supporting the initiation need to represent at least 25% of total production.

8.3.2 The Content of a Request for Initiation of a CVD Investigation

An application shall include sufficient evidence of the existence of:

(a) A subsidy and, if possible, its amount;

(b) Injury; and

(c) A causal link between the subsidized imports and the alleged injury.

The application shall contain information as is reasonably available to the applicant on (Art. 11.2 SCM):

(a) The identity of the applicant;

(b) The description of the allegedly subsidized product;

(c) The existence, amount and nature of the subsidy in question; and

(d) The injury to a domestic industry caused by subsidized imports.

In *China–GOES*, the Panel explained that an IA must satisfy itself as to the adequacy of evidence presented which does not have to be conclusive (§§ 7.54ff.). In making this determination, the IA will be balancing two competing interests, namely the interest of the domestic industry in securing the initiation of an investigation and the interest of respondents in ensuring that investigations are not initiated on the basis of frivolous or unfounded suits (§ 7.54). The evidence supplied must relate to financial contribution, benefit, and nature of subsidy (e.g., its specificity) (§ 7.62): for example, mentioning US subsidies to sponsors of healthcare plans were judged *de jure* unspecific; the fact that 26 years had passed by from subsidization to the launching of the application was judged too long a time for a reasonable IA to conclude that the evidence submitted was sufficient to launch an investigation (§ 7.69). The same was true for challenged tax breaks, since 15 years had passed by since the US law providing them had lapsed (§ 7.78).

8.3.3 Compulsory Consultations

A special feature of a CVD investigation is the requirement to enter into consultations with the exporting government (Art. 13 SCM). Consultations should be held as soon as possible after an application has been accepted, and in any event before the initiation of any investigation. The aim is to clarify the situation as to the matters referred to in the application and to arrive at a mutually agreed solution, if possible. Furthermore, throughout the period of investigation, WTO Members whose products are the subject of the investigation are to be afforded a reasonable opportunity to continue consultations. The Agreement emphasizes that no affirmative determination, whether preliminary or final, may be made without reasonable opportunity for consultations (Art. 13.2 SCM, and footnote 44). The Agreement adds that the provisions regarding consultations are not intended to prevent the authorities of a WTO Member from proceeding expeditiously with regard to initiating the investigation, reaching preliminary or final determinations, whether affirmative or negative, or from applying provisional or final measures, in accordance with the provisions of this Agreement.

8.3.4 Initiation of an Investigation

The Agreement clarifies that simple assertion, unsubstantiated by relevant evidence, cannot be considered sufficient to meet its requirements. The IA shall review the accuracy and adequacy of the evidence provided in the application to determine whether the evidence is sufficient to justify the initiation of an investigation. If, in special circumstances, the IA decides to initiate an investigation without having received a written application by or on behalf of a domestic industry for the initiation of such investigation, it shall proceed only if it has sufficient evidence of the existence of a subsidy, injury and causal link to justify the initiation of an investigation.

In case of initiation at the request of the domestic industry, the IA will also need to examine whether the domestic industry filing the application had standing to do so. An investigation shall not be initiated unless the authorities have determined that the application was supported by those domestic producers whose collective output constitutes more than 50% of the total production of the like product produced by that portion of the domestic industry expressing either support for or opposition to the application. In addition, a second threshold needs to be met: the Agreement provides that no investigation shall be initiated when domestic producers expressly supporting the application account for less than 25% of total production of the like product produced by the domestic industry (Art. 11.4 SCM). Investigations shall, except in special circumstances, be concluded within one year. Art. 11.11 SCM states that an investigation shall in no case take more than 18 months from its initiation.

In *Mexico–Olive Oil*, the Panel addressed some of the issues concerning initiation. In this case, there was a dispute between the two parties regarding the timing of the initiation: the EU held the view that the investigation had been initiated when the competent authority had signed the document initiating the process, whereas Mexico submitted that, according to its own law, an investigation is not been initiated before the signed act has been published. The Panel agreed with Mexico that municipal law should be the criterion for deciding this issue (§§ 7.21ff., and especially 7.30). The same Panel dismissed a challenge by the EU to the effect that Mexico had not allowed for sufficient time to consult (in the Panel's calculation there were only 13 days between the invitation for consultations, and the initiation of investigation, § 7.42), arguing that no obligation (to allow sufficient time) existed in the SCM Agreement. Finally, the Panel found that Mexico had violated its obligations under Art. 11.11 SCM by extending the investigation beyond the 18 month-period prescribed in the SCM Agreement (§ 7.123).

8.3.5 Due Process Obligations

The content of Art. 12 SCM reproduces is almost identical to Art. 6 AD. The quintessential requirement imposed on an IA is to ensure even-handedness (due process) when performing its tasks, since, during the investigation process, different interests will be represented: on the one hand the foreign exporters and domestic consumers, and, on the other, the domestic industry. For example, an IA is required, by virtue of Art. 15.1 SCM, to perform an objective examination of the matter before it. In its report on *EC–Countervailing Measures on DRAM Chips*, the Panel quoted (§§ 7.271–7.276) from a report issued in the area of antidumping: in *US–Hot-Rolled Steel*, the AB provided its understanding of the term "objective examination" (§ 193):

> The term 'objective examination' aims at a different aspect of the investigating authorities' determination. While the term 'positive evidence' focuses on the facts underpinning and justifying the injury determination, the term 'objective examination' is concerned with the investigative process itself. The word 'examination' relates, in our view, to the way in which the evidence is gathered, inquired into and, subsequently, evaluated; that is, it relates to the conduct of the investigation generally. The word 'objective', which qualifies the word 'examination', indicates essentially that the 'examination' process must conform to the dictates of the basic principles of good faith and fundamental fairness. 'In short, an "objective examination" requires that the domestic industry, and the effects of dumped imports, be investigated in an unbiased manner, without favouring the interests of any interested party, or group of interested parties, in the investigation. The duty of the investigating authorities to conduct an 'objective examination' recognizes that the determination will be influenced by the objectivity, or any lack thereof, of the investigative process.

This is not the only due process clause in the SCM Agreement. WTO Members investigating the necessity to impose CVDs have to respect due process in numerous other instances: interested members, and all other interested parties (e.g., the exporter, the domestic industry) must be given notice of the information which the authorities require, and ample opportunity to present in writing all evidence which they consider relevant in respect of the investigation in question. Subject to the requirement to protect confidential information, evidence presented in writing by one party shall be made available promptly to the others. Interested members and interested parties also shall have the right, upon justification, to present information orally. Thus, the authorities shall whenever practicable provide timely opportunities for all interested members and interested parties to see all information that is:

(a) Relevant to the presentation of their cases, that is

(b) Not confidential, and that is

(c) Used by the authorities in a CVD investigation, and to prepare presentations on the basis of this information.

Decisions by the IA can only be based on the written record. Except in the case of a determination based on facts available, the authorities have to satisfy themselves as to the accuracy of the information supplied by interested members or interested parties upon which their findings are based. This may be done through on-the-spot verifications or through investigations on the premises of a company of its records if:

(a) The company so agrees; and

(b) The WTO Member in question is notified and does not object.

Subject to the requirement to protect confidential information, the IA shall make the results of any such investigations available, or shall provide disclosure thereof to the firms to which they pertain and may make such results available to the applicants. The Panel in *US–Countervailing Duty Investigation on DRAMs* took the view that a WTO Member should either object to the verification taking place on its soil, or not, but that it cannot be considered to have objected to the verification if it simply expressed concerns about certain aspects of the conduct of the verification. The Panel found that the right of objection cannot be extended to encompass a right to dictate the specific procedures to be followed during the investigation proceedings. The Panel further disagreed that an outright refusal to allow for a verification visit to take place leads to the application of facts available: whether that is so, will actually depend as much on the IA, and whether it has itself acted in a reasonable, objective and impartial manner (§§ 7.404–407).

The authorities shall, before a final determination is made, inform all interested members and interested parties of the essential facts under consideration which form the basis for the decision whether to apply definitive measures: the disclosure should take place in sufficient time for the parties to defend their interests (Art. 12.8 SCM). Any information which is by nature confidential (for example, because its disclosure would provide a competitor with significant competitive advantage, or because its disclosure would have a significantly adverse effect upon a person supplying the information or upon a person from whom the supplier acquired the information), or which is provided on a confidential basis by parties to an investigation shall, upon "good cause" shown, be treated as such by the authorities (Art. 12.4 SCM). A non-confidential summary of confidential information must be furnished, unless if, exceptionally so, a summary is not possible (Art. 12.4.1 SCM).[58] Confidential information shall not be disclosed without specific permission of the party submitting it. If the IA finds that a request for confidentiality is not warranted, and if the supplier of the information is either unwilling to make the information public or to authorize its disclosure in generalized or summary form, the IA may disregard such information, unless it can be demonstrated to its satisfaction from appropriate sources that the information is correct (Art. 12.4.2 SCM). Requests for confidentiality should not be arbitrarily rejected. The IA may request the waiving of confidentiality only regarding information relevant to the proceedings.

Panels will, typically, adopt specific procedures to deal with the provision and dissemination of business confidential information (BCI) in a particular case. For example, the Panel in *Korea–Commercial Vessels* set out in a detailed attachment how the panel would deal with BCI in this case. The most extreme form of 'confidential treatment' occurred in *EC and Certain Member States–Large Civil Aircraft*. A customary request had been tabled to the Panel to adopt special procedures to protect confidential information, but in this case it was highly sensitive business information (HSBI) that had to be protected. All information supplied was locked into one personal computer (PC) which had been locked into one room in the WTO Headquarters; its USB key entries had been sealed and no entry of a key was possible. Parties and third parties could check the information in the PC followed by a camera, and only the Legal Counsel of companies could get into the room (since, these individuals are subjected to their Bar ethical rules). Only the WTO Secretariat could enter the room and check information without being followed by a camera.

8.3.6 Duty to Cooperate and Recourse to Facts Available

Art. 12.7 SCM allows the IA to make determinations on the basis of the facts available in case any interested member or interested party refuses access to, or otherwise does not provide, necessary information within a reasonable period or significantly impedes the investigation. It is interesting to note that, although the language is identical to that of the AD Agreement (Art. 6.8), the SCM Agreement does not contain an annex similar to Annex II to the AD Agreement. Nevertheless, in *EC–Countervailing Measures on DRAM Chips,* the Panel was of the view that

---

[58] The Panel in *Mexico–Olive Oil*, found that Mexico had violated its obligations under Art. 12.4.1 SCM by not requesting a non-confidential summary from the party that had supplied confidential information (§§ 7.100–101).

an IA was entitled to expect a high degree of cooperation from interested parties, and would be entitled to draw adverse inferences from a refusal to cooperate with the authorities, even in the absence of a provision equivalent to Annex II AD, § 7. It concluded that (§ 7.245):

> Article 12.7 identifies the circumstances in which investigating authorities may overcome a lack of information, in the response of the interested parties, by using "facts" which are otherwise "available" to the investigating authority.

This report distinguishes between questions relating to the weight given to various pieces of information and evidence in general, on the one hand, and a situation in which information that was requested was not provided and other information available had to be used, on the other. The Panel rejected Korea's argument that the EU had given undue weight to the documents, and that its reading of these documents was improperly colored by the alleged failure of Korea to provide these documents itself (§ 7.249). This report reveals two instances where recourse to Art. 12.7 SCM is legitimate:

> (a) If the requested party provides false information. In the case at hand, Korea had denied that high-level government officials took part in a meeting, and subsequently, full proof that the meeting took place and was attended by such high-level people became available. In the eyes of the Panel, the EU had had legitimate recourse to Art. 12.7 SCM, and looked for information from secondary sources, since necessary information had not been disclosed (§ 7.254);

> (b) If the requested party provides insufficient information, and no information at all when subsequently requested: in the case at hand, Korea provided the EU IA with a one-page excerpt from a 200–page report. The EU took the view that the report was quite relevant to the investigation, and requested additional information, but did not obtain any information (additional to the one-page excerpt). The Panel took the view that, in light of Korea's response, the EU could legitimately have had recourse to information from secondary sources (§ 7.259).

8.3.7 Judicial Review of CVD Decisions

Art. 23 SCM requires each WTO Member to provide for review of all administrative actions relating to the final determinations of CVD investigations and sunset review. This may be done through a judicial, arbitral, or administrative tribunals. However, the review tribunals and procedures must be independent of the IA.

8.4 STANDARD OF REVIEW

The AB, in *US–Lead and Bismuth II*, was confronted with the issue of whether the standard of review in the context of the SCM Agreement should be identical to that practiced in the WTO AD (Art. 17.6 AD) or, conversely, whether the generic standard of review enshrined in Art. 11 DSU was applicable in the context of the SCM Agreement as well. The AB ruled that, in the absence of specific language mandating an exception (similar to that embedded in Art. 17.6 AD), the generic standard of review was applicable in the SCM Agreement context as well (§§ 44–51). Note however, that in a subsequent case, the Panel in *US–Softwood Lumber VI*, did not consider it (§ 7.17):

> either necessary or appropriate to conduct separate analyses of the USITC determination.

involving a single injury determination with respect to both subsidized and dumped imports, under the two Agreements. The Panel indicated that, given the similarity of the CVD-, and the AD-process, inconsistent results should be avoided. In other words, the standard of review should be the same when examining an injury determination in a CVD case, and an AD case (§ 7.18):

> We consider this result appropriate in view of the guidance in the Declaration of Ministers relating to Dispute Settlement under the AD and SCM Agreements. While the Appellate Body has clearly stated that the Ministerial Declaration does not require the application of the Article 17.6 standard of review in countervailing duty investigations, it nonetheless seems to us that in a case such as this one, involving a single injury determination with respect to both subsidized and dumped imports, and where most of Canada's claims involve identical or almost identical provisions of the AD and SCM Agreements, we should seek to avoid inconsistent conclusions.

So far, this case, remains an isolated incident and is quite idiosyncratic anyway because of the single injury determination that was performed by the IA for both dumped and subsidized imports.

8.5 NO DOUBLE DIPPING

CVDs are discussed in Part III of the SCM Agreement, whereas countermeasures in Part II. Footnote 35 to the SCM Agreement reads:

> The provisions of Part II or III may be invoked in parallel with the provisions of Part V; however, with regard to the effects of a particular subsidy in the domestic market of the importing Member, only one form of relief (either a countervailing duty, if the requirements of Part V are met, or a countermeasure under Articles 4 or 7) shall be available. The provisions of Parts III and V shall not be invoked regarding measures considered non-actionable in accordance with the provisions of Part IV. However, measures referred to in paragraph 1(a) of Article 8 may be

investigated in order to determine whether or not they are specific within the meaning of Article 2. In addition, in the case of a subsidy referred to in paragraph 2 of Article 8 conferred pursuant to a programme which has not been notified in accordance with paragraph 3 of Article 8, the provisions of Part III or V may be invoked, but such subsidy shall be treated as non-actionable if it is found to conform to the standards set forth in paragraph 2 of Article 8.

It follows that WTO Members can initiate a CVD investigation and imposed CVDs and at the same time request from a Panel to find that it has suffered adverse effects as a result of an actionable subsidy (and/or that a prohibited subsidy had been bestowed). In that case, if the subsidizer refuses to withdraw the adverse effects or the prohibited subsidy, it might (assuming a request to this effect) be authorized to impose countermeasures. When doing so, it must deduct the amount of CVDs already in place. In other words, the SCM Agreement does not allow for double dipping.[59]

9. INSTITUTIONAL ISSUES

The Committee on Subsidies and Countervailing Measures (SCM Committee) is established by virtue of Art. 24 SCM. Its tasks are described in this provision and include the establishment of a Permanent Group of Experts (PGE) to assist a Panel, if requested, under Article 4(5) SCM with regard to whether the measure in question is a prohibited subsidy, and to provide advisory opinions on the existence and nature of any subsidy if so requested by the Committee or a Member in relation to its own subsidy. To date, the PGE has never been requested to intervene in the context of a dispute concerning the provision of a prohibited subsidy.

In addition, Art. 25 SCM requires all WTO Members to notify any "subsidy" as defined under the SCM Agreement to the SCM Committee. Art. 25.3 SCM requires that the content of the notifications "should be sufficiently specific to enable other Members to evaluate the trade effects and to understand the operation of the notified subsidy programs." To that end, it specifies specific information that must be included with the notification. A full and complete list of all subsidy programs must be provided every three years by each WTO Member, with updates in the intervening years. Art. 25.7 SCM makes clear that notification of a measure does not prejudge its legal status. In recent years, the US and other WTO Members have raised concerns about the incompleteness of certain WTO Members' notifications (e.g., China). Art. 25.8 SCM allows any WTO Member to make a written request for information on the nature and extent of any subsidy granted or maintained by another Member, or for an explanation of the reasons as to why a particular measure was not noti-

---

[59] Bhagwati and Mavroidis (2004).

fied. Finally, as was the case with AD, a WTO Member must provide semi-annual updates to the SCM Committee on its CVD practices (Art. 25.11 CVD).

QUESTIONS AND COMMENTS

Negotiating History: The negotiating history of the SCM Agreement[60] supports two main findings: first, the Agreement was possible because of the rapprochement between the EU and the US administrations regarding their attitude towards subsidies.[61] The latter was in the 1980s quite hostile to the idea of government intervention in the life of business. In 1992, President Clinton comes to power and with him in his advisors groups proponents of a different philosophy: there is good and bad regulation, good and bad deregulation.[62] This sounds more European than the previous credo, and it is this change in US attitude that facilitated the advent of the SCM Agreement.

US and the Dollar/Gold Parity: The US back in 1971 wanted the following to be a prohibited export subsidy:[63]

> special government measures to offset, in whole or in part, the price disadvantages on exports that result from its own or other countries' exchange rate adjustment.

1971 is of course the year the US had unilaterally decided to throw the Bretton Woods system of fixed parities to the dustbin of history by simply pressing the "delete" function. The US has defended the exactly opposite position in recent years following the allegedly willful undervaluation of the reminbi, China's currency.

Should We Outlaw Subsidies? The negotiating objective is not necessarily an economist's dream: economists would rather be looking at economy wide effects; subsidies are viewed by economists as an instrument whereby governments, at least in a perfect competition model,[64] subsidize foreign consumers: a reduction in the marginal cost of foreign firms (which may be the consequence of a subsidy) in general reduces prices for the domestic firms. Hence, many economists have made the point that instead of imposing countervailing measures to offset subsidization, governments affected by foreign subsidies should be sending a 'thank you note' to the subsidizing govern-

---

[60] Croome (1995); McDonough (1993); Hoekman and Mavroidis (1996a); Wouters and Coppens (2010).

[61] Horlick and Clarke (1994).

[62] D'Andrea Tyson (1992).

[63] Proposal by the US, Supplementary List of Practices that Constitute an Export Subsidy, INT(73)58, June 26, 1973.

[64] In non-perfect competition markets subsidies granted by governments to monopolies may not necessarily benefit consumers wherever they may be, as the beneficiary-monopolist may use the subsidy (perversely and rationally at the same time) to maximize its profit by setting the price somewhere between the market price and the reservation price (i.e., monopoly price). Ostensibly, even when there are few industries competing on the world stage, these firms may still have incentives to price their products above the market price without entering into any tacit or explicit agreement.

ment.⁶⁵ Fundamentally, if the purpose of trade agreements is to address negative external effects stemming from the unilateral definition and exercise of trade policies, then one might wonder whether the treatment of subsidies fits this idea: subsidies produce both positive- and negative external effects; foreign consumers would be the first to write a thank you-note to subsidizers, whereas foreign producers of competing goods (and not producers in the downstream industry using the subsidized good as input for the production of their final product) would be, in principle, hurt. Should not then the SCM Agreement reflect on both effects and recommend anti-subsidy action accordingly?

In similar vein, Sykes (2003a) pertinently asks why outlaw local content-when the same is not done with respect to production subsidies while the two subsidy schemes can have similar effects on the market.⁶⁶ There are some counter-arguments here: Green and Trebilcock (2010) and Coppens (2012) have offered a wide defense of the current regulatory regime; Potipiti (2006) offers one example where banning export subsidies might be the sensible thing to do; she shows how in a world where trade and transportation costs decrease over time export sectors grow while import competing sectors decline. Consequently, export sectors attract new entrants and investment that erodes the protection rent associated with export subsidies. It follows that the government rent from paying export subsidies declines as well, and under similar conditions governments might opt to ban export subsidies. Potipiti's point is well taken yet it is clear that the author makes no case for an agreement to ban subsidies, much like Brou and Ruta (2011) do not make this case: they describe unilateral behavior. With the notable exception of predatory subsidization,⁶⁷ economists generally caution against far-reaching disciplines on subsidies. For all these reasons, one might legitimately wonder whether it was sensible to move away from the benign attitude that the GATT had espoused towards subsidies into today's more binding context.

Pass Through: Grossman and Mavroidis (2007), and (2007c) have taken issue with the decisions of the AB in the privatization cases. In their view, the price paid is simply irrelevant when it comes to deciding whether a benefit continues to exist: at the heart of their disagreement with the AB's decision lies their understanding of the term 'benefit'; they argue that the only interpretation consistent with the aims and objectives of those who drafted the Agreement is one that attributes benefit whenever a firm's competitive position is advantaged relative to what it would have been but for the government's financial contribution (an understanding consistent with the negotiating history and the overall context of the SCM Agreement, as we saw

---

⁶⁵ In the absence of any other distortion and if—and this is a big if—such a subsidy will reduce welfare in the two countries combined. The foreign country may lose or gain. The domestic economy may also lose or gain. It all depends on their strategic interaction.

⁶⁶ Of course local content-and production subsidies can have different effects: a production subsidy could for example lead to exports only without any effect on domestic goods, whereas local content subsidies will increase demand for domestic goods. They could also nonetheless, have very similar effects and this is the reason why Sykes' remark is pertinent.

⁶⁷ Theoretically, it could be the case that subsidies be predatory and thus hurt competition, and not just competitors. In the real world, this looks like a highly unlikely scenario.

above). To achieve this objective, it makes no sense to interpret 'benefit' in terms of the financial wealth of the owners of a firm. Rather, the potentially adverse effects of a subsidy on producers in an importing country can be avoided only if a subsidy is deemed to exist whenever a government's financial contribution impacts the competitive situation in an industry. And the price at which a change in ownership takes place has no bearing on the subsequent competitive conditions. Consequently, no presumption that the benefit has passed through is legitimate either. It is through an investigation that national authorities will determine whether pass through of subsidies has indeed been the case. Events that occur subsequent to the payment of a subsidy may render *infra*-marginal an investment that was formerly unprofitable. If an investment becomes *infra*-marginal, it is impossible to argue that the subsidy is the cause of on-going injury. In such circumstances, the injury would be present even if the subsidy had never been paid. This is the test that WTO adjudicating bodies should apply to determine whether pass through has occurred or not.

Chapter 16

Safeguards

■ ■ ■

1. THE LEGAL DISCIPLINE

WTO Members can lawfully impose safeguards in the form of tariffs, quotas, or tariff quotas if they can show that, as a result of unforeseen developments, imports have risen, and caused injury to the domestic industry producing the like product. Actually, the unforeseen developments-requirement does not figure anywhere in the WTO Agreement on Safeguards (SG); it is reflected in Art. XIX GATT only. It is the AB that introduced this requirement through case law. The AB held that, with respect to the imposition of safeguards, the sources of law are the sum of Art. XIX GATT and the SG Agreement.[1] We quote from its report on *Argentina–Footwear* (§ 81):

> Therefore, the provisions of Article XIX of the GATT 1994 *and* the provisions of the *Agreement on Safeguards* are *all* provisions of one treaty, the *WTO Agreement*. They entered into force as part of that treaty at the same time. They apply equally and are equally binding on all WTO Members. And, as these provisions relate to the same thing, namely the application by Members of safeguard measures, the Panel was correct in saying that "Article XIX of GATT and the Safeguards Agreement must *a fortiori* be read as representing an *inseparable package* of rights and disciplines which have to be considered in conjunction." Yet a treaty interpreter must read all applicable provisions of a treaty in a way that gives meaning to *all* of them, harmoniously. And, an appropriate reading of this "inseparable package of rights and disciplines" must, accordingly, be one that gives meaning to *all* the relevant provisions of these two equally binding agreements. (emphasis and italics in the original).

There are thus, four requirements that must be cumulatively met:
- Increased quantities of imports
- As a result of unforeseen developments
- That have caused or threaten to cause serious injury to the domestic industry producing the like product

---
[1] Wauters (2010) provides an excellent overview of the Agreement.

- In the sense that a causal link between the increased quantity of imports and the serious injury (threat of injury) is (can be) established

A WTO Member must appoint an investigating authority (IA) to conduct an investigation into the matter. WTO law requires that certain procedural and due process requirements be followed during the course of the investigation.

Unlike the other two instruments of contingent protection (AD and CVD), safeguard measures are not imposed against imports from a particular trading partner. Instead, they must be applied in a non-discriminatory manner to all imports. There is one exception: until December 2013, a special safeguard mechanism exists whereby a WTO Member may impose a special safeguard only against imports from China.

A number of other important differences, as compared to AD and CVD measures, exist: safeguard measure must be progressively liberalized after a year; WTO Members imposing a safeguard must agree on adequate means of compensation with affected trading partners once the safeguard exceeds three years; safeguards also cannot be renewed over and over again, but instead must be terminated after a fixed period of time and not be re-introduced for another fixed period of time.

2. THE RATIONALE FOR THE LEGAL DISCIPLINE

According to Maruyama (1989) the first formal safeguard mechanism was included in the 1942 US–Mexico Reciprocal Trade Agreement.[2] The US would, according to the clause, be allowed to pull back if US negotiators excessively reduced tariffs:

> The 'escape clause' is aimed at providing temporary relief for an industry suffering from serious injury, or the threat thereof, so that the industry will have sufficient time to adjust to the freer international competition.[3]

This was the negotiating rationale. The GATT safeguard clause was modeled after this clause that it reproduced almost verbatim.[4] And, in this vein, the GATT Panel in *Hatters' Fur Sales*[5] held that Art. XIX had

---

[2] US Stat. 833 (1943).

[3] S. Rep. No 1298, 93d Cong., 2nd Sess. 119 (1974). Or to borrow from Segal (2011): trade produces winners and losers, as capital and labor get reallocated to the sectors in which countries excel. Since the winners win more than the losers lose, openness is to the nation's overall benefit—even though the autoworker in Ohio who was put out of work after his factory closed may not share in that benefit. Safeguards are about the autoworker in Ohio. Whether it is sound policy, is something that we will be discussing in what follows.

[4] Bronckers (1985); Jackson (1969); Stewart and Brilliant (1993).

[5] GATT Doc. No. GATT/551–3 at p. 21.

been enacted in order to provide temporary relief and not to help develop an industry.[6]

Because a safeguard is imposed as a "safety valve" measure and not in response to "unfair" trade practices, it is subject to more strict disciplines than the other contingent protection measures (AD, CVD) designed to address unfair trade practices. This gives rise to certain notable differences (e.g., the duration with which a safeguard may be imposed, compensation required, etc.)

3. COVERAGE OF THE LEGAL DISCIPLINE

3.1 A TYPOLOGY OF SAFEGUARD MEASURES

There is no exhaustive or even indicative list of safeguards provided in the SG Agreement or the GATT. Based on the notifications by WTO Members to the Safeguards Committee, it appears that ad valorem tariff increases are the most widely used safeguards instrument. Almost as popular are tariff quotas. Specific tariff increases are third on the ranking. Quantitative restrictions are a distant fourth only.[7] "Voluntary export restraints" (VERs) are now officially illegal under the SG Agreement (Art. 11.2 SG):

> The phasing out of measures referred to in paragraph 1(b) shall be carried out according to timetables to be presented to the Committee on Safeguards by the Members concerned not later than 180 days after the date of entry into force of the WTO Agreement. These timetables shall provide for all measures referred to in paragraph 1 to be phased out or brought into conformity with this Agreement within a period not exceeding four years after the date of entry into force of the WTO Agreement, subject to not more than one specific measure per importing Member, the duration of which shall not extend beyond 31 December 1999.

Paragraph 1(b) cited in the quoted passage explicitly refers to VERs. The notorious "Leutwiler report"[8] makes references to intense negotiations during the Tokyo round on this score where the EU and the US tried in vain to persuade the rest of the membership to explicitly provide for country-specific safeguards. In the absence of formal agreement, some

---

[6] By the same token, Art. XIX GATT serves a different purpose than Art. XXVIII GATT: this latter provision is not meant to provide relief limited in time. As we will see *infra*, the advent of the SG Agreement specified the time limits within which safeguards can be lawfully imposed, in line with the original idea underlying Art. XIX GATT which, however, did not contain specific time limits as does Art. 8 SG.

[7] WTO Doc. G/L/936 of October 29, 2010.

[8] A report prepared by experts at the request of the GATT named after the Chairman of the group, see Trade Policies for a Better Future: Proposals for Action, GATT: Geneva, at pp. 42ff.; see also Stewart *et al.* (1993) at pp. 1761ff.

GATT contracting parties, upon request, would "voluntarily" agree to limit their exports towards particular destinations.[9] The legality of VERs was never formally challenged before a GATT Panel.[10] During the Uruguay round, a number of exporting nations requested that the practice of VER be explicitly outlawed. Art. 2.2 SG makes it legally impossible to have recourse to discriminatory VERs nowadays, since:

> Safeguard measures shall be applied to a product being imported irrespective of its source.

Art. 11.1(b) SG explicitly outlaws recourse to VER. It reads:

> Furthermore, a Member shall not seek, take or maintain any voluntary export restraints, orderly marketing arrangements or any other similar measures on the export or the import side. These include actions taken by a single Member as well as actions under agreements, arrangements and understandings entered into by two or more Members. Any such measure in effect on the date of entry into force of the WTO Agreement shall be brought into conformity with this Agreement or phased out in accordance with paragraph 2.

A footnote to this provision reads:

> An import quota applied as a safeguard measure in conformity with the relevant provisions of GATT 1994 and this Agreement may, by mutual agreement, be administered by the exporting Member.

A CU[11] may impose safeguard measures, either as a single unit, or on behalf of one of its members. The AB has acknowledged this possibility in its report on *Argentina–Footwear (EC),* (§ 108). When a CU imposes a measure on behalf of one of its members, footnote 1 to the SG Agreement specifies that all the requirements for the determination of serious injury or threat thereof shall be based on the conditions existing in that member and the measure shall be limited to that member as well. The question thus, arises whether, when safeguards are imposed at the CU-level on behalf of a single member of the CU, restrictions on imports from CU partners will be imposed as well. A parallel question is whether members of an FTA can include imports from their FTA partners when imposing safeguards. This question has been addressed in case law in instances involving safeguards imposed by Argentina (a member of MERCOSUR, a CU), and the US (a member of NAFTA, an FTA). Both Argentina and the US had excluded from the scope of their safeguards measures, imports

---

[9] Sometimes referred to as voluntary restraint agreements (VRA), or even, orderly market arrangement (OMA).

[10] AB, *US–Wheat Gluten*, § 98.

[11] Art. 2 SG, footnote 1. FTAs have no common external trade policy, hence, its members will continue to apply safeguards individually.

from the other CU/FTA partners. Before we proceed to the case law responses, recall that the last sentence of footnote 1 to the SG Agreement provides that:

> Nothing in this Agreement prejudges the interpretation of the relationship between Article XIX and paragraph 8 of Article XXIV of GATT 1994.

3.2 THE CONDITIONS FOR LAWFUL IMPOSITION OF SAFEGUARDS

The AB, in *US–Line Pipe*, advanced a distinction between:

(a) The right to impose a safeguard; and

(b) The lawful application of a safeguard.

For a right to exist, a WTO Member must ensure that it has met all of the requirements for a lawful imposition . For an application to be lawful, the safeguard measure may be applied only to the extent necessary to counteract the resulting damage (§§ 83–84):

> A WTO Member seeking to apply a safeguard measure will argue, correctly, that the right to apply such measures must be respected in order to maintain the domestic momentum and motivation for ongoing trade liberalization. In turn, a WTO Member whose trade is affected by a safeguard measure will argue, correctly, that the application of such measures must be limited in order to maintain the multilateral integrity of ongoing trade concessions. The balance struck by the WTO Members in reconciling this natural tension relating to safeguard measures is found in the provisions of the *Agreement on Safeguards*.
>
> This natural tension is likewise inherent in two basic inquiries that are conducted in interpreting the *Agreement on Safeguards*. These two basic inquiries are: first, is there a right to apply a safeguard measure? And, second, if so, has that right been exercised, through the application of such a measure, within the limits set out in the treaty? These two inquiries are separate and distinct. They must not be confused by the treaty interpreter. One necessarily precedes and leads to the other. First, the interpreter must inquire whether there is a right, under the circumstances of a particular case, to apply a safeguard measure. For this right to exist, the WTO Member in question must have determined, as required by Article 2.1 of the *Agreement on Safeguards* and pursuant to the provisions of Articles 3 and 4 of the *Agreement on Safeguards*, that a product is being imported into its territory in such increased quantities and under such conditions as to cause or threaten to cause serious injury to the domestic industry. Second, if this first inquiry leads to the conclu-

sion that there is a right to apply a safeguard measure in that particular case, then the interpreter must next consider whether the Member has applied that safeguard measure 'only to the extent necessary to prevent or remedy serious injury and to facilitate adjustment', as required by Article 5.1, first sentence, of the *Agreement on Safeguards*. Thus, the right to apply a safeguard measure—even where it has been found to exist in a particular case and thus can be exercised—is not unlimited. Even when a Member has fulfilled the treaty requirements that establish the right to apply a safeguard measure in a particular case, it must do so 'only to the extent necessary . . . (italics in the original).

3.2.1 Unforeseen Developments

The AB in *Argentina–Footwear (EC)* held that the legal basis for adding "unforeseen developments" to the statutory requirements for lawfully imposing safeguards was provided by the letter of Art. 1 SG, which states that safeguard measures will be understood to be the measures provided for in Art. XIX GATT (§§ 83, 84, 93 and 94). The GATT Panel in *Hatters' Fur Sales* held that (p. 10):

> the term 'unforeseen development' should be interpreted to mean developments occurring after the negotiation of the relevant tariff concession which it would not be reasonable to expect that the negotiators of the country making the concession could and should have foreseen at the time when the concession as negotiated.

It is not, hence, so much the development that has to be unforeseen (in this case, the change in fashion), but rather the damaging effect on the domestic industry of such a change. This case related to the withdrawal of a concession by the US on women's fur hats and hat bodies. The members of the Working party agreed that the fact that hat styles had changed did not constitute an unforeseen development within the meaning of Art. XIX GATT, but that the effects of this development (§ 12):

> particularly the degree to which the change in fashion affected the competitive situation, could not reasonably be expected to have been foreseen by the United States authorities in 1947, and that the condition of Article XIX that the increase in imports must be due to unforeseen developments and to the effect of the tariff concessions can therefore be considered to have been fulfilled.

In *Argentina–Footwear (EC)*, the AB considered unforeseen developments to be (§ 92):

> a circumstance which must be demonstrated as a matter of fact.

What needs to be demonstrated is not merely the existence of unforeseen developments, but rather the existence of a logical link between the unforeseen developments and the resulting increase in imports for each of the products subject to the safeguard measure: this was clearly stated by the AB in *US–Steel Safeguards* (§§ 318–319, 322). Unforeseen developments and increased imports are, nevertheless, two distinct matters, as was clearly stated in the Panel report in *Argentina–Preserved Peaches* (§§ 7.17–18).

In *Korea–Dairy*, the AB held that "unforeseen" should be read as synonymous to "unexpected", as opposed to "unpredictable" which would be synonymous to "unforeseeable" (§ 84). So a distinction should be drawn between unforeseen and unforeseeable. The Panel in *Argentina–Preserved Peaches*, reflecting prior case law by the AB, found that developments should be unforeseen at the time when concessions were made (§§ 7.26–28).

The AB, in *US–Lamb*, imposed a procedural requirement: in the order imposing safeguard measures, an IA must demonstrate that the requirement of an unforeseen development has been met; failure to demonstrate is fatal (§§ 72–73). In *US–Steel Safeguards*, the US IA conducted a multi-stage review in which it first issued a report on the safeguards investigation and then followed up by adding its findings on the existence of unforeseen developments. The Panel held that in the case of a multi-stage review, there is no violation of WTO rules if the IA adds its findings on unforeseen developments at a later stage, provided that such findings precede the application of the safeguard measure (§ 10.58).

The Panel in *Argentina–Preserved Peaches* found that demonstration of unforeseen developments required a reasoned explanation as to why such developments were unforeseen. In its words (§ 7.33):

> A mere phrase in a conclusion, without supporting analysis of the existence of unforeseen developments, is not a substitute for a demonstration of fact. The failure of the competent authorities to demonstrate that certain alleged developments were unforeseen in the foregoing section of their report is not cured by the concluding phrase.

The AB, in *US–Steel Safeguards*, held that it did not suffice that a WTO Member considered data which could be relevant; it must also explain how such data satisfied the unforeseen developments-requirement (§§ 279ff., and especially 329). The Panel in *US–Steel Safeguards* concluded that, whether an explanation is sufficient and adequate will depend on the circumstances of the case (§ 10.115); in this case, the US IA had prepared a special report (referred to as the "Second Supplementary Report" in the Panel report) which focused on unforeseen developments (§ 10.116). Still, the measure was judged to be WTO-inconsistent, since, in the eyes of the Panel, the IA had failed to provide a sufficient, adequate and reasoned explanation linking the possible unforeseen developments to the specific increase in imports of the products covered by the measure (§ 10.122). The Panel found that the US IA had referred to a plausible set of circumstances concerning the Asian and Russian financial crises at the end of the 1990s, and the strong US dollar and economy (§ 10.121). It had not examined the actual circumstances in the case at hand that could have given rise to unforeseen developments and this is why the US, in the Panel's view, had acted inconsistently with the requirements of the SG Agreement. Had the US managed, in other words, to connect increased imports in the US market to the financial crises abroad and the strong US dollar, it would have prevailed; it did not, and it lost.[12]

3.2.2 Increased Quantities of Imports

Art. 2.1 SG provides that for safeguards to be imposed, a product must be imported in such increased quantities, absolute or relative to domestic production so as to cause serious injury.[13] Note the difference between the SG-, and the AD Agreement in this respect: in the safeguards-context, increased imports constitute an independent condition for imposition of a measure, similar to a finding of dumping or subsidization in the AD context; without an increase in imports, no safeguard measure. In the AD-context, the requirement to demonstrate increased (dumped) imports is not an independent condition, but rather part of the overall injury-analysis. Recall also that, as Art. 3.2 AD clearly indicates, and as Panels and the AB have consistently emphasized, not one or several of these factors can necessarily give decisive guidance; in short, AD measures may be imposed even in the absence of an increase in imports, something that can never happen in the SG-context. There are two additional, albeit less important, differences between the AD- and the SG Agreements:

> (a) The increase in imports in the SG-context must be determined in absolute terms, or in terms of imports relative to production, rather than to production or consumption as is the case in the AD-context;
>
> (b) While the increase in imports in the SG-context is not qualified as necessarily having to be significant (as in the AD-context), the increase has to be of such a nature that it is capable of causing serious injury.

---

[12] The AB upheld, see § 330 of its report.

[13] Economic theory suggests that imports per se can never be a cause of injury, for they represent the difference between consumption and domestic production at a given price-level: imports thus, are a proximate-, and not the ultimate cause of injury. Sykes (2003) has correctly criticized the SG Agreement for being economically naïve in this respect. One possible way to avoid this issue is to interpret the term increased imports as a pure procedural requirement, and also require from IAs to also investigate why imports have risen. Such an approach has been advanced by Grossman and Mavroidis (2007d). This understanding of the term has not been accepted in case law as we will discover in our discussion of the increased imports-requirement.

In *Argentina–Footwear (EC)*, the AB ruled that Panels should look at trends instead of isolated transactions or absolute numbers based on an end-point to end-point comparison (§ 129). It used the term "trend" probably to denote an effort to collect information and attempt to spot a pattern.[14] In the same report, the AB emphasized that if an increase occurred early on in the presented data and was followed by a decrease, then the increased imports-requirement might not be satisfied; it is necessary for the competent authorities to focus on recent imports (§ 130). The AB held that trends of imports should be "recent, sudden, sharp and significant" enough, both quantitatively and qualitatively, so as to cause serious injury (§ 131):

> We recall here our reasoning and conclusions above on the meaning of the phrase 'as a result of unforeseen developments' in Article XIX:1(a) of the GATT 1994. We concluded there that the increased quantities of imports should have been 'unforeseen' or 'unexpected'. We also believe that the phrase 'in such increased quantities' in Article 2.1 of the *Agreement on Safeguards* and Article XIX:1(a) of the GATT 1994 is meaningful to this determination. In our view, the determination of whether the requirement of imports 'in such increased quantities' is met is not a merely mathematical or technical determination. In other words, it is not enough for an investigation to show simply that imports of the product this year were more than last year—or five years ago. Again, and it bears repeating, not just *any* increased quantities of imports will suffice. There must be '*such* increased quantities' as to cause or threaten to cause serious injury to the domestic industry in order to fulfil this requirement for applying a safeguard measure. And this language in both Article 2.1 of the *Agreement on Safeguards* and Article XIX:1(a) of the GATT 1994, we believe, requires that the increase in imports must have been recent enough, sudden enough, sharp enough, and significant enough, both quantitatively and qualitatively, to cause or threaten to cause 'serious injury'. (italics and emphasis in the original).

The AB in its report on *US–Steel Safeguards*, in an effort to underscore that trends matter, held that even a decrease at the end of the investigating period cannot detract from a finding that increased imports occurred if this is what the overall picture suggests (§ 367):

> We agree with the United States that Article 2.1 does not require that imports need to be increasing at the time of the determination. Rather, the plain meaning of the phrase 'is being imported

---

[14] In statistics, trend analysis would be employed to detect behavior that would otherwise be hidden by noise (irrelevant information) in a time series. This is probably not what the AB had in mind here.

in such increased quantities' suggests merely that imports must have increased, and that the relevant products continue 'being imported' in (such) increased quantities. We also do not believe that a decrease in imports at the end of the period of investigation would necessarily prevent an investigating authority from finding that, nevertheless, products continue to be imported 'in such increased quantities'.

According to the AB view expressed in the same report, what is important in such a case is the explanation to be provided by the IA as to why in the presence of a recent decrease in imports, the increased imports-condition has nevertheless been met (§§ 368, 370). The Panel in *Argentina–Preserved Peaches* was of the view that an overall decrease of imports (not examined in terms of the relative changes in domestic production) between the start and the end of the reference period implies that the increased imports-requirement is not satisfied, unless an adequate and reasoned explanation to the contrary has been provided to this effect (§§ 7.60–61). The Panel in *US–Steel Safeguards* held that an absolute increase in imports, provided that it is recent, sudden, sharp and significant enough so as to cause injury, satisfies the requirements of Art. 2.1 SG, even if the increase has not been examined in relative terms (§ 10.234). This conclusion will not be disturbed by a finding that an increase in absolute terms has been accompanied by an equally strong, or stronger increase of domestic production and a flourishing domestic industry, in which case there would be no relative increase, and there may not be any causation of serious injury (§ 10.234). Similarly, the Panel was of the view that (§ 10.218):

> as a legal matter, a decrease in absolute terms does not invalidate the sufficiency of a relative increase.

The Panel in *US–Steel Safeguards* understood "sudden" to be synonymous with some sort of emergency and a complement to the unforeseen developments-requirement: together they underline the highly exceptional character of safeguards (§ 10.166). The same Panel provided in its report graphic illustrations of trends in imports that were considered to satisfy and not satisfy the requirements of Art. 2.1 SG. Case 1 (reflected in § 10.179 of the Panel report), and Case 2 (§ 10.202) are instances where, in the Panel's view, the graphic representation of imports does not satisfy the requirements of Art. 2.1 SG, essentially because the most recent events had not been taken into account (§§ 10.183, 10.209). Case 3 (§ 10.212), and Case 4 (§ 10.222) are instances where, in the Panel's view, the graphic representation does satisfy the requirements of Art. 2.1 SG.

SEC. 3 COVERAGE OF THE LEGAL DISCIPLINE 513

Case 1

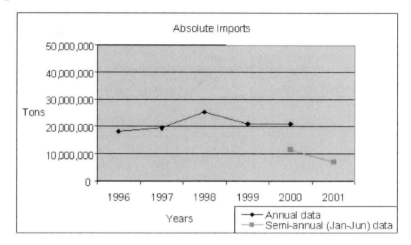

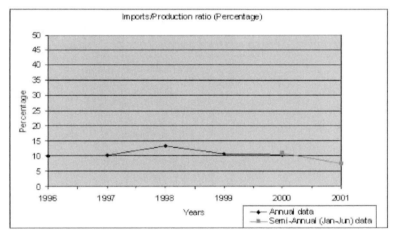

Case 2

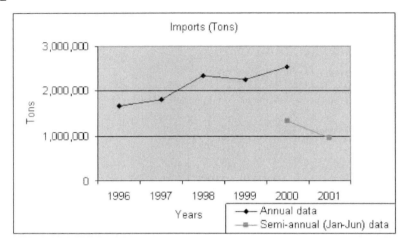

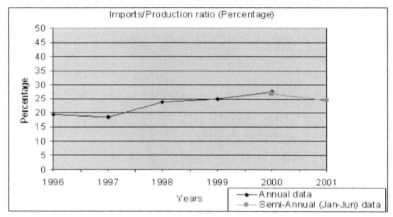

Case 3

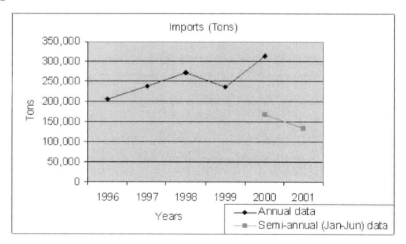

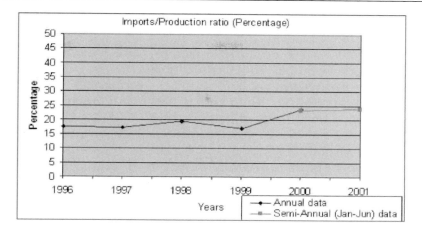

Case 4

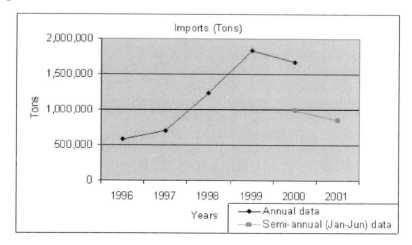

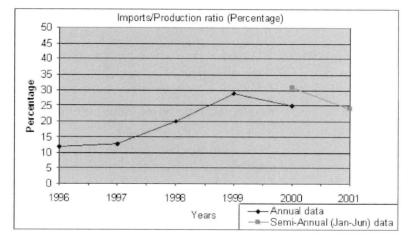

The SG Agreement does not provide for the length of the investigation period, a fact noted by the Panel in *Argentina–Preserved Peaches* (§ 7.50). In the absence of legislative guidance, the AB has stepped in and provided some clarifications: in *Argentina–Footwear (EC)*, it held that the investigation period should not only end in the recent past, but should be the very recent past (§ 130). The Panel in *US–Line Pipe* concluded that a five-year period of investigation was justified (§ 7.201). In practice, the period of investigation for examining increased imports tends to be the same as that for examining serious injury. This is different from the practice in a dumping-, or subsidization-context, where the period of investigation for dumping or subsidization is generally shorter (normally one year) than the period for determining material injury (normally three years). The Panel in *US–Line Pipe* explained and justified this different practice in the safeguards context in the following manner (§ 7.209):

> We are of the view that one of the reasons behind this difference is that, as found by the Appellate Body in *Argentina—Footwear Safeguard*, 'the determination of whether the requirement of imports "in such increased quantities" is met is not a merely mathematical or technical determination'. The Appellate Body noted that when it comes to a determination of increased imports 'the competent authorities are required to consider the trends in imports over the period of investigation'. The evaluation of trends in imports, as with the evaluation of trends in the factors relevant for determination of serious injury to the domestic industry, can only be carried out over a period of time. Therefore, we conclude that the considerations that the Appellate Body has expressed with respect to the period relevant to an injury determination also apply to an increased imports determination. (italics in the original).

3.2.3 Injury to the Domestic Industry Producing the Like Product

<u>Serious injury</u>: The SG Agreement allows for the imposition of safeguard measures if a WTO Member has shown either serious injury, or threat of (serious) injury. Serious injury is defined in Art. 4.1 SG as:

> a significant overall impairment in the position of the domestic industry.

Imposing a safeguard measure requires proving the existence of "serious injury", rather than the weaker "material injury"-standard required in antidumping investigations; this reading is probably warranted because safeguards are not a response to unfair trade, but rather a breather because of the (unexpected) failure of the domestic industry to face foreign competition, the causal link between import surge and injury.[15] The same provision (Art. 4.1 SG) states that threat of serious injury shall be understood to mean serious injury that is clearly imminent, adding that a determination of the existence of a threat shall be based on facts, and not merely on allegation, conjecture or remote possibility (Art. 4.1(b) SG). The SG Agreement contains a definition of threat of serious injury:

> Threat of serious injury shall be understood to mean serious injury that is clearly imminent, in accordance with the provisions of paragraph 2. A determination of the existence of a threat of serious injury shall be based on facts and not merely on allegation, conjecture or remote possibility.

The AB in *US–Lamb* provided its understanding of the terms "injury" and "threat of injury" and the difference between them in the following terms (§§ 124–125):

> The standard of 'serious injury' set forth in Article 4.1(a) is, on its face, very high. Indeed, in *United States—Wheat Gluten Safeguard*, we referred to this standard as 'exacting'. Further, in this respect, we note that the word 'injury' is qualified by the adjective 'serious', which, in our view, underscores the extent and degree of 'significant overall impairment' that the domestic industry must be suffering, or must be about to suffer, for the standard to be met. We are fortified in our view that the standard of 'serious injury' in the *Agreement on Safeguards* is a very high one when we contrast this standard with the standard of 'material injury' envisaged under the *Antidumping Agreement*, the *Agreement on Subsidies and Countervailing Measures* (the '*SCM Agreement*') and the GATT 1994. We believe that the word 'serious' connotes a much higher standard of injury than the word 'material'.
>
> Moreover, we submit that it accords with the object and purpose of the Agreement on Safeguards that the injury standard for the application of a safeguard measure should be higher than the injury standard for antidumping or countervailing measures, since, as we have observed previously:
>
>> [t]he application of a safeguard measure does not depend upon 'unfair' trade actions, as is the case with antidumping or countervailing measures. Thus, the import restrictions that are imposed on products of exporting Members when a safeguard action is taken must be seen, as we have said, as extraordinary. And, when construing the prerequisites for

---

[15] The original US regulations on safeguards (US Section 201 of the 1974 Trade Act) specified that imports must be a more (or no less) important source of injury than any other factor for it to constitute a substantial cause: this standard required listing the potential sources of injury, separating them and quantifying their respective impact before permitting trade relief.

taking such actions, their extraordinary nature must be taken into account.

Returning now to the term 'threat of serious injury', we note that this term is concerned with 'serious injury' which has not yet occurred, but remains a future event whose actual materialization cannot, in fact, be assured with certainty. We note, too, that Article 4.1(b) builds on the definition of 'serious injury' by providing that, in order to constitute a 'threat', the serious injury must be 'clearly imminent'. The word 'imminent' relates to the moment in time when the 'threat' is likely to materialize. The use of this word implies that the anticipated 'serious injury' must be on the very verge of occurring. Moreover, we see the word 'clearly', which qualifies the word 'imminent', as an indication that there must be a high degree of likelihood that the anticipated serious injury will materialize in the very near future. We also note that Article 4.1(b) provides that any determination of a threat of serious injury 'shall be based on facts and not merely on allegation, conjecture or remote possibility' (emphasis added). To us, the word 'clearly' relates also to the factual demonstration of the existence of the 'threat'. Thus, the phrase 'clearly imminent' indicates that, as a matter of fact, it must be manifest that the domestic industry is on the brink of suffering serious injury. (italics in the original).

Panels have consistently examined whether an adequate, reasoned and reasonable explanation has been provided by the authorities for their findings of a significant overall impairment of the industry concerned. In *US–Lamb*, the AB highlighted the need to examine the adequacy of the IA's explanation and reasoning in light of some alternative plausible explanation of the facts (§ 106):

Panels must, therefore, review whether the competent authorities' explanation fully addresses the nature, and, especially, the complexities, of the data, and responds to other plausible interpretations of that data. A panel must find, in particular, that an explanation is not reasoned, or is not adequate, if some alternative explanation of the facts is plausible, and if the competent authorities' explanation does not seem adequate in the light of that alternative explanation. Thus, in making an 'objective assessment' of a claim under Article 4.2(a), panels must be open to the possibility that the explanation given by the competent authorities is not reasoned or adequate.

In this vein, the Panel in *Argentina–Preserved Peaches* considered the temporal focus of the competent authorities' evaluation of the data in making their determination of a threat of serious injury. It then inquired into whether the explanation was adequate in the light of any plausible alternative explanation of the facts (§ 7.104). The failure of the Argentine IA to discuss alternative explanations led to the condemnation of its practices (§§ 7.116–117). To reach the conclusion whether injury has occurred, the SG Agreement requires from an IA to evaluate all relevant factors that it specifically mentions, namely (Art. 4.2(a) SG):

> (a) The rate and amount of the increase in imports of the product concerned in absolute and relative terms;
>
> (b) The share of the domestic market taken by increased imports;
>
> (c) Changes in the level of sales;
>
> (d) Production by the domestic industry;
>
> (e) Its productivity;
>
> (f) Its capacity utilization;
>
> (g) Its profits and losses; and
>
> (h) The situation regarding employment.

Unlike the AD and SCM Agreements, the SG Agreement does not contain a sentence to the effect that no single factor provides decisive guidance (along the lines of Art. 3.4 AD and Art. 15.4 SCM). Despite this absence, the AB nevertheless concluded in *US–Lamb* that no decisive importance should be accorded to one factor, even if this factor is profits which could be quite telling for the state of health of the domestic industry:

> [P]rofits are simply one of the relevant factors mentioned in Article 4.2(a) and to accord that factor decisive importance would be to disregard the other relevant factors . . .

although it did acknowledge in the same report that:

> it will be a rare case, indeed, where the relevant factors as a whole indicate that there is a threat of serious injury, even though the "majority of firms in the industry" is not facing declining profitability.[16]

Similar to the interpretation given by Panels and the AB with respect to the obligation to examine the 15 and 16 factors enumerated in Arts. 3.4 AD and 15.4 SCM Agreement respectively, the AB considered that an IA is required to always examine and evaluate, at the very least, these eight factors (§ 136). In addition, in the AB's view, Art. 4.2(a) SG requires from an IA to evaluate all other objective and quantifiable factors that are relevant to the situation of the industry concerned (§ 136).The AB, in its report on *Argentina–Footwear (EC)*, emphasized that, in addition to a technical examination regarding the impact of all the listed factors and any other relevant factors, an IA must also examine the overall position of the domestic industry (§ 139).

---

[16] *US–Lamb*, footnote 99.

Whereas, in the AD/CVD-context,[17] price analysis (in the sense of comparison of prices between imported and domestic goods) is required as part of the injury analysis, no similar requirement exists in the safeguards-context: instead a more general evaluation of the conditions under which foreign goods are being imported is required; indeed, price is not mentioned as a relevant factor among the list of factors appearing in Art. 4.2(a) SG. The Panel in *Korea–Dairy* explicitly rejected the argument that the requirement to conduct price analysis was implied by Art. 2.1 SG in order to establish that increased imports entered the country under such conditions as to cause serious injury (§§ 7.51–52). What exactly this means is difficult to decipher; most likely, the Panel wanted to signal that if the final order imposing safeguards is overall reasonable, absence of price analysis will not detract from its solidity. While no price analysis is required for a safeguard to be imposed lawfully, this does not imply that price effects of the imports may be ignored altogether. The Panel in *US–Wheat Gluten* found that price may be a relevant factor that needs to be examined, and may even be quite important in a causation analysis as part of the conditions of competition (§ 8.109).

Threat of injury: An IA invoking threat of injury is required to demonstrate that, absent safeguards, injury will happen imminently, that is, in the very near future. A demonstration that injury is clearly imminent must be based on facts and not merely on allegation, conjecture or remote possibility (Art. 4.1(b) SG). The AB, in its report on *US–Lamb,* understood this requirement to mean that it must be manifest that the domestic industry is on the brink of suffering serious injury (§ 125). We again quote the relevant language in the report:

> ... The word 'imminent' relates to the moment in time when the 'threat' is likely to materialize. The use of this word implies that the anticipated 'serious injury' must be on the very verge of occurring. Moreover, we see the word 'clearly', which qualifies the word 'imminent', as an indication that there must be a high degree of likelihood that the anticipated serious injury will materialize in the very near future. We also note that Article 4.1(b) provides that any determination of a threat of serious injury 'shall be based on facts and not merely on allegation, conjecture or remote possibility' (emphasis added). To us, the word 'clearly' relates also to the factual demonstration of the existence of the 'threat'. Thus, the phrase 'clearly imminent' indicates that, as a matter of fact, it must be manifest that the domestic industry is on the brink of suffering serious injury.

The Panel in *Argentina–Preserved Peaches* found that an IA must demonstrate at least a 'projection' that there is strong likelihood that injury will happen; otherwise, it will not have met the requirements of the

---

[17] See Art. 3 AD, and Art. 15 SCM.

SG Agreement with respect to the threat of serious injury-standard. The capacity of imports to cause serious injury, which the authorities found to exist, was not, in this Panel's view, enough (§ 7.122). In other words, serious injury must not simply be the *possible* consequence of increased imports; it must be the *likely* consequence. What is, consequently, required from an IA, is to perform a fact-based assessment of the likelihood of imports increasing and a projection of what is about to occur.

There is, of course, unavoidable tension between requesting a future-oriented study (similar to that required for threat of injury to be determined) and, at the same time, obliging the IA to come up with hard data, hence the established likelihood-standard. This is the reason why all that is requested from an IA is to provide adequate justification for its final findings. To do that, it should, in the AB's view (*US–Lamb*, § 137) examine recent data, since:

> data relating to the most recent past will provide competent authorities with an essential, and, usually, the most reliable, basis for a determination of a threat of serious injury.[18]

However, as was emphasized by the AB, recent data should not be examined in isolation from the data for the entire period of investigation, but rather, in its context (§§ 136–138).

The AB in *US–Line Pipe* addressed the question whether an IA can, using the same set of facts, show serious injury and threat of serious injury at the same time. It was addressing a claim to the effect that a discrete finding of either injury or threat of injury was required for a lawful imposition of safeguard measures. The Panel had taken the view that a discrete finding was necessary, since, in its view, the same set of facts could not simultaneously support a finding of injury and a finding of threat of injury. Adopting a textual interpretation, the AB reversed the Panel in this respect and held that a discrete finding was not required by the Agreement. In doing so, the AB took the view that the threat of injury-standard was a lower threshold than the serious injury-standard. What was important, in the AB's view, for the right to impose a safeguard measure to exist, was that at least a threat of injury be established (§§ 169–172). In its words, "serious injury is the realization of threat of injury" (§ 169).

Industry producing the like product: Injury or threat of injury must be suffered by the domestic industry producing the like product. Art. 4.1(c) SG provides that, in determining injury, a domestic industry shall be understood to mean the producers as a whole of the "like or directly competitive products" operating within the territory of a member, or those whose collective output of the like or directly competitive products consti-

---

[18] The question regarding the type of data on which the threat of injury should be based must be dissociated from the standard of review of Panels dealing with similar issues.

tutes a major proportion of the total domestic production of those products. While the AD and SCM Agreements contain a definition of the term "like product", the SG Agreement does not. The AB expressed its views on this term in a safeguards dispute in the context of the now defunct Agreement on Textiles and Clothing (ATC). *US–Cotton Yarn* concerned the conditions under which safeguards could be imposed. The AB found that the term 'like products' referred to two products which were competitive if they were commercially interchangeable, or if they offered alternative ways of satisfying the same consumer demand. It was the capacity of products to compete in the same market which mattered in the eyes of the AB (§ 96). Because of the qualifier "directly" appearing before the term "competitive products", the AB was of the view that (§ 98):

> a safeguard action will not extend to protecting a domestic industry that produces unlike products which have only a remote or tenuous competitive relationship with the imported product..[19]

The Panel in *US–Lamb* went so far as to state that (§ 7.117):

> This being said, it is clear on the face of the *Safeguards Agreement* that the product coverage of a safeguard investigation can potentially be broader than in an antidumping or countervail case, to the extent that 'directly competitive' products are involved. In our view, this apparent additional latitude that exists under the *Safeguards Agreement* may be related to the basic purpose of the *Safeguards Agreement* and GATT Article XIX, namely to provide an effective safety valve for industries that are suffering or are threatened with serious injury caused by increased imports in the wake of trade liberalization. (italics in the original).

The AB in *US–Cotton Yarn* explained that the term "domestic industry of the like or directly competitive product" should be interpreted in a product-oriented (as opposed to producer-oriented) manner. It thus expressed its preference for demand-side criteria and relegated the relevance of supply-side considerations (§ 86). In its report on *US–Lamb*, the AB confirmed this point (§ 94). The fact that there is a high degree of vertical integration between an input producer and a producer of the final like product is not relevant in defining the domestic industry producing the like product (AB, *US–Lamb*, § 94). In this case, the US had argued that producers of the input (live lambs) may under certain circumstances be considered part of the domestic industry producing the final product (lamb meat) investigated. It had, accordingly, included in its safeguards investigation of imports of lamb meat not only the domestic producers of lamb meat (the breakers and packers) but also the growers and feeders of live lamb in the US. The US IA had considered that this approach was

---

[19] In fact, the AB, in its report on *US–Cotton Yarn*, referred explicitly (§ 91) to its report in *Korea–Alcoholic Beverages* which had been adjudicated under Art. III GATT.

justified (§ 89). The AB, like the Panel before it (§§ 7.71–77, 7.118), in no unclear terms rejected this argument concluding that it is not permitted to include input producers as part of the industry producing the like product under Art. 4.1(c) SG (§ 90). The AB, thus, concluded that, by expanding the scope of the domestic industry so as to include producers of other products, namely, live lambs, the USITC had defined its domestic industry inconsistently with Art. 4.1(c) SG: it should have limited only to packers and breakers of lamb meat (§§ 95–96).

The Panel in *US–Steel Safeguards* held that the product definition must be such that it allows for the possibility to conduct a meaningful causation analysis. In this case, the US IA had relied on data that sometimes referred to the wider CCFRS (certain carbon flat rolled steel products) category, and sometimes not (§ 10.358). On its own admittance, reliance on combined data could sometimes involve double-counting. The improper product definition led the Panel to find that the US had acted inconsistently with its obligations to demonstrate causality under Art. 4.2(b) SG (§§ 10.416–417). In other words, if the product definition is too broad, no meaningful analysis of the conditions of competition is possible, and the causation requirement cannot be met. More to the point, the Panel in *Argentina–Footwear (EC)* observed that in case of broad definition (§ 8.261):[20]

> the statistics for the industry and the imports as a whole will only show averages, and therefore will not be able to provide sufficiently specific information on the locus of competition in the market.

Recall that the domestic industry covers the domestic producers as a whole, or those whose collective output constitutes a major proportion of the total domestic product (Art. 4.1(c) SG). In *US–Lamb*, the AB held that the data used had to be sufficiently representative of the domestic industry so as to allow factually accurate determinations about that industry (§ 131). The AB has also held that it is not necessary for an IA to gather data from the whole of the industry producing the like or directly competitive product; it suffices that it has before it data from a statistically valid sample so that they are sufficiently representative to give a true picture of the particular domestic industry in question. Absent such data, the findings risk being found inconsistent with the SG Agreement (§ 132).

3.2.4 Causal Link Between Increased Imports and Injury

A determination that increased imports caused or are threatening to cause serious injury may only be made where the investigation demonstrates the existence of a causal link between the increased imports and serious injury: Art 4.2(b) SG makes it clear that, when factors other than

---

[20] On this issue, see also the Panel report on *US–Steel Safeguards* at § 10.378.

increased imports are causing injury to the domestic industry, injury not caused by increased imports shall not be attributed to them. There is an important body of WTO case law on this issue under the AD-, and SCM Agreements which contain very similar provisions and its relevance for the SG-context has been explicitly acknowledged by the AB in its report on *US–Line Pipe* (§ 214). Recall that case law stands for the proposition that, under the non-attribution requirement, an IA must separate and distinguish the effects of increased imports from the effects that other factors might have had on the state of its domestic industry producing the like or directly competitive product; it is only after having complied with this requirement, that the causal link between increased imports and injury can be established.

In *US–Wheat Gluten*, the AB rejected the argument that an IA must establish that increased imports alone are the cause of serious injury (§ 79); rather, the obligation to impose safeguard measures so as to counteract only that part of injury caused by increased imports is, in the AB's view, an obligation resulting from Art. 5.1 SG which concerns the application of safeguards (and not the right, as such, to impose them). The AB has made clear that there is a logical/temporal sequence between the two sentences of Art. 4.2 SG, in the sense that, one cannot reach the conclusion that serious injury has been caused by imports, unless one has first complied with the non-attribution requirement. In its report on *US–Lamb*, the AB pertinently ruled to this effect (§ 180):

> the "causal link" between increased imports and serious injury can only be made after the effects of increased imports have been properly assessed, and this assessment, in turn, follows the separation of the effects caused by all the different causal factors.[21]

Two questions arise with respect to the non-attribution requirement:

(a) How will separation occur? and

(b) What happens post-separation?

The first question was addressed by the AB its report on *US–Lamb* (§ 181):

> We emphasize that the method and approach WTO Members choose to carry out in the process of separating the effects of the other causal factors is not specified by the *Agreement on Safeguards*. What the Agreement requires is simply that the obligation in Article 4.2 must be respected when a safeguard measure is applied. (italics in the original).

The Panel in *US–Steel Safeguards* observed that quantification of the portion of the injury caused by specific factors might on occasion be desirable (§ 10.336). The same Panel went on to consider that, in certain cir-

---

[21] See also the AB reports in *US–Wheat Gluten* at § 70, and *US–Line Pipe* at § 215.

cumstances, quantification may even be necessary in order to establish non-attribution explicitly on the basis of a reasoned and adequate explanation without however explaining when this should be the case (§§ 10.340–342).

It follows that the methodology to separate the effects of various factors is not, in the eyes of the WTO adjudicating bodies, prejudged by the Agreement[22] and quantification of their impact might on (undefined) occasions be necessary.

Two Panels (*US–Wheat Gluten*, and *US–Lamb*) discussed the second question, namely what should be done post-separation. They took the view that, once the effects of other factors had been separated and distinguished from the effects of the imports, an IA was required to determine that the imports, in and of themselves, were responsible for the serious injury. The AB, in *US–Wheat Gluten*, summarized the Panel's approach in § 66, and rejected it in § 79. We quote:

> It seems to us that the Panel arrived at this interpretation through the following steps of reasoning: first, under the first sentence of Article 4.2(b), there must be a 'causal link' between increased imports and serious injury; second, the non-'attribution' language of the last sentence of Article 4.2(b) means that the effects caused by increased imports must be distinguished from the effects caused by other factors; third, the effects caused by other factors must, therefore, be excluded totally from the determination of serious injury so as to ensure that these effects are not 'attributed' to the increased imports; fourth, the effects caused by increased imports alone, excluding the effects caused by other factors, must, therefore, be capable of causing serious injury.
>
> . . .
>
> For these reasons, we agree with the first and second steps we identified in the Panel's reasoning; however, we see no support in the text of the *Agreement on Safeguards* for the third and fourth steps of the Panel's reasoning. (italics in the original).

All this might seem quite complicated, especially since the AB has left unresolved the question whether imports, post-separation, must in and of themselves cause serious injury. It seems though, that the need to provide an adequate and reasoned explanation as to the impact of other factors on the state of the domestic industry emerges as the prime obligation of the IA. The AB, held as much, in *US–Line Pipe* (§ 217). In this

---

[22] Although the methodology is not prejudged by legislative *fiat*, it is difficult to see how separation can happen without recourse to economics. We briefly discuss at the end of this section how regression simulation and in some detail the decomposition approach can help in this respect referring to the work of Kelly (1988), Irwin (2003), and Grossman (1986).

vein, in *US–Wheat Gluten*, the AB found that the US had failed to respect Art. 4.2(b) SG by not properly accounting for the increased (US) industry capacity, as the data revealed that this factor may have played a very important role in the deteriorating state of the industry (§ 89). According to the AB, the US IA had not adequately evaluated the complexities of this issue, in particular, whether the increases in average capacity during the investigative period were causing injury to the domestic industry simultaneously with increased imports (§§ 90–91). Similarly, in *US–Lamb*, the AB was of the view that, in the absence of any meaningful explanation of the nature and extent of the injurious effect of other factors, the US IA had failed to ensure that it had not attributed to increased imports injury which had actually been caused by other factors (§ 186). A failure to provide a reasoned and adequate explanation demonstrating that a causal link existed between increased imports and serious injury was also the basis for the Panel finding in *US–Steel Safeguards* (§§ 10.418ff.) that the US order imposing safeguards on nine product categories was inconsistent with Art. 4.2(b) SG.

So imports must not be in and of themselves the sole cause for injury and what matters is whether a reasoned statement concerning causality has been provided by the IA. Nevertheless, a causal link between imports and serious injury must anyway be established post-separation. In § 68 of its report in *US–Wheat Gluten*, the AB took the view that a causal link referred to a relationship of cause and effect, such that increased imports contributed to bringing about, producing, or inducing the serious injury (§ 68); it went on to state that a genuine and substantial relationship between cause and effect must exist for the causality-requirement to be met (§ 69):

> Article 4.2(b) presupposes, therefore, as a first step in the competent authorities' examination of causation, that the injurious effects caused to the domestic industry by increased imports *are distinguished from* the injurious effects caused by other factors. The competent authorities can then, as a second step in their examination, attribute to increased imports, on the one hand, and, by implication, to other relevant factors, on the other hand, 'injury' caused by all of these different factors, including increased imports. Through this two stage process, the competent authorities comply with Article 4.2(b) by ensuring that any injury to the domestic industry that was *actually* caused by factors other than increased imports is not 'attributed' to increased imports and is, therefore, not treated as if it were injury caused by increased imports, when it is not. In this way, the competent authorities determine, as a final step, whether 'the causal link' exists between increased imports and serious injury, and whether this causal link involves a genuine and substantial relationship of

cause and effect between these two elements, as required by the *Agreement on Safeguards*. (italics and emphasis in the original).

The US domestic legislation has espoused the substantial cause-standard[23] the consistency of which with the WTO has been tangentially only discussed in case law so far. Although the AB has yet to issue a definitive ruling, the US causation analysis has, in all cases so far, been found to be WTO-inconsistent. In addition, certain statements by the AB and the Panel in their respective reports in *US–Lamb* and *US–Line Pipe* suggest that, if challenged as such, the substantial cause-standard will be found wanting. In *US–Lamb*, the AB observed (§ 184):

> Although an examination of the relative causal importance of the different causal factors may satisfy the requirements of United States law, such an examination does not, for that reason, satisfy the requirements of the Agreement on Safeguards.

In *US–Line Pipe*, the Panel was of the view that the US substantial cause-standard merely assessed the injurious effects of the other factor at issue against the injurious effects of increased imports and the remaining other factors, and, thus, reached the following conclusion (§ 7.289):

> We do not consider that such an analysis allows an investigating authority to determine whether there is "a genuine and substantial relationship of cause and effect" between the serious injury and the increased imports.

But what does an authority need to do in order to establish a genuine and substantial relationship? In *Argentina–Footwear (EC)*, the AB agreed with the following analysis by the Panel, as to what was required to comply with the causation requirement of Article 4.2(b) SG (§ 145):

> ... we will consider whether Argentina's causation analysis meets these requirements on the basis of (i) whether an upward trend in imports coincides with downward trends in the injury factors, and if not, whether a reasoned explanation is provided as to why nevertheless the data show causation; (ii) whether the conditions of competition in the Argentine footwear market between imported and domestic footwear as analysed demonstrate, on the basis of objective evidence, a causal link of the imports to

---

[23] The decision of December 23, 1977 (97–1077) by the US Court of Appeals for the Federal Circuit (CAFC) re: *Gerald Metals Inc.* described as follows the substantial cause-standard which is reflected in US statutes: "... the statute requires the injury to occur "by reason of" the LTFV (less than fair value) imports. This language does not suggest that an importer of LTFV imports goods can escape countervailing duties by finding some tangential or minor cause unrelated to the LTFV goods that contributed to the harmful effects on domestic market prices. By the same token, this language does not suggest that the Government satisfies its burden of proof by showing that the LTFV goods themselves contributed only minimally or tangentially to the material harm.... Hence, the statute requires adequate evidence to show that the harm occurred "by reason of" the LTFV imports, not by reason of a minimal or tangential contribution to material harm caused by LTFV goods." (pp. 9–10 of the decision).

any injury; and (iii) whether other relevant factors have been analysed and whether it is established that injury caused by factors other than imports has not been attributed to imports.

In other words, in the AB's view, a causation analysis involves a three-step analysis of:

(a) Correlation in trends;

(b) The conditions of competition between the imports and domestic like products, and

(c) The effects of other factors on the domestic industry.

Correlation is not causality, but absence of correlation could be fatal to causality-analysis: in *Argentina–Footwear (EC)*, the AB referred with approval to the following statement by the Panel establishing a negative presumption in case of an absence of correlation (§ 144):

> While such a coincidence [between an increase in imports and a decline in the relevant injury factors] by itself cannot prove causation (because, *inter alia*, Article 3 requires an explanation—i.e., 'findings and reasoned conclusions'), its absence would create serious doubts as to the existence of a causal link, and would require a very compelling analysis of why causation still is present.

In this vein, the Panel in *US–Steel Safeguards* distinguished between instances where there was coincidence between increased imports and injury, and instances where no coincidence existed: the Panel accepted, in this latter context, that there may be a time lag between the increase in imports and the manifestation of their effects on the domestic industry (§ 10.310). The Panel was, however, of the view that there are temporal limits to the extent of this time lag, depending on the industry (§ 10.312):

> Generally speaking, the more rigid the market structure associated with a particular industry, the more likely a lag in effects would exist, at least in relation to some factors. Conversely, the more competitive the market structure, the less tenable it is that lagged effects could be expected.

The same Panel considered that an additional explanation from the IA was required when there was no time-coincidence between increased imports and injury (§ 10.303). The Panel in *Argentina–Footwear (EC)* held that, in addition to a trends/correlation analysis, a causation analysis required an examination of the conditions of competition between the imported products and the like or directly competitive products (§ 8.250). While this may imply a price analysis, this was not necessarily so, in this Panel's view, as much depended on the product in question (§ 8.251):

> We note in this regard that there are different ways in which products can compete. Sales price clearly is one of these, but it is

certainly not the only one, and indeed may be irrelevant or only marginally relevant in any given case. Other bases on which products may compete include physical characteristics (e.g., technical standards or other performance-related aspects, appearance, style or fashion), quality, service, delivery, technological developments consumer tastes, and other supply and demand factors in the market. In any given case, other factors that affect the conditions of competition between the imported and domestic products may be relevant as well. It is these sorts of factors that must be analysed on the basis of objective evidence in a causation analysis to establish the effect of the imports on the domestic industry.[24]

To conclude, assuming that an investigating authority has:

(a) Examined all relevant factors that might be causing injury;

(b) Separated and distinguished the effects caused by increased imports from those caused by other factors; and

(c) Has found that there exists a causal link between increased imports and serious injury or threat thereof,

it has complied with its substantive obligations under the causality-requirement, and can lawfully impose safeguards.

3.3 PROVISIONAL SAFEGUARDS

Provisional measures can be imposed in accordance with Art. 6 SG:

(a) In cases where delay would cause damage difficult to repair;

(b) A preliminary determination has been made to the effect that there is clear evidence that increased imports have caused, or are threatening to cause serious injury;

(c) For a period of no more than 200 days; and

(d) In the form of tariff increases.

The period of application of provisional safeguard measures shall be counted as part of the period of application of the final measures. Unlike the AD/CVD-context, the SG Agreement does not contain any minimum period of time between initiation of the investigation and imposition of provisional measures.

3.4 APPLICATION OF DEFINITIVE SAFEGUARDS

3.4.1 Application Only to the Extent Necessary

Art. 5.1 SG requires from WTO Members to:

---

[24] Note, however, that the Panel in *US–Steel Safeguards*, considered that price was an important, if not the most important factor, when analyzing conditions of competition (§ 10.320).

apply safeguard measures only to the extent necessary to prevent or remedy serious injury and to facilitate adjustment.

In *US–Line Pipe*, the AB held that, by virtue of this provision, an IA, following separation of the effects caused by imports from those caused by other factors, can apply the safeguard only up to the level necessary to address the part of injury caused by increased imports. Assume, for example, that it can be shown that, increased imports account for 20% of the total injury suffered; a WTO Member, by virtue of Art. 5.1 SG, can impose safeguards to counteract the 20%, and not the total amount of injury suffered. The facts in *US–Line Pipe* were as follows: when imposing safeguards, the USITC had identified six factors, other than increased imports, as possible causes contributing to serious injury. The USITC further found that one of the six factors, namely, declining demand in the oil and gas sector, had actually contributed to serious injury. However, since increased imports had a greater impact on injury than this factor, the USITC, in application of the substantial cause-standard, imposed safeguards to counteract all of the injury caused to the US domestic industry (AB, *US–Line Pipe*, §§ 203, 207). This USITC determination was judged inconsistent with the US' obligation under Art 5.1 SG: in reaching this conclusion, the AB began by explaining that its prior rulings on the obligation to separate the effects of various factors simultaneously causing injury were pertinent only to address the issue whether a right to impose a safeguard exists (§§ 242–243). The AB then went on to explain why, post-separation, a WTO Member must apply safeguards only to the extent necessary to remedy the part of injury caused by increased imports; that is, separation of effects also in a way serves the purpose to highlight the ceiling that safeguards cannot violate. In its view, textual reasons (the wording of Art. 5.1 SG), contextual reasons (the wording of other SG provisions closely relating to the subject-matter of Art. 5.1 SG), as well as the object and purpose of the SG Agreement supported this view (§§ 249–250, 252, 257–258). The AB thus concluded that Art. 5.1 SG required WTO Members to impose safeguards only to the extent necessary to counteract injury caused by increased imports (§ 260). Yet, absent quantification of the contribution to injury, it will be hard to imagine how the necessity-requirement will be respected in practice.

3.4.2 Application on Non–Discriminatory Basis, Bar Quota Modulation

Safeguards can only be imposed on non-discriminatory basis (Art. 2.2 SG). The only exception to this statement is "quota modulation" provided for in Art. 5.2(b) SG. To understand how quota modulation works a short detour into the overarching discipline embedded in Art. 5 SG is necessary. Art. 5.1 SG deals with safeguards in the form of QRs and reads:

such a measure shall not reduce the quantity of imports below the level of a recent period which shall be the average of imports in the last three representative years for which statistics are available, unless clear justification is given that a different level is necessary to prevent or remedy serious injury.

If imports increased during the last three years from say 100, to 150 in year two, to 200 tons in year three, at least 150 tons should be allowed to enter the country after imposition of a safeguard. There is of course a question about the meaning of the term "representative"; it could be argued that, in the case of a sudden and sharp increase in imports in the last year of the period of investigation, this last year was not representative of normal import volumes, but rather the result of some unforeseen developments. Excluding this last year from the representative period would of course entail serious implications for the minimum amount of allowable imports. Restricting imports by imposing a QR which lowers the amount of imports to below the average of the last three representative years (in our example, anything below 150 tons), is possible if justification is given that such a different level is necessary to prevent or remedy serious injury (Art. 5.1 SG). The need for justification in this particular situation, led the AB to conclude, in *Korea–Dairy* (§§ 99, 103) and *US–Line Pipe* (§ 234), that in all other situations (that is, cases where the safeguard measures do not take the form of QRs, or in the case of QRs, respect the average level-requirement) there is no need for an authority to provide an explanation of why the level of the measure is actually necessary to prevent or remedy serious injury (§ 99). So, while there is a substantive obligation to ensure compliance with the necessity-requirement, there is no procedural obligation to demonstrate that compliance indeed occurred. The AB underscored this point in *US–Line Pipe* (§ 234). In the same report, the AB added that a justification of the measure, while not required as such, would in any case be the incidental effect of the required reasoned and adequate explanation of causal link-analysis under Art. 3.1 SG, and Art. 4.2(b) SG (§ 236).

When safeguard measures are imposed in the form of QRs, they shall, by virtue of Art. 5.2 SG, be allocated to supplying WTO Members by reference to their share in the import market during a previous representative period. Article 5.2(a) SG does not specify the representative period. Case law has not discussed this point either. Consequently, when a quota is privileged, trade within the quota will not be conducted on MFN basis, but in respect of historic market shares, as is the case under Art. XIII GATT.

Moreover, WTO Members can depart from the obligation to respect historic market shares in their import market, and target the relatively more efficient sources of supply (the "mavericks"), by allocating to them quotas which are less than their historic market share; they can, thus, target those WTO Members which have increased their market share more rapidly: this is what "quota modulation" under 5.2(b) SG amounts to. According to this provision, quota modulation can take place where a clear demonstration has been given to the Committee on Safeguards that:

(a) Imports from certain WTO Members have increased in disproportionate percentage in relation to the total increase of imports of the product concerned during the representative period;

(b) The reasons for the departure from the historic patterns have been justified; and

(c) The conditions of such departure are equitable to all suppliers of the product concerned.

The duration of any such measure shall not extend beyond the initial period of four years. Such targeted safeguard measures may only be used in the case of a finding of current serious injury and not in the case of a threat of serious injury. It is noteworthy that the SG Agreement does not provide that the Committee has to authorize such a departure from historical patterns, it must merely be informed.

The obligations discussed above only apply in cases where the safeguard measure takes the form of a QR. They do not apply in cases where a safeguard measure takes the form of tariff increases. In *US–Line Pipe*, the Panel rejected the argument by Korea that tariff quotas are a form of quotas/quantitative restrictions and could thus benefit from this regime (§ 7.69).

3.5 THE DURATION OF SAFEGUARDS

A safeguard measure can be imposed for an initial period of up to four years (Art. 7.1 SG). It can be extended for a maximum four years more if it has been determined that:

(a) The safeguard measure continues to be necessary to prevent or remedy serious injury; and

(b) There is evidence that the industry is adjusting.

Such an extended measure may not be more restrictive than it was at the end of the initial period (Art. 7.4 SG in fine). Eight years is the maximum period for a continued imposition of a safeguard measure (Art. 7.3 SG). However, an exception exists for developing countries which are allowed to maintain a safeguard measure for a maximum period of ten years (Art. 9.2 SG). During this time, the measure must be progressively liberalized at regular intervals, unless the measure has been imposed for a period not exceeding one year (Art. 7.4 SG). The SG Agreement provides for a mandatory review of any safeguard measure which has been in place for more than three years, at the latest before the mid-term of this measure. If appropriate, the measure is to be withdrawn or the pace of liberalization increased.

The imposition of a safeguard measure must be followed by no imposition of safeguards in the same product-market for an equal time period; this is the "dynamic use constraint" imposed by Art. 7.5 SG: for example, if country A takes safeguard action in the area of cars for eight years, it has to desist from a safeguard action with respect to cars for the eight years following the expiry of the original safeguard measure. This period is halved for developing countries (Art. 9.2 SG). This grace period shall in any case not be shorter than two years, even if the measure itself was applied for a shorter period of time, except in the case of very short safeguard measures of less than six months (up to 180 days), provided the conditions in Art. 7.6 SG have been met. Bagwell and Staiger (2005) note that, because of the dynamic use constraint imposed in the SG Agreement, WTO Members will have the incentive to strategically choose the sectors where they will take protective action. This point is well taken and very true in a world where safeguards are the only way to protect a market. In practice, however, it could be the case that a WTO Member, sequences the imposition of safeguards by an imposition of AD duties in the same market.[25]

3.6 COMPENSATION

Art. 8 SG provides that, before imposing safeguard measures, WTO Members must enter into negotiations with the affected Members, the object of which is to compensate them for damage suffered as a result of the imposition of safeguards (Art. 8.1 SG). Assuming that there is no agreement within 30 days, the affected Member(s) can withdraw substantially equivalent concessions or other obligations, unless the Council for Trade in Goods (CTG) by consensus-voting disapproves of such action; withdrawal should occur at the latest 90 days following imposition of the safeguard, and the CTG should be given at least 30 days to react (Art. 8.2 SG).

The term "affected parties", appearing in Art. 8.1 SG, is not specified any further in the SG Agreement. There is, however, a link between Art. 8.1 SG, and Art. 12.3 SG, which refers to consultations with those WTO Members having a substantial interest as exporters of the product concerned: the Panel (§ 8.206) and the AB (§ 146) in *US–Wheat Gluten* explicitly referred to the link between these two provisions. In light of their approach on this issue, it seems safe to conclude that the term "affected parties" should cover the WTO Members having a substantial interest as exporters of the product. Consequently, only a subset of the WTO Member-

---

[25] See, for example, WTO Docs. G/SG/N/8/EEC/2, G/SG/N/10/EEC/2, and G/SG/N/11/EEC/2/Suppl. 1 of March 16, 2004.

ship will be entitled to suspend concessions in case of disagreement as to the adequate means of trade compensation to be paid.[26]

The obligation to compensate can be avoided if a WTO Member proposes a safeguard action, the maximum duration of which will not exceed three years, if two conditions have been met (Art. 8.3 SG):

(a) The measure has been taken as a result of an absolute increase in imports; *and*

(b) The measure was taken in conformity with the provisions of the SG Agreement.

The question is, of course, who determines whether the measure conforms with the provisions of the SG Agreement? The law does not explicitly decide this issue. In *US–Steel Safeguards*, the EU first published a list of products on which additional duties were going to be levied as of the third birthday of the US safeguard measure, or the fifth day following the date of a decision by the WTO DSB that the measure is incompatible with the WTO Agreement, if that is earlier.[27] In this case the US repealed the steel safeguard shortly after the AB had issued its report, and even before the DSB had had a chance to adopt the report. The announced EU countermeasures were abandoned shortly thereafter.

3.7 SPECIAL AND DIFFERENTIAL TREATMENT FOR DEVELOPING COUNTRIES

A safeguard measure is not to be applied against imports from developing countries where their share of imports does not exceed 3% of the total in the importing market (or 9% cumulatively, that is, where products originate in various developing countries): this is what Art. 9 SG dictates. If imports from developing countries have been excluded on the basis of Art. 9 SG, an IA must establish in a clear manner that imports from sources other than the excluded developing countries fulfilled all the conditions for the imposition of a measure (AB, *US–Steel Safeguards*, § 472).

3.8 STANDARD OF REVIEW

The SG Agreement does not contain a specific provision dealing with standard of review. Consequently, all disputes arising under this agreement should be adjudicated in light of the generic standard of review included in Art. 11 DSU, that is, they must make an objective assessment of the matter before them. The AB accepted as much in its report on *US–Cotton Yarn* (§ 74). The term "objective assessment" is far from being clear. The AB, in its report on *US–Lamb*, explained that, in order to make

---

[26] Although the term 'substantial interest' is not defined any further, one could plausibly make arguments to the effect that it should be constructed in a manner consistent with the term 'principal supplying interest' appearing in Art. XXVIII GATT.

[27] See Council Regulation (EC) No.131/2002 of June 13, 2002.

an objective assessment of the matter before it, a Panel must satisfy itself that an IA has evaluated all relevant facts before it, and has provided an adequate and reasoned explanation for its overall findings (§§ 103–107). In this vein, the AB, in its report on *US–Cotton Yarn*, added that Panels cannot base their determination on evidence which did not exist when the investigation took place. If they do, they violate ipso facto Art. 11 DSU (§ 78). In *US–Lamb*, the AB explained that, the impossibility to perform *de novo* review should not be understood by Panels as equivalent to total deference to the findings by an IA. To the contrary, they must actively review the determinations by an IA (§§ 106–107):

> We wish to emphasize that, although panels are not entitled to conduct a *de novo* review of the evidence, or to substitute their own conclusions for those of the competent authorities, this does not mean that panels must simply accept the conclusions of the competent authorities. To the contrary, in our view, in examining a claim under Article 4.2(a), a panel can assess whether the competent authorities' explanation for its determination is reasoned and adequate only if the panel critically examines that explanation, in depth, and in the light of the facts before the panel. Panels must, therefore, review whether the competent authorities' explanation fully addresses the nature, and, especially, the complexities, of the data, and responds to other plausible interpretations of those data. A panel must find, in particular, that an explanation is not reasoned, or is not adequate, if some alternative explanation of the facts is plausible, and if the competent authorities' explanation does not seem adequate in the light of that alternative explanation. Thus, in making an 'objective assessment' of a claim under Article 4.2(a), panels must be open to the possibility that the explanation given by the competent authorities is not reasoned or adequate.
>
> In this respect, the phrase '*de novo* review' should not be used loosely. If a panel concludes that the competent authorities, in a particular case, have not provided a reasoned or adequate explanation for their determination, that panel has not, thereby, engaged in a *de novo* review. Nor has that panel substituted its own conclusions for those of the competent authorities. Rather, the panel has, consistent with its obligations under the DSU, simply reached a conclusion that the determination made by the competent authorities is inconsistent with the specific requirements of Article 4.2 of the *Agreement on Safeguards*. (italics in the original).

The Panel in *US–Steel Safeguards* drew a distinction between the standard of review to be applied by Panels when evaluating the right to apply a safeguard measure, and the standard to be applied when evaluating the application of the measure itself. In its view, in the latter case, a Panel's examination can be more intrusive than in the former (§§ 10.25–27):

> The Panel is of the view that the standard of review applicable in the present dispute must be seen in light of the distinction between the first and second enquiry that the Panel must perform when assessing a Member's compliance with the requirements of the *Agreement on Safeguards* and Article XIX of GATT 1994. When assessing a Member's compliance with its obligations pursuant to Articles 2, 3 and 4 of the *Agreement on Safeguards* and Article XIX of GATT, the Panel is not the initial fact finder. Rather, the role of the Panel is to 'review' determinations and demonstrations made and reported by an investigating authority.
>
> The situation is different in the context of the second enquiry when assessing whether the measures were applied only to the extent necessary to prevent the serious injury caused by increased imports. In that situation, it is before the Panel, during the WTO dispute settlement process, that the importing Member is forced for the first time to respond to allegations relating to the level and extent of its safeguard measures. For us, this is clear from the following statement of the Appellate Body in *US—Line Pipe*:
>
>> [I]t is clear, therefore, that [...] Article 5.1, including the first sentence, does not oblige a Member to justify, at the time of application, that the safeguard measure at issue is applied 'only to the extent necessary'.
>
> Article 5.1 does not establish a general procedural obligation to demonstrate compliance with Article 5.1, first sentence, at the time a measure is applied.
>
> In that second enquiry, the Panel is thus reviewing whether the measures 'as applied' comply with the requirements of Articles 5, 7, 8 and 9 of the *Agreement on Safeguards* on the basis of the evidence and arguments put forward by the parties during the WTO dispute settlement process. (italics in the original).

4. SPECIAL SAFEGUARD REGIME WITH RESPECT TO CHINA

The accession of China to the WTO introduced a special country-specific safeguards regime for imports of Chinese products. Three types of "safeguards" measures may be imposed on products from China:[28]

---

[28] On this issue, see Bown (2010).

(a) A normal MFN safeguard measure taken under the SG Agreement (an ordinary safeguard). The rules of the SG Agreement apply;

(b) A special China-specific transitional safeguard measure (a transitional safeguard). The provisions governing such a transitional safeguard are set forth in China's Accession Protocol[29] and the Report of the Working Party on the Accession of China;[30]

(c) A textile specific safeguard measure to textile products from China (a textile safeguard). The rules governing such textile safeguards are set forth in the Report of the Working Party on the Accession of China.[31]

WTO Members are not allowed to impose simultaneously a textile- and a transitional safeguard.[32] On the other hand, simultaneous application of an ordinary- and a specific or transitional safeguard is not explicitly outlawed: the EU notified the initiation of such a double China-specific, and ordinary safeguard investigation on mandarins from China. In the end, only an ordinary safeguard was imposed, with a China-specific quota.[33]

The transitional period during which this regime is applicable is 12 years, that is, until December 10, 2013.[34] The transitional safeguard measure is not imposed on an MFN-basis, but targets only Chinese products. A transitional safeguard may be imposed:

in cases where products of Chinese origin are being imported into the territory of any WTO Member in such increased quantities or under such conditions as to cause or threaten to cause market disruption to the domestic producers of like or directly competitive products.[35]

The conditions of increased imports, market disruption, causation and domestic producers of like or directly competitive products are very similar to those set forth in Art. 2 SG. At first sight, it appears that the important difference is the use of the term "market disruption", instead of serious injury. China's Accession Protocol seems to equate market disruption with material injury, which can be demonstrated by examining the volume of imports, their price effects and the effect on the state of the domestic industry:[36]

---

[29] See WTO Doc. WT/L/432 at p. 9, §§ 1–9.
[30] See WTO Doc.WT/MIN (01)/3, section 13, §§ 245–250.
[31] Idem at §§ 241–242.
[32] See § 242(g) of the Report of the Working Party on the Accession of China.
[33] WTO Docs. G/SG/N/6/EEC/2, and G/SG/N/8/EEC/Suppl.1.
[34] China's Accession Protocol, Section 16 § 9.
[35] China's Accession Protocol, Section 16 § 1.
[36] China's Accession Protocol, Section 16 § 4.

Market disruption shall exist whenever imports of an article, like or directly competitive with an article produced by the domestic industry, are increasing rapidly, either absolutely or relatively, so as to be a significant cause of material injury, or threat of material injury to the domestic industry. In determining if market disruption exists, the affected WTO Member shall consider objective factors, including the volume of imports, the effect of imports on prices for like or directly competitive articles, and the effect of such imports on the domestic industry producing like or directly competitive products.

The term "are increasing" is notably different from the corresponding term appearing in the SG Agreement. Trends will not suffice to satisfy this criterion; the Panel in *US–Tyres (China)* found that imports must continue to be increasing at the moment the investigation takes place and the AB upheld this finding (§ 134):

The use of the present continuous tense "are increasing" also suggests that imports follow an upward trend, in that they have increased in the past and continue to increase at present.

China appealed the Panel finding that the requirement above would be satisfied when imports have been increasing in the five-year period preceding the investigation; in China's view the investigation should focus only on the most recent period. The AB saw nothing in the Chinese Protocol of Accession (Arts. 16§ 1 and 16§ 4) to support this argument. It consequently upheld the Panel finding in this respect (§ 149). It follows that imports must be increasing when the investigation is being conducted but the increase could be relative to the beginning of the investigation period. Moreover, there is no need for sharp, rapid increases as the AB noted (§ 158), in fact even if the rate of increase is dropping the requirements for imposing a safeguard will have been met as long as imports are increasing in absolute terms (§ 167). The AB further held that the term "material injury" appearing in 16§ 4 of the Chinese Protocol of Accession is a lower standard than the term "serious injury" appearing in the SG Agreement without specifying how much lower (§ 183). The Panel however, had explained in detail the US standard which in a nutshell required from Chinese imports to have contributed significantly to the injury of the US domestic industry. We quote from § 7.150 of the report:

To determine whether the Section 421 causation standard is inconsistent with the United States' WTO obligations, we must establish what that causation standard actually means. It is well established that, when ascertaining the meaning of domestic legislation, a panel might refer to evidence of the consistent application of that law. In its defence, the United States has produced evidence to the effect that the "contributes significantly" definition is equivalent to the Protocol's "significant cause" standard because of consistent USITC practice requiring the demonstration of a "direct and significant causal link" between the rapidly increasing imports and the market disruption. In particular, the United States refers to the following extract from the USITC Report in the *Tyres* case:

> The third statutory criterion for finding market disruption is whether the rapidly increasing imports are a significant cause of material injury or threat of material injury. The term "significant cause" is defined in section 421(c)(2) of the Trade Act of 1974 to mean "a cause which contributes significantly to the material injury of the domestic industry, but need not be equal to or greater than any other cause." The legislative history of section 406 describes the significant cause standard as follows:

Under this standard, the imports subject to investigation need not be the leading or most important cause of injury or more important than (or even equal to) any other cause, so long as a direct and significant causal link exists. Thus, if the ITC finds that there are several causes of the material injury, it should seek to determine whether the imports subject to investigation are a significant contributing cause of the injury or are such a subordinate, subsidiary or unimportant cause as to eliminate a direct and significant causal relationship. (italics in the original).

Both the Panel (§§ 7.160ff.) as well as the AB (§§ 200ff.) found the US standard consistent with the US WTO obligations in this respect. The AB upholding the Panel's findings in this respect, held that the non-attribution language included in Art. 4.2 SG should find application here as well, the absence of specific language to this effect in the Chinese Protocol of Accession notwithstanding (§ 200).

Transitional safeguards may only be imposed for such period of time as may be necessary to prevent or remedy market disruption, but no maximum time period is provided for.[37] Similarly, the measure may be applied only to the extent necessary to prevent or remedy market disruption.[38] Note that none of the specific disciplines concerning quantitative restrictions as set forth in Art. 5 SG are explicitly mentioned. The Report of the Working Party on the Accession of China adds in § 246(g) that, except for good cause, a grace period of one year has to be respected following the completion of a previous investigation. It appears that this rule does not prohibit the initiation of a new investigation at the time of expiration of the measure.

---

[37] China's Accession Protocol, Section 16 § 6.
[38] *Id.*, Section 16 § 3.

Provisional measures may be applied in critical circumstances, where delay would cause damage, which would be difficult to repair, following a preliminary determination of increased imports, market disruption and a causal link. The maximum period of time for the application of provisional measures is 200 days.[39] As is the case for ordinary safeguards, a WTO Member imposing a transitional safeguard will have to compensate China, by allowing it to suspend an equivalent level of concessions. But China is not entitled to exercise that right during the first two years of the measure, in cases where the measure was adopted following a finding of relative increase of imports, and during the first three years, in case of a finding of absolute increase in imports.[40] There is no requirement that the measure must have been taken in a WTO-consistent manner in order to be able to enjoy a free ride for three years, as was the case in the SG Agreement. Moreover, under the SG Agreement, a relative increase would not have sufficed to escape payment, as only in case of an absolute increase, and a measure taken in conformity with the provisions of the SG Agreement, can the right to compensation be suspended for three years.

From a procedural point of view, a consultation phase precedes the adoption of safeguard measures. It may lead to a bilateral agreement, and, accordingly, China might agree to exercise self-restraint and take such action to prevent or remedy the market disruption.[41] If bilateral consultations do not lead to an agreement within 60 days, a WTO Member may withdraw concessions, or simply limit imports of the Chinese product in question. The Committee on Safeguards has to be notified of any request for consultations, and of the decision to impose measures. Before taking action, a WTO Member must conduct an investigation pursuant to procedures previously established and made available to the public.[42] Due process rights, such as public notice, an adequate opportunity for interested parties to submit their views and evidence, including through a public hearing, are respected; moreover, a written notice setting forth the reasons for the measure, its scope, and duration, must be provided by the WTO Member taking the measure.[43]

In *US–Tyres (China)* the Panel reproduced the standard of review applicable in safeguard cases and added what in its view were idiosyncratic elements that it had to take account of when dealing with a China-special safeguard. The AB (§§ 123–124), in upholding the Panel report, also reproduced the standard of review, noting the following:

---

[39] *Id.*, Section 16 § 7.
[40] *Id.*, Section 16 § 6.
[41] China's Accession Protocol, Section 16 § 2.
[42] See § 246(a) of the Report of the Working Party on the Accession of China.
[43] China's Accession Protocol, Section 16 § 5.

In *US—Lamb*, the Appellate Body provided guidance on how panels should assess the conclusions of national investigating authorities under Article 4.2(a) of the *Agreement on Safeguards*:

> A panel must find, in particular, that an explanation is not reasoned, or is not adequate, if some *alternative explanation* of the facts is plausible, and if the competent authorities' explanation does not seem adequate in the light of that alternative explanation. Thus, in making an "objective assessment" of a claim under Article 4.2(a), panels must be open to the possibility that the explanation given by the competent authorities is not reasoned or adequate. (original emphasis)

In articulating the standard of review that it applied in this dispute, the Panel referred to, and quoted from, the above guidance of the Appellate Body, and made certain additional statements. Importantly, the Panel recalled that the standard of review to be applied by a panel in a given case is also a function of the substantive provisions of the specific covered agreement that is at issue in the dispute, and thus "must be understood in the light of the obligations of the particular covered agreement at issue". The Panel noted that, under Paragraph 16.4 of China's Accession Protocol, an investigating authority is required to "consider objective factors" in determining whether market disruption exists, and that, under Paragraph 16.5, the importing Member "shall provide written notice of the decision to apply a measure, including the reasons for such measure". The Panel further observed that "a panel's standard of review is necessarily distinct from the substantive and procedural obligations of the investigating authority." On this basis, the Panel considered that, in order to review whether the reasoning of the USITC was adequate, the Panel was required to "assess whether the reasoning provided by the USITC in its determination seem[ed] adequate in light of plausible alternative explanations of the record evidence or data advanced by China in this proceeding." The USITC made an affirmative determination that certain passenger vehicle and light truck tyres from China are being imported into the United States in such increased quantities or under such conditions as to cause market disruption. In the present case, the Panel was therefore required to assess whether the USITC provided a reasoned and adequate explanation to support this determination. (italics and emphasis in the original).

A second type of transitional safeguard is the safeguard against the effects of another WTO Member's safeguards action against China: In case of significant trade diversion, caused by the imposition of a transitional safeguard by a WTO Member on a particular type of product originating in China, a third WTO Member may withdraw concessions, or otherwise limit imports from China, only to the extent necessary to prevent or remedy such diversions.[44] The Report of the Working Party on China's Accession clarifies (§ 248) the criteria that would have to be examined in order to determine trade diversion caused by another WTO Member's transitional safeguard, *inter alia*:

(a) The increase in market share of imports from China;

(b) The nature or extent of the action taken or proposed;

(c) The increase in volume of imports from China due to the action taken;

(d) Conditions of demand and supply in the importing WTO Member for the products at issue; and

(e) The volume of exports from China to the WTO Member imposing the original transitional safeguard.

The trade diversion-safeguard is closely linked to the original transitional safeguard, as it has to be reviewed in case of a change to the original transitional safeguard, and must be terminated at the latest 30 days following expiration of the original transitional safeguard (§§ 249–250). There is no obligation to compensate.

The textile safeguard is a product-cum-country-specific safeguard: only Chinese textile products come under its purview. The Report of the Working Party on China's Accession contains the rules governing this type of safeguard (§ 242). The textile safeguard regime remained applicable until December 31, 2008. The products covered, textiles and apparel, are essentially those that were previously covered by the now defunct ATC. The textile safeguards mechanism is a two-stage process and combines a sort of voluntary export restraint by China, with a possibility of imposing a safeguard in case China does not comply with this restraint. A WTO Member may request consultations with China, if it believes that Chinese textile imports were threatening to impede the orderly development of trade; it would need to provide China with a detailed factual statement of reasons and justifications supported by current data of:

(a) The existence or threat of market disruption; and

(b) The extent to which products of Chinese origin have provoked the market disruption.

Consultations should be held within 30 days, and a mutually satisfactory solution should be reached within 90 days following the request. Immediately following the request for consultations, China is required to hold its shipments of the textile products in question to the WTO Member (requesting consultations) to a level no greater than 7.5% (6% for wool

---

[44] China's Accession Protocol, Section 16 § 8.

product categories) above the amount entered during the first 12 months of the most recent 14 months preceding the month in which the request for consultations was made. It follows that the request for consultations triggers a self-imposed restraint on exports. If the consultations do not lead to a solution after 90 days, the voluntary restraint may be turned into a safeguard measure by the importing WTO Member limiting imports of the Chinese textile products in question to the same level (7.5%). This safeguard measure can stay in place for a maximum period of one year, but there are no rules prohibiting the re-application of a new measure on the same products at the end of this period [§ 242(e), (f)]. No investigation is required, nor is there any obligation to notify any WTO body of these textile safeguards.

5. PROCEDURAL REQUIREMENTS

A WTO Member may apply a safeguard measure only following an investigation by its IA pursuant to procedures previously established and made public (Art. 3.1 SG). Art. 3.1 SG requires from an IA of a WTO Member to provide public notice to all interested parties regarding the initiation of investigation; to provide all such parties with the opportunity to present evidence, and their views, and to respond to the presentations of other parties; and to conduct the investigation in accordance with procedures previously established and made public.

5.1 INITIATION

The SG Agreement is silent on the initiation phase and does not subject the decision to initiate an investigation to any procedural or substantive conditions. Unlike other contingent protection instruments no distinction is drawn between self-initiated (ex officio), and investigations upon the request of a private party. What is clear is that, contrary to the AD and SCM Agreements, there are no standing requirements reflected in the SG Agreement, and no other threshold conditions that must be met for an investigation to be lawfully launched. There is no need to show preliminary evidence of increased imports resulting from unforeseen developments, nor that imports might be causing injury to the domestic industry. It suffices that the IA has decided to initiate the process.

5.2 THE PERIOD OF INVESTIGATION (POI)

The SG Agreement does not provide any guidance on the POI to be used when evaluating serious injury. According to the Panel in *US–Wheat Gluten*, any determination of serious injury must pertain to the recent past (§ 8.81).

5.3 AN ACTIVE INVESTIGATING AUTHORITY

In marked difference to its jurisprudence in the AD- and SCM-context, the AB in *US–Wheat Gluten* made it clear that an IA cannot remain passive and rely on the interested parties to raise a factor other than the eight listed factors as relevant (§§ 55–56):

> However, in our view, that does not mean that the competent authorities may limit their evaluation of 'all relevant factors', under Article 4.2(a) of the *Agreement on Safeguards*, to the factors which the interested parties have raised as relevant. The competent authorities must, in every case, carry out a full investigation to enable them to conduct a proper evaluation of all of the relevant factors expressly mentioned in Article 4.2(a) of the *Agreement on Safeguards*. Moreover, Article 4.2(a) requires the competent authorities—and not the interested parties—to evaluate fully the relevance, if any, of 'other factors'. If the competent authorities consider that a particular 'other factor' may be relevant to the situation of the domestic industry, under Article 4.2(a), their duties of investigation and evaluation preclude them from remaining passive in the face of possible short-comings in the evidence submitted, and views expressed, by the interested parties. In such cases, where the competent authorities do not have sufficient information before them to evaluate the possible relevance of such an 'other factor', they must investigate fully that 'other factor', so that they can fulfil their obligations of evaluation under Article 4.2(a).
>
> Thus, we disagree with the Panel's finding that the competent authorities need only examine 'other factors' which were 'clearly raised before them as relevant by the interested parties in the domestic investigation' (emphasis added). However, as is clear from the preceding paragraph of this Report, we also reject the European Communities' argument that the competent authorities have an open-ended and unlimited duty to investigate all available facts that might possibly be relevant. (italics in the original).

5.4 PROVISION OF ACCESS TO THE FILE

There is no express provision guaranteeing interested parties "access to the file" apart from the very general need to provide reasonable public notice to all interested parties. Nor does the SG Agreement contain any disclosure obligations (compare Arts. 6.4, and 6.9 AD). The AB has used the general nature of the obligations as a basis for introducing the essential aspects of practically all of the procedural aspects of the more detailed AD and CVD provisions into the SG Agreement. We quote from the report in *US–Wheat Gluten* (§§ 53–55):

We turn, therefore, for context, to Article 3.1 of *Agreement on Safeguards*, which is entitled 'Investigation'. Article 3.1 provides that 'A Member may apply a safeguard measure only following an investigation by the competent authorities of that Member . . .' (emphasis added). The ordinary meaning of the word 'investigation' suggests that the competent authorities should carry out a 'systematic inquiry' or a 'careful study' into the matter before them. The word, therefore, suggests a proper degree of activity on the part of the competent authorities because authorities charged with conducting an inquiry or a study—to use the treaty language, an 'investigation'—must actively seek out pertinent information.

The nature of the 'investigation' required by the *Agreement on Safeguards* is elaborated further in the remainder of Article 3.1, which sets forth certain investigative steps that the competent authorities 'shall include' in order to seek out pertinent information (emphasis added). The focus of the investigative steps mentioned in Article 3.1 is on 'interested parties', who must be notified of the investigation, and who must be given an opportunity to submit 'evidence', as well as their 'views', to the competent authorities. The interested parties are also to be given an opportunity to 'respond to the presentations of other parties'. The *Agreement on Safeguards*, therefore, envisages that the interested parties play a central role in the investigation and that they will be a primary source of information for the competent authorities.

In that respect, we note that the competent authorities' 'investigation' under Article 3.1 is not limited to the investigative steps mentioned in that provision, but must simply 'include' these steps. Therefore, the competent authorities must undertake additional investigative steps, when the circumstances so require, in order to fulfil their obligation to evaluate all relevant factors. (italics in the original).

5.5 CONFIDENTIAL INFORMATION

Art. 3.2 SG incorporates the requirement to protect confidential information, much like Arts. 6.5 AD, and 12.4 SCM do: It may not be disclosed without the permission of the party submitting it.

5.6 PUBLICATION AND NOTIFICATION

The SG Agreement does not impose any detailed publication requirements: while Arts. 12 AD and 22 SCM contain specific obligations concerning public notice of the initiation of the investigation and the measures taken, both provisional and final, all that Art. 3.1 SG requires is that the investigation includes reasonable public notice to all interested parties, and that the authorities publish a report setting forth their findings and reasoned conclusions on all pertinent issues of fact and law. This obligation is not specified any further. The Panel in *US–Steel Safeguards*, took the view that Art. 3.1 SG does not require from an IA to send draft findings to interested parties (§ 10.64–65). The absence of an explicit, or a clear and unambiguous, explanation of the pertinent issues of fact and law was considered WTO-inconsistent by the AB. The complainant (EU) argued that the US had not fully justified how it had met the unforeseen developments-requirement; on appeal, the AB took the view that for compliance with Art. 3.1 SG to be achieved, a WTO Member must set forth findings and reasoned conclusions on all pertinent issues of facts and law, since this was the only basis (along with requirements under Art. 4 SG) upon which Panels can base their findings (§ 299). The US had argued that failure to explain a pertinent issue of fact or law, in its order imposing safeguards, should not amount to a Panel finding that no investigation of this particular issue had been conducted at all. The AB disagreed, and held that such a finding was appropriate, in light of the absence of a reasoned explanation in conformity with Art. 3.1 SG.

A separate notification requirement is included in Art. 12 SG: it requires that the WTO Safeguards Committee be duly notified, in a timely manner, of decisions to initiate a safeguard investigation (Art. 12.1(a) SG). The same duty exists with respect to the decision to impose provisional measures, impose or extend definitive measures, as well as all findings of injury or threat thereof caused by increased imports (Art. 12.1(b) SG, and Art. 12.1(c) SG). The duty to notify is accompanied by the obligation to do so immediately upon making such a finding or taking such a decision. The AB, in *US–Wheat Gluten,* held that the ordinary meaning of the term "immediately" implies certain urgency (§§ 105–106). The requirement of Art. 12.2 SG to provide the Safeguards Committee with all pertinent information on a number of matters has been considered to be different and less demanding than the requirement of Art. 3.1 SG in fine, to publish a report setting forth an IA's findings and reasoned conclusions on all pertinent issues of fact and law (Panel, *Korea–Dairy*, § 7.125). According to the AB (*Korea–Dairy*), a notification which does not set forth the findings on all of the injury factors mentioned in Art. 4.2 SG, does not include all pertinent information on serious injury (§ 109). Arts 12.2, and 12.3 SG explain that a WTO Member, which is about to apply or extend a safeguard measure, shall provide the WTO Safeguards Committee with all pertinent information including, *inter alia,* evidence of injury, or threat thereof, and information on the proposed measure and its expected duration (Art. 12.2 SG); at the same time, it shall provide all interested WTO Members with the possibility to engage in consultations prior to the imposition of the safeguard measure (Art. 12.3 SG). The aim of these consultations is to allow affected WTO Members to review the notified information, exchange views on the measure proposed, and reach an understanding on the ways to maintain a substantially equivalent level of concessions or adequate trade compensation (Art. 12.3 SG). The AB, in *Korea–Dairy*, agreed with the view of the Panel, that the notification serves, essentially, a transparency and information purpose (§ 111):

> We think that the notification serves essentially a transparency and information purpose. In ensuring transparency, Article 12 allows Members through the Committee on Safeguards to review the measures. Another purpose of the notification of the finding of serious injury and of the proposed measure is to inform Members of the circumstances of the case and the conclusions of the investigation together with the importing country's particular intentions. This allows any interested Member to decide whether to request consultations with the importing country which may lead to modification of the proposed measure(s) and/or compensation.

Notifications under Art. 12.2 SG, concerning findings of injury or threat thereof, and of the decision to take a measure as a result, have to be made prior to the application of the measure, and in sufficient time before its application, in order to allow for meaningful consultations. The AB, in *US–Line Pipe*, confirmed that WTO Members must provide interested parties with enough time so as to ensure that consultations will be meaningful: the AB held that the US, by providing Korea with less than 20 days for consultations, violated its obligations under Art. 12.3 SG (§§ 107, and 111–113). With respect to a notification concerning the initiation of an investigation, the AB held in *US–Wheat Gluten* that a delay of 16 days was not consistent with the requirements of the SG Agreement; with respect to notification concerning findings of injury caused by increased imports, the AB held that a delay of 26 days was not consistent with the requirements of the SG Agreement either (§§ 111, 112 and 116). In both cases, the limited content of the notification was an important element in considering that the notification could have been made sooner. On the other hand, with respect to notifications concerning a decision to apply or extend a safeguard, the AB held that the passage of 5 days between the date when a decision was taken and its notification was not in contravention of the SG Agreement (§ 129). Similarly, the Panel in *Korea–Dairy* found that a delay of 14 days for the limited notification of the initiation of an investigation, 40 days for notifying the injury finding, and 24 days for the decision to apply a measure, was inconsistent with Art. 12.1 SG(§§ 7.134, 7.136 and 7.145). The AB, in *US–Line Pipe*, made clear that a violation of the duty to notify a proposed safeguard measure and provide adequate time for consultations to affected parties (under Art. 12 SG) ipso facto amounted to a violation of the obligation included in Art. 8.1 SG. It thus read Arts. 8.1 and 12.3 SG together (§§ 116–119).

6. INSTITUTIONAL ISSUES

A Committee on Safeguards is established, and its tasks are described in Art. 13 SG. WTO Members will notify this committee of their safeguard measures and the latter can assist them with all matters regarding imposition of safeguards. This committee performs a transparency function since it is the depository of safeguards and periodically issues documents reporting on the status of notifications, measures in place, etc.

QUESTIONS AND COMMENTS

The Rationale for Safeguards: Compare the views expressed by Horn and Mavroidis (2003), Saggi (2010), and Sykes (1990), (2003), (2006).

Unforeseen Developments: Saggi (2010) held that, its definitional weaknesses notwithstanding, this requirement is needed in the SG Agreement: in his view, any time tariff concessions have been made, other things equal, the quantity of imports will increase. Hence, absent the "unforeseen developments"-requirement, WTO Members will be taking with one hand what they will be giving with the other, since they will (almost) always be in position to satisfy the increased imports-requirement. This argument is reinforced by an empirical paper authored by Crowley (2010).

VERs: There were admittedly few, if any, incentives to mount a legal challenge: the requesting state would not normally attack a practice it had requested; and the country limiting its exports was, at the very least, adjusting itself in a comfortable second-best, as the work of Smith and Venables (1991) has demonstrated: in the absence of the expectation to capture the totality of a market, it would raise its price to that of competition, and would pocket 'monopoly rents'. This could be the outcome of a mere increase in the price of goods exported, or because exporters might have the incentive to 'trade up', that is to move from low- to high value goods and increase product differentiation. Empirical work suggests that it is consumers in the importing market that will be burdened with the payment of higher prices.[45] And one should not totally discount the probability that a non-observable consideration had been paid for a promise to limit exports. The absence of a formal condemnation notwithstanding, a series of good arguments could be advanced in support of the view that VERs violate Art. XI GATT (since they effectively amount to a quantitative restriction), assuming of course that they could be attributed to a government.

---

[45] Berry et al. (1999); Kostecki (1987); Hindley (1980).

Chapter 17

Agriculture

■ ■ ■

1. THE LEGAL DISCIPLINE

The Agreement on Agriculture (AG) is one of the more complicated WTO Agreements, but this should not come as a surprise given the sensitivity of many WTO Members to liberalizing trade in agricultural products. The AG's very existence is proof of this point; after all, why is a separate sectoral agreement needed, if not because of the "politicization" of farm policy?

The Agreement contains disciplines on several dimensions:

First, it requires that all protection imposed at the border are expressed in the form of tariffs, with two exceptions:

(1) WTO Members may employ a special safeguard mechanism under certain circumstances. This special safeguard may be employed when: (a) price falls below a certain reference level, or (b) imports surge beyond a certain threshold, with the threshold level dependent on the current level of "import penetration" within a market.

(2) WTO Members can continue to employ non-tariff measures with respect to "special treatment" cases listed in Annex 5 AG.

Second, the Agreement imposes several disciplines on domestic subsidies provided to the agricultural sector. These are divided into a series of "color" boxes.

- The Green Box is a set of permissible domestic subsidies. Some of them have a limited impact on trade (e.g., subsidies for research, disease control, *infra*structure). Others constitute important policy concerns (e.g., food security, structural adjustment assistance, environmental programs).
- The Blue Box is a set of permissible domestic subsidies specifically designed to limit production of agricultural goods.
- With the exception of certain subsidies considered to be de minimis and certain subsidies allowed for development purposes, all other subsidies fall under the Amber Box. Commitments are to be made to lower the level of Amber Box subsidies, i.e., the total Aggregative Measure of Support (AMS).

Third, the Agreement allows for certain forms of export subsidies for agricultural products. Therefore, it constitutes an exception to the SCM Agreement provisions prohibiting export subsidies. However, commitments must be made to reduce these subsidies.

We will explain each of these obligations in greater depth in this Chapter. Note that developing and least-developed countries incur fewer obligations than developed countries. In addition, WTO Members must follow certain transparency requirements.

2. THE RATIONALE FOR THE LEGAL DISCIPLINE

The rationale for the disciplines imposed by the Agreement on Agriculture has to do with the resolve of trading nations to bring farm trade within the disciplines of the GATT. The GATT did not regulate goods by sector. Instead, as we saw in the previous Chapters, disciplines were imposed on all goods. Specific GATT provisions addressed farm trade: Art XI.1 GATT prohibits quantitative restrictions, but Art XI.2 GATT reflects an exception for farm products.[1] As the Executive Secretary of the GATT once observed, though Art XI.2 GATT was "largely tailor-made to United States requirements [. . .] the tailors cut the cloth too fine."[2] In similar a vein, Art.XVI.3 GATT regulates export subsidies for primary (farm) products; this provision aims at discouraging the subsidization of primary goods, and allows subsidization only to the extent that the subsidizing GATT contracting party does not end up with more than an "equitable share of the world market".

Why was it necessary to regulate farm trade and not other goods? And why did nations not exchange tariff concessions on farm goods over the years? It was possible, of course, for nations to exchange tariff concessions during the trade rounds that took place during the GATT years, but similar exchanges were infrequent. Following the traumatic experience in World War II, many countries sought to become self-sufficient in food production and adopted corresponding farm policies. For example, the US sought and and obtained a waiver in 1955[3] in order to address the surplus of many farm products. Through this waiver, the US was essentially free to control imports in order to be able to heavily subsidize its farm production.[4] Other GATT contracting parties also managed to keep their farm policies immune from legal challenges, either through waivers (Belgium

---

[1] See the relevant discussion in Chapter 2.

[2] Eric Wyndham–White, quoted in Dam (1970, p. 260).

[3] GATT Doc. BISD 3S/32 ff.

[4] Over the years, the US reduced subsidization and became more hawkish in farm talks. "Deficiency payments" (that is, support from the federal government tied to prices and the production of specific crops) were replaced by direct payments in 1996; the US Food, Conservation and Energy Act (FCE) of 2008 guaranteed a stream of income to farmers (decoupled from production) until 2012, and the Average Crop Revenue Election (ACRE) programme of the same year, ensured cash flows irrespective of price volatility. See Gardner (2002), (2009), Orden (2009), and Blandford and Orden (2011).

and Luxembourg), or through special clauses in their protocol of accession (Switzerland). Besides quantitative restrictions and high tariffs on imports, public policy in most developed countries included price and supply management tools, seen as appropriate and necessary to maintain the viability of rural and agrarian communities and ensure adequate food supply. For some agricultural products (e.g., rice in Japan) market access for imports was effectively non-existent. The result was that many agricultural import markets became highly insulated.[5]

The EU's agricultural policy, the notorious Common Agricultural Policy (CAP) aimed at ensuring self-sufficiency in farm goods.[6] . It used a system of subsidies to increase domestic production, and 'variable levies' to fend off imports of farm goods in the EU market: duties varied inversely to world prices, that is, the higher the world price, the lower the levy (and correspondingly, the lower the world price, the higher the levy).[7] As a result, "Fortress Europe" came into existence for the European farm market.[8] In addition, the EU adopted various export subsidies. European farmers faced high cost structures but could maintain high prices due to the largely closed market: world market prices were consistently lower than the European prices; therefore, without export subsidies, European farm goods would not find buyers in world markets (where prices were consistently lower than the EU prices).[9] GATT contracting parties sought to reduce protection of farm markets through discussions about farm protectionism: for example, a GATT Committee issued a document calling for moderation of the protection, but it fell short of making specific proposals.[10] Although many questioned whether the legality of certain protection schemes, such as the variable import levies, complied with the GATT, few legal challenges were raised. Josling *et al.* (1996, pp. 71ff)

---

[5] Recall the Haberler report discussed in Chapter 6. Brink (2011) offers a discussion on this score. He perceptively points to the fact that the current structure in the AG Agreement corresponds to Haberler's distinction between measures aimed at discouraging imports, at encouraging exports, and at encouraging domestic production as well.

[6] The EU was not alone in championing such an objective. See, e.g., Gopinath (2011) describing how India also sought self-sufficiency. One might legitimately cast doubt on the wisdom of similar policies in light of the multitude of sources of farm supplies around the world and the rather impossibility to face cartelized practices. Other justifications offered for regulation of farm trade heard in policy circles include the unusual price instability, preservation of lifestyle, or the cost for farmers in LDCs. The validity of the first two grounds is questionable: If it is lifestyle we care about why not simply adopt decoupled income payments? Price instability becomes less of a concern with scientific progress. At the end of the day, a lot of intervention is the pure outcome of political economy factors.

[7] Some variable duties were as high as 480% *ad valorem*, see p. 84 in Committee on Finance, United States Finance, Summary and Analysis of H.R. 10710—The Trade Reform Act of 1973, February 26, 1974, US Government Printing Office, Washington D.C., 1974) states US exports to world grew twice as much as towards EU 1961–1970.

[8] Balassa (1975) offers a great discussion on farm protectionism in Europe.

[9] Josling and Swinbank (2011) correctly deduce that we are in presence of one instrument too many: the combination of variable levies and export subsidies made the need for other domestic support mechanisms redundant.

[10] GATT Doc. BISD 10s/135ff.

have argued that the US, at least, was reluctant to issue a challenge because of its larger foreign policy objective of encouraging European integration: The CAP was viewed as integral part of the EU integration process, and therefore, even though the US might have had qualms about the legality of certain CAP measures, it did not want to do anything that might put the wider process at risk. The unwillingness of the US to destabilize the European integration process thus probably explains why EU farm policy remained unchallenged for so long: If the US did not take the first step, who would?

It turned out that the answer was Uruguay. In 1962, Uruguay launched in 1962 a complaint against fifteen GATT contracting parties,[11] whereby it challenged, inter alia, the consistency of variable import levies with the GATT rules. However, the Panel's deliberations were inconclusive in this respect (§ 17):

> The Panel was faced with a particular difficulty in considering the status of variable import levies or charges. It noted the discussion which took place at the nineteenth session of the CONTRACTING PARTIES on this subject during which it was pointed out that such measures raised serious questions which had not been resolved. In these circumstances the Panel has not considered it appropriate to examine the consistency or otherwise of these measures under the General Agreement.[12]

Consequently, the Panel did not make any recommendations regarding the consistency of variable import levies with the GATT rules. It did, nonetheless, acknowledge their detrimental effect on the export interests of Uruguay. We read, for example, in pp. 135–136 of the report where the Panel discusses the complaint against the Netherlands:

> However, in respect of the *variable import levies*, the Panel considers that, having regard to the nature of the measures and the interest which Uruguay has in the products in question, there are *a priori* grounds for assuming that those measures could have an adverse effect on Uruguayan exports. (italics in the original).

Eventually, the US did chalenge the consistency of the CAP with the GATT in the 1980s. However, the majority of these GATT Panel reports remained un-adopted, and thus, of limited legal value. By refusing to adopt them, the EU demonstrated its will to continue to protect its farmers.

---

[11] Uruguayan Request to Article XXIII, Report adopted on November 16, 1962, GATT Doc. BISD 11s/95ff.

[12] Some later GATT discussions though, reveal that variable duties that exceeded the level of bound duties would be deemed illegal, see GATT Doc AG/M/3, p. 63 (1984).

Several factors, however, pushed the EU towards becoming more flexible in its agricultural trade policy.[13] Europeans became alarmed about the high percentage that farm protection represented in the EU budget. Other European industries became increasingly dissatisfied that the EU could not secure as much in the way of trade gains for other sectors on account of EU farm protectionism.[14] In addition, Europe's trading partners stepped up their resolve to open up the lucrative EU market. In the Uruguay Round, a coalition of exporters of agricultural products—the so-called "Cairns group"[15]—provided the necessary stimulus to push for a worldwide liberalization of agricultural trade.[16] The AG Agreement was a milestone in that finally farm goods would come under the purview of the multilateral rules. Art. 20 AG addresses this point:

> Recognizing that the long-term objective of substantial progressive reductions in support and protection resulting in fundamental reform is an ongoing process, Members agree that negotiations for continuing the process will be initiated one year before the end of the implementation period, taking into account:
>
> (a) the experience to that date from implementing the reduction commitments;
>
> (b) the effects of the reduction commitments on world trade in agriculture;
>
> (c) non-trade concerns, special and differential treatment to developing country Members, and the objective to establish a fair and market-oriented agricultural trading system, and the other objectives and concerns mentioned in the preamble to this Agreement; and
>
> (d) what further commitments are necessary to achieve the above mentioned long-term objectives.[17]

---

[13] Various contributions in Swinnen (2008) discuss the most recent reforms in the EU farm policy, whereas Swinnen (2009) discusses the evolution in farm protection in the Europe in the 19th and 20th century.

[14] In Marchetti and Mavroidis (2011) we provided some evidence to the effect that the EU services lobby was not prepared to sit back and postpone services liberalization in the name of EU farm protectionism, although key political European figures thought otherwise. Compare Swinbank (2009).

[15] The Cairns Group comprised 19 agricultural exporting countries and borrowed its name from the Australian city where the original founders first met. The group was originally composed of Argentina, Australia, Brazil, Canada, Chile, Colombia, Fiji, Hungary, Indonesia, Malaysia, New Zealand, Philippines, Thailand, and Uruguay. Later Hungary and Fiji left the group and Bolivia, Costa Rica, Guatemala, Paraguay, South Africa, Pakistan and Peru joined. See Breene (1993).

[16] On the negotiation of the agreement on agriculture, see Olsen (2005). For an excellent survey of the WTO AG, see McMahon (2006).

[17] In *Canada–Dairy* (§§ 7.25 and 7.26) the Panel accepted as much arguing that this agreement was a framework for further liberalization. Yeutter (1998, p.73) sums it up perfectly when quoting Carole Brookins, a prominent agricultural economist:

> The Agreement was a remarkable achievement, bringing agricultural trade under the rules and disciplines of the GATT for the first time. No one should underestimate the value of full tariffication, nor the initial steps made towards eliminating export subsidies. In fact, the great tragedy for the agricultural sector and for the whole world economy is the nearly half century of

3. COVERAGE OF THE LEGAL DISCIPLINE

3.1 THE AGREEMENT IN A NUTSHELL

The main features of the Agreement on Agriculture are the following:

Border Measures: Art. 4 AG requests from WTO Members to convert all non-tariff border measures (such as import quotas, or variable levies) into tariffs. This is the notorious "tariffication" process of border farm protection.[18] WTO Members undertook the obligation to have their overall tariff protection (following tariffication) reduced by 36% over a 10–year period (for developed countries) or 24% over a 10–year period (for developing countries). LDCs are not required to make commitments. While WTO Members retain some discretion as to which sectors will suffer bigger and which smaller tariff reductions, the AG Agreement requests that a minimum of 15% tariff reduction be implemented for each product category (10% for developing countries). Tariffs will be the only form of protection of farm goods as WTO Members cannot introduce new non-tariff measures following the advent of the WTO. WTO Members also agreed to allow foreign producers to gain at least 3% of their import markets (to rise up to 5% by the end of the implementation period) as a result of the reduction of the border protection.

Domestic support: WTO Members agreed on a common metric to calculate domestic support for the farm sector: the Aggregate Measurement of Support (AMS).[19] They also agreed on a base period for calculating AMS (1986–1988). All forms of domestic support are classified, as we saw supra, in three categories ("boxes"): the Green, Blue, and Amber Boxes. Each WTO Member must notify the WTO of its programs coming under each one of the three boxes. Although the agreement contains fairly detailed criteria for notification, disagreements might arise across members as to the designation of a particular national program.[20] The Green Box (Annex 2) includes programs that are not at all, or are minimally distorting, such as agricultural research and are exempted from reduction commitments. The Blue Box includes production-limited support for either crop or livestock production and are not subject to reduction commitments as long as they meet the criteria of Art. 6.5 AG. The Amber Box includes measures that do not come under the exempted categories (Blue Box, Green Box, de minimis payments, and development payments) and

---

time lost in getting this job started. If we had begun this process in 1947 when the GATT began its work in reducing industrial tariffs, we would have a 50 year 'adjustment' period to transition down to full open markets in agriculture by 1997. And what a difference that would have made.

[18] The Illustrative list of measures that must be converted to tariffs includes variable import levies, and minimum import prices (Art. 4.2 AG); see Panagariya (2005).

[19] The AMS was based, but does not correspond to entirely, the OECD Producer Subsidy Equivalent (PSE), which we discuss in more detail *infra*.

[20] As a result, disputes might be initiated before the WTO: in *US–Upland Cotton*, for example, Brazil successfully challenged the US designation of production flexibility contract (PFC) as fully decoupled, and therefore, green box-consistent.

must be capped. WTO Members are requested to reduce their support from the established baseline over a 6–year period (Arts. 1(a), 6 AG, and Annex 3 to the AG Agreement) by 20% (developed countries); and by 13.3% over a 10–year period (developing countries). LDCs are not required to make commitments. WTO Members enjoy flexibility and can decide to decrease protection in one agricultural commodity, while increasing it somewhere else as long as they can abide by their overall reduction obligation.

De minimis payments: Under this provision (Art. 6.4 AG), WTO Members are allowed to use domestic subsidies up to 5% (10% for developing countries) of the total value of domestic agricultural production.

Export subsidies: WTO Members undertake product (or group of products)-specific commitments, in the form of commitments to reduce both budgetary outlays and the quantity of exports receiving export subsidies. If a WTO Member qualifies as developed country, it must reduce export subsidies over a 6–year period by 21% in terms of volume of products that receive subsidies, and 36% in terms of cash value of these subsidies (Arts. 8–10 AG). Developing countries enjoy a 10–year period during which they must reduce 2/3 the size of what is required from developed countries (*i.e.*, a 14% in terms of volume of products that receive subsidies, and 24% in terms of cash value of these subsidies). LDCs are not required to make commitments.

WTO Members undertake some other, specific obligations (such as time-limited due restraint, export prohibition, transparency requirements and obligations vis-à-vis the net food importing developing countries).

3.2 THE RELATIONSHIP BETWEEN THE AG AND THE SCM AGREEMENTS

Export farm subsidies can be tolerated as long as they respect the agreed caps, whereas non-farm export subsidies are outright illegal. The relationship between the SCM- and the AG Agreements is key in understanding the extent of the exception. Art 21.1 AG reads:

> The provisions of GATT 1994 and of other Multilateral Trade Agreements in Annex 1A to the WTO Agreement shall apply subject to the provisions of this Agreement.

In *Canada–Dairy*, the parties disagreed whether Canada had exceeded its commitments on exports of milk, assuming the scheme was viewed by the Panel as an export subsidy. The Panel (§§ 7.20ff.) held that WTO Members must observe both the AG- and the SCM-disciplines, since the former does not constitute a "safe harbor" for measures inconsistent with the SCM. This point was made even clearer by the AB in its report on *US–Upland Cotton*. The AB faced, inter alia, an appeal by the US concerning the consistency of the so-called "Step 2 payments" with the AG and SCM (§ 514):

> Under the program, marketing certificates or cash payments (collectively referred to by the Panel as "user marketing (Step 2) payments") are issued to eligible domestic users and exporters of eligible upland cotton when certain market conditions exist such that United States cotton pricing benchmarks are exceeded. "Eligible upland cotton" is defined as "domestically produced baled upland cotton which bale is opened by an eligible domestic user ... or exported by an eligible exporter". An "eligible domestic user" of upland cotton is defined under the regulations as:
>
>> A person regularly engaged in the business of opening bales of eligible upland cotton for the purpose of manufacturing such cotton into cotton products in the United States (domestic user), who has entered into an agreement with CCC to participate in the upland cotton user marketing certificate program.

Brazil did not contest that the US was in compliance with its obligations under Art. 6.3 AG (which imposes a cap on total spending). It contested, nevertheless, the consistency of the US payments with the SCM Agreement, arguing that such payments, which amounted to local content subsidies, were inconsistent with Art. 3.1(b) SCM.

The AB agreed with the Panel that Art. 21.1 AG applies in three situations (§ 532):

> where, for example, the domestic support provisions of the *Agreement on Agriculture* would prevail in the event that an explicit carve-out or exemption from the disciplines in Article 3.1(b) of the *SCM Agreement* existed in the *text* of the *Agreement on Agriculture*. Another situation would be where it would be impossible for a Member to comply with its domestic support obligations under the *Agreement on Agriculture* and the Article 3.1(b) prohibition simultaneously. Another situation might be where there is an explicit authorization in the text of the *Agreement on Agriculture* that would authorize a measure that, in the absence of such an express authorization, would be prohibited by Article 3.1(b) of the *SCM Agreement*. (italics in the original).

The AB then added that (§ 550):

> In providing such domestic support, however, WTO Members must be mindful of their other WTO obligations, including the prohibition in Article 3.1(b) of the *SCM Agreement* on the provision of subsidies that are contingent on the use of domestic over imported goods. (italics in the original).

Thus, whenever it is possible for a WTO Member to simultaneously comply with both the AG and the SCM Agreements, it should do so. As a result, in this situation, the AB outlawed the US Step 2 payments (§ 552).[21] However, in the three scenarios sketched out by the AB above, where it is impossible for a WTO Member to comply with both the provisions of the AG and SCM Agreements or where an explicit carve-out exists in the text, then AG trumps SCM.

3.3 PRODUCT COVERAGE

Art. 2 AG states that this Agreement applies to all products included in Annex 1. This Annex provides a list of the products coming under the purview of AG Agreement: it covers HS Chapters 1–24, except for fish and fish products, plus a number of other more detailed headings which are not exhaustively mentioned in Annex 1. Schedule of concessions are based on the list of products mentioned in Annex 1, annexed to the AG Agreement (Annex 1) and form an integral part thereof (Art. 21.2 AG). The AB in its report on *EC–Export Subsidies on Sugar*, confirmed that the WTO Members' schedules of concession have to adhere to the disciplines included in the AG Agreement (§§ 224–226).

4. BORDER MEASURES ON AGRICULTURAL GOODS

4.1 THE TARIFFICATION REQUIREMENT

Arts. 4.1 and 4.2 AG request from WTO Members to express all their pre-Uruguay Round border farm protection in tariffs. Footnote 1 (to Art. 4.2 AG) includes an indicative list of measures that come under the purview of this provision:

> These measures include quantitative import restrictions, variable import levies, minimum import prices, discretionary import licensing, non-tariff measures maintained through state-trading enterprises, voluntary export restraints, and similar border measures other than ordinary customs duties, whether or not the measures are maintained under country-specific derogations from the provisions of GATT 1947, but not measures maintained under balance-of-payments provisions or under other general, non-agriculture-specific provisions of GATT 1994 or of the other Multilateral Trade Agreements in Annex 1A to the WTO Agreement.

WTO Members often use specific duties to protect their own farm production. In *Chile–Price Band*,[22] WTO adjudicating bodies contributed

---

[21] Eventually the US settled the case by agreeing to pay a lump sum to Brazil for technical capacity-purposes, and subsequently the payments stopped, Brink (2011) at pp. 38ff.

[22] Bagwell and Sykes (2007) discuss the case.

some important clarifications regarding the interpretation of the discipline included in Art. 4.2 AG. The question facing the Panel was whether a scheme which had not been explicitly included in footnote 1 should still be the subject of tariffication. At issue in the case was a Chilean measure which operated as buffer between domestic prices and international prices aiming to ensure some margin of fluctuation between the two. The duty imposed on imports was distinguished into two parts: an ad valorem duty, and a specific duty (the price band) that was determined by comparing a reference price to the upper or lower threshold of a band (determined annually). The Panel held that the obligation to tariffy includes, but is not limited to, quantitative restrictions (§ 7.29), variable import levies, and minimum import prices (§§ 7.36, 7.41, 7.46 and 7.48–65). The AB confirmed the Panel's finding in this respect (§ 262) and added that measures that should have been converted and were not cannot be maintained after the WTO Agreement entered into force (§ 207). They thus requested from Chile to convert the price band into a tariff.[23]

Following the tariffication process, WTO Members will enter into their Schedules of Concessions any tariff commitments to be made for each agricultural good; they are obliged not to apply a tariff that exceeds any tariff bindings made (Art. 4.1 AG).

4.2 EXCEPTIONS TO BOUND TARIFF RATE

For agricultural products, there are, nevertheless, two specific exceptions to the rule that the applied tariff rate for a given agricultural good must not exceed the bound tariff rate listed on the Schedule of Concessions:

1. In accordance with the procedures of Art. 5 AG, a WTO Member can adopt a provisional safeguard provision (called 'special safeguard provision');

2. WTO Members can continue to apply non-tariff measures with respect to the so-called 'special treatment' cases referred to in Annex 5.

4.2.1 Special Safeguard Mechanism

WTO Members must denote in their schedule of concessions the products that will benefit from the special safeguard provision with the acronym 'SSG'. For such products, once a trigger is met, a WTO Member may levy an additional duty until the end of the year in which it has been imposed. The two scenarios that can trigger the enactment of the additional duty under the special safeguard mechanism are:

---

[23] Bagwell and Sykes (2007) question the solidity of this approach since the band could lead to lower duties as well. Compare McMahon (2011).

(1) When the volume of imports for a particular good exceeds a trigger level (calculated in accordance with Art. 5.4 AG). Note that the trigger level is dependent on the share of imports as a percentage of overall total domestic consumption of the good during the preceding three years and is expressed as a percentage of the average quantity of imports for that good over the preceding three years. (Please read Art. 5.4 AG for the specific details.) Under this scenario, the additional duty cannot exceed one-third of the duty applied during the year when safeguard action is taken (Art. 5.4 AG).

(2) When the price of the good concerned falls below a trigger price equal to the average 1986–1988 reference price (expressed as the cost-insurance-freight (c.i.f.) unit value of the product concerned, per Art. 5.1(b) AG). Under this scenario, the exact amount of the additional duty that is permissible will depend on the size of the difference between the current c.i.f. price and the trigger price.

So, contrary to other goods, safeguards on farm goods may be imposed automatically if WTO Members have ex ante reserved their right to make use of this possibility. Note that 39 WTO Members have indicated that they will be making use special safeguards on 6,156 products.[24]

Art. 5.9 AG expresses a view that the special safeguard mechanism is not meant to be a permanent feature of the trading system. Instead, it is meant to last as the reform process described in Art. 20 AG is ongoing. As no end date is in sight for this process, however, it is safe to assume that the special safeguard mechanism will remain in place for the foreseeable future. Finally, even if the special safeguard mechanism were to disappear, the generic safeguards clause that we discussed in Chapter 16 would remain available for agricultural products. In that sense, the special safeguard clause serves only as an additional protective mechanism with an easier-to-meet standard for compliance.

4.2.2 Special Treatment Cases

Additional protection can be imposed on "special treatment" cases as well. WTO Members can do that with respect to "designated products"[25], if the following conditions have been cumulatively met:

(a) Imports of the designated products comprised less than 3% of the domestic consumption during the agreed base period (1986–1988);

(b) No export subsidies have been provided to the designated products since the beginning of the agreed base period;

(c) Effective production-restricting measures are applied to the primary agricultural product;

---

[24] Finger (2010) discusses the special safeguard clause in detail.

[25] These products are designated with the symbol 'ST–Annex 5' in Section I–B of Part I of a Member's Schedule.

(d) Minimum access opportunities corresponding to 4% of the base period domestic consumption, and increasing by 0.8% per year for the remainder of the implementation period shall be afforded.[26]

Special treatment can extend beyond the end of the 10th year following the beginning of the implementation period,[27] if (a) successful negotiations have been undertaken to this effect and (b) such negotiations were completed during this time period (Annex 5, §§ 8–10). Korea and the Philippines have negotiated to this effect for rice. When special treatment ceases to exist, the applied protection must be tariffied and will be subjected to reduction commitments provided for in Annex 5, § 6.

4.3 COMMITMENTS TO REDUCE THE OVERALL LEVEL OF AGRICULTURAL TARIFFS

In addition to agreeing to comply with the bound tariff rates made, WTO Members also undertook commitments to reduce the overall level of tariffs on agricultural goods. Recall that developed countries agreed to average tariff reductions of 36% (with a minimum of 15% *per* product) over a period of six years; developing countries agreed to average tariff reductions of 24% (with a minimum of 10%) over a period of 10 years; LDCs were not required to undertake reduction commitments.

5. DOMESTIC SUBSIDIES FOR AGRICULTURE

Various WTO Members enact a plethora of domestic subsidy programs to support their farmers and the agricultural sector overall. One of the achievements of the Uruguay Round was that the AG Agreement devised a common metric for calculating and grouping such subsidies. Although this has been criticized for creating a number of legal loopholes for certain domestic agricultural subsidy programs, it nevertheless has led to a means through which such subsidies can be negotiated using a common parlance and framework.

5.1 THE ADVENT OF AMS

Given the variety of forms that domestic agricultural subsidies may take on, before one can negotiate the level of such subsidies, one needs to devise a common metric for expressing the level of such subsidies. The common metric agreed upon in the AG is what is known as the Aggregate Measure of Support (AMS).

---

[26] They would be guaranteed through tariff quotas (TRQs), the utilization rate of which was however, disappointing due probably you the high in quota-rate, see Laborde and Martin (2011).

[27] Art. 1(f) AG states that implementation period 'means the six-year period commencing in the year 1995, except that, for the purposes of Article 13, it means the nine-year period commencing in 1995'.

WTO Members must calculate their Total AMS[28] (Art. 1(h) AG) which should be distinguished from product-specific AMS. Any reduction commitments made will be based on this calculation. Recall that WTO Members can raise product-specific AMS, and still be within the bounds of their contractual obligations, provided that their Total AMS has been reduced by the agreed amount.

The AMS is based on the PSE, the producer subsidy equivalent[29], an index of domestic farm protection elaborated by the OECD.[30] As revised by the OECD in 1990, a PSE is defined as:

> The annual monetary value of gross transfers from consumers and taxpayers to agricultural producers, measured at the farm-gate level, arising from policy measures that support agriculture, regardless of their nature, objectives or impact on farm production or income.[31]

Annex 3 explains the specifics for the calculation of the AMS. The AMS covers the so-called Amber Box. This box has no specified content; it covers whatever is not included in the other two boxes and exceptions mentioned in the AG Agreement.

There are four categories of payments that are excluded from the calculation of the AMS:

- Payments relating to development needs (available to developing countries only) (Art. 6.2 AG);
- De minimis payments (Art. 6.4 AG);
- Direct payments for production-limiting programmes (Blue Box measures) (Art. 6.5 AG);
- Green Box measures (Annex 2).

---

[28] During the Doha Round negotiations, the term Final Bound Total AMS (FBTAMS) was privileged.

[29] The subsidy-equivalent of a given policy instrument is the payment per unit of output that a government would have to pay domestic producers in order to generate the same impact on production as that measure, say an import tariff. The notion of subsidy-equivalent stems from economic theory in the 1970s aiming at evaluating effects of tariffs. For a comprehensive analysis of this concept, see Corden (1971).

[30] In 1982, the OECD Ministerial Council decided that farm policies should be reformed and that farm trade should be integrated in the multilateral disciplines. Farm protection was quite asymmetric across OECD members and worse polymorphous. The OECD members were consequently, in search of a common metric, a common base for their policy dialogue, a consistent and comparable method to evaluate the incidence of farm policies. This is where and why the PSE was born.

[31] Idem at p. 22.

5.2 EXCEPTIONS FROM CALCULATIONS OF AMS

5.2.1 Development Subsidies

Note first that this exemption is available only for developing countries. Three types of payments are excluded:

- Investment subsidies that are generally available;
- Agricultural input subsidies, which are generally available to low income, or resource poor-producers;
- Support to encourage diversification from growing illicit narcotic crops.[32]

Orden *et al.* (2011) cite evidence of wide use of this possibility. India, for example, has included under this heading subsidies on fertilizer, electricity, and irrigation.

5.2.2 De minimis Payments

The Agreement on Agriculture distinguishes between support that is product-specific and that which is not product-specific. With respect to the former, payments below 5% of the relevant WTO Member's total value of production of a "basic agricultural product" during the relevant year,[33] are exempted. Art. 1(b) AG defines basic agricultural product, as:

> the product as close as practicable to the point of first sale as specified in a Member's Schedule and in related supporting material.

With respect to forms of domestic support that are not specific to any given product, WTO Members can exempt from the calculation of AMS payments up to 5% of the value of their total farm production. Art. 6.4(b) AG makes it clear that the figures are adjusted to 10% (for both categories) for WTO Members that are developing countries.

5.2.3 Direct Payments for Production–Limiting Programs (Blue Box Measures)

Art. 6.5 AG identifies three situations where a WTO Member can legitimately exempt direct payments under production-limiting programs from the calculation of its AMS (and hence, the Amber Box):

- Direct payments are based on fixed area and yields;
- Direct payments are made on 85% or less of the base level of production; or

---

[32] This category is often referred to in literature as the 'development box', Brink (2011) at pp. 29ff.

[33] Throughout the Agreement, the term 'year', in relation to specific commitments of a Member, refers to the calendar, financial or marketing year specified in the Schedule relating to that Member (Art. 1(i) AG).

Sec. 5   Domestic Subsidies for Agriculture

- Livestock payments that are made on a fixed number of head.

5.2.4   Green Box Measures

The Green Box is spelled out in Annex 2 AG, which exempts from the calculation of AMS (and hence, from the Amber Box) twelve measures of support funded through a government program which does not have the effect of price support (§ 1).[34] The rationale for the exclusion of 12 government services included in Annex 2 is that they have no, or have minimal trade-distorting effects.[35] To avoid any misunderstandings as to the exhaustive character of programmes featured in Annex 2, Art. 7.2 AG makes it clear that any programme which does not satisfy the criteria specified in Annex 2 must be included in the calculation of the total AMS. Art. 7.1 AG, moreover, requires that any measure initially characterized as a Green Box measure must continue to conform to the criteria for exclusion on an ongoing basis. The schemes excluded from the calculation of the AMS come under the following headings:

(a) <u>General Services</u>: This includes payments relating to:
- General research
- Pest and disease control
- Training services, both general and specialist
- Extension and advisory services
- Inspection services (e.g., health, safety, grading, and standardization)
- Marketing and promotion services
- Infrastructure services: Note that this can be for a wide variety of services (e.g., electricity, roads, water supply, market and port facilities, etc.), but they only include expenditures directed to the provision or construction of capital works only and not direct payments to producers.

(b) <u>Food Security</u>: For payments to be excluded under this heading, the volume and accumulation of stocks must be pre-determined. Government purchases for food security stock must be made at current market prices. Sales from the stock must also be made at no less than current market prices.

(c) <u>Domestic Food Aid</u>: it must take the form of direct provision of food to those in need, subject to clearly-defined criteria related to nu-

---

[34] There is no workable definition of what is a non-distorting subsidy and this is probably the reason why negotiators felt that an indicative list would better reflect their intentions, compare Brink (2011) pp. 31ff.

[35] Stancanelli (2009, p.32) mentions that, during the negotiations, the EU insisted in including hectare and cattle herd payments in the 'green box; since this was very much a measure at the core of the CAP reform'. It seems that the extent of the green box was influenced by similar concerns. Stancanelli (2009) discusses the various proposals regarding green box entries of the key players during the Uruguay round in pp.27ff.

tritional objectives. Government purchases for food aid supply must be made at current market prices and must be made transparent.

(d) <u>Direct Payments to Producers</u>: Any direct payments must be government-funded and must not be more than minimally trade-distorting. In addition, any direct payment must conform to the criteria in the various dealing with specific categories of direct payments that follow.

> To illustrate what constitutes a direct payment, an example may be helpful. If the government provides a pest control service to a farmer, this falls under the heading "General Services". However, if a government makes a direct payment to compensate the producer for any crops culled to control pests, then such payments come under this "Direct Payments to Producers" heading. Consequently, the cost of supplying the service to the farmer comes under the heading "General Services", whereas the direct payment to producer would come under this and the following headings and have to comply with them in order to be excluded from the calculation of AMS.

(e) <u>Decoupled Income Payments</u>: Eligibility for such payments can be established on clear criteria, such as, income, status as producer or land-owner, production level etc. Payments should not be related to production, factors or production or prices. The AB in *US–Upland Cotton* provided some clarifications regarding the disciplines imposed on decoupled income payments. The report reflects a brief but very informative presentation of the legal framework applicable to decoupled income payments as reflected in Annex 2 (§ 325):

> Paragraph 6 of Annex 2, entitled "[d]ecoupled income support", seeks to decouple or de-link direct payments to producers from various aspects of their production decisions and thus aims at neutrality in this regard. Subparagraph (b) decouples the payments from production; subparagraph (c) decouples payments from prices; and subparagraph (d) decouples payments from factors of production. Subparagraph (e) completes the process by making it clear that no production shall be required in order to receive such payments. Decoupling of payments from production under paragraph 6(b) can only be ensured if the payments are not related to, or based upon, either a positive requirement to produce certain crops or a negative requirement not to produce certain crops or a combination of both positive and negative requirements on production of crops.

The AB was called upon to review the Panel's finding that the US production flexibility contract payments were inconsistent with Annex 2, § 6(b). The AB describes the contentious US law as follows (§ 311):

> The production flexibility contract program dispensed with the requirement that producers continue to plant upland cotton in order to receive payments; instead, payments would generally be made regardless of what the producer chose to grow, and whether or not the producer chose to produce anything at all. However, there were limits to this planting flexibility. Specifically, payments were reduced or eliminated if fruits and vegetables (other than lentils, mung beans, and dry peas) were planted on upland cotton base acres, subject to certain other exceptions.

The AB formulated the issue before it in the following manner (§ 312):

> The question before us in this appeal thus concerns a measure with a partial exclusion combining planting flexibility and payments with the reduction or elimination of the payments when the excluded crops are produced, while providing payments even when no crops are produced at all." (emphasis in the original).

The Panel had originally found that the US measure at hand was not a decoupled income payment pursuant to Annex 2, § 6(b). The AB upheld the Panel's findings in this respect for the following reasons (§ 329):

> We agree with the Panel that a partial exclusion of some crops from payments has the potential to channel production towards the production of crops that remain eligible for payments. In contrast to a total production ban, the channelling of production that may follow from a partial exclusion of some crops from payments will have *positive* production effects as regards crops eligible for payments. The extent of this will depend on the scope of the exclusion. We note in this regard that the Panel found, as a matter of fact, that planting flexibility limitations at issue in this case "significantly constrain production choices available to PFC and DP payment recipients and effectively eliminate a significant proportion of them". The fact that farmers may continue to receive payments if they produce nothing at all does not detract from this assessment because, according to the Panel, it is not the option preferred by the "overwhelm-

ing majority" of farmers, who continue to produce some type of permitted crop. In the light of these findings by the Panel, we are unable to agree with the United States' argument that the planting flexibility limitations only negatively affect the production of crops that are excluded. (emphasis in the original).

Note that the US had not required production of any kind in order to make the decoupled income payments; when reading §§ 329–331, one is left with the impression that the decision to produce was a private decision by US farmers. It seems that the AB was led to this conclusion in light of the extent of the partial exclusion: the US scheme required producers not to produce fruits and vegetables, but did not impose an absolute ban on production of farm goods. Because, in its view, the exclusion was not substantial, the AB was led to believe that:

> because the opportunity for farmers to receive payments for producing crops, while less or no such payments are made to farmers who produce excluded crops, provides an incentive to switch from producing excluding crops to producing eligible for payments. (§ 331 *in fine*).

In the AB's view, hence, these payments were not sufficiently decoupled.

(f) <u>Payments for Income Insurance and Income Safety Net</u>: These payments aim to compensate farmers for losses of income. They can legitimately be excluded from the calculation of AMS, if the loss corresponds to at least 30% of the income (made during a reference period), and provided that the compensation does not exceed 70% of the income lost.

(g) <u>Natural Disasters Relief</u>: These include not only payments made to compensate farmers for losses from natural disasters (including disease outbreaks, pest manifestations, nuclear accidents, and war) but also government payments for crop insurance schemes related to natural disasters. Such payments can legitimately be excluded from the calculation of the AMS if the production loss is at least 30% of the production during a reference period, and provided that the compensation aims to cover losses only.

(h) <u>Structural Adjustment Assistance Provided Through Producer Retirement Programs</u>: Payments are legitimately exempted, if they are conditioned upon the total and permanent retirement of the beneficiaries.

(i) <u>Structural Adjustment Assistance Provided Through Resource Retirement Programs</u>: Payments are legitimately exempted, provided that the land will be set aside for at least three years.

(j) <u>Investment Aid</u>: Payments can be exempted if farmers suffer from objectively demonstrated structural disadvantages which are not based on the type/volume of production, are not related to prices, and provided that they take place only as long as necessary to overcome the mentioned disadvantages.

(k) <u>Environmental Programmes</u>: Payments are exempted to the extent that they are limited to the cost of compliance with the government programme.

(l) <u>Regional Assistance</u>: Payments are exempted, if they are generally available to all producers in a disadvantaged region, and are limited to the costs that the producer must undertake because of the location of its production.

5.3 CALCULATION OF AMS (AND EMS)

All remaining domestic protection falls under the AMS. Annex 3 explains how the AMS will be calculated:[36]

(a) The AMS covers both product-specific and non-product-specific payments;

(b) Product-specific payments cover market price support, non-exempt direct payments, and any other subsidy, except, of course, for those that are explicitly exempted (§ 1 of the Annex). Payments at both the national level and the sub-national level will be taken into account (§ 3). Payments by farmers will be deducted (§ 4);

(c) Non-product-specific payments will be expressed in one (non-product specific) AMS in monetary terms (§ 1);

(d) Market price support will be calculated by multiplying the quantities of products eligible to receive it by the difference between the fixed external reference price and the applied administered price. Items such as storage costs will not be part of the calculation (§ 8). The base period (reference period) for the calculation will be 1986–1988, and, for net exporting countries it is the f.o.b. (free on board) price that matters, whereas for net importing countries, it is the c.i.f. (cost, insurance, freight) price that will be used (§ 9);

(e) Non-exempt direct payments will be calculated, either in the same manner as market price support, or by using budgetary outlays (§ 10) Art. 1(c) AG makes it clear that the term 'budgetary outlays' covers revenue foregone as well. If non-exempt direct payments have been

---

[36] As can be seen the WTO and the OECD definitions are not identical. Critically, the OECD definition uses an evolving market benchmark to calculate the subsidy-equivalent whereas the WTO AMS a defined, static base period. For a comprehensive discussion in the differences, see Diakosavvas (2002).

based on non-price factors, then they will be measured by reference to budgetary outlays only (§ 12);

(f) Product-specific AMS will be expressed in monetary terms (§ 6), as close as possible to the first point of sale (§ 7).

When the calculation of AMS is impracticable, support to producers will be calculated through recourse to the Equivalent Measurement of Support (EMS), which is defined in Art. 1(d) AG:

> "Equivalent Measurement of Support" means the annual level of support, expressed in monetary terms, provided to producers of a basic agricultural product through the application of one or more measures, the calculation of which in accordance with the AMS methodology is impracticable, other than support provided under programmes that qualify as exempt from reduction under Annex 2 to this Agreement, and which is:
>
> (i) with respect to support provided during the base period, specified in the relevant tables of supporting material incorporated by reference in Part IV of a Member's Schedule; and
>
> (ii) with respect to support provided during any year of the implementation period and thereafter, calculated in accordance with the provisions of Annex 4 of this Agreement and taking into account the constituent data and methodology used in the tables of supporting material incorporated by reference in Part IV of the Member's Schedule.

Recourse to EMS was made in a very limited number of cases only. Calculation of AMS is to be made in accordance with Art. 1 AG, and Annex 3, but in some instances the 1986–1988 external reference price for the supported product was not available in the constituent data and methodology (that is, the supporting tables included by reference in each Member's Schedule of Concessions, in Part VI, the so-called "AGST Tables"): One explanation was that a product was not traded by that particular country during that particular reference period, hence no external reference price was recorded. In such instances, the notifying Member used the proxy-approach, (i.e., the EMS), in order to evaluate the level of support granted to the product, for notification purposes. Argentina, for example, used EMS for the calculation of its support on tobacco.[37]

Annex 4 explains the calculation of EMS: in parallel with the AMS, product specific-EMS will be derived from a multiplication of the applied administered price by the quantities eligible for budgetary outlays, and will be calculated as close as possible to the first point of sale. Non-exempt direct payments will be calculated in the same manner as in AMS.

---

[37] WTO Doc. G/AG/N/ARG/24 of April 25, 2006.

Consider the following example: In the EU, a system of minimum import prices was in place for beef and cereals. Such prices depended on various factors, such as:

(a) Tariff protection;

(b) Production controls;

(c) The EU intervention price (a price decided by the EU ministers for agriculture normally on a yearly basis, which corresponds to the applied administered price as indicated in § 8 of Annex 3); and

(d) Export subsidies.

The system of minimum import prices was aimed at restricting supply to the domestic (EU) market, thus keeping domestic prices higher than the world price. The AMS calculation for beef and cereals was estimated to be the value of support of the volume of production multiplied by the difference between the EU intervention price and world price (for the base period between 1986 and 1988). Assuming for example, that the intervention price for wheat is €200 per tonne, the world price is €100 per tonne, and the total wheat production in the EU is 1,000,000 tones, the EU AMS for wheat is €10,000,000.[38]

5.4 COMMITMENTS TO REDUCE TOTAL AMS

Developed countries have agreed to reduce their total AMS by 20% by the end of a period of six years; developing countries have agreed to reduce their total AMS by 13.3% by the end of a period of ten years; LDCs must bind their AMS support level (if applicable), but were not required to make any reduction commitments.

6. AGRICULTURAL EXPORT SUBSIDIES

The original GATT contained no provisions on export subsidies for farm goods. It was only in 1955 with the adoption of Art. XVI.3 GATT that an initial attempt was made to regulate agricultural export subsidies. Art. XVI.3 GATT sanctioned export subsidies that led to the subsidizing country obtaining more than an equitable share of the world market, but stopped short of outlawing export subsidies altogether. In the GATT-era, in *EC–Refunds on Exports of Sugar*, the Panel held that a reference period of the last three years could be appropriately used to decide on whether the 'equitable share'-requirement embedded in Art. XVI.3 GATT had been met or surpassed. The situation changed with the entry into force of the SCM Agreement and the outright ban on export subsidies. The AG Agreement constitutes an exception from this ban.

The term "export subsidy" is defined in Art. 1(e) AG as:

---

[38] For a concrete application, see the AB report on Korea–Various Measures on Beef (§§ 90ff.).

subsidies contingent upon export performance, including the export subsidies listed in Article 9 of this Agreement.

Art. 9.1 AG contains a list of export subsidies to which reduction commitments are to be applied:

(a) the provision by governments or their agencies of direct subsidies, including payments-in-kind, to a firm, to an industry, to producers of an agricultural product, to a cooperative or other association of such producers, or to a marketing board, contingent on export performance;

(b) the sale or disposal for export by governments or their agencies of non-commercial stocks of agricultural products at a price lower than the comparable price charged for the like product to buyers in the domestic market;

(c) payments on the export of an agricultural product that are financed by virtue of governmental action, whether or not a charge on the public account is involved, including payments that are financed from the proceeds of a levy imposed on the agricultural product concerned or on an agricultural product from which the exported product is derived;

(d) the provision of subsidies to reduce the costs of marketing exports of agricultural products (other than widely available export promotion and advisory services) including handling, upgrading and other processing costs, and the costs of international transport and freight;

(e) internal transport and freight charges on export shipments, provided or mandated by governments, on terms more favourable than for domestic shipments;

(f) subsidies on agricultural products contingent on their incorporation in exported products.

In *Canada–Dairy*, the AB held that the cost of production could serve as benchmark to determine whether a payment has in fact been made within the meaning of Art. 9.1(c) AG. In *EC–Export Subsidies on Sugar*, the AB clarified its understanding of the terms "financed", and "by virtue of governmental action" appearing in Art. 9.1(c) AG: (§§ 236–237):

Addressing the word "financed", the AB held that this word generally refers to the "mechanism" or "process" by which financial resources are provided, such that payments are made. Article 9.1(c), by stating "whether or not a charge on the public account is involved", expressly provides that the government itself need not provide the resources for producers to make payments. Instead, payments may be made and funded by private parties.

With respect to the words "by virtue of", the AB has previously held that there must be a "nexus" or "demonstrable link" between the governmental action at issue and the financing of payments. The AB clarified that not every governmental action will have the requisite "nexus" to the financing of payments. For instance, the AB held that the "demonstrable link" between "governmental action" and the "financing" of payments would not exist in a scenario in which "governmental action ... establish[es] a regulatory framework merely *enabling* a third person freely to make and finance 'payments'." In this situation, the link between the governmental action and the financing of payments would be "too tenuous", such that the "payments" could not be regarded as "financed by virtue of governmental action" within the meaning of Article 9.1(c). Rather, according to the AB, there must be a "tighter nexus" between the mechanism or process by which the payments are financed (even if by a third person) and governmental action. In this respect, the AB clarified that, although governmental action is essential, Article 9.1(c) contemplates that "payments may be financed by virtue of governmental action even though significant aspects of the financing might not involve government." Thus, even if government does not fund the payments itself, it must play a sufficiently important part in the process by which a private party funds "payments", such that the requisite nexus exists between "governmental action" and the "financing". The alleged link must be examined on a case-by-case basis, taking account of the particular character of the governmental action at issue and its relationship to the payments made. (italics and emphasis in the original).

It follows that the form of financing is immaterial; a tight nexus must be established between the government action and the financing of the payments. It is not the case that any nexus will do: a framework that merely enables third persons to make payments, it is not enough, in the AB's view, for the scheme to be subjected to the disciplines of Art. 9.1 AG. This case law is reminiscent of our discussions regarding attribution of a practice to government that we entertained in Chapter 2 when discussing *Japan–Semiconductors*. The same logic would suggest that although legal compulsion is not necessary, practice will not be attributed to a government unless the latter has provided individuals with incentives to act in a particular way. Unfortunately, this test suffers from the imprecisions that we discussed already in Chapter 2. The AB went on to apply this test to the growers of 'C Sugar' in its report on *EC–Export Subsidies on Sugar* where it used the term "incentives" as criterion to attribute behaviour to the EU. The facts of the case are reflected in § 2 of the report:

> EC Regulation 1260/2001 is valid for the marketing years 2001/2002 to 2005/2006 and establishes, *inter alia*: quotas for

sugar production; an intervention price for raw and white sugar, respectively; a basic price and a minimum price for beet for quota sugar production; quota (that is, "A" and "B") sugar as well as non-quota (that is, "C") sugar; import and export licensing requirements; producer levies; and preferential import arrangements. Furthermore, the EC sugar regime provides "export refunds" to its sugar exporters for certain quantities of sugar, other than C sugar. These "refunds", which are direct export subsidies, cover the difference between the European Communities' internal market price and the prevailing world market price for sugar. Non-quota sugar (that is, C sugar) must be exported, unless it is carried forward, but no "export refunds" are provided for such exports. (italics in the original).

The AB upheld the Panel's finding that the EU regime be considered an export subsidy in the sense of Art. 9.1(c) AG (§§ 238–239):

Turning to the specific circumstances of the present dispute, we note that, in its finding that "payments" in the form of sales of C beet below its total cost of production are "financed by virtue of governmental action", the Panel relied on a number of aspects of the EC sugar regime. The Panel considered, *inter alia*, that: the EC sugar regime regulates prices of A and B beet and establishes a framework for the contractual relationships between beet growers and sugar producers with a view to ensuring a stable and adequate income for beet growers; C beet is invariably produced together with A and B beet in one single line of production; a significant percentage of beet growers are likely to finance sales of C beet below the total cost of production as a result of participation in the domestic market by making "highly remunerative" sales of A and B beet; the European Communities "controls virtually every aspect of domestic beet and sugar supply and management", including through financial penalties imposed on sugar producers that divert C sugar into the domestic market; the European Communities' Sugar Management Committee "overviews, supervises and protects the [European Communities'] domestic sugar through, *inter alia*, supply management"; the growing of C beet is not "incidental", but rather an "integral" part of the governmental regulation of the sugar market; and C sugar producers "*have incentives* to produce C sugar so as to maintain their share of the A and B quotas", while C beet growers "have an incentive to supply as much as is requested by C sugar producers with a view to receiving the high prices for A and B beet and their allocated amount of . . . C beet".

We agree with the Panel that, in the circumstances of the present case, all of these aspects of the EC sugar regime have a direct bearing on whether below-cost sales of C beet are financed by virtue of governmental action. As a result, we are unable to agree with the European Communities' first argument on appeal, namely, that the Panel applied a test under which an Article 9.1(c) subsidy was deemed to exist "simply because [governmental] action 'enabled' the beet growers to finance and make payments". Rather, we believe that the Panel relied on aspects of the EC sugar regime that go far beyond merely "enabling" or "permitting" beet growers to make payments to sugar producers. Indeed, in our view, there is a tight nexus between the European Communities' "governmental action" and the financing of payments in the case before us. We have no doubt that, without the highly remunerative prices guaranteed by the EC sugar regime for A and B beet, sales of C beet could not take place profitably at a price below the total cost of production. (italics and emphasis in the original).

Art. 3.3 AG reads:

Subject to the provisions of paragraphs 2(b) and 4 of Article 9, a Member shall not provide export subsidies listed in paragraph 1 of Article 9 in respect of the agricultural products or groups of products specified in Section II of Part IV of its Schedule in excess of the budgetary outlay and quantity commitment levels specified therein and shall not provide such subsidies in respect of any agricultural product not specified in that Section of its Schedule.

This obligation is compounded by Art. 8 AG which reads:

Each Member undertakes not to provide export subsidies otherwise than in conformity with this Agreement and with the commitments as specified in that Member's Schedule.

It is thus clear from the text of Art. 3.3 AG that WTO Members have accepted disciplines with respect to both scheduled goods (that is, goods that they have included in their schedules of concessions), and unscheduled goods (that is, goods that they have not included in their schedules of concessions). There is a difference though:

(a) With respect to the former, they have entered commitments with respect to both the volume of exports, and the maximum subsidization:

- Developed countries agreed to a reduction by 21% of the volume of exports, and 36% of budgetary outlays over a period of 6 years, and for incorporated/processed products, they agreed to a reduction of only budgetary outlays by 36% (Art. 11 AG);
- Developing countries agreed to a reduction equalling 2/3 of the reduction required by developed countries, over a period

of 10 years, and, by virtue of Art. 9.4 AG, they have been granted an exception during the implementation period with respect to certain marketing and internal transportation services.

- No commitments have been requested of LDCs.

(b) With respect to unscheduled goods, WTO Members cannot provide any export subsidy.[39]

It follows that WTO Members had an incentive to schedule goods if subsidization was practised in the base period of 1986–1990, and if they intended to continue subsidizing thes goods. All commitments are product-specific. The AB, in *US–FSC* held (§§ 151–152) that the nature of commitments assumed with respect to scheduled goods is some sort of limited authorization, which will instantly turn into a prohibition when the thresholds established in the relevant schedule of concessions have been met.

Art. 10 AG is the anti-circumvention provision included in the Agreement. It contains four paragraphs, each of them dealing with a specific subject-matter:

- Art. 10.1 AG reflects the general rule that export subsidy commitments should not be circumvented;
- Art. 10.2 AG reflects the willingness of WTO Members to eventually develop international disciplines on export credits, export credit guarantees, and insurance programmes;
- Art. 10.3 AG deals with the allocation of burden of proof in cases where a WTO Member claims that its exports exceeding its commitments have not been subsidized;
- Finally, Art. 10.4 AG deals with international food aid: it provides that aid must not be tied to commercial exports of farm products, and must be carried out in accordance with international standards, namely, the 'Principles of Surplus Disposal and Consultative Obligations', including, where appropriate, the system of Usual Marketing Requirements (URM) established by the FAO (Food and Agriculture Organization).

In *US–Upland Cotton*, the AB had to decide on the relationship between the general prohibition of circumvention (Art. 10.1 AG), and the more specific provision regarding export credits (and guarantees) included in Art. 10.2 AG. Art. 10.2 AG reads:

> Members undertake to work toward the development of internationally agreed disciplines to govern the provision of export credits, export credit guarantees or insurance programmes and, after

---

[39] The AB held as much in its report on *US–FSC* at §§ 145–146. In *EC–Export Subsidies on Sugar*, it confirmed that, pursuant to Art. 9 AG, WTO Members are required to make both budgetary outlay-and quantity reduction-commitments (§ 193).

agreement on such disciplines, to provide export credits, export credit guarantees or insurance programmes only in conformity therewith.

The US and Brazil presented divergent arguments regarding the interpretation of this provision. The US contended that, in light of the wording of Art. 10.1 AG, export credit guarantees were "carved out" from the discipline included in Art. 10.1 AG; Brazil later claimed that this should not be the case. The three member-division of the AB deciding the dispute could not agree on this issue. The majority sided with Brazil, and held that, until disciplines have been elaborated, export credit guarantees must observe the existing discipline included in Art. 10.1 AG (§§ 607ff. and especially 616, 626–627). One member of the AB expressed a rare minority dissenting opinion. In that person's view, Art. 10.2 AG should be regarded as carve out from the obligation included in Art. 10.1 AG. According to the minority view, until disciplines have been worked out, WTO Members incur no obligation with respect to export credits, export credit guarantees, and insurance programmes (§§ 631–641).

Case law has also dealt with the interpretation of Art. 10.3 AG: WTO Members exporting beyond the committed quantity must establish that the surplus exports have not benefited from export subsidies. The AB has consistently held (*Canada–Dairy*, § 75; *US–Upland Cotton*, § 645) that all the complaining party needs to establish is the quantitative part of its claim, i.e., that the subsidizing state has exported quantities beyond its export quantity reduction commitments. The burden of proof will then shift to the subsidizing state to demonstrate that its exports have not benefited from subsidies mentioned in Art. 9.1 AG. In *US–Upland Cotton*, the AB took distance from the Panel's findings in this respect, and held that Art. 10.3 AG does not apply to unscheduled goods (§ 652):

> We disagree with the Panel's view that Article 10.3 applies to *unscheduled* products. Under the Panel's approach, the only thing a complainant would have to do to meet its burden of proof when bringing a claim against an *unscheduled* product is to demonstrate that the respondent has exported that product. Once that has been established, the respondent would have to demonstrate that it has not provided an export subsidy. This seems to us an extreme result. In effect, it would mean that any export of an unscheduled product is *presumed* to be subsidized. In our view, the presumption of subsidization when exported quantities exceed the reduction commitments makes sense in respect of a *scheduled* product because, by including it in its schedule, a WTO Member is reserving for itself the right to apply export subsidies to that product, within the limits in its schedule. In the case of *unscheduled* products, however, such a presumption appears inappropriate. Export subsidies for both un-

scheduled agricultural products and industrial products are completely prohibited under the *Agreement on Agriculture* and under the *SCM Agreement*, respectively. The Panel's interpretation implies that the burden of proof with regard to the same issue would apply differently, however, under each Agreement: it would be on the respondent under the *Agreement on Agriculture*, while it would be on the complainant under the *SCM Agreement*. (italics and emphasis in the original).

Referring to prior case law, the AB held in *US–Upland Cotton*, that not only actual, but also threat of circumvention might suffice for a violation of Art. 10 AG: mere possibility that circumvention might occur at some point in the future as a result of government behaviour does not nevertheless, fall within the meaning of threat of circumvention; the AB held that a likelihood-standard that an event might occur must be complied with (§§ 704, 710, and 713).[40]

7. OTHER COMMITMENTS

7.1 PEACE CLAUSE

In Art. 13 AG, commonly referred to as the Peace Clause, WTO Members agreed that during the implementation period, compliance with the obligations imposed under the Green Box, the Blue Box and Arts. 8–10 AG meant *ipso facto* compliance with the WTO. Hence, WTO Members agreed to not impose CVDs against similar measures nor raise non-violation complaints against such measures. As we saw in *US–Upland Cotton*, following the end of the implementation period, exports subsidies must comply not only with the AG-but also with the SCM requirements. Consequently, the Peace Clause provision is best understood as a time-bound exception to Art. 21 AG.[41]

7.2 NET FOOD–IMPORTING DEVELOPING COUNTRIES

The commitments under the Agreement, and the export commitments in particular, might have a negative impact on net food importing countries, since they will not be in a position to procure farm goods in favourable (i.e., subsidized) terms. Two provisions aim at addressing the situation:

First, Art. 16 AG requires that developed countries take action in accordance with the 'Decision on Measures Concerning the Possible Negative Effects of the Reform Programme on Least Developed and Net Food Importing Developing Countries'. This Decision aims to ensure that LDCs and net food importing developing countries will not be negatively affect-

---

[40] Orden *et al.* (2011, pp. 402ff.), in general, and Nassar (2011) pp. 223ff. with respect to Brazil.

[41] See Bown and Meagher (2010).

ed by the commitments undertaken as a result of the successful conclusion of the Uruguay round. More specifically, it calls for a review of the level of food aid established periodically by the Committee on Food Aid under the Food Aid Convention; the initiation of negotiations in order to establish a level of food aid commitments sufficient to meet the needs of net food importers; the adoption of guidelines to ensure that increasing proportions of basic foodstuffs will be provided in fully grant form; an agreement by developed countries to help, through technical advice, increase the productivity in net food importing countries.[42] The Committee on Agriculture has established a list of countries that will benefit from such initiatives. Originally, it included all LDCs plus 19 developing countries: Barbados, Botswana, Cuba, Côte d'Ivoire, Dominican Republic, Egypt, Honduras, Jamaica, Kenya, Mauritius, Morocco, Pakistan, Peru, Saint Lucia, Senegal, Sri Lanka, Trinidad and Tobago, Tunisia, and Venezuela). Subsequently, the list has been updated, with 10 new developing countries added: Dominica, Gabon, Grenada, Jordan, Maldives, Mongolia, Namibia, Saint Kitts and Nevis, Saint Vincent and the Grenadines, and Swaziland.[43]

Second, Art. 12 AG requires any WTO Member with lawful recourse to export restrictions (Art. XI.2(a) GATT) to pay due consideration to importing Members' food security. To this effect, the WTO Member restricting exports must notify the Committee on Agriculture of similar measures, and consult, if requested, with those negatively affected.

7.3 TRANSPARENCY REQUIREMENTS

WTO Members undertake, by virtue of Art. 18 AG, to promptly notify the Committee on Agriculture of all matters of interest to the reform programme. That is, WTO Members must notify everything of interest to their commitment with respect to tariffication, domestic subsidies, and export subsidies. Recall that with respect to subsidies characterized as Green Box measures, for example, WTO Members must ensure that their measures remain during their lifetime within the parameters of Annex 2.

8. INSTITUTIONAL ISSUES

8.1 COMMITTEE ON AGRICULTURE

The Committee on Agriculture was established pursuant to the Agreement on Agriculture and is responsible for its administration. All WTO Members, as well as observers to the WTO, participate therein. It meets four times a year, but (additional) special sessions can be arranged.

---

[42] Schoenbaum (2011) offers a very persuasive explanation why changing circumstances matter here more than elsewhere.

[43] WTO Doc. G/AG/5/Rev. 9 of April 6, 2011.

The Committee oversees implementation of commitments undertaken during the Uruguay Round.

8.2 THE COTTON INITIATIVE

Four WTO Members, namely, Benin, Burkina Faso, Chad, and Mali, tabled a proposal in 2003 to the WTO General Council, arguing that they must be compensated for damages suffered by subsidies paid by developed WTO Members on production of cotton, and also requested that cotton subsidies be withdrawn. Given the very high dependence of these poor African economies on cotton exports, it was agreed that cotton was a special issue. The WTO General Council decision of August 1, 2004 (reflecting the so-called 'July package') contained a specific reference to this issue and called for action:

> the General Council reaffirms the importance of the Sectoral Initiative on Cotton and takes note of the parameters set out in Annex A within which the trade-related aspects of this issue will be pursued in the agriculture negotiations. The General Council also attaches importance to the development aspects of the Cotton Initiative and wishes to stress the complementarity between the trade and development aspects. The Council takes note of the recent Workshop on Cotton in Cotonou on 23–24 March 2004 organized by the WTO Secretariat, and other bilateral and multilateral efforts to make progress on the development assistance aspects and instructs the Secretariat to continue to work with the development community and to provide the Council with periodic reports on relevant developments.
>
> Members should work on related issues of development multilaterally with the international financial institutions, continue their bilateral programmes, and all developed countries are urged to participate. In this regard, the General Council instructs the Director General to consult with the relevant international organizations, including the Bretton Woods Institutions, the Food and Agriculture Organization and the International Trade Centre to direct effectively existing programmes and any additional resources towards development of the economies where cotton has vital importance.

The Cotton Sub–Committee was established on November 19, 2004, with the mandate to focus on cotton as a specific issue in the wider negotiations on liberalization of trade in farm goods. WTO Members, as well as countries that have observer status in the WTO, were welcome to participate. This organ operates in close cooperation with the WTO General Council, the Trade Negotiations Committee (TNC), and the Ministerial Conference.

QUESTIONS AND COMMENTS

Green Box: These schemes have been increasing over the years but not in all countries: Brazil and Japan, for example report no increase in this respect. Orden et al. (2011, pp. 408ff.) calculate that they represent 20% of the production value in EU, and US (2008) and 40% for the same period in Brazil, China and India. Other developing countries have not made much use of Green Box measures essentially because the areas in which they are most interested (extension services, research, soil conservation, pest and disease control) contain limits with which they find difficult.[44]

Art. 10.2 AG: Do you agree with the majority or the minority opinion expressed in *US–Upland Cotton*?

Decoupled Income Payments: In your view is the ruling in *US–Upland Cotton* correct?

Variable Import Levies: In case the question concerning their consistency with the WTO were brought today before a Panel, what would you think the outcome would be?

---

[44] Compare in this respect the experiences of India, China, and African countries discussed in Dhar (2009), Xie (2009), and Oduro (2009) respectively.

CHAPTER 18

THE AGREEMENT ON TEXTILES AND CLOTHING

■ ■ ■

1. THE LEGAL DISCIPLINE

Trade in textiles is now governed by the disciplines discussed in the previous Chapters. This has not always been the case though: Textiles were brought into the multilateral trading system through the WTO Agreement on Textiles and Clothing (ATC). In this Chapter we will hence be reviewing the discipline imposed by the ATC.

2. THE RATIONALE FOR THE LEGAL DISCIPLINE

Before the advent of the ATC, which was negotiated during the Uruguay round, textile and clothing quotas were negotiated bilaterally and governed by the rules of the Multi–Fibre Arrangement, the notorious MFA.[1] The MFA was signed in 1974 between some developed and 31 developing countries, and essentially imposed a worldwide system of bilateral quotas. In fact, since 1961 (i.e., even before the MFA came into being), international trade in textiles and clothing had been virtually excluded from the normal rules and disciplines of the GATT. It was governed by a system of discriminatory restrictions, which deviated from the basic GATT principles, and remained in force until the WTO Agreements came into effect on 1 January 1995. It was negotiated because of concerns in developed countries over rising imports.[2] Art 1 MFA states:

> To achieve the expansion of trade, the reduction of barriers to such trade and the progressive liberalization of world trade in textile products, while at the same time ensuring the orderly and equitable development of this trade and avoidance of disruptive effects in individual markets and on individual lines of production of both importing and exporting countries.

The MFA was a four-year arrangement which was subsequently renewed. MFA IV was supposed to lapse by 1991. The impossibility to con-

---

[1] For a comprehensive account on the history of MFA, see Bagchi (2001).
[2] US ITC, The History and Current Status of Multifiber Arrangement, USITC Pub. No 850 (1978).

clude the Uruguay round by that time though led trading partners to renew it so as to ensure a time-wise coincidence between the end of the MFA and the advent of the WTO. The Arrangement could be summarily described as follows: a Textiles Surveillance Body (TSB) was established (Art. 11), composed of a Chairman and eight members (an equal number of delegates from textile-importing and textile-exporting countries). Participants were textiles experts from countries participating in the Arrangement and consequently, one could legitimately raise doubts as to their impartiality when administering the MFA.[3] The expectation probably was that by appointing delegates from countries with divergent interests, useful and legitimate (e.g., representative) compromises could be reached. The TSB received notifications of all existing QRs which, if not notified, were deemed contrary to the Arrangement (Art. 2). Notified QRs had to be eliminated, unless if, through bilateral negotiations (and agreements), parties agreed to limit trade so as to avoid the risk of market disruption, as defined in Annex A to the Arrangement (sharp increase of imported products offered at prices substantially below those of comparable domestic goods). Agreements had to include "base levels" and "growth rates". It was through similar bilateral agreements that a quota-system was imposed on textiles-trade. Participants agreed to refrain from introducing new restrictions, unless such action could be justified through recourse to Art. 3: if imports caused market disruption. There was nonetheless no need for injury determination in order to determine whether market disruption existed; contrary to the standard GATT-safeguard clause, restrictions could be placed in the presence of difference across domestic prices and prices of imported goods, irrespective of whether the domestic industry was injured at all, or the reasons for injury.[4]

A best-endeavours clause was included, to the effect that interests of developing countries would be taken into account (Art. 6).[5] Disputes regarding the operation of the Arrangement would be brought to the TSB. Participants were free to subsequently take their dispute further and request the establishment of a GATT Panel. In such case, however, the Panel would have to take into account the conclusions of the TSB (Art. 11.10). The TSB would report to the Textiles Committee. The Textiles Committee was established and all participants in the Arrangement had a representative therein. It would receive an annual report from TSB and overview the operation of the MFA. The MFA entered into force on January 1, 1974. Gradually, some liberalization occurred: estimates based on 1990 data indicate that close to 11% of world trade in textiles and 35% in clothing were covered by the MFA. On November 1, 1994, the MFA

---

[3] Tang (1998) at pp. 180ff.

[4] Low (1993) pp. 108ff.

[5] The International Textiles and Clothing Bureau (ITCB) was established in the mid-eighties to serve as ante-chambre where developing countries could meet and coordinate their policies, see Dickerson (1995) at pp. 379ff.

counted 39 participants, eight of which should be described as "importers", and of these Austria, Canada, the EU, Finland, Norway and the US continued to apply restrictions, Japan and Switzerland having dropped them in the meantime.[6] The MFA was a world-wide cartel where consumers' interests were not represented at all.[7]

The MFA was, on its face, inconsistent with various GATT rules (including, Art. XI, Art. XIX, and Art. I GATT as well, since, in practice, the quotas were country-specific). The inconsistency however, was healed by the fact that it benefitted from a *de facto* waiver.[8] The Arrangement Regarding International Trade in Textiles (as is the official title of the MFA) was adopted and published in the BISD Series (21S/3): although no formal waiver was ever requested, GATT contracting parties behaved as if the Arrangement amounted to a de facto waiver, and never challenged its consistency with the multilateral rules. The MFA was eventually replaced in 1995 by the ATC. The ATC[9] was signed along with the other Uruguay Round agreements, and replaced the MFA. It was a transitional agreement aimed at the elimination of existing quotas and the introduction of trade in textiles and clothing into the GATT disciplines: its basic objective was thus to integrate textiles-trade into the multilateral disciplines. During the Uruguay Round, in the TNC meeting of April 1989, a decision was taken to this effect. It relevantly read in § 2:[10]

> Substantive negotiations will begin in April 1989 in order to reach agreement within the time-frame of the Uruguay Round on modalities for the integration of this sector into GATT, in accordance with the negotiating objective; . . . such modalities for the process of integration into GATT on the basis of strengthened GATT rules and disciplines should inter alia cover the phasing out of restrictions under the Multi-fibre Arrangement.

3. COVERAGE OF THE LEGAL DISCIPLINE

3.1 THE OBJECTIVES SOUGHT

The objective sought through the enactment of the ATC was to undo the restrictions imposed by the MFA. Art. 1.1 ATC captures this point:

---

[6] The Results of the Uruguay Round of Multilateral Trade Negotiations, Market Access for Goods and services: Overview of the Results, The GATT: Geneva, 1994.

[7] Dickerson (1995) at pp. 490ff.

[8] Actually, even the MFA was on occasion judged insufficient by some importing countries: Dickerson (1995, pp. 87ff.) discusses the US attempts to move to an even more restrictive regime with the discussion of the 'Jenkins Bill'.

[9] The drafting history of this agreement is explained in detail in Bagchi (2001, pp. 224ff.), and Raffaelli and Jenkins (1995), see also Croome (1995).

[10] Raffaelli and Jenkins (1995).

This Agreement sets out provisions to be applied by Members during a transition period for the integration of the textiles and clothing sector into GATT 1994.

The Panel in *US–Underwear* stated in a similar vein (§ 7.19):

> the overall purpose of the ATC is to integrate the textiles and clothing sector into GATT 1994. Article 1 of the ATC makes this point clear. To this effect, the ATC requires notification of all existing quantitative restrictions (Article 2 of the ATC) and provides that they will have to be terminated by the year 2004 (Article 9 of the ATC). The ATC allows adoption of new restrictions in addition to those notified under Article 2 of the ATC for products not yet integrated into GATT 1994 pursuant to Article 2.6 to 2.8 of the ATC only exceptionally and in accordance with the relevant provisions of the ATC or in accordance with the relevant provisions of GATT 1994.[11]

3.2 THE MEANS IN A NUTSHELL

The ATC imposes two main obligations:

(a) To integrate textiles trade into the multilateral rules within a pre-defined calendar; and

(b) To avoid from introducing any new restrictions, unless by respecting the strict conditions embedded in Art.6 ATC.

Besides these two obligations, the ATC:

(a) Requests from exporting WTO Members to continue to administer their restrictions;

(b) Includes anti-circumvention provisions; and

(c) Assigns to the TMB the responsibility to administer the Agreement: WTO Members agreed to notify the newly established Textiles Monitoring Body (TMB) their quotas and abolish them within 10 years, that is, by 1 January 2005. Art. 9 ATC underscores the transitional character of the TMB as well which has also ceased to exist as of January 1, 2005. After that date, it is only through tariffs that textiles goods are protected.

3.3 PRODUCT COVERAGE

Art. 1.7 ATC explains that the product coverage of the ATC is elaborated in the Annex to the Agreement. The Annex includes the relevant HS-classifications at the 6 digit-level (Chapters 51–63, and some products

---

[11] The AB in this case, as well as the Panel in *US–Cotton Yarn* (§ 7.73) went so far as to state that the MFA was no legal context, in the VCLT-sense of the term, for the interpretation of the ATC.

in Chapters 30–49, and 64–96), and also states a list of products on which no transitional safeguard can be imposed.

3.4 THE INTEGRATION PROCESS

3.4.1 Integration in Ten Years

The integration process is explained in Art. 2 ATC: WTO Members must integrate the products listed in the Annex into the rules of GATT over the ten-year period; it will be carried out progressively in three periods. All covered products must have been integrated into the GATT rules at the end of the ten-year period.[12] The first period began on January 1, 1995 with the integration of products representing not less than 16% of Members' total 1990 imports (of all products included in the product coverage appearing in the Annex); the second period began on January 1, 1998, and WTO Members undertook the obligation to integrate a further 17% (of the same total); the third period started on January 1, 2002, and a further 18% (of the same total) was integrated. On January 1, 2005, all remaining products (amounting up to 49% of the same total) were integrated, and the ATC, as a result, ceased to exist. WTO Members enjoyed substantial discretion with respect to the products that they would be integrating in each of the three periods. All existing restrictions had to be notified however, otherwise they could not benefit from the transitional regime included in the ATC. The restrictions notified were assumed to correspond to the totality of existing restrictions. The MFA-growth rates were increased on January 1, 1995 by a factor of 16% for the first period, and the new growth rate was applied annually. The growth rate for the first period was then increased by 25% for the second period (starting on January 1, 1998), and was further increased by 27% for the third, and last period, beginning on January 1, 2002.

3.4.2 No New Restrictions

Art. 2.4 ATC made clear that WTO Members could not enter any new restrictions, unless in conformity with the multilateral rules (essentially, by invoking the safeguard mechanism included in Art. 6 ATC). The Panel in *Turkey–Textiles* explicitly acknowledged this understanding of the integration process (§§ 9.68–9.69): in this vein, it held that, since Turkey had notified no restrictions, it could not introduce any new ones, unless in conformity with the ATC and other relevant GATT provisions; Turkey thus could either invoke Art. 6 ATC, or another appropriate GATT provision, like Art. XXIV, to this effect though it would have to comply with the requirements included in this provision (§ 9.78).

---

[12] Das (2001, pp. 104ff.) offers a concise description of the ATC.

3.5 SPECIAL TRANSITIONAL SAFEGUARD MECHANISM

Art. 6 ATC protects a WTO Member against surges in imports during the transition period from products which had not yet been integrated into GATT and which were not already under quota, if, as a result of a surge, its domestic industry producing the like product had been damaged. A WTO Member wishing to invoke this provision, had to:

(a) Determine that total imports of a specific product were causing serious damage, or actual threat thereof, to its domestic industry; and

(b) Decide to which individual Member(s) this serious damage could be attributed.

The purpose of the special transitional safeguard mechanism was explained in the Panel report in *US–Underwear* (§§ 7.23–24):

> The overall purpose of Article 6 of the ATC is to give Members the possibility to adopt new restrictions on products not already integrated into GATT 1994 pursuant to Article 2.6 to 2.8 of the ATC and not under existing restrictions, i.e., not notified under Article 2.1 of the ATC. Article 6 of the ATC, in our view, establishes a three-step approach which has to be followed for a new restriction to be imposed.

The interested WTO Member had to then seek consultations with the exporting Member(s). Safeguard measures could be applied on a selective, country-by-country basis, irrespective of whether an agreement has been reached, (between the importing and the exporting Members), or not (within a sixty days-consultation process). The quota imposed could not be lower than the actual level of imports for the exporting country during a recent reference period (twelve months); safeguard measures could remain in place for up to three years. If, however, a safeguard measure was in place for over a year, the growth rate should be at least 6%. WTO Members were required to notify the TMB if they wished to retain the right to use the special transitional safeguard mechanism (Art. 6.1 ATC). Fifty-five WTO Members chose to retain this right and most of them provided lists of products for integration. Nine WTO Members, namely, Australia, Brunei Darussalam, Chile, Cuba, Hong Kong, Iceland, Macau, New Zealand and Singapore decided not to maintain the right to use the special transitional safeguard mechanism. The special safeguard was invoked on 24 occasions in 1995 (all by the US); 8 times in 1996 (Brazil 7, US); 2 times in 1997 (both by the US); and 10 times in 1998 (Colombia 9, US 1).

Safeguard measures could be invoked, either because an import surge had caused, or because it threatened to cause damage. The Panel in *US–Underwear* explained that the two notions were distinct, and that consequently a separate type of analysis was required in order to demonstrate damage, or threat of damage. The facts of the case were as follows: on March 27, 1995, the US had requested consultations with Costa Rica on trade in cotton and man-made fibre underwear under Art. 6.7 ATC. At the same time, the US provided Costa Rica with a Statement of Serious Damage, dated March 1995 (the 'March Statement'), on the basis of which it had proposed the introduction of a restraint on imports of underwear from Costa Rica. Notice of the request for consultations, the proposed restraint and the proposed restraint level was published in the US Federal Register on April 21, 1995. Consultations were held, but the US and Costa Rica failed to negotiate a mutually acceptable settlement. The US subsequently invoked Art. 6.10 ATC, and introduced a transitional safeguard measure in respect of cotton and man-made fibre underwear imports from Costa Rica on June 23, 1995. The measure was, by its terms, to be valid for a period of twelve months, effective March 27, 1995 (i.e., the date of the request for consultations). The TMB found that the US had failed to demonstrate serious damage to its domestic industry: it did not reach consensus on the existence of an actual threat of serious damage though, and similarly failed to make any findings on the effective date of application of the US restraint. Accordingly, the TMB recommended that the US and Costa Rica hold further consultations with a view to resolving the matter. In the absence of any settlement, the parties reverted to the TMB, which confirmed its earlier findings and considered its review of the matter completed. Although further consultations took place between the US and Costa Rica in November 1995, no agreement was reached. In December 1995, Costa Rica invoked the dispute settlement provisions. One of the questions before the Panel was whether a separate analysis was required for a finding of damage and/or threat of damage. The Panel rejected the US argument that no separate analysis was required in the following terms (§ 7.55).[13] The Panel further rejected the US argument that it had acted consistently with its obligations under the ATC, when it established that damage had indeed occurred. In its view, the US-analysis suffered from serious weaknesses, since it was predicated on a review of the situation of:

> only one or two companies of indeterminate size or market share out of an industry consisting of 395 establishments. (§ 7.45).

However, the Panel refrained from making a finding on this point of law. It found that the factors listed in Art. 6.3 ATC did not provide sufficient and exclusive guidance and the Panel was therefore not in a position to conclude that the US had failed to demonstrate serious damage or actual threat thereof.

---

[13] Recall however, that subsequently, in the case law concerning contingent protection WTO adjudicating bodies adopted the opposite point of view, that is, that the same facts can be used to support findings of threat of injury and of injury as well without imposing a requirement for separate analysis.

Damage or threat of damage has to be suffered by the domestic industry producing the like and/or directly competitive product (Art. 6.2 ATC). The interpretation of the term "like and/or directly competitive product" was discussed in the Panel and AB report on *US–Cotton Yarn*. On December 24, 1998, the US filed a request for bilateral consultations with Pakistan, pursuant to Art. 6.7 ATC, on its proposed safeguard measure. The US attached to this request its Report of Investigation and Statement of Serious Damage or Actual Threat Thereof: Combed Cotton Yarn for Sale: Category 301 (December 1998), (the 'Market Statement'), which formed the basis for the proposed safeguard measure. The Market Statement set out the results of the investigation of the conditions prevailing in the US market for yarn. It defined the domestic industry and concluded that increased imports had caused serious damage, and actual threat thereof, to the domestic industry, and that this damage and threat were attributable to Pakistan. The US held bilateral consultations with Pakistan in February 1999, which did not result in a mutually agreed solution. Subsequently, the US imposed the transitional safeguard measure at issue in this dispute in the form of a quantitative restriction on Category 301 imports of yarn from Pakistan. The safeguard measure was made effective for one year as of March 17, 1999, and was extended twice, each time for one further year, effective March 17, 2000, and March 17, 2001, respectively. The TMB reviewed the matter, pursuant to Arts. 6.10 and 8.10 ATC, in April and in June 1999. The TMB concluded on both occasions that the US had not demonstrated successfully that yarn was being imported into its territory in such increased quantities as to cause serious damage, or actual threat thereof, to its domestic industry producing the like and/or directly competitive product. Accordingly, the TMB recommended that the safeguard measure introduced by the US on imports of yarn from Pakistan be rescinded. On August 6, 1999, the US informed the TMB that it believed its action was justified under the provisions of Art. 6 ATC, and that it would hence maintain the safeguard measure. The US and Pakistan held a further round of consultations in November 1999 but failed to reach a mutually agreed solution. On April 3, 2000, Pakistan requested the establishment of a Panel. One of the questions before the Panel was whether captive consumption should be excluded from the definition of the industry producing the like product, as the US had argued. The AB rejected the US argument, while explaining at the same time its understanding of the like product-analysis (§§ 99–101):

> We will now examine whether, in this case, yarn produced by the vertically integrated fabric producers of the United States for their own captive consumption is directly competitive with the imported yarn for the purposes of Article 6.2 of the *ATC*. The United States argues that such yarn is not directly competitive because it is not offered for sale on the market except when the

captive production is "out of balance", and even then only in *de minimis* quantities. In addition, vertically integrated fabric producers are not dependent on the merchant market for meeting any of their requirements of yarn except to a *de minimis* extent. In the United States' view, these factors are clearly reflected in the very low and stable rate of yarn sold or purchased by vertically integrated fabric producers to or from the merchant market over the last several years.

We are unable to subscribe to this static view which makes the competitive relationship between yarn sold on the merchant market and yarn used for internal consumption by vertically integrated producers dependent on what they choose to do at a particular point in time.

If the competitive relationship between the two products is properly considered, it will be clear that they are "directly competitive" within the meaning of that term in Article 6.2.

The attribution of damage to a particular country (Art. 6.4 ATC) is the last step for lawful imposition of transitional safeguard under the ATC: it requires an assessment that an import surge caused injury to the domestic industry producing the like product. The AB held as much in its report in *US–Cotton Yarn* (§§ 112–115). Total damage (or threat thereof) must be attributed proportionately to the exporting WTO Member, that is, in accordance with the damage caused by its exports to a given (importing) market (AB, *US–Cotton Yarn*, § 119). The AB acknowledged that the attribution-analysis could be done in various ways. Art. 6.4 ATC provided some information concerning the elements (levels of imports, market share, prices, etc.) that had to be taken into account in the context of this analysis. For the rest, case law added that the investigating authority of the importing state must perform a comparative analysis, whereby it would compare the effects of imports from various sources (§§ 122–123, *US–Cotton Yarn*, AB). The requirement to perform comparative analysis was echoed by the Panel in *US–Underwear* (§ 7.49).

The WTO Member proposing to take safeguard action has to request consultations with the affected Members, informing them about the results of its investigation (Art. 6.7 ATC). The request for consultations (as well as all relevant factual information regarding the investigation process) had to be communicated to the Chairman of the TMB. If parties reached an agreement, they had to communicate it to the TMB (Art. 6.8 ATC). Details of the agreement had to be communicated to the TMB (Art. 6.9 ATC); even in absence of agreement though, a WTO Member could, nonetheless, go ahead and apply a safeguard (Art. 6.10 ATC). In this case, either the importing-or the affected Member(s) could refer the matter to the TMB and request a review. The TMB should promptly examine the matter and make appropriate recommendations to the Members concerned (Art. 6.11 ATC).

Art. 6.10 ATC allowed WTO Members to impose safeguards within 30 days following the 60 days-consultation period. Art. 3.5(i) MFA states that the restraint could be instituted:

> for the twelve-month period beginning on the day when the request was received by the participating exporting country or countries.

The question arose whether the importing state could retroactively impose safeguards at that stage: Costa Rica argued that the US had retroactively applied restrictions in violation of Art. 6.10 ATC; restrictions were introduced on June 23, 1995 for a period of 12 months starting on March 27, 1995, which was the date of the request for consultations under Art. 6.7 ATC. Thus, the question before the Panel was whether the ATC should be interpreted as prohibiting a practice which was explicitly recognized under the MFA, and if so, what should be the appropriate date from which the restraint period is to be calculated under the ATC. The AB, having dismissed the relevance of MFA as context to the ATC as we saw *supra*, held in its report in *US–Underwear* that WTO Members should not be imposing safeguards in retroactive manner (p. 14):

> we believe that, in the absence of an express authorization in Article 6.10, *ATC*, to backdate the effectivity of a safeguard restraint measure, a presumption arises from the very text of Article 6.10 that such a measure may be applied only prospectively.

The Panel in *US–Underwear*, held that a violation of Art. 6 ATC amounted *ipso facto* to a violation of Art. 2.4 ATC (§ 7.71).

3.6 OBLIGATIONS OF WTO MEMBERS DURING THE TRANSITION PERIOD

The ATC entrusted exporting WTO Members with the responsibility to administer the restrictions during the transition period. Any changes in practices, rules or procedures were subject to consultations with a view to reaching mutually acceptable solutions (Art. 4 ATC). Art. 5 ATC contained the rules and procedures concerning circumvention of the quotas through trans-shipment, re-routing, false declaration of origin, or falsification of official documents. WTO Members should establish the necessary legal provisions and/or administrative procedures to address and take action against circumvention. When sufficient evidence was available, possible recourse might have included the denial of entry of goods.

4. INSTITUTIONAL ARRANGEMENTS: THE TMB

The TMB was the successor to the TSB. It was composed of delegates by both exporting and importing countries and had the power to recommend ways to end disputes brought to its attention (Arts 8.8–10 of the ATC).[14] The TMB was established in order to supervise the implementation of the ATC and to examine all measures taken under it, to ensure that they were in conformity with the rules. It was a quasi-judicial, standing body, and consisted of a Chairman and ten members, discharging their function on an ad personam basis, and taking all decisions by consensus: participation in the TMB was in function of criteria similar to those guiding participation in the TSB: representativeness of the WTO Membership; proportionate participation of textiles-importing-, as well as textiles-exporting WTO Members. Recall that the TMB would be notified of all restrictions and requested to pronounce on their consistency of the ATC. The question arose in practice whether Panels were bound by the TMB recommendations, or whether they were free to decide the issue: in its report on *Turkey–Textiles*, the Panel held that some deference to the TMB was appropriate, but underlined that it was not bound by its recommendations (§§ 9.85):

> We consider, based on the interpretation by the Appellate Body in *Guatemala—Cement* with regard to the relationship between the DSU and the Antidumping Agreement, that the provisions of the ATC (providing jurisdiction to the TMB to examine measures applied pursuant to the ATC) and the provisions of the DSU (providing jurisdiction for panels to interpret any covered agreement, including the ATC) may both apply together. Therefore even if the TMB has jurisdiction to determine what constitutes a "new" measure in the sense of the ATC and whether a violation of the ATC has taken place, we remain convinced that a panel is entitled to interpret the ATC to the extent necessary to ascertain whether Turkey benefits from a defence to India's claims under Articles XI and XIII of GATT based on the provisions of the ATC.

The TMB ceased to exist at the end of the transitional period envisaged in the ATC, that is, as of January 1, 2005.

QUESTIONS AND COMMENTS

MFA, a US Initiative: Bagchi (2001) attributes the advent of the MFA to an alliance that Richard Nixon, then candidate for the US Presidency, struck with the US textiles lobby. He quotes (p. 73) the following 1968 speech by candidate Nixon:

---

[14] Tang (1998) at pp. 187ff.

> As President my policy will be ... to assure prompt action to effectively administer the existing Long Term Cotton Textile Agreement. Also, I will promptly take the steps necessary to extend the concept of international trade agreement to all other textile articles involving wool, manmade fibres and blends.

MFA, a Costly Option: the MFA was a costly instrument, since consumers were deprived of cheap goods and forced to purchase domestic, expensive substitutes. Deardorff and Stern (1998, pp.20ff.) attempt a quantification of the barriers resulting from MFA and show how high protection was during the MFA years. Demelo and Tarr (1992) for example, estimated that the US could have enjoyed a welfare gain between $7–15 billion by removing all textiles and apparel quotas. Kathuria et al. (2003) discuss welfare implications for exporters and especially India: it is true that India could capture monopoly rents as a result of the passage of the MFA; gains from export rents though were offset by losses in exports to unrestricted markets and efficiency losses resulting from inability to put resources to their best uses. The economic evidence and the ensuing case against the MFA is thus overwhelming. Wolf et al. (1984, p. 136) captured it best when they stated:

> The MFA is a monument to diplomatic compromise, political appeasement and bureaucratic obfuscation. A defence can hardly be made in economic terms.

CHAPTER 19

TECHNICAL BARRIERS TO TRADE

■ ■ ■

1. THE LEGAL DISCIPLINE

A vast array of technical regulations and standards apply to products within any market. They may serve legitimate regulatory purposes (e.g., consumer protection, product safety, environmental protection, technical harmonization, etc.); they may also act as non-tariff barriers to protect domestic industries if enacted in an arbitrary and/or discriminatory manner. The TBT Agreement regulates the enactment and use of technical regulations and standards to ensure that they are genuinely useful and do not become an excuse for protectionism.

The TBT Agreement covers "technical regulations", "standards", and "conformity assessment". The first two establish specific characteristics of a product (e.g., design, function, size, label, packaging etc.) as well as its related process and production method. The key difference between the two is that conformity with a standard is voluntary, but conformity with a technical regulation is mandatory. "Conformity assessment" covers procedures (e.g., testing, verification, certification, etc.) that ensure that a product conforms to the established technical regulation or standard.

The TBT Agreement requires from WTO Members to follow relevant international standards when adopting measures coming under its aegis, assuming that such exist and are appropriate in light of the objectives pursued. If this is not the case, a WTO Member may have recourse to unilateral action, provided that the measures adopted are applied in a non-discriminatory manner and respect the necessity-principle.

2. THE RATIONALE FOR THE LEGAL DISCIPLINE

During the Tokyo Round, a Code on Technical Barriers to Trade (TBT) was agreed upon which called for the avoidance of using unnecessary standards. Participation in the TBT Code, however, was optional. The sheer rise in the number of technical regulations, and standards worldwide (and especially in Europe where consumer protection provided the impetus for strict regulation of its industry)[1] persuaded negotiators in the Uruguay Round that the time had come to add a binding multilateral

---

[1] Vogel (1997).

agreement to the existing rules. Public health, environmental- and consumer protection are the most frequent reasons for imposing technical regulations and standards at the national level. These are areas the regulation of which has, at least in some parts of the world, been heavily influenced by scientific progress. Regulation at the national level is not however, always immune to political-economy considerations, and as a result, there is no guarantee that the end product will be a first-best regulatory response to an existing distortion.[2] Büthe and Mattli (2011, p. 135) offer the following example of regulatory capture by domestic lobbies:

> A Japanese product standard ... adopted in 1986 by the Consumer Product Safety Association (CPSA) at the request of the nascent Japanese ski manufacturing industry, required that skis sold in Japan would have to comply with particular product design specifications in order to get a consumer safety seal. None of the major foreign manufacturers met the standard. The CPSA sought to justify the introduction of the ski standard by arguing that Japanese snow is 'different' from snow in other (ski-exporting) countries.

In order to avoid rent-seeking behavior from domestic lobbies, a certain degree of cooperation might be warranted.

3. COVERAGE OF THE LEGAL DISCIPLINE

3.1 THE RELATIONSHIP WITH THE GATT

Art. 2.2 TBT provides an indicative list of legitimate objectives for technical regulations and standards; it mentions national security, the prevention of deceptive practices, protection of human health or safety, animal or plant life or health, or the environment.

The TBT Agreement is an Annex 1A agreement (of the WTO Agreement); its relationship with the GATT is addressed in the General Interpretative Note to Annex 1A. In *EC—Asbestos*, the AB, reversing the Panel in this respect, concluded that a measure, which revealed the characteristics of a technical regulation, and thus, simultaneously fell under the TBT and the GATT should have been reviewed under the TBT Agreement, and not under the GATT (as the Panel had originally done). The subsequent Panel report in *EC–Sardines* contains an even more explicit reflection of this approach (§§ 7.14–16):

---

[2] Kono (2006) for example, observes that it is democracies that typically create non-tariff barriers (NTBs). In his analysis, by increasing the transparency of some policies relative to others, democracy induces politicians to replace transparent trade barriers (such as tariffs) with less transparent ones (such as NTB). He tests his hypothesis using a sample of 75 countries and concludes that democracy leads to lower tariffs, higher core NTBs, and even higher quality NTBs. In his view, democracy promotes optimal obfuscation that allows politicians to protect their markets while maintaining a veneer of liberalization. Compare Milner (1988).

... If we were to determine that the EC Regulation is not inconsistent with the provisions of the TBT Agreement invoked by Peru, it requests that we examine its claims in respect of Article III:4 of the GATT 1994.

In addressing the issue of the order of analysis, we have taken into account earlier considerations of this question. We recall the AB's statement in *EC—Bananas III* which stated that the panel "should" have applied the Licensing Agreement first because this agreement deals "specifically, and in detail" with the administration of import licensing procedures. The AB noted that if the panel had examined the measure under the Licensing Agreement first, there would have been no need to address the alleged inconsistency with Article X:3 of the GATT 1994. The AB suggests that where two agreements apply simultaneously, a panel should normally consider the more specific agreement before the more general agreement.

Arguably, the TBT Agreement deals "specifically, and in detail" with technical regulations. If the AB's statement in EC—Bananas III is a guide, it suggests that if the EC Regulation is a technical regulation, then the analysis under the TBT Agreement would precede any examination under the GATT 1994. Moreover, Peru, as the complaining party, requested that we first examine its claim under Article 2.4 of the TBT Agreement followed by Article 2.2 if we find that the EC Regulation is consistent with Article 2.4. And similarly, only if we were to find that the EC Regulation is consistent with Article 2.2 does Peru ask us to consider its claim under Article 2.1. In the event that we were to find that the EC Regulation is consistent with the TBT Agreement, Peru requests that we examine its claim under Article III:4 of the GATT 1994. We note that the European Communities did not contest Peru's request regarding this sequencing analysis.

On appeal, the AB did not reverse the order of analysis. Subsequent Panel reports (*US–Tuna II (Mexico)*; *US–Clove Cigarettes*; *US–COOL*) have followed this order of analysis and it is now commonplace that Panels will start reviewing claims under the TBT Agreement and eventually, if need be, review them under the GATT as well.

In the next Chapter, we will discuss a particular class of technical regulations and standards, known as sanitary and phytosanitary standards. With respect to this class of measures, Art. 1.5 TBT makes clear that the WTO agreement that governs these measures (known as the Agreement on Sanitary and Phytosanitary Standards, or SPS Agreement) takes precedence.

3.2 DEFINITIONS

The TBT Agreement governs three types of measures:

- Technical regulations
- Standards
- Conformity assessment procedures

The term "technical regulation" is defined in Annex 1, § 1 of the TBT Agreement as follows:

> Document which lays down product characteristics or their related processes and production methods, including the applicable administrative provisions, with which compliance is mandatory. It may also include or deal exclusively with terminology, symbols, packaging, marking or labeling requirements as they apply to a product, process or production method.

Reviewing its prior jurisprudence on the issue (§§ 67–72, *EC–Asbestos*), the AB defined technical regulation in its report on *EC–Sardines* in the following manner (§§ 175–176):

> In doing so, we set out *three criteria* that a document must meet to fall within the definition of "technical regulation" in the *TBT Agreement*. *First*, the document must apply to an identifiable product or group of products. The *identifiable* product or group of products need not, however, be expressly *identified* in the document. *Second*, the document must lay down one or more characteristics of the product. These product characteristics may be intrinsic, or they may be related to the product. They may be prescribed or imposed in either a positive or a negative form. *Third*, compliance with the product characteristics must be mandatory. (emphasis in the original)[3]

Compliance with a technical regulation is mandatory for a product to gain access to a given market, whereas it is voluntary when it comes to standards.

In *EC–Asbestos*, however, the AB held that even when the words used in a document are of hortatory nature, we could still be in presence of a technical regulation if the latter (§ 68):

> has the *effect* of prescribing or imposing one or more 'characteristics'—'features', 'qualities', 'attributes', or other 'distinguishing mark. (emphasis in the original).

In this vein, the Panel in *US–COOL* went on to examine whether a letter sent by US Secretary of Agriculture Vilsack, which contained unambiguously hortatory language, could be considered as technical regula-

---

[3] See also the Panel report in *US–COOL* at § 7.147.

tion. In this case, Canada and Mexico had challenged a US measure imposing compulsory labeling indicating the origin of imported goods (such as bovine meet and pork).[4] The US measure established four categories: category A refered to beef wholly produced and slaughtered in the US, whereas category D covered beef produced and slaughtered abroad. There were two in between categories, B, and C the functionality of which is explained in § 7.697 of the report:

> We recall that meat falling within the scope of categories B and C is required to carry labels indicating "product of the US, Country X" (Label B) and "product of Country X, the US" (Label C). As described above in Section VII.C.1(b)(i), Label B refers to meat derived from animals born in Country X, and raised and slaughtered in the United States, whereas Label C refers to meat derived from animals imported for immediate slaughter (i.e. animals born and raised outside the United States). Labels B and C are therefore differentiated by the order of country names indicated on the label.

Secretary Vilsack issued a letter implementing the US statute which read, in part, as follows (§ 7.123):

> I am suggesting ... that the industry *voluntarily* adopt the following practices to ensure that consumers are adequately informed about the source of food products: ... processors should *voluntarily* include information about what production steps occurred in each country when multiple countries appear on each label. ... Even if products [that are otherwise exempt] are subject to curing, smoking, broiling, grilling, or steaming, *voluntary* labeling would be appropriate. ... (emphasis in the original).

The Panel went ahead and examined whether the statute's language notwithstanding this letter could be considered as technical regulation. It concluded in the negative since it found no empirical evidence suggesting it operated as such (§§ 7.188ff.).

In *US–Tuna II (Mexico)*, the Panel held that a US legislation which did not impose the label "dolphin-safe" on imports of tuna but which conditioned its lawful use upon meeting certain criteria was a technical regulation and not a standard (§§ 7.100ff., and especially 7.120 and 7.131). A separate opinion issued by one member of the Panel stressed that the measure would be a "technical regulation" only if imported goods had to carry the label "dolphin-safe"; this was not the case here and, consequently, the challenged measure was a standard (§§ 7.146ff.). On appeal, the AB (§§ 172–199) endorsed the majority view and held that the US measure was indeed a technical regulation although tuna could be marketed in the US market without carrying the label "dolphin-safe". In the AB's view

---

[4] For detailed description of the goods concerned see § 7.78 of the Panel report.

what mattered was that goods had to follow the statutory requirements (and had no discretion at all to this effect); otherwise they could not legitimately be considered "dolphin-safe".

Usually, a technical regulation defines specific product characteristics, such as size, shape, design, functions, performance, labeling or packaging, as well as related process and production standards. The AB, interpreting the identification-requirement, has emphasized that there is no obligation that a particular product be explicitly mentioned in the body of the technical regulation; it suffices that a product can be identified. Therefore, omissions are not fatal (*EC–Sardines*, §§ 180, 183). In that case, although the challenged regulation did not explicitly identify 'sardinops sagax' as one of the types of sardines that was covered, it was quite clear, in the AB's view, that the scope of the regulation covered this type of sardines as well. In the AB's view, what matters is whether a means of identification of a product has been provided (§§ 190–191).

A conformity assessment procedure refers to the procedures for ensuring conformity with a technical regulation or standard.

3.3 SCOPE OF APPLICATION

The provisions within the TBT Agreement are applicable to any technical regulation, standard, or conformity assessment procedure enacted by central government bodies. With respect to bodies at the local government level and also non-governmental bodies within the territory of a WTO Member, the TBT Agreement requests that the central government of WTO Members take "reasonable measures" to ensure compliance with the provisions of the Agreement, except with respect to notification requirements (Arts. 3.1, 4.1, and 7.1 TBT). The central government of WTO Members also may not take measures which require or encourage local government level and also non-governmental bodies to act in a manner that is inconsistent with the requirements for technical regulations, standards, and conformity assessment procedures (Arts. 3.4, 4.1, and 7.4 TBT).

3.4 GENERAL PRINCIPLES APPLICABLE TO TECHNICAL REGULATIONS AND STANDARDS

Before we discuss the specific case law, we highlight some of the common principles applicable to both technical regulations and standards:

- Where relevant international standards exist or where their completion is imminent, WTO Members shall use them as basis for their technical regulations and standards, unless such international standards would be ineffective or inappropriate for the fulfillment of a legitimate policy objective. (Art. 2.4 TBT for technical regulations; Annex 3, § F for standards)

- Non-discrimination: Imports shall receive treatment no less favorable than that accorded to "like" products produced domestically and in any other country. (Art. 2.1 TBT for technical regulations; Annex 3, § D for standards)
- Whenever appropriate, technical regulations and standards shall be specified based on product characteristics in terms of performance rather than design or descriptive characteristics. (Art. 2.8 TBT for technical regulations; Annex 3, § I for standards)
- In addition, certain *ex ante* and *ex post* transparency requirements must be met with respect to notification, opportunities for comment, and publication of technical regulations and standards. (Arts. 2.5, 2.9, and 2.12 TBT for technical regulations; Annex 3, §§ L–P for standards)

We turn now to a more detailed discussion of several of these obligations, beginning with technical regulations. Note that conformity assessment procedures are bound by their own set of requirements, to which we will turn after our discussion of technical regulations and standards.

4. TECHNICAL REGULATIONS

The AB in *EC–Sardines* has made clear that a technical regulation is a measure that fulfills the following three criteria cumulatively (§§ 175–176):

- It applies to a product or an identifiable group of products, but this need not be expressly identified;
- It lays down one or more characteristics of the product, which may be intrinsic or related to the product, and which may be prescribed or imposed in a positive or negative form;
- It is mandatory.

Recall that technical regulations must respect three disciplines:

1) They must be non-discriminatory;
2) They must be necessary to achieve a particular objective; and
3) They must be pursuing a legitimate objective.

These disciplines must be cumulatively met (Arts 2.1 and 2.2 TBT). In addition, WTO Members are expected to fulfill certain transparency requirements with respect to their technical regulations.

4.1 CONFIRMITY WITH INTERNATIONAL STANDARDS, IF POSSIBLE

Art. 2.4 TBT mandates the use of international standards, except under certain circumstances:[5]

> Where technical regulations are required and relevant international standards exist or their completion is imminent, Members shall use them, or the relevant parts of them, as a basis for their technical regulations except when such international standards or relevant parts would be an ineffective or inappropriate means for the fulfillment of the legitimate objectives pursued, for instance because of fundamental climatic or geographical factors or fundamental technological problems.

The term "international standard" is not defined at all, except for a reference in Annex 1 to the effect that:

> Standards prepared by the international standardization community are based on consensus. This Agreement covers also documents that are not based on consensus.

The concept of the "international standardization community" is not further elaborated upon. In its Annexes, however, the TBT Agreement makes explicit reference to one such community: the ISO (International Organization for Standardization). Subsequent case law has recognized, for example, naming standards employed by organizations such as the Codex Alimentarius Commission.[6] In case of disagreement, it will be up to Panels to decide whether a "document" can be considered as an international standard. In principle, even an ISO-standard would have to be accepted as an international standard by a Panel, since nowhere in the Agreement does it curtail the Panels' discretion to this effect.

The Explanatory Note in Annex 1 to the TBT states that the TBT Agreement covers "documents" that are not based on consensus.[7] In this vein, in *EC–Sardines* (§ 225),[8] the AB rejected an argument advanced by the EU that only standards adopted by unanimity are international standards. The AB held that even standards adopted without consensus

---

[5] International standardization is one of the objectives of the TBT Agreement, prominently featuring in its Preamble.

[6] See, e.g., *EC–Sardines*.

[7] The Explanatory Note in Annex 1 of the TBT Agreement reads: "The terms as defined in ISO/IEC Guide 2 cover products, processes and services. This Agreement deals only with technical regulations, standards and conformity assessment procedures related to products or processes and production methods. Standards as defined by ISO/IEC Guide 2 may be mandatory or voluntary. For the purpose of this Agreement standards are defined as voluntary and technical regulations as mandatory documents. Standards prepared by the international standardization community are based on consensus. This Agreement covers also documents that are not based on consensus".

[8] Horn and Weiler (2007). In *EC–Sardines*, the AB, upholding the Panel's findings in this respect, confirmed that the definition of "standard" in § 2 of Annex 1 to the TBT is relevant not only for domestic (that is, non-compulsory), but for international standards as well (§ 220).

are recognized as international standards and can still qualify as standard under Art. 2.4 TBT Agreement.

The 2000 TBT Committee Decision[9] which included six principles that should be observed when international standards are elaborated. § 1 of the Decision reads:

> The following principles and procedures should be observed, when international standards, guides and recommendations (as mentioned under Articles 2, 5 and Annex 3 of the TBT Agreement for the preparation of mandatory technical regulations, conformity assessment procedures and voluntary standards) are elaborated, to ensure transparency, openness, impartiality and consensus, effectiveness and relevance, coherence, and to address the concerns of developing countries.

§ 8 of the Decision explains in more detail how the TBT Committee understood the "consensus" principle to apply:

> All relevant bodies of WTO Members should be provided with meaningful opportunities to contribute to the elaboration of an international standard so that the standard development process will not give privilege to, or favour the interests of, a particular supplier/s, country/ies or region/s. Consensus procedures should be established that seek to take into account the views of all parties concerned and to reconcile any conflicting arguments.

Note that neither the Panel nor the AB in *EC–Sardines* paid any lip service to the 2000 TBT Committee Decision, making it clear that consensus is not required for a document to rise to the level of an international standard.

WTO Members will have to base their regulatory interventions on international standards, only to the extent that the latter are relevant to the objective they are pursuing. In *EC–Sardines*, the AB understood the term "basis" as, at the very least, entailing that a technical regulation should not be contradictory to the relevant international standard. The AB also pointed out that all relevant parts of an international standard, not only some of them, must form the basis of a technical regulation (§§ 248 and 250). WTO Members can deviate from an international standard if it is ineffective or inappropriate for the attainment of a sought objective. As noted above, Art. 2.2 TBT contains an illustrative list of potential legitimate objectives for a measure.

In *EC–Sardines*,[10] the AB clarified a number of important issues, including the meaning of "ineffective or inappropriate" and which party car-

---

[9] Decision by the Committee on Principles for the Development of International Standards, Guides and Recommendations in Relation to Articles 2, 5 and Annex 3 of the Agreement, WTO Doc. G/TBT/9 of November 13, 2000.

[10] We discuss the facts in detail *infra*.

ries the burden-of-proof of demonstrating that this is the case with respect to an international standard. At issue in the case was the EU's rules concerning which fish could be labeled as "sardines" when sold in the European market. Before going into the details of the case, one should be aware that several species of fish exist that are referred to by some as sardines. *Sardina pilchardus Walbaum* ("*Sardina pilchardus*"), is found mainly around the coasts of the eastern North Atlantic Ocean, in the Mediterranean Sea, and in the Black Sea, *i.e.*, the area where EU fishermen normally fish. *Sardinops sagax* is found mainly in the eastern Pacific Ocean, along the coasts of Peru and Chile.

An EU Council Regulation[11] set forth common marketing standards for preserved sardines, allowing products to carry the name "sardine" commercially only when they conform to the following four requirements:

(a) They must be covered by CN codes 1604 13 10 and ex 1604 20 50;

(b) They must be prepared exclusively from fish of the species "*Sardina pilchardus Walbaum*";

(c) They must be pre-packaged with any appropriate covering medium in a hermetically sealed container; and, finally,

(d) They must be sterilized by appropriate treatment.

In 1978, the Codex Alimentarius Commission of the United Nations Food and Agriculture Organization (FAO) and the World Health Organization (WHO) adopted a worldwide standard for preserved sardines and sardine-type products.[12] This standard (CODEX STAN 94–1981, Rev.1–1995) covers preserved sardines or sardine-type products prepared from 21 fish species, and among them *Sardina pilchardus* and *Sardinops sagax*. Section 6.1.1 of the CODEX standard regulated the name that the 21 mentioned species could legitimately carry in the following manner:

(a) "Sardines" to be reserved exclusively for *Sardina pilchardus Walbaum;* or

(b) "X sardines" of a country, a geographic area, the species, or the common name of the species in accordance with the law and custom of the country in which the product is sold, and in a manner not to mislead the consumer.

The parties did not disagree that the EU had deviated from the international standard: under the CODEX standard, Peruvian exports of *Sardinops sagax* could be labeled "Peruvian sardines" but the EU regulation expressly forbid it from using the term "sardines." Peruvian producers feared that marketing its exports under a different name would ad-

---

[11] (EEC) 2136/89 of 21 June 1989 laying down common marketing standards for preserved sardines, 1989, OJ L212/79.

[12] Besides addressing naming conventions, the CODEX STAN 94–1981, Rev.1–1995 also regulates matters such as presentation, essential composition and quality factors, food additives, hygiene and handling, labeling, sampling, examination and analyses, defects and lot acceptance.

versely affect its interests. Peru therefore filed a complaint that the EU had unjustifiably deviated from the international standard reflecting the denomination of sardines in violation of the TBT Agreement.

The EU argued that, since the product coverage between the international standard and the EU technical regulation was not identical, the former was not relevant for the latter: the international standard covered the marketing of 21 fish species while the EU technical regulation only covered the marketing of one of them. The AB rejected this argument: Since the EU technical regulation had legal implications for the marketing of the other 20 species covered by the international standard, the AB held that the international standard was relevant for the EU technical regulation (§§ 222ff).

The AB then had to examine whether the EU deviation was authorized because the international standard was ineffective or inappropriate for the EU's regulatory objective. To do so, the AB first had to decide the meaning of the term "ineffective or inappropriate" (§ 285):

> [W]e noted earlier the Panel's view that the term "ineffective or inappropriate means" refers to two questions—the question of the *effectiveness* of the measure and the question of the *appropriateness* of the measure—and that these two questions, although closely related, are different in nature. The Panel pointed out that the term "ineffective" "refers to something which is not 'having the function of accomplishing', 'having a result', or 'brought to bear', whereas [the term] 'inappropriate' refers to something which is not 'specially suitable', 'proper', or 'fitting' ". The Panel also stated that:
>
>> Thus, in the context of Article 2.4, an ineffective means is a means which does not have the function of accomplishing the legitimate objective pursued, whereas an inappropriate means is a means which is not specially suitable for the fulfillment of the legitimate objective pursued ... The question of effectiveness bears upon the *results* of the means employed, whereas the question of appropriateness relates more to the *nature* of the means employed.
>
> We agree with the Panel's interpretation. (emphasis in the original)[13]

The AB then had to respond to the question who carries the burden of proof to demonstrate that the standard at hand was ineffective or inap-

---

[13] In *US–Tuna II (Mexico)* the Panel addressed an argument by Mexico to the effect that the US had violated its obligations under the TBT by deviating from an international standard (the AIDCP standard, discussed in more detail below). The Panel held that the invoked standard was not as effective as the US chosen means since it did not address both of the concerns advanced by the US as the underlying rationale for adoption of its measure (§§ 7.721 ff., and especially 7.726).

propriate. On this question, the AB reversed the Panel and held that the burden falls on the complainant to prove that the international standard is appropriate and effective (§ 282). In the AB's view, the complainant was not placed at disadvantage through its allocation of the burden of proof; it could easily acquire the necessary information regarding the EU standard through the various transparency obligations embedded in the TBT Agreement, and critically through the enquiry points that the TBT Agreement requires from WTO to establish in order to inform traders about their standards (Art. 10 TBT). Even if this was not enough, Peru anyway became accustomed with the EU standard, in the AB's view, through the litigation process. The AB also referred to its case law under the SPS Agreement (*EC–Hormones*) where it had decided a similar issue in this manner, and saw no reason to decide otherwise in the context of the TBT Agreement. Curiously though, although it reversed the Panel, it still found in favor of Peru based on evidence that Peru had submitted before the Panel where the allocation of burden of proof had been different (§ 290).

4.2 NON–DISCRIMINATION

Art. 2.1 TBT sets forth the principle of non-discrimination applicable to technical regulations:

> Members shall ensure that in respect of technical regulations, products imported from the territory of any Member shall be accorded treatment no less favourable than that accorded to like products of national origin and to like products originating in any other country.

Art. 2.1 TBT encapsulates both the principles of MFN treatment and national treatment. As we have seen in the context of the GATT, certain terms carry specific meanings with respect to these provisions. Below, we elaborate on the case law that has evolved with respect to the concepts of a "like product" and less favorable treatment as interpreted in the context of Art. 2.1 TBT.

4.2.1 Like Products

WTO Members must, by virtue of the non-discrimination discipline, not afford imported goods less favorable treatment than that afforded to domestic like products. In *US–Tuna II (Mexico)*, and *US–Clove Cigarettes*, two Panels were requested to provide their understanding of the term.

The *US–Clove Cigarettes* dispute concerned a challenge brought by Indonesia against the US over the Family Smoking Prevention Tobacco Control Act of 2009 that banned clove cigarettes. Indonesia alleged that Section 907 of this law prohibited the production or sale in the US of cigarettes containing certain additives, including clove, but would continue to permit the production and sale of other cigarettes, including cigarettes containing menthol. Indonesia alleged that Section 907 was inconsistent with Art. 2 TBT. The question arose whether clove cigarettes and menthol cigarettes were like products.

In *US–Tuna II (Mexico)*, Mexico challenged a series of US measures which established the conditions for use of a "dolphin-safe" label on tuna products. The documentary evidence that a producer had to provide in order to be considered for the label varied depending on the geographic area where the tuna had been harvested and the fishing method used. In Mexico's view, these measures were inconsistent with Art. 2.1 TBT. The Panel was asked to pronounce on the likeness of two tuna products harvested in different geographic locations. It held that (§§ 7.225–226):

> The TBT Agreement applies to a limited set of measures, and our understanding of its terms, including the terms "like products" must be informed by this context. As expressed in the preamble of the TBT Agreement, this Agreement reflects the intention of the negotiators to:
>
>> "[E]nsure that technical regulations and standards, including packaging, marking and labelling requirements, and procedures for assessment of conformity with technical regulations and standards do not create unnecessary obstacles to trade."
>
> To the extent that Article 2.1 contributes to avoiding "unnecessary obstacles to trade" arising from undue discrimination with respect to technical regulations, it seeks to preserve the competitive opportunities of products originating in any Member, in relation to technical regulations. Thus, the term "like products" under Article 2.1 of the TBT Agreement may be similarly understood as relating to "the nature and extent of a competitive relationship" between and among products.
>
> We further note, as the Appellate Body did in relation to Article III:4 of the GATT 1994, that this does not necessarily imply that Members may not draw any regulatory distinctions, under Article 2.1 of the TBT Agreement, between products that have been determined to be like products. The question of the treatment to be given to products that are like is addressed separately in the requirement of not affording treatment less favourable, which we consider in the next Section of our Report.

In *US–Clove Cigarettes*, the Panel held that (§§ 7.244–247):

> As we have explained, we believe that such legitimate objective must permeate and inform our likeness analysis. In the weighing of these criteria, we have therefore carefully considered the relevance of those traits that are significant for the public health objective of Section 907(a)(1)(A), i.e., to reduce youth smoking.

We consider that our basic approach to "likeness" in this case is consistent with a very helpful hypothetical presented by the United States at the second meeting of the Panel, and reiterated in response to a question from the Panel:

> "Certain products may be considered like in certain contexts but not in others. For example, as the United States noted at the Second Substantive Meeting with Panel, cups made from paper, plastic and aluminum might be considered 'like' products regardless of these physical differences with respect to a tax or other fiscal measure. They all serve the same end-use of holding liquids, and may be viewed as interchangeable by consumers in this context. The different materials used in the cups may be considered to be less important in the like product analysis in this situation. However, the same cups might not be considered 'like' with respect to a measure regulating products that can be used safely in microwave ovens. In that case, the different materials used to make the cups would be more relevant, as aluminum may not be safely used in a microwave. This difference would effect whether consumers viewed each cup as suitable for use in a microwave and would be relevant to measures regulating which cups could be used in microwaves. In this context, the different materials used would be significant differences among the cups. The particular measure at issue is relevant to whether the different physical properties of the cup mean that one cup is not 'like' another cup."

We think that clove cigarettes and menthol cigarettes may be considered "like" in certain contexts but not in others. For example, these two kinds of cigarettes might not be considered "like" in the context of a hypothetical measure regulating products on the basis of characteristics that clove cigarettes and menthol cigarettes do not have in common, for example whether they contain eugenol (clove cigarettes do, and most menthol cigarettes do not). Along the same lines, they might not be considered "like" in the context of a hypothetical tax or fiscal measure based on the type of tobacco they contain (clove cigarettes tend to contain Java sun-cured tobacco, menthol cigarettes do not). However, these same two types of cigarettes might be considered "like" in the context of other measures that regulate products on the basis of characteristics that clove and menthol cigarettes do have in common, for example a hypothetical measure distinguishing between various tobacco products on the basis of whether or not those products are carcinogenic (which clove cigarettes and menthol cigarettes both are).

The measure at issue in this case plainly regulates cigarettes on the basis of a characteristic that clove cigarettes and menthol cigarettes have in common, which in the words of Section 907(a)(1)(A), is the shared characteristic that they "contain, as a constituent . . . or additive, an artificial or natural flavor . . . or an herb or spice . . . that is a characterizing flavor". In the context of this particular measure, which regulates tobacco products on the basis of this particular characteristic—which may be regarded as perhaps the defining feature of each type of product—we find it very difficult to see how clove cigarettes and menthol cigarettes would not be considered to be "like". As discussed in our findings, we are aware that there are certain differences between clove cigarettes and menthol cigarettes. These differences may well lead to the conclusion that these two products are not "like" in the context of different measures. However, in the context of the measure at issue in this dispute, these differences are less significant, and less relevant. In other words, contrary to what the United States argues, those differences do not relate to the public health objective of the measure at issue and therefore, are not relevant to the like product analysis in this case. In our view, the similarities related to the public health objective of Section 907(a)(1)(A) are highly relevant to the like product analysis in the circumstances of this case.

The two Panel reports offer two divergent approaches: The former suggests that likeness will be a matter of competitive relationship implying that it is the market that will decide this point. The latter suggests that an inquiry into the aims of the challenged measure is appropriate in order to conclude whether two goods are like or not. On appeal, the AB rejected the notion that the aims of the law are a valid criterion for consideration, as suggested by the Panel in *US–Clove Cigarettes*. The AB (§§ 110–120) held that likeness is function of the competitive relationship between two products in the market which could be informed by regulatory concerns (e.g., health risks). In addition, it underscored that likeness and DCS-relationship must exist at least in some part of the market and not necessarily throughout the market (§§ 142–143).[14]

4.2.2 Less Favorable Treatment

In *US–Clove Cigarettes*, the Panel made it clear that it was (§ 7.269):

---

[14] The AB did not clarify if the health risks that matter are risks perceived by consumers or by the adjudicators. Contrary to the Panel though, it did not mention the aims of the law as relevant criterion though.

. . . required to consider whether the detrimental effect(s) can be explained by factors or circumstances *unrelated to the foreign origin of the product* . . . (emphasis in the original)[15]

On appeal, the AB upheld this view (§§ 175ff.), further adding that less favorable treatment (LFT) does not exist if the detrimental impact is the outcome of pursuing legitimate objectives.

At issue in *US–COOL* was an American technical regulation requiring traders to indicate origin for cattle and hogs, with respect to their birth, raising and slaughter (so that a good could have more than one origin) (§ 240). This requirement applied to both domestic and foreign livestock (§ 239). Upstream suppliers had to indicate the origin to retailers and needed to observe recordkeeping requirements (§ 242). For labeling-origin purposes, the regulation permitted the use of four categories:

- A, wholly obtained (e.g., born, raised, and slaughtered) in US;
- B, one of the stages of production occurs only in the US;
- C, imported for immediate slaughter in the US;
- D, wholly obtained abroad (§ 243).

Livestock categorized as A and D reflected only one country on their country-of-origin label (COOL). Livestock categorized as B and C reflected all the countries where a production stage had occurred on their COOL (§ 245). Commingled meat referred to "covered commodities (of the same type) presented for retail sale in a consumer package that had been prepared from raw material sources having different origins." Therefore, commingled A and B livestock would B; B and C would be B as well, etc. (§ 246). The question was whether the technical regulation for labeling the origin of livestock afforded less favorable treatment to certain imports.

In assessing whether LFT had been afforded through this measure, the AB first noted:

> In assessing even-handedness, a panel must "carefully scrutinize the particular circumstances of the case, that is, the design, architecture, revealing structure, operation, and application of the technical regulation at issue (§ 271).

Following a long discussion (§§ 287ff.), the AB applied this test to the specifics of the case as follows:

> In sum, our examination of the COOL measure under Article 2.1 reveals that its recordkeeping and verification requirements impose a disproportionate burden on upstream producers and pro-

---

[15] The same attitude is evidenced in the *Panel report in US–Tuna II (Mexico)* at § 7.375, as well as in *US–COOL* § 7.313: the last report went so far as to explicitly state that Art. III.4 GATT was legal context for the interpretation of the LFT-requirement under the TBT Agreement, §§ 7.234ff.

cessors, because the level of information conveyed to consumers through the mandatory labelling requirements is far less detailed and accurate than the information required to be tracked and transmitted by these producers and processors. It is these same recordkeeping and verification requirements that "necessitate" segregation, meaning that their associated compliance costs are higher for entities that process livestock of different origins. Given that the least costly way of complying with these requirements is to rely exclusively on domestic livestock, the COOL measure creates an incentive for US producers to use exclusively domestic livestock and thus has a detrimental impact on the competitive opportunities of imported livestock. Furthermore, the recordkeeping and verification requirements imposed on upstream producers and processors cannot be explained by the need to convey to consumers information regarding the countries where livestock were born, raised, and slaughtered, because the detailed information required to be tracked and transmitted by those producers is not necessarily conveyed to consumers through the labels prescribed under the COOL measure. This is either because the prescribed labels do not expressly identify specific production steps and, in particular for Labels B and C, contain confusing or inaccurate origin information, or because the meat or meat products are exempt from the labelling requirements altogether. Therefore, the detrimental impact caused by the same recordkeeping and verification requirements under the COOL measure can also not be explained by the need to provide origin information to consumers. Based on these findings, we consider that the regulatory distinctions imposed by the COOL measure amount to arbitrary and unjustifiable discrimination against imported livestock, such that they cannot be said to be applied in an even-handed manner. Accordingly, we find that the detrimental impact on imported livestock does not stem exclusively from a legitimate regulatory distinction but, instead, reflects discrimination in violation of Article 2.1 of the *TBT Agreement*. (§ 349, italics in the original).

In other words, the technical regulation afforded less favorable treatment to certain importers, not because domestic goods were favored over imports (i.e., not because category A was advantaged over category D), but because the technical regulation advantaged purely-domestic goods over goods where only a single stage of production had been conducted domestically (i.e., category A over categories B and C).

In *US–Tuna II (Mexico)*, a question arose as to whether less favorable treatment of tuna could arise even if the technical regulation specified differential treatment not on the basis of national origin. In that case, Mexico asserted that its tuna products were treated less favorably on account of the US regulation subjecting tuna to different requirements for obtaining a "dolphin-safe" certification on the basis of whether the tuna was fished inside or outside the Eastern Tropical Pacific (ETP).[16] The Panel found that the difference in certification requirements did not constitute LFT, as the regulation was origin-neutral and Mexican tuna fishermen could fulfill the necessary requirements needed to obtain the certification (§§ 7.377–7.378). The AB reversed the Panel, noting:

> An enquiry into whether a measure comports with the "treatment no less favourable" requirement in Article 2.1 does not hinge on whether the imported products could somehow get access to an advantage, for example, by complying with all applicable conditions. Rather, as explained above, a determination of whether imported products are accorded "less favorable treatment" within the meaning of Article 2.1 of the TBT Agreement calls for an analysis of whether the contested measure modifies the conditions of competition to the detriment of imported products. Contrary to what the Panel appears to have assumed, the fact that a complainant could comply or could have complied with the conditions imposed by a contested measure does not mean that the challenged measure is therefore consistent with Article 2.1 of the TBT Agreement.

The AB criticized the Panel for failing to take into account that a measure may be *de facto* inconsistent with Art. 2.1 TBT even if it is origin-neutral. It reiterated its command in *US–Clove Cigarettes* that a Panel must "scrutinize the particular circumstances of the case, that is, the design, architecture, revealing structure, operation, and application of the technical regulation at issue, and in particular, whether that technical regulation is even-handed" (§ 225). The AB then proceeded to examine whether the regulation modified the conditions of competition to the detriment of Mexican products and whether the measure was properly calibrated to fulfill the US regulatory objective, before concluding that the regulation amounted to LFT (§ 297):

> [W]e conclude that the United States has not demonstrated that the difference in labelling conditions for tuna products containing tuna caught by setting on dolphins in the ETP, on the one hand, and for tuna products containing tuna caught by other fishing methods outside the ETP, on the other hand, is "calibrated" to the risks to dolphins arising from different fishing methods in different areas of the ocean. It follows from this that the United States has not demonstrated that the detrimental impact of the US measure on Mexican tuna products stems exclusively from a legitimate regulatory distinction. We note, in particular,

---

[16] In order to obtain "dolphin-safe" label certification, tuna caught within the ETP was subject to more stringent requirements than tuna caught outside of the ETP.

that the US measure *fully* addresses the adverse effects on dolphins resulting from setting on dolphins in the ETP, whereas it does "not address mortality (observed or unobserved) arising from fishing methods other than setting on dolphins outside the ETP."

4.2.3 Necessity

The TBT Agreement requires WTO Members to ensure that technical regulations should not be enacted unless they are necessary and, if enacted, they should not be more trade restrictive than necessary to achieve the stated regulatory objective. This is captured in Art. 2.2 TBT:

> Members shall ensure that technical regulations are not prepared, adopted or applied with a view to or with the effect of creating unnecessary obstacles to international trade. For this purpose, technical regulations shall not be more trade-restrictive than necessary to fulfill a legitimate objective, taking account of the risks non-fulfillment would create.

The necessity requirement, therefore, requires a two-part analysis:

- First, an analysis of the risks in the event no regulatory intervention takes place, in order to determine whether the regulatory intervention is necessary at all;
- Second, if intervention is judged necessary, an analysis of whether the chosen means are more trade-restrictive than necessary to reach the stated legitimate objective.

Interventions based on international standards are, by virtue of Art. 2.5 TBT, presumed necessary to achieve a legitimate objective.[17]

In *US–Tuna II (Mexico)*, the Panel underscored that the appropriate level of protection is the exclusive privilege of WTO Members who are sole responsible to define it. The Panels' function is simply to review the legitimacy of the means employed to reach the objectives (§ 7.622). In that case, the US insisted on use of its own "dolphin-safe" labeling scheme and did not allow for a less-stringent scheme stemming from the Agreement on International Dolphin Conservation Program (AIDCP) to be used. Both the US and Mexico were parties to the AIDCP, a multilateral convention aimed at reducing dolphin mortality. The Panel concluded that the US scheme would be less trade-restrictive if it had used its own scheme in conjunction with the AIDCP scheme; it therefore found the US to be in violation of the necessity principle of Art. 2.2 TBT(§§ 7.601 ff). On appeal, the AB disagreed that the two schemes used in conjunction would have achieved US objectives "to the same extent" as use of the US scheme alone and reversed (§§ 328–31). Left unquestioned was the legitimacy of

---

[17] The Panel in *US–Clove Cigarettes* held that this provision (Art. 2.5 TBT) creates a rebuttable presumption (§ 7.331).

the US regulatory objective; the WTO's role was simply to examine whether a less trade-restrictive measure would have allowed the US to fulfill those objectives, with the AB concluding that it did not.

In *US–COOL*, the Panel found that the US regulatory scheme violated the necessity requirement as it did not clearly accomplish the objective that was sought. The scheme sought to provide consumers with clearer and more detailed information about the product. However, the Panel found that it might instead cause consumer confusion regarding which step of production was undertaken in which country in instances where different stages of production had taken place in different countries. In other words, because the regulation did not achieve the objective sought (but was instead dis-servicing it), the Panel found the US measure to be unnecessary (§§ 7.684ff. and especially 7.697 and 7.708ff.). The same report held that the fact that the requirement to demonstrate origin was imposed only on some products, but not others that might be characterized as DCS, was not demonstrative of the measure's protectionist intent; the necessity test does not include a consistency requirement across products. (§§ 7.682–683). Finally, the Panel held that, in interpreting the necessity-requirement in the TBT-context, it would be inspired by the case law interpretation of the same term in the GATT- and the SPS-context (§§ 7.667ff.).

The AB upheld this view. We quote § 378 from *US–COOL*, which reproduces § 322 of the AB report in *US–Tuna II (Mexico)*:

> [A]n assessment of whether a technical regulation is "more trade-restrictive than necessary" within the meaning of Article 2.2 of the *TBT Agreement* involves an evaluation of a number of factors. A panel should begin by considering factors that include: (i) the degree of contribution made by the measure to the legitimate objective at issue; (ii) the trade-restrictiveness of the measure; and (iii) the nature of the risks at issue and the gravity of consequences that would arise from non-fulfilment of the objective(s) pursued by the Member through the measure. In most cases, a comparison of the challenged measure and possible alternative measures should be undertaken. In particular, it may be relevant for the purpose of this comparison to consider whether the proposed alternative is less trade restrictive, whether it would make an equivalent contribution to the relevant legitimate objective, taking account of the risks non-fulfilment would create, and whether it is reasonably available. (footnote omitted)

4.2.4 Legitimate Objectives

The TBT includes an illustrative list of legitimate objectives: national security requirements; the prevention of deceptive practices; protection of human health or safety, animal or plant life or health, or the environment. Panels, when assessing similar risks, can take into account available scientific and technical information, related processing technology or the intended end-uses of products. WTO Members have of course the right to determine themselves the legitimate policies they want to pursue, and this is but an indicative list. In *US–Gasoline*, a case in which an American regulation of gasoline for environmental purposes was at issue, the AB noted (p. 29):

> WTO Members have a large measure of autonomy to determine their own policies on the environment (including its relationship with trade), their environmental objectives and the environmental legislation they enact and implement. So far as concerns the WTO, that autonomy is circumscribed only by the need to respect the requirements of the *General Agreement* and the other covered agreements. (italics in the original)[18]

A deferential attitude towards the regulating WTO Member is also evidenced in the Panel report in *US–COOL*. In this case, nevertheless, the Panel did impose a limit when finding that the regulating state could not be self-contradictory when pursuing objectives that it can unilaterally decide (§§ 7.611ff.). On appeal, the AB laid out the test to decide if an objective qualifies as legitimate (§ 372):

> With respect to the determination of the "legitimacy" of the objective, we note first that a panel's finding that the objective is among those listed in Article 2.2 will end the inquiry into its legitimacy. If, however, the objective does not fall among those specifically listed, a panel must make a determination of legitimacy. It may be guided by considerations that we have set out above, including whether the identified objective is reflected in other provisions of the covered agreements.

WTO Members are, by virtue of Art. 2.3 TBT, obliged to set aside technical regulations where the circumstances that gave rise to their adoption no longer exist. Technical regulations should, whenever feasible, be drafted in terms of performance requirements (Art. 2.8 TBT).[19]

---

[18] In *US–Clove Cigarettes*, the Panel held that banning clove cigarettes on allegedly public health grounds (reduce smoking by youth) should be upheld; it cautioned the complainant (Indonesia) that claims to the effect that the defendant acted in bad faith (enacted the law on grounds other than those invoked) are associated with a very demanding burden of persuasion (§§ 7.335ff.). In *US–Tuna II (Mexico)*, the Panel held that protection of animal life is not limited to endangered species only but to any animal irrespective whether it qualifies as endangered species or not (§ 7.437).

[19] In *US–Clove Cigarettes*, the Panel dismissed an argument by Indonesia to the effect that Art. 2.8 TBT required from WTO Members to provide a certain level of specificity. In its view, the only requirement there is to opt for performance requirements if appropriate (§§ 7.473ff.).

4.2.5 Transparency

The TBT Agreement also imposes certain procedural obligations on WTO Members enacting technical regulations. Except for cases of urgency, WTO Members are required to respect both *ex ante* and *ex post* transparency requirements when enacting technical regulations:

(a) Art. 2.5 TBT, and Art. 2.9 TBT impose on WTO Members an *ex ante* transparency obligation, namely a duty to notify the WTO of their upcoming technical regulations and upon request, provide a justification for them;[20]

(b) Art. 2.12 TBT requests from WTO Members to allow a "reasonable interval" between notification of their proposed technical regulation and its entry into force.[21] In *US–Clove Cigarettes*, the Panel found that a US decision to allow for an interval of three months only was in violation of this provision (§§ 7.563 ff.). To reach this conclusion, the Panel relied on a Decision by the TBT Committee[22] which had incorporated § 5.2 of the Doha Ministerial Decision which pertinently read in part: ". . . the phrase 'reasonable interval' shall be understood to mean normally a period of not less than 6 months, except when this would be ineffective in fulfilling the legitimate objectives pursued." In this Panel's view, the Doha Ministerial Decision was in line with Art. IX.2 of the WTO Agreement, in that it helped fill a gap in the original text, and hence, should be taken into account.[23] The notification requirement is less burdensome with respect to technical regulations adopted at the local government level or by non-governmental bodies (Art. 3.2 TBT): no notification is required if the content is substantially the same with that of previous notifications of the central authority;[24]

(c) Art. 10 TBT obliges WTO Members to establish enquiry points, through which interested parties can request information about the upcoming or already in force technical regulations;

---

[20] Failure to notify the list of products covered by a technical regulation by the US led the Panel in *US–Clove Cigarettes* to conclude that it had violated its obligations under Art. 2.9.2 TBT (§ 7.550).

[21] In *US–Clove Cigarettes* (§ 290), the AB produced the test for compliance with Art. 2.12 TBT: the complainant must show that the period is unreasonable; then burden shifts to regulator who will be asked to show that (a) an urgent situation reflected in Art. 2.10 TBT has arisen; (b) the producers of other WTO Members can adjust within a shorter period, or (c) a shorter period would be ineffective for the regulating state and would not allow it to reach its objectives.

[22] WTO Doc. G/TBT/1/Rev. 8 of May 23, 2002.

[23] The AB discussing the appeal against the Panel report in *US–Clove Cigarettes* endorsed the Panel's view upheld this view (§ 290).

[24] In exceptional circumstances, Art. 2.10 TBT explicitly exempts WTO Members from their obligations under Art. 2.9. In *US–Clove Cigarettes*, the Panel held that Art. 2.10 TBT can only be invoked as justification for deviations from obligations under Art. 2.9 TBT since, we quote 'we see no situation in which a WTO Member's actions would fall within the scope of both obligations at the same time' (§ 7.502).

(d) Finally, Art. 2.11 TBT imposes a publication requirement for all technical regulations adopted.

5. STANDARDS

The term "standard" is defined in Annex A to the TBT Agreement in the following manner:

> Document approved by a recognized body, that provides, for common and repeated use, rules, guidelines or characteristics for products or related processes and production methods, with which compliance is not mandatory. It may also include or deal exclusively with terminology, symbols, packaging, marking or labeling requirements as they apply to a product, process or production method.[25]

Nowadays, there is a variety of standards in fields ranging from toothbrushes to sustainable forest management. Standards can be national, or regional. Marx (2011) and Schepel (2005) discuss the significant increase in recent years in standard-setting which, as mentioned *supra*, covers a sizeable part of world trade: standards are set by standardizing bodies which can be at different levels of government (federal, local etc.), and even non-governmental. Art. 4.1 TBT states that WTO Members must ensure that their central government standardizing bodies are bound by the disciplines included in the Code of Good Practice which appears in Annex 3 of the TBT Agreement and to take all reasonable measures to ensure that local and/or non-governmental standardizing bodies adhere to it as well.[26]

Compliance with the Code of Good Practice amounts *ipso facto* to compliance with the principles of the TBT Agreement (Art. 4.2 TBT).

Included in the Code of Good Practice are both the non-discrimination and necessity principles. §§ D–E reads:

> In respect of standards, the standardizing body shall accord treatment to products originating in the territory of any other Member of the WTO no less favorable than that accorded to like products of national origin and to like products originating in any other country.
>
> The standardizing body shall ensure that standards are not prepared, adopted or applied with a view to, or with the effect of, creating unnecessary obstacles to international trade.

In addition, § F of the Code of Good Practice also commands WTO Members to adopt national standards on the basis of international stand-

---

[25] Sykes (1995) provides a comprehensive account.

[26] Standards are of course set by the market as well as for example, the Microsoft-experience has amply demonstrated.

ards when they exist or their completion is imminent, unless the international standards would be ineffective or inappropriate.

The Code of Good Practice also includes a series of provisions designed to foster transparency:

§ J: Standardizing bodies should publish at least once every 6 months their work programme;

§ L: WTO Members should allow 60 days, if possible, to lapse between adoption and entry into force of the standard;

§ M: *Ex ante* transparency is required in the sense that draft standards must be made available to interested parties to comment upon;

§ N: Comments received on draft standards should be, if appropriate, taken into account when drafting the final text;

§ O: All standards must be published;

§ P: Standardizing authorities should provide, if requested, information about their work programme.

Finally, the Code of Good Practice includes certain provisions, unique to the standards context, designed to encourage further creation of standards at the international level:

§ G: To further harmonization among nationally defined standards, (national) standardizing bodies are encouraged to participate in the work of international standardizing bodies;

§ H: National standardizing bodies should avoid duplication of the work done at the international level;

§ K: Standardizing bodies should join the ISONET (the ISO information network).

Standards can be issued as briefly mentioned above not only by recognized governmental bodies but also by private entities. We refer to the latter as "private standards". The question arises whether similar entities would have to respect (any of) the obligations embedded in the TBT Agreement. The question is highly relevant nowadays in light of the proliferation of private standards. Recall that under Art. 4.1 TBT, WTO Members:

> ... shall take such reasonable measures as may be available to them to ensure that local government and non-governmental standardizing bodies within their territories, as well as regional standardizing bodies of which they or one or more bodies within their territories are members, accept and comply with this Code of Good Practice. In addition, Members shall not take measures which have the effect of, directly or indirectly, requiring or encouraging such standardizing bodies to act in a manner inconsistent with the Code of Good Practice. The obligations of Members with respect to compliance of standardizing bodies with the

provisions of the Code of Good Practice shall apply irrespective of whether or not a standardizing body has accepted the Code of Good Practice.

During the Fifth Triennial Review, many WTO Members expressed their concern regarding the emergence of private standards and the ensuing obstacles to international trade. As a result, a plea for effective compliance with the Code of Good Practice was re-iterated.[27]

6. CONFORMITY ASSESSMENT

Conformity assessment is defined in § 3 of Annex 1 to the TBT Agreement as follows:

> Any procedure used, directly or indirectly, to determine that relevant requirements in technical regulations or standards are fulfilled.
>
> *Explanatory note*
>
> Conformity assessment procedures include, *inter alia*, procedures for sampling, testing and inspection; evaluation, verification and assurance of conformity; registration, accreditation and approval as well as their combinations.

Arts. 5–7 TBT contain the basic obligations that must be assumed by "central government bodies" which must be applied to "local government bodies", "non-governmental bodies" and "international and regional systems", by virtue of Arts. 7–9 TBT. All these terms are defined in Annex 1 to the TBT as follows:

> § 4 International body or system
>
> Body or system whose membership is open to the relevant bodies of at least all Members.
>
> § 5 Regional body or system
>
> Body or system whose membership is open to the relevant bodies of only some of the Members.
>
> § 6 Central government body
>
> Central government, its ministries and departments or any body subject to the control of the central government in respect of the activity in question.
>
> > Explanatory note:
> >
> > In the case of the European Communities the provisions governing central government bodies apply. However, regional bodies or conformity assessment systems may be es-

---

[27] WTO Doc. G/TBT/13 at § 25.

tablished within the European Communities, and in such cases would be subject to the provisions of this Agreement on regional bodies or conformity assessment systems.

§ 7 Local government body

Government other than a central government (e.g. states, provinces, Länder, cantons, municipalities, etc.), its ministries or departments or any body subject to the control of such a government in respect of the activity in question.

§ 8 Non-governmental body

Body other than a central government body or a local government body, including a non-governmental body which has legal power to enforce a technical regulation.

Whereas WTO Members must ensure that central government bodies behave in accordance with the TBT Agreement described above when performing conformity assessment (Art. 6 TBT), they are expected to only take reasonable measures available to them in order to ensure that local- and non-government bodies behave in similar manner: Art. 22.9 DSU is clear in this respect. WTO Members are free to design their own conformity assessment-procedures, which must respect the necessity-requirement, in the sense that they should not be more trade-restrictive than what is required to achieve their objective (Art. 5.1.2 TBT); they must further be published (Art. 5.8 TBT), and explained in detail to interested parties (Art. 5.2 and 5.6 TBT). Once they have enacted their conformity assessment procedures, they must provide interested WTO Members with access to them. Art. 5.1.1 TBT reads:

> WTO Members are obliged to give access to foreign suppliers to their facilities, under the same conditions applied to domestic producers, to have the conformity of their products with the technical regulation or standard at hand assessed.[28]

Conformity assessment can be performed in relation to specific products, or in relation to the activity of conformity assessment. Products will be typically tested in laboratories, inspected by inspection bodies, and certified by certification bodies. Metrological and accreditation bodies will review the activities performed by laboratories, inspection- and certification bodies. The ISO/IEC have developed a glossary of the various procedures and activities related to conformity assessment. Two highly relevant examples are the ISO Committee on Conformity Assessment (CASCO), and the ISO/IEC Guide 2 (1991)[29] Conformity assessment for prod-

---

[28] In practice, reference is also made to 'legal metrology', that is, the regulatory requirements for measurements and measuring instruments: it aims to ensure the appropriate quality and credibility of measurements related to official controls in the areas of health, safety and the environment, see Lesser (2007).

[29] ISO/IEC 17000, International Standard, ISO 2004, Geneva.

ucts can be performed by the producer itself (called "first party assessment"), the purchaser or a conformity assessment body on its behalf ("second party assessment"), or a body independent from both the producer and the purchaser ('third party assessment').

When it comes to testing of products itself, the ISO/IEC Guide 2 distinguishes between the following activities:

- Sampling
- Testing
- Inspection
- Evaluation of conformity
- Verification of conformity
- Assurance of conformity
- Certification
- Supplier's declaration of certification
- Approval
- Registration

When it comes to procedures in relation to the activity of conformity assessment, the ISO/IEC guide 2 distinguishes between the following activities:

- Accreditation (of an entity entrusted to carry out tasks relating to conformity assessment);
- Registration (of an accredited entity);
- Metrology (i.e., science of measurement).

This last point deserves some additional explanation: In fact, all sorts of issues can affect conformity assessment. Some are counter-intuitive, such as, say, the expression of weight in kilograms and pounds.[30] This is why the Convention du Mètre established the "Bureau International des Poids et des Mesures" (International Bureau of Weights and Measures). This intergovernmental organization today has 55 members and 34 associate members, and its mandate is to provide the basis for a single, coherent system of measurements throughout the world.

The need for cooperation in this area is evident, but then again cooperation requires some sort of acceptance of each other's standard. There is a specific provision dealing with recognition (and we discuss it in the next sub-section). Beyond recognition, the TBT Agreement aims to contribute to increasing the quality of standards worldwide and also the technical capacity regarding conformity assessment procedures. The TBT Committee has organized a number of events aiming at developing technical ca-

---

[30] De Bièvre et al. (2011).

pacity in this area especially among those in need for expertise.[31] Moreover, the TBT Agreement specifically refers to "accreditation" as means to verify the competence of entities entrusted with conformity assessment in the exporting WTO Member (Art. 6.1.1). Assuming this can be achieved, transaction costs regarding conformity assessment are substantially reduced. Similar agreements however, are usually signed across WTO Members with similar levels of development. Accreditation bodies are working towards harmonizing international practices in this context. WTO Members are, more generally, encouraged to participate in the work of international bodies aiming at harmonizing conformity assessment procedures (Art. 5.5 TBT) or to opt for recognition that we discuss immediately after.

WTO Members must also use relevant guides and recommendations issued by international standardizing bodies as basis for the elaboration of their conformity assessment procedures (Art. 5.4 TBT). This obligation kicks in if positive assurance is required that products conform to technical regulations or standards and relevant guides or recommendations by international standardizing bodies exist. A WTO Member may deviate from this obligation if the guides or recommendations are "inappropriate". The last sentence of this provision (Art. 5.4 TBT) includes an indicative list of what might constitute an "inappropriate" guide or recommendation:

- Prevention of deceptive practices;
- Protection of environment;
- National security;
- Protection of human health or safety;
- Fundamental problems regarding infrastructure;
- Climatic factors;
- Technological problems.

This list will be completed over the years through the notifications-system established through the TBT Agreement. WTO members notifying a conformity assessment procedure must indicate the objective sought as well as the rationale for it (Arts. 5.62, and 5.7.1 TBT). Eventually, thanks to similar notifications, the WTO Membership will have a more complete picture regarding instances where guides and recommendations issued by standardizing bodies are considered "inappropriate".[32]

Over the years, conformity assessment procedures have been streamlined. OECD (2000) concluded that deregulation of the approval process

---

[31] See for example, WTO Docs. G/TBT/9 of November 13, 2000; G/TBT/M/33/Add.1 of October 21, 2004; G/TBT/35 of May 24, 2005; and G/TBT/38/Add. 1 of June 6, 2006.

[32] The TBT Committee established in 1996 a 'Technical Working Group on ISO/IEC Guides Relating to Articles 5 and 6 of the Agreement' (WTO Doc. G/TBT/M/6 of December 6, 1996 at § 14); it met three times in 1998 and the basic conclusions were compiled in a document (WTO Doc. G/TBT/W/43). The work and relevance of the ISO/IEC Guides has been discussed in every Triennial Review so far, see for example WTO Doc. G/TBT/26 of November 13, 2009.

has led to increasing competition across approving agencies and thus, decreasing costs of approvals. The contribution by the TBT Committee in this respect should not be underestimated. Through its forum on 'good regulatory practice' it has significantly promoted rational behavior when it comes to regulating areas coming under the mandate of the TBT Agreement.

7. RECOGNITION

WTO Members are encouraged to recognize each other's technical regulations as equivalent (Art. 2.7 TBT). Recognition could be unilateral, or two (or more) WTO Members could sign a mutual recognition agreement (MRA) regarding the manner in which conformity with technical regulations can be assessed. In fact, WTO Members are encouraged to sign MRAs (Art. 6.3 TBT). Entering into an MRA usually entails that the products of the exporting state do not have to undergo conformity assessment in the importing state in order to ensure that they meet the relevant regulatory requirements. Any time an MRA has been agreed, any WTO Member which takes the view that it can comply with its requirements can legitimately request that it benefits from its extension: it will of course, have to assume the burden to prove equivalence between its own regulation and that of the MRA-partners. WTO Members must provide recognition if they are satisfied that conformity with applicable technical regulations and/or standard in another WTO Members is equivalent to their own (Art. 6.1 TBT). This provision deals only with recognition by central government bodies, and mentions "equivalence" not "equation." Hence what matters is not absolute identity between two procedures but whether conformity has been achieved to the satisfaction of the recognizing WTO Member. WTO Members are encouraged to enter into consultations in order to achieve equivalence (Art. 6.1.1 TBT).

The WTO must be notified of all MRAs (Art. 10.7 TBT). More than a hundred agreements have been notified so far. The TBT Committee, in its Fourth Triennial Review, discussed some of the many reasons why agreements are being signed almost exclusively across "like-minded" countries. Among the reasons highlighted by the TBT Committee are concerns about differences in development levels and the lower (opportunity) cost of negotiating similar agreements, etc.[33]

Recognition can also take place on voluntary basis. In this vein, Art. 9.2 TBT is relevant, and it reads:

> Members shall take such reasonable measures as may be available to them to ensure that international and regional systems for conformity assessment in which relevant bodies within their territories are members or participants comply with the provisions

---

[33] WTO Doc. G/TBT/19 at § 39.

of Articles 5 and 6. In addition, Members shall not take any measures which have the effect of, directly or indirectly, requiring or encouraging such systems to act in a manner inconsistent with any of the provisions of Articles 5 and 6.

8. SPECIAL AND DIFFERENTIAL TREATMENT FOR DEVELOPING COUNTRIES

Developed WTO Members must:

(a) By virtue of Art. 11 TBT assist developing countries in the preparation of technical regulations, standards etc.;

(b) By virtue of Art. 12 TBT take account of the special development, financial and trade needs of developing country Members when enacting technical regulations, standards and conformity assessment procedures, with a view to ensuring that they do not create unnecessary obstacles to the exports of developing countries. The same Article explains that WTO Members should not expect developing countries to base their own technical regulations or standards on international standards, if the latter are not necessarily conducive to their development needs.

In *US–Clove Cigarettes*, the Panel held that the fact that Indonesia had raised its concerns before the US authorities adopting a technical regulation, and the fact that key officials in the US government had debated the concerns raised was enough for the US to be deemed in compliance with its obligations under this provision, even though at the end it did not endorse any of them (§§ 7.644 ff.).

9. INSTITUTIONAL ISSUES

Art. 13 TBT established a TBT Committee that is entrusted with the responsibility to overview the operation of the Agreement. The TBT Committee is quite unique across the other WTO Committees in some respects: Participation in the Committee is often entrusted to technical experts (often with scientific expertise) and not to typical trade delegates. Its mandate extends to a variety of issues; and it has been quite successful both in advancing the "lawmaking" agenda, as well as in settling disputes.[34] In the context of the TBT, initiatives have been taken to reduce the problems posed on international trade as a result of regulatory diversity across WTO Members. Pursuant to Art. 15.3 TBT, the TBT Committee has been conducting annual reviews discussing implementation of transparency provisions (notifications), technical assistance, and disputes involving the TBT Agreement. As of the end of the first three years, and at the end of every following three year-period, it has been conducting a review with the aim of proposing any necessary adjustments to the TBT

---

[34] Horn et al. (2012).

Agreement. The Triennial Reviews are conducted with a view to (Art. 15.4 TBT):

> Recommending an adjustment of the rights and obligations of this Agreement where necessary to ensure mutual economic advantage and balance of rights and obligations, without prejudice to the provisions of Article 12.[35]

The TBT Committee, in its Fourth Triennial Review of the Operation and Implementation of the TBT Agreement issued a report[36] in which, *inter alia*, it advanced the following priorities:

> (a) Good regulatory practice (in the sense that a decision whether there is need to regulate should always precede a decision to regulate) must be encouraged;
>
> (b) The use of Supplier's Declaration of Conformity (SDoc) should also be encouraged in order to avoid unnecessary costs with respect to conformity assessment;
>
> (c) Unilateral recognition of results of foreign conformity assessment (Art. 6.1 TBT) should also take place more frequently, if possible, as should participation of foreign conformity assessment bodies in domestic conformity assessment procedures (Art. 6.4 TBT); finally,
>
> (d) The document supports the conclusion of MRAs, and notes the conclusion of voluntary MRAs between domestic and foreign conformity assessment bodies (individual laboratories, certification and inspection bodies.

Discussions on good regulatory practice continued in the Fifth Triennial Review.[37] Discussions also have been initiated regarding "regulatory cooperation" across WTO Members, which is defined as follows:

> Regulatory cooperation between Members is, in essence, about reducing *unnecessary* regulatory diversity; it is also about limiting the costs associated with *necessary* regulatory diversity. Regulatory cooperation is premised on the notion that it is possible to remove unnecessary regulatory diversity without preventing Members from achieving their legitimate policy objectives. When fruitful, cooperation between Members—in various forms and configurations—can contribute to the reduction of unnecessary barriers to trade. (emphasis in the original)[38]

Regulatory cooperation is actively promoted by the WTO TBT Committee. Some of it of course, already exists embedded in various TBT pro-

---

[35] Recall that this provision deals with special and differential treatment for developing countries.

[36] WTO Doc. G/TBT/19 of November 14, 2006. For a more recent report on this score, see WTO Doc. G/TBT/26.

[37] WTO Doc. G/TBT/13 of November 13, 2009.

[38] WTO Doc. G/TBT/W/340.

visions such as international standards, equivalence, conformity assessment etc. Some cooperation already takes place at regional level such as the FTA between China and New Zealand, or the regulatory cooperation schemes between Australia and New Zealand, and between the EU and the US. The latter has already been discussed extensively in the TBT Committee[39] and focuses on three issues: the "Regulatory Cooperation Roadmap"(sector-specific agreements on a series of goods such as autos, drugs and medical devices); the US Office of Management and Budget (OMB) and EU Commission dialogue on good regulatory practices (transparency, impact assessment, etc.); and, the Regulatory Cooperation Forum (senior-level meetings on issues such as new technology, safety of goods etc.). The discussions take place under the aegis of the Transatlantic Economic Council (TEC), a body established to direct economic cooperation between the EU and the US.

On the other hand, a number of disputes, aptly named "specific trade concerns" (STCs) are routinely submitted to the TBT Committee. So far, over 300 hundred have been submitted.[40] Based on these submissions, the following may be observed:

- The majority of STCs concern requests for further clarification, followed by claims of non-compliance with the necessity-requirement, transparency-related claims, and the use of international standards.
- Of the claims, technical regulations are the most often challenged instrument followed by conformity assessment procedures.
- Approximately two-thirds of all STCs have been raised once or twice before the TBT Committee; a quarter of them have been raised 3–5 times; and 12% have been raised more than 5 times.
- Public health, environmental protection, and the prevention of deceptive practices are the three stated objectives of the instruments most often challenged.
- 39% of all measures challenged originate in the Asia–Pacific, 25% in the EU, 16% in Latin America, 15% in North America, 11,4% in the Middle East and 3% in Africa.[41]

The fact that only a handful of the submitted STCs have reached the Panel-stage is testimony of the good work at the Committee-level that has managed to resolve the majority of them.[42]

---

[39] WTO Doc. G/TBT/W/287 of March 11, 2008.

[40] The TBT Committee will periodically issue documents that refer to all of them, see for example, WTO Doc. G/TBT/29 of March 8, 2011.

[41] WTO Doc. G/TBT/GEN/74/Rev. 8 of June 1, 2011.

[42] Horn et al. (2013) discuss in detail the record in this respect. Lang and Scott (2009) discuss the works of the TBT Committee in more comprehensive manner, and not simply its activities relating to settlement of disputes.

The WTO Secretariat has, in concert with WTO Members, taken active steps to provide much needed transparency with respect to measures coming under the purview of the TBT Agreement. Most notable is the establishment of the TBT Information Management System (TBT IMS)[43] which allows users to obtain information on measures notified to the TBT Committee, on conformity assessment procedures, enquiry points etc.

A Panel adjudicating a dispute coming under the TBT Agreement may, at the request of a party or on its own initiative, establish an expert group to assist it on issues of technical nature (Art. 14.2 TBT). Annex 2 to the TBT Agreement sets out in detail the procedure to be followed on this score. The mandate of TBT-experts is thus limited to questions of technical nature only. So far, nevertheless, Panels have not made use of this opportunity.

QUESTIONS AND COMMENTS

Cost Shifting: Staiger and Sykes (2011) show how "large" nations may have an incentive to impose discriminatory product standards against imported goods once border instruments are constrained and how inefficiently stringent standards may emerge under certain circumstances even if regulatory discrimination is prohibited. It follows that economic operators established in large, lucrative markets will, other things equal, enjoy an advantage that those exporting to their market will have to pay for.

Political Economy of International Standards: There is an increasing political economy literature discussing standard setting in similar bodies. Domestic standard-setting institutions will try to influence standard-setting at the international level and promote national choices. Büthe and Mattli (2011, pp. 11ff.) got it probably right when arguing that technical expertise is necessary but not sufficient conditions in the quest for preeminence in international standard setting bodies; it is 'timely information and effective representation of domestic interest that confer the critical advantage in these regulatory processes, determining who wins and who loses'.

***EC–Sardines* and International Standards**: Horn and Weiler (2007), in our view, have validly criticized the approach of the AB. They question whether, in light of the current allocation of the burden of proof, traders will have the incentive to be forthcoming when it comes to providing information regarding their standards; arguably, they will have an incentive to be circumspect. In this vein, they question whether it is possible at all for the complainant to know why the defendant took the view that the international standard was ineffective or inappropriate: this could be classic case of private information and in light of the incentives described above, could remain private for some time. Curiously though, the AB's construction of Art. 2.4 TBT does not put into question the legitimacy of international standards: the very

---

[43] Available at http://tbtims.wto.org.

low burden of persuasion imposed on Peru is the reason. Quoting from Horn and Weiler (2007):

> In the dispute Peru submitted evidence suggesting that "sardines" by itself or combined with the name of a country or region is a common name for *Sardinops sagax* in the EC. Peru here referred to three dictionaries/publications, two of which produced in cooperation with, or with support by, the European Commission, and one prepared by the OECD. But it should be noted that this evidence does not directly show that consumers would not confuse *Sarinops sagax*, if labeled as "Peruvian Sardines", with *Sardina pilchardus*. On the contrary, it might perhaps be argued that the existence of these lexica suggests that the classification of fish is not a simple matter, and that consequently there are reasons to suspect that consumers might be confused about the different species of fish. Hence, it is strictly speaking not clear what these publications say about consumer perceptions.

Technical Regulation: Do you agree with the definition of the term by the AB in *US–Tuna II (Mexico)*? If yes, what would be the impact of this definition on the understanding of the term 'standard'?

Less Favorable Treatment: In *US–COOL*, the Panel evaluated econometric evidence in order to reach the conclusion that *de facto* discrimination had been afforded to imported goods, e.g., that imported goods were granted LFT than domestic like goods in contravention of Art. 2.1 TBT. The question before the Panel was whether certain country of origin labeling requirements on meat and meat products imposed additional costs on imports. An econometrics study (by Informa Economics, a consultancy) had been submitted to the Panel, which found that costs were indeed being imposed on foreign goods that did not have to be bore by domestic goods: this was the case because, in the Panel's view, imported goods had to face higher segregation costs (corresponding to costs associated with verification of the origin of the various stage of production of beef). The Panel refused to accept the reliability of the study, since in its words it (§ 7.499):

> is silent on its methodology and the sample considered.

The complainants submitted another study prepared by Prof. Sumner (University of California at Davis). Sumner had compared Canadian meat prices and market shares in two scenarios: one where COOL requirements were present, and one where they were not; he found that US retailers were willing to pay significantly less for Canadian meat in the first scenario, simply because of the ensuing compliance costs with the COOL-requirements. In his view, this was the reason why the market share for Canadian meat had been reduced. There were also other studies submitted estimating the impact of the COOL requirements on imports by both the US (Department of Agriculture) and Canada (Sumner): these studies reached opposite results. The Panel made it clear that it was going to limit its review of the case to the econometrics expertise already supplied, and that it was not going to request its own expertise as it could have done by virtue of Art. 13 DSU. In this vein, the Panel held that that the study prepared by Sumner made a *prima facie* case that the request to comply with the COOL requirements resulted in de facto discrimination. In its words, the study (§ 7.542):

> makes a prima facie case that the COOL measure negatively and significantly affected the import shares and price basis of Canadian livestock.

In its view, the study submitted by the US was not sufficiently robust and as a result did not refute the prima facie case established by Sumner's study (§ 7.543–545):

> In fact, the 13 estimated equations for the cattle analysis do not show sufficient consistency to reach a robust conclusion. According to the USDA Econometric study, the COOL variable and its impact are never significant. However, the impact of economic recession is only negative and significant in a limited number of specifications and even in those cases only at a relatively low level of precision, i.e. at a 90% instead of the usual 95% level of confidence. This means that the USDA Econometric Study does not provide a sufficiently robust explanation that any negative impact is attributable to economic recession rather than to the COOL measure. In addition, any finding of the USDA Econometric Study with regard to the economic recession variable and its impact is called into question by potential multicollinearity, which the study failed to address.
>
> As regards hogs, the USDA Econometric Study merely refers to certain features of the hog market, i.e. US-based pricing and Canadian hog's inventory decline, but this cannot substitute for a proper and robust econometric analysis.
>
> Hence, the USDA Econometric Study does not rebut the prima facie case for a negative and significant COOL impact established by the Sumner Econometric Study.

CHAPTER 20

SANITARY AND PHYTO–SANITARY MEASURES

■ ■ ■

1. THE LEGAL DISCIPLINE

The Agreement on Sanitary and Phytosanitary Measures (SPS Agreement) deals with measures to ensure food safety, to prevent the entry of pests and other disease-carrying organisms, and to regulate the risks from additives, contaminants, and toxins. Each WTO Member is allowed to set its own standards and regulations, but must do so in a way that does not constitute an arbitrary or unjustifiable discrimination on trade.

The SPS Agreement encourages WTO Members to use international standards, guidelines, and recommendations, where they exist, to set their rules and regulations. A WTO Member may establish its own SPS measure provided it is: (a) non-discriminatory, (b) based on scientific evidence; (c) necessary to achieve the stated objective; and (d) consistent with other SPS measures adopted by the WTO Member. In instances where there is scientific uncertainty, a WTO Member is allowed to apply a SPS measure based on a "precautionary" principle, provided certain steps are taken to ensure that this measure is temporary and that steps are being taken to resolve the uncertainty.

Therefore, the legal discipline governing a SPS measure differs, depending upon the category under which it falls. These include SPS measures:

- based on international standards;
- that justifiably deviate from an international standard and result in a higher level of protection;
- established where no international standard exists;
- based on a precautionary principle

We will discuss the law as it applies for each of these categories of SPS measures.

2. THE RATIONALE FOR THE LEGAL DISCIPLINE

The SPS Agreement seeks to ensure that regulations are not used as an excuse for protectionism. This is achieved, *inter alia*, through an emphasis on relying upon internationally agreed-upon standards and scientific evidence.

Scientific evidence at the domestic level can serve as some sort of buffer against political economy type of pressure.[1] This is why it has been included as a requirement upon which SPS measures must be based, if they are to deviate from an international standard or in instances where no such standard exists.[2]

3. COVERAGE

3.1 THE RELATIONSHIP WITH THE GATT AND THE TBT

The relationship between TBT and SPS is regulated in Art. 1.5 TBT: SPS takes precedence over TBT. As to the relationship between SPS and GATT, our discussion in the previous Chapter regarding the relationship between TBT and the GATT is applicable here as well. Therefore, it follows that SPS takes precedence over TBT which takes precedence over GATT.

3.2 SCOPE OF MEASURES COVERED

Annex A to the SPS Agreement defines SPS measures as follows:

Any measure applied:

(a) to protect animal or plant life or health within the territory of the Member from risks arising from the entry, establishment or spread of pests, diseases, disease-carrying organisms or disease-causing organisms;

(b) to protect human or animal life or health within the territory of the Member from risks arising from additives, contaminants, toxins or disease-causing organisms in foods, beverages or feedstuffs;

(c) to protect human life or health within the territory of the Member from risks arising from diseases carried by animals, plants or products thereof, or from the entry, establishment or spread of pests; or

(d) to prevent or limit other damage within the territory of the Member from the entry, establishment or spread of pests.

---

[1] But on occasion, it can also serve as means for pressure when the holder of scientific evidence requests regulation in accordance with say its patent.

[2] In the TBT-context, available scientific information is relevant in assessing the risk resulting from non-fulfillment of a legitimate objective mentioned in Art. 2.2 TBT; there is nevertheless, no obligation to base technical regulations or standards on science.

> Sanitary or phytosanitary measures include all relevant laws, decrees, regulations, requirements and procedures including, *inter alia*, end product criteria; processes and production methods; testing, inspection, certification and approval procedures; quarantine treatments including relevant requirements associated with the transport of animals or plants, or with the materials necessary for their survival during transport; provisions on relevant statistical methods, sampling procedures and methods of risk assessment; and packaging and labelling requirements directly related to food safety.

In *Australia–Apples*, New Zealand challenged an Australian measure aimed to protect apples from "fire blight and apple leafcurling midge" (ALCM). At the outset, the AB discussed whether the Australian measure was suitably understood as SPS-measure, holding (§ 173):

> Whether a measure is "applied . . . to protect" in the sense of Annex A(1)(a) must be ascertained not only from the objectives of the measure as expressed by the responding party, but also from the text and structure of the relevant measure, its surrounding regulatory context, and the way in which it is designed and applied. For any given measure to fall within the scope of Annex A(1)(a), scrutiny of such circumstances must reveal a clear and objective relationship between that measure and the specific purposes enumerated in Annex A(1)(a).

The Panel in *EC–Approval and Marketing of Biotech Products*,[3] held that the purpose of an SPS measure can be expressed in terms of requirement, or in terms of a procedure that should be followed (§ 7.149).

As is the case under the TBT Agreement, WTO Members can either use international standards, or proceed unilaterally and enact their own SPS measures. However, unlike the TBT Agreement, no distinction is made between technical regulations and standards.

Also, as is the case with the GATT, only measures attributable to a government can come under the purview of the SPS Agreement. However, WTO Members are required to take reasonable measures to ensure that bodies other than governmental bodies will also observe the SPS Agreement (Art. 13 SPS).[4]

---

[3] This case dealt with an EU moratorium that would severely hamper, if not prohibit altogether the marketing and commercialization of genetically modifies organisms (GMOs) in the EU market. It did not contain any revelations regarding the construction of case law, but did manage to occupy literature because of the manner in which it understood the relationship between WTO-and public international law. See the contributions by Broude (2007), Conrad (2007), Davies (2007), Footer (2007), Howse and Horn (2009), and Perez (2007).

[4] This provision is reminiscent of the federal clause embedded in Art. XXIV.12 GATT. Assuming the case law there applies here *mutatis mutandis*, one should expect that WTO Members will be acting in accordance with this provision by adhering to their constitutional powers.

3.3 KEY QUESTIONS IN EXAMINING A SPS MEASURE

Once it has been determined that a particular government measure qualifies as a SPS measure under WTO law, the next issue is to determine the provisions of the SPS Agreement that apply. To that end, we suggest that it helps to understand the answers to two sets of questions in the context of the SPS measure being examined:

(a) Is there an international standard that is applicable? If so, does the SPS measure deviate from the international standard?

(b) Is there sufficient scientific evidence regarding the existence and extent of the relevant risk that the SPS measure seeks to mitigate?

Based on the answers to the first set of questions, we divide SPS measures into those which are based on international standards and those which are undertaken "unilaterally" either because no international standard exists or because a WTO Member chooses to deviate from that standard. Of the unilateral SPS measures, a sub-category exists based on the answer to the second question—these are "precautionary" SPS measures undertaken in instances of insufficient scientific evidence. In what follows, we will examine each of the legal requirements with respect to each of these categories in turn.

4. SPS MEASURES BASED ON INTERNATIONAL STANDARDS

4.1 THE PRIMACY OF INTERNATIONAL STANDARDS

As is the case under the TBT Agreement, where an international standard exists, WTO Members must use that international standard, assuming it is effective and appropriate and will thus help them reach their objectives. Art. 3.1 SPS reads to this effect:

> Members shall base their sanitary or phytosanitary measures on international standards, guidelines or recommendations, where they exist, except as otherwise provided for in this Agreement, and in particular in paragraph 3.

The AB in *EC–Hormones (US)*[5] had the opportunity to explain its understanding of the rationale for Art. 3.1 SPS (§ 177):

> ... In generalized terms, the object and purpose of Article 3 is to promote the harmonization of the SPS measures of Members on as wide a basis as possible, while recognizing and safeguarding, at the same time, the right and duty of Members to protect the life and health of their people. The ultimate goal of the harmonization of SPS measures is to prevent the use of such measures

---

[5] This case concerned a sales ban on hormone treated beef imposed by the EU which affected largely US exports of beef where cows are often subjected to growth hormones.

for arbitrary or unjustifiable discrimination between Members or as a disguised restriction on international trade, without preventing Members from adopting or enforcing measures which are both "necessary to protect" human life or health and "based on scientific principles", and without requiring them to change their appropriate level of protection.

In the same case, the AB held that the term "based on", appearing in Art. 3.1 SPS, does not impose on WTO Members a requirement of absolute conformity between the regulatory intervention and the relevant international standard; rather, WTO Members, when basing their interventions on an international standard, still retain the discretion to use some (and not other) elements included in it. The EU in that case had banned the sale of hormone-treated beef (both domestic and imported) on the ground that such beef was dangerous to human health. However, the EU regulation contravened a relevant international standard that had been adopted to this effect. The AB had to address the extent to which the EU was required to shape its SPS measure in absolute conformity with the relevant international standard. It disagreed with the Panel, which had held that absolute conformity was required (§ 177). In reaching this conclusion, the AB took the view that the intention of the parties (the framers of the SPS Agreement) was not to vest international standards with broad powers such as to require absolute conformity between them, on the one hand, and national SPS measures, on the other (§ 165). The AB nevertheless did not cite any preparatory work to support its view.

There is a statutory presumption that international standards respect the necessity-requirement (Art. 3.2 SPS). In *EC–Hormones (US)*, the AB specified that the presumption of conformity established by Art. 3.2 SPS is rebuttable (§ 170). There is no case so far where this presumption has been defeated.

4.2 WHO ISSUES INTERNATIONAL STANDARDS?

The SPS Agreement, in parallel with the TBT Agreement, does not provide a definition to evaluate which standards are acknowledged as international standards.

However, in contrast to the TBT Agreement, the SPS Agreement does explicitly identify several standard-setting institutions under Art. 3.4 SPS. These institutions include the Codex Alimentarius Commission, the International Office of Epozootics, and the International Plant Protection Convention. Standards set forth by these organizations are explicitly deemed international standards. This list of institutions is an indicative list. That is to say, standards originating in institutions other than those mentioned in Art. 3.4 SPS can be recognized as international standards as well.

Annex A, § 3 SPS pertinently reads:

(a) For food safety, the standards, guidelines and recommendations established by the Codex Alimentarius Commission relating to food additives, veterinary drug and pesticide residues, contaminants, methods of analysis and sampling, and codes and guidelines of hygienic practice;

(b) For animal health and zoonoses, the standards, guidelines and recommendations developed under the auspices of the International Office of Epizootics;

(c) For plant health, the international standards, guidelines and recommendations developed under the auspices of the Secretariat of the International Plant Protection Convention in cooperation with regional organizations operating within the framework of the International Plant Protection Convention; and

(d) For matters not covered by the above organizations, appropriate standards, guidelines and recommendations promulgated by other relevant international organizations open for membership to all Members, as identified by the Committee."

The SPS Committee can identify which other standards by which institutions are relevant as well.[6]

4.3 DEVIATING FROM INTERNATIONAL STANDARDS

Recall that Art. 3.1 SPS makes explicit reference to Art. 3.3 SPS, in allowing for WTO Members to deviate from an international standard. Art. 3.3 SPS reads:

Members may introduce or maintain sanitary or phytosanitary measures which result in a higher level of sanitary or phytosanitary protection than would be achieved by measures based on the relevant international standards, guidelines or recommendations, if there is a scientific justification, or as a consequence of the level of sanitary or phytosanitary protection a Member determines to be appropriate in accordance with the relevant provisions of paragraphs 1 through 8 of Article 5. Notwithstanding the above, all measures which result in a level of sanitary or phytosanitary protection different from that which would be achieved by measures based on international standards, guidelines or recommendations shall not be inconsistent with any other provision of this Agreement.

A footnote to this provision reads:

---

[6] At the time of writing, no other institution has been identified by the SPS Committee. The door is, of course, always open. Eventually, one could see, for example, the International Health Regulations of the WHO, or the Cartagena Protocol coming under the purview of Annex A § 3(d). Panels as well, in the absence of action by the WTO SPS committee, have the inherent power to identify institutions in this context.

> For the purposes of paragraph 3 of Article 3, there is a scientific justification if, on the basis of an examination and evaluation of available scientific information in conformity with the relevant provisions of this Agreement, a Member determines that the relevant international standards, guidelines or recommendations are not sufficient to achieve its appropriate level of sanitary or phytosanitary protection.

In short, deviation can occur if:

> (a) WTO Members may choose a level of sanitary or phyto-sanitary protection higher than that provided for in the international standard if there is scientific justification to this effect; or
>
> (b) Following risk assessment (Art. 5 SPS), a WTO Member decides on its appropriate level of protection and this is different from that provided for in the international standard.

Whereas Art. 3.3 SPS clearly indicates that a WTO Member must comply with Art. 5 SPS whenever it has recourse to option (b), no similar obligation is imposed when recourse to option (a) is made. However, the last sentence of Art. 3.3 SPS requires that in case of a deviation from an international standard, irrespective of whether recourse is made to option (a) or (b), WTO Members must ensure consistency with the other provisions of the SPS Agreement. The question arose in *EC–Hormones (US)* whether a WTO Member still needed to perform a risk assessment when choosing option (a). The AB responded in the affirmative (§§ 175 and 177).

The question who bears the burden of proof when the regulating state has deviated from an international standard was first discussed in the SPS-context and it is this case law that inspired the ruling in *EC–Sardines*. The Panel in *EC–Hormones (US)* had originally found that the burden rested with the deviating party (the EU) to prove that its deviation from the relevant international standard was justified under the SPS (§§ 8.86ff.). The AB disagreed and reversed this finding. In its view, WTO Members that choose not to use an international standard should not be penalized for their decision to do so (§ 102). Therefore, it held, it is up to the complainant to establish that the regulating Member could have attained its objectives by sticking to the international standard, and that, consequently, no need for deviation was warranted (§§ 104 and 172).

5. UNILATERAL SPS MEASURES

If a WTO Member decides to deviate from an international standard, or if no international standard exists, then it can adopt a unilateral SPS measure. Such SPS measures must, in principle, be:

(a) Non-discriminatory;
(b) Based on scientific evidence;
(c) Necessary to achieve the stated objective; and

(d) Consistent (with other SPS measures adopted by the same WTO Member).

These four requirements must be cumulatively met. Failure to meet any one of these conditions will lead to a SPS measure to be deemed WTO-inconsistent. We will examine all these requirements one by one in what follows.

5.1 NON–DISCRIMINATION

WTO Members must, by virtue of Art. 2.3 SPS, respect non-discrimination when adopting SPS measures:

> Members shall ensure that their sanitary and phytosanitary measures do not arbitrarily or unjustifiably discriminate between Members where identical or similar conditions prevail, including between their own territory and that of other Members. Sanitary and phytosanitary measures shall not be applied in a manner which would constitute a disguised restriction on international trade.

The terms "like product" or "less favorable treatment" that we have encountered in numerous provisions regarding non-discrimination are missing here. This provision is reminiscent of the chapeau of Art. XX GATT and a similar test should apply here as well. This point of view is strengthened by the fact that Art. 2.4 SPS makes explicit reference to Art. XX(b) GATT: it states that SPS measures conforming to the SPS Agreement shall be deemed to be in accordance with Art. XX(b) GATT as well. Although case law has not developed this point any further, the presumption of legality established here seems to be irrebuttable.

5.2 SCIENTIFIC EVIDENCE[7]

Art. 2.2 SPS reads:

> Members shall ensure that any sanitary or phytosanitary measure is applied only to the extent necessary to protect human, animal or plant life or health, is based on scientific principles and is not maintained without sufficient scientific evidence, except as provided for in paragraph 7 of Article 5.[8]

In *EC–Hormones (US)*, the AB held that this provision must be read in tandem with Art. 5.1 SPS, which provides for the obligation to ensure that SPS measures are based on risk assessment (§ 250). These two provisions, according to the AB, aim to strike the appropriate balance between the interest to promote world trade, and the interest to protect life

---

[7] See the excellent analysis of earlier WTO case law on this score by Trebilcock and Soloway (2002), and Sykes (2006a).

[8] This paragraph reflects the "precautionary principle", which we discuss *infra*.

and the health of humans (*Australia–Salmon*, § 177).⁹ The AB has explicitly acknowledged, in its report on *Australia–Salmon* that Art. 5.1 SPS is lex specialis to Art. 2.2 SPS (§ 180):

> ... the Panel considered that Article 5.1 may be viewed as a specific application of the basic obligations contained in Article 2.2 of the *SPS Agreement* ... We agree with this general consideration and would also stress that Articles 2.2 and 5.1 should constantly be read together. Article 2.2 informs Article 5.1: the elements that define the basic obligation set out in Article 2.2 impart meaning to Article 5.1.

The AB added in the same report that a violation of Art 2.2 of the SPS amounted *ipso facto* to a violation of Art 5.1 and vice-versa (§ 138).

Both provisions request that SPS measures be "based" on scientific evidence: in its report on *EC–Hormones (US)*,¹⁰ the AB explained that the term "based" suggests that there must be a rational connection between the (science-based) risk assessment and the SPS measure eventually adopted, in the sense that the former must reasonably support the latter (§ 193):

> ... We believe that Article 5.1, when contextually read as it should be, in conjunction with and as informed by Article 2.2 of the *SPS Agreement*, requires that the results of the risk assessment must sufficiently warrant—that is to say, reasonably support—the SPS measure at stake. The requirement that an SPS measure be "based on" a risk assessment is a substantive re-

---

⁹ Garcia (2006) offers a comprehensive analysis of this dispute.

¹⁰ There are already two WTO disputes recorded on this issue (*EC–Hormones (US)*; *US–Suspended Concession*). The original dispute dates back in the '80s and the narrative has been reflected in the excellent account by Meng (1990). In the late '70s and early '80s, EU member states did not have a common attitude towards hormones but to different degrees worried about (some) hormones because of the so called 'hormone scandals'. In 1981 the first ban on use of some hormones at EU-wide basis was promulgated and covered thyrostatics and stilbenes but there was not agreement with respect to all other hormones. Between 1981–1984 additional research was conducted, the result of which was that natural hormones did not represent any risk to human health; the need to continue examining synthetic hormones was underlined. In 1985 formal rules of control were adopted. In the same year a ban on all hormones was also adopted (the results of scientific studies notwithstanding): the Commission chose Art. 43 of the Treaty as appropriate legal basis and this provision; this provision allowed for adoption of legal instruments on qualified majority (e.g., dissenting votes notwithstanding). UK and Denmark dissented (Ireland abstained); US introduced a legal complaint before the ECJ (85/469/EEC). It partly prevailed and the Court declared the legal instrument null and void but accepted the legal basis. The ban on hormones was re-enacted (by 'healing' the vice observed this time) in 1988 and the ban on all hormones was re-imposed. The US requested the establishment of a technical experts group to examine the consistency of the EU measure under the provisions of the Tokyo round TBT Code. The EU refused the US request (this was the time when trading nations could still block the establishment of a Panel and this is the only recorded cases where a refusal was expressed), and the US imposed countermeasures as a result, without prior authorization by the GATT contracting parties. The EU agreed to a GATT Panel but only in order to examine the consistency of the US countermeasures with the GATT. The result of the disagreement was that no Panel was ever established in the GATT-era.

quirement that there be a rational relationship between the measure and the risk assessment. (italics in the original).[11]

Scientific evidence will need to point to a "risk", and consequently, a risk assessment must take place. Before we discuss the understanding of the term "risk assessment" though, it is probably warranted to explain how the WTO adjudicating bodies have understood the terms "risk", "scientific evidence", and the requirement to "base" risk assessment on scientific evidence. The AB, in *EC–Hormones (US)*, explained that the risk must be identifiable, and not a mere hypothetical possibility (§ 186):

> In one part of its Reports, the Panel opposes a requirement of an "identifiable risk" to the uncertainty that theoretically always remains since science can *never* provide *absolute* certainty that a given substance will not *ever* have adverse health effects. We agree with the Panel that this theoretical uncertainty is not the kind of risk which, under Article 5.1, is to be assessed. (emphasis in the original).

In an oft-quoted passage, the AB stated (§ 187):

> It is essential to bear in mind that the risk that is to be evaluated in a risk assessment under Article 5.1 is not only risk ascertainable in a science laboratory operating under strictly controlled conditions, but also risk in human societies as they actually exist, in other words, the actual potential for adverse effects on human health in the real world where people live and work and die.[12]

In the same case, the AB held that SPS measures need not be based solely on the prevailing opinion in the relevant scientific field in order to satisfy the statutory requirements included in Arts. 2.2 and 5.1 SPS: SPS measures based on minority scientific opinions could very well be WTO-consistent (§ 194). In *US–Suspended Concession*,[13] the AB held that evi-

---

[11] This view has been repeatedly confirmed in case-law. The AB, for example, in *Japan–Agricultural Products II* held that, as per Art 5.2 SPS, a legal requirement is imposed on WTO Members to provide a rational relationship between the SPS measure enacted, and the available scientific evidence that exists (§ 84). See the relevant analysis by Dunoff (1999) and (2006).

[12] In this vein, the Panel in its report on *Japan–Apples* (Article 21.5–US), dismissed the relevance of two studies presented to it, because they did not correspond to natural conditions (§§ 8.65 and 8.140ff).

[13] This is the sequel to *EC–Hormones (US)*. Following the condemnation of its practices, the EU did not change its conduct and did not implement the findings of the WTO adjudicating bodies. The US was authorized to impose countermeasures (suspension of tariff concessions according to Art. 22.6 DSU) against the EU, which it did. Years later, the EU initiated a new Panel against the US, arguing that it had subsequently complied with the rulings and that the US should withdraw its countermeasures as a result. An astonishing Panel report found that the EU was right and that, while the disagreement between the two parties persisted as to whether implementation had occurred, the US should stop imposing countermeasures immediately; if it wanted to resurrect the imposition of countermeasures, the US would have, according to this Panel, to initiate a new dispute. Luckily, this Panel was overturned by the AB in the case discussed here: the AB held that countermeasures lawfully remain in place until either the parties to the dispute have agreed that implementation had indeed occurred, or a multilateral ruling to

dence will be considered scientific if it respects the standards of the relevant scientific community (§ 591). In *Australia–Apples*, the AB held that this standard is further distinguished into two steps (§ 215):

> Thus, in its discussion of the standard of review that applies to a panel reviewing a risk assessment under Article 5.1 of the *SPS Agreement*, the Appellate Body identified two aspects of a panel's scrutiny of a risk assessment, namely, scrutiny of the *underlying scientific basis* and scrutiny of the *reasoning of the risk assessor based upon such underlying science*. (italics in the original).

It went on to hold that the first step was particularly important whenever regulation was based on minority scientific opinions (§ 221):

> We note that the first aspect, the panel's review of the scientific basis of the risk assessment, may be particularly relevant in cases where the importing Member has relied on minority scientific opinions in conducting a risk assessment. In such cases, the question whether such opinions constitute "legitimate" science from respected and qualified sources according to the standards of the relevant scientific community may have greater prominence.

The term "risk assessment" is defined in Annex A § 4 to the SPS Agreement:

> *Risk assessment*—The evaluation of the *likelihood* of entry, establishment or spread of a pest or disease within the territory of an importing Member according to the sanitary or phytosanitary measures which might be applied, and of the associated potential biological and economic consequences; or the evaluation of the *potential* for adverse effects on human or animal health arising from the presence of additives, contaminants, toxins or disease-causing organisms in food, beverages or feedstuffs. (italics in the original).

There are, thus, two kinds of risk assessment:[14] all risks arising from the presence of additives, contaminants, toxins or disease-causing organisms in food, beverages or feedstuffs, must be assessed and their potential effects on human or animal life evaluated (Risk assessment I); on the other hand, as far as pests or diseases are concerned, the SPS Agreement provides for assessment of the likelihood of a pest or disease entering, establishing and spreading and the associated potential biological and economic consequences (Risk assessment II). Whereas the potential effects must be assessed in Risk assessment I, it is the likelihood of a pest enter-

---

this effect had been issued; the unilateral declaration of the party interested in seeing measures against it to be removed does not suffice, held the AB quite correctly. Compare the analysis by Hoekman and Trachtman (2010).

[14] Gruszczynski (2010) offers a very comprehensive discussion of WTO case law regarding risk assessment.

ing a particular market that must be assessed in Risk assessment II. There are different evidentiary standards associated with the two terms (potential, likelihood), and thus, with the two types of risk assessment. In *EC–Hormones (US)*, the AB articulated its understanding of the term "likelihood" and "potential" (§§ 123–124) and determined that "likelihood" was a more demanding standard than "potential" (§§ 183–184):

> Interpreting [paragraph 4 of Annex A of the *SPS Agreement*], the Panel elaborates risk assessment as a two-step process that "should (i) *identify* the *adverse effects* on human health (if any) arising from the presence of the hormones at issue when used as growth promoters *in meat* . . . , and (ii) if any such adverse effects exist, *evaluate* the *potential* or probability of occurrence of such effects".
>
> . . . Although the utility of a two-step analysis may be debated, it does not appear to us to be substantially wrong. What needs to be pointed out at this stage is that the Panel's use of "probability" as an alternative term for "potential" creates a significant concern. The ordinary meaning of "potential" relates to "possibility" and is different from the ordinary meaning of "probability". "Probability" implies a higher degree or a threshold of potentiality or possibility. It thus appears that here the Panel introduces a quantitative dimension to the notion of risk. (emphasis in the original).

Consequently, the standard with respect to Risk assessment II is more demanding.

In its report on *Australia–Salmon*, the AB provided its understanding of the duty to perform a risk assessment in the following terms (§ 121):

> . . . a risk assessment within the meaning of Article 5.1 must:
>
> (1) *identify* the diseases whose entry, establishment or spread a Member wants to prevent within its territory, as well as the potential biological and economic consequences associated with the entry, establishment or spread of these diseases;
>
> (2) *evaluate the likelihood* of entry, establishment or spread of these diseases, as well as the associated potential biological and economic consequences; and
>
> (3) evaluate the likelihood of entry, establishment or spread of these diseases *according to the SPS measures which might be applied*. (emphasis in the original).

In *US–Suspended Concession*, the AB explained the sequential steps that Panels should take whenever they face a challenge against the legality of a risk assessment (§ 598):

Looking at the Panel's analysis of whether the European Communities specifically assessed the risks arising from the consumption of meat from cattle treated with oestradiol–17ß, we note that a significant portion of the Panel's reasoning consists of summaries of the responses of the experts. It is only after summarizing the experts' responses that the Panel describes some of the issues discussed in the 1999 Opinion. Given the applicable standard of review and the role of the Panel that is determined by it, the Panel's analysis should have proceeded differently. The Panel should have first looked at the European Communities' risk assessment. It should then have determined whether the scientific basis relied upon in that risk assessment came from a respected and qualified source. The Panel should have sought assistance from the scientific experts in confirming that it had properly identified the scientific basis underlying the European Communities' risk assessment or to determine whether that scientific basis originated in a respected and qualified source. The Panel should also have sought the experts' assistance in determining whether the reasoning articulated by the European Communities on the basis of the scientific evidence is objective and coherent, so that the conclusions reached in the risk assessment sufficiently warrant the SPS measure. Instead, the Panel seems to have conducted a survey of the advice presented by the scientific experts and based its decisions on whether the majority of the experts, or the opinion that was most thoroughly reasoned or specific to the question at issue, agreed with the conclusion drawn in the European Communities' risk assessment. This approach is not consistent with the applicable standard of review under the *SPS Agreement.* (italics in the original).

In *US–Suspended Concession*, the AB faced the following facts (§ 536):

Before we proceed to examine the European Communities' claims, we briefly summarize some of the relevant facts of this case. We note that Codex has adopted an international standard for oestradiol–17ß, based on evaluations carried out by JECFA [the Joint FAO/WHO Expert Committee on Food Additives]. The European Communities asserts that it has determined a higher level of protection than that which would be achieved under Codex's standard. According to the European Communities, its level of protection is "no (avoidable) risk, that is a level of protection that does not allow any unnecessary addition from exposure to genotoxic chemical substances that are intended to be added deliberately to food." The European Communities also notes that it has performed a risk assessment for meat from cattle treated with oestradiol–17ß for growth-promotion purposes. This risk assessment consists of the 1999, 2000, and 2002 Opinions, as supported by 17 studies conducted between 1998 and 2001. The European Communities further explains that its SPS measure—that is, the import and marketing ban applied pursuant to Directive 2003/74/EC—was taken in the light of the higher level of protection that it determined for itself and is properly based on its risk assessment.

In its risk assessment, the EU had assessed not only the risk from growth hormones, but also the risk resulting from abuse or misuse in the administration of hormones; such risk apparently exists when "good veterinary practices" are not observed. The Panel had summarily dismissed the relevance of this assessment, and the AB, in total disagreement with the Panel in this respect, reversed its findings: in its view the risk originating in the administration of hormones can of course, be included (§ 545ff. and especially §§ 553–555). It added that, in case various factors contribute to a risk, there is no obligation to disentangle their effects (§ 562).

In *Japan–Apples*, the issue was whether the SPS Agreement prejudges the methodology that should be used in the context of risk assessment. The AB found that the agreement does not impose a particular methodology to this effect (§ 204). In the same report, the AB, confirming prior case-law on this issue, held that the obligation to base measures on risk assessment entails that the WTO Member wishing to enact an SPS measure cannot carry out a risk assessment in a manner that precludes phyto-sanitary measures, other than the one already in place, to be considered. The AB found (§ 209) that Japan had violated its obligations under the SPS Agreement by conducting a risk assessment justifying the measure it had in place, without, however, inquiring into the possibility of other, potentially applicable, measures. In this regard, the AB concluded that although the SPS Agreement does not require a particular methodology be applied, it does require that the chosen methodology be specific to (in close connection with) the factual situation investigated.

The AB explained in its report on *EC–Hormones (US)* that a WTO Member can base its measures on a risk assessment performed either by another WTO Member or by an international organization (§ 190). In the same report, the AB reversed a finding by the Panel to the effect that Arts. 2.2 and 5.1 SPS impose a minimum procedural requirement, in the sense that a WTO Member adopting an SPS measure must provide evidence that it did base its measure on scientific evidence at the time when the measures had been originally adopted. In this case, the Panel had found no evidence in the body of the EC regulation (reflecting the SPS measure), or in its preamble, that the EU had indeed based its measure on science and, consequently, held that it had violated its obligations under the SPS Agreement. The AB disagreed (§§ 188–190): in its view, no such obligation can be discerned from the SPS Agreement. The Agreement imposes transparency obligations, that much is for sure, and maybe the AB held that these requirements in and of themselves suffice; WTO Members must, pursuant to § 1 of Annex B to the SPS Agreement, ensure:

> that all sanitary and phytosanitary regulations which have been adopted are published promptly in such a manner as to enable interested Members to become acquainted with them.

§ 3 of the same Annex further requires from WTO Members to introduce "enquiry points" whereby interested parties can request (and obtain) information regarding the SPS measures. Consequently, even in absence of procedural requirements, WTO Members will be violating their obligations (§ 3 of the Annex) if they do not provide adequate information regarding the basis of their measures: were one to take the view that WTO Members have complied with this provision by providing, say, meaningless or unhelpful information, this would deprive § 3 of the Annex of its "*effet utile*".

Assuming existence of risk, it is for WTO Members, depending on their risk aversion, to decide whether to intervene or not. WTO adjudicating bodies cannot prejudge the level of risk aversion that a given society unilaterally sets. In the WTO-era, the AB reaffirmed this point in the most unambiguous terms in *EC–Hormones (US)* (§ 186):

> To the extent that the Panel purported to require a risk assessment to establish a minimum magnitude of risk, we must note that imposition of such a quantitative requirement finds no basis in the SPS Agreement. A panel is authorized only to determine whether a given SPS measure is 'based on' risk assessment.

In order to reach this finding, the AB dissociated the notion of "risk assessment" from that of "risk management": The latter is often used to denote the level of risk that a given society is prepared to live with. Therefore, risk management naturally follows risk assessment, in the sense that, assuming knowledge as to the distribution or probabilities that an event might occur, a given society, depending on its risk aversion, will define the level of protection that it deems appropriate. It is following this logic that the Panel in *EC–Hormones (US)* accepted the distinction between risk management and risk assessment; the AB however, on formal grounds (lack of explicit reference to risk management in the SPS Agreement), dismissed its relevance altogether (§ 181). And yet, a few paragraphs further down, as we saw *supra*, the AB accepted (§ 186) that WTO Members can unilaterally set their appropriate level of protection that Panels cannot disturb.¹⁵ This is in line with Annex A to the SPS Agreement where § 5 reads:

> *Appropriate level of sanitary or phytosanitary protection*—The level of protection deemed appropriate by the Member establishing a sanitary or phytosanitary measure to protect human, animal or plant life or health within its territory. (italics in the original)

The Preamble to the SPS Agreement also in relevant part reads:

> without requiring Members to change their appropriate level of protection of human, animal or plant life or health.

5.3 THE NECESSITY–REQUIREMENT

The necessity-requirement is set out in Art. 5.6 SPS:

> ... Members shall ensure that such measures are not more trade-restrictive than required to achieve their appropriate level of sanitary or phytosanitary protection, taking into account technical and economic feasibility.

A footnote to Art. 5.6 SPS further specifies:

> For purposes of paragraph 6 of Article 5, a measure is not more trade-restrictive than required unless there is another measure, reasonably available taking into account technical and economic feasibility, that achieves the appropriate level of sanitary or phytosanitary protection and is significantly less restrictive to trade.

In *Australia–Salmon*, the question was whether an Australian measure banning, on health grounds, imports of salmon not treated in a particular manner was consistent with various provisions of the SPS Agreement, and, *inter alia*, whether it was necessary in the sense of Art. 5.6 SPS.¹⁶ The AB provided the test that should be applied by WTO adjudicating bodies in order to establish a violation of Art. 5.6 SPS in the following terms (§ 194):

> We agree with the Panel that Article 5.6 and, in particular, the footnote to this provision, clearly provides a three-pronged test to establish a violation of Article 5.6. As already noted, the three elements of this test under Article 5.6 are that there is an SPS measure which:
>
> (1) is reasonably available taking into account technical and economic feasibility;

---

[15] The AB went so far as to accept that WTO Members can opt for zero risk (which it is doubtful if it ever exists).

[16] Garcia (2006).

(2) achieves the Member's appropriate level of sanitary or phytosanitary protection; and

(3) is significantly less restrictive to trade than the SPS measure contested.

These three elements are cumulative in the sense that, to establish consistency with Article 5.6, all of them have to be met. If any of these elements is not fulfilled, the measure in dispute would be inconsistent with Article 5.6.[17]

In *Australia–Apples*, the AB explained that its quest for a reasonably available, significantly less restrictive measure was meant to be an intellectual exercise aimed at establishing whether the necessity-requirement had been adhered to (§ 363):

> Compliance with this requirement is tested through a comparison of the measure at issue to possible alternative measures. Such alternatives, however, are mere conceptual tools for the purpose of the Article 5.6 analysis. A demonstration that an alternative measure meets the relevant Member's appropriate level of protection, is reasonably available, and is significantly less trade restrictive than the existing measure suffices to prove that the measure at issue is more trade restrictive than necessary. Yet this does not imply that the importing Member must adopt that alternative measure or that the alternative measure is the only option that would achieve the desired level of protection

The judicial review is limited to an evaluation of the means that are employed to reach ends that cannot be put into question. Dealing with the interpretation of the term "appropriate level of protection", quoted *supra*, the AB held that the choice of the level of protection logically precedes the choice of the instrument that will eventually be used: a WTO Member first defines its appropriate level of protection, and only then will choose the instrument to achieve the level sought (§§ 200, 201, 203). In § 199 it went so far as to state:

> We do not believe that Article 11 of the DSU, or any other provision of the DSU or of the *SPS Agreement*, entitles the Panel or the AB, for the purpose of applying Article 5.6 in the present case, to substitute its own reasoning about the implied level of protection for that expressed consistently by Australia. The determination of the appropriate level of protection, a notion defined in paragraph 5 of Annex A, as "the level of protection deemed appropriate by the Member establishing a sanitary . . . measure", is a *prerogative* of the Member concerned and not of a panel or of the AB.

---

[17] See also the AB report in *Japan–Agricultural Products II* (§ 95), and § 8.162 of the Panel report in *Japan–Apples (Article 21.5–US)*.

Repeating prior case law, it went on to say that a WTO Member could therefore decide to accept zero risk when defining its policies:

> ... As stated in our Report in *European Communities–Hormones*, the "risk" evaluated in a risk assessment must be an ascertainable risk; theoretical uncertainty is "not the kind of risk which, under Article 5.1, is to be assessed." This does not mean, however, that a Member cannot determine its own appropriate level of protection to be "zero risk". (italics in the original).

In the same report, the AB explains that WTO Members have no obligation to express their appropriate level of protection in quantitative terms. However, some degree of precision is required, otherwise it will be impossible to determine whether they have complied with other relevant provisions of the SPS Agreement: unless expressed in precise enough terms, the quest for the relationship between the measure chosen and the level of protection sought will be severely hindered and, consequently, a WTO adjudicating body, facing a claim under Art. 5.6 SPS, might find it impossible to carry out its task. To avoid this, WTO Members are required to define with precision (albeit, not necessarily in quantitative terms) their level of protection (§ 206):

> We thus believe that the *SPS Agreement* contains an implicit obligation to determine the appropriate level of protection. We do not believe that there is an obligation to determine the appropriate level of protection in quantitative terms. This does not mean, however, that an importing Member is free to determine its level of protection with such vagueness or equivocation that the application of the relevant provisions of the *SPS Agreement,* such as Article 5.6, becomes impossible. It would obviously be wrong to interpret the *SPS Agreement* in a way that would render nugatory entire articles or paragraphs of articles of this Agreement and allow Members to escape from their obligations under this Agreement. (italics in the original).

In the same report, the AB held that if a WTO Member fails to determine the appropriate level of protection (or when it does so with insufficient precision), Panels can fill the gap: a review of the SPS measure employed will help them to establish the appropriate level of protection (§ 207). In other words, the absence of a definition of the level of protection, or insufficient precision, is not fatal for the regulating state.

5.4 CONSISTENCY

Art. 5.5 SPS reflects the consistency-requirement:

> ... each Member shall avoid arbitrary or unjustifiable distinctions in the levels it considers to be appropriate in different situ-

ations, if such distinctions result in discrimination or a disguised restriction on international trade.

WTO case-law (AB, *EC–Hormones (US)*, §§ 212, 238) has established that this provision should be read together with Art. 2.3 SPS, which, as we saw *supra*, requires non-discriminatory behavior across WTO Members. In *Australia–Salmon*, the AB went one step further and explained that a violation of Art. 5.5 SPS *ipso facto* entails a violation of Art. 2.3 SPS as well (§ 252).[18] Whereas the latter part (across WTO Members) seems easier to grasp, the former part (across situations) is far from being a walk in the park for the adjudicator. A benchmark is required in order to establish comparability across situations. Case-law has contributed some clarifications on this score. The AB held in *EC–Hormones (US)* that, for a violation of Art. 5.5 SPS to be established, a complaining party must satisfy a three prong-test (§§ 214–215):

> Close inspection of Article 5.5 indicates that a complaint of violation of this Article must show the presence of three distinct elements. The first element is that the Member imposing the measure complained of has adopted its own appropriate levels of sanitary protection against risks to human life or health in several different situations. The second element to be shown is that those *levels of protection* exhibit arbitrary or unjustifiable differences ("distinctions" in the language of Article 5.5) in their treatment of different situations. The last element requires that the arbitrary or unjustifiable differences result in discrimination or a disguised restriction of international trade. We understand the last element to be referring to the *measure* embodying or implementing a particular level of protection as resulting, in its application, in discrimination or a disguised restriction on international trade.
>
> We consider the above three elements of Article 5.5 to be cumulative in nature; all of them must be demonstrated to be present if violation of Article 5.5 is to be found. In particular, both the second and third elements must be found. The second element alone would not suffice. The third element must also be demonstrably present: the implementing measure must be shown to be applied in such a manner as to result in discrimination or a disguised restriction on international trade. The presence of the second element—the arbitrary or unjustifiable character of differences in *levels of protection* considered by a Member as appropriate in differing situations—may in practical effect operate as a

---

[18] Note, however, that under Art. 6 SPS, WTO Members do not need to apply their SPS measures against all exports when a pest or a disease has surfaced which necessitated the adoption of the SPS measure. Pest-free and disease-free areas can legitimately be excluded. The terms "pest- or disease-free area" and "area of low pest or disease" are further detailed in §§ 6–7 of Annex A to the SPS Agreement.

"warning" signal that the implementing *measure* in its application *might* be a discriminatory measure or *might* be a restriction on international trade disguised as an SPS measure for the protection of human life or health. Nevertheless, the measure itself needs to be examined and appraised and, in the context of the differing levels of protection, shown to result in discrimination or a disguised restriction on international trade. (emphasis in the original).

To perform this test, the complaining party needs to first establish comparability across situations. In §§ 217ff. of its report on *EC–Hormones (US)*, the AB, applying this test, held that the EU had violated Art. 5.5 SPS by banning sales of hormone-treated beef, and not banning sales of hormone-treated pork. Nevertheless, the only element of comparability was that pork and beef were probably DCS goods in the EU market. The AB did not deem it necessary to also examine whether risks from consumption of hormone-treated beef are comparable to those presented by hormones-treated chicken. This report implicitly establishes that DCS-relationship is an element of comparability.[19] The AB explained in the same report that the letter and the spirit of Art. 5.5 SPS does not require from WTO Members to guarantee an absolute uniformity across the various appropriate levels of protection that they pursue. In its view, Art. 5.5 SPS should be properly understood as a legal prohibition of arbitrary or unjustifiable discrimination (§ 213):

> The objective of Article 5.5 is formulated as the "achieving [of] consistency in the application of the concept of appropriate level of sanitary or phytosanitary protection". Clearly, the desired consistency is defined as a goal to be achieved in the future.... Thus, we agree with the Panel's view that the statement of that goal does not establish a *legal obligation* of consistency of appropriate levels of protection. We think, too, that the goal set is not absolute or perfect consistency, since governments establish their appropriate levels of protection frequently on an *ad hoc* basis and over time, as different risks present themselves at different times. It is only arbitrary or unjustifiable inconsistencies that are to be avoided. (italics and emphasis in the original).

Subsequently, in *Australia–Salmon*, the AB offered another benchmark for comparability (§§ 146 and 152):

> the Panel was correct in stating that situations can be compared under Article 5.5 if these situations involve *either* a risk of entry, establishment or spread of the same or a similar disease, *or* a

---

[19] Horn and Mavroidis (2003a).

risk of the same or similar "associated potential biological and economic consequences".

. . .

we believe that for situations to be comparable under Article 5.5, it is sufficient for these situations to have in common a risk of entry, establishment or spread of *one* disease of concern. There is no need for these situations to have in common a risk of entry, establishment or spread of *all* diseases of concern. (emphasis in the original).

Therefore, similarity of the disease or of the associated risk also provides a comparability-element. The question nonetheless, remains whether the test should be confined to the DCS-category of goods or not. In *Australia–Salmon,* the AB introduced the term "warning signals", which refers to elements or properties of particular SPS measures that could be relevant in establishing a violation of Art. 5.5 SPS. The quantity and quality of such warning signals will ultimately prove to be the decisive factor in determining whether Art. 5.5 SPS has been violated: substantial difference in the level of protection across two comparable situations (§ 164), and/or violation of Art. 5.1 SPS (§ 166), could serve as warning signals.[20]

On June 22, 2000, WTO Members adopted Guidelines which provide some clarification on the scope of the obligation assumed under Art 5.5 of the SPS Agreement[21]: WTO Members must, in order to observe their consistency-obligation, indicate the level of protection which they consider appropriate, and also indicate if there is a difference in the level of protection under consideration and levels already determined by the regulating WTO Member in different situations. WTO Members must further compare the level of protection now being sought with that already considered in previous situations which contain sufficient common elements so as to render the two situations comparable.[22] We read on p. 4 of the Guidelines:

What a Member is comparing are the levels of protection against the risks posed . . . Characterizing risks as "similar" must include a comparison of both the relevant likelihood and the corresponding consequences.

6. PRECAUTIONARY SPS MEASURES

WTO Members can, in accordance with Art. 5.7 SPS, provisionally adopt SPS measures on the basis of available information, even in the absence of scientific backing. However, in instances in which such provi-

---

[20] Evidence of this attitude can also be detected in § 240 of the AB's report on *EC–Hormones (US)*.

[21] WTO Doc G/SPS/15 of July 18, 2000.

[22] See p. 3 of the Guidelines, op. cit. under A4.

sional measures are enacted, a WTO Member is under an obligation to collect information that will enable it to perform a risk assessment within a reasonable period of time.

Underlying Art. 5.7 SPS is the concept of the "precautionary principle." This is the notion that under certain circumstances where the scientific evidence is not forthcoming, a government may nevertheless be under an obligation to take precautionary actions to safeguard the public interest. For example, in the immediate aftermath of the Fukushima Daichi nuclear disaster resulting from the Tohoku Earthquake of 2011, several countries moved to impose temporary import bans on agricultural products from northeastern Japan. Although the scientific evidence was not yet forthcoming that consumption of such products would be harmful, governments felt that precautionary measures were necessary. Art. 5.7 SPS provides the means to take such steps while safeguarding trade-related interests by preventing governments from abusing such measures to protect domestic interests.

Note that Art. 5.7 SPS does not explicitly refer to the "precautionary principle." Nevertheless, WTO adjudicating bodies have held that this concept is reflected within this provision. In *EC–Hormones (US)*,[23] the AB noted the following regarding the relevance of the "precautionary principle" in the WTO legal order (§§ 123–125):

> (a) The precautionary principle is reflected in Art. 5.7 SPS, but is also reflected in other SPS provisions such as the preamble and Art. 3.3 SPS. Hence, the precautionary principle is not exhaustively reflected in Art. 5.7 SPS;
>
> (b) The status of precautionary principle under customary international law is unclear;[24]
>
> (c) WTO Panels should keep precautionary principle in mind when interpreting the SPS; but
>
> (d) The precautionary principle does not override the explicit wording of specific SPS provisions.

The relationship between Art. 5.7 SPS on one hand, and Art. 2.2 SPS (the obligation to base measures on scientific evidence) on the other, was addressed by various AB reports, and not always in a consistent manner. In *Japan–Agricultural Products II*[25] the AB held (§ 80):

> ... Article 5.7 allows Members to adopt provisional SPS measures "[I]n cases where relevant scientific evidence is insuffi-

---

[23] Mercurio and Shao (2010) offer an analysis of this dispute as well as all of the WTO case law on precaution.

[24] In *EC–Approval and Marketing of Biotech Products*, the Panel, when dealing with the EU regime for approval of genetically modified organisms (GMOs) even cited the International Tribunal of the Law of the Sea (ITLOS) as support for its finding that the precautionary principle had an uncertain status under customary international law (§ 7.89).

[25] See Dunoff (2006) for an excellent account of this dispute.

cient" and certain other requirements are fulfilled. Article 5.7 operates as a qualified exemption from the obligation under Article 2.2 not to maintain SPS measures without sufficient scientific evidence. An overly broad and flexible interpretation of that obligation would render Article 5.7 meaningless. (emphasis in the original).

In *Japan–Apples*, the AB went one step further: In its view, if science is well settled on an issue, recourse to precaution is unwarranted. In a sense, the AB sees a firewall between scientific evidence and precaution (§ 184):

> The application of Article 5.7 is triggered not by the existence of scientific uncertainty, but rather by the insufficiency of scientific evidence. The text of Article 5.7 is clear: it refers to 'cases where relevant scientific evidence is insufficient', not to 'scientific uncertainty'. The two concepts are not interchangeable. Therefore, we are unable to endorse Japan's approach of interpreting Article 5.7 through the prism of 'scientific uncertainty'.[26]

It follows, that, in the early cases discussed by the AB, a measure can either be based on science or on Art. 5.7 SPS, and that recourse to the latter is appropriate in cases of scientific insufficiency, but not of scientific uncertainty.

In *US–Suspended Concession*, the AB re-visited prior case-law, distanced itself from it and adopted a more coherent approach on this issue. In this case, an international standard for growth hormones existed, from which the EU had deviated in seeking higher protection. The AB implicitly held that there should be no firewall between science and precaution, since science normally proceeds incrementally, and only rarely do we experience paradigm shifts (§ 703). In its view, nothing should stop WTO Members from challenging the orthodoxy of an accepted scientific acquis. In this vein, the presence of an international standard is no presumption that recourse to Art. 5.7 SPS is impossible. It could very well be the case, as indeed was the case in this particular dispute, that the regulating state seeks a level of protection higher than that achieved by the international standard in place (§§ 627ff. and in particular § 697). Moreover, distancing itself from a Panel ruling to this effect, the AB held, that when an international standard exists, there is no need to demonstrate a critical mass of evidence to support a measure based on Art. 5.7 SPS. In its words (§ 725):

> In concluding that it is "not convinced" that the ultra-sensitive assay study referred to by the European Communities "call[s] into question the fundamental precepts of previous knowledge" in relation to the effect of the five hormones on pre-pubertal chil-

---

[26] See also § 188 of this report.

dren, the Panel applied an excessively high threshold in relation to the new scientific evidence which is required to render previously sufficient scientific evidence "insufficient" within the meaning of Article 5.7. Irrespective of whether the Panel was itself persuaded by the Klein study, the Panel erred to the extent that it considered that a paradigmatic shift in the scientific knowledge was required in order to render the scientific evidence relied by JECFA now "insufficient" within the meaning of Article 5.7. The "insufficiency" requirement in Article 5.7 does not imply that new scientific evidence must entirely displace the scientific evidence upon which an international standard relies. It suffices that new scientific developments call into question whether the body of scientific evidence still permits of a sufficiently objective assessment of risk.

WTO case law has also dealt with the mechanics of the compliance with Art. 5.7 SPS.[27] The AB, in its report on *Japan–Agricultural Products II* established a four-prong test that must be met in its entirety for a measure to be deemed consistent with Art. 5.7 SPS (§ 89):

Article 5.7 of the *SPS Agreement* sets out four requirements which must be met in order to adopt and maintain a provisional SPS measure. Pursuant to the first sentence of Article 5.7, a Member may provisionally adopt an SPS measure if this measure is:

(1) imposed in respect of a situation where "relevant scientific information is insufficient"; and

(2) adopted "on the basis of available pertinent information".

Pursuant to the second sentence of Article 5.7, such a provisional measure may not be maintained unless the Member which adopted the measure:

(1) "seek[s] to obtain the additional information necessary for a more objective assessment of risk"; and

(2) "review[s] the ... measure accordingly within a reasonable period of time.

These four requirements are clearly cumulative in nature and are equally important for the purpose of determining consistency with this provision. Whenever *one* of these four requirements is not met, the measure at issue is inconsistent with Article 5.7. (emphasis in the original).

---

[27] Foster (2011) offers a construction not espoused by case law and discusses how allocation of the burden of proof (reversal of the burden of production of proof) can help reduce the potential of error when adjudicating disputes regarding the application of the precautionary principle. Compare this with the current understanding in case law of the allocation of burden of proof as explained in Grando (2009).

The term "reasonable period of time" was discussed in the AB report on *Japan–Agricultural Products II*. There, the AB held that this term will have to be interpreted on a case by case basis. In this particular case, four years of inaction by Japan subsequent to the adoption of a measure under Art. 5.7 SPS was deemed to be unreasonable (§ 93). In the same dispute, the AB held that the additional information sought during the reasonable period of time must be germane in conducting a risk assessment (§ 92). Case law has so far not addressed the question of whether precautionary measures must still observe the non-discrimination obligation (Art. 3.2 SPS), the consistency-(Art. 5.5 SPS), and the necessity-requirements (Art. 5.6 SPS). The text of Art. 5.7 SPS does not absolve WTO Members from the obligation to observe these three obligations but does not compel them to observe them either. The *travaux préparatoires* unfortunately do not shed enough light on this issue: some of the negotiating history of this provision[28] suggests that it was drafted to deal with emergency situations, such as an outbreak of a disease. This is by now water under the bridge: the AB, in its report on *EC–Hormones (US)*, extended Art. 5.7 SPS to cover precautionary measures which do not necessarily have to be taken as a matter of urgency.

7. CONTROL PROCEDURES

Art. 8 SPS reads:

Members shall observe the provisions of Annex C in the operation of control, inspection and approval procedures, including national systems for approving the use of additives or for establishing tolerances for contaminants in foods, beverages or feedstuffs, and otherwise ensure that their procedures are not inconsistent with the provisions of this Agreement.

Annex C requires that any procedure to check the fulfillment of SPS measures be undertaken and completed without undue delay and in no less favorable manner for imported products than for like domestic products; that the procedure is published and communicated upon request; that confidentiality-requirements will observe NT; that control-requirements be limited to what is reasonable and necessary; that equitable fees, if at all, are imposed on inspected products; and, finally, that procedures for complaints shall be introduced.

The SPS Agreement encourages WTO Members to conclude MRAs between themselves which must nevertheless respect the non-discrimination obligation, as reflected in Art. 4 SPS: WTO Members not party to an MRA, can request that the MRA be extended to them, if they can establish that their regulatory framework is equivalent to those of the

---

[28] GATT Docs. MTN.GNG/NG5/WGSP/7 of November 20, 1990, and MTN.GNG/NG5/WGSP/17 of April 30, 1990.

MRA-partners. A SPS Committee Decision sheds some light on Art. 4 SPS.[29] This decision makes it clear that equivalence can be accepted for measures relating to a specific product or categories of products or a system-wide basis, hence the coverage can be quite extensive; that a reliable communication channel must be established between the exporting (requesting equivalence) and the importing WTO Member: the latter should provide information regarding its level of protection and justification of its SPS measures, while the former should cooperate in supplying information regarding its scientific capacity, the product-related infrastructure etc.; trade should not be interrupted only because a request for equivalence has been tabled; WTO Members should participate in the ongoing work of international institutions harmonizing standards, such as the Codex Alimentarius Commission, in equivalence-related work by the World Organization for Animal Health, and in the framework of the International Plant Protection Convention. It does not detail any further how the MFN-requirement will be complied with in presence of equivalence (unilateral or MRA) but does mention the word "confidence" a number of times: this word is unquantifiable and this property in and of itself makes the MFN-requirement a tough to meet test for outsiders (as is the case in the TBT Agreement).

Art. 7 SPS (which is further detailed in Annex B to the SPS Agreement) reads:

> Members shall notify changes in their sanitary or phytosanitary measures and shall provide information on their sanitary or phytosanitary measures in accordance with the provisions of Annex B.

To this effect § 1 of Annex B requires that all SPS measures be published. The AB held, in its report on *Japan–Agricultural Products II*, that the term "laws, decrees or ordinances" (appearing in § 1 of Annex B) should be interpreted broadly, so that all SPS measures are covered, and not just those that can formally be characterized as such. In its view, what matters is the objective sought through this provision: to ensure that all SPS measures are published, irrespective of their qualification under domestic law (§§ 105–106).

8. SPECIAL AND DIFFERENTIAL TREATMENT FOR DEVELOPING COUNTRIES

Art. 10 SPS contains the special and differential treatment provision of the Agreement, and essentially follows the TBT-recipe in this respect: Where there is scope for a phased introduction of a SPS measures, longer time frames for compliance should be given to products from developing countries. By the same token, the Doha Ministerial Declaration calls for

---

[29] WTO Doc. G/SPS/19/Rev. 2 of July 23, 2004.

the passage of a certain period of time between the enactment of a measure and its entry into force so that foreign producers can adjust to the new regulatory reality and not be caught off-guard. In addition, the SPS Committee is permitted to grant specified, time-limited exceptions in whole or in part from obligations under the Agreement to developing countries, upon request from such countries.

9. EXPERTISE IN SPS-RELATED DISPUTE ADJUDICATION

Since SPS measures must, in principle, be based on scientific evidence, it is to be expected that scientific experts might be called to explain regulatory interventions if need be before WTO adjudicating bodies; since scientific disagreements are not uncommon, judges might be called to resolve similar disagreements. Art. 11.2 SPS urges Panels to have recourse to experts when dealing with SPS issues, stating in relevant part that "a panel *should* seek advice from experts" (emphasis added).

This expression is in slight contrast to the formulation privileged in Art. 13.2 DSU which reflects the generic provision regarding recourse to expertise

> Panels [. . .] *may* consult experts to obtain their opinion on certain aspects of the matter. With respect to a factual issue concerning a scientific or other technical matter raised by a party to a dispute, a panel *may* request an advisory report in writing from an expert review group. (emphases added).

Although the wording of Art.11.2 SPS suggests a slightly more imperative tone, it is nonetheless within the discretion of a Panel to decide whether or not to have recourse to experts. If they do opt to have recourse to expertise, then Panels must respect Art. 11.2 SPS:

> In a dispute under this Agreement involving scientific or technical issues, a panel should seek advice from experts chosen by the panel in consultation with the parties to the dispute. To this end, the panel may, when it deems it appropriate, establish an advisory technical experts group, or consult the relevant international organizations, at the request of either party to the dispute or on its own initiative.

Two issues have occupied case law so far: first, in *Japan–Agricultural Products II*, the question arose whether an expert opinion extending beyond an argument[30] advanced by one of the parties could still be of legal

---

[30] A claim consists of a statement to the effect that particular practice is WTO-inconsistent (factual matter) as well as the legal basis that is allegedly being violated (legal matter). Arguments are (logical) constructions aiming to substantiate a claim. WTO Members, when litigating, are required to present all their claims at the moment they request the establishment of a Panel (Art. 6.2 DSU); they can add arguments to support their claims during the Panel proceedings, see the Chapters on Dispute Settlement.

relevance to the Panel. More precisely, the US had claimed that Japan's measures violated the necessity-requirement, arguing that Japan could have used another less trade-restrictive measure. Experts confirmed the US point of view; in doing that, they pointed, however, to an alternative measure, other than that advanced by the US, which, in their view, constituted an option even less restrictive: the US had advanced the argument that Japan should have used "testing by product" instead of the measure privileged by Japan; the experts argued that Japan should have used "sorption levels", a measure that had not at all been discussed by the US in its pleadings. The Panel accepted the claim by the US and held that Japan had not complied with its obligations under Art. 5.6 SPS. The AB reversed this finding on the ground that, in the absence of an argument by the US to this effect, the Panel did not have the legal authority to find against Japan for an argument advanced by the experts only (§§ 125ff.). The AB probably equated the expertise regarding sorption levels as a claim that had not been lawfully introduced by the US; in this case, even if the US had endorsed the supplied expertise, it would be running afoul of its obligations under Art. 6.2 DSU since the claim was introduced after the establishment of the Panel.

Second, case law has dealt with the selection of experts. Expertise has been routinely sought by Panels dealing with challenges against SPS measures. Panels privilege experts affiliated with the institutions explicitly mentioned in the SPS Agreement (Office International des Epizooties, International Plant Protection Convention, Codex Alimentarius Commission): in *Australia–Salmon*, the Panel selected four experts after consultations with the Office International des Epizooties (§§ 6.1ff.); in *Japan–Agricultural Products II*, the Panel chose three experts after soliciting suggestions from the Secretariat of the International Plant Protection Convention (§§ 6.1ff.). In *EC–Hormones (US)*, the Panel initially requested the parties to the dispute to name one expert each. It then named two experts (from a list prepared by the Codex Alimentarius Commission and the International Agency for Research on Cancer) and one additional expert in the area of carcinogenic effects of hormones (§§ 6.1ff.). The EU appealed the fact that one of the experts was a national of a third party and had ties with the pharmaceutical industry. The AB dismissed the EU argument and held that (§ 148):

> once the panel has decided to request the opinion of individual scientific experts, there is no legal obstacle to the panel drawing up, in consultation with the parties to the dispute, ad hoc rules for those particular proceedings.

Until *US–Suspended Concession*, there had never been a case when experts had been selected against the will of one of the parties to the dispute; but in this case, the EU objected to the appointment of two experts on the grounds that they had real or perceived conflicts of interest that should have disqualified them from assisting the panel, in particular, because (§§ 416–424):

> (a) They were both affiliated with JEFCA, the institution that had elaborated the international standard that the EU had criticized and from which it had deviated;
>
> (b) One of them had taken a position on the issue in the dispute, and the other had received research money from the pharmaceutical industry.

The AB established, for the first time, that due process considerations should guide the selection of panelists (§ 436); it further recalled the disclosure obligations that selected experts must observe in order to ensure that due process has been complied with (§ 438). It went on to confirm the Panel's rejection of the EU claims regarding point (b) above (§ 455). The AB, however, found that the Panel should not have selected the two experts because of their institutional affiliation with JEFCA, the standard which the EU had been criticizing (§ 469). The AB went on to find that the Panel had violated the EU's due process rights, and in doing so, failed to perform an objective assessment of the matter before it as required by Art. 11 DSU (§§ 481–482); it added that all subsequent findings by the Panel could be invalidated because of this choice, but still went on and examined them one by one (§ 484).

Finally note that a Panel does not need to explicitly refer to all expertise received by experts to observe its duty to perform an objective assessment of the matter before it (Art. DSU). In *Australia–Apples*, the AB pertinently held (§ 275):

> Regarding the Panel's treatment of the evidence, we consider that its role as the trier of facts requires it to review and consider all the evidence that it receives from the parties or that it seeks pursuant to Article 13 of the DSU. Nonetheless, as the Appellate Body explained in *EC–Hormones*, a panel cannot be expected to refer to all the statements made by the experts it consulted. To reproduce every statement made by the experts in the report is neither a necessary nor a sufficient condition for a panel to perform its function in accordance with Article 11 of the DSU. Article 11 requires a panel, in its reasoning on a given issue, to weigh and balance all the relevant evidence, including testimony by the experts. A panel may reproduce the relevant statements by the experts, but still fail to make an objective assessment of the facts under Article 11 if it then fails to properly assess the significance of these statements in its reasoning, as the Appellate Body found in *US/Canada–Continued Suspension*. Conversely, a panel that does not expressly reproduce certain statements of its appointed experts may still act consistently with Article 11, especially when the panel's reasoning reveals

that it has nevertheless assessed the significance of these statements or that these statements are manifestly not relevant to the panel's objective assessment of the facts and issues before it. (italics in the original).

10. STANDARD OF REVIEW

The AB, in *EC–Hormones (US)*, held that WTO adjudicating bodies, when dealing with cases coming under the purview of the SPS Agreement must apply the standard of review set out in Art. 11 DSU. Recall nevertheless, that in *EC–Asbestos* and in case law regarding the interpretation of Art. XX GATT, the AB has held that a more deferential standard is warranted if the objective is the protection of human health. One would expect a similar attitude towards at least those SPS measures that aim to protect public health.

11. INSTITUTIONAL ISSUES

WTO Members have established an SPS Committee which provides a regular forum for consultations among WTO Members, and, in general, is in charge of the administration of the SPS Agreement. It aims to provide transparency regarding national SPS measures, provide clarifications of the SPS Agreement (like the Decision on Art. 4 and the Guidelines regarding Art. 5.5 SPS), promote regulatory cooperation across WTO Members, international harmonization, and also, if possible resolve disputes. In parallel with the TBT Agreement, it has established an online forum providing detailed information regarding national measures.[31] It recently launched the SPS Notification Submission System (NSS) which enabled WTO Members to fill out and submit notifications online. The online submission system was designed to ensure that notifications would become more complete and accurate. Since the WTO was set up, governments have shared in the context of the SPS Committee information with each other on over 10,000 SPS measures that they have implemented on food safety and animal and plant health.[32]

QUESTIONS AND COMMENTS

Precaution: in an elaborate document prepared for the European Scientific Technology Observatory (ESTO), Stirling (2001) argues that precaution should be a response to yet a distinct concept, ignorance. Ignorance is but one element in a wider context. The starting-point is a distinction between knowledge about likelihoods and knowledge about outcomes. The former can be further distinguished between firm likelihood, shaky likelihood, and no basis for probabilities. The latter can be distinguished in a continuum of outcomes, set of discrete outcomes, and outcomes poorly defined. Depend-

---

[31] http://spsims.wto.org.
[32] http://www.wto.org/english/news_e/news11_e/sps_19oct11_e.htm.

ing on the combination between the various elements of the two variables, we can end up with a state of uncertainty, ambiguity, or ignorance. Uncertainty is the state where there is a continuum of outcomes, but we have no basis for probabilities; ambiguity is the state where outcomes are poorly defined but we have a firm, or at the very least, a basis of probabilities; finally, ignorance is the state where we have no basis for probabilities and outcomes are poorly defined. In epistemic terms, scenario analysis is recommended in cases of uncertainty, sensitivity analysis in cases of ambiguity, and precaution in cases of ignorance. Precaution emerges as the scientific approach to address incommensurability, that is, the situation where one compares apples to oranges. Should precaution in WTO parlance be confined to cases of ignorance and incommensurability only? Or should we understand precaution as an antidote to uncertainty and ambiguity as well?

Appropriate Level of Protection: The discretion of WTO Members to set their appropriate level of protection has been respected in all but one case: *Japan–Apples*.[33] Japan imposed a series of measures to ban trade of apples originating in the US, fearing that some of them might suffer from "fire blight". The challenged measure consisted of nine prohibitions or requirements (§§ 8.5ff). Among these was the prohibition on importing apples from US states other than Oregon and Washington, certification-requirements, and the prohibition of exports, if fire blight had been detected in a neighboring geographical area. According to the Japanese regulator, in the absence of a total embargo on imports, the risk that the disease would spread was very much alive. Fire blight affects apples, and not human life. There was no evidence that apples infected with fire blight had been exported to Japan, although there was evidence of a shipment of infected apples to the separate customs territory of Taiwan, Penghu, Kinmen, and Matsu;[34] However, the apples shipped to Taiwan, Penghu, Kinmen, and Matsu had not been infected with fire blight, but rather with another disease ("codling moth"). Japan claimed that it possessed sufficient scientific evidence that risk did exist: the record shows that apples infected with fire blight had been exported to New Zealand in the early twentieth century, to the United Kingdom in the 1950s, and to Egypt a little later. Scientific evidence showed (with a considerable degree of confidence) that the disease had been transmitted because of the nature of the trade involved (trade in root stocks, that is, in apple trees and not in apples). The trade involved in *Japan–Apples* dispute concerned apples and not apple trees. The expertise provided to the Panel suggested that the risk of completing the pathway (and thus, transmitting the disease) was negligible. The Panel rejected the US argument that it was required to confine its review only to mature, symptom-less apples, since only such apples were being exported to Japan; the Panel held that the risk (because of human error) that immature, symptom-full apples be exported to Japan should also be taken into account. In the experts' view, however, even if this were the case, the risk would still be negligible because the disease could only be transmitted through birds flying from infected apples to uninfected apple trees. Rely-

---

[33] Neven and Weiler (2007) have provided an excellent, critical account of this dispute.
[34] See § 160 of the AB report and footnote 289.

ing on the guidance of the experts on this point, the Panel explicitly accepted that there was negligible risk. It still went ahead, nevertheless, and found that there was no rational or objective relationship between the measure and the relevant scientific evidence: in light of the negligible risk identified on the basis of the scientific evidence and the nature of elements composing the measure, the Panel concluded that the Japanese measure was clearly disproportionate (§§ 8.198–199). Note that the Panel did not reach its finding in this respect based on Art. 5.6 SPS (which reflects the necessity-requirement). It decided to exercise judicial economy in this respect. It held that the measure was inconsistent with Art. 2.2 SPS, since there was no scientific evidence to support it, although it accepted that risk, albeit negligible, did exist. The AB endorsed the idea that in light of the negligible risk, the challenged measure was disproportionate (§§ 160 and 163ff) and thus, in violation of Art. 2.2 SPS. Zero risk was accepted in *EC–Hormones (US)*, while negligible risk, for sure higher than zero risk, was not enough to base SPS measures in Japan–Apples. What in your view justifies this discrepancy?

Legitimate Regulation: At one end of the spectrum we could imagine cases where risk assessment has not provided us with responses either way, but where the scientific process is well under way. At the other end, we could envision cases where there is public anxiety even if it is caused by flimsy reasons, such as dissemination through the mass media of irresponsible information, and even worse sometimes in order to advance domestic producers' interests. There should be no doubt that the former end of the spectrum should be covered, but how far down the road should we go towards the latter? This issue is highly debated by scholars from different disciplines, and it is hard to come up with the "correct" response, assuming there is one. Slovic (2000), an eminent psychologist, states for example:

> Human beings have invented the concept of 'risk' to help them understand and cope with the dangers and uncertainties of life. Although these dangers are real, there is no such thing as 'real risk' or 'objective risk'.

The affect heuristic certainly simplifies our life. Quoting from Kahneman (2011, p.140):

> ... people who had received a message extolling the benefits of a technology also changed their beliefs about its risks. Although they had received no relevant evidence, the technology they now liked more than before was also perceived as less risky.

In the words of Haidt (2001) "the emotional tail wags the rational dog". On the other hand, Sunstein (2002), (2003), and Kuran and Sunstein (1999) warn against populist excesses: they name "availability cascade" a chain of events which might originate in media and lead up to public panic. Kuran and Sunstein (1999) discuss a couple of incidents where regulation was totally baseless and unfounded and might have also done public health a disservice. They criticize public intervention absent serious scrutiny of the legitimacy of public anxiety. Kahneman (2011) takes a seemingly conciliatory attitude here but *de facto* sides with Slovic when he states (p. 144):

> I share Sunstein's discomfort with the influence of irrational fears and availability cascades on public policy in the domain of risk. However, I also share Slovic's belief that widespread fears, even if they are unreasonable, should not be ignored by policy makers. Rational or not, fear is painful and debilitating, and policy makers must endeavor to protect the public from fear, not only from real dangers.

Expert Testimony: The US Ninth Circuit, for example, held on remand in the *Daubert*[35] litigation that expert testimony should not be merely relevant but that it should be fit to the requirements of the litigation where it has been offered. The fit-requirement is "higher than bare relevance" but "lower than the standard of correctness".[36] Thus, courts will not be deprived of useful information while ensuring that they will not be lost in useless, confusing details either. In this vein, *Daubert* requires a thorough analysis of the expert's economic model, which should not be admitted if it does not apply to the specific facts of the case. "Relevant evidence" is defined in Rule 401 of the Federal Rules of Evidence (US) as:

> evidence having any tendency to make the existence of any fact that is of consequence to the determination of the action more probable or less probable.

US Courts further examine the qualifications of the experts.[37] In *Berlyn, Inc v. Gazette*, for example, a district court excluded the testimony of an expert, who was an experienced newspaper executive, on the relevant market in question, for the simple reason that he was not an economist or an attorney and had never published anything related to economics or antitrust:

> general business experience unrelated to antitrust economics does not render a witness qualified to offer an opinion on complicated antitrust issues such as defining relevant markets.[38]

---

[35] *Daubert v. Merrell Dow Pharm, Inc.*, 509 U.S. 579, 588–589 (1993). See also Sykes (2006).

[36] *Daubert v. Merrell Dow Pharmaceuticals, Inc.*, 43 F.3d 1311, 1321 (9th Cir. 1995); See also, *In re Linerboard Antitrust Litigation*, 497 F.Supp.2d 666, 673 (E.D.Pa 2007); *United States v. Ford*, 481 F.3d 215, 220 n. 6 (3d Cir. 2007). *United States v. Williams*, 2007 WL 1643197, 3 (3d Cir., 2007).

[37] *Paoli R.R. Yard PCB Litig.*, 35 F.3d 717 (3d Cir. 1994); *Raskin v. Wyatt Co.*, 125 F.3d 55, 66 (2d Cir. 1997).

[38] *Berlyn Inc. v. Gazette Newspapers, Inc.*, 214 F. Supp. 2d 530, 536 (D. Md. 2002).

CHAPTER 21

TRADE RELATED INVESTMENT MEASURES (TRIMs)

■ ■ ■

1. THE LEGAL DISCIPLINE

The TRIMs Agreement requires that WTO Members, when regulating investments within their jurisdiction, must not impose investment measures that violate Arts. III and XI GATT. By way of an Illustrative List annexed, the TRIMs Agreement specifically outlaws instruments such as export performance requirements and local content requirements.

2. THE RATIONALE FOR THE LEGAL DISCIPLINE

On account of growing foreign investment worldwide, GATT Members considered it necessary to add this agreement for essentially two reasons: On the one hand, it would anyway provide some clarity judged necessary with respect to the two types of investment-related instruments mentioned *supra*; on the other, the advent of this Agreement was considered a precursor for a more "comprehensive" agreement on trade and investment.

3. COVERAGE OF THE LEGAL DISCIPLINE

3.1 NO COMPREHENSIVE TREATMENT OF INVESTMENT IN THE GATT

The GATT Panel in *Canada–FIRA* clarified that protection of investors is not addressed by the GATT.[1] The GATT requires WTO Members to abolish two types of investment measures:

(a) local content requirements (Art. III.5 GATT), and
(b) export performance requirements (Arts. XI GATT).

---

[1] See the discussion in Chapter 8.

3.2 MEASURES COMING UNDER THE PURVIEW OF TRIMS

Art. 2.1 TRIMs prohibits WTO Members from applying any investment measure that is inconsistent with Art. III, or Art. XI GATT. An Illustrative List annexed to TRIMs provides the following examples of measures that are inconsistent with Art. III or Art. XI GATT:

(a) Local content requirements;

(b) Export performance requirements;

(c) Trade balancing requirements;

(d) Foreign exchange balancing restrictions, and

(e) Restrictions on an enterprise's export or sale for export of products.

WTO Members must phase out similar measures during a transitional period, assuming that they have notified the WTO of these measures. A longer transition period is available to developing countries. The content of the Illustrative List is inspired by the plain text of GATT provisions, and by the relevant case law as well. It follows that the TRIMs facilitates the work of WTO adjudicating bodies, since it identifies specific types of trade-related investment measures (other than local content that is explicitly included in the body of Art. III GATT) that are considered to be inconsistent with GATT Article III or XI. The Panel in *India–Autos* (§ 7.157) held that the Illustrative List:[2]

> provides additional guidance as to the identification of certain measures considered to be inconsistent with Articles III:4 and XI:1 of the GATT 1994.

Assuming a measure challenged falls under the Illustrative List, it will be ipso facto judged WTO-inconsistent; the judge will not have to see to what extent it violates a specific provision. The *Indonesia–Autos* Panel ruled to this effect (§ 14.83):

> An examination of whether the measures [in question] are covered by Item (1) of the Illustrative List ... will not only indicate whether they are trade-related but also whether they are inconsistent with Article III:4 and thus in violation of Article 2.1 of the TRIMs Agreement.

3.2.1 Art. III GATT–Type Measures Included in the Illustrative List

The following measures could come under this heading:

(a) Required purchase or use by an enterprise of products of domestic origin or from any domestic source; or

---

[2] See Bagwell and Sykes (2007a).

(b) Requirements to the effect that an enterprise's purchases or use of imported products be limited to an amount related to the volume or value of local products that it exports.

In *Indonesia–Autos*, the Panel ruled on the legality of an Indonesian car programme, linking tax benefits for cars manufactured in Indonesia to local content-requirements, and linking customs duty benefits for imported components of cars manufactured in Indonesia to similar local content requirements. The Panel found that these were indeed local content-requirements which had a significant impact on investment in the automotive sector (§ 14.80), and that they were trade-related, because they affected trade (§ 14.82). The Panel also found that compliance with the requirements for the purchase and use of products of domestic origin was necessary to obtain the tax and customs duty benefits and that such benefits were advantages within the meaning of the illustrative list (§§ 14.89–91). As a result, the Panel ruled that the local content-requirements imposed by Indonesia violated the TRIMs Agreement (§ 14.91).

3.2.2 Art. XI GATT–Type Measures Included in the Illustrative List

Three categories of measures come under the purview of Art. XI.1 GATT:

(a) The importation by an enterprise of products used in or related to its local production, generally in an amount related to the volume or value of local production that it exports;

(b) The importation by an enterprise of products used in or related to its local production by restricting its access to foreign exchange to an amount related to the foreign exchange inflows attributable to the enterprise;

(c) The exportation or sale for export by an enterprise of products.

All these measures are (in varying degree) export-related performance requirements. The *India–Autos* litigation[3] involved the review of an Indian trade balancing-measure: the import (by domestic car manufacturers) of parts and components necessary for the production of cars was conditioned on a certain FOB-(free on board) value of exports of cars and components over the same period; if the statutory thresholds had not been met, no imports would occur. The legislation thus gave an incentive to Indian car manufacturers to export (so that they could profit from cheap inputs). The Panel addressed this measure in the following manner (§§ 7.277–7.278):

> [As of the date of the establishment of the trade balancing condition,] there would necessarily have been a practical threshold to the amount of exports that each manufacturer could expect to

---

[3] Bagwell and Sykes (2007a) discuss this case.

make, which in turn would determine the amount of imports that could be made. This amounts to an import restriction. The degree of effective restriction which would result from this condition may vary from signatory [of a memorandum of understanding with the Indian government] to signatory depending on its own projections, its output, or specific market conditions, but a manufacturer is in no instance free to import, without commercial constraint, as many kits and components as it wishes without regard to its export opportunities and obligations. The Panel therefore finds that the trade balancing condition[,] . . . by limiting the amount of imports through linking them to an export commitment, acts as a restriction on importation, contrary to the terms of Article XI:1.

Having found that the trade balancing requirements violated Art. XI.1 GATT, the *India–Autos* Panel invoked the principle of judicial economy and concluded that it was not necessary to analyze the measures under the TRIMs Agreement as well (§§ 7.323–7.324).

3.3 OBLIGATIONS DURING AND AFTER THE TRANSITIONAL PHASE

Art. 5.2 TRIMs provides for three different transition periods during which WTO Members, according to their level of development, must phase out WTO-inconsistent measures that the Council on Trade in Goods (CTG) had been notified of:

(a) Developed country Members were required to eliminate their WTO-inconsistent measures by January 1, 1997;

(b) Developing country Members were required to eliminate their WTO-inconsistent measures by January 1, 2000;

(c) LDCs were required to eliminate their WTO-inconsistent measures by January 1, 2002.[4]

Art. 5.1 TRIMs subjects to prior notification all measures that can benefit from the transitional period established: new measures introduced within 180 days before the entry into force of the Agreement shall not profit from the transitional period (Art. 5.4 TRIMs). During the transitional period, a WTO Member could not modify the terms of any WTO-inconsistent measure (Art. 5.4 TRIMs): this is the standstill-obligation imposed on WTO Members with respect to all notified TRIMs. Some developing countries were unable to eliminate WTO-inconsistent measures during the transitional period, and made use of the possibility provided in

---

[4] The transition period for LDCs was extended until 2012 by virtue of Annex F of the Hong Kong Ministerial Declaration, see *infra* for more detail.

the TRIMs Agreement (Art. 5.3) to request extension of the deadline for compliance from the CTG.[5]

3.4 PROCEDURAL OBLIGATIONS

WTO Members must (Art. 6.2 TRIMs):

notify the Secretariat of the publications in which TRIMs can be found, including those applied by regional and local governments and authorities within their territories.

The purpose of this obligation is to ensure transparency. This transparency obligation covers both WTO-consistent and WTO-inconsistent measures.

3.5 SPECIAL AND DIFFERENTIAL TREATMENT

The TRIMs Agreement provides for special and differential treatment by making available longer transitional periods in order to eliminate notified TRIMs to developing countries and LDCs. Following negotiations, it was agreed during the Hong Kong Ministerial Conference (2005) that additional measures were required. Annex F of the Hong Kong Ministerial Decision[6] reflects these new measures:

(a) LDCs were allowed to maintain existing TRIMs until the end of a new transition period lasting for seven years:

(i) The transitional period may be extended by decision of the CTG, in light of the individual financial, trade, and development needs of the Member in question;

(ii) LDCs would have to notify the CTG within 2 years of their TRIMs, their notification duty starting on January 17, 2006;

(b) LDCs were further allowed to introduce new TRIMs:

(i) The duration of the new TRIMs shall not exceed 5 years, and they could be renewed subject to review and decision by the CTG;

(ii) To this effect, LDC will have to notify the CTG of their new TRIMs within 6 months of their adoption;

(iii) The CTG is encouraged to give positive consideration to such notifications.

---

[5] Extensions were granted to Argentina, Colombia, Malaysia, Mexico, Pakistan, Thailand (until December 31, 2003), Philippines (June 30, 2003), and Romania (May 31, 2003).

[6] Decision adopted on December 18, 2005, see WTO Doc. WT/MIN(05)/DEC of December 22, 2005.

3.6 THE RELATIONSHIP BETWEEN TRIMS AND THE GATT

Several WTO Panels have dealt with measures challenged under both GATT and Art. 2.1 TRIMs. In analyzing the legal relationship between GATT and TRIMs, a preliminary issue is whether there is a conflict between the two agreements. Recall that, according to the General Interpretive Note to Annex 1A of the WTO Agreement, when a conflict exists between a provision of the GATT and a provision of another agreement in Annex 1A, (like TRIMs), the provision of the other agreement "shall prevail to the extent of the conflict". In the event of a conflict between provisions of GATT and TRIMs, the provisions of the TRIMs would, therefore, prevail. The term "conflict" is not defined any further. As we saw in the previous Chapters, the originally narrow understanding of the term conflict, quickly gave way to the concept of *lex specialis*: According to this interpretative principle, even if no genuine conflict between two provisions in two different agreements exists, a transaction which potentially could be submitted under two different agreements should always be submitted to the one that regulates in more detail the transaction at hand. There have been disagreements, nevertheless, in earlier case law as to which of the two (GATT, TRIMs) is the more specific agreement. For example, in *Indonesia–Autos,* the Panel reflects the view that TRIMs is the more specific agreement (§ 14.63):

> first examine[d] the claims under the TRIMs Agreement since the TRIMs Agreement is more specific than Article III:4 [of the GATT] as far as the claims under consideration are concerned.

However, in *Canada–Autos,* while the Panel accepted (§ 10.63):

> that a claim should be examined first under the agreement which is the most specific with respect to that claim . . .

it concluded that TRIMs could not be (§ 10.63):

> properly characterized as being more specific than Article III:4 in respect of the claims raised by the complainants in the present case.

In the same vein, in *India–Autos*, the Panel stated that, as a general matter, it might be difficult to characterize the TRIMs Agreement as necessarily more specific than the relevant GATT provisions (§ 7.157). The Panel analyzed the measures in question under the GATT first, partly because India, the responding party, encouraged the Panel to refrain from evaluating the consistency of the challenged measures with the relevant provisions of the TRIMs Agreement (§ 7.158). The order of analysis of the various claims presented should not, in principle, affect the outcome, assuming that an examination under the TRIMs will follow that under the GATT; nevertheless, as the Panel itself implicitly recognized, the situation could be different in case judicial economy has been exercised. In this case, the outcome of the dispute could be different had a Panel examined the challenged measure under the more detailed agreement (TRIMs) as well (§§ 7.158–161).[7]

There has been a drastic change in the attitude of the WTO adjudicating bodies since the *EC–Sardines* case. In that report, the AB made it abundantly clear that WTO adjudicating bodies should always start from the agreement regulating a matter in a more specific manner; by privileging the TBT over the GATT (§ 204), and hinting that the GATT is the default agreement, one should expect that Panels now confronted with this issue, will start their analysis from the claims under TRIMs.

3.7 THE RELATIONSHIP WITH OTHER ANNEX 1A AGREEMENTS

The legal relationship between TRIMs and other Annex 1A agreements was discussed in a case involving a measure challenged under TRIMs Agreement and the SCM Agreements. In *Indonesia–Autos*, the Panel concluded that measures challenged under both TRIMs and the SCM must be reviewed under both agreements. The Panel examined whether there was conflict between the two agreements. In its view, the General Interpretive Note did not apply to the relationship between TRIMs and SCM (§ 14.49). It used a narrow definition of the term "conflict" to arrive at its final judgment. It held that (§ 14.55):

> there is no general conflict between the SCM Agreement and the TRIMs Agreement.

It thus moved on and applied the two agreements cumulatively to the transaction before it.

4. INSTITUTIONAL ISSUES

A Committee on Trade–Related Investment Measures (TRIMs Committee) is established by virtue of Art. 7 TRIMs. The main task of the TRIMs Committee is to monitor the operation and implementation of the TRIMs Agreement. It further provides a forum for consultations among WTO Members on trade and investment issues. The TRIMs Committee reports annually to the CTG.

5. TRADE AND INVESTMENT RE–VISITED

The inevitable conclusion from the discussion above is that the WTO, as it now stands, does not deal with investment in comprehensive manner. A Working Group was, nevertheless, established soon after the advent of the WTO to discuss this issue. It lived, alas, a short life and did

---

[7] For examples of judicial economy, see the Panel reports on *Indonesia–Autos* (§ 14.93); *India–Autos* (§ 7.324); *EC—Bananas III* (§ 7.185); and *Canada–Autos* (§ 10.91).

not manage to bring its mandate to conclusion. Attempts to multilateralize investment protection have also taken place outside the WTO, most notably within the OECD where the Multilateral Agreement on Investment (MAI) was launched. This initiative too was not led to fruitful conclusion. As a result, investment protection nowadays takes place within bilateral investment treaties (BITs), regional schemes, and PTAs.

5.1 THE WORKING GROUP ON TRADE AND INVESTMENT

Following an initial discussion in the Singapore Ministerial Conference (1996), WTO Members agreed at the Doha Ministerial Conference (November 2001), to undertake negotiations on trade and investment beginning in 2003.[8] The scope of these negotiations was not initially defined. The negotiators nonetheless, recognized the interrelationship between trade and investment and decided to start the negotiating process on a clean slate.[9] During the Cancun Mid–Term Review meeting (September 2003), which was supposed to signal that trading partners were half way towards the successful conclusion of the Doha round, the WTO Membership took the dramatic decision to stop the negotiation on trade and investment.[10] As a result, the WTO Membership abandoned the negotiating group on trade and investment.[11] We quote from a decision adopted by the WTO General Council on August 1, 2004:

> Relationship between trade and investment, interaction between trade and competition policy and transparency in government procurement: the Council agrees that these issues, mentioned in the Doha Ministerial Declaration in paragraphs 20–22, 23–25 and 26 respectively, will not form part of the Work Programme set out in that Declaration and therefore no work towards negotiations on any of these issues will take place within the WTO during the Doha Round.[12]

5.2 ATTEMPTS TO MULTILATERALIZE OUTSIDE THE WTO

The only attempt to multilateralize investment protection conducted under the aegis of the WTO was a failure: negotiated at the OECD, the MAI was intended to be eventually "exported" to the WTO. The MAI would have removed barriers to investment, provided protection against

---

[8] WTO Doc. WT/MIN(01)/DEC/1 of November 20, 2001 at § 20.

[9] WTO Working Group on the Relationship between Trade and Investment, WTO Doc. WT/WGTI/W/7 of 18 September 1997. See the excellent analysis of Koulen (2001).

[10] Along with the negotiation on trade and competition.

[11] See Trachtman (1998) on the issue of linkage between trade and investment, and Sauvé and Wilkie (2000) on the negotiation in the WTO.

[12] WTO, Doha Work Programme, Decision Adopted by the General Council on 1 August 2004 (2004) WTO Doc. WT/L/579 at § 3.

expropriation and measures diminishing its value, and instituted a dispute settlement system. The MAI deserves a short narrative: in 1992, the OECD Investment Committee started its preparatory work.[13] The mandate for the negotiations was to achieve a multilateral framework for investment, with high standards of investment liberalization and protection. Negotiators further aimed at providing an effective dispute settlement system that would be accessible to OECD and non-OECD Members. The negotiations formally began in September 1995, continued until April 1998 and extended into the fall of 1998. The 29 OECD Members as well as the Commission of the EU participated in the negotiations. Participation was not confined to OECD Members only:

(a) Eight non-OECD Members participated as observers: Argentina; Brazil; Chile; Estonia; Hong Kong, China; Latvia; Lithuania; and the Slovak Republic;

(b) Other (than the eight who acquired observer-status) non-OECD Members were informed on a regular basis about the status and substance of the negotiations.

The negotiators felt the time was ripe for a global framework for investment, mainly because foreign direct investment (FDI) grew 14 times between 1973 and 1996 (from $25 to $350 billion), significantly faster than growth in international trade.[14] The MAI was a very ambitious project. Unlike the regime envisaged by most bilateral investment treaties, the MAI purported to cover the pre-establishment phase as well.[15] Hence, the MAI included provisions on privatization, behaviour of monopolies, and the temporary entry and stay of key personnel, such as investors, managers, and experts. It had three pillars:

(a) Investment liberalization;

(b) Investment protection; and

(c) Dispute settlement.

With respect to the first and the second pillars, the MAI enshrined the principle of non-discrimination:

(a) First, the MAI signatories committed to treat foreign investors and their investments no less favourably than they treat their own (NT);

(b) Second, the MAI signatories agreed not to distinguish between investors and investments of other MAI parties (MFN).

With respect to the third pillar, the MAI contained provisions on cross-border transfer of funds, fair and equitable treatment, and the

---

[13] Karl (1998) and Daly (1998) for an insider's narrative on the MAI. See also Trebilcock, Howse and Elliason (2012) who provide a slightly different account.

[14] See on this score, Trebilcock, Howse and Elliason (2012).

[15] On this issue, see the comprehensive analysis in Sacerdotti (1997), and also in Sauvé and Wilkie (2000).

standard of compensation in case of expropriation. The coverage of the MAI was quite broad: FDI, portfolio investment, and rights under contract formed part of its subject matter. The MAI negotiations provoked a series of negative reactions and the project was abandoned in late 1998.

5.3 INVESTMENT PROTECTION IN BITs AND PTAs

The absence of success in the MAI-and the WTO Trade and Investment negotiations, as well as the current limited ambit of TRIMs, amount to absence of multilateral protection of investors who are currently protected through BITs, or through investment provisions in PTAs, such as NAFTA Chapter 11[16] or the EU. Inclusion of investment in PTAs deserves particular mention: A recent study by Horn et al. (2010) shows that investment protection prominently figures among many PTAs signed by the two main hubs (EU, US) and a series of spokes. It is remarkable that many developing countries are eager to sign investment protection provisions with capital exporting countries in the context of PTAs: Horn et al. (2010) show that 12 out of 14 PTAs signed between 1992 and 2008 by the EU with a host of developing nations contain provisions relating to investment protection. Moreover, in 8 of these schemes the language chosen was clearly binding, thus ensuring, enforcement of property rights. The US included provisions relating to investment protection in 11 out of 14 PTAs signed, of which all 11 contain binding language. In another recent study Kotschwar (2010) analyzes investment provisions in 52 PTAs and concludes that it is flexibility that drives the inclusion of investment provision in PTAs. If right, then the possibility for concluding an international agreement would be severely hampered. It is probably high time that the WTO reflects seriously on why this has been the case. This is of course part of a wider discussion concerning the discrepancy between the multilateral and the preferential agenda that the Doha Round should have entertained but did not.

QUESTIONS AND COMMENTS

ITO and Investment: Investment was not regulated in comprehensive manner in the Havana Charter. Two provisions (Arts. 11 and 12) in Chapter III entitled "Economic Development and Reconstruction" deal with this issue, and the placement of investment-related provisions in this Chapter probably denotes the over-arching objective that investment regulation should serve. The regime was thus not geared towards protecting property rights, although this would have been the natural outcome; it was more thought as a tool to promote economic development faithful to the *"dirigiste"* spirit of the ITO. The provisions were all of hortatory language leaving ample discretion to interested parties to adopt specific measures the content of which is not specified ex ante:

---

[16] 32 International Legal Materials 289 (1993).

(a) ITO Members could reflect on the appropriateness to sign bilateral or even multilateral agreements protecting international investment, the possibility for one multilateral agreement being retained;

(b) In the meantime, they should strive to provide foreign investors with equitable treatment, the parameters of the treatment remaining unspecified.

Two more specific provisions were included in the ITO Charter:

(a) ITO Members should reflect on avoiding double taxation as means to promote international investment;

(b) They should further reflect on the appropriateness to avoid discriminating against foreign investors (the benchmark of comparison being domestic investors).

Again the language was hortatory. Anyway, the non-advent of the ITO[17] meant the *de facto* irrelevance of these provisions. By virtue of Art. XXIX GATT, GATT contracting parties undertook to observe, pending the entry into force of the ITO, to the fullest extent possible the general principles of Chapters I–VI of the Havana Charter.

Renegotiating the TRIMs: The CTG was required to review the TRIMs by January 1, 2000 (Art. 9 TRIMs) to:

consider whether the Agreement should be complemented with provisions on investment policy and competition policy.

The review process began in 1999 and is still on-going. There is no consensus on the need to amend the Agreement. While developing countries are seeking greater flexibility to apply TRIMs for development purposes, developed countries generally would like to see the current balance of rights and obligations maintained.

MAI: Why in your view did the MAI initiative fail?

---

[17] Irwin et al. (2008); Jackson (1969); Wilcox (1949).

CHAPTER 22

GOVERNMENT PROCUREMENT

■ ■ ■

1. THE LEGAL DISCIPLINE

The Agreement on Government Procurement (GPA) is a plurilateral agreement. Its signatories commit that certain (governmental, non-governmental) entities, which they have included in their lists of concessions, will purchase on a non-discriminatory basis from suppliers originating in other signatories.

2. THE RATIONALE FOR THE LEGAL DISCIPLINE

There are undisputed gains from trade liberalization in the GP market: although the importance of the government procurement market tends to be over-stated sometimes,[1] it is far from negligible;[2] a 2001 OECD study[3] shows that, on average, the size of the government procurement market (besides defence-related spending, and compensation to employees) for all OECD Members is roughly 7.57% of their national incomes; the WTO webpage calculates it at $1.6 trillion for 2008.

3. COVERAGE OF THE LEGAL DISCIPLINE

3.1 A PLURILATERAL AGREEMENT

The GPA is one of the original four plurilateral agreements. As a result, the GPA is binding only upon those WTO Members which have adhered to it. The main discipline imposed though the GPA is non-discrimination when committed entities purchase goods; by virtue of Art. III.8 GATT, Members are not bound by the NT-obligation with respect to

---

[1] According to the WTO DG, the new GPA package agreed in the Doha round would result in gains in market access between $80–100 billion annually, but this of course depends on a number of parameters that are unknown or relatively little known at this moment. It is only normal of course for the DG to opt for a high number in an effort to persuade trading nations to join the GPA, see WTO Doc. WT/MIN(11)/5 of November 18, 2011 at p. 6.

[2] See for example, Francois et al. (1997) who calculated the welfare implications of liberalization in the GP market for the US.

[3] OECD, The Size of Government Procurement Markets, www.oecd.org/dataoecd/34/14/18845927.pdf (2001): the OECD, Paris. Note that the OECD study refers to the contestable market, that is, the part of the government procurement market that is open to foreign bidders and not to the overall market, which could be substantially higher.

government purchasing. By the same token, Art. XIII GATS excludes national treatment from government procurement in the services sector. Signatories to the GPA, consequently, have brought, with respect to their list of covered entities, government procurement back into the realm of national treatment. There were questions asked regarding the legal relevance of MFN in the GP-context:[4] the Panel in *EC–Commercial Vessels* held that this should not be the case. Looking into the negotiating history of the relevant legal instruments, it concluded that, with respect to government procurement, GATT contracting parties aimed to introduce a caveat to both the MFN—as well as the national treatment obligation (§§ 7.85–87):

> In support of its reading of "all matters referred to in paragraphs 2 and 4 of Article III", Korea argues that this phrase was inserted during the Geneva Session of the ITO Preparatory Committee in 1947 in order to extend the grant of MFN treatment to all matters dealt with in those paragraphs regardless of whether national treatment is provided for in respect of such matters. We note in this respect that during that session of the ITO Preparatory Committee, the United States made a proposal to amend the text of what was then draft Article 14 (general most-favoured-nation treatment) of the ITO Charter by replacing the phrase "with respect to all matters in regard to which national treatment is provided for in Article 15" (national treatment) with "with respect to all matters referred to in paragraphs 1,2,3, and 4 of Article 15".
>
> . . . At the time the United States made this proposal, paragraph 5 of Article 15, which eventually became paragraph 8 of Article 18 of the Havana Charter and of Article III of the GATT, provided that the national treatment obligations would not apply to government procurement. . . . Therefore, we fail to see how this . . . can support the position taken by Korea in this dispute that a measure expressly removed from the scope of the national treatment obligation in Article III can nevertheless be among the "matters referred to in paragraphs 2 and 4 of Article III".
>
> It is noteworthy in this regard that in a discussion on draft Article 18.8(a) of the Havana Charter corresponding to Article III:8(a), it was observed at a meeting in February 1948 that:
>
>> ". . . the Sub–Committee had considered that the language of paragraph 8 would except from the scope of Article 18 [national treatment] <u>and hence from Article</u> 16 [MFN treatment], laws, regulations and requirements governing purchases effected for governmental purposes where resale was only incidental . . . ".

---

[4] Arrowsmith (2005).

This clearly suggests that negotiators understood that the reference to government procurement in Article 18.8(a) would also apply in the context of the MFN clause (Article 16).

Thus the relevant drafting history that we are aware of shows that the exclusion of government procurement from the national treatment article would also apply to the MFN clause.

The WTO GPA is not the first agreement in this area; it is a successor agreement to the Tokyo round GPA.[5] According to Agreement Establishing the WTO (Art. XII.3), participation in a plurilateral agreement shall be governed by the provisions of each such agreement. Art. XXIV.2 GPA reserves the right to participate in the GPA to WTO Members only. The modalities of the accession procedures are reflected in a WTO document prepared to this effect:[6] A Working Party will be established where all signatories will participate and discuss the term s of accession for the acceding country; at the end of negotiations, a (final) report will be submitted to the GPA Committee,[7] which will decide by consensus on the request for accession.

3.2 THE GPA MEMBERSHIP

The following WTO Members are signatories to the GPA: Armenia,[8] Canada; Chinese Taipei,[9] the EU;[10] Hong Kong, China; Iceland; Israel; Japan; Korea; Liechtenstein; Netherlands with respect to Aruba; Norway; Singapore; Switzerland; and the US. The GPA is dominated by developed countries. So far, Armenia and Chinese Taipei are the only developing countries that have joined the GPA so far. To encourage participation by developing countries, Art. V.3 GPA provides:

> With a view to ensuring that developing countries are able to adhere to this Agreement on terms consistent with their development, financial and trade needs, the objectives listed in paragraph 1 shall be duly taken into account in the course of negotiations with respect to the procurement of developing countries to be covered by the provisions of this Agreement. Developed countries, in the preparation of their coverage lists under the provi-

---

[5] On the history of GPA, see Blank and Marceau (1997).

[6] WTO Doc. WTO/GPA/1, Annex 2.

[7] Each signatory has a delegate participating in the GPA Committee. An indicative timeframe for accession negotiations has been agreed upon (WTO Doc. GPA/W/109/Rev.2). The GPA Committee has also agreed on a check-list of issues for the provision of information by the applicant governments (WTO Doc. GPA/35).

[8] Armenia joined the GPA on September 15, 2011.

[9] On December 9, 2008, the Committee on Government Procurement adopted a decision inviting Chinese Taipei to accede to the plurilateral agreement—ending their accession negotiations. Chinese Taipei finally joined the GPA on July 15, 2009.

[10] On the enlargement of the EU from 15 to 25 and the corresponding accession of its 10 new Members to the GPA, see WTO Doc. GPA/78 of May 4, 2004; on the enlargement of the EU from 25 to 27 (accession of Bulgaria and Romania to the GPA), see WTO Doc. GPA/90 of December 11, 2006.

sions of this Agreement, shall endeavour to include entities procuring products and services of export interest to developing countries.

There are other provisions as well which are meant to encourage participation of developing countries to the GPA: Art. V (Special and Differential Treatment) for example, contains a number of best endeavors-clauses calling on GPA signatories to take into account the need of developing countries to safeguard their balance of payments position; to promote the establishment of domestic industries; to support their industrial units; and to encourage their development through arrangements among developing countries. Albania, China, Georgia, Jordan, Kyrgyz Republic, Moldova, Oman and Panama are formally in the process of acceding to the GPA. Four WTO Members have provisions in their respective Protocols of Accession to the WTO regarding accession to the GPA: Croatia, the Former Yugoslav Republic of Macedonia, Mongolia, and Saudi Arabia.[11] Twenty-one WTO Members have observer status in the GPA Committee: Albania, Argentina, Australia, Bahrain, Cameroon, Chile, China, Colombia, Croatia, Georgia, Jordan, the Kyrgyz Republic, Moldova, Mongolia, New Zealand, Oman, Panama, Saudi Arabia, Sri Lanka, Turkey and Ukraine. Four intergovernmental organizations also have observer status: IMF, International Trade Centre (ITC), OECD, and UNCTAD.

3.3 THE ENTITIES COVERED

WTO Members joining the GPA can decide on how much they want to liberalize their procurement markets: Art. I GPA makes it clear that the GPA disciplines apply only to entities committed by the signatories and inscribed to this effect in an appendix to the GPA:

> This Agreement applies to any law, regulation, procedure or practice regarding any procurement by entities covered by this Agreement, as specified in Appendix 1.

Appendix 1, which forms an integral part of the GPA, is divided into five Annexes and reflects the commitments of each GPA signatory with respect to:

(a) Central government entities (Annex 1);

(b) Sub-central government entities (Annex 2);

(c) All other entities that procure in accordance with the provisions of this Agreement (Annex 3);

(d) Entities procuring services (Annex 4);

(e) Entities procuring construction services (Annex 5).

Whereas the first three Annexes refer to covered entities, the last two refer to types of contracts that the covered entities can sign. Each GPA signatory will reflect its entities for which it agrees to abide by the GPA

---

[11] WTO Doc. GPA/92 of December 13, 2007.

obligations. Hence, the GPA covers entities procuring both goods and services, albeit the latter in a limited manner.[12] A parallel process aiming to liberalize procurement in the services markets is underway but has not led to a fruitful conclusion yet. Under Art. XIII.1 GATS, procurement of services is neither subject to MFN (Art. I GATS), nor to specific commitments (Art. XVI GATS, and Art. XVII GATS). Art. XIII.2 GATS explains that multilateral negotiations should take place within two years from the entry into force of the Agreement Establishing the WTO with the aim of liberalizing the government procurement market for services. In March 1995, the GATS Rules Working Party was established which has been in place ever since. According to the Guidelines and Procedures for the Negotiations on Trade in Services (established in WTO Doc. S/L/93), WTO Members should, *inter alia*, complete negotiations under Art. XIII GATS before negotiating specific commitments. The mandate was re-affirmed in the Hong Kong Ministerial Declaration (2005).[13] The EU has taken the initiative and proposed the elements of an agreement;[14] so far, however, negotiations have been inconclusive.[15] So with the exception Annexes 4 and 5 to the GPA, there are no multilateral disciplines regarding government procurement in the services market.

It is not the case that any purchasing by the entities covered will *ipso facto* have to respect the disciplines included in the GPA. WTO Members will specify in each Annex the relevant threshold-value: contracts worth a value above the established threshold-value will have to respect the GPA-disciplines. Art. I.4 GPA reads in this respect:

> this Agreement applies to any procurement contract of a value of not less than the relevant threshold specified in Appendix I.[16]

The GPA does not provide for one valuation method to be used by all GPA signatories at all times. Instead, it stipulates criteria to be used when establishing the valuation method. As a result, some discretion is left with the signatories. To cement the obligation reflected in Art. I.4 GPA, Art. II.3 GPA relevantly provides that:

> the selection of the valuation method by the entity shall not be used, nor shall any procurement requirement be divided, with the intention of avoiding the application of this Agreement.

---

[12] Bronckers (1997). At the 1996 Singapore Ministerial Conference, another multilateral track aiming at the liberalization of the government procurement market was established: the Working Group on Transparency in Government Procurement. It was been inactive following a decision to this effect at the Cancun meeting, that is, the Mid-term review of the Doha round (2004).

[13] See Annex C of the Declaration.

[14] See WTO Doc. S/WPGR/M/54 of 20 June 2006.

[15] See S/WPGR/17 of 16 November 2007, and WTO Doc. S/WPGR/M/60 of 17 January 2008.

[16] The usual threshold values used are 130,000 SDR (special drawing rights) for goods and services, and 5,000,000 SDR for construction services procured by Annex 1 entities. Higher thresholds have been used for some entities covered by Annexes 2 and 3.

3.4 NON–DISCRIMINATION

Art. III GPA reflects the non-discrimination obligation; it requires from GPA signatories to treat foreign suppliers no less favorably than they treat their domestic suppliers in the context of government purchasing:

> With respect to all laws, regulations, procedures and practices regarding government procurement covered by this Agreement, each Party shall provide immediately and unconditionally to the products, services and suppliers of other Parties offering products and services of the Parties, treatment no less favourable than:
>
> (a) that accorded to domestic producers, services and suppliers; and
>
> (b) that accorded to products, services and suppliers of any other Party.[17]

Art. III.3 GPA clarifies that:

> the provisions of paragraphs 1 and 2 shall not apply to customs duties and charges of any kind imposed on or in connection with importation, the method of levying such duties and charges, other import regulations and formalities, and measures affecting trade in services other than laws, regulations, procedures and practices regarding government procurement covered by this Agreement.

This clarification is necessary in order to leave no doubt that imported goods will have to pay the import duty that has been agreed upon through negotiations. Each WTO Member is free to unilaterally define the origin of the supplier, and apply its definition in a manner consistent with the NT-obligation. Art. IV.2 GPA requests that, when the negotiations on the WTO Agreement on Rules of Origin are completed to:

> take the results of that work programme and those negotiations into account in amending paragraph 1 as appropriate.

As is the case in both the GATT and the GATS, the GPA contains a list of exceptions to the Agreement, set out in Art. XXIII. Art. XXIII.1 GPA refers to national security, while Art. XXIII.2 GPA reflects the list of general exceptions.[18] The schedules of concessions under the GPA often contain General Notes at the end which might provide for a number of additional exceptions, including from the obligation not to discriminate; this practice has developed, although the GPA nowhere mentions that

---

[17] Domestic laws, on the other hand, will regulate the behavior of suppliers. As Wood (1997) points out, antitrust might have an important role to play in this respect. Recall nonetheless, that there is nothing like a world competition law, so regulation in this respect could be asymmetric across countries.

[18] See the discussion in Chapter 12.

signatories can legitimately introduce such clauses in their schedules.[19] Modifications of schedules are possible by virtue of Art. XXIV.6 GPA: to this effect, the Member requesting modification will notify its new concession and, assuming no objection has been raised within 30 days, the concession will be modified accordingly.[20]

3.5 AWARDING A CONTRACT

3.5.1 The Procedure

The GPA distinguishes between four different modes following which a decision to award a contract will be taken:

(a) Open tendering procedures, whereby, by virtue of Art. VII.3(a) GPA, any interested party may apply and participate in a competition to win a government procurement contract;

(b) Selective tendering procedures, whereby only few suppliers are invited by the procuring entity to participate (provided that Art. X GPA, and Art. VII.3(b) GPA, have been respected). To ensure that these procedures will not serve as a gateway to protectionist behavior, the procuring entities are required to invite the maximum number of entities to submit a tender. Art. VIII GPA includes safeguards to ensure that conditions for qualification do not discriminate against foreign suppliers. Moreover, by virtue of Art. IX.9 GPA, procuring entities are required to publish on a yearly basis the list of suppliers that qualify for these procedures, as well as the criteria that new suppliers are required to meet for their inclusion in the list. The selective procedure allows for a stage for negotiations with suppliers even after the submission of bids provided that this intent is clearly mentioned in the invitation to participate. This is important because it makes the GPA more flexible in comparison to other regimes (for example the EU Public Sector Procurement Directive) and more comparable to the EU Utilities Directive and the Defence and Security Directive;

(c) Limited tendering procedures, whereby an entity may, by virtue of Art. VII.3(c) GPA, contact suppliers individually provided that the conditions included in Art. XV GPA have been respected. Art. XV GPA reserves this possibility to cases of urgency, or cases where no response to an open and/or selective procedure has been registered, or cases where the product or service purchased can only be purchased from one supplier;

(d) Negotiations between the procuring entity and economic operators under the strict conditions expressed in Art. XIV GPA (for example,

---

[19] A signatory can of course, assuming the relevant conditions have been met, take exemption from the obligation not to discriminate for health, national security, etc. reasons. A General Note does not serve this purpose though.

[20] It is not infrequent that an objection is raised, see, for example, objections to Canada's modifications in WTO Doc. GPA/92 of December 13, 2007.

when it is clear that no one tender is the most advantageous and subject to the non-discrimination discipline).

3.5.2 Kicking the Process Off: The Invitation to Submit

Covered entities wishing to procure must, according to Art. IX.1 GPA, publish an invitation to participate for all cases of intended procurement which is covered by the GPA ("tender notice"): through this document, they will inform all GPA signatories of the imminent procurement. The tender notice must reflect all elements referred to in Art. IX.6 GPA:

> (a) The nature and quantity of the procurement as well as an estimate of timing;
> (b) Whether the procedure is open, selective or whether it will involve negotiation;
> (c) Date for starting delivery;
> (d) Address and deadline for submission;
> (e) Address of the entity awarding the contract;
> (f) Economic and technical requirements;
> (g) The amount and terms of payment;
> (h) Whether offers concern purchase, lease, etc.

A summary of the notice of initiation must be published in one of the official languages of the WTO, that is, English, French, or Spanish (Art. IX.8 GPA). In the "tender documentation" (Art. XII GPA), the procuring entity will be further required to provide all information necessary to the suppliers in order to prepare their proposals: this includes technical specifications (if applicable), as well as the criteria under which the contract will be awarded; parties to the GPA are requested, by virtue of Art. VI GPA, when drawing technical specifications reflecting the characteristics of the products or services to be procured (such as quality, performance, safety and dimensions, packaging, etc.), to ensure that their requirements:

> shall not be prepared, adopted or applied with a view to, or with the effect of, creating unnecessary obstacles to trade.

In the same vein, Art. VI.2 GPA reads:

> Technical specifications prescribed by procuring entities shall, where appropriate: (a) be in terms of performance rather than design or descriptive characteristics; and (b) be based on international standards, where such exist . . .

3.5.3 Awarding the Contract

Art. XVIII.1 GPA obliges GPA signatories to publish, within 72 days from the award of a contract, a statement where they indicate, *inter alia*, the winning supplier. They do not necessarily have to award the contract to the lowest bidder; they could very well award it to the supplier who, in their judgment, tabled the most advantageous offer. Consequently, procuring entities retain substantial authority when deciding on the winning party and their decisions can hardly, assuming no arbitrariness is involved, be put into question. In the absence of case law on this specific issue, we can safely presume that WTO adjudicating bodies will adopt a standard similar to that adopted in contingent protection instruments, that is, neither de novo review, but not total deference either. There is no obligation imposed on procuring entities to include the rationale for the award of the contract in their decision;[21] only if requested by an unsuccessful supplier must an entity provide the reasons that led it to award the contract to a particular supplier (Art. XVIII.2 GPA).

3.6 THE NEW GPA

The negotiations on a new GPA were de-linked from the Doha Round-package. The negotiators managed to agree on a new text in 2006,[22] but as of mid-2013, it has not yet entered into force. The reason for its non-entry into force is that the parties in December 2006, struck an informal agreement that the revised GPA text would not come into force until there was also a mutually satisfactory conclusion in the coverage negotiations, and not before thirty days after 2/3 of the Membership had deposited their instrument of ratification.[23] The GPA has not been much of a success when it comes to inducing participation, as membership remains essentially limited to the OECD countries (and Chinese Taipei). The new revised GPA contains four additional elements aiming at streamlining special and differential treatment and ensuring that developing countries can benefit from market liberalization, that enough room is made to recognize idiosyncratic elements due to their current level of development, but also that their deviations from obligations will not become a permanent theme. To this effect, a series of provisional—that is, time-bound—measures, such as price preferences, are at the disposal of developing countries intended to facilitate their accession to the GPA;[24] recourse to similar measures can take place provided that there is prior demonstration that they correspond to specific development needs; reciprocity (across commitments by developed and developing countries) is the key in negotiating similar measures.[25]

---

[21] Arrowsmith (2005) provides an authoritative explanation of this issue.

[22] WTO Doc. GPA/W/297 of December 11, 2006.

[23] WTO Doc. GP/112 of December 16, 2011.

[24] Mattoo (1997) borrowing from theoretical work in this area had identified the absence of price preferences as one of the reasons why developing countries might legitimately want to abstain from joining the GPA: absent a scheme to this effect, bidding companies might have an incentive to collude in the absence of meaningful competition from local companies.

[25] For an extensive discussion of the new GPA provisions dealing with special and differential-treatment, see Müller (2011).

3.7 TRANSPARENCY

Besides the transparency-requirements with respect to the announcing and the award of contracts, WTO Members of the GPA must, by virtue of Art. XIX.5 GPA, collect and provide, on an annual basis, statistics on their procurements covered by the GPA.[26] A Working Group on Transparency in Government Procurement was established in 1996 and produced some interesting work regarding transparency in this context regarding for example, the scope of procurement, the various procurement methods etc.[27] This group has been inactive since 2004 following the decision in Cancun (2003).

4. ENFORCING THE GPA

4.1 CHALLENGE PROCEDURES

Art. XX GPA reflects the obligation to establish a forum to entertain disputes between private parties and the entities concerned. The rationale behind this provision has to do with the general feeling of uneasiness that surrounded the remedy recommended in the "Trondheim" dispute (*Norway–Trondheim Toll Ring*) in the GATT years, and the resolve to ensure that effective remedies against violations would be provided for in the WTO GPA. The facts of the case are described adequately in § 4.1 of the report:

> The basic facts of the case before the Panel are that in March 1991 the Norwegian Public Roads Administration awarded a contract relating to electronic toll collection equipment for a toll system around the city of Trondheim to a Norwegian company, Micro Design, after single tendering the procurement with that company. The central point of difference between the two parties to the dispute was whether, in single tendering the procurement, Norway had met the requirements of Article V:16(e) of the Agreement. Norway maintained that the single tendering of the contract was justifiable under these provisions, since the contract was for research and development and the part of the contract which it considered covered by the Agreement was for the procurement of prototypes which had been developed in the course of and for that research and development contract. Furthermore, Norway contended that it had complied with the requirements in the headnote to Article V:16. The United States maintained that Article V:16(e) was not applicable since, in its view, the objective of the contract was not research and development but the procurement of toll collection equipment. Moreo-

---

[26] See, for example, Norway's notification for 2006 (WTO Doc. GPA/88/Add. 1 of March 12, 2007), and Hong Kong, China's for the same year (WTO Doc. GPA/91 of October 9, 2007).

[27] See WTO doc. WT/WGTGP/W/32 of May 23, 2002, a compilation of the various discussion topics by the WTO Secretariat.

ver, the United States disputed that research and/or development had been required to produce these products, that the products could justifiably be characterised as prototypes and that Norway had met the requirements in the headnote to Article V:16.

The US complained that Norway, by not publishing the tender document, had violated its obligations under the GPA and hence for this reason alone had wrongfully awarded the contract to the Norwegian company. It was a rather obvious violation (since the contract concerned the construction of the toll ring system and not research and development) and the Panel had no problem establishing that Norway had indeed violated its obligations under the GPA (§§ 4.14ff.) But then came the question of what the consequence should be for Norway; in what way should it bring its measures into compliance? The US had requested that it be allowed to negotiate compensation with Norway based on lost opportunities. One thing was clear: it would be next to impossible to calculate precise compensation since, in the absence of transparency regarding the tender, any company by any GPA signatory could in principle have won.[28] The Panel, against this background, decided to request from Norway to promise that it would never commit a similar sin and left it there[29] (§§ 4.26ff.):

> In the light of the above, the Panel did not consider that it would be appropriate for it to recommend that Norway negotiate a mutually satisfactory solution with the United States that took into account the lost opportunities of United States companies in the procurement or that, in the event that such a negotiation did not yield a mutually satisfactory result, the Committee be prepared to authorise the United States to withdraw benefits under the Agreement from Norway with respect to opportunities to bid of equal value to the Trondheim contract. The Panel had recognised, however, that nothing prevented the United States from pursuing these matters further in the Committee or from seeking to negotiate with Norway a mutually satisfactory solution provided that it was consistent with the provisions of this and other GATT agreements.
>
> . . .
>
> On the basis of the findings set out above, the Panel <u>concluded</u> that Norway had not complied with its obligations under the Agreement on Government Procurement in its conduct of the procurement of toll collection equipment for the city of Trond-

---

[28] This is probably an exaggeration since not all companies have identical endowments. It is, however, probably true for a smaller segment of all potential candidates, assuming competition in the relevant market. See, on this score, Mavroidis (1993).

[29] What in public international law parlance is known as 'guarantees of non-repetition', see Mavroidis (1993).

heim in that the single tendering of this procurement could not be justified under Article V:16(e) or under other provisions of the Agreement.

The Panel <u>recommends</u> that the Committee request Norway to take the measures necessary to ensure that the entities listed in the Norwegian Annex to the Agreement conduct government procurement in accordance with the above findings. (emphasis in the original).

This is where the GPA "challenge procedures" come in. They are meant to provide:

> non-discriminatory, timely, transparent and effective procedures enabling suppliers to challenge alleged breaches of the Agreement arising in the context of procurements in which they have, or have had, an interest. (Art. XX.2 GPA).

Consequently, private parties will have direct access to the national fora established to adjudicate GPA-related disputes. Private parties must exercise their rights by relatively short deadlines (no less than 10 days from the time when the basis of the complaint is known or reasonably should be known, according to Art. XX.5 GPA). Complaints shall be heard 'by a court or by an impartial and independent review body' (Art. XX.6 GPA). Art. XX.7 GPA regulates the remedies that should be recommended, if a challenge procedure has been successfully invoked by a private party:

> Challenge procedures shall provide for:
>
> (a) rapid interim measures to correct breaches of the Agreement and to preserve commercial opportunities. Such action may result in suspension of the procurement process. However, procedures may provide that overriding adverse consequences for the interests concerned, including the public interest, may be taken into account in deciding whether such measures should be applied. In such circumstances, just cause for not acting shall be provided in writing;
>
> (b) an assessment and a possibility for a decision on the justification of the challenge;
>
> (c) correction of the breach of the Agreement or compensation for the loss of damages suffered, which may be limited to costs for tender preparation or protest.

Although the GPA does not set a limit for the completion of the procedures, it does request (Art. XX.8 GPA) that "the challenge procedure shall normally be completed in a timely fashion."[30] The GPA challenge

---

[30] Georgopoulos (2000) discusses Greece's experience enforcing government procurement.

procedures leave substantial discretion to signatories to "flesh out" the various steps involved.[31]

4.2 WTO DISPUTE SETTLEMENT

Art. XXII GPA also makes it clear that, in principle, the DSU is applicable for disputes arising in the GPA-context as well. Of course, as briefly discussed in Chapter 1, the WTO dispute settlement is a state-to-state-forum where private parties have no standing. Art. XXII.4 GPA contains the standard terms of reference to be used by interested parties, unless of course they agree to special terms. Interestingly, and in contradiction with the DSU rules, Art. XXII.7 GPA does not allow for cross-retaliation. Practice reveals only a few cases where recourse to the WTO dispute settlement procedures was judged necessary:

(a) In *Japan–Procurement of a Navigation Satellite*, the EU requested consultations arguing that tender specifications by a Japanese entity contravened various GPA rules. The Japanese Ministry of Transportation, an entity covered by the GPA, wanted to purchase a satellite and the technical specifications issued to this effect, explicitly referred to a US system used for air traffic management. During consultations, an arrangement was reached between the complainant and the defendant whereby the latter agreed to establish a cooperative arrangement between the Ministry and an EU agency guaranteeing the inter-operability of the two (the European and the US) systems;[32]

(b) In *US–Procurement*, the EU and Japan challenged the consistency of a US state law prohibiting covered entities from awarding contracts to companies originating in states doing business with Myanmar. This measure was designed to ban companies doing business with a regime which, in the eyes of the Massachusetts government, was in violation of the most fundamental human rights. Following unsuccessful consultations, a panel was established at the request of the complainants. However, shortly thereafter, a US court set aside the law. The Panel was suspended and since no party to the dispute requested, within in a year, that it be reconvened, its authority under Art. 12.12 DSU, lapsed;[33]

(c) In *Korea–Procurement*, the US claimed that Korea had not respected its obligations under the GPA when constructing the Inchon International Airport. Following unsuccessful consultations, the dispute was submitted to a panel which ruled that the Korean procuring entity was not covered by the GPA disciplines. No appeal against the Panel report was launched.

---

[31] The EU Remedies Directive for example, the EU domestic instrument to this effect, provides for a mandatory standstill period and an automatic suspension, see Priess and Friton (2011).

[32] WTO Doc. GPA/M/8.

[33] WTO Docs. WT/DS88/5 and WT/DS95/5 and WT/DSB/M/49. See Linarelli (2011).

5. INSTITUTIONAL ISSUES

A GPA Committee has been established, where each signatory is represented. This body discusses all issues coming under the purview of the GPA, as well as accessions/withdrawals from the GPA (Art. XXI GPA). It issues an annual report pursuant to Art. XXIV.7(a) GPA.

QUESTIONS AND COMMENTS

Remedies: What should be the remedy in the Trondheim litigation discussed *supra*, in your view?

Why did Countries not Liberalize their GP Market Unilaterally? Evenett and Hoekman (2007) have expressed the view that the Keynesian idea that an increase in national income due to rise in government expenditure was greater the smaller the share of goods produced outside the country, was prevailing in the late 1940s. It was thus originally decided that government procurement would not be part of the GATT disciplines.[34] Over the years, government procurement became a formidable weapon at the disposal of national industrial policy. It is remarkable that even serious integration initiatives, like the EU, could not easily tame the will of governments to keep this market to local suppliers only: Messerlin's study (2001) of the EU market shows that at the wake of the great expansion of the EU from 15 to 25 and then 27 member states, its government procurement market was largely segmented, with national champions dominating national markets.

GPA and Developing Countries: Mattoo (1997) advances a series of good reasons explaining why developing countries have so far refused to join: Many of them might, on occasion, be requested to pay supra-competitive prices since, because of the "smallness" of their market, they might not be attracting enough competitors when issuing tenders and those participating might have a strong incentive to collude. It is true that participation in the GPA, under assumptions, might help WTO Members to induce pro-competitive behavior, it should not nevertheless, be considered to be a perfect substitute for effective competition laws.[35] The reasons for not joining are not necessarily the same across WTO Members: Wang (2011) for example, goes so far as to suggest lack of political momentum in China favoring accession to the GPA in light of the difficulty in measuring the pros and the cons, the commitment to join in the Chinese Protocol of Accession notwithstanding; Chakravarthy and Dawar (2011) argue that political economy explains India's reluctance.

---

[34] We are still lacking a theoretical paper discussing the possibility to understand commitments under the GPA through the lenses of terms of trade. And yet there are some reasons to believe that this could be the case: the two main procurement markets negotiating in the context of the GPA (EU, US) are quite symmetric, and reciprocity of market access commitments is an important consideration in the negotiations; on this last point, see Anderson (2011) and WTO Committee on Government Procurement, Modalities for the Negotiations on Extension of Coverage and Elimination of Discriminatory Measures and Practices, WTO Doc. WT/GPA/79 of July 19, 2004.

[35] Anderson, Kovacic, and Müller (2011); Georgopoulos (2000); Wood (1997). Similar results are reported in the empirical study regarding the government procurement provisions in the EC–CARIFORUM agreement by Dawar and Evenett (2011).

Chapter 23

The Advent and Integration Model of GATS

■ ■ ■

1. REGULATION OF TRADE IN SERVICES BEFORE THE ADVENT OF GATS

Trade in services was regulated in the years before the advent of the GATS through bilateral and regional schemes.[1] During this period, the US first developed a comprehensive regulation of its own services market, and had also concluded a number of treaties of Friendship, Commerce, and Navigation (FCN) which regulated relations across countries with respect to specific services, such as, aviation, shipping and communications.[2] Besides that, the US had concluded two PTAs that included chapters on services trade:

(a) the US–Israel Free Trade Agreement, and
(b) the Canada–US Free Trade Agreement.[3]

The former was non-binding with respect to services trade, the parties undertaking however, the obligation to adhere to certain core principles. Section 1401 of the latter limited its applicability to specific sectors only.

The EU was the only entity with experience in negotiating the liberalization of trade in services. Its integration process included comprehensive obligations regarding liberalization of trade in services. The EU was imposing a requirement to liberalize trade in services on all countries which were prepared to sign association agreements with a view to accession to the EU. The EU had similar arrangements with countries that did not adhere to the EU: the EEA (European Economic Area), an association between the EU and Iceland, Liechtenstein, and Norway is a good exam-

---

[1] It took some time before we reached this stage. As Bhagwati (1989) mentions, in early economic analysis services were considered non-tradable (the implication being that if at all an international agreement should cover investment only).

[2] Brock (1982) at pp. 236ff. The US stopped negotiating FCNs already in the fifties.

[3] See Nyahoho (1990) on the impact that this agreement had on the GATS negotiation. Krommenacker (1987) mentions an agreement between Japan and the US (implemented on April 1, 1987) concerning the possibility for lawyers from the two countries to work in each other's territory under strict conditions specified in the agreement.

ple. As is the case with the US, the EU did not have any North–South agreements aiming at liberalizing trade in services.

There was also some industry-specific cooperation: the International Telecommunications Unions (ITU) allocates broadcasting frequencies; the Bank for International Settlements (BIS) discusses and sets standards on international banking regulation and supervision; the International Civil Aviation Organization (ICAO) administers agreements on civil aviation; the International Maritime Organization (IMO) is in charge of agreements on shipping. Within the OECD, the Code of Liberalisation of Current Invisible Operations, and the Code of Liberalisation of Capital Movements have contributed towards reducing restrictions on current invisible transactions and transfers, as well as abolishing some restrictions on cash flows.

The absence of a genuine multilateral scheme was no obstacle to the fast increase of the volume of services traded. A number of reasons help explain this:

(a) technology (e.g., the telecoms revolution) made it possible to perform a wide variety of services at a distant geographical location opening up the road to trade opportunities: trade analysts in Washington D.C could, for example, have access to data maintained in various parts of the world;[4]

(b) the increasing connection between goods and services, since many services were inputs to goods, and liberalization of trade in goods *ipso facto* amounted to liberalization of trade in services as well;

(c) The shift in employment from manufacturing to services in most OECD countries;[5]

(d) The trend towards greater specialization in services and the ensuing gains in productivity.

The IMF data suggest that in the late 1970s, that is, before the discussion to liberalize started gaining pace, trade in services was in the vicinity of $400 billion, or close to 1/5 of world trade in goods.[6] However, what is more noticeable is that trade in services (as recorded at that time) doubled between 1960 and 1970, and once again between 1970 and 1975, and this upward trend more or less continued after 1975 as well. The World Bank data suggest the following:

---

[4] It is not only for example, through the advances in telecoms that services could by-pass national frontiers. It is also the service-product itself that benefitted from technological advances and incorporated elements un-bestowed to it previously.

[5] Brock (1982) cites statistics to the effect that in the US in 1981, 72% of the non agricultural population was engaged in service activities (63% in 1961). This was not just a US phenomenon: in Japan the corresponding numbers were 49 and 37%.

[6] Balance of Payments Statistics, IMF, Washington, vol. XXXII, 1981, part 2. McCulloch (1990, p. 331) mentions that in GATT's estimate, the value of world trade of services for 1988 rose up to $600 billion.

Table 23.1 Global Trade Flows, 1980 and 1992 (US $billion and percentage)[7]

	1980	1992	Average annual change
Total trade in services	358	931	8.3
OECD (shares in parentheses)	283 (79%)	765 (82%)	8.6
Rest of world	75 (21%)	166 (18%)	6.8
Services as share of goods *and* services	17.0	22.0	2.2
OECD	18.8	22.7	1.6
Rest of world	12.7	19.2	3.5

Table 23.2 Shares in Global Service Exports and Relative Specialization, 1980 and 1992[8]

Country group	Travel		Transport		All Other	
	1980	1992	1980	1992	1980	1992
Share in global trade:						
OECD members	71.6	77.9	78.4	81.8	80.2	84.6
Developing countries	21.8	17.3	16.5	12.5	15.3	11.7
Relative specialization:						
OECD members	1.01	0.96	1.10	1.02	1.13	1.06
Developing countries	0.93	1.12	0.65	0.82	0.65	0.74
Small LDCs (1 million people or less)	2.19	3.45	1.19	1.85	0.39	1.11

If trade in services was growing in the absence of a comprehensive framework à la GATS, why bother negotiating one? Brock (1982) speaks of a trend of new protectionism. In his words (Brock, 1982, p. 234):

---

[7] Source: World Bank, data pertain only to countries reporting to the IMF.
[8] Idem.

Restrictive measures under consideration in a number of countries in telecommunications, data processing and information services have already created much uncertainty in the business community about the future ability of firms to utilise communication and data-processing facilities; it has hurt investments and reduced trade opportunities. If the trend of increasing barriers to trade in services continues unchecked, trade opportunities could be markedly reduced and the international trading system could be seriously harmed.

2. THE ROAD TO PUNTA DEL ESTE AND THE FORMAL NEGOTIATION OF GATS

2.1 THE 1982 MINISTERIAL DECISION

In 1982, encouraged by the fact that the Tokyo Round contained scattered provisions on services, the US attempted to introduce the negotiation of a services agreement at the Ministerial Conference held in Madrid (from 24 to 29 November and attended by some 70 Ministers from the 88 GATT member countries). But its push was largely unsuccessful;[9] a coalition of developing countries with some help from France resisted the idea. At that time, the USTR, William E. Brock, had already served before in the Banking Committee of the US Senate, and is, for this reason, quite immersed in this discussion. The US did not leave, nonetheless, the Ministerial Conference totally empty-handed. It managed to secure reference to services trade in the Ministerial Declaration:

The CONTRACTING PARTIES decide:

1. To recommend to each contracting party with an interest in services of different types to undertake, as far as it is able, national examinations of the issues in this sector.

2. To invite contracting parties to exchange information on such matters among themselves, *inter alia*, through international organizations such as GATT. The compilation and distribution of such information should be based on as uniform a format as possible.

---

[9] Croome (1995 at pp. 118ff.) reports that hostility of developing countries against this subject was such that, in the early 1980s at least, no meeting could be held in the GATT premises nor could the GATT Secretariat participate in the meetings wherever held. Brock is quoted in Deese (2007 p. 98) stating: "key states just naturally reacted against US proposals because they were coming from the United States". In the same vein, it is reported that Brazilian Ambassador Maciel complained to DG Dunkel that GATT Secretariat staffer Jacques Nussbaumer was having in visible place in his office binders with the title 'Trade in Services'. Such headings (titles) were impermissible in his view and should be immediately modified. Viewed from this perspective the coalition between developed and developing countries that later helped launch the services negotiation in the Uruguay Round (the Café au Lait group that we discuss *infra*) must have been a blessing for the US position, if it did not have its blessing altogether.

3. To review the results of these examinations, along with the information and comments provided by relevant international organizations, at their 1984 Session and to consider whether any multilateral action in these matters is appropriate and desirable.[10]

2.2 THE CG 18

Simultaneously with its efforts to obtain a binding agreement to negotiate on trade in services, the US tried to push its services agenda through the Consultative Group of Eighteen (CG 18) as well, a GATT organ. The role and function of this organ is often overlooked in literature. CG 18 was some sort of a harbinger for global governance: representatives of the IMF attended part of the group's third meeting in June 1976. And the US choice is not accidental. It wanted to secure a "soft" agreement in the context of CG 18, an organ not entrusted with decision making powers that could serve as a pathway to a binding decision. The US did not want to burn any bridges: It would take the time necessary to bring a critical mass of GATT players on board; almost all of them participated in CG 18.[11]

The group discussed trade in services in October 1979 and in March 1981. The GATT Secretariat was asked by CG 18 to prepare documents which it did on essentially conceptual issues.[12] The CG 18 then would deliberate on the basis of the submitted information. Although it did not have the authority to decide on inclusion of this item in the agenda for the new round, two things are clear: first, it was in favour of a new round, and second, it did not oppose the inclusion of services among the negotiating items.[13]

---

[10] GATT Doc. BISD 29th Supplement at pp. 21–22, italics in the original. The GATT CONTRACTING PARTIES (in block letters) was the highest organ of the GATT. It could decide on everything coming under the GATT mandate and had the authority to establish subsidiary bodies necessary for the functioning of the GATT. All GATT contracting parties (in low case this term indicates the GATT 'membership') participated in the CONTRACTING PARTIES which decided by consensus. See also the Appendix in Feketekuty (1988). In his view, the aforementioned decision was the best Brock could get in order to keep the ball rolling.

[11] Marchetti and Mavroidis (2011).

[12] For example, GATT Doc. CG.18/W/45 of October 10, 1980.

[13] The mandate of CG 18 was renewed in November 1976 for another year, and in November 1977 the GATT Council decided to extend the mandate until the end of the Tokyo Round and to take a decision then on the group's future. In the group's report on its activities to the GATT Council in 1979 (L/4869), having reviewed its activities over the previous four years, it recommended to the GATT Council that it should be established as a permanent GATT body. The GATT Council accepted this recommendation and reconfirmed the group's mandate, with no changes in its substance. GATT Doc. L/4869 records the strong belief of the group that "the GATT should have at its disposal a small but representative group which would permit existing and emerging trade policy issues to be discussed in confidence among responsible officials from capitals and thus facilitate an effective concertation of policies in the trade field". The group died alas, a slow death, as a result of the impossibility to convene when it moved from 18 to 22 permanent members with many others knocking on the door. The idea for an Executive Committee somewhere in the GATT structure, nonetheless, did not die altogether. Although CG 18 has not

The US also put together informal gatherings of trade ministers where even the DG of the GATT, Arthur Dunkel, participated. Dunkel was of the view that the trading community was probably unprepared for a new round after such a short time following the end of the tumultuous Tokyo Round, but was quite distressed to see the expansion and extension of the MFA (Multi–Fibre Agreement) as well as the numerous unilateral actions of dubious GATT-consistency by leading WTO Members. He is quoted to have held the view that in the early 1980s there were real problems in international trade relations and that:

> the answer to them lies in negotiation, not in further breaches of the rules which must weaken the whole trading system.[14]

In Dunkel, the US had an ally arguing in favour of a new round. It was for the US to capture the moment and ensure that services would be part of the new agenda. CG 18 was one step in that direction.

2.3 INVOLVING THE OECD

The US international initiatives did not stop here. Already in October 1978, it had proposed that the OECD Trade Committee study this issue in sufficient detail. In 1979, the Trade Committee started to work. In a Declaration on Trade Policy, OECD members agreed to:

> pursue their efforts to reduce or abolish obstacles to the exchange of goods and services.[15]

The Secretary of the OECD, Emile van Lennep, was no novice in this discussion. Already as of 1971 he had started work on this score by appointing a group of eminent people to evaluate the pros and cons of an agreement in services.[16] The GATT and the OECD became the two main fora where the US was pushing its initiative for a new, more comprehensive round where negotiations on trade in services would have their place. The OECD is in a way an ante-chamber to the GATT: developed countries could use the former to coordinate the policies that they would subsequently advocate in the latter.

In 1987, the OECD produced a comprehensive document that detailed the main elements of an agreement on trade in services, the so-called "Elements of a Conceptual Framework for Trade in Services".[17]

---

reconvened in the 1990s, there were attempts to re-establish it under different names: during the time of DG Ruggiero, some of its members met regularly under the new name 'Invisibles'. Even this group failed to survive the test of time and never convened after the failure to agree in Seattle.

[14] Croome (1995) at p. 17.

[15] See Activities of the OECD in 1980 (1981) at p. 93. See also Drake and Nicolaidis (1992) at pp. 50ff.

[16] Bill Eberle from US business, Bertil Ohlin, the Swedish Nobel Prize economist and former Minister, Sir Richard Powell, from the UK Board of Trade, and the US economist, Harald Malmgren participated in this group.

[17] Elements of a Conceptual Framework for Trade in Services, the OECD: Paris, France.

This document included a non-exhaustive list of items that would have to be included in an eventual agreement covering trade in services.

2.4 THE JARAMILLO GROUP

In early November 1984, the US requested the establishment of a GATT Working Party on Trade in Services, but its request was refused.[18] The US did not lose all the way. On November 30, 1984 it managed a rather "minor" victory, when it secured the following decision by the CONTRACTING PARTIES:

The CONTRACTING PARTIES,

Noting:

that a number of contracting parties with an interest in services have undertaken and circulated national examinations of the issues in this sector, and that other such examinations are recommended; and that the process of carrying out the Ministerial decision highlights the complexity of the issues involved, In pursuance of the 1982 Ministerial decision on services,

Agree to the following arrangements within GATT:

1. That the Chairman of the CONTRACTING PARTIES will organize the exchange of information provided for in the Ministerial Decision on issues in the services sector, essentially on the basis of national examinations, which could refer to any considerations in the area of services which appear relevant to the contracting party concerned, and the compilation and distribution of such information based on as uniform a format as possible;

2. The GATT Secretariat will provide the support necessary for this process;

3. The Chairman of the CONTRACTING PARTIES will keep the Council informed of the progress made and report to the CONTRACTING PARTIES;

4. The CONTRACTING PARTIES decide to review the results of these examinations, along with the information and comments provided by relevant international organizations, at their next regular session and to consider whether any multilateral action in these matters is appropriate and desirable.[19]

This decision was taken at the 40th session of the GATT CONTRACTING PARTIES. It essentially provided for an information exchange mechanism; the desirability of any further action would be decided at a later stage. Ambassador Jaramillo of Colombia, who played a ra-

---

[18] GATT Doc. C/M/183.
[19] GATT Doc. L/5762 published in GATT Doc. BISD 31st Supplement at p. 16.

ther important role in bringing around the GATS, had already been appointed as head of a working group aimed at providing the context to discuss the information mechanism that had been established through the 1982 Ministerial Declaration. Naturally the group was named after him and became known as the "Jaramillo Group".[20] The Jaramillo Group proceeded with the examination of national studies regarding trade in services. Between January 1985 and August 1986, the group reviewed 16 national studies submitted from various countries, namely, Australia, Belgium, Canada, Denmark, European Community, Finland, France, Germany, Italy, Japan, Netherlands, Norway, Sweden, Switzerland, United Kingdom, and the US.[21] Note however, that there is not one single study concerning developing countries. This does not mean however, that developing countries were absent from the process.[22] The GATT Secretariat prepared a very useful document summing up the main questions raised by the various trading partners during this process. This document reveals to considerable extent the attitude (aggressive/defensive) of the various GATT contracting parties.[23] The sequence was, hence, as follows:

> (a) in 1982 the Ministerial Decision allowed for national studies to be conducted by those willing and opened the door to their examination in the 1984 session;
>
> (b) following the rejection of the US proposal to establish a Working Party on Services, the Jaramillo Group sees the light of day and it is in this context that national studies conducted in accordance with the 1982 Ministerial Decision were examined;
>
> (c) in 1984, the CONTRACTING PARTIES institutionalized the information exchange mechanism (in essence, the review of national studies) and *ipso facto* the Jaramillo Group.

During the extraordinary session of the GATT CONTRACTING PARTIES in September 1985,[24] it was decided to establish a Senior Officials Group (SOG) to discuss the modalities of a new round in which trade in services could have been included.[25] Dunkel made appeal to a group of

---

[20] Jaramillo (1994) who explains in sufficient detail the mandate and practice of the group.

[21] GATT Doc. MIN(86)/4 of September 15, 1986.

[22] See for example, the many questions that Argentina and others posed on the occasion of the presentation of national studies by Denmark, Germany, Italy, Norway, and Switzerland, GATT Doc. MDF/W/23 of February 7, 1985.

[23] GATT Doc. MDF/W/58 of November 26, 1985.

[24] Bradley (1987) at pp. 78ff. The GATT Council was an organ that had not been foreseen in the original GATT. It was established through a decision by the CONTRACTING PARTIES (GATT Doc. BISD 9S at pp. 8–9). It was meant to undertake the tasks of the GATT CONTRACTING PARTIES in between their (annual) sessions. Like the GATT Council, the GATT CONTRACTING PARTIES was deciding by consensus. However, in theory at least, it could decide most issues by the majority of the votes cast (Art. XXV GATT). It is impossible to know whether the US would push for voting. It did nonetheless, signalled its interest to decide this issue at the highest level, and not simply in the context of an informal group.

[25] Bradley (1987) at p.79.

experts[26] with no affiliation to the GATT and asked them to provide a diagnosis of the major issues in trade relations and also suggest their medicine. The group was composed of seven personalities: Bill Bradley (US Senator and member of the US Senate Finance Committee, SFC); Pehr Gyllenhammar (Chairman of Volvo); Guy Ladreit de Lacharrière (Vice President of the International Court of Justice, ICJ); Fritz Leutwiler (Chairman of the Swiss National Bank, and President of the Bank for International Settlements); I.G. Patel (London School of Economics); Mario Henrique Simonsen (ex Minister of Finance for Brazil); and Sumito Djojohadikusumo (ex Minister of Trade and Industry of Indonesia). Leutwiler acted as Chairman and the group produced the "Leutwiler report".[27] It provided those arguing in favor of including services in the trading system with an encouragement:

> An attempt to extend a rule-based approach to new areas of economic relations while permitting the rules of trade in goods to continue to decay would lack credibility.[28]

The next year, at the 41st session of the GATT contracting parties, a Preparatory Committee was established in order to prepare the next round of multilateral trade negotiations.[29] In his report to the Session of Contracting Parties at ministerial level, this is how Ambassador Jaramillo summarized the state of the negotiations on the need to add trade in services in the agenda of the upcoming round:

> In my own view, the meetings had gone a long way towards examining the relevant aspects of the issues under discussion and in addressing the themes and concepts to which various delegations had drawn attention. The discussions which had taken place in connection with the presentations by representatives of other international organizations had also provided an opportunity to deal with development aspects, with some key sectoral activities, and with the rôle, of transnational corporations in services. Clearly, however, in the absence of national examinations from developing contracting parties, and perhaps of some other

---

[26] This was only the second time in GATT history that the GATT turned to outside experts. In 1958, a group of experts was established under the Chairmanship of Gottfried Haberler (Harvard), Roberto de Oliveira Campos, a Brazilian economist and Minister of state, and two Nobel prize winners in economics, James Meade and Jan Tinbergen. Together they produced a report called Trends in International Trade which discussed the state of international trade during that period. GATT Doc. L/794/Add. 1 of March 14, 1958.

[27] See Bradley (1987) at pp. 60ff. The US got some help from the participants in the so called Leutwiler report (or report of the seven wise men), a group of seven eminent persons who discussed the future of the GATT and recommended that the possibility for bringing trade in services under the aegis of the GATT be explore. The report, the official name of which was Trade Policies for a Better Future, has been reprinted in 24 International Legal Materials 716 (1985).

[28] This passage is cited in Croome (1995) at pp. 19–20. Croome provides a comprehensive discussion of the report.

[29] GATT Doc. BISD 32, at p. 10.

elements of information on specific subjects which might be thought desirable, the documentation at hand could not be said to be exhaustive. Therefore, it would be wise at this stage to leave open the possibility for examining any new information which could be made available. Moreover, while the exchange of information had been useful, I did not find that there was a consensus on which to base recommendations to the CONTRACTING PARTIES on the question of the appropriateness and desirability of multilateral action on services.

A number of options were open under the terms of reference of the Decision of CONTRACTING PARTIES of November 1985. Consultations were held among a large number of delegations and at informal meetings convened to discuss the matter. These consultations lead to the conclusion that an attempt to draft a text of agreed recommendations for adoption by Ministers would not be useful, given the divergencies of views which existed.

On the other hand, many delegations considered that a clear statement of positions by individual delegations would assist CONTRACTING PARTIES in gauging the situation and in identifying some points of convergence concerning the central question of the appropriateness, desirability and modalities for any possible multilateral action on services.

At the meeting of 29 August 1986, there were statements by some delegations in which they expressed their views on the state of the deliberations and indicated that some elements of convergence between previously opposed views were emerging that seemed to show that a solution in the field of services might be possible. Other delegations expressed scepticism about some aspects of these statements. In this situation I felt that it would be for Ministers at this meeting to tackle the issue in an effort to reach a solution satisfactory to all contracting parties. Accordingly, the meeting of 29 August 1986 recommended that Ministers take fully into account all statements made at that meeting (which are recorded in MDF/36), those made at the meeting of 27 and 30 June 1986 (MDF/35) as well as all the work undertaken under the Agreed Conclusions of 1984 and the November 1985 Decision of the CONTRACTING PARTIES. I would suggest that all these elements might be used as a basis on which efforts way be undertaken at this Session to work towards consensus.[30]

As a new round of multilateral trade negotiations was being agreed, there was still uncertainty as to whether trade in services would be part of it.

---

[30] GATT Doc. MIN(86)/4 of September 15, 1986.

2.5 PUNTA DEL ESTE (1986)

This is how an official GATT document describes the situation at the moment when ministers were convening in Punta del Este:

> Although in a limited way the General Agreement does touch upon some of these industries—for instance, film quotas are the subject of Article IV—the work of the GATT since its inception has been almost wholly concerned with trade in goods. Discussion on whether the GATT should take up the question of trade in services in a serious way and, perhaps, evolve some framework of rules and disciplines began in the early 1980s. The United States promoted the idea prior to the Ministerial Meeting of November 1982. The Ministers decided upon a programme of work which provided for the exchange of information on national examinations of issues in the services sector, and for a review of the results of such examination, so as to determine whether any multilateral action was appropriate and desirable.
>
> The 1982 Ministerial decision was further elaborated by a decision of the November 1984 Session of Contracting Parties. In line with that decision, a series of meetings were held during 1985 and early 1986 to facilitate the exchange of information on issues in the services sector. This exchange was, for the most part, based upon sixteen national examinations presented by Australia, Belgium, Canada, Denmark, the European Communities, Finland, France, the Federal Republic of Germany, Italy, Japan, the Netherlands, Norway, Sweden, Switzerland, the United Kingdom and the United States.
>
> To assist the meetings, the Secretariat prepared an analytical summary of the information contained in the national studies. It also prepared summaries of information made available by a number of international organizations which had conducted work in the services area. The discussions in the meetings provided an opportunity for all delegations to comment on the studies and on the information provided by relevant international organizations.
>
> The discussions on the national examinations were concentrated on four main areas. The first concerned the general characteristics of services and included consideration of the problem of defining the term itself. In addition, thought was given to the importance of services in the world and in national economies. The second area of discussion was concerned with basic concepts relating, *inter alia*, to "traded" or "tradeable" services, and to statistical problems and methodologies. It was generally recognized

that available data is inadequate and that international comparisons can therefore be misleading.

The third point of discussion concerned national and international regulations governing individual service sectors and problems identified in relation to international transactions in services. The national studies had noted many types of regulations applying to services in their respective countries and some of them emphasized the growing number of measures, usually of a regulatory nature, which acted as constraints on the development of international trade in services. Some delegations drew attention to the national objectives, often of a non-economic character, served by some regulations.

The meetings also looked at the issues raised in the studies in connection with possible multilateral action on services. At the November 1985 Session of Contracting Parties, it was decided to continue the exchange of information and that Contracting Parties would consider recommendations at their next Session—in fact, the Ministerial Meeting.

Although, by the Summer of 1986, a considerable amount of detailed examination of the various studies had taken place, there remained major differences between the Contracting Parties. Some believed that the GATT should now move on to a new, more concrete, phase of work with the clear objective of creating general and particular trade rules for services. Some were unconvinced but prepared to take the process further while others felt that the exchange of information should continue as before. Some countries continued to feel strongly that the GATT had other important priorities apart from the issue of services, in particular because the GATT rules on trade in goods were being so severely abused.

These countries have contended that the GATT is not the competent international institution to deal with trade in services. In the context of a new round, some countries were concerned that there might be a 'trade-off' between concessions affecting trade in goods for concessions—or progress—in a negotiation affecting trade in services. Some countries have made clear that the idea of a new trade round only makes sense to them if the subject of trade in services is part of it: especially so, given the growing economic importance of the sector and the present lack of internationally agreed trade rules and disciplines. Equally, they do not accept the arguments against the GATT's competence to deal with trade in services.

In these circumstances, it has not proved possible for a set of agreed recommendations to be devised for transmission to the

Ministerial Meeting. Instead, Ambassador Jaramillo of Colombia, who has chaired the Services meetings, will make a report to the Meeting on his own responsibility and it will be for Ministers to decide if, or how, services should be treated in a new trade round. It should be noted that the matter was also raised in the Preparatory Committee and proposals for negotiations in this area have been put forward by some delegations, in the context of the documentation transmitted by the Preparatory Committee to the Ministerial Meeting.[31]

The US continued to increase the pressure on its trading partners. It is the emergence of the "Café au Lait" group,[32] a group of both developed and developing countries which managed to overcome the North–South divide and put together a compromise, which gathered momentum and ultimately provided the basis for the agreement on the extent of the negotiating agenda.

The agreed multilateral trade negotiations (MTN) covered the area of trade in goods as well as TRIPs, and came under Part I of the Ministerial Declaration of Punta del Este; the GATS came under Part II and as such it was not part of the "single undertaking" approach.[33] This is how the final decision reads with respect to services:

> Ministers also decide, as part of the Multilateral Trade Negotiations, to launch negotiations on trade in services.
>
> Negotiations in this area shall aim to establish a multilateral framework of principles and rules for trade in services, including elaboration of possible disciplines for individual sectors, with a view to expansion of such trade under conditions of transparency and progressive liberalization and as a means of promoting economic growth of all trading partners and the development of developing countries. Such framework shall respect the policy objectives of national laws and regulations applying to services and shall take into account the work of relevant international organizations.
>
> GATT procedures and practices shall apply to these negotiations. A Group of Negotiations on services is established to deal with these matters. Participation in the negotiations under this Part of the Declaration will be open to the same countries as under Part I. GATT secretariat support will be provided, with technical support from other organizations as decided by the Group of Negotiations on Services.

---

[31] GATT Doc. GATT/1395 at pp. 22–24.
[32] See the detailed account by Narlikar (2003).
[33] GATT Doc. MTN.GNS/2 of November 25, 1986.

The Group of Negotiations on Services shall report to the Trade Negotiations Committee.[34]

The decision to initiate the negotiations on liberalization of trade in services was taken in Punta del Este in an *ad hoc* intergovernmental meeting, parallel to the session of the GATT Contracting Parties where a decision on a new round of negotiations on trade in goods in the GATT was simultaneously adopted.[35] For Brazil, and India a separate track was the maximum they would accept.[36] Part II of the Punta del Este Ministerial Declaration also provided for the organization of negotiations. It was decided in this regard that:

(a) the GATT procedures and practices would apply to services negotiations as well;[37] and

(b) negotiations would be conducted by the Group of Negotiations on Services (GNS), which would report to the Trade Negotiations Committee (TNC, the body supervising the progress in the Uruguay Round where all national delegations participate).[38] The GNS held its first meeting on October 27, 1986 under the chairmanship of Ambassador F. Jaramillo (Colombia).[39]

3. NEGOTIATING THE GATS

3.1 ORGANIZATION OF THE NEGOTIATIONS AND THE PLAYERS INVOLVED

To honor their mandate, the negotiators established, besides the GNS, which was the main forum for negotiating trade in services and where all GATT contracting parties participated, a number of sectoral working groups which were meeting regularly and periodically submitted reports to the GNS.[40] These groups were: labor mobility, construction and

---

[34] GATT Doc. MIN.DEC, September 20, 1986 at p. 7. Although it was the Colombian delegation that proposed that services come under Part II as compromise solution, it was after the Indian delegation had accepted this idea in a meeting that the two delegations had organized.

[35] GATT Doc. MTN.GNS/W/3 at § 4.

[36] Randhawa (1987) at pp. 164ff.

[37] In the eyes of many developing countries, this reference to the GATT was perceived as acknowledgement that decisions in the services-context would be taken by consensus, as was the case in GATT, Randhawa (1987) at p. 165.

[38] The TNC would meet every six months and when meetings occurred in non-ministerial sessions it would be chaired by DG Dunkel. Three bodies were established and were hierarchically below the TNC: the GNS, the GNG (Group of Negotiations on Goods), and the SB (Surveillance Body). The GNG was superfluous as its tasks duplicated those of the TNC. The SB had the task to ensure that countries participating in the Uruguay Round lived up to their promises for standstill and rollback, that is, to not introduce new restrictions, and to initiate the process of liberalization as agreed during the Round. Subjecting the GNS to the TNC is another argument in favour of those who believed that no firewall was established between the two negotiations (goods, services) with the Punta del Este Declaration, see Marconini (1990).

[39] See GATT Doc. MTN.GNS/1 of November 3, 1986.

[40] See, for example, GATT Doc. MTN.GNS/36/Add. 1 of July 24, 1990.

engineering services, maritime transport services, land transport services, air transport services, telecommunications services. These groups were established later on at various stages of the negotiation. Participation in all these groups was open to all WTO Members.

When the negotiators met for the first time in Geneva, they realized that the negotiation had not been adequately prepared and that more time was needed to this effect.[41] The mandate itself could hardly be characterized as far-reaching; still, initially at least services looked like a negotiation too far.

The US wanted a meaningful, comprehensive agreement in services:[42] although the possibility for variable geometry was not totally excluded *ab initio*, the US wished to include all Uruguay Round participants in the negotiation and was to this effect, prepared to make concessions to LDCs in order to facilitate their participation. It was opposed though to widespread free riding and was not prepared to extend this courtesy to developing countries that did not qualify as LDCs.[43] The (eventual) GATS should, in the US view, be a multilateral agreement where everybody except for the LDCs would be requested to make a substantial liberalization effort, that is, all sectors should be included in national offers except for those for which exceptions had been negotiated.[44] The EU as well was in favor of a comprehensive agreement.[45] Its overall negotiating objective was to considerable extent a function of its willingness to preserve its CAP. The most active other OECD countries were Australia, Canada, New Zealand, and Japan. They had more or less symmetric strategies in the sense that they were in favour of including some specific sectors, while being adamant on excluding others. Unfortunately, their "ins" and "outs" were not identical and this was one of the factors that made the negotiation on MFN quite hard. Developing countries are divided into two camps. The reluctant players, that is, those that see no reason why the negotiation should take place in the first place. For them, the opening up of the OECD farm- and textile-markets should be the focus of this round, and adding to these negotiating items could oper-

---

[41] *Idem*.

[42] Self (1989). Hindley (1987) mentions that originally the US government toyed with the idea of concessions only in non-factor services, that is, services that can be supplied from a supplier in country A to a buyer in country B without relocation of either seller or buyer. It is after lobbying by US services industries that the US espoused the idea of concessions in the realm of right of establishment as well.

[43] The EU on the other hand, could happily live with a special and differential treatment à la GATT, probably hoping that such an offer would tone down the requests for developing countries for reforming its farm policy, see Paemen and Bentsch (1995, pp. 132ff).

[44] See Berg (1987) at pp. 14ff.

[45] A key negotiator for a member state (von Dewitz, Germany) went in record stating that "from a negotiating point of view it is preferable to put as much as possible into the basket which contains the subjects for negotiations. The more comprehensive such subjects, the easier to reach a reasonably balanced exchange of concessions between the negotiating partners", von Dewitz (1987) at p. 479.

ate as diversion of the attention from the real focus.[46] Moreover, they believed that there was not much in for them anyway. Which services could they export to the rest of the world? They held that their competitive advantage was in the goods sectors, not in services.[47] And those services of interest to them (like tourism) were liberalized anyway. They adopted a passive, if not destructive attitude towards the negotiation, at least early on.[48] None better than the then Indian Ambassador Shukla can sum up the way they felt following the Punta del Este Ministerial Declaration:

> In the negotiations that led to Punta del Este, developing countries were able to ensure that their concerns were taken into account in the following manner. First, the respect of the policy objectives behind national regulations was explicitly recognized in the Punta del Este mandate, which to a great extent alleviated the fears of developing countries. Second, development was stated as the ultimate goal of the negotiations, in other words whatever rules and disciplines were to emerge should promote the development of developing countries. Thus, the recognition of the development objective was to meet the concern that the element of equity could be ignored or inequity increased, as a result of the negotiations. Finally, the subject matter of the negotiations was defined as 'trade in services', which meant some kind of narrowing down of the scope of negotiations. If a broad coverage had been intended, the mandate would have been framed in terms of negotiations on services or negotiations on transactions of services. Instead, the Ministerial Declaration refers to trade, which is natural for a forum that basically deals with trade matters and not with the whole body of transactions that are associated with any economic activity. Those are the basic principles of the Punta del Este Declaration, which were designed to take care of the concerns of developing countries. It is interesting that the mandate does not speak of liberalization per se as the goal of negotiations. It aims at expansion of trade, not liberalization, of expansion of trade as an instrument for the growth of all trading partners and for the development of developing countries. That is the central goal of the multinational framework that must evolve.[49]

---

[46] Gill (1988).

[47] Although some economists were quite positive when arguing that exports of developing countries would expand over the years, see Sapir (1987).

[48] Randhawa (1987) noted that probably some developing countries feared a GATT-like approach to services which, in the eyes of developing countries, was not about equitable growth. The same author notes that the Punta del Este Declaration does mention development in the context of its paragraphs on services and thus, development becomes a centrepiece of the negotiation and not an afterthought (as in the GATT-context).

[49] Shukla (1989) at p. 171.

The main point is that at this stage (some) developing countries were not prepared to talk right of establishment, that is, an investment-type agreement, hence the focus on trade in services. It is only at a later stage that, following a change in personnel as well, India saw the potential in the agreement and became the most fervent supporter of Mode IV. To achieve that, concessions would have to be made. Then, there were those developing countries (like those participating in the Café au Lait group) which saw export opportunities at least with respect to some sectors, and/or which were prepared to do trade-offs between services and goods.

In the aftermath of Punta del Este, developed countries favored an agreement with full coverage within the auspices of the GATT, while developing countries favored an agreement with partial coverage outside of the GATT. The Café au Lait group advocated an intermediate position of partial coverage under the auspices of the GATT. By the end of the Uruguay Round, participants agreed to the Café au Lait group's position.

3.2 REACHING CONSENSUS

It is commonplace across commentators that the GATS general framework, as we know it, was largely negotiated in 1990 (and then, marginally so, after the first six months of 1991), that is the year following the unsuccessful Brussels meeting.[50] Dunkel had to resurrect the negotiating process traumatized by the failure in Brussels. To this effect, he proposed the following modus operandi in his "Dunkel Draft":

9. While much intensive work was done in Brussels it is my understanding that the issues to be settled in the area of services remain, in general, those set out on pages 328 to 382 of W/35/Rev.1.

10. I suggest that participants now make arrangements to restart negotiations on services. When doing so, I suggest that they ask themselves what can usefully be done at the present stage. In this respect, it would appear that there is agreement among participants to undertake work in three specific areas: the framework, initial commitments and sectoral annexes. My own suggestion is that consultations be held during which participants should first be given an opportunity (a) to take stock of the situation by assessing where we are in the negotiations on initial commitments, the framework text and on the annexes and (b) to explain how they see further developments in this work in terms of priorities and interrelationships.

11. I suggest that participants should also identify technical work that can be done in the coming weeks in each of the three

---

[50] Reyna (1993) who discusses in detail the negotiating record, and Marchetti and Mavroidis (2011) citing various sources.

main elements of the negotiations on services—commitments, framework and annexes. Such technical work might relate for example to the clarification and evaluation of offers and to the establishment of appropriate negotiating procedures, to further examination of arrangements and agreements of a general character for which exceptions from m.f.n. provisions might be sought, and to specific modalities for the application of m.f.n. in particular sectors.[51]

The next DG, Peter D. Sutherland, played an important role in "bullying" the final push and bringing the overall package to a successful conclusion. In his statement to TNC, he highlighted the remaining issues to be resolved and requested from negotiators to focus there:

> Yesterday's meeting of Heads of Delegation discussed the negotiations on Services, focusing on the few outstanding textual issues and on the remaining problems in Maritime Transport, Audiovisual Services and in particular Financial Services. Quite apart from the substance of these problems, was struck by the consciousness of the overwhelming pressure of time; however complex the substance may be, further delay will make their solution harder, not easier—because all solutions have to be multilateral.
>
> The time factor is particularly evident today, which is the deadline agreed by the GNS for the submission of draft final schedules and final lists of MFN exemptions. Revised schedules and exemption lists are being submitted and circulated every day, but many of these schedules are still heavily conditional often for perfectly understandable reasons and there are far too many outstanding. We have to remember the sheer logistical problems of circulating schedules which are submitted late, and of having them examined in capitals. I have asked Ambassador Hawes to focus on these questions at this afternoon's meeting of the GNS.[52]

There was some late friction: the EU, surprisingly for many, changed its attitude on maritime transport days before the final agreement, requesting now exclusion of this sector from the package. The rationale that the EU offered for its change of heart had to do with its disagreements with the US regarding the extent of "cabotage": In its view, the US opted for a very expansive understanding of the term, making it impossible to successfully negotiate a compromise.

This led services negotiators back to the room where the Annex on Negotiations on Maritime Transport Services was concluded. For all prac-

---

[51] GATT Doc. MTN.TNC/W/69 of February 26, 1991.
[52] GATT Doc. NUR 077 of November 26, 1993.

tical purposes, negotiations on maritime transport were postponed for a later day, that is, after the entry of the Uruguay Round package. It is thanks to this final compromise that reportedly was achieved one hour before the gavel in the hands of Peter D. Sutherland marking the end of the round went down, that the GATS had been finally agreed.[53]

4. THE INTEGRATION MODEL OF GATS

The GATS covers, in principle, all minus two services: services in the exercise of governmental authority and traffic rights have been explicitly excluded from the coverage of GATS. This does not mean that WTO Members have to make commitments on each and every sector mentioned in the CPC list: a positive list-approach has been privileged, whereby WTO Members will indicate the sectors where they will undertake commitments. Whereas the number of sectors where commitments have been undertaken could be described as the extensive margin, the intensity of commitments (intensive margin) could vary per sector/per Member. WTO Members might open up to an unlimited number of new banks, or to a specific number, or not at all. Accession to GATS means that WTO Members must accept a set of obligations (called "general obligations"), while remaining free to accept "specific commitments" with respect to the sectors where they wish to undertake liberalization commitments. The dichotomy between general obligations and specific commitments is an element idiosyncratic to the GATS; in a sense, the set of general obligations is the compulsory intensive margin that binds all WTO Members. Commitments will be entered with respect to the four modes of supply, that is, the four modes through which services are being traded. Commitments are not retroactive. They bind WTO Members as of the advent of the WTO (January 1, 1995, or the date at which a sector-specific agreement has entered into force). Challenges to the effect that commitments have not been respected can be mounted with respect to "measures affecting trade in services" using the procedures established in the DSU. It could be the case that it is unclear whether a measure falls under GATT or GATS and since the two agreements reflect drastically different standards for consistency as we will detail *infra*, the relationship between the two agreements is crucial in correctly subjecting a transaction to one or the other.

4.1 COVERAGE OF GATS

4.1.1 All Encompassing Minus Two

In the area of trade in goods as we saw, there are two sector-specific agreements: the Agreement on Agriculture (AG), and the Agreement on

---

[53] Negotiations on basic telecoms, financial services and maritime transport were concluded in the late 1990s. Mickey Kantor, the USTR, gave his own account of the last moments of the negotiation, see 'The World Trade Agreement: The Turning Point; A Call from Clinton, and Then a Deal', Business Day, December 16, 1993.

Textiles and Clothing (ATC). Both follow the same technique with respect to coverage: Annex 1 AG and the Annex to ATC contain an exhaustive list of all HS classifications that come under their purview. Consequently, there should be no disputes regarding the coverage of these agreements. To the extent that a good comes under one of the HS classifications mentioned in the respective annexes, it should be subjected to the disciplines of the relevant agreement. The rest of the GATT does not evidence a similar technique with respect to coverage: it covers in principle all goods, but does not contain a definition of the term 'good'. The GATT context, nonetheless, is quite helpful in clarifying this issue: international trade negotiations take place using the HS classifications as common language for all goods traded. In this vein, the HS classifications exhaust the class of goods that are covered by the GATT.

We witness a similar approach when discussing this issue in GATS. The end outcome was far from obvious in the beginning though. Sampson (1989, p. 136) put it quite appropriately when stating:

> As services encompass such a heterogeneous group of economic activities, the formulation of a definition of the services sector ... is conceptually difficult. One approach has been to define services residually as being activities that are neither manufacturing, mining nor agriculture. Sometimes, services are described as non-storables or intangibles. While service industries do deal with intangibles, there are exceptions. A number of economic activities with tangible outputs such as construction, publishing, films or public utilities are, none the less, commonly considered as being services. The residual and intangible nature of services is, however, quite unhelpful in attempting to find a multilateral framework within which to identify issues for the negotiators. Given the sensitive nature of some services and the lack of a natural scientific definition there are a number of key questions which confront negotiators in defining trade in services.

What Sampson is succinctly describing is of course, a well know problem. The Treaty Establishing the European Community defined services as activities that are not considered goods. Art. 57 of the Treaty on the Functioning of the European Union (TFEU) which is now in force, defines services in the following manner:

Article 57

(ex Article 50 TEC)

Services shall be considered to be 'services' within the meaning of the Treaties where they are normally provided for remuneration, *in so far as they are not governed by the provisions relating to freedom of movement for goods, capital and persons.*

'Services' shall in particular include:

(a) activities of an industrial character;

(b) activities of a commercial character;

(c) activities of craftsmen;

(d) activities of the professions.

Without prejudice to the provisions of the Chapter relating to the right of establishment, the person providing a service may, in order to do so, temporarily pursue his activity in the Member State where the service is provided, under the same conditions as are imposed by that State on its own nationals. (emphasis added).

Initially, there were proposals advocating a definition of services as residual category à la TFEU (activities that do not belong to the primary or secondary sector), and a classification as regulated sectors (e.g., financial services, transport, and telecommunication), public—(e.g., health, education, defence, administration), business—(e.g., consulting, advertising), and personal services (e.g., hairdressers). Since personal and public services had not traditionally been the object of trade transactions, the discussion, those in favour of the distinction argued, should focus on the other two categories.[54]

Finally, Art. I.3(b) GATS was agreed: it defines the term "services" as follows:

> any service in any sector except services supplied in the exercise of governmental authority.

The term "any" in this provision suggests that all services are covered with the exception of those services that qualify as services "supplied in the exercise of governmental authority". § 2 of the Annex on Air Transport Services adds the second and last exception to the coverage of GATS: air traffic rights.

Coverage is important since it circumscribes the ambit of services where commitments can (but do not have to) be entered.

4.1.2 Services Supplied in the Exercise of Governmental Authority

Art. I.3(b) GATS reads as follows:

> 'a service supplied in the exercise of governmental authority' means any service which is supplied neither on a commercial basis, nor in competition with one or more service suppliers.

---

[54] GATT Doc. MTN.GNS/8 of May 6, 1987. It is during these exchanges that the first conceptualization of the modes of supply of services took place (see § 14 of the document).

Services which are simultaneously supplied on a non-commercial basis and without competing with other service suppliers fall outside the sectoral scope of the GATS and are, therefore, not subject to the provisions of the GATS. These two terms, "commercial basis", and "competition", raise new interpretative issues. The GATS uses the term "commercial basis" elsewhere as well: Art. IV.1(a) refers to access to technology on a commercial basis. A relatively similar expression is to be found in the GATS Annex on Financial Services, where a "public entity" is defined as:

> not including an entity principally engaged in supplying financial services on commercial terms.

"Supply of a service" is defined in GATS (Art. XXVIII) as including:

> the production, distribution, marketing, sale and delivery of a service.

It follows that the manner in which the service is produced, distributed, marketed or even delivered has to be taken into account, too. It is usually the case that a commercial activity is commercial because of the pursuance of profit, which emerges as the key element to distinguish between commercial- and non-commercial activities. Hence, both the characteristics of the single activity and the supplier should be considered. Regarding the latter, the supplier's profit intention becomes crucial in order to assess the commerciality of the business being undertaken.

The expression "in competition with" is undefined in the GATS. It is worth noting, in this regard, that the GATS makes use of the term "competition" in different contexts: two examples are offered by Art. XVII GATS (National Treatment), as well as Art. VIII GATS (Monopolies and Exclusive Service Suppliers). It seems quite reasonable to conclude that this term captures a situation where services belong to the same relevant market (more or less in the anti-trust sense of the term). Note to this effect that Art. I.3(c) GATS does not refer to competition with "like" service suppliers. Rather, it refers to "competition with one or more service suppliers".

Note nevertheless, that, by virtue of §§ 1(b) and (c) of the Annex on Financial Services, activities forming part of a statutory system of social security or public retirement plans are to be considered as services supplied in the exercise of governmental authority, provided those activities are not conducted in competition with a public entity or a financial service supplier. Nothing in this Annex states that the service has to be provided on a non-commercial basis as well.

Art. I.3(b) GATS does not require a harmonized understanding of its coverage across WTO Members: public services are unilaterally defined by each WTO Member and definitions change over time. It should not come as a surprise to see, for example, that education as such is considered a public service by some WTO Members, whereas only elementary education is considered a public service by yet another group of WTO Members.

4.1.3 Air Transport Services

By virtue of § 2 of the Annex on Air Transport Services, which is an integral part of the GATS (Art. XXIX GATS), the Agreement does not apply to measures affecting:

(a) traffic rights, however granted; or

(b) practices directly related to the exercise of traffic rights, except as provided in § 3 of this Annex.

The term "traffic rights" is defined in § 6 of the same Annex in the following manner:

"Traffic rights" mean the right for scheduled and non-scheduled services to operate and/or to carry passengers, cargo and mail for remuneration or hire from, to, within, or over the territory of a Member, including points to be served, routes to be operated, types of traffic to be carried, capacity to be provided, tariffs to be charged and their conditions, and criteria for designation of airlines, including such criteria as number, ownership, and control.

The term practices "directly related to the exercise of traffic rights" appearing in § 2(b) is not defined any further. § 3 of the Annex however enumerates the three practices that are not covered by this term (and which, consequently, are subjected to GATS disciplines):

(a) aircraft repair and maintenance services;

(b) the selling and marketing of air transport services; and

(c) computer reservation system (CRS) services.

These three activities are explained in further detail in § 6 of the Annex. § 5 of the Annex mandates a periodic review, at least every five years, of developments in the air transport sector as well as the operation of the Annex, with a view to considering the possible further application of the GATS to this sector.

4.1.4 Social Security, BITs, Labor Mobility, Judicial and Administrative Assistance

Towards the end of the Uruguay Round, negotiations confronted the applicability of GATS to certain categories of measures, namely:

(a) Measures relating to social security, including those pursuant to bilateral agreements on the avoidance of double contributions to, and/or double benefits from social security systems;

(b) Measures relating to judicial and administrative assistance between governments, including those pursuant to international agreements on such matters;

(c) Measures relating to the settlement of disputes pursuant to bilateral investment agreements (BITs);

(d) Measures relating to the entry and stay of natural persons, including those pursuant to international agreements on labor mobility; and

(e) Measures relating to the entry and temporary stay of natural persons pursuant to bilateral agreements on entry and temporary stay of agricultural workers on a seasonal basis; working holidays and young workers programmes; programmes for the exchange of University professors and school teachers; and cultural affairs.

The discussions were pursued after the conclusion of the Uruguay Round, and in March 1995, the CTS agreed to adopt the conclusion of the Sub–Committee on Services concerning measures relating to judicial and administrative assistance, according to which none of the provisions of the GATS would apply to such measures. On the other hand, no common understanding regarding the other types of measures under consideration could be achieved. In any case, none of them has been explicitly excluded from the scope of the GATS.[55]

4.2 POSITIVE LIST, NEGATIVE LIST

The US had in mind an investment agreement-model, that is, an agreement where in principle at least, all services sectors would be covered and eventually, exceptions would be negotiated. This position nonetheless, was soon abandoned: the US delegate proposed that participants to the GNS should notify anonymously to the GATT Secretariat those sectors that they believed should be subjected to the rules and disciplines of the framework agreement. It is on the basis of these anonymous notifications that the GATT Secretariat would prepare a consolidated list of all sectors notified, which should constitute a point of departure from which the negotiation on sectoral coverage could be launched.[56] The EU had explicitly declared that it would oppose any unilateral exclusion of sectors from the obligations of the agreement to be negotiated.[57] Following the Montreal Ministerial Declaration, the EU notified its interest to present an indicative list of sectors of interest for submission to the GNS, and the

---

[55] See Issues Relating to the Scope of the GATS—Report by the Chairman of the Sub–Committee on Services (WTO doc. S/C/1) and the report of the meeting of the CTS held on March 1, 1995 (S/C/M/1), §§ 14 and 15.

[56] GATT Doc. MTN.GNS/W/37 at § 7 and 13. The US opposed eventually the idea of negotiating disciplines on shipping (maritime transport) and was not very sympathetic to the idea of opening up its banking market. The EU was sympathetic to the idea of concessions between likeminded countries only, see GATT Doc. MTN.GNS/W/77 of October 19, 1989. So was Switzerland, see Croome (1995) at p. 126.

[57] GATT Doc. MTN.GNS/18 at § 10. As we will see *infra*, when we discuss the conference held at Montreal for the Mid Term Review (MTR), the EU did not want to discuss disciplines on the audiovisual sector but did not want to exclude it either: it held that this sector had idiosyncratic elements that distinguished it from any other services sector.

US agreed to do the same.[58] The EU started with an initial list of sectors to be negotiated, making it clear nonetheless that it would be eventually adding new sectors at a later stage:

> The Community has already undertaken a preliminary internal examination of sectoral specificities. From this examination it appears that an <u>initial</u> list of sectors which it will wish to refer to in the context of this examination, and without prejudice to the coverage of the final agreement, would include:
>
> > Audiovisual services
> >
> > Banking and securities-related activities
> >
> > Business services
> >
> > Construction
> >
> > Insurance
> >
> > Telecommunications and Information Services
> >
> > Tourism
> >
> > Transport
>
> The Community may wish to refer to other sectors in the course of the Group of Negotiations on Services' examination of sectoral specificities.[59]

Developing countries privileged asymmetric commitments by the various participants.[60] They voiced their wish that the agreement covers (at the very least) sectors where they held comparative advantage, that is labour intensive industries.[61] India and Brazil opted for a positive list-approach, that is, commitments should be made in sectors appearing in a "list of different sectors in which the participants would be interested",[62] but explicitly opposed the inclusion of the right to establishment in the discussion arguing that such a right belongs to an investment- and not a trade agreement. In the words of the Brazilian delegate:

> The suggestion to apply the theoretical principles of comparative advantage to trade in services gives evidence, in effect, to some inherent contradictions which surface quite clearly in the light of an expanded definition of trade in services advanced by the sup-

---

[58] GATT Doc. MTN.GNS/22 of May 18, 1989 at §§ 33–34.

[59] GATT Doc. MTN.GNS/W/56 of May 25, 1989.

[60] See for example, the views of the Peruvian delegation in § 44 of GATT Doc. MTN.GNS/30 of February 8, 1990. For a reaction, see, for example, the views expressed by the US delegate at § 50 of GATT Doc. MTN.GNS/27.

[61] GATT Doc. MTN.GNS/7.

[62] GATT Doc. MTN.GNS/8, and MTN.GNS/W/4 of March 11, 1987 at §§ 13ff. Opting for a positive list has of course repercussions for future negotiations: liberalization is easier in case commitments have been already made in a previous round, and the positive list approach resulted (for many trading nations) in commitments in a few sectors only.

porters of the free-trade approach. Their definition would go beyond services that can actually cross borders and would include the notion of "establishment" or "presence" in the foreign market by the provider of services which cannot be shipped or transmitted by telecommunication. Such a notion of movement of capital and labour across frontiers would hardly conform though with the key assumption of the international immobility of factors of production, a central tenet of the classical theory of free-trade.

The idea put forward in some quarters that establishment should be a "right" to be ensured in foreign markets to the provider of services is by itself in contradiction with the right of States to regulate the entry of foreign investment and the conditions of establishment of foreign enterprises; such a right has been expressly acknowledged by the international community, at the United Nations level, by the Charter of Economic Rights and Duties of States and, at the regional level, by the OECD member countries when dealing with the question of national treatment for foreign controlled enterprises.[63]

Croome (1995, p. 126), an insider, since as member of the GATT Secretariat he participated in many meetings during this time, mentions three reasons explaining why many (essentially developing, but also developed) countries were opposed to the inclusion of some sectors:

> Some sectors were seen as special for reasons similar to those which have traditionally affected GATT negotiations on good. Just as agriculture and textiles have enjoyed long-standing protection in many countries, service sectors such as shipping in the United States, film making in Western Europe and banking in India have been given help and protection against foreign competition, and can count on the support of local lobbies. Some sectors have characteristics that are recognized as needing close oversight by governments: financial services such as banking and insurance are obvious examples, in which 'prudential' considerations will require that they be regulated to prevent fraud or reckless behaviour. A third possible reason to exclude a sector might be that it was already governed by an international agreement that seemed adequate. From an early stage, it became obvious that there could be a halfway house between inclusion and exclusion of a sector, through negotiation of a special

---

[63] GATT Doc.MTN.GNS/3 at §§ 27–28. The first discussions on the right of establishment date from the pre-Punta del Este days. The delegate of Canada is recorded saying back in 1985: "The right of establishment was one issue that would have to be looked at in detail: services were delivered in a different manner from goods, sometimes requiring a presence which might necessitate rules regarding the right to conduct business. While recognizing that establishment had not been covered by GATT rules, Canada was keeping an open mind regarding all issues concerning how service firms conducted business and what constituted trade in services." See GATT Doc. MDF/10 of May 21, 1985.

agreement for that sector which would add to, or subtract from, the general rules to be included in the framework for services. This was to be another key element in the outcome of the Round.[64]

Paemen[65] and Bentsch (1995) refer to a "secret" meeting where delegates from the EU, Sweden and a host of developing countries (Argentina, Brazil, Egypt, India, Jamaica) participated where the so called "weekend text" was produced.[66] In its first comprehensive proposal the EU did include provisions allowing for positive list.[67] And Falkenberg (1997, p. 461), one of the EU negotiators, provided confirmation that for pragmatic reasons the EU was led to endorse the positive list-approach:

> Adopting a negative-list approach; I do not believe that countries will make commitments they do not intend to make by a simple presentational trick. I believe rather on the contrary that the approach followed in GATS has allowed many countries to list commitments which would otherwise have taken no commitment at all. It is the best means to achieve progressively higher levels of liberalization which is the major GATS objective.

The "weekend text" formed the basis of the Montreal Declaration which opened the door to a positive list-approach. The next question was where should trading nations draw inspiration from in preparing a list of services that would find their way to the negotiating table. Following numerous discussions and research of relevant practice on this score, the GATT Secretariat took the view that the UN Central Product Classification (CPC)-list was the most appropriate for the purposes of negotiating the GATS:

> First, international transactions do not pertain to activities, as these are primarily statistical constructions. Second, the provision of a service may require a producer (supplier) to move to the location of the consumer (recipient). While a product-based system does not specifically include *factor* flows (e.g. movement of labour and capital) these are covered to the extent that they actually produce a service product. Services that require factor movement to be provided internationally have thus been included in the proposed reference list, as appears necessary at this

---

[64] Croome (1995, p. 127) notes that the third rationale offered here was quickly dismissed: discussions with the ICAO, the ITU, and UNCTAD, made the trading nations aware of the fact that while national treatment and transparency were key elements in all agreements coming under the aegis of these three institutions in the pre-GATS era, MFN was not: typically, the agreements would take the form 'of tightly-drawn bilateral deals based on strict reciprocity'.

[65] Hugo Paemen, a high EU Commission official, was one of the leading EU negotiators during the Uruguay Round.

[66] Marconini (1990) goes so far as to describe the EU stance as that of a consistent mediator between the US and developing countries throughout the process.

[67] GATT Doc. MTN.GNS/W/105, see Arts. XIX and XX in this document.

stage from paragraph 4 of the Montreal Ministerial Declaration. Utilisation of a product-based system will also allow foreign provision to be related to domestic production. Furthermore, a focus on products allows a higher degree of disaggregation and precision to be attained should it become necessary, at a later stage, when examining the nature of transactions (e.g. specificity of purpose) or the sectoral implications of various concepts. Finally, a product-based system meets the objective of achieving the highest degree of concordance with existing and proposed systems for recording statistics on services trade and production.[68]

The CPC classification provided the basis on which WTO Doc. W/120 was prepared, that is, the document that provides the classification of the services coming under the aegis of the GATS.[69]

4.3 GENERAL OBLIGATIONS, AND SPECIFIC COMMITMENTS

The GATS distinguishes between "General Obligations and Disciplines" (Part II of the Agreement) and "Specific Commitments" (Part III of the Agreement). While the latter are applicable only to the sectors explicitly identified in Members' schedules, the former apply in principle to all service sectors regardless of whether the Member has made a specific commitment. Trading nations reached an agreement on this dichotomy early during the negotiation.[70] The original agreement to distinguish between general framework and specific commitments notwithstanding, divergences across developed and developing nations continued well after the Montreal Ministerial Conference. Croome (1995, p. 246) mentions a paper submitted by Brazil, Egypt, and India (and some other developing countries) which:

> argued that the mandate of GNS did not go beyond negotiating the general framework of rules and principles, leaving any negotiation of specific commitments to the years after the Round was concluded.

There were two angles to this issue intimately linked to each other:

(a) What should be content of the framework?

(b) How much of the GATT could usefully be incorporated in the services context?

In the eyes of the USTR at least, the usefulness of the GATT principles was limited: sectoral agreements were necessary in order to adjust the GATT principles to elements idiosyncratic in the various services

---

[68] GATT Doc. MTN.GNS/W/50 of April 13, 1989 at § 6.

[69] Note that the EU statistical office, the Eurostat, was compiling its data on services form early on in a CPC-compatible manner, see GATT Doc. MTN.GNS/W/22 of October 22, 1987.

[70] Croome (1995) at pp. 260ff.

markets.[71] The EU, implicitly at least, endorsed this view. In mid–1990, the EU tabled a proposal calling for a general framework that would include provisions on the basic GATT concepts (MFN, NT), as well as on all GATT instruments of contingent protection (antidumping-, AD; countervailing duties, CVD; and safeguards).[72] Besides MFN, the eventual compromise is reminiscent of the GATT but only in name. NT is part of the GATS legal arsenal, but is legally relevant only when specific commitments have been entered, and only to the extent that no deviation from it has been included in the schedule of concessions; it is not an obligation that applies to all services irrespective whether a commitment has been made.[73] The Table below classifies the various GATS provisions under general obligations and specific commitments:[74]

Generally applicable	Applicable only to committed sectors
Article II (MFN) Note: Subject to MFN exemptions, and not applicable to government procurement of services (as per Article XIII)	
Article III:1 (Transparency—publication) "[publication of] all relevant measures of general application which pertain to or affect the operation of this Agreement"	Article III:3 (Transparency—notification) "[measures] which significantly affect trade in services covered by its specific commitments under this Agreement"
Article III:4 (Transparency—Respond to requests for information) "... respond promptly to all requests by any other Member for specific information on any of its measures of general application or international agreements within the meaning of paragraph 1"	Article III:4 (Transparency—Establishment of enquiry points) "Each Member shall also establish one or more enquiry points to provide specific information to other Members, upon request, on all such matters as well as those subject to the notification requirement in paragraph 3"

---

[71] Gao (2008) has endorsed this view, that is, that the sectoral disciplines functioned as some sort of a reality check for provisions negotiated in the abstract and coming under the aegis of the general framework.

[72] GATT Doc. MTN.GNS/W/105 of June 18, 1990.

[73] On the negotiation of NT, see Sampson (1988), and Viganó (1988).

[74] The next Chapter is dedicated to a detailed discussion of these provisions.

Generally applicable	Applicable only to committed sectors
Article IV:2 (Increasing Participation of Developing Countries—Establishment of contact points) *"Developed country Members, and to the extent possible other Members, shall establish contact points within two years from the date of entry into force of the WTO Agreement to facilitate the access of developing country Members' service suppliers to information, related to their respective markets, concerning . . ."*	
Article VI:2 (Domestic Regulation—domestic review mechanisms) *". . . [review and remedies for] administrative decisions affecting trade in services."*	Article VI:1 (Domestic Regulation—reasonable, objective and impartial administration of all measures of general application) *"In sectors where specific commitments are undertaken . . ."*
	Article VI:3 (Domestic Regulation—information on the status of authorization applications) *"Where authorization is required for the supply of a service on which a specific commitment has been made . . ."*
	Article VI:5 (Domestic Regulation—licensing and qualification requirements and technical standards) *"In sectors in which a Member has undertaken specific commitments, pending the entry into force of disciplines developed in these sectors pursuant to paragraph 4 . . ."*
	Article VI:6 (Domestic Regulation—procedures to verify the competence of professionals) *"In sectors where specific commitments regarding professional services are undertaken . . ."*

Generally applicable	Applicable only to committed sectors
Article VII (Recognition) "... a Member may recognize the education or experience obtained, requirements met, or licenses or certifications granted in a particular country..."	
Article VIII:1 (Monopolies and Exclusive Service Suppliers—Respect of MFN) "[ensure that monopolies do not] act in a manner inconsistent with that Member's obligations under Article II and specific commitments."	Article VIII:1 (Monopolies and Exclusive Service Suppliers—Respect of specific commitments) "[ensure that monopolies do not] act in a manner inconsistent with that Member's obligations under Article II and specific commitments."
	Article VIII:2 (Monopolies and Exclusive Service Suppliers—supply of service outside the scope of the monopoly) "Where a Member's monopoly supplier competes, either directly or through an affiliated company, in the supply of a service outside the scope of its monopoly rights and which is subject to that Member's specific commitments, the Member shall ensure that such a supplier does not abuse its monopoly position to act in its territory in a manner inconsistent with such commitments."
Article IX:2 (Business Practices—consultations) "enter into consultations with a view to eliminating practices referred to in paragraph 1 ..."	
Article XI:1 (Payments and Transfers—current transactions) "... not apply restrictions on international transfers and payments for current transactions relating to its specific commitments."	Article XI:2 (Payments and Transfers—capital transactions) "... not impose restrictions on any capital transactions inconsistently with its specific commitments regarding such transactions, except under Article XII or at the request of the Fund."

Generally applicable	Applicable only to committed sectors
	Article XII:1 (Restrictions to Safeguard the Balance of Payments) "In the event of serious balance-of-payments and external financial difficulties or threat thereof, a Member may adopt or maintain restrictions on trade in services on which it has undertaken specific commitments, including on payments or transfers for transactions related to such commitments."
Article XV:2 (Subsidies—consultations) "Any Member which considers that it is adversely affected by a subsidy of another Member may request consultations with that Member on such matters. Such requests shall be accorded sympathetic consideration."	
	Article XVI (Market Access) "1 . . . each Member shall accord services and service suppliers of any other Member treatment no less favourable than that provided for under the terms, limitations and conditions agreed and specified in its Schedule. "2. In sectors where market-access commitments are undertaken, the measures which a Member shall not maintain or adopt . . . unless otherwise specified in its Schedule . . .
	Article XVII (National Treatment) "In the sectors inscribed in its Schedule, and subject to any conditions and qualifications set out therein . . . "

SEC. 4 THE INTEGRATION MODEL OF GATS

Generally applicable	Applicable only to committed sectors
	Article XVIII (Additional Commitments) *"Members may negotiate commitments with respect to measures affecting trade in services not subject to scheduling under Articles XVI or XVII, including those regarding qualifications, standards or licensing matters. Such commitments shall be inscribed in a Member's Schedule."*
Annex on Telecommunications (Transparency—paragraph 4) *"In the application of Article III of the Agreement, each Member shall ensure that relevant information on conditions affecting access to and use of public telecommunications transport networks and services is publicly available, including . . . "*	Annex on Telecommunications (Access to and use of Public Telecommunications Transport Networks and Services—paragraph 5) *"Each Member shall ensure that any service supplier of any other Member is accorded access to and use of public telecommunications transport networks and services on reasonable and non-discriminatory terms and conditions, for the supply of a service included in its Schedule. This obligation shall be applied, inter alia, through paragraphs (b) through (f)."*

4.4 THE MODES OF SUPPLY

4.4.1 The Current Regime

The GATS does not define 'services', but includes a definition of 'trade in services' as the supply of a service through four different modes. "Supply of a service" is further defined in Art. XXVIII GATS as including the production, distribution, marketing, sale and delivery of a service. A thorough understanding of the modes of supply is crucial for two reasons: on the one hand, by case law construction, in order to decide whether a measure affects trade in services requires inquiring into how the services at issue are supplied (including that is, through which of the four modes of supply identified in the GATS); on the other hand, as hinted in Art. XVI GATS and clarified in the Guidelines for the Scheduling of Specific Commitments under the GATS (the "Scheduling Guidelines"),[75] limita-

---

[75] WTO Doc. S/L/92. The original documents, produced and circulated by the GATT Secretariat towards the end of the Uruguay Round were entitled Scheduling of Initial Commitments in Trade in Services: Explanatory Note (MTN.GNS/W/164), dated 3 September 1993, and an Addendum 1, carrying the same title, and dated 30 November 1993. These two documents were revised by the Committee on Specific Commitments and the revised version entitled Guidelines for the Scheduling of Specific Commitments under the General Agreement on Trade in Services, were adopted by the CTS on March 23, 2001 (WTO doc. S/L/92). It is understood, as indicated in

tions on market access and NT must be entered not only on a sector-by-sector but also on a mode-by-mode basis. The four modes of supply envisaged are (Art. I.2 GATS):

(a) cross-border supply (Mode 1);

(b) consumption abroad (Mode 2);

(c) commercial presence (Mode 3); and

(d) temporary presence of natural persons as suppliers of services (Mode 4).

4.4.2 How Did We Get Here?

Negotiators struggled the first years trying to define trade in services, the manner in which services would be traded. Negotiators profited in this respect from writings by academics: Sampson and Snape (1985), and Bhagwati (1987) came up with similar categorizations of the modes of supply. They distinguished between four modes of supply:

(a) Mobile Provider / Immobile User: the former moves to the latter, e.g., an attorney supplies services in a foreign market;

(b) Mobile User / Immobile Provider: the latter moves to the former, e.g., a client purchases attorney service in the attorney's market;

(c) Mobile User / Mobile Provider: either the former moves to the latter's market or vice-versa;

(d) Long Distance: physical presence is not essential, e.g., an attorney sends his expertise by fax or email.

Modes (a), (b), and (d) found their way into the GATS. Mode (c) did not since it is anyway subsumed in (a) or (b). Based on these ideas, the EU[76] first, and Switzerland[77] subsequently, submitted comprehensive proposals that reflect almost verbatim the four modes of supply as we now know them in the GATS text. It did not happen overnight though: developing countries opposed the right of establishment (and hence what eventually became Mode 3). India siding with the Café au Lait submissions, shifted towards a quid pro quo between migration and investment: it would be prepared to accept right of establishment in exchange for a promise by developed countries to allow workforce migration.[78] From then onwards it was all downhill. First, § 4 of the Montreal Ministerial Declaration read:

---

a footnote to document S/L/92, that schedules of specific commitments in force prior to the date of document S/L/92 have been drafted according to documents MTN.GNS/W/164 and MTN.GNS/W/164/Add.1.

[76] GATT Doc. MTN.GNS/W/105.

[77] GATT Docs. MTN.GNS/W/69 of September 15, 1989, and MTN.GNS/W/102 of June 7, 1990.

[78] Marchetti and Mavroidis (2011) document this point in detail.

Work on definition should proceed on the basis that the multilateral framework may include trade in services involving cross-border movement of services, cross-border movement of consumers, and cross-border movement of factors of production where such movement is essential to suppliers. However, this should be examined further in the light of, *inter alia*, the following:

(a) Cross-border movement of service and payment.
(b) Specificity of purpose.
(c) Discreteness of transactions.
(d) Limited duration.[79]

Then, in a document issued by the GATT Secretariat after Montreal and before Brussels, and awkwardly entitled "Elements for a Draft Which Could Permit Negotiations to Take Place for the Completion of All Parts of the Multilateral Review",[80] the distinction between movement of production factors and right of establishment is made. It should consequently, come as no surprise at all that, the Dunkel Draft, which came really close to the final text, explicitly acknowledged the right of establishment without subjecting it to any particular conditions. It stated in Art. 1:

For the purposes of this Agreement, trade in services is defined as the supply of a service:

(a) from the territory of one Party into the territory of any other Party;

(b) in the territory of one Party to the service consumer of any other Party;

(c) through the presence of service providing entities of one Party in the territory of any other Party;

(d) by natural persons of one Party in the territory of any other Party.

4.4.3 Cross–Border Supply (Mode 1)

Mode 1 is defined in GATS as the supply of services:

> from the territory of one Member into the territory of any other Member.

The consumer remains in his or her home territory, the supplier is located in a different territory (from where the export is made), and it is actually the service which crosses national borders. This situation arises when the service can be either embodied in a transportable medium (e.g. DVDs, CD–ROMs, written material), or be sent across the border through telecommunications networks. International transport (e.g. freight

---

[79] GATT Doc. MTN.TNC/11 of April 21, 1989.
[80] GATT Doc. MTN.GNS/28 of December 18, 1989.

transport services) would also constitute a case of cross-border supply. This mode of supply is conceptually similar to the traditional notion of trade in goods, where both the consumer and the supplier remain in their respective territories when the product is delivered. The definition of this mode has been discussed in the Panel report in *Mexico–Telecoms*. In this case, the US challenged Mexican regulations that required long distance carriers serving customers outside Mexico (calling into Mexico) to purchase interconnection services from licensed concessionaires in Mexico based on prices negotiated by the largest such concessionaire, that is, in the case at hand, Telmex. The US argued that these provisions violated Mexico's specific commitments on market access, as well as its commitments under the GATS Annex on Telecommunications and the Telecommunications Reference Paper (TRP) concluded at the end of the negotiations on basic telecommunications (February 1997). Before proceeding to an analysis of Mexico's policies in light of the TRP, the Panel had first to determine the nature and extent of Mexico's specific commitments. The US contended that Mexico's practices were unlawful because they contravened Mexico's commitments on the cross-border supply of basic telecommunication services from the US into Mexico, through US carriers, something that seems to have been taken for granted by the Panel, as we see in § 7.42 of its report:

> More generally, a supplier of services under the GATS is no less a supplier solely because elements of the service are subcontracted to another firm, or are carried out with assets owned by another firm. What counts is the service that the supplier offers and has agreed to supply to a customer. In the case of a basic telecommunications service, whether domestic or international, or supplied cross-border or through commercial presence, the supplier offers its customers the service of completing the customer's communications. Having done so, the supplier is responsible for making any necessary subsidiary arrangements to ensure that the communications are in fact completed. The customer typically pays its supplier the price of the end-to-end service, regardless of whether the supplier contracts with, or uses the assets of, another firm to supply the services.

Mexico on its part argued that the US telecom operators were not in fact supplying services in the Mexican territory to Mexican consumers, but were rather supplying telecom services in the US market to US consumers. According to Mexico, the US suppliers were in fact handing off the calls originated in the US market at the Mexican border for completion by Mexican operators. The Panel did not side with Mexico. The quoted excerpt was included under the heading "(b) Are the services at issue supplied cross-border?", appearing on p. 144 of the Panel report: it leaves no doubt that the Panel was indeed contemplating a transaction whereby a US carrier supplies cross-border telephone services to its customers, and not the sale of termination services from Mexico to the United States. Indeed, with respect to this latter element of the telephone service, the Panel makes the point that it is immaterial whether it is being subcontracted (outsourced) by the US carrier.

The defining feature of Mode 1 is that the supplier and its customer are not present in the same territory. It is worth recalling § 26 of the Scheduling Guidelines, which states that the modes

> are essentially defined on the basis of the *origin of the service supplier and consumer,* and the *degree and type of territorial presence* which they have at the moment the service is delivered.

In this dispute, however, this was not how the mode of supply was understood.[81] Case law has also shed light on the so-called "technological neutrality" of modes of supply, particularly of Mode 1. This notion is not developed in the text of the GATS and was introduced in the negotiations on Basic Telecommunications with a view to clarifying the scope of specific commitments on those services. The thrust of this notion, which translated in a Chair's note at the time, is that, unless otherwise noted in the sector column of the schedule of specific commitments, any basic telecom service listed in the sector column may be provided through any means of technology (e.g. cable, wireless, satellites, Internet).[82] In considering whether the US had violated its commitments on market access for the cross-border supply of gambling services, the Panel in *US–Gambling* looked into the notion of technological neutrality (§ 6.280–§ 6.287). The Panel was actually trying to interpret the meaning of the term "none", inscribed in the market access column (for Mode 1) in the US schedule.[83] Noting that the definition of Art. I.2(a) GATS does not contain any indication as to the means that can be used to supply services cross-border, the Panel stated that in its view:

> the GATS does not limit the various technologically possible means of delivery under mode 1 (§ 6.281).

Furthermore, by looking at the relevant paragraphs and examples of the Scheduling Guidelines, the Panel concluded in § 6.285 that:

> ... mode 1 under the GATS encompasses all possible means of supplying services from the territory of one WTO Member into the territory of another WTO Member. Therefore, a market access commitment for mode 1 implies the right for other Members' suppliers to supply a service through all means of delivery,

---

[81] Interestingly, § 26, which was § 18 of the Uruguay Round Scheduling Guidelines (MTN.GNS/W/164) is not even mentioned in the Panel report.

[82] Notes for Scheduling Basic Telecom Services Commitments, Note by the Chairman, Group on Basic Telecommunications, document S/GBT/W/2/Rev.1, dated January 16, 1997.

[83] We discuss this term in detail in Chapter 25. Suffice to state for the time being that whenever this term appears in a schedule, the scheduling WTO Members promises to erect no barriers to trade.

whether by mail, telephone, Internet etc., unless otherwise specified in a Member's Schedule. We note that this is in line with the principle of "technological neutrality", which seems to be largely shared among WTO Members. Accordingly, where a full market access commitment has been made for mode 1, a prohibition on one, several or all means of delivery included in this mode 1 would be a limitation on market access for the mode.

In § 6.287, the Panel summed up its thinking on this matter:

To sum up, we conclude that mode 1 includes all means of delivery. We are of the view that when a Member inscribes the word "None" in the market access column of its schedule for mode 1, it commits itself not to maintain measures which prohibit the use of one, several or all means of delivery under mode 1 in a committed sector or sub-sector. This is especially so in sectors and sub-sectors where cross-border supply is effected essentially if not exclusively through the Internet.

4.4.4 Consumption Abroad (Mode 2)

The second mode of supply is defined in GATS as the supply of services in the territory of one Member to the service consumer of any other Member. In this case, the consumer consumes services in the territory of another Member, presumably, but not necessarily, in the territory where the supplier is located. Tourist activities, visits to museums and theatres, medical treatment obtained abroad, language courses taken abroad, are typical examples of this mode of supplying services. According to the Scheduling Guidelines, activities such as ship and aircraft repair abroad, where only the property of the consumer moves or is situated abroad, are also covered by this mode of supply.[84]

Discussions during the 1997 negotiations on financial services showed that some uncertainties remained in the mind of WTO Members as to whether physical movement was indeed needed in order to be consuming services abroad, particularly with the expansion of transactions carried out through electronic means such as the internet. This raises the more conceptual issue regarding the distinction between Mode 1 and Mode 2: in the context of the negotiations on financial services that led to the Fifth Protocol, negotiators became aware of the fact that there was not necessarily a firewall between the two Modes.[85] The problem was originally explained in the following terms: as indicated in the guidelines

---

[84] WTO Doc. S/L/92, at § 29.

[85] The WTO Secretariat exposed the issue for the first time in document S/FIN/W/9, and then contributed to the discussion during the negotiations held in 1997, by writing a couple of informal communications, dated June 24, and July 3, 1997. These informal communications were later attached to document S/FIN/W/14 and to the Scheduling Guidelines (S/L/92).

used by WTO Members to schedule their specific commitments on market access and national treatment, the modes of supply

> are essentially defined on the basis of the origin of the service supplier and consumer, and the degree and type of territorial presence which they have at the moment the service is delivered.[86]

In both Modes 1 and 2, the supplier is not present within the territory of the Member that has undertaken the commitment, i.e., the consumer's country of origin.[87] So, in accordance with those guidelines, the distinction between Mode 1 and Mode 2 would therefore hinge upon whether the service is delivered within the territory of the Members making the commitment (e.g. Switzerland) or whether the service is delivered to a Swiss consumer outside Switzerland. The perceived ambiguity is due to the fact that, in light of the explanation provided in the Scheduling Guidelines, the delivery of a financial service very often does not require the physical presence of the consumer. Technological advances, notably the Internet, have made it possible to deliver a financial service almost anywhere in the world:

> Once the physical presence of the consumer ceases to be a benchmark for determining the place of delivery of a service, it becomes extremely difficult to determine in an unambiguous manner where a service is delivered.[88]

In essence, what is at stake here is whether a cross-border financial services transaction should be classified as a Mode 1 or a Mode 2 transaction. It is clear that the question becomes particularly relevant when different levels of commitment have been undertaken for both modes of supply, which is often the case, with more liberal commitments having been undertaken in general for Mode 2. If both modes of supply were unbound, Switzerland (to continue with our example) would be entitled to introduce any restrictions on market access or national treatment, thus preventing either the non-established suppliers from supplying services into Swiss territory or Swiss consumers from acquiring services abroad. If both modes of supply were fully bound, it would be unlawful for Switzerland to prevent a foreign non-established supplier from reaching a consumer

---

[86] This explanation is contained in paragraph 18 of the scheduling note written by the *GATT Secretariat* at the request of *Uruguay Round* participants (MTN.GNS/W/164, dated September 3, 1993). WTO Members reviewed these scheduling guidelines in 2001, but that statement was not modified (see paragraph 26 of document S/L/92).

[87] But note that when it comes to telecoms, this solution is probably ill-equipped to find application. Recall *Mexico–Telecoms*: in that case the commitment would have been entered by Mexico (cap its termination rates), that is, the WTO Member where the supplier originates. The fact however, that for technical reasons the telecoms solution should be idiosyncratic does not put into question the validity and applicability of this rule in other transactions.

[88] See Informal Note of the GATT Secretariat, dated June 24, 1997, annexed to the document Indicative Checklist of Issues for Discussion, Note by the WTO Secretariat, WTO Doc. S/FIN/W/14, of May 17, 1999.

within Switzerland or to prevent its own consumers from getting services abroad. At the time of the negotiations on financial services, in 1997, Members discussed several options to deal with this alleged problem:

> (a) all financial transactions (between non-resident suppliers and resident consumers) that take place inside the territory of the Members making the commitment could be classified as Mode 1;
>
> (b) Mode 1 transactions could be defined as those that take place under the laws of the Member making the commitment, while Mode 2 transactions could be defined as those that take place under the laws of the foreign country from which the service is supplied;
>
> (c) the supply of services accompanied by solicitation could be defined as Mode 1, Mode 2 being the fallback option if the former were not the case;
>
> (d) any measure applicable to the supplier of the service could be classified under Mode 1, any measure applicable to the consumer would fall under Mode 2;
>
> (e) Modes 1 and 2 could be merged.

The place where the consumer uses the service may hold the key to solving this puzzle. Distinguishing between Modes 1 and 2 may depend on where final use of the service takes place. If the consumer uses the (essential part of the) service in question in its own territory, then the transaction should fall under Mode 1; while if the consumer uses the (essential part of the) service in question in the territory of any other Member, then the activity should fall under Mode 2.

4.4.5 Commercial Presence (Mode 3)

The third and fourth modes of supply, commercial presence and presence of natural persons, concern the supply of services through the movement and establishment of the suppliers in the territory of the consumer. The main difference between these two modes of supply resides in the entity that supplies the service: Mode 3 is defined in GATS as the supply of a service

> by a service supplier of one Member, through *commercial presence* in the territory of any other Member.

"Commercial presence" is further defined in Art. XXVIII(d) GATS as:

> any type of business or professional establishment, *including* through (i) the constitution, acquisition or maintenance of a juridical person, or (ii) the creation or maintenance of a branch or a representative office, within the territory of a Member for the purpose of supplying a service. (emphasis added).

Mode 3, hence, concerns supply of services through legal persons only, although what constitutes a business or professional establishment is not more clearly defined. Nevertheless, the concrete forms of commercial presence mentioned in this definition are illustrative, which can be interpreted as an effort by the GATS framers to accommodate the many types of business or professional establishments permitted across WTO Members. According to Art. XXVIII(l) GATS, juridical person means any legal entity duly constituted or otherwise organized under the applicable law, whether for profit or otherwise, and whether privately-owned or governmentally-owned, including any corporation, trust, partnership, joint venture, sole proprietorship or association. It is also clear from this definition that a commercial presence may result from a *de novo* establishment (e.g. a foreign bank establishing a new, wholly-owned branch or subsidiary that competes with domestic firms) or from the acquisition, in whole or in part, of an already existing domestic firm.[89] If a service supplier does not have the status of a juridical person under the law of the Member where it is established, but has rather constituted commercial presence in the form of a branch or representative office, it nevertheless qualifies as a service supplier under Mode 3.[90] In the case of the supply of services through commercial presence, the element defining the origin of service is the origin of its supplier, which in turn, is defined on the basis of the origin of the juridical and/or natural persons that own or control that commercial presence. As expressed in Art. XXVIII(m) GATS:

> "juridical person of another Member" means a juridical person which is either:
>
> (i) constituted or otherwise organized under the law of that other Member, and is engaged in substantive business operations in the territory of that Member or any other Member; or
>
> (ii) in the case of the supply of a service through commercial presence, owned or controlled by:
>
> > 1. natural persons of that Member; or
> >
> > 2. juridical persons of that other Member identified under subparagraph (i);

More specifically, according to Art. XXVIII(n) GATS, a "juridical person" is

---

[89] The reference to maintenance of commercial presence may be relevant, for example, in situations where the measures taken before the WTO inception continued to have effect in the present.

[90] Footnote 12 to Article XXVIII(g), "service supplier", states that "[w]here the service is not supplied directly by a juridical person but through other forms of commercial presence such as a branch or a representative office, the service supplier (i.e. the juridical person) shall, nonetheless, through such presence be accorded the treatment provided for service suppliers under the Agreement. Such treatment shall be extended to the presence through which the service is supplied and need not be extended to any other parts of the supplier located outside the territory where the service is supplied."

(i) "owned" by persons of a Member if more than 50 per cent of the equity interest in it is beneficially owned by persons of that Member;

(ii) "controlled" by persons of a Member if such persons have the power to name a majority of its directors or otherwise to legally direct its actions;

(iii) "affiliated" with another person when it controls, or is controlled by, that other person; or when it and the other person are both controlled by the same person;

When it comes to commercial presence, determining the origin of a foreign service supplier is not an easy task, particularly because subsidiaries of many transnational corporations are usually in multiple ownership or control relationships with one another. For example, a company headquartered in Germany may control a subsidiary in the US, which in turn may control a subsidiary in Canada. Is the subsidiary in Canada a service supplier originating in the US or Germany? Faced with this situation, GATS jurisprudence has made it clear that what is required is to identify the immediate controlling juridical or natural person, not the ultimate one. In *Canada–Autos* (§ 10.257), the Panel stated (in a point that was not disputed by Canada on appeal) that:

In our view, DaimlerChrysler Canada Inc. is a service supplier of the United States within the meaning of Article XXVIII(m)(ii)(2) of the GATS, because it is controlled by DaimlerChrysler Corporation, a juridical person of the United States according to sub-paragaph (i) of Article XXVIII(m). What is relevant, therefore, is that DaimlerChrysler Corporation is a juridical person of the United States. The fact that, in turn, DaimlerChrysler Corporation may be controlled by a juridical person of another Member is not relevant under Article XXVIII of the GATS. In order to define a "juridical person of another Member" Article XXVIII(m) of the GATS does not require the identification of the ultimate controlling juridical or natural person: it is sufficient to establish ownership or control by a juridical person of another Member, defined according to the criteria set out in subparagraph (i).

4.4.6 Presence of Natural Persons (Mode 4)

Art. I GATS defines Mode 4 as:

the supply of a service by a service supplier of one Member, through presence of natural persons of a Member in the territory of any other Member.

Art. XXVIII GATS further defines a service supplier as any person that supplies a service, and, in turn, a person means either a natural or a juridical person: Mode 4 though, always involves a natural person supplying a service in the host country. The natural person is not necessarily the service supplier for the sake of the definition in Art. I GATS; depending on the nature of the transaction, the service supplier may be another natural person, or even a juridical person. In each case it is vital to identify the service supplier, on whom the obligations in the GATS are bestowed.[91] It is the Annex on Movement of Natural Persons Supplying Services under the Agreement which specifies the two types of natural persons that are covered: those who are (themselves) service suppliers; and those who are employed by a service supplier. The first type (natural persons who are service suppliers of a Member), involves only one and the same person, who is present and supplies a service in the territory of another Member. This would cover a self-employed person who is remunerated directly for the supply of a service by customers in the host country. The natural person must be the national (or permanent resident) of a Member other than that in which he or she is present to supply the service, i.e. the natural person must be of different origin from the host Member's perspective. The second type concerns natural persons of a Member who are employed by a service supplier of a Member. In other words, a distinction is made between the natural person and the service supplier. According to Art. XXVIII(g) and (j) of the GATS, a service supplier can be either a natural person or, more commonly in this context, a juridical person, but it will be that person's employee who is present and delivers the service in the host Member.

The natural person and the service supplier need to be nationals of another WTO Member, i.e. they must be of foreign origin from the perspective of the host country, but not necessarily from the same Member or origin. In other words, as nationally-owned service companies are not service suppliers of another Member, any foreign natural persons they employ are therefore not covered by Mode 4. Distinguishing between service suppliers and employees of service suppliers is crucial, particularly when a national service company is involved. As developed here, Mode 4 covers foreigners who are themselves the service supplier and foreigners employed by a foreign service supplier, but not foreigners who are employees of a national service company or individual.

The Annex on Movement of Natural Persons Supplying Services under the Agreement provides additional elements that aim at clarifying the

---

[91] It is also important to determine the origin of the Mode 4 service supplier, since the main substantive provisions of the GATS, i.e. MFN (Art. II), market access (Art. XVI) and NT (Art. XVII), focus on "service suppliers of any other Member". This is hardly surprising, as it is only service suppliers of other WTO Members, and not a Member's own suppliers or the suppliers of a non-Member, that are eligible for the treatment provided under the GATS. Relevant origin definitions are found in Art. XXVIII GATS. A "natural person of another Member" is a natural person who resides in the territory of a WTO Member and who is either a national or, in certain circumstances, a permanent resident of that other Member. For the purpose of services traded through Mode 4, a "juridical person of another Member" is a juridical person constituted or otherwise organized under the law of that other Member and engaged in substantive business operations in the territory of a WTO Member.

scope of Mode 4. For example, it is this document which makes it clear that Mode 4 covers temporary presence of natural persons. It further specifies that the GATS does not apply to measures regarding citizenship, residence or employment on a permanent basis. The GATS, nevertheless, does not make reference to a specific timeframe to determine what might constitute temporary presence: pursuant to the Scheduling Guidelines, each WTO Member should specify in its schedule of specific commitments the permitted duration of stay for the categories of natural persons included therein. In a sense, everything is temporary and one can legitimately wonder what the counterfactual here can be. At the end of the day, what matters is the length of stay mentioned in the commitments entered under Mode 4 in national schedules.

The Annex on Movement of Natural Persons Supplying Services under the Agreement also states that:

> the Agreement shall not apply to measures affecting natural persons seeking access to the employment market of a Member.

It further clarifies that, regardless of their obligations under the GATS, Members are free to regulate the entry and stay of individuals in their territory, provided that the measures concerned:

> are not applied in such a manner as to nullify or impair the benefits accruing to any Member under the terms of a specific commitment.

It also provides that the operation of visa requirements only for natural persons of certain Members, but not for others, is not per se regarded as nullifying or impairing such benefits.

Table 23.3   Modes of Supply

Supplier Presence	Other Criteria	Mode
Service supplier <u>not present</u> within the territory of the Member	Service delivered <u>with in</u> the territory of the Member, from the territory of another Member	CROSS–BORDER SUPPLY (Mode 1)
	Service delivered <u>outside</u> the territory of the Member, in the territory of another Member, to a service consumer of the Member	CONSUMPTION ABROAD (Mode 2)

Service supplier <u>present</u> within the territory of the Member	Service delivered within the territory of the Member, through the commercial presence of the supplier	COMMERCIAL PRESENCE (Mode 3)
	Service delivered within the territory of the Member, with supplier present as a <u>natural</u> person	PRESENCE OF NATURAL PERSON (Mode 4)

4.5 NON–RETROACTIVITY OF OBLIGATIONS ASSUMED UNDER THE GATS

In *EC–Bananas III*, the EU argued that, because its import licensing regime pre-dated the entry into force of GATS, it could not be subjected to review by the Panel. The Panel disagreed. In its view (§ 7.308) for a measure to be subject to review under the GATS it has, independently of its entry into force, to produce (legal) effects after January 1, 1995. The AB (§ 235–237) upheld this view:

> The European Communities also raises the question whether the Panel erred in giving retroactive effect to Articles II and XVII of the GATS, contrary to the principle stated in Art. 28 of the *Vienna Convention*. Art. 28 states the general principle of international law that "[u]nless a different intention appears from the treaty or is otherwise established, its provisions do not bind a party in relation to ... any situation which ceased to exist before the date of entry into force of the treaty ...". The Panel stated in its finding on this issue that:
>
>> ... the scope of our legal examination includes only actions which the EC took or continued to take, or measures that remained in force or continued to be applied by the EC, and thus did not cease to exist after the entry into force of the GATS. Likewise, any finding of consistency or inconsistency with the requirements of Articles II and XVII of GATS would be made with respect to the period after the entry into force of the GATS.
>
> The Panel stated, further, in a footnote to this finding, that
>
>> "the EC measures at issue may be considered as continuing measures, which in some cases were enacted before the entry into force of the GATS but which did *not* cease to exist

after that date (the opposite of the situation envisaged in Art. 28)".

The European Communities argues that the continuing situation at issue here is not the continued existence of Regulation 404/93 and other related regulations, but is, instead, the alleged discrimination against and among foreign service suppliers. The European Communities maintains that *de facto* discrimination is a fact at a particular point in time, and does not necessarily continue for as long as a law remains in force. The European Communities argues that the Panel based its finding with respect to *de facto* discrimination on data related to 1992, that is, before the entry into force of the GATS on 1 January 1995. In the view of the European Communities, there is no basis for the assumption that this factual data relating to 1992, even if correct, continued to exist after the entry into force of the GATS. In the absence of evidence to the contrary, the European Communities argues, it should be concluded that the *de facto* discrimination in 1992 was a situation which ceased to exist before the entry into force of the GATS. Consequently, the European Communities contends that the non-retroactivity principle in Art. 28 of the *Vienna Convention* applies in this case, and that this invalidates the Panel's conclusion of inconsistency of the EC import licensing regime with Articles II and XVII of the GATS.

It is, however, evident from the terms of its finding that the Panel concluded, as a matter of fact, that the *de facto* discrimination did continue to exist after the entry into force of the GATS. This factual finding is beyond review by the AB. Thus, we do not reverse or modify the Panel's conclusion in § 7.308 of the Panel Reports." (italics and emphasis in the original).

In the absence of a distinction by the AB, this ruling is pertinent for both general obligations assumed under, and specific commitments made in the GATS.

4.6 MEASURES AFFECTING TRADE IN SERVICES

Art. I.1 GATS states that the GATS:

applies to measures by Members affecting trade in services.

The term "measure affecting trade in services" is further explained (Art. XXVIII(c) GATS):

measures by Members affecting trade in services" include measures in respect of (i) the purchase, payment or use of a service; (ii) the access to and use of, in connection with the supply of a service, services which are required by those Members to be offered to the public generally; (iii) the presence, including commercial presence, of persons of a Member for the supply of a service in the territory of another Member.

The wording makes it clear that the list of the three types of measures is of indicative nature. Recourse to case law is thus, warranted in order to understand how the contract has been completed so far. The AB, in *EC–Bananas III*, opted for a wide understanding of the class of measures that are capable of affecting trade in services (§ 220):

> In our view, the use of the term 'affecting' reflects the intent of the drafters to give a broad reach to the GATS. The ordinary meaning of the word 'affecting' implies a measure that has 'an effect on', which indicates a broad scope of application. This interpretation is further reinforced by the conclusions of previous panels that the term 'affecting' in the context of Article III of the GATT is wider in scope than such terms as 'regulating' or 'governing'. . . . We also note that Article I:3(b) of the GATS provides that ' "services" includes *any service* in *any sector* except services supplied in the exercise of governmental authority' (emphasis added), and that Article XXVIII(b) of the GATS provides that the ' "supply of a service" includes the production, distribution, marketing, sale and delivery of a service'. There is nothing at all in these provisions to suggest a limited scope of application for the GATS. . . . For these reasons, we uphold the Panel's finding that there is no legal basis for an *a priori* exclusion of measures within the EC banana import licensing regime from the scope of the GATS. (italics and emphasis in the original).

The AB was upholding a finding by the Panel that there:

> is no legal basis for an *a priori* exclusion of measures within the EC banana import licensing regime from the scope of GATS (§ 220 of the AB report).

However, a wide understanding of the term does not imply that no review at all is necessary by a court when deciding whether a *measure is indeed affecting* trade in services. This issue was discussed in the *Canada–Autos* litigation. The Panel, when asked to review whether a duty free exemption was a measure affecting trade in services, reproduced, faithfully in its view, the approach taken in *EC–Bananas III*, and decided (§ 10.234) that there is no *a priori* basis for exclusion of a measure. Consequently, the Panel did not conduct a market analysis to substantiate whether the measure at hand was indeed affecting trade in services: the question before it was whether a Canadian measure reserving some advantages to a particular sub-set of all car distributors in Canada was consistent with GATS. The AB disagreed with the Panel's findings. In its view, its prior statement to the effect that the term measure affecting trade in services is prone to wide understanding, should not be equated with a total absence of judicial review aiming to establish whether a measure had indeed affected trade in services. In the AB's view (§ 152):

> [T]he fundamental structure and logic of Art. I:1, in relation to the rest of the GATS, require that determination of whether a measure is, in fact, covered by the GATS must be made before the consistency of that measure with any substantive obligation of the GATS can be assessed.

The AB went even further and provided a legal test to decide whether a measure is indeed affecting trade in services. As reflected in § 155 of the report:

> ... we believe that at least two key legal issues must be examined to determine whether a measure is one 'affecting trade in services': first, where there is 'trade in services' in the sense of Art. I:2; and, second, whether the measure in issue 'affects' such trade in services within the meaning of Art. I:1.

In further explaining its method, the AB took the view (§ 157) that the first leg of its two-prong test requires inquiring into whether the services at issue are supplied through any of the four modes of supply that constitute the definition of trade in services in Art. I GATS. In the present dispute, since Canada did not challenge the fact that foreign suppliers were established in its market, the AB found that the first leg of the test had been satisfied. With respect to the second leg of the test, the AB developed its argument in two stages:

> (a) first, since some measures can be scrutinized under both GATT and GATS, it is imperative to explain how exactly a particular measure affects trade in goods or in services (§§ 160–1). This first step was particularly important, since Canada had argued that the challenged measures affected only trade in goods;
>
> (b) second, it noted that, in the instant case, the Panel had not examined any evidence relating to the provision of wholesale trade services of motor vehicles in the Canadian market. The Panel had assumed a particular market situation without any actual review of the market (§§ 164–5). Absent such a review, the Panel's findings had to be rejected as totally unsubstantiated. Assumptions are simply "not good enough", in the AB's eyes (§ 166). The Panel should, in the AB's view have examined who supplies such services and how such services are supplied.

In *US–Gambling,* both the Panel and the AB emphasized the distinction between the measure of a Member and its effect. In this case, the US had in place a number of federal and state laws which outlawed the remote supply of gambling, including internet gambling. The US laws in place were non-discriminatory, i.e. they banned internet gambling irrespective of whether the service supplier was national (US supplier) or foreign. The US however, had taken full specific commitments on the cross-border supply of "other recreational services (except sporting)", i.e. without indicating any limitation in its schedule of commitments.[92] Antigua and Barbuda complained that the US, in the absence of limitations in its schedule, could not restrict internet gambling services originating in Antigua's territory. The Panel eventually ended up accepting this claim. To do this however, the Panel had to identify what was the measure at issue and whether it was a measure affecting trade in services.[93] In fact, presumably because of the difficulty of identifying all measures potentially at issue, Antigua challenged the "total prohibition" resulting from the application of an unidentified number of measures, at different government levels, in the US. Both the Panel and the AB rejected Antigua's position, emphasizing the distinction between the measure of a Member and its effect. As explained by the AB, what Antigua was challenging was the collective effect of the operation of several state and federal laws of the US (§ 124). In accordance with Article 6.2 of the DSU, nevertheless, only a specific measure, that is, the source of the alleged prohibition, may be challenged under the WTO; otherwise, the respondent would not be in a position to prepare adequately its defence (§ 125). The AB therefore upheld the Panel's finding that without demonstrating the source of the prohibition, a complainant may not challenge a total prohibition as a measure per se in dispute settlement proceedings under the GATS (§ 126).

A measure is understood to be any measure taken by central, regional or local governments and authorities, as well as non-governmental bodies in the exercise of powers delegated by central, regional or local governments or authorities, whether in the form of a law, regulation, rule, procedure, decision, administrative action, or any other form.[94] Therefore, governments can, in principle, be held accountable in the WTO for decisions or actions affecting trade in services by sub-central governments (states, provinces, cantons, municipalities, etc.) and even non-governmental bodies exercising delegated powers (e.g. professional associations, stock exchanges, associations allocating Internet domain names). The GATS makes it clear though that central governments are not fully responsible for the enforcement of measures at sub-central levels or by non-governmental entities. Art. I.3(a) GATS states to this effect:

> [i]n fulfilling its obligations and commitments under the Agreement, each Member shall take such reasonable measures as may be available to it to ensure their observance by regional and local

---

[92] The Panel additionally found that "other recreational services (except sporting)" included gambling services.

[93] The Panel actually looked at three federal statutes preventing certain interstate and international activities involving betting, and eight states laws.

[94] Arts. I.3(a), and XXVIII(a) GATS.

governments and authorities and non-governmental bodies within its territory.

This clause is reminiscent of Art. XXIV.12 GATT, the federal clause, and for this reason, the case law to this provision should, in principle, be relevant here as well. The GATT Panel in *US–Malt Beverages* clarified that the burden of proof to show whether Art. XXIV.12 GATT has been complied with rests with the complainant and not with the defendant federal state.[95] The GATT Panel in *Canada–Provincial Liquor Boards (US)* held that Art. XXIV.12 GATT is not an exception to the other GATT provisions since it merely qualified the obligation to implement the GATT.[96] In the same vein, the GATT Panel in *Canada–Gold Coins* held that Art. XXIV.12 GATT does not limit the applicability of the GATT but merely the obligation of federal governments to implement the GATT.[97] This Panel ruled that:

> The basic principle embodied is ... that in determining which measures to secure the observance of the provisions of the General Agreement are 'reasonable' within the meaning of Article XXIV:12, the consequences of their non-observance by the local government for trade relations with other contracting parties are to be weighed against the domestic difficulties of securing observance.[98]

4.7 THE RELATIONSHIP BETWEEN GATT AND GATS

In *Canada–Periodicals,* the issue arose whether the Canadian Excise Tax Act should come under the purview of GATT or GATS since, as Canada had argued, the tax (equal to 80% of the value of all the advertisements contained in the so-called split-run magazines) was imposed on a service (advertising), and was therefore only subject to the disciplines of the GATS. Canada further argued that the measure at hand could only be reviewed under the national treatment obligation of the GATS (Art. XVII) in respect of which no specific commitments on advertising had been taken. Both the Panel and the AB disagreed with the Canadian argument, stating that the measure at hand was affecting trade in goods as well. On the wider issue regarding the frontier between GATT and GATS, the AB provided a rather non-committal statement (p. 19):

> The entry into force of the GATS, as Annex 1B of the *WTO Agreement*, does not diminish the scope of application of the GATT 1994. Indeed, Canada concedes that its position 'with respect to the inapplicability of the GATT would have been exactly

---

[95] §§ 5.78–5.80.
[96] § 5.36.
[97] § 64.
[98] § 69. This report remains un-adopted and hence, of limited legal value.

the same under the GATT 1947, before the GATS had ever been conceived'.

We agree with the Panel's statement:

> The ordinary meaning of the texts of GATT 1994 and GATS as well as Art. II:2 of the WTO Agreement, taken together, indicates that obligations under GATT 1994 and GATS can co-exist and that one does not override the other.
>
> We do not find it necessary to pronounce on the issue of whether there can be potential overlaps between the GATT 1994 and the GATS, as both participants agreed that it is not relevant in this appeal. (italics in the original).

In short, in *Canada–Periodicals*, the AB held that the obligations of both agreements can co-exist. In *EC–Bananas III*, the EU defended the view that GATT and GATS cannot overlap, as a matter of principle. The Panel disagreed essentially because, in its view, in the absence of overlap, WTO Members would easily be in a position to circumvent their WTO obligations. The Panel offered the following example to highlight its view at § 7.283:

> For example, a measure in the transport sector regulating the transportation of merchandise in the territory of a Member could subject imported products to less favourable transportation conditions compared to those applicable to like domestic products. Such a measure would adversely affect the competitive position of imported products in a manner which would not be consistent with that Member's obligation to provide national treatment to such products. If the scope of GATT and GATS were interpreted to be mutually exclusive, that Member could escape its national treatment obligation and the Members whose products have been discriminated against would have no possibility of legal recourse on account that the measure regulates 'services' and not goods.

In § 7.285, the Panel defined the scope of application of the GATS in the following terms:

> [N]o measures are excluded a priori from the scope of the GATS as defined by its provisions. The scope of the GATS encompasses any measure of a Member to the extent it affects the supply of a service regardless of whether such measure directly governs the supply of a service or whether it regulates other matters but nevertheless affects trade in services.

Based on this interpretation of the scope of the GATS, the Panel in *EC–Bananas III* concluded that there was (§ 7.286):

no legal basis for an a priori exclusion of measures within the EC banana import licensing regime from the scope of the GATS.

The AB upheld this finding, since in its view, the use of the term "affecting" reflected the intent of the drafters to give a broad reach to the Agreement, in any case broader than would have been the case if expressions such as regulating or governing would have been privileged. In its view then, there is nothing that suggests limited scope for the GATS (p. 220); moreover, the AB reaffirmed that in certain circumstances GATT and GATS may overlap. At the same time, it made it clear that, although a measure could simultaneously fall under the GATT and the GATS, it could not be the case that the same facet of the measure challenged could simultaneously be scrutinized under both agreements. The AB distinguished between three categories of measures:

(a) those affecting trade in goods as goods, and therefore falling exclusively under the GATT;

(b) those affecting the supply of services as services, therefore falling exclusively under the GATS; and,

(c) thirdly, those that, in principle, could fall under both. It is this latter category that is of interest to our discussion (p 221):

there is yet a third category of measures that could be found to fall within the scope of both the GATT 1994 and the GATS. These are measures that involve a service relating to a particular good or service supplied in conjunction with a particular good. In all such cases in this third category, the measure in question could be scrutinized under both the GATT 1994 and the GATS. However, while the same measure could be scrutinized under both agreements, the specific aspects of that measure examined under each agreement could be different. Under the GATT 1994, the focus is on how the measure affects the goods involved. Under the GATS, the focus is on how the measure affects the supply of the service or the service suppliers involved. Whether a certain measure affecting the supply of a service related to a particular good is scrutinized under the GATT 1994 or the GATS, or both, is a matter that can only be determined on a case-by-case basis.

QUESTIONS AND COMMENTS

Genesis: Marchetti and Mavroidis (2011) provide a comprehensive account of the GATS negotiations and an attempt to assign property rights to the various GATS provisions. Specific aspects of the negotiations have been discussed in various papers, most notably in Arkell (1990), Brittan (2000), Das (2006), Feketekuty (1988a), Gibbs and Mashayekhi (1991), Hoekman (1995), Richardson and Scheele (1989), and Self and Zutshi (2003).

Economics of Trade in Services: There are few papers on this issue, Ethier and Horn (1991) are one of the pioneers.

US Financial Services and GATS: The role of "American Express Co." in getting the multilateral negotiation on trade in services off the ground is pivotal and needs some further explanation. Yoffie (1990) is the author of the standard work in this context. In his account, the company adopted a *Vince Lombardi*-strategy, named after the famous football coach, and described in the following terms by Joan Spero, Vice President for International Corporate Affairs:

> The best defence was a good offense. The company did not want to be a passive observer of events. On the contrary the fundamental principle guiding American Express' actions was that 'if you don't like the environment, you should try to change it'.

US Division of Competences: All along the negotiation, the US was troubled by an inter-agency conflict: the US Treasury was competent to negotiate financial services and taxation, while the USTR had competence on everything else. This distribution of competences was not inconsequential as far as the GATS negotiation was concerned: theoretically, the US Treasury could have left the negotiating room if it had not been satisfied with the offers of the various trading partners; it was negotiating in self-contained manner where trade-offs were possible only with respect to financial services. In other words, if the US Treasury felt that counter-offers on financial services by the other trading nations were not satisfactory, that would signal the end of the negotiation on this sector as far as the US was concerned. The USTR could, on the other hand, decide on trade-offs not only between various services, but also across services and goods or even TRIPs. The inter-agency play between USTR and US Treasury would turn to be one of the keys in determining the US approach at various stages of the negotiation.

Mexico–Telecoms: Neven and Mavroidis (2007) have critically analysed the Panel report in *Mexico-Telecoms* noting:

> if one applies this line of reasoning to the transaction considered by the Panel, we are led to conclude that US operators do not provide a cross-border service under mode 1, since both the supplier (US carrier) and the consumer (US residents) are indeed physically present in the same territory.... As indicated above, an international call from the US to Mexico can be seen as the bundle of two strict complements, namely a routing from the US subscriber to the border and a termination within Mexico. The US operator sells the bundle to a US subscriber and purchases one element of the bundle (one input) from a Mexican operator. From this perspective, Mexican operators are thus selling one service (termination) to a foreign firm. In other words, they are producing a service using domestic inputs and selling it to a foreign undertaking. This is literally a mode 1 type of supply, but in this perspective the supplier is the Mexican operator that terminates the call (and not the US operator, as

deemed by the Panel.) Hence, the Panel ends up imposing a discipline on the exports of Mexican services, making sure in particular that such services are sold at prices that reflect cost.

Neven and Mavroidis conclude that the only cross border supply involved in this case is that of export of termination calls by Telmex (core supplier) to the US operators (another supplier), and not between a supplier and a final consumer envisaged by the Panel. In their view, hence, the Panel was looking into the wrong schedule.

Technological Neutrality: Did the Panel in *US-Gambling* get it right? It seems that when the negotiation took place internet gambling was technologically impossible. How then could the US ever make commitments to this effect? Also, check the following passage:

> a prohibition on one, several or all means of delivery included in this mode 1 would be a limitation on market access for the mode. (§ 6.285).

Did, in your view, the Panel expand the list of market access limitations contained in Art. XVI:2 GATS with this statement?

Chapter 24

General Obligations

...

1. GENERAL OBLIGATIONS: IDENTIFICATION AND FUNCTION

An exhaustive list of general obligations in GATS includes:

Art. II GATS:	MFN
Art. III GATS:	Transparency
Art. IIIbis GATS:	Disclosure of confidential information
Art. IV GATS:	Increasing participation of developing countries
Art. V GATS:	Economic integration
Art. Vbis GATS:	Labor markets integration agreements
Art. VI GATS:	Domestic regulation
Art. VII GATS:	Recognition
Art. VIII GATS:	Monopolies and exclusive service suppliers
Art. IX GATS:	Business practices
Art. X GATS:	Emergency safeguard measures
Art. XI GATS:	Payments and transfers
Art. XII GATS:	Restrictions to safeguard the balance of payments
Art. XIII GATS:	Government procurement
Art. XIV GATS:	General exceptions
Art. XIVbis GATS:	Security exceptions
Art. XV GATS:	Subsidies

General obligations bind WTO Members irrespective whether they have agreed to make sector-specific commitments in a particular sector. A WTO Member must, for example, respect MFN, even if it has decided not to open up say its economic consultancy market at all; it must treat all WTO Members in the same manner by denying market access to all of them. Some of these obligations apply only to the sectors where specific commitments have been undertaken (e.g. disciplines on licensing and qualification requirements in Art. VI GATS, some notification obligations in Art. III GATS, obligations on international payments and transfers in Art. XI GATS); others constitute in fact specific negotiating mandates to develop multilateral disciplines in those areas (e.g. Art. X GATS, Art. XIII GATS, Art. XV GATS, and Art. VI.4 GATS).

2. MFN

2.1 THE LEGAL DISCIPLINE

Art. II.1 GATS imposes on WTO Members the obligation to accord unconditionally and automatically to any service and/or services suppliers of other WTO Members treatment no less favorable than the treatment they accord to like services and like services suppliers from any other country.

2.2 THE RATIONALE FOR THE LEGAL DISCIPLINE

MFN is the insurance policy that negotiators bought in order to avoid concession erosion. But what if no commitments at all have been made? Assume that a WTO Member that made no commitments at all, subsequently opens up its market and accepts a service supplier. Any service supplier originating in a WTO Member who can demonstrate that is a like service supplier (to the one admitted) will have to be granted market access as well. In this scenario, it cannot be that concession erosion explains the MFN obligation, since no concession has been made in the first place; it is the appurtenance to WTO that explains why benefits must be extended to all WTO Membership in this case.

2.3 COVERAGE

The MFN requests from WTO Members to treat like services (and services suppliers) in a non-discriminatory manner; in this vein, any advantage granted must be extended automatically and unconditionally to all like services and services suppliers.

2.3.1 Likeness of Services (and Services Suppliers)

In *Canada–Autos*, the Panel dealt with the issue whether "manufacture beneficiaries" and "non-manufacture beneficiaries" are like services suppliers "regardless of whether or not they have production facilities in Canada". The issue before the Panel was whether the mode of supply influences likeness. The Panel (§§ 10.247–248) responded in the negative:

> The complainants argue, and Canada does not contest, that manufacturer beneficiaries and non-manufacturer-beneficiaries provide "like" services and are "like" service suppliers, irrespec-

tive of whether their services are supplied with respect to motor vehicles imported by the manufacturer beneficiaries or with respect to motor vehicles imported by non-manufacturer-beneficiaries, and regardless of whether or not they have production facilities in Canada.

We agree that to the extent that the service suppliers concerned supply the same services, they should be considered "like" for the purpose of this case.

It bears repetition that WTO Members can, of course, differentiate when scheduling their commitments between different modes: they might be more liberal for example, under Mode 1 and less so under Mode 3 or Mode 4. Hence, if at all this ruling will be pertinent assuming no such distinctions have been made in a national schedule of commitments. This finding was not appealed.[1]

In *EC–Bananas III*, the issue was whether the EU had violated this provision through its categorization of distributors of bananas: the "Operator Category Rules", whereby the EU authorities would classify suppliers of bananas into two categories, A and B, depending on the origin of the bananas they would be distributing, and would further allocate to category B operators (distributing bananas originating in ACP countries) 30% of the licences for importing third-country and non-traditional ACP bananas at in-quota tariff rates. These were the "Hurricane Licences", whereby only operators who include or directly represent EU or ACP producers or producer organizations affected by a tropical storm were eligible for allocation of hurricane licences (which operated thus, as means of compensation). The Panel held that the various distributors involved were all like suppliers (§ 7.322):

> Fourth, in our view, the nature and the characteristics of wholesale transactions as such, as well as of each of the different subordinated services mentioned in the headnote to section 6 of the CPC, are "like" when supplied in connection with wholesale services, irrespective of whether these services are supplied with respect to bananas of EC and traditional ACP origin, on the one hand, or with respect to bananas of third-country or non-traditional ACP origin, on the other. Indeed, it seems that each of the different service activities taken individually is virtually the same and can only be distinguished by referring to the origin of the bananas in respect of which the service activity is being performed. Similarly, in our view, to the extent that entities provide these like services, they are like service suppliers.

This finding was not appealed.

---

[1] See the analysis of Mattoo (2000).

2.3.2 Less Favorable Treatment

Art. XVII GATS, which deals with national treatment explicitly provides that its coverage extends to both *de jure*-, as well as *de facto*-discrimination.[2] This is not the case in the context of Art. II GATS, which reads:

> With respect to any measure covered by this Agreement, each Member shall accord immediately and unconditionally to services and service suppliers of any other Member treatment no less favourable than that it accords to like services and service suppliers of any other country.

The question arises whether the difference in language was intended, whether in other words, Art. II GATS should be limited to cases of *de jure* discrimination, or whether it should be construed so as to expand to cases of *de facto* discrimination as well. The AB in *EC–Bananas III* put such doubts to rest by holding that the latter should be the case (§§ 229–234):

> The European Communities appeals the Panel's finding:
>
>> ... that the obligation contained in Art. II:1 of GATS to extend "treatment no less favourable" should be interpreted *in casu* to require providing no less favourable conditions of competition.
>
> The critical issue here is whether Art. II:1 of the GATS applies only to *de jure*, or formal, discrimination or whether it applies also to *de facto* discrimination.
>
> The Panel's approach to this question was to interpret the words "treatment no less favourable" in Art. II:1 of the GATS by reference to paragraphs 2 and 3 of Art. XVII of the GATS. The Panel said:
>
>> ... we note that the standard of "no less favourable treatment" in § 1 of Art. XVII is meant to provide for no less favourable conditions of competition regardless of whether that is achieved through the application of formally identical or formally different measures. Paragraphs 2 and 3 of Art. XVII serve the purpose of codifying this interpretation, and in our view, do not impose new obligations on Members additional to those contained in § 1. In essence, the "treatment no less favourable" standard of Art. XVII:1 is clarified and reinforced in the language of paragraphs 2 and 3. The ab-

---

[2] Art. XVII GATS reads in part (§§ 2 and 3) as follows: A Member may meet the requirement of § 1 by according to services and service suppliers of any other Member, either formally identical treatment or formally different treatment to that it accords to its own like services and service suppliers. Formally identical or formally different treatment shall be considered to be less favourable if it modifies the conditions of competition in favour of services or service suppliers of the Member compared to like services or service suppliers of any other Member.

sence of similar language in Art. II is not, in our view, a justification for giving a different ordinary meaning in terms of Art. 31(1) of the Vienna Convention to the words "treatment no less favourable", which are identical in both Articles II:1 and XVII:1.

We find the Panel's reasoning on this issue to be less than fully satisfactory. The Panel interpreted Art. II of the GATS in the light of Panel reports interpreting the national treatment obligation of Art. III of the GATT. The Panel also referred to Art. XVII of the GATS, which is also a national treatment obligation. But Art. II of the GATS relates to MFN treatment, not to national treatment. Therefore, provisions elsewhere in the GATS relating to national treatment obligations, and previous GATT practice relating to the interpretation of the national treatment obligation of Art. III of the GATT 1994 are not necessarily relevant to the interpretation of Art. II of the GATS. The Panel would have been on safer ground had it compared the MFN obligation in Art. II of the GATS with the MFN and MFN-type obligations in the GATT 1994.

Articles I and II of the GATT 1994 have been applied, in past practice, to measures involving *de facto* discrimination. We refer, in particular, to the Panel report in *EEC–Imports of Beef from Canada*, which examined the consistency of EEC regulations implementing a levy-free tariff quota for high quality grain-fed beef with Art. I of the GATT 1947. Those regulations made suspension of the import levy for such beef conditional on production of a certificate of authenticity. The only certifying agency authorized to produce a certificate of authenticity was a United States agency. The Panel, therefore, found that the EEC regulations were inconsistent with the MFN principle in Art. I of the GATT 1947 as they had the effect of denying access to the EEC market to exports of products of any origin other than that of the United States.

The GATS negotiators chose to use different language in Art. II and Art. XVII of the GATS in expressing the obligation to provide "treatment no less favourable". The question naturally arises: if the GATS negotiators intended that "treatment no less favourable" should have exactly the same meaning in Articles II and XVII of the GATS, why did they not repeat paragraphs 2 and 3 of Art. XVII in Art. II? But that is not the question here. The question here is the meaning of "treatment no less favourable" with respect to the MFN obligation in Art. II of the GATS. There is more than one way of writing a *de facto* non-discrimination provision. Art. XVII of the GATS is merely one of many provisions in the WTO Agreement that require the obligation of providing "treatment no less favourable". The possibility that the two Articles may not have exactly the same meaning does not imply that the intention of the drafters of the GATS was that a *de jure*, or formal, standard should apply in Art. II of the GATS. If that were the intention, why does Art. II not say as much? The obligation imposed by Art. II is unqualified. The ordinary meaning of this provision does not exclude *de facto* discrimination. Moreover, if Art. II was not applicable to *de facto* discrimination, it would not be difficult—and, indeed, it would be a good deal easier in the case of trade in services, than in the case of trade in goods—to devise discriminatory measures aimed at circumventing the basic purpose of that Article.

For these reasons, we conclude that "treatment no less favourable" in Art. II:1 of the GATS should be interpreted to include *de facto*, as well as *de jure*, discrimination. We should make it clear that we do not limit our conclusion to this case. We have some difficulty in understanding why the Panel stated that its interpretation of Art. II of the GATS applied "in casu". (italics in the original).

The Panel had concluded that "the vast majority of operators who include or directly represent EC or ACP producers are service suppliers of EU (or ACP) origin", and the AB agreed that this fact led to the finding that the EU practice was inconsistent with Art. II GATS (§§ 242–245):

> The European Communities argues that the aim of the operator category system, in view of the objective of integrating the various national markets, and of the differing situations of banana traders in the various Member States, was not discriminatory but rather was to establish machinery for dividing the tariff quota among the different categories of traders concerned. In the view of the European Communities, the operator category system also serves the purpose of distributing quota rents among the various operators in the market. The European Communities emphasizes, furthermore, that the principle of transferability of licences is used in order to develop market structures without disrupting existing commercial links. The effect of the operator category rules, the European Communities argues, is to leave a commercial choice in the hands of the operators.
>
> We do not agree with the European Communities that the aims and effects of the operator category system are relevant in determining whether or not that system modifies the conditions of competition between service suppliers of EC origin and service suppliers of third-country origin. Based on the evidence before it, the Panel concluded "that most of the suppliers of Complainants'

origin are classified in Category A for the vast majority of their past marketing of bananas, and that most of the suppliers of EC (or ACP) origin are classified in Category B for the vast majority of their past marketing of bananas". We see no reason to go behind these factual conclusions of the Panel.

We concur, therefore, with the Panel's conclusion that "the allocation to Category B operators of 30 per cent of the licences allowing for the importation of third-country and non-traditional ACP bananas at in-quota tariff rates creates less favourable conditions of competition for like service suppliers of Complainants' origin and is therefore inconsistent with the requirement of Article XVII of GATS". We also concur with the Panel's conclusion that the allocation to Category B operators of 30 per cent of the licences for importing third-country and non-traditional ACP bananas at in-quota tariff rates is inconsistent with the requirements of Article II of the GATS.

With respect to the latter, it similarly held (§§ 247–248):

With respect to Article II of the GATS, the European Communities argues that there is no *de facto* discrimination since there is no indication in the hurricane licence rules that operators that are not ACP-owned or -controlled cannot own or represent ACP producers on the same basis as ACP or EC-owned or -controlled operators.

Once again, we do not accept the argument by the European Communities that the aims and effects of a measure are relevant in determining its consistency with Articles II or XVII of the GATS. We note that under the EC hurricane licence rules, only operators who include or directly represent EC or ACP producers or producer organizations affected by a tropical storm are eligible for allocation of hurricane licences. The Panel made a conclusion of fact that "the vast majority of operators who 'include or directly represent' EC or ACP producers are service suppliers of EC (or ACP) origin". Given this factual finding, we do not reverse the Panel's conclusions in paragraphs 7.393 and 7.397 of the Panel Reports.

In the same report, the AB explicitly rejected the relevance of the aims and effects-standard of review in the context of claims under Art. II GATS (§§ 240–241):

The European Communities argues that the EC licensing system for bananas is not discriminatory under Articles II and XVII of the GATS, because the various aspects of the system, including the operator category rules, the activity function rules and the special hurricane licence rules, "pursue entirely legitimate policies" and "are not inherently discriminatory in design or effect".

We see no specific authority either in Art. II or in Art. XVII of the GATS for the proposition that the "aims and effects" of a measure are in any way relevant in determining whether that measure is inconsistent with those provisions. In the GATT context, the "aims and effects" theory had its origins in the principle of Art. III:1 that internal taxes or charges or other regulations "should not be applied to imported or domestic products so as to afford protection to domestic production". There is no comparable provision in the GATS. Furthermore, in our Report in *Japan— Alcoholic Beverages*, the Appellate Body rejected the "aims and effects" theory with respect to Art. III:2 of the GATT 1994. The European Communities cites an unadopted Panel report dealing with Art. III of the GATT 1947, *United States—Taxes on Automobiles*, as authority for its proposition, despite our recent ruling." (italics in the original).

In accordance with Art. II.1 GATS, WTO Members incur the obligation to accord treatment no less favourable than that accorded to like service or service supplier of other WTO Members automatically and unconditionally. There is little doubt that the term automatically essentially imposes on WTO Members the obligation to waste no time extending a benefit already granted to a service or service supplier. The term "unconditionally" was discussed by the Panel in *Canada–Autos*: it held that a WTO Member cannot discriminate across WTO Members, that is, it cannot impose conditions additional to those imposed the first time it granted an advantage, when a request for re-extension of the same advantage comes from another WTO Member. We quote from §§ 10.23–10.24:

> Art. I:1 requires that, if a Member grants any advantage to any product originating in the territory of any other country, such advantage must be accorded "immediately and unconditionally" to the like product originating in the territories of all other Members. We agree with Japan that the ordinary meaning of "unconditionally" is "not subject to conditions". However, in our view Japan misinterprets the meaning of the word "unconditionally" in the context in which it appears in Art. I:1. The word "unconditionally" in Art. I:1 does not pertain to the granting of an advantage per se, but to the obligation to accord to the like products of all Members an advantage which has been granted to any product originating in any country. The purpose of Art. I:1 is to ensure unconditional MFN treatment. In this context, we consider that the obligation to accord "unconditionally" to third countries which are WTO Members an advantage which has been granted to any other country means that the extension of

that advantage may not be made subject to conditions with respect to the situation or conduct of those countries. This means that an advantage granted to the product of any country must be accorded to the like product of all WTO Members without discrimination as to origin.

In this respect, it appears to us that there is an important distinction to be made between, on the one hand, the issue of whether an advantage within the meaning of Art. I:1 is subject to conditions, and, on the other, whether an advantage, once it has been granted to the product of any country, is accorded "unconditionally" to the like product of all other Members. An advantage can be granted subject to conditions without necessarily implying that it is not accorded "unconditionally" to the like product of other Members. More specifically, the fact that conditions attached to such an advantage are not related to the imported product itself does not necessarily imply that such conditions are discriminatory with respect to the origin of imported products. We therefore do not believe that, as argued by Japan, the word "unconditionally" in Art. I:1 must be interpreted to mean that making an advantage conditional on criteria not related to the imported product itself is per se inconsistent with Art. I:1, irrespective of whether and how such criteria relate to the origin of the imported products.

2.4 DEVIATIONS FROM MFN

There are two categories of exceptions to the MFN in GATS: first, exceptions that a WTO Member can enlist in a document (the MFN Exceptions List) that it deposits with the WTO; second, the GATS provisions that justify deviations from Art. II GATS.[3]

2.4.1 MFN Exemptions (Listed Exemptions)

The first grounds is captured in Art. II.2 GATS which in relevant part reads:

> A Member may maintain a measure inconsistent with § 1 provided that such a measure is listed in, and meets the conditions of, the Annex on Art. II Exemptions.

The Annex on Art. II GATS Exemptions states that no new exemptions can be added to the original ones (that is, those inserted before January 1, 1995) unless recourse has been made to the waiver provisions (Art. IX.3 GATS). During the Uruguay Round, a decision was taken to

---

[3] The difference with the GATT regime is thus the MFN exemptions: the possibility offered to WTO Members to indicate which WTO Members will not benefit from MFN treatment for reasons other than those mentioned in the various GATS provisions justifying deviations from MFN.

extend the deadline for notification of MFN exemptions, since negotiations on telecommunications, financial services and maritime transport did not conclude in time.[4] In this vein, the Annex on Negotiations on Maritime Transport Services provides, for example, in its § 1:

> Art. II and the Annex on Art. II Exemptions, including the requirement to list in the Annex any measure inconsistent with most-favoured-nation treatment that a Member will maintain, shall enter into force for international shipping, auxiliary services and access to and use of port facilities only on:
>
> (a) the implementation date to be determined under § 4 of the Ministerial Decision on Negotiations on Maritime Transport Services; or,
>
> (b) should the negotiations not succeed, the date of the final report of the Negotiating Group on Maritime Transport Services provided for in that Decision.

On July 3, 1996 the negotiators decided to suspend the process and, as a result, did not issue a final report.[5] Consequently, for those WTO Members which made commitments by that time, MFN is relevant, and for those that did not, MFN is not relevant.

A note was prepared by the GNS explaining what an exemption from MFN entails, and also describing the manner in which exemptions should be listed by those interested.[6] Although similar notes are of limited legal value (since, they at best qualify as supplementary means of interpretation in the VCLT-sense of the term), they are useful documents in that they denote the attitude and understanding of negotiators on specific issues. This note reads in pertinent part:

> 3. ... a Member may take such exemptions only once. The procedures in the attachment to the Annex make it clear that the exemptions can only be sought prior to the adoption of the text of the GATS. Any exemptions sought later could only be granted in accordance with the procedures set out in paragraph 4 of Article XXIV.
>
> 4. The attachment to the Annex on Article II exemptions specifies the information which must be provided on each exemption sought. It makes it very clear that the essential element in describing a measure is the treatment inconsistent with paragraph 1 of Article II. However, in many cases the MFN exemption lists submitted to date do not describe such treatment clearly. In many instances they merely refer to the entire law, regulation or agreement under which the treatment is accorded. It should be emphasised that MFN exemptions should describe clearly the

---

[4] WTO Docs. S/L/8 and S/L/9 of 24 July 1995.
[5] WTO Doc. S/L/24.
[6] JOB no 2061 of September 15, 1993.

treatment inconsistent with the MFN obligations, regardless of the legal basis for such treatment (law, regulation or agreement), in order to ensure that other members understand accurately the discrimination involved in an exemption. An additional reference to such legal basis may be useful for transparency purposes but would not constitute an essential part of the listing of the exemption. Furthermore, it would be possible, according to the MFN exemption annex, to include measures which are not codified either in a law or a regulation as long as the treatment inconsistent with Article II is clearly described. It should also be noted that Article II and the Annex, as they stand, do not rule out the listing of measures which are to be applied in the future.

5. An MFN exemption relieves a Member only from its obligation under paragraph 1 of Article II, according to which it is required to extend the most favourable treatment it accords to any country to all other Members of the GATS. An exemption does not relieve a Member from its obligations or commitments under any other provision of the GATS. Therefore if a Member takes an MFN exemption in a sector where specific commitments are undertaken, the exemption would allow that Member to deviate from its obligations under paragraph 1 of Article II but not from its commitments under Articles XVI or XVII. Accordingly, a Member undertaking a market access or a national treatment commitment in a sector must accord the stated minimum standard of treatment specified in its schedule to all other Members. Therefore, an MFN exemption in such a case would only allow the Member to extend to certain countries treatment which is more favourable than that specified in the schedule; extending treatment less favourable than that specified in its schedule would constitute a violation of the Member's commitments under Articles XVI or XVII, which cannot be justified by the exemption.

Example: A Member binds a limitation on the participation of foreign capital (not more than 49 per cent) in the banking sector. An exemption from MFN in that case would only allow that Member to extend more favourable treatment to certain countries (e.g. waive the limitation and allow 100 per cent foreign ownership), but not less favourable treatment (e.g. a limitation of foreign capital participation to 20 per cent).

Table 24.1: MFN-exemptions by sector

Sector or sub-sector	Number of Exemptions	Number of Members with Exemptions	Intended Duration	
All sectors	82	44	73:	Indefinite

Sector or sub-sector	Number of Exemptions	Number of Members with Exemptions	Intended Duration	
			4:	Subject to the duration of the agreement concerned
			2:	Ten years
			1:	Eleven years
			1:	Temporary
			1:	Until the time of full membership of Cyprus in the EU
Professional services	19	13	19:	Indefinite
Other business services	9	8	8:	Indefinite
			1:	Five years
Postal services	1	1	1:	Indefinite
Telecommunication services	19	12	17:	Indefinite
			2:	Ten years
Audiovisual services	102	44	95:	Indefinite
			5:	Subject to the duration of the agreement concerned
			1:	Ten years, automatically extended for the same period
			1:	Activated in the event of any other Member maintaining exemptions which provide for unreasonable unilateral action
Construction and related engineering services	2	2	1:	Indefinite
			1:	Subject to the duration of the

Sector or sub-sector	Number of Exemptions	Number of Members with Exemptions	Intended Duration	
				agreement concerned
Distribution services	3	3	3:	Indefinite
Education services	1	1	1:	Indefinite
Financial services	51	27	48:	Indefinite
			2:	Subject to the duration of the agreement concerned
			1:	Ten years
Health related and social services	2	2	2:	Indefinite
Tourism and travel related services	4	4	4:	Indefinite
Recreational, cultural and sporting services	5	4	5:	Indefinite
All transportation services	3	1	3:	Indefinite
Water transport services:				
—Maritime transport	64	28	48:	Indefinite
			7:	Near future, while the objective pursued takes root
			3:	Subject to the duration of the agreement concerned
			5:	Ten years, among which two are renewable
			1:	until the date on which notice of termination by one of the parties ends

Sector or sub-sector	Number of Exemptions	Number of Members with Exemptions	Intended Duration	
—Internal waterways transport	10	9	10:	Indefinite
Air transport	28	24	27:	Indefinite
			1:	Five years
Space transport	1	1	1:	Indefinite
Land transport services:				
—Generic land transport	13	10	12:	Indefinite
			1:	Subject to the duration of the agreement concerned
—Rail transport	4	4	4:	Indefinite
—Road transport	42	34	37:	Indefinite
			2:	Subject to the duration of the agreement concerned
			2:	Exemptions needed until multilateral liberalization of road transport services, taking into account regional specificity and environmental effects of road transport, will have been agreed upon
			1:	To be reviewed 12 years after entry into force of the bilateral agreement between Switzerland and EC

Sector or sub-sector	Number of Exemptions	Number of Members with Exemptions	Intended Duration	
—Pipeline transport	1	1	1:	Indefinite
Services auxiliary to all modes of transport	1	1	1:	Indefinite

The WTO Members adopted a Decision on Procedures for the Certification of Terminations, Reductions, and Rectifications of Article II (MFN) Exemptions.[7] This document, as its title makes it clear, lays out the procedure to follow for rectifying, reducing the impact of, and terminating notified exemptions. The term "rectification" in WTO parlance amounts to anodyne changes which do not affect the intrinsic value of the notified exemption. At any rate, it is impossible for WTO Members to expand a notified exemption through this instrument. It pertinently reads:

> Modifications in the authentic texts of lists of Article II exemptions which consist of terminations, reductions of the scope or level of existing exemptions, or rectifications or changes of a purely technical character that do not alter the substance of the existing exemptions, shall take effect by means of certification.
>
> Terminations of Article II (MFN) exemptions
>
> A Member intending to terminate any of its Article II exemptions prior to its termination date shall notify the Council for Trade in Services. Such a notification shall contain information on the reasons for the intended termination, as well as the date of entry into force of the termination. The Secretariat shall issue a communication to all Members to the effect that the termination of the Article II exemption has been certified, indicating the date of entry into force of the termination.
>
> Reductions and Rectifications of Article II (MFN) exemptions
>
> A Member intending to reduce the scope or level of its existing exemptions, or to rectify or make changes of a purely technical character that do not alter the substance of such exemptions, shall submit to the Secretariat for circulation to all Members a draft list of Article II Exemptions clearly indicating the details of the modifications. The draft list containing the modifications shall enter into force upon the conclusion of a period of 45 days from the date of its circulation by the Secretariat, or on a later date specified or to be specified by the modifying Member provided no objection has been raised by any other Member. At the end of the 45–day period, if no objection has been raised, the

---

[7] WTO Docs. S/L/105 and S/L/106 of June 11, 2002.

Secretariat shall issue a communication to all Members to the effect that the certification procedure has been concluded, indicating the date of entry into force of the modifications.

Any Member wishing to object to the proposed modifications shall submit a notification to that effect to the Secretariat for circulation to all Members. A Member making an objection should identify the specific elements of the modifications which gave rise to that objection. A Member shall not cite loss of preferential treatment as the basis for objection. The objecting Member(s) and the modifying Member shall enter into consultation as soon as possible and shall endeavour to reach a satisfactory solution of the matter within 45 days after the expiry of the period in which objections may be made. When an objection has been notified, this procedure shall be deemed concluded upon the withdrawal of the objection by the objecting Member or the expiry of the period in which objections may be made, whichever comes later. When more than one objection has been notified, this procedure shall be deemed concluded upon the withdrawal of the objections by all objecting Members or the expiry of the period in which objections may be made, whichever comes later. The withdrawal of any objection shall be communicated to the Secretariat, which shall issue a communication informing all Members of the withdrawal of the objection(s) and the conclusion of the certification procedure, indicating the date of entry into force of the modifications.

If as a result of the consultations mentioned in paragraph 4, the draft list of Article II Exemptions originally submitted for certification were to be modified, the modifying Member shall reinitiate the procedure described in paragraph 3.

Review

Following the lapse of three years from the date of entry into force of these procedures, the Council for Trade in Services shall, at the request of any Member, review the operation of these procedures. In such a review, the Council for Trade in Services may agree to amend these procedures.

Exemptions should terminate on the date provided for in the exemption itself. In the event of termination, the Member terminating should notify the CTS of the event. In principle, they should all terminate after ten years, and, in any event, they should constitute the subject-matter of negotiation in subsequent rounds. § 3 of the Annex on Article II Exemptions assigns to the CTS the competence to review all exemptions for a period extending beyond five years, and also states that the first such review would take place five years after the advent of the WTO. Consequently, it is not the case, as is sometimes erroneously stated, that exemptions will lapse after ten years anyway. Three reviews have been completed so far[8] and during those reviews there was a brief discussion on existing exemptions (some of which have by now run for over 10 years) without decisions to terminate them. As a result, some exemptions continue to be applied more than fifteen years after the advent of the GATS.

2.4.2 GATS Provisions Justifying a Deviation From MFN

There are several GATS provisions to this effect:

- General exceptions (Art. XIV GATS);
- Security exception (Art. XIVbis);
- PTAs (Art. V GATS);
- Labour Markets Integration Agreements (Art. Vbis);
- Special and differential treatment for developing countries.

We discuss them in detail in Chapter 26 since they constitute exceptions not only to general obligations but also to specific commitments.

3. DOMESTIC REGULATION

3.1 THE LEGAL DISCIPLINE

Art. VI GATS[9] figures among the general obligations although it concerns obligations that WTO Members have entered through specific commitments. Namely, WTO Members are required to administer all measures of general application affecting trade in services in a reasonable, objective and impartial manner. They must also establish independent fora to review administrative decisions affecting trade in services. In addition, pending the adoption of common disciplines regarding qualifications and standards,[10] they must not apply legislation which is non-transparent, or unnecessary. Finally, they must establish adequate procedures in order to verify the competence of (foreign) services suppliers wishing to access the market of professional services.

3.2 THE RATIONALE FOR THE LEGAL DISCIPLINE

Regulatory diversity substantially increases transaction costs and thus, impedes trade liberalization. This is a particularly acute issue in the services context where the overwhelming majority of trade barriers are of regulatory nature. The Work Programme established through Art. VI.4 GATS aims to rationalize and harmonize (to some extent) domestic

---

[8] WTO Docs. S/C/M/51 of March 2, 2001; S/C/M/79 of August 16, 2005; JOB/SERV/29 of October 11, 2010; JOB/SERV/30 of October 11, 2010; and JOB/SERV/31 of October 15, 2010.

[9] On this score, see the excellent analysis in Delimatsis (2008).

[10] Art. VI.4 GATS entrusts the Council for Trade in Services (CTS) with the competence to prepare disciplines in an effort to ensure that qualification requirements, standards and licensing requirements do not constitute unnecessary obstacles to international trade (Work Programme).

regulation. Pending its conclusion, WTO Members have agreed to adopt not only non-discriminatory but also necessary measures (to achieve their objectives): this obligation echoes that embedded in the TBT Agreement and we refer the reader to the discussion in Chapter 19.

3.3 COVERAGE

3.3.1 Reasonable, Objective, and Impartial Administration

The language used is reminiscent of that in Art. X GATT. In fact, two of the three terms (reasonable, impartial) are identical. It is thus to be expected that GATS case law in this respect will be inspired by the existing jurisprudence in the context of Art. X GATT. Recall that, in *Dominican Republic–Import and Sale of Cigarettes*, the Panel made it clear that not only positive actions, but omissions too can come under scrutiny in the context of the review regarding the consistency of a specific law, regulation etc. with Art. X.3 GATT (§ 7.379).[11]

3.3.2 Judicial Review of Domestic Regulation

Art. VI.2 GATS requires from WTO Members to establish an independent forum to judge in an impartial manner cases affecting trade in services. Individual (foreign) services suppliers will have access to such fora, which must review domestic laws, regulations etc. affecting trade in services, and provide for appropriate remedies, whenever warranted. Such fora should be independent of the agency entrusted with the challenged decision, and where this has not been the case, the WTO Member concerned must ensure that the procedure established provides in fact for an objective and impartial review: thus, an obligation of result, and not an obligation of specific conduct is established through this provision. Note that, this paragraph, contrary to the other paragraphs in Art. VI GATS, does not explicitly refer to specific commitments: hence, its coverage extends to general obligations as well.

The jurisprudence under Art. X GATT which contains identical language serving the same functionality as this provision should be pertinent here as well.[12]

3.3.3 The Work Programme and the Transitional Obligations

The Work Programme aims at establishing that measures relating to qualification requirements and procedures, technical standards, and licensing requirements do not constitute unnecessary barriers to trade in services. Regulatory diversity will, as a result, be preserved; it will, however, be based on agreed criteria. To this effect, the CTS is called to establish disciplines aimed at guaranteeing that the three aforementioned cat-

---

[11] See the discussion in Chapter 11.
[12] See Chapter 11.

egories of measures are based on objective and transparent criteria; are not more burdensome than necessary to ensure the quality of the service; and that, in the case of licensing requirements, they do not in themselves constitute a restriction on the supply of the service. The only relevant work in this field so far has been undertaken in the context of professional services and, more specifically, in the accountancy sector.[13] A Working Party was established which prepared guidelines for mutual recognition of accountancy qualifications. The guidelines issued are of non-binding nature and do not preclude the use of alternative methods. The model advanced[14] requests from WTO Members wishing to enter into a mutual recognition agreement (in accordance with Art. VII GATS) with another WTO Member, whereby it will acknowledge that its accountants are fulfilling the criteria imposed by its domestic legislation, to promptly notify the GATS Council. They must also afford adequate opportunity for other interested Members to negotiate their accession to such an agreement or arrangement or to negotiate comparable ones with it. Finally, WTO Members, whenever appropriate, shall base their decisions on recognition on mutually agreed criteria. The CTS also adopted the Disciplines on Domestic Regulation in the Accountancy Sector,[15] a document which includes the obligations of WTO Members in the accountancy sector, even if no specific commitments have been undertaken. The language in this document too is hortatory.

On April 26, 1999, WTO Members adopted a decision to establish a Working Party on Professional Services that would expand its mandate beyond the accountancy sector:

1. A Working Party on Domestic Regulation shall be established and the Working Party on Professional Services shall cease to exist.

2. In accordance with § 4 of Art. VI of the GATS, the Working Party shall develop any necessary disciplines to ensure that measures relating to licensing requirements and procedures, technical standards and qualification requirements and procedures do not constitute unnecessary barriers to trade in services. This shall also encompass the tasks assigned to the Working Party on Professional Services, including the development of general disciplines for professional services as required by § 2 of the Decision on Disciplines Relating to the Accountancy Sector (S/L/63).

3. In fulfilling its tasks the Working Party shall develop generally applicable disciplines and may develop disciplines as appropriate for individual sectors or groups thereof.

---

[13] See WTO Docs. S/WPPS/W/1, W/12, W/12/Rev. 1, W/14, and W/14/Rev.1.
[14] See WTO Doc. S/WPPS/W/12/Rev. 1, Annex at p. 7.
[15] See WTO Doc. S/L/64 of 17 December 1998.

4. The Working Party shall report to the Council with recommendations no later than the conclusion of the forthcoming round of services negotiations.[16]

So far, this Working Group has not agreed on disciplines in any sector. Pending the adoption of disciplines by the CTS in other sectors, WTO Members will, in accordance with Art. VI.5(a) GATS, have to abstain from introducing measures which do not respect the spirit of Art. VI.4 GATS, in all sectors where they have undertaken specific commitments. Consequently, WTO Members must ensure that their legislation in the field of qualification / licensing requirements and technical standards is based on objective and transparent criteria, is not more burdensome than necessary to ensure the quality of the service, and, in case of licensing, does not constitute a restriction on the supply of the service.

4. RECOGNITION

4.1 THE LEGAL DISCIPLINE

The GATS does not define "recognition", other than to distinguish between unilateral and bilateral (Art. VII.1 GATS). It does state though that recognition should, but does not have to, be based on multilaterally agreed criteria; WTO Members agree to cooperate within international organizations and non-governmental organizations (NGOs) with a view to establishing common standards (Art. VII.5 GATS).[17] Recognition cannot serve as means of discrimination across WTO Members (Art. VII.3 GATS). To this effect, that is, in order to guarantee that recognition does not *de facto* amount to discrimination, Art. VII.2 GATS requests from those who have either unilaterally recognized or are members of a bilateral (mutual) recognition agreement (MRA) to afford adequate opportunities to all other WTO Members who wish to benefit from this. Art. VII.2 GATS does not impose an obligation of result (i.e., petitioners must accede to an MRA), but an obligation of specifc conduct (i.e., petitioners will be afforded adequate opportunity (whatever this means) to negotiate accession to an existing agreement, to negotiate a comparable agreement, or to demonstrate that their own qualifications should also be recognized). To cement this obligation, Art. VII.4 GATS requests from all WTO Members to notify all existing recognition measures, the opening of any negotiation on recognition, as well as recognition outcomes. Recognition finally, cannot serve as "a disguised restriction on trade in services" (Art. VII.3 GATS).

---

[16] See WTO Doc. S/L/70 of 28 April 1999.
[17] Pursuant to the Decision on Professional Services adopted by Ministers at the end of the Uruguay Round, in May 1997 the WTO Working Party on Professional Services issued non-binding guidelines for the negotiation of mutual recognition agreements or arrangements (see WTO document S/L/39, dated 28 May 1997).

4.2 THE RATIONALE FOR THE LEGAL DISCIPLINE

Recognition guarantees market access while allowing those participating in similar arrangements to reap gains from innovation.[18]

4.3 NON–DISCRIMINATION

Art. VII GATS explicitly states that the WTO Member that has recognized the regulatory standards of another WTO Member must afford adequate opportunities to the demandeur to present its case. Recognition provisions regarding financial services is discussed in GATS Annex on Financial Services, § 3(b): the demandeur must demonstrate the existence of specific circumstances, namely:

> ... [the existence of] equivalent regulation, oversight, implementation of such regulation, and, if appropriate, procedures concerning the sharing of information between the parties to the agreement or arrangement.

5. TRANSPARENCY

5.1 THE LEGAL DISCIPLINE

The transparency obligation in the GATS context operates at three different levels: first, WTO Members must promptly publish all relevant measures of general application which pertain to, or affect the operation of GATS (Art. III.1 GATS); second, WTO Members must inform on a periodical basis the CTS of all new laws, regulations or administrative guidelines which significantly affect trade in services covered by its specific commitments under the GATS (Art. III.3 GATS); third, WTO Members will have to respond to requests by other Members for specific information on any of their measures of general application by establishing inquiry points to this effect (Art. III.4 GATS). A WTO Member can, under Art. III.5 GATS, notify GATS-relating legislation adopted by another WTO Member.

5.2 THE RATIONALE FOR THE LEGAL DISCIPLINE

This provision is, essentially, driven by transaction costs-related arguments, as already discussed in Chapter 11.

5.3 COVERAGE

There has been no case law under GATS further explaining the terms appearing in this provision. There is however, GATT case law under Art. X GATT dealing with the term measures of general application which, in

---

[18] See the discussion in Chapter 19.

light of the similar function of the two provisions, could serve as guidance for the understanding of this term.[19]

6. COMPETITION–RELATED DISCIPLINES

6.1 THE LEGAL DISCIPLINE

Arts. VIII and IX GATS impose specific obligations on all WTO Members as to the treatment of monopolies (and exclusive services suppliers), and restrictive business practices (RBPs). The disciplines included in Arts. VIII and IX GATS are, with respect to trade in telecommunications services, further detailed in the so-called Telecommunications Reference Paper (TRP). Arts. VIII and IX GATS essentially request from WTO Members to ensure that their monopolies and exclusive services suppliers will not operate in a manner that is MFN-inconsistent and will not abuse their monopoly position so as to jeopardise the trade value of specific commitments made (Art. VIII GATS); it is also recognized that practices other than abusing a monopoly position may restrain competition, and, to this effect, WTO Members are required to consult with a view to eliminating such practices, assuming a request to this effect has been submitted to them by an affected WTO Member (Art. IX GATS). There is, nonetheless, no clear-cut obligation to eliminate such practices: Art. IX GATS imposes an obligation to consult (upon request) with a view to eliminating such practices, without requesting that elimination be necessarily the case.

6.2 THE RATIONALE FOR THE LEGAL DISCIPLINE

Multilateral acknowledgement that trade can be impeded through private restraints as well, exists since the days of the International Trade Organization (ITO): Chapter V of the ITO dealt with a series of RBPs that would run counter to the objective to liberalize trade[20]. Chapter V is not, in principle, legally irrelevant, since WTO Members incur a best-endeavors obligation to respect its spirit, by virtue of Art. XXIX GATT. The advent of the WTO, and the discontinuation of the Working Party on the Inter-relationship between Trade and Competition Policies would, however, cast severe doubt on the continued relevance of this provision. Moreover, Art. XXIX is a GATT and not a GATS provision. The framers of GATS felt though, that the rationale for Chapter V of the ITO was meritorious: some (sectoral) liberalization commitments would *de facto* have to be carried out by private operators, and not by state entities. This was especially the case in the field of telecommunications, where, following privatization of this sector in some quarters, it is private operators that would be requested to sell access to network (its duplication being, at

---

[19] See the relevant discussion in Chapter 11.
[20] See Irwin et al. (2008).

least at this stage of technological progress, too costly). Absent the negotiation of specific disciplines that would require WTO Members to ensure that their private operators behave in a particular manner, the whole liberalization edifice would risk being reduced to irrelevance and redundancy. This thinking led the GATS framers to the negotiation of the TRP. This is not a telecoms-specific concern, though. Private operators can hinder market access in other fields as well, wherever incumbents enjoy market power and have either been entrusted with (regulatory) authority which, if abused, can lead to impediments on market access, or where market access impediments are simply the result of absence of enforcement of national antitrust law.

6.3 THE COVERAGE OF THE LEGAL DISCIPLINE

Art. VIII.2 GATS refers to one RBP only, that is, abuse of monopoly position. The Panel in *Mexico–Telecoms*[21] discussed, *inter alia*, this term. This case essentially evolved around one question: under what conditions could foreign telecom operators terminate calls in Mexico? The US had argued that the Mexican regulation of termination charges was not in conformity with the obligations contained in the TRP. It argued in particular that termination charges were not cost oriented and that Mexico had set up a cartel of telecom operators. Within Mexico, local networks (operating the last mile, that is, terminating international calls) were typically provided by Telmex, the telecom monopolist. Long distance services within Mexico (between cities or regions) had been opened to competition and at the time the dispute arose, there were as many as 27 long distance carriers operating in the country, including Telmex. Long distance carriers could not however be controlled by foreign operators, ownership being limited to 49% (according to the Mexican telecom regulation, in line with appropriate specific limitations on commitments taken by Mexico within GATS). Some of them were still partly owned by US operators or associated with them. In this environment, the completion of international calls requires the connection of networks operated by different firms.[22] In order to offer outgoing calls, say to the US, long distance carriers in Mexico needed to connect to a firm operating in the US. Similarly, in order to provide international service to Mexico to their domestic subscribers, US operators needed a connection to a Mexican operator in order to terminate the calls. The US presented a series of claims under the TRP; in one of them, it claimed that price discrimination by Telmex was inconsistent with Mexico's obligations under the TRP. The Panel agreed, and also found that differential pricing by an entity covered by Art. VIII GATS could constitute a violation of the said provision since it might run counter to Art. II GATS (§§ 7.133 and 7.137):

---

[21] See Neven and Mavroidis (2007).
[22] Given that in addition none of the Mexican carriers controlled a foreign network.

The traditional "accounting rate revenue division procedure" based on a negotiated rate resulted in pricing which, in practice, depended on many factors other than cost, including the dynamics of different bilateral negotiations. When the supplier, public or private, had monopoly rights within a Member's territory, any different pricing of services that occurred on the basis of a Member's territory might also, under GATS Art. VIII:1, lead to MFN inconsistencies under GATS Art. II. Under Art. VIII:1, a Member "shall ensure that any monopoly supplier of service in its territory does not, in the supply of the monopoly service in the relevant market, act in a manner inconsistent with that Member's obligations under Art. II [MFN] and specific commitments." This possible inconsistency with the MFN principle was the particular concern that was addressed in the Understanding, which speaks of "differential rates" being inherent in accounting rates.

. . .

Based on this delineation of the "accounting rates" that are within the scope of the Understanding, we can make several observations. First, not all international interconnection pricing was excluded from dispute settlement by the Understanding, only traditional accounting rate regimes with "differential rates". Second, the exclusion was from dispute settlement, not from the substantive obligations of the GATS, including its schedules of commitments. Third, the explicit aim of the exclusion was the MFN obligation under GATS Art. II. Other obligations or specific commitments in the GATS, such as Section 2 of Mexico's Reference Paper were not specified. Fourth, not all traditional accounting rate regimes would be MFN inconsistent, even if they were not cost-oriented. In order to demonstrate the MFN inconsistency of a traditional accounting system regime, one would have to show that the rate is either a "measure" of a Member, or that it falls within a Member's obligations under Art. VIII:1 on monopolies, and that different rates for different international routes amount to treatment less favourable with respect to one "like service" compared to another "like service". Finally, the existence of the Understanding demonstrates that, even though negotiators considered at length the issue of rates for international interconnection, they chose not to adopt wording that would have expressly excluded certain types of interconnection from the scope of the Reference Paper.(emphasis in the original).

7. PAYMENTS AND TRANSFERS

7.1 THE LEGAL DISCIPLINE

WTO Members cannot apply restrictions on international transfers and payments for current transactions which relate to their specific commitments (Art. XI GATS). They can do so only at the request of the IMF, or in order to safeguard a balance of payments crisis (Art. XII GATS).

7.2 THE RATIONALE FOR THE LEGAL DISCIPLINE

Absent this provision, the value of specific commitments made by WTO Members would have been severely undermined, since the incentive to provide services in a market which did not guarantee international payments for services supplies could be severely undermined. The Panel report on *US–Gambling* confirmed this understanding of the function of this provision in the following terms (§ 6.442):

> ... Art. XI plays a crucial role in securing the value of specific commitments undertaken by Members under the GATS. Indeed, the value of specific commitments on market access and national treatments would be seriously impaired if Members could restrict international transfers and payment for service transactions in scheduled sectors. In ensuring, *inter alia*, that services suppliers can receive payments due under services contracts covered by a Member's specific commitment, Art. XI is an indispensable complement to GATS disciplines on market access and national treatment. At the same time, the Panel is of the view that Art. XI does not deprive Members from regulating the use of financial instruments, such as credit cards, provided that these regulations are consistent with other relevant GATS provisions, in particular Art. VI." (italics in the original).

7.3 COVERAGE

The obligation to guarantee international payments for current transactions kicks in only as far as specific commitments are concerned. Art. XI GATS is irrelevant as far as fields where no specific commitments have been made.

8. BALANCE OF PAYMENTS

8.1 THE LEGAL DISCIPLINE

Art. XII GATS is an exception to Art. XI GATS: it allows for restrictions on international payments for current transactions on balance of payments (BoP) grounds, if such restrictions comply with its various requirements. As far as developing countries are concerned, the requirements are more relaxed, since they can invoke this provision any time they fall below the level of financial reserves adequate for the implementation of their program of economic development.

8.2 THE RATIONALE FOR THE LEGAL DISCIPLINE

The inclusion of this provision functions as an insurance policy, in the sense that it induces commitments while guaranteeing that those committing will not be held to ransom if they face in the future BoP problems.

8.3 COVERAGE

WTO Members that have recourse to Art. XII GATS must, by virtue of Art. XII.2 GATS, ensure consistency of their measures with the IMF Articles. They cannot discriminate among WTO Members, and they must avoid unnecessary damage to the commercial, economic and financial interests of any other Member. Measures must be temporary and necessary to address a BoP crisis, and must be phased out as soon as the circumstances which gave rise to their adoption cease to exist. The General Council must be notified, whereas the WTO Member concerned will have to consult promptly with the Committee on Balance of Payments (Art. XII.4/5 GATS). When adopting similar measures, a WTO Member should not aim to protect a particular service sector. It can, nonetheless, prioritize those service sectors that are essential to its economic development (Art. XII.3 GATS).

9. GATS RULES

Soon after the advent of the WTO, a Working Group was established to negotiate disciplines on provisions of the GATS that were left incomplete at the negotiation stage, namely, Art. X GATS (Emergency Safeguard Measures), Art. XIII GATS (Government Procurement), and Art. XV GATS (Subsidies). The name of the group is GATS Rules. At the moment of writing, the group has not managed to conclude its mandate, although two of the three provisions included a deadline for the completion of the work (3 years for Art. X, and 2 years for Art. XIII GATS respectively).

QUESTIONS AND COMMENTS

Likeness: What in the AB analysis in *EC–Bananas III* provides, in your view, support in favor of the thesis that discrimination (between ACP- and non ACP nationals) is the result of the EU measure?

Listed Exemptions: What in your view, should the allocation of burden of proof be in case there is disagreement about one of the listed exemptions? Should it be identical to that when for example, Art. XIV GATS has been invoked?

Recognition: Beviglia–Zampetti (2000), (2000a), Nicolaidis (2000), and Nicolaidis and Trachtman (2000) all discuss the conditions under which recognition can be extended on non-discriminatory basis. Marchetti and Mavroidis (2012) provide a taxonomy of existing recognition agreements.

Telecoms Reference Paper: We reproduce below the full text of the TRP as agreed on April 24, 1996:

Scope

The following are definitions and principles on the regulatory framework for the basic telecommunications services.

Definitions

Users mean service consumers and service suppliers.

Essential facilities mean facilities of a public telecommunications transport network or service that

(a) are exclusively or predominantly provided by a single or limited number of suppliers; and

(b) cannot feasibly be economically or technically substituted in order to provide a service.

A major supplier is a supplier which has the ability to materially affect the terms of participation (having regard to price and supply) in the relevant market for basic telecommunications services as a result of:

(a) control over essential facilities; or

(b) use of its position in the market.

1. Competitive safeguards

1.1 Prevention of anti-competitive practices in telecommunications

Appropriate measures shall be maintained for the purpose of preventing suppliers who, alone or together, are a major supplier from engaging in or continuing anti-competitive practices.

1.2 Safeguards

The anti-competitive practices referred to above shall include in particular:

(a) engaging in anti-competitive cross-subsidization;

(b) using information obtained from competitors with anti-competitive results; and

(c) not making available to other services suppliers on a timely basis technical information about essential facilities and commercially relevant information which are necessary for them to provide services.

2. Interconnection

2.1 This section applies to linking with suppliers providing public telecommunications transport networks or services in order to allow the users of one supplier to communicate with users of another supplier and to access services provided by another supplier, where specific commitments are undertaken.

2.2 Interconnection to be ensured

Interconnection with a major supplier will be ensured at any technically feasible point in the network. Such interconnection is provided.

(a) under non-discriminatory terms, conditions (including technical standards and specifications) and rates and of a quality no less favourable than that provided for its own like services or for like services of non-affiliated service suppliers or for its subsidiaries or other affiliates;

(b) in a timely fashion, on terms, conditions (including technical standards and specifications) and cost-oriented rates that are transparent, reasonable, having regard to economic feasibility, and sufficiently unbundled so that the supplier need not pay for network components or facilities that it does not require for the service to be provided; and

(c) upon request, at points in addition to the network termination points offered to the majority of users, subject to charges that reflect the cost of construction of necessary additional facilities.

2.3 Public availability of the procedures for interconnection negotiations

The procedures applicable for interconnection to a major supplier will be made publicly available.

2.4 Transparency of interconnection arrangements

It is ensured that a major supplier will make publicly available either its interconnection agreements or a reference interconnection offer.

2.5 Interconnection: dispute settlement

A service supplier requesting interconnection with a major supplier will have recourse, either:

(a) at any time or

(b) after a reasonable period of time which has been made publicly known

to an independent domestic body, which may be a regulatory body as referred to in paragraph 5 below, to resolve disputes regarding appropriate terms, conditions and rates for interconnection within a reasonable period of time, to the extent that these have not been established previously.

3. Universal service

Any Member has the right to define the kind of universal service obligation it wishes to maintain. Such obligations will not be regarded as anticompetitive *per se*, provided they are administered in a transparent, non-discriminatory and competitively neutral manner and are not more burdensome than necessary for the kind of universal service defined by the Member.

4. <u>Public availability of licensing criteria</u>

Where a licence is required, the following will be made publicly available:

(a) all the licensing criteria and the period of time normally required to reach a decision concerning an application for a licence and

(b) the terms and conditions of individual licences.

The reasons for the denial of a licence will be made known to the applicant upon request.

5. <u>Independent regulators</u>

The regulatory body is separate from, and not accountable to, any supplier of basic telecommunications services. The decisions of and the procedures used by regulators shall be impartial with respect to all market participants.

6. <u>Allocation and use of scarce resources</u>

Any procedures for the allocation and use of scarce resources, including frequencies, numbers and rights of way, will be carried out in an objective, timely, transparent and non-discriminatory manner. The current state of allocated frequency bands will be made publicly available, but detailed identification of frequencies allocated for specific government uses is not required.

CHAPTER 25

SPECIFIC COMMITMENTS

■ ■ ■

1. THE LEGAL DISCIPLINE

With respect to some (or all) service appearing in the CPC and each mode of supply, WTO Members can undertake specific commitments concerning market access and/or national treatment. They can further undertake additional commitments to this effect.

2. THE RATIONALE FOR THE LEGAL DISCIPLINE

This is the outcome of the decision to adopt a "positive list" approach whereby WTO Members can make commitments with respect to the services sectors they choose to liberalize (while incurring general obligations for all services irrespective whether they have entered a specific commitment).

3. COVERAGE

3.1 ISSUES COMMON TO MARKET ACCESS, NATIONAL TREATMENT, AND ADDITIONAL COMMITMENTS

3.1.1 The List of Services Where Commitments Will Be Entered

WTO Members agreed to base their commitments on W/120 (WTO Doc. MTN.GNS/W/120, 'The Services Sectoral Classification List') which, as we saw in Chapter 23, was modelled after the UN CPC list. To understand the logic of W/120[1] it is imperative that we first take a look into the underlying logic of CPC. § 33 of the Introductory Note to the CPC explains the manner in which taxonomy operates under the CPC-system:

> The coding system of CPC is hierarchical and purely decimal. The classification consists of **sections** (identified by the first dig-

---

[1] One might legitimately ask whether W/120 was necessary at all since the CPC list could have been used as such. The added value of the W/120 is threefold: it clarifies which air transport services are covered by the GATS (Art. I.2 GATS excludes air traffic rights but does not explain where exactly commitments can be entered); with respect to financial services, W/120 follows a different taxonomy from CPC (espousing to a large extent a proposal tabled by the EU); W/120, unlike CPC, also includes widespread 'Other' categories at the end of services sectors.

it), **divisions** (identified by the first and second digits), **groups** (identified by the first three digits), **classes** (identified by the first four digits) and **sub-classes** (identified by all five digits, taken together). The codes for the sections range from 0 through 9 and each section may be divided into nine divisions. At the third digit of the code each division may, in turn, be divided into nine groups which then may be further divided into nine classes and then again into nine sub-classes. In theory, this allows for 65,610 categories. In practice however, there are 10 sections, 69 divisions, 293 groups, 1,050 classes and 1,811 sub-classes. The code numbers in CPC consist of five digits without separation of any kind between digits. (emphasis added).

CPC numbers are modelled after, but do not precisely correspond to, the HS classification for goods. Commitments are customarily made at 2, 3, 4, and 5 digit levels. In contrast to the goods-regime, however, WTO Members can disaggregate or carve out definitions at any digit-level. For instance, if a WTO Member wishes to enter a commitment at the 3 digit-level, but on a narrower basis than that reflected in the CPC, it can simply state so in its schedule of commitments (usually, by introducing an asterisk in the category where it wishes to make its narrower commitment). Absent language to the opposite, a commitment at the 3 digit-level covers services at the 4 and 5 digit-level as well. The AB decided as much in *US–Gambling* (§ 200):

> As the CPC is a decimal system, a reference to an aggregate category must be understood as a reference to all of the constituent parts of that category. Put differently, a reference to a three-digit CPC Group should, in the absence of any indication to the contrary, be understood as a reference to all the four-digit Classes and five-digit Sub-classes that make up the group; and a reference to a four-digit Class should be understood as a reference to all of the five-digit Sub-classes that make up that Class.

In the same report, the AB held that the CPC list is exhaustive (there are no services beyond those covered in the list), and that its various categories are mutually exclusive (§ 172): one particular service cannot belong to two different headings. The AB held that, the broad language used in sector 10 of the CPC (where the categories "recreational services", "sporting", and "entertainment services" were included) notwithstanding, gambling and betting services, the issue at dispute between Antigua and Barbuda on the one hand, and the US on the other, could only fall, if at all, within one of those service categories (§ 180).

There are differences between W/120 and the CPC. In the words of the AB:

> W/120 is a much more aggregated classification list than the one found in the CPC. Whereas W/120 contains 12 sectors (11 and

one "other") and more than 150 subsectors, the CPC classification scheme is comprised of 10 Sections, 69 Divisions, 295 Groups, 1,050 Classes and 1,811 Subclasses. (*US–Gambling*, § 200).

The question, thus, might (and did) arise which of the two documents (W/120, CPC) will prevail in case of conflict. In its report on *EC–Bananas III*, the AB made it clear that the CPC classification was crucial in classifying services without going any further (§§ 224–226). In *Canada–Autos*, the Panel held that the CPC number prevails in case of discrepancy between the literal heading of a schedule and the number. The question before the Panel was whether Canada had undertaken commitments on wholesale trade services of motor vehicles (§§ 10.278–282):

Japan argues that Canada's Schedule of Specific Commitments includes wholesale trade of motor vehicles either under the general entry "B. Wholesale trade services" or under the more specific entry "Sale of motor vehicles including automobiles and other road vehicles", United Nations Provisional Central Product Classification (CPC) number 6111. Japan also points out that under "B. Wholesale trade services", Canada lists a limitation for the state of Saskatchewan applying to "sale of motor vehicles". According to Japan, by inserting this limitation Canada is implying that its commitments on wholesale trade services also include wholesale services for motor vehicles. Canada responds that its entry "B. Wholesale trade services" expressly refers to CPC 622, which excludes distribution of motor vehicles and that the insertion of a limitation with respect to motor vehicles is a scheduling error. It also points out that CPC entry "6111" is inscribed under the heading "C. Retail services" and therefore should be read as a commitment only on retail services for motor vehicles.

We note that the CPC entry 622 (Wholesale trade services) does not have a sub-heading for motor vehicles, and that sub-heading 62282 (Wholesale trade services of transport equipment other than motor vehicles, motorcycles and bicycles) expressly excludes motor vehicles. In our view, the fact that Canada has inscribed a limitation applying to motor vehicles with respect to the entry "Wholesale trade services (622)" in its schedule does not in itself constitute sufficient evidence to conclude that it has undertaken a commitment on wholesale trade services of motor vehicles.

Nevertheless, Canada has also listed in its schedule of commitments an entry for "Sale of motor vehicles including automobiles and other road vehicles" with an explicit reference to CPC number 6111. In the United Nations Provisional Central Product

Classification, the entry "6111 Sale of motor vehicles including automobiles and other road vehicles" includes two sub-headings: "61111 Wholesale trade services of motor vehicles"; and "61112 Retail sales of motor vehicles". In our view, if Canada had meant to limit this commitment only to retail services it should have inscribed entry 61112 (Retail sales of motor vehicles) in its schedule rather than 6111 (Sale of motor vehicles).

We note that there is a discrepancy between the inclusion of the whole CPC entry 6111 and the heading of the commitment ("C. Retailing services") in page 48 of Canada's schedule. However, the fact that entry 6111 has been listed under the heading <u>C. Retailing services</u> does not constitute sufficient evidence to exclude a commitment with respect to wholesale trade services of motor vehicles. If the heading were to prevail, the systemic impact would be that all unqualified CPC numbers in Members' schedules of commitments, referring to clearly and precisely defined subsectors, would be undermined, at least when their combination with headings is inconsistent. For these reasons we consider that the description of the CPC should prevail and that the commitments contained in page 48 of Canada's schedule also apply to wholesale trade of motor vehicles.

We find therefore that, by inscribing the CPC entry "6111 Sale of motor vehicles including automobiles and other road vehicles" in its schedule of specific commitments, Canada has undertaken a commitment also covering "61111 Wholesale trade services of motor vehicles".

Recall that the HS has been acknowledged to have the value of legal context by the AB (*EC–Chicken Cuts*) and, consequently, by virtue of Art. 31 VCLT, it must always be taken into account, whenever an issue regarding the interpretation of a commitment arises. W/120, by contrast, has been considered to be supplementary means of interpretation, which means that recourse to it will be made only under the restrictive conditions of Art. 32 VCLT: the AB held as much in its report on *US–Gambling*.[2]

3.1.2 The 1993 and 2001 Scheduling Guidelines

The AB succinctly discussed the content and function of the Scheduling Guidelines[3] report on its *US–Gambling* report in the following man-

---

[2] Mavroidis (2008) explains the difference in treatment by the fact that whereas the HS Convention is an international agreement to which many WTO Members have adhered, W/120 is a Secretariat document.

[3] WTO Members used, for the purposes of scheduling their commitments made during the Uruguay Round, the 1993 Scheduling Guidelines WTO Doc. (MTN.GNS/W/164 and Add. 1) which was a WTO Secretariat Note that had been circulated to the negotiators. Its purpose was to facilitate the on-going negotiations. On March 23, 2001, the WTO Members formally WTO

ner: the 1993 Scheduling Guidelines address two questions, namely, what items should be included, and how included items should be scheduled. The main thrust of the Scheduling Guidelines is described in the following terms in the AB report (§ 173):

> Since schedules, including footnotes, headnotes and attachments, are a record of legal commitments, nothing should appear in them which a Member does not intend to be legally binding. A schedule contains the following main types of information: a clear description of the sector or sub-sector committed, limitations to market access, limitations to national treatment, and additional commitments other than market access and national treatment. If a Member undertakes a commitment in a sector then it must indicate for each mode of supply that it binds in that sector:
>
> — what limitations, if any, it maintains on market access;
>
> — what limitations, if any, it maintains on national treatment; and
>
> — what additional commitments, relating to measures affecting trade in services not subject to scheduling under Articles XVI and XVII, it may decide to undertake under Art. XVIII.
>
> Where commitments do not cover the entire national territory, the entry should describe the geographical scope of measures taken according to Art. I:3(a)(i). If attachments are used, clear reference should be made to the part of the schedules they refer to (i.e. definitions in the first column, market access commitments in the second column, national treatment commitments in the third column and additional commitments in the fourth column).
>
> Exchange control restrictions are subject to the general disciplines of Articles XI (Payments and Transfers) and XII (Restrictions to Safeguard the Balance of Payments) of the GATS. There is no requirement in the GATS to schedule a limitation to the effect that the cross-border movement of goods associated with the provision of a service may be subject to customs duties or other administrative charges. Such measures are subject to the disciplines of the GATT.

Doc. S/L/91.adopted in the context of the CTS a new document prepared by the WTO Secretariat: S/L/92: this document (the 2001 Scheduling Guidelines) contains no substantive change or deviation from the 1993 Scheduling Guidelines; it re-states the 1993 Scheduling Guidelines and adds a few Annexes and a list of illustrative list of limitations to National Treatment. It is the successor document to the 1993 Scheduling Guidelines. It follows that the 1993 Scheduling Guidelines are relevant for commitments made during the Uruguay Round, whereas the 2001 Scheduling Guidelines are currently being used for commitments made during the Doha Round.

The two documents (1993, 2001 Guidelines) are legally distinct and the later in time document cannot be used to interpret the previous version. The AB, in *US–Gambling* thwarted a claim by Antigua to this effect (§ 193):

> Although the 2001 Guidelines were explicitly adopted by the Council for Trade in Services, this was in the context of the negotiation of *future* commitments and in order to assist in the preparation of offers and requests in respect of such commitments. As such, they do not constitute evidence of Members' understanding regarding the interpretation of *existing* commitments. Furthermore, as the United States emphasized before the Panel, in its Decision adopting the 2001 Guidelines, the Council for Trade in Services explicitly stated that they were to be "non-binding" and "shall not modify any rights or obligations of the Members under the GATS".(emphasis in the original).

The legal relevance of the (1993 and 2001) Scheduling Guidelines is addressed in the text of this document. The first paragraph of the 1993 Scheduling Guidelines states:

> This note is intended to assist in the preparation of offers, requests and national schedules of initial commitments. Its objective is to explain, in a concise manner, how commitments should be set out in schedules in order to achieve precision and clarity. It is based on the view that a common format for schedules as well as standardization of the terms used in schedules are necessary to ensure comparable and unambiguous commitments. The note cannot answer every question that might occur to persons responsible for scheduling commitments; it does attempt to answer those questions which are most likely to arise. The answers should not be considered as an authoritative legal interpretation of the GATS.

By the same token, the decision (WTO Doc. S/L/91) adopting the 2001 Scheduling Guidelines reads:

> 1. To adopt the Guidelines for the Scheduling of Specific Commitments under the General Agreement on Trade in Services contained in document S/CSC/W/30 as a non-binding set of guidelines.
>
> 2. Members are invited to follow these guidelines on a voluntary basis in the future scheduling of their specific commitments, in order to promote their precision and clarity.

3. These guidelines shall not modify any rights or obligations of the Members under the GATS.[4]

Two WTO Panels have dealt with the issue of the legal value of the (1993 and 2001) Scheduling Guidelines. Both Panels held that the Scheduling Guidelines have important ramifications in the interpretation of GATS. While doing that however, the two Panels have reached irreconcilable conclusions on this issue: the report in *Mexico–Telecoms* reflects the view that the Scheduling Guidelines are an integral part of the Travaux Préparatoires of GATS (§§ 7.66–7.67) and classified them under Art. 32 VCLT. The Panel in *US–Gambling* held that the Scheduling Guidelines form an integral part of the context in the sense of Art. 31 VCLT (§ 6.82). The AB settled the score in its report in *US–Gambling*. It rejected the Panel's view that they should be considered as context in the VCLT-sense of the term (§§ 174–175), and held that they should be understood as supplementary means of interpretation, in the sense of Art. 32 VCLT (§ 196). Consequently, recourse to the Scheduling Guidelines is now a matter of discretion for the WTO judge.

3.1.3 The Level of Commitments

WTO Members can vary the level of commitments by introducing in the respective columns of Arts. XVI and XVII GATS one of the following three indications:

(a) **None**: this means that that it does not impose any limitation;[5]

(b) **Unbound**: this means that no commitment has been entered;

(c) **Other**: the WTO Member at hand will introduce specific language to describe its commitment.[6]

The 2001 Scheduling Guidelines contain two more levels of commitments: "no commitment technically feasible" (§ 47), and "special cases" (§§ 48 and 49). The first of these two categories can be discarded since, as the 2001 Scheduling Guidelines mention, in similar cases WTO Members will simply introduce the term "unbound". Assuming that the liberalization of the service at hand becomes eventually technically feasible, new negotiations will have to take place to define the level of commitment. The second category (special cases) is *de facto* (that is, in the scheduling practice of WTO Members) merged with the category commitment with

---

[4] A WTO Secretariat Note underscores that the 2001 Scheduling Guidelines were not enacted with the aim to affect the balance of rights and obligations as struck by the framers of GATS (§ 4 in WTO Doc. S/CSC/W/12 of 10 October 1997).

[5] This reading of the term 'none' has been confirmed by the Panel in § 6.279 of its report in *US–Gambling*.

[6] According to the terminology used in the 2001 Scheduling Guidelines, the first category is known as full commitment (§§ 42 and 43); the second, no commitment (§ 46); and the third, commitment with limitations (§§ 44 and 45). Occasionally, WTO Members use variations of these inscriptions. The Panel in *China-Electronic Payment Services* found nothing wrong with a Chinese commitment stating 'unbound except . . .' (§ 7.650 and footnote 848).

limitations. The following example cited in the 2001 Scheduling Guidelines proves this point (§ 48):

> It could be argued that a reservation for a residence requirement, a nationality condition or a commercial presence requirement under cross border trade amounts to an "unbound". However in some cases there is clearly an advantage in inscribing those requirements instead of the term "unbound" in that trading partners have the certainty that there are no other limitations with respect to the cross border mode (see also § 14 on residency requirements and § 12 on nationality requirements).

3.1.4 Horizontal and Sector–Specific Commitments

WTO Members may enter both horizontal as well as sector-specific commitments. The 2001 Scheduling Guidelines in § 37 define the term horizontal commitment as follows:

> A horizontal commitment applies to trade in services in all scheduled services sectors unless otherwise specified. It is in effect a binding, either of a measure which constitutes a limitation on market access or national treatment or of a situation in which there are no such limitations. Where measures constituting limitations are referred to, the commitment should describe the measure concisely, indicating the elements which make it inconsistent with Articles XVI or XVII. In order to avoid repetition, it is desirable to enter these commitments in a separate section at the beginning of the schedule according to the four modes of supply. Such a section could be entitled: "Horizontal commitments applicable to sectors listed in the sectoral part of the schedule". Some horizontal measures may be specific to only one mode of supply:

> <u>Example</u>: Legislation may refer to foreign investment, formation of corporate structures or land acquisition regulations. Such measures affect above all <u>commercial presence</u>.

> <u>Example</u>: Legislation may stipulate requirements regarding entry, temporary stay and right to work of natural persons; the categories of natural persons covered by a particular offer may also be specified. Such measures affect above all the <u>presence of natural persons</u>.

> Other horizontal measures may affect more than one mode of supply:

> <u>Example</u>: Legislation may provide for tax measures which are contrary to national treatment and not covered by Art. XIV(d). Such measures would normally affect the supply of services in several modes.

A sector-specific commitment is defined in § 39 of the 2001 Scheduling Guidelines:

> A sector-specific commitment applies to trade in services in a particular sector. If in the context of such a commitment, a measure is maintained which is contrary to Articles XVI or XVII, it must be entered as a limitation in the appropriate column (either market access or national treatment) for the relevant sector and modes of supply; the entry should describe the measure concisely, indicating the elements which make it inconsistent with Articles XVI or XVII.

3.1.5 Clarification of Commitments Entered

The WTO Membership realized soon after the end of the Uruguay Round negotiation that it was, on occasion, very difficult (if not a quixotic test altogether) to understand what precisely had been committed. There was general dissatisfaction with the scheduling approach followed early on. The dissatisfaction centred around specific commitments made in the movement of natural persons, maritime services, financial services, and basic telecommunications: the WTO Membership decided that it was imperative to clarify their scope. Negotiations took place to this effect under the aegis of the WTO Committee on Specific Commitments. An unofficial note prepared by the WTO Secretariat (WTO Doc. S/CSC/W/33 of June 3, 2002) states that the intent was to put some order in the jungle of subsequent schedules arising from the so-called extended negotiations.[7] Two approaches were developed that could be used: the "replacement option", or the "accumulation option". The content of each option is explained in S/CSC/W/33 in the following terms:

> In some cases the new instrument replaced the pre-existing one (replacement method), while in other cases the new instrument supplemented or partially modified the pre-existing schedule (accumulation method). The replacement method resulted in all of a Member's commitments in force in a sector being embodied in a single instrument. The accumulation method resulted in all of a Member's commitments in force in a sector being contained in more than one instrument, which then needed to be read together.
>
> . . .
>
> Only 58 Members maintain GATS commitments in a single document. For each of the 86 Members that have made changes to their original Uruguay Round or accession schedules, the total number of documents containing commitments that are, or have

---

[7] This term refers to the negotiations held after the successful conclusion of the Uruguay Round, that is, between 1995–1997.

been, in force varies between two and seven. This multiplicity of documents might result in difficulties in determining the legal status of a Member's commitments under the GATS. In such cases, to obtain a complete and accurate picture of such legal status it is necessary to look at the original schedule, together with subsequent documents modifying it, and assess how the various documents relate to each other.

There was legitimate fear that, when entering a new commitment, WTO Members would not be improving or clarifying their old commitments, but instead, backtracking on their previous engagements. Could WTO Members do that? The response to this question should be no, unless if they were to respect the disciplines enshrined in Art. XXI GATT (explained *infra*). §§ 7–9 of WTO Doc. S/CSC/W/33 issued to this effect underscored this point:

> During discussions in the Committee, Members raised the question of the preservation of legal certainty of existing commitments. In principle, the new schedule would not be expected to reduce the level of commitments in an old schedule. The mandate for the negotiation of specific commitments is indicated in § 1 of GATS Art. XIX, which states that

> "... Members shall enter into successive rounds of negotiations, beginning not later than five years from the date of entry into force of the WTO Agreement and periodically thereafter, with a view to achieving a progressively higher level of liberalization. Such negotiations shall be directed to the reduction or elimination of the adverse effects on trade in services of measures as a means of providing effective market access."

> Using almost identical language, § 1 of the Guidelines and Procedures for the Negotiations states that "the negotiations shall aim to achieve progressively higher levels of liberalization of trade in services through the reduction or elimination of the adverse effects on trade in services of measures as a means of providing effective market access.

Having established that no backtracking is possible, the remaining question is how does one monitor that no such thing has occurred? §§ 15 and 16 of WTO Doc. S/CSC/W/33 sketch out the following response:

> In the case of accumulation, a link between commitments in old and new schedules is needed. It would be necessary therefore to define clearly in the Sixth Protocol how the new commitments in each attached schedule would affect existing commitments. Therefore, in presenting an offer that modifies existing commitments, it would be desirable for the Member to indicate in detail the relationship between the proposed changes in the offer and

the existing commitments. Once the offer becomes final, this relationship would need to be made explicit in the language of the Sixth Protocol incorporating the new schedule.

A question raised during the Committee discussions concerned the preservation of the legal certainty of existing commitments. Since the method of accumulation of schedules implies that some commitments would be left unaltered in old schedules, and not replicated in new schedules to be attached to the Sixth Protocol, the issue of preserving commitments would seem relevant only in the case of changes to existing commitments. Changes brought about by the new schedule would presumably override the original inscriptions on the same subject. The principle in Art. 30 of the Vienna Convention on the Law of Treaties, designed to resolve conflicts between provisions of successive treaties on the same subject-matter, gives some guidance on this issue. Whether a proposed change in an offer constitutes an "improvement" and thereby does not impair the existing commitment is a question subject to Members' determination throughout the negotiations; in that sense there is a built-in mechanism for the preservation of existing commitments.

3.2 MARKET ACCESS

3.2.1 Six Measures Prohibited, in Principle

Art. XVI.2 GATS prohibits, in principle, recourse to six types of measures:

(a) limitations on the number of suppliers;

(b) limitations on the total value of service transactions or assets;

(c) limitations on the total number of service operations or on the total quantity of service output;

(d) limitations on the total number of natural persons that may be employed;

(e) measures which restrict or require specific types of legal entity or joint venture;

(f) limitations on the participation of foreign capital.

Exceptions to the prohibition are possible, as the wording of Art. XVI.2 GATS makes clear. To this effect, nevertheless, WTO Members will have to indicate in their schedule of concessions one (or more) of the limitations mentioned above. Limitations and restrictions mentioned in Art. XVI.2 GATS can be entered with respect to one or more mode(s) of supply of the service concerned (Art. VI.2 GATS). Absent indication to this effect, recourse to any of these measures is impermissible. The negotiating record seems to indicate that the measures included were among the most frequently observed obstacles to trade in services.[8] Consequently, negotiators pushing for trade liberalization in services decided to prohibit them on a priority basis.

The 1993 Scheduling Guidelines make it clear that minimum requirements do not come under the purview of Art. XVI GATS; non-discriminatory licensing requirements do not come under its purview either. The Table below provides an illustration of limitations on market access:

Market Access Limitations	Example
(a) Limitations on the number of service suppliers whether in the form of numerical quotas, monopolies, exclusive service suppliers or the requirements of an economic needs test;	Licences for new restaurants subject to economic needs test based on population density.
(b) Limitations on the total value of service transactions or assets in the form of numerical quotas or the requirement of an economic needs test;	Foreign bank subsidiaries limited to x per cent of total domestic assets of all banks.
(c) Limitations on the total number of service operations or on the total quantity of service output expressed in terms of designated numerical units in the form of quotas or the requirement of an economic needs test[a];	Restrictions on the broadcasting time available for foreign films.
(d) Limitations on the total number of natural persons that may be employed in a particular service sector or that a service supplier may employ and who are necessary for, and directly related to, the supply of a specific service in the form of numerical quotas or the requirement of an economic needs test;	Foreign labour should not exceed x per cent of the work force and/or not account for more than y per cent of total wages.
(e) Measures which restrict or require specific types of legal entity or joint venture through which a service supplier may supply a service;	Commercial presence excludes repre-

---

[8] Marchetti and Mavroidis (2011).

Market Access Limitations	Example
	sentative offices.
(f) Limitations on the participation of foreign capital in terms of maximum percentage limit on foreign share-holding or the total value of individual or aggregate foreign investment.	Foreign equity participation in domestic insurance companies should not exceed x per cent.

3.2.2 Art. XVI GATS: An Exhaustive List of Market Access Restrictions?

The Panel in *US–Gambling* held that Art. XVI.2 GATS is an exhaustive list (§ 6.318):

> The ordinary meaning of the words, the context of Art. XVI, as well as the object and purpose of the GATS confirm that the restrictions on market access that are covered by Art. XVI are only those listed in § 2 of this Article.

In § 6.327 of the same report, the Panel held that qualitative (as opposed to quantitative) restrictions should not be caught by Art. XVI GATS since so much is made clear in the 1993 Scheduling Guidelines. In § 6.331 of the same report, the Panel took the view that zero quotas, although not explicitly mentioned in Art. XVI.2 GATS, are covered by Art. XVI GATS. The rationale is as follows:

> The fact that the terminology embraces lesser limitations, in the form of quotas greater than zero, cannot warrant the conclusion that it does not embrace a greater limitation amounting to zero.

This view was confirmed in *China–Electronic Payment Services*: the US had requested consultations with China with respect to certain restrictions and requirements maintained by China pertaining to electronic payment services for payment card transactions and the suppliers of those services. The US had alleged that China permitted only a Chinese entity (China Union Pay) to supply electronic payment services for payment card transactions denominated and paid in renminbi in China. Service suppliers of other Members could only supply these services for payment card transactions paid in foreign currency. China further required that all payment card processing devices be compatible with that entity's system, and that payment cards should bear that company's logo. It further ensured that the Chinese entity has guaranteed access to all merchants in China that accept payment cards, while services suppliers of other Members were obliged to negotiate for access to merchants. The US alleged that China was acting inconsistently with its obligations under Arts. XVI and XVII GATS (§ 7.202ff.). The Panel dismissed the US claims under Art. XVI GATS holding that, a measure that operates as limitation, but is not explicitly included in the body of this provision, is not in violation of GATS (§ 7.635).

3.2.3 Art. XVI GATS and Domestic Services Suppliers

Following the example set in 1993, the 2001 Scheduling Guidelines read:

> The list is exhaustive and includes measures which may also be discriminatory according to the national treatment standard (Art. XVII). In other words, all measures falling under any of the categories listed in Art. XVI:2 must be scheduled, whether or not such measures are discriminatory according to the national treatment standard of Art. XVII.

The Panel, in its report on *US–Gambling*, dealt with a series of US federal and state laws which prohibited the supply of internet gambling in a non-discriminatory manner: Neither US- nor foreign services suppliers were allowed to supply similar services. The Panel accepted the argument advanced by Antigua and Barbuda that, in the absence of indicating restrictions in its schedule of concessions, the US was effectively in violation of its commitments. In doing that, the Panel effectively ruled that the limitations included in Art. XVI GATS apply not only to foreign, but to domestic suppliers as well. The Panel found that a series of US federal and state measures which regulate the supply of services by foreign and domestic suppliers alike, violated Art. XVI GATS. Some examples of such laws are: in § 6.365, the Panel outlawed the "Wire Act" (federal statute) which reads in pertinent part:

> Whoever being engaged in the business of betting or wagering knowingly uses a wire communication facility for the transmission in interstate or foreign commerce of bets and wagers or information assisting in the placing of bets or wagers or any sporting event or contest, or for the transmission of a wire communication which entitles the recipient to receive money or credit as a result of bets or wagers shall be fined under this title or imprisoned not more than two years, or both;

In § 6.373, the Panel found that the "Travel Act" (federal statute), which reads in a quasi-identical manner with the Wire Act, and punishes those who travel and practice foreign or interstate commerce, or use the mail with intent to distribute the proceeds of, or promote establish, carry on, facilitate unlawful activities, to be WTO-inconsistent. In § 6.380, the Panel reached the conclusion that the Illegal Gambling Business Act (IGBA) to be WTO-inconsistent. The IGBA reads in pertinent part:

> Whoever conducts, finances, manages, supervises, directs or owns all or part of an illegal gambling business shall be fined under this title or imprisoned not more than five years, or both.

The AB agreed with the Panel's analysis (§ 265).

3.2.4 Relationship With Art. VI GATS (Domestic Regulation)

The Panel in *US–Gambling* held that the two provisions are mutually exclusive (§ 6.305):

> Under Art. VI and Art. XVI, measures are either of the type covered by the disciplines of Art. XVI or are domestic regulations relating to qualification requirements and procedures, technical standards and licensing requirements subject to the specific provisions of Art. VI. Thus, Articles VI:4 and VI:5 on the one hand and XVI on the other hand are mutually exclusive.

The 1993 Scheduling Guidelines on the other hand, read:

> If approval procedures or licensing and qualification requirements contain any of the limitations specified in Art. XVI, they should be scheduled as market access limitations.

The Panel, in its report on *US–Gambling* dealt with the following US state measure (§ 18–10–103 of the Colorado Revised Statutes):

> (1) A person who engages in gambling commits a class 1 petty offense.
>
> (2) A person who engages in professional gambling commits a class 1 misdemeanor. If he is a repeating gambling offender, it is a class 5 felony.

The Panel found that this measure was not inconsistent with Art. XVI GATS, since, in its view, it was not covered by Art. XVI GATS. In its view, it was:

> ... not directed at 'service suppliers' for the purpose of Art. XVI.2(a) nor to 'service operations and 'service output' for the purposes of Art. XVI.2(c). ... Antigua has not adduced any evidence to indicate that the supply of gambling services by the Internet or by any other means included in mode 1 is prohibited.[9]

3.3 NATIONAL TREATMENT (NT)

A WTO Member may accord services and services suppliers of other WTO Members treatment no less favourable than that accorded to their own services (and services suppliers), assuming it has entered a commitment to this effect in its schedule.

---

[9] § 6.382 of the Panel report, see also §§ 6.397, 6.401 and 6.405 which reflect the similar findings.

3.3.1 The Test of Compliance With Art. XVII GATS

The Panel in *EC–Bananas III* developed a four-prong test to establish inconsistency of a particular measure with Art. XVII GATS (§ 7.134). In this case, the US claimed that the EU was in violation of its obligations under the GATS since it was treating EU distributors of bananas more favorably than their foreign counterparts. The Panel held that the following elements should be cumulatively present for the claim to succeed: first, that the EU had undertaken a specific commitment in the relevant sector and mode of supply (distribution of bananas); second, that the EU had adopted a measure that affected the supply of services in the sector and the mode of supply concerned; third, the measure at hand was applied to foreign and domestic like services and/or services suppliers; and fourth, the measure afforded to foreign services/services suppliers treatment less favorable than that afforded to their domestic counterparts. On appeal, the AB followed the same approach (§§ 241ff. and especially § 244). The question whether a specific commitment had been made, is a factual issue. The response is to be found in the schedules of concessions of a WTO Member. The term *"measure affecting trade in services"* should be interpreted, as already noted in Chapter 23, in accordance with the AB's ruling in *Canada–Autos*: the party carrying the burden of proof should at least establish who provides the service concerned and how he/she is affected by the measure adopted. We turn to the interpretation of the last two conditions in what immediately follows.

3.3.2 Like Services/Services Suppliers

The Panel in *EC–Bananas III* held that, to the extent that services are like, those providing them are like services suppliers. The marketplace becomes, in the eyes of this Panel, the defining criterion to establish likeness between two services/services suppliers (§ 7.322):

> Fourth, in our view, the nature and the characteristics of wholesale transactions as such, as well as of each of the different subordinated services mentioned in the headnote to section 6 of the CPC, are "like" when supplied in connection with wholesale services, irrespective of whether these services are supplied with respect to bananas of EC and traditional ACP origin, on the one hand, or with respect to bananas of third-country or non-traditional ACP origin, on the other. Indeed, it seems that each of the different service activities taken individually is virtually the same and can only be distinguished by referring to the origin of the bananas in respect of which the service activity is being performed. Similarly, in our view, to the extent that entities provide these like services, they are like service suppliers.

On appeal, the AB dismissed the relevance of the "aims and effects"-test (as argued by the EU) (§§ 240–241).[10]

3.3.3 Less Favorable Treatment (LFT)

The Panel in *EC–Bananas III* dealt with the following issue: the EU had in place a licensing scheme which distinguished between category A and category B operators depending on whether they had had in a previous representative period marketed bananas originating in ACP— (African, Caribbean, Pacific) or, in dollar zone-countries. Distributors who marketed (predominantly) ACP-bananas were considered to be category B; those that marketed dollar zone-bananas belong to category A. The major characteristics of the licensing scheme are reflected in the Panel report:

> the operator category rules apply to service suppliers regardless of their nationality, ownership or control. (§ 7.324);

Import licenses were tradable and transferable (§ 7.336): category A operators were allocated 66.5% of the licenses required for the importation of dollar zone bananas, and category B operators, 30% of the same licenses. Category B operators received 30% of licenses, regardless of their record in importing dollar zone-bananas in the previous representative period. License transferees are usually category A operators who are forced to pay a premium in order to be in a position to sell dollar zone-bananas (§ 7.336):

> given that license transferees are usually Category A operators who are most often service suppliers of foreign origin and since license sellers are usually Category B operators who are most often service suppliers of EC (or ACP) origin, we conclude that service suppliers of the Complainants' origin are subject to less favourable conditions of competition in their ability to compete in the wholesale services market for bananas than service suppliers of EC (or ACP) origin.

In the Panel's view the allocation of the 30% quota constituted more favourable treatment than that reserved to A distributors (§ 7.341). The AB (§§ 242–244) upheld the Panel's findings in this respect:

> We do not agree with the European Communities that the aims and effects of the operator category system are relevant in determining whether or not that system modifies the conditions of competition between service suppliers of EC origin and service suppliers of third-country origin. Based on the evidence before it, the Panel concluded "that most of the suppliers of Complainants' origin are classified in Category A for the vast majority of their

---

[10] The Panel in *China–Electronic Payment Services* confirmed that it is the competitive relationship of services at issue that matters to define likeness (§ 7.702ff.).

past marketing of bananas, and that most of the suppliers of EC (or ACP) origin are classified in Category B for the vast majority of their past marketing of bananas". We see no reason to go behind these factual conclusions of the Panel.

We concur, therefore, with the Panel's conclusion that "the allocation to Category B operators of 30 per cent of the licences allowing for the importation of third-country and non-traditional ACP bananas at in-quota tariff rates creates less favourable conditions of competition for like service suppliers of Complainants' origin and is therefore inconsistent with the requirement of Art. XVII of GATS". We also concur with the Panel's conclusion that the allocation to Category B operators of 30 per cent of the licences for importing third-country and non-traditional ACP bananas at in-quota tariff rates is inconsistent with the requirements of Art. II of the GATS.

3.3.4 *De Jure* and *De Facto* LFT

Art. XVII.2 GATS states that a WTO Member will meet its obligations under Art. XVII GATS, if it accords:

> either formally identical treatment or formally different treatment to that it accords to its own like services and service suppliers.

Case law (AB, *EC–Bananas III* at §§ 244 ff.) has understood this provision as covering both *de jure* as well as *de facto* discrimination.

3.4 ADDITIONAL COMMITMENTS

3.4.1 The Content

WTO Members can, by virtue of Art. XVIII GATS, make specific commitments, additional to those made under Arts. XVI, and Art. XVIII GATS. The language of Art. XVIII GATS is open-ended: although this provision contains a list of measures that could come under its purview, its wording makes it clear that the included list is of indicative character:

> Members may negotiate commitments with respect to measures affecting trade in services not subject to scheduling under Articles XVI or XVII, including those regarding qualifications, standards, or licensing matters. Such commitments shall be inscribed in a Member's Schedule.

The value added of Art. XVIII GATS is especially in the short run: it was felt that additional commitments could be entered that would reduce the transaction costs in the supply of services, until the disciplines provided for in Art. VI GATS have been elaborated.[11] Art. XVIII GATS makes it clear that the measures coming under its purview, cannot be scheduled under Arts. XVI, and/or XVII GATS. Additional commitments can, in principle, be taken in any services sector. So far, additional commitments have been undertaken by many WTO Members in various sectors: accounting; auditing and book-keeping; architectural; distribution; engineering and integrated engineering; entertainment; financial; medical and dental; maritime transport; taxation; and telecoms.[12] The types of measures that have been expressed in terms of additional commitments vary: in telecoms, for example, the most common inscriptions relate to interconnection, universal service obligations (USO), allocation of the use of scarce resources; in other sectors, the most frequent inscriptions relate to licensing provisions. The majority of additional commitments are in three sectors: telecoms, maritime transport, and financial services.

3.4.2 Scheduling Additional Commitments

The 2001 Scheduling Guidelines how scheduling of additional commitments occurs:

> A Member may, in a given sector, make commitments with respect to measures affecting trade in services not subject to scheduling under Articles XVI and XVII. Such commitments can include, but are not limited to, undertakings with respect to qualifications, technical standards, licensing requirements or procedures, and other domestic regulations that are consistent with Art. VI. Additional commitments are expressed in the form of undertakings, not limitations. In the schedule, the Additional Commitments column would only include entries where specific commitments are being undertaken, and need not include those modes of supply where there are no commitments undertaken or any entries at all where no Art. XVIII undertakings are made.

Consequently, what matters is that the language introduced is specific enough to provide an adequate representation of what has been committed. Examples of additional commitments have been included in Attachment 1 to the WTO Doc. S/CSC/W/34. We quote here a few typical illustrations:

(a) <u>Publication of measures of general application—Art. III</u>

> The Government will publish the rules and regulatory policy regarding further competition in the field of basic telecommunication services.

---

[11] On this score, see a document prepared by the WTO Secretariat, which aims to establish, *inter alia*, the common understanding of negotiators regarding the rationale for Art. XVIII GATS, see WTO Doc. S/CSC/W/34 of July 16, 2002.

[12] See WTO Doc. S/CSC/W/34 at p. 2.

Where a licence is required, the following will be made publicly available: (a) all the licensing criteria and the period of time normally required to reach on decision concerning an application for a licence and (b) the terms and conditions of individual licenses.

(b) <u>Decision review procedures—Art. VI: 2(a)</u>

Appeals against the decisions of the Authority may be filed in the High Court.

(c) <u>Authorization procedures—Art. VI: 3 and 4</u>

Applications for new products will be reviewed and responded to within three months of receipt of the completed documentation; and applications for products that have already been approved for other financial institutions will be reviewed and responded to within 15 days of receipt of completed documentation.

Applicants will be informed of results in writing no later than 30 days after submission of their applications.

The Authorities will make their best endeavours to consider within 6 months complete applications for licenses ... to respond without undue delay to requests for information by applicants ...

Appropriate authorities will fully utilize the existing mechanisms available to them to respond expeditiously to accommodate innovations in securities products, while ensuring the most appropriate supervision of markets from prudential viewpoints.

(d) <u>Qualification requirements and procedures and licensing requirements—Art.VI:4</u>

The foreign service supplier must be a world class operator with extensive international experience.

With respect to the assets of Employees' Pension Funds (hereinafter referred to as "Funds") qualified by appropriate authorities to be managed by discretionary investment management service suppliers, the eight-year qualification requirement with respect to the required duration of the Funds following their establishment is reduced to three years.

Regulatory Authority may grant licences for satellite based services on following conditions: (a) Frequency clearance by Board, (b) Security and sovereignty regulations, (c) Availability of ITUT/R standards, (d) resolution of cross-border communication issues; and (e) resolution of Customs procedures.

The Government will grant recognition of AFLA to the following: i. the service provider is qualified as a lawyer in his/her home jurisdiction(s), and ii. the service provider as practiced as a qualified lawyer for at least 5 years in his/her home jurisdiction(s)....

Licensing conditions, for all subsectors, may provide the application of the universal service principles as defined by the regulatory authority.

For the liberalization of these services, the Government requires any telecommunications services supplier to: ... contribute to the national training and research endeavour in the telecommunications field.

(e) <u>Procedures to verify competence of professionals—Art. VI:4 and 6</u>

Foreign architects licensed under their home country's law may acquire an architect license by passing a simplified examination which covers only two of the regular test's six subjects: architectural laws and regulations and architectural design.

The qualifying examination to determine the competence and ability to supply the service for the purposes of registration with the professional bodies will be conducted in the English language.

To the extent that no specific exemption has been taken to this effect, additional commitments must be provided on a non-discriminatory basis.

4. MODIFICATION OF SCHEDULES

Art. XXI GATS epitomizes the idea that the GATS is about maintaining a level of reciprocally negotiated concessions. Art. XXI GATS is the corresponding provision to Art. XXVIII GATT. It provides WTO Members with the possibility to modify the content of their specific commitments, or withdraw a specific commitment altogether upon payment of compensation. Art. XXI GATS differs from its GATT-provision in some important respects:

(a) First, when a WTO Member wants to modify its schedule of commitments, it will have to notify the CTS of its intent to do so. Contrary to what happens under GATT though, the notifying WTO Member will have to, in principle, negotiate not only with a select group of countries (those holding initial negotiating rights, the principal supplying interest-countries, and those having a substantial interest in the modifying Member's market), but with all WTO Members which in principle qualify as 'affected Members';

(b) Second, compensation has to be offered to all affected WTO Members on an MFN-basis. If there is disagreement as to the amount of compensation, the matter has to be referred to binding arbitration;

no modification can occur, unless the compensation has been paid, in conformity with the findings of the arbitration;

(c) Third, the timing of modification is different: modification in GATS can occur, in accordance with Art.XXI.1 GATS, only after three years have lapsed from the date of the entry into force of a commitment.

The US did not implement the findings, and Antigua and Barbuda requested authorization to suspend equivalent concessions. The Arbitrator found that the damage done to Antigua and Barbuda was $21 million.[13] Antigua and Barbuda did not suspend concessions. Subsequently, the US government notified the CTS of its interest to exclude "gambling and betting services" from the sector column of its schedule. The ensuing negotiations that took place were between the US and seven WTO Members that declared themselves to be "affected members" as per Art. XXI.2(a) GATS: Antigua and Barbuda (the complainant), Canada, Costa Rica, the EU, India, Japan, and Macao, China. Three of the affected members (EU, Canada, and Japan) reached an agreement with the US. From the remaining four affected members, only Costa Rica submitted a request for referral to the arbitration within the negotiated deadline (January 28, 2008). A sole arbitrator (Lars Annell, former ambassador for Sweden at the WTO) was appointed to adjudicate this dispute. Had none of the affected members requested the establishment of an arbitral procedure, then the US would have been free to modify their schedule (Art. XXI.3(b) GATS). Antigua and Barbuda joined in the arbitration two days later. India and Macao, China decided not to join in. Costa Rica withdrew its arbitration request on February 27, 2008 and eventually reached an agreement with the US on March 4, 2008. This left Antigua and Barbuda as the last affected member still participating in the arbitration. The arbitration was suspended 13 times, as each time parties preferred to negotiate bilaterally at the margin of the procedure. Following repeated failures to negotiate a deal, the arbitration procedure resumed. It was suspended for the last time until the end of 2009 and never resumed after that.

5. INTERPRETATION OF COMMITMENTS

In *US–Gambling*, the AB had the opportunity to provide its understanding on the manner in which commitments should be interpreted. As briefly argued above, the litigation revolves around one issue: what were the US commitments with respect to internet gambling? The US schedule read as follows:

---

[13] WTO doc. WT/DS285/ARB.

Sector or subsector		Limitations on market access	
10.	RECREATIONAL, CULTURAL, & SPORTING SERVICES		
A.	ENTERTAINMENT SERVICES (INCLUDING THEATRE, LIVE BANDS AND CIRCUS SERVICES)	1)	None
		2)	None
		3)	None
		4)	Unbound, except as indicated in the horizontal section
B.	NEWS AGENCY SERVICES	1)	None
		2)	None
		3)	None
		4)	Unbound, except as indicated in the horizontal section
C	LIBRARIES, ARCHIVES, MUSEUMS AND OTHER CULTURAL SERVICES	1)	None
		2)	None
		3)	None
		4)	Unbound, except as indicated in the horizontal section
D.	OTHER RECREATIONAL SERVICES (except sporting)	1)	None
		2)	None
		3)	The number of concessions available for commercial operations in federal, state and local facilities is limited
		4)	Unbound, except as indicated in the horizontal section

The AB upheld the Panel's finding that the VCLT was relevant for the interpretation of the US commitment (§ 162ff.). The Panel, borrowing from the AB jurisprudence regarding the interpretation of tariff concessions under the GATT where the AB ruled that the general rules of treaty interpretation set out in the VCLT are applicable, made a similar point with respect to GATS commitments (§ 6.45). The AB further held that the GATS, the rest of the WTO Agreement, the schedule of the US, as well as the schedules of other WTO Members constituted context to the US commitment (§ 178). The AB went on to state that, in light of its structure, it could never be the case that one service figures under two classifications (§ 180). The AB found it impossible to decide on the extent of the commitment made by the US by relying solely on the elements of Art. 31 VCLT. It thus, felt that reliance to Art. 32 VCLT was necessary. To this effect, it had to first identify the supplementary means that it would be using. The agreement of the parties to the dispute on this issue facilitated its task: it held that both W/120 and the 1993 Scheduling Guidelines were preparatory work in the sense of Art. 32 VCLT on gambling services (§ 196). In an effort to underscore the relevance of W/120, the AB noted that WTO Members were expected to follow it when scheduling their commitments (§ 204). The AB noted (§ 202) that the CPC Class that corresponds to "Sporting services" (9641) does not include gambling and betting services. Rather, it is under the Class "Other recreational services" (9649) that the Sub-class for gambling and betting services (96492) falls. With all the elements thus established, the AB proceeded to find that the US were in violation of their obligations since they had not imposed any restrictions on the cross border supply of gambling services (§§ 203–206):

> It is reasonable to assume that the parties to the negotiations expected the same technique to be applied to *exclude* a discrete service from the scope of a commitment, when the commitment is made in a subsector identified in W/120 and the excluded service is more disaggregated than that subsector.
>
> In our view, the requisite clarity as to the scope of a commitment could not have been achieved through mere omission of CPC codes, particularly where a specific sector of a Member's Schedule, such as sector 10 of the United States' Schedule, follows the structure of W/120 in all other respects, and adopts *precisely* the same terminology as used in W/120. As discussed above, W/120 and the 1993 Scheduling Guidelines were prepared and circulated at the request of parties to the Uruguay Round negotiations for the express purpose of assisting those parties in the preparation of their offers. These documents undoubtedly served, too, to assist parties in reviewing and evaluating the offers made by others. They provided a common language and structure which, although not obligatory, was widely used and relied upon. In such circumstances, and in the light of the specific guidance provided in the 1993 Scheduling Guidelines, it is reasonable to assume that parties to the negotiations examining a sector of a Schedule that tracked so closely the language of the same sector in W/120 would—absent a clear indication to the contrary—have expected the sector to have the same coverage as the correspond-

ing W/120 sector. This is another way of stating that, as the Panel observed, "unless otherwise indicated in the Schedule, Members were assumed to have relied on W/120 and the corresponding CPC references."

Accordingly, the above excerpt from the 1993 Scheduling Guidelines, together with the linguistic similarities between the two subsectors, provide strong support for interpreting subsector 10.D of the United States' Schedule as corresponding to subsector 10.D of W/120, notwithstanding the absence of CPC codes in the United States' Schedule. Subsector 10.D of W/120, in turn, corresponds to Class 964 of CPC, along with its sub-categories.

We observe that another element of the preparatory work of the GATS suggests that the United States itself understood the Scheduling Guidelines in this way and sought to comply with them in the drafting of its GATS Schedule. Several drafts of the United States' Schedule included the following cover note:

[E]xcept where specifically noted, the scope of the sectoral commitments of the United States corresponds to the sectoral coverage in the Secretariat's Services Sectoral Classification List (MTN.GNS/W/120, dated 10 July 1991). (italics in the original).

The ultimate finding of the AB is reflected in § 213:

Based on our reasoning above, we reject the United States' argument that, by excluding "sporting" services from the scope of its commitment in subsector 10.D, the United States excluded gambling and betting services from the scope of that commitment. Accordingly, we *uphold*, albeit for different reasons, the Panel's finding, in § 7.2(a) of the Panel Report, that:

> ... the United States' Schedule under the GATS includes specific commitments on gambling and betting services under subsector 10.D." (emphasis in the original).

QUESTIONS AND COMMENTS

Classification of Services: The following can serve as an illustration of how different services have been classified in W/120:

A. Professional Services

    a.   Legal Services   861

    b.   Accounting, auditing and book-keeping services   862

    c.   Taxation Services   863

    d.   Architectural services   8671

	e.	Engineering services	8672
	f.	Integrated engineering services	8673
	g.	Urban planning and landscape architectural services	8674
	h.	Medical and dental services	9312
	i.	Veterinary services	932
	j.	Services provided by midwives, nurses, physiotherapists and para-medical personnel	93191
	k.	Other	
C.	Telecommunication services		
	a.	Voice telephone services	7521
	b.	Packet-switched data transmission services	7523**
	c.	Circuit-switched data transmission services	7523**
	d.	Telex services	7523**
	e.	Telegraph services	7522
	f.	Facsimile services	7521**+7529**
	g.	Private leased circuit services	7522**+7523**
	h.	Electronic mail	7523**
	i.	Voice mail	7523**
	j.	On-line information and data base retrieval	7523**
	k.	electronic data interchange (EDI)	7523**
	l.	enhanced/value-added facsimile services, including store and forward, store and retrieve	7523**
	m.	code and protocol conversion	n.a.
	n.	on-line information and/or data processing (including transaction processing)	843**
	o.	other	

N.B.: The (**) indicates that the service specified constitutes only a part of the total range of activities covered by the CPC concordance (e.g. voice mail is only a component of CPC item 7523).

Is the List Included in Art. XVI.2 GATS Exhaustive? Siegel (2002) has taken the view that the interpretation of the Panel, to the effect that the list of measures appearing in Art. XVI.2 GATS is exhaustive, is wrong, for a number of reasons:

(a) <u>first</u>, because the wording of Art. XVI.1 GATS, that is, the immediate context to Art. XVI.2 GATS, mentions, beyond limitations, terms and conditions as the three elements that can be used in order to regulate the opening of a particular market to foreign competition. The reading of Art. XVI GATS by the Panel in *US–Gambling* effectively reads out terms and conditions. This outcome runs afoul the VCLT, in the name of which this, and all other WTO panels, have performed their interpretative tasks;

(b) <u>second</u>, footnote 8 to the GATS provides support to the argument that the list of Art. XVI.2 GATS is not exhaustive. According to this footnote, a WTO Member making commitments under Mode 1, cannot restrict capital movement (to and from its territory) necessary to realize cross border supply of the service at hand; moreover, a WTO Member making commitments under Mode 3, cannot restrict capital movement (to its territory) necessary to realize commercial presence in its market. A literal reading of this footnote supports the view that, when making commitments under Modes 2 and 4, WTO Members can, of course, restrict capital movement. The restriction of capital movement however, is not enlisted in Art. XVI.2 GATS. Hence, the list of Art. XVI.2 GATS cannot be considered exhaustive for this reason.

Art. XVI GATS: Mavroidis (2006a) has argued that the *US–Gambling* Panel's view regarding the applicability of Art. XVI GATS to domestic suppliers is unwarranted for both legal, as well as policy grounds: being part of an international agreement the purpose of which is to liberalize trade in general, one would expect that Art. XVI GATS should concern exclusively the conditions under which foreign services and services suppliers should be granted market access in a given market. Moreover, the first sentence of Art. XVI GATS says as much:

> . . . each Member shall accord services and service suppliers of any *other* Member treatment no less favourable . . . (emphasis added).

Do you agree with this view? Does Art. XX GATS help you resolve this question? In the same vein, the Panel report in *China–Electronic Payment Services* held that there is "scheduling primacy" of Art. XVI over Art. XVII GATS (§ 7.664). How do you understand this point?

National Treatment: Mattoo (2000) explains the limits of non-discrimination, and full commitments on national treatment.

CHAPTER 26

EXCEPTIONS

■ ■ ■

1. PREFERENTIAL TRADE AGREEMENTS (PTAS)

Pursuant to Art. V GATS, WTO Members may lawfully grant prefernces for services trade to PTA partners. PTA partners must have agreed to liberalize substantially all services sectors between them without raising new protection towards non-participants and must have notified the WTO of their resolve to proceed this way.

1.1 COVERAGE

PTAs in the GATS-context borrow some, but not all, the GATT disciplines on PTAs:

(a) There is an internal requirement that members of a PTA must observe (Art. V.1 GATS): They must ensure that their PTA has "substantial sectoral coverage", and that discrimination (in the sense of Art. XVII GATS) has been abolished, except for what is necessary under Arts. XI, XII, XIV, and XIVbis GATS;

(b) There is also an external requirement (Art. V.4 GATS), to the effect that members of a PTA must not raise the level of barriers applicable to outsiders;

(c) There is further a notification requirement (Art. V.7 GATS): All PTAs must be notified to the Committee on Regional Trade Agreements (CRTA).

There are, on the other hand, some features which are specific to PTA in the realm of services:

(a) There is only one form of PTA in GATS, and it looks more like an FTA rather than a CU, since no obligation to pursue a common external commercial policy is imposed on the members of the PTA by virtue of Art. V GATS;

(b) The multilateral review is looser than in the GATT-context, since the CRTA must take into account the contribution of the PTA to the wider economic integration between the members of the PTA (Art. V.2 GATS);

(c) Assuming a member of the PTA has to withdraw a concession in order to comply with the PTA rules, the negotiations under Art. XXI

GATS (modification of schedules) will be initiated. In such negotiations (Art. XXI GATS), built-in compensation cannot be taken into account (Art. V.8 GATS). Outsiders (services suppliers originating in WTO Members which are not participating in the PTA) will be benefiting from the PTA, if they have substantive business operations within the territory of one of the members of the PTA.

"Substantial sectoral coverage" is explained in a footnote to Art. V.1 GATS:

> This condition is understood in terms of number of sectors, volume of trade affected and modes of supply. In order to meet this condition, agreements should not provide for the *a priori* exclusion of any mode of supply.

1.2 A PROFILE OF NOTIFIED PTAS

The level of intra-PTA liberalization varies. Marchetti and Roy (2009) conclude that PTAs that involve the US have the most comprehensive coverage and deepest level of commitments, although there are, generally speaking, no Mode 4 commitments; important sectors, such as maritime cabotage and broadcasting services are excluded; and disciplines are limited to the federal government-level (*i.e.*, state-level policies are not covered.) A list of PTAs with services commitments have been notified to the CRTA can be found on the WTO website at http://www.wto.org/english/tratop_e/region_e/rta_participation_map_e.htm.

2. LABOUR MARKETS INTEGRATION AGREEMENTS

Art. V*bis* GATS reads:

> This Agreement shall not prevent any of its Members from being a party to an agreement establishing full integration of the labour markets between or among the parties to such an agreement, provided that such an agreement:
>
> (a) exempts citizens of parties to the agreement from requirements concerning residency and work permits;
>
> (b) is notified to the Council for Trade in Services.

This provision as well is an exception to MFN only. In contrast to Art. V GATS, Art. V*bis* GATS does not deal with integration processes with substantial sectoral coverage; it is just labor markets that are being integrated. This provision was introduced at the request of Nordic European countries, which have traditionally had this type of arrangements between them. So far the following arrangements have been notified to the WTO:

S/C/N/34	2.12.96	[*Denmark*]	Notification pursuant to Art. V*bis* of the General Agreement on Trade in Services
S/C/N/35	2.12.96	[*Iceland*]	Notification pursuant to Art. V*bis* of the General Agreement on Trade in Services
S/C/N/36	2.12.96	[*Norway*]	Notification pursuant to Art. V*bis* of the General Agreement on Trade in Services
S/C/N/37	2.12.96	[*Sweden*]	Notification pursuant to Art. V*bis* of the General Agreement on Trade in Services
S/C/N/38	2.12.96	[*Finland*]	Notification pursuant to Art. V*bis* of the General Agreement on Trade in Services

3. GENERAL EXCEPTIONS

3.1 AN EXHAUSTIVE LIST

Art. XIV GATS mentions five grounds, recourse to which can justify GATS-inconsistent behaviour. This provision is an exception to all obligations assumed under GATS as the introductory sentence of this provision makes clear:

> *Nothing* in this Agreement shall be construed to prevent the adoption or enforcement by any Member of measures. (emphasis added).

The Panel in *US–Gambling* confirmed that this provision is an exception to both general obligations as well as specific commitments (§ 6.528):

> Art. XIV allows Members to derogate from their obligations under GATS (including *any* specific commitments they may have undertaken) subject to the conditions stipulated in that Article. (emphasis added).

The five grounds mentioned in the body of Art. XIV GATS are:

(a) Necessary for the protection of public morals and public order;

(b) Necessary for the protection of animal plant life or health;

(c) Necessary for the protection of laws not inconsistent with GATS;

(d) Inconsistent with Art. XVII GATS and relating to effective imposition and collection of taxes;

(e) Inconsistent with Art. II GATS and relating to double taxation.

There is no need to indicate in the schedule of concessions measures coming under the purview of Art. XIV GATS (AB, *US–Gambling*, §§ 268ff.).

3.2 A TWO–TIER TEST (À LA GATT)

A measure must be provisionally justified under a particular sub-paragraph and also be applied in non-discriminatory manner as required by the chapeau, otherwise it cannot be justified under Art. XIV GATS. The AB in *US–Gambling* endorsed (§§ 292ff.) the Panel's findings on this score (§ 6.449).

3.3 PUBLIC ORDER

The Panel in *US–Gambling* accepted that legislation put in place to address organized crime, money laundering, fraud and other criminal activities, and risks to children given the availability of remotely supplied gambling and betting services could come under Art. XIV(a) GATS and qualify as public order (§ 6.479ff.). The AB upheld this finding, stating that the fundamental interests of a society can come under the public order exception (§§ 296ff.). In this case, the AB clarified the standard of review to be applied by a WTO adjudicating body when confronting this issue. In its view, although the ends sought are not justiciable, the relative importance of the regulatory objective pursued matters and should be taken into account. This means that the standard of review will be more deferential towards the regulating state when important public order concerns are at stake, and less so when mundane invocations are made. The contribution of the means used to the realization of the end sought must be taken into account as well: the question to ask is to what extent the means chosen helps the regulating state achieve its stated aims. Finally, the restrictive impact of the means used on international commerce is pertinent information. Therefore, a Panel must make sure that there is no other alternative which is both less restrictive and reasonably available to the intervening WTO Member (§§ 306–308):

> The process begins with an assessment of the "relative importance" of the interests or values furthered by the challenged measure. Having ascertained the importance of the particular interests at stake, a panel should then turn to the other factors that are to be "weighed and balanced". The AB has pointed to two factors that, in most cases, will be relevant to a panel's determination of the "necessity" of a measure, although not necessarily exhaustive of factors that might be considered. One factor

is the contribution of the measure to the realization of the ends pursued by it; the other factor is the restrictive impact of the measure on international commerce.

A comparison between the challenged measure and possible alternatives should then be undertaken, and the results of such comparison should be considered in the light of the importance of the interests at issue. It is on the basis of this "weighing and balancing" and comparison of measures, taking into account the interests or values at stake, that a panel determines whether a measure is "necessary" or, alternatively, whether another, WTO-consistent measure is "reasonably available".

The requirement, under Art. XIV(a), that a measure be "necessary"—that is, that there be no "reasonably available", WTO-consistent alternative—reflects the shared understanding of Members that substantive GATS obligations should not be deviated from lightly. An alternative measure may be found not to be "reasonably available", however, where it is merely theoretical in nature, for instance, where the responding Member is not capable of taking it, or where the measure imposes an undue burden on that Member, such as prohibitive costs or substantial technical difficulties. Moreover, a "reasonably available" alternative measure must be a measure that would preserve for the responding Member its right to achieve its desired level of protection with respect to the objective pursued under § (a) of Art. XIV.

In the same report, the AB also clarified the allocation of the burden of proof when an Art. XIV GATS defence is raised. Overturning the Panel's findings in this respect, the AB held that the original burden of proof rests with the WTO Member raising the defence. Assuming it has made a prima facie case, the burden of proof shifts to the other party (the original complainant), which will now have to demonstrate that the use of another, less restrictive (but equally effective) measure could have been privileged. Assuming the existence of such a measure has been confirmed, the burden of proof will shift again to the party raising the Art. XIV GATS-defense. This time however, it will have to demonstrate that this measure (e.g., the less-restrictive alternative) was not reasonably available to it (§§ 309–311):

> It is well-established that a responding party invoking an affirmative defence bears the burden of demonstrating that its measure, found to be WTO-inconsistent, satisfies the requirements of the invoked defence. In the context of Art. XIV(a), this means that the responding party must show that its measure is "necessary" to achieve objectives relating to public morals or public order. In our view, however, it is not the responding party's burden to show, in the first instance, that there are no rea-

sonably available alternatives to achieve its objectives. In particular, a responding party need not identify the universe of less trade-restrictive alternative measures and then show that none of those measures achieves the desired objective. The WTO agreements do not contemplate such an impracticable and, indeed, often impossible burden.

Rather, it is for a responding party to make a prima facie case that its measure is "necessary" by putting forward evidence and arguments that enable a panel to assess the challenged measure in the light of the relevant factors to be "weighed and balanced" in a given case. The responding party may, in so doing, point out why alternative measures would not achieve the same objectives as the challenged measure, but it is under no obligation to do so in order to establish, in the first instance, that its measure is "necessary". If the panel concludes that the respondent has made a prima facie case that the challenged measure is "necessary"—that is, "significantly closer to the pole of 'indispensable' than to the opposite pole of simply 'making a contribution to' "—then a panel should find that challenged measure "necessary" within the terms of Art. XIV(a) of the GATS.

If, however, the complaining party raises a WTO-consistent alternative measure that, in its view, the responding party should have taken, the responding party will be required to demonstrate why its challenged measure nevertheless remains "necessary" in the light of that alternative or, in other words, why the proposed alternative is not, in fact, "reasonably available". If a responding party demonstrates that the alternative is not "reasonably available", in the light of the interests or values being pursued and the party's desired level of protection, it follows that the challenged measure must be "necessary" within the terms of Art. XIV(a) of the GATS.

3.4 MEASURES AIMED AT SECURING COMPLIANCE WITH LAWS

The Panel report in *US–Gambling* explained, in §§ 6.538 and 6.539 of its report, its understanding of the type of measures that could legitimately come under Art. XIV(c) GATS in the following manner:

> ... the reference to 'secure compliance' in Art. XIV means that the measures for which justification is sought must 'enforce' the relevant laws and regulations. Second, it indicates that the measures for which justification is sought must enforce 'obligations' contained in the laws and regulations rather than merely ensure attainment of the objectives of those laws and regulations.

As for the degree to which a measure must 'secure compliance' with obligations under other laws and regulations, we note that the panel in *Korea—Various Measures on Beef* recognized that a measure need not be designed *exclusively* to 'secure compliance' with the justifying law. Rather, the panel in that case accepted that it was sufficient if a measure was put in place, at least *in part*, in order to secure compliance with the justifying legislation. (italics and emphasis in the original).

3.5 COMPLIANCE WITH THE CHAPEAU OF ART. XIV GATS

The chapeau of Art. XIV GATS reads:

Subject to the requirement that such measures are not applied in a manner which would constitute a means of arbitrary or unjustifiable discrimination between countries where like conditions prevail, or a disguised restriction on trade in services, nothing in this Agreement shall be construed to prevent the adoption or enforcement by any Member of measures.

In *US–Gambling*, the AB held that the chapeau requires from WTO Members to behave in a consistent manner across (comparable) situations. In the case at hand, it faced an argument by Antigua and Barbuda to the effect that the US was not acting in a non-discriminatory manner when, through some legislative documents such as the Wire Act, the Travel Act and the IGBA, it was prohibiting remote gambling for both domestic and foreign suppliers, whereas, through another legislation, the Interstate Horseracing Act (IHA), it allowed only US suppliers to supply remote gambling services. The AB upheld a Panel finding to the effect that such treatment was indeed discriminatory and in violation of the requirements under the chapeau of Art. XIV GATS (§§ 348ff. and especially 351 and 356). In doing that, the AB made it clear that the complainant, in order to establish discriminatory treatment, must show evidence of patterns of enforcement and not mere individual instances of differential treatment (§ 356).

4. NATIONAL SECURITY

Art. XIV*bis* GATS makes it clear that a WTO Member can justifiably deviate from any obligation it has assumed under the GATS in order to protect its national security interests. The negotiating history reveals no objection regarding the inclusion of this clause in the GATS. Indeed, participants found it unreasonable to request from contracting parties to continue to do business with firms that transferred all or part of their profits from their sales to the enemy. And of course, this provision echoes Art.

XXI GATT.[1] This provision makes it clear that nothing in the GATS could be construed so as to prevent WTO Members from refusing to furnish any information the disclosure of which would prejudice their national security; or prevent them from taking any action relating to services carried out directly or indirectly for the purpose of provisioning a military establishment, or relating to fissionable or fusionable materials (or the materials from which they are derived), or taken in time of war or other emergency in international relations; or prevent them from taking actions in pursuance of their obligations under the UN Charter for the maintenance of international peace and security. WTO Members making use of this provision must immediately inform the CTS of the measures undertaken as well as of their termination.

QUESTIONS AND COMMENTS

Special and Differential Treatment: The GATS does not reflect the GATT approach to special and differential treatment, according to which, all developing countries (bar the distinction between developing countries and least developed countries, LDCs) are entitled to the same treatment; the GATS aims to customize flexibility depending on the particular endowments of specific addressees. This is why various provisions (e.g., Art. III GATS) contain paragraphs that specifically address concerns by developing countries.

Burden of Proof: Do you agree with the allocation of burden of proof in *US–Gambling*?

PTAs: How do you understand the term "substantial sectoral coverage"? Assume for example that a PTA covers all sectors but the commitments made are shallow. Would that satisfy this requirement?

Public Order: Do you agree with the inclusion of this term in Art. XIV GATS? If yes, would you recommend it for inclusion in Art. XX GATT as well? If yes, is there a need to add anything else in either provision?

---

[1] Marchetti and Mavroidis (2011).

CHAPTER 27

TRIPS: INTRODUCTION AND BASIC PRINCIPLES

■ ■ ■

1. OVERVIEW OF THE TRIPS AGREEMENT

The Agreement on Trade–Related Aspects of Intellectual Property Rights (TRIPS Agreement) is considered to be one of the most significant, and most controversial, outcomes of the Uruguay Round negotiations. It is significant because, by incorporating the global intellectual property (IP) regime into the trade regime, the TRIPS Agreement significantly expanded both the scope of the trade regime and the range of enforcement actions in dealing with global IP problems. It also tangibly interlinked the two areas. A new quiver has been added to the arsenal of measures that a country can use to threaten, or effect, retaliation for a breach of a trade obligation: the withdrawal of IP rights.

The TRIPS Agreement is also one of the most controversial outcomes of the Uruguay Round negotiations. The terms of the Agreement are considered, by some, to undermine other public welfare interests—in development, public health, indigenous rights, food production, biodiversity (to name just a few). Some have openly questioned whether the terms actually help facilitate trade and innovation, as its proponents claim, or whether they merely seek to enshrine a set of rules that largely benefit corporations located predominantly in industrialized countries, at the expense of others, especially in the developing world. These questions are complex, and their answers vary depending on industry dynamics. Nevertheless, the passion with which these questions have been debated suggests the influential impact of the TRIPS Agreement in the span of its short existence.

The TRIPS Agreement itself is divided into seven parts:

(a) Part I discusses the *general obligations* and *principles* applicable to all parties to the TRIPS Agreement.

(b) Part II elaborates on the *specific standards* concerning the availability, scope, and use of IP rights. Seven categories of intellectual property are mentioned in the agreement itself: copyright, trademarks, patents, geographical indications, industrial designs, layout-designs of integrated circuits, and undisclosed information (which is often synonymous with trade secrets). Because the TRIPS Agreement incorporates by reference provisions of earlier international IP treaties (e.g., the Berne, Paris, and Rome Conventions), these provisions are also considered substantive obligations of the Agreement.

(c) Part III focuses on the *enforcement* of IP rights, including specific institutional, procedural, and remedial obligations with respect to a WTO member's civil and criminal justice system, as well as its border controls.

(d) Part IV contains a single article concerning the *acquisition* and *maintenance* of IP rights and related *inter partes* procedures, such as the opposition, revocation, and cancellation of IP rights.

(e) Part V lists *transparency* requirements to which WTO members must adhere with respect to reporting about their IP regimes, as well as the principles governing any *dispute settlement* proceedings that may arise from the Agreement.

(f) Part VI provides *transitional* allowances for developing and least-developed countries and sets forth principles concerning *technical co-operation*.

(g) Finally, Part VII establishes the *institutional arrangements* to oversee the Agreement.

Before discussing the details enshrined within the TRIPS Agreement, it is important that we situate it in the appropriate context. First, from a historical perspective, the move to regulate IP at the international level is not new. Unlike the GATS, a robust international system for regulating IP existed prior to the TRIPS Agreement. To name just two, the Paris Convention, governing patents, dates back to 1883, while the Berne Convention, governing copyright, dates back to 1886. The substantive commitments contained within the TRIPS Agreement should not be seen as entirely new. Instead, they are a combination of existing long-standing obligations with a set of new obligations. What is radical about the change triggered by the advent of TRIPS is, first, that these obligations now are subject to binding dispute settlement, and second, that they now apply to a much broader set of countries.

Second, while we will focus heavily on the TRIPS Agreement, the story does not end with the signing of the Marrakesh Agreement. Instead, it continues robustly. As Gervais (2007) suggests, the policy debate in the years following the advent of TRIPS have consisted of three narratives. The first is a set of *addition narratives*, where industrialized countries, dissatisfied with incomplete elements of the Agreement, have sought to clarify or expand the protections afforded IP producers. This has been done most vividly through a series of preferential trade agreements, as well as the recently-concluded Anti–Counterfeiting Trade Agreement (ACTA). They have resulted in a creation of a series of "TRIPS-plus" commitments and norms, shared among an exclusive set of WTO members.

The second is a set of *subtraction narratives*, where developing countries and civil activists, dissatisfied with the costs imposed by TRIPS, have sought to clarify or limit the scope of its applicability. Its proponents have been actively at odds with those favoring the addition narratives. Their most obvious triumph was the WTO's November 2001 issuance of the Doha Declaration on the TRIPS Agreement and Public Health, offering clarification on the flexibility that WTO members possess to gain access to essential medicines. This issue will be discussed in greater detail in Chapter 30. In addition, those involved in fostering this narrative have vastly expanded their efforts to highlight awareness of the costs of implementing the TRIPS Agreement for developing countries and to push for the emergence of alternative competing norms in other forums (such as the Convention on Biodiversity).

The third is the more recent emergence of a set of *calibration narratives*, which contends that the relationship between IP protection and other desirable outcomes is complex and context-specific. As such, the higher protection standards mandated by the TRIPS Agreement are not desirable or undesirable per se, but instead must be calibrated based on the particular resource endowment of the country at issue. In this narrative version, the challenge is not so much one of further fostering or resisting certain norms, but rather learning how to calibrate the implementation of TRIPS obligations appropriately so as to foster one's national interests.

It is within this context that the debate about the TRIPS Agreement and the appropriate role to be played by the trade regime in regulating IP protection has taken place. In recent years, attempts to introduce greater IP protection have been greeted with public backlash, not only within developing countries, but also by constituents within some of the industrialized countries that traditionally have championed efforts to expand the scope of IP protection. The outcry against the Protect IP Act and the Stop Online Piracy Act in the US in early 2012 was emblematic of this backlash. Billed as efforts to combat counterfeit drugs, to protect the IP of content creators, and to safeguard American jobs, the bills instead triggered fears that legal measures would impact online speech, innovation, and the efficacy of websites negatively; their consideration was postponed. Mass protests occurred in several European countries against the ACTA in early 2012, leading the European Parliament to reject the treaty in July 2012. In December 2012, the European Commission confirmed that it would withdraw its appeal to the European Court of Justice. This effectively confirmed that the EU would not join the ACTA, despite being an original signatory to it, due to public outcry during the ratification process. By the end of 2012, only Japan has ratified the ACTA.[1] More battles over the extension of IP protection are likely to emerge in coming years.

2. THE ADVENT OF THE TRIPS AGREEMENT

While international agreements on intellectual property date back to the 1880s, intellectual property did not play a prominent role in the original GATT. Article XX(d) did afford GATT Members a general exception to adopt or enforce measures "necessary to secure compliance with laws or regulations which are not inconsistent with the provisions of this Agreement, including those relating to [. . .] the protection of patents, trade marks, copyrights, and the prevention of deceptive practices." But, the original GATT did not include detailed substantive provisions about the levels of protection necessary for different forms of IP. Nor did it enumerate specific enforcement obligations. By and large, GATT Members were given the freedom to shape their own IP regimes as they saw fit.

How then did the global trade regime emerge as the primary regulator of international rules on IP? Why did the TRIPS Agreement emerge as an outcome of the Uruguay Round negotiations?

Beginning in the 1960s, the United States and other developed countries began expressing concerns over the growing global trade in counterfeit goods. Increasingly, these countries sought ways to raise the standard of IP protection and enforcement worldwide. In 1967, the Stockholm Convention led to the creation of the World Intellectual Property Organization (WIPO) as a specialized agency under the United Nations. WIPO served as the principal body for administering international IP issues, including oversight of updated versions of the Paris Convention for the Protection of Industrial Property (1967) and Berne Convention for the Protection of Literary and Artistic Works (1971).

WIPO, however, proved to be a disappointment for developed countries. Attempts to use WIPO to raise the substantive requirements for IP protection proved to be less than successful. Even where substantive requirements were successfully embedded within agreements, developed countries bemoaned WIPO's inability to bind developing countries to these requirements. Because WIPO members were not required to sign on to all WIPO agreements, important developing countries were not parties to several key agreements.

The United States and European Community therefore began exploring the possibility of shifting international IP negotiations to the GATT in order to attain broader IP protection requirements. The first attempt to

---

[1] Within the US, the ACTA is the subject of a debate as to whether Congressional ratification is necessary. The Executive Branch has asserted that the treaty qualifies as a Congressional–Executive Agreement, which does not require Senate approval, with the State Department's Legal Advisor citing the PRO IP Act (15 U.S.C. 8113(a)) as providing prior Congressional consent.

do so was during the Tokyo Round (1973–79). Developed countries pushed for the inclusion of rules that would address the trade in counterfeits. However, this first attempt was unsuccessful as the negotiating parties failed to agree on a common set of rules. Efforts nonetheless continued. A draft agreement on measures to discourage the importation of counterfeit goods was produced, and the 1982 Ministerial Declaration included instructions for the GATT Council to explore the appropriateness of taking action under the GATT framework to address counterfeit goods.

The Punta del Este Declaration launching the Uruguay Round resulted in a significant broadening of this mandate. Industrialized countries, in particular the US and Japan, pushed for the negotiations to cover all IP rights rather than address simply counterfeit goods.[2] Some developing countries resisted this idea, arguing that negotiations should occur only where there was a clearly proven trade distortion, as was the case with counterfeits. The final Declaration, however, included a broadly-worded mandate to negotiate "trade-related aspects of intellectual property rights, including trade in counterfeit goods." It charged the negotiations "to clarify GATT provisions and *elaborate as appropriate new rules and disciplines*" "[i]n order to reduce the distortions and impediments to international trade, . . . , and to ensure that measures and procedures to enforce intellectual property rights do not themselves become barriers to legitimate trade."[3]

As a result of this charge, the US, EC, Japan, and other industrialized countries tabled broad-reaching negotiating proposals. These proposals covered multiple forms of IP, outside of trademarks, and included specific requirements for enforcement. Some developing countries objected to the broadened scope of negotiations, arguing that the talks should be confined to trade-distortions resulting from counterfeiting. Others continued to push for WIPO as the appropriate forum for drafting new rules.

As the negotiations continued, the proposals put forth by industrialized countries continued to persist in the bracketed draft text used as the basis for negotiations. Developed countries held firm to their desire to seek a broad-based agreement, especially in light of the strengthened dispute settlement regime that was to result from the Uruguay Round talks. Negotiations continued until the end of the Round, but in the end, developed countries were successful in achieving their objectives. The major concession to developing countries was the inclusion of transitional periods, but not exclusion from certain substantive requirements altogether. Thus, the TRIPS Agreement, in its current form, was born.

The rationale for why developed countries would push for such an arrangement is clear. IP-related goods are an increasingly important part of their exports. As terms of trade have shifted, developed countries increas-

---

[2] See GATT Doc. PREP.COM(86)SR/3 of 11 April 1986.
[3] See GATT Doc. MIN.DEC of 20 September 1986, at pp. 7–8.

ingly find their competitive advantage to be in innovation-driven industries, such as software, pharmaceutical, semiconductor, and entertainment. Stronger IP protection and enforcement ensures that these industries are able to capture greater profits in foreign markets over a longer period. Moreover, these industries have powerful lobbying efforts. Had governments in developed countries relented during the Uruguay Round IP negotiations, they would have paid a political price.

However, the rationale for why developing countries agreed to the TRIPS Agreement arrangement is more debatable. One explanation is that they envisaged it as part of a grand bargain. In exchange for lower tariffs and greater market access achieved in other parts of the agreement (as well as increased protection from unilateral sanctions resulting from the creation of a mandatory dispute settlement process), developing countries were willing to concede on intellectual property and other areas. This explanation suggests that developing countries were cognizant of the potential costs imposed by the TRIPS Agreement. Nevertheless, they thought that the benefits achieved elsewhere outweighed the costs.

A second explanation is based on similar lines, but suggests that developing countries miscalculated, and therefore, underestimated, the costs. A number of developing countries, particularly the least-developed ones, have few innovation-driven industries of their own. Their economies also lack the counterfeit manufacturers or generic pharmaceutical companies that would benefit from lax IP protection. Thus, they saw the TRIPS negotiations outcome as one affecting the distribution of rents to competing foreign producers—but not one in which their own industries had much at stake. By viewing the negotiations through this lens, a subset of developing countries failed to properly account for how much the strengthened IP regime would increase the volume of rents that foreign firms could capture from their consumers. Moreover, these governments also failed to properly calculate the negative social externalities arising from these increased rents. As a result, they signed onto an agreement thinking there were lower costs than was the actual case.

A third explanation rests on entirely different lines. This explanation suggests that developing countries believed increased IP protection and enforcement was in their interest because of resulting gains in investment, technology transfer, and productivity gains. Moreover, they believed that a strengthened IP regime would allow them to better develop innovation-driven industries, allowing them to move up the global value chain. Thus, they willingly signed onto the agreement.

A final explanation suggests that the strength of the TRIPS Agreement is exaggerated. While the agreement is quite detailed in its obligations on laws providing IP protection, as we will see, it is considerably less detailed in the areas of enforcement. Thus, developing countries can mitigate the negative costs and externalities arising from the agreement through under-enforcement. This explanation suggests that developing countries, aware of this informal opt-out possibility, readily agreed to the terms as drafted.

These explanations are not entirely mutually exclusive. Because governments are not transparent about their negotiating behavior, it is hard to discern exactly why developing countries agreed to the agreement that resulted. How much of it was power politics at the international level? What was the impact of domestic politics? Did these governments properly calculate their interests? Were they outmaneuvered during the actual course of the Uruguay Round negotiations? In the ensuing years, a rich debate has emerged as to what exactly led to the TRIPS Agreement's formation, from the standpoint of developing countries. As will be noted below, intervening developments suggest that the rationale (and the TRIPS Agreement's impact) has varied across developing countries, and therefore, it may not be correct to think of them as a collective entity with necessarily shared interests.

What is clear is that the emergence of the TRIPS Agreement represented a significant triumph for industrialized countries. After years of having their efforts to increase IP protection stalled at WIPO and earlier GATT talks, they managed to prevail with a much more comprehensive agreement than imaginable two decades earlier. Going forward, trade and IP would be forever intertwined.

3. RATIONALES FOR THE TRIPS AGREEMENT

The original argument for including IP provisions in the GATT regime centered around the distorting effects of counterfeits on legitimate trade. The existence of counterfeits of a given good has a "crowding out" effect on the sale of the legitimate good, even if one assumes that a certain percentage of the purchasers of a counterfeit good would not have purchased the legitimate good at the legitimate, rather than counterfeit, price point. Because government actions in providing IP protection and enforcement directly affect the availability of counterfeit goods, attempts to regulate such actions are characterized as attempts to remedy or limit trade distortions.

The case for inclusion of measures to address areas outside of counterfeiting is harder to explain. Why should the global trade regime care to regulate patents or copyright or geographical indications? Proponents for the broad coverage of the TRIPS Agreement argue that IP laws essentially function as a potential barrier to trade, in a manner similar to other non-tariff barriers. Left unregulated, each country will set its IP laws at a level ideal for the welfare implications of its own domestic producers and consumers, without regard for the welfare externalities imposed on others. As was the case with tariffs, unilateral setting of levels of IP protection and enforcement can spiral into a Prisoner's Dilemma situation whereby countries impose their externalities upon one another in a non-cooperative manner. Inclusion of international IP regulations within a trade agreement is a means of escaping this situation. By mandating an appropriate level of IP protection and enforcement by each trade partner, we arrive at a welfare-enhancing outcome superior to the outcome in an unregulated state.

This characterization of intellectual property therefore suggests that the rationale for the TRIPS Agreement is based on a similar version of the *terms of trade theory* used to explain other outcomes from the Uruguay Round negotiations. But how correct is it? To some extent, as is the case with services, we are still somewhat unclear about the size of the (negative) externalities associated with the unilateral setting of IP policies. Moreover, the TRIPS Agreement, as designed, does not fully ameliorate these externalities. Rather, it introduces its own set of externalities for consideration in this equation. Hence, it is not altogether clear that the terms of trade theory fully explains the rationale for the TRIPS Agreement, even if it is a plausible one.

An even more fundamental issue with the terms of trade theory is the issue of whether it is appropriate to analogize IP protection to tariff protection. Panagariya (1999) and others have argued that the analogy does not hold. Whereas tariff liberalization clearly results in efficiency gains, Panagariya argues that TRIPS produces efficiency results of a dubious nature and results in negative redistribution effects between rich developed countries and poor developing countries. Thus, he and other opponents question whether the TRIPS Agreement actually produces the welfare-enhancing outcome suggested by the terms of trade theory.

The alternative theory considered for goods and services, the *commitment theory*, is fairly unpersuasive in this context. While the TRIPS Agreement does require irreversible buy-in to certain IP protection norms, the theory is undermined in at least two ways. First, recall that the commitment theory suggests that a government, faced with an unpopular but desirable choice, will use international agreements to "tie its hands" and force it to embrace the choice. It then uses the international agreement as an excuse in order to minimize the negative political fallout from its decision. The problem herein lies with the fact that we find scant evidence that governments for whom the TRIPS outcome was politically unpopular, thought that the outcome was nonetheless desirable and therefore wanted to tie down their own hands. Second, the notion of commitment is undermined in part by the flexibilities contained within the enforcement sections of TRIPS. They raise the question of how much actual commitment was achieved, at least with respect to certain parts of the agreement. Nevertheless, commitment theory is not altogether unhelpful. It may explain particular instances of behavior, especially where a government sides with domestic producers at the expense of consumers when adopting certain TRIPS obligations.

What many opponents of the TRIPS Agreement contend is that there is no sound rationale for the agreement. Instead, they argue that the agreement is a welfare-reducing one with negative redistribution consequences. It allows corporations in rich countries to capture an unjustified and disproportionate share of rents from citizens in developing countries, without providing a commensurate benefit. This characterization of the TRIPS Agreement relies heavily on a *political economy* explanation, where governments, at a domestic level, are captured by the interests of multinational corporations, and countries, at an international level, are engaged in a regime where the outcomes are dictated largely by the interests of developed countries. The result is what some have termed "the tragedy of TRIPS."[4]

In the intervening years, however, it is not altogether clear that the costs for developing countries have been nearly as large as some had feared in the immediate aftermath of the Uruguay Round. Certainly, some constituencies within developing countries have suffered losses—as is also true of certain constituencies within developed countries. The resulting change in the price and availability of pharmaceuticals is one often-cited area of economic loss for certain constituencies. But it is far from clear that the TRIPS Agreement has caused across-the-board losses for all developing countries.

Instead, the evidence suggests a much more nuanced story. Some developing countries have effectively learned to take advantage of the TRIPS Agreement to their benefit. For example, after winning a dispute against a developed country, developing countries have used the suspension of TRIPS obligations under "cross-retaliation" quite effectively in order to put pressure on the larger developed country to comply, rather than simply ignore, the ruling. After prevailing in *US–Gambling*, Antigua effectively used such a threat. More recently, Brazil has also used such a threat to induce US compliance following *US–Upland Cotton*.

Also, to date, litigation losses suffered by developing countries as a result of WTO disputes on TRIPS commitments have not spread across a wide range of developing countries. Instead, they have been concentrated in a fairly narrow subset of Members—*e.g.*, China, India, and Argentina. The defendants in TRIPS-related litigation, therefore, have tended to be robust emerging economies, rather than truly impoverished least developed countries.

---

[4] Gerhart (2007) uses this phrase to contend that existing institutional settings, which privilege the nation-state, prevent the shaping of intellectual property policies which properly balance the interests of knowledge producers and knowledge users, and therefore fail to advance global public welfare sufficiently. For another critical account, see Sell (2003).

In addition, developed countries are not the only WTO Members that are using the threat of WTO litigation, based on TRIPS provisions, to stymie regulatory efforts which run counter to their exporters' interests. In the June 2011 meeting of the TRIPS Council, certain Latin American countries—such as Honduras and the Dominican Republic—used the trademark provisions in the TRIPS Agreement to attack proposed Australian legislation on cigarette packaging that their domestic producers opposed. For more and more WTO Members, including developing countries, TRIPS is simply another tool to be used to promote their economic and systemic interests.

All this suggests that viewing the rationale for the TRIPS Agreement through a North–South, developed-developing country lens is likely to be incorrect and outdated. The impact of the TRIPS Agreement has varied greatly across developing countries, and hence, the rationale for the Agreement is likely to be just as varied.

4. AN OVERVIEW OF THE TRIPS AGREEMENT

Before examining the detailed substantive obligations contained within the TRIPS Agreement, it is worth taking a step back to understand the Agreement as a whole. Like the other Uruguay Round agreements, the TRIPS Agreement only confers obligations and rights to WTO Members. Corporations and individuals within the WTO Members must work through their government in order to address any concerns they may have about implementation of the Agreement in other jurisdictions.

4.1 A BASELINE AGREEMENT FOR PARTIAL HARMONIZATION

The TRIPS Agreement provides considerable leeway to individual WTO Members in terms of how they seek to administer their IP laws and regimes. However, it does mandate a certain level of harmonization of the substantive and procedural rights related to IP within WTO Members. Generally speaking, these can be divided into three categories:

First, with regards to national IP laws, the TRIPS Agreement seeks to *establish certain minimum "floors" in terms of the standard of protection* that must be afforded by WTO Members. For example, the Agreement mandates that certain categories of marks must be afforded protection under national trademark laws. It leaves it open to individual WTO Members to decide whether additional marks, outside of those mentioned in the Agreement, should also be afforded protection. Another example is how the TRIPS Agreement treats copyright term. The Agreement mandates a minimum length of time for which copyright must apply. It leaves open to WTO Members whether they wish to grant terms longer than that specified in the Agreement.

Second, the TRIPS Agreement also seeks to *establish minimum requirements for the enforcement of IP laws* by national officials, to ensure that the laws do not simply exist on the books unenforced. Specifically, governments are required, at a minimum, to provide certain types of authority to their judicial and administrative officials in their handling of IP infringement cases. The Agreement also specifies a minimum set of circumstances under which criminal procedures and remedies must be in place in domestic law. In addition, it also mandates that certain measures be available for Customs and law enforcement officials to take when dealing with IP infringing goods. However, provided these minimums are met, the exact nature of judicial authority and the exact allocation of enforcement resources against specific types of IP infringement are left up to the discretion of WTO Members.

Third, the TRIPS Agreement seeks to *delineate a series of minimum procedural requirements* that must be followed by WTO Members when administering their IP regimes and adjudicating IP related cases. For example, WTO Members are required to provide for judicial review of administrative decisions. Another example is the procedures specified in the Agreement concerning the seizure of suspected IP infringing goods by Customs. Again, the TRIPS Agreement leaves open to WTO Members the possibility of enacting additional procedural safeguards beyond those enumerated in the Agreement.

Most significantly, the TRIPS Agreement makes the WTO dispute settlement system available as a means of enforcing these obligations contained within each of the three above-mentioned categories. As a result, national IP laws and national enforcement regimes are subject to the oversight of an international adjudicatory body with actual enforcement ability. This development significantly strengthened the ability of an individual WTO Member to ensure that their trading partners establish the minimum agreed-upon international IP standards. Therefore, while the TRIPS Agreement is certainly not the first time that countries have sought to harmonize their IP laws, it is undoubtedly the most impactful.

4.2 TRANSITIONAL PERIODS FOR IMPLEMENTATION

Because of the complexities involved in overhauling a domestic IP regime to comply with baseline standards mandated by the TRIPS Agreement, WTO Members agreed to provide each other with a transition period to implement the necessary changes. The length of the transition period varied depending on whether the WTO Member was classified as an industrialized country, developing country, or least developed country (LDC).

Regardless of their classification, all WTO Members are now required to abide by two conditions during the transition period. First, Art. 65.5 TRIPS mandates that during the transition period, no changes in laws, regulations, or practice can be made which resulted in a "lesser degree of consistency" with the provisions of the Agreement. In other words, a WTO Member can not temporarily lower its IP protection during the transition period. Originally, the requirement of Art. 65.5 TRIPS did not extend to LDCs. However, the non-backsliding obligation was extended to LDCs in the TRIPS Council (discussed *infra* under Institutional Arrangements) decision of 29 November 2005, which extended the general transition period for LDCs.[5]

Second, Art. 70.8 TRIPS requires that all WTO Members must make available a "mailbox" process for the filing of applications by pharmaceuticals and agricultural chemical products during the transition period. Companies that avail themselves of this "mailbox" process are allowed to preserve priority and novelty for their applications during the transition period. Therefore, once the transition ends, their applications can be evaluated to determine whether they meet the patentability standards of the revised regime. If they do, then the Member is required to grant protection for the remainder of the patent term, with the term having commenced on the date of the initial filing. In addition, Art. 70.9 TRIPS stipulates that any product subject to the "mailbox" filing process which obtains marketing approval shall be granted exclusive marketing rights for a period of up to five years, or until the product patent application is either granted or rejected, whichever period is shorter

Industrialized countries were given a transition period of one year. Therefore, on January 1, 1996, the TRIPS Agreement entered into force in these countries. Developing countries were given a longer transition period of five years. This transition period was also given to transition economies, officially defined as any WTO Member "which is in the process of transformation from a centrally-planned into a market, free-enterprise economy, and which is undertaking structural reform of its intellectual property system and facing special problems in the preparation and implementation" of IP laws and regulations. Such countries were given until January 1, 2000 to comply with the Agreement.

In addition, for developing countries, Art. 65.4 TRIPS extends an additional transition period of five years for the extension of product patent protection to "areas of technology not so protectable on the general date of application" of the Agreement. Therefore, for example, India was given until January 1, 2005 to extend product patent protection for pharmaceuticals, because it did not offer product patents for pharmaceuticals when TRIPS became applicable.

Note that the WTO has not traditionally relied upon any official classification (such as the UN classification) for determining whether a member is a "developing country." While in theory, this may be a potential

---

[5] *See* WTO Doc. IP/C/40 of 30 November 2005 at § III, para. 5.

source of conflict, in reality, it did not present a problem. No TRIPS-related complaints were filed during the transition period in which a WTO Member's classification was at issue.

The same approach, however, is not true when it comes to the classification of least-developed countries (LDCs). Here, the WTO has traditionally accepted the UN's list of LDCs as determined and occasionally modified by the UN General Assembly.[6] LDCs were originally given a transition period of ten years, set to expire on January 1, 2006. In 2002, the TRIPS Council decided to extend the transition period for LDCs' protection of pharmaceutical products until January 1, 2016.[7] The General Council also provided that the obligations of LDCs under Art. 70.9 TRIPS regarding exclusive marketing rights shall be waived for pharmaceutical products until January 1, 2016.[8]

Then, in November 2005, with the LDC transition period set to expire for all non-pharmaceutical products, the TRIPS Council decided to further extend the transition period for non-pharmaceutical products until July 1, 2013.[9] There is much speculation that this transition period will be further extended as the July 2013 deadline date approaches. Note that once a WTO Member is no longer classified as a LDC by the UN, it is no longer able to avail itself of the transition period.

4.3 IMPLEMENTATION FLEXIBILITY

As noted above, the TRIPS Agreement serves as a *baseline* agreement. The Agreement grants wide latitude to each individual WTO Member on how it chooses to implement its obligations in order to conform to the baseline requirements. Art. 1.1 TRIPS states: "Members shall be free to determine the appropriate method of implementing the provisions of this Agreement within their own legal system and practice."

WTO Members are also free to exceed the baseline requirements so long as such laws do not contravene the provisions of the TRIPS Agreement itself (Art. 1.1 TRIPS). However, they are not obliged to do so. A WTO Member may choose to implement IP laws above the minimum standards set forth in TRIPS for several reasons: First, such laws may already have been in place prior to TRIPS. Second, a Member may decide to raise its IP protection in a given area unilaterally due to political lobbying from certain domestic constituencies and/or policy decisions made by the executive and legislative branches. Third, a Member may be pressured to do so unilaterally by another country, as part of an ongoing bilateral trade dialogue. Fourth, it may be required to do so as a result of obligations incurred in another bilateral or plurilateral trade agreement.

---

[6] For the current list, see http://www.unohrlls.org/en/ldc/related/62/.
[7] *See* WTO Doc. IP/C/25 of July 1, 2002.
[8] *See* WTO Doc. WT/L/478 of 12 July 2002.
[9] *See* WTO Doc. IP/C/40 of 30 November 2005.

Finally, it may consider it simply good policy to do so. Any provision above the minimum standard set forth in TRIPS is commonly referred to as a *TRIPS-plus* provision.

In *India–Patents (US)*, the AB confirmed that a government's choice of implementation is subject to review by the WTO. At issue in *India–Patents (US)* were the transition requirements of Art. 70.8 and 70.9 TRIPS discussed above. Recall that Art. 70.8 TRIPS requires that if a WTO Member did not provide for patent protection for pharmaceutical and agricultural chemical products as of the date of entry into force, then it must establish a "mailbox" system to allow interested parties to preserve novelty and priority with respect to their applications during the transition period. In other words, the WTO Member making use of a transition period must accord interested pharmaceutical and agricultural chemical companies a mechanism to deposit their patent applications, to be evaluated once the transition period ended. Art. 70.9 TRIPS further required that the WTO Member grant exclusive marketing rights with respect to such applications for a period of five years or until the patent is granted or rejected, whichever is shorter.

India originally met its obligations through the Patents Ordinance 1994, promulgated by the President on December 31, 1994. Under the Indian Constitution, when the Parliament is not in session, the President is permitted to promulgate laws if the President considers it necessary. However, the authority of such laws lapses six weeks after Parliament reconvenes. Therefore, the Patent Ordinance 1994 expired on March 26, 1994. However, Parliament failed to pass subsequent legislation re-establishing the mailbox system and granting exclusive marketing rights. During this time, the Indian government directed its patent offices to continue receiving patent applications for pharmaceutical and agricultural chemical products and to set them aside as if the mailbox system still operated. India also noted that it received no requests for exclusive marketing rights for such products following the lapse of the Patents Ordinance 1994.

The US filed a complaint against India, alleging that India was in violation of its obligations under Arts. 70.8 and 70.9 TRIPS because it did not have a formal mailbox system and did not pass any legislation mandating the grant of exclusive marketing rights for patent applicants that took advantage of this system. India retorted that it was in compliance since it had issued "administrative instructions" for its patent office to comply with Art. 70.8 TRIPS. India argued that it was not obliged to implement its obligations through legislation, especially in light of the discretion accorded to it by Art. 1.1 TRIPS to determine the appropriate method for implementation in the context of its legal system.

The Panel and Appellate Body in *India–Patents (US)* rejected this argument. The Appellate Body affirmed that "Members are free to determine how best to meet their obligations under the TRIPS Agreement within the context of its own legal systems." (§ 59). However, it also confirmed that the implementation approach is subject to review (§§ 59–71).[10] A Member must stand ready to prove that its approach meets its obligations under the TRIPS Agreement given its domestic legal regime.

4.4 STRUCTURE OF THE TRIPS AGREEMENT

The TRIPS Agreement is broken down into a number of constituent parts: Part I contains the Agreement's general provisions and outlines its basic principles. In the remainder of the Chapter, we will focus on three of these basic principles:

- National treatment
- Most favored nation treatment
- Exhaustion

The first two principles should be very familiar to you by now; we will focus our discussion on specifics related to the TRIPS Agreement. The third principle is unique to the IP context, and we will explain it in greater detail *infra*.

Part II is the substantive heart of the TRIPS Agreement. It contains the key provisions establishing the minimal baseline standards concerning the availability, scope and use of IP rights, as established in the Agreement. Part Two is broken down into eight sections:

- Section 1 concerns Copyright and Related Rights (to be discussed in Chapter 28)
- Section 2 concerns Trademarks (to be discussed in Chapter 29)
- Section 3 concerns Geographical Indications (GIs). This volume does not discuss this topic in-depth, but GIs are defined under Art. 22.1 TRIPS as markers "which identify a good as originating in the territory of a [WTO] Member, or a region or locality in that territory, where a given quality, reputation or other characteristic of the good is essentially attributable to its geographic origin."
- Section 4 concerns Industrial Designs. As this section is limited to only two Articles, we do not discuss it in-depth. Art. 25 TRIPS requires protection of independently created industrial designs that are new or original. Art. 26 TRIPS stipulates the duration and scope of the right to protection, as well as limitations to exceptions.
- Section 5 concerns Patents (to be discussed in Chapter 30)
- Section 6 concerns Layout Designs of Integrated Circuits. This is a specialized topic that we do not discuss in this volume.

---

[10] On this score, see also the Panel report in *India–Patents (EC)*, §§ 7.41–7.42.

- Section 7 concerns the Protection of Undisclosed Information. Although it contains only one provision, Art. 39 TRIPS has featured prominently in ensuing debates over TRIPS and TRIPS-plus provisions, particularly over access to medicines. We therefore discuss it in Chapter 30.
- Section 8 concerns the Control of Anti–Competitive Practices in Contractual Licenses. Art. 40 TRIPS clarifies that nothing in the TRIPS Agreement prevents WTO Members from taking action in their domestic legislation against the use of IP which would result in anti-competitive practices.

Part III of the Agreement contains requirements with respect to the enforcement of IP rights. We will discuss elements contained within this Part in Chapter 31. The remainder of the Agreement (Parts IV–VIII) contain provisions regarding transition periods, institutional arrangements, dispute settlement, etc. We highlight certain of these provisions in this and other subsequent Chapters.

5. NATIONAL TREATMENT

In the next three sections, we focus on three basic principles that underlie the TRIPS Agreement which are featured in Part One of the Agreement. We begin our discussion by examining the concept of national treatment in the context of the TRIPS Agreement.

5.1 THE LEGAL DISCIPLINE

Art. 3.1 TRIPS requires WTO Members to accord to the nationals of other Members treatment no less favorable than that it accords to its own nationals, with respect to matters affecting the availability, acquisition, scope, maintenance, and enforcement of IP rights, as well as those matters affecting the use of IP rights specifically addressed in the TRIPS Agreement.

The preamble to the TRIPS Agreement recognizes that IP rights are private rights. Art. 1.3 TRIPS also explicitly states that the treatment provided for in the Agreement is one which should be accorded by a WTO Member to the nationals of all other WTO Members. "Nationals" are defined as "those natural or legal persons that would meet the eligibility for protection" provided for in earlier treaties covering the given IP subject area (*e.g.*, the Paris Convention (1967) for industrial property; the Berne Convention (1971) for literary and artistic works; the Rome Convention for the works of performers, producers of phonograms, and broadcasting organizations; and the Treaty on Intellectual Property in Respect of Integrated Circuits).[11]

The national treatment requirement is subject to the exceptions already provided in the Paris Convention (1967), the Berne Convention (1971), the Rome Convention, and the Treaty on Intellectual Property in Respect of Integrated Circuits. With respect to performers, producers of phonograms, and broadcasting organizations, the national treatment requirement applies only to rights provided under the TRIPS Agreement.

5.2 THE RATIONALE FOR THE LEGAL DISCIPLINE

Prevention of *concession erosion* serves as a rationale for national treatment in the TRIPS Agreement, as is true also of the GATT and GATS. Essentially, WTO Members seek to ensure that the rights granted by TRIPS cannot be diminished through subsequent favorable treatment of nationals vis-à-vis foreigners. Absent such a guarantee, WTO Members would be reluctant to offer concessions in the first place.

However, the language of the national treatment obligation in Art. 3.1 TRIPS is more complicated than that found in Art. XVI GATS. This is because the concept of national treatment in the international IP regime pre-dates the TRIPS Agreement, extending as far back as the late 19th Century. National treatment clauses are to be found in pre-TRIPS IP agreements. The agreements, however, permit certain exceptions to the national treatment rule. For example, the Berne Convention permits exceptions for the protection of applied art and industrial design, copyright term, and the resale royalty right.[12] Because the framers of TRIPS sought to create a regime which incorporated, rather than replaced, pre-existing IP agreements, the agreement needed to contain language recognizing that the exceptions to the national treatment rule found in the pre-existing agreements continued to hold. Thus, Art. 3.1 TRIPS begins with the general language stating the concept of national treatment, but then subjects it to the exceptions already existing in the other agreements.

Finally, Art. 3.1 TRIPS states that the national treatment obligation with respect to the rights of performers, producers of phonograms, and broadcasting organizations extend only to the subject matter covered in the TRIPS Agreement, namely Art. 14. The reason for this language may not be obvious to an outsider unfamiliar with the international IP regime. This sentence was inserted in the late stages of the TRIPS negotiations.[13] It reflects the divergent views toward the IP protection granted to performers, phonograph producers, and broadcasters between Anglo–

---

[11] A separate footnote defines nationals of a separate customs territory Member of the WTO to mean "persons, natural or legal, who are domiciled or who have a real and effective industrial or commercial establishment in that customs territory."

[12] See Berne Convention (1971), Arts. 2(7), 7(8), and 14*ter*(2) respectively.

[13] On this score, see Gervais (2008).

American common law countries and civil law countries. In the former, the protection for these categories of subject matter is extended through copyright. In the latter, however, the protection is done through a concept of "neighboring rights." Goldstein and Hugenholtz (2010), among others, provides an explanation of the difference between the two. For current purposes, it is sufficient to note that the language was considered necessary in order for the TRIPS Agreement to maintain a neutral stance between these competing modes of protection. The restriction to rights specifically covered within TRIPS is because the Rome Convention recognizes rights beyond those elaborated in Art. 14 TRIPS. The language, in effect, deems that a WTO Member that is a party to the Rome Convention (*e.g.*, the EU) need not grant full national treatment to broadcasters, performers, and phonograph producers to nationals of WTO Members that are not party to the Rome Convention (*e.g.*, the US). Instead, national treatment need only be extended to obligations covered within Art. 14 TRIPS, and not the full slate of Rome Convention rights.

5.3 COVERAGE OF THE LEGAL DISCIPLINE

5.3.1 Relationship to Other International IP Agreements

Art. 2 TRIPS clarifies that nothing in the TRIPS Agreement shall derogate from the existing obligations that WTO Members may have with one another under four existing IP agreements: the Paris, Berne, and Rome Conventions and the Treaty on Intellectual Property in Respect of Integrated Circuits (IPIC Treaty). As a result, to understand the scope of the coverage of the national treatment principle, we need to first understand the principle, as applied, in these other agreements. The text of each follows below:

Art. 2(1) of the Paris Convention (1967) governing the protection of industrial property states:

> Nationals of any country of the Union shall, as regards the protection of industrial property, enjoy in all the other countries of the Union the advantages that their respective laws now grant, or may hereafter grant, to nationals; all without prejudice to the rights specifically provided for by this Convention. Consequently, they shall have the same protection as the latter, and the same legal remedy against any infringement of their rights, provided that the conditions and formalities imposed upon nationals are complied with.

Art. 5(1) of the Berne Convention (1971) for the protection of literary and artistic works states:

> Authors shall enjoy, in respect of works for which they are protected under the Convention, in countries of the Union other than the country of origin, the rights which their respective laws

do now or may hereafter grant to their nationals, as well as the rights specifically granted by this Convention.

Art. 5(1) of the IPIC Treaty states:

... [E]ach Contracting Party shall, in respect of the intellectual property protection of layout-designs (topographies), accord, within its territory, (i) to natural persons who are nationals of, or are domiciled in the territory of, any of the other Contracting Parties, and (ii) to legal entities which or natural persons who, in the territory of any other Contracting Parties, have a real and effective establishment for the creation of layout-designs (topographies) or the protection of integrated circuits, the same treatment that it accords its own nationals.

Finally, Art. 2 of the Rome Convention provides for national treatment for performers, phonograph producers, and broadcasting organizations, subject to the protection specifically granted, and the limitations specifically provided for, in the Convention. These provisions elaborating on these limitations follow below:

Art. 4, which requires national treatment for performers, states:

Each Contracting State shall grant national treatment to performers if any of the following conditions is met: (a) the performance takes place in another Contracting State; (b) the performance is incorporated in a phonogram which is protected under Article 5 of this Convention; and (c) the performance, not being fixed on a phonogram, is carried by a broadcast which is protected under Article 6 of this Convention.

Art. 5(1), which requires national treatment for phonograph producers, states:

Each Contracting State shall grant national treatment to producers of phonograms if any of the following conditions is met: (a) the producer of the phonogram is a national of another Contracting State (criterion of nationality); (b) the first fixation of the sound was made in another Contracting State (criterion of fixation); (c) the phonogram was first published in another Contracting State (criterion of publication).

Art. 6(1), which requires national treatment for broadcasting organization, states:

Each Contracting State shall grant national treatment to broadcasting organizations if either of the following conditions is met: (a) the headquarters of the broadcasting organization is situated in another Contracting State; (b) the broadcast was transmitted from a transmitter situated in another Contracting State.

One question which arises is whether violation of the national treatment provisions of any of these agreements could be subject to WTO dispute settlement. In *US–Section 211 Appropriations Act*, the AB answered the question in the affirmative, at least with respect to the Paris Convention (§ 238).

> "by virtue of Article 2.1 of the TRIPS Agreement, Article 2(1) of the Paris Convention (1967), as well as certain other specified provisions of the Paris Convention (1967), have been incorporated into the TRIPS Agreement and, thus, the WTO Agreement. Consequently, these obligations of countries of the Paris Union under the Paris Convention (1967) are also now obligations of all WTO Members, whether are countries of the Paris Union or not, under the WTO Agreement, and thus, are enforceable under the DSU."

One should note that the national treatment language of Art. 3.1 TRIPS differs slightly from the national treatment language of the Paris Convention and the IPIC Treaty. Art. 3.1 TRIPS uses the "treatment no less favorable" formulation also used in the GATT and the GATS. In theory, at least, a WTO Member could provide less favorable treatment to its nationals than to foreigners and still be in compliance with Art. 3.1 TRIPS. By contrast, Art. 2(1) of the Paris Convention requires that parties provide "the *same* treatment . . . and the *same* legal remedy." Art. 5(1) of the IPIC Treaty also requires that a signatory provide "the *same* treatment that it accords its own nationals." So far, this tension between the national treatment language in TRIPS and that in the Paris Convention and the IPIC Treaty has not been resolved through any dispute settlement case. However, it was noted by the Panel in *US–Section 211 Appropriations Act*, which then proceeded to punt on the issue. It simply stated (§ 8.126 fn. 140):

> "We do not purport to determine whether the expression 'treatment no less favourable' means 'the same protection . . . and the same legal remedy.' However, given the common objective of according non-discriminatory treatment to foreign nationals in respect of protection of intellectual property, a finding of inconsistency under Article 3.1 could also lead to the same finding under Article 2.1 of the TRIPS Agreement in conjunction with Article 2(1) of the Paris Convention (1967)."

The odds that a future Panel would act to resolve this discrepancy in language are small. Essentially, it would require the Panel to face a dispute where a WTO Member highlights this issue on behalf of another Member's domestic constituency, at the expense of its own nationals, who are being advantaged. It is difficult, if not impossible, to fathom why any WTO Member would do so. Nevertheless, it is worth highlighting that a tension does exist, in theory, between the national treatment formulation of TRIPS and that of the international IP agreements which it incorporates.

5.3.2 Relationship to the GATT

A second question concerns the relationship of Art. 3.1 TRIPS with Article III:4 GATT concerning national treatment for goods. The Panel, in *US–Section 211 Appropriations Act*, remarked that a "major difference between the national treatment principle as set forth in Article 3.1 of the TRIPS Agreement and Article III:4 of the GATT 1994 is that the national treatment attaches to the intellectual property right holder under Article 3.1 whereas it attaches to the goods under Article III:4." Despite this difference, however, the Panel (§ 8.129) opined that "[i]n construing Article 3.1 of the TRIPS Agreement, Article III:4 can serve as a useful context."

The AB then confirmed the validity of this approach (§ 242). It declared that "the jurisprudence of Article III:4 of the GATT 1994 may be useful in interpreting the national treatment obligation in the TRIPS Agreement." Therefore, while the national treatment right attaches differently, one should not consider Art. 3.1 TRIPS in isolation, but rather in context with Art. III:4 GATT.

5.3.3 Conditional Reciprocity

A third question is whether Art. 3.1 TRIPS permits WTO Members to make national treatment conditional. Can Country A attach a condition that it will grant IP rights to nationals of Country B only if Country B reciprocates by granting such rights to nationals of Country A? The essence of the national treatment principle is that this answer should be no. However, we have already hinted at several instances where exceptions are granted within the TRIPS Agreement to allow for conditional reciprocity.

Some of these exceptions are clearly spelled out in the language of the TRIPS Agreement itself. For example, on the rights accorded to performers, phonograph producers, and broadcasting organizations, Art. 3.1 TRIPS clearly limits the extension of national treatment to those rights delineated in the TRIPS Agreement itself, in Art. 14 TRIPS. For other non-TRIPS-delineated IP rights, a WTO Member may legally attach a condition that the rights holder be a national of a WTO Member that is party to the Rome Convention.

Thus, the EU (which is a member of the Rome Convention) may not accord more extensive IP protection to its own performers over American, Japanese, or Indian performers when it comes to the broadcast of a live performance, because this right is clearly spelled out in Art. 14.1 TRIPS. However, it may accord advantages to its own broadcasters over American broadcasters for any right not spelled out in Art. 14.2 TRIPS because the U.S. is not a party to the Rome Convention. It may not, however, accord similar advantages to its own broadcasters over Japanese or Indian broadcasters, because both Japan and India are also parties to the Rome Convention. To do so would violate the Rome Convention. By extension, it would then also violate Art. 2.2 TRIPS which states that nothing in TRIPS may derogate from existing obligations that members may have to each other under the Rome Convention.

Not all of the exceptions permitting conditional reciprocity are spelled out so clearly in the text of the TRIPS Agreement itself. Consider the issue of copyright term. Art. 12 TRIPS sets forth a minimum term that all WTO Members are required to provide. However, some WTO Members provide for terms beyond this minimum. Is such a WTO Member required to allow all foreign nationals to receive this extended copyright term? Must it provide full national treatment? The answer is no. Recall that Art. 3.1 TRIPS is subject to the exceptions as provided in the Paris, Berne, and Rome Conventions, as well as the IPIC Treaty. Art. 7(8) of the Berne Convention serves as an exception to the national treatment rule for copyright term. It states that "unless the legislation of that country otherwise provides, the term shall not exceed the term fixed in the country of origin of the work." As a result, the WTO Member may attach a reciprocity condition for the provision of copyright term beyond the minimum set forth in Art. 12 TRIPS.

Therefore, in analyzing whether conditional reciprocity is permitted, one needs to look not only at the text of the TRIPS Agreement itself, but also the text of the Paris, Berne, and Rome Conventions as well as the IPIC Treaty. Only if an exception is not provided for in any of these agreements does the principle of unconditional national treatment apply.

The cases where the issue of conditional reciprocity has surfaced most clearly are the two *EC–Trademark and Geographical Indications* disputes. These were challenges brought by the US (DS174) and Australia (DS 290) to the EC regulation for the protection of geographical indications (GIs) for agricultural products and foodstuffs. This was done through Council Regulation (EEC) No. 2801/92 and its subsequent amendments. Article 12(1) of the Regulation contained conditional language stating:

> "Without prejudice to international agreements, this Regulation may apply to an agricultural product or foodstuff from a third country provided that:
>
> — the third country is able to give guarantees identical or equivalent to those referred to in Article 4,
>
> — the third country concerned has inspection arrangements and a right to objection equivalent to those laid down in this Regulation,

— the third country concerned is prepared to provide protection equivalent to that available in the Community to corresponding agricultural products or foodstuffs coming from the Community."

Article 12(3) of the Regulation further spelled out that the European Commission would examine, at the request of the country concerned, whether a third country satisfies the equivalence conditions and offers guarantees within the meaning of Article 12(1), and only where its finding was in the affirmative would GI protection be granted.

The Panel first tackled the question of whether the conditions laid out in Article 12 did, in fact, apply to WTO Members.[14] After finding that they did (DS174 § 7.102; DS290 § 7.152), the Panels in both cases ruled this conditionality to be impermissible and in violation of the national treatment obligations of Art. 3.1 TRIPS. The Panel in the US report noted (§§ 7.139–140):

> "The Panel considers that those conditions modify the effective equality of opportunities to obtain protection with respect to intellectual property in two ways. First, GI protection is not available under the Regulation in respect of geographical areas located in third countries which the Commission has not recognized under Article 12(3). The European Communities confirms that the Commission has not recognized any third countries. Second, GI protection under the Regulation may become available if the third country in which the GI is located enters into an international agreement or satisfies the conditions in Article 12(1). Both of those requirements represent a significant 'extra hurdle' in obtaining GI protection that does not apply to geographical areas located in the European Communities. The significance of the hurdle is reflected in the fact that currently no third country has entered into such an agreement or satisfied those conditions.
>
> Accordingly, the Panel finds that the equivalence and reciprocity conditions modify the effective equality of opportunities with respect to the availability of protection to persons who wish to obtain GI protection under the Regulation, to the detriment of those who wish to obtain protection in respect of geographical areas located in third countries, including WTO Members. This is less favourable treatment."

Outside of the exceptions permitted under Art. 3.1 TRIPS, including those within the cross-referenced WIPO conventions, conditional reciprocity for IP protection is clearly not allowed.

---

[14] The European Community noted that Article 12(1) included the opening qualifier "without prejudice to international agreements" and that the phrase "international agreements" extended to the WTO agreements. Therefore, it argued that Article 12(1) of the EC Regulation did not apply to WTO Members, but only to third parties. (DS174 § 7.41–43; DS290 § 7.89–94). This argument was rejected.

5.3.4 *De Jure* vs. *De Facto* Discrimination

Violation of the national treatment obligation of Art. 3.1 TRIPS can take one of two forms: *de jure* discrimination and *de facto* discrimination. In *Canada–Patent Protection of Pharmaceutical Products*, the Panel (§ 7.94) explicitly highlighted this difference:

> "Discrimination may arise from explicitly different treatment, sometimes called '*de jure* discrimination', but it may also arise from ostensibly identical treatment which, due to differences in circumstances, produces differentially disadvantageous effects, sometimes called '*de facto* discrimination'."

With respect to *de jure* discrimination, the AB appears to suggest that very little leeway will be given for IP laws, governed by the TRIPS Agreement, which explicitly differentiate in their treatment of domestic and foreign nationals. In *US–Section 211 Appropriations Act*, the Panel and AB considered the legality of the *de jure* discrimination found in Section 211(a) of the US Omnibus Appropriations Act of 1998. That section required foreign nationals who are successors-in-interest to go through an additional proceeding on top of the OFAC licensing procedures that both U.S. and foreign nationals are required to go through. In other words, foreign nationals faced two proceedings, whereas US nationals faced only one. The US argued that the likelihood of a foreign national having to overcome both hurdles was small (§ 265), and that US nationals, despite facing only one proceeding, were subject similarly to a court-imposed doctrinal limitation (§ 257). Both the Panel and the AB rejected this argument. The AB concluded that "even the *possibility*" of a foreign national having to face an additional hurdle renders the law "*inherently less favourable*" (§ 265). With this declaration, it is highly unlikely that any *de jure* discriminatory law would be able to survive a national treatment challenge.

With respect to *de facto* discrimination, however, the situation is different. In *Canada–Patent Protection of Pharmaceutical Products*, the Panel (§ 7.104) suggested that *de facto* discrimination consists of two elements:

> One is the question of *de facto* discriminatory effect—whether the actual effect of the measure is to impose differentially disadvantageous consequences on certain parties. The other, related to the justification for the disadvantageous effects, is the issue of purpose—not an inquiry into the subjective purposes of the officials responsible for the measure, but an inquiry into the objective characteristics of the measure from which one can infer the existence or non-existence of discriminatory objectives.

The use of this approach can be seen in the two *EC–Trademark and Geographical Indications* disputes. The Panel in those cases noted that the EC Regulation being challenged, on its face, contained "formally identical provisions vis-à-vis the nationals of different Members, with respect to the availability of GI protection." (DS 174 § 7.172; DS 290 § 7.206). Nevertheless, it drew on a series of GATT national treatment cases, including *US–Section 337*and *Korea–Various Measures on Beef*, to declare that it would evaluate whether *de facto* discrimination existed on the basis of an "effective equality of opportunities" standard. The Panel further declared that it would focus on the "fundamental thrust and effect" of the Regulation (DS 174 § 7.176; DS 290 § 7.210). On the basis of this examination, the Panel found that the EC Regulation did, in effect, discriminate between European and foreign nationals in its protection of geographical indications, in violation of Art. 3.4 TRIPS.

6. MOST FAVORED NATION (MFN) TREATMENT

6.1 THE LEGAL DISCIPLINE

Art. 4 TRIPS requires that with regard to the protection of intellectual property, a WTO Member shall accord MFN treatment to the nationals of all WTO Members for "any advantage, favour, privilege, or immunity" accorded to the national of *any other country*. However, there are four exemptions to the MFN principle for "any advantage, favour, privilege, or immunity" accorded by a WTO Member deriving from: (1) international agreements on judicial assistance or law enforcement of a general nature; (2) rights granted under the Berne Convention (1971) or Rome Convention provisions based on the treatment accorded in another country; (3) rights of performers, phonograph producers, and broadcasting organizations not provided under the TRIPS Agreement; and (4) rights deriving from pre-TRIPS international agreements on IP.

6.2 THE RATIONALE FOR THE LEGAL DISCIPLINE

The rationale for MFN obligation in TRIPS is similar to that of the GATT and GATS. It acts as a guard against *concession erosion*. Without the MFN provision, negotiators would fear that the value of their current concessions might erode with time as their counterparts make further concessions to other trading partners in subsequent negotiations. The MFN obligation ensures against that possibility.

One other rationale for inclusion of the MFN obligation is to ensure consistency across the different agreements concluded in the Uruguay Round. The principle of MFN is viewed as one of the fundamental blocks of the international trade regime. If regulation of international IP rights was to be included as part of the regime, it was important for the principle to be embedded within the TRIPS Agreement.

6.3 COVERAGE OF THE LEGAL DISCIPLINE

6.3.1 General Remarks

Art. 4 TRIPS represents the first time that the MFN obligation has been included in a multilateral international IP agreement. Previously, the MFN obligation had appeared only in bilateral IP agreements. The MFN principle is nowhere to be found in the Paris, Berne, or Rome Conventions or the IPIC Treaty cross-referenced by the TRIPS Agreement. This is because negotiators thought it was unlikely that a country would grant more favorable treatment to foreign nationals over its own nationals. Therefore, historically, they have emphasized the national treatment obligation as a way of ensuring that their nationals received the most favorable treatment. However, events in the early 1990s raised the possibility that a country might be willing to grant more favorable treatment to foreign nationals than its own nationals. As a result, negotiators thought it was important to include the MFN obligation as part of the TRIPS Agreement.[15]

Note that the language of Art. 4 TRIPS applies the MFN principle in relation to benefits accorded to nationals of any other country, regardless of whether or not that country is a WTO Member. This ensures that nationals of WTO Members be granted the best possible treatment accorded to foreign nationals. Hence, a WTO Member may not grant more favorable concessions to nationals of a non-WTO Member without extending such concessions to nationals of all WTO Members as well.

Also, note that because of Art. 1.2 TRIPS, the MFN obligation (as well as the national treatment obligation) attaches only to the privileges and immunities with respect to the IP rights that are covered in the TRIPS Agreement (i.e., those covered under Sections 1 through 7 of Part II of TRIPS). This means that any additional "new" IP-related rights created outside of the TRIPS framework—for example, requirements for domain name protection enshrined within a preferential trade agreement between WTO Members—do not fall under the purview of the MFN obligation. However, the MFN obligation does extend to higher protection of TRIPS-covered IP rights (*e.g.*, an extension of copyright or patent term) resulting from a preferential trade agreement.

The importance of the MFN principle was underscored by the AB in *US–Section 211 Appropriations Act* (§ 297):

> Like the national treatment obligation, the obligation to provide most-favoured-nation treatment has long been one of the cornerstones of the world trading system. For more than fifty years, the obligation to provide most-favoured-nation treatment in Article I of the GATT 1994 has been both central and essential to assur-

---

[15] On this score, see Sell (1998); Abbott et al. (2007).

ing the success of a global rules-based system for trade in goods. Unlike the national treatment principle, there is no provision in the Paris Convention (1967) that establishes a most-favoured-nation obligation with respect to rights in trademarks or other industrial property. However, the framers of the TRIPS Agreement decided to extend the most-favoured nation obligation to the protection of intellectual property rights covered by that Agreement. As a cornerstone of the world trading system, the most-favoured-nation obligation must be accorded the same significance with respect to intellectual property rights under the TRIPS Agreement that it has long been accorded with respect to trade in goods under the GATT. It is, in a word, fundamental.

6.3.2 Exceptions to the MFN Principle

Four exceptions exist with respect to the MFN principle of Art. 4 TRIPS. Below, we discuss each in greater depth.

First, a carve-out is made in Art. 4(a) TRIPS with respect to "international agreements on judicial assistance or law enforcement of a general nature and not particularly concerned to the protection of intellectual property." Thus, even if such an agreement has bearing on the enforcement of IP rights, MFN treatment need not be extended so long as the agreement is of a general nature. The main significance of this provision is its implication for transnational prosecution of IP crimes and cross-border issues in civil IP cases. Certain countries have signed bilateral agreements for law enforcement cooperation and judicial assistance. Art. 4(a) TRIPS ensures that obligations extended under such agreements to certain countries, for example, with respect to cross-border cooperation on the provision of evidence or on extradition, need not be extended to all other WTO Members.

Second, Art. 4(b) TRIPS creates an exception for benefits "granted in accordance with the provisions of the Berne Convention (1971) or the Rome Convention authorizing that the treatment accorded be a function not of national treatment but of the treatment accorded in another country." One example of where this exception applies is Art. 7(8) of the Berne Convention, discussed earlier in the national treatment discussion. Recall that Art. 7(8) permits a party to the Berne Convention to shorten the term of protection for a foreign national to a period equal in length to the term of protection in its own country. Thus, protection need not be extended on MFN terms. Art. 3(b) TRIPS also validates the less-than-MFN terms of Art. 2(7) of the Berne Convention concerning the protection of works of applied art and industrial designs and models and of Art. 14*ter* concerning the *droit de suite*, or the inalienable right to an interest in any sale of a work of art or manuscript subsequent to the first transfer by the author of the work. It also permits the less-than-MFN terms associated with rights granted under the Rome Convention which are not discussed in the TRIPS Agreement.

Third, Art. 4(c) TRIPS allows an exception "in respect of the rights of performers, producers of phonograms and broadcasting organizations not provided under this Agreement." This provision permits WTO Members that are parties to the Rome Convention to not extend MFN treatment of rights granted under the Rome Convention to WTO Members that are not parties to the Rome Convention, outside of the rights specifically mentioned in Art. 14 TRIPS. The same also holds true with respect to rights granted under the WIPO Performances and Phonograms Treaty not mentioned in TRIPS.

Finally, the exception permitted in Art. 4(d) TRIPS is perhaps the most far-reaching of the four. It exempts any advantage, favor, privilege, or immunity "deriving from international agreements related to the protection of intellectual property which entered into force prior to the entry into force of the WTO Agreement." However, such agreements must be notified to the TRIPS Council, and the pre-existing IP agreement may not "constitute an arbitrary or unjustifiable discrimination against nationals of other Members."

Essentially, this provision permits the continuance of regional IP arrangements which existed prior to TRIPS. Examples include the EU, the Andean Community, NAFTA, and MERCOSUR, all of which have made notifications to the TRIPS Council. Art. 4(d) TRIPS permits WTO Members that are parties to such an arrangement to continue to engage in differentiated treatment on IP matters for nationals of other parties to the arrangement, without having to accord MFN treatment to nationals of parties not subject to the arrangement. Note that with respect to both the EU and MERCOSUR, the TRIPS Council notification also explicitly grandfathers any *future* IP integration measure from the MFN obligations of Art. 4 TRIPS.[16]

7. EXHAUSTION

Exhaustion refers to the principle of when a product is placed on a market such that the owner of the IP no longer has rights of distribution over it. Once exhaustion occurs, the product may be re-sold without the IP right-holder's permission. As will be discussed below, countries have applied the principle of exhaustion differently.

7.1 THE LEGAL DISCIPLINE

Art. 6 TRIPS explicitly states that for the purposes of dispute settlement, subject to the national treatment and MFN provisions of the TRIPS

---

[16] See WTO Doc. IP/N/4/EEC/1 of 29 January 1996. See also WTO Docs. IP/N/4/ARG/1, IP/N/4/BRA/1, IP/N/4/PRY/1, IP/N/4/URY/1, all of 14 July 1998.

Agreement, nothing in the Agreement shall limit the discretion of WTO Members to regulate the international exhaustion of IP rights.

7.2 RATIONALE FOR THE LEGAL DISCIPLINE

Because different countries apply the exhaustion principle differently, this issue was one of the more contentious points of the TRIPS Agreement negotiations.[17] Art. 6 TRIPS reflects a compromise reached which agreed that the TRIPS Agreement would not allow for this matter to be discussed or settled through WTO litigation.

7.3 COVERAGE OF THE LEGAL DISCIPLINE

There are endless variations of exhaustion regimes. For the sake of simplicity, we will describe three ideal types: (1) national exhaustion; (2) international exhaustion; or (3) regional exhaustion. Note that in reality, the exhaustion regimes of some WTO Members reflect a combination of these ideal types. All three ideal types, as well as their variants, are permissible under the TRIPS Agreement, so long as they abide by the national treatment and MFN obligations.

National exhaustion refers to the principle that the distribution right is said to be exhausted only when a product is offered for sale on the market on the territory of a given country with the consent of the IP right-holder. To illustrate national exhaustion, consider a scenario where a right-holder has released a product for sale in Country A but not Country B. If Country B abides by national exhaustion, then the product cannot be imported into Country B from Country A. The distribution right for the good has not been exhausted. Among the countries that abide by national exhaustion principle are the US, Morocco, and Honduras.

The main rationale for national exhaustion is that it allows a right-holder to differentiate by price across different markets. Supporters of national exhaustion make two arguments in its favor. First, they contend that it better fosters innovation. By allowing the innovator more flexibility in how to time entry and set prices across markets, the policy grants the innovator greater control over how it recovers the costs of innovation and seeks profits across markets. Second, they contend that it encourages IP right-holders to provide greater access to products in less developed countries at more affordable prices. Without national exhaustion, an IP right-holder may fear that the release of a product in a less developed country at a cheaper price would flood back to the developed country's market through parallel importation. Based on this fear, the right-holder would price the product at the same price in the developing country to stifle the parallel importation risk. This would increase cost and reduce access in the developing country.

---

[17] On this score, see Gervais (2008).

By contrast, international exhaustion refers to the principle that the distribution right is said to be exhausted when a product is offered for sale on the market on the territory of any country with the consent of the IP right-holder. Returning to our earlier example, if Country B abides by international exhaustion, then the distribution right of the owner has exhausted once the product is offered for sale in Country A. The product can be legally imported into Country B from Country A. Among the WTO Members that practice international exhaustion are India, Hong Kong, Chile, Argentina, South Africa, and Singapore.

Supporters of international exhaustion argue that it fosters the benefit of open markets because it prevents a IP right-holder from segmenting markets. As a result, once a product is offered for sale legitimately anywhere, it can be imported into a market. This forces the IP right-holder to set price across the global market, rather than seeking to extract greater rents through price differentiation across markets. Supporters contend that such an approach enhances consumer welfare, through lower prices and increased consumer choice.

A third approach is that of regional exhaustion. Countries that have entered into regional arrangements may rely on this approach. Essentially, it treats all the markets of the regional entity as a single market for the purposes of exhaustion. Once a product has been offered for sale legitimately in any of the markets of a country belonging to the regional entity, the distribution right is said to be exhausted. Returning to our example, if Country A and Country B had a regional trade arrangement and Country B abided by regional exhaustion, then the first sale in Country A exhausts the distribution right in Country B. However, if Country A fell outside of its regional trade arrangement, then the first sale in Country A would not exhaust the distribution right.

Note that the flexibility contained in Art. 6 TRIPS is subject to certain limitations based on other provisions in the TRIPS Agreement. The most important are the two already discussed in this Chapter: the national treatment obligation of Art. 3 TRIPS and the MFN obligation of Art. 4 TRIPS. A country must apply the same principle of exhaustion for its own nationals and foreign nationals. It also cannot apply different exhaustion rules vis-à-vis different WTO members.

However, a WTO Member is allowed to apply different exhaustion rules for different forms of IP. Therefore, a WTO Member may decide to apply national exhaustion to patents but international exhaustion for trademarks and copyright.

8. INSTITUTIONAL ARRANGEMENTS

Art. 68 TRIPS mandated the creation of the Council for Trade-Related Aspects of Intellectual Property Rights, commonly referred to as the TRIPS Council. Its duties as charged are as follows:

> The Council for TRIPS shall monitor the operation of this Agreement and, in particular, Members' Compliance with their obligations hereunder, and shall afford Members the opportunity of consulting on matters relating to the trade-related aspects of intellectual property rights. It shall carry out other such responsibilities as assigned to it by the Members, and it shall, in particular, provide any assistance requested by them in the context of dispute settlement procedures.

Specifically, the TRIPS Council monitors and reviews the IP laws and regulations of all WTO members. Art. 63.2 TRIPS requires WTO Members to notify all new IP laws and regulations to the TRIPS Council as well as subsequent amendments. In addition, Art. 63.1 TRIPS requires that WTO Members make available "final judicial decisions and administrative rulings of general application . . . pertaining to the subject matter of this Agreement (the availability, scope, acquisition, enforcement and prevention of the abuse of intellectual property rights)."

Membership on the TRIPS Council is open to the representatives of all WTO Members. In addition, certain international organizations are granted regular observer status within the Council. Along with WIPO, these include the Food and Agriculture Organization (FAO), the International Monetary Fund (IMF), the International Union for the Protection of New Varieties of Plants (UPOV), the Joint UN Programme on HIV/AIDS (UNAIDS), the Organization for Economic Cooperation and Development (OECD), the United Nations, the United Nations Conference on Trade and Development (UNCTAD), the World Bank, and the World Customs Organization (WCO). In addition, the World Health Organization (WHO) is granted ad hoc observer status, as is the African Regional Industrial Property Organization (ARIPO) and the African Intellectual Property Organization (OAPI) on a meeting-by-meeting basis.

As part of its work, the TRIPS Council engages in regular review of the IP laws, regulations, judicial decisions, and administrative rulings of WTO Members. During the review process, members may submit questions to the WTO Member under review. These range from requests for additional information to clarifications concerning laws, regulations, judicial decisions, and/or administrative rulings. The WTO Member under review must then provide written answers to these questions, which are made publicly available through the WTO website. This process provides WTO Members with a mechanism to monitor compliance with the TRIPS

Agreement of other Members as well as a forum to discuss any emerging concerns.

In addition, the TRIPS Council may also be called upon as a forum to discuss any issues that arise under the TRIPS Agreement. This direction is embedded within the language of Art. 68 TRIPS, which directs the Council to monitor the *operation* of the Agreement. In June 2010, for example, the TRIPS Council undertook a special review of the system implementing Paragraph Six of the Doha Declaration on TRIPS and Public Health, a topic mentioned in passing above and which will be discussed *infra*. The Doha Declaration also formally established the Special Session of the TRIPS Council as a negotiating body charged with negotiations for a multilateral system for notification and registration for geographical indications for wines and spirits.[18] In addition, the TRIPS Council has also issued important decisions on the extension of the transition periods for implementing TRIPS obligations for least-developed countries[19] and on technology transfer.[20] The former is pursuant to a mandate given to the Council in Art. 66.1 TRIPS.

In recent years, the Council has met three times a year—in March, June, and October. Each year, it publishes an Annual Report, which details any notifications made under the provisions of the TRIPS Agreement, any reviews made by the Council of national laws and regulations, and any items for review on the TRIPS Council agenda. Examples of items under recent review include (a) the relationship between the TRIPS Agreement and the Convention on Biological Diversity; and the protection of traditional knowledge and folklore; (b) the application of provisions on the section on geographical indications; and (c) technical cooperation.[21] In addition, as of March 2010, the Council also agreed to keep as a regular agenda item a discussion of non-violation and situation complaints.

QUESTIONS AND COMMENTS

Intellectual Property Rights and Development: Economists have tried to measure the relationship between intellectual property rights and economic development. Fink and Maskus (2005) have been among the leaders of this effort. The evidence is mixed, and it is difficult to discern what is driving what. Moreover, it becomes difficult to discern whether other policies or factor endowments are necessary pre-conditions for IP policy to have a positive impact. To what extent should we be concerned about the TRIPS Agreement having a positive normative basis for development?

---

[18] On this score, see, for example, WTO Doc. TN/IP/M/25 of 31 May 2010 and WTO Doc. TN/IP/M/26 of 20 October 2010.

[19] *See* WTO Doc. IP/C/40 of 30 November 2005 and WTO Doc. IP/C/25 of 1 July 2002.

[20] *See* WTO Doc. IP/C/28 of 20 February 2003.

[21] *See* WTO Doc. IP/C/56 of 10 November 2010.

Critical Legal Theories of TRIPS: Chang (2002) has suggested that the TRIPS Agreement is an attempt by powerful industrialized countries to "kick away the ladder." Essentially his argument is that most industrialized countries have, at one stage or another, engaged in policies, including those involving the borrowing of intellectual property, to advance their economy. Now that they have succeeded, they are using legal instruments, such as the TRIPS Agreement, to prevent developing countries from using the same strategies that they once employed. What do you think of this description?

Unexpected Outcomes: Brewster (2011) contends that regardless of one's overall normative take on the TRIPS Agreement, the Agreement contains surprising benefits for certain developing countries. These include the fact that it provides some smaller developing countries with means to retaliate against larger countries with whom such countries would hold normally little leverage. For example, Antigua has threatened to not observe certain IP rights with respect to American copyright producers in the US–Gambling case.

It's All Local and Yet Global: Kapczynksi (2009) has demonstrated how efforts to harmonize IP standards have triggered a backlash in the domestic political economy of certain countries, such as India. While we may think of these as local movements, they are also part of a larger transnational movement. The same may be true of the recent efforts to rollback IP protection in the US and EU. While the efforts to stop ACTA in the EU were certainly locally-led, they were also fuelled in part by trans-national NGOs and inspired by the success of the anti-PIPA/SOPA movement in the U.S. Is the fight over international IP essentially a struggle between competing ideological camps that is being replayed in various jurisdictions?

"Locking In" Levels of Protection: Should efforts such as ACTA be thought of as efforts by pro-IP industries to "lock in" a certain standard of protection through treaty law? In essence, the relevant question is whether the presence of a treaty will make it harder for a future legislature to undo a certain level of IP protection because they would not want to have their actions violate the country's treaty obligations. Do you think this question matters in the minds of most legislators?

Institutional Arrangements: To what extent should the advent of the TRIPS Agreement be considered a reflection of the failed governance arrangements of other prior institutions, such as the World Intellectual Property Organization? If you believe this to be the case, then what role, if any, do you think these institutions, which continue to operate without major governance reform, should play in the governance of international intellectual property rights?

Multilateral versus Bilateral Negotiation of IP Rights: Industrialized countries, and in particular, the US, have recognized the difficulty of advancing any additional protection for IP rights in the WTO and are moving increasingly to plurilateral trade negotiations to secure TRIPS-plus provisions. Yet, because of the absence of a PTA exception to the MFN rule in

TRIPS, the nature of these bilateral negotiations is very different in the IP context than in the case of goods and/or services. Essentially, a concession given to the US will need to be given to all other countries. This opens the door to accusations of "free riding" against certain countries that may be using WTO Members that are more active in PTA negotiations to obtain positive concessions for its IP-dependent industries. It also increases the stake of the IP negotiations in PTAs for countries that are being asked to raise their standards to TRIPS-plus+ levels.

CHAPTER 28

COPYRIGHT

■ ■ ■

1. THE LEGAL DISCIPLINE

The TRIPS Agreement draws much of the Berne Convention for the Protection of Literary and Artistic Works (1971) into the WTO dispute settlement regime, with the exception of moral rights. For certain subject matter (*e.g.*, computer programs, database compilations), it also clarified the conditions under which such works should be afforded IP protection. It also confers rental rights for computer programs and cinematographic works, under certain conditions. TRIPS marks the first time that rental rights are explicitly conferred in an international agreement. Moreover, it clarified the term of protection for works not associated with a natural person (*e.g.*, a work by a corporation). Finally, TRIPS clarifies the conditions under which exceptions and limitations may be placed on copyright, author's rights, and neighboring rights.

2. THE RATIONALE FOR THE LEGAL DISCIPLINE

Norms for the international copyright regime have existed since the drafting of the initial Berne Convention in 1886 and have been amended on several occasions since then. However, the Berne Convention has lacked a mechanism for interpretation and enforcement. Negotiators wanted to give greater teeth to enforcing the Berne Convention (1971) by drawing it into the WTO dispute settlement regime. At the same time, developed countries had major differences in how they chose to afford protection to different categories of works. This was especially true with respect to the subject matter covered by the Rome Convention. The TRIPS provisions therefore reflect a compromise, in part, between common law and civil law countries, leaving flexibility in many instances for each WTO Member to implement the regime that it saw fit.

The provisions also reflect the desire of certain developed countries to preserve their existing regime in certain areas. For example, Japan sought to preserve its equitable remuneration system for producers of phonograms, while the US sought to ensure that the fair use doctrine of its copyright law would not be undermined by TRIPS. The provisions also reflect a desire to clarify the applicable scope of protection in certain contexts. One area, for example, is the protection to be accorded to works not associated with a natural person in civil law countries. Finally, the provisions seek to standardize the rules for creating exceptions and limitations for protection, and therefore, create a means to challenge national legislation enacting such exceptions and limitations.

3. COVERAGE OF THE LEGAL DISCIPLINE

3.1 PRELIMINARY REMARKS

Two major legal traditions exist for protecting literary and artistic works. One is the tradition of copyright, associated primarily with common law countries such as the US, UK, Australia, Canada, India, and other members of the British Commonwealth. The other is the tradition of author's right and neighboring rights, associated primarily with civil law countries such as those in continental Europe and Latin America.

The two traditions have different philosophical underpinnings.[1] The copyright tradition is based on a utilitarian philosophical outlook, in which protection for a given creative work is extended if it will stimulate further production of creative works. Benefits and costs figure heavily into the trade-off analysis to be undertaken by authorities in deciding the proper balance of copyright protection. In contrast, the author's right and neighboring rights tradition is based on a philosophy of natural rights. According to this tradition, individual authors are entitled, as a right and as a matter of justice, to protection for their creative works. Authorities intervene only when necessary in order to prevent socially-harmful outcomes.

Despite stemming from different philosophical traditions, the differences between the two regimes are not as extreme as one might believe. Ginsburg (1990) and others have shown that the actual underpinnings of different countries' laws are mixed; copyright laws reflect some natural rights principles, while author's right and neighboring rights laws also reflect some utilitarian principles. An important reason for the narrowing of differences between the laws of the two different traditions is the Berne Convention, which dates back to 1886. The Berne Convention decreed a set of minimum substantive rules, forcing the laws of the different traditions to converge on certain international norms.

Still some differences do persist. One is in the accordance of rights to performers, phonograph producers, and broadcasters. In the US and other common law countries, this is done through copyright. However, in civil law countries, this is done through the doctrine of neighboring rights. The Rome Convention serves as the pre-TRIPS international agreement on this matter. Its parties include many major civil law countries, as well as a few common law countries, such as the UK, that effectively provide similar protection as mandated by the Rome Convention through copyright.

---

[1] For a short, but insightful, view on this score, see Goldstein and Hugenholtz (2010).

The US, notably, is not a signatory. Works protected as neighboring rights under the Rome Convention enjoy shorter terms of protection and scope of rights, but as Goldstein and Hugenholtz (2010) points out, in most instances, this difference is symbolic rather than of economic consequence.

The Uruguay Round negotiations on copyright should be understood within this context. First, most developed countries, which were (and still remain) the primary creators of literary and artistic works seeking IP protection, shared a common interest in enhancing the enforcement mechanism for the Berne Convention regime. On this front, they largely succeeded by bringing the bulk of the Berne Convention provisions into the realm of the WTO's dispute settlement regime. Second, countries sought greater clarification on some subject matter issues. In a few of these areas, they successfully managed to achieve convergence, but in many areas they did not. Third, in many areas, countries simply sought to maintain the flexibility to continue with their pre-existing regime. The exact wording of the provisions contained in Arts. 9–14 TRIPS reflects these competing negotiating interests, which were decided primarily among developed countries themselves in the Uruguay Round.

3.2 RELATIONSHIP TO THE BERNE CONVENTION

A major achievement of the TRIPS Agreement was the fact that it brought much of the Berne Convention (1971) under the dispute settlement mechanism established through the Uruguay Round. Previously, countries had few means to enforce compliance with Berne Convention obligations. Art. 9.1 TRIPS clarified that with respect to Arts. 1–21 of the Berne Convention (1971) as well as the 1971 Appendix to the Convention.

An important exception to this incorporation into the dispute settlement regime is Art. 6*bis* of the Berne Convention, which concerns moral rights. In many countries, an author's rights consist of a set of economic rights and a set of moral rights. Even after the economic rights are transferred, the moral rights of a work remain with the author. The moral rights discussed in Art. 6*bis* of the Berne Convention include the right to claim authorship of the work and to object to any distortion, mutilation, or modification of the work. The desire to exclude moral rights from TRIPS came largely at the insistence of the US, which argued that such rights were not trade-related. However, the US, more practically, likely was also concerned that its implementation of the Berne Convention may not have been in full compliance with art. 6*bis* of Berne, and did not want the issue to be subject to dispute settlement.

3.3 SCOPE OF COVERAGE

Art. 2 of the Berne Convention contains a non-exhaustive list of categories of works that are to be accorded protection.

"The expression 'literary and artistic works' shall include every production in the literary, scientific, and artistic domain, whatever may be the mode or form of its expression such as books, pamphlets or other writings; lectures, addresses, sermons and other works of the same nature; dramatic or dramatico-musical works; choreographic works and entertainment in dumb show; musical compositions with or without words; cinematographic works to which are assimilated works expressed by a process analogous to cinematography; works of drawing, painting, architecture, sculpture, engraving and lithography; photographic works to which are assimilated works expressed by a process analogous to photography; works of applied art; illustrations, maps, plans, sketches and three-dimensional works relative to geography, topography, architecture or science."

This provision is incorporated into the TRIPS Agreement, by way of Art. 9.1 TRIPS. Hence, negotiators did not think it necessary to delineate a list of categories of protected works in the Agreement.

What is interesting is that, instead, negotiators chose to state clearly what may not be protected. Art. 9.2 TRIPS represents the first time that an international agreement states clearly what falls outside of scope of copyright. It declares: "Copyright protection shall extend to expressions and not to ideas, procedures, methods of operation or mathematical concepts as such." This notion of establishing an ideas / expression dichotomy draws inspiration from US copyright law. The notion of excluding methods of operation and mathematical concepts first surfaced in a Japanese proposal concerning copyright protection for computer program works, but its scope was later extended during the negotiations to apply generally.[2]

Art. 10.1 TRIPS establishes for the first time in an international copyright treaty that computer programs are protectable subject matter. It requires that computer programs shall be protected as literary works under the Berne Convention (1971). Although many countries already provided protection to software at the time of the negotiations, some countries argued that software, or at least certain types, should not be considered a literary work since it did not meet the standard of originality necessary for protection. The debate was especially contentious around the issue of object code, which is a collection of source code instructions that serves a functional purpose. Some countries had opted to offer modalities of protection, by treating computer programs as an applied art or by granting a *sui generis* regime.[3] Art. 10.1 TRIPS effectively settled this debate, by mandating that all WTO Members treat both the source and ob-

---

[2] On this score, see Gervais (2008) who details the rationale for this change.

[3] For example, France applied the concept of applied arts, while Brazil and South Korea adopted *sui generis* regimes. See Correa (2007).

ject code forms of software as literary works. This represented a triumph for the US and other developed countries with major software industries. Interestingly, Japan had sought the inclusion of a clarification that protection did not extend to "any programming language, rule, or algorithm" used for computer programs. Rather than including such a clarification, the negotiators opted for a more general statement of principle, which is reflected in Art. 9.2 TRIPS.

The scope of coverage is also clarified in Art. 10.2 TRIPS, which notes that compilations of data or other material, "which by reason of the selection or arrangement of their contents constitute intellectual creations shall be protected as such" but "without prejudice to any copyright subsisting in the data or material itself." In other words, IP protection should be extended to databases and other collections of works, such as encyclopedias or anthologies, provided they meet the test of demonstrating creativity in the selection or arrangement of data or other materials. This is without regard to whether the underlying data or material is already in the public domain or even subject to copyright protection, although Art. 10.2 TRIPS clarifies that the treatment of such data or material shall not be affected. Prior to TRIPS, the issue of how databases should be treated was unclear, as Art. 2(5) of the Berne Convention mandates protection of only "collections of literary and artistic works." Art. 10.2 TRIPS broadens the scope of coverage by including data explicitly. It also imposed a lower threshold for originality. Whereas Art. 2(5) of the Berne Convention required that the collection demonstrate originality in its selection *and* arrangement of content, Art. 10.2 TRIPS states that the intellectual creation may result from either the selection *or* arrangement of content.

3.4 RENTAL RIGHTS

Also addressed by TRIPS is the issue of rental rights, meaning the right of an author or his or her successor in title to authorize or prohibit the commercial rental to the public of originals or copies of a copyrighted work. The TRIPS Agreement is the first time that this right has been recognized in an international copyright agreement. Art. 11 TRIPS states that WTO Members must, at a minimum, provide for rental rights for computer programs, so long as the program itself is an essential object of the rental. Art. 11 TRIPS also obliges WTO Members to provide rental rights for cinematographic works, if "rental has led to widespread copying of such works which is materially impairing the exclusive right of reproduction conferred in that Member on authors and their successor in title."

The language of the exceptions in both instances is worth a closer examination. Regarding computer programs, Art. 11 TRIPS notes that the obligation to provide rental rights "does not apply to rentals where the program itself is not the essential object of the rental." Thus, it would not apply to computer programs used in microprocessors in a rental car. The essential object of the rental is the vehicle and the provision of transportation, rather than the computer program itself. However, it would apply to rentals of a laptop with pre-loaded software. In that case, the essential object of the rental is to obtain access to the computer program.

Regarding cinematographic works, WTO Members are required to provide rental rights only when two thresholds are met: (1) there is widespread copying; and (2) the copying materially impairs the exclusive right of reproduction of the right-holder. This language is somewhat vague and reflects compromises reached during the course of the negotiations. Left unresolved is the issue of what constitutes "widespread copying" and "material impairment."

Finally, note that Art. 11 TRIPS applies only to commercial rentals. Therefore, non-profit rentals and public lending fall outside of the scope of the provision. However, even if there is no fee involved in the transaction, one must be prepared to demonstrate that no commercial advantage resulted from the rental.

The issue of rental rights for phonogram producers emerges separately in Art. 14.4 TRIPS. That provision requires that WTO Members provide rental rights to "producers of phonograms and any other rights holders in phonograms" subject to two limitations noted above: (1) the "essential object of the rental" requirement; and (2) the "commercial rental" limitation. However, Art. 14.4 TRIPS contains a carve-out exception for any WTO Member which, on April 15, 1994, "has in force a system of equitable renumeration for the rental of phonograms." Such countries are permitted to maintain their equitable renumeration system, rather than provide for rental rights, subject to the condition that "the commercial rental of phonograms does not lead to the material impairment of the exclusive rights of reproduction of rights holders." The most prominent WTO Member to utilize such a system is Japan, which pushed for this carve-out.

3.5 TERM OF PROTECTION

The pre-TRIPS Berne Convention provided for a minimum term of protection for literary and artistic works of the life of the author plus fifty years. However, exceptions exist for cinematographic works, anonymous or pseudonymous works, and photographic works and works of applied art.

For works by a natural person, Art. 12 TRIPS leaves in place the general Berne Convention minimum standard of "life plus fifty years." Note that this is a minimum. Certain countries, including the US and the EU members, have extended copyright term to periods beyond this length. In post-TRIPS trade agreements, they have also obliged certain trading partners to adopt longer terms of protection.

What Art. 12 TRIPS resolves is the debate over whether protection can be extended to works for which the author is not a natural person. The most common example is where the author is a corporation. It is also true of instances where the work is a collective work or where the author is truly anonymous. Art. 12 TRIPS requires that in such instances, the term "shall be no less than 50 years from the end of the calendar year of the authorized publication." It also clarifies that where authorized publication does not occur within 50 years from the making of work, the term shall expire "50 years from the end of the calendar year of the making."

Art. 14.5 TRIPS further requires that the minimum term of protection to be accorded to performers and producers of phonograms shall be 50 years computed from the end of the calendar year in which the fixation was made or the performance took place. This is an extension of the minimum term required under the Rome Convention. However, Art. 14.5 TRIPS left the term of protection for broadcasting organizations at 20 years.

3.6 RELATED RIGHTS

The differences between WTO Members that follow the copyright tradition and those that do not are most apparent when it comes to the rights of performers, producers of phonograms, and broadcasting organizations. Many civil law countries have treated such rights under the notion of neighboring rights, rather than viewing them on par with author's rights. Most common law countries, on the other hand, make no distinction and therefore treat such rights as copyright. As a result, the TRIPS Agreement adopts the rubric of "related rights" in discussing these rights.

The language of Art. 14 TRIPS, which addresses such rights, is important. Recall that with respect to the rights of performers, producers of phonograms, and broadcasting organizations, WTO Members are only required to provide national treatment and MFN treatment for the obligations explicitly discussed in Art. 14 TRIPS. Two of these obligations have already been discussed above—rental rights of phonogram producers (Art. 14.4 TRIPS); and the term of protection for all three categories (Art. 14.5 TRIPS).

The other obligations are as follows: Art. 14.1 TRIPS requires WTO Members to grant performers the right to prevent: (a) unauthorized fixation of an unfixed performance; (b) reproduction of an unauthorized fixation of an unfixed performance; (c) unauthorized broadcast of a performance by wireless means; and (d) the unauthorized communication to the public of a live performance. Art. 14.2 TRIPS obliges WTO Members to grant phonograph producers "the right to authorize or prohibit the direct or indirect reproduction of their phonograms." Finally, Art. 14.3 TRIPS requires WTO Members to grant broadcasting organizations the right to prohibit the following acts when undertaken without their authorization:

(a) fixation of broadcasts, (b) the reproduction of fixations of broadcasts, (c) the rebroadcasting by wireless means of broadcasts, and (d) the communication to the public of television broadcasts. However, a Member is exempt from the obligations of Art. 14.3 TRIPS if it recognizes copyright protection with regard to broadcast programs, with the possibility of preventing the acts mentioned in the provision, subject to the provisions of the Berne Convention (1971).

Art. 14 TRIPS draws heavily from the Rome Convention, which is the primary pre-TRIPS international agreement addressing such rights. However, note that the Rome Convention, unlike the Berne Convention (1971), is not incorporated into the TRIPS Agreement itself. With respect to the first three paragraphs of Art. 14 TRIPS (*i.e.*, those provisions discussed in the paragraph immediately preceding), Art. 14.6 TRIPS explicitly grants WTO Members the authority to apply any of the "conditions, limitations, exceptions, and reservations permitted by the Rome Convention." Among the exceptions denoted in Art. 7(1) of the Rome Convention are: (a) private use; (b) use of short excerpts in connection with the reporting of current events; (c) ephemeral fixation by a broadcasting organization by means of its own facilities and for its own broadcasts; and (d) use solely for the purpose of teaching or scientific research.

Finally, note that the rights of performers and phonogram producers were subsequently updated after TRIPS in the 1996 WIPO Performances and Phonograms Treaty (WPPT). Not all WTO Members, however, have signed on to the WPPT. Note that the MFN and national treatment obligations apply for those WTO Members that have implemented the WPPT.[4]

One important difference between Art. 14 TRIPS and the WPPT is its definition of what constitutes a performance. The TRIPS Agreement does not provide for an actual definition. However, the rights of performers are addressed in Art. 14.1 TRIPS, and Art. 14.6 TRIPS authorizes WTO Members to apply limitations contained within the Rome Convention with respect to that provision. Thus, WTO Members may confine their obligations to the Rome Convention's definition of a performance. That definition covers only "literary and artistic works." Excluded are performances of expressions of folklore. This category is covered in the definition in Article 2(a) of the WPPT. One debated question, therefore, is whether performances of expressions of folklore are covered by Art. 14.1 TRIPS. A strict reading of the limitation imposed by Art. 14.6 would suggest that it does not, but the issue has yet to be considered by a Panel.

---

[4] The same is true of WTO Members that have implemented the 1996 WIPO Copyright Treaty.

3.7 LIMITATIONS AND EXCEPTIONS: THE THREE-STEP TEST

What limitations or exceptions can a WTO Member legally impose to the protections that are required under the copyright and related rights provisions of the TRIPS Agreement? Can, for example, governments carve out an exception for "fair use," a fundamental principle of US copyright law? What about a situation where an educational textbook seeks to use copyrighted materials, but the pricing necessary to obtain its use is exorbitant? Can the government allow for the use of compulsory licensing? We close our discussion of this chapter by highlighting the rules that the TRIPS Agreement lays out on limitations and exceptions to the obligations imposed.

Recall again that Art. 9.1 TRIPS, along with Art. 2.2 TRIPS, specifically incorporate Articles 1–21 of the Berne Convention. Contained within these articles are a number of provisions allowing for exceptions to the rights conferred by the Berne Convention. For example, Article 10(1) of the Berne Convention permits the use of quotations from newspaper articles and periodicals in the form of press summaries, provided the work has already been lawfully made available to the public and the extent of the quotation does "not exceed that justified by the purpose." Article 10(2) of the Berne Convention contains an exception for teaching, and Article 10*bis*(2) contains an exception for current events reporting. Moreover, the press and broadcasters are permitted, by way of Article 10*bis*(1), to reproduce newspaper articles, periodical articles, and broadcasts "on current economic, political or religious topics" so long as the source is clearly indicated. They are also permitted, by way of Article 2(2), to reproduce lectures and addresses delivered in public. All of these exceptions granted by the Berne Convention are therefore preserved under the TRIPS Agreement.

In addition, Art. 9(2) of the Berne Convention grants an exception to the right of reproduction for literary and artistic works "in certain special cases, provided that such reproduction does not conflict with a normal exploitation of the work and does not unreasonably prejudice the legitimate interests of the work." This language serves as a clear source of inspiration for Art. 13 TRIPS, which reads: "Members shall confine limitations or exceptions to exclusive rights to certain special cases which do not conflict with a normal exploitation of the work and do not unreasonably prejudice the legitimate interests of the right holder."

In light of the similar language between the provisions, and the fact that the exceptions and limitations contained within the Berne Convention continue to apply, there is a question as to what is the applicable scope of Art. 13 TRIPS. A narrow interpretation would be to argue that its scope is limited to new rights conferred by the TRIPS Agreement which were not discussed in the Berne Convention (*e.g.*, rental rights). A broader interpretation, however, would be to argue that its scope is that of all other exclusive rights outside of the right of reproduction. This would include the existing rights contained within the Berne Convention—*e.g.*, the right of translation (Art. 8 of the Berne Convention), the right of public performance (Art. 11), the right of broadcasting and other forms of public communication (Art. 11*bis*), the right of public recitation—as well as the new rights conferred by the TRIPS Agreement.

In *US–Section 110(5) Copyright Act*, the Panel (§ 6.80) expressly rejected the narrow interpretation: "In our view, neither the express wording nor the context of Article 13 or any other provision of the TRIPS Agreement supports the interpretation that the scope of application of Article 13 is limited to the exclusive rights newly introduced under the TRIPS Agreement." Thus, the conditions imposed by Art. 13 TRIPS should be considered applicable to the scope of copyright and related rights conferred within the entire TRIPS Agreement, including those parts of the Berne Convention incorporated within.

At issue in *US–Section 110(5) Copyright Act* was whether two exemptions contained within Section 110(5) of the US Copyright Act were permissible under Art. 13 TRIPS. The two exemptions allowed, under certain conditions, the playing of radio and television music in certain public places (*e.g.*, bars, shops, restaurants, etc.) without the payment of a royalty fee. The first exemption, known as the "homestyle" exemption, applied to establishments other than a food service or drinking establishment, such as a retail shop. Provided an establishment had less than 2,000 gross square feet, the exemption applied. In addition, if it exceeded this size, provided that it used only equipment commonly used within homes (*i.e.*, no more than 6 loudspeakers, of which no more than 4 were in any single room; no more than 4 audiovisual devices of a screen size less than or equal to 55 inches, of which no more than 1 was in any single room), the exemption also applied. The second exemption, known as the "business" exemption, applied to food service or drinking establishments, such as restaurants and bars. Similar requirements for the exemption existed, except that the square footage cut-off for such establishments was set at 3,750 gross square feet.

In adjudicating this case, the Panel established the use of a three-step test to determine whether an exception fell within the permissible scope of Art. 13 TRIPS. The Panel (§ 6.174) declared that three cumulative conditions must be met:

"(1) the limitations or exceptions are confined to certain special cases;

(2) they do not conflict with a normal exploitation of the work; and

(3) they do not unreasonably prejudice the legitimate interests of the right holder."

Based on these conditions, the Panel concluded that the "business" exemption did not meet the criteria of the three-step test (§ 6.266), but that the "homestyle" exemption did (§ 6.272).

The Panel's treatment of each of the three steps is worth a closer look. Regarding the first criteria, the Panel (§ 6.112) explained:

> "In our view, the first condition of Article 13 requires that a limitation or exception in national legislation should be clearly defined and should be narrow in its scope and reach. On the other hand, a limitation or exception may be compatible with the first condition even if it pursues a special purpose whose underlying legitimacy in a normative sense cannot be discerned. The wording of Article 13's first condition does not imply passing a judgment on the legitimacy of the exceptions in dispute. However, public policy purposes stated by law-makers when enacting a limitation or exception may be useful from a factual perspective for making inferences about the scope of a limitation or exception or the clarity of its definition."

The Panel (§ 6.111) noted that the exception need not "be justified in terms of a legitimate public policy purpose in order to fulfill the first condition." Furthermore, in considering whether an exception or limitation is confined to "certain special cases," the Panel (§§ 6.107–6.110) noted that the restriction must fall under the normal dictionary definitions of each of these three terms.

Regarding the second criteria, the Panel (§ 6.187) adopted a dynamic approach to interpreting what constitutes a "normal exploitation" of the work.

> We base our appraisal of the actual and potential effects on the commercial and technological conditions that prevail in the market currently or in the near future. What is a normal exploitation in the market-place may evolve as a result of technological developments or changing consumer preferences. Thus, while we do not wish to speculate on future developments, we need to consider the actual and potential effects of the exemptions in question in the current market and technological environment.

The Panel (§§ 6.177–6.178) recognized that part of this analysis involved an inquiry into whether the exception or limitation impinged on "areas of the market in which the copyright owner would ordinarily expect to exploit the work, but which are not available for exploitation because of this exemption." Nevertheless, it refused to limit its inquiry to simply this analysis. Instead, the Panel (§ 6.180) suggested that in determining what constitutes a "normal exploitation," one should "consider, in addition to those forms of exploitation that currently generate significant or tangible revenue, those forms of exploitation which, with a certain degree of likelihood and plausibility, could acquire considerable economic or practical importance."

Finally, on the third criteria, the Panel in *US–Section 110(5) Copyright Act* also addressed the meaning of "legitimate interests" and "unreasonably prejudice"—the two critical terms in the third step of the test. On "legitimate interests," the Panel (§ 6.227) explained:

> In our view, one—albeit incomplete and thus conservative—way of looking at legitimate interests is the economic value of the exclusive rights conferred by copyright on their holders. It is possible to estimate in economic terms the value of exercising, e.g., by licensing, such rights. That is not to say that legitimate interests are necessarily limited to this economic value.

While the Panel (§ 6.223) did not explain what outside of an economic value analysis applies, the Panel suggested that interests are broader than simply economic advantage.

> "The ordinary meaning of the term 'interests' may encompass a legal right or title to a property or to use or benefit of a property (including intellectual property). It may also refer to a concern about a potential detriment or advantage, and more generally to something that is of some importance to a natural or legal person. Accordingly, the notion of 'interests' is not necessarily limited to actual or potential economic advantage or detriment."

In addition, the Panel (§ 6.224) declared that legitimacy "relates to lawfulness from a legal positivist perspective, but it has also the connotation of legitimacy from a more normative perspective." Thus, in determining what is legitimate, one should consider not only the law but also "the context of calling for the protection of interests that are justifiable in the light of the objectives that underlie the protection of exclusive rights."

As for what constitutes "unreasonable prejudice," the Panel was less than clear. It (§ 6.229) simply stated: "In our view, prejudice to the legitimate interests of right holders reaches an unreasonable level if an exception or limitation causes or has the potential to cause an unreasonable loss of income to the copyright owner." What is considered unreasonable, however, is left unaddressed.

Finally, we note that exceptions and limitations on copyright and related rights for public interest purposes are not required by the TRIPS Agreement, other than to the extent required by the Berne Convention provisions discussed above. In that sense, while Art. 13 TRIPS allows for the possibility of further exceptions and limitations, it is, in essence, a limiting provision. To be considered legitimate, any other legislation authorizing exceptions or limitations must meet the requirements of the three-step test. Thus, Art. 13 TRIPS serves the purpose of providing WTO Members a means to challenge a public interest exception, rather than mandating that such interests be protected.

QUESTIONS AND COMMENTS

Harmonization: To what extent is the TRIPS Agreement responsible for the harmonization of copyright standards across trading partners? For many of the GATT years, the Berne Convention did not include a major party: the US. The US did not accede to the Berne Convention until 1989, largely out of two concerns: certain formalities such as the copyright notification requirement for all works, and the provision of moral rights. The former were eliminated as a result of the Berne Convention Implementation Act of 1989, which occurred prior to the completion of the TRIPS Agreement. The latter were carved out of dispute settlement proceedings. With respect to a large trading country such as the US, did the TRIPS Agreement requirements for harmonization really result in major changes? Or were the decisions to make such changes already taken beforehand and simply enshrined within the Agreement? In other words, when we talk about the TRIPS Agreement facilitating harmonization, do we really mean that the Agreement forced smaller countries to conform to the standards of their larger trading partners, rather than the Agreement forced key countries to resolve differences among themselves and agree on a common standard?

Digital Millennium Copyright Act (DMCA): The DMCA is the legislation passed the US Congress to implement the WIPO Copyright Treaty and the WIPO Performances and Phonograms Treaty. The DMCA included provisions prohibiting the circumvention of digital "access controls" and "copy controls" that a copyright owner may have implemented in order to safeguard access to a copyrighted work through technologies such as password encryption. The DMCA also exempted service providers from liability provided they conformed with certain "notice and takedown" requirements. These standards have since been promulgated globally by the US through its free trade agreements. This move has been met with criticism from some non-governmental organizations, such as the Electronic Frontier Foundation and the Chilling Effects Clearinghouse, that contend that provisions within the DMCA have a "chilling effect" on free expression.

Folklore / Traditional Cultural Expression: The issue of how to protect folklore and other modes of traditional cultural expression is one that has rankled some who contend the TRIPS Agreement does not provide adequate means for protecting creative works outside of Western societies. Using copyright to protect folklore can be difficult on several accounts: Copyright laws often require that the work be fixed in a tangible medium; however, folklore is preserved often through intangible forms such as oral retellings of stories. Copyright laws also require that the work be original; however, originality is difficult to establish when there is no written record of the evolution of folklore over time. WIPO issued a set of Draft Articles for the Protection of Traditional Expression in July 2011.

CHAPTER 29

TRADEMARKS

■ ■ ■

1. THE LEGAL DISCIPLINE

The TRIPS Agreement clarifies the international law governing the regulation of trademarks in a number of important ways. The Agreement specifies what types of marks must be protected by WTO Members, which include trademarks as well as service marks. It also specifies a minimum set of rights to be conferred upon owners of a trademark. The Agreement sets a minimum term of protection of seven years and mandates that WTO Members must allow for a system of regular renewals. Furthermore, TRIPS imposes an absolute ban on compulsory licensing of trademarks. While WTO Members may make registration contingent on the use of a mark, the TRIPS Agreement imposes certain limitations on the use requirement. In addition, it further limits the scope of special requirements that a WTO Member may place on the use of a trademark. Finally, the TRIPS Agreement subjects provisions of the Paris Convention regulating the protection of marks to the WTO dispute settlement process.

2. THE RATIONALE FOR THE LEGAL DISCIPLINE

Prior to the TRIPS Agreement, international rules governing national trademark regimes existed within the Paris Convention (1967). However, the Paris Convention provided much discretion to individual countries on how they went about implementing their regimes. A major driving force behind the trademark section of the TRIPS Agreement is to reduce this discretion, and therefore, provide for greater uniformity among trading partners.

Recall that a key reason why developed countries wanted to draw the international IP regime into the international trade regime was to provide greater leverage to address the issue of trade in counterfeit goods. While strengthening national trademark regimes is a prong of that strategy, it should not be seen as necessarily the most important one. Even though counterfeit goods always involve the violation of trademarks, the main innovation of the TRIPS Agreement, with respect to addressing counterfeit goods, was the inclusion of an enforcement section (discussed *infra* in Chapter 31) subject to the WTO's dispute settlement proceedings. Thus, the trademarks section of the TRIPS Agreement focused more on the desire to obtain greater certainty of rules, rather than directly addressing counterfeiting concerns.

3. COVERAGE OF THE LEGAL DISCIPLINE

3.1 PARIS CONVENTION (1967) OBLIGATIONS

Before expounding on the new obligations created within the TRIPS Agreement, we first quickly summarize the relevant pre-TRIPS Paris Convention obligations. Recall that these obligations are incorporated into the TRIPS Agreement by way of Art. 2.1 TRIPS, which requires that WTO Members comply with Arts. 1–12 and 19 of the Paris Convention.

Art. 4 of the Paris Convention provides that any person who has filed for a trademark shall enjoy a priority period of six months in all other countries that had acceded to the Paris Convention. Art. 5C requires that a country can only cancel a trademark registration due to non-use of the trademark after a "reasonable period, and then only if the person concerned does not justify his inaction." It also clarifies that a country may not invalidate a trademark because of "use in a form differing in elements which do not alter the distinctive character of the mark in the form in which it was registered." Furthermore, a country shall allow co-proprietors of a mark to use the mark concurrently on identical or similar goods, so long as such use does not mislead the public and is not contrary to the public interest. In addition, Art. 7*bis* allows for the registration of collective marks. Art. 6*bis* also allows countries to establish a system for designating well-known marks, if it so desires.

Art. 6(1) of the Paris Convention states that the filing of a trademark registration application shall take place at the national level, with Art. 6(3) confirming that the national systems are independent of each other. Art. 6*quinquies* provides that if a trademark is registered in its country of origin, it shall be considered as accepted for filing and protected as is in all other countries of the Paris Convention. However, a country may refuse to recognize a trademark registered in its country of origin because of one of three grounds spelled out in Art. 6*quinquies*: (1) if it infringes on rights acquired by third parties in the country; (2) if it is devoid of any distinctive character; or (3) if it is contrary to morality or public order. In addition, Art. 10*bis* of the Paris Convention permits a country to refuse recognition on unfair competition grounds. However, Art. 6(2) of the Convention notes that an application may not be rejected nor may a mark be invalidated on the grounds that "filing, registration, or renewal has not been effected in the country of origin" of the mark. In other words, a person or corporation is not required to maintain a valid trademark registration in its home country before seeking to register the mark elsewhere.

Art. 8 of the Paris Convention requires that each country protect trade names, without any obligation of filing or registration. Trade names are the name by which a firm operates or the name by which a commercial product or service is known. This requirement applies, regardless of whether or not the trade name forms part of a trademark. However, again, Art. 10*bis* allows for an exception to this requirement on unfair competition grounds.

Obligations concerning the seizure of unlawful goods are spelled out in Arts. 9 and 10 of the Paris Convention. A government is required to seize goods which unlawfully bear a trademark or trade name that is registered and protected in that country as well as goods which bear a false indication regarding its source or the identity of the producer. However, these obligations apply only to goods being imported into the country and not goods in transit.

Finally, Art. 6*ter* of the Convention requires that countries prohibit the registration of flags, state emblems, official signs, and official hallmarks of other countries and also of international organizations.

The main impact of Art. 2.1 TRIPS, which incorporates these Paris Convention provisions into the TRIPS Agreement, is that it raises the cost of non-compliance. Prior to the TRIPS Agreement, a country had little recourse to take action against another country that failed to meet its Paris Convention obligations. After TRIPS, a WTO Member could now subject a non-compliant Member to WTO dispute settlement. The possibility that this process may eventually result in authorized trade sanctions dramatically increases the leverage that a country has to compel its trading partners to comply with its Paris Convention obligations.

3.2 PROTECTABLE SUBJECT MATTER

One of the clarifications offered by the TRIPS Agreement is a definition of what constitutes a trademark. This issue was not addressed in the Paris Convention or any prior international agreement. Art. 15.1 TRIPS lays forth the criterion that "[a]ny sign, or any combination of signs, capable of distinguishing the goods or services of one undertaking from those of another, shall be capable of constituting a trademark." The key feature emphasized here is distinctiveness. This may be inherent in the mark itself, or it may be acquired through use.[1] Note that the criterion denoted in Art. 15.1 does not require that the mark convey any information about the source of the good or service. It must simply distinguish the good or service as distinct from other goods and services.

Art. 15.1 TRIPS includes an illustrative list of potential signs that may acquire distinctiveness: "words including personal names, letters, numerals, figurative elements and combinations of colors as well as any combination of such signs." However, this is simply an illustrative, rather

---

[1] However, WTO Members do not need to grant protection to marks where the distinctiveness is acquired through use. Art. 15.1 TRIPS uses a "may" rather than "shall" formulation in discussing protection of signs that are not inherently distinctive.

than exhaustive, list. That is to say, signs which are not explicitly mentioned in this list may also be deemed protectable. Nor does it require a WTO Member to register every sign of the categories mentioned in the list. In *US–Section 211 Appropriations Act*, the AB (§§ 154–55) clarified:

> Article 15.1 defines which signs or combinations of signs are *capable of* constituting a trademark. These signs include words such as personal names, letters, numerals, figurative elements and combinations of colours, as well as any combination of such signs. This definition is based on the distinctiveness of signs as such, or on their distinctiveness as acquired through use. If such signs are capable of distinguishing the goods or services of one undertaking from those of other undertakings, then they become *eligible for* registration as trademarks. To us, the title of Article 15.1—'Protectable Subject Matter'—indicates that Article 15.1 embodies a *definition* of what can constitute a trademark. WTO Members are obliged under Article 15.1 to ensure that those signs or combinations of signs that meet the distinctiveness criteria set forth in Article 15.1—and are, thus, *capable of constituting a trademark*—are *eligible for registration* as trademarks within their domestic legislation.
>
> ... Identifying certain signs that are *capable of* registration and imposing on WTO Members an obligation to make those signs *eligible for* registration in their domestic legislation is not the same as imposing on those Members an obligation to register *automatically* each and every sign or combination of signs that are *capable of* and *eligible for* registration under Article 15.1. This Article describes which trademarks are 'capable' of registration. It does not say that all trademarks that are capable of registration 'shall be registered.' This Article states that such signs or combinations of signs 'shall be *eligible* for registration' as trademarks. It does not say that they 'shall be registered'. To us, these are distinctions with a difference. And, as we have said, supporting these distinctions is the fact that the title of this Article speaks of subject matter as 'protectable', and not of subject matter 'to be protected'. In this way, the title of Article 15 expresses the notion that the subject matter covered by the provision is subject matter that *qualifies* for, but is not necessarily *entitled to*, protection.

Art. 15.1 TRIPS grants WTO Members flexibility as to whether or not it will protect non-visual signs. It allows Members to establish a requirement that signs be visually perceptible. As a result, WTO Members have different rules about whether non-visual marks, such as scent marks or sound marks, may be protected.

Finally, note that one important expansion of protectable subject matter in the TRIPS Agreement is its requirement that WTO Members protect service marks. This requirement did not exist in the Paris Convention.[2] In addition, Art. 15.4 TRIPS expands the terms of Art. 7 of the Paris Convention to include service marks. That provision states that the "nature of the good or service to which a trademark is to be applied shall in no case form an obstacle to the registration of the trademark." Furthermore, Art. 16.2 TRIPS clarifies that Art. 6*bis* of the Paris Convention, dealing with well-known marks, also applies to service marks.

3.3 GROUNDS FOR DENIAL OF PROTECTION

As noted above, the Paris Convention specifies a number of grounds that a country may use to deny trademark protection. Art. 10 of the Paris Convention permits countries to reject protection if doing so would violate unfair competition principles. Art. 6*bis* requires that a country prohibit a third party from registering a well-known trademark, and Art. 6*ter* requires that a country prohibit the registration of state emblems, flags, and official hallmarks of nations as well as those of international organizations. Finally, Art. 6*quinques*(B) laid out three conditions under which a country may reject registration of a mark registered in its country of origin. These include infringement of the prior rights of others, lack of distinctive character, and where refusal is justified on moral or public order grounds.

These grounds for refusal continue to be valid. In Art. 15.2 TRIPS, negotiators chose to include a sentence clarifying that Art. 15.1 "shall not be understood to prevent a Member from denying registration of a trademark on other grounds, provided that they do not derogate from the provisions of the Paris Convention (1967)."

The wording of Art. 15.2 TRIPS, however, is quite vague, as it does not elaborate on what would constitute a derogation from the provisions of the Paris Convention. This question surfaced in *US–Section 211 Appropriations Act*. The EC argued that the proper reading of Art. 15.2 TRIPS is that it limited the valid grounds for denial of protection to the conditions expressly mentioned in the Paris Convention and the TRIPS Agreement. The US argued otherwise. Both the Panel and the AB sided with the US. The AB (§ 177) noted that "a condition need not be expressly mentioned in the Paris Convention (1967) in order not to 'derogate' from it." Instead, the AB defined derogation as occurring only "if the denial were on grounds that are inconsistent with the provisions of that Convention."

As a result of this ruling, WTO Members continue to have much flexibility in defining the conditions under which they may evaluate the dis-

---

[2] With respect to service marks, Art. 6*sexies* of the Paris Convention explicitly states that countries "shall not be required to provide for the registration of such marks."

tinctiveness requirement of Art. 15.1 TRIPS. So long as the condition does not violate the provisions of the Paris Convention or TRIPS Agreement, it remains permissible.

3.4. MINIMUM RIGHTS CONFERRED UPON THE OWNER OF A MARK

Another important clarification provided by the TRIPS Agreement is the scope of rights to which the owner of a protected mark is entitled. This was not elaborated upon in the Paris Convention. Instead, Art. 10*bis* of the Paris Convention simply required that countries protect against unfair competition, including prohibiting acts which "create confusion," contain "false allegations," or "mislead the public." However, the Paris Convention does not require that specific rights be granted to the owner of a registered mark.

Art. 16.1 TRIPS requires that all WTO Members must grant the owner of a registered mark "the exclusive right to prevent all third parties not having the owner's consent from using in the course of trade identical or similar signs for goods or services which are identical or similar to those in respect of which the trademark is registered where such use would result in a likelihood of confusion." In other words, Art. 16.1 specifically grants a right to owners of a protected mark to take action against infringers of its mark. However, it is subject to the limitation that the infringement must take place "in the course of trade."

Art. 16.1 introduces the "likelihood of confusion" as an international standard for evaluating claims of trademark infringement. Note that this is a looser standard that that required by the Art. *6bis* of the Paris Convention. The owner of the mark need not provide proof that the alleged infringing act caused actual confusion nor need it show that the act actually misled members of the public. Rather, the burden on the mark owner is simply to show that the act is *likely* to cause confusion. Furthermore, Art. 16.1 TRIPS requires that Members adopt a presumption of a likelihood of confusion where an identical sign is used for identical goods or services.

In *US–Section 211 Appropriations Act*, the AB (§ 186) clarified that "Article 16 confers on the *owner* of a registered trademark an internationally agreed minimum level of 'exclusive rights' that all WTO Members must guarantee in their domestic legislation." That is to say, WTO Members may confer further rights beyond that required by Art. 16 TRIPS. In addition, the AB, in *EC–Trademarks and Geographical Indications*, (§ 7.602) further clarified that the meaning of "exclusive right" goes beyond the notion of a "right to 'exclude' others." Instead, subject to a limited set of exceptions, WTO members must only grant the owner alone the right to prevent all third parties from undertaking certain acts concerning the mark without the owner's consent.

The language of Art. 16.1 grants flexibility to each WTO Member regarding how the provision's requirement is to be implemented. One area of flexibility is how Members choose to define the "owner" of a registered mark. In analyzing this question in *US–Section 211 Appropriations Act*, the AB (§ 187) held:

> "As used in this treaty provision, the ordinary meaning of 'owner' can be defined as the proprietor or the person who holds the tile or dominion of the property constituted by the trademark. We agree with the Panel that this ordinary meaning does not clarify how the ownership of a trademark is to be determined. Also, we agree with the Panel that Article 16.1 does not, in express terms, define how ownership of a registered trademark is to be determined. Article 16.1 confers exclusive rights on the 'owner', but Article 16.1 does not tell us who the 'owner' is."

Another area of flexibility is with respect to the definition of similarity. Note that Art. 16.1 TRIPS confers an exclusive right with respect to "identical or similar signs for goods or services." While the meaning of identical is difficult to dispute, there is ample flexibility in how WTO Members choose to define "similar" in their law. So far, the issue of what is permissible has yet to be addressed in WTO dispute settlement.

Finally, Art. 21 TRIPS provides an owner of a registered trademark with the right to assign the trademark without transferring the business associated with the trademark. This provision reflects a principle commonly referred to as the "free assignability" of trademarks. Art. 21 eliminates an exception provided for in Art. 6*quater* of the Paris Convention which allowed countries to maintain a business transfer requirement.

However, two points are worth noting with regard to the right provided in Art. 21. First, the provision explicitly refers to *registered* trademarks. Therefore, WTO Members are free to maintain the business transfer requirement for unregistered trademarks. Second, in addition to permitting a business transfer requirement, Art. 6*quater* of the Paris Convention allows countries to maintain as a second condition that the owner of the mark transfer the underlying goodwill of the mark when assigning a trademark. On this condition, Art. 21 TRIPS is silent. While the issue of whether a WTO Member may maintain this condition has not been adjudicated, it appears that the proper reading of Art. 21 TRIPS is that it does not provide for a complete "free assignability" right. Rather, WTO Members are only required to provide *registered* trademark owners with the right of assignment without requiring transfer of the business associated with the mark.

3.5 TERM OF PROTECTION

Under the Paris Convention, there is no mandated minimum term of protection for trademarks. Art. 18 TRIPS requires that WTO Members provide for a minimum term of at least seven years in their national law. It also requires that Members provide for a renewal process, whereby each renewal is also for a minimum term of at least seven years.

Since TRIPS, several WTO Members have signed on to other international agreements which require a term of protection of ten years. For example, the Madrid Protocol establishes an international system for registering marks, provides for an initial term of ten years (Art. 6(1)) and renewal terms of ten years (Art. 7). As of this writing, 83 parties have signed onto the Protocol.[3] In addition, the Trademark Law Treaty also mandates, in Art. 13(7), a minimum term of protection of ten years for the initial registration and subsequent renewals. As of this writing, there are 45 contracting parties to the Treaty.[4]

Art. 18 TRIPS also requires that WTO Members allow for an indefinite number of renewals of a trademark, provided that the mark continues to meet the validity requirements under national law. Thus, unlike patents or copyrights, a trademark does not fall into the public domain after an established period of time.

3.6 LIMITATIONS ON CANCELLATION OF A TRADEMARK

Under Art. 5C(1) of the Paris Convention, a registered mark may be cancelled if the trademark is not used "after a reasonable period" and the owner fails to "justify his inaction." Among the rationales for such a condition are to prevent individuals from simply squatting on certain marks (and thereby raising the costs of using certain marks), to eliminate unjustified grants of IP protection, and to lower the administrative costs of national trademark offices. However, the language of Art. 5C(1) of the Paris Convention is quite vague. This gave countries much flexibility in how they chose to administer the cancellation of registered trademarks. Art. 19 TRIPS seeks to limit this flexibility by clarifying the conditions under which a WTO Member may cancel protection of a registered mark.

Art. 19.1 TRIPS requires that a WTO Member must grant the owner of a registered mark an uninterrupted period of at least three years for using the mark before it may be cancelled. Note that Art. 5C(1) of the Paris Convention had no fixed time period, but rather only spoke of a "reasonable period." Art. 19.2 TRIPS also defines use of a trademark by another person, other than the owner, as a valid use of the mark, so long as this is subject to the control of the trademark's owner.

In addition, the TRIPS Agreement further elaborates on the Paris Convention by clarifying that certain circumstances constitute justifica-

---

[3] Note that not all of the parties to the Madrid Protocol are WTO Members (*e.g.*, Iran). A complete list of signatories is provided on the WIPO website.

[4] As of this writing, not all of the parties to the Trademark Law Treaty are WTO Members. A complete list of signatories is provided on the WIPO website.

tion for non-use of a trademark. The category of permissible circumstances is quite broad. According to Art. 19.1 TRIPS, non-use is justified whenever circumstances arise "independently of the will of the owner of the trademark which constitute an obstacle to the use of the trademark." This includes import restrictions on the good or service associated with the trademark, as well as any other form of government requirements on the good or service. Therefore, as long as the good or service is regulated in some form (*e.g.*, through an approval process), Art. 19.1 TRIPS renders it significantly difficult for a government to cancel trademark protection.

Finally, note that Art. 15.3 TRIPS specifies that "actual use of a trademark shall not be a condition for filing of an application for registration." It further clarifies that an application "shall not be refused solely on the ground that intended use has not taken place before the expiry of a period of three years from the date of application." In other words, WTO Members may not enact a requirement that a mark have already been used before it is granted protection. Instead, the clock for counting the period of non-use may only begin to tick after an application is filed.

3.7 LIMITATIONS ON COMPULSORY LICENSING AND OTHER GOVERNMENT REQUIREMENTS

Art. 21 TRIPS prohibits WTO Members from enacting any form of compulsory licensing of a trademark. This prohibition is absolute. Unlike patents, where compulsory licensing may occur when it is in the public interest, no such exception exists for trademarks. In addition, negotiators from developed countries sought to limit other forms of requirements that governments, particularly from developing countries, had placed on trademark owners. For example, prior to TRIPS, a government seeking to promote a generic form of a product (*e.g.*, pharmaceutical, fertilizer, foodstuff) over a branded version may have required that the trademark owner display the generic name for a product along with the trademark on the product. It may have also regulated the font size of the trademark name as well as the generic name. Another example is where a government requires that a trademark be used in conjunction with another mark. This type of requirement was frequently used when a developing country sought to force a foreign trademark owner to engage in a joint venture partnership or licensing arrangement with a local party.

Art. 20 TRIPS states that the use of a trademark "in the course of trade shall not be unjustifiably encumbered by special circumstances." It then provides an illustrative list of such circumstances: (a) "use with another trademark"; (b) "use in a special form"; or (c) "use in a manner detrimental to its capability to distinguish the goods or services of one undertaking from those of other undertakings." However, Art. 20 TRIPS clarifies that a Member may require that the trademark distinguishing a good or service be displayed in conjunction with the mark of the producer of the good or service, so long as such a requirement does not link the two marks.

Note that Art. 20 TRIPS only limits the ability of WTO Members to set special conditions for the use of a trademark by its owner. It does not apply to preferential programs that may involve requirements on the use of a trademark but in which participation is optional rather than mandatory. This type of situation was at issue in *Indonesia–Autos*. Indonesia established a National Car Program which sought to promote the development of Indonesia's automobile industry. The Program designated certain Indonesian automobile companies as a "Pioneer" company. Cars produced by such companies could be designated as a "national motor vehicle" provided certain requirements were met. Such cars were exempt from a luxury sales tax, and the parts and components used to assemble the car were exempt from import duties. Among the requirements set forth was that the national motor vehicle must use a trademark acquired by an Indonesian company, whether that company be a joint venture or wholly-owned Indonesian company.

The US (§§ 14.277–14,278) argued that this amounted to a "special requirement" under Art. 20 TRIPS. In order to qualify for "national motor vehicle" designation, a foreign car company had to engage in a joint venture with an Indonesian "Pioneer" car company and allow the joint venture to acquire its trademark. This effectively encumbered the ability of the foreign car company to use the acquired trademark elsewhere. Furthermore, foreign trademark holders which did not enter into such an arrangement were placed at a competitive disadvantage since they could not enjoy the benefits given to a "national motor vehicle." The Panel (§ 14.277) rejected these arguments. It held that so long as an arrangement was voluntary, it could not amount to a special requirement. Furthermore, the Panel (§ 14.278) remarked that ineligibility for certain benefits did not amount to a "special requirement" under the meaning of Art. 20 TRIPS.

3.8 EXCEPTIONS

Finally, Art. 17 TRIPS elaborates on the conditions under which a WTO Member may impose an exception legally: "Members may provide limited exceptions to the rights conferred by a trademark, . . . , provided that such exceptions take account of the legitimate interests of the owner of the trademark and of third parties."

Note that there are two important conditions denoted in Art. 17 TRIPS. First, any exception must be "limited." To date, no WTO Member has brought forward a dispute which has resulted in an interpretation of the meaning of "limited" in the context of Art. 17 TRIPS. However, note that the wording of Art. 17 TRIPS is identical to that of Art. 30 TRIPS, which authorize exceptions to the exclusive rights conferred upon a patent. The term "limited exception" in that context has been interpreted in *Canada–Patent Protection for Pharmaceutical Products* (§ 7.30) to "connote a narrow exception—one which makes only a small diminution of the rights in question." Whether a Panel interpreting Art. 17 TRIPS would choose to adopt the same interpretation is open to future resolution.

Second, any exception must take into account the "legitimate interests" of the trademark owner and other third parties. Again, the meaning of what constitutes a "legitimate interest" has not been interpreted in the Art. 17 TRIPS context. However, the term has been interpreted in other non-trademark contexts. In *Canada–Patent Protection for Pharmaceutical Products*, the Panel (§ 7.69), in interpreting the Art. 30 TRIPS exceptions language for patents, declared that the "term must be defined in a way that it is often used in legal discourse—as a normative claim calling for protection of interests that are 'justifiable' in the sense that they are supported by relevant public policies or other social norms." Furthermore, in *US–Section 110(5) Copyright Act*, the Panel (§ 6.224) noted that "one—albeit incomplete and thus conservative—way of looking at legitimate interests is the economic value of the exclusive rights conferred . . . on their holders." These other interpretations may prove informative of how the term will be interpreted in the Art. 17 TRIPS context.

Art. 17 TRIPS specifically mentions one illustrative example which would qualify as a legitimate exception: "fair use of descriptive terms." This occurs when a term is used for identification or informative purposes. For example, one may employ a protected mark when describing information concerning a particular person, the origin of a particular good or service, or qualitative aspects of a particular good or service.

QUESTIONS AND COMMENTS

Generic marks: The possibility exists that use of a term becomes so commonplace that it acquires a certain generic quality. For example, think of terms such as "Xerox" or "Kleenex" being used to describe certain activities or products. Although the TRIPS Agreement does not refer to generic marks explicitly, Art. 15 TRIPS does require that the mark be for a "sign, or any combination of signs, capable of distinguishing the goods or services of one undertaking from those of other undertakings." What does this suggest, if anything, about the discretion of WTO Members to afford trademark protection to terms that acquire a certain generic quality? Compare the language of Art. 15 TRIPS with Art. 6*quinques* of the Paris Convention which allows its Members to deny trademark protection when a mark is "devoid of any distinctive character, or consist exclusively of signs or indications which may serve, in trade to designate the kind [of good] or have become customary in the current language or in the bona fide and established practices of the trade of the country where protection is claimed."

Well–Known Mark Registries: Certain countries have attempted to resolve the issue as to what constitutes a well-known mark by establishing a registry. In some instances, these efforts have been met with concern by trading partners that do not employ a registry. The International Trademark Association (INTA) has called for the establishment of certain best practices by countries that employ a well-known mark registry, including: publication of the adopted rules for the criteria and procedures for applications to join the registry, opposition and cancellation procedures for interested third-parties, and protection of business-sensitive information submitted in conjunction with an application or with a request opposing an application or seeking cancellation.

Internet Domain Names: With the proliferation of internet domains in the 1990s, controversies arose over whether domain names were subject to trademark protection. The Internet Corporation for Assigned Names and Numbers (ICANN) emerged as a non-profit organization to oversee an international registry of domain names. WIPO recommended that domain name disputes be resolved through ICANN, which developed the Uniform Dispute Resolution Policy (UDRP) to administer such disputes. Under the UDRP, ICANN has the authority to "cancel, transfer, or otherwise make changes to domain name registrations" through an administrative decision in instances where a party has registered and is using a domain name in "bad faith" and the domain name is "identical or confusingly similar" to a trademark or service mark in which a complainant has rights.

CHAPTER 30

PATENTS AND UNDISCLOSED INFORMATION

■ ■ ■

The patents and undisclosed information sections of Part II of the TRIPS Agreement are arguably the most controversial elements of the Agreement. They represent an expansion of patent rights under international law with significant repercussions, particularly in the areas of public health and food. The provisions themselves are the result of extensive negotiations between developed and developing countries, and between developed countries themselves. Many have criticized the provisions as an accommodation of the interests of pharmaceutical companies and agricultural chemical companies. Some have decried these provisions of TRIPS as reflective of the captured interests of US and European negotiators. Left paying the price, critics contend, are the poor in developing countries. In response, governments in developed countries and companies have argued that the provisions are necessary for strengthening patent protection to spur greater innovation especially given the costs and uncertainty involved in developing pharmaceuticals. Without strengthened laws guaranteeing global protection for innovation, supporters of the TRIPS provisions argue that the pace of development of new medicines and agricultural chemicals would slow dramatically.

Subsequent to the Agreement itself, the provisions have been subject to extensive examination—in WTO dispute settlement proceedings, in TRIPS Council, in other multilateral fora, and in policy and academic circles. They have also been subject to clarification and revision, as reflected in the Doha Declaration on the TRIPS Agreement and Public Health, discussed *infra*, and the TRIPS Council decision of November 30, 2005 extending the deadline for least-developed countries.

In addition, since the TRIPS Agreement was concluded, several other developments have affected the landscape: First, as already discussed elsewhere in this book, we have witnessed a growth of preferential trade agreements. Many of the PTAs signed by developed countries, and in particular, the United States, have included TRIPS-plus provisions impacting pharmaceuticals and agricultural chemicals. We will provide a few examples of such provisions in this chapter.

Second, since 1995, we have seen the growth of important intermediaries, such as the William J. Clinton Foundation and its Clinton Health Access Initiative. By acting as an intermediary, such groups allow for the pooling of efforts across countries in order to obtain economies of scale and greater negotiating leverage vis-à-vis corporations. As a result, they have played a key role in impacting the price negotiations for pharmaceutical drugs for developing countries and in increasing access to such drugs in developing countries. Because of their work, some of the negative price-related effects of strengthened IP protection have been effectively mitigated.

Third, perhaps more than any other issue within the TRIPS Agreement, civil society has reacted strongly to the public health issues raised by the patents and undisclosed information sections of the Agreement. There is greater awareness of the impact of these provisions, at least among a certain class of well-educated citizens within developed countries, than that of other provisions within the TRIPS Agreement. Non-profit organizations ranging from Médecins Sans Frontières (Doctors Without Borders) to Oxfam have all spoken out against this section of the TRIPS Agreement and engaged in public awareness campaigns. In addition, student-led efforts, such as Universities Allied for Essential Medicines, have raised awareness on campuses and attempted to change norms and practices for university patenting and licensing.

What is the impact of these developments? Arguably, this section of the TRIPS Agreement has witnessed the most dynamic evolution of any section resulting from the Uruguay Round. At the same time, it offers an interesting case study into the both possibilities and the limits of mobilizing civil society to shape the evolution of international trade law. Below, we detail the initial legal requirements and the subsequent developments in greater detail.

1. THE LEGAL DISCIPLINE

A patent is an exclusive right conferred by a government upon an inventor or the inventor's assignee. In exchange for a right to prevent others from making, using, selling, or distributing the invention without permission, the holder of the patent is required to disclose information about the invention to the public. As a result of this public disclosure, the information within the public domain expands and others are able to build upon past inventions.

The process by which a government evaluates a patent request varies by country, as do the standards employed. In the United States, for example, there is a requirement that a patent be new, non-obvious, and useful or industrially applicable. In other countries, certain subject matter may not be patented. Finally, some countries lack patent regimes altogether. The TRIPS Agreement is an attempt to impose similar standards, to the extent possible, across countries.

The patent regime should be thought of as a series of trade-offs. On the one hand, sufficient incentives need to be provided to encourage innovation and the disclosure of the findings from that innovation. On the other hand, society must also keep in mind certain public interests and social costs that arise from conferring a patent. The legal discipline therefore entails an elaboration of the rights conferred as well as conditional exceptions that may be applied.

Art. 27 TRIPS clarifies what subject matter may be protected by a patent. It also mandates that all national laws use a similar set of evaluative criteria. Governments are to evaluate a patent request on the basis of its novelty, involvement of an inventive step, and industrial applicability. In addition, Art. 27 TRIPS also clarifies categories of inventions that may be excluded from patentability.

One of the important principles of international trade law is the concept of non-discrimination. Art. 27 TRIPS also clarifies how this principle is to be applied within the context of patents. Art. 28 TRIPS then details the exclusive rights that are to be conferred upon an owner of a patent. As noted above, in exchange for these rights, the patent holder is required to disclose information about the invention to the public. The disclosure standard that a government must require is stipulated in Art. 29 TRIPS.

The TRIPS Agreement, however, protects the ability of WTO Members to make exceptions to the exclusive rights conferred upon the patent holder. The conditions which these exceptions must meet are spelled out in Art. 30 TRIPS. In addition, Art. 31 TRIPS lays out the conditions under which a WTO Member may use compulsory licensing, a situation where the government compels the right holder to grant the right to another, say in order to produce a pharmaceutical drug. On the one hand, these articles provide flexibilities to WTO Members to prevent the patent regime from stifling other competing public interests. On the other hand, they are designed to standardize, to the extent possible, the conditions under which exceptions apply and compulsory licensing may be employed.

Finally, the TRIPS Agreement also introduces requirements for the protection of undisclosed information in Art. 39. Among the items afforded protection are what is commonly referred to as trade secrets in some jurisdictions, confidential business information, and test data submitted for regulatory approval for pharmaceuticals and agricultural chemicals. The last of these, in particular, has generated much controversy due to the data exclusivity provisions that have been introduced in national laws in response to Art. 39 TRIPS and subsequent free trade agreements.

2. THE RATIONALE FOR THE LEGAL DISCIPLINE

Prior to the TRIPS Agreement, the Paris Convention (1967) provided some international rules governing the regulation of patents. Yet, the

Paris Convention was notoriously vague. It did not specify what constituted patentable subject matter nor did it mandate a term of protection. These flexibilities, coupled with the lack of an effective enforcement mechanism, allowed countries to shape their patent regimes to accommodate their own national priorities. To the chagrin of multinational companies in developed countries, several developing countries exempted certain subject matter, such as pharmaceuticals, from patent protection. Others limited the scope of patent protection, to say only process patents for pharmaceuticals.

The patent and undisclosed information sections of the TRIPS Agreement were an effort by developed countries to remedy this situation, in response to counterfeiting and the inability to secure patent protection in overseas markets. Developed countries sought to ensure that their producers' goods would receive proper patent protection in developing countries, by mandating that all WTO Members adopt certain minimum standards for patent protection. They also sought to introduce standards regulating undisclosed information, for instances where patent protection was not available or needed to be supplemented. Moreover, they demanded a clear set of uniform rules for the types of exceptions that governments could establish and for when governments could employ compulsory licensing procedures. As a whole, the TRIPS Agreement can be seen as a means to limit the discretion and flexibility of countries in shaping their patent regimes.

Despite this commonality of interests between producers in the major developed countries, there were some important differences between the United States, the European Community, Japan, and Switzerland. Parts of the language should be understood as compromise efforts to bridge these differences. On the whole, however, the Agreement accomplishes much of what the leading executives within the pharmaceutical companies of these countries lobbied for and sought—a more robust and expansive patent regime, coupled with a strengthened enforcement regime.[1]

The question remains why developing countries would be willing to proceed with these terms. The questions raised in Chapter 27 are equally applicable in this context. India and Brazil, along with a few other developing countries, did raise their opposition to many of the patent-related proposals forthcoming from developed countries. At the end of the day, however, much of the strong language in the developed countries' proposals held, with flexibility provided in the form of transition periods for developing countries.

In that sense, the rationale for the legal discipline, from the perspective of developing countries, can only be understood from the context of the Uruguay Round as a whole. The different explanations posited in

---

[1] On this point, see Sell (2003), among others.

Chapter 27 are equally applicable here. Was this part of a "grand bargain"? Or did countries simply "miscalculate" the impact? Or was there a genuine belief that stronger patent protection would spur greater innovation and be positive for economic development? Each of these explanations has earned its own share of supporters and detractors over the years.

What is clear is that, among the WTO legal disciplines, the soundness of the rationale for this section is among the most widely debated. Indeed, the debate on TRIPS and public health, discussed *infra*, was an attempt to reexamine the rationale, leading to a clarification and recalibration of the terms of the legal discipline. While the fundamental architecture is unlikely to change radically, the prospects for further reexamination and recalibration is certainly possible, as the legal discipline evolves.

3. COVERAGE OF THE LEGAL DISCIPLINE

3.1 PARIS CONVENTION (1967) PROVISIONS

As was true of trademarks, the TRIPS Agreement, by way of Art. 2.1 TRIPS, incorporates the relevant obligations concerning patents reflected in Arts. 1–12 and 19 of the Paris Convention. Again, the main innovation here is the fact that these obligations are now subject to the WTO dispute settlement process. This raises the cost of non-compliance by WTO Members.

However, as noted above, the TRIPS Agreement involved a much more extensive rewriting of the international law governing the regulation of patents than was the case with trademarks. In addition, non-compliance with the patent provisions of the Paris Convention has not been a major problem. As a result, the relevant patent-related provisions of the Paris Convention have not been the subject of much controversy. However, it is worth quickly highlighting a few of these obligations below, as they remain obligations under the TRIPS Agreement.

Art. 4 of the Paris Convention provides that any person who has duly filed for a patent in one of the countries shall enjoy a right of priority in the other countries for a designated period of twelve months. This period begins from the date of the filing of the application. In addition, Art. 4G of the Paris Convention clarifies that if the examination of a patent reveals multiple inventions, the applicant may divide the application into divisional applications and preserve the right of priority. The applicant may also, on his own initiative, divide the application and preserve the right of priority, if permitted to do so by the national laws of the country in which he is seeking patent protection.

Art. 4F of the Paris Convention provides certain limitations on the grounds for not providing priority or rejecting a patent application. Specifically, no country "may refuse a priority or a patent application on the ground that the applicant claims multiple priorities, even if they originate in different countries, or on the ground that an application claiming one or more priorities contains one or more elements that were not included in the application or applications whose priority is claimed, provided that, in both cases, there is unity of invention within the meaning of the law of the country."

Also, the patent regimes of each WTO Member are considered to be independent. Art. 4*bis* of the Paris Convention explicitly states that patents applied for in various countries shall be considered independent of patents obtained for the same invention in other countries.

The Paris Convention also contains a number of provisions concerning issues such as compulsory licensing, local working requirements for a patent, and importation of patented articles. These issues are all addressed within the TRIPS Agreement itself. Therefore, we discuss them below rather than in this section. In many instances, the TRIPS Agreement provisions clarify and/or further limit the Paris Convention provisions.

3.2 PROTECTABLE SUBJECT MATTER AND PERMITTED EXCEPTIONS

The TRIPS Agreement resulted in a more precise definition of the subject matter for which a WTO Member must provide patent protection. Prior to TRIPS, the concept of patentability was left up to each country to decide. Art. 1(4) of the Paris Convention, for example, contained a vague and extremely flexible definition of patents; it simply stated that "[p]atents shall include the various kinds of industrial patents recognized by the laws of the countries of the Union" followed by a few illustrative examples.

Art. 27.1 TRIPS states that subject to certain exceptions, to be discussed *infra*, WTO Members must make patents available "for any inventions, whether products or processes, in all fields of technology, provided they are new, involve an inventive step and are capable of industrial application." This sentence is worth highlighting on several fronts.

First, the sentence does not define what constitutes an "invention." Instead, the TRIPS Agreement preserves the flexibility of a WTO Member to decide this question. This question surfaces in a number of areas. For example, legislatures and courts in a number of WTO Members have been or will be asked to consider whether or not human genes are patentable. One of the questions at stake is whether the discovery of a sequence of human genes, which occurs naturally, constitutes an invention. Another example is the issue of the "second indication" of a pharmaceutical product. The second indication refers to a second use of a drug, outside of the original use for which it was intended. For example, Amgen's ligand inhibitor, denosumab (commonly known as Xgeva), was originally intended for postmenopausal women with osteoporosis who are at risk of a bone fracture, but also found to be effective for preventing skeletal-related problems in patients with bone metastases from solid tumors. A question arises as to whether the discovery of the second indication constitutes an invention and is independently patentable. Different WTO Members have resolved these questions differently, and the flexible language of Art. 27.1 TRIPS permits them to do so.

Second, Art. 27.1 TRIPS mandates the patenting of both products and processes. The latter refers to an act, operation, step, or sequence thereof performed on a specific subject matter to obtain a physical result. For example, it may refer to the process of manufacturing a certain product. TRIPS requires that a WTO Member not only allow for the patentability of the end product, but also the process of obtaining it.

Third, the sentence requires that the national law of WTO Members on patentability include three evaluative criteria: (1) novelty, (2) involvement of an inventive step; and (3) industrial applicability. A footnote to this sentence clarifies that the second criteria may be deemed by a Member to be synonymous with the term "non-obvious" and that the third criteria may be deemed to be synonymous with the term "useful." This footnote, in essence, ensures that criteria laid forth in US patent law are in compliance with this provision. Provided the three criteria are met, the WTO Member must grant a patent to the product or process, unless certain exceptions apply.

These exceptions are spelled out in the remainder of Art. 27 TRIPS. Art. 27.2 TRIPS permits WTO Members to enact exceptions for the patentability of certain inventions if "necessary to protect the *ordre public* or morality." Among the examples given are exceptions to "protect human, animal, or plant life or health" and "to avoid serious prejudice to the environment." Several points are worth noting about this sentence as well.

First, Art. 27.2 TRIPS makes clear that any WTO Member seeking to enact this exception must do so on the level of an individual invention. As a result, a WTO Member cannot subject an entire category of products to a blanket Art. 27.2 TRIPS exception. For example, a country cannot refuse to grant patents to all pharmaceuticals simply because of a need to protect human health. Instead, it must consider each individual pharmaceutical invention independently.

Second, Art. 27.2 TRIPS borrows heavily from the exceptions language of Art. XX GATT and Art. XIV GATS. However, it is not identical. As a result, one open question for debate is the extent to which the jurisprudence involving the other non-TRIPS exceptions applies to the interpretation of Art. 27 TRIPS. In particular, note that the "necessity" formulation found in certain provisions of Art. XX GATT and Art. XIV GATS continues to hold true in Art. 27.2 TRIPS, but that unlike these other provisions, Art. 27.2 is not subject to a blanket chapeau requiring that the exceptions measure not constitute an arbitrary or unjustifiable discrimination between countries.

Third, the English language version of Art. 27.2 TRIPS makes explicit use of the French term, *ordre public*, rather than the English term, public order. The two terms have different connotations under their legal traditions. It is important that Art. 27.2 TRIPS be interpreted exclusively under the French tradition of *ordre public*, rather than under the public order standard that applies, for example, in Art. XIV GATS.

In addition to the exceptions permitted under Art. 27.2 TRIPS, an additional set of exceptions are also enumerated in Art. 27.3 TRIPS. Unlike Art. 27.2 TRIPS, however, the exceptions spelled out in Art. 27.3 TRIPS are categorical exceptions. As a result, a WTO Member can enact a categorical ban in its patent law and need not consider the exception on an invention-by-invention basis. The categories spelled out in Art. 27.3 TRIPS as excludable from patentability are:

- Diagnostic, therapeutic and surgical methods for the treatments of humans or animals;
- Plants and animals, other than micro-organisms; and
- Essentially biological processes for the production of plants or animals, other than non-biological and microbiological processes.

However, if a WTO Member chooses not to allow patenting of plants, then it is required by Art. 27.3(b) TRIPS to provide for the protection of plant varieties by an effective *sui generis* system. An example of such a system is that which was established by the International Convention for the Protection of New Plant Varieties (UPOV Convention).

The patenting of plant varieties is an extremely controversial topic as it affects the issue of food production, particularly with respect to use of seeds by farmers. Those in favor of providing enhanced IP protection have argued that it helps spur greater research and innovation into disease-resistant seeds and more efficient seeds, thereby increasing global food production. However, opponents argue that allowing plant varieties to be patented advantages large corporations, such as Monsanto, at the expense of small farmers. Yet, the issue is not simply a developed country versus developing country one. During the Uruguay Round negotiations, the EC pushed heavily for language along the lines of the Art. 27.3(b) exception, as plant and animal varieties are excluded under the European Patent Convention. What resulted is the categorical exception permitted under Art. 27.3, along with an acknowledgement that implementation of such an exception is optional for WTO Members.

3.3 TERM OF PROTECTION

The TRIPS Agreement also resulted in harmonization across WTO Members regarding the length of a patent term. Prior to TRIPS, patent terms differed across countries. Furthermore, countries disagreed about how the patent term should be calculated. Some based their calculation on the filing date of the patent, while others based it on the date that the patent was granted.

Art. 33 TRIPS requires WTO Members to provide that the "term of protection available for a patent shall not end before the expiration of twenty years counted from the filing date." The Agreement also includes a footnote clarifying the situation for those WTO Members which do not grant patents originally but instead base it on the system of others. For such countries, the period may be based on the filing date in the system of the original grant.

Note that the provision is silent as to how WTO Members are to conduct their patent review and regulatory approval processes. In those regards, WTO Members maintain much flexibility. Art. 33 TRIPS only discusses the first date when the term of protection is allowed to expire. It does not discuss when the effective date of protection (*i.e.*, the date when a right holder is allowed to obtain damages for patent infringement) must begin. Members are allowed to specify that the effective date begins only after the patent is granted. Thus, while Art. 33 TRIPS requires a patent term of 20 years, the effective period of protection is likely to be much shorter.

Also, Members are under no obligation to extend the term of a patent to compensate for delays in the regulatory approval process. Developing countries rejected efforts to include language to this effect by developed countries. However, such language is included in many of the post-TRIPS preferential free trade agreements concluded by the US.

Many countries, including the US, amended their patent laws in order to bring changes in their patent term into compliance with Art. 33 TRIPS. In *Canada–Patent Term of Protection*, the AB clarified that the requirement applied to all patents which are in effect at the time that the obligation entered into force. It rejected Canada's argument that Art. 33 TRIPS applied only to new patent grants, and not previously-granted patents still in force.

3.4 EXCLUSIVE RIGHTS CONFERRED ON THE PATENT OWNER

Art. 28 TRIPS clarifies the exclusive rights that must be conferred to the owner of a patent by a WTO Member. Owners of a product patent must be accorded the exclusive right "to prevent third parties not having the owner's consent from the acts of: making, using, offering for sale, selling, or importing for these purposes that product." Owners of a process patent must be accorded the exclusive right "to prevent third parties not having the owner's consent from the act of using the process and from the acts of: making, using, offering for sale, selling, or importing for these purposes that process." In addition, all patent owners shall also have the exclusive right "to assign, or transfer by succession, the patent and to conclude licensing contracts."[2] With regard to importation, a footnote makes clear that Art. 28 TRIPS must be read in conjunction with Art. 6 TRIPS, concerning exhaustion.

Art. 28 TRIPS resulted in a harmonization of a set of minimum exclusive rights to be enjoyed by the holder of a granted patent in WTO Members. It is these exclusive rights which provide a patent owner with the ability to exploit his or her invention for gain.

3.5 NON–DISCRIMINATION PRINCIPLE

While the principle of non-discrimination is clearly elaborated in Arts. 3–4 TRIPS, negotiators considered it necessary to identify in Art. 27.1 TRIPS three specific ways in which a WTO Member could not discriminate in its provision of patent rights. Subject to the Art. 27 TRIPS exceptions mentioned above, WTO Members are forbidden from discriminating on the basis of:

- Place of invention
- Field of technology; and
- Whether products are imported or locally produced

Art. 27.1 TRIPS makes clear that the obligation to not discriminate applies to both the availability and enjoyment of patent rights. In other words, a WTO Member may not discriminate in either its granting of patent rights or its enforcement of patent rights.

Why are these three specific elaborations necessary? The first, non-discrimination with regard to the place of invention, ensures that a WTO Member cannot impose a requirement that patent rights are made available only when the inventive activity takes place on the Member's territory. Such a condition arguably would not violate national treatment principles (at least, with respect to de jure discrimination). Yet, it would seriously disadvantage foreign inventors. Art. 27.1 TRIPS therefore clarifies that a territoriality requirement with respect to invention is forbidden.

The principle of non-discrimination with respect to the field of technology is already reflected in the first sentence of Art. 27.1 TRIPS emphasizing that "patents shall be available for any inventions . . . in all fields of technology." Thus, the need to reemphasize this point in the non-

---

[2] Note that as the provision is drafted, this exclusive right to assignment must be provided only to owners of a granted patent. It does not have to be granted to applicants whose patents have not yet been granted.

discrimination sentence is to ensure that no discrimination occur in the enforcement of patents based on the field of technology. In other words, WTO Members cannot simply grant a patent for a particular area (*e.g.*, pharmaceuticals) but then discriminate through under-enforcement.

The third elaboration is designed to address of whether WTO Members may discriminate on the basis of where an invention is produced. Art. 27.1 TRIPS makes clear that Members may not. In other words, Members may not condition enforcement of patent rights on local production of the patented product.

In *Canada–Pharmaceutical Patents*, a WTO Panel clarified that the non-discrimination principle extends to Art. 30 TRIPS, which concerns exceptions to the exclusive rights conferred upon the patent owner. That is to say, any legally-permitted exceptions may not be discriminatory. In addition, it is widely believed that the principle also extends to the use of compulsory licensing. Both topics are discussed, *infra*.

3.6 DISCLOSURE CONDITIONS ON PATENT APPLICANTS

Underlying the patent system is a trade-off: In exchange for enjoying certain exclusive rights for a limited period, patent owners are required to disclose their claimed invention. After the term of protection expires, the public at large may take advantage of this disclosure for its own use. This allows for knowledge, which would otherwise be kept secret, to be disseminated into the public domain. In principle, this should result in a public externality gain, as individuals and corporations can build off the knowledge of others.

This system, however, only works if the information being disclosed is sufficient for others to understand the invention. Otherwise, the public will grant the inventor an exclusive period to reap the gains of the invention without reaping anything in exchange. To ensure that this trade-off occurs, Art. 29 TRIPS stipulates the disclosure standard that must be set by WTO Members in their national patent laws. It states: "Members shall require that an applicant for a patent shall disclose the invention in a manner sufficiently clear and complete for the invention to be carried out by a person skilled in the art and may require the applicant to indicate the best mode for carrying out the invention known to the inventor at the filing date or, where priority is claimed, at the priority date of the application."

Art. 29 TRIPS also allows Members the option of requiring that a patent applicant disclose information concerning its corresponding foreign applications and grants. This flexibility is especially important for WTO Members with weaker capacities in their patent offices. As a result of this provision, such patent offices may rely on the work of other Members' patent offices to help inform their own work. For example, if a patent application is denied in another country, a Member may require that the applicant disclose information regarding the denial. The same requirement may hold true in the case of a patent grant or revocation.

3.7 EXCEPTIONS TO THE RIGHTS CONFERRED

A WTO Member, however, may wish to make certain exceptions to the exclusive rights granted for a patent. Art. 30 TRIPS grants Members the right to allow for such exceptions. At the same time, it establishes three conditions that must be met, whenever such an exception is allowed under the law of a WTO Member. First, the exception must be "limited." Second, it must not "unreasonably conflict with a normal exploitation of the patent." Third, it must also "not unreasonably prejudice the legitimate interests of the patent owner." A caveat is included which states that in applying an exception, a Member is to take into account "the legitimate interests of third parties."

In *Canada–Pharmaceutical Patents*, the Panel (§ 7.20) clarified that the "three conditions are cumulative, each being a separate and independent requirement that must be satisfied. Failure to comply with any one of the three conditions results in the Article 30 exception being disallowed." The Panel also further clarified each of the three requirements.

The two sides to the dispute—Canada and the EC—offered competing arguments as to the meaning of the first requirement: that an exception be limited. Canada (§ 7.27) argued that the word "limited" should be "interpreted according to the conventional dictionary definition, such as 'confined within definite limits', or 'restricted in scope, extent, amount'." On the other hand, the EC (§ 7.28) asserted that the word "limited" "connotes a narrow exception, one that could be described by words such as 'narrow, small, minor, insignificant or restricted.' " In assessing the requirement, the EC argued that the Panel should assess the impact of the exceptions measure on the exclusionary rights granted to a patent owner rather than the restrictiveness of the measure.

The Panel (§§ 7.30–7.31) sided largely with the EC:

"The Panel agreed with the EC that, as used in this context, the word 'limited' has a narrower connotation than the rather broad definitions cited by Canada. Although the word itself can have both broad and narrow definitions . . . the narrower definition is the more appropriate when the word 'limited' is used as part of the phrase 'limited exception'. The word 'exception' by itself connotes a limited derogation, one that does not undercut the body of rules from which it is made. When a treaty uses the term 'limited exception', the word 'limited' must be given a meaning separate from the limitation implicit in the word 'exception' itself. The term 'limited exception' must therefore be read to connote a narrow exception—one which makes only a small diminution of the rights in question.

The Panel agreed with the EC interpretation that 'limited' is to be measured by the extent to which the exclusive rights of the patent owner have been curtailed. The full text of Article 30 refers to 'limited exceptions to the exclusive rights conferred by a patent'. In the absence of other indications, the Panel concluded that it would be justified in reading the text literally, focusing on the extent to which legal rights have been curtailed, rather than the size or extent of the economic impact. In support of this conclusion, the Panel noted that the following two conditions of Article 30 ask more particularly about the economic impact of the exception, and provide two sets of standards by which such impact may be judged. The term 'limited exceptions' is the only one of the three conditions in Article 30 under which the extent of the curtailment of rights as such is dealt with."

However, the Panel (§ 7.32) added a caveat:

"The Panel does not agree, however, with the EC's position that the curtailment of legal rights can be measured by simply counting the number of legal rights impaired by an exception. A very small act could well violate all five rights provided by Article 28.1 and yet leave each of the patent owner's rights intact for all useful purposes. To determine whether a particular exception constitutes a limited exception, the extent to which the patent owner's rights have been curtailed must be measured."

The second condition of Art. 30 TRIPS is that an exception must not "unreasonably conflict with a normal exploitation of the patent." The Panel (§ 7.55) interpreted the term "normal exploitation of the patent" to mean the right of the patent owner "to exclude all forms of competition that could detract significantly from the economic returns anticipated from a patent's grant of market exclusivity." It further added that "[t]he specific forms of patent exploitation are not static, of course, for to be effective exploitation must adapt to changing forms of competition due to technological development and the evolution of marketing practices." In other words, the term is to be interpreted dynamically. Moreover, as to what constitutes "normal," the Panel (§ 7.54) held that the term should be understood to combine two meanings: (1) "an empirical conclusion about what is common within a relevant community" and (2) "a normative standard of entitlement."

Finally, the Panel in *Canada–Pharmaceutical Patents* also interpreted the meaning of what constitutes a "legitimate interest." Note that this term is used in both the third condition—that the exception must "not unreasonably prejudice the legitimate interests of the patent owner"—as well as the caveat to Art. 30 TRIPS requiring WTO Members to consider the "legitimate interests of third parties" when implementing an exception. The Panel (§ 7.68) rejected the EC's argument that the term, with respect to the third condition, should be equated to the legal interests defined in Art. 28(1) TRIPS (*i.e.*, the exclusive rights which are required to be conferred under the TRIPS Agreement). Instead, the Panel (§ 7.69) held that "the term must be defined in a way that it is often used in legal discourse—as a normative claim calling for protection of interests that are 'justifiable' in the sense that they are supported by relevant public policies or other social norms."

What then are some possible exceptions that a WTO Member may provide as a result of Art. 30 TRIPS? One is to provide a parallel imports exception, meaning that one may import a product that has been put on the market of another country with the consent of the patent owner. This type of exception is explicitly contemplated in the footnote to Art. 28.1 TRIPS.

Another is to provide an exception for non-commercial use, such as for teaching purposes. A third is to provide an exception for research and experimental use. For example, Art. 27.b of the EU's Community Patent Convention permits "acts done for experimental purposes relating to the subset-matter of the patented invention." An exception for experimental use is important for encouraging further innovation based on the disclosure of the invention.

One final exception worth discussing more extensively is an exception allowing for the use of a patent for purposes of seeking regulatory approval for the marketing of a product prior to the expiration of a patent. The most widely known version of such an exception is the so-called "Bolar exception" for pharmaceuticals.[3] It allows potential generic producers of a patented pharmaceutical to use the invention to seek regulatory approval of the generic version of the product so that it can be sold shortly after the expiration of the patent. At issue in the *Canada–Pharmaceutical Patents* dispute was whether Canada's version of the Bolar exception was permissible under Art. 30 TRIPS. Canada's Patent Act allowed third parties, prior to the expiration of a patent, to produce a product, without the patent holder's consent, under two circumstances. First, a third party was allowed to do so for regulatory review purposes. In other words, the third party was allowed to produce the patented product to the extent necessary in order to gain the information needed to obtain regulatory approval of the third party's version of the product (*e.g.*, test data). Second, a third party was also allowed to do so for stockpiling purposes. This allowed the third party to manufacture and store the product so that it is able to sell the product shortly after the expiration of the patent. In *Canada–Pharmaceutical Patents*, the Panel held that an

---

[3] This exception is named after the US case, *Roche Products Inc. v. Bolar Pharmaceutical Co.*, 733 F.2d 858 (Fed. Cir. 1984).

exception for regulatory review purposes was permissible, but that an exception for stockpiling purposes violated Art. 30 TRIPS (§ 7.36).

One issue that has arisen is whether the non-discrimination principle of Art. 27.1 TRIPS applies to Art. 30 TRIPS. Recall that Art. 27.1 TRIPS guarantees that patent rights be enjoyable "without discrimination as to the place of invention, the field of technology and whether products are imported or locally produced." A question arises as to whether an exception, targeted at a particular industry, would violate Art. 27.1 TRIPS.

In *Canada–Pharmaceutical Patents*, the Panel (§ 7.91–7.93) explicitly rejected Canada's argument that the non-discrimination requirement of Art. 27.1 TRIPS did not apply to exceptions under Art. 30 TRIPS. It explained:

> "Article 27.1 prohibits discrimination as to enjoyment of 'patent rights' without qualifying that term. Article 30 exceptions are explicitly described as 'exceptions to the exclusive rights conferred by a patent' and contain no indication that any exemption from non-discrimination rules is intended. A discriminatory exception that takes away enjoyment of a patent right is discrimination as much as is discrimination in the basic rights themselves."

However, a question arises as to whether an exception may be targeted for a specific industry, or whether such an exception would constitute discrimination as to the field of technology. Dinwoodie and Dreyfus (2009), among others, have proposed that industry-specific exceptions be permissible, so long as a WTO Member defending such an exception be allowed to rebut a showing of disparate treatment by demonstrating a legitimate purpose. The Panel in *Canada–Pharmaceutical Patents* appears to endorse this approach. It (§ 7.92) further clarified "it is not true that Article 27 requires all Article 30 exceptions to be applied to all products" and that "Article 27 does not prohibit bona fide exceptions to deal with problems that may exist only in certain product areas." Thus, regulatory approval measures for a certain industry are permissible under the Art. 30 TRIPS exception.

To reiterate, exceptions to the exclusive rights mandated by Art. 28 TRIPS are allowed so long as they meet the three conditions set forth in Art. 30 TRIPS. However, the validity of such exceptions is to be considered on a case-by-case basis. So long as future Panels choose to continue abiding by the approach established in *Canada–Pharmaceutical Patents*, an assessment of the three conditions will involve numerous assessments which vary depending on the context. To name but a few such assessments, a Panel will need to determine: (a) to what extent the exception curtails the exclusive rights of the patent holder; (b) what is "unreasonable", (c) what is "normal", and (d) what are "legitimate interests." Thus, Art. 30 TRIPS should be considered to provide only a certain set of guidelines which vary depending on circumstances and which are likely to evolve over time.

3.8 COMPULSORY LICENSING

Enacting an exception under Art. 30 TRIPS is one way to limit the rights of the patent holder. Another way to do so is through a compulsory license. This refers to a situation in which the government forces the holder of a patent (or another exclusive right) to grant that right to the government or another entity. For example, in order to address concerns over the supply of a patented drug, a government might choose to grant a compulsory license so that other manufacturers can produce the drug.

Prior to TRIPS, compulsory licensing was only briefly addressed in international agreements. Art. 5A(2) of the Paris Convention noted that each country had the right to take legislative measures for providing the grant of a compulsory license "to prevent the abuses which might result from the exercise of the exclusive rights conferred by the patent." Art. 5A(3) requires that two years must pass from the grant of the first compulsory license before authorities may institute proceedings for forfeiture or revocation of a patent. Finally, Art. 5A(4) requires that at least four years pass from the date of filing of a patent and three years pass from the date of the grant of the patent before a compulsory licensing can be granted for failure to "work" a patent. The requirements of Art. 5A of the Paris Convention continue to apply under the TRIPS Agreement, which incorporates these provisions.

However, what the TRIPS Agreement accomplishes, with respect to compulsory licensing, is much more ambitious. Art. 31 TRIPS establishes a common set of additional rules for the use of a compulsory license by a WTO Member. By and large, the TRIPS Agreement preserves the flexibility of WTO Members to determine the circumstances under which a compulsory license may be applied. It offers an illustrative list of such circumstances: for example, national emergencies, a case of extreme urgency, public non-commercial use, or remedy of an anti-competitive practice. WTO Members, however, need not limit the use of compulsory license to such circumstances.

The only field of technology where WTO Members are not given flexibility to define the circumstances for use of a compulsory license is semiconductor technology. Art. 31(c) TRIPS explicitly confines the use of a compulsory license of a patent related to semiconductor technology to two situations: (1) "public non-commercial use" and (2) "to remedy a practice determined after judicial or administrative process to be anti-competitive."

For all other fields of technology, Art. 31 TRIPS simply presents a checklist of conditions that must be met whenever a compulsory license is granted.

First, except under certain circumstances, Art. 31(b) TRIPS requires that the proposed user of a compulsory license have engaged in prior negotiations with the right holder. Specifically, the provision requires that the proposed user have "made efforts to obtain authorization from the right holder on reasonable commercial terms and conditions and that such efforts have not been successful within a reasonable period of time." As this provision has not been subject to any dispute settlement proceedings, no interpretation of "reasonableness" has been offered in this context.

Prior negotiation is not required under the following circumstances: (1) where a compulsory license is granted to remedy an anti-competitive practice determined by a judicial or administrative authority; (2) "in the case of a national emergency or other circumstances of extreme urgency"; and (3) "in cases of public non-commercial use," meaning instances where the proposed user is the government or a government contractor. In both the second and third circumstances, the right holder is to be informed. In the second circumstance, notification must be made "as soon as reasonably possibly"; in the third circumstance, it must be done "promptly."

Second, Art. 31(c) TRIPS requires that the scope and duration of any compulsory license "shall be limited to the purpose for which it was authorized." The requirement regarding scope means that the compulsory license must be proportional. It cannot be used for other purposes beyond the authorized purpose. The requirement regarding duration means that once the original authorized purpose is accomplished and the original circumstances are unlikely to recur, the compulsory license must terminate. In other words, systems which automatically grant a compulsory license until the end of a patent term are unlikely to be permissible.

Third, the compulsory licensing must be non-exclusive and non-assignable, according to Art. 31(d) and (e) TRIPS, respectively. That is to say that a compulsory license cannot deny the patent owner from being able to use the patent. Furthermore, a party who is the user of a compulsory license cannot assign this right to another party. An exception is made for the "enterprise or goodwill" in respect of which the compulsory license was granted.

Fourth, Art. 31(h) TRIPS requires that WTO Members establish a mechanism by which the right holder is "paid adequate remuneration in the circumstances of each case, taking into account the economic value of the authorization." That is to say, that the patent holder must be compensated for the use of the patent through a compulsory license. However, the only limitation placed by TRIPS on the value of the compensation is that it be "adequate." This meaning of this term has not been defined in any dispute. It is likely that it would vary on a case-by-case basis.

Note that the existence of the possibility of a compulsory license alone reduces the leverage that the patent holder has in negotiations over the use of the patent. If a patent holder holds out from granting a voluntary license because it is dissatisfied with the commercial terms being offered, it faces the threat that the government may step in and grant a compulsory license. So long as the remuneration terms being offered by a potential user are above what could be considered "adequate," the patent holder should be inclined eventually to grant a voluntary license rather than continually hold out for better terms.

Fifth, TRIPS also requires that WTO Members establish a system of "judicial review or other independent review" for compulsory licenses. Art. 31(i) TRIPS requires that judicial review apply to decisions to grant or renew a compulsory license, while Art. 31(j) TRIPS requires that it also apply to the terms of remuneration paid to the patent holder. The use of the term "other independent review" as an alternative to judicial review is due to the fact that in many countries, compulsory licensing decisions are made and also reviewed by administrative bodies. What Art. 31 TRIPS requires is that the entity reviewing these decisions be separate and independent from that which made the decision.

This checklist of conditions applies to all compulsory licenses or other non-voluntary uses of a patent. In addition, three additional conditions apply for dependent patents. A dependent patent is one where the use of a patent (known as the second patent) depends on authorization to use another patent (known as the first patent). In such circumstances, Art. 31(l) TRIPS requires that:

(i) "the invention claimed in the second patent shall involve an important technical advance of considerable economic significance in relation to the invention claimed in the first patent;

(ii) the owner of the first patent shall be entitled to a cross-license on reasonable terms to use the invention claimed in the second patent and

(iii) the use authorized in respect of the first patent shall be non-assignable except with the assignment of the second patent."

The exact scope of the requirements of Art. 31(j) has yet to be determined. Note the use of several terms—"considerable economic value" and "reasonable terms"—whose interpretation can vary across WTO Members and whose meanings have yet to be determined in a WTO dispute. Nevertheless, Art. 31(j) does impose additional requirements on the use of compulsory licenses for dependent patents.

Like Art. 30 TRIPS, a question also arises as to whether the non-discrimination principles underlying Art. 27.1 TRIPS apply in the context of Art. 31 TRIPS. Although the question has never been explicitly the subject of a dispute, the Panel decision in *Canada–Pharmaceutical Pa-*

tents is widely believed to provide support for answering this question in the affirmative. In that dispute, the Panel (§ 7.91) described as "acknowledged fact" the notion that "the Article 31 exception for compulsory licences and government use is understood to be subject to the non-discrimination rule of Article 27.1."

Furthermore, there is the question of whether a compulsory license may be limited to a particular industry without violating the Art. 27.1 TRIPS principle of non-discrimination with respect to the field of technology. While no Panel has ever considered this question, there is widespread support that such compulsory licenses are permissible. First, the Panel's jurisprudence in *Canada–Pharmaceutical Patents*, which allows for limited-scope exceptions so long as they cover the applicable problem area, is often seen as suggesting that a similar principle holds true in the context of limited-scope compulsory licenses. Second, the Doha Declaration on the TRIPS Agreement and Public Health, discussed *infra*, explicitly contemplates the use of a compulsory license for a particular area, pharmaceuticals.

A dispute has arisen over the question of whether the non-discrimination principle of Art. 27.1 TRIPS is violated when a compulsory license arises due to a patent owner's failure to work a patent locally. In *Brazil–Patent Protection*, the US challenged a provision of Brazil's 1996 Industrial Property Law allowing for such compulsory licenses. Brazil's law allowed its authorities to issue a compulsory license in the event that a patent was not "worked" in Brazil within three years of the patent's issuance. The law defined a patent as being "worked" if the patented invention was manufactured in Brazil or the patented process was used in Brazil. The US contended that linking compulsory licensing with a local working requirement violated the non-discrimination principle of Art. 27.1 TRIPS, which stipulates that patent rights shall be enjoyable without discrimination as to "whether products are imported or locally produced." However, the question of whether Brazil's measures violated Art. 27.1 TRIPS was not resolved by a WTO Panel. Instead, Brazil and the US notified the WTO that the parties had reached a mutually-agreed solution based on bilateral consultations.

Overall, as a result of the TRIPS Agreement, additional international rules have been put in place regarding compulsory licensing. While these rules still leave considerable flexibility for a country to grant a compulsory license, they do standardize, and therefore restrict, the use beyond what was allowed prior to TRIPS. Nevertheless, the threat of a compulsory license does present many governments with significant leverage when negotiating with a patent holder over price, volume, release date, or other elements of a patent-protected product.

3.9 PROTECTION OF TEST DATA NECESSARY FOR REGULATORY APPROVAL

The requirements discussed above were all established in the patents section of the TRIPS Agreement, *i.e.*, Section 5 of Part II of the Agreement. They have been extremely controversial because the provisions, as a whole, have triggered an expansion in the scope of patent protection for a number of subject matter, such as pharmaceuticals and agricultural products. As discussed in the Introduction, this extension of protection has major implications on public health, food security, and other public policy matters. These have been of particular concern in developing countries.

The patent section of the TRIPS Agreement is not the only section that gives rise to concern. The other section, closely linked with respect to many patented products, is Section 7 of Part II of the TRIPS Agreement, entitled "Protection of Undisclosed Information." This section concerns the protection of confidential information within the control of a legal person as well as data submitted to government authorities for regulatory approval.

The section consists of only one provision, Article 39. However, this provision should be considered as having two distinct components. Art. 39.2 TRIPS concerns the regulation of undisclosed information, or what is commonly referred to as a trade secret in many WTO Members' jurisdictions. Art. 39.3 TRIPS concerns the regulation of undisclosed test data submitted to regulatory authorities as a condition of approval for marketing of a pharmaceutical or agricultural chemical product. We begin by first discussing the latter, which is, by far, the more controversial.

Before elaborating on the requirements of Art. 39.3 TRIPS in detail, it is important to understand first why such a section exists at all within the TRIPS Agreement. As noted above, the provision deals only with pharmaceuticals and agricultural chemicals. For these products, most governments will require that the producer of such products obtain regulatory approval first, before being allowed to market the product for sale. This is because of concerns about human health, animal health, the environment, and possibly other issues.

Governments may choose to test the product directly. More commonly, they may require that the producer submit the results of its own test data verifying the safety of the product for government authorities to review. The production of this test data is often a major cost to the manufacturer. Consider, for example, the costs involved to test a pharmaceutical. The drug company must set up a whole series of clinical trials, for which it must recruit subjects, monitor results, and synthesize the data. It also expends effort preparing its regulatory submission and discussing its trial results with regulatory authorities.

The first party to seek regulatory approval has no choice but to produce the test data necessary to gain approval. But governments have a range of options for policies on how to deal with subsequent parties which also seek marketing approval. Many governments allow for a streamlined process for any subsequent party that claims to have produced a product identical to the first party's product. For such parties, the government may require that it only prove that its product is identical. It need not produce any additional test data. Instead, it can rely on the test data submitted by the first party. The rationale for a government adopting this type of policy approach is two-fold: First, it avoids a wasteful duplication of resources. Second, it allows for faster entry to market of competitor products, which in turn lower costs to the benefit of consumers. Note that a government can implement variants of the policy described above. For example, it may choose to allow for reliance on test data only after the passage of a certain amount of time. This type of policy is known as one which grants a "data exclusivity" period.

Companies that were likely to be first movers in a product market argued that a reliance policy without a sufficiently long "data exclusivity" period was unfair. Essentially, they had invested extensively in the costs of gathering their test data, and their competitors were being allowed to "free ride" off their investment. On the other hand, many policy activists argued in favor of allowing for continued flexibility of policies allowing for reliance on test data. If a generic or low-cost manufacturer can prove that its product is identical, they argued, why should it expend unnecessary resources to gather test data when authorities have already approved a competitor's identical product? Allowing for reliance would help keep prices low, ensuring greater access to essential drugs and allowing farmers to afford agricultural chemicals.

Prior to the TRIPS Agreement, the issue of how such test data should be regulated was not discussed in any international agreement. Art. 39.3 TRIPS attempts to deal with these issues, at least with respect to pharmaceuticals and agricultural chemicals. However, it should be noted that this issue only emerges when the pharmaceutical or agricultural chemical is either: (a) not protected by patent, or (b) given regulatory approval close to the expiration of its patent term. Otherwise, the exclusive rights granted under the patent renders the issue irrelevant for the duration of the patent term.

Art. 39.3 TRIPS reads as follows:

Members, when requiring, as a condition of approving the marketing of pharmaceutical or of agricultural chemical products which utilize new chemical entities, the submission of undisclosed test or other data, the origination of which involves considerable effort, shall protect such data against unfair commercial use. In addition, Members shall protect such data against disclosure, except where necessary to protect the public, or unless steps are taken to ensure that the data are protected against unfair commercial use.

Note that there are a number of terms here which are left ambiguous. This reflects, in part, the difficulty negotiators had in arriving at acceptable language on this provision. As one might expect, Art. 39.3 TRIPS sparked considerable controversy with some developing countries. The ambiguous language leaves sufficient room for flexibility in the implementation of this requirement.

First, note that the provision only applies to the regulatory approval process for a pharmaceutical or agricultural chemical which contains a "new chemical entity." This term is left undefined, and was introduced only in the later stages of the Uruguay Round negotiations. What is considered a "new chemical entity" is left up to the interpretation of each WTO Member.[4] However, what are clearly excluded by the term are situations where the pharmaceutical or agricultural chemical is simply of a different dosage or administered in a different manner.

Second, note that the provision only applies to test data whose origination required "considerable effort." Again, the standards for defining this term are left to the discretion of each WTO Member. Presumably, clinical trials involving some investment of resources should meet the standard.

Third, Art. 39.3 TRIPS only protects the data against "unfair commercial use." This is an important qualification, and the boundaries of this qualification are left for each WTO Member to define. Art. 39.3 TRIPS does not forbid the use of this data for non-commercial purposes. Thus, the data may be used by government authorities to assess the safety and efficacy of the product. It may also be used for public policy purposes. However, WTO Members are given flexibility to define what is "unfair."

Many developed countries have interpreted Art. 39.3 TRIPS to suggest that were a second producer allowed to free ride off the first producer's investments in testing its research and development soon thereafter, this would be "unfair." Thus, they have chosen to confer a period of "data exclusivity." Recall that this is a period of time whereby no other company may rely on the test data to obtain marketing approval for an identical product. The US and EU have also demanded that countries signing a preferential trade agreement implement similar data exclusivity provisions. Such provisions effectively prevent generic versions of pharmaceu-

---

[4] On the negotiating history, see Gervais (2007). For example, in the US, the Food and Drug Administration defines a "new chemical entity" as one which does not contain an "active moiety," or molecule responsible for the physiological or pharmacological action of the drug, that has been previously approved by the FDA.

ticals (or agricultural chemicals) from being marketed for the data exclusivity period.[5] As a result, they have been highly controversial.

Other developing countries have interpreted the concept of "unfair commercial use" more liberally. In particular, some countries do not directly examine the test data, but simply rely on the fact that the pharmaceutical or agricultural chemical has been approved in another jurisdiction (most likely, the US, EU, or Japan) for its regulatory review. In such countries, the authorities may simply ask that the second producer show that its product is identical, often meaning bio-equivalent, to the product already approved overseas. Once this is shown, they will grant regulatory approval for the second manufacturer's product. These countries argue that neither the regulatory authorities nor the second manufacturer, in effect, ever "use" the data. What they have relied upon is the foreign approval rather than the data itself. Thus, their practice, they argue, is in compliance with Art. 39.3 TRIPS.

Finally, note that Art. 39.3 TRIPS binds WTO Members to a non-disclosure obligation regarding the test data. That is to say, government authorities cannot disclose the data to other individuals, corporations, or the public at large. This is subject to two exceptions. First, authorities may disclose data in the event that it is "necessary to protect the public." While the language grants sufficient flexibility to WTO Members to interpret this phrase, it would likely be subject to the necessity test imposed on other GATT and GATS exceptions. Second, authorities may disclose data if "steps are taken to ensure that the data are protected against unfair commercial use." Again, the debate over what constitutes "unfair commercial use" emerges in this context. In addition, the burden of proof would fall on the WTO Member to illustrate the steps that it has taken to implement guarantees against such use.

3.10 TRADE SECRETS AND CONFIDENTIAL INFORMATION

The other component of Art. 39 TRIPS concerns undisclosed information that is lawfully within the control of a natural or legal person. Such information is sometimes referred to as "trade secrets" or "confidential information" within the national laws of WTO Members.

Prior to the TRIPS Agreement, the only provision in an international agreement which could be considered to regulate this subject matter was Art. 10*bis* of the Paris Convention. That article concerned unfair competition broadly. It required that countries that were party to the Convention provide "effective protection against unfair competition" defined as "[a]ny

---

[5] Of course, the generic pharmaceutical or agricultural chemical manufacturer could engage in its own clinical tests to gather the data necessary to obtain regulatory approval. However, because of the costs involved, most do not do so. Therefore, the data exclusivity provision serves as an effective bar.

act of competition contrary to honest practices in industrial or commercial matters." Presumably, the unauthorized use of a competitor's trade secrets / confidential information falls into this category. As such, Art. 10*bis* of the Paris Convention could be read as requiring "effective protection" against such acts.

The TRIPS Agreement attempts to situate Section 7 by noting that the requirements of Article 39 are elaborations on the "effective protection" required by Art. 10*bis* of the Paris Convention rather than new international obligations. This is done in three ways.

First, Art. 39.2 TRIPS clarifies the characteristics of information which must be afforded effective protection. Such information must meet three requirements. (1) It must be secret, meaning that "it is not, as a body or in the precise configuration or assembly of its components, generally known among or readily accessible to persons within the circles that normally deal with this kind of information." Note that the test requires a comparison against the knowledge of others skilled in dealing with this information, rather than that of the public at large. (2) It must have commercial value because it is secret. (3) It "has been subject to reasonable steps under the circumstances, by the personal lawfully in control of the information, to keep it secret."

Second, provided the three criteria for the type of information are met, Art. 39.2 TRIPS defines the type of protection which must be accorded. WTO Members must grant persons possessing such information "the possibility of preventing the information lawfully within their control from being disclosed to, acquired by, or used by others without their consent in a manner contrary to honest commercial practices." Note that this requirement does not require the original bearer of the information to identify the source of the violation. A WTO Member may be in violation simply if it can be shown that it did not enact measures to prevent such measures from being used, even if it is unclear to the aggrieved how others came to be privy to this information.

Finally, whereas the Paris Convention leaves the definition of "honest practice in industrial or commercial matters" to the discretion of individual countries, a footnote to Art. 39.2 TRIPS provides an illustrative list of what is meant by "honest commercial practice." That term "shall mean at least practices such as breach of contract, breach of confidence and inducement to breach, and includes the acquisition of undisclosed information by third parties who knew, or were grossly negligent in failing to know, that such practices were involved in the acquisition." Note that the use of an "at least" formulation means that what is defined is a minimum set of practices, but that WTO Members are free to elaborate beyond this set. Finally, note that the definition requires the use of a gross negligence standard, whose meaning is set according to national law.

4. TRIPS AND PUBLIC HEALTH

In short, while Art. 10*bis* of the Paris Convention could be read to require protection of trade secrets and other forms of confidential business information, Art. 39.2 TRIPS clarifies the scope of this protection. As a result, its inclusion was seen as beneficial to many industrial entities.

A major concern that has emerged over the TRIPS Agreement is its impact on access to pharmaceuticals in developing countries. Prior to the TRIPS Agreement, a number of countries did not have patent laws in place. Others, such as India, had enacted a patent law, but its law did not grant patent protection to pharmaceutical products. Moreover, many countries did not have laws requiring protection of undisclosed test data for pharmaceuticals. As a result, many developing countries were able to obtain medicines for their national health programs relatively cheaply.

Why does the existence of a patent law and data protection regulation impact drug prices? Without patent protection, soon after the original innovator's drug appears on the market, a generic pharmaceutical manufacturer is able to introduce a lower-cost generic version of the same drug. However, with patent protection, generic manufacturers are forbidden from entering the market until after the term of protection for the patent expires. Moreover, with the enactment of data protection laws, generic manufacturers are forbidden from relying on the innovator's test data results for gaining market approval until after the term of data protection expires. This further delays the entry of generic drugs from the market.

The branded version of a drug is sold at a price higher than the generic version, and sometimes, several times higher. Branded manufacturers explain this difference as resulting from a need to recoup the cost of innovation and to defray the innovation costs of unsuccessful products in its product portfolio. Critics, however, point to this difference as the company's exploitation of the monopoly power of its patent to extract rents on behalf of shareholders.

What is clear is that the introduction of a generic version of a drug creates downward price pressure on the branded manufacturer. With countries signing onto the TRIPS Agreement, it became more difficult for generic drugs to gain access to certain markets. How did the TRIPS Agreement change the equation? Under the TRIPS Agreement, any developing country not classified as a least developed country (LDC) is required under the TRIPS Agreement to implement a patent regime by 2000.[6] By 2005, at the very latest, all such countries were obliged to provide patent protection for pharmaceuticals.[7] After such a regime is im-

---

[6] *See* Art. 65.2 TRIPS.

[7] *See* Art. 65.4 TRIPS which grants an additional five-year transition period to a developing country that is obliged "to extend patent protection to areas of technology not so protectable in its territory on the general date of application of the Agreement for that Member."

plemented, so long as the branded manufacturer seeks patent protection, a generic alternative may not be placed on the market prior to the expiration of the patent term. In addition, the TRIPS Agreement requires countries to protect undisclosed test data. While there is no required length of protection specified in Art. 39 TRIPS, a data protection regulation may further impede the introduction of a generic drug.

The lack of a generic alternative on the market reduces competition, which allows for higher prices to be charged for the patented drug. This raises the cost for a government's national health program. A developing country which is not a LDC is presented with a series of uncomfortable choices: It can spend more in order to allow its citizens to access medicines under its public health program—an option which it may not be able to afford fiscally. Or it can pass on the higher costs to its citizens through charging more for medicines through its public health program—an option that may be difficult politically. Or it can ration access to more expensive medicines for certain parts of the population—another difficult option politically. All options require some part of the population to pay a cost, whether fiscally or through public health outcomes or both, for implementing the TRIPS Agreement.

This impact is not limited to simply those developing countries not classified as LDCs. Although LDCs are given a transitional reprieve from implementing the patent obligations of the TRIPS Agreement through Art. 66 TRIPS and subsequent extensions issued by the TRIPS Council, LDCs may be negatively impacted nevertheless. This is because many LDCs do not have indigenous manufacturing capabilities for pharmaceuticals. Instead, they need to import generic drugs from other developing countries, such as India. However, with India and other developing countries obliged to implement patent protection for pharmaceuticals by 2005, the incentives for generic manufacturers to produce a generic alternative to a branded drug diminisheds. Thus, even countries not required to implement TRIPS obligations for pharmaceuticals may find themselves hurt by a diminished supply of generic drugs. This, in turn, also raises costs, leading to the similar unwanted policy trade-offs in LDCs.

Pharmaceutical companies and their supporters argue that the benefits of patent protection are necessary in order to create incentives to develop drugs for treating diseases that affect populations primarily within the developing world. If a generic drug manufacturer is allowed to piggyback off the results of the original innovator soon afterwards, the financial returns to the innovator become so minimal that it makes little sense for them to focus their drug development efforts on such diseases. They recognize that the TRIPS Agreement may create a near-term welfare loss in certain countries, but argue that this loss is more than offset by the longer-term innovation gains. Critics, on the other hand, point to alternative arrangements, such as prize funds, which can introduce incentives for innovation at a lower social welfare cost.[8]

In the eyes of many public health activists, the TRIPS Agreement essentially is allowing pharmaceutical companies to gain at the expense of the sick in developing countries. By increasing the difficulty of accessing generic pharmaceuticals, decreasing competition, and increasing prices, critics argue that the Agreement legitimizes a wealth transfer from developing countries and their citizens to pharmaceutical companies and their shareholders. Not surprisingly, the TRIPS Agreement has become a favorite scapegoat for denying access to essential medicines for the global poor.

Without a doubt, millions in the developing world continue to lack access to affordable medicines for infectious diseases such as malaria and tuberculosis as well as life-threatening diseases such as HIV/AIDS. But how much is the TRIPS Agreement to blame?

Supporters of the TRIPS Agreement have responded that the Agreement is not the primary cause of lack of access to essential medicines. Instead, they contend that the lack of political leadership, social norms, and structural barriers within developing countries are much more important causes. Moreover, they point to the various flexibilities built into the TRIPS Agreement allowing for governments to employ exceptions to ensure access to affordable medicines. Foremost among these are the provisions within Art. 31 TRIPS, discussed *supra*, allowing for compulsory licensing of a patented invention to a third party or a government agency without the patent holder's consent. In addition, Art. 6 TRIPS, discussed in Chapter 27, allows countries to use parallel importation as a tool to take advantage of cost differences across markets to import lower-priced patented products.

However, at the time of the Doha Ministerial in 2001, there was continued uncertainty over how these flexibilities would be interpreted. Of particular alarm for many developing countries was the response of the United States and its pharmaceutical manufacturers to South Africa's Medicines and Substance Control Act of 1997. The Act emphasized the ability of the South African government to use compulsory licensing and parallel importation as tools to improve access to drugs, particularly to combat HIV/AIDS. However, American pharmaceutical manufacturers alleged that the Act, as written, violated the TRIPS Agreement and pressured their government to take action.[9]

---

[8] A prize fund sets aside a fixed sum of money, or a prize, to reward an innovator that develops a drug treatment with proven health care outcomes. Thus, innovators are guaranteed a certain reward for their research and development efforts and need not rely on reaping the gains of patent protection to recoup their costs.

[9] For more detail about this episode, see Bombach (2001).

As a result, many developing countries, especially those in Africa, felt that it was important to provide clarification on the issue of how the flexibilities within the TRIPS Agreement may be used for public health concerns. This resulted in the Doha Declaration on the TRIPS Agreement and Public Health, adopted on 14 November 2001.[10] This declaration attempted to strike a balance. On the one hand, it recognized "the gravity of the public health problems affecting many developing and least-developed countries, especially those resulting from HIV/AIDS, tuberculosis, malaria, and other epidemics" and the need for the TRIPS Agreement "to be part of the wider national and international action to address these problems."[11] On the other hand, it also recognized that "intellectual property protection is important for the development of new medicines" while recognizing "the concerns about its effects on prices."[12]

The Declaration, in paragraph 4, declared: "We agree that the TRIPS Agreement does not and should not prevent members from taking measures to protect public health. Accordingly, while reiterating our commitment to the TRIPS Agreement, we affirm that the Agreement can and should be interpreted and implemented in a manner supportive of WTO members' right to protect public health, and in particular, to promote access to medicines for all. In this connection, we reaffirm the right of WTO members to use, to the full, the provisions in the TRIPS Agreement, which provide flexibility for this purpose."

The next paragraph of the Declaration then goes on to clarify:

5. Accordingly, . . . , we recognize that these flexibilities include:

[. . .]

b. Each member has the right to grant compulsory licenses and the freedom to determine the grounds upon which such licenses are granted.

c. Each member has the right to determine what constitutes a national emergency or other circumstances of extreme urgency, it being understood that public health crises, including those relating to HIV/AIDS, tuberculosis, malaria and other epidemics, can represent a national emergency or other circumstances of extreme urgency.

d. The effect of the provisions in the TRIPS Agreement that are relevant to the exhaustion of intellectual property rights is to leave each member free to establish its own regime for such exhaustion without challenge, subject to the MFN and national treatment provisions of Articles 3 and 4.

---

[10] See WTO Doc. WT/MIN(01)/DEC/2 of 20 November 2001.
[11] See *id.* at paras. 1–2.
[12] See *id.* at para. 3.

Through the Doha Declaration on the TRIPS Agreement and Public Health, WTO Members reaffirmed that each Member is empowered to use compulsory licensing and parallel importation to address public health issues and access to medicines. How exactly did the Declaration clarify any legal ambiguities? Recall that the TRIPS Agreement permits the use of compulsory licensing, but sets forth limitations. In particular, Art. 31(b) TRIPS requires that a WTO Member first seek to obtain authorization from the right holder prior to issuing a compulsory licensing. However, Art. 31(b) also allows for an exception for "in the case of a national emergency or other circumstances of extreme urgency." Prior to the Doha Declaration, what constitutes a "national emergency" or a "circumstance of extreme urgency" was left ambiguous. Therefore, it was unclear whether the Art. 31(b) exception could apply to public health crises. Paragraph 5(c) of the Declaration clarified that the terms are to be defined unilaterally by each WTO Member. It further clarifies that public health crises can fall into the category of "national emergency" or "circumstance of extreme urgency." Therefore, a WTO Member could seek to use a compulsory license without first seeking the authorization of the right holder for a pharmaceutical product to address public health issues.

Furthermore, Paragraph 5(d) of the Doha Declaration also clarified that so long as the law governing parallel importation complied with the MFN and national treatment requirements of the TRIPS Agreement, it could not be challenged. This too underscored the ability of WTO Members to address public health and access to medicines issues through flexibilities contained within the TRIPS Agreement.

Importantly, the Doha Declaration also extended the transition period for LDCs for implementing any of the TRIPS Agreement obligations for patents and the protection of undisclosed information for pharmaceutical products until 1 January 2016.[13] In doing so, the Doha Declaration makes it easier for LDCs to continue to provide cheaper generic versions of drugs for their populations.

One issue which was not settled at the Doha Ministerial itself was what to do about those countries that lacked pharmaceutical manufacturing capabilities. Such countries are not able to take full advantage of TRIPS flexibilities such as compulsory licensing. Even were the government to issue a compulsory license, there is no means by which to make the drug domestically. One might think that such countries could import a generic version of the drugs from overseas. But the TRIPS Agreement made it more difficult to do so. First, if the product is under patent protection elsewhere, then a generic alternative is not readily available on the market. Second, the TRIPS Agreement places strict limitations on the use of compulsory licensing for exporting purposes. Art. 31(f) TRIPS specifically states that products made under compulsory licensing must be

---

[13] See *id.* at para. 7.

"predominantly for the supply of the domestic market." Thus, if Country A is without pharmaceutical manufacturing capabilities, it cannot simply request that Country B, which has manufacturing capabilities, issue a compulsory license in order to produce the patented drug to export back to Country A. Were Country B to do so, it would violate Art. 31(f) TRIPS. Instead, Country A must find another country in which the desired drug is not under patent protection and which has manufacturing capabilities from which it can import a cheaper version of the drug. Because of the TRIPS Agreement, after 2005, the only countries likely to be able to export to Country A are LDCs.[14] However, few LDCs have pharmaceutical manufacturing capabilities. Therein lies the problem recognized in Paragraph Six of the Doha Declaration.

Paragraph Six of the Doha Declaration instructed the TRIPS Council to find a solution to this problem and report back to the General Council. The answer arrived at by WTO Members is commonly referred to as the "Paragraph Six solution," its informal name. Formally, the solution took the form of a Decision of the General Council of 30 August 2003 and is entitled "Implementation of Paragraph Six of the Doha Declaration on the TRIPS Agreement and Public Health."[15]

The Paragraph Six solution amounts to three legal waivers designed to make it easier for a WTO Member to import cheaper generic versions of a medicine made under compulsory licensing if a Member is unable to manufacture the drug itself. Note that any WTO Member, and not just LDCs, may avail itself of the option to import a pharmaceutical product through this procedure so long as prior notification is given to the TRIPS Council.[16] The three waivers are as follows:

First, as noted above, Art. 31(f) TRIPS specifically states that products made under compulsory licensing must be "predominantly for the supply of the domestic market." This obligation is waived for the exporting Member when it issues a compulsory license for purposes of production of a pharmaceutical product(s) for export to an eligible importing WTO Member.[17] Note that while the Art. 31(f) TRIPS obligation is waived, the Decision imposes several requirements on the exporting country. These include: (a) it must produce "only the amount necessary to

---

[14] This is because, as noted above, Art. 65 TRIPS requires that all developing countries, which are not LDCs, implement patent regimes by 2000, with an extension to 2005 for extending protection to any areas of technology not so protectable on the general date of application of the TRIPS Agreement.

[15] See WTO Doc. WT/L/540 and Corr. 1 of 1 September 2003.

[16] Under the Decision, an "eligible importing Member" is defined as "any least developed country Member, and any other Member that has made a notification to the Council for TRIPS of its intention to use the system as an importer, it being understood that a Member may notify at any time that it will use the system in whole or in a limited way." Thus, LDCs are not required to give notification, but non-LDC WTO Members must first notify the TRIPS Council. See *id.* at para. 1(b) (citation omitted).

[17] Note the definition of an "eligible importing Member" in the previous footnote.

meet the needs of the eligible importing Member(s)," (b) products produced under the compulsory license must be clearly identified and distinguished "through special packaging and/or special colouring or shaping of the products themselves" to the extent that this distinction is possible, and (c) it must post on a website information about the quantities being shipped and the special distinguishing characteristics.[18]

Second, recall that Art. 31(h) TRIPS requires that the right holder be paid adequate remuneration in the circumstances of each case. The Decision clarifies that only the exporting Member must pay compensation when issuing the compulsory license to produce the medicine for export. Any obligation of the importing Member to pay remuneration under Art. 31(h) is waived.[19] This is to avoid double payment for the compulsory license.

Third, the export constraint imposed by Art. 31(f) TRIPS is waived for developing countries and LDCs that are party to a regional trade agreement within the meaning of Art. XXIV GATT, as long as at least half of the membership of the agreement is classified as a LDC by the United Nations as of 30 August 2003. This is to allow such developing countries to make use of economies of scale, both for the purpose of enhancing purchasing power with regards to pharmaceuticals as well as for the development of local production capabilities.[20]

Note that the Paragraph Six solution does not require that a WTO Member use the system to import only in times of national emergencies or other circumstances of extreme urgency. However, some WTO Members have voluntarily announced that they would use the system in only this limited way.[21] Still others have voluntarily announced that they will not use the system at all.[22]

The waivers contained within the Paragraph Six solution of 2003 were meant to be a temporary solution. A proposal was put forth by the TRIPS Council that the waivers be directly translated as a formal amendment to the TRIPS Agreement.[23] In its Decision of 6 December 2005, the General Council agreed to do so, with the condition that the Protocol Amending the TRIPS Agreement would take effect upon its acceptance by two-thirds of the Members of the WTO, in accordance with paragraph 3 of Article X of the WTO Agreement.[24] As of the date of this writing, however, the required ratification by two-thirds of WTO Mem-

---

[18] See WTO Doc. WT/L/540 and Corr. 1 of 1 September 2003 at para. 2.
[19] See *id.* at para. 4.
[20] See *id.* at para. 6.
[21] These WTO Members include Hong Kong, Israel, Korea, Kuwait, Macao, Mexico, Qatar, Singapore, Chinese Taipei, Turkey, and the United Arab Emirates.
[22] These WTO Members include Australia, Canada, the members of the European Union, Japan, New Zealand, Switzerland, and the United States.
[23] See WTO Doc. IP/C/41 of 6 December 2005.
[24] See WTO Doc. WT/L/641 of 8 December 2005.

bers of the Protocol has yet to be achieved. Thus, the temporary waiver of August 2003 remains in force.

Following the August 2003 Decision, a few countries have implemented regimes allowing them to facilitate the export of affordable generic medicines to developing countries. The most high profile of these regimes is Canada's Access to Medicines Regime (CAMR), implemented in 2005. CAMR includes a list of eligible importing WTO Members, eligible medicines for export, product quality and safety requirements, requirements for distinguishing characteristics of products produced under CAMR, royalties, dispute settlement, and statutory review.[25] In addition to Canada, other WTO Members that have amended their Patent Law and/or regulations to set forth procedures for using compulsory licensing for export of pharmaceuticals include China,[26] Croatia,[27] the European Union,[28] Hong Kong China,[29] India,[30] South Korea,[31] and Switzerland.[32] Japan and Ecuador also have clarified that procedures exist under its domestic law.[33]

So far, the Paragraph Six solution has been used only once, by Rwanda to import a new triple combination HIV/AIDS drug, Apo–TriAvir, from Canada through CAMR.[34] This lack of use has drawn concern from public health activists. In its October 2010 meeting, the TRIPS Council itself convened a review of the Paragraph Six system and its impact. Some have criticized the Paragraph Six system as achieving less impact for developing countries than may have been originally promised. Others contend that the problem lies with capacity-building and that more results will be forthcoming as developing countries become more adept at taking advantage of the system.[35]

---

[25] For more information about CAMR, see www.camr-rcam.gc.ca. Developing countries which are not WTO Members are also eligible to import pharmaceutical products under CAMR upon request.

[26] See Art. 50 of China's Patent Law which authorizes the State Council and relevant patent administration authorities to issue a compulsory license for export of pharmaceuticals for public health purposes.

[27] See Croatia's Act on Amending the Patent Act of December 2009

[28] See Regulation (EC) No. 816/2006 of the European Parliament and of the Council.

[29] See Patent Amendment Ordinance 2007, passed on 30 November 2007 and which took effect on 22 February 2008.

[30] See Section 92A of the Indian Patents (Amendment) Act of 2005.

[31] In 2005, South Korea enacted Article 107(1)(v) of its Patent Act and amended the Regulation on Expropriation and Licensing of Patents to provide statutory grounds and set forth procedures. The Regulation was further amended in July 2010.

[32] See Article 40(d) of Switzerland's revised Patent Act which entered into force on 1 July 2008.

[33] See WTO Doc. IP/C/M/64 at paras. 177–182.

[34] See WTO Doc. IP/N/9/RWA/1 and WTO Doc. IP/N/10/CAN/1.

[35] Since 2003, the WTO itself has conducted multiple workshops on TRIPS and public health, including a joint workshop on pricing and procurement practices for medicines with the WIPO and the World Health Organization (WHO).

The efforts of activists to push for the Doha Declaration and the subsequent Paragraph Six solution illustrate the ability to mobilize civil society to impact the development of international trade law. Without a doubt, these clarifications have impacted the behavior of large multinational pharmaceutical companies and governments in developed countries. Yet, the continued reluctance of WTO Members to take advantage of the flexibilities clarified through the Doha Declaration and the Paragraph Six solution also illustrates the inherent limits of legal clarifications. What is clear is that so long as public health crises continue to plague WTO Members, the impact of the TRIPS Agreement on access to affordable medicines within the developing world will continue to receive close scrutiny in the years ahead.

QUESTIONS AND COMMENTS

Weak Patent Regimes as a Barrier to Trade: Maskus (2005) estimates, based on a model that he formulates, that the strengthening of patent rights would lead manufacturing imports by large developing countries to expand by between $14.7 billion and $24.2 billion per year. He notes that this leads to two important conclusions. First, weak patent regimes are significant barriers to manufacturing trade, particularly for goods reliant upon intellectual property. Second, countries with strong imitation capabilities benefit most from imposing such barriers in that they avoid the negative effects on their terms of trade that would emerge from eliminating such barriers.

Efficacy of the Paragraph Six Solution: What do you make of the fact that very few countries have availed themselves of this process? Is this a testament to the fact that developed countries, by virtue of other trade instruments (e.g., preferential market access given through GSP programs, etc.), still hold considerable leverage over developing countries, thereby creating a "chilling effect"? Or is this a testament to the fact that there has been little need to resort to this process in recent years, due to the lack of large-scale public health emergencies and the emergence of other intermediaries to help mitigate the negative consequences of the TRIPS Agreement?

Pharmaceutical Company Responses to Compulsory Licensing by Developing Countries: Beginning in November 2006, Thailand began issuing compulsory licenses on a spate of patented drugs, including antiretrovirals for the treatment of AIDS, an anti-platelet drug for the treatment of heart disease, and several cancer drugs. After Thailand announced that it was issuing a compulsory license on Abbott Pharmaceutical's AIDS drug, Kaletra, in January 2007, Abbott responded by announcing that it would withdraw an application to sell seven new drugs in Thailand, including its latest AIDS drugs. This was met with public indignation. Yet, Abbott's decision is outside of the purview of the TRIPS Agreement, as it does not regulate the responses of private companies to decisions by countries to exercise their rights pursuant to the TRIPS Agreement.

CHAPTER 31

ENFORCEMENT OF IP RIGHTS

■ ■ ■

As the preceding Chapters have discussed, the TRIPS Agreement contains a set of minimum obligations for the protection of different forms of intellectual property. Part of the significance of the TRIPS Agreement is that, unlike previous international agreements on IP, the Agreement also attempts to provide for certain standards concerning the enforcement of these obligations. These are detailed in Part III of the Agreement.

This Chapter provides an overview of these enforcement provisions. In reading through these obligations, one should be attentive to four issues: First, the forum in which IP rights are enforced differs across WTO Members. Some rely more heavily on judicial proceedings, whereas others rely more on administrative proceedings. In addition, the structure of the judiciary differs across WTO Members. In some, there are specialized courts for intellectual property with judges trained particularly in the subject. In others, IP litigation is handled through the regular court docket. Finally, there are differences between civil law and common law jurisdictions. Part III of the Agreement was drafted with a need to respect many of these differences. Bear these differences in mind as you think about why the language of the obligations is structured as it is.

This leads then to a second issue: Because of these differences, the negotiating parties were not able to reach exact agreement on many enforcement questions. Instead, some of the provisions in Part III are left purposely vague. As a result, one should pay careful attention to the exact terminology used in the provisions. Many of the obligations contain terms which are not defined precisely. For example, Art. 41 TRIPS speaks of "effective action" but leaves unanswered the question of what is effective versus ineffective. This means that there is much room for further interpretation by the Dispute Settlement Body. Until such guidance is provided by the Appellate Body, there is also much room for disagreement among WTO Members as to whether one is fully complying with enforcing the TRIPS Agreement.

Third, the areas on which negotiating parties were able to reach agreement were often on procedural matters. Parties did not necessarily want to require a certain forum for enforcement or mandate the use of remedies in certain circumstances. What they could agree on were the proper procedures for adjudicating IP-related disputes. However, you may want to ask: To what extent does the strengthening of procedural obligations improve one's ability to enforce one's IP rights? Or is this more akin to "empty window dressing"? At the end of the day, while the TRIPS Agreement certainly goes further than its predecessors, just how much does it strengthen IP enforcement?

Fourth, Reichman and Lange (1998), Yu (2011) and others have described the enforcement provisions as the "Achilles heel" of the TRIPS Agreement. This description as the weak link arises from the ambiguous and flexible language in this section of the Agreement. As you read the text of the provisions themselves, consider just how easy or difficult it is for a WTO Member to get away with lax enforcement. Is it possible for a country to simply put the laws on the books, but fail to give proper protection to foreign IP right-holders in order to advantage their own domestic producers or consumers? Are certain countries better positioned to circumvent TRIPS than others? Also, pay attention to the role that WTO dispute settlement may play in clarifying the TRIPS enforcement obligations, and to the difficult geopolitical and institutional issues that may be entangled in these disputes.

1. THE LEGAL DISCIPLINE

Part III of the TRIPS Agreement mandates that each WTO Member adopt certain enforcement procedures, as specified in this Part of the Agreement, "so as to permit effective action against any act of infringement of intellectual property rights covered by this Agreement." Among these are a set of civil and administrative procedures and remedies, border measures, and criminal procedures. Also included are provisions mandating that judicial authorities have the authority to order injunctive relief. These provisions are detailed below. In many instances, the enforcement provisions require that judicial, administrative, or other authorities be given certain authority under a WTO Member's national law, but leave it to the discretion of such authorities as to whether or not they wish to exercise this newly-mandated authority.

2. THE RATIONALE FOR THE LEGAL DISCIPLINE

The problem confronting IP right-holders prior to the TRIPS Agreement was two-fold: On one level, many countries' laws provided what some right-holders would consider to be "inadequate" protection, or simply failed to provide any protection at all. The various obligations required in Part II of the TRIPS Agreement were designed to address this first problem. However, simply because a country adopted laws on its books did not mean that they would necessarily enforce them. The obligations contained within Part III of the TRIPS Agreement are designed to address this second problem.

What types of problems do IP right-holders face in terms of enforcement? Depending on the country, they run the gamut. One set of problems concerns resources. The police, faced with other pressing crimes, may refuse to dedicate resources to enforce IP laws. As a result, counterfeit and pirated goods are sold right out in the open. Similarly, customs authorities may refuse to dedicate resources to train inspectors to check for counterfeit or pirated goods at the borders. Another problem concerns the disposal of seized goods. The police or customs may seize counterfeit and pirated goods, but then release them back into channels of commerce after a fine is paid. Yet, another set of problems concerns legal remedies. The punishment for committing IP crimes, such as the level of fines, may be set too low, allowing counterfeiters and pirates to simply build them into the cost of doing business. As a result, the laws fail to act as a meaningful deterrent.

Part III of the Agreement reflects the efforts of developed countries to address these problems. This is to ensure that the concessions obtained within Part II of the Agreement were not devalued through lax enforcement. Having been "burned" by the lax enforcement provisions of prior international IP agreements, developed countries were determined to repeat this mistake. Hence, they bargained hard for a comprehensive set of enforcement obligations.

Much of what underlies the enforcement provisions of the TRIPS Agreement reflects an American conception of what is necessary for proper enforcement: preliminary injunctions, pre-trial discovery, etc.[1] However, not all WTO Members' national legal systems are well suited to incorporate elements of the American system. Therefore, parts of the enforcement provisions reflect a desire to provide sufficient flexibility for WTO Members to incorporate these concepts within their own legal regimes.

In addition, developing countries expressed a concern that TRIPS should not oblige them to commit enforcement resources beyond what they were capable of providing. Nor should it force them to prioritize IP enforcement efforts above other law enforcement efforts. Therefore, balanced against some countries' desire to strengthen IP enforcement regime is a counter-desire of others to maintain sufficient flexibility in the allocation of resources across law enforcement activities.

American and European negotiators recognized that if they were to succeed in their efforts to obtain a more robust enforcement section, they needed to make some concessions to developing countries' concerns. However, they worried that these competing concerns of developing countries would dilute the impact of this section. In the end, for some provisions, rather than agreeing upon specific levels of enforcement, the negotiators chose to make the obligation outcome-specific. That is to say, they simply determined what the outcomes of the enforcement measures should be,

---

[1] On this score, see Gervais (2008).

without prescribing what countries needed to do to achieve these outcomes.

Therefore, unlike other parts of the WTO regime, it is difficult to say that there is a single underlying rationale for the enforcement provisions within the TRIPS Agreement. On one level, they can be seen as an instrument to reduce uncertainty about the value of concessions. The value of an IP-related obligation that a country makes varies greatly depending on the efforts that a country devotes toward enforcing that obligation. As a result, negotiating parties faced considerable uncertainty about the benefits of the IP concessions extracted from others. Standardizing enforcement obligations, in effect, reduces this uncertainty and allows parties to better anticipate the expected value of certain TRIPS obligations. Thus, one reason for the enforcement provisions is to facilitate bargaining and set expectations. Where possible, this was done through concrete requirements prescribing exactly how IP laws are to be enforced. Where this was not possible, outcomes-based obligations were established.

On another level, they can also be seen as an instrument to bring developing countries onboard to the notion of incorporating IP-based rules within the trade regime. Recall that at the start of the Uruguay Round, it was not obvious that the results of the round would include anything as robust as the TRIPS Agreement. Some developing countries, such as India, strongly resisted. By granting them some flexibility in how they enforced their TRIPS obligations—and agreeing upon only vaguely-described outcomes—developed countries made the TRIPS Agreement more palatable to developing countries.

Finally, one further way of conceptualizing the rationale for the legal discipline is that they were intended as a placeholder for further evolution. Developed countries were determined to obtain guarantees of greater enforcement from their trading partners. Yet, they recognized that the differences in IP enforcement were enormous and could not be eliminated overnight. Therefore, they simply did what they could to standardize wherever possible. Where it was not, they put down placeholders, leaving it open for the meaning of the provisions to evolve through future adjudications and negotiations.

3. COVERAGE OF THE LEGAL DISCIPLINE

The Preamble to the TRIPS Agreement captures the balance sought within Part III of the TRIPS Agreement. It acknowledges the negotiating parties' recognition of "the need for new rules and disciplines concerning . . . the provision of effective and appropriate means for the enforcement of trade-related intellectual property rights, taking into account differences in national legal systems." On the one hand, this is an explicit recognition of the inadequacy of the pre-TRIPS international IP rules on enforcement. New rules were necessary in order to ensure the efficacy of the IP laws available. On the other hand, the preamble statement also reflects the desire for flexibility, as evident in the acknowledgement of different national legal systems and the placement of the adjective "appropriate" following "effective." With this in mind, we turn to the specific legal provisions.

3.1 GENERAL OBLIGATIONS

Art. 41 TRIPS sets forth the general obligations expected of WTO Members. We start by highlighting three provisions within this article:

1. Members shall ensure that enforcement procedures as specified in this Part are available under their law so as to permit effective action against any act of infringement of intellectual property rights covered by this Agreement, including expeditious remedies to prevent infringements and remedies which constitute a deterrent to further infringements. These procedures shall be applied in such a manner as to avoid the creation of barriers to legitimate trade and to provide for safeguards against their abuse.

2. Procedures concerning the enforcement of intellectual property rights shall be fair and equitable. They shall not be unnecessarily complicated or costly, or entail unreasonable time limits or unwarranted delays.

. . .

5. It is understood that this Part does not create any obligation to put in place a judicial system for the enforcement of intellectual property rights distinct from that for the enforcement of the law in general, nor does it affect the capacity of Members to enforce their law in general. Nothing in this Part creates any obligation with respect to the distribution of resources as between enforcement of intellectual property rights and the enforcement of law in general.

Several points from these provisions are worth highlighting. First, Art. 41.1 TRIPS reflects a desire that a WTO Members' enforcement regime be comprehensive. It makes clear that the regime must cover any IP-infringing act covered by the TRIPS Agreement.

Second, Art. 41.1 TRIPS also establishes a standard for the remedies available under the enforcement regime. The language here is a clear example of the outcomes-based obligation discussed above. The remedies must be "expeditious," and importantly, they must achieve two outcomes: (1) to prevent infringements, where actions can be taken by authorities to do so (for example, with respect to seized goods or by imposing preliminary injunctions); and (2) to constitute a deterrent to further infringements. With respect to the latter, the provision leaves open to each WTO

Member how it wishes to achieve this outcome—whether through civil, administrative, and/or criminal penalties. What is important is that the outcome is obtained.

Third, Art. 41.2 TRIPS guards against the possibility of an enforcement regime being overly cumbersome for an IP holder seeking to enforce its rights. It mandates that the procedures must not be overly complicated or costly. It also guards against the possibility that enforcement efforts are unreasonably long, due to procedural rules or delays. These provisions act as a check against national legal systems where IP laws exist but where it is difficult to obtain legal judgments enforcing them.

However, cast against these two provisions is Art. 41.5 TRIPS. This provision makes clear that WTO Members may handle IP enforcement matters through their standard judicial system rather than create any specialized IP courts or tribunals to expedite the processing of such cases. WTO Members are also not obliged to allocate extra funding to meet their TRIPS enforcement obligations. Thus, to the extent that the enforcement obligations cannot be met because of resource constraints, it is acceptable to not meet these obligations. However, if no demonstrable increase in resources is necessary to effectuate an obligation, then WTO Members are bound to do so.

Consider an example of Country A where IP infringement cases take a notoriously long time to move through the courts, much to the dissatisfaction of right-holders in Country B. Depending on the rationale for this delay, Country A may or may not be obliged to make any changes as a result of Art. 41 TRIPS. If the delay is because the judicial system is overburdened and all cases face a long wait time, then Country A is not obligated to create a specialized court for IP cases just to expedite them. Nor is Country A required to supply more judges or prosecutors to address IP cases. Art. 41.5 TRIPS makes this clear. On the other hand, if the long delay is due to procedural rules and not resource constraints, then Country A cannot seek refuge under Art. 41.5 TRIPS and instead will be obliged to make changes per Art. 41.2 TRIPS.

The inclusion of Art. 41.5 TRIPS came at the insistence of Indian negotiators, who wanted to make sure that TRIPS would not hold developing countries accountable for implementation problems due to resourcing difficulties.[2] It means that when examining the plausibility of a TRIPS enforcement action against any WTO Member, one needs to take a comprehensive look at the resources devoted to law enforcement and the judiciary in general. Defendants may attempt to seek cover through Art. 41.5 TRIPS by arguing that enforcement problems arise from resource constraints, so complainants need to be prepared to demonstrate otherwise.

---

[2] On this score, see Correa (2007).

The other means through which a defendant may attempt to seek cover is through the vague language contained in these provisions. Art. 41.1 TRIPS requires that enforcement procedures are available so as to permit effective action—but the notion of what is "effective" is left undefined. As we will see, this notion of "effectiveness" and the problems created by this vague language are also found elsewhere in the TRIPS Agreement. By leaving this term open for future interpretation by WTO dispute settlement, the provision creates immense uncertainty for potential complainants. How will Panels test effectiveness, and therefore, what types of evidence need to be submitted to demonstrate "ineffectiveness"? Until this question is resolved, the evidentiary bar for proving an Art. 41.1 TRIPS violation is difficult to ascertain.

Similarly, the issue of what constitutes "a deterrent to prevent further infringement" is also left unclear. No law can reasonably be expected to prevent all further recurrences of the undesirable activity. But deterrence theorists argue that laws and enforcement regimes can certainly affect the propensity of individuals to undertake the undesirable action. If one believes that individual behavior is to some extent affected by rational calculations, then this certainly is true. But how then is one to prove when a law fails to constitute a deterrent? Importantly, this question is also left open for future interpretation.

Art. 41.2 TRIPS also contains a number of vague terms. Consider these three: (1) "unnecessarily" complicated or costly; (2) "unreasonable" time delay; and (3) "unwarranted" delays. Again, the meaning of what is "unnecessary," "unreasonable," or "unwarranted" in the context of a particular WTO Members' judicial system is left open to interpretation based on the facts at hand. As a result, the evidentiary burden for proving an Art. 41.2 TRIPS violation is similarly difficult to ascertain.

While the above discussion has focused on the core principles and uncertainties embedded within Art. 41 TRIPS, we should note that Art. 41 TRIPS also contains several obligations related to procedural issues. These obligations apply regardless of the avenue through which judicial enforcement is pursued—whether civil, administrative, and/or criminal. Art. 41.3 TRIPS requires that decisions on the merits "be based only on evidence in respect of which parties were given an opportunity to be heard." This implies the requirement to create a judicial system, which, if not directly adversarial in nature, is at least open with respect to the disclosure of evidence. Art. 41.3 TRIPS also obliges WTO Members to make decisions on the merits available to the parties in the case.[3] In addition, Art. 41.4 TRIPS requires that WTO Members provide for judicial review of the legal aspects of administrative decisions.

---

[3] Art. 41.3 TRIPS expresses a preference that these decisions are delivered in writing and reasoned.

Therefore, despite a professed respect for differences across national legal systems and an emphasis on outcomes, the TRIPS Agreement does push towards greater standardization—at least with respect to certain procedural elements. This point will become even more evident as we examine the specific obligations imposed for the different channels through which IP enforcement may be pursued.

3.2 CIVIL AND ADMINISTRATIVE PROCEDURES AND REMEDIES

IP infringement cases are most commonly pursued through either civil or administrative actions. The choice between the two depends on the national legal system. While in many WTO Members, action against infringing activity is pursued through a civil lawsuit, in some WTO Members, this is more commonly done through seeking administrative enforcement. The largest economy in which administrative enforcement plays an important role is China, which has a dual track regime whereby a right-holder can seek administrative or civil action against an infringer.

Art. 42 TRIPS requires that WTO Members "shall make available to right holders civil judicial procedures concerning the enforcement any intellectual property right covered by this Agreement." The AB (§ 215), in *US—Section 211 Appropriation Act*, stated that the term "make available" meant "that 'right holders' are entitled . . . to have access to civil judicial proceedings that are effective in bringing about the enforcement of their rights covered by the Agreement." Note, however, that this definition still leaves open the question of what constitutes effectiveness, as was the case with Art. 41.1 TRIPS.

The issue of who is a "right holder" was also at issue in *US—Section 211 Appropriations Act*. The US argued that term should be understood to be synonymous with the "owner" of the intellectual property right. The Panel disagreed, and the AB (§ 217) confirmed that the term is to be construed more broadly. While it includes the owner, it also encompasses any other person "who has the legal standing to assert rights." A footnote to Art. 42.1 TRIPS notes that this category is not limited to natural persons, but also includes federations and associations.

While the TRIPS Agreement requires civil judicial proceedings, it is agnostic on the question of whether a WTO Member is allowed to complement it with administrative proceedings. Art. 49 TRIPS simply states that "[t]o the extent that any civil remedy can be ordered as a result of administrative procedures on the merits of the case," such procedures must conform to those required of civil judicial procedures in the TRIPS Agreement. What then are these procedural requirements? What follows below is a discussion of several of them:

Art. 42 TRIPS states that the following are required to ensure "fair and equitable procedures":

- Defendants shall have the right to written notice which is timely and contains sufficient detail, including the basis of the claims.
- Parties shall be allowed to be represented by independent legal counsel, and
- [P]rocedures shall not impose overly burdensome requirements concerning mandatory personal appearances.
- Parties shall be duly entitled to substantiate their claims and to present all relevant evidence.

In addition, all WTO Members must "provide a means to identify and protect confidential information, unless this would be contrary to existing constitutional requirements."

What happens though when the evidence necessary to substantiate an infringement claim is in the hands of the alleged infringer? Different national legal systems have different rules with respect to civil discovery procedures. The TRIPS Agreement does not attempt to standardize these rules. However, Art. 43.1 TRIPS makes clear that WTO Members must provide judicial authorities with the authority to compel production of evidence subject to two qualifications: (1) "a party has presented reasonably available evidence to support its claims," and (2) a party "specified evidence relevant to substantiation of its claims which lies in the control of the opposing party." Note though that the concepts of what is "reasonably available" and what is "relevant" are left undefined.

If a party does not produce the evidence upon receipt of a court-issued request, without good reason, then Art. 43.2 TRIPS notes that WTO Members have the option to "accord judicial authorities the authority to make preliminary and final determinations, . . . , on the basis of the information presented to them." This is not required, but Art. 43.2 TRIPS clarifies that where such authority is granted, judicial authorities may factor into their decision the information contained within the adversely-affected party's complaint or allegations.

In addition, Art. 47 TRIPS clarifies that WTO Members have the option to provide judicial authorities with the power to order an infringer to provide information about "the identity of third persons involved in the production and distribution of the infringing goods or services and of their channels of distribution." This requirement is not mandatory. However, it is important because often times the infringer caught is part of a complex supply chain. Unless the production source of the infringed good or service and the distribution sources are disrupted, it is unlikely that the infringing activity will cease. An infringer may be compelled to reveal this information to the right holder, so that the right holder may be able to pursue further action against other parts of the supply chain.

The TRIPS Agreement also contains an important set of requirements with respect to remedies. Art. 45 TRIPS notes that "judicial authorities shall have the authority to order the infringer to pay the right holder damages adequate to compensate for the injury the right holder has suffered" as well as the right holder's expenses, including appropriate attorney's fees. However, if the party requesting the enforcement action is found to have "abused enforcement procedures," then Art. 48 TRIPS also requires that judicial authorities be given the authority to order the applicant to pay the defendant's expenses, including appropriate attorney's fees.

In addition, the TRIPS Agreement also mandates the availability of remedies concerning the disposal of infringing goods. Such a provision was deemed necessary because right-holders found themselves frustrated that infringers, in some jurisdictions, after paying the appropriate civil or administrative penalty, were able to repossess the infringing good. The infringer could simply build the likelihood of incurring a penalty into the cost of doing business.

Art. 46 TRIPS states the following:

> In order to create an effective deterrent to infringement, the judicial authorities shall have the authority to order that goods that they have found to be infringing be, without compensation of any sort, disposed of outside the channels of commerce in such a manner as to avoid harm caused to the right holder, or unless this would be contrary to existing constitutional requirements, destroyed. The judicial authorities shall also have the authority to order that materials and implements the predominant use of which has been in the creation of the infringing goods be, without compensation of any sort, disposed of outside the channels of commerce in such a manner as to minimize the risks of further infringements.

Correa (2007) and others have described this as an overly strong sanction. They assert that the sanction "may lead to significant economic waste and be socially questionable, especially in developing countries."[4] Instead, perhaps, infringing goods—such as counterfeit clothes and shoes—would be better put to use if supplied to charities or socioeconomically-disadvantaged groups.

Art. 46 TRIPS does recognize the potential waste in the sanction. Following the sentences excerpted above, it adds the following guiding principle: "In considering such requests, the need for proportionality between the seriousness of the infringement and the remedies ordered as well as the interests of third parties shall be taken into account." However, it makes clear that with respect to counterfeit trademark goods, "the simple removal of the trademark unlawfully affixed shall not be sufficient, other than in exceptional cases, to permit the release of the goods into the

---

[4] See Correa (2007) at p. 428.

channels of commerce." A Panel in *China–Intellectual Property Rights* has expounded on the interpretation of the term "exceptional cases." Because this dispute concerns border measures and a similar term is used in Art. 59 TRIPS, the Panel's interpretation of this term is discussed *infra* in the section on border enforcement measures.

Why did the drafters consider it necessary to insert this last sentence about the disposal of counterfeit trademark goods? Consider the case of a well-made coat with an infringing designer logo. Critics would argue that ordering the destruction of the coat simply because of the infringing logo is wasteful. There are many poor people who could use a well-made coat. Why not just simply remove the logo and then give away the coat or sell it for an inexpensive price? Proponents of the provision argue that if this were allowed, there is too high a risk that the coat would find its way back into the hands of the counterfeiters. The main cost of the infringing good itself is the coat, not the logo. Counterfeiters would simply wait for the next batch of fake logos, affix it to the coat, and then sell it again. To counter the problem requires attacking the source, which is to order the destruction of the coat altogether.

At the end of the day, the TRIPS Agreement requires that judicial authorities be given the power to order such remedies, but leaves the decisions up to the adjudicators themselves. Judges can weigh the competing interests and decide what is proper. Art. 46 TRIPS does not mandate the use of such remedies, but it does seek to ensure that it is among the set of remedial options available.

Besides allowing IP right holders to seek damages and the destruction of infringing goods, the TRIPS Agreement also mandates that WTO Members must provide for injunctive relief as a remedy for infringement. An injunction usually takes the form of a court order requiring that a party stop engaging in infringing activity. It may take one of two forms: (1) a preliminary injunction, meaning that it is temporary and subject to further review at a later point in time, or (2) a permanent injunction. The former is discussed in Art. 50 TRIPS, whereas the latter is discussed in Art. 44 TRIPS. We will discuss the latter first, before turning to the former.

The requirement that judicial authorities must be provided with the authority to issue a permanent injunction is enshrined within Art. 44.1 TRIPS. Because the concept of an injunction is not universal across jurisdictions, the provision provides a definition ("an order to desist from an infringement") and offers an example.[5] WTO Members are given discretion to determine the breadth of circumstances in which an injunction may be issued. For example, Members need not accord judicial authorities

---

[5] Following the definition, the provision reads, "*inter alia*, to prevent the entry into the channels of commerce in their jurisdiction of imported goods that involve the infringement of an intellectual property rights immediately after customs clearance of such goods."

the power to issue injunctions in instances where the "protected subject matter [was] acquired or ordered by a person prior to knowing or having reasonable grounds to know that dealing in such subject matter would entail the infringement of an intellectual property right."

Negotiators from both developed and developing countries also sought to limit the use of injunctive relief against government action.[6] Art. 44.2 TRIPS allows WTO Members to restrict the scope of remedies in the case of government use or use by third parties authorized by the government (*e.g.*, compulsory license) to payment of remuneration in accordance with Art. 31(h) TRIPS. Also, if the remedies are "inconsistent" with a WTO Member's laws, then Art. 44.2 mandates that, at a minimum, declaratory judgments and "adequate" compensation must be available. Note that the issue of what is to be considered adequate has yet to be interpreted by WTO adjudication.

In addition to permanent injunctions, the TRIPS Agreement also provides for temporary injunctions, or what Art. 50 TRIPS terms "provisional measures." WTO Members must provide judicial authorities with the power to issue such measures in order to:

(a) to prevent an infringement of any intellectual property right from occurring, and in particular to prevent the entry into the channels of commerce in their jurisdiction of goods, including imported goods immediately after customs clearance;

(b) to preserve relevant evidence in regard to the alleged infringement.

Art. 50.2 TRIPS clarifies that the preliminary injunction may be issued without notice to the alleged infringer. It notes that this may be appropriate "where any delay is likely to cause irreparable harm to the right holder, or where there is demonstrable risk of evidence being destroyed." However, Art. 50.4 TRIPS requires that the affected party "shall be given notice, without delay after the execution of the measures at the latest" and be afforded a right to be heard upon request. In addition, where the preliminary injunction is revoked or later found to be unwarranted because there was no infringement, Art. 50.7 TRIPS stipulates that judicial authorities shall have the authority to order the party that sought the injunction to pay "appropriate compensation for any injury caused by these measures." Art. 50.8 TRIPS clarifies that these requirements apply to preliminary injunctions issued through both civil judicial procedures as well as administrative procedures. For example, injunctions requested of Customs authorities may fall into the latter category.

---

[6] On this score, see Gervais (2008).

3.3 BORDER MEASURES

Part III of the TRIPS Agreement also contains a series of requirements with respect to measures taken at the border to enforce intellectual property rights. Recall that concerns about cross-border enforcement of counterfeit goods sparked the impetus to include an intellectual property agreement within the Uruguay Round, so it is not surprising that this section is fairly robust.

Art. 51 TRIPS marks the first time that international legal rules concerning border enforcement of IP rights were established. The first sentence of the article reads:

> Members shall, . . . , adopt procedures to enable a right holder, who has valid grounds for suspecting that the importation of counterfeit trademark or pirated copyright goods may take place, to lodge an application in writing with competent authorities, administrative or judicial, for the suspension by the customs authorities of the release into free circulation of such goods.

This sentence is worth examining closer, for several reasons.

First, the requirement applies only to counterfeit trademark goods and pirated copyright goods. These are defined as follows: Counterfeit trademark goods "shall mean any goods, including packaging, bearing without authorization a trademark which is identical to the trademark validly registered in respect of such goods, or which cannot be distinguished in its essential aspects from such a trademark, and which thereby infringes the rights of the owner of the trademark in question under the law of the country of importation." Pirated copyright goods "shall mean any goods, which are copies made without the consent of the right holder or person duly authorized by the right holder in the country of production and which are made directly or indirectly from an article where the making of that copy would have constituted an infringement of a copyright or a related right under the law of the country of importation." Note that this is different than requiring that border enforcement measures be applicable against all forms of trademark and copyright infringement. Instead, Art. 51 TRIPS is required only in instances of counterfeiting and piracy. WTO Members may, but are not required, to apply border enforcement measures to other forms of IP infringement.

Second, the requirement only applies to border enforcement against *imports* of counterfeit trademark goods and pirated copyright goods. The provision does not require that a WTO Member implement any border measures to guard against the export of such goods. Nor does the TRIPS

Agreement require that border measures be applied to goods in transit.[7] Again, a WTO Member may, but is not required, to do so.

Third, the provision does not require WTO Members to proactively inspect a portion of imported goods for IP infringement. Instead, the burden falls on the right holder to identify imports suspected of counterfeiting or piracy. What Art. 51 TRIPS requires is that in instances where a right holder does so, the WTO Member must have a procedure set up through which the right holder may file a written application asking for intervention by customs authorities of any suspected imports. Specifically, Art. 51 TRIPS requires that customs officials suspend the release of the suspected goods into free circulation. Generally, this takes the form of detention.

Fourth, this application is to be made to "competent authorities." This term is used because the authority that determines whether the suspected good is validly detained or should be released varies, depending on the WTO Member. Most often, the authority is either a judicial or an administrative official. In some instances, it may be a trained customs official. The provision simply requires that the authority be "competent."

Art. 52 TRIPS further clarifies the details of the application to be made. It states that any right holder making such a request must provide "adequate" evidence to satisfy the competent authorities of a *"prima facie"* case of infringement. In addition, the right holder must "supply a sufficiently detailed description of the goods to make them readily recognizable by the customs authorities."

In order to guard against the abuse of this procedure, Art. 53.1 TRIPS allows WTO Members to provide the competent authorities with the authority to require that an applicant pay a "security or equivalent assurance." However, the provision cautions that deposit required should not "unreasonably deter recourse" to border enforcement procedures.

After the suspected infringing goods have been detained by customs, the importer and the applicant are to be "promptly" notified, per Art. 54 TRIPS. Art. 57 TRIPS further mandates that both parties be given the opportunity to inspect the goods, subject to a qualification for the protection of confidential information.

Art. 55 TRIPS provides that the suspected infringing goods may be detained for up to ten working days in order to allow a party to initiate judicial or administrative proceedings. This time limit may be extended

---

[7] A dispute concerning the application of TRIPS border enforcement measures for goods in transit is *EU—Seizure of Generic Drugs in Transit* (DS408 filed by India, and DS409 filed by Brazil). As of the time of this writing, the parties to the dispute were still formally in consultations.

for another ten working days in "appropriate cases." If no such proceedings are initiated, then the goods are to be released by customs.[8]

If a proceeding is initiated, then there is no strict time limit for deciding the merits of the case. Art. 55 TRIPS provides for a vague guideline that this decision be made within a "reasonable period." The defendant is to be accorded a right of review, which includes a right to be heard.

If the imported goods[9] are found to be infringing, then Art. 59 TRIPS establishes that WTO Members must provide for the remedy to destroy or dispose of the infringing good in accordance with Art. 46 TRIPS, discussed *supra*. In other words, WTO Members are to treat the disposal of infringing goods seized at the borders in the same way as those seized within its borders. One additional requirement is added, which is that the infringing good should not be re-exported in an unaltered state, other than in "exceptional circumstances."

Recall that a similar exception for "exceptional" cases is used in Art. 46 TRIPS. The meaning of "exceptional" was explored in the *China–Intellectual Property Rights* dispute, which concerned Chinese border measures. In that dispute, China's Customs Regulations provided that where the infringing goods confiscated at the border cannot be used for social public welfare undertakings and where the right holder has no intention to buy it, Chinese Customs was authorized to auction the good "after eradicating the infringing features." The US argued that China's actions were inconsistent with Art. 59 TRIPS, as it incorporates Art. 46 TRIPS which prohibits release of the good after the simple removal of the trademark. China responded that because it afforded the right holder the opportunity to comment, the release was subject to more than the simple removal of the trademark. Even were that not the case, China further argued that its actions fell under the "exceptional" circumstances exception, since it occurred infrequently and only "usual" and "out-of-the ordinary" circumstances.

The Panel (§ 7.390) ruled against China's proposed definition of "exceptional" since it failed to "explain *in what way* a case must be different from other cases" in order to fall under the exception granted by the provision. The meaning of the exception, the Panel (§ 7.391) declared, "must be interpreted in light of the objective of the Article, namely, 'to create an

---

[8] In instances where a WTO Member extends the border enforcement measures beyond counterfeit trademark and pirated copyright goods, the requirements of Art. 53.2 TRIPS may apply. That provision covers "the release of goods involving industrial designs, patents, layout-designs or undisclosed information." Art. 53.2 TRIPS stipulates that in order to obtain the release of such goods after the period provided for in Art. 55 TRIPS has expired, the owner, importer, or consignee shall post a security in an amount sufficient to protect the right holder of infringement. It adds: "Payment of such security shall not prejudice any other remedy available to the right holder, it being understood that the security shall be released if the right holder fails to pursue the right of action within a reasonable period of time."

[9] In *China–Intellectual Property Rights*, the Panel (§ 7.224) confirmed that "there is no obligation to apply the requirements of Article 59 to goods destined for destination."

effective deterrent to infringement.'" It added that "such cases must be narrowly circumscribed in order to satisfy the description of 'exceptional'" and therefore, "the application of the relevant provision must be rare, lest the so-called exception become the rule, or at least ordinary."

What happens, though, if the detained good is found not to be infringing? In the event of a "wrongful detention," Art. 56 TRIPS states, "Relevant authorities shall have the authority to order the applicant to pay the importer, the consignee, and the owner of the goods appropriate compensation for any injury caused to them through the wrongful detention of goods." Note that the intent of this provision is to indemnify parties against economic loss. It is not to guard against abuse, as there need not be a showing of bad faith or malicious intent.

Note that the enforcement obligations within TRIPS do not oblige WTO Members to require that their customs authorities proactively inspect imported goods for counterfeiting and piracy. Some do allow for *ex officio* action, whereby customs officials will inspect a small proportion of imports. If this is the case, then Art. 58 TRIPS clarifies that such procedures should comply with the timing and notification provisions required within this section of the Agreement.

3.4 CRIMINAL PROCEDURES

Finally, the TRIPS Agreement also stipulates a set of criminal enforcement measures for intellectual property infringement. This is viewed by some IP right holders as critical because infringers may be more deterred by the threat of criminal sanctions than civil or administrative sanctions. The former are more likely to impose a personal cost on the infringer, whereas the latter impose largely an economic cost, which can be built into the cost of doing business.

The scope of IP infringement for which criminal measures must be made available was the subject of disagreement during the Uruguay Round negotiations. Some Members demanded that criminal measures be made available for any infringement, while others wanted to limit them to willful commercial infringements affecting the "public order."[10] The negotiating parties agreed on the following language, enshrined in Art. 61 TRIPS: "Members shall provide for criminal procedures and penalties to be applied at least in cases of willful trademark counterfeiting or copyright piracy on a commercial scale."

The definition of what constitutes trademark counterfeiting and copyright piracy is the same as that set forth in Art. 51 TRIPS, which defined the scope of the border enforcement provisions. Note that Art. 61 TRIPS, unlike Art. 51 TRIPS, adds two additional qualifiers:

---

[10] On this score, see Gervais (2008).

First, the counterfeiting or piracy must be willful. This term has been understood to be similar to the *mens rea* element found in the criminal law of common law countries such as the US. In *China–Intellectual Property Rights*, the Panel (§ 7.523) noted that the word focuses "on the infringer's intent" and "reflects the criminal nature of the enforcement procedures at issue." It confirmed that "[t]here is no need to make [criminal] penalties available with respect to acts of infringement committed without the requisite intent."

Second, the counterfeiting or piracy must be occurring on a commercial scale. The meaning of the term "commercial scale" was examined closely by the Panel in *China–Intellectual Property Rights*. The United States asserted that the term encompassed all commercial activity, with the exception of trivial and *de minimis* activities. The Panel (§ 7.553) disagreed with the American definition, while also rejecting China's interpretation of the term as "a significant magnitude of infringement activity." Instead, the Panel (§ 7.576–77) held that the "precise benchmark in each case depends on the product and the market to which the phrase relates. . . . Therefore, counterfeiting or piracy 'on a commercial scale' refers to counterfeiting or piracy carried on at the magnitude or extent of typical or usual commercial activity with respect to a given product in a given market."

Third, the scope of coverage defined in Art. 61 TRIPS is a minimum standard. WTO Members are free to expand criminal measures to a wider range of IP infringing activities, such as patent infringement.[11] Moreover, they are free to eliminate the willfulness or commercial scale requirement, if they so wish.

Fourth, Art. 61 TRIPS further requires that the remedies available under a WTO Member's laws for criminal IP infringement include "imprisonment and/or monetary fines sufficient to provide a deterrent, consistently with the level of penalties applied for crimes of a corresponding gravity." An earlier draft proposal during the Uruguay Round negotiations required that available remedies include both imprisonment and monetary fines, but this was watered down to require that a WTO Member's criminal law provide at least one of the two discussed remedies.[12] One might ask what is the use of having just monetary fines as a criminal remedy? After all, couldn't an infringer just as easily build the expected cost of criminal fines into its cost of doing business, as is the case with available civil and administrative remedies? The answer, some believe, is that a deterrent component still exists because of a greater stigma associ-

---

[11] This is made clear by the last sentence of Art. 61 TRIPS, which states: "Members may provide for criminal procedures and penalties to be applied in other cases of infringement of intellectual property rights, in particular where they are committed wilfully and on a commercial scale."

[12] See Gervais (2008).

ated with being criminally sanctioned and the possibility of further restrictions placed on those found criminally guilty.[13]

Art. 61 TRIPS further adds that "remedies available shall also include the seizure, forfeiture and destruction of the infringing goods and of any materials and implements the predominant use of which has been in the commission of the offence." However, the use of such remedies may be limited to "appropriate circumstances," a term which is left undefined. As a result, WTO Members have much discretion as to when they wish to apply such remedies in criminal cases.[14]

In *China–Intellectual Property Rights*, the United States challenged China's use of thresholds to determine whether criminal punishment was available for illegal activities related to trademark counterfeiting or copyright infringement. These thresholds varied depending on the type of activity. They were numerical in nature and concerned the amount of monetary gain, the monetary volume of the operation, and/or the number of pieces of the infringing good of the defendant. The US was not challenging the use of thresholds per se. Instead, the US argued that the thresholds as set by China were too high and failed to consider enough factors to capture the TRIPS requirement of applying criminal measures to all cases on a commercial scale.

The Panel (§ 7.523) ruled that to in order to prove such an argument, the complainant needs to submit evidence which establishes that the defendant's laws "actually function to exclude a category of infringement that meets the 'commercial scale' standard." Recall that, in the same case, the Panel established that the term "commercial scale" is to be understood in a product- and market-specific context. Because the US "did not provide adequate data demonstrating what constituted a commercial scale in the specific situation of China's marketplace," the Panel (§ 7.614) ruled against the US.[15]

The *China–Intellectual Property Rights* ruling suggests that in order for a WTO Member to prevail on an Art. 61 TRIPS claim related to the question of whether another Member's criminal laws extends to all cases of a commercial scale, it must be willing to invest substantially in gathering evidence related to product and market conditions in the other Member's economy. Unless it does so, it is unlikely to prevail. It remains to be seen whether Members will be willing to devote the resources necessary

---

[13] For example, being convicted of a crime may be grounds for denying certain licenses.

[14] Unlike Art. 46 TRIPS which discusses the use of these remedies in the context of civil enforcement measures (and Art. 59 TRIPS which extends these remedies to border enforcement measures), Art. 61 TRIPS does not contain an explicit requirement that the use of such remedies be consistent with existing constitutional requirements. However, this difference may be insignificant due to the "appropriate circumstances" language of Art. 61 TRIPS.

[15] The Panel (§ 7.523) noted that "the information that was provided [by the US] was too little and too random to demonstrate a level that constitutes a commercial scale for any product in China."

for future Art. 61 TRIPS cases. To date, no other disputes on this provision have been filed following *China–Intellectual Property Rights*.

4. POST–TRIPS DEVELOPMENTS: THE ANTI–COUNTERFEITING TRADE AGREEMENT (ACTA)

Despite the efforts to standardize the nature of IP rights enforcement through TRIPS, the effectiveness of IP enforcement continues to vary widely across WTO Members. Deere (2009), in a study of developing countries, highlighted a range of challenges: Despite having more authority available as a result of TRIPS, the judicial system continues to be "slow, disorganized, and under-resourced for a whole range of national laws—not just IP." The same is true of administrative officials; despite the increased powers accorded them as a result of TRIPS obligations, they continue to be under-resourced in many countries and lack sufficient capacity. In addition, she finds that the absence of a prior culture of private IP rights creates further difficulties. Most importantly, in some WTO Members, there is an absence of political will. Officials may turn a blind eye toward illicit infringing activities because they are an important source of local employment, or because they are simply bought off through bribery.

All of this has contributed to a sense of frustration among foreign IP right-holders. The *China–Intellectual Property Rights* ruling further underscored the difficulties of using WTO litigation to enforce TRIPS obligations. As noted above, the Panel's ruling highlighted the necessity of aggregating product- and/or market-specific information to prevail on challenges to the under-inclusiveness of a Member's Art. 61 TRIPS obligations, at least with respect to demonstrating "commercial scale." This is a costly and time-consuming endeavor, and one that right-holders have been reluctant to undertake. This is true even for China, which is arguably the market where counterfeiting and piracy have contributed to the most significant economic losses.

In light of these trends, a collection of WTO Members embarked on a plurilateral agreement designed to enhance the framework for enforcing IP rights within their jurisdictions. The WTO Members involved in this effort were primarily developed countries, with a select number of developing countries that had previously concluded free trade agreements with the US and/or EU. They included: Australia, Canada, the EU member states, Japan, Korea, Mexico, Morocco, New Zealand, Singapore, Switzerland, and the United States. This effort culminated in the Anti–Counterfeiting Trade Agreement (ACTA), a finalized text of which was release in December 2010.

As of the time of this writing, the ACTA is still undergoing a process of approval by the Members involved in the negotiation. The ACTA was signed by all the negotiating parties except for the EU member states,

Switzerland, and Mexico in October 2011; the EU and Mexico signed the agreement in 2012. The ACTA is open for further signature by any WTO Member, including those who did not participate in its negotiations, until May 2013. After that date, any WTO Member wishing to join must be approved by a committee established by ACTA. As of now, it appears unlikely that any additional Member will choose to sign.

The ACTA will take effect only after six nations ratify the treaty. In October 2012, Japan became the first country to ratify the agreement. The Executive Branch of the US having taken the position that Congressional approval of the agreement is unnecessary because it is a Congressional–Executive agreement for which Congress provided approval *ex ante*. The ratification process has run into intense opposition in a number of countries. As of this writing, it appears unlikely that the EU will ratify ACTA, due to concerns being raised in a number of its member states. In July 2012, Mexico's legislature also passed a resolution calling on the country's new President to nullify Mexico's signature of the treaty.

Like Part III of the TRIPS Agreement, the ACTA contains a set of required measures concerning civil enforcement, border measures, and criminal enforcement. In addition, there is a section on the enforcement of IP rights in the digital environment. Such provisions are not part of the TRIPS Agreement but have been included in the IP chapters of subsequent free trade agreements signed by WTO Members.

The provisions of the ACTA seek to clarify and/or expand upon the obligations found in the TRIPS Agreement. As was the case with TRIPS, the ACTA has been subject to much praise and also much criticism, depending on the constituency. Critics have argued that the ACTA is an unnecessary further pursuit of an IP-maximalist agenda. They have been particularly concerned about the efforts by the US to standardize approaches toward enforcement efforts on the internet and the willingness of the parties to fragment the global enforcement regime by establishing the ACTA Committee outside of the WTO. Proponents argue that the ACTA is a much-needed updating of the TRIPS enforcement procedures, especially considering that many infringing activities are now taking place through channels, such as the internet, which were not of important focus to the Uruguay Round negotiators. As to the criticism of regime fragmentation, proponents respond that this is a practical reality given the unwillingness of certain WTO Members to add IP issues to the WTO's negotiations agenda.

Should most parties to the negotiations adopt the ACTA (an outcome that may be in doubt, depending on reactions to the fact that as of this writing, the EU is unlikely to ratify the agreement), the provisions will have a noticeable impact on the further standardization of global IP enforcement efforts. The parties to the negotiations collectively constitute more than fifty percent of world trade. As a result, the ACTA will represent the most significant updating of the international trade rules on IP enforcement since TRIPS. Its provisions will effectively serve as a framework for a global TRIPS-plus enforcement regime adopted by a select set of WTO Members.

QUESTIONS AND COMMENTS

The Rise of National Opposition to Further Multilateral IP Enforcement Treaties: Why do you think that meaningful opposition groups in developed countries, including the EU and US, have arisen in the past few years to new initiatives such as the ACTA? After all, domestic industries in their countries would benefit from such treaties. Is it on account of their own personal experiences domestically, with issues such as copyright, which has led them to see the demands of their own IP industries as excessive? Or is it because they have developed greater sympathy for the plight of individuals in developing countries? If the latter, do you think this will be specific to IP, or do you think it will extend to other core areas of concern (*e.g.,* agriculture)?

Special 301: One of the motivating factors for the Uruguay Round talks was the need to establish stronger legal disciplines in order to forestall having GATT members "take matters into their own hands" through using unilateral measures. The US however continues to employ a Special 301 process in which it evaluates its trade partners' IP practices, including those for enforcement, annually. This results in an annual report in which "problematic" countries are "named and shamed" through their inclusion on a "Watch List" or "Priority Watch List." What do you make of such a practice? What purpose does it serve? How effective is it? For the most egregious parties, the process requires that the US government take action, including possibly filing a WTO case.

Local Protectionism: For large developing countries, in particular China, do you think most of the IP enforcement problems being ascribed to it are the result of "willful strategy" on the part of the central government? Or if that goes too far, then is it simply reflective of "willful neglect"? How much do you think this is a matter of local governments seeking to protect local jobs—even if they arise out of illegitimate industries—and actively defying the central government's command to enforce IP laws versus this being a concerted effort on the part of all levels of government to take advantage of the weak enforcement provisions of the TRIPS Agreement?

Chapter 32

From GATT to the WTO: History of Adjudication in the Multilateral Trading System & Presentation of the WTO DSU

■ ■ ■

1. THE (ORIGINAL) GATT

The GATT did not contain any elaborate dispute settlement mechanism, since the GATT was conceived to be an agreement coming under the institutional umbrella of the ITO; it is in the ITO Agreement that negotiators had regulated dispute settlement procedures.[1] There were only two provisions in the GATT dealing with dispute settlement (Arts. XXII and XXIII), and they reflect a two stage-procedure, whereby GATT contracting parties would first consult and, assuming no fruitful consultations, they could refer their dispute to the GATT contracting parties, that is, the highest organ comprising all countries participating in the GATT.[2]

Art. XXII.1 GATT required that each contracting party, when requested to this effect, had to afford adequate opportunity for consultations. Art. XXIII.1 GATT provided that if any contracting party considered that any benefit directly or indirectly accruing to it under the GATT was being nullified or impaired by another party, it could make written representations or proposals to that other party. In principle, thus, there is an overlap between the subject-matter of Art. XXII.1 GATT, and Art. XXIII.1 GATT, although the wording across the two provisions is not identical: the wording of the former seems to be substantially wider than that of the latter. An early GATT decision (GATT Doc. BISD 9S/20) made it clear that GATT contracting parties could use the two provisions alternatively; what mattered was that recourse to consultations had been made, before a request to review the matter by the GATT contracting parties (the Panel procedure) could be lawfully launched. The wording of Art. XXIII.1 GATT was unambiguous in this respect: review by the GATT contracting parties could take place only if no satisfactory adjustment between the consulting contracting parties could take place within a reasonable period of time.

---

[1] See Irwin et al. (2008).
[2] The GATT contracting parties, in practice, adopted their decisions by consensus.

Assuming unsuccessful consultations, the complaining party could be authorized under Art. XXIII.2 GATT, to refer the matter to the GATT contracting parties, who were required to investigate the matter before them and make appropriate recommendations: Art. XXII.2 GATT authorized the GATT contracting parties acting jointly, at the request of a contracting party, to consult on matters which were not resolved through Art. XXII.1 GATT consultations. For this to happen though, the defendant had to be in agreement. Assuming a finding of violation of the GATT, the party concerned would be required to implement the recommendations by bringing its measures into compliance with its obligations. For this to happen though, once again, the report of the Panel would have to be adopted, that is, the defendant would have to agree to its adoption. The term "adoption" of Panel report refers to the process whereby, usually at the request of the complainant, the GATT contracting parties would decide whether or not to adopt a Panel report. Un-adopted reports could not serve as basis to request implementation from their addressees. In Chapter 1, we saw how the legal value of adopted and un-adopted panel reports has been clarified in WTO case-law. In theory, not only the defendant, but any other GATT contracting party could block adoption of a Panel report. In practice, there is no such reported case, as Hudec (1993) mentions.

Assuming adoption of the report and lack of implementation, the CONTRACTING PARTIES could authorize the complaining party to suspend the application of tariff concessions or other GATT obligations vis-à-vis the party found to be acting inconsistently with its obligations under the Agreement. For this to occur, a request to this effect would first have to be submitted and the agreement of the defendant was once again required. Hence, in a nutshell, a complainant should:

(a) Request from the defendant bilateral consultations. The defendant had to adhere to such a request;

(b) Consultations could lead to a resolution of the dispute. If not however, the complainant could refer the matter to the GATT contracting parties;

(c) Assuming that the report that was adopted by the GATT contracting parties found in favour of the complainant, the defendant would be requested to bring its measures into compliance with its obligations;

(d) If no compliance occurred, the complainant could be authorized by the GATT contracting parties to suspend concessions (that is, raise its tariff protection) vis-à-vis the recalcitrant GATT contracting party up to an amount equivalent to the damage suffered.

2. PANEL PROCEDURES

Practice developed in a different way: Disputes would be submitted to a Panel of three (in the majority of occasions) or five (sometimes) experts, who would decide on the issue and submit a report to the GATT contracting parties. We quote from Palmeter and Mavroidis (2004):

> Early dispute settlement in GATT reflected its diplomatic roots. In fact, the process initially was referred to as "conciliation," not as dispute settlement. It all began with a complaint in the summer of 1948 by the Netherlands against Cuba which presented the question, did the most-favored-nation obligation of Article I apply to consular taxes. The matter was referred to the chairman, who ruled that Article I did apply. From these early beginnings of rulings by the chairman, disputes later came to be referred to working parties which consisted of the complaining party, the party complained against, and any others that had an interest. Eventually, the parties directly involved were dropped, and a three or five-member panel process was adopted, using neutral panelists rather than representatives of parties with an interest in the issue.
>
> Most of the advocates before panels and most of the panelists themselves—the "judges"—were diplomats, not lawyers, and as Robert Hudec (1993, p. 12) has observed, "Legal rulings were drafted with an elusive diplomatic vagueness." The goal of the process, as Davey (1987) observes, was more to reach a solution mutually agreeable to the parties than to render a decision in a legal dispute.

Panel practice exists since the fifties. At the conclusion of the Tokyo Round, the GATT contracting parties adopted the Understanding on Notification, Consultation, Dispute Settlement and Surveillance of 28 November 1979 (hereinafter, the 1979 Understanding), which included an Annex setting out an Agreed Description of the Customary Practice of the GATT in the Field of Dispute Settlement. The Understanding and the Agreed Description implicitly reflect the satisfaction of the GATT contracting parties with Panel practice, and their willingness to pursue dispute settlement in the years to come in this manner. The Agreed Description reflects the first official account of Panel practice in the GATT years. We quote in relevant part:

> Panels set up their own working procedures. The practice for the panels has been to hold two or three formal meetings with the parties concerned. The panel invited the parties to present their views either in writing and/or orally in the presence of each other. The panel can question both parties on any matter which it considers relevant to the dispute. Panels have also heard the

views of any contracting party having a substantial interest in the matter, which is not directly party to the dispute, but which has expressed in the Council a desire to present its views. Written memoranda submitted to the panel have been considered confidential, but are made available to the parties to the dispute. Panels often consult with and seek information from any relevant source they deem appropriate and they sometimes consult experts to obtain their technical opinion on certain aspects of the matter. Panels may seek advice or assistance from the secretariat in its capacity as guardian of the General Agreement, especially on historical or procedural aspects. The secretariat provides the secretary and technical services for panels.[3]

3. THE LATER GATT YEARS

The GATT contracting parties over the subsequent years dealt in more detail with specific aspects of dispute settlement. For example, in 1982, focusing on implementation this time, the GATT adopted a decision including a requirement to the effect that:

> The contracting party to which such a recommendation [i.e., to bring a challenged measure into conformity with GATT] has been addressed, shall report within a reasonable specified period on action taken or on its reasons for not implementing the recommendation or ruling by the CONTRACTING PARTIES.[4]

Additional steps of marginal, if any value added, were taken in a Decision on Dispute Settlement Procedures on November 30, 1984.[5] The most significant change comes with the adoption of the Montreal Rules that grew out of the December 1988 Ministerial Conference in the Canadian city where the progress of the Uruguay Round was being evaluated. The Montreal Rules were officially adopted by the GATT contracting parties in April 1989.[6] They formed the basis of what eventually became the WTO Understanding on Rules and Procedures Governing the Settlement of Disputes (DSU). It was agreed to apply the Montreal Rules:

> on a trial basis from 1 May 1989 to the end of the Uruguay Round in respect of complaints brought during that period under Article XXII or XXIII.[7]

The Montreal Rules placed time limits on consultations, and provided for the automatic establishment of a Panel. Parties would be required to reply to a request of consultations within 10 days, and to agree to enter

---

[3] GATT Doc. BISD 26S/215ff.
[4] GATT Doc. BISD 29S/13.
[5] GATT Doc. BISD 31S/9.
[6] GATT Doc. BISD 36S/61, Improvements to the GATT Dispute Settlement Rules and Procedures, Decision of 12 April 1989.
[7] Id..

into consultations in good faith in no less than 30 days. In the absence of an agreement to consult and the holding of timely consultations, the complaining party could proceed directly to request the establishment of a Panel. If consultations failed to settle the dispute within 60 days of the request, the complaining party could request the establishment of a Panel:

> if the complaining party so requests, a decision to establish a panel or a working party shall be taken at the latest at the Council meeting following that at which the request first appeared as an item on the Council's regular agenda, unless at that meeting the Council decides otherwise.[8]

A Panel would be established anyway at the meeting of the GATT Council following that where the request had been first put on the agenda, unless if the GATT Council decided otherwise. For the GATT Council to decide otherwise however, all parties including the complainant would have to decide otherwise. In other words, the system had changed from one that required "positive consensus" to establish a Panel to a system of "negative consensus" that required consensus not to establish a Panel. The passage to negative consensus in the Montreal Rules-setting occurred only with respect to Panel establishment, and not with respect to adoption of panel reports or authorization to impose countermeasures. It is the advent of the DSU that marked the extension of the passage to negative consensus in the other two areas as well.

Hudec's (1993) study shows that from 1947 to 1992, the losing party eventually accepted the results of an adverse panel report in approximately 80% of the cases.[9] Moreover, the percentage would have been even higher (close to 90%), if it was not for Panel practice in the 1980s. During that period, parties blocked adoption with increasing frequency, probably because trading partners moved to the adjudicating table issues that they could not agree upon while negotiating. For example, a number of the Panel decisions during this period dealt with farm policy, a contentious issue for which further legal obligations would be developed during the Uruguay Round.[10]

Hudec's study points to one case only where the defendant refused to establish a Panel: the case concerned the first hormones dispute between the EU and the US, and a Panel was not ultimately established due to the disagreement between them regarding the composition of the panel (one party privileging a scientists-only Panel, whereas the other opting for a normal Panel composed of trade experts and, if warranted, scientists as well).[11] The only time that a request for authorization to impose counter-

---

[8] Id.
[9] Hudec (1993) at p. 278.
[10] Swinbank and Tanner (1996).
[11] Meng (1990).

measures was submitted, it was granted.[12] The trading partners were living in a *de facto* world of compulsory third party adjudication.[13]

4. THE WTO DISPUTE SETTLEMENT UNDERSTANDING (DSU)

4.1 MAJOR DEPARTURES FROM THE GATT SYSTEM

The passage from the GATT to the WTO signalled, through the adoption of the DSU three major changes: first, the creation of the AB, charged with hearing appeals on questions of law from panel rulings; second, the extension of negative consensus: as of January 1, 1995, the vote of the complainant suffices for a Panel/AB to be established (Arts. 6.1 & 17.14 DSU), their reports to be adopted (Arts. 16.4 & 17.14 DSU), and (eventually) for a request for countermeasures to be authorized (Art. 22.6 DSU); third, the WTO adjudicating bodies become the exclusive forum to adjudicate disputes under the WTO covered agreements (Art. 23.2 DSU). Disputes regarding the operation of any of the WTO covered agreements have to be resolved through recourse to the procedures embedded in the DSU.

4.2 STATE TO STATE LITIGATION

The administration of disputes is entrusted to the Dispute Settlement Body (DSB), where representatives of all WTO Members participate. Disputes cannot be initiated ex officio, since there is no authority assigned to a supra-national entity (a watchdog) to initiate complaints against WTO Members; disputes are launched at the sole initiative of a WTO Member.

Private parties, however, do not have standing before the WTO. It is up to individual WTO Members to draw national instruments of "diplomatic protection" whereby they will explain the conditions under which they will agree to represent the interests of their citizens (be it moral, or physical persons) before the WTO. The conditions under which a WTO Member agrees to do so is a question of national law which escapes the scrutiny of WTO law.[14] The WTO DSU is applicable from the time a WTO Member has decided to pursue a dispute before the multilateral forum (Art. 1 DSU).

---

[12] GATT Doc. BISD 4S/31: the GATT contracting parties authorized Netherlands to apply a limit of 60,000 metric tons on imports of wheat flour from the United States during the calendar year 1956.

[13] The Legal Affairs Division was established in 1982 and thus expert advice was being channelled to Panels.

[14] Mavroidis and Zdouc (1998) discuss two of the most prominent instruments of diplomatic protection, the US Section 301, and the EU TBR (Trade Barriers Regulation).

4.3 AN EXCLUSIVE FORUM

Art. 23 DSU reads:

1. When Members seek the redress of a violation of obligations or other nullification or impairment of benefits under the covered agreements or an impediment to the attainment of any objective of the covered agreements, they shall have recourse to, and abide by, the rules and procedures of this Understanding.

2. In such cases, Members shall:

> (a) not make a determination to the effect that a violation has occurred, that benefits have been nullified or impaired or that the attainment of any objective of the covered agreements has been impeded, *except through recourse to dispute settlement in accordance with the rules and procedures of this Understanding*, and shall make any such determination consistent with the findings contained in the panel or AB report adopted by the DSB or an arbitration award rendered under this Understanding; (emphasis added).

First, the Panel in *EC–Commercial Vessels* noted its double purpose:

(a) to ensure that WTO Members will seek to redress violations of the WTO Agreement through recourse to the DSU procedures and will thus avoid unilateral action; and

(b) to also ensure that WTO Members will use exclusively the DSU procedures when trying to redress violations of the WTO Agreement and will not have recourse to the dispute settlement procedures of other fora.

Then, the AB endorsed this view. In *US–Certain EC Products*, it understood this provision as banning unilateral definitions of illegality (§ 111):

> Article 23.1 of the DSU imposes a general obligation on Members to redress a violation of obligations or other nullification or impairment of benefits under the covered agreements only by recourse to the rules and procedures of the DSU, and not through unilateral action. Subparagraphs (a), (b) and (c) of Article 23.2 articulate specific and clearly-defined forms of prohibited unilateral action contrary to Article 23.1 of the DSU. There is a close relationship between the obligations set out in paragraphs 1 and 2 of Article 23. They all concern the obligation of Members of the WTO not to have recourse to unilateral action. (. . .)."

Then, in *US–Suspended Concession*, the AB expanded on this idea (§ 371):

... Article 23.1 lays down the fundamental obligation of WTO Members to have recourse to the rules and procedures of the DSU when seeking redress of a violation of the covered agreements. Article 23 restricts WTO Members' conduct in two respects. First, Article 23.1 establishes the WTO dispute settlement system as the exclusive forum for the resolution of such disputes and requires adherence to the rules of the DSU. Secondly, Article 23.2 prohibits certain unilateral action by a WTO Member. Thus, a Member cannot unilaterally: (i) determine that a violation has occurred, benefits have been nullified or impaired, or that the attainment of any objective of the covered agreements has been impeded; (ii) determine the duration of the reasonable period of time for implementation; or (iii) decide to suspend concessions and determine the level thereof.

Jackson (1969) notes that, although the possibility to submit trade-related disputes to the International Court of Justice (ICJ) was in principle open to GATT contracting parties, no use of it was ever made. Art. 23.2 DSU thus eliminated this theoretical possibility.

4.4 TWO PHASES OF ADJUDICATION

Adjudication in the WTO system echoes the GATT system and is divided into two phases: one in principle bilateral, and one multilateral. The bilateral phase consists of consultations between the complainant and the defendant. When requesting consultations, the complainant has to notify the WTO as to the subject-matter of the dispute. Other WTO Members wishing to join as co-complainants can do so, provided that the defendant accepts their request (Art. 4.11 DSU).

Assuming that the parties reach no solution during the consultations-stage, the complainant can request the establishment of a Panel to adjudicate the dispute. This second phase of adjudication is multilateral and consists of two parts: the first is the Panel procedures, and the second, the procedure before the AB. Whereas the three person panels are ad hoc adjudicating bodies, the composition of which depends, in principle, on the will of the parties to the dispute, the AB is composed of seven judges appointed on four years terms, renewable once. Panels have competence to review the factual record and the legal issues before them, whereas the AB's review is limited to the latter. Panels are assisted by members of the WTO Secretariat (usually lawyers, and occasionally economists as well).

Assuming that the AB (or the Panel, in situations where the report has not been appealed) accepts the original complaint, the defendant will be requested to implement the judgment. Implementation should, if possible, occur immediately, although this is hardly ever the case. Instead, defendants are granted an implementation period, that is either agreed bilaterally, or through recourse to binding arbitration. Disagreements as to whether implementation has truly occurred might arise. In such cases, the dispute is referred to a compliance Panel the task of which is to determine whether implementation occurred. If the compliance Panel (and eventually the AB) hold that no implementation has occurred, the complainant can request authorization to suspend concessions. Following authorization, the complainant will have the right to raise its bound duties to the level necessary to inflict on the defendant damage equal in value to the damage the complainant suffered as a result of the practice that was found to be illegal.

4.5 THE TYPES OF LEGAL COMPLAINTS

The WTO DSU reproduces the GATT-regime that distinguishes between: violation complaints (Art. XXIII.1a GATT); non-violation complaints (Art. XXIII.1b GATT); and situation complaints (Art. XXIII.1c GATT). The DSU has added however, some extra detail with respect to non-violation and situation complaints (Art. 26 DSU).

4.5.1 Violation Complaints

Art. XXIII.1(a) GATT reads as follows:

If any contracting party should consider that any benefit accruing to it directly or indirectly under this Agreement is being nullified or impaired or that the attainment of any objective of the Agreement is being impeded as the result of

(a) the failure of another contracting party to carry out its obligations under this Agreement . . .

Hence, through a violation complaint, a WTO Member alleges that the defendant has violated the WTO Agreement. This category comprises the vast majority of complaints submitted to the WTO so far.[15] On its face, Art. XXIII.2 GATT seems to require from the complainant to prove, beyond violation of a GATT provision, that a benefit accruing to it had been nullified or impaired. Standing GATT case law however has made it clear that any time the complaining party has managed to prove violation of the GATT there was ipso facto a prima facie case that a benefit accruing to it had indeed been nullified or impaired.[16] In fact, so far there has never been a case where this presumption has been effectively rebutted.[17]

---

[15] Horn et al. (2011).

[16] See on this score Jackson (1969).

[17] In the WTO-era, in *EC–Bananas III (Article 21.5–Ecuador) (Second Recourse)*, the AB repeated that there is a presumption of nullification and impairment any time a provision has been violated (§§ 469ff.).

4.5.2 Non–Violation Complaints

Non-violation complaints (NVCs) are described in Art. XXIII.1b GATT:

> If any contracting party should consider that any benefit accruing to it directly or indirectly under this Agreement is being nullified or impaired or that the attainment of any objective of the Agreement is being impeded as the result of
>
> . . .
>
> (b) the application by another contracting party of any measure, whether or not it conflicts with the provisions of this Agreement
>
> . . .

In Art. 26 DSU, the founding fathers reflected some of the jurisprudential evolution in the context of NVCs: the defendant, following a successful complaint, does not have to withdraw the challenged measure; instead, a mutually agreed solution is encouraged. Recourse to an arbitration in order to quantify the damage is an option; suggestions by the Arbitrator entrusted with the task to determine the level of nullified benefits are non-binding on their addressee.

The rationale for NVCs has to do with the explicit (in Art. XXIII GATT) acknowledgement that benefits (from trade liberalization) accruing to the various WTO Members can be nullified as a result of either a GATT-inconsistent or GATT-consistent behaviour. In a way, NVC are an application of the good faith (*bona fides*) principle, in the sense that, by adhering to the WTO, a Member should not only abstain from GATT-inconsistent, but also from GATT-consistent behavior, to the extent that the latter might nullify benefits from trade liberalization. The key issue how far does the good faith obligation extend to? The aggravating factor is the incompleteness of the GATT contract. There are a number of areas that affect trade and have not been explicitly dealt with in the GATT, and the question arises whether a WTO Member is liable for any (lawful) measure it might adopt which even tangentially might influence the value of a tariff promise it has previously made.

Case law has tried to provide some responses to this question. First, the 1990 Panel report in *EEC–Oilseeds I* provided the rationale for NVCs (§§ 144 and 148):

> The idea underlying [the provisions of Article XXIII:1(b)] is that the improved competitive opportunities that can legitimately be expected from a tariff concession can be frustrated not only by measures proscribed by the General Agreement but also by measures consistent with that Agreement. In order to encourage contracting parties to make tariff concessions they must therefore be given a right of redress when a reciprocal concession is

impaired by another contracting party as a result of the application of any measure, whether or not it conflicts with the General Agreement.

. . .

The Panel considered that the main value of a tariff concession is that it provides an assurance of better market access through improved price competition. Contracting parties negotiate tariff concessions primarily to obtain that advantage. They must therefore be assumed to base their tariff negotiations on the expectation that the price effect of the tariff concessions will not be systematically offset. If no right of redress were given to them in such a case they would be reluctant to make tariff concessions and the General Agreement would no longer be useful as a legal framework for incorporating the results of trade negotiations.

The aforementioned Panel dealt with a (legal) subsidy scheme granted by the EU. Subsidies have a rather direct nexus with prices, since a benefiting producer could use the proceeds to lower its price. All NVCs launched during the GATT-era shared similar facts: the complainant claimed that a subsidy paid subsequent to a negotiated concession was nullifying benefits accruing to it.[18] The question is what conduct other than payment of subsidies can form the subject-matter of an NVC?

The AB in *EC–Asbestos, inter alia,* faced an argument advanced by the EU that an NVC could not be used against health-based trade-obstructing measures justified under Art. XX GATT. In the EU's view, a measure could not, on the one hand, be explicitly permitted under a GATT provision and still induce the liability of the regulating state. The AB dismissed this argument (§§ 188–189):

> The European Communities also contends that the Panel erred in finding that Article XXIII:1(b) applies to measures which pursue health, rather than commercial, objectives and which can, therefore, be justified under Article XX(b) of the GATT 1994. Once again, we look to the text of Article XXIII:1(b), which provides that "the application by another Member of any measure" may give rise to a cause of action under that provision. The use of the word "any" suggests that measures of all types may give rise to such a cause of action. The text does not distinguish between, or exclude, certain types of measure. Clearly, therefore, the text of Article XXIII:1(b) contradicts the European Communities' argument that certain types of measure, namely, those with health objectives, are excluded from the scope of application of Article XXIII:1(b).

---

[18] See Petersmann (1991) for an exhaustive discussion on this score.

In any event, an attempt to draw the distinction suggested by the European Communities between so-called health and commercial measures would be very difficult in practice. By definition, measures which affect trade in goods, and which are subject to the disciplines of the GATT 1994, have a commercial impact. At the same time, the health objectives of many measures may be attainable only by means of commercial regulation. Thus, in practice, clear distinctions between health and commercial measures may be very difficult to establish. Nor do we see merit in the argument that, previously, only "commercial" measures have been the subject of Article XXIII:1(b) claims, as that does not establish that a claim cannot be made under Article XXIII:1(b) regarding a "non-commercial" measure. (emphasis in the original).

Standing GATT/WTO case-law has clarified that, for a WTO Member to successfully launch an NVC, it must demonstrate that an action:

(a) had been taken, the WTO-consistency of which is not in dispute;

(b) occurred after a tariff concession had been agreed;

(c) could not have been reasonably anticipated by the complainant;

(d) reduced the value of the concession.[19]

Whenever these four conditions have been cumulatively met, panels have always accepted the NVC submitted by the complaining party.

Points (a) and (b) above are factual issues. Point (d) would require causality-analysis. So far GATT/WTO case-law has not contributed much on this score: since most of it dealt with subsidies, Panels took it for granted that beneficiaries would use the subsidy-proceedings to lower their prices and, thus, make it harder for imports to penetrate the market. The economic rationality of such an approach is, of course, highly questionable.[20]

With respect to point (c), the Panel in *Japan–Film* held that the moment when the challenged measure occurred should serve as benchmark for the allocation of the burden of proof (§§ 10.79–81):

We consider that the issue of reasonable anticipation should be approached in respect of specific "measures" in light of the following guidelines. First, in the case of measures shown by the United States to have been introduced subsequent to the conclusion of the tariff negotiations at issue, it is our view that the United States has raised a presumption that it should not be held to have anticipated these measures and it is then for Japan

---

[19] See for example, the GATT Panel report in *EEC–Oilseeds I*.

[20] One might for example, ask the question why did not such investments take place before the subsidy had been paid if they were profitable? It is highly unlikely that all beneficiaries were simultaneously suffering from liquidity constraint.

to rebut that presumption. Such a rebuttal might be made, for example, by establishing that the measure at issue is so clearly contemplated in an earlier measure that the United States should be held to have anticipated it. However, there must be a clear connection shown. In our view, it is not sufficient to claim that a *specific* measure should have been anticipated because it is consistent with or a continuation of a past *general* government policy. As in the *EEC–Oilseeds* case, we do not believe that it would be appropriate to charge the United States with having reasonably anticipated all GATT-consistent measures, such as "measures" to improve what Japan describes as the inefficient Japanese distribution sector. Indeed, if a Member were held to anticipate all GATT-consistent measures, a non-violation claim would not be possible. Nor do we consider that as a general rule the United States should have reasonably anticipated Japanese measures that are similar to measures in other Members' markets. In each such instance, the issue of reasonable anticipation needs to be addressed on a case-by-case basis.

Second, in the case of measures shown by Japan to have been introduced prior to the conclusion of the tariff negotiations at issue, it is our view that Japan has raised a presumption that the United States should be held to have anticipated those measures and it is for the United States to rebut that presumption. In this connection, it is our view that the United States is charged with knowledge of Japanese government measures as of the date of their publication. We realize that knowledge of a measure's existence is not equivalent to understanding the impact of the measure on a specific product market. For example, a vague measure could be given substance through enforcement policies that are initially unexpected or later changed significantly. However, where the United States claims that it did not know of a measure's relevance to market access conditions in respect of film or paper, we would expect the United States to clearly demonstrate why initially it could not have reasonably anticipated the effect of an existing measure on the film or paper market and when it did realize the effect. Such a showing will need to be tied to the relevant points in time (i.e., the conclusions of the Kennedy, Tokyo and Uruguay Rounds) in order to assess the extent of the United States' legitimate expectations of benefits from these three Rounds. A simple statement that a Member's measures were so opaque and informal that their impact could not be assessed is not sufficient. While it is true that in most past non-violation cases, one could easily discern a clear link between a product-specific action and the effect on the tariff concession that it allegedly impaired, one can also discern a link between general measures affecting the internal sale and distribution of products, such as rules on advertising and premiums, and tariff concessions on products in general.

Third, for our purposes, we consider the conclusion of the tariff negotiations in the three Rounds to be as follows: In the case of the Kennedy Round, it appears that tariff negotiations continued until the very end of the Round and thus we will consider the date of the conclusion of the Round, i.e., 30 June 1967, as the relevant date. In the case of the Tokyo Round, the conclusion of the Round was 12 April 1979, although the relevant Protocol was formally dated 30 June 1979. We will address where appropriate the US argument that the negotiations on film tariff reductions ended earlier. In the case of the Uruguay Round, tariff negotiations were substantially completed as of 15 December 1993, although the formal end of the Round occurred on the signing of the WTO Agreement in Marrakesh on 15 April 1994. Accordingly, we will use the date of 15 December 1993 as the conclusion of the Uruguay Round tariff negotiations.

Actions that took place before the exchange of concessions will be presumed to be known by the complainant; conversely, actions that took place after the exchange of concessions, will be presumed to be unknown to it. In the case at hand, the Japanese measures were all in place before film concessions had been exchanged between Japan and the US, and the US lawyers did not manage to rebut the presumption.

4.5.3 Situation Complaints

A situation complaint was originally defined in Art. XXIII.1(c) GATT:

If any contracting party should consider that any benefit accruing to it directly or indirectly under this Agreement is being nullified or impaired or that the attainment of any objective of the Agreement is being impeded as the result of

(c) the existence of any other situation . . .

It is hard to imagine what could come under Art. XXIII.1(c) GATT, that is not already covered by Art. XXIII.1(a), or by Art. XXIII.1(b) GATT. Hence, it is not surprising that throughout the GATT years there is no case law in this respect. There is only one exception: a 1982 request for consultations by the EU (against Japan), the so-called "Japanese way of life" litigation,[21] which however never led to the establishment of a Panel. Some claims were made in the context of *Japan–Film* but were not discussed in any comprehensive manner.

---

[21] Bronckers (1987).

Art. 26.2 DSU deals with situation complaints in more detailed manner: it makes it clear that the DSU is applicable to situation complaints up to the stage of the proceedings where the report has been circulated to WTO Members. The practical significance of this provision is that there is no negative consensus with respect to the adoption of the report, and with respect to a request to authorize countermeasures, as far as situation complaints are concerned.

QUESTIONS AND COMMENTS

Non–Violation Complaints: Do you agree with the Panel report in *EC–Asbestos*? Where would you draw the line yourself between permissible and impermissible NVCs?

Situation Complaints: Is there room for this type of complaints?

Exclusive Forum: What are the pros and cons in your view of establishing an exclusive forum to litigate disputes coming under the purview of the WTO?

Bob Hudec: His 1993 book made a strong case to the effect that the manner in which disputes were being adjudicated during the GATT years best explains the passage to negative consensus. Do you agree with this view?

Instruments of Diplomatic Protection: What are the pros and cons of scrutinizing private claims before agreeing to represent them at a WTO Panel, instead of agreeing to representing them all?

CHAPTER 33

CONSULTATIONS

■ ■ ■

1. THE REQUEST FOR CONSULTATIONS

The term "dispute" is not defined in the DSU. The DSU is concerned with administering resolution of disputes however the latter are defined by WTO Members. Consultations represent the first step towards resolving a dispute. Reminiscent of early GATT years, where a rather diplomatic resolution of disputes was privileged (at least in practice), the consultations-stage comprises bilateral meetings between complainant and defendant. The first act is the submission of a formal request for consultations. Requests for consultations should be in writing (Art. 4.4 DSU) and should be copied to the DSB, and to the relevant Councils and Committees: for example, if a dispute concerns an alleged illegal imposition of antidumping duties, the DSB, the Council for Trade in Goods, and the Antidumping Committee will have to be notified thereof.

The request for consultations should specify the articles of the relevant WTO agreements under which consultations are sought (provisions of procedural nature). Art. 4.4 DSU requires that the complaining party:

> give the reasons for the request including identification of the measures at issue and an indication of the legal basis for the complaint.[1]

This provision requests from WTO Members to identify the factual matter that forms the subject-matter of consultations and the claims raised.[2]

2. NO PANEL WITHOUT CONSULTATIONS

Consultations are the *sine qua non* for an (eventual) submission of a dispute to the Panel process. A Panel will not be lawfully established unless if consultations were held and were fruitless; or, if the defending party declined to respond to a request for consultations within 10 days from

---

[1] Panels will routinely examine whether there is parallelism in the subject matter that is being raised before them, and that discussed during the consultations-stage, and in case an issue does not appear in the request for consultations they might decline to review it (see the discussion in next Chapter).

[2] Legal arguments might of course, be shaped during the consultations-stage (and different legal advisors might have differing views as to the appropriate legal basis anyway). What matters at the stage of request is the identification of the factual matter, and hence, the accent in Art. 4.4 DSU on this point is highly appropriate.

its receipt; or, assuming a positive response, it declined to consult within 30 days (Art. 4.3 DSU).[3] Consultations can, in theory, go on for an idefinite period of time, but the complainant can submit a request for Panel establishment 60 days after consultations had been initiated (Art. 4.6 DSU).

3. MULTILATERAL DEFENSE

The DSU contains three provisions that aim at eliminating firewalls between bilateral consultations and the multilateral system:

- First, Art. 4.4 DSU obliges all WTO Members wishing to enter into consultations with another WTO Member to make their request in writing and notify the WTO to this effect, so that the WTO Membership is aware of the content of consultations;
- Second, assuming an agreement has been reached at the consultations-stage between the interested parties, the DSB must be notified thereof, and it is at the DSB where its consistency with the WTO will be discussed (Arts. 3.5, 3.6 DSU). Consulting parties are under the duty to ensure that all agreements reached at the consultations-stage are WTO-consistent (Art. 3.6 DSU);
- Third, Art. 4.11 DSU allows interested WTO Members to request to join in consultations. To this effect, interested parties will have to make their interest known within the statutory deadline, and they must also secure the agreeement of the defendant as well.

4. CONFIDENTIALITY REQUIREMENTS

According to Art. 4.6 DSU, consultations are confidential. No public record of the consultations exists as a result. If no agreement is reached, a WTO Member cannot rely on admissions of inconsistency made by the other WTO Member during the consultations-stage, to substantiate its claims before a Panel. Art. 4.6 DSU reads to this effect:

> Consultations shall be . . . without prejudice to the rights of any Member in any further proceedings.

---

[3] The AB had the opportunity to provide its understanding regarding the interpretation of Art. 4.3 DSU in its report in *Mexico–Corn Syrup (Article 21.5–US)*. In that case, a compliance Panel (Art. 21.5 DSU) had been established by the DSB without prior consultations. Mexico did not object at the time the Panel was established, and did not object before the Panel either. It raised the issue for the first time on appeal, arguing that the Panel should have addressed ex officio whether consultations had been held prior to the request for establishment. The AB held, in § 35 of its report, that Mexico had effectively waived its right for consultations by not objecting at the DSB meeting to the establishment of the Panel; the Panel did not have to address the issue whether consultations were held sua sponte.

5. THE OUTCOME OF CONSULTATIONS

Consultations might lead to an agreement, a partial agreement, or not resolve the issue at all. If the latter happens, it will be up to the complainant to weigh the options and, eventually, submit the dispute to a Panel. If a total or partial agreement has been reached, it must be WTO-consistent (Art. 3.5 DSU), and the DSB must be notified (Art. 3.6 DSU). Similar agreements are referred to as mutually agreed solutions (MAS).

QUESTIONS AND COMMENTS

Bargaining in the Shadow of Law: Busch and Reinhardt have been studying in a very detailed manner the outcomes and the political economy of consultations. A number of factors, ranging from the rather "intimate" nature of consultations (flexibility, few participants, no detailed legal constraints) help explain, in their view, the success rate at the consultations-stage, see Busch and Reinhardt (2001), (2002) and (2005). Guzman and Simmons (2005) offer some insights as to the conditions under which a party might privilege an early settlement or decide to go all the way and submit a dispute to a Panel.

Original Complainants: The data in Horn et al. (2011) reveals that developing countries have a tendency to join in consultations more often than OECD members. Would that say something about search costs associated with detecting illegal trade barriers?

Admissions of Guilt: In your view can a Panel close its eyes to admissions of guilt made during the consultations-stage simply because of Art. 4.6 DSU?

Duration of Consultations: The data in Horn et al. (2011) shows that on average consultations last for more than seven months. Why in your view do not complainants request establishment of a Panel the 61st day counting from the date of initiation of consultations?

CHAPTER 34

PANEL PROCEEDINGS

■ ■ ■

1. THE REQUEST FOR ESTABLISHMENT OF A PANEL

1.1 THE TEST FOR COMPLIANCE WITH THE STATUTORY REQUIREMENTS

Panels will be established at the latest at the DSB meeting following that at which the item was first placed on the agenda (Art. 6.1 DSU). Art. 6 DSU prejudges both the form and the content of a request for establishment: it must always be in writing, and it must contain a statement as to whether consultations were held, as well as the facts alleged to be inconsistent with the WTO, and the legal provisions against which they run afoul. It is addressed to the DSB. More specifically, Art. 6.2 DSU requires that, with respect to the content, a request for establishment:

> shall ... identify the specific measures at issue and provide a brief summary of the legal basis of the complaint sufficient to present the problem clearly.

In *Brazil–Desiccated Coconut*, the AB explained the rationale for Art. 6.2 DSU (§ 186):

> A panel's terms of reference are important for two reasons. First, terms of reference fulfill an important due process objective—they give the parties and third parties sufficient information concerning the claims at issue in the dispute in order to allow them an opportunity to respond to the complainant's case. Second, they establish the jurisdiction of the panel by defining the precise claims at issue in the dispute.

In *Korea–Dairy*, the AB provided the legal standard for consistency with Art. 6.2 DSU:

> Identification of the treaty provisions claimed to have been violated by the respondent is always necessary both for purposes of defining the terms of reference of a panel and for informing the respondent and the third parties of the claims made by the complainant; such identification is a minimum prerequisite if the legal basis of the complaint is to be presented at all. But it may not always be enough. There may be situations where the simple

listing of the articles of the agreement involved may, in the light of attendant circumstances, suffice to meet the standard of *clarity* in the statement of the legal basis of the complaint. However, there may also be situations in which the circumstances are such that the mere listing of treaty articles would not satisfy the standard of Article 6.2. This may be the case, for instance, where the articles listed establish not one single, distinct obligation, but rather multiple obligations. In such a situation, the listing of articles of an agreement, in and of itself, may fall short of the standard of Article 6.2 (§ 124, emphasis in the original).

And later:

... whether the mere listing of the articles claimed to have been violated meets the standard of Article 6.2 must be examined on a case-by-case basis. In resolving that question, we take into account whether the ability of the respondent to defend itself was prejudiced, given the actual course of the panel proceedings, by the fact that the panel request simply listed the provisions claimed to have been violated (§ 127).

In *Korea–Dairy*, the AB established the distinction between claims and arguments holding that only the former need to appear in the request for establishment of a Panel (§ 139):

[A] party to a dispute settlement proceeding may not introduce a new claim during or after the rebuttal stage. Indeed, any claim that is not asserted in the request for the establishment of a panel may not be submitted at any time after submission and acceptance of that request. By *"claim"* we mean a claim that the respondent party has violated, or nullified or impaired the benefits arising from, an identified provision of a particular agreement. Such a *claim of violation* must, as we have already noted, be distinguished from the *arguments* adduced by a complaining party to demonstrate that the responding party's measure does indeed infringe upon the identified treaty provision. Arguments supporting a claim are set out and progressively clarified in the first written submissions, the rebuttal submissions and the first and second panel meetings with the parties. Both "claims" and "arguments" are distinct from the "evidence" which the complainant or respondent presents to support its assertions of fact and arguments. (emphasis in the original).[1]

The listing of provisions is thus, a threshold issue and sometimes even that might not be enough.[2] The same is true when it comes to identi-

---

[1] See also, the AB report in *EC–Bananas III* (§§ 141, 143 and 145).

[2] In *Korea–Dairy*, the AB explained that identification of the particulart paragraph or sub-paragraph of a provision might be necessary if a certain provision contains various paragraphs

fying the factual issue. The AB in *US–Carbon Steel* had to deal with, *inter alia*, the following: The EU had challenged a US measure as well as "certain aspects of the sunset review procedure which led to it", and "the implementing regulations and interim final rules issued by the DOC". The US complained that the reference to "certain aspects" was not precise enough, and that, as a result, the claims relating to this term should be excluded from the Panel's review. The Panel agreed with the US claim, and the AB upheld the Panel's finding (§ 171). The Panel in *US–Continued Suspension* rejected the claim by the EU that mere reference in its request for establishment to a dispute which incorporated specific legal instruments sufficed for it to raise before the Panel a claim with respect to these instruments. In the case at hand, the complainant was challenging the consistency of zeroing in a series of cases handled by the US; it mentioned the cases in the request without referring to the particular instrument that it was challenging. In the words of the Panel (§ 7.51):

> In this regard, we see a significant difference between the issue presented in those cases and the one before us in this dispute. The issue in this case does not concern the description of the legal instrument that embodies the challenged measure. Rather, the issue here is the identification of the measure itself. Hence, we do not consider the references to *Argentina—Footwear* and *Canada—Wheat* pertinent.

In *EC–IT Products*, the Panel held that amendments to a measure specified in the request can legitimately come under the jurisdiction of the Panel, if the expression of the measure was wide enough, the subsequent amendment does not change the essence of the challenged measure, and the resolution of the amendment is necessary for the resolution of the dispute (§§ 7.140–146).

The AB opened the door to the possibility to clarify claims reflected in a request for establishment of a Panel, through recourse to the first submission of the complainant (*Korea–Dairy*, §§ 127 and 132):

> As we have said previously, compliance with the requirements of Article 6.2 must be demonstrated on the face of the request for the establishment of a panel. Defects in the request for the establishment of a panel cannot be "cured" in the subsequent submissions of the parties during the panel proceedings. Nevertheless, in considering the sufficiency of a panel request, submissions and statements made during the course of the panel proceedings, in particular the first written submission of the complaining party, may be consulted in order to confirm the meaning of the words used in the panel request and as part of the assess-

---

that reflect different obligations (§§ 127ff.). See also the AB report in *US–Continued Zeroing* at §§ 161–169.

ment of whether the ability of the respondent to defend itself was prejudiced. Moreover, compliance with the requirements of Article 6.2 must be determined on the merits of each case, having considered the panel request as a whole, and in the light of attendant circumstances.

. . .

We are confirmed in this view by our reading of the European Communities' first written submission to the Panel. This submission clearly addresses United States law, as such, governing the likelihood determination. Section 6 of the submission, entitled "Claims", is divided into four subsections. Subsection 6.2 deals with the determination to be made in a sunset review, and in part 6.2.2 of that subsection, headed "US laws and practice", the European Communities alleges, *inter alia*, that United States law is inconsistent with the United States' obligations under Article 21.3 of the *SCM Agreement*." (italics in the original).[3]

1.2 THE LEGAL CONSEQUENCE FOR VIOLATING ART. 6.2 DSU

A claim that does not respect the requirements of Art. 6.2 DSU lies outside the terms of reference of the Panel. In *US–Lamb*, for example, the Panel did not extend its review of the legal challenge beyond claims advanced by the complainant (§ 5.21).[4] The absence of a legal challenge by the defendant to this effect does not affect this issue: Panels have the competence to review their own competence to adjudicate a particular dispute. The Panel in *US–AD Act of 1916* pertinently stated to this effect that (§ 6.71):

... the Panel considers that it has the 'competence of its competence', i.e., that it may determine whether a given claim can be addressed, irrespective of the positions expressed by the parties on the issue.[5]

The AB in *EC–Bananas III* underscored this view where it held (§ 142):

---

[3] The Panel in *Colombia–Ports of Entry* used the first submission to interpret the request for establishment (§ 7.33). Although there is no obligation to do so, claims regarding the consistency of a request for establishment with Art. 6.2 DSU, will usually be raised in the form of a request for a preliminary ruling. See, for example, §§ 7.1ff. of the Panel report in *EC–Trademarks and Geographical Indications*.

[4] In *Canada–Autos,* the Panel refused to entertain a claim which had not been properly included in the request for establishment; it still however, examined it on the merits, assuming arguendo that it was properly before it before condemning it altogether (§§ 10.132–134).

[5] In similar vein, there is no need for the defendant to contest for the Panel to examine whether a claim comes under its terms of reference, see the Panel report in *Colombia–Ports of Entry* at § 7.47.

We recognize that a panel request will usually be approved automatically at the DSB meeting following the meeting at which the request first appears on the DSB's agenda. As a panel request is normally not subjected to detailed scrutiny by the DSB, it is incumbent upon a panel to examine the request for the establishment of the panel very carefully to ensure its compliance with both the letter and the spirit of Article 6.2 of the DSU.

In *Mexico–Corn Syrup (Article 21.5–US)*, the AB went one step further and argued that panels must (as opposed to "should") address the issue of their own competence (§ 36).

1.3 ATTENDANT CIRCUMSTANCES

The Panel in *EC–Tube or Pipe Fittings* used the term "vague claim" to distinguish an imprecise claim that had been submitted to it from a claim that had not even been identified in the request for establishment of a Panel: in its view, in the latter case, the claim is outside the terms of reference of the Panel (§ 7.14); in the former case, the WTO Member complaining, must show that it suffered prejudice because of the vagueness in the formulation of the claim (§ 7.10, and § 7.22).[6] The AB has understood that prejudice might not exist because of "attendant circumstances" that we discuss in what follows.

1.3.1 Claims on Provisions Incorporated in Cited Provisions

In *Korea–Various Measures on Beef*, the request for establishment did not explicitly reflect provisions the inconsistency of which with the WTO had been invoked: Australia had included in its request claims under Arts. 3, 6 and 7 AG. It then moved on and presented before the Panel claims on Annex 3 of the same agreement, and claims relating to schedule LX, that is Korea's schedule reflecting its commitments on farm products. Korea objected that the invoked provisions had not been explicitly identified in the request. The Panel ruled that the claims were within its terms of reference and moved on to review them on the merits. Korea appealed. The AB rejected the Korean claims stating that Art. 6 AD explicitly refers to commitments, and hence to Schedule LX which had thus been directly incorporated by reference into the claims presented (§ 83). Annex 3 was also judged to be within the terms of reference because Arts. 3 and 6 refer to Art. 1(a)(ii) which refers to Annex 3 (§ 87).

---

[6] Originally, there were some examples to the opposite: the Panel in *US–Suspended Concession* held that there is no prejudice requirement in the body of Art. 6.2 DSU (§§ 7.65–66). These were isolated incidents that stopped once the AB settled the issue in favor of a prejudice-test to decide if a claim was properly before a Panel.

1.3.2 Provision Not Adequately Cited, but Claim Explained in Submission

The Panel in *Mexico–Antidumping Measures on Rice* faced an argument by Mexico that the US request for establishment was falling short of the requirements of Art. 6.2 DSU since, the US had failed to include the specific paragraphs of Art. VI GATT that they were complaining about. Art. VI GATT, it is uncontested, includes paragraphs which impose different obligations. The US request read as follows (§ 7.29):

> Article VI of the GATT 1994 and Articles 1, 3.1, 3.2, 3.4, 3.5, and 4.1 of the AD Agreement because Mexico based its injury and causation analyses on only six months of data for each of the years examined; failed to collect or examine recent data; failed to properly evaluate the relevant economic factors; failed to base its determination on a demonstration that the dumped imports are, through the effects of dumping, causing injury within the meaning of the AD Agreement; and failed to base its injury determinations on positive evidence or to conduct objective examinations of the volume of dumped imports, the effect of those imports on prices in the domestic market of like products, and the impact of the imports on domestic producers of those products.

The Panel acknowledged that Art. VI GATT imposes various obligations on WTO Members. It held, however, that Mexico did not suffer any damage as a result, since the US in their request had sufficiently explained their claims so as not to leave room for doubt as to which paragraphs it was complaining about (§§ 7.29–7.31).[7]

1.3.3 Provision Not Adequately Cited, but Obligations Are Interlinked

In *Thailand–H–Beams*, Poland alleged that (§ 89, AB report):

> Thai authorities have made a determination that Polish imports caused injury to the Thai domestic industry, in the absence of, *inter alia*, "positive evidence" to support such a finding and without the required "objective examination" of enumerated factors such as import volume, price effects, and the consequent impact of such imports on the domestic industry, in contravention of Article VI of GATT 1994 and Article 3 of the Antidumping Agreement.

---

[7] In *EC–Selected Customs Matters*, the US was challenging hundreds of customs administration-related measured adopted by the EU. It did not list each one of them in its request. The Panel held that the US should at least have referred to the areas of customs administration to which the specific measures belonged. Otherwise, it would consider that the US had not satisfied the requirements of Art. 6.2 DSU (see the analysis leading to the ruling in § 7.31).

Thai authorities have made a determination of dumping and calculated an alleged dumping margin in violation of Article VI of GATT 1994 and Article 2 of the Antidumping Agreement.

Thai authorities initiated and conducted this investigation in violation of the procedural and evidentiary requirements of Article VI of GATT 1994 and Articles 5 and 6 of the Antidumping Agreement.

It is undisputed that Arts. 2, 3 and 5 AD reflect distinct obligations. With respect to Art. 3 AD, the AB essentially accepted wholeheartedly the finding by the Panel holding that Art. 3.1 informs all other paragraphs included in Art. 3 and thus accepted that the claim was within its terms of reference (§ 90). With respect to Art. 5 AD, the AB held that, in light of the "interlinked" nature of the obligations reflected in this provision, a generic reference to the procedural requirements included in Art. 5 AD suffices for the purposes of meeting the requirements of Art. 6.2 DSU (§ 93): Art. 5 AD refers to the various steps explaining the conditions under which an investigation is lawfully launched.[8]

1.3.4 Provision Not Adequately Cited, but Matter Was Discussed in WTO Committee

In *US–Lamb,* the complainants included in their request for establishment references to Arts. 2, 3, and 4 SG. All these provisions contain sub-paragraphs that impose distinct obligations. Before the Panel the complainants argued on a series of sub-paragraphs of these provisions that were not explicitly mentioned in the request. The Panel noted that the defendant suffered no damage as a result, since all these claims had already been discussed between complainants and defendant before the WTO Safeguards Committee (§§ 5.32ff).

1.3.5 WTO Practice

In the AB report in *US–OCTG*, Argentina was challenging a determination by the US antidumping authority which was based on a virtually irrefutable presumption under "US law as such" (§ 158). The US had argued that Argentina was challenging only the determination at hand and not the underlying US statute and, consequently, the Panel should not have entertained the Argentine claims in this respect. The AB however, held that, by virtue of standing WTO-practice, the words "as such" appearing in the request, should leave no room for doubt that Argentina was challenging the US law at hand as well (§§ 165–172).

---

[8] Some Panels like *US–Line Pipe* seem to privilege a more stringent standard and refused to examine whether obligations are interlinked, satisfying themselves that a claim lied outside their terms of reference if it had not been individually identified (§ 7.123).

1.3.6 Trade Custom

In *EC–Computer Equipment (LAN)*, the US argued that all LAN equipment was properly before the Panel (the request for establishment did not refer to particular products other than a reference to LAN equipment), whereas the defendant (EU) argued that the Panel should narrow its review to only a sub-category of LAN. Both the Panel and the AB, siding with the US, held that by trade custom, reference to LAN equipment covers all LAN equipment-products (§ 70).

1.3.7 Contribution to Vagueness by the Party Challenging It

In *Thailand–H–Beams*, the AB dealt with a Thai complaint about the treatment of claims presented by Poland under Art. 2 AD (see the discussion *supra*). The AB rejected the claim advanced by Thailand on two grounds, one of which was that Poland's deficiencies were partly due to the non-cooperative attitude of Thailand (§ 91).

1.4 MOOT CLAIMS

In *EC–Sardines*, the appellant had initially raised a claim but made no arguments to support the claim throughout the process. The AB held that the claim became moot (§ 136). It is possible nevertheless, that the complainant has included a claim in its request for establishment of the Panel, it does not pursue it in its first submission to the Panel, and yet the complainant might decide to pursue this claim at a later stage of the proceedings. The AB in *EC–Bananas III* held that Panels should go ahead and review the claims (§ 147).

2. THE COMPOSITION OF PANELS

When a Panel is established, there is no decision as to the panelists, that is, the individuals who will decide on the dispute brought before them. Panelists (always three as of January 1, 1995) will, in principle, be selected from a "roster" which is kept by the WTO Secretariat. WTO Members can propose their nominees for the roster. It has been the case though, that non-roster Panelists have served in a Panel. Following the establishment, the WTO Secretariat will organize a meeting with the parties to the dispute in order to select Panelists. The initiative to propose Panelists lies clearly with the Secretariat and WTO Members cannot oppose proposals but for compelling reasons (Art. 8.6 DSU).

If no agreement (or, if only partial agreement) between the parties is reached within 20 days from the establishment of the Panel, the DG of the WTO will, at the request of either party, nominate the Panelist or

Panelists missing (Art. 8.7 DSU).⁹ Absent a request, the search for commonly agreed Panelists can continue beyond the statutory (20 days) deadline. It is not impossible that a citizen of a party to the dispute serves as Panelist (Art. 8.3 DSU), although this is a rarity in WTO practice.

3. THE TERMS OF REFERENCE (TOR)

Art. 7.1 DSU reflects the standard TOR which apply by default, that is, unless parties otherwise agree. It reads:

> To examine, in light of the relevant provisions in (name of the covered agreement(s) cited by the parties to the dispute), the matter referred to the DSB by (name of party) in document ... and to make such findings as will assist the DSB in making the recommendations or in giving the rulings provided for in that/those agreement(s).

Special terms of reference were agreed only in *Brazil–Desiccated Coconut* (§ 10.288).

4. SOURCES RESTRAINING A PANEL'S JURISDICTION

Securing compliance with Art. 6.2 DSU does not in and of itself prescribe the ambit of a Panel's jurisdiction. The latter can be prejudged on other grounds as well. Some of these grounds are explicitly mentioned in the DSU; others have developed through case law. In practice, claims regarding a Panel's jurisdiction to adjudicate a particular dispute are usually raised as a preliminary question,[10] although they can (and sometimes they must) be raised in different stages of the panel process: for example, a mutually agreed solution which is concluded half way through the Panel process cannot take the form of a preliminary issue. In *US–Carbon Steel*, the AB confirmed the Panel's decision to reject a claim by the US concerning the Panel's terms of reference, which was first presented at the interim review-stage. In the AB's view, such late challenge was running counter to due process considerations. The AB however, did not exclude the possibility that other jurisdictional claims, unrelated to the

---

[9] Horn and al. (2011) find this to have occurred in at least 60% of all Panels established. In *US–Large Civil Aircraft (Second Complaint)*, the DDG replaced the DG in selecting Panelists (§ 1.5).

[10] WTO law does not prescribe what kind of issues can take the form of a preliminary question. Practice shows that a wide variety of issues are raised as a preliminary question. Palmeter and Mavroidis (2004), and Waincymer (2002) show that issues regarding the jurisdiction of a Panel are frequently raised at this stage of the dispute. Preliminary rulings are normally incorporated in the final Panel report. Very rarely they have been issued separately. In *Canada–Wheat Exports and Grain Imports*, the Panel issued a separate preliminary ruling in order to clarify the scope of the matter before it, in light of the divergence of views among the parties to the dispute on this issue (WTO Doc. WT/DS276/8). The Panel in *Australia–Apples* folowed a similar attitude, see WTO Doc. WT/DS367/7.

terms of reference, could be raised at any stage during the proceedings (§ 123):

> In considering this issue, we recall that we have consistently held that, in the interests of due process, parties should bring alleged procedural deficiencies to the attention of a panel at the earliest possible opportunity. In this case, we see no reason to disagree with the Panel's view that the United States' objection was not raised in a timely manner. At the same time, however, as we have observed previously, certain issues going to the *jurisdiction* of a panel are so fundamental that they may be considered at any stage in a proceeding. In our view, the Panel was correct, therefore, in turning to consider its terms of reference and in satisfying itself as to its jurisdiction with respect to this matter. (emphasis in the original).

4.1 A PANEL'S AUTHORITY LAPSES

This is the only legislative source restraining a Panel's jurisdiction: Art. 12.12 DSU makes it clear that, upon request of one of the parties to the dispute, a Panel may suspend its work for a period up to 12 months. It suffices that the complainant has requested suspension, and, if no new request to resume has been tabled within the 12 month-period, the Panel's authority will lapse.

4.2 SUBJECT MATTER IN CONSULTATIONS AND REQUEST FOR ESTABLISHMENT

During the GATT years (*US–Salmon*, §§ 332–338) Panels refused to examine claims that did not feature in the request for consultations. The AB confirmed this principle in *US–Certain EC Products* (§ 70). In determining whether an issue has been discussed during consultations, a Panel might choose to turn to examine the actual records of the consultation as evidence. For example, the Panel in *US–Upland Cotton* took such an approach. The AB, however, disagreed with this attitude. In its view, what matters is the request for consultations which is public anyway, since it has to be notified at the WTO (§§ 286–287). In *US–Shrimp (Thailand)*, the AB held that precise and exact identity between the subject-matter of consultations and panel proceedings is unnecessary, if the essence of the dispute has not been modified (§ 293):

> The Appellate Body has also explained that "*[a]s long as the complaining party does not expand the scope of the dispute*, [it would] hesitate to impose too rigid a standard for the 'precise and exact identity' between the scope of the consultations and the request for the establishment of a panel, as this would substitute the request for consultations for the panel request". The Appellate Body has also held that a "precise and exact identity"

of measures between the two requests is not necessary, "provided that the 'essence' of the challenged measures had not changed." In our view, whether a complaining party has "expand[ed] the scope of the dispute" or changed the "essence" of the dispute through the inclusion of a measure in its panel request that was not part of its consultations request must be determined on a case-by-case basis. (emphasis in the original).

4.3 RES JUDICATA

In *India–Autos*, India argued that the US had already raised some of the issues in a previous Panel, *India–Quantitative Restrictions*; consequently, in India's view, the second Panel was prohibited from discussing the same issues by virtue of *res judicata*. The Panel first explained its understanding of the term *res judicata* in the following terms (footnote 335):

> While there may be variations in the exact understanding of the doctrine depending on the jurisdiction concerned or commentators' interpretation of its scope, it can be noted that *res judicata* is broadly understood to encompass three elements: a final decision, on a given issue, between the same parties. Black's Law Dictionary defines *res judicata* as follows:

> "A matter adjudged; a thing judicially acted upon or decided; a thing or matter settled by judgment. Rule that a final judgment rendered by a court of competent jurisdiction on the merits is conclusive as to the rights of the parties and their privies, and, as to them, constitutes an absolute bar to a subsequent action involving the same claim, demand or cause of action. (...) And to be applicable, requires identity in thing sued for as well as identity of cause of action, of persons and parties to action, and of quality in persons for or against whom claim is made. The sum and substance of the whole rule is that a matter once judicially decided is finally decided (...)". (italics in the original).

It then went on to explain under what conditions, in its view, *res judicata* could be accepted as a factor restraining its jurisdiction if there was identity between the measures, the claims pertaining to them, and the parties in two different disputes (§§ 7.66, 7.94–95). It refused to apply it in this case, since the subject-matter in the two disputes was not identical (§ 7.94).

4.4 MUTUALLY AGREED SOLUTIONS (MAS)

The Panel in *India–Autos* faced the argument by India that a claim was inappropriately before it since the EU (complainant) and India (defendant) had already reached an MAS:[11] India was supposed to remove a series of measures which formed the basis of the complaint by the EU. The schedule for the removal of the measures concerned was particularly pertinent since, as India indicated and the EU had accepted, India was supposed to eliminate the measures by April 2001, that is, more than 6 months after the establishment of the Panel. The Panel found that no MAS had been concluded with respect to some of the measures before it, but had it been the case, it would have refrained from exercising jurisidction (§§ 7.116–124).

In *EC–Bananas III (Article 21.5–Ecuador II)*, the Panel faced an argument by the EU that, Ecuador was legally barred from bringing a compliance challenge against it, since they had concluded together the "Bananas Understanding". The Panel decided that Ecuador was not barred from challenging the EU measures (§ 7.75):

(a) the Bananas Understanding provided only for a means, i.e. a series of future steps, for resolving and settling the dispute;

(b) the adoption of the Bananas Understanding was subsequent to recommendations, rulings and suggestions by the DSB; and

(c) parties had made conflicting communications to the WTO concerning the Bananas Understanding.

The panel went on to state that, in light of its conclusions above, the Bananas Understanding would not bar Ecuador from challenging the EU measures, even if it qualified as a mutually agreed solution (§ 7.135).

4.5 AGREEMENTS BETWEEN PARTIES AS TO THE AMBIT OF THEIR DISPUTE

Agreements between the parties as to the ambit of their dispute should be distinguished from MAS in that they constitute no agreement as to what a Panel should judge. In *Brazil–Aircraft (Article 22.6–Brazil)*, the Panel noted that an agreement had been concluded between the two parties at a DSB meeting not to seek countermeasures pending the report by the compliance Panel on whether implementation had occurred. In its view, this agreement was binding on the parties to the dispute, and it did not include any findings on this issue (§ 3.8).

4.6 ESTOPPEL

The Panel in *Argentina–Poultry Antidumping Duties* discussed a claim by Argentina whether Brazil was estopped from submitting a dis-

---

[11] An MAS can be reached at any stage of the process: in *Japan–Quotas on Laver* for example, an MAS between Korea and Japan was reached only 4 days before the issuance of the interim report, that is, some weeks after the issuance of the descriptive part of the panel report. It was notified to the Panel which concluded its work by reporting that an MAS had effectively been reached (see §§ 14ff. in WTO Doc. WT/DS323/R).

pute to a WTO Panel on an issue that had previously formed the subject-matter of a dispute before a MERCOSUR panel. The Panel in §§ 7.37–39 stated the three conditions for lawful application and rejected the claim because the conditions had not been fulfilled in this case:

> Argentina has also argued that Brazil is estopped from pursuing the present WTO dispute settlement proceedings. Argentina asserts that the principle of estoppel applies in circumstances where (i) a statement of fact which is clear and unambiguous, and which (ii) is voluntary, unconditional, and authorized, is (iii) relied on in good faith. We asked Argentina to explain exactly how it considers that these three conditions are satisfied in this case. In particular, we asked Argentina to identify the relevant "statement of fact" made by Brazil, and to describe how Argentina had relied on it in good faith. Argentina replied:
>
> . . .
>
> We do not consider Argentina's response sufficient to establish that the three conditions it identified for the application of the principle of estoppel are fulfilled in the present case. Regarding the first condition identified by Argentina, we do not consider that Brazil has made a clear and unambiguous statement to the effect that, having brought a case under the MERCOSUR dispute settlement framework, it would not subsequently resort to WTO dispute settlement proceedings. In this regard, we note that the panel in *EEC (Member States)–Bananas I* found that estoppel can only "result from the express, or in exceptional cases implied consent of the complaining parties". We agree. There is no evidence on the record that Brazil made an express statement that it would not bring WTO dispute settlement proceedings in respect of measures previously challenged through MERCOSUR. Nor does the record indicate exceptional circumstances requiring us to imply any such statement. In particular, the fact that Brazil chose not to invoke its WTO dispute settlement rights after previous MERCOSUR dispute settlement proceedings does not, in our view, mean that Brazil implicitly waived its rights under the *DSU*. This is especially because the Protocol of Brasilia, under which previous MERCOSUR cases had been brought by Brazil, imposes no restrictions on Brazil's right to bring subsequent WTO dispute settlement proceedings in respect of the same measure. We note that Brazil signed the Protocol of Olivos in February 2002. Article 1 of the Protocol of Olivos provides that once a party decides to bring a case under either the MERCOSUR or WTO dispute settlement forums, that party may not bring a subsequent case regarding the same subject-matter in the other forum. The Protocol of Olivos, however, does not

change our assessment, since that Protocol has not yet entered into force, and in any event it does not apply in respect of disputes already decided in accordance with the MERCOSUR Protocol of Brasilia. Indeed, the fact that parties to MERCOSUR saw the need to introduce the Protocol of Olivos suggests to us that they recognised that (in the absence of such Protocol) a MERCOSUR dispute settlement proceeding could be followed by a WTO dispute settlement proceeding in respect of the same measure.

Regarding the third condition, we note that Argentina failed to quote the entirety of the relevant author's text. Quoted in full, the third condition reads "there must be reliance in good faith upon the statement either to the detriment of the party so relying on the statement or to the advantage of the party making the statement". Citing the same author, another panel has asserted that "[e]stoppel is premised on the view that where one party has been induced to act in reliance on the assurances of another party, in such a way that it would be prejudiced were the other party later to change its position, such a change in position is 'estopped', that is precluded". In our view, merely being inconvenienced by alleged statements by Brazil is not sufficient for Argentina to demonstrate that it was induced to act in reliance of such alleged statements. There is nothing on the record to suggest to us that Argentina actively relied in good faith on any statement made by Brazil, either to the advantage of Brazil or to the disadvantage of Argentina. There is nothing on the record to suggest that Argentina would have acted any differently had Brazil not made the alleged statement that it would not bring the present WTO dispute settlement proceedings. In its abovementioned response to Question 66, which was specifically addressing this issue, Argentina simply stated that it "is now suffering the negative impact of [Brazil's] change of position" (regarding its earlier practice of not pursuing WTO cases following MERCOSUR rulings in respect of the same subject-matter), without explaining further the nature of that "negative impact". Argentina's vague assertion regarding "negative impact" is not sufficient to demonstrate that it was induced to act in reliance on the alleged statement by Brazil, and that it is now suffering the negative consequences of the alleged change in Brazil's position. For these reasons, we reject Argentina's claim that Brazil is estopped from pursuing the present WTO dispute settlement proceedings." (italics in the original).

In *US–Sunset Review Carbon Steel*, an interested private party had not raised an issue before the US domestic authority during an antidumping investigation. Subsequently, Japan raised this issue before the WTO proceedings. The Panel declined to examine the Japanese claim, because it had not been properly raised (by the private party) before the US authorities; in the Panel's eyes, Japan was estopped from raising before a Panel an issue not raised by a private party in the context of an antidumping investigation which led to a WTO panel procedure. The AB disagreed with the Panel's view on this issue. In its view, Japan was not estopped from raising this claim before the Panel, simply because the Japanese private party had failed to do so before the US investigating authority (§§ 130–132).

4.7 DIRECT EFFECT OF WTO LAW IN DOMESTIC LEGAL ORDERS

In *Mexico–Anti-dumping Measures on Rice*, Mexico claimed that the Panel should not review the consistency of Mexican practices with WTO law (in the case at hand, the consistency of an antidumping imposition), because all international agreements were self-executing in Mexico. The Panel rejected this argument; in its view, the self-executing character of WTO law in the Mexican legal order did not *ipso facto* guarantee that WTO law would be applied in a WTO-consistent manner, since national adjudicating bodies still retained discretion in this respect (§ 7.224).

5. THE MEASURE BEFORE THE PANEL

The measure challenged is defined in the request for establishment of a Panel assuming the conditions for the request have been observed, and the Panel's jurisdiction does not suffer from one of the vices described in the Section above. Case law has contributed two additional refinements: Panels' review will be influenced if the challenged measure is legislation and depending on whether it is of mandatory or discretionary nature; Panels' review will also be influenced if the measure is still in force when the proceedings are held or not.

5.1 MANDATORY VERSUS DISCRETIONARY LEGISLATION

Until the issuance of the Panel report in *US–Section 301 Trade Act*, an absolute dichotomy between mandatory- and discretionary legislation had been developed in case law: the former referred to a situation where government agents were obliged to follow a pattern; under the latter, government agents retained discretion. The foundation of the Panel in *US–Section 301 Trade Act* is that some provisions of the WTO Agreement (like Art. 23 DSU) give rise to an obligation to ensure that even discretionary legislation do not threaten a WTO violation (§ 7.54): hence, state responsibility ultimately flows from the particular nature of the treaty provision.

The subsequent AB report in *US–AD Act of 1916* narrowed down this finding in two important ways: <u>first</u>, it held that only discretion vested in the executive branch of the government matters for the purposes of this distinction; <u>second</u>, for discretionary legislation to be judged WTO-inconsistent, it must be:

> of such a nature or of such a breadth as to transform the 1916 Act into discretionary legislation, as this term has been understood for purposes of distinguishing between mandatory and discretionary legislation.

The issue took another twist in the AB report in *US–Section 211*. There the AB faced the argument by the EU that the US legislation at hand, the discretionary character of which was acknowledged in the Panel report, was imposing an "extra hurdle" on foreign nationals in violation of the national treatment obligation protected under the TRIPs Agreement. The AB reversed the Panel's findings that the legislation could not be scrutinized by a WTO adjudicating body because it was discretionary precisely because they had to go through an extra hurdle (§§ 256, 259–260 and 267–268). The extra hurdle is described in § 256:

> That "extra hurdle" is this. United States nationals who are successors-in-interest must go successfully only through the OFAC procedure. In the circumstances addressed by Section 211, they are not subject to the constraints imposed by Section 211(a)(2). In contrast, non-United States successors-in-interest not only must go successfully through the OFAC procedure, but also find themselves additionally exposed to the "extra hurdle" of an additional proceeding under Section 211(a)(2). In sum, United States nationals face only *one* proceeding, while non-United States nationals face *two*. It is on this basis that the European Communities claims on appeal that Section 211(a)(2), as it relates to successors-in-interest, violates the national treatment obligation in the TRIPS Agreement and the Paris Convention (1967).

In essence, in this report, the AB reversed the allocation of burden of proof requesting from the defendant to demonstrate that discretion would always be exercised in WTO-consistent manner.

In *US–Sunset Review Carbon Steel*, the AB dealt with an administrative instrument issued by the US executive agency (the "Sunset Policy Bulletin" describing how sunset reviews should be operated by US agencies, discussed in § 84 of the report). The parties to the dispute disagreed as to the justiciability of the Bulletin, the US arguing that it was issued for administrative convenience only and, at any rate, it could not be considered to be mandatory legislation. The AB held that the distinction between mandatory- and discretionary legislation should be viewed as an analytical tool. As a result, its application might vary from case to case (§ 93). It reversed the Panel's findings that the Bulletin was not challengeable as such because it is not a mandatory legislation (§ 100). It did so, based on the fact that the Panel:

(a) looked only at the introductory language of the legislation at hand;

(b) did not examine specific provisions of the Bulletin and compare them with the corresponding statutory and regulatory provisions; and

(c) did not examine to what extent the Bulletin's provisions were normative in nature, nor the extent to which the US agency (USDOC) itself treated them as binding (§ 99).

In a related dispute (*US–OCTG*), the AB confirmed that the Bulletin was a measure properly before the Panel (§§ 187ff.). Subsequently, the AB was confronted with the issue of the justiciability of the Bulletin yet again in *US–Anti-dumping Measures on OCTG*. In finding that the US had violated its obligations under the AD Agreement, the Panel had reviewed 206 cases, the overwhelming majority of which had been decided by reference to the waiver procedures (included in the Bulletin), which the AB had already found in previous cases to be inconsistent with the requirements of the AD Agreement. The Panel's decision boils down to this rationale: by applying consistently a WTO-inconsistent procedure (by virtue of the Bulletin's prescription), the US was in violation of its obligations under the WTO. The AB rejected the Panel's findings. In its view (§§ 203ff.), the Panel hastily rushed to conclusions; absent an inquiry into the rationale of the US domestic authority's decisions (all 206 of them), its conclusions were unfounded. The AB did not explain why the rationale for the US investigating authority's decisions mattered, since the methodology used was illegal anyway, as the AB itself ruled in previous cases. The AB further did not explain how can a Panel inquire into the rationale of these cases without actually performing *de novo* review, which it cannot anyway, as the AB has ruled in prior case-law.

5.2 MEASURES CHALLENGED MUST BE IN EFFECT WHEN THE PANEL IS ESTABLISHED

The Panel in *India–Autos* clarified that measures in existence or that have been in existence are properly before a Panel (§ 7.26). The panel clarified that a distinction should be drawn between actual, and future, or hypothetical measures (that is, measures not in existence when the panel was established), which could not be reviewed by a Panel (§ 7.34).[12] Case law has made it clear that Panels retain the legal power to make findings on the consistency of measures which are no longer in effect, but will refrain from making a recommendation to the WTO Member concerned to bring its measures into compliance with its WTO obligations, if the WTO-

---

[12] This is akin to stating that Panels do not issue advisory opinions.

inconsistent measure is not in force anymore: the removal of the challenged measure restrains the Panel's jurisdiction to issue a recommendation, but not the Panel's competence to pronounce on its WTO-consistency.[13] We quote from § 7.124 of the report in *Chile–Price Band System*:

> Article 19.1 DSU does not prevent us from making *findings* regarding the consistency of an expired provisional safeguard measure, if we were to consider that the making of such finding is necessary 'to secure a positive solution' to the dispute. We would not, however, formulate *recommendations* with regard to those measures. (emphasis in the original).

What if the challenged measure has been modified subsequent to the establishment of the Panel? The AB dealt with such a case in *Chile–Price Band System*. The AB held that the measure, as amended, is the measure that should be considered, assuming that the terms of reference are broad enough to cover both the original measure, as well as its modified version (§ 139). We read in § 144:

> [T]he demands of due process are such that a complaining party should not have to adjust its pleadings throughout dispute settlement proceedings in order to deal with a disputed measure as a 'moving target.' If the terms of reference in a dispute are broad enough to include amendments to a measure—as they are in this case—and if it is necessary to consider an amendment in order to secure a positive solution to the dispute—as it is here—then it is appropriate to consider the measure *as amended* in coming to a decision in a dispute. (emphasis in the original).

In *EC–Chicken Cuts*, the AB, applying this test, refused to extend the Panel's mandate to two EU regulations which had been enacted after the Panel had been established, which made no reference at all to the measures properly before the Panel, and which had a partial only overlap with the original measures. In the AB's view, the measures could not be considered as amendments (§ 156).

6. RIGHTS AND DUTIES OF PARTIES APPEARING BEFORE PANELS

6.1 COMPLAINANTS AND DEFENDANTS

Art. 1 DSU reads:

---

[13] In *EC–Bananas III (Article 21.5–Ecuador) (Second Recourse)*, the AB repeated this statement, holding that measures not in force can be the subject-matter of consultations as well, if their effect survives their expiration: in this case the Panel and the AB were dealing with previously bestowed subsidies the effect of which had allegedly survived their withdrawal.

... rules and procedures of this Understanding shall ... apply to consultations and the settlement of disputes between Members ...

In *EC–Bananas III*, the participation of the US (complainant) was challenged because the US was not exporting bananas to the EU market. The AB held that there is no legislative requirement that legal interest be shown for the quality of complainant to be conferred: the US could act as complainant since all WTO Members have an interest in promoting the enforcement of the multilateral rules; even in the absence of trade damage, a WTO Member can lawfully bring a complaint before the WTO and challenge practices by another Member (§§ 132, and 136–138). This caselaw has not been put into question ever since.[14]

In the same dispute, the question arose whether a WTO Member may appoint a private counsel to represent it in the proceedings.[15] The AB, in its report, categorically denied that WTO law was imposing any disciplines on the composition of delegations appearing before WTO adjudicating bodies (§§ 10 and 12). In *EC–Tariff Preferences*, the EU raised the issue whether, as a matter of principle, the same legal counsel could represent simultaneously a complaining party and a third party and if so, under what conditions (§ 7.3). The Panel, stating that legal counsels must abide by the ethical rules of the Bar where they belong (§ 7.10), stated that the EU did not manage to persuade the Panel that concerns regarding breach of confidentiality were an issue in the present dispute (§ 7.12). It thus did not put into question the participation of the legal counsel. The liberty regarding the composition of a national delegation is not limited to legal counsel: Indonesia named an industry representative in its delegation during the proceedings that led to the report on *Korea–Certain Paper* (§ 7.12).

Complainants and defendants have the right to make submissions to Panels (that we discuss *infra* in the sections on Evidence) and are under the duty to cooperate (which we discuss *infra* when discussing the right of Panels to seek information).

6.2 THIRD PARTIES

Any WTO Member having a substantial interest in a dispute, and having notified the DSB of that interest, may be heard by a Panel and may make written submissions to it (Art. 10 DSU). The DSU is silent on the timing of the request. The GATT Council adopted a decision whereby the request should be tabled during the DSB session establishing the Panel, or within ten days from this date (Doc. C/COM/3, of June 27, 1994). There are cases of WTO Members who notified after the 10 day-

---

[14] See for example, the AB report in *US–Section 211* (§§ 301–319).

[15] See the detailed analysis in Palmeter and Mavroidis (2004) on this score. See also, Sacerdoti (2005), and Waincymer (2002), and Van den Bossche (2005).

deadline and still could participate as third parties.¹⁶ We note the following GATT Council Chairman's Statement of June 1994 discussed notification within a ten-day period following the establishment of a panel:

> Delegations in a position to do so, should indicate their intention to participate as third party in a panel proceeding at the Council session which establishes the panel. Others who wish to indicate a third party interest should do so within the next ten days."¹⁷

As the AB explained in *Chile–Price Band System* (§ 163), third parties cannot make claims before a Panel, and a complainant cannot rely on them to do so on its behalf.¹⁸ An explicit finding to this effect is to be found in § 5.11 of the GATT Panel report on *EEC–Parts and Components*. The Panel had faced an argument by the defendant that its anti-circumvention provisions were justified through recourse to Art. XX(d) GATT, but no argument as to their potential justifiability under Art. VI GATT. An argument to this effect had been however, raised by a third party. The Panel refused to examine the claim of the third party, noting:

> In conformity with the practice of panels not examine exceptions under the General Agreement which have not been invoked by the contracting party complained against (see, e.g., BSID 31S/74) and not to examine issues brought only by third parties (cf. L/6514, page 15 and the references therein), the Panel decided not to examine whether the anti-circumvention duties could be justified under Article VI of the General Agreement.

Third parties may not appeal a Panel report, but can participate in AB proceedings (Art. 17.4 DSU).

Third parties are entitled to receive the first written submissions of the parties to a dispute made during the first meeting of the Panel (Art. 10.3 DSU). They may also present their views at a session of the first substantive meeting of the Panel (Appendix 3.6 to the DSU). The possibility for "enhanced third party rights" arose in *EC–Bananas III*, when a number of developing countries, which were appearing as third parties before the Panel, requested that they be permitted to attend all meetings (§ 7.4).¹⁹ The Panel, in light of the fact that the export revenue for a series of developing countries risked being heavily affected by the outcome of

---

¹⁶ See §§ 6.1–9 of the Panel report in *Turkey–Rice*.

¹⁷ Third Party Participation in Panels, Statement by the Chairman of the Council, document C/COM/3 of 27 June 1994, at p. 1. The question of formalizing a ten-day notification requirement remains the subject of proposals in the context of the DSU negotiations (Panel report in *EC–Export Subsidies on Sugar (Australia)*, § 2.2). See also *EC–IT Products* at § 7.73: in this case, a request to participate that was tabled 3 months after the establishment of the Panel and one day after its composition was expressed and accepted (§ 7.75).

¹⁸ Nothing, however, can stop a complainant from incorporating in its submission in support of its claims an argument by a third party.

¹⁹ In *US–Large Civil Aircraft (Second Complaint)*, the Panel held that it is for the party requesting enhanced rights to carry the associated burden of proof (§ 7.16).

this dispute, agreed to the request and allowed them to participate in the second meeting as well, but denied third parties' participation at the interim review-stage (§§ 7.8 and 7.9). In *EC–Hormones*, two separate Panels composed of the same members were established to examine the same measures by the EU; the complainant (Canada, US) to the first Panel was third party to the second Panel established. The two Panels decided to give both Canada and the US access to all information submitted, including written second submissions (§ 8.15). The AB upheld this decision (§ 154).

The Panel in *US–1916 Act (EC)* (a dispute between the EU and the US) reflects a request by Japan, which was the complainant in parallel proceedings on the same issue, to be granted enhanced third party rights (§ 6.33). Japan cited the ruling of the *EC–Hormones* case to substantiate its request. The Panel denied the request, finding that particular circumstances existed in *EC–Hormones* that did not exist in the *US–1916 Act* cases (§ 6.35):

> their highly technical and factually intensive nature, as well as the fact that the panels had decided to hold one single meeting with the parties and the experts.

On appeal, the AB affirmed the Panel's approach, stating however (§ 150) that the Panel's discretion was subject to appellate review. The issue arose again in *EC–Tariff Preferences*. The Panel issued a formal decision in this respect echoing the solution in *EC–Bananas III* because of the similarities across the two cases (WTO Doc. WT/DS246/R, Annex A, Page A–1).

The submissions of third parties will normally be briefly discussed in the "Findings" part of reports. There are few exceptions: a good illustration to this effect is provided by the AB report in *EC–Bed Linen (Article 21.5–India)*, which dedicated a very lengthy and detailed discussion of submissions by a third party (§§ 140ff.).

6.3 AMICI CURIAE

In *US–Shrimp*, two environmental organizations filed amicus curiae briefs. The Panel noted that under Art. 13 DSU, it alone had the authority to seek information from any source. As it had not sought information from the organizations submitting the briefs, it declined to take them into account. The Panel noted that if any of the parties wished to put forward all or parts of the amicus briefs as its own documents, the Panel would be willing to accept them. On appeal, the AB reversed the Panel's finding that the term "seek" prohibited the Panel from considering information that it had not solicited on its own initiative. The AB held that this term did not prevent Panels from exercising discretion and considering unsolicited submissions from non-governmental organizations and private persons (§§ 107 and 108).

The Panel in *Australia–Salmon (Article 21.5–Canada)* decided to accept unsolicited information: it had received a letter from "Concerned Fishermen and Processors", an NGO. It cited Art. 13.1 DSU as the legal basis conferring it authority to accept similar briefs (§§ 7.8–9). The Panel in *EC–Asbestos* rejected a brief by an NGO only because it had been filed after the interim review stage, that is, at such a late stage of the proceedings that it could no longer be taken into account (§ 8.14).

Even a WTO Member can participate as amicus. A WTO Member cannot, by virtue of Art. 17.4 DSU, participate as third party before the AB, if it has not participated as third party before the Panel. In *EC–Sardines*, Morocco decided to file an amicus brief before the AB, since it had not participated before the Panel. Since the identity of amici is nowhere prejudged, its brief was well received.

7. THE DUTY OF THE PANEL: TO PERFORM AN OBJECTIVE ASSESSMENT

Panels are required to make an objective assessment of the matter before them (Art. 11 DSU):

> The function of panels is to assist the DSB in discharging its responsibilities under this Understanding and the covered agreements. Accordingly, a panel should make an objective assessment of the matter before it, including an objective assessment of the facts of the case and the applicability of and conformity with the relevant covered agreements, and make such other findings as will assist the DSB in making the recommendations or in giving the rulings provided for in the covered agreements. Panels should consult regularly with the parties to the dispute and give them adequate opportunity to develop a mutually satisfactory solution.

To this effect, they are equipped with an arsenal of instruments: they organize the process where evidence will be submitted, and have the right to seek information from any source they deem appropriate, including the parties to the dispute. The latter are under the right to cooperate and their incentive to do so is compounded by the possibility that Panels have to draw inferences from un-cooperative behavior. The Panel's duty of objective assessment is justiciable.

7.1 WORKING PROCEDURES

Panels will adopt their Working Procedures, which are modelled after Appendix 3 of the DSU. Art. 12.1 DSU makes it clear that panels, after consulting the parties to the dispute can adopt working procedures which are not consonant with Appendix 3. Working procedures adopted by a Panel are binding: in *EC–Selected Customs Matters*, the Panel rejected evidence submitted after the interim review stage, holding that it was at odds with Art. 12.1 of its Working Procedures, as well as the letter and the spirit of Art. 15.2 DSU (§ 6.6). The AB, in *US–Stainless Steel (Mexico)*, held that, it was concerned with a 3 hours delay in the delivery of the submission by the United States (the defendant), but did not issue a formal ruling in this respect (§§ 163–164). In *US–Upland Cotton (Article 21.5–Brazil)*, the US twice submitted belatedly its brief, and twice Brazil requested from the Panel to disregard the belatedly submitted briefs. The Panel declined to do that, claiming that nothing in the DSU or its Working Procedures would authorize such action, but requested from the US to respect the deadlines in the reamining part of the procedures (§§ 8.21ff., and especially, at § 8.26).

Panels will typically organize two meetings with the parties. Parties are invited to present two written submissions (first written submission and rebuttal) and further present their views orally during the meetings with the panel.[20] Beyond their two submissions however, the parties can also raise preliminary questions, or contest aspects of the procedure that, in their view, do not respect the provisions of the DSU.

According to Art. 14.1 DSU, and §§ 1, and 2 of Appendix 3 to the DSU, Panel sessions are closed to the public and its deliberations are confidential. That is, only the parties to the dispute, the third parties, the members of the Panel and the WTO Secretariat assigned to provide support to a particular panel can assist. They can be open to the public, assuming an agreement between the parties to the dispute to this effect. In *US–Continued Suspension* and *Canada–Continued Suspension*, the parties to the dispute agreed to open up the process to the public. The panel agreed to their request, although the meeting with third parties would still take place behind closed doors, since third parties did not agree to opening up the process.[21] If one of the parties to the dispute does not agree, there will be no opening up of the process: Antigua's disagreement meant that no open hearing was held during the proceedings in *US–Gambling (Article 22.6–US)* (Panel report, § 2.29). For the same reason no open hearing was scheduled during the proceedings in *US–Upland Cotton (Article 21.5–Brazil)* (Panel report, § 8.20). There is one stage of the Panel process that cannot open to public though: to preserve the confidentiality of the proceedings, panel reports are to be drafted without the presence of the parties to the dispute (Art. 14.2 DSU).

---

[20] In *Colombia–Ports of Entry*, the Working Procedures provided for the timeliness of submission of preliminary objections as well (§ 7.16).

[21] WTO Docs. WT/DS310/8 and WT/DS321/8 of August 2, 2005. A public hearing was also agreed in *US–Continued Zeroing* as well, where a public viewing took place via a real time closed-circuit television broadcast.

Panel submissions shall also be treated as confidential (Art. 18 DSU): they will be handed to other parties to the dispute (and, eventually, third parties) only. Nothing prohibits a WTO Member from disclosing its own submissions to the public.

A party to a dispute cannot however, provide one version of its submission to a Panel and a different version to the parties to the dispute, because it fears a confidentiality breach. In *Korea–Certain Paper*, Korea wanted to supply a (confidential) version of its submission to a Panel, and a shorter, non-confidential version of its submission to the complainant, Indonesia. Korea submitted that such an action was necessary since Indonesia had included representatives of its domestic paper industry in its delegation, and Korea was afraid that these individuals would not abide by the same standards as public officials. The Panel rejected Korea's request. In its view, were Korea to submit different versions of its pleadings to the panel and Indonesia, it would have, in the eyes of the Panel, *ipso facto* violated the DSU provisions with respect to *ex parte* communications (§§ 7.12–17).

7.2 RESPECTING THE INSTITUTIONAL BALANCE

Art. 3.2 DSU reads:

The dispute settlement system of the WTO is a central element in providing security and predictability to the multilateral trading system. The Members recognize that it serves to preserve the rights and obligations of Members under the covered agreements, and to clarify the existing provisions of those agreements in accordance with customary rules of interpretation of public international law. *Recommendations and rulings of the DSB cannot add to or diminish the rights and obligations provided in the covered agreements.* (emphasis added).

The Panel in *Turkey–Textiles* dealt with the issue whether a TMB decision binds a Panel which is subsequently called to deal with the same issue. It held that Panels can decide an issue independently of the content of the TMB decision (§ 8.92). In the context of the same dispute, the issue arose whether Panels should be reviewing the consistency of a PTA with the WTO rules. The argument advanced by the defendant (Turkey) was that this could not be the case since the consistency of a PTA with the multilateral rules came under the purview of the CRTA. In Turkey's view, Panels should refrain from addressing such issues until the CRTA has issued its final report. Both the Panel and the AB rejected this argument. The AB held that WTO adjudicating bodies can go ahead and comprehensively review the consistency of a PTA with the multilateral rules (§ 58ff.). This issue was discussed again by the panel in its report in *In-*

dia–*Quantitative Restrictions* (§§ 5.93–94). India[22] had imposed a quantitative restriction which it was trying to justify through recourse to the BOP Committee. At the time of the establishment of the Panel, the BOP Committee had not reached any decision on the issue. The Panel first explained that, assuming it had ruled first on the issue, nothing would prevent the BOP Committee from reaching a different conclusion on the same issue; conversely, in case the BOP Committee had already decided the issue, it could see no reason why it would not take the conclusions reached into account. On appeal, the AB upheld (§ 99 and 105).

7.3 NON ULTRA PETITA

By virtue of the maxim "*non ultra petita*", a judge cannot adjudicate issues not submitted by the parties. In *US–Certain EC Products*, the AB reversed the Panel's findings on issues which had not been put properly before it: in the case at hand, the complainant had not presented any claims under Art. 23.2(a) DSU, and this omission notwithstanding, the Panel went on and pronounced on the consistency of the defendant's actions with the mentioned legal basis; the AB reversed (§ 115). Whereas a judge is, of course, free to use its own arguments to reach a conclusion (that is, a judge is not bound by the sum of arguments submitted by the parties to a dispute), a judge cannot make claims for either party. The only permissible exception to this maxim is the authority of Panels to enquire into their competence to adjudicate a dispute, even in absence of a specific claim to this effect. The AB, in its report on *Mexico–Corn Syrup (Article 21.5–US)*, noted to this effect (§ 36):

> Second, panels have to address and dispose of certain issues of a fundamental nature, even if the parties to the dispute remain silent on those issues. In this regard, we have previously observed that "[t]he vesting of jurisdiction in a panel is a fundamental prerequisite for lawful panel proceedings." For this reason, panels cannot simply ignore issues which go to the root of their jurisdiction—that is, to their authority to deal with and dispose of matters. Rather, panels must deal with such issues—if necessary, on their own motion—in order to satisfy themselves that they have authority to proceed.

7.4 EXERCISING JUDICIAL ECONOMY

Recall that under Art. 11 DSU:

> The function of panels is to assist the DSB in discharging its responsibilities under this Understanding and the covered agreements. . . . [A panel] should make such other findings as will as-

---

[22] Ironically, India was involved in both cases (this one and *Turkey–Textiles*) and argued once in favor of extending the Panel's jurisdiction to cover issues also entrusted to WTO Committees and once against similar extension.

sist the DSB in making the recommendations or in giving the rulings . . .

Arguably, this could happen even if a Panel does not address all claims before it. The AB originally endorsed the practice of judicial economy by Panels in *US–Wool Shirts and Blouses*:

> A panel need only address those claims which must be addressed in order to resolve the matter in issue in the dispute.

This attitude has been maintained across Panel reports ever since. In *EC–Sardines*, for example, the Panel re-visited prior case law, and on this basis decided to discuss claims under the TBT Agreement and exercise judicial economy on claims under the GATT (§§ 7.147–152). The AB has urged Panels to explicitly state the claims that they will not be addressing on grounds of judicial economy (§ 117, *Canada–Autos*):

> we are bound to add that, for purposes of transparency and fairness to the parties, a panel should, however, in all cases, address expressly those claims which it declines to examine and rule upon for reasons of judicial economy. Silence does not suffice for these purposes.

Panel practice, however, has been quite consistent and Panels usually exercise judicial economy; there are scarce examples to the opposite: in *US–Lamb*, the Panel decided (§ 7.119) to address all claims advanced by the complaining party to a dispute, notwithstanding that their earlier findings were sufficient to establish violation and sustainable under judicial economy considerations.

Because of the frequent exercise of judicial economy, the order of examining claims matters. Early WTO case law evidences an attitude to examine first claims under the more general (as opposed to specific) WTO agreement: in *India–Autos*, where claims under both the GATT and the TRIMs had been submitted, the Panel examined first the claims under the GATT and exercised judicial economy with respect to the remaining claims (§§ 7.157–162). Over the years however, Panels have changed their attitude and, usually, started their review from the specific agreement: the report in *EC–Sardines* emerges as the catalyst (§§ 7.15–16).[23]

7.5 *DE NOVO* REVIEW

This term was first used in the context of contingent protection instruments (antidumping, countervailing, safeguards) to indicate that Panels should check whether, based on the facts before it, an investigating authority reached a reasonable conclusion. In *EC–Hormones*, the AB

---

[23] For confirmation, see the Panel report on Turkey–Rice, where the Panel stated that it would examine claims under the AG-, and ILA Agreements ahead of claims under the GATT (§§ 7.48ff.).

established the standard that Panels should follow across cases irrespective of the subject-matter (§ 117):

> So far as fact-finding by panels is concerned, their activities are always constrained by the mandate of Article 11 of the DSU: the applicable standard is neither *de novo* review as such, nor "total deference", but rather the "objective assessment of the facts". Many panels have in the past refused to undertake *de novo* review, wisely, since under current practice and systems, they are in any case poorly suited to engage in such a review. On the other hand, "total deference to the findings of the national authorities", it has been well said, "could not ensure an 'objective assessment' as foreseen by Article 11 of the DSU". (italics in the original).

Consequently, the Panels' role as trier of facts is not reduced to redundancy. To the contrary: not performing a *de novo* review means that Panels, assuming they have been satisfied with the factual basis on which a decision by a domestic investigating authority rests, should not re-open the whole investigation and should limit themselves in asking the question whether the ultimate finding by the domestic authority is a reasonable one. The AB further clarified this position in *US–Cotton Yarn*, where it was asked to pronounce on whether the Panel applied the correct standard of review in a dispute where Pakistan was challenging the consistency of a transitional safeguard on imports of textile products from Pakistan (§§ 78–79):

> In our view, a *panel* reviewing the due diligence exercised by a Member in making its determination under Article 6 of the *ATC* has to put itself in the place of that Member at the time it makes its determination. Consequently, a panel must not consider evidence which did not exist *at that point in time*. A Member cannot, of course, be faulted for not having taken into account what it could not have known when making its determination. If a panel were to examine such evidence, the panel would, in effect, be conducting a *de novo* review and it would be doing so without having had the benefit of the views of the interested parties. The panel would be assessing the due diligence of a Member in reaching its conclusions and making its projections with the benefit of hindsight and would, in effect, be reinvestigating the market situation and substituting its own judgment for that of the Member. In our view, this would be inconsistent with the standard of a panel's review under Article 11 of the DSU.
>
> Moreover, if a Member that has exercised due diligence in complying with its obligations of investigation, evaluation and explanation, were held responsible before a panel for what it *could not have known* at the time it made its determination, this would

undermine the right afforded to importing Members under Article 6 to take transitional safeguard action when the determination demonstrates the fulfillment of the specific conditions provided for in this Article. (italics and emphasis in the original).

The AB dismissed an argument advanced by the US to the effect that the Panel's disagreement with the overall conclusion of the US domestic authority amounted to the Panel effectively engaging in a *de novo* review (*US–Lamb*, § 107). In the same report, it provided the standard that has been quoted ever since (§ 103):

> Thus, an "objective assessment" of a claim under Article 4.2(a) of the *Agreement on Safeguards* has, in principle, two elements. First, a panel must review whether competent authorities have evaluated *all relevant factors*, and, second, a panel must review whether the authorities have provided a *reasoned and adequate explanation* of how the facts support their determination. Thus, the panel's objective assessment involves a *formal* aspect and a *substantive* aspect. The formal aspect is whether the competent authorities have evaluated "all relevant factors". The substantive aspect is whether the competent authorities have given a reasoned and adequate explanation for their determination. (italics and emphasis in the original).

7.6 REWEIGHING THE EVIDENCE

Panels can re-weigh the evidence submitted to them, and do not have to attach the importance that parties to the dispute have attached to it. The AB, in *US–Carbon Steel*, clarified this issue beyond doubt (§ 146):

> It is clear, from these statements, that the Panel took account of, and did not disregard, the evidence placed before it by the European Communities. Accordingly, bearing in mind that Article 11 does not oblige panels to attach to a particular piece of evidence the same weight as the party submitting that evidence, we see no reason to disturb the Panel's treatment of the Sunset Policy Bulletin and the SAA in its assessment of the meaning of United States law.

The AB again confirmed this point in *EC–Bed Linen (Article 21.5–India)* (§ 177).

7.7 REFUSAL TO TAKE INTO ACCOUNT BELATEDLY SUBMITTED EVIDENCE

The AB in *EC–Sardines* stated that a Panel which refuses to take into account evidence submitted for the first time during the interim review-stage is not violating its duty under Art. 11 DSU (§ 301). This issue must be examined in conjunction with the schedule included in adopted Panel Working Procedures.

7.8 DISCRETION TO EXERCISE THE RIGHT TO SEEK INFORMATION

In *US–Carbon Steel*, the AB held that Art. 13 DSU confers a right to Panels to seek information, and not an obligation to do so (§ 153). This approach has been confirmed in subsequent reports as well: in *EC–Bed Linen (Article 21.5–India)* for example, India claimed that the Panel, by deciding not to exercise its rights under Art. 13 DSU (the right to seek information), had ipso facto violated its obligations under Art. 11 DSU. The AB rejected India's argument (§ 166). In *US–Upland Cotton (Article 21.5–Brazil)*, the Panel held that it was not bound by a request from a party to a dispute to exercise its rights under Art. 13 DSU. In the case at hand, Brazil had asked the Panel to request some information from the US which Brazil thought was important to its case. The Panel did not share Brazil's view on the importance of the information, and declined to exercise its rights under Art. 13 DSU (§§ 8.4ff.).

7.9 DISCOVERY POWERS

7.9.1 Calling Upon Experts

Art. 13 DSU reads:

> Each panel shall have the right to seek information and technical advice from *any individual or body which it deems appropriate*. However, before a panel seeks such information or advice from any individual or body within the jurisdiction of a Member it shall inform the authorities of that Member. A Member should respond promptly and fully to any request by a panel for such information as the panel considers necessary and appropriate. Confidential information which is provided shall not be revealed without formal authorization from the individual, body, or authorities of the Member providing the information. (emphasis added).

Art. 13.2 DSU specifies that this right includes the possibility for Panels to request information from "expert review groups", established in accordance with the procedures included in Annex 4 to the DSU.[24] In *EC–Selected Customs Matters*, the Panel refused to acquiesce to a request by the EU to call upon experts, because the other party (US) stated that, calling upon experts, was not a necessary step for the panel to decide on the case before it (§§ 7.81–83).

---

[24] So far no recourse to this procedure has been recorded. Recourse to individual experts has occurred, especially in the SPS-context, see Grando (2009).

7.9.2 Questions to the Parties

Panels can address questions to the parties (Appendix 3, § 8). In practice, a questionnaire will customarily be forwarded to the parties during and following the first and second meetings. Although oral responses do take place, Panels insist on receiving written responses as well. Responses to the questions constitute part of the record.[25] WTO Members will have to respond to the questions asked, by virtue of the duty to cooperate[26] that they must incur (Art. 13.1 DSU).

The AB, in *India–Patents (US)*, explained that, when having recourse to its discovery powers, a Panel must ensure that it does so within the context of the claims presented; it cannot use its discovery powers to alter the claims submitted (§ 94). In *Japan–Agricultural Products II*, the Panel faced a claim by the US to the effect that the challenged Japanese measure was unnecessarily restrictive, and, thus, in violation of Art. 5.6 SPS. To support its claim, the US advanced the argument that Japan could have used one particular method, which was arguably less-restrictive than that chosen, and still reach its objective. The Panel was not persuaded by the US argument in this respect and requested expert advice. Experts demonstrated that there was another method (not suggested by the US) which clearly was less restrictive than, and as effective as, the method used by Japan. The Panel, on these grounds, moved on to find that Japan had violated its obligations under Art. 5.6 SPS. The AB reversed the Panel's findings, since in its view, the Panel could not have based itself on the method suggested by the experts since the US had not suggested this method in its submission (§§ 123–130). In subsequent jurisprudence, and more specifically in *EC–Hormones (US)*, the AB took the view that confining a Panel to the arguments presented by the parties to the dispute might put into question its ability to respect its legal duty to perform an objective assessment. Panels should be free to develop their own reasoning, independently of the arguments advanced by the parties but within the ambit of the claims submitted (§ 156):

> ... Panels are inhibited from addressing legal claims falling outside their terms of reference. However, nothing in the DSU limits the faculty of a panel freely to use arguments submitted by any of the parties—or to develop its own legal reasoning—to support its own findings and conclusions on the matter under its consideration. A panel might well be unable to carry out an objective assessment of the matter, as mandated by Article 11 of the DSU, if in its reasoning it had to restrict itself solely to arguments presented by the parties to the dispute. Given that in

---

[25] In practice, parties to a dispute can address questions to each other through the chair. The responses will form part of the record as well. However, this is a right acknowledged to parties and not part of a Panel's discovery powers, see Palmeter and Mavroidis (2004).

[26] The AB in *Canada–Aircraft* made it clear that the duty to cooperate is not contingent upon a prior prima facie demonstration that a violation has been committed (§§ 185, 192).

this particular case both complainants claimed that the EC measures were inconsistent with Article 5.5 of the *SPS Agreement*, we conclude that the Panel did not make any legal finding beyond those requested by the parties. (italics in the original).

7.9.3 Drawing Inferences From Non–Cooperative Attitude by the Parties

Panels lack the legal powers to compel disclosure of information from the parties; they can, however, draw inferences where a party has refused to provide certain information. In *Canada–Aircraft*, Canada refused to provide information sought by the Panel, and the Panel decided this point against Canada, arguing that Canada was compelled to cooperate (Art. 13.1 DSU), and that non-cooperation was not void of consequences; the Panel's finding was upheld by the AB (§ 203):

> Clearly, in our view, the Panel had the legal authority and the discretion to draw inferences from the facts before it—including the fact that Canada had refused to provide information sought by the Panel.

7.10 REVIEWING COMPLIANCE WITH ART. 11 DSU

7.10.1 The Generic Standard of Review

In *EC–Hormones (US)*, the AB held that the question whether a Panel has adhered to the discipline embedded in Art. 11 DSU is a legal issue and, hence, can form the subject-matter of an appeal. In the same report, the AB clarified that the standard of review applicable to claims regarding Art. 11 DSU is quite demanding: Panels must commit an egregious error for a violation of Art. 11 DSU to occur (§ 133):

> Clearly, not every error in the appreciation of evidence . . . may be characterized as a failure to make an objective assessment of the facts . . . The duty to make an objective assessment of the facts is, among other things, an obligation to consider the evidence presented to a panel and to make factual findings on the basis of that evidence. The deliberate disregard or, or refusal to consider, the evidence submitted to a panel is incompatible with a panel's duty to make an objective assessment of the facts. The willful distortion or misrepresentation of the evidence put before a panel is similarly inconsistent with an objective assessment of the facts. "Disregard" and "distortion" and "misrepresentation" of the evidence, in their ordinary signification in judicial and quasi-judicial processes, imply not simply an error of judgment in the appreciation of evidence but rather an *egregious error that calls into question the good faith of a panel*. A claim that a panel disregarded or distorted the evidence submitted to it is, in effect, a

claim that the panel, to a greater or lesser degree, denied the party submitting the evidence fundamental fairness, or what in many jurisdictions is known as due process of law or natural justice. (italics and emphasis in the original).

In *US–Wheat Gluten*, the AB held that difference of opinion does not suffice (§§ 151):

In assessing the panel's appreciation of the evidence, we cannot base a finding of inconsistency under Article 11 simply on the conclusion that we might have reached a different factual finding from the one the panel reached. Rather, we must be satisfied that the panel has exceeded the bounds of its discretion, as the trier of facts, in its appreciation of the evidence. As is clear from previous appeals, we will not interfere lightly with the panel's exercise of its discretion." (emphasis in the original).[27] [28]

7.10.2 Finding *Ultra Petita*

The AB in *Chile–Price Band System* held that Panels violate their duty under Art. 11 DSU when they rule beyond what has been requested from the parties to the dispute (*ultra petita*) (§ 173).

7.10.3 Judicial Economy

The AB, in *EC–Poultry*, held that Panels do not violate Art. 11 DSU when they decide to exercise judicial economy (§ 135). Not any exercise of judicial economy is lawful, however: In *EC–Export Subsidies on Sugar*, the AB found that a Panel which exercised judicial economy in a manner that prejudiced the rights of a WTO Member, has disrespected its obligations under Art. 11 DSU. The AB did not put into question the discretion of Panels to exercise judicial economy; it imposed limits, however, on its exercise. In the case at hand, the Panel had found that the EU practices were inconsistent with the provisions of the WTO Agreement on Agriculture. Having done that, it declined, in the name of judicial economy, to also find that the EU practices were also in violation of the provisions of the WTO SCM Agreement. The latter agreement, however, prescribes that Panels must recommend that WTO Members withdraw prohibited subsidies with immediate effect. A similar recommendation is not reflected in the WTO Agreement on Agriculture. As a result, the Panel, by exercising judicial economy, did not make a recommendation to the effect that the EU withdraws its subsidy. Thus, it deprived the complainants of a remedy. The AB thus, found that the Panel violated Art. 11 DSU (§§ 334–335).

---

[27] See also the AB reports in *EC–Sardines* at § 299, and *Dominican Republic–Import and Sale of Cigarettes* (§ 84).

[28] The AB refused to find that a Panel which had made a wrong, but inconsequential for its overall finding, statement was in violation of Art. 11 DSU, see *EC–Chicken Cuts*, at § 186.

7.10.4 *De novo* Review

In *US–Countervailing Duty Investigation on DRAMs*, the AB reviewed the manner in which the Panel had exercised its discovery powers: it had examined whether certain pieces of evidence were sufficient to establish conclusions that the investigating authority did not draw (at least, not solely on the basis of this evidence); it also failed to examine the evidence in its totality. In the AB's view, this Panel had improperly engaged in *de novo* review and had thus violated Art. 11 DSU (§§ 185–190).

7.10.5 Improper Examination of the Factual Record

In *Canada–Periodicals*, the AB reversed a Panel finding on the grounds that the Panel had not properly examined the factual record before it. Although the AB did not explicitly cite Art. 11 DSU when reversing the Panel's finding, it is clear that it found that the Panel had not performed an objective assessment of the matter before it (p. 21). A Panel violates Art. 11 DSU by not examining submitted evidence in its totality (AB, *US–Continued Zeroing*, § 348). But, omitting information based on submitted evidence from the Panel does not necessarily lead to a violation of Art. 11 DSU: in *US–COOL* (§ 321ff. and especially in § 323) the AB held as much arguing that it could be the case that similar evidence was immaterial for the purposes of resolving a dispute (as indeed was information submitted regarding COOL discounts).

7.10.6 Absence of Reasoning

In *US–Countervailing Duty Investigation on DRAMs*, the AB held that the absence of reasoning by the Panel to explain its decision to rejct submitted evidence was tantamount to a violation of Art. 11 DSU (§ 189).

7.10.7 Inconsistent Reasoning

In *US–Wheat Gluten*, the AB faced an allegation that the Panel on the one hand saw deficiencies in the US report imposing safeguard measures, and, on the other, found that the same report was consistent with the US obligations under the WTO. In its view, in light of the former finding, the latter conclusion was simply inappropriate. Under the circumstances, the AB found that the Panel had violated its duty to perform an objective assessment of the matter before it (§ 161).[29]

7.10.8 Panels Cannot Rely on Ex Post Facto Justifications

In *US–Wheat Gluten*, the Panel reached its conclusions on the consistency of a safeguard action imposed by the USITC in part by using information which was not properly before it when it undertook its investigation. The Panel did not disturb these findings. Relying on *ex post facto*

---

[29] See also the AB report in *US–OCTG* at §§ 200ff., and especially 209–210.

justifications which were not reflected in the investigation-record, is not, in the AB's view, exercise of judicial review in conformity with Art. 11 DSU (§ 162).

7.10.9 Violating Due Process

In *US–Suspended Concession*, the AB found that the Panel had violated its duty to perform an objective assessment by violating the complainant's (the EU) due process rights: the EU had objected to the appointment of two experts that the Panel had selected, since they had participated in the the elablorations of an international standard that the EU was deviating from. In the AB's view, these two experts should not have been appointed at all, in light of their affiliation with the institution (JEFCA) that had elaborated the standard; by appoitning them, the Panel had violated the due process rights of the EU (§ 481), and in doing that, it did not eprform an objective assessment of the matter before it (§ 482).

8. EVIDENCE

Parties to a dispute are entrusted with the submission of factual evidence and they can count on the WTO adjudicating bodies to apply the law. In practice, nonetheless, the parties to a dispute will invariably offer their understanding of the applicable law in support of their factual claims.

8.1 TIMELY SUBMISSION OF EVIDENCE

The Panel's Working Procedures, which are modelled after Appendix 3 to the DSU, will usually regulate the time limits for lawful submission of evidence. In the absence of a specific provision to this effect, the WTO adjudicating bodies can still decide whether evidence was lawfully submitted or not. In the absence of regulation, submission of evidence for the first time at the interim review-stage can legitimately be rejected by panels: the AB ruled as much in *EC–Sardines* (§ 301).

In *US–Gambling*, Antigua complained that the US had raised its defence under Art. XIV GATS only in its second written submission to the Panel. The AB first, explained that, in accordance with Art. 3.10 DSU, WTO Members, irrespective whether they are complainants or defendants, must respect due process when participating in dispute settlement proceedings (§§ 370–371). Antigua had not protested before the Panel, but only before the AB. In light of the fact that Antigua did not raise the issue before the Panel, and since it was handed the opportunity to respond anyway to the US defence, the AB held that the Panel had not violated Art. 11 DSU (§§ 275–276).

8.2 NO *EX PARTE* COMMUNICATIONS

Art. 18 DSU makes it plain that *ex parte* communications with the members of the Panel are prohibited. As a result, parties to a dispute must share between them all information that they have communicated to the Panel. In this vein, in *Turkey–Rice*, the Panel rejected the submission of documents that Turkey would not submit to the other party to the dispute (§§ 7.100ff.).

8.3 ALLOCATION OF BURDEN OF PROOF

Burden of proof is usefully distinguished into burden of production (who must bring forward evidence?), and burden of persuasion (how much evidence is necessary for the burden to shift to the other party?).

8.3.1 Burden of Production

In *US–Wool Shirts and Blouses*, the AB fist held that the party making a claim carries the associated burden to produce the necessary proof (§ 14).

> It is a generally accepted canon of evidence in civil law, common law, and, in fact, most jurisdictions, that the burden of proof rests upon the party, whether complaining or defending, who asserts the affirmative of a particular claim or defence. If that party adduces sufficient evidence to raise a presumption that what is claimed is true, the burden then shifts to the other party, who will fail unless it adduces sufficient evidence to rebut the presumption.

In this vein, the party invoking an exception carries the burden of proof to show that it meets its requirements: in *India–Autos*, India invoked Art. XVIII GATT to justify, on balance of payments (BOP)-grounds its quantitative restriction in place. India was responding to a claim by the US that its measures were in violation of Art. XI GATT, a claim which, in the eyes of the Panel, the US had proved (§§ 7.285–292). Recall nevertheless, that both in *EC–Sardines* (Chapter 19), as well as in *EC–Tariff Preferences* (Chapter 6), the burden of proof was not assigned to the party invoking the exception.

8.3.2 Burden of Persuasion

In *US–Wool Shirts and Blouses*, the AB held (as we saw above) that the party making a claim must make a prima facie case (§ 14). In subsequent cases, Panels have understood the requirement "to make a prima facie case" as equivalent to raising a presumption that what is claimed is true (US–Stainless Steel, at § 6.2). The Panel in *Mexico–Taxes on Soft Drinks* ruled that the duty of the complainant to make a prima facie case is not affected by the defendant's decision not to challenge the claims and arguments made: Mexico had chosen not to raise any defence against some of the claims advanced by the US. The Panel held that Mexico's inaction did not amount to admission that the US had made a prima facie case; the Panel went on and examined to what extent a prima facie case had been made, the absence of a Mexican response notwithstanding (§§ 8.16ff.). In *US–Zeroing (Korea)*, the US did not advance arguments against Korea's claims that zeroing violates WTO; the Panel did not equate the absence of response to victory for Korea but moved on to examine the quality of prior case law on zeroing and only then found for Korea (§§ 7.34ff.).

Assuming a prima facie case has been made, the burden of proof will shift to the other party which will have to effectively refute the presumption: the Panel in *Thailand–H–Beams,* for example, requested (§ 7.49) from Thailand to provide effective refutation against Poland's prima facie case. In practice, WTO Panels will not raise a flag anytime a presumption has been created; they will make a global evaluation based on what has been pleaded before them by the parties to the dispute (AB, *Korea–Dairy*, § 145):

> no provision in the DSU . . . that requires a panel to make an explicit ruling on whether the complainant has established a *prima facie* case of violation before a panel may proceed to examine the respondent's defence and evidence. (italics in the original)

The Panel, in *US–1916 Act (EC),* concluded that if the evidence submitted by complainant and defendant was in equipoise, then the defendant prevails (§ 6.58):

> If, after having applied the above methodology, we could not reach certainty as to the most appropriate court interpretation, i.e. if the evidence remains in equipoise, we shall follow the interpretation that favours the party against which the claim has been made, considering that the claimant did not convincingly support its claim.

9. THE OUTCOME OF THE PANEL PROCESS

9.1 INTERIM REVIEW

Panels will issue an interim review report (Art. 15 DSU) shortly before the circulation of the final report to the parties to the dispute. Parties to dispute have the legal right to comment on the interim report. Practice varies: usually, parties prefer to comment only on factual aspects of the report and ensure that their claims and arguments have been properly reflected therein. There are exceptions, however: In *US–Steel Safeguards*, the parties to the dispute made extensive comments that led the Panel to even complete omissions in the interim report spotted by the parties to the dispute (§§ 9.27ff). In the overwhelming majority of cases so far, the interim and the final report are similar; at best, there are few (and, usually, un-important) differences between them. The Panel report in *Korea–Certain Paper* is a very notable exception to this practice: the part of the final report on circumspection (§§ 7.110ff.) was substantially modified after the interim review had been issued.

The Panel, in *US–Steel Safeguards*, noted that interim reports are confidential (§ 9.41). This understanding is based on the interpretation of Art. 14 DSU according to which Panel deliberations without any further distinctions are confidential.

9.2 THE FINAL REPORT

9.2.1 The Form

Panel reports are divided in two parts: the factual part, where the claims and arguments of parties to the dispute (including those made by third parties) are reflected, and, the findings, where the Panel, recounting in summary form the claims and arguments made by the parties to the dispute, provides its legal evaluation of the dispute before it. At the end of the findings part, Panels will reflect their conclusions.

9.2.2 The Obligation to Provide a Reasoned Explanation for the Findings

Art. 12.7 DSU requires from Panels to set out the basic rationale for their findings:

> ... the report of the panel shall set out the findings of fact, the applicability of relevant provisions and the basic rationale behind any findings and recommendations that it makes.

In *US–Lamb*, the AB explained its understanding of this provision (§ 106):

> We wish to emphasize that, although panels are not entitled to conduct a *de novo* review of the evidence, nor to *substitute* their own conclusions for those of the competent authorities, this does *not* mean that panels must simply *accept* the conclusions of the competent authorities. To the contrary, in our view, in examining a claim under Article 4.2(a), a panel can assess whether the competent authorities' explanation for its determination is reasoned and adequate *only* if the panel critically examines that explanation, in depth, and in the light of the facts before the panel. Panels must, therefore, review whether the competent authorities' explanation fully addresses the nature, and, especially, the complexities, of the data, and responds to other plausible inter-

pretations of that data. A panel must find, in particular, that an explanation is not reasoned, or is not adequate, if some *alternative explanation* of the facts is plausible, and if the competent authorities' explanation does not seem adequate in the light of that alternative explanation. Thus, in making an "objective assessment" of a claim under Article 4.2(a), panels must be open to the possibility that the explanation given by the competent authorities is not reasoned or adequate. (italics and emphasis in the original)

The term "basic rationale" was further explained in the AB report in *Mexico–Corn Syrup (Article 21.5–US)*:

> In our view, the duty of panels under Article 12.7 of the DSU to provide a "basic rationale" reflects and conforms with the principles of fundamental fairness and due process that underlie and inform the provisions of the DSU. In particular, in cases where a Member has been found to have acted inconsistently with its obligations under the covered agreements, that Member is entitled to know the reasons for such finding as a matter of due process. In addition, the requirement to set out a "basic rationale" in the panel report assists such Member to understand the nature of its obligations and to make informed decisions about: (i) what must be done in order to implement the eventual rulings and recommendations made by the DSB; and (ii) whether and what to appeal. Article 12.7 also furthers the objectives, expressed in Article 3.2 of the DSU, of promoting security and predictability in the multilateral trading system and of clarifying the existing provisions of the covered agreements, because the requirement to provide "basic" reasons contributes to other WTO Members' understanding of the nature and scope of the rights and obligations in the covered agreements.

Consequently, this duty requires from Panels to actively research whether other, alternative explanations are better suited to the case before them, and to explain to the addressees of the report what should be done in terms of implementation.

9.2.3 Dissenting Opinions

The majority of Panel reports are adopted unanimously, all three panelists subscribing to the final outcome. Occasionally, there have been cases where Panelists have expressed dissenting opinions. Dissenting opinions have to, by virtue of Art. 14.3 DSU, be anonymous. A dissenting opinion, in practice, can be the result of a disagreement with the overall outcome, or with the reasoning followed, or with both. The Panel report in *US–Carbon Steel* offers a good illustration of the former (§§ 10.1ff.); the Panel reports in *US–Softwood Lumber V* (§§ 9.1ff), and *US–Suspended*

Concession (§§ 9.1ff) offer examples of the second category. The Panel report in *US–Zeroing (EC)* is a good example of a dissenting opinion where the dissenter disagreed with both the reasoning and the outcome (§§ 9.1ff.).

9.2.4 Timely Circulation of Panel Reports

The DSU contains a specific provision (Art. 12.9) which makes it plain that Panel reports should be circulated no longer than six months counting from the establishment of the Panel,[30] and in exceptional circumstances the deadline for issuance of the Panel report can be extended to nine months. In practice, they are issued much later than the statutory deadlines prescribe.[31] It is not unusual though, that Panels actively aim at reducing the duration of the process before them: to this effect, Panels have, for example, rejected the issuance of a separate report (requested under Art. 9.2 DSU, in the case of a multiple complaint) because such issuance would affect the timeliness of the issuance of the final report.[32]

9.2.5 Adoption of Panel Reports

Art. 16.4 DSU reads:

Within 60 days after the date of circulation of a panel report to the Members, the report shall be adopted at a DSB meeting unless a party to the dispute formally notifies the DSB of its decision to appeal or the DSB decides by consensus not to adopt the report. If a party has notified its decision to appeal, the report by the panel shall not be considered for adoption by the DSB until after completion of the appeal. This adoption procedure is without prejudice to the right of Members to express their views on a panel report.

Footnote 7 to Art. 16.4 DSU clarifies that:

If a meeting of the DSB is not scheduled within this period at a time that enables the requirements of paragraphs 1 and 4 of Article 16 to be met, a meeting of the DSB shall be held for this purpose.

Reports will be adopted by negative consensus, and the defendant might find it appropriate to signal, at the DSB meeting, its disagreement with the report. Mexico, for example, expressed in very explicit terms, its disagreement with the rationale and the findings of the report in *Mexico–Telecoms* when it was presented for adoption (WTO Doc. M/170 of 6 July 2004). Reports will be adopted, unless appealed within the statutory

---

[30] According to the same provision, in case of urgency, a Panel report should be circulated within three months from the date of establishment of the Panel.

[31] Horn et al. (2011) provide precise numbers for Panel duration from 1995–2010.

[32] See, for example, §§ 7.3–6 of the report in *US–Offset Act (Byrd Amendment)*.

deadlines (Art. 16.4 DSU). There is only WTO Panel report that has never been adopted: *EC–Bananas III (Article 21.5–EC)*. The EU had requested establishment of this compliance Panel, and had no interest in seeing it adopted. Since anyway, suspension of concessions had been authorized against it in parallel proceedings, the EU did not request that an item be placed on the agenda to the effect that this report be adopted; in the same vein, the complainants in the original dispute did not place a similar request either.

9.2.6 Special Procedures for Least Developed Countries (LDC)

Art. 24 DSU reads:

1. At all stages of the determination of the causes of a dispute and of dispute settlement procedures involving a least-developed country Member, particular consideration shall be given to the special situation of least-developed country Members. In this regard, Members shall exercise due restraint in raising matters under these procedures involving a least-developed country Member. If nullification or impairment is found to result from a measure taken by a least-developed country Member, complaining parties shall exercise due restraint in asking for compensation or seeking authorization to suspend the application of concessions or other obligations pursuant to these procedures.

2. In dispute settlement cases involving a least-developed country Member, where a satisfactory solution has not been found in the course of consultations the Director–General or the Chairman of the DSB shall, upon request by a least-developed country Member offer their good offices, conciliation and mediation with a view to assisting the parties to settle the dispute, before a request for a panel is made. The Director–General or the Chairman of the DSB, in providing the above assistance, may consult any source which either deems appropriate.

Chad made a third party submission in *US–Upland Cotton (Article 21.5–Brazil)*. The Panel took note, in accordance with this provision, of the fact that Chad is an LDC, and invited Chad to also make an oral statement as well (§ 8.29).

9.3 MULTIPLE COMPLAINTS

Art. 9.1 DSU allows for the possibility to establish a single Panel when different complaints relate to the same subject-matter. Merging into one Panel[33] does not necessarily mean that one Panel report will even-

---

[33] Panel proceedings can also be synchronized (without being merged). In *EC–Bananas III (Article 21.5–Ecuador) (Second Recourse)*, the AB upheld the Panel's decision not to synchronize

tually come out of the process: at the request of one of the parties, separate reports for each complaint submitted could be issued (Art. 9.2 DSU). Panels, assuming no request to the opposite has been tabled by a party to the dispute, enjoy discretion in deciding whether a single report should be issued or not: the commonality of claims might justify one report. This was the Panel's view expressed in § 9.40 of its report in *US–Steel Safeguards*. Parties to the dispute have the right to request issuance of separate reports. Assuming such a request has been submitted, Panels must, in principle, adhere to it (Art. 9.2 DSU). The AB, in its report on *US–Offset Act (Byrd Amendment)*, dealt with the question whether, under specific circumstances a request for separate reports could be answered in the negative. It noted that a request for separate reports must be made in a timely manner. In the case at hand, the AB ruled that the US request was untimely since it was submitted two months after the issuance of the descriptive part of the Panel report. Moreover, the US did not show any damage resulting from the issuance of a single report and thus the AB found nothing wrong with the Panel's decision to reject the US request (§§ 313–316). Art. 9.3 DSU states that, if multiple Panels have been established, to the extent possible the same Panelists serve in all Panels and the schedule is harmonized so that the end result will be coherent.

QUESTIONS AND COMMENTS

Art. 23.2 DSU: Canada and the US are members of the WTO and of NAFTA. Sometimes they bring their disputes before NAFTA and sometimes before the WTO. Art. 23.2 DSU makes it clear that all trade disputes shall be submitted to the WTO. Are Canada and the US violating Art. 23.2 DSU any time they submit a trade dispute to a NAFTA Panel?

The Role of the WTO Secretariat in Dispute Settlement: Nordström (2005) discusses the influence of the Secretariat in drafting Panel reports. Inside US Trade, October 3, 2008, discussed one of the Panel report on zeroing, noting:

> Sources close to respondents argued that disagreements on zeroing between panels and the Appellate Body is due to the influence of the WTO Rules' Division, which advises panelists in cases involving interpretations of the AD Agreement. Those advisers tend to favor the use of zeroing, according to these sources.

Annex A of the WTO Staff Regulations reads:

Participation of staff members in the WTO dispute settlement process

---

two Panel proceedings as requested by the EU because in the absence of synchronicity the EU rights had not been negatively affected anyway.

34. When paragraph VI:4(c) of the Rules of Conduct for the Understanding on Rules and Procedures Governing the Settlement of Disputes (hereafter called the "Rules of Conduct" and contained in WT/DSB/RC/1) is applicable (i.e. when staff members are considered to assist in a dispute), staff members shall disclose to the Director–General the information required to be disclosed by paragraph VI:2 of the Rules of Conduct, as well as any information regarding their participation in earlier formal consideration of the specific measure at issue in a dispute under any provisions of the WTO Agreement, including through formal legal advice under Article 27.2 of the Understanding on Rules and Procedures Governing the Settlement of Disputes, as well as any involvement with the dispute as an official of a WTO Member government or otherwise professionally, before having joined the Secretariat. The Director–General shall consider any such disclosures in deciding on the assignment of members of the Secretariat to assist in a dispute. When the Director–General, in the light of that consideration, including of available Secretariat resources, decides that a potential conflict of interest is not sufficiently material to warrant non-assignment of a particular member of the Secretariat to assist in a dispute, the Director–General shall inform the panel of that decision and of the relevant supporting information.

35. If a staff member becomes the object of a complaint regarding material violation of the Rules of Conduct, pursuant to Article VIII:11, the Director–General shall provide any evidence submitted in respect thereof to the staff member who is the subject of such evidence. The Director–General shall consult with the person who is the subject of the evidence and the panel and shall, if necessary, take appropriate disciplinary action in accordance with *Staff Regulation* 11.1."

Freedom of Information Act (FOIA): Can the US simultaneously respect the FOIA and the confidentiality requirements embedded in the DSU?

Sources of Law: Mavroidis (2008) discusses the sources of law that WTO Panels have used since the advent of the WTO.

Rules of Conduct: The full text of the Rules of Conduct applicable to Panelists (but also to members of the WTO Secretariat, AB members, experts who testify) is included in WTO Doc. WT/DSB/RC/1 of December 11, 1996.

Institutional Balance: In *US–Softwood Lumber IV*, the Panel faced an awkward situation: it was called on to review a challenge by Canada to the effect that, the US, by not using one of the benchmarks included in Art. 14 SCM to calculate the benefit Canadian producers of soft lumber had received, had violated its obligations under the SCM; in Canada's view, the list included in Art. 14 SCM was exhaustive. Art. 14 SCM, which deals with the calculation of benefit, pre-supposes the existence of a market price, but such a price did not exist in Canada. The US had used a benchmark other than those referred to in Art. 14 SCM, precisely because none of the benchmarks included therein was appropriate for the case at hand. The Panel signalled the issue, but refused to play legislator, and found against the defendant (US). The AB reversed the Panel, in principle, arguing that one could legitimately use other benchmarks. In your view, did the Panel, the AB or both respect Art. 3.2 DSU in this case?

Remand Authority: Exercise of judicial authority can be highly problematic though, in case the AB reverses the Panel's findings, see Palmeter (1998) and his plea to introduce remand authority in the WTO.

Expert Review Groups: Why, in your view have we seen not one signle expert review group established since the advent of the WTO?

Expert Testimony before Panels: This is the agreed procedure for inviting expert witnesses to the Panel proceedings in *EC–Asbestos*:

Nature of advice

On the basis of the first submissions from both parties, the Panel will determine the areas in which it wants to seek expert advice.

Selection of experts

The Panel will seek expert advice from individual experts. Experts are under the Panel's authority. They shall serve in their individual capacities and not as government representatives, nor as representatives of any organization. The opinions they provide shall be advisory only. The number of experts the Panel will select will be determined in light of the number of issues on which advice will be sought, as well as by how many of the different issues each expert can provide expertise on. The Panel will solicit suggestions of possible experts from the Secretariat of [the appropriate international body] and, subsequently, from the parties. The parties should not contact the individuals suggested. The Panel will not appoint experts who are nationals of either the complaining or the defending party involved in the dispute unless the parties agree with such appointment or in the event the Panel considers that otherwise the need for specialized expertise cannot be fulfilled. The parties are, however, free to include in their delegations the experts of their choice and may, of course, submit evidence produced by any expert they deem appropriate. The Secretariat will seek brief curricula vitae from the individuals suggested. To the extent available, they will be provided to the parties. The parties will have the opportunity to comment on and make known to the Panel any compelling objections to any particular expert under consideration. After consideration of the parties' comments, the Panel will inform the parties of the experts it has selected.

Written questions to experts

The Panel will prepare specific questions for the experts. These will first be provided to the parties.

The parties will have the opportunity to comment on the proposed questions, or to suggest additional ones, before the questions are sent to the experts. After consideration of the parties' comments and suggestions, the Panel will inform the parties of the questions it has sent to the experts. The experts will be provided with all relevant parts of the parties' submissions on a confidential basis. The experts will be requested to provide responses in writing. Copies of these responses will be provided to the parties and to each of the experts. The parties will have the opportunity to comment in writing on the responses from the experts. The parties' comments on the experts' responses will be provided to the experts. The panel may, at any time, submit additional questions to the experts. The descriptive part of the Panel's report will include a section with the Panel's questions to the experts and a summary of their answers. The experts will be able to review their statements as reflected in the Panel's report before the report becomes final.

Meeting with experts

If the Panel decides it opportune, or a party so requests, a meeting with experts, immediately prior to the second substantive meeting, may be held. The purpose of this meeting would be for the experts to express their opinions orally and for the panel and parties to ask specific questions to the experts.

The verbatim transcript of the meeting with experts will be submitted to the parties and the experts for correction. Once corrected, it will be attached to the Panel's final report.

Expert advice Timetable

Receipt of names of possible experts from [*appropriate international body*], and immediate transmission thereof to the parties:	[1 week before first substantive meeting]
Receipt of names of possible additional experts from the parties:	[date of first substantive meeting]
Transmission to the parties of a consolidated list of suggested experts with available *curricula vitae* and draft questions:	[2 weeks]
Receipt from the parties of comments on the list of suggested experts and on the draft questions:	[1 week]

Notification of selection of experts to the parties, and provision of questions to experts and the parties:	[1 week]
Receipt of written responses from experts and transmission of the responses to the parties:	[4 weeks]
Receipt of comments on experts' responses from the parties:	[2 weeks]
Possible meeting with experts:	[two days before the second substantive meeting]

CHAPTER 35

THE APPELLATE BODY

■ ■ ■

1. THE NOTICE OF APPEAL

Art. 16.4 DSU reads:

Within 60 days after the date of circulation of a panel report to the Members, the report shall be adopted at a DSB meeting unless a party to the dispute formally notifies the DSB of its decision to appeal or the DSB decides by consensus not to adopt the report. If a party has notified its decision to appeal, the report by the panel shall not be considered for adoption by the DSB until after completion of the appeal. This adoption procedure is without prejudice to the right of Members to express their views on a panel report.[1]

Rule 20 of the AB Working Procedures (WP)[2] makes it plain that the notice of appeal must be made in writing within the time-frame established in Art. 16.4 DSU.[3] In § 2, Rule 20 reflects the substantive content of a notice of appeal, which must include: the title of the Panel report under appeal; the name of the party to the dispute filing the Notice of Appeal; the service address, telephone and facsimile numbers of the party to the dispute; and a brief statement of the nature of the appeal, including the allegations of errors in the issues of law covered in the Panel report and legal interpretations developed by the panel. In *US–Countervailing Measures on Certain EC Products*, the AB held that the notice of appeal does not simply trigger the process; it also serves the purpose to inform the appellee about the allegations of error that the Panel, in the appel-

---

[1] A footnote to this provision reads: "if a meeting of the DSB is not scheduled within this period at a time that enables the requirements of paragraphs 1 and 4 of Article 16 to be met, a meeting of the DSB shall be held for this purpose."

[2] The AB has adopted its own WP that it applies (with small variations) across cases. The current version is reproduced in WTO Doc. WT/AB/WP/6 of August 16, 2010. See also WTO Doc. WT/AB/WP/W/11 of July 27, 2010, where the AB Secretariat explains the modifications in the WP following consultations with stakeholders. Rule 20 WP is comprehensively discussed in the AB report in *EC–Bananas III (Article 21.5–Ecuador) (Second Recourse)* at § 267.

[3] Practice suggests that the 60 day-deadline can be extended by agreement between the parties to a dispute. In *US–Zeroing (EC)*, the Panel report was circulated on October 31, 2005. The parties tabled a joint request on November 25 of the same year (see WTO Doc. WT/DS294/1), whereby they agreed that the DSB adopt the Panel report on January 31, 2006 that is more than 90 days after its circulation. The justification offered in the joint request was that the delegations were busy preparing the Ministerial Conference (December 2005, Hong Kong, China). The DSB agreed and adopted the joint request, although Art. 16.4 DSU makes no provision for flexibility.

lant's view, has committed (§ 62).[4] The AB has understood the function of a notice of appeal in a manner similar to its case-law on the function of a request for establishment of a panel (Art. 6.2 DSU). In *Chile–Price Band System*, the AB explicitly stated that claims are not lawfully before the AB, unless they have been included with sufficient clarity in the notice of appeal (§ 182):

> In our view, this distinction between claims and legal arguments under Article 6.2 of the DSU is also relevant to the distinction between "allegations of error" and legal arguments as contemplated by Rule 20 of the *Working Procedures*. Bearing this distinction in mind, we do *not* agree with Argentina that Chile's arguments regarding the order of analysis chosen by the Panel amount to a separate "allegation of error" that Chile *should have*—or *could have*—included in its Notice of Appeal. In fact, we do not see, nor has Argentina explained, what *separate* "allegation of error" could have been made, or what legal basis for such "allegation of error" there could have been. Rather than making a separate "allegation of error", Chile has, in our view, simply set out a *legal argument* in support of the issues it raised on appeal relating to Article 4.2 of the *Agreement on Agriculture* and Article II:1(b) of the GATT 1994. (italics and emphasis in the original).

Consequently, a claim that has not been included in the notice of appeal will not be entertained by the AB (AB, *EC–Bananas III*, § 152). In *EC–Bananas III (Article 21.5–Ecuador) (Second Recourse)* though, the AB held that failure to mention which provisions have been wrongly interpreted and which paragraphs of the Panel report the complainant attacks are fatal only if the appellee's rights have been impaired. In the instant case, the appellee's rights, in the AB's views, had not been impaired, since the US had reacted in detail to all arguments made at the hearing (§ 283).

In the AB's view, claims regarding its jurisdiction are of such fundamental nature, that they could be raised before it, even if they do not appear in the notice of appeal (AB, *US–Offset Act (Byrd Amendment)*, § 208).

Claims do not have to substantiated in the notice of appeal; this will be done at a later stage through submissions by the parties (AB, *US–Shrimp*, § 95). The sufficiency of the substantive content of a notice of appeal will be judged on a case by case basis. Generic statements, however, will not suffice. The AB, in its report on *US–Offset Act (Byrd Amendment)*, held that similar statements do not sufficiently inform the appellee about the issues at stake (§ 200). In this vein, although a reference to the "Conclusions and Recommendations" section of a Panel report would

---

[4] In similar vein, in *US–Large Civil Aircraft (2nd Complaint)*, the AB held in § 681 that the Notice of Appeal serves two purposes, namely to initiate the process and to inform the appellee of the breadth and width of the appeal so it can effectively exercise its rights (due process).

normally not suffice to satisfy the adequacy requirements of the notice of appeal, it could exceptionally do so if this section includes the rationale behind the conclusions and recommendations reached (AB, *US–Countervailing Measures on Certain EC Products*, § 70).[5]

The DSU does not classify appeals in any particular way.[6] Practice however, reveals that WTO Members have had recourse to "conditional appeals". In *US–FSC (Article 21.5–EC)*, the appellant (EU) requested the AB to rule on two of its claims, only in case the AB would reverse the Panel's findings, where the complainant had prevailed (§§ 253–255). In *EC–Bed Linen (Article 21.5–India)*, the AB explained that it would not rule on conditional appeals in case the conditions for the appeal had not been met (§ 100).

If no appeal has been launched, the Panel's findings are the last word on an issue. Assuming however, that only a portion of the Panel's findings has been appealed, the question arises as to the legal value of the un-appealed panel findings; the AB dealt with this issue in *EC–Bed Linen (Article 21.5–India)*. It held that un-appealed Panel findings must be treated as final resolution of the dispute, since the final report that will be adopted at the DSB will consist of both the un-appealed and the appealed Panel findings (§ 93).

2. ESTABLISHMENT OF THE AB DIVISION

2.1 A PERMANENT BODY

The AB has seven members appointed for an initial term of four years, renewable once (Arts. 17.1, Art. 17.2 DSU).[7] As with Panels, the AB has its own administrative and legal support (Art. 17.7 DSU); a WTO official with the rank of Director is heading the AB Secretariat.

2.2 THE SELECTION PROCESS

A Preparatory Committee was established (where delegates at the DSB could participate) in order to decide on the selection process for the members of the AB. Following a recommendation by this body, the DSB decided that an organ be established comprising the DG of the WTO, and the Chairmen of the General Council, the DSB, the CTG, the CTS, and the TRIPS Council. This organ would be receiving propositions for nomi-

---

[5] A Notice of Appeal may be amended. To this effect, a request must be made and the AB will decide taking into account the incidence on the time-table as well as the interests of the other parties to the dispute (Rule 23bis WP).

[6] Within five days from the submission of a Notice of Appeal, a party to the dispute other than the original appellant can introduce its own appeal called Notice of Other Appeal, for an illustration, see *US–Large Civil Aircraft (2nd Complaint)* § 687.

[7] To ensure continuity, the term of some of the members of the first AB was cut short (six instead of eight years), so that some of the members of the original AB could serve as the 'institutional memory' of the AB and thus provide a link between the first and the second AB.

nations by WTO Members, and, at the end, propose to the DSB its nominees. It is the DSB that would appoint the members of the AB.[8] Candidates must correspond to the qualitative requirements described in Art. 17.3 DSU:

> The AB shall comprise persons of recognized authority, with demonstrated expertise in law, international trade and the subject matter of the covered agreements generally. They shall be unaffiliated with any government. The AB membership shall be broadly representative of membership in the WTO. All persons serving on the AB shall be available at all times and on short notice, and shall stay abreast of dispute settlement activities and other relevant activities of the WTO. They shall not participate in the consideration of any disputes that would create a direct or indirect conflict of interest.

The EU and the US have always had a national each in the AB since 1995. The remaining members are nationals of various WTO Members, but geographical considerations are by and large respected (Africa, Asia, Latin America have always had one members each in the AB).

2.3 DUTIES AND RESPONSIBILITIES OF MEMBERS OF THE AB

The duties and responsibilities of the members of the AB are only briefly described in the DSU; they are described in detail in the AB Working Procedures. Art. 17.9 DSU is the legal basis acknowledging the authority of the AB to draw its own WP. The WP were issued in early 1996, shortly after the members of the first AB were appointed[9] and have been amended several times ever since, without however substantial modifications.[10] According to Rule 2 of the WP, a member shall not accept any employment nor pursue any professional activity that is inconsistent with his/her duties and responsibilities; it shall exercise his/her office without accepting or seeking instructions from any international, governmental, or non-governmental organization or any private source; and it shall be available at all times and on short notice. Rules 8–11 of the WP impose disclosure obligations to all members who might be conflicted and thus not in position to serve on a particular dispute. Annex II to the WP cements the disclosure obligations.

The AB elects its Chairman (Rule 5 WP).

---

[8] WTO Doc. WT/DSB/1.
[9] WTO Doc. WT/AB/WP/1 of February 15, 1996.
[10] WTO Doc. WT/AB/WP/4 of May 1, 2003.

2.4 THE AB DIVISION

Art. 17.1 DSU states that three rotating members of the AB (a division) will hear a case. The formula for selection of a division is not reflected in the DSU or in the WP, and is unknown to the wider public (Rule 6 WP).[11] A presiding member for each division will be selected (Rule 7 WP). Although a division hears and decides a particular case (Rule 3 WP), a practice of collegiality has developed. In an effort to promote consistency and coherence in decision-making, Rule 4 WP reflects the so-called collegiality-requirement: according to its § 3, the members of a division will exchange views with members of the AB who do not participate in their division, on the resolution of the dispute before them. The final decision of course will be taken by the members of the division alone.

3. SOURCES RESTRAINING THE JURISDICTION OF THE AB

3.1 WITHDRAWAL OF THE APPEAL

Rule 30(1) WP makes it clear that an appeal can be withdrawn at any time after the AB was convened. In such a case, the AB will refrain from adjudicating the dispute and will inform the DSB accordingly.

3.2 MUTUALLY AGREED SOLUTIONS (MAS)

It could very well be the case that the parties to the dispute reach an amiable solution during the process before the AB. In this case, they must respect the discipline of Art. 3.6 DSU, and notify their MAS to the AB. Rule 30(2) WP requests that the AB be notified of the MAS, but does not request that proceedings be stopped with immediate effect. As is the case in Panel practice, the AB will review whether the notified MAS settles the whole or part of the dispute only.

4. THE PARTIES BEFORE THE AB

4.1 APPELLANT, APPELLEE

Only parties to the dispute, not third parties, may appeal a Panel report (Art. 17.4 DSU). The party appealing the report is the appellant and the party defending it is the appellee. In practice the original complainant and the original defendant can be either or both appellant and appellee to each other's submission, since they can appeal different portions of the Panel report.

---

[11] Anecdotally, it seems that on its appointment, each member of the AB receives a number. A combination of three numbers, rotating according to a *secret formula*, will hear appeals as they are coming to the AB. For example, numbers 1, 2 and 5 will hear appeal against DS 1, numbers 2, 6 and 9 will hear appeals against DS 2 and so on. What is unknown is the *formula* for rotating the divisions.

4.2 THIRD PARTIES

Only WTO Members can, in light of the wording of Arts. 10, and 17.4 DSU, be third parties. A WTO Member can participate as third party before the AB, only if it has notified its interest to participate as third party before the Panel (Art. 17.4 DSU).[12] Rule 24 WP explains the rights of third parties:

> Any third party may file a written submission, stating its intention to participate as third participant in the appeal and containing the grounds and legal arguments in support of its position, within 25 days after the date of the filing of the Notice of Appeal.

A third participant who has filed a written submission may appear before the AB (Rule 27(3) WP).

4.3 AMICI CURIAE

In *US–Lead and Bismuth II*, the AB accepted that an individual can qualify as an amicus (§ 41). In *US–Shrimp*, the AB accepted three amici curiae representing various NGOs. In *EC–Sardines*, Morocco, a WTO Member, requested to participate as amicus; it had not participated as third party in the Panel proceedings. The AB, against the objections of the appellee (Peru) accepted the brief of Morocco (§§ 161–167). The AB has based its decisions to invite participation by amici on Rule 16.1 WP which allows it to "fill the gaps" in its procedures. We quote, for example, from § 107 of its report in *US–Shrimp*:

> ... If, in the exercise of its sound discretion in a particular case, a panel concludes *inter alia* that it could do so without "unduly delaying the panel process", it could grant permission to file a statement or a brief, subject to such conditions as it deems appropriate. The exercise of the panel's discretion could, of course, and perhaps should, include consultation with the parties to the dispute. (italics in the original).

In *US–Lead and Bismuth II*, the AB explained that, in the absence of an explicit prohibition, adjudicating bodies were in principle, free to accept amici-participation, assuming that such participation did not run afoul the DSU (§ 39). In *EC–Asbestos*, the AB issued a communication inviting outsiders to express their interest to participate in the proceedings.

---

[12] The Definitions Section of the WP distinguishes between third parties and third participants. Third party, in accordance with the WP: 'means any WTO Member who has notified the DSB of its substantial interest in the matter before the panel pursuant to paragraph 2 of Article 10 of the DSU.' Third participant, in the same document: 'means any third party that has filed a written submission pursuant to Rule 24(1); or any third party that appears at the oral hearing, whether or not it makes an oral statement at that hearing.' The distinction is pertinent in light of the fact that some third parties might decide not to file before the AB. Third participants are hence, a sub-set of third parties: any third participant must be a third party; the opposite is not necessarily true, however.

This was the first official invitation to this effect.[13] The AB based its legal authority to invite amici briefs on Rule 16(1) WP.[14] Following this initiative, a number of WTO Members requested and convened a special meeting of the WTO General Council where, the vast majority of the WTO Membership, took issue and criticized the AB's initiative.[15] The AB accepted no amicus briefs submitted to it in *EC–Asbestos*.[16] Practice evidences other cases as well where the AB has not accepted briefs by amici. Usually, the AB will justify its decision to reject a brief submitted to it, although it does not have to do so: for example, in *US–Steel Safeguards*, the AB explained that, the reason for its decision not to accept an NGO brief, had to do with the fact that the brief submitted concerned a question which had not been reflected in the claims before it (§ 268); in *US–Lead and Bismuth II*, the AB rejected two briefs because they would not help it reach its final conclusions anyway (§ 42).[17] On the other hand, the AB (and panels for the same reasons) has no discretion whether to accept amici submissions, if they have been incorporated (attached to) in the briefs of a party to the dispute. In § 89 of the AB report in *US–Shrimp* we read:

> We consider that the attaching of a brief or other material to the submission of either appellant or appellee, no matter how or where such material may have originated, renders that material at least *prima facie* an integral part of that participant's submission. On the one hand, it is of course for a participant in an appeal to determine for itself what to include in its submission. On the other hand, a participant filing a submission is properly regarded as assuming responsibility for the contents of that submission, including any annexes or other attachments. (italics in the original).

The AB has clarified that participation of amici in proceedings depends on the discretion of WTO adjudicating bodies to which a request to this effect has been submitted (*US–Lead and Bismuth II*, §§ 40–42). Consequently, amici are not at par with WTO Members when it comes to access to dispute settlement proceedings (AB, *US–Shrimp*, § 101).

---

[13] The second time an official invitation was issued to members of the civic society to participate in proceedings occurred in DS 327, the dispute between the European Community and the United States on the EC-policy with respect to imports of hormone-treated beef (September 2005). It should be noted that in DS 327, the invitation was not to simply send a brief, but to be physically present in (some stages of) the proceedings.

[14] WTO Doc. WT/DS135/9 of November 8, 2000.

[15] WTO Doc. WT/GC/M/60 of January 23, 2001.

[16] For a detailed narrative, see Mavroidis (2004).

[17] Practice also evidences cases where the AB has accepted amici briefs: see, for example, § 160 of the AB report in *EC–Sardines*.

4.4 PASSIVE OBSERVERS

In *EC–Asbestos*, Zimbabwe requested to participate as passive observer to an AB session, that is, to attend the oral hearing without filing a third party submission. In the absence of a negative reaction to this effect by the parties to the dispute, the AB agreed. Zimbabwe had participated as third party before the Panel but had not manifested its interest to participate as third party before the AB (§ 7).

5. THE DUTY OF THE AB

The AB is under the duty to make an objective assessment of the matter before it. As we explain *infra*, although the DSU does not impose on the AB a similar duty (Art. 11 DSU is addressed to Panels only), the AB has imposed this duty on itself. Nevertheless, there is a limitation: the AB may only uphold, modify or reverse the legal findings and conclusions of a Panel (Art. 17.3 DSU); in *US–Certain EC Products*, the AB stated that its mandate cannot extend beyond these three functions (§ 92). When the AB upholds a Panel's finding, it states its agreement with both the rationale and the final outcome; when it reverses a Panel's finding, the AB disagrees with the outcome anyway, and most, probably, with the rationale as well; and when the AB modifies the Panel's findings, it will uphold the outcome, albeit for reasons other than those invoked by the Panel. One should not neglect the imperative embedded in Art. 17.6 DSU either:

> An appeal shall be limited to issues of law covered in the panel report and legal interpretations developed by the panel.[18]

Consequently, the AB will uphold, reverse, or modify Panel findings by addressing legal issues only: it is within these confines that its duty to perform an objective assessment of the matter before it must be assessed.

5.1 WORKING PROCEDURES

The AB, as mentioned *supra*, has enacted its own WP which regulate the process before it.

---

[18] A good example is offered by the report on *US–Certain EC Products*: the AB addressed a claim by the defendant that a particular measure was adopted after the consultations had ended and hence was not properly before the Panel. The AB held that Panel findings on a factual issue are not properly before it (§ 90 and § 97). Not taking into account relevant facts nevertheless, is a legal issue: in *US–Countervailing Duty Investigation on DRAMs*, the Panel, based on a series of factual observations, had found that the US had not properly demonstrated government involvement, a key issue in deciding whether a subsidy had indeed been paid by the Korean government to specific producers. In doing so, the Panel had on the one hand, omitted to examine some of the evidence in the record without explaining its decision to do so, and, also, omitted to examine the evidence in its totality. The AB held that this approach was not consonant with the Panel's duty to ask as an objective trier of facts and, consequently, reversed the Panel's findings (§§ 185–190).

5.2 OBJECTIVE ASSESSMENT

Whether the AB has abided by its self-imposed standard to perform an objective assessment is hard to tell given that it decides in last resort. In *EC–Hormones*, the AB stated that it will not disturb every Panel finding with which it disagrees (§ 132):

> Under Article 17.6 of the DSU, appellate review is limited to appeals on questions of law covered in a panel report and legal interpretations developed by the panel. . . . Determinations of the credibility and weight properly to be ascribed to (that is, the appreciation of) a given piece of evidence is part and parcel of the fact finding process and is, in principle, left to the discretion of the panel as the trier of facts.

In *Korea–Alcoholic Beverages*, the AB rejected a claim by Korea relating to the weight that the Panel had given to evidence before it and refused to (§ 160):

> second-guess the panel in appreciating either the evidentiary value of such studies or the consequences, if any, of alleged defects in those studies.

The AB has no remand authority: It cannot send a case back to the original Panel and ask it to re-consider. The absence of remand is particularly problematic in cases where the original Panel exercised judicial economy: assuming this has been the case, and that the AB reverses the Panel's findings, the complainant will have to re-introduce its claims to a new Panel and start the process all over again.[19] To prevent this from being the case, the AB has occasionally employed a technique that it calls 'completing the analysis'.

In §§ 117–118 of its report in *Australia–Salmon*, the AB, regrouping all of its prior case-law on the issue, went on to state that, when the factual record before it is sufficient, it will go ahead and complete the analysis. In *US–Wheat Gluten*, the AB reversed the causation analysis proposed by the Panel and its conclusions with regard to the ambit of the US obligation to notify a safeguard measure; it then went on to complete the analysis based on the factual information before it (§§ 80 and 127). A similar approach was followed by the AB in *US–Carbon Steel*, where the AB declined to complete the analysis in light of the lack of clarity as to factual aspects of the case (§ 138).[20]

In *Canada–Periodicals*, Canada had successfully appealed the Panel's conclusions regarding the first sentence of Art. III.2 GATT (like products) and persuaded the AB to overturn the Panel's findings in this respect. The Panel, however, had also concluded that, in light of its decision

---

[19] On this issue, see the comprehensive analysis in Palmeter (1998).
[20] See also the AB report in *Canada–Autos* in § 133.

as to the first sentence, it need not consider Art. III.2, second sentence GATT (directly competitive or substitutable products), and this aspect of its decision was not appealed. Canada argued that the AB lacked jurisdiction to consider any issues beyond what had been appealed. The AB disagreed (p. 21):

> As the legal obligations in the first and second sentences are two closely-linked steps in determining the consistency of an internal tax measure with the national treatment obligations of Article III:2, the AB would be remiss in not completing the analysis of Article III:2. In the case at hand, the Panel made legal findings and conclusions concerning the first sentence of Article III:2, and because we reverse one of those findings, we need to develop our analysis based on the Panel Report in order to issue legal conclusions with respect to Article III:2, second sentence, of the GATT 1994.

In *EC–Asbestos*, the AB reversed the Panel's findings with respect to the non-applicability of the TBT Agreement. Although the factual record before it arguably sufficed for the AB to complete the analysis under the TBT Agreement, the AB declined to do that. The stated reason for its decision, was that the TBT Agreement and Art. III GATT (which was used as an alternative basis by Canada for its claims) are not part of a logical continuum. Citing *Canada–Periodicals*, the AB held that, whereas Art. III.1, and Art. III.2 GATT are part of such a continuum, this is not the case between Art. III GATT on one hand, and the TBT on the other (§§ 79–82). Consequently, the AB will go ahead and rule on issues not dealt with by the Panel if:

> (a) it judges that the factual record before it was adequate to do so; and
>
> (b) it establishes that there is a logical continuum between the claims before it.[21]

The question has arisen, quid in case where the AB has overturned a Panel finding but has been unable to complete the analysis? In *US–Softwood Lumber IV*, the AB reversed the Panel's findings on the Canadian claims under Art. 14(d) SCM. It felt however, that it did not have adequate factual record before it to complete the analysis. As a result, it decided to make no findings at all as to the consistency of the US alternative benchmark with the Art. 14(d) SCM. We quote the relevant passage from § 167 of the report:

> (a) <u>reverses</u> the Panel's consequential finding, in paragraph 7.65 of the Panel Report, that the United States acted inconsistently with Articles 10, 14, 14(d) and 32.1 of the *SCM Agreement* with

---

[21] Compare the AB report in *US–Continued Zeroing* at § 187.

respect to USDOC's determination of the existence and amount of benefit in the underlying countervailing duty investigation;

(b) <u>finds,</u> however, that there is not a sufficient factual basis to complete the analysis as to whether, under Article 14(d) of the *SCM Agreement*, USDOC was justified in using a benchmark other than private prices in Canada, and as to whether such benchmark relates or refers to, or is connected with, prevailing market conditions in Canada, (including price, quality, availability, marketability, transportation and other conditions of purchase or sale), and, therefore, <u>does not make findings</u> on whether USDOC's determination of the existence and amount of benefit in the underlying countervailing duty investigation is consistent or inconsistent with Articles 14 and 14(d) of the *SCM Agreement*, or on whether the imposition of countervailing duties based on that determination is consistent or inconsistent with Articles 10 and 32. 1 of the *SCM Agreement*. (underlining and italics in the original).[22]

5.3 DISCOVERY POWERS

Rule 28 WP reads:

(1) At any time during the appellate proceeding, including, in particular, during the oral hearing, the division may address questions orally or in writing to, or request additional memoranda from, any participant or third participant, and specify the time-periods by which written responses or memoranda shall be received.

(2) Any such questions, responses or memoranda shall be made available to the other participants and third participants in the appeal, who shall be given an opportunity to respond.

(3) When the questions or requests for memoranda are made prior to the oral hearing, then the questions or requests, as well as the responses or memoranda, shall also be made available to the third parties, who shall also be given an opportunity to respond.

It follows that the AB has discovery powers that it will exercise through questions to the parties to a dispute.

6. DUTY OF PARTIES

The duty to cooperate is spelled out in Rule 29 WP in the following terms:

Where a participant fails to file a submission within the required time-periods or fails to appear at the oral hearing, the division

---

[22] See also the AB report in *Canada–Dairy* at § 104.

shall, after hearing the views of the participants, issue such order, including dismissal of the appeal, as it deems appropriate.

7. EVIDENCE

7.1 THE APPELLANT'S SUBMISSION(S)

According to Rule 21(1) WP, following the notice of appeal, the appellant will send its submission within the specified time-limits. The appellant's submission will have to be transmitted to the WTO Secretariat and proof of service will be affixed to each one of them (Rule 18 WP). The AB, in *EC–Sardines*, explained that the appellant can withdraw and re-file its appeal, if it is to clarify some issues and no new issues are added, since due process is not impaired (§ 145).

7.2 THE APPELLEE'S SUBMISSION

Rule 22 WP is the corresponding provision to Rule 21 WP and regulates the time of filing as well as the content of the appellee's submission. In *US–Countervailing Measures on Certain EC Products*, the EU requested the right to add to its original submission to the AB. To this effect, it requested from the AB, to modify the procedure, as it had the discretion to do per Rule 16(1) WP, and allow it to deposit an additional brief. The AB acquiesced to this request, but provided the US with the possibility to submit an additional notice of appeal (§§ 52 and 64).

7.3 MEETING WITH THE PARTIES

Upon receipt of the notice of appeal, the AB will organize an oral hearing with the parties (as a general rule, 30 days after the date of the filing of the notice of appeal). There is normally only one meeting of the parties with the AB (Rule 27 WP). In practice, the AB will ask questions to the parties which, in turn, are usually prepared to respond on the spot. The record before the AB comprises not only the written submissions, but also the responses provided orally to the AB during the hearing. The AB will set the time-limits during which a written version of the responses orally given (plus responses to questions not answered during the oral hearing) must be submitted to it. Responses to the questions asked by the AB will form part of the record and will be transmitted to other parties to the dispute (Rule 28 WP).

7.4 NO *EX PARTE* COMMUNICATIONS

Ex parte communications are not permitted (Art. 18 DSU). Rule 19 WP further clarifies that this prohibition binds not only members of the division, but all members of the AB.

7.5 PROCEEDINGS ARE CONFIDENTIAL

Proceedings before the AB are confidential (Art. 17.10 DSU).

7.6 TIMELY CIRCULATION OF AB REPORTS

The AB should complete its work within 60 days from the date a party to the dispute formally notifies its notice of appeal. This period can be extended, if the AB cannot finish its work within the set time-limit, but under no circumstances should it exceed 90 days (always counting from the date of filing of the notice of appeal). Of course, the time-limits will be adjusted to the extent that a covered agreement so provides: this is for example, the case when a dispute involves a challenge against a prohibited subsidy. Annex I to the WP provides a (tentative) time-table which also explains the individual steps taken during the appellate process. We quote:

	General Appeals	Prohibited Subsidies Appeals
	Day	Day
Notice of appeal	0	0
Appellant's submission	0	0
Notice of Other Appeal	5	2
Other appellant(s)' submission(s)	5	2
Appellee(s)' submission(s)	18	9
Third participant(s)' submission(s)	21	10
Third Participant(s)' notification(s)	21	10
Oral hearing	30–45	15–23
Circulation of appellate report	60–90	30–60
DSB meeting for adoption	90–120	50–80

In practice, in case the AB believes that it will exceed the statutory time-limits, it will issue a "deeming letter" requesting the acquiescence of the parties to the dispute.[23]

---

[23] WTO Doc. WT/DS381/13 of April 16, 2012.

8. THE AB REPORT

8.1 DISSENTING OPINIONS

Rule 3(2) WP, provides that members of the AB will make every effort to ensure that decisions will be reached by consensus. A decision, however, can be taken by a majority vote among the members of the division. Dissenting opinions expressed by members of the AB shall be, in accordance with Art. 17.11 DSU, anonymous. Practice so far evidences that the overwhelming majority of reports have been unanimously supported by the AB Division that issued them. There are few cases where a member of the AB has dissented: in *US–Upland Cotton*, for example, one member of the AB dissented on the interpretation of Art. 10.2 AG (§§ 63ff.). In *EC–Asbestos*, a separate but concurring opinion was expressed (that is, not a dissenting opinion): one member of the AB issued the opinion which pointed to the same overall conclusion (§§ 149–154).

8.2 JUDICIAL ECONOMY

The AB shall address all issues raised in the appeal (Art. 17.12 DSU). There are cases however, where the AB exercising judicial economy, refrained from ruling on some issues: it did so when, in its view, it had provided the DSB with the necessary material to ensure resolution of the dispute before it. An appropriate illustration is provided by § 127 of the report in *US–Cotton Yarn*:

> We finally turn to the United States' appeal against the Panel's interpretation that Article 6.4 requires attribution to all Members the imports from whom cause serious damage or actual threat thereof. In this respect, we note that the scope of this dispute is defined by Pakistan's claims before the Panel. Pakistan claimed that the United States acted inconsistently with Article 6.4 because it "attributed serious damage to imports from Pakistan without making a comparative assessment of the imports from Pakistan and Mexico and their respective effects". The Panel considered it necessary, in its reasoning, to rule on the broader interpretative question of whether Article 6.4 requires attribution to all Members the imports from whom cause serious damage or actual threat thereof. The United States also appeals the Panel's interpretation on this broader question. However, our findings resolve the dispute as defined by Pakistan's claims before the Panel. We, therefore, do not rule on the issue of whether Article 6.4 requires attribution to all Members the imports from whom cause serious damage or actual threat thereof. In these circumstances, the Panel's interpretation on this question is of no legal effect.

Practice reveals that, the AB has occasionally moved and addressed issues not strictly before it and, thus, expressed its view on a particular legal issue as an *obiter dictum* (that is, a finding that is not necessary for the resolution of the dispute). For example, parts of the report in *US–Steel Safeguards* reflect a long *obiter dictum* (§§ 485ff.).

8.3 NO APPEAL AGAINST AB REPORTS

Absent negative consensus, the DSB will adopt both the AB report (and the un-appealed Panel findings) 30 days following the circulation of the AB report to the WTO Membership (Art. 17.14 DSU).[24] Once the AB report has been adopted, the WTO Member concerned will be requested to implement it within a reasonable period of time. There is no possibility to further appeal an AB report.

8.4 THE LEGAL VALUE OF AB REPORTS

There is nothing like stare decisis in WTO law. This does not mean however, that AB reports are void of any precedence-value. In *US–Stainless Steel (Mexico)*, the AB re-visited all prior case law, and held that it expected Panels to follow prior AB findings dealing with the same issue (§§ 158–162):

> It is well settled that Appellate Body reports are not binding, except with respect to resolving the particular dispute between the parties. This, however, does not mean that subsequent panels are free to disregard the legal interpretations and the *ratio decidendi* contained in previous Appellate Body reports that have been adopted by the DSB. In *Japan—Alcoholic Beverages II*, the Appellate Body found that:
>
>> [a]dopted panel reports are an important part of the GATT *acquis*. They are often considered by subsequent panels. They create legitimate expectations among WTO Members, and, therefore, should be taken into account where they are relevant to any dispute.
>
> In *US–Shrimp (Article 21.5–Malaysia)*, the Appellate Body clarified that this reasoning applies to adopted Appellate Body reports as well. In *US–Oil Country Tubular Goods Sunset Reviews*, the Appellate Body held that "following the Appellate Body's conclusions in earlier disputes is not only appropriate, but is what would be expected from panels, especially where the issues are the same."
>
> Dispute settlement practice demonstrates that WTO Members attach significance to reasoning provided in previous panel and Appellate Body reports. Adopted panel and Appellate Body re-

---

[24] So far, all AB reports have been adopted.

ports are often cited by parties in support of legal arguments in dispute settlement proceedings, and are relied upon by panels and the Appellate Body in subsequent disputes. In addition, when enacting or modifying laws and national regulations pertaining to international trade matters, WTO Members take into account the legal interpretation of the covered agreements developed in adopted panel and Appellate Body reports. Thus, the legal interpretation embodied in adopted panel and Appellate Body reports becomes part and parcel of the *acquis* of the WTO dispute settlement system. Ensuring "security and predictability" in the dispute settlement system, as contemplated in Article 3.2 of the DSU, implies that, absent cogent reasons, an adjudicatory body will resolve the same legal question in the same way in a subsequent case.

In the hierarchical structure contemplated in the DSU, panels and the Appellate Body have distinct roles to play. In order to strengthen dispute settlement in the multilateral trading system, the Uruguay Round established the Appellate Body as a standing body. Pursuant to Article 17.6 of the DSU, the Appellate Body is vested with the authority to review "issues of law covered in the panel report and legal interpretations developed by the panel". Accordingly, Article 17.13 provides that the Appellate Body may "uphold, modify or reverse" the legal findings and conclusions of panels. The creation of the Appellate Body by WTO Members to review legal interpretations developed by panels shows that Members recognized the importance of consistency and stability in the interpretation of their rights and obligations under the covered agreements. This is essential to promote "security and predictability" in the dispute settlement system, and to ensure the "prompt settlement" of disputes.

The Panel's failure to follow previously adopted Appellate Body reports addressing the same issues undermines the development of a coherent and predictable body of jurisprudence clarifying Members' rights and obligations under the covered agreements as contemplated under the DSU. Clarification, as envisaged in Article 3.2 of the DSU, elucidates the scope and meaning of the provisions of the covered agreements in accordance with customary rules of interpretation of public international law. While the application of a provision may be regarded as confined to the context in which it takes place, the relevance of clarification contained in adopted Appellate Body reports is not limited to the application of a particular provision in a specific case.

We are deeply concerned about the Panel's decision to depart from well-established Appellate Body jurisprudence clarifying the interpretation of the same legal issues. The Panel's approach has serious implications for the proper functioning of the WTO dispute settlement system, as explained above. Nevertheless, we consider that the Panel's failure flowed, in essence, from its misguided understanding of the legal provisions at issue. Since we have corrected the Panel's erroneous legal interpretation and have reversed all of the Panel's findings and conclusions that have been appealed, we do not, in this case, make an additional finding that the Panel also failed to discharge its duties under Article 11 of the DSU. (italics in the original).

And in *US–Continued Zeroing*, it expounded this approach (§ 362):

Following the Appellate Body's conclusions in earlier disputes is not only appropriate, it is what would be expected from panels, especially where the issues are the same. This is also in line with a key objective of the dispute settlement system to provide security and predictability to the multilateral trading system. The Appellate Body has further explained that adopted panel and Appellate Body reports become part and parcel of the *acquis* of the WTO dispute settlement system and that "ensuring 'security and predictability' in the dispute settlement system, as contemplated in Article 3.2 of the DSU, implies that, absent cogent reasons, an adjudicatory body will resolve the same legal question in the same way in a subsequent case." Moreover, referring to the hierarchical structure contemplated in the DSU, the Appellate Body reasoned in *US—Stainless Steel (Mexico)* that the "creation of the Appellate Body by WTO Members to review legal interpretations developed by panels shows that Members recognized the importance of consistency and stability in the interpretation of their rights and obligations under the covered agreements." The Appellate Body found that failure by the panel in that case to follow previously adopted Appellate Body reports addressing the same issues undermined the development of a coherent and predictable body of jurisprudence clarifying Members' rights and obligations under the covered agreements as contemplated under the DSU. (italics in the original).

A good example of the Panels' attitude is provided by the report in *US–Shrimp and Sawblades*. Noting in § 7.25 that it was dealing with yet another zeroing case, and in § 7.28 that the AB had already condemned zeroing on numerous occasions, the Panel noted first in § 7.29 that although the WTO legal order did not know of a formal stare decisis, still the AB had cautioned failure by Panels to follow previously adopted AB reports addressing the same issue. In § 7.30 the Panel invoked the consistent line of AB reports condemning zeroing; in § 7.31, it went on to hold that, by invoking this case law, China had adduced *prima facie* evidence;

since the US did not manage to rebut the prima facie case made by China, the latter prevailed in the dispute.

There are few instances where Panels did not follow rulings by the AB. In *EC–Commercial Vessels*, for example, the Panel refused to adhere to the AB's understanding of Art. 18.1 AD, as expressed in its *US–Offset Act (Byrd Amendment)* report. A series of Panels have distanced themselves from the AB's outlawing of the zeroing practice in antidumping investigations.[25] However, on appeal of these cases, the AB has consistently referred to its own prior reports. Only in a few select cases has the AB departed from prior case law.[26]

QUESTIONS AND COMMENTS

Scrutinizing the Output by the AB: The ALI reporters' studies is the one forum that critically reviews all reports issued by the AB (as well as unappealed Panel reports) since 2000. The authors' papers are available at www.ali.org.

Secret Formula to Select the AB Division: Are there any good reasons why, in your view, the formula for selecting an AB division should be kept secret?

Completing the Analysis: Does the AB, when it completes the analysis, ipso facto deprive WTO Members of a two instances-adjudication?

AB Members Selection: How would you choose the members of your ideal AB? What kind of expertise would you take into account on a priority basis? Would geographical considerations matter in your choice?

The AB Mandate: Do you agree with the idea that all the AB should do is to assist parties to resolve their dispute? Do you see a head on collision between this idea and the creation of jurisprudence in the WTO context?

Completing the Contract: Horn, Maggi and Staiger (2010) provide their understanding of the WTO judge: it is the entity entrusted with the completion of an incomplete contract. Do you agree that this is the function of the WTO judge and how does it tie with Art. 3.7 DSU?

---

[26] For an illustration, see the treatment of pass through in successive AB reports as reported in Grossman and Mavroidis (2007), and (2007c).

CHAPTER 36

ALTERNATIVE PROCEEDINGS

■ ■ ■

1. ALTERNATIVE DISPUTE SETTLEMENT PROCEEDINGS

Two alternative (to the usual procedure, that is, Panel/AB) procedures are reflected in the DSU:

(a) Art. 5 DSU provides for the possibility of recourse to mediation and good offices;

(b) Art. 25 DSU provides for the possibility to have recourse to arbitration.

Only one case so far has been adjudicated under Art. 25 DSU, whereas there is no reported case adjudicated under Art. 5 DSU.

2. ARBITRATION UNDER ART. 25 DSU

Art. 25.1 DSU states:

Expeditious arbitration within the WTO as an alternative means of dispute settlement can facilitate the solution of certain disputes that concern issues that are clearly defined by both parties.

Arbitration under Art. 25 DSU can thus be used as a substitute to the usual procedure. In *US–Section 110(5) Copyright Act (Article 25)*, however, the EU and the US established an arbitration under Art. 25 DSU and requested from the Arbitrators to deal with one issue only: the quantification of the damage suffered by the EU as a result of the violation of the TRIPs by the US: a WTO Panel, *US–Section 110(5) Copyright Act,* had already found the US practices to be in violation of the TRIPs Agreement and the US did not appeal the Panel report. Instead, the parties to the dispute agreed to submit to arbitration under Art. 25 DSU the question mentioned above. Hence, in this case, recourse to the procedure embedded in Art. 25 DSU was designed as a substitute for a specific part of the usual procedure: the quantification of nullification and impairment. Art. 22.6 DSU deals with this aspect of the procedure, and the question arose whether in light of the fact that Art. 22.6 DSU deals specifically with this issue, arbitration under Art. 25 DSU could overlap with Art. 22.6 DSU. The Arbitrators in their report on *US–Section 110(5) Copyright*

Act (Article 25) took the view that nothing in the DSU stopped them from entertaining the request of the parties to the dispute (§§ 2.4–6).

2.1 THE IDENTITY OF THE ARBITRATORS

Art. 25 DSU does not discuss the identity of the Arbitrators. The parties to the dispute in *US–Section 110(5) Copyright Act (Article 25)* decided to name as Arbitrators the members of the original Panel:

> The arbitration shall be carried out by the original panel. Should any of the members of the original panel not be available for the arbitration, and the parties to the arbitration do not agree on a replacement, the parties shall request the Director–General of the WTO to appoint a replacement within one week of the request.[1]

2.2 PARTIES TO AN ART. 25 DSU ARBITRATION?

Besides the parties requesting the establishment of arbitration, third parties as well can participate in arbitration under Art. 25 DSU. However, the agreement of the parties to the dispute is necessary (Art. 25.3):

> Other Members may become party to an arbitration proceeding only upon the agreement of the parties which have agreed to have recourse to arbitration.

2.3 NO CONSULTATIONS REQUIRED

There is no need to hold bilateral consultations.

2.4 NOTIFICATION REQUIREMENTS

Art. 25.2 DSU imposes an obligation on all WTO Members wishing to have recourse to Art. 25 DSU to notify the WTO Membership of their intentions to do so:

> Agreements to resort to arbitration shall be notified to all Members sufficiently in advance of the actual commencement of the arbitration process.

2.5 JURISDICTION

In *US–Section 110(5) Copyright Act (Article 25)*, the Arbitrators held that they had the legal right to consider their jurisdiction.[2] In their words (§ 2.1):

---

[1] WTO Doc. WT/DS160/15. Two members of the original Panel were unavailable. Since the parties to the dispute could not agree on replacements, the DG appointed the remaining two members, see WTO Doc. WT/DS160/ARB25/1 at § 1.3.

[2] WTO Doc. WT/DS/160/ARB25/1.

Whereas the DSB establishes panels or refers matters to other arbitration bodies, Article 25 provides for a different procedure. The parties to this dispute only had to *notify* the DSB of their recourse to arbitration. No decision is required from the DSB for a matter to be referred to arbitration under Article 25. In the absence of a multilateral control over recourse to that provision, it is incumbent on the Arbitrators themselves to ensure that it is applied in accordance with the rules and principles governing the WTO system. As recalled by the AB in *United States—AD Act of 1916,* it is a widely accepted rule that an international tribunal is entitled to consider the issue of its own jurisdiction on its own initiative. The Arbitrators believe that this principle applies also to arbitration bodies. In case there be any question as to the jurisdiction of the Arbitrators to deal with this dispute, we provide brief reasons for our conclusion that we do have the necessary jurisdiction. (italics in the original).

2.6 DESIGNING THE PROCEDURES

Art. 25.2 DSU states that:

except as otherwise provided in this Understanding, . . . the parties . . . shall agree on the procedures to be followed.

Art. 25.4 DSU further states that:

Articles 21 and 22 of this Understanding shall apply *mutatis mutandis* to arbitration awards. (italics in the original).

In *US–Section 110(5) Copyright Act (Article 25)*, the Arbitrators mentioned explicitly that they did not feel bound by Art. 22 DSU (§ 4.19):[3]

The Arbitrators note that they have been appointed under Article 25 of the DSU. As a result, they do not feel constrained by a number of obligations imposed on arbitrators in Article 22.6 proceedings. Unlike Article 22.6, which closely relates to compliance (or absence thereof) at the end of the reasonable period of time, Article 25 is silent as to the date on which a matter referred to arbitration should be assessed. However, the Arbitrators are aware that they are not called upon to consider the level of EC benefits which may still be nullified or impaired after the end of the implementation period, but to consider the level of EC benefits which are being nullified or impaired as a result of the current application of Section 110(5)(B). General practice under the DSU has been to consider the facts of a case as at the date of establishment of the panel. In the absence of any specification in our mandate, we believe that it should be assumed that the parties wanted us to assess the level of benefits nullified or impaired

---

[3] WTO Doc. WT/DS160/ARB25/1.

on the date the matter was referred to us. In other words, we must determine the level of nullification or impairment of EC benefits over a one-year period ending as closely as possible to 23 July 2001.[4]

2.7 BURDEN OF PROOF

Formally, there is no complainant requesting an Art. 25 DSU Arbitration; issues are defined by both parties (Art. 25.1 DSU). In *US–Section 110(5) Copyright Act (Article 25)*, the Arbitrators' task was facilitated in this respect, since the parties had already agreed that the EU would be first providing its own methodology regarding the quantification of the nullification and impairment that it had suffered as a result of the WTO-inconsistent behavior adopted by the US. In §§ 4.4–5 of the report, the Arbitrators explain that, it was for the US to make a prima facie case that the EU methodology was not appropriate; upon demonstration, the burden of proof would shift back to the EU to rebut the US claims.

2.8 EVIDENCE

In *US–Section 110(5) Copyright Act (Article 25)*, requested information was submitted after the imposed deadline.. Arbitrators showed flexibility and agreed to accept it for the reasons quoted below (§§ 1.17–21):

> First, in a case where relevant information was scarce, and given the time-frame within which the Arbitrators were supposed to complete their work, any additional information was welcome at any time and a priori important in the light of the Arbitrators' duty to provide an objective assessment of the facts.
>
> Second, the additional information was adduced by the United States as part of a rebuttal of EC arguments contained in its reply to questions of the Arbitrators, as agreed with the Arbitrators at the hearing. The Arbitrators note that the EC did not claim that the exhibits were not related to the rebuttal of EC arguments contained in its reply to questions from the Arbitrators.
>
> Finally, whilst the US justification for its production of exhibits US ARB–25 and US ARB–26 was belated, in its response the European Communities did in fact deal with the substance of these exhibits. As the Chairman noted in his letter of 19 September 2001 to the parties, the EC has thus not been deprived of the opportunity to comment on the US exhibits.
>
> Given these special circumstances, the Arbitrators hold that exhibits US ARB–25 and US ARB–26 are admitted in the procedure. As far as the substance of these pieces of evidence is con-

---

[4] The agreed procedures were reflected in WTO Doc. WT/DS160/15.

cerned, the Arbitrators will revert to it as necessary in the course of this award.

2.9 CONFIDENTIAL INFORMATION

In *US–Section 110(5) Copyright Act (Article 25)* the Arbitrators were inspired by the AB case law regarding the treatment of confidential information (§ 1.24):

> "In the absence of specific requests from the parties as to how confidentiality of business confidential information should be preserved, the Arbitrators will rely generally on the practice of the AB on this matter. To the extent that confidential information may appear as such in the award in order to support the findings of the Arbitrators, the Arbitrators decided that two versions of the award would be prepared. One, for the parties, would contain all the information used in support of the determinations of the Arbitrators. The other, which would be circulated to all Members, would be edited so as not to include the information for which, after consultation with the parties, the Arbitrators would conclude that confidentiality for business reasons was sufficiently warranted. The information which the Arbitrators would consider to be business confidential would be replaced by "x".

2.10 DISCOVERY POWERS OF ARBITRATORS

In *US–Section 110(5) Copyright Act (Article 25)* the Arbitrators sought information from two of the US collective management organization, the American Society of Authors, Composers and Publishers (ASCAP), and the Broadcast Music Inc. (BMI). Before doing so, however, the Arbitrators consulted the parties on the questions to be asked to the two outside sources. The parties did not object to the Arbitrators seeking such information. The Arbitrators further agreed that the parties might comment on any information submitted by ASCAP and BMI.[5]

2.11 THE LEGAL EFFECT OF THE ARBITRAL AWARD

Art. 25.3 DSU makes it clear that arbitration awards cannot be appealed:

> The parties to the proceeding shall agree to abide by the arbitration award.

In this vein, the parties to the arbitration on *US—Section 110(5) Copyright Act (Article 25)* have reflected their agreement to abide by the award in the following terms:

---

[5] See § 1.9 of the WTO Doc. WT/DS160/ARB25/1.

The parties agree that the award of the arbitrator shall be final, and they shall accept it as the level of nullification or impairment for purposes of any future proceedings under Article 22 of the DSU related to this dispute.[6]

3. GOOD OFFICES, CONCILIATION AND MEDIATION

WTO Members can voluntarily have recourse to good offices, conciliation and mediation. The DG of the WTO (Art. 5.6 DSU) may ex officio offer his good services to assist WTO Members to settle a dispute. There is no practice in this respect so far.

4. DISPUTE RESOLUTION OUTSIDE OF THE DSU

On two occasions so far, WTO Members followed ad hoc procedures not embedded in the DSU, in order to resolve their disputes. On October 16, 2002, Philippines, Thailand and the EU requested mediation from the DG of the WTO. As the hereby reproduced document makes it clear (WTO Doc. WT/GC/66), the mediation requested was not mediation under Art. 5 DSU:

<u>Communication from the Director–General</u>

The following communication, dated 10 October 2002, has been received by the Chairman of the General Council from the Director–General with the request that it be circulated to delegations.

I would like to inform you that on 4 September 2002, the Philippines, Thailand and the European Communities (hereafter the "requesting Members") have jointly requested mediation by myself or by a mediator designated by me with their agreement.

The purpose of the requested mediation process is "to examine the extent to which the legitimate interests of the Philippines and Thailand are being unduly impaired as a result of the implementation by the European Communities of the preferential tariff treatment for canned tuna originating in ACP states. In the event that the mediator concludes that undue impairment has in fact occurred, the mediator could consider means by which this situation may be addressed."

The requesting Members have held three rounds of consultations, but could not reach a mutually acceptable solution. Although the requesting Members consider that the matter at issue is not a "dispute" within the terms of the DSU, they agree that I

---

[6] WTO Doc. WT/DS160/ARB25/1.

or the mediator designated by myself could be guided by procedures similar to those envisaged for mediation under Article 5 of the DSU, as described in a communication by the Director–General on Article 5 of the DSU (WT/DSB/25).

I wish to inform you that I have accepted the request for mediation and, with the agreement of the requesting Members, have nominated Deputy Director–General Mr. Rufus H. Yerxa as mediator in this case. Mr. Yerxa will receive Secretariat support, as appropriate. I will notify you once Mr. Yerxa completes the mediation process or when the requesting Members decide to terminate the process.

The report of the mediator even today remains confidential and has not been issued as a WTO document in the WT/DS series. The only official evidence that a report was indeed circulated to the parties is to be found in WTO Doc. WT/GC/66/add. 1 of December 23, 2002, which in relevant part, reads:

> On 20 December 2002, Mr. Yerxa informed me that, on that date, he completed his work in accordance with the timetable agreed to by the requesting Members. Mr. Yerrxa also informed me that the requesting Members had agreed that the Mediator's conclusions would remain confidential.

Based on the circulated report, the parties to the dispute managed to reach an amiable solution, the content of which however, remains confidential as well. WTO Doc. WT/GC/71 of August 1, 2003 is the official evidence that a solution was indeed reached:

> We wish to inform you that an amicable outcome has been reached among the parties concerned based on the Advisory Opinion of the Mediator.
>
> We would like to take this opportunity once more to thank you for your invaluable assistance, and in particular the unstinting efforts of Mr. Yerxa and the Secretariat, in having contributed to the successful outcome of this mediation.

On June 5, 2003, the Council Regulation (EC) No. 975/2003 (on opening and providing for the administration of a tariff quota for imports of canned tuna covered by CN codes 1604.14.11, 1604.14.18 and 1604.2070)[7] was adopted. This regulation implements through a tariff quota the report of the mediator.

The story of the Bananas arbitration is different. The parties to the dispute made it clear that the arbitration sought, to examine whether the EU proposals with respect to the import treatment of bananas would be WTO-consistent, was not an Art. 5 DSU mediation. Still the award of the

---

[7] Official journal of the European Union L 141/1ff. of June 7, 2003.

Arbitrator was circulated as a WTO Doc., albeit not in the DS series, as is usually the case with dispute settlement documents: it was circulated as WTO Doc. WT/L/616 on August 1, 2005. The Arbitrator had been appointed by the DG (§§ 1 and 6).[8]

QUESTIONS AND COMMENTS

Extra–WTO Procedures: what is the legal value of settlements occurring through mechanisms such as those used in the Canned Tuna- and the Bananas-disputes?

Alternative Proceedings: why is there so scarce use of the procedures under Arts. 5 and 25 DSU in your view?

---

[8] The Arbitrators were two members of the AB, and the former Canadian Ambassador who at the time when the Arbitral Body was established was in private practice.

CHAPTER 37

ENFORCEMENT

■ ■ ■

1. RECOMMENDATIONS AND SUGGESTIONS

A ruling, that is, a finding of inconsistency is the necessary condition[1] for Panels to recommend that the WTO Member concerned brings its measures into compliance with the WTO. Panels may also suggest ways to do so.[2] Art. 19.1 DSU reads:

> Where a panel or the AB concludes that a measure is inconsistent with a covered agreement, it shall recommend that the Member concerned bring the measure into conformity with that agreement. In addition to its recommendations, the panel or AB may suggest ways in which the Member concerned could implement the recommendations.

1.1 RECOMMENDATIONS

WTO Panels, with the caveat of pronouncing on a measure that has already expired, must issue a recommendation every time the complainant has successfully met its burden of proof.[3] Art. 19 DSU leaves WTO adjudicating bodies no discretion as to the substantive content of a recommendation, which is inflexible: the author of the illegal act must bring its measures into compliance.[4] As a result, a recommendation leaves its

---

[1] Recall our discussion in Chapter 34: a recommendation is not necessary in case the challenged measure is no longer in place. To this effect, in *US–Certain EC Products*, the AB ruled that (§ 81): "The Panel erred in recommending that the DSB request the United States to bring into conformity with its WTO obligations a measure which the Panel has found no longer exists." Subsequent Panels (*India–Autos* §§ 8.14ff.) have confirmed this view.

[2] There is of course no need for a ruling of inconsistency in case an NVC (or a situation complaint) has been lodged. In similar cases a recommendation (and/or suggestion) will be issued any time the conditions for the successful invocation of the two types of complaints have been met. The AB as well can recommend and/or suggest under the same conditions as Panels.

[3] In *US–Large Civil Aircraft (2nd Complaint)*, the Panel refused to issue a recommendation (although it had established the inconsistency of the challenged measure with the WTO) because the recommendation issued at the first complaint was still operative, § 8.6.

[4] See, for example, § 7.24 of the Panel report in *EC–Commercial Vessels*, where the Panel rejected a request by Korea to recommend 'that the European Communities immediately cease any further disbursements of illegal funding'. In its view, the only recommendation it could make is (eventually) that the defendant bring its measures into compliance with its obligations. There is one exception so far: in *US–Suspended Concession*, the AB recommended "that the Dispute settlement Body request the United states and the European Communities to initiate Article 21.5 proceedings without delay in order to resolve their disagreement as to whether the European Communities has removed the measure found to be inconsistent in *EC–Hormones* and whether the application of the suspension of concessions by the United States remains legally valid." (§ 737).

addressees with substantial discretion as to what needs to be done for compliance to be achieved.[5] The need for discretion when it comes to implementing a report by a WTO adjudicating body, has been best described in the panel report in *US–Section 301 Trade Act*:

> The obligation on Members to bring their laws into conformity with WTO obligations is a fundamental feature of the system and, despite the fact that it affects the internal legal system of a State, has to be applied rigorously. At the same time, enforcement of this obligation must be done in the least intrusive way possible. The Member concerned must be allowed the maximum autonomy in ensuring such conformity and, if there is more than one lawful way to achieve this, should have the freedom to choose that way which suits it best (§ 7.102).

A recommendation will be part of a DSB decision addressed to the WTO Member concerned, and is binding upon its addressee.

1.2 SUGGESTIONS

Through a suggestion, Panels will suggest ways to implement an adverse finding. Art. 19 DSU states that suggestions are meant to facilitate the implementation of recommendations: the Panel in *US–Stainless Steel (Mexico)* refused to issue a suggestion, because it had previously refused to issue a recommendation, since the challenged measure had already expired (§ 8.5). Suggestions can be requested by the complaining party, but Panels do not have to grant them. In *US–Lead and Bismuth II* the Panel faced a request by the EU:

> to suggest that the United States amend its countervailing duty laws to recognize the principle that a privatization at market prices extinguishes subsidies. (§ 8.2).

Since however, the EU had not identified the specific provision of US law, the Panel declined to make a suggestion to the effect requested. In *US–Stainless Steel*, Korea requested the Panel to suggest that the US revoke the antidumping order in place. The Panel refused to accept Korea's claim, stating:

> Article 19.1 of the DSU allows but does not require a panel to make a suggestion where it deems it appropriate to do so. (§ 7.8)

The Panel however added that, in its view, revocation of the antidumping order would be one way for the US to bring their measures into compliance but not the only way to do so (§ 7.10). In *EC–Pipe Fittings*, the Panel held that (§ 8.11):

> By virtue of Article 19.1 of the *DSU*, a panel has discretion to ("may") suggest ways in which a Member could implement the

---

[5] The WTO Member concerned cannot of course continue and/or repeat the same behavior.

recommendation that the Member concerned bring the measure into conformity with the covered agreement in question. Clearly, however, a panel is by no means required to make a suggestion should it not deem it appropriate to do so. Thus, while we are free to suggest ways in which we believe the European Communities could appropriately implement our recommendation, we decide not to do so in this case.[6]

In *Guatemala–Cement I*, Mexico, requested the Panel to recommend that Guatemala revoke the measure and also:

> refund those anti-dumping duties already collected. (§ 8.1).

The Panel declined, noting that Art. 19.1 DSU requests from Panels to recommend that the Member bring its measures into conformity (§ 8.2). The Panel did note at the same time that Art. 19.1 DSU authorized it to suggest ways in which the Member concerned could bring its measure into conformity. With regard to Mexico's request concerning revocation, the Panel stated that, since it had concluded that the entire investigation rested on an insufficient basis and therefore never should have been initiated:

> we suggest that Guatemala revoke the existing anti-dumping measure on imports of Mexican cement, because, in our view, this is the only appropriate means of implementing our recommendation. (§ 8.6).

The same issue came up again during the proceedings of *Guatemala–Cement II*. Mexico again requested revocation of duties and reimbursement of illegally perceived duties. The Panel repeated its position that it had discretion to provide for suggestions, even in presence of a specific request by the complaining party to this effect (§ 9.5). It then went on to briefly remind the particular circumstances of the case at hand: the investigation should have never been initiated on the basis of the available information; illegalities were committed during the investigation; no finding that dumping occurred which caused injury was supported by the available evidence (§ 9.6). In light of all this, the Panel could:

> not perceive how Guatemala could properly implement our recommendation without revoking the anti-dumping measure at issue in this dispute. (§ 9.6)

The Panel report in *Argentina–Poultry Antidumping Duties* faced the same issue, that is, a request from Brazil to suggest revocation of the Argentine order imposing antidumping duties. The Panel had previously found that Argentina had violated its obligations:

> (a) by determining that there was sufficient evidence to initiate an investigation when this was not the case;

---

[6] See also the Panel report in *US–Softwood Lumber IV (Article 21.5)* at § 5.6.

(b) by having recourse to best information available in violation of Art. 6.8 AD;

(c) by making an improper comparison between normal value and export price;

(d) by failing to make an objective examination of the injury factors; and

(e) by de-respecting the causality-requirement.

In the Panel's view, in light of the extent of Argentina's violations, a revocation of duties imposed was well in order (§§ 8.5ff.). In *Mexico–Steel Pipes and Tubes*, the Panel found that Mexico had violated a series of provisions referring to various stages of the investigation, and thus, revocation of duties was appropriate remedy (§§ 8.12–13). In its report on *US–1916 Act (Japan)*, the Panel, although it recognized that the remedy that Japan requested it to suggest (that the US repeal its law found to be inconsistent with the WTO) was not the only way that the US could bring its measures into compliance (since, the panel itself accepts that an amendment of the law could probably suffice), it still went on to make the suggestion as requested by Japan, noting that its suggestion should be understood as one of the ways in which the US could bring its measures into conformity with the WTO (§ 6.292). The Panel report in *EC–Export Subsidies on Sugar* is the only case so far where a Panel suggested, although it was not requested to do so by the complaining parties. It justified its decision to suggest by underscoring the interests of the many developing countries participating in the process (§§ 8.3–5).

In *US–Anti-dumping Measures on OCTG*, the AB faced a challenge by Mexico to the effect that the Panel had violated its obligations under Art. 11 DSU by refusing to suggest when requested to do so (§§ 8.15–18). The AB rejected this argument, holding that Panels have discretion to suggest and are not required to do so (§ 189).[7]

All reports so far have consistently held that suggestions are not binding on their addressees, who can legitimately choose another (than the suggested) way to implement the recommendation addressed to them. In *EC–Bananas III (Article 21.5–Ecuador) (Second Recourse)*, the AB went one step further and held that implementing a suggestion creates no presumption that compliance has been achieved (§ 325).

---

[7] Note, that with respect to export subsidies, there is an explicit requirement in the SCM Agreement that they must be withdrawn without delay. In such cases, the recommendation to bring the measures into compliance will be accompanied by a request that the export subsidy be withdrawn without delay (Art. 4.7 SCM). The AB in *US–FSC (Article 21.5–EC)* stated that a defense to the effect that citizens have a right for an orderly transition cannot validly be raised against the obligation to withdraw immediately an illegal subsidy (§§ 223–224 and 229).

2. REASONABLE PERIOD OF TIME (RPT)

The addressee of a recommendation and/or suggestion will have to bring its measures into compliance with the WTO within a reasonable period of time (RPT). The RPT can be defined either by agreement between the parties to the dispute, or through recourse to arbitration.

2.1 BILATERAL AGREEMENT ON THE EXTENT OF THE RPT

Agreement on the extent of the RPT can be tacit, if the proposal by the party requested to implement is not objected to by the other party or parties (Art. 21.3(a) DSU), or explicit (Art. 21.3(b) DSU).

2.2 ARBITRATION

Art. 21.3(c) DSU deals with the situation where parties to the dispute cannot agree on the extent of the RPT. In this case, recourse can be made to arbitration and the RPT will be:

> a period of time determined through binding arbitration within 90 days after the date of adoption of the recommendations and rulings. In such arbitration, a guideline for the arbitrator should be that the reasonable period of time to implement panel or AB recommendations should not exceed 15 months from the date of adoption of a panel or AB report. However, that time may be shorter or longer, depending upon the particular circumstances.

2.2.1 The Identity of the Arbitrator

Footnote 2 to Art. 21.3(c) DSU reads:

> The expression "arbitrator" shall be interpreted as referring either to an individual or a group.

Footnote 1 to the same provision reads:

> If the parties cannot agree on an arbitrator within ten days after referring the matter to arbitration, the arbitrator shall be appointed by the Director–General within ten days, after consulting the parties.

In practice, it is usually the DG who appoints the Arbitrator. In *US–COOL (Article 21.3(c))*, for example, we read in § 65 that in the face of disagreement among the parties as to the identity of the Arbitrator, the DG appointed a former AB member. A rare example to the opposite is provided in the arbitration in *Japan–DRAMS (Korea) (Article 21.3(c))*, where the parties agreed on a member of the AB (§ 3). In all cases submitted to arbitration so far, the Arbitrator has been an acting member of the AB, and in some of them, e.g., in *US–Gambling (Article 21.3(c))*, in *US–COOL (Article 21.3(c))*, and in *EC–Chicken Cuts (Article 21.3(c))*, the

Arbitrator was a former AB member (Claus–Dieter Ehlermann, Giorgio Sacerdoti, and James Bacchus, respectively).

2.2.2 The Task of the Arbitrator

The Arbitrator in *US–Offset Act (Byrd Amendment) (Article 21.3(c))* provided his understanding of the mandate entrusted to him:

> it is *not* part of my mandate to determine or even to suggest the manner in which the United States is to implement the recommendations and rulings of the DSB (§ 48, emphasis in the original).
>
> . . .
>
> . . . my task is not to look at *how* implementation will be carried out, but to determine *when* it is to be done. (§ 53, emphasis in the original).

In even clearer terms, the Arbitrator in *EC–Chicken Cuts (Article 21.3(c))* stated:

> with respect to the implementing measure, my task focuses on the *when*, not the *what*. (§ 49, emphasis in the original).[8]

The Arbitrator does not start from a clean slate though. The DSU contains some guidance helpful to determine when implementation should occur: the Arbitrator is requested to define an RPT because immediate compliance, which is the over-riding objective, is impracticable (art. 21.3 DSU); the RPT should not exceed fifteen months, but it can be longer or shorter depending on particular circumstances (Art. 21.3(c) DSU).

In *US–COOL (Article 21.3(c))*, the Arbitrator confirmed that its task was to determine when and not how implementation should occur; the means at the disposal of the implementing state would, nevertheless, influence the time of implementation. In the case at hand, the US had submitted that it could implement the rulings either through legislative or through regulatory (administrative) action. The Arbitrator respected the US view, and did examine the required time for either option, but still held that the US could reach implementation within 10 months irrespective of the option chosen (§§ 68–98).

2.2.3 Deciding on the RPT

The RPT is measured from the date when a report (Panel, or AB, as the case may be) was adopted.[9] The Arbitrator in *EC–Chicken Cuts (Article 21.3(c))* held that the absence of any implementation efforts by the EU in the four months between the adoption of the AB report and the request

---

[8] See on this score, § 47 of the award in *Brazil–Retreaded Tyres (Article 21.3(c))*.

[9] For an explicit confirmation, see *US–OCTG Sunset Reviews (Article 21.3(c))* at § 22, and *EC–Chicken Cuts (Article 21.3(c))* at § 84.

for arbitration under Art. 21.3(c) DSU were a pertinent factor that should be taken into account in the measurement of the RPT (§§ 66ff.). That is, WTO Members cannot use the non-request for arbitration as pretext for staying idle during the implementation period.

In § 34 of the report in *Chile–Price Band System (Article 21.3(c))*, the Arbitrator stated that the statutory 15 month period is but a guideline and that what matters in order to measure the RPT each time is the existence of attendant *"circumstances"*:

> Article 21.3(c) provides for an arbitrator a "guideline" of a maximum of 15 months from the date of adoption of the panel and AB reports when establishing a "reasonable period of time" for implementation. Notwithstanding this "guideline", I must ultimately be informed, as Article 21.3(c) instructs, by the "particular circumstances" of a given case, which may counsel in favour of shorter or longer periods. As previous arbitrators have observed, the controlling principle is that the "reasonable period of time" should be "the shortest period possible within the legal system of the Member to implement the relevant recommendations and rulings of the DSB", in the light of the "particular circumstances" of the dispute.[10]

The Arbitrator in *US–Hot–Rolled Steel (Article 21.3(c))* explained that looking into attendant circumstances is similar to establishing a reasonableness-test (§ 25):

> In sum, a "reasonable period" must be interpreted consistently with the notions of flexibility and balance that are inherent in the concept of "reasonableness", and in a manner that allows for account to be taken of the particular circumstances of each case.

At any rate, the RPT must not serve the purpose of providing breathing space for the industry which will be affected as a result of the imminent compliance.[11]

It is for the implementing Member to demonstrate that its proposed period of implementation is reasonable.[12] In *US–Offset Act (Byrd Amendment) (Article 21.3(c))*, the Arbitrator held (§ 44) that it is for the implementing party to establish that the proposed RPT is the shortest period possible; absent demonstration, the Arbitrator will judge based on evidence submitted by the parties to the dispute. In *Colombia–Ports of Entry (Article 21.3 (c))*, belated submitted evidence (first time at the oral hearing) was judged acceptable, as long as it was not new evidence. The belat-

---

[10] See also *US–Offset Act (Byrd Amendment) (Article 21.3(c))* at § 41.

[11] §§ 92ff. of the report of the Arbitrator in *EC–Export Subsidies on Sugar (Article 21.3 DSU(c))*.

[12] § 31 of *US–Gambling (Article 21.3(c))*.

edly submitted evidence in this case was a summary of evidence that had already been submitted (§ 58).

In this vein, the means necessary to achieve implementation (will it place through administrative or through legislative action?) can be of importance; it is to be expected that the former can take place in a shorter time (§ 49, *Canada–Pharmaceutical Patents (Article 21.3(c)*; § 38, *Chile–Price Band System (Article 21.3(c))*.[13] In *US–Offset Act (Byrd Amendment) (Article 21.3(c))*, the Arbitrator clarified that when recourse to legislative activity is required, the calendar of the legislative body could be relevant (§ 70). The Arbitrator in *Brazil–Retreaded Tyres (Article 21.3(c))* did not (§ 68):

> consider that implementation through the judiciary can be *a priori* excluded from the range of permissible action that can be taken to implement DSB recommendations and rulings and bring about compliance with a Member's obligations under the covered agreements. (italics in the original).

Yet, when defining the RPT, he did not stick to the period of time proposed by Brazil (21 months from the date of the adoption of the AB report), but, instead, argued in favor of an expedited judicial review that the Brazilian government had already requested from its national Supreme Court (12 months, § 91).

In *US–Stainless Steel (Mexico) (Article 21.3(c))*, the Arbitrator held that holding elections was not an issue in deciding on the extent of the RPT when administrative action is called for which can start irrespective of whether elections are held (§ 62).

The complexity of the implementation process (that is whether a series of new statutes is required, or whether a simple repeal of the statute suffices) is relevant (§ 50, *Canada–Pharmaceutical Patents (Article 21.3(c))*). In *Chile–Price Band System (Article 21.3(c))*, the Arbitrator added that information about the measure aimed to ensure implementation is necessary (§ 37), although the legal issue regarding its consistency with the WTO is beyond the Arbitrator's mandate. The Arbitrator in *US–Offset Act (Byrd Amendment) (Article 21.3(c))* stated that the fact that a WTO Member is required to implement international obligations is not a complexity-factor (§ 70).

The legally binding—as opposed to the discretionary—nature of the implementing procedures will also weigh in the Arbitrator's mind, the former weighing in heavier than the latter (§ 51, *Canada–Pharmaceutical Patents (Article 21.3(c))*).

---

[13] In *Chile–Price Band System (Article 21.3(c))* the Arbitrator took into account pre-legislative activity although similar activity was not legally required (§ 42).

If the WTO Member requested to implement an adverse ruling is a developing country, then the Arbitrator will usually define a longer RPT (*Chile–Alcoholic Beverages (Article 21.3(c))* § 45). In *US–OCTG Sunset Reviews (Article 21.3(c))*, the Arbitrator rejected the relevance of Argentina's developing country-status since, in his view, when a legislative change is required for compliance to be achieved, it is immaterial if the complainant is a developing or a developed country (§ 52). This should not mean that a complainant enjoying developing country-status cannot secure a shorter (than otherwise) RPT. To do so however, the developing country requesting a shorter RPT, will have to establish why being a developing country makes it harder to accept a lengthier RPT. The Arbitrator in *US–Gambling (Article 21.3(c))* for example, refused to shorten the RPT simply because Antigua (the complainant) invoked its status as developing country: Antigua had argued that the US practices led a number of Antiguan workers to un-employment and a continuation of such practices for a long period would be equally harmful. Antigua however, submitted no data to substantiate its claims, and the Arbitrator, in the absence of such a submission, refused to adhere to its request (§ 62). The Arbitrator in *EC–Export Subsidies on Sugar (Article 21.3 (c))* accepted that information provided by Brazil with respect to the number of jobs in the sugar industry (Brazil was attacking subsidies on sugar provided by the EU) was relevant and persuasive. He consequently decided to take into account the developing country-status of Brazil and shorten the RPT (§§ 99ff.).[14] In *Chile–Price Band System (Article 21.3(c))* both complainant and defendant were developing countries, and the Arbitrator decided not to account for this factor in the calculation of the RPT (§ 56).

The role of the measure found to be inconsistent with WTO rules in a particular society in the shaping of domestic policies might also influence the definition of RPT. The Arbitrator in *Chile–Price Band System (Article 21.3(c))* held as much (§ 48):

> I am of the view that the PBS is so fundamentally integrated into the policies of Chile, that domestic opposition to repeal or modification of those measures reflects, not simply opposition by interest groups to the loss of protection, but also reflects serious debate, within and outside the legislature of Chile, over the means of devising an implementation measure when confronted with a DSB ruling against the original law. In the light of the longstanding nature of the PBS, its fundamental integration into the central agricultural policies of Chile, its price-determinative regulatory position in Chile's agricultural policy, and its intricacy, I find its unique role and impact on Chilean society is a relevant factor in my determination of the "reasonable period of time" for implementation.

---

[14] See also *EC–Chicken Cuts (Article 21.3(c))* at §§ 81ff.

In *US–COOL (Article 21.3(c))*, the Arbitrator noted (in the passage leading to § 121) that Art. 2.12 TBT requires an RPT between publication and entry into force of technical regulations. This provision aims to provide traders with the necessary time to adjust to the new norms. The RPT should be 6 months at least, we saw in Chapter 19. Since the complainants however, had argued that they did not need this extra time, the Arbitrator refused to take it into account when calculating the reasonable period within which the US should implement the recommendations and ruling of the AB; in doing that, the Arbitrator rejected a US claim to this effect.

A final award will be issued within 90 days from the date of adoption of recommendations and rulings (Panel or AB report as the case may be). In *Colombia–Ports of Entry (Article 21.3 (c))*, we note that the final report that the award was issued later than the statutory deadline; the parties had agreed to the extension.

3. COMPLIANCE PANELS

If during the RPT no implementing activities at all take place, then the complaining party can request authorization to suspend concessions, which we discuss *infra*. If, on the other hand, implementing activities do take place, one can distinguish between two situations:

(a) the complaining party agrees that the author of the illegal act has adequately implemented its WTO obligations; or

(b) the complaining party does not agree that this has indeed been the case.[15]

The agreement in the first case marks the end of the matter, assuming that no third WTO Member objects to the implementation. In the second case, the original complainant can request the establishment of a compliance Panel as per Art. 21.5 DSU to decide on whether compliance occurred or not. The rationale for a compliance Panel has to do with the resolve of WTO Members to ensure that no unilateral definitions of illegality will take place after the advent of the WTO (Art. 23.2 DSU)

3.1 THE IDENTITY OF THE PANELISTS

The Panel will be composed by the members of the original Panel, if possible. If not, the parties to the dispute and, ultimately in case of disagreement, the DG of the WTO, will compose the Panel: for example, in *US–Softwood Lumber V (Article 21.5–Canada)*,[16] a member of the original Panel subsequently became Deputy Director General (DDG) of the WTO,

---

[15] There is a third (rather unlikely) situation where the parties to the dispute agree that implementing activities that took place were inadequate. In this case as well, the injured party can request authorization to suspend concessions.

[16] § 1.5.

and had to withdraw from the Panel and be replaced. In *US–Upland Cotton (Article 21.5–Brazil)*, the US requested from the DG not to nominate Panelists who were nationals of third parties, and the EU challenged this request, and asked the Panel to make a finding or ruling on the propriety of the Panel's composition (§ 8.27). In the EU's view, the US was abusing the system, since it had not objected to Panelists who were nationals of third parties during the original Panel stage. The DG decided to call only one of the three original Panelists back to service and to nominate two new Panelists.[17] The Panel ultimately declined to rule on the EU request arguing that it lacks the authority to this effect (§ 8.28).

3.2 DURATION

A compliance Panel should complete its work within 90 days, unless if members of the Panel realize that they need more time and have informed the parties to the dispute.

3.3 NO NEED FOR CONSULTATIONS

The AB, when confronted with this issue in its *Mexico–Corn Syrup (Article 21.5–US)* report, decided not to address it (§ 65). Note nonetheless, that, in this case, both the Panel and the AB proceeded to review the case before them, the absence of consultations between the parties to the dispute notwithstanding.

3.4 REQUEST FOR ESTABLISHMENT OF A COMPLIANCE PANEL[18]

The applicability of Art. 6.2 DSU has by now been endorsed by the AB. In *US–FSC (Article 21.5–EC II)*, the AB took the view that Art. 6.2 DSU is generally applicable in Art. 21.5 DSU proceedings. In § 62, the AB explained in detail the minimum requirements for a lawful request to establish a compliance Panel:

> First, the complaining party must cite the recommendations rulings that the DSB made in the original dispute as well as any preceding Article 21.5 proceedings, which, according to the complaining party, have not yet been complied with. Secondly, the complaining party must either identify, with sufficient detail, the measures already taken to comply with those recommendations and rulings, as well as any omissions or deficiencies therein, or state that *no* such measures have been taken by the implementing Member. Thirdly, the complaining party must pro-

---

[17] See EU third party submission, A–57ff. on the report §§ 6ff., and especially at § 7. Only one of the three Panelists selected (Matus, Chile) had acted as Panelist in the original Panel. The other two members of the original Panel (Rosati, Poland, and Moulis, Australia), although both available, were replaced by Perez Motta, Mexico, and Ahn, Korea at the compliance-stage.

[18] The content of a request to establish a compliance Panel is comprehensively discussed in the Panel report in *US–Zeroing (EC) (Article 21.5–EC)* at § 8.25.

vide a legal basis for its complaint, by specifying how the measure taken, or not taken, fail to remove the WTO-inconsistencies found in the previous proceedings, or whether they have brought about new WTO-inconsistencies. (emphasis in the original).

In *EC–Bananas III (Article 21.5–Ecuador) (Second Recourse)*, the AB held that conclusion of an Understanding among the parties to the dispute does not necessarily signal the end of the proceedings if the Understanding is about future action and no implementation has occurred at the time of the request (§§ 218–222).

3.5 STANDING

In *EC–Bananas III (Article 21.5–US)*, the Panel held that the US had legal interest and standing before it since it had been an original complainant in the dispute; in the Panel's view, it would be for the EU to rebut this presumption, not for the US to prove it (§ 7.34). The EU also submitted that the item concerning compliance of the EU with the WTO had been withdrawn from the DSB agenda, and had been re-introduced only four years later against its objection, and that this was proof that the US had conceded that the EU had complied with the WTO, and was, consequently, barred from entering a compliance challenge (§ 7.410). The Panel dismissed this argument since the US had stated after the withdrawal and before the re-introduction of the item in the DSB agenda that it had not been satisfied with the implementation efforts of the EU (§ 7.430).

3.6 SEQUENCING

By "sequencing" we understand that a WTO Member can request authorization to impose countermeasures only in case it has first secured a report by a compliance Panel that no implementation took place during the implementation period.[19] There are reported cases in the first years of WTO practice, however, where a request for authorization to suspend concessions did not follow a report by a compliance Panel. The most notable case is *EC–Bananas III*. The US had requested authorization to suspend concessions vis-à-vis the EU since, in its view, the latter had not brought its measures into compliance during the RPT. The EU argued that compliance had indeed occurred during the RPT. The EC further argued that, in case of disagreement between the parties, a compliance Panel would have to first pronounce on the absence of compliance before the complainant could legitimately request suspension of concessions. In the US view, if the deadline mentioned in Art. 22.2 DSU had lapsed, it would have lost its right to request authorization to suspend concessions:

---

[19] There is, of course, no need to have recourse to a compliance panel, if both parties agree that no implementation ever took place. Recourse to a compliance panel is necessary only in case there is disagreement between the parties to the dispute as to whether implementation occurred.

this provision states that a request for countermeasures can lawfully be submitted within 20 days after the end of the RPT. The US went ahead and requested authorization for suspension of concessions within 20 days from the end of the RPT, without submitting its dispute as to whether compliance had occurred to a compliance Panel.[20] Four days later, Ecuador (the other complainant) requested the establishment of a compliance Panel to rule on whether the EU had indeed complied during the reasonable period of time.[21] Consequently, two parallel procedures were established. The EU requested from the Arbitrators to suspend their proceedings until the compliance Panel had first ruled whether compliance had indeed occurred or not. The Arbitrators in *EC–Bananas III (Article 22.6–US)* rejected this point (§ 2.9):

> In a letter dated 22 February 1999, the European Communities requested that we suspend this arbitration proceeding until 23 April 1999, i.e. until 10 days or so after the date set for the completion of the pending proceedings brought by Ecuador and the European Communities pursuant to Article 21.5 of the DSU in respect of the revised EC banana import regime. However, in light of Article 22.6 of the DSU, which requires that an arbitration thereunder "shall be completed within 60 days after the date of expiry of the reasonable period of time", or 2 March 1999, we decided that we were obligated to complete our work in as timely a fashion as possible and that a suspension of our work would accordingly be inappropriate.

As a result, the report by the Arbitrators determining the level of concessions to be suspended was circulated on April 9, 1999 whereas three days later, that is, on April 12, 1999, the compliance Panel established at the request of Ecuador circulated its report where it found that the EU had not complied with its obligations during the RPT (*EC–Bananas III (Article 21.5–Ecuador)*).

A different approach was followed by the Panel in *US–Certain EC Products*: When confronted with the same issue, the Panel made it clear that a request for suspension of concessions can only be authorized if a compliance Panel has first ruled that no compliance occurred during the RPT. However, in the Panel's view, an Arbitrator requested to determine the level of concessions to be suspended could also determine whether compliance occurred (§§ 6.92–94).

WTO Members have, ever since, either through agreement or informally so, always sought recourse to compliance Panels before they tabled a request for authorization to impose counter-measures. During the DSU

---

[20] WTO Doc. WT/DS27/43 of January 14, 1999.
[21] WTO Doc. WT/DS27/44 of January 18, 1999.

Review,[22] a number of proposals have been made to ensure that sequencing will in the future be explicitly reflected in the DSU.

3.7 THE MANDATE OF COMPLIANCE PANELS

In *Canada–Aircraft (Article 21.5–Brazil)*, following condemnation, Canada revised its original TPC programme. The complainant (Brazil) was not in agreement with Canada as to the adequacy of its implementing efforts. The dispute was submitted to a compliance Panel, the report of which was appealed. On appeal, the AB provided its understanding of the mandate of a compliance Panel (§ 37):

> ... in our view, the obligation of the Article 21.5 Panel, in reviewing 'consistency under Article 21.5 of the DSU, was to examine whether the new measure—the revised TPC programme–was 'in conformity with', 'adhering to the same principles of' or 'compatible with' Article 3.1(a) of the *SCM Agreement*. In short, both the DSU and the Article 21.5 Panel's terms of reference required the Article 21.5 Panel to determine whether the revised TPC programme involved prohibited export subsidies within the meaning of Article 3.1(a) of the *SCM Agreement*. (italics in the original).

The AB confirmed its understanding of this issue in § 88 of its report in *US–Shrimp (Article 21.5–Malaysia)*. It seems clear that a compliance Panel's mandate is limited to the new measure (the measure taken to comply with the WTO adjudicating body's findings). Omissions as well can form the subject-matter of a compliance Panel: the AB clarified, in its report on *US–Softwood Lumber IV (Article 21.5–Canada)*, that what matters is an evaluation whether compliance has been achieved and that, in this perspective, a WTO Member might be requested to omit some actions (§ 67). The complainant cannot use a compliance Panel to expand its challenge: the AB in *EC–Bed Linen (Article 21.5–India)* held that a claim which challenges a measure which is not taken to comply with the original Panel's recommendation is not properly before a compliance panel (§ 78).

Compliance panels will be confronted with legal challenges concerning the consistency of measures taken during the RPT. The question has arisen in practice, whether a Panel can legitimately take into account events that occurred after the expiry of the RPT. In *Australia–Automotive Leather II (Article 21.5–US)*, Australia withdrew a subsidy, which the original Panel had found to be inconsistent with the WTO; Australia granted a loan on non-commercial terms to a beneficiary company instead specifically conditioned upon the repayment of the original subsidy. Australia had argued before the Panel that the loan at hand was not a meas-

---

[22] Mavroidis (2004a) discusses the proposals on sequencing tabled during the DSU review.

ure taken to comply with the recommendation of the original panel. The compliance Panel disagreed: the "particularly close relationship" between the original subsidy and the loan sufficed for the compliance Panel to extend its mandate to the loan itself (§§ 6.1ff. and especially § 6.5). This attitude has been confirmed in subsequent Panels and by the AB itself (§§ 75ff., *US–Softwood Lumber IV (Article 21.5–Canada)*).[23]

Compliance panels might even review measures that occurred after their establishment. In *Australia–Salmon (Article 21.5–Canada)*, the complaining party requested that a measure not identified in the request for establishment be nonetheless reviewed by the compliance Panel. The Panel agreed that there might be good reasons why it might be willing to review measures taken after its establishment (§ 28):

> We do not consider that measures taken subsequently to the establishment of an Article 21.5 compliance panel should *per force* be excluded from its mandate. [. . .] In compliance panels we are of the view that there may be different and, arguably, even more compelling reasons [than before an original panel] to examine measures introduced during the proceedings. As noted earlier, compliance is often an ongoing or continuous process and once it has been identified as such in the panel request, as it was in this case, any 'measure taken to comply' can be presumed to fall within the panel's mandate, unless a genuine lack of notice can be pointed to.(italics in the original).

A similar attitude is evidenced in the Panel report in *Japan–Apples (Article 21.5–US)*.[24]

Compliance panels are not required to issue recommendations. They do not need to recommend that the WTO Member bring its measures into compliance since, all they are requested to do is decide whether the Member concerned has already brought its measures into compliance: the Panel *US–FSC (Article 21.5–EC II)* made this point clear (§§ 7.39–46). Note, however, that the Panel in *EC–Bananas III (Article 21.5–Ecuador)*

---

[23] In this case, following its condemnation by the WTO, the US adopted a US Section 129 Review of the CVDs imposed, whereby it tried to implement the recommendations by the WTO Panel. A little later, the US adopted the first administrative review of CVDs on the same product which had entered the US market after the date of establishment of the original Panel. The US declared that the first assessment review was not a measure taken to comply. However, the Panel disagreed. The AB confirmed the Panel's approach, in light of the nexus between the Section 129 determination and the first assessment review (§§ 79ff. and especially § 90). In *US–Zeroing (EC) (Article 21.5–EC)*, the Panel held that it will review reviews of the original measure that had not been identified in the Panel request if they had been adopted in order to comply with the original recommendation, see §§ 8.127ff. See also § 77 of the AB report in *US–Softwood Lumber IV (Article 21.5–Canada)*. In *Japan–Apples (Article 21.5–US)*, the Panel decided to use the same experts as the original Panel who provided scientific expertise (§ 6.1) in order to address the new measures taken during the RPT before it.

[24] See §§ 8.21 ff.; see also *US–Upland Cotton (Article 21.5–Brazil)* at §§ 9.21ff. The Panel in *EC–Bananas III (Article 21.5–US)* refused to examine measures which had occurred after its establishment, since it could not establish a particular close relationship, § 6.5.

not only recommended, but even suggested a tariff only system for bananas that would enable the EU to bring its measures into compliance (§§ 6.156–157).

3.8 THE STANDARD OF REVIEW OF COMPLIANCE PANELS

Compliance Panels have to abide by the standard of review embedded in Art. 11 DSU.

3.9 COMPLIANCE PANEL REPORTS CAN BE APPEALED

A report by a compliance Panel can be appealed.

3.10 MORE THAN ONE COMPLIANCE PANELS IN THE SAME DISPUTE?

Practice reveals that a second compliance Panel can be effectively established in the context of the same original dispute: *Brazil–Aircraft (Article 21.5–Canada II)* is an appropriate illustration.[25]

4. COMPENSATION AND THE SUSPENSION OF CONCESSIONS

4.1 A PREFERENCE FOR COMPLIANCE (RETALIATION, ONLY IF NECESSARY)

Art. 22.1 DSU reads:

Compensation and the suspension of concessions or other obligations are temporary measures available in the event that the recommendations and rulings are not implemented within a reasonable period of time. However, neither compensation nor the suspension of concessions or other obligations is preferred to full implementation of a recommendation to bring a measure into conformity with the covered agreements. Compensation is voluntary and, if granted, shall be consistent with the covered agreements.

Art. 22.8 DSU underscores this point:

The suspension of concessions or other obligations shall be temporary and shall only be applied until such time as the measure found to be inconsistent with a covered agreement has been removed, or the Member that must implement recommendations or rulings provides a solution to the nullification or impairment

---

[25] See also *EC–Bananas III (Article 21.5–Ecuador II)*.

of benefits, or a mutually satisfactory solution is reached. In accordance with paragraph 6 of Article 21, the DSB shall continue to keep under surveillance the implementation of adopted recommendations or rulings, including those cases where compensation has been provided or concessions or other obligations have been suspended but the recommendations to bring a measure into conformity with the covered agreements have not been implemented.

The statutory preference is hence for compliance ("property rules"), compensation and suspension of other concessions ("liability rules") being temporary means until compliance has been achieved. The Arbitrators in *EC–Bananas III (Article 22.6–US)* held that the purpose of countermeasures is to induce compliance (§ 6.3):

> Accordingly, the authorization to suspend concessions or other obligations is a temporary measure pending full implementation by the Member concerned. We agree with the United States that this temporary nature indicates that it is the purpose of countermeasures to *induce compliance.* (emphasis in the original).

4.2 THE FORMS OF RETALIATION

Art. 22.1 DSU mentions three forms of retaliation until compliance is achieved: compensation, suspension of concession, and suspension of other obligations.

4.3 COMPENSATION

The form of compensation is not prejudged in the DSU. Compensation has been agreed only once: following the condemnation of US copyright practices in *US–Section 110(5) Copyright Act*, the EU and the US agreed to submit their dispute concerning the compensation to be paid to arbitration under Art. 25 DSU.[26]

4.4 SUSPENSION OF CONCESSIONS

Art. 22.2 DSU reads:

> If the Member concerned fails to bring the measure found to be inconsistent with a covered agreement into compliance therewith or otherwise comply with the recommendations and rulings within the reasonable period of time determined pursuant to paragraph 3 of Article 21, such Member shall, if so requested, and no later than the expiry of the reasonable period of time, enter into negotiations with any party having invoked the dispute settle-

---

[26] The Arbitrator orders the US to pay an annual sum over $1,000,000 to the EU on annual basis until compliance were achieved, see the discussion of the case in Grossman and Mavroidis (2007a).

ment procedures, with a view to developing mutually acceptable compensation. If no satisfactory compensation has been agreed within 20 days after the date of expiry of the reasonable period of time, any party having invoked the dispute settlement procedures may request authorization from the DSB to suspend the application to the Member concerned of concessions or other obligations under the covered agreements.

Suspension of concessions means suspension of tariff concessions. The WTO Member wishing to impose countermeasures will first have to draw a list of concessions to be suspended. It will have to respect two disciplines when doing so:

(a) it will have to follow the procedure included in Art. 22.3 DSU, whereby it will have first to seek suspension in the same sector(s) in which the violation occurred and, assuming it believes that such action is not practicable or effective, in a different sector covered by the same agreement or, eventually, in a different sector covered by another agreement (cross-retaliation).[27] Assuming the WTO Member decides to take action under a different sector (than that in which violation has been found), it will have to justify its decision to do so;

(b) It will also have to ensure that there is equivalence between the proposed suspension of concessions and the damage suffered as a result of the defendant's practices (Art. 22.4 DSU).

If an agreement can be found between the parties to the dispute, then the proposed list will be applied; if not the requesting WTO Member can request the establishment of an Arbitrator (usually, the members of the original Panel, and if this solution is impossible, it is the DG of the WTO who will appoint the missing Arbitrator(s)) that will decide on whether the two conditions mentioned above have been met (Art. 22.6 DSU).

4.4.1 The Conditions for Lawful Recourse to Cross-Retaliation

A "sector" is defined in the following terms in Art. 22.3 DSU:

with respect to goods, all goods;

with respect to services, a principal sector as identified in the current "Services Sectoral Classification List" which identifies such sectors;

with respect to trade-related intellectual property rights, each of the categories of intellectual property rights covered in Section 1,

---

[27] The Arbitrators on *US–Gambling (Article 22.6–US)* authorized Antigua to retaliate in TRIPs, against a violation that had occurred in the services context (§ 5.8). The Arbitrators took the view that, the difference in bargaining power across the two parties to the dispute, largely justified their choice to allow cross-retaliation (§ 4.114).

or Section 2, or Section 3, or Section 4, or Section 5, or Section 6, or Section 7 of Part II, or the obligations under Part III, or Part IV of the Agreement on TRIPS.

An "agreement" is, for the purposes of Art. 22.3 DSU, the GATT with respect to trade in goods, the GATS with respect to trade in services, and the TRIPS with respect to trade in intellectual property rights. WTO Members can request suspension of concessions in a different sector (and/or, eventually, agreement), only if it believes that suspending concessions in the same sector is not practicable or effective. Moving to suspension of concessions under a different agreement is referred to as "cross-retaliation". The question has arisen in practice whether the decision by a WTO Member to cross-retaliate should be justiciable, or, conversely, whether it should be the exclusive privilege of the WTO Member taking this decision. In *EC—Bananas III (Ecuador) (Article 22.6–EC)*, Ecuador requested authorization to suspend concessions under TRIPS, although the EU had refused to comply with its obligations under the GATT. Ecuador had clearly stated in its request that it wanted to suspend concessions only in the fields of GATS and TRIPS, justifying its choice in the following terms:

> The economic cost of withdrawal of concessions in the goods sector alone would have a greater impact on Ecuador than on the EC, and in proceeding in that way Ecuador would only succeed in further accentuating the imbalance in their trade relations, already seriously injured by the nullification and impairment of benefits for which the European Communities alone are responsible. This nullification or impairment of benefits amounts to over 50 per cent of all exports of goods by the EC to Ecuador. The great majority of these exports consist of capital goods and raw materials that are essential for the Ecuadorian economy.
>
> Since the withdrawal of concessions in the goods sector is at present not practicable or effective, and the circumstances are sufficiently serious to justify fully Ecuador exercising its rights under Article 22, Ecuador requests authorization to suspend concessions and other obligations under the GATS and TRIPS Agreements.
>
> For the reasons given above, Ecuador proposes to suspend concessions or obligations stemming from the trade-related intellectual property rights in the following categories set out in Part II of the TRIPS Agreement:
>
> > Section 1: Copyright and related rights, *Article 14: Protection of performers, producers of phonograms (sound recordings) and broadcasting organizations*

Section 3: Geographical indications

Section 4: Industrial designs

Ecuador also proposes to suspend concessions and obligations in the following subsector in its Schedule of specific commitments:

4. Distribution services

B. Wholesale trade services (CPC 622)

In addition, Ecuador reserves the right to suspend tariff concessions or other tariff obligations granted in the framework of the GATT 1994 in the event that these may be applied in a practicable and effective manner.

The suspension of concessions or other obligations will apply to the following EC member States: Austria, Belgium, Finland, France, Germany, Greece, Ireland, Italy, Luxembourg, Portugal, Spain, Sweden and the United Kingdom. (italics in the original).[28]

The Arbitrators, in *EC–Bananas III (Ecuador) (Article 22.6–EC)*, did not accept the list presented by Ecuador. In their view, they retained discretion to review it and amend it (§ 52, § 101, §§ 125–126, and §§ 167–170):

> It follows from the choice of the words "if that party considers" in subparagraphs (b) and (c) that these subparagraphs leave a certain margin of appreciation to the complaining party concerned in arriving at its conclusions in respect of an evaluation of certain factual elements, i.e. of the practicability and effectiveness of suspension within the same sector or under the same agreement and of the seriousness of circumstances. However, it equally follows from the choice of the words "in considering what concessions or other obligations to suspend, the complaining party shall apply the following principles and procedures" in the chapeau of Article 22.3 that such margin of appreciation by the complaining party concerned is subject to review by the Arbitrators. In our view, the margin of review by the Arbitrators implies the authority to broadly judge whether the complaining party in question has considered the necessary facts objectively and whether, on the basis of these facts, it could plausibly arrive at the conclusion that it was not practicable or effective to seek suspension within the same sector under the same agreements, or only under another agreement provided that the circumstances were serious enough.
>
> . . .

---

[28] WTO Doc. WT/DS27/52 of November 9, 1999.

In the light of the foregoing considerations, it is our view that the degree of practicability and effectiveness of suspension of concessions under the GATT may vary between different categories of products imported from the European Communities to Ecuador. We conclude that the European Communities has not established that suspension of concessions with respect to primary goods and investment goods is both practicable and effective for Ecuador in this case. However, with respect to consumer goods, we conclude that Ecuador has not followed the principles and procedures of Article 22.3 in considering that suspension of concessions on consumer goods is not practicable or effective for it in this case.

. . .

Ecuador submitted the statistics that display the inequality between Ecuador and the European Communities in support of its argumentation that circumstances are serious enough to justify suspension across agreements: Ecuador's population is 12 million, while the EC's population is 375 million. Ecuador's share of world merchandise trade is below 0.1 per cent, whereas the EC's world merchandise trade share is in the area of 20 per cent. In terms of world trade in services, the EC's share is 25 per cent, while no data are available for Ecuador because its share would be so small. The GDP at market prices in 1998 was US$20 billion for Ecuador and US$7,996 billion for the 15 EC member States. In 1998, the EC's GDP per capita is US$22,500, whereas per capita income is US$1,600 in the case of Ecuador.

In our view, these figures illustrate the considerable economic differences between a developing WTO Member and the world's largest trader. We believe that these differences confirm our considerations above that it may not be practicable or effective for Ecuador to suspend concessions or other obligations under the GATS or with respect to all product categories under the GATT. However, to some extent, the same rationale could hold true also for suspension of obligations under the TRIPS Agreement by a developing country Member in a situation involving a substantial degree of economic inequality between the parties concerned.

. . .

The counterfactual we have chosen is a global tariff quota equal to 2.553 million tonnes (subject to a 75 Euro per tonne tariff) and unlimited access for ACP bananas at a zero tariff (assuming the ACP tariff preference would be covered by a waiver). Since the current quota on tariff-free imports of traditional ACP bananas is in practice non-restraining, this counterfactual regime would have a similar impact on prices and quantities as the current EC regime. However, import licences would be allocated differently in order to remedy the GATS violations.

We calculated the effect on relevant Ecuadorian imports of the revised EC banana regime, compared with the counterfactual described in the previous paragraph, based on the assumption that the aggregate volume of EC banana imports is the same in the two scenarios. This implies that EC banana production and consumption, and the f.o.b., c.i.f., wholesale and retail prices of bananas, also are the same in the two scenarios. This in turn implies that the aggregate value of wholesale banana trade services after the f.o.b. point, and the aggregate value of banana import quota rents, are the same in the two scenarios. Both of those values are readily calculated from the price and quantity data made available to us. The only difference between the scenarios is in the shares of those aggregates that are enjoyed by Ecuador and other goods and service suppliers.

We assume the volume of Ecuador's banana exports to the EC would increase (at the expense of other suppliers) to the level of its best-ever exports during the past decade, that the share of those bananas distributed in the EC by Ecuadorian service suppliers would rise to 60 per cent, and that the proportion of those distributed bananas for which Ecuadorian service suppliers are given import licences would rise to 92 per cent (assuming that the remaining 8 per cent of the available import licences are those reserved for newcomers, consistent with the assumption used in the US/EC Bananas III arbitration).

Using the various data provided and our knowledge of the current quota allocation and what it would be under the WTO-consistent counterfactual chosen by us, we determine that the level of Ecuador's nullification and impairment is US$201.6 million per year.

In § 173, the Arbitrators indicated where suspension of concessions should take place:

> Consequently, and consistent with past practice in arbitration proceedings under Article 22, we suggest to Ecuador to submit another request to the DSB for authorization of suspension of concessions or other obligations consistent with our conclusions set out in the following paragraphs:
>
>> Ecuador may request, pursuant to paragraph 7 of Article 22, and obtain authorization by the DSB to suspend concessions or other obligations of a level not exceeding US$201.6 million per year which we have estimated to be equivalent within the meaning of Article 22.4 to the level of nullifica-

tion and impairment suffered by Ecuador as a result of the WTO-inconsistent aspects of the EC import regime for bananas.

Ecuador may request, pursuant to subparagraph (a) of Article 22.3, and obtain authorization by the DSB to suspend concessions or other obligations under the GATT concerning certain categories of goods in respect of which we have been persuaded that suspension of concessions is effective and practicable. Notwithstanding the requirement set forth in Article 22.7 that arbitrators "shall not examine the nature of the concessions or other obligations to be suspended", we note that in our view these categories of goods do not include investment goods or primary goods used as inputs in Ecuadorian manufacturing and processing industries, whereas these categories of goods do include goods destined for final consumption by end-consumers in Ecuador. In making its request for suspension of concessions with respect to certain product categories, we note that, consistent with past practice in arbitration proceedings under Article 22, Ecuador should submit to the DSB a list identifying the products with respect to which it intends to implement such suspension once it is authorized.

Ecuador may request, pursuant to subparagraph (a) of Article 22.3, and obtain authorization by the DSB to suspend commitments under the GATS with respect to "wholesale trade services" (CPC 622) in the principal sector of distribution services.

To the extent that suspension requested under the GATT and the GATS, in accordance with subparagraphs (b) and (c) above, is insufficient to reach the level of nullification and impairment indicated in subparagraph (a) of this paragraph, Ecuador may request, pursuant to subparagraph (c) of Article 22.3, and obtain authorization by the DSB to suspend its obligations under the TRIPS Agreement with respect to the following sectors of that Agreement:

> (i) Section 1: Copyright and related rights, Article 14 on "Protection of performers, producers of phonograms (sound recordings) and broadcasting organisations";
>
> (ii) Section 2: Geographical indications;
>
> (iii) Section 3: Industrial designs.

Furthermore, footnote 59 in the text reads:

> We would expect that a request by Ecuador under subparagraph (a) of Article 22.3 for suspension of concessions under the GATT with respect to the product categories just mentioned would be at least of the amount identified in paragraph 99 above.

§ 99 of the report to which footnote 59 refers, reads in pertinent form:

> We believe that the discrepancy between the statistics submitted by the parties concerning Ecuadorian imports of consumer goods of EC origin results, at least in part, from the different ways in which the parties categorise products into, e.g. consumer goods, primary goods or investment goods. We note that, according to Ecuador's own statistics, imports of consumer goods from the European Communities amount to at least US$60.8 million.

Hence Ecuador was authorized to impose countermeasures worth $60.8 million in the field of goods, and was free to choose between countermeasures in the area of services or TRIPS for the remaining part leading up to $201.6 million. The standard of review that the Arbitrators applied in *EC–Bananas III (Ecuador) (Article 22.6–EC)* was couched in the following terms (§ 50):

> the margin of review by the Arbitrators implies the authority to broadly judge whether the complaining party in question has considered the necessary facts objectively and whether, on the basis of these facts, it could plausibly arrive at the conclusion that it was not practicable or effective to seek suspension within the same sector.

In *US–Upland Cotton (Article 22.6–US)*, the Arbitrators held that they would be actively checking whether it was impractical or ineffective to suspend concessions in the same agreement before authorizing cross-retaliation (§§ 5.128ff.). The same report states that cross-retaliation is practicable if the proposed action is available (§ 5.73).

4.4.2 The Legal Constraint of Art. 22.4 DSU

Any time suspension of concessions is sought, WTO Members have to respect Art. 22.4 DSU which calls for equivalence between the proposed level of suspension of concessions and the level of nullification and impairment suffered by the injured party:

> The level of the suspension of concessions or other obligations authorized by the DSB shall be equivalent to the level of the nullification or impairment.

Recall that as briefly stated *supra*, in case of disagreement between the parties, recourse will be made to Arbitrators who will determine the level of concessions to be suspended (Art. 22.6 DSU).

<u>The Task of the Arbitrators</u>: Art. 22.7 DSU requests from the Arbitrators to ensure that the level of proposed countermeasures corresponds to the damage suffered by the party requesting authorization to adopt countermeasures. The Arbitrators in *US–Gambling (Article 22.6–US)* held that the benchmark to calculate the number can be provided by a counterfactual, whereby the author of the illegal act is presumed to have acted in a WTO-consistent manner (§§ 3.14ff.). The Arbitrators have consistently understood that their task is to come up with a number; in case of disagreement with the proposed list, they should reduce the requested amount of concessions to be suspended. In this vein, the Arbitrators in *EC–Bananas III (Ecuador) (Article 22.6–EC)*, stated (§§ 52ff.):

> [W]e note that, if we were to find the proposed amount . . . not to be equivalent, we would have to estimate the level of suspension we consider to be equivalent to the nullification or impairment suffered by Ecuador. This approach is consistent with Article 22.7 of the DSU which emphasizes the finality of the arbitrators' decision. . . .
>
> We recall that this approach was followed in the US/EC arbitration proceeding in EC—Bananas III and the arbitration proceedings in EC—Hormones, where the arbitrators did not consider the proposed amount of suspension as equivalent to the nullification or impairment suffered and recalculated that amount in order to be able to render a final decision."[29]

The Arbitrators cannot adjudicate to the requesting party more than what it has applied for since, in such case, they would be acting in violation of the maxim non ultra petita.

<u>Working Procedures</u>: An Annex in *US–Offset Act (Byrd Amendment) (Article 22.6–EC)* reflects the procedures followed by the Arbitrator (pp. 50–51):[30]

> The Arbitrator will follow the normal working procedures of the DSU where relevant and as adapted to the circumstances of the present proceedings, in accordance with the timetable it has adopted. In this regard,
>
> the Arbitrator will meet in closed session;
>
> the deliberations of the Arbitrator and the documents submitted to it shall be kept confidential. However, this is without prejudice to the parties' disclosure of statements of their own positions to the public, in accordance with Article 18.2 of the DSU;

---

[29] See also *Canada–Aircraft Credits and Guarantees (Article 22.6–Canada)*.

[30] This is a typical case, and similar procedures have been followed in other Art. 22.6 DSU cases.

at any substantive meeting with the parties, the Arbitrator will ask the United States to present orally its views first, followed by the party(ies) having requested authorization to suspend concessions or other obligations;

each party shall submit all factual evidence to the Arbitrator no later than in its written submission to the Arbitrator, except with respect to evidence necessary during the hearing or for answers to questions. Derogations to this procedure will be granted upon a showing of good cause, in which case the other party(ies) shall be accorded a period of time for comments, as appropriate;

the parties shall provide an electronic copy (on a computer format compatible with the Secretariat's programmes) together with the printed version (6 copies) of their submissions, including the methodology paper, on the due date. All these copies must be filed with the Dispute Settlement Registrar, [. . .]. Electronic copies may be sent by e-mail to [. . .]. Parties shall provide 6 copies and an electronic version of their oral statements during any meeting with the Arbitrator or no later than noon on the day following any such meeting.

except as otherwise indicated in the timetable, submissions should be provided at the latest by 5.00 p.m. on the due date so that there is a possibility to send them to the Arbitrator on that date. As is customary, distribution of submissions to the other party(ies) shall be made by the parties themselves;

if necessary, and at any time during the proceedings, the Arbitrator may put questions to any party to clarify any point that is unclear. Whenever appropriate, a right to comment on the responses will be granted to the other party(ies);

any material submitted shall be concise and limited to questions of relevance in this particular procedure.

Parties have the right to determine the composition of their own delegations. Delegations may include, as representatives of the government concerned, private counsel and advisers. Parties shall have responsibility for all members of their delegations and shall ensure that all members of their delegations act in accordance with the rules of the DSU and these Working Procedures, particularly in regard to confidentiality of the proceedings. Parties shall provide a list of the participants of their delegation prior to, or at the beginning of, any meeting with the Arbitrator.

to facilitate the maintenance of the record of the arbitration, and to maximize the clarity of submissions and other documents, in particular the references to exhibits submitted by parties, parties shall sequentially number their exhibits throughout the course of the arbitration.[31]

Third Parties: Art. 22.6 DSU makes no specific provision for third parties. In practice, requests have been rejected in some cases: e.g., *Brazil–Aircraft (Article 22.6–Brazil)*, §§ 2.4–6; *EC–Bananas III (Article 22.6–EC)*, § 2.8. Requests have been accepted in *EC–Hormones (Article 22.6–EC)*, and *EC–Hormones (US) (Article 22.6–EC)*, at § 7. Summing up prior practice in this respect, the Arbitrators in *US–Gambling (Article 22.6–US)* rejected the EU request to appear as third party stating that, in the absence of an explicit DSU provision to this effect, third party participation would largely depend on the agreement of the parties to the dispute; there was no agreement in this case (§ 2.31).

Allocation of the Burden of Proof: Summarizing past practice, the Arbitrators in their report on *US–1916 Act (EC) (Article 22.6–US)* discussed this issue as follows (§ 3.2):

> The burden of proof in Article 22.6 arbitrations, as in regular WTO dispute settlement, is by now well established. As stated by the arbitrators in *EC—Hormones (US) (Article 22.6—EC)*:
>
>> "WTO Members, as sovereign entities, can be *presumed* to act in conformity with their WTO obligations. A party claiming that a Member has acted *inconsistently* with WTO rules bears the burden of proving that inconsistency. The act at issue here is the US proposal to suspend concessions. The WTO rule in question is Article 22.4 prescribing that the level of suspension be equivalent to the level of nullification and impairment. The EC challenges the conformity of the US proposal with the said WTO rule. It is thus for the EC to prove that the US proposal is inconsistent with Article 22.4. Following well-established WTO jurisprudence, this means that it is for the EC to submit arguments and evidence sufficient to establish a *prima facie* case or presumption that the level of suspension proposed by the US is *not* equivalent to the level of nullification and impairment caused by the EC hormone ban. Once the EC has done so, however, it is for the US to submit arguments and evidence sufficient to rebut that presumption. Should all arguments and evidence remain in equipoise, the EC, as the party bearing the original burden of proof, would lose.
>
>> The same rules apply where the existence of a specific *fact* is alleged . . . It is for the party alleging the fact to prove its existence.

---

[31] In *US–Upland Cotton (Article 22.6–US)*, the Arbitration was suspended and then resumed (§§ 1.21–22).

The duty that rests on *all* parties to produce evidence and to collaborate in presenting evidence to the arbitrators—an issue to be distinguished from the question of who bears the burden of proof—is crucial in Article 22 arbitration proceedings. The EC is required to submit evidence showing that the proposal is *not* equivalent. However, at the same time and as soon as it can, the US is required to come forward with evidence explaining how it arrived at its proposal and showing why its proposal *is* equivalent to the trade impairment it has suffered . . . (emphasis and italics in the original).

A presumption is thus, established, that the proposed list has respected Art. 22.4 DSU which will hold true unless effectively challenged.[32] It is, consequently, for the original defendant to rebut the consistency of the proposed list with Art. 22 DSU: in case it is successful, the authorized level of suspensions will be lower than that requested; in case it does not, the authorized level will correspond to that requested.

Discovery Powers: Art. 22.6 DSU contains no language regarding discovery powers of the Arbitrators. This did not stop the Arbitrators in *US–Gambling (Article 22.6–US)* from requesting data from the IMF, and the Eastern Central Caribbean Bank (ECCB), in order to properly evaluate the claims before them (§ 2.32).

Duty to Cooperate / Drawing Inferences: In *US–Offset Act (Byrd Amendment) (EC) (Article 22.6–US)*, the Arbitrators requested factual information from the parties in dispute. With respect to elasticity of substitution, the Arbitrators drew inferences from the fact that the US did not submit the requested elasticities. As a result, the Arbitrators used in their model the values submitted by the requesting parties. In recognition of the fact that different aggregation methodologies existed, they decided to vary the elasticity values submitted by the requesting parties by 20%. Therefore, three different sets of simulations were performed: one using the submitted elasticities, and one each for values that are 20% lower and 20% higher than these elasticities.

Punitive Damages: In *EC–Bananas III (Ecuador) (Article 22.6–EC)* the Arbitrators held that the purpose of suspending concessions should be to induce compliance by the recalcitrant WTO Member. However, in their view, the quest for compliance-inducing mechanisms cannot lead to calculations that would neglect Art. 22.4 DSU. Punitive damages, for example, could induce compliance; in the Arbitrators' view, nonetheless, recourse to punitive damages was, by virtue of Art. 22.4 DSU, excluded (§ 6.3). In *Canada–Aircraft Credits and Guarantees (Article 22.6–Canada)* though, without stating that they were suggesting punitive damages, the Arbitrators revised their authorized level upwards by adding a 20% mark-up,

---

[32] See also § 2.8 in *Canada—Aircraft Credits and Guarantees (Article 22.6–Canada)*

because Canada had officially stated that it would maintain its subsidy programme irrespective of the Arbitrators' decision (§ 3.49):

> Recalling Canada's current position to maintain the subsidy at issue and having regard to the role of countermeasures in inducing compliance, we have decided to adjust the level of countermeasures calculated on the basis of the total amount of the subsidy by an amount which we deem reasonably meaningful to cause Canada to reconsider its current position to maintain the subsidy at issue in breach of its obligations. We consequently adjust the level of countermeasures by an amount corresponding to 20 per cent of the amount of the subsidy as calculated in Section III.E above, i.e.:
>
> US$206,497,305 x 20% (US$41,299,461) = US$247,796,766.

Retroactive Remedies: In the overwhelming majority of cases, Arbitrators have recommended prospective remedies, stating that the obligation to compensate kicks in from the point in time when the RPT expired. In *EC–Hormones (US) (Article 22.6–EC)*, for example, the Arbitrators held that the damage inflicted should be calculated from the end of the RPT (§ 38). Similar conclusions are to be found, for example, in *EC–Bananas III (Ecuador) (Article 22.6–EC)*, as well as in *Brazil–Aircraft (Article 22.6–Brazil)*. In *Australia–Automotive Leather II* however, the Panel reached the opposite conclusion:

> ... we do not believe that Article 19(1) of the DSU, even in conjunction with Article 3(7) of the DSU, requires the limitation of the specific remedy provided for in Article 4(7) of the SCM Agreement to purely prospective action.

So far, this remains an isolated case.

Indirect Benefits: In *EC–Bananas III (Ecuador) (Article 22.6–EC)*, the US had claimed that it should be compensated for lost profits; in its view, the EU, by blocking imports into its market of bananas originating in Mexico, was ipso facto blocking exports of US fertilizers to Mexico. The Arbitrators decided against the US claim in this respect: the EU could be held liable for trade in bananas lost by Mexican exporters, but not for trade in fertilizers lost by US exporters (§§ 6.12–14):

> We are of the view that the benchmark for the calculation of nullification or impairment of US trade flows should be losses in US exports of goods to the European Communities and losses by US service suppliers in services supply in or to the European Communities. However, we are of the opinion that losses of US exports in goods or services between the US and third countries do not constitute nullification or impairment of even *indirect* benefits accruing to the United States under the GATT or the GATS for which the European Communities could face suspension of

concessions. To the extent the US assessment of nullification or impairment includes lost US exports defined as US content incorporated in Latin American bananas (e.g. US fertilizer, pesticides and machinery shipped to *Latin America and US capital or management service*s used in banana cultivation), we do not consider such lost US exports for calculating nullification or impairment in the present arbitration proceeding between the European Communities and the United States.

As for goods used as inputs, this conclusion is also consistent with the rules of origin for goods. The WTO Agreement on Rules of Origin contains some disciplines, but otherwise leaves discretion to WTO Members to devise rules for the determination of the country of origin of goods during a transitional period until the work programme for the harmonization of non-preferential rules of origin is completed. WTO Members typically determine the origin of agricultural products based on the place of production. In principle, every banana has the origin of the country where it was grown. For purposes of WTO rules it is irrelevant whether goods or services (e.g. fertilizer, machinery, pesticides, capital and management services) used as intermediate inputs in the cultivation of bananas and their delivery up to the f.o.b. stage are of US origin even if US content should amount to a significant part of the end-product's value. Also under US rules of origin bananas grown in Puerto Rico or Hawaii are US products regardless of the percentage of foreign input incorporated in them or used for their cultivation. Our conclusion also reflects the fact that the requirements of Articles I and XIII of GATT are tied to the origin of goods.

It would be wrong to assume that there is no further recourse within the framework of the WTO dispute settlement system to claim compensation or to request authorization to suspend concessions equivalent to the level of the nullification or impairment caused with respect to bananas of Latin American origin, including incorporated inputs of whatever kind or origin. A right to seek redress for that amount of nullification or impairment does exist under the DSU for the WTO Members which are the countries of origin for these bananas, but not for the United States. In fact, a number of these WTO Members have been in the recent past, or are currently, in the process of exercising their rights under the DSU. Moreover, our concern with the protection of rights of other WTO Members is in conformity with public international law principles of sovereign equality of states and the non-interference with the rights of other states. Consequently, there is no right and no need under the DSU for one WTO Member to claim compensation or request authorization to suspend concessions for the nullification or impairment suffered by another WTO Member with respect to goods bearing the latter's origin or service suppliers owned or controlled by it. (emphasis in the original).

Only Value Added Matters: The Arbitrators in *EC–Bananas III (Ecuador) (Article 22.6–EC)* captured this point in §§ 6.18ff.:

> If we were to allow for such *"double-counting"* of the same nullification or impairment in arbitration proceedings under Article 22.6 of the DSU with different WTO Members, incompatibilities with the standard of "equivalence" as embodied in paragraphs 4 and 7 of Article 22 of the DSU could arise. Given that the same amount of nullification or impairment inflicted on one Member cannot simultaneously be inflicted on another, the authorizations to suspend concessions granted by the DSB to different WTO Members could exceed the overall amount of nullification or impairment caused by the Member that has failed to bring a WTO-inconsistent measure into compliance with WTO law. Moreover, such cumulative compensation or cumulative suspension of concessions by different WTO Members for the same amount of nullification or impairment would run counter to the general international law principle of proportionality of countermeasures.
>
> In view of the fact that initially five WTO Members participated in the original *Bananas III* dispute, the problem of *"double-counting"* nullification or impairment is more than a theoretical possibility. Despite the ambiguity in the wording of Article 22.6 of the DSU, we as Arbitrators in this arbitration proceeding involving only the United States do not exclude the possibility that other original complainants may request authorization from the DSB to suspend concessions towards the European Communities at a later point in time (assuming that the revised regime should prove to be WTO-inconsistent). Therefore, in addition to the need to preserve the rights of other WTO Members under Article 22.6 of the DSU, we also believe that the calculation of the level of nullification or impairment suffered by other original complainants in the *Bananas III* dispute is not within our terms of reference in this arbitration proceeding between the European Communities and the United States only.
>
> We consider that not only goods or service inputs in banana cultivation but also services that add value to bananas after harvesting up to the f.o.b. stage should be excluded from the calculation of nullification or impairment that the United States is entitled to claim in the present arbitration proceeding. We realize that the use of this f.o.b. cut-off point as well as of origin rules is

somewhat arbitrary. The globalization of the world economy means that products increasingly "incorporate" as intermediate inputs many goods and services of different origins. While it may be necessary to develop more sophisticated rules in this regard in the future, we believe that the line we have drawn is appropriate in this particular case, which involves the suspension of concessions. We imply no limitations on the extent of WTO obligations for this or other cases by this decision.

In response to the foregoing section B, which was contained in our Initial Decision, the United States argues that the export of packaging materials should be treated differently because such materials are not an input to banana production per se. However, in our view, to the extent that the packaging is part of the value of the exported bananas as of the f.o.b. stage, the reasoning set out above clearly applies. (italics and emphasis in the original).

Litigation Costs Are Not Recoverable: In *US–1916 Act (EC) (Article 22.6–US)*, the Arbitrators made it clear that legal fees paid cannot be recovered by the winning complainant (§ 5.76).

Calculating Suspension Following a GATS–Violation: In *EC–Bananas III (Ecuador) (Article 22.6–EC)*, the Arbitrators clarified that, for the purposes of estimating the damage from a violation of the GATS, the origin of the goods does not matter; what matters is the amount of trade lost by foreign distributors (§§ 6.25–26):

In our view, what matters for purposes of the calculation of nullification or impairment under the GATS, in light of the EC's commitments on "wholesale trade services", is that, according to the UN CPC descriptions quoted above, the *principal* services rendered by wholesalers relate to reselling merchandise, accompanied by a variety of related, *subordinated* services, such as, maintaining inventories of goods; physically assembling, sorting and grading goods in large lots; breaking bulk and redistribution in smaller lots; delivery services; refrigeration services; sales promotion services. We consider that this rather broad variety of *principal* and *subordinated* services should constitute the benchmark against which the United States could possibly claim nullification or impairment for losses in its actual or potential trade with the European Communities.

We would also emphasize that, according to Article XXVIII(b) of the GATS, the "supply of a service" (e.g. wholesaling) includes "the production, distribution, marketing, sale and delivery of a service". We also recall that, pursuant to Articles XXVIII(d,f,g,l,m,n) of the GATS, the origin of a service supplier is defined on the basis of its ownership and control. Therefore, for the calculation of nullification or impairment by reference to losses of actual or potential service supply, it does not matter whether the lost services relate to trade in bananas from the United States, or from third countries, to the European Communities, or to bananas wholesaled within the European Communities, provided that the service suppliers harmed are commercially present in the European Communities and US-owned or US-controlled. These considerations are subject to our conclusion above that it is the right of those WTO Members which are the countries of origin of bananas to claim nullification or impairment for actual or potential losses in the supply of service transactions that add value to bananas up to the f.o.b. stage, and that such claims cannot be made by the United States under Article 22.6 of the DSU.

Prohibited Subsidies: Art. 4.10 SCM reads:

> In the event the recommendation of the DSB is not followed within the time-period specified by the panel, which shall commence from the date of adoption of the panel's report or the AB's report, the DSB shall grant authorization to the complaining Member to take appropriate countermeasures, unless the DSB decides by consensus to reject the request.

Footnote 9 further explains the term appropriate:

> This expression is not meant to allow countermeasures that are disproportionate in light of the fact that the subsidies dealt with under these provisions are prohibited.

Note that Art. 4.10 SCM, contrary to Art. 22.4 DSU, does not use the term "equivalent", but instead the term "appropriate". In *EC–Bananas III (Ecuador) (Article 22.6–EC)*, the Arbitrators noted that the term "equivalent" captures a relation between the level of concessions to be suspended and the level of nullification and impairment (§ 6.5):

> However, we note that the ordinary meaning of *"appropriate"*, connoting "specially suitable, proper, fitting, attached or belonging to", suggests a certain degree of relation between the level of the proposed suspension and the level of nullification or impairment, where as we stated above, the ordinary meaning of *"equivalent"* implies a higher degree of correspondence, identity or stricter balance between the level of the proposed suspension and the level of nullification or impairment. Therefore, we conclude that the benchmark of equivalence reflects a stricter standard of review for Arbitrators acting pursuant to Article 22.7 of the WTO's DSU than the degree of scrutiny that the standard of *appropriateness*, as applied under the GATT of 1947 would have suggested. (emphasis in the original).

In *Brazil–Aircraft (Article 22.6–Brazil)*, the Arbitrators added that in the case of a prohibited subsidy, appropriate countermeasures should be calculated using as benchmark the amount of subsidy paid (§§ 3.54–3.60):

> Our interpretation of the scope of the term "appropriate countermeasures" in Article 4 of the SCM Agreement above shows that this would not be the case. Indeed, the level of countermeasures simply corresponds to the amount of subsidy which has to be withdrawn. Actually, given that export subsidies usually operate with a multiplying effect (a given amount allows a company to make a number of sales, thus gaining a foothold in a given market with the possibility to expand and gain market shares), we are of the view that a calculation based on the level of nullification or impairment would, as suggested by the calculation of Canada based on the harm caused to its industry, produce higher figures than one based exclusively on the amount of the subsidy. On the other hand, if the actual level of nullification or impairment is substantially lower than the subsidy, a countermeasure based on the actual level of nullification or impairment will have less or no inducement effect and the subsidizing country may not withdraw the measure at issue.

> Brazil also claimed that countermeasures based on the full amount of the subsidy would be highly punitive. We understand the term "punitive" within the meaning given to it in the Draft Articles. A countermeasure becomes punitive when it is not only intended to ensure that the State in breach of its obligations bring its conduct into conformity with its international obligations, but contains an additional dimension meant to sanction the action of that State. Since we do not find a calculation of the appropriate countermeasures based on the amount of the subsidy granted to be disproportionate, we conclude that, a fortiori, it cannot be punitive.

> We note that Brazil also claimed that Canada could not request the right to take countermeasures in the amount of the subsidy because it chose to take countermeasures in the form of suspension of concessions or other obligations and, pursuant to Article 22.4 of the DSU, such measures must be equivalent to the level of nullification or impairment.

> We read the provisions of Article 4.11 of the SCM Agreement as special or additional rules. In accordance with the reasoning of the AB in Guatemala—Cement, we must read the provisions of the DSU and the special or additional rules in the SCM Agreement so as to give meaning to all of them, except if there is a conflict or a difference. While we agree that in practice there may be situations where countermeasures equivalent to the level of nul-

lification of impairment will be appropriate, we recall that the concept of nullification or impairment is absent from Articles 3 and 4 of the SCM Agreement. In that framework, there is no legal obligation that countermeasures in the form of suspension of concessions or other obligations be equivalent to the level of nullification or impairment.

On the contrary, requiring that countermeasures in the form of suspension of concessions or other obligations be equivalent to the level of nullification or impairment would be contrary to the principle of effectiveness by significantly limiting the efficacy of countermeasures in the case of prohibited subsidies. Indeed, as shown in the present case, other countermeasures than suspension of concessions or obligations may not always be feasible because of their potential effects on other Members. This would be the case of a counter-subsidy granted in a sector where other Members than the parties compete with the products of the parties. In such a case, the Member taking the countermeasure may not be in a position to induce compliance.

We are mindful that our interpretation may, at a first glance, seem to cause some risk of disproportionality in case of multiple complainants. However, in such a case, the arbitrator could allocate the amount of appropriate countermeasures among the complainants in proportion to their trade in the product concerned. The "inducing" effect would most probably be very similar.

For the reasons set out above, we conclude that, when dealing with a prohibited export subsidy, an amount of countermeasures which corresponds to the total amount of the subsidy is "appropriate".

The same approach was followed in the Arbitrators' report on *US–FSC (Article 22.6–US)*. In this case however, the Arbitrators held that, had they followed an injury-test and linked the level of appropriate countermeasures to the level of injury suffered by the EU, they would have ended up with the same result anyway (§§ 5.56–57). This approach was abandoned in *US–Upland Cotton (Article 22.6–US)*: as stated in Chapter 15, the Arbitrators linked the level of appropriate countermeasures to the damage suffered by the complainant.

<u>Applying Suspended Concessions</u>: The DSU does not contain any provisions regarding the application of authorized suspension of concessions.[33] There is no obligation to notify the DSB of the application of authorized suspension of concessions. Practice shows that, on occasion, it has been requested, from the WTO Member authorized to suspend con-

---

[33] Malacrida (2008).

cessions, to notify the DSB of the final list that it will apply. We read, for example, from p. 4 of the WTO Doc. WT/DSB/M/59 (June 3, 1999), where a discussion took place on the US request to suspend concessions in the context of *EC–Bananas III*:

> The Chairman noted the statement made by the United States that the list of products subject to the suspension was in a press release and would be published in the Federal Register. Although the United States had referred to the requirements under Article 22.7 of the DSU, he noted that there was not much disagreement on this issue. He nevertheless asked the United States to circulate a copy of the press release containing the list of products at the end of the meeting.

On occasion, however, this has not happened: Mexico, for example, suspended concessions vis-à-vis the US following the Byrd Amendment-litigation, and never notified the WTO about it; the discussion before the DSB, nonetheless, leaves no doubt that Mexico had indeed suspended concessions: following authorization to suspend concessions (WTO Doc. WT/DSB/M/178 of January 17, 2005 at p. 16), Mexico decided to suspend concessions (Diario Oficial de la Federacion, August 17, 2005; WTO Docs. WT/DSB/M/194 of August 26, 2006 at p. 5; WT/DSB/M/196 of August 31, 2005 at p.6). Mexico modified the original suspension (Diario Oficial de la Federacion, September 13, 2006, and December 12, 2006), without notifying the DSB.

4.4.3 The Arbitrators' Decision: First and Last Resort

Art. 22.7 DSU pertinently provides that:

The parties shall accept the arbitrator's decision as final.

The Arbitrators in *EC–Bananas III (Ecuador) (Article 22.6–EC)* confirmed (§ 2.12) that Art. 22.7 DSU precludes the possibility to appeal the Arbitrators' award.

4.5 SUSPENSION OF OTHER OBLIGATIONS

In *Brazil–Aircraft (Article 22.6–Brazil)*, Brazil requested authorization to suspend concessions under the ILA, that is, it did not wish to suspend tariff concessions. The Arbitrators authorized it, provided that it would respect Art. 22.4 DSU (§ 4.1):

> For the reasons set out above, the Arbitrators decide that, in the matter *Brazil—Export Financing Programme for Aircraft*, the suspension by Canada of the application to Brazil of tariff concessions or other obligations under GATT 1994, the Agreement on Textiles and Clothing and the Agreement on Import Licensing Procedures covering trade in a maximum amount of C$344.2 million per year would constitute appropriate countermeasures

within the meaning of Article 4.10 of the SCM Agreement. (italics in the original).

As a result of a bilateral agreement reached, Brazil did not exercise this option. The question arose again during the proceedings in *US–AD Act 1916 (EC)*. Having secured a ruling that the US AD Act 1916 was WTO-inconsistent, and faced with non-compliance by the US during the RPT, the EU submitted to the US its proposal to adopt mirror legislation. In the absence of agreement with the US, the EU tabled the same request before the Arbitrators (under Art. 22.6 DSU) who were asked to pronounce on whether the proposed mirror legislation satisfied the requirements of Art. 22 DSU. The Arbitrators responded in the negative. In their view, the EU should be permitted to suspend concessions equivalent to the amount of nullification and impairment suffered each time the US AD Act 1916 was applied against EU economic operators. It was prohibited, however, from adopting mirror legislation since a similar measure would not be WTO-consistent because the equivalence between damage suffered and suspension of concessions could not be *ex ante* guaranteed and thus, Art. 22.4 DSU would have been violated as a result (*US–AD Act 1916 (Article 22.6–US)*, §§ 7.3–9).

5. MONITORING COMPLIANCE FOLLOWING RETALIATION

Art. 21.6 DSU reads:

The DSB shall keep under surveillance the implementation of adopted recommendations or rulings. The issue of implementation of the recommendations or rulings may be raised at the DSB by any Member at any time following their adoption. Unless the DSB decides otherwise, the issue of implementation of the recommendations or rulings shall be placed on the agenda of the DSB meeting after six months following the date of establishment of the reasonable period of time pursuant to paragraph 3 and shall remain on the DSB's agenda until the issue is resolved. At least 10 days prior to each such DSB meeting, the Member concerned shall provide the DSB with a status report in writing of its progress in the implementation of the recommendations or rulings.

The above-cited Art. 22.8 DSU underscores this point holding that retaliatory measures must be withdrawn when compliance has been achieved: assuming that there is agreement between complainant(s) and respondent that compliance has indeed occurred, the item will be removed from the agenda, and recourse to suspension of concessions will be terminated as well; assuming that there is agreement that no compliance has occurred, the complainant has the right to continue suspending the authorized concessions; problems might arise in case there is disagreement between the complainant and the defendant as to whether compliance has occurred.

Art. 22.8 DSU was interpreted for the first time in *Canada–Suspended Concession*.[34] It is worth recounting the facts as they were summarized in §§ 2.1–7 of the Panel report:

> On 13 February 1998, the DSB adopted the Panel and Appellate Body reports in *EC—Hormones*. In doing so, the DSB recommended that the European Communities bring the measures at issue into conformity with WTO rules. The Arbitrator appointed pursuant to Article 21.3(c) of the DSU determined that the European Communities should have a "reasonable period of time" until 13 May 1999 to comply with the recommendations. On 26 July 1999, Canada obtained from the DSB the authorization to suspend obligations up to the level of 11.3 million Canadian Dollars per year. The arbitrators acting pursuant to Article 22.6 of the DSU had previously determined this level to be equivalent to the level of nullification or impairment (Article 22.4 of the DSU) suffered by Canada at the time of its recourse to arbitration in May 1999. On 1 August 1999 and pursuant to the DSB's authorization, Canada introduced import duties in excess of bound rates to imports from the European Communities by imposing a 100% ad valorem rate of duty on a list of articles that are the products of certain EC Member States.

> The original measures in the *EC—Hormones (Canada)* dispute were provided in Directive 96/22/EC, which prohibited the administering to farm animals of substances having a thyrostatic action or substances having an oestrogenic, androgenic, or gestagenic action as well as the placing on market of meat from such animals. On 22 September 2003, the European Communities adopted Directive 2003/74/EC of the European Parliament and of the Council amending Council Directive 96/22/EC concerning the prohibition on the use in stockfarming of certain substances having a hormonal or thyrostatic action and of beta-agonists. The Directive was published and entered into force on 14 October 2003. It provides for a permanent prohibition on oestradiol–17ß and a provisional prohibition on testosterone, progesterone, trenbolone acetate, zeranol and melengestrol acetate.

> Prior to the adoption of the Directive 2003/74/EC, and in order to comply with the recommendations and rulings of the DSB and the covered agreements, the European Communities initiated and funded a number of specific scientific studies and research

---

[34] This is a parallel case to *US–Continued Suspension*.

projects for the purpose of conducting risk assessment(17 in total). The Scientific Committee on Veterinary Measures relating to Public Health (SCVPH), an independent experts committee established under EC legislation, reviewed the results of these studies and other publicly available information as well as the data it collected from various sources including CODEX/JECFA, and published its opinion entitled "Assessment of Potential Risks to Human Health from Hormones Residues in Bovine meat and Meat Products" ("the 1999 SCVPH Opinion") on 30 April 1999. The SCVPH subsequently reviewed this Opinion on two occasions and adopted review reports on 3 May 2000 ("the 2000 SCVPH Opinion") and on 10 April 2002 (the 2002 SCVPH Opinion). The SCVPH Opinions address six hormonal substances: oestradiol–17ß, testosterone, progesterone, trenbolone acetate, zeranol and melengestrol acetate.

In light of these Opinions, which the European Communities contends are risk assessments, the European Communities prohibited the placing on the market of meat and meat products from animals that have been treated with oestradiol–17ß for growth promotion purposes on the grounds that there was a substantial body of evidence showing that its residues are both carcinogenic and genotoxic. With respect to testosterone, progesterone, trenbolone acetate, zeranol and melengestrol acetate, the European Communities introduced the same measure on a provisional basis on the grounds that the available pertinent scientific information reflected in the above-mentioned SCVPH Opinions showed the existence of risks, but all the information and data necessary to conduct a more objective and complete risk assessment were insufficient or missing.

On 27 October 2003, the European Communities notified to the DSB the adoption, publication and entry into force of the Directive. In the same communication, the European Communities explained that it considers itself to have fully implemented the recommendations and rulings of the DSB in the *EC—Hormones* dispute and as a consequence, it considers the Canada's suspension of concessions vis-à-vis the European Communities to be no longer justified.

Canada disagreed in the DSB meeting held on 7 November 2003 that the new Directive was based on science and stated that it would not remove the retaliatory measures vis-à-vis the European Communities.

The measure challenged by the European Communities is the suspension of concessions and other obligations under the covered agreements, continued without recourse to the procedures under the DSU, after the European Communities' adoption of Directive 2003/74/EC on 22 September 2003 amending Council Directive 96/22/EC concerning the prohibition on the use in stock-farming of certain substances having a hormonal or thyrostatic action and of beta-agonists. The measure is provided in Canada's European Union Surtax Order and is enforced as of 1 August 1999. The EC's Directive was published and entered into force on 14 October 2003. The EC stated in its notification to the Dispute Settlement Body (DSB) that it has fully implemented the recommendations and rulings of the DSB in the dispute *European Communities—Measures Concerning Meat and Meat Products (Hormones)* (WT/DS48/AB/R, WT/DS48/R/CAN)." (italics in the original).

Canada disagreed with the EU when the latter argued that it had complied with its obligations. The Panel held that Canada was wrong (§§ 7.228–232):

> Indeed, the question before us in the context of Article 23.2(a) is not whether the European Communities has actually removed the measure found to be inconsistent, but whether it notified a measure which has not yet been subject to dispute settlement. As noted above, the European Communities notified a new piece of legislation and Canada itself recognizes that the measure is different and challenges its legality on different legal and factual grounds than it challenged the legality of the original measure for which it received an authorization to suspend concessions or other obligations from the DSB. Since this is a different measure, it is logical under Article 23 that Canada's prior authorization to suspend concessions or other obligation do not apply to this measure.

> Canada considers that the EC argument that a notification of a new measure is sufficient to invalidate the DSB authorization to suspend concessions, if accepted, would allow the simple adoption and notification by one Member of a "compliance measure" automatically to render WTO-inconsistent an otherwise WTO-consistent measure of another Member. Under such a regime, a Member against whom suspension of concessions has been authorized could buy itself considerable periods of relief through the announcement of a measure that barely differed from the one originally found to be inconsistent with its WTO obligations. This would clearly not contribute to the objectives of inducing prompt compliance and ensuring the security and predictability of the multilateral trading system.

> First, we believe that not only scam legislation, but also any other implementing measures could lead to recurrent litigations.

One could envisage that, in a complex case, a Member could notify in good faith an implementing measure which would be subsequently found not to fully comply with the original recommendations and ruling of the DSB. This Member would have to submit a revised measure which could, once again, be challenged and found to comply only partly with the covered agreements. Such repeated inconsistencies could have to do with the fact that, pursuant to Article 19.1 of the DSU, panels and the Appellate Body may only recommend that the Member concerned bring its legislation into conformity with the covered agreement(s) found to be breached, and may only make non-binding suggestions regarding ways in which the Member concerned could implement their recommendations. Since Members remain free to implement recommendations and rulings as they deem appropriate, differences in the interpretation of the recommendations of the DSB cannot be excluded, which can result in old inconsistencies remaining in the implementing measure or in new ones creeping into it.

Second, we recall that our findings are limited to the facts of this particular case. In this case, the European Communities has adopted Directive 2003/74/EC at the outcome of a lengthy and complex internal decision-making process. The Panel notes in this respect that the Commission proposal was submitted in 2000 and 2001 and that the procedure for the adoption of the Directive was the procedure provided for in Article 251 of the Treaty establishing the European Community. This procedure involved a number of steps, including an Opinion of the European Parliament (1 February 2001), a Common Position of the Council of the European Union (20 February 2003) and finally a Decision of the European Parliament (2 July 2003), a Decision of the Council of the European Union (22 July 2003) and an adoption by the European Parliament and the Council of the European Union on 22 September 2003. Without prejudice to the question whether Directive 2003/74/EC is actually based on the three opinions of the Scientific Committee on Veterinary Measures relating to Public Health (SCVPH) of 1999, 2000 and 2002 within the meaning of the SPS Agreement, the Panel notes that this Directive expressly refers to those opinions and that, as a result, they were part of the process that led to the adoption of the Directive. The Panel also notes the efforts of the European Communities to have the conformity of its measure reviewed under the DSU. Even if the EC implementing legislation were ultimately found not to comply with the SPS Agreement, the Panel considers that it shows all the signs of an implementing measure having gone through all the formal process required for its adoption and showing, on its face, all the signs of a measure adopted in good faith.

We therefore conclude that Canada made a "determination" within the meaning of Article 23.2(a) in relation to Directive 2003/74/EC.

The AB totally reversed the Panel in this respect. It held that concessions can be legitimately suspended until a multilateral finding has been secured pronouncing their inconsistency with the multilateral rules (§ 306). This is so because, in the AB's view, the simple removal of a WTO-inconsistent measure does not necessarily lead to implementation of multilateral rulings (§ 309). Consequently, the EU could not benefit from the good faith principle, as the Panel had argued (§ 315). The US and Canada could continue to suspend concessions until a new multilateral finding occurred that declared the defendant to have implemented the multilateral ruling (§ 384). The AB further recommended that the DSB requests from the parties to the dispute to initiate an Art. 21.5 DSU proceedings in order to resolve this dispute (§ 737).

QUESTIONS AND COMMENTS

Property vs. Liability Rules: Pascal Lamy, when he was EU Commissioner for Trade, that is, before he was appointed DG of the WTO, was quoted saying that, as long as a WTO Member is prepared to pay (that is, be subjected to suspension of concessions), it can lawfully continue to violate the WTO agreement (European Union Press and Communications Service, No 3036, May 23, 2000). Is this view consonant with Art. 22 DSU?

Cross–Retaliation: Robert Zoellick (ex-USTR), in a visit to Brazil, was confronted with a question regarding the possible US reaction in case Brazil were to impose lawful suspension of concessions under TRIPS (that is, cross-retaliate). Zoellick quickly pointed out that Brazil might be facing countermeasures itself in that case. The US could be removing some GSP benefits. We quote:

> There's always a danger in trade relations—these things start to slip out of control. You know, keep in mind, Brazil sells about two and a half million dollars under a special preference program to the United States, under the GSP. We have been working with Brazil because of the problems of intellectual property violations here, which could lead to their removal. It did in the case of Ukraine. So, I think it is dangerous for people to go down these paths because one retaliates, and all of the sudden you might find out that something else happens. We have felt—in the case of intellectual property rights—that Brazil is trying. We've decided to give time to work, to try. But, one decides to retaliate, well, who knows, maybe others will too. (Transcript of Joint Press Availability, Deputy Secretary of State, Robert B. Zoellick, and Brazilian Finance Minister Antonio Palocci, Ministry of Finance, Brasilia, Brazil, October 6, 2005).

In your view is Zoellick's reaction in line with US obligations under the WTO? In the same subject, do you agree with the award of the Arbitrators in *EC–Bananas III (Ecuador) (Article 22.6–EC)* that Ecuador should not be the sole judge when deciding the sector where it would withdraw concessions? Does it square with the wording of Art. 22.3 DSU?

Tradable Remedies: Bagwell et al. (2005) have defended the Mexican proposal, arguing that there is probably room for tradable remedies in the WTO: A complaining party that prevails in a WTO litigation should be in position to auction off its right to suspend concessions. In their extended model, the author of the illegal act could participate in the auction, and such participation reduces the scope for auction failure. Do you agree with their argument? Is there a downside?

Retroactive Remedies: Does Art. 19 DSU make them a legal impossibility in your view?

Compliance Panels: In light of the wording of the DSU, could it ever be the case that two compliance Panels be established in the context of the same dispute?

Sub-optimal Remedies: Ethier (2001) has advanced the following idea: in light of the uncertainty as to who will be defendant in eventual disputes, WTO partners agreed to provide for a compulsory third party adjudication (which will essentially decide on winners/losers) and, at the same time agreed to less stringent (than otherwise) remedies in case a violation has been established. In its view, such an understanding of the remedies-régime in the WTO is consistent with the incentives trading partners had at the moment when the WTO agreement (a largely incomplete and immune to ambiguity contract) entered into force. Do you agree with this view?

Claw-back Statutes: During the *US–1916 Act (EC)*, and *US–1916 Act (Japan)* litigation, in order to avoid long delays, Japan and the EU enacted *claw-back statues* (Japan: Law No 162 (2004), see also Department of International Trade and Commerce—Judicial Affairs, Commentary on Damage Recovery Law Pertaining to the Antidumping Act of 1916 in the US, vol. 32, no 12; the EU: Council Regulation (EC) No. 2238/2003 of December 15, 2003, OJ L 333/1 (December 20, 2003). This legislation authorized Japanese and EU parties against whom a US judgment had been rendered under the US 1916 Act to sue in Japan and the EU in order to recover their losses. Are these two claw-back statutes consistent with the WTO, in your view?

Implementation: The Panel report in *US–Softwood Lumber VI (Article 21.5–Canada)* held that, implementation could be achieved without addressing the various points raised by the Panel with respect to the consistency of the original measure with the WTO (§ 7.12): the US was found to be in violation of its obligations under the WTO and more, specifically, in violation of Art. 3.7 AD and 15.7 SCM (§ 7.5). The US was requested to implement the original Panel rulings. Under US procedures (Section 129), the competent authority re-visited its original determination. Without making any substantive changes, it simply re-focused the argument in the justification, and presented a new report as its implementing measure. Canada disagreed. It took the view that it is impossible to comply without introducing a new measure. The Panel disagreed with Canada (§ 8.1). To reach its final conclusion, the Panel accepted that the manner in which the US authority had now interpreted the same factual evidence was enough for a finding of implementation. The fact that Canada had presented alternative explanations about the data which, in the Panel's view, were reasonable, was not enough for the Panel to change its position on this issue (§§ 7.27, 7.50, 7.56). Do you agree with this Panel report?

Becker: Becker (1968) links enforcement to the welfare implications in case of enforcement (or non-enforcement): assuming certainty that violations will always be detected and pursued, tough punishments (e.g., "I will shoot you if you steal a chewing gum") are very close to guaranteeing enforcement of contractual obligations. However, such punishments go against some basic legal principles, such as the proportionality principle. More importantly, it is simply not the case that all violations of the WTO agreement are done abusively so: the WTO agreement is a sufficiently incomplete contract to make room for legitimate disagreements as to its precise scope. And it is not always the case that a solution provided by a WTO adjudicating body is the correct one: we run the risk of enforcing Type I errors. On credibility of threat, see also Schelling (1960). Where do you stand on this discussion?

Strong Adjudication, Weak Legislation: Barfield (2001) has argued that the internal flaw is between the WTO consensus-plagued inefficient rule-making procedures and its highly efficient dispute settlement system—an imbalance that creates pressure to "legislate" new rules through adjudication. Barfield goes on to suggest two ways out of this flaw: The Director-General should be given the prerogative to remove controversial or "political" disputes from the docket; additionally, a blocking minority of WTO Members should be entitled to overrule a decision by the WTO adjudicating bodies. The author thus supports strong enforcement of some but critically not all WTO obligations.

Efficient Breach of Contract: Schwarz and Sykes (2002) claim that the WTO remedies-system should provide victorious plaintiffs with expectation damages. By this, they mean to capture a situation which places the promisee in as good a position as it would have been if the promisor had performed. If the promisor is obliged to make the promisee no worse off than it would have been had the contract been fulfilled and can fulfill this obligation even while breaking the contract, then the resulting breach is efficient.

Prices and Sanctions: Cooter (1984) states that remedies could be prices or sanctions. Goal of sanction is to deter, goal of price is to allow the illegal behavior, when gains from activity outweigh losses (assuming a price has been paid). Where would you classify WTO remedies in Cooter's taxonomy?

Contingent Liberalization Commitments: From a more practical perspective, Lawrence (2003) has proposed the introduction of contingent liberalization commitments as a means to secure enforcement. We quote from p. 87:

> In this approach, WTO Members would be given the option of offering a preauthorizing compensation mechanism during the Doha round negotiations. These offers would be included in the multilateral negotiations. If a country's offer is accepted, in the event it is later found to have violated the agreement and failed to come into compliance, winning plaintiffs would be authorized to select an equivalent package of concessions from the defendant's commitments. Countries could choose from several options in making their CLCs. They could indicate a willingness to provide (selective) financial compensation, they could agree to provide across-the-board (most favoured nation) tariff cuts to generate additional trade equal to the value of the infraction, or they could agree to liberalize certain sectors on an MFN basis. Since the sectors to be covered would be negotiated, in the multilateral setting, countries specializing in particular exports (for example, textiles) could form alliances to ensure that products of interest to them would be included in the commitments of important trading partners.

INDEX

References are to Pages

A

AB Division, 380, 993–95, 1004
AB Secretariat, 993
AB Working Procedures, 991–98, 1001–03
Acceptance, 29–31, 41–2, 81–2, 127, 148, 365, 408, 481, 602, 619, 946
Accession of Greece to the European Communities, 144–45
Accession of Portugal and Spain to the European Communities, 145
Access to File, 399, 408
Access to Medicines, 824, 896–97
Accumulation Option, 781
Acquis, 35, 221, 651, 1005–06
Additional Commitment(s), 773–82, 790–93
Additional Duty(ies), 101, 332, 534, 558
Adequate Opportunity(ies), 262, 265, 540, 761–63, 925, 966
Adjustment Cost(s), 287
Administrative Review, 346, 367, 374–77, 485–89, 1031
Ad valorem, 83, 91–96, 102–03, 196, 229–31, 365, 457, 471, 482, 488, 505, 551, 558, 1054
Adverse Effects, 423–24, 439, 451, 456, 460, 467–68, 498, 501, 611, 638–40, 782
Adverse Inference, 401, 406, 496
Affirmative Waiver, 379
African, Caribbean and Pacific (ACP), 23, 44, 52, 100, 132, 148, 179, 745–49, 768, 788–90, 1014, 1037
African Growth and Opportunity Act (AGOA), 47, 135, 185–87
Aggregate Measurement of Support (AMS), 549, 554, 560–69
Agreement on Antidumping (AD), 331–421
Agreement between the EEC and Egypt, 147
Agreement Establishing the WTO, 1, 29, 42, 91, 103, 679
Agreement on Agriculture (AG), 33, 37, 72, 92, 94, 168, 436, 549–79, 707, 976, 992
Agreement on [Application of] Sanitary and Phyto–sanitary Measures (SPS), 37, 132, 595, 604, 612, 629–61, 973–75, 1057
Agreement on Government Procurement (GPA), 34, 40–41, 218, 675–88
Agreement on International Dolphin Conservation Program (AIDCP), 603, 611

Agreement on Rules of Origin (ROO), 37, 125–26, 132, 680, 1046
Agreement on Safeguards (SG), 503–48
Agreement on Subsidies and Countervailing Measures (SCM), 38, 423–501, 555–57
Agreement on Technical Barriers to Trade (TBT), 37, 593–627, 630
Agreement on Textiles and Clothing (ATC), 37, 522, 542, 581–92, 708, 971
Agreement on Trade–Related Aspects of Intellectual Property Rights (TRIPs), 33–38, 809–42, 893–901
Agreement on Trade–Related Investment Measures (TRIMs), 37, 661–73
Agricultural Chemicals, 869–71, 888–91
Agricultural Products, 95, 130, 550–59, 570–76, 650, 830, 888, 1046
Agricultural Subsidies, 560
Aid for Trade, 192–93
Aims and Effects, 233, 246, 748–50, 789
Aircraft Repair and Maintenance Services, 711
Air Transport Services, 38, 703, 709, 711, 773
All Others Rate, 371
All Relevant Factors, 465, 519, 529, 544–45, 972,
Amber Box, 549, 554, 561–63
Ambiguity, 659, 727, 1047, 1059
American Selling Price (ASP), 202
Amicus Curiae, 965
Annex on Air Transport Services, 38, 709, 711
Annex on Article II GATS Exemptions, 751
Annex on Financial Services, 710, 763
Annex on Negotiations on Maritime Transport Services, 38, 706, 752
Annex on Movement of Natural Persons Supplying Services under the Agreement, 38, 327, 731–32, 781
Annex on Telecommunications, 38, 721, 724
Anti–circumvention, 257, 348, 428, 433, 447, 574, 584, 964
Anti–counterfeiting Trade Agreement (ACTA), 810–12, 841, 921–23
Antidumping, 101–02, 331–421
Antidumping Committee (ADP Committee), 394, 417
Appellate Body (AB), 991–1008
Appropriate Countermeasures, 451–455, 1049–52

Appropriate Level of Protection, 611, 633, 635, 643–46, 659
Arbitrary or Unjustifiable Discrimination, 313, 629, 633, 648, 836,
Arbitration, 793–94, 931–33, 1009–14, 1021–26, 1033–54
ASEAN, 150, 162, 171, 176–78
Association of Industrial Producers of Leather, Leather Manufactures and Related Products (ADICMA), 271–77
Attendant Circumstances, 946–52, 1023

B

Balance of Payments (BOP), 36, 59, 69, 72–83, 241, 259, 267, 557, 678, 720, 743, 767–68, 777, 979
Balance of Payments Committee (WTO) (BOP Committee), 73, 969
Bananas Understanding, 956
Bangkok Agreement, 176, 180, 183–84
Barter Trade, 76
Base Period, 554, 559–74
Basic Agricultural Product, 562, 568
Basic Telecommunication, 38, 724–25, 769–71, 781
Berne Convention, 810, 812, 824–26, 830–35, 843–55
Best Information Available (BIA), 365, 392, 401–07, 481, 1020
Bilateral Investment Treaties (BITs), 670–72, 711–12
Blue Box, 549, 554, 561–62, 576
Bolar Exception, 882
Bona Fides, 385, 934
Budgetary Outlay, 555, 567–73
Built–in Compensation, 146, 802
Burden of Persuasion, 149, 613, 626, 979–80
Burden of Production, 652, 979
Business Confidential Information (BCI), 275, 399, 495, 1013
Byrd Amendment, 365, 372, 385–86, 426, 456–57, 983–85, 992, 1008, 1022–24, 1041, 1044, 1052

C

Cafe au Lait Group, 692, 701, 705, 722
Cairns Group, 553
Cancun Mid–Term Review, 670
Capacity Utilization, 353, 519
Cascade Tax, 220
Causality, 362, 373, 420, 465, 478, 523–29, 936, 1020
Causation, 66, 199, 353–54, 363–64, 392, 464–66, 472–83, 512, 520–28, 537–38, 950, 999
Central Product Classification (CPC), 707, 715–16, 745, 773–76, 788, 796–98, 1036, 1039, 1048
Central Registry of Notifications (CRN), 282

Certification, Modification and Rectification of Schedules, 99–101
Challenge Procedures, 684–87
Changed Circumstances Review, 374–75, 485–89
Chapeau, 285, 289–93, 311–16, 338–39, 399–400, 439, 458, 636, 804, 807, 876
Chapter V (ITO), 764–65
Clean Air Act (US), 304
Classification of/for Goods, 115, 774
Cobden–Chevalier, 131
Code of Good Practice, 615–17
Codex Alimentarius Commission, 600, 602, 633–34, 654–56
Collapsing, 347–48, 368
Commercial Presence, 722–24, 728–33, 780, 784, 799
Commitment Theory, 55, 816
Committee on Food Aid, (FAO) 577
Committee on Import Licensing, 200–01
Committee on Regional Trade Agreements (CRTA), 137, 139–49, 162 801–02, 968
Committee on Trade and Development (CTD), 13, 140, 162, 171, 190–93
Committee on Trade–Related Investment Measures, 669
Common Agricultural Policy (CAP), 551
Common Trust Fund, 191
Commonwealth, 152, 844
Compensation, 88–89, 103–13, 146, 372, 468, 504, 533–47, 566, 675, 685–86, 793–94, 802, 885, 899, 912–14, 1032–61
Competitive Safeguards, 769
Compliance Panel, 1026–32, 1059
Completing the Analysis, 999–1000
Compromise, 57, 403, 582, 592, 701–07, 837, 843, 848, 872
Compulsory Licensing, 851, 857, 865–87, 895–901
Computed Value, 202, 206
Computer Reservation System (CRS), 711
Concession Diversion, 121
Concession Erosion, 121, 257, 744, 825, 833
Conciliation, 201, 927, 984, 1014
Confidential Information, 200, 206, 275–77, 389, 398–401, 494–95, 545, 743, 888–93, 911, 916, 973, 1013
Confidentiality, 206, 942, 967–68, 1013–1042
Conformity Assessment, 593–601, 617–25
Consensus, 705–07
Consistency, 147–60, 646–49
Constructed Normal Value, 335–40, 398–99
Consular Taxes, 927
Consultation, 491–92, 941–43, 954–55, 1010, 1027
Consultative Group of 18 (CG 18), 213, 693–94
Consumption Abroad, 722–32
Contingent Protection, 78, 170, 332, 410, 420, 504–05, 543, 587, 683, 717, 970
Continued Dumping and Subsidies Offset Act (CDSOA), 372, 386, 426

Convention on Biological Diversity (CBD), 23, 27
Convention on International Trade in Endangered Species of Wild Fauna and Flora (CITES), 23, 287, 290, 304
Copyright, 843–55
Cost Insurance Freight (C.I.F.), 203, 559, 567, 1038
Cost–Oriented Rates, 770
Council for Trade in Goods (CTG), 6, 43, 105–14, 140, 264, 533, 666–73, 941, 993
Council for Trade in Services (CTS), 7, 43, 56, 140, 757–59, 778, 802
Counterfeiting, 810, 813, 858, 872, 918–23
Countervailing Duties (CVD), 101–02, 423–99
Covered Agreement, 39, 121, 280, 409, 541, 591, 613, 930–32, 953, 966–68, 982, 994, 1003, 1006–07, 1017–19, 1024, 1032–34, 1054, 1057
Critical Shortage, 68–70
Cross Border Supply, 722–42, 796–99
Cross–notification, 264, 282
Cross–retaliation, 687, 817, 1034–40, 1058
Cumulation, 358, 382–83, 563, 781–83
Currency, 76–83, 343, 376, 442, 446–47, 499, 785
Customary International Law, 650
Customs Classification, 92, 129
Customs Cooperation Council (CCC), 90, 556
Customs Union (CU), 121, 137–48
Customs Valuation, 96–97, 197–214

D

Data Exclusivity, 871, 889–91
Decision Concerning Article XXI of the General Agreement, 321, 326
Decision on Measures Concerning the Possible Negative Effects of the Reform Programme on Least Developed and Net Food Importing Developing Countries, 576–77
Decision on Texts Relating to Minimum Values and Imports by Sole Agents, Sole Distributors and Sole Concessionaires, 202
Declaration on the TRIPs Agreement and Public Health, 31, 811, 869, 896–98
Decoupled Income Payment, 551, 564–66, 579
Deductive Value, 203–06
Deemed Waiver, 379
De Facto Discrimination, 124, 626–27, 734, 746–49, 790, 832–33
De Facto Export Subsidies, 447–51
De Minimis, 228–29, 349–50, 359, 369, 382, 470–72, 488–90, 554–55, 562, 589, 919
De Novo Review, 403, 409, 412, 535, 683, 961, 970–72, 977, 981

Department of Commerce (DOC) (US), 377–80, 419, 442, 487–88, 961, 1001
Deputy Director General (DDG), 953, 1015, 1026
Designated Product, 559
Designated Representative (DR), 467
Destination principle, 219
Devaluation, 82, 193, 375–76, 398
Developing Countries, 165–97, 534, 576–77, 622, 654–55
Direct Effect, 578, 959
Directly Competitive or Substitutable (DCS), 225–32
Director–General, 7–8, 97, 99, 984, 986, 1010, 1014–14, 1021, 1060
Disciplines on Domestic Regulation in the Accountancy Sector, 761
Discovery Powers, 973–75, 1001, 1013, 1044
Discretionary Legislation, 959–61
Dispute Settlement Body, 38, 168, 903, 1017, 1056
Dispute Settlement Understanding, 6, 38–39, 930–39
Dissenting Opinion, 346, 575, 982–3, 1004
Doha Development Agenda (DDA), 191
Doha Round 4, 31, 89, 97–98, 132, 192, 213–14, 367, 373, 561, 670, 672, 675, 679, 683, 777, 1061
Domestic Regulation, 759–62, 787
Domestic Subsidies, 560–69
Double Jumping, 135
Double Remedies, 426–27
Double Taxation, 431–32, 673, 804
Drug Arrangements, 127–28, 187–89
Dual Retail System, 241, 301–02
Dual Rule Approach, 133
Due Allowance, 342–44
Due Process, 398–401, 493–95, 978
Dumping, 334–49
Dumping Margin, 344–46
Dunkel, 7, 692–96, 702, 705,
Dunkel Draft, 723
Duty to Cooperate, 344, 401–07, 495–96, 963, 974, 1001, 1044
Dynamic Use Constraint, 533

E

Effective Refutation, 980
Effects Doctrine, 81, 307
Enabling Clause, 138–40, 162–74, 187–94
Enhanced Integrated Framework (EIF), 192
Enhanced Third Party Rights, 964–65
Enquiry Point, 604, 614, 625, 643, 717
Entrustment or Direction, 433–34
Environmental Protection Agency (EPA), 304
Equipoise, 980, 1043
Equitable Share, 311, 550, 569
Equivalent Measurement of Support (EMS), 568
Escape Clause, 504

Essential Facts, 407–08, 494
Estoppel, 956–59
European Economic Area (EEA), 156, 689
European Free Trade Association (EFTA), 24, 155–57
Eurostat, 716
Everything But Arms (EBA), 134, 174, 179, 185
Ex Factory, 343
Exhaustible Natural Resource, 69, 79, 213, 292, 303–08, 317
Expedited Review, 371, 483
Expert Advice, 930, 974, 987–88
Explanatory Note (HS), 116, 270, 600, 617
Export Credit, 42, 446–47, 574–75
Export Performance, 447–49, 473, 478, 570, 663–64
Export Price, 62–67, 78, 81, 331–408
External Requirement, 139–46, 801
Export Subsidies, 447–51, 569–76
Extra Hurdle, 831, 960
Ex–Works Price, 134

F

Fair Use, 843, 851, 867,
Fall–Back Method, 201, 206
Final Determination, 269, 354, 364–67, 380, 407–08, 482–96, 911
Fire Blight, 631, 659
Fiscal Monopolies, 259
Food and Agriculture Organization (FAO), 24, 52, 309, 574, 578, 602, 839
Food Security, 549, 566, 577, 888
Foreign Direct Investment (FDI), 161, 221, 671–72
Foreign Exchange Contract (FOREX), 208
Foreign Sales Corporations (FSC), 430, 437, 453
Framework Agreement, 100, 712
Framework Group, 212
Freedom of Information Act (FOIA), 986
Free on Board (F.O.B), 203, 567, 665, 1038, 1046–49
Free Trade Area (FTA), 137–62, 171–73, 184, 196, 506–07, 624, 801
Free Trade Area Between Canada and the US (CUSFTA), 142
Friendship, Commerce, and Navigation (FCN), 88, 689
Full Commitment, 779, 799

G

Gas Guzzler, 233, 246
GATS Rules Working Party, 679
GATT Acquis, 35, 221, 1005
GATT Secretariat, 62, 213, 216, 323, 692–727
General Agreement on Tariffs and Trade (GATT), 1–6, 925–939
General Exceptions, 285–317, 803–07
General Infrastructure, 432

Generalized System of Preferences (GSP), 167–96, 901, 1058
Generally Accepted Accounting Principles (GAAP), 206, 337
General Obligation (GATS), 716–21, 743–71, 907–10
General or Local Short Supply, 311
Generic Drugs 893–94
Genetically Modified Organism (GMO), 631, 650
Geneva, 3–4, 115, 136, 703
Genuine and Substantial Relationship, 363, 526–27
Geographical Indications, 809, 815, 823, 840, 1036, 1039
Gulf Cooperation Council (GCC), 157, 162, 173
Good Cause, 202, 399–401, 495, 539, 1042
Good Faith, 385, 404, 471, 493, 929, 934, 957–58, 975, 1057–58
Good Offices, 12, 984, 1009, 1014
Government Procurement Agreement (GPA), 973–88
Graduation, 168–69, 230
Grandfathering, 34, 131
Granger Causality, 420
Great Depression, 1, 60, 87
Green Box, 549, 554, 561–67, 576–79
Gross Domestic Product (GDP), 69, 1037
Gross National Product (GNP), 161
Group of Negotiations on Goods (GNG), 702
Group of Negotiations on Services (GNS), 701–16, 752

H

Harmonization, 37, 593, 616, 632, 658, 818–19, 855, 877–78, 1046
Harmonized Formula, 97
Harmonized System (HS), 10, 45–46, 72, 87, 90–93, 221–22
Havana Charter, 2, 138, 224, 309, 672–73, 676
Havana Conference, 136, 220, 224
Head–counting, 27
Headnote, 684–85, 745, 777, 788
Headquarters Agreement, 6, 8
Historic Market Share, 80, 531
HIV/AIDS, 835, 895–96, 900
Horizontal Commitment, 780
HS Committee, 92–93, 116
Hull, Cordell, 3, 122, 135–36
Human, Animal, or Plant Life or Health, 293–99
Human Health, 5, 239, 286, 594, 612, 620, 633, 638, 640, 658, 875, 888, 1055
Hurricane Licence, 745, 749–50

I

Illegal Gambling Act (IGBA), 786, 807
Immediate Context, 799

Immediately and Unconditionally, 126–31, 680, 746, 750
Impediment, 2, 381, 404, 459–60, 765, 813, 931
Implementation Period, 553–54, 560, 574, 576, 932, 1011, 1023, 1028
Imperial Preferences, 2, 34, 122, 131, 135–36
Import Licensing Agreement (ILA), 38, 66, 197–201, 1052
Import Surge, 517, 586, 589,
Incomplete Contract, 1008, 1060
Increased Quantities, 503, 507, 510–16, 537, 541, 588
Independent Entity, 211
Indirect Benefits, 1045
Infant Industry, 69, 73, 77–78, 349, 362
Inference, 203, 350, 361, 401, 406, 411, 434, 496, 853, 966, 975, 1044
Informal Group of Experts (IGE), 482–83
Information Technology (IT), 90
Information Technology Agreement (ITA), 92, 98
Initiation, 364, 368, 370, 377, 380–81, 386–403, 484–93, 529, 537, 539, 543, 545, 577, 682, 943
Inspection, 96–97, 197–214, 563, 617–19, 631, 647, 653, 830
Institutional Balance, 74, 968–69, 986
Integrated Circuits, 809, 823–27
Integrated Database (IDB), 283
Integrated Framework (IF), 13, 40, 53, 192
Intellectual Property in Respect of Integrated Circuits (IPIC) Treaty, 825–34
Interconnection, 117, 724, 766, 770, 791
Interested Parties, 168, 203, 344, 371, 381, 393, 399–408, 434, 471, 483, 486, 493–96, 543–46, 614–16, 643, 687, 822, 942, 971
Intergovernmental Commodity Agreement, 308–10
Interim Review, 274, 953, 966–67, 978, 980–81
Internal Requirement, 139–43, 801
International Bovine Meat Agreement (IBM), 40–41
International Chamber of Commerce (ICC), 52, 211
International Civil Aviation Organization (ICAO), 690, 715
International Cocoa Organization (ICCO), 308
International Coffee Organization (ICO), 308
International Commodity Agreement (ICA), 308, 310
International Convention for the Abolition of Import and Export Prohibitions and Restrictions (World Economic Conference of 1927), 316
International Copper Study Group (ICSG), 308
International Cotton Advisory Committee (ICAC), 308

International Court of Justice (ICJ), 324, 697, 932
International Dairy Agreement, 40–41
International Federation of Inspection Agencies (IFIA), 52, 209–11
International Grains Council (IGC), 24, 308
International Jute Study Group (IJSG), 308
International Law Commission (ILC), 453
International Lead and Zinc Study Group (ILZSG), 308
International Maritime Organization (IMO), 690
International Monetary Fund (IMF), 2, 6, 24, 51–52, 74–83, 192, 678, 690–93, 767–68, 839, 1044
International Nickel Study Group (INSG), 308
International Office of Epozootics, 633
International Olive Oil Council (IOOC), 308
International Organization for Standardization (ISO), 24, 53, 600
International Rubber Study Group (IRSG), 308
International Standard, 593, 598, 600–04, 611, 616, 624–35, 641, 651–52, 657, 862, 978
International Study Groups (ISG), 308
International Sugar Organization (ISO), 308
International Telecommunications Union (ITU), 52, 690
International Textiles and Clothing Bureau (ITCB), 582
International Trade Centre (ITC), 24, 191–92, 678
International Trade Commission (US ITC), 382, 410–11, 419, 497, 523, 530, 539, 541, 581, 977
International Trade Organization (ITO), 2–5, 75, 141, 232, 245, 672–76, 764, 925
International Tribunal of the Law of the Sea (ITLOS), 650
International Tropical Timber Organization (ITTO), 308
Internet Gambling, 736–37, 742, 786, 794
Interstate Horseracing Act (IHA), 807
Investigating Authority (IA), 331, 339, 342, 350, 354, 360–61, 365, 373, 380–416, 424, 433, 439, 442, 473–504, 512, 527–29, 541, 544, 961, 971, 977
Investment, 663–73
Invisibles, 694
Invoice Price, 201, 203, 208

J

Jenkins Bill, 583
Joint Integrated Technical Assistance Programme (JITAP), 192
Judicial Economy, 94, 199, 260, 660, 668–69, 969–70, 976, 999, 1004–05

K

Kemp–Wan, 161
Kennedy Round, 4, 97, 105, 166, 169, 333, 938
Known Factors, 362–63, 466, 478–79
Korean Unfair Competition Act, 301–02

L

Last Mile, 765
Laws, Regulations, and Decisions of General Application, 268–69
Least Developed Countries (LDC), 11–14, 46, 115, 134–35, 168–69, 174–95, 471, 550–77, 666–67, 691–703, 808, 810, 819–21, 840, 869, 893–99, 984
Legal Affairs Division (WTO), 8, 930
Legal Interest, 276–77, 882, 963, 1028
Legal Personality, 6, 51
Legitimate Expectations, 92–93, 937, 1005
Lesser Duty Rule, 364–65, 373–74, 482
Less Than Fair Value (LTFV), 527
Leutwiler Report, 505
Lex specialis, 218, 637, 668
Licensing, 197–213, 865–66, 884–88
Likelihood, 238, 254, 278–79, 359, 378–91, 474, 490, 518–21, 576, 639–40, 649, 658, 854, 862, 912
Like Product, 129, 232–40, 355–58, 516–23, 604–07
Like Service, 744–46, 766, 770, 788–90
Like Services Supplier, 710, 744–49, 770, 788–90
Limited Tendering Procedures, 681
Linear Reduction, 97
Liquid Crystal Display (LCD), 273–74
Listed Exemptions, 751–59, 768
Litigation Costs, 1048
Local Content 134, 218, 223, 423, 443, 446, 500, 556, 663–65
Logistics Performance Index (LPI), 214
London Conference, 72, 136
Lomé Convention, 44, 148, 310

M

Mandatory Legislation, 960–61
Marine Mammal Protection Act (US), 286
Maritime Transport, 703, 706–07, 712, 752, 755, 791
Market Access, 773–87
Market Disruption, 537–42, 582
Marketing Board, 258–59, 570
Market Share, 80, 107–08, 243–44, 353, 360, 442, 452–64, 473, 531–32, 542, 587, 626, 1050
Marshall–Lerner Condition, 82, 193
Material Injury, 333, 349, 358–62, 407, 411, 446, 470, 474–75, 483, 516, 537–39

Material Retardation, 349, 362, 370
Measure Affecting Trade in Services, 734–37, 788
Mediation, 1009, 1014–15
Memorandum of Understanding (MOU), 51–53, 64–65
Mercosur, 162, 173, 312–13, 419, 506, 836, 957–58
METI (Ministry of Economy, Trade and Industry), 64
Mid–Term Review (MTR), 670, 679, 712
Minimum Access Opportunities, 560
Minimum Customs Value, 202
Minimum Import Price, 62–63, 128, 554–58, 569
Ministerial Conference, 6, 8, 14, 19–31, 43, 49, 98, 190–91, 207, 578, 667, 670, 69, 692, 716, 928, 991
MITI (Ministry of International Trade and Industry), 64
Mixing Requirement, 218
Mode 1, 722–28, 732, 741–45, 787, 799
Mode 2, 722, 726–28, 732
Mode 3, 722, 728–29, 733, 745, 799
Mode 4, 722, 730–33, 745, 802
Model Bilateral Agreement on Mutual Administrative Assistance in Customs Matters, 207
Mode of Supply, 724–26, 744, 773, 777, 780, 788, 802
Modification, 99–112, 242, 309, 547, 681, 757–58, 793–94, 802, 845, 991, 1025
Montreal Ministerial Declaration, 712, 716
Moral Rights, 843–45, 855
Most Favored Nation (MFN), 121–35, 833–36
Multi–Fibre Agreement (MFA), 581–92, 694
Multilateral Trade Negotiations (MTN), 4, 97–98, 145, 213, 583, 697–701
Multiple Complaints, 984–85
Mutually Agreed Solution (MAS), 100, 466, 492, 588, 887, 934, 943, 953, 955–56, 995
Mutual Recognition Agreement (MRA), 621–23, 653–54, 761–62

N

National Security, 319–29
National Treasure, 79, 285, 303
National Treatment (NT), 215–49
Natural Disaster, 168, 311, 566
Necessity, 611–12, 644–46
Negative Consensus, 32, 467, 929–30, 939, 983, 1005
Negative Integration, 286
Negotiating Group on Maritime Transport Services (NGTMS), 752
Neighboring Rights, 826, 843–45, 849
Netting Back, 343
New Shipper, 346, 369–71
New Commitment, 782
No Commitment, 574, 715, 744, 779, 791

No Commitment Technically Feasible, 779
Non Adimpleti Contractus, 115
Non–Application, 48–51
Non–Attribution, 362, 465, 469, 472, 474, 478–80, 524–25, 539
Non–Factor Service, 703
Non–Governmental Organization (NGO), 25, 762, 841, 855, 966, 994, 997
Non–Market Economies (NME), 340–41
Non Ultra Petita, 969, 1041
Normal Value (NV), 331–46, 365–69, 387–89, 397–403, 408, 1020
North American Free Trade Area (NAFTA), 135, 141, 149, 160–61, 300–01, 506, 672, 836, 985
Notice of Appeal, 991–1003
Non–Tariff Barrier (NTB), 4, 170, 593–94, 815

O

Objective Examination, 44, 350, 395–98, 424, 470–71, 493, 950, 1020
Obligation of Result, 378, 408, 760, 762
Obligation of Specific Conduct, 760
Observer, 8, 19–26, 77, 193, 577–78, 671, 678, 741, 839, 998
Office International des Epizooties (OIE), 52, 656
Offshoring, 133–34, 419
Open Tendering Procedures, 681
Operator Category Rules, 748–49, 789
Oral Hearing, 304, 351, 996, 998, 1001–03
Orderly Market Arrangement (OMA), 506
Ordinary Course of Trade, 96, 334–39, 406–07
Organization for Economic Cooperation and Development (OECD), 24, 53, 135, 169, 214, 220, 554, 561, 567, 620, 626, 670–71, 675, 678, 683, 690–91, 694, 703, 714, 839, 943
OECD Trade Committee, 694
Other Restrictive Regulations of Commerce, 142–43
Ottoman Empire, 136
Outsourcing, 133

P

Panel Proceedings, 945–89
Paragraph Six Solution, 898–901
Parallel Importation, 837, 895–97
Paris Convention, 810–12, 824–28, 835, 857–74, 884, 891–93, 960
Part IV, 166, 321, 497, 568, 573, 810, 1035
Particular Market Situation, 334–36, 464, 736
Passive Observer, 741, 998
Pass Through, 252, 437–39, 500–01, 1008
Patents, 870–901
Payments and Transfers, 719, 743–44, 767, 777
Percentage Criterion, 126

Period of Application, 199, 484, 529
Period of Investigation (POI), 393–98, 543–44
Permanent Group of Experts (PGE), 451, 498
Permissible Interpretation, 409, 414–15
Pharmaceuticals, 865, 869–79, 882, 887–901
Plurilateral Trade Agreement, 5–12, 31, 39–54, 821
POI Recommendation, 394–97
Positive Consensus, 929
Positive Evidence, 349–50, 376–81, 395–98, 424, 459, 470–74, 493, 950
Precautionary Principle, 629, 636, 650–52
Predatory Pricing, 333
Preferential Rules of Origin, 126, 134, 1046
Preferential Trade Agreement (PTA), 137–63
Preliminary Question, 304, 953, 967
Preliminary Ruling, 948, 953
Pre–shipment Inspection, 195–214
Prevailing Market Conditions, 439–40, 1001
Prevention of Deceptive Practices, 594, 612, 620, 624, 812
Price Discrimination, 418, 765
Price Suppression, 352–53, 363, 458–66, 473, 479–80
Price Undercutting, 352, 458–62, 477
Price Undertaking, 170, 363, 365–66, 408, 481–82
Prima Facie, 5, 81, 116, 131, 149, 231, 273, 298–99, 354, 418, 627, 805–06, 916, 933, 974, 979–80, 997, 1007–13
Primarily Aimed, 306
Primarily Concerned, 112
Principal Supplying Interest (PSI), 104–11, 534
Prison Labor, 285, 292, 303
Private Investor–Test, 436
Privatization, 40, 437–38, 486–88, 500, 671, 764, 1018
Process and Production Method (PPM), 287, 593
Producer Subsidy Equivalent (PSE), 554, 561
Production Flexibility Contract (PFC), 554, 565
Productivity, 134, 193–95, 353, 360–62, 473, 478, 519, 577, 690, 814
Profits, 134, 241, 261, 319, 337–43, 353, 360, 399, 407, 420–21, 473, 519, 807, 814, 837, 1045
Prohibited Subsidies, 445–56
Prospective Assessment, 366
Prospective Remedies, 1045
Protect IP Act (PIPA), 841
Protective Application, 229–31, 316
Protocol of Accession, 9, 11, 34, 62, 289, 538, 551, 688
Provisional Duties, 364–67, 483–84
Provisional Measures, 363–68, 480–84, 529, 540
Provisional Safeguards, 529

Public Body, 423, 427–35
Public Health, 893–901
Public Hearing, 540, 967
Public Morals, 59, 79, 286, 292–93, 803–05
Public Notice, 71, 376, 391, 399, 408, 540–45
Public Order, 207, 255, 278, 292, 803–08, 858, 876, 918
Publication, 200, 207, 211, 267–80, 377, 418, 545–48, 599, 615, 626, 667, 717, 791, 827, 849, 868, 937, 1026, 1055
Punitive Damages, 452–55, 1044
Punta del Este, 692–705, 714, 813

Q

Quantitative Restriction (QR), 59–85, 102, 106–07, 109, 174, 263, 435, 505, 532, 548–541, 558, 584, 588, 785, 975
Quorum, 26–9
Quota Modulation, 530–32

R

Ratification, 4, 316, 683, 811, 899, 922
Rational Connection, 306, 637,
Reasonableness, 279, 383, 467, 885, 1023
Reasonable Period of Time (RPT), 1021–26
Reasonably Available 291, 296–302, 387, 390, 398, 491, 612, 644–45, 805–06
Reciprocal Trade Agreements Act (RTAA), 2
Reference Period, 80, 512, 566–68, 586
Refund, 272, 275, 366–68, 416–17, 447, 483, 572, 1019
Regional Cumulation, 135
Regional Trade Agreement (RTA), 39, 137, 899
Regulatory Cooperation Forum, 624
Regulatory Cooperation Roadmap, 624
Reimbursement, 416
Remand Authority, 987, 999
Rental Rights, 847–48
Replacement Option, 781
Report of the Working Party on the Accession of China, 537–42
Request–Offer, 97
Research and Development (R&D), 468, 684–85, 890, 895
Residual Rate, 370–71
Res Judicata, 955
Restrictive Business Practice (RBP), 764–65
Restrictive Regulations of Commerce, 142–43
Retaliation, 1032–61
Retroactive Remedies, 417, 1045, 1059
Retrospective Assessment, 366–68
Review Session, 311, 340, 446
Revocation, 124, 375, 378, 391, 810, 880, 884, 1018–20
Ricardo, David, 55, 134

Risk Assessment, 208, 631, 635–46, 646, 650, 653, 660, 1055
Risk Management, 643
Roll–Call, 27, 320
Rome Convention, 810, 824–50
Rules of Conduct, 986
Rules of Origin, 37, 125–26, 132–35, 144, 179, 182, 195, 680, 1046
Rules of Procedure for Sessions of the Ministerial Conference and the General Council, 25–28

S

SCM Agreement, 223, 267, 317, 352–56, 366, 375–78, 385, 401, 410, 414, 423–500, 517–24, 543, 550, 555–57, 569, 576, 669, 948, 976, 1000–01, 1020, 1030, 1045, 1050–53
Safeguards Committee (WTO), 505, 546, 951
Same Level of Trade, 342–43, 458
Same Person Methodology, 487–88
Sampling, 346–58, 36–72, 483, 602, 617–19, 631–34
Scheduled Goods, 573–75
Schedule of Concessions, 10, 88, 93, 96, 101, 113, 263, 557–58, 568, 574, 717, 783, 786, 804
Scheduling Guidelines, 721, 725–27, 732, 776–97
Scientific Evidence, 237, 294, 630–44, 650–52, 659–60
Section 201 [of the 1974 Trade Act (US)], 517
Section 301 [of the 1974 Trade Act (US)], 930
Section 751(c) [of the Tariff Act of 1930 (US)], 377
Sectoral Approach, 98
Sector–specific Commitment, 743, 780–81
Security Exception, 142, 245, 254, 319, 743, 759
Selective Tendering Procedures, 681
Self–contained, 741
Self–executing, 959
Self–election, 168
Selling General and Administrative Expenses (SG & A), 335–41, 399, 407
Senior Officials Group (SOG), 696
Separate Customs Territory, 8–9, 14, 19, 54, 125, 160, 659, 825
Sequencing, 1028–30
Sequential Enforcement, 453
Serious Prejudice, 424, 456–68, 479–82, 875
Services Sectoral Classification, 773, 797, 1034
Singapore Ministerial Conference, 98, 214, 670, 679
Singer–Prebisch Thesis, 166, 193
Single Undertaking, 34–40, 333, 701
Situation Complaint, 840, 933, 938–39, 1017

Smoot–Hawley, 2, 60, 91
So as to Afford Protection (SATAP), 216, 223, 225, 228–32, 235, 240, 245–46, 750
Social Security, 220–23, 710–12
Société Générale de Surveillance (SGS), 208–10
Special 301, 923
Special and Differential Treatment, 12, 40, 131, 165–96, 206–07, 212–14, 534, 553, 622–23, 654–55, 667, 683, 703, 759, 808
Special Care, 475
Special Case, 357, 779, 851–53
Special Safeguard Provision (SSG), 558
Special Terms of Reference, 323, 326, 953
Special Transitional Safeguard Mechanism (ATC), 586–90
Special Treatment, 174, 549, 559–60
Specific Commitment, 773–99
Specific Duties, 94–95, 557
Specificity, 82, 440, 443–45, 491, 613, 716, 723, 756
Specific Trade Concern (STC), 624
Standards for the Classification, Grading or Marketing of Commodities, 70
Standard of Review, 278–81, 378–81, 409–16, 496–97, 534–36, 658, 975–76, 1032
Standstill, 666, 687, 702
Stare Decisis, 1005–07
State Owned Commercial Bank (SOCB), 429, 441
State Owned Enterprise (SOE), 428, 437
Statistically Valid Sample, 347, 523
Step 2 Payments, 556–57
Stockholm Convention, 24, 812
Stumpage Arrangement, 432
Sub–Committee on LDCs, 13, 191
Substantial Cause, 517, 527, 530
Substantial Interest (SI), 107–14, 533–34, 793, 928, 963, 996
Substantially All Trade, 137–43, 162
Substantially Equivalent Concessions, 111–14
Substantial Sectoral Coverage, 802–08
Substantial Transformation, 126
Suggestion, 1017–20
Sunset Policy Bulletin (US), 960–72
Sunset Review, 376–84, 489–90
Suspension of Concessions, 984, 1017, 1028–29, 1032–58
Swiss Formula, 97, 107

T

Tariff Classification, 91–93, 117, 126, 129, 225, 232–38, 273, 477
Tariff Escalation, 39
Tariffication, 89, 553–54, 757–58, 577
Tariff Quota (TRQ), 83, 123, 149, 332, 503–05, 532, 560, 747, 1015, 1037
Tax Occulte, 220

Technical Assistance, 12–13, 21, 40, 191–94, 208, 212, 214, 622
Technical Committee, 204, 207
Technical Criterion, 126
Technical Regulation, 37, 593–631, 1026
Technological Neutrality, 725–26, 742
Telecommunications Reference Paper (TRP), 724, 764–71
Telmex, 724, 742, 765
Tempest, 134
Temporary Defence Mechanism (TDM), 426
Terms of Reference (TOR), 953
Terms of Trade, 55–56, 132–34, 161, 193, 213, 247, 688, 813, 816, 901
Territoriality–Principle, 431
Textiles Committee, 582
Textiles Monitoring Body (TMB), 584–91, 968
Textiles Surveillance Body (TSB), 582, 591
Third Country Price, 335–36
Third Party, 38, 336, 341, 407, 619, 656, 861, 882, 895, 930, 963–66, 984, 996–98, 1027, 1043, 1059
Threat of Injury, 334, 359–61, 367, 390, 410, 470, 474–76, 484, 504, 517, 520–21, 587
Tiered Cuts, 97
Tokyo Round, 35, 75, 97, 104, 197, 201, 206–07, 212–13, 282, 333, 427, 463, 505, 593, 637, 677, 692–94, 813, 927, 938
Total Deference, 409–10, 535, 683, 971
Trade Association, 385
Trade Barriers Regulation (TBR), 930
Trade Damage, 279
Trade Diversion, 135, 142, 161–62, 541–42
Trade Effects, 63–67, 83, 226, 235, 323, 452–59, 474, 498
Trade Facilitation, 214
Trade in Tasks, 133, 419
Trade Negotiations Committee (TNC), 97, 207, 578, 583, 702, 706, 723
Trade Policy Review Mechanism (TPRM), 6, 33, 35, 39–40, 141, 268
Trade Secrets, 891–93
Trademarks, 857–68
Trademark Law Treaty, 864
Traffic Rights, 707–11, 773
Transaction Value, 201–06
Transit, 251–55, 327, 859, 916
Transparency, 199–200, 211–12, 264, 267–83, 407–08, 577, 614–15, 684, 763–64
Travaux Préparatoires, 95, 653, 779
Travel Act (US), 786, 807
Treaty Establishing the European Community (ECT), 708
Treaty on the Functioning of the European Union (TFEU), 708–09
Trend Analysis, 511
Trier of Facts, 480, 657, 971, 976, 998–99
TRIPS Agreement (Agreement on Trade–Related Aspects of Intellectual Property), 783–923
TRIPS Council, 839–40
Turtle Excluding Device (TED), 287

U

Unbound, 87–88, 96, 123, 418, 727, 779–80, 795
Uncertainty, 67, 105, 264, 361, 376–83, 629, 638, 646, 651, 659, 692, 698, 895, 906, 909, 1059
Understanding on Rules and Procedures Governing the Settlement of Disputes, 6, 38–39, 930–39
Unfair Trade, 78, 332–33, 425, 505, 516–17
Understanding Regarding Export Restrictions and Charges, 213
Unforeseen Developments, 503, 508–12, 531, 546, 548
United Nations (UN), 24, 42, 52, 174, 309, 319, 324, 714, 812, 839, 899
United Nations Conference on Trade and Development (UNCTAD), 52, 167, 191–92, 214, 678, 715, 839
United Nations Convention on the Law of the Sea (UNCLOS), 304
United Nations Development Programme (UNDP), 24, 52, 192
UN Security Council Resolution, 502 321
Universal Service, 770–71, 793
Universal Service Obligation (USO), 791
Unscheduled Goods, 574–75

V

Vienna Convention on Consular Relations, 6
Vienna Convention on the Law of Treaties, 29, 91, 93, 116, 316, 353, 414–15, 584, 747, 752, 776, 779, 783, 795–96, 799
Violation Complaint, 933
Voluntary Export Restraint (VER), 59–60, 506, 542, 557
Voluntary Restraint Agreement (VRA), 435, 506

W

Waiver, 42–48
Wassenaar Arrangement, 328–29
Webb Pomerene Act (US), 81
Weighted Average (WA), 145, 335, 339, 345, 369, 483
WIPO Copyright Treaty (WRT), 850, 855
WIPO Performances and Phonograms Treaty (WPPT), 836, 850, 855
Wire Act (US), 786, 807
Working Party on Notifications Obligations and Procedures, 283
Working Group on Other Barriers to Trade, 311
Working Group on the Accession of the United Arab Republic, 320
Working Party (WP), 9–11, 34, 54–56, 72, 80, 85, 127, 141–47, 166, 211–32, 259, 264, 283, 340, 446, 508, 677–679, 761–64, 929
Working Party on Professional Services, 761–62
Working Party on China's Accession, 537–42
Work Programme for Small Economies, 191
World Bank (WB), 2, 25, 51, 53, 192, 214, 690–91, 839
World Health Organization (WHO), 25, 602, 634, 641, 839, 900
World Trade Report, 134, 146
WTO Committee on Specific Commitments, 721, 781
WTO Law Advisory Centre, 194
WTO Secretariat, 7–10, 39, 99, 105, 141, 194, 200, 211, 282–83, 495, 578, 625, 684, 726–27, 776–81, 791, 932, 952, 967, 985–86, 1002
Wyndham–White, 7, 114, 550

Y

Yeutter, Clayton, 553

Z

Zeroing, 344, 346, 947, 980, 985, 1007–08
Zoellick, Robert, 37, 1059